PHILIP'S

ROAD ATLAS

2025 EASY TO READ MULTISCALE EUROPE

CONTENTS

II Legend to map symbols

III Driving regulations

1 Key to route planning map pages

2 Route planning maps

24 Key to road map pages · Distance table

26 Road maps of Europe

201 Index to road maps

Inside back cover **Map of high-speed rail network**

www.philips-maps.co.uk

First published in 1998 by Philip's,
a division of Octopus Publishing Group Ltd
www.octopusbooks.co.uk
Carmelite House, 50 Victoria Embankment, London EC4Y 0DZ
An Hachette UK Company
www.hachette.co.uk

Thirtieth edition 2024
First impression 2024
ISBN 978-1-84907-660-9 spiral-bound
ISBN 978-1-84907-659-3 paperback

 **Ordnance Survey Licensed Data**
This product includes mapping data licensed from
Ordnance Survey®, with the permission of the
Controller of His Majesty's Stationery Office
© Crown copyright 2024. All rights reserved.
Licence number AC0000851689

 is a registered Trade Mark of the Northern Ireland Department of
Finance and Personnel. This product includes mapping data licensed from
Ordnance Survey of Northern Ireland®, reproduced with the permission of
Land and Property Services under delegated authority
from the Controller of His Majesty's Stationery Office, © Crown Copyright 2024.

All enquiries should be addressed to the Publisher.

While every reasonable effort has been made to ensure that the information compiled in
this atlas is accurate, complete and up-to-date at the time of publication, some of this
information is subject to change and the Publisher cannot guarantee its correctness or
completeness.

The information in this atlas is provided without any representation or warranty, express
or implied and the Publisher cannot be held liable for any loss or damage due to any use or
reliance on the information in this atlas, nor for any errors, omissions or subsequent changes
in such information.

The representation in this atlas of any road, drive or track is not evidence of
the existence of a right of way.

The maps of Ireland on pages 26 to 30 are based upon the Crown Copyright and are
reproduced with the permission of Land & Property Services under delegated authority from
the Controller of His Majesty's Stationery Office, © Crown Copyright and database right
2020, PMLPA No 100503, Ordnance Survey Ireland/Tailte Éireann Permit No. 9296
© Tailte Éireann/Government of Ireland

Tailte Éireann Clárachan, Luacháil
Suirbhéireacht
Registration, Valuation,
Surveying

Cartography by Philip's
Copyright © Philip's 2024

Printed in Dubai

The UK's best-selling Europe atlases
Data from Nielsen Total Consumer Market 2023

David Ionut / Shutterstock

Legend to road maps
pages 26–200

⑦ ⑧	**Motorway with junctions** – full, restricted access
◇ ◆	services, rest area
]┅┅[═ ═ ═	tunnel, under construction
▬ ▌	**Toll Motorway** – with toll barrier
▬▬▬	**Pre-pay motorway** – 'vignette' must be purchased before travel
━━━ ━ ━	**Principal trunk highway** – single / dual carriageway
➤┅┅┤ ═ ═ ═	tunnel, under construction
━━━ ━ ━	**Other main highway** – single / dual carriageway
─── ─ ─	**Other important road, other road**
E25 A49	**European road number, motorway number**
135	**National road number**
▼ Col Bayard 1248 ▲	**Mountain pass**
▬▬◀	**Scenic route, gradient** – arrow points uphill
○ 143 ○	**Distances** – in kilometres
	major
● 28 ●	
	minor
─>─ ─ ─<─	**Principal railway with tunnel**
🚢	**Ferry route**
·············	**Short ferry route**
▬·▬·▬	**International boundary, national boundary**
〰〰	**National park, natural park**
1754▲	**Spot height**
Sevilla	**World Heritage town**
Verona	**Town of tourist interest**
■ ◉	**City or town with Low Emission Zone**

✈	**Airport**
🏛	**Ancient monument**
⚲	**Beach**
🏰	**Castle or house**
⌂	**Cave**
✦	**Other place of interest**
❁	**Park or garden**
✝	**Religious building**
⛷	**Ski resort**
🎡	**Theme park**
⊕	**World Heritage site**

Legend to route planning maps
pages 2–23

▬✶▬	**Motorway with selected junctions**
▬⊓⊓⊓▬	tunnel
▪▪▪▪▪	under construction
▬▬▬	**Toll motorway**
▬▬▬	**Pre-pay motorway**
━━━	**Main through route**
───	**Other major road**
───	**Other road**
25	**European road number**
56	**Motorway number**
55	**National road number**
○ 56 ○	**Distances** – in kilometres
▬▬▬	**International boundary**
─ ─ ─	**National boundary**
─ ⚓ ─ LE HAVRE	**Car ferry and destination**
≍	**Mountain pass**
✈	**International airport**
1089 ▲	**Height** (metres)

		Town – population
MOSKVA	▣ ◼	5 million +
BERLIN	▢ ◻	2–5 million
MINSK	◌ ◻	1–2 million
Oslo	◉ ⦿	500000–1 million
Aarhus	⊙ ◉	200000–500000
Turku	◎ ◎	100000–200000
Gävle	⊙ ◎	50000–100000
Nybro	○ ◎	20000–50000
Ikast	○ ●	10000–20000
Skjern	○ ●	5000–10000
Lillesand	○ ●	0–5000

The green version of the symbol indicates towns with Low Emission Zones

---

Scale · pages 26–181

1:753 800
1 inch = 12 miles
1 cm = 7.5km

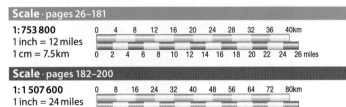

0 4 8 12 16 20 24 28 32 36 40km
0 2 4 6 8 10 12 14 16 18 20 22 24 26 miles

Scale · pages 182–200

1:1 507 600
1 inch = 24 miles
1 cm = 15km

0 8 16 24 32 40 48 56 64 72 80km
0 4 8 12 16 20 24 28 32 36 40 44 48 52 miles

Scale · pages 2–23

1:3 200 000
1 inch = 50.51 miles
1 cm = 32km

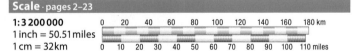

0 20 40 60 80 100 120 140 160 180 km
0 10 20 30 40 50 60 70 80 90 100 110 miles

Driving regulations

The information below is for drivers visiting for fewer than 12 months, as different rules will apply for residents.

Vehicle Fitting headlamp converters or beam deflectors when taking a right-hand-drive car to a country where driving on the right (every country in Europe except the UK and Ireland) is compulsory. A national vehicle plate is required when taking a vehicle abroad. The (GB) identifier was replaced by (UK) in September 2021 and is no longer valid. If you are driving a UK registered vehicle within the EU and its number plate does not include a UK identifier and the Union flag, you will need to attach a UK sticker. Outside the EU and in Cyprus, Malta and Spain, a UK sticker is required even if your number plate includes a UK identifier. A UK sticker isn't required in Ireland.

Vehicle documentation All countries require that you carry a vehicle registration document (V5C), hire certificate (VE103) or letter of authority for the use of someone else's vehicle, full driving licence/International Driving Permit and insurance documentation (and/or Green Card outside the EU – see also "Insurance" below). Minimum driving ages are often higher for people holding foreign licences. Drivers of vehicles over three years old should ensure that the MOT is up to date and take the certificate with them.

Travel documentation All UK visitors' passports should be valid for at least six months. Some non-EU countries also require a visa. UK nationals may visit the EU Schengen area countries for up to 90 days in a 180-day period without a visa. A UK EHIC (UK European Health Insurance Card) or a UK GHIC (UK Global Health Insurance Card) will allow you to access state provided healthcare when visiting an EU country. They are available from the NHS website https://services.nhsbsa.nhs.uk/cra/start. Not all healthcare in the EU is free so you should also ensure you also have suitable travel insurance. In future, the GHIC card may cover additional countries outside the EU but it is not currently valid in Norway, Iceland, Liechtenstein or Switzerland.

Insurance Third-party cover is compulsory across Europe. Most insurance policies give only basic cover when driving abroad, so you should check that your policy provides at least third-party cover for the countries in which you will be driving and upgrade it to the level that you require. You might be forced to take out extra cover at the frontier if you cannot produce acceptable proof that you have adequate insurance.

Licence A photo licence is preferred. If you have an old-style paper driving licence or are visiting countries outside the EU, you may need to carry an IDP (International Driving Permit). Some non-EU countries may only recognise one of the three available types of IDP (1926, 1949 or 1968) so the correct one should be obtained, see www.gov.uk/driving-abroad/international-driving-permit. If planning to hire a car abroad, you should check in advance if the hire company wish to check your licence for endorsements and permitted vehicles categories. If so, visit www.gov.uk/view-driving-licence to create a digital code (valid for 72 hours) that allows your licence details to be shared. For more information, contact the DVLA (0300 790 6802), www.dft.gov.uk/dvla.

Motorcycles It is compulsory for all motorcyclists and passengers to wear crash helmets in all countries. In France it is compulsory for them to carry reflective jackets.

Other In countries in which reflective jackets are compulsory, one for each person should be carried in the passenger compartment (or motorcycle panniers). Warning triangles should also be carried here. The penalties for infringements of regulations vary considerable between countries. In many, the police have the right to impose on-the-spot fines (ask for a receipt). Serious infringements, such as exceeding the blood-alcohol limit, can result in immediate imprisonment. Please note that driving regulations often change and it has not been possible to include the information for all types of vehicle. The figures given for capitals' populations are for the entire metropolitan area.

Symbols

- 🏛 Motorway
- ▲ Dual carriageway
- ▲ Single carriageway / expressway
- 🚗 Surfaced road
- 🚗 Unsurfaced / gravel road
- 🏘 Urban area
- 🕐 Speed limit in kilometres per hour (kph)
- 🔴 Seat belts
- 👶 Children
- 🍷 Blood alcohol level
- △ Warning triangle
- ⬛ First aid kit
- 💡 Spare bulb kit
- 🔥 Fire extinguisher
- ⊖ Minimum driving age
- 📄 Additional documents required
- 📱 Mobile phones
- **LEZ** Low Emission Zone
- 🔦 Dipped headlights
- ❄ Winter driving
- ★ Other information

Andorra Principat d'Andorra (AND)

Area 468 sq km (181 sq miles)
Population 85,000 **Capital** Andorra la Vella (22,000)
Languages Catalan (official), French, Castilian and Portuguese **Currency** Euro = 100 cents
Website http://visitandorra.com

🏛	▲	▲	🏘
🕐 n/a	90	60/90	50

- 🔴 Compulsory
- 👶 Under 10 and below 150 cm must travel in an EU-approved restraint system adapted to their size in the rear. Airbag must be deactivated if a child is in the front passenger seat.
- 🍷 0.05% △ 2 compulsory ⬛ Recommended
- 💡 Compulsory 🔥 Recommended ⊖ 18
- 📱 Only allowed with hands-free kit
- 🔦 Compulsory for motorcycles during day and for other vehicles during poor daytime visibility
- ❄ Snow chains must be carried or winter tyres fitted 1 Nov–15 May
- ★ On-the-spot fines imposed
- ★ Visibility vests compulsory
- ★ Wearers of contact lenses or spectacles should carry a spare pair

Austria Österreich (A)

Area 83,859 sq km (32,377 sq miles)
Population 8,941,000 **Capital** Vienna / Wien (1,960,000) **Languages** German (official) **Currency** Euro = 100 cents **Website** www.austria.info/en

🏛	▲	▲	🏘
🕐 130	100	100	30–50

If towing trailer under 750kg / over 750 kg

🕐 100/80	100/80	100/70	50

Minimum speed on motorways 60 kph

- 🔴 Compulsory
- 👶 Under 14 and under 135cm cannot travel as a front or rear passenger unless they use a suitable child restraint; under 14 over 150cm must wear adult seat belt. Airbags must be deactivated if a rear-facing child seat is used in the front.
- 🍷 0.049% · 0.01% for professional drivers or if licence held less than 2 years
- △ Compulsory 💡 Recommended 🔥 Recommended
- ⬛ Compulsory ⊖ 18 (16 for motorbikes up to 125cc)
- 📄 Paper driving licences must be accompanied by photographic proof of identity.
- 📱 Only allowed with hands-free kit
- **LEZ** Several cities and regions have LEZs affecting HGVs that ban non-compliant vehicles, impose speed restrictions and night-time bans. Trucks in categories N1 to N3 must display an environmental badge (Umwelt-Pickerl) in these areas.
- 🔦 Compulsory for motorcycles and in poor visibility for other vehicles. Headlamp converters compulsory for right-hand drive vehicles
- ❄ Winter tyres compulsory 1 Nov–15 Apr. Snow chains only permitted if road is fully covered by snow or ice.
- ★ On-the-spot fines imposed
- ★ Radar detectors and dashcams prohibited
- ★ To drive on motorways or expressways, a motorway sticker must be purchased at the border or main petrol station. These are available for 10 days, 2 months or 1 year. Vehicles 3.5 tonnes or over must purchase an on-board unit in order to pay a mileage-based toll.
- ★ Visibility vests compulsory
- ★ When traffic flow ceases on a motorway or dual carriageway, vehicles are required to form a corridor between lanes for use by emergency services.

HELP ME, PLEASE!

If you're in a difficult situation and need local help, then the following words and phrases might prove useful if language is a problem:

🇬🇧	🇫🇷	🇪🇸	🇮🇹	🇩🇪
Do you speak English?	Parlez-vous anglais?	¿Habla usted inglés?	Parla inglese?	Sprechen Sie Englisch?
Thank you (very much)	Merci (beaucoup)	(Muchas) Gracias	Grazie (mille)	Danke (sehr)
Is there a police station near here?	Est-ce qu'il y a un commissariat de police près d'ici?	¿Hay una comisaría cerca?	C'e' un commissariato qui vicino?	Gibt es ein Polizeirevier hier in der Nähe?
I have lost my passport.	J'ai perdu mon passeport.	He perdido mi pasaporte	Ho perso il mio passaporto.	Ich have meinen Reisepass verloren.
I have broken down.	Je suis tombé en panne	Mi coche se ha averiado.	Ho un guasto.	Ich habe eine Panne.
I have run out of fuel.	Je suis tombé en panne d'essence.	Me he quedado sin gasolina.	Ho terminato la benzina.	Ich habe kein Benzin mehr.
I feel ill.	Je me sens malade.	Me siento mal.	Mi sento male.	Mir ist schlecht.

Belarus (BY)

Area 207,600 sq km (80,154 sq miles)
Population 9,384,000
Capital Minsk (2,049,000)
Languages Belarusian, Russian (both official)
Currency Belarusian ruble = 100 kopek
Website www.belarus.by/en/government

🏛	⚠	▲	🏘
🕐 110	90	90	60[1]

If towing trailer under 750kg

🕐 90	70	70	50

[1] In residential areas limit is 20 kph • Vehicle towing another vehicle 50 kph limit • If full driving licence held for less than 2 years, must not exceed 70 kph

- Compulsory in front seats, and rear seats if fitted
- Under 12 not allowed in front seat and must use appropriate child restraint
- 0.00% △ Compulsory ⊞ Recommended
- Recommended 🔺Recommended ⊖ 18
- Visa, 1968 International Driving Permit, green card recommended, local health insurance. Even with a green card, local third-party insurance may be imposed at the border.
- Only allowed with a hands-free kit
- Compulsory during the day in poor visibility or if towing or being towed. Headlamp converters compulsory for right-hand drive vehicles
- Winter tyres compulsory 1 Dec–1 Mar; snow chains recommended
- ★ A temporary vehicle import certificate must be purchased on entry and driver must be registered
- ★ It is illegal for vehicles to be dirty
- ★ Many road signs use only the Cyrillic alphabet
- ★ On-the-spot fines imposed
- ★ Radar-detectors prohibited
- ★ To drive on main motorways an on-board unit must be acquired at the border or a petrol station in order to pay tolls. See www.beltoll.by/index.php/en

Belgium Belgique (B)

Area 30,528 sq km (11,786 sq miles)
Population 11,914,000
Capital Brussels/Bruxelles (2,110,000)
Languages Dutch, French, German (all official)
Currency Euro = 100 cents
Website www.belgium.be/en

🏛	⚠	▲	🏘
🕐 120[1]	120[1]	90[2]	50[3]

Over 3.5 tonnes

🕐 90	90	70[2]–90	50[3]

[1] Minimum speed of 70 kph may be applied in certain conditions on motorways and some dual carriageways. [2] 70 kph in Flanders. [3] 20 kph in residential areas, 30 kph near some schools, hospitals and churches, and in designated cycle zones.

- Compulsory
- All under 18s under 135 cm must wear an appropriate child restraint. Airbags must be deactivated if a rear-facing child seat is used in the front.
- 0.05% • 0.02% professional drivers
- △ Compulsory
- ⊞ Recommended (compulsory for vehicles registered in Belgium)
- 🔺 Recommended (compulsory for vehicles registered in Belgium)
- Recommended ⊖ 18
- Only allowed with a hands-free kit
- **LEZ** LEZs in operation in Antwerp, Brussels and Ghent. Preregistration necessary and fees payable for most vehicles.
- Mandatory at all times for motorcycles and during the day in poor conditions for other vehicles
- Winter tyres permitted 1 Oct to 31 Apr. Snow chains only permitted if road is fully covered by snow or ice. Vehicles with studded tyres restricted to 90 kph on motorways/dual carriageways and 60 kph on other roads.

- ★ If a tram or bus stops to allow passengers on or off, you must not overtake
- ★ Motorcyclists must wear fully protective clothing
- ★ On-the-spot fines imposed
- ★ Radar detectors prohibited
- ★ Sticker indicating maximum recommended speed for winter tyres must be displayed on dashboard if using them
- ★ Visibility vest compulsory
- ★ When a traffic jam occurs on a road with two or more lanes in the direction of travel, motorists should move aside to create a path for emergency vehicles between the lanes.

Bosnia & Herzegovina
Bosna i Hercegovina (BIH)

Area 51,197 km² (19,767 mi²) **Population** 3,808,000 **Capital** Sarajevo (555,000) **Languages** Bosnian/Croatian/Serbian **Currency** Convertible Marka = 100 convertible pfenniga **Website** www.fbihvlada.gov.ba/english/index.php

🏛	⚠	▲	🏘
🕐 130	100	80	50

- Compulsory
- Under 12s must sit in rear using an appropriate child restraint. Under-2s may travel in a rear-facing child seat in the front only if the airbags have been deactivated.
- 0.03% • no person under the influence of alcohol may travel in front seats.
- △ 2 compulsory ⊞ Recommended
- Recommended 🔺Compulsory for LPG vehicles
- ⊖ 18
- Original vehicle registration and ownership papers.
- Only allowed with hands-free kit
- Compulsory for all vehicles at all times
- Winter tyres compulsory 15 Nov–15 Apr; the use of snow chains is compulsory in thick snow or if indicated by road signs.
- ★ GPS must have fixed speed camera function deactivated; radar detectors prohibited.
- ★ On-the-spot fines imposed
- ★ Visibility vest, tow rope or tow bar recommended

TOP TIP

In Austria and Germany, if traffic on a dual carriageway or motorway ceases to flow, vehicles are required move aside to form a corridor for use by emergency services.

Bulgaria Bulgariya (BG)

Area 110,912 sq km (42,822 sq miles)
Population 6,828,000
Capital Sofia (1,287,000)
Languages Bulgarian (official), Turkish
Currency Lev = 100 stotinki
Website www.government.bg/en

🏛	⚠	▲	🏘
🕐 140	120	90	50

If towing trailer

🕐 100	90	70	50

Over 3.5 tonnes

🕐 100	90	80	50

- Compulsory
- Under 3s not permitted in vehicles with no child restraints; 3–10 year olds must sit in rear in an appropriate restraint. Rear-facing child seats may be used in the front only if the airbag has been deactivated.
- 0.05% △ Compulsory
- ⊞ Compulsory 🔘Recommended
- 🔺 Compulsory ⊖ 18
- Photo driving licence preferred; a paper licence must be accompanied by an International Driving Permit.
- Only allowed with a hands-free kit
- Compulsory
- Winter tyres compulsory. Snow chains should be carried from 1 Nov–1 Mar. Max speed with chains 50 kph
- ★ GPS must have fixed speed camera function deactivated
- ★ On-the-spot fines imposed
- ★ A vignette is required to drive on motorways and main roads. These can be purchased at the border. Digital e-vignettes can be obtained from terminals at border checkpoints or online in advance: https://tollpass.bg/en
- ★ Visibility vest compulsory

Croatia Hrvatska (HR)

Area 56,538 km² (21,829 mi²)
Population 4,169,000
Capital Zagreb (1,107,000)
Languages Croatian
Currency Euro = 100 cents
Website https://vlada.gov.hr/en

🏛	⚠	▲	🏘
🕐 130	110	90	50

If towing

🕐 90	90	80	50

Lower speed limits for newly qualified drivers; please check before travelling

- Compulsory if fitted
- Children under 12 not permitted in front seat and must use appropriate child seat or restraint in rear. Children under 2 may use a rear-facing seat in the front only if the airbag is deactivated.
- 0.05% • 0.00 % for drivers under 24 and professional drivers
- △ Compulsory (2 if towing) ⊞ Compulsory
- Compulsory except for xenon or LED lights
- 🔺 Recommended ⊖ 18
- Only allowed with hands-free kit
- Compulsory in reduced visibilty and at all times from the last weekend in October until the last weekend in March
- From 15 Nov to 15 Apr, winter tyres must be fitted, snow chains and shovel must be carried in vehicle. Winter tyres must have minimum tread of 4mm
- ★ Motorway tolls can be paid in cash or by credit or debit card. An electronic toll collection system is also available, for details see www.hac.hr/en
- ★ On-the-spot fines imposed
- ★ Radar detectors prohibited
- ★ Visibility vest compulsory

Czechia Česko (CZ)

Area 78,864 sq km (30,449 sq miles)
Population 10,706,000 **Capital** Prague/Praha
(1,318,000) **Languages** Czech (official), Moravian
Currency Czech Koruna = 100 haler
Website https://vlada.cz/en

🏛	⚠	▲	🏭
⊙ 130	110/80[1]	90	50

If towing

⊙ 80	80	80	50

[1]80 kph on urban expressways.

🚗 Compulsory

🧒 Children under 36 kg and 150 cm must use appropriate child restraint. Only front-facing child retraints are permitted in the front in vehicles with airbags fitted. Airbags must be deactivated if a rear-facing child seat is used in the front.

🍷 0.00% △ Compulsory 🚦 Compulsory

🚦 Compulsory 🦺 Recommended

⊖ 18 (17 for motorcycles under 125 cc)

🪪 Licences with a photo preferred. Paper licences should be accompanied by an International Driving Permit.

📵 Only allowed with a hands-free kit

LEZ Two-stage LEZ in Prague for vehicles over 3.5 and 6 tonnes. Permit system.

🔦 Compulsory at all times

❄ Winter tyres compulsory 1 Nov–31 Mar if roads are icy/snow-covered or snow is expected. Also if winter equipment sign (circular blue sign with white car and snowflake) is displayed. Minimum tread depth 4mm.

★ GPS must have fixed speed camera function deactivated; radar detectors prohibited

★ On-the-spot fines imposed

★ Replacement fuses must be carried

★ Spectacles or contact lens wearers must carry a spare pair in their vehicle at all times

★ Vehicles up to 3.5 tonnes require e-vignette for motorway driving, available for 1 year, 30 days, 10 days. https://edalnice.cz/en. Vehicles over 3.5 tonnes are subject to tolls and must carry an electronic tag https://mytocz.eu/en

★ Visibility vest compulsory

Denmark Danmark (DK)

Area 43,094 sq km (16,638 sq miles)
Population 5,947,000 **Capital** Copenhagen /
København (1,370,000) **Languages** Danish (official)
Currency Krone = 100 øre
Website www.visitdenmark.com

🏛	⚠	▲	🏭
⊙110-130[1]	80	80	50[2]

If towing

⊙ 100	80	80	50[2]

[1]Over 3.5 tonnes 80 kph [2]Central Copenhagen 40 kph

🚗 Compulsory

🧒 Under 135cm must use appropriate child restraint; in front permitted only in an appropriate rear-facing seat with any airbags disabled.

🍷 0.05% △ Compulsory 🚦 Recommended

🚦 Recommended 🦺 Recommended ⊖ 18

📵 Only allowed with a hands-free kit

LEZ Aalborg, Aarhus, Copenhagen/Frederiksberg and Odense. Older diesel-powered trucks, buses, vans and cars may not enter unless they have been retrofitted with a compliant particulate filter. Pre-registration required. Non-compliant vehicles banned. https://miljoezoner.dk/en

🔦 Must be used at all times

❄ Studded tyres may be fitted 1 Nov–15 April, if used on all wheels

★ On-the-spot fines imposed ★ Radar detectors prohibited ★ Visibility vest recommended

★ Tolls apply on the on the Storebælt and Øresund bridges

Estonia Eesti (EST)

Area 45,100 sq km (17,413 sq miles)
Population 1,203,000
Capital Tallinn (427,000)
Languages Estonian (official), Russian
Currency Euro = 100 cents
Website www.valitsus.ee/en

🏛	⚠	▲	🏭
⊙ n/a	90[1]	90	50

[1]In summer, the speed limit on some dual carriageways may be raised to 100/120 kph. The limit on ice roads varies between 10kph and 70 kph according to ice thickness.

🚗 Compulsory if fitted

🧒 Children too small for adult seatbelts must wear a seat restraint appropriate to their size. Rear-facing safety seats must not be used in the front if an air bag is fitted, unless this has been deactivated.

🍷 0.02%

△ 2 compulsory

🚦 Recommended (compulsory for company cars)

🚦 Recommended 🦺 Compulsory

⊖ 18

📵 Only allowed with a hands-free kit

🔦 Compulsory at all times

❄ Winter tyres are compulsory from Dec–Mar; dates may be extended in severe weather. Studded winter tyres are allowed from 15 Oct–31 Mar, but this can be extended to start 1 October and/or end 30 April

★ A toll system is in operation in Tallinn

★ On-the-spot fines imposed

★ Radar detectors prohibited

★ 2 wheel chocks compulsory

★ Visibility vest compulsory

Finland Suomi (FIN)

Area 338,145 sq km (130,557 sq miles)
Population 5,615,000
Capital Helsinki (1,328,000)
Languages Finnish, Swedish (both official)
Currency Euro = 100 cents
Website https://valtioneuvosto.fi/en/frontpage

🏛	⚠	▲	🏭
⊙100-120	80-100	80-100[1]	20/50

Vans, lorries and if towing

⊙ 80	80	60	20/50

[1]100 in summer • If towing a vehicle by rope, cable or rod, max speed limit 60 kph • Maximum of 80 kph for vans and lorries • Speed limits are often lowered in winter

🚗 Compulsory

🧒 Below 135 cm must use a child restraint or seat

🍷 0.05%

△ Compulsory 🚦 Recommended

🚦 Recommended 🦺 Recommended

⊖ 18

📵 Only allowed with hands-free kit

🔦 Must be used at all times

❄ Winter tyres compulsory Dec–Feb

★ On-the-spot fines imposed

★ Radar-detectors are prohibited

★ Visibility vest compulsory

France (F)

Area 551,500 sq km (212,934 sq miles)
Population 68,522,000
Capital Paris (11,142,000)
Languages French (official), Breton, Occitan
Currency Euro = 100 cents
Website www.gouvernement.fr/en

🏛	⚠	▲	🏭
⊙ 130	110	80	50

On wet roads or if full driving licence held for less than 3 years

⊙ 110	100	70	50

above 3.5 tonnes gross

⊙ 90	80	80	50

50kph on all roads if fog reduces visibility to less than 50m

🚗 Compulsory in front seats and, if fitted, in rear

🧒 Children up to age 10 must use suitable child seat or restraint and may only travel in the front if: • the vehicle has no rear seats • no rear seatbelts • the rear seats are already occupied by children up to age 10 • the child is a baby in a rear facing child seat and the airbag is deactivated.

🍷 0.05% • 0.02% if full driving licence held for less than 3 years • All drivers/motorcyclists are required to carry an unused breathalyser though this rule is not currently enforced.

△ Compulsory

🚦 Recommended

🚦 Recommended

⊖ 18 (16 for motorbikes up to 125cc)

📵 Use permitted only with hands-free kit. Must not be used with headphones or earpieces

LEZ An LEZ operates in the Mont Blanc tunnel and such zones are being progressively introduced across French cities. Non-compliant vehicles are banned during operating hours. Crit'Air stickers must be displayed by compliant vehicles. See http://certificat-air.gouv.fr/en

🔦 Compulsory in poor daytime visibility and at all times for motorcycles

❄ In mountainous areas (marked by signs), winter tyres must be fitted or snow chains available 1 Nov to 31 March

★ GPS must have fixed speed camera function deactivated; radar-detection equipment is prohibited

★ Headphones or earpieces must not be used for listening to music or making phone calls while driving.

★ Motorcyclists and passengers must have four reflective stickers on their helmets (front, back and both sides) and wear CE-certified gloves.

★ On-the-spot fines imposed

★ Tolls on motorways. Electronic tag needed if using automatic tolls.

★ Visibility vests, to be worn on the roadside in case of emergency or breakdown, must be carried for all vehicle occupants and riders.

★ Wearers of contact lenses or spectacles should carry a spare pair

---

TOP TIP

In most countries, signs show the European road number in white on a green background alongside the appropriate national road number. However, in Sweden and Belgium only the E-road number will be shown.

Germany Deutschland (D)

Area 357,022 sq km (137,846 sq miles)
Population 84,220,000
Capital Berlin (3,571,000)
Languages German (official)
Currency Euro = 100 cents
Website www.bundesregierung.de/breg-en

🏛	▲	▲	🏭
⏱ 130¹	130¹	100	50

If towing

⏱ 80	80	80	50

¹recommended maximum • 50kph if visibility below 50m

- 🚗 Compulsory
- 👶 Aged 3-12 and under 150cm must use an appropriate child seat or restraint and sit in the rear. Children under 3 must be in a suitable child restraint and may travel in a rear-facing seat in the front if airbags are deactivated.
- 🍷 0.05% • 0.00% for professional drivers, under 21s and those with less than 2 years full licence
- △ Compulsory
- ➕ Compulsory
- 🔦 Recommended
- 🦺 Recommended
- ⊖ 18
- 📱 Use permitted only with hands-free kit – also applies to drivers of motorbikes and bicycles
- **LEZ** Many cities have or are planning LEZs (Umweltzone). Vehicles must display a 'Plakette' sticker, indicating emissions category. Proof of compliance needed to acquire sticker. Non-compliant vehicles banned. www.umwelt-plakette.de/en
- 💡 Compulsory during poor daytime visibility and tunnels; recommended at other times. Compulsory at all times for motorcyclists.
- ❄ Winter tyres compulsory in all winter weather conditions; snow chains recommended
- ★ GPS must have fixed speed camera function deactivated; radar detectors prohibited
- ★ On-the-spot fines imposed
- ★ Tolls on autobahns for lorries
- ★ Visibility vest compulsory

Greece Ellas (GR)

Area 131,957 sq km (50,948 sq miles)
Population 10,498,000
Capital Athens / Athina (3,154,000)
Languages Greek (official)
Currency Euro = 100 cents
Website www.visitgreece.gr

🏛	▲	▲	🏭
⏱ 130	110	90	50

If towing

⏱ 90–100	80–90	80	50

- 🚗 Compulsory in front seats and, if fitted, in rear
- 👶 Under 12 or below 135cm must use appropriate child restraint. In front if child is in rear-facing child seat, any airbags must be deactivated.
- 🍷 0.05% • 0.02% for professional drivers or drivers with less than 2 years full licence
- △ Compulsory
- ➕ Compulsory
- 🔦 Recommended
- 🦺 Compulsory
- ⊖ 18
- 📱 Only allowed with a hands-free kit
- 💡 Compulsory during poor daytime visibility and at all times for motorcycles
- ❄ Snow chains permitted on ice- or snow-covered roads. Max speed 50 kph.
- ★ On-the-spot fines can be imposed but not collected by the police
- ★ Radar-detection equipment is prohibited
- ★ Tolls on several newer motorways.

Hungary Magyarorszàg (H)

Area 93,032 sq km (35,919 sq miles)
Population 9,670,000
Capital Budapest (1,775,000)
Languages Hungarian (official)
Currency Forint = 100 filler
Website https://abouthungary.hu

🏛	▲	▲	🏭
⏱ 130	110	90	50¹

If towing or if over 3.5 tonnes

⏱ 80	70	70	50¹

¹30 kph zones have been introduced in many cities

- 🚗 Compulsory
- 👶 Under 150cm and over 3 must be seated in rear and use appropriate child restraint. Under 3 allowed in front only in rear-facing child seat with any airbags deactivated.
- 🍷 0.00%
- △ Compulsory ➕ Recommended
- 🔦 Recommended 🦺 Recommended
- ⊖ 17
- 📱 Only allowed with a hands-free kit
- **LEZ** Budapest is divided into zones with varying restrictions on HGVs
- 💡 Compulsory during the day outside built-up areas; compulsory at all times for motorcycles
- ❄ Snow chains compulsory where conditions dictate. Max speed 50 kph.
- ★ Tolls apply to many motorways and are administered through an electronic vignette system with automatic number plate recognition https://nemzetiutdij.hu/en/
- ★ On-the-spot fines issued
- ★ Radar detectors prohibited
- ★ Tow rope recommended
- ★ Visibility vest recommended

Iceland Ísland (IS)

Area 103,000 sq km (39,768 sq miles)
Population 361,000
Capital Reykjavik (140,000)
Languages Icelandic
Currency Krona = 100 aurar
Website www.government.is

🏛	🚗	🚗	🏭
⏱ n/a	90	80	50

- 🚗 Compulsory in front and rear seats
- 👶 Children up to 135 cm must use suitable child seat or restraint. Up to 150cm must not sit in front seat unless airbag is deactivated.
- 🍷 0.05%
- △ Compulsory ➕ Recommended
- 🔦 Recommended 🦺 Recommended
- ⊖ 17
- 📱 Only allowed with a hands-free kit
- 💡 Compulsory at all times
- ❄ Winter tyres compulsory c.1 Nov–14 Apr (variable). Snow chains may be used when necessary.
- ★ Driving off marked roads is forbidden
- ★ Highland roads are not suitable for ordinary cars and many are unusable in winter
- ★ On-the-spot fines imposed

TOP TIP

Contact details. Make sure you have all relevant emergency helpline numbers with you, including emergency services, breakdown assistance, the local British consulate and your insurance company. There are links to embassies and consulates around the world from the Foreign Office website: www.fco.gov.uk
The European emergency telephone number (equivalent of 999) is 112.

Ireland Eire (IRL)

Area 70,273 sq km (27,132 sq miles)
Population 5,324,000 **Capital** Dublin (1,458,000)
Languages Irish, English (both official)
Currency Euro = 100 cents **Website** www.gov.ie/en

🏛	▲	▲	🏭
⏱ 120	100	80	50¹

If towing

⏱ 80	80	80	50¹

¹Dublin and other areas have introduced 30 kph zones

- 🚗 Compulsory where fitted. Driver responsible for ensuring passengers under 17 comply
- 👶 Children under 150cm and 36 kg must use appropriate child restraint. Airbags must be deactivated if a rear-facing child seat is used in the front.
- 🍷 0.05% • 0.02% for novice and professional drivers
- △ Recommended (compulsory for HGVs and buses)
- ➕ Recommended
- 🔦 Recommended 🦺 Recommended
- ⊖ 17 (16 for motorbikes up to 125cc; 18–24 for over 125cc according to power).
- 📱 Only allowed with a hands-free kit
- 💡 Compulsory in poor visibility
- ★ Driving is on the left
- ★ GPS must have fixed speed camera function deactivated; radar detectors prohibited
- ★ On-the-spot fines imposed
- ★ Tolls are being introduced on some motorways; the M50 Dublin has barrier-free tolling with number-plate recognition. Tolls can be paid in cash or with an electronic toll tag; not all toll stations accept cards. www.etoll.ie/driving-on-toll-roads/information-for-visitors

Italy Italia (I)

Area 301,318 sq km (116,338 sq miles)
Population 61,022,000 **Capital** Rome / Roma (4,298,000) **Languages** Italian (official)
Currency Euro = 100 cents **Website** www.italia.it

🏛	▲	▲	🏭
⏱ 130	110	90	50

If towing

⏱ 80	70	70	50

When wet

⏱ 110	90	80	50

Some motorways with emergency lanes have speed limit of 150 kph

- 🚗 Compulsory in front seats and, if fitted, in rear
- 👶 Children under 150cm must use appropriate child restraint. In front, if child is in rear-facing child seat, any airbags must be deactivated. For foreign-registered cars, the country of origin's legislation applies.
- 🍷 0.05% • 0.00% for professional drivers or with less than 3 years full licence
- △ Compulsory ➕ Recommended
- 🔦 Recommended 🦺 Recommended
- ⊖ 18 (14 for mopeds, 16 up to 125cc)
- 📱 Only allowed with hands-free kit
- **LEZ** Italy has many LEZs with varying standards and hours of operation. Milan and Palermo operate combined LEZ and urban road toll schemes.
- 💡 Compulsory outside built-up areas, in tunnels, on motorways and dual carriageways and in poor visibility; compulsory at all times for motorcycles
- ❄ Winter tyres or snow chains compulsory 15 Oct–15 Apr in certain areas where signs indicate. Max speed with snow chains 50 kph
- ★ On-the-spot fines imposed
- ★ Radar-detection equipment is prohibited
- ★ Tolls on motorways. Blue lanes accept credit cards; yellow lanes restricted to holders of Telepass pay-toll device.
- ★ Visibility vest compulsory

Kosovo Republika e Kosoves / Republika Kosovo (RKS)

Area 10,887 sq km (4203 sq miles)
Population 1,964,000 **Capital** Pristina (162,000)
Languages Albanian, Serbian (both official), Bosnian, Turkish, Roma
Currency Euro (Serbian dinar in Serb enclaves)
Website http://kryeministri-ks.net/en

⏱ 110–130   100   80   50

- 🔧 Compulsory
- 👶 Under 12 must sit in rear seats in an appropriate restraint
- 🍷 0.01%
- △ Compulsory
- 🧰 Compulsory
- 💡 Compulsory
- 🦺 Compulsory
- ⊖ 18
- 📇 International Driving Permit recommended, locally purchased third-party insurance (green card is not recognised). Visitors from many non-EU countries also require documents with proof of ability to cover costs and valid reason for visiting.
- 📱 Only allowed with a hands-free kit
- 💡 Compulsory at all times
- ❄ Winter tyres or snow chains compulsory in poor winter weather conditions

Latvia Latvija (LV)

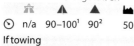

Area 64,589 sq km (24,942 sq miles)
Population 1,822,000
Capital Riga (870,000)
Languages Latvian (official), Russian
Currency Euro = 100 cents
Website www.mk.gov.lv/en

⏱ n/a   90–100[1]   90[2]   50

If towing

⏱ n/a   80   80   50

[1]100 on designated roads only during 1 Mar–1 Nov. • [2]80 on gravel roads. In residential areas limit is 20kph

- 🔧 Compulsory in front seats and if fitted in rear
- 👶 Children under 150cm must use suitable child restraint
- 🍷 0.05% • 0.02% with less than 2 years experience
- △ Compulsory
- 🧰 Recommended
- 🦺 Recommended
- 💡 Recommended
- ⊖ 18
- 📱 Only allowed with hands-free kit
- 💡 Must be used at all times all year round
- ❄ Winter tyres:compulsory 1 Dec–1 Mar on all vehicles up to 3.5 tonnes. Studded tyres allowed 1 Oct–30 Apr.
- ★ On-the-spot fines can be imposed but not collected by the police
- ★ Radar-detection equipment prohibited
- ★ Visibility vests recommended

TOP TIP

Check the adjustments required for your headlights before you go. Beam deflectors are a legal requirement if you drive in Europe. They are generally sold at the ports, on ferries and in the Folkestone Eurotunnel terminal, but be warned – the instructions can be a little confusing!
The alternative is to ask a local garage to do the job for you before you go. If you choose this, then make sure you shop around as prices for undertaking this very simple task vary enormously.

Lithuania Lietuva (LT)

Area 65,200 sq km (25,173 sq miles)
Population 2,656,000
Capital Vilnius (854,000)
Languages Lithuanian (official), Russian, Polish
Currency Euro = 100 cents
Website https://lrv.lt/en

⏱ 130/110[1]   120/110[1]   70–90   50[2]

If towing

⏱ 90   90   70–90   50

If licence held for less than two years

⏱ 100   90   70–80   50

[1]Apr–Oct / Nov–Mar [2]20kph in some residential areas

- 🔧 Compulsory
- 👶 Under 12 or below 135 cm not allowed in front seats unless in suitable restraint; under 3 must use appropriate child seat. A rear-facing child seat may be used in front only if airbags are deactivated.
- 🍷 0.04% • 0.00% if full licence held less than 2 years
- △ Compulsory
- 🧰 Recommended
- 🦺 Recommended
- 💡 Recommended
- ⊖ 18
- 📇 Licences without a photograph must be accompanied by photographic proof of identity, e.g. a passport
- 📱 Only allowed with a hands-free kit
- 💡 Must be used at all times
- ❄ Winter tyres compulsory 10 Nov–10 Apr
- ★ On-the-spot fines imposed
- ★ Visibility vest recommended

Luxembourg (L)

Area 2,586 sq km (998 sq miles)
Population 661,000
Capital Luxembourg (133,000)
Languages Luxembourgian / Letzeburgish (official), French, German
Currency Euro = 100 cents
Website http://luxembourg.public.lu/en

⏱ 130/110[1]   90   90   50[2]

If towing

⏱ 90   75   75   50[2]

If full driving licence held for less than 2 years, must not exceed 75 kph • [1]110 in wet weather • [2]30 kph zones are progressively being introduced. 20 kph in zones where pedestrians have priority.

- 🔧 Compulsory
- 👶 Children under 3 must use an appropriate restraint system. Airbags must be disabled if a rear-facing child seat is used in the front. Children 3–18 and/or under 150 cm must use a restraint system appropriate to their size. If over 36kg a seatbelt may be used in the back only.
- 🍷 0.05%, 0.02% for young drivers, drivers with less than 2 years experience and drivers of taxis and commercial vehicles
- △ Compulsory
- 🧰 Recommended
- 🦺 Recommended
- 💡 Recommended
- ⊖ 18
- 📱 Use permitted only with hands-free kit
- 💡 Compulsory for motorcyclists and for other vehicles in poor visibility and in tunnels. Outside urban areas, full-beam headlights are compulsory at night and in poor visibility.
- ❄ Winter tyres compulsory in winter weather
- ★ On-the-spot fines imposed
- ★ Visibility vest recommended

North Macedonia Severna Makedonija (NMK)

Area 25,713 sq km (9,927 sq miles)
Population 2,131,000
Capital Skopje (607,000)
Languages Macedonian (official), Albanian
Currency Denar = 100 deni
Website

⏱ 130   110[1]   80   50

[1]If road reserved for motor vehicles, otherwise 80 • Lower limits apply to newly qualified drivers

- 🔧 Compulsory
- 👶 Between 2 and 12 not allowed in front seats; under 5 must use an appropriate child restraint. Under 2 allowed in front seat in a rear-facing child seat if airbags are deactivated.
- 🍷 0.05% • 0.00% for business, commercial and professional drivers and with less than 2 years experience
- △ Compulsory
- 🧰 Recommended
- 🦺 Recommended
- 💡 Recommended; compulsory for LPG vehicles
- ⊖ 18 (16 with parental supervision, 16 for mopeds)
- 📇 International Driving Permit and green card recommended
- 📱 Use not permitted whilst driving
- 💡 Compulsory at all times
- ❄ Winter tyres or snow chains compulsory 15 Nov–15 Mar. Max speed 50 kph for vehicles using snow chains
- ★ GPS must have fixed speed camera function deactivated; radar detectors prohibited
- ★ Novice drivers are subject to restricted driving hours
- ★ On-the-spot fines imposed but paid later
- ★ Tolls apply on many roads
- ★ Tow rope recommended
- ★ Visibility vest recommended and should be kept in the passenger compartment and worn to leave the vehicle in the dark outside built-up areas

Moldova (MD)

Area 33,851 sq km (13,069 sq miles)
Population 3,251,000
Capital Chisinau (779,000)
Languages Moldovan / Romanian (official)
Currency Leu = 100 bani
Website www.moldova.md

⏱ n/a   110   80   50[1]

[1]20kph in some residential areas

- 🔧 Compulsory in front seats and, if fitted, in rear seats
- 👶 Under 12 not allowed in front seats and must use an appropriate child restraint in the back
- 🍷 0.00%
- △ Compulsory
- 🧰 Recommended
- 🦺 Recommended
- 💡 Recommended
- ⊖ 18
- 📇 If not the vehicle owner, bring written permission from the owner, translated into Romanian and legalised; valid insurance (green card).
- 📱 Only allowed with hands-free kit
- 💡 Must use dipped headlights at all times 1 Nov–31 Mar
- ❄ Winter tyres compulsory 1 Nov–31 Mar
- ★ On-the-spot-fines imposed
- ★ Vehicles not registered in Moldova require a vignette. These may be purchased from MAIB (Moldova-Agroindbank) branches or online https://evinieta.gov.md

Montenegro Crna Gora (MNE)

Area 14,026 sq km, (5,415 sq miles)
Population 602,000 **Capital** Podgorica (186,000)
Languages Serbian (of the Ijekavian dialect)
Currency Euro = 100 cents **Website** www.gov.me/en

🏛	⚠	▲	⛰
🕓 100	100	80	50

80kph speed limit if towing a caravan

- 🛞 Compulsory in front and rear seats
- 👶 Under 12 not allowed in front seats. Under-5s must use an appropriate child seat.
- 🍷 0.03% · 0.01% if aged up to 24 or licence held for less than 1 year.
- △ Compulsory
- 🧰 Recommended
- 🧯 Recommended
- 🔦 Recommended
- ⊖ 18
- 🪪 1968 International Driving Permit (1949 IDP may not be recognised); original vehicle registration document; vehicle insurance valid in Montenegro (green card recommended)
- 📵 Prohibited
- 🔆 Must be used at all times
- ❄ Winter tyres compulsory 15 Nov–31 Mar.
- ★ On-the-spot fines imposed
- ★ Tolls in the Sozina tunnel between Lake Skadar and the sea. Toll charged on the open section of new A1 motorway (not yet completed)
- ★ Visibility vest recommended

Netherlands Nederland (NL)

Area 41,526 sq km (16,033 sq miles)
Population 17,464,000
Capital Amsterdam 1,166,000 · administrative capital 's-Gravenhage (The Hague) 2,390,000
Languages Dutch (official), Frisian
Currency Euro = 100 cents
Website www.government.nl

🏛	⚠	▲	⛰
🕓 100–130	80/100	80/100	50

- 🛞 Compulsory
- 👶 Under 3 must travel in the back, using an appropriate child restraint; 3–18 and under 135cm must use an appropriate child restraint. A rear-facing child seat may only be used in front if airbags are deactivated.
- 🍷 0.05% · 0.02% if full licence held less than 5 years and for moped riders under 24.
- △ Compulsory
- 🧰 Recommended
- 🧯 Recommended
- 🔦 Recommended
- ⊖ 18
- 📵 Only allowed with a hands-free kit
- LEZ LEZs for diesel vehicles operate in many Dutch cities. Restrictions depend on vehicle's Euro emissions standard. For information see https:// www.milieuzones.nl/english
- 🔆 Recommended in poor visibility and on open roads. Compulsory for motorcycles.
- ★ On-the-spot fines imposed
- ★ Radar-detection equipment is prohibited
- ★ Trams have priority over other traffic. You must wait if a bus or tram stops in the middle of the road to allow passengers on or off.

TOP TIP

Fuel is generally most expensive at motorway service areas and cheapest at supermarkets. However, these are usually shut on Sundays and Bank Holidays. So-called '24 hour' regional fuel stations in France generally accept payment by UK credit card these days, but some drivers still occasionally report difficulties.

Norway Norge (N)

Area 323,877 sq km (125,049 sq miles)
Population 5,598,000
Capital Oslo (1,071,000)
Languages Norwegian (official), Lappish, Finnish
Currency Krone = 100 øre
Website www.norway.no/en/uk

🏛	⚠	▲	⛰
🕓 80–100	80	80	30/50

If towing trailer with brakes

🕓 80	80	80	50

If towing trailer without brakes

🕓 60	60	60	50

- 🛞 Compulsory in front seats and, if fitted, in rear
- 👶 Children shorter than 135cm or lighter than 36kg must use appropriate child restraint. Children under 4 must use child safety seat or safety restraint (cot). A rear-facing child seat may be used in front only if airbags are deactivated.
- 🍷 0.02% △ Compulsory 🧰 Recommended
- 🧯 Recommended 🔦 Recommended
- ⊖ 18 (heavy vehicles 18/21)
- 📵 Only allowed with a hands-free kit
- 🔆 Must be used at all times
- ❄ Winter tyres with at least 3mm tread compulsory during winter. Studded tyres may be used 1 Nov until first Sunday after Easter (15 Oct–1 May in Nordland, Troms, and Finnmark). There is a fee for using studded tyres within city boundaries of Oslo, Bergen and Trondheim. Vehicles under 3.5 tonnes must carry snow chains if snow or ice is expected.
- ★ On-the-spot fines imposed
- ★ Radar-detectors are prohibited
- ★ Tolls apply on some bridges, tunnels and access roads into Bergen, Haugesund, Kristiensand, Oslo, Stavangar, Tonsberg, Trondheim and others. Most use electronic fee payment collection only https:// www.autopass.no/en/user/foreign-vehicles/
- ★ Some of the higher mountain passes can experience snowfall and ice even if conditions are warm at lower altitudes, particularly in spring and autumn.
- ★ Visibility vest compulsory

Poland Polska (PL)

Area 323,250 sq km (124,807 sq miles)
Population 37,992,000
Capital Warsaw / Warszawa (1,795,000)
Languages Polish (official)
Currency Zloty = 100 groszy
Website www.poland.travel/en

🏛	⚠	▲	⛰
🕓 140	120[1]/100	100[1]/90	20/50/60[2]

if towing

🕓 80	80	70	20/50/60[2]

[1]Expressway, indicated by signs with white car on blue background · [2]residential / built-up area / built-up area 2300–0500

- 🛞 Compulsory in front seats and, if fitted, in rear
- 👶 Under 12 and below 150 cm must use an appropriate child restraint. A rear-facing child seat may be used in front only if airbags are deactivated.
- 🍷 0.02% △ Compulsory 🧰 Recommended
- 🧯 Recommended 🔦 Compulsory
- ⊖ 18 (mopeds and motorbikes under 125cc – 16)
- 📵 Only allowed with a hands-free kit
- 🔆 Compulsory for all vehicles
- ❄ Snow chains permitted only on roads completely covered in snow
- ★ On-the-spot fines imposed
- ★ Radar-detection equipment is prohibited
- ★ Vehicles under 3.5 tonnes pay tolls on some motorways https://etoll.gov.pl/en/light-vehicles · www.tolls.eu/poland
- ★ Visibility vests compulsory

Portugal (P)

Area 88,797 sq km (34,284 sq miles)
Population 10,223,000
Capital Lisbon / Lisboa (2,986,000)
Languages Portuguese (official)
Currency Euro = 100 cents
Website www.visitportugal.com/en

🏛	⚠	▲	⛰
🕓 120[1]	90/100	90	50/20

If towing

🕓 100[1]	80	70	50/20

[1]50kph minimum; 90kph max if licence less than 1 year

- 🛞 Compulsory in front seats and, if fitted, in rear
- 👶 Under 12 and below 135cm must travel in the rear in an appropriate child restraint; rear-facing child seats permitted in front for under 3s only if airbags deactivated
- 🍷 0.05% · 0.02% for professional drivers or if full licence held less than 3 years
- △ Compulsory 🧰 Recommended
- 🧯 Recommended 🔦 Recommended
- ⊖ 18
- 🪪 IDP required if you have old-style paper licence, photographic proof of identity must be carried at all times
- 📵 Only allowed with hands-free kit
- LEZ Lisbon's LEZ has a minimum entry requirement of emission standard Euro 3 for the central zone and Euro 2 for the outer zone between 0700 and 2100.
- 🔆 Compulsory for motorcycles, compulsory for other vehicles in poor visibility and tunnels
- ★ On-the-spot fines imposed
- ★ Radar detectors and dash-cams prohibited
- ★ Some motorways use traditional toll booths (green lanes are reserved for auto-payment users) but others may only be used by vehicles registered with an automated billing system. www.portugaltolls.com/en
- ★ Visibility vest compulsory
- ★ Wearers of spectacles or contact lenses should carry a spare pair

Romania (RO)

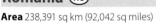

Area 238,391 sq km (92,042 sq miles)
Population 18,326,000 **Capital** Bucharest / Bucuresti (1,785,000) **Languages** Romanian (official), Hungarian
Currency Romanian leu = 100 bani
Website https://romaniatourism.com

🏛	⚠	▲	⛰

Cars and motorcycles

🕓 130	100	90	50

If towing

🕓 120	90	80	50

If full driving licence has been held for less than one year, speed limits are 20kph lower than those listed above.

- 🛞 Compulsory
- 👶 Under 12s not allowed in front and must use an appropriate restraint in the rear
- 🍷 0.00%
- △ Compulsory 🧰 Compulsory
- 🧯 Compulsory 🔦 Compulsory
- ⊖ 18
- 🪪 Green card recommended
- 📵 Only allowed with hands-free kit
- 🔆 Compulsory outside built-up areas, compulsory everywhere for motorcycles
- ❄ Winter tyres compulsory Nov–Mar if roads are snow- or ice-covered, especially in mountainous areas
- ★ Compulsory electronic road tax can be paid for at the border, post offices and some petrol stations and on-line www.roviniete.ro/en
- ★ On-the-spot fines imposed
- ★ Visibility vest compulsory

Russia Rossiya (RUS)

Area 17,075,000 sq km (6,592,800 sq miles)
Population 141,699,000
Capital Moscow / Moskva (12,641,000)
Languages Russian (official), and many others
Currency Russian ruble = 100 kopeks
Website www.visitrussia.org.uk

🏛	⚠	▲	🏭
🕐 110	90	90	60/20

If licence held for under 2 years

🕐 70	70	70	60/20

- 🦺 Compulsory if fitted
- 👶 Under 8 must use suitable child restraint in front and rear seats; under 12 must use suitable child restraint in front seat
- 🍷 0.03 %
- △ Compulsory
- 🔲 Compulsory
- 💡 Compulsory
- 🔺 Compulsory
- ⊖ 18
- 📇 1968 International Driving Permit with Russian translation, visa, green card may not be accepted – check with insurance company before travel,, International Certificate for Motor Vehicles
- 📱 Only allowed with a hands-free kit
- 🔆 Compulsory during the day outside built-up areas
- ❄ Winter tyres compulsory 1 Dec–1 Mar
- ★ On-the-spot fines imposed but must be paid later
- ★ Picking up hitchhikers is prohibited
- ★ Radar detectors/blockers prohibited
- ★ Road tax payable at the border
- ★ Some toll roads, mainly payable in cash

Serbia Srbija (SRB)

Area 77,474 sq km, 29,913 sq miles
Population 6,693,000
Capital Belgrade / Beograd (1,405,000)
Languages Serbian
Currency Dinar = 100 paras
Website www.srbija.gov.rs

🏛	⚠	▲	🏭
🕐 130	100	80	50

If towing

🕐 80	80	80	50

Speed limits vary so check local signage

- 🦺 Compulsory in front and rear seats
- 👶 Age 3–12 must be in rear seats and use an appropriate child restraint; under 3 in rear-facing child seat permitted in front only if airbag deactivated
- 🍷 0.029% • 0.00% for commercial drivers, motorcyclists, or if full licence held less than 1 year
- △ Compulsory
- 🔲 Recommended
- 💡 Recommended
- 🔺 Recommended
- ⊖ 18
- 📇 International Driving Permit recommended, insurance that is valid for Serbia or locally bought third-party insurance
- 📱 Only allowed with a hands-free kit
- 🔆 Compulsory
- ❄ Winter tyres compulsory 1 Nov–1 Apr for vehicles up to 3.5 tonnes. Carrying snow chains compulsory in winter as these must be fitted if driving on snow-covered roads when signs indicate.
- ★ 3-metre tow rope or bar and spare wheel compulsory
- ★ On-the-spot fines imposed
- ★ Radar detectors prohibited
- ★ Tolls on motorways
- ★ Visibility vest compulsory

Slovakia Slovenska Republika (SK)

Area 49,012 sq km (18,923 sq miles)
Population 5,425,000
Capital Bratislava (720,000)
Languages Slovak (official), Hungarian
Currency Euro = 100 cents
Website https://slovakia.travel/en

🏛	⚠	▲	🏭
🕐 130/90[1]	90	90	50

[1] rural roads / urban roads

- 🦺 Compulsory
- 👶 Under 12 or below 150cm must be in rear in appropriate child restraint
- 🍷 0.00%
- △ Compulsory
- 🔲 Recommended
- 💡 Recommended
- 🔺 Recommended
- ⊖ 18
- 📱 Only allowed with a hands-free kit
- 🔆 Compulsory at all times
- ❄ Winter tyres compulsory when snow or ice on the road
- ★ On-the-spot fines imposed
- ★ Radar-detection equipment is prohibited
- ★ Tow rope recommended
- ★ Electronic vignette required for motorways, validity: 1 year, 30 days, 10 days https://eznamka.sk/en
- ★ Visibility vests recommended

Slovenia Slovenija (SLO)

Area 20,256 sq km (7,820 sq miles)
Population 2,100,000
Capital Ljubljana (538,000)
Languages Slovene
Currency Euro = 100 cents
Website www.slovenia.info/en

🏛	⚠	▲	🏭
🕐 130	110	90	50[1]

If towing

🕐 80	80	80	50[1]

[1] 30 kph and 20 kph zones are increasingly common in cities. 50 kph in poor visibility or with snow chains

- 🦺 Compulsory
- 👶 Below 150cm must use appropriate child restraint. A rear-facing baby seat may be used in front only if airbags are deactivated.
- 🍷 0.05% • 0.00% for commercial drivers, under 21s or with less than one year with a full licence
- △ Compulsory
- 🔲 Recommended
- 💡 Recommended
- 🔺 Recommended
- ⊖ 18 (motorbikes up to 125cc – 16, up to 350cc – 18)
- 📇 Licences without photographs must be accompanied by an International Driving Permit
- 📱 Only allowed with hands-free kit
- 🔆 Must be used at all times
- ❄ From 15 Nov to 15 Mar winter tyres must be fitted or snow chains must be carried ready for use in icy conditions. Winter tyres also compulsory in wintry conditions beyond those dates.
- ★ On-the-spot fines imposed
- ★ Radar detectors prohibited
- ★ An e-vignette must be purchased before a vehicle can enter a toll road, https://evinjeta.dars.si/en
- ★ Visibility vest recommended

Spain España (E)

Area 497,548 sq km (192,103 sq miles)
Population 47,223,000 **Capital** Madrid (6,714,000)
Languages Castilian Spanish (official), Catalan, Galician, Basque **Currency** Euro = 100 cents
Website www.spain.info/en

🏛	⚠	▲	🏭
🕐 120[1]	100[1]	90	50[1]

Passenger cars & vans with trailers, vehicles below 3.5 t

🕐 90	80	80	50[1]

[1] Urban motorways and dual carriageways 80 kph. 20 kph zones are being introduced in many cities

- 🦺 Compulsory
- 👶 Up to 12 years or below 135cm must use an appropriate child restraint and sit in the rear, unless all rear seats being used by other children. Rear-facing baby seat permitted in front only if airbag deactivated.
- 🍷 0.05% • 0.03% if less than 2 years full licence or if vehicle is over 3.5 tonnes or carries more than 9 passengers
- △ 2 compulsory (one for in front, one for behind)
- 🔲 Recommended 💡 Compulsory
- 🔺 Recommended. Compulsory for buses and LGVs
- ⊖ 18 (16 for motorbikes up to 125cc)
- 📱 Only allowed with a hands-free kit. Headphones and earpieces not permitted
- **LEZ** Many Spanish cities have LEZs, restricting access to vehicles which meet specific emission requirements. Advance registration is required. See https://urbanaccessregulations.eu/countries-mainmenu-147/spain
- 🔆 Compulsory for motorcycles and for other vehicles in poor daytime visibility and in tunnels
- ❄ Snow chains compulsory in areas indicated by signs
- ★ On-the-spot fines imposed
- ★ Radar-detection equipment is prohibited
- ★ Spare wheel compulsory
- ★ Tolls on motorways ★ Visibility vest compulsory

Sweden Sverige (S)

Area 449,964 sq km (173,731 sq miles)
Population 10,536,000 **Capital** Stockholm (1,679,000)
Languages Swedish (official), Finnish
Currency Swedish krona = 100 ore
Website https://sweden.se

🏛	⚠	▲	🏭
🕐 70–120	70	70	30–50

If towing trailer with brakes

🕐 80	80	70	50

- 🦺 Compulsory in front and rear seats
- 👶 Under 135cm must use an appropriate child restraint and may sit in the front only if airbag is deactivated; rear-facing baby seat permitted in front only if airbag deactivated.
- 🍷 0.02% △ Compulsory 🔲 Recommended
- 💡 Recommended 🔺 Recommended ⊖ 18
- 📇 Licences without a photograph must be accompanied by photographic proof of identity, e.g. a passport
- 📱 Only allowed with hands-free kit
- **LEZ** Many Swedish cities have LEZs restricting access for lorries and buses; a small area of central Stockholm also restricts cars https://urbanaccessregulations.eu/countries-mainmenu-147/sweden-mainmenu-248
- 🔆 Must be used at all times
- ❄ 1 Dec –31 Mar and in wintry conditions outside these dates, winter tyres, anti-freeze screenwash additive and shovel compulsory
- ★ On-the-spot fines imposed ★ Radar-detection equipment is prohibited ★ Tolls on some roads and charges to use some bridges. ★ Tow rope recommended ★ Visibility vest recommended

Switzerland Schweiz (CH)

Area 41,284 sq km (15,939 sq miles)
Population 8,564,000 **Capital** Bern (134,000)
Languages French, German, Italian, Romansch
(all official) **Currency** Swiss Franc = 100 centimes /
rappen **Website** www.myswitzerland.com/en-gb

🕐	⚠	▲	🏔
120	80–100	80	50

If towing

🕐			
80	80	80	50

- 🦺 Compulsory 👶 Up to 12 years or below 150 cm must use an appropriate child restraint. A rear-facing child seat may only be used in the front if the airbag is deactivated.
- 🍷 0.05%, but 0.01% for commercial drivers or with less than 3 years with a full licence
- △ Compulsory 🔲 Recommended
- 🧯 Recommended 🔦 Recommended
- 🚫 18 (mopeds up to 50cc – 16)
- 📱 Only allowed with a hands-free kit
- 🦺 Compulsory
- ❄ Winter tyres recommended Nov–Mar; snow chains compulsory in designated areas in poor winter weather
- ★ All vehicles under 3.5 tonnes must display a vignette on the windscreen. These are valid for one year and can be purchased at border crossings, petrol stations, post offices and online https://switzerlandtravelcentre.com/en/gbr/offer/vignette. Vehicles over 3.5 tonnes are subject to a heavy vehicle charge https://via.admin.ch/shop/dashboard.
- ★ GPS must have fixed speed camera function deactivated; radar detectors prohibited
- ★ On-the-spot fines imposed
- ★ Picking up hitchhikers is prohibited on motorways
- ★ Spectacles or contact lens wearers must carry a spare pair in their vehicle at all times
- ★ Visibility vests recommended

Turkey Türkiye (TR)

Area 774,815 sq km (299,156 sq miles)
Population 83,593,000 **Capital** Ankara (5,636,000)
Languages Turkish (official), Kurdish
Currency New Turkish lira = 100 kurus
Website www.mfa.gov.tr/default.en.mfa

🕐	⚠	▲	🏔
120	90	90	50

Motorbikes

🕐			
80	70	70	50

- 🦺 Compulsory if fitted
- 👶 Under 150 cm and below 36kg must use suitable child restraint. Under 3s can only travel in the front in a rear facing seat if the airbag is deactivated. Children 3–12 may not travel in the front seat.
- 🍷 0.05% immediate confiscation of licence if over limit • 0.00% for professional drivers and if towing trailer or caravan
- △ 2 compulsory (one in front, one behind)
- 🔲 Compulsory 🧯 Recommended
- 🔦 Compulsory 🚫 18
- 🪪 1968 International Driving Permit advised, and required for use with licences without photographs, or UK licence with notarised copy in Turkish; note that Turkey is in both Europe and Asia, green card/UK insurance that covers whole of Turkey or locally bought insurance.
- 📱 Only allowed with a hands-free kit
- 🦺 Compulsory in poor daytime visibility
- ★ On-the-spot fines imposed
- ★ GPS must have fixed speed camera function deactivated; radar detectors prohibited
- ★ Tolls on several motorways and the Bosphorus bridges; electronic payment required by purchasing HGS vignette or pre-payment card from Post Offices or service stations.
- ★ Winter tyres recommended

Ukraine Ukraina (UA)

Area 603,700 sq km (233,088 sq miles)
Population 43,306,000
Capital Kiev / Kyviv (3,010,000)
Languages Ukrainian (official), Russian
Currency Hryvnia = 100 kopiykas
Website www.kmu.gov.ua/en

🕐	⚠	▲	🏔
130	110	90	20/50

If driving licence held less than 2 years, must not exceed 70 kph. 50 kph if towing another vehicle.

- 🦺 Compulsory in front and rear seats
- 👶 Under 12 and below 145cm must use an appropriate child restraint and sit in rear
- 🍷 0.02% – if use of medication can be proved. Otherwise 0.00%.
- △ Compulsory
- 🔲 Compulsory
- 🧯 Compulsory
- 🔦 Compulsory
- 🚫 18
- 🪪 1968 International Driving Permit, green card (check that insurance is recognised in Ukraine).
- 📱 Only allowed with a hands-free kit
- 🦺 Compulsory in poor daytime visibility and from 1 Oct–30 Apr
- ❄ Winter tyres compulsory Nov–Apr in snowy conditions
- ★ On-the-spot fines imposed
- ★ Visibility vest compulsory

United Kingdom (GB)

Area 241,857 sq km (93,381 sq miles)
Population 68,138,000
Capital London (9,541,000)
Languages English (official), Welsh (also official in Wales), Gaelic
Currency Sterling (pound) = 100 pence
Website www.gov.uk

🕐	⚠	▲	🏔
112	112	96	48

If towing

🕐			
96	96	80	48

Several cities have introduced 32 kph (20 mph) zones away from main roads

- 🦺 Compulsory in front seats and if fitted in rear seats
- 👶 Under 3 must use appropriate child restraint in front and rear; 3-12 or under 135cm must use appropriate child restraint in front, in rear must use appropriate child restraint or seat belt if no child restraint is available (e.g. because two occupied restraints prevent fitting of a third).
- 🍷 0.08% (England, Northern Ireland, Wales) • 0.05% (Scotland)
- △ Recommended
- 🔲 Recommended
- 🧯 Recommended
- 🔦 Recommended
- 🚫 17 (16 for mopeds)
- 📱 Only allowed with hands-free kit
- 🏷 London's LEZ and ULEZ (ultra-low emission zone) operate by number-plate recognition; non-compliant vehicles face hefty daily charges. Foreign-registered vehicles must register.
- ★ Driving is on the left
- ★ On-the-spot fines imposed
- ★ Smoking is banned in all commercial vehicles
- ★ Tolls on some toll motorways, bridges and tunnels

TOP TIPS FOR STAYING SAFE

1 Plan your route before you go.
That includes the journey you make to reach your destination and any excursions or local journeys you make while you're there.

2 Take extra care at junctions when you're driving on the 'right side' of the road. Be careful if you are reversing out of a parking space on the street, as things will feel in the wrong place. If driving in a group, involve everybody in a quick 'junction safety check'. Having everyone call out a catchphrase such as "DriLL DriLL DriLL" (Driver Look Left) at junctions and roundabouts is a small but potentially life-saving habit.

3 Remember that you will be subject to the same laws as local drivers. Claiming ignorance will not be accepted as an excuse.

4 Take fatigue seriously. The European motorway network makes it easy to cover big distances but you should also make time for proper breaks (15 minutes every two hours). If possible, share the driving and set daily limits for driving hours.

5 Expect the unexpected. Styles of driving in your destination country are likely to be very different from those you know in the UK. Drive defensively and certainly don't get involved in any altercations on the road.

6 Drink-driving limits across Europe are generally lower than those in the UK. Bear this in mind if you're flying to a destination before hiring a car and plan to have a drink on the plane. Drivers who cause collisions due to drinking are likely to find their insurance policy will not cover them.

7 Don't overload your car, however tempting the local bargains may appear. Make sure you have good all-round visibility by ensuring you don't pile up items on the parcel shelf or boot, and keep your windscreen clean.

8 Always wear a seatbelt and ensure everyone else on board wears one. Check specific regulations regarding the carriage of children: in some countries children under the age of 12 may not travel in the front of the car.

9 Don't use your mobile phone while driving. Even though laws on phone use while driving differ from country to country, the practice is just as dangerous wherever you are.

10 When you're exploring on foot, be wise to road safety as a pedestrian. You may get into trouble for 'jay-walking' so don't just wander across a road. Use a proper crossing, but remember that drivers may not stop for you! Don't forget that traffic closest to you approaches from the LEFT.

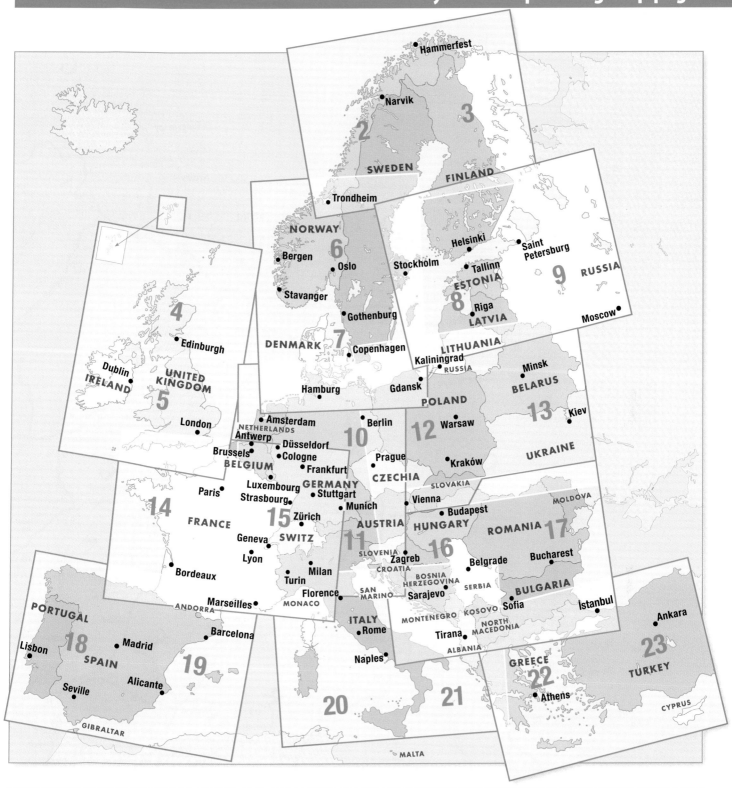

Map key numbers shown on the map: 1, 2, 3, 4, 5, 6, 7, 8, 9, 10, 11, 12, 13, 14, 15, 16, 17, 18, 19, 20, 21, 22, 23

MOTORWAY VIGNETTES Some countries require you to purchase (and in some cases display) a vignette before using certain classes of road

In Austria you will need to purchase and display a vignette on the inside of your windscreen. These may be purchased at border crossings and petrol stations. Digital vignettes are also available. More details from www.asfinag.at/en/toll/vignette/

In Belarus all vehicles over 3.5 tonnes and cars and vans under 3.5 tonnes registered outside the Eurasion Economic Union are required to have a BelToll unit installed. This device enables motorway tolls to be automatically deducted from the driver's account. http://beltoll.by/index.php/en/

In Bulgaria a vignette is required to drive on motorways and main roads. These can be purchased at the border. Digital e-vignettes can be obtained from terminals at border checkpoints or online in advance: www.bgtoll.bg/en

In Czechia vehicles up to 3.5 tonnes require an e-vignette for motorway driving, these are available for periods of 1 year, 30 days or 10 days https://edalnice.cz/en. Vehicles over 3.5 tonnes are subject to tolls and must carry an electronic tag https://mytocz.eu/en

In Hungary tolls apply to many motorways and are administered through an electronic vignette system with automatic number plate recognition https://nemzetiutdij.hu/en

In Moldova vehicles not registered in Moldova require a vignette. These may be purchased from MAIB (Moldova-Agroindbank) branches or online https://evinieta.gov.md

In Slovakia an electronic vignette is required for motorways, validity: 1 year, 30 days, 10 days. https://eznamka.sk/en

In Slovenia an e-vignette must be purchased before a vehicle can enter a toll road https://evinjeta.dars.si/en

In Switzerland all vehicles under 3.5 tonnes must display a vignette on the windscreen. These are valid for one year and can be purchased at border crossings, petrol stations, post offices and online https://switzerlandtravelcentre.com/en/gbr/offer/ vignette. Vehicles over 3.5 tonnes are subject to a heavy vehicle charge https://via.admin.ch/shop/dashboard.

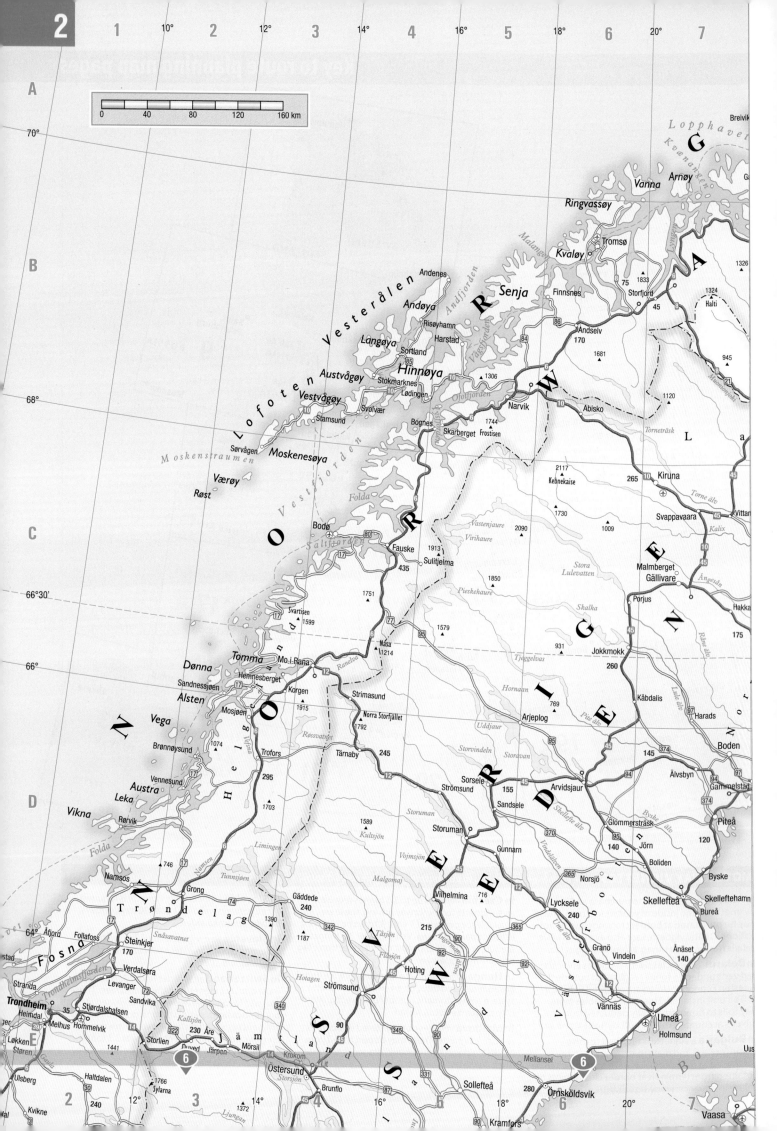

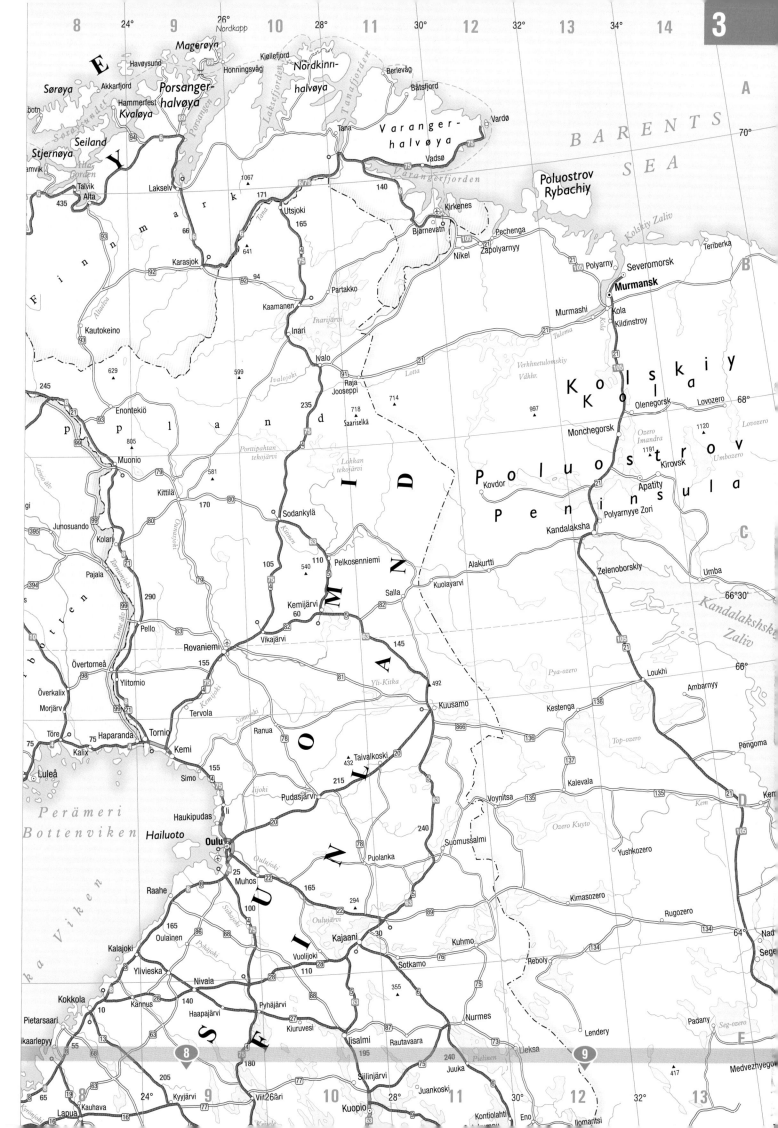

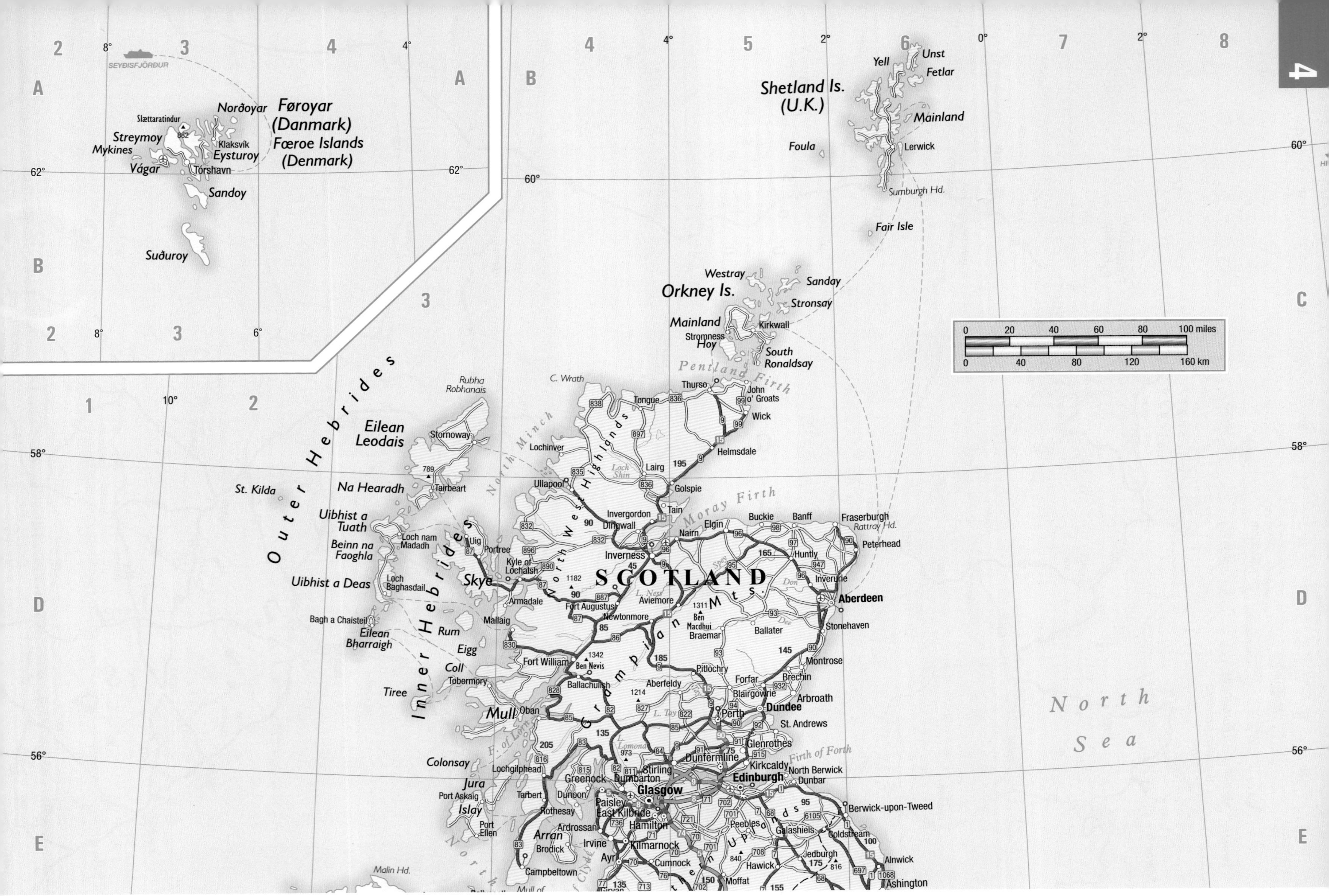

North Sea

100 miles
160 km

Shetland Is.
(U.K.)

Unst
Fetlar
Yell
Mainland
Lerwick
Foula
Sumburgh Hd.
Fair Isle

Orkney Is.
Westray
Sanday
Stronsay
Mainland
Kirkwall
South Ronaldsay
Stromness
Hoy

Pentland Firth
John o' Groats
Wick
Thurso
Helmsdale
99
99
C. Wrath
Tongue
836
Lairg
195
Golspie
836
Loch Shin
Durness
Moray Firth
836
897
Invergordon
96
Tain
Dingwall
Nairn
Elgin
Buckie
Banff
Huntly
97
96
Fraserburgh
Peterhead
Rattray Hd.
90
Inverurie
Aberdeen
Stonehaven

North Minch
Lochinver
Ullapool
838
832
832
890
890
Inverness
Newtonmore
Aviemore
Ben Macdhui 1311
Ballater
Braemar
Dee
145
Montrose
Brechin
Forfar
Arbroath
St. Andrews
Blairgowrie
Perth
Dundee
SCOTLAND
M t s.
Aberfeldy
185
L. Tay
822
94
Glenrothes
915
Kirkcaldy
North Berwick
Dunbar
Firth of Forth
Edinburgh
Dunfermline
Stirling
973
811
L. Lomond
135
Dumbarton
Glasgow
Hamilton
East Kilbride
Paisley
Greenock
Dunoon
205
Rothesay
Ardrossan
Irvine
Kilmarnock
Cumnock
713
Brodick
Campbeltown
Ayr
77 135
736

Berwick-upon-Tweed
Coldstream
Kelso
Jedburgh
175 816
Galashiels
Peebles
840
Hawick
Moffat
150
701
702

Alnwick
Ashington
1068
697
155

Rubha Robhanais
Stornoway
838
Tarbert
789
Eilean Leodais
Na Hearadh
Uibhist a Tuath
Beinn na Faoghla
Loch nam Madadh
Uibhist a Deas
Loch Baghasdail
Eilean Bharraigh
Bagh a Chaisteil
St. Kilda

Outer Hebrides
Inner Hebrides

Portree
Uig
871
Skye
Kyle of Lochalsh
830
Armadale
Mallaig
Fort William
828
Ben Nevis 1342
Ballachulish
Fort Augustus
85
87
Loch Ness
90
Oban
Mull
Tobermory
Coll
Rum
Eigg
Tiree
Colonsay
Jura
Islay
Port Askaig
Port Ellen
Lochgilphead
Tarbert
Arran
Jura
816
83
Mull of Kintyre

Grampian
1182
1214
827
90
887
887

Malin Hd.

Føroyar
(Danmark)
Færoe Islands
(Denmark)
Norðoyar
Klaksvík
Eysturoy
Streymoy
Tórshavn
Slættaratindur 882
Mykines
Vágar
Sandoy
Suðuroy
SEYÐISFJØRÐUR

62°
60°
0°
2°
4°
56°
58°

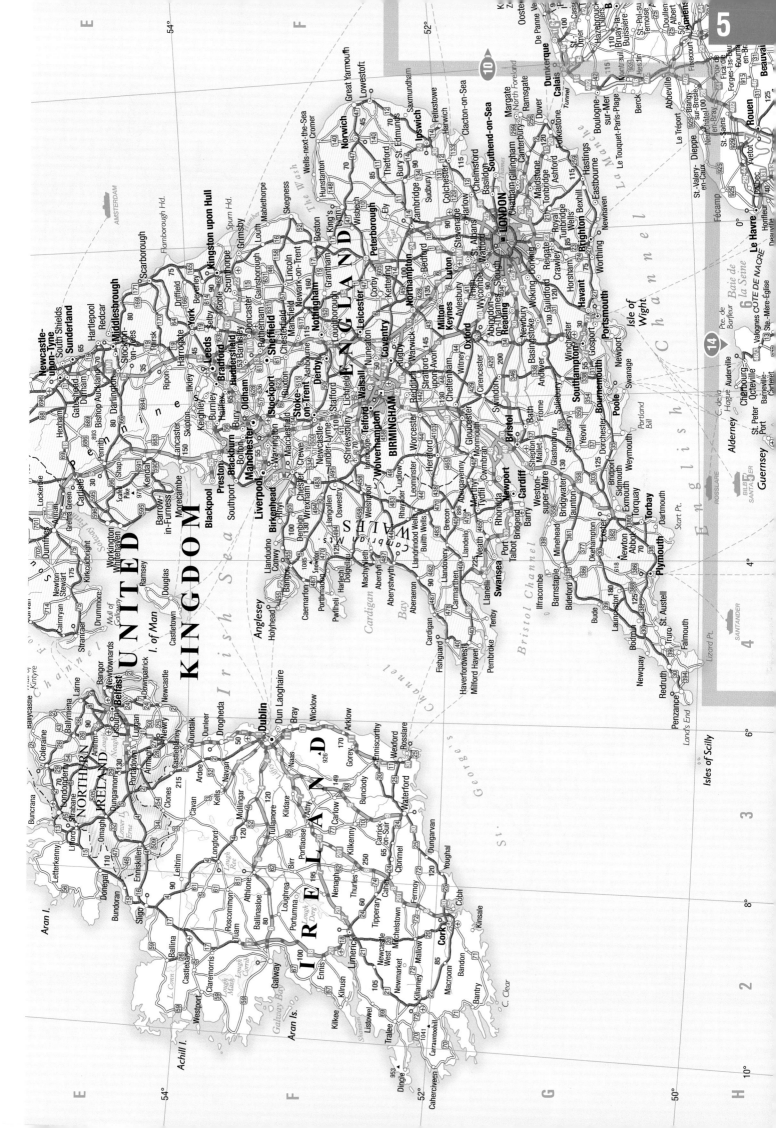

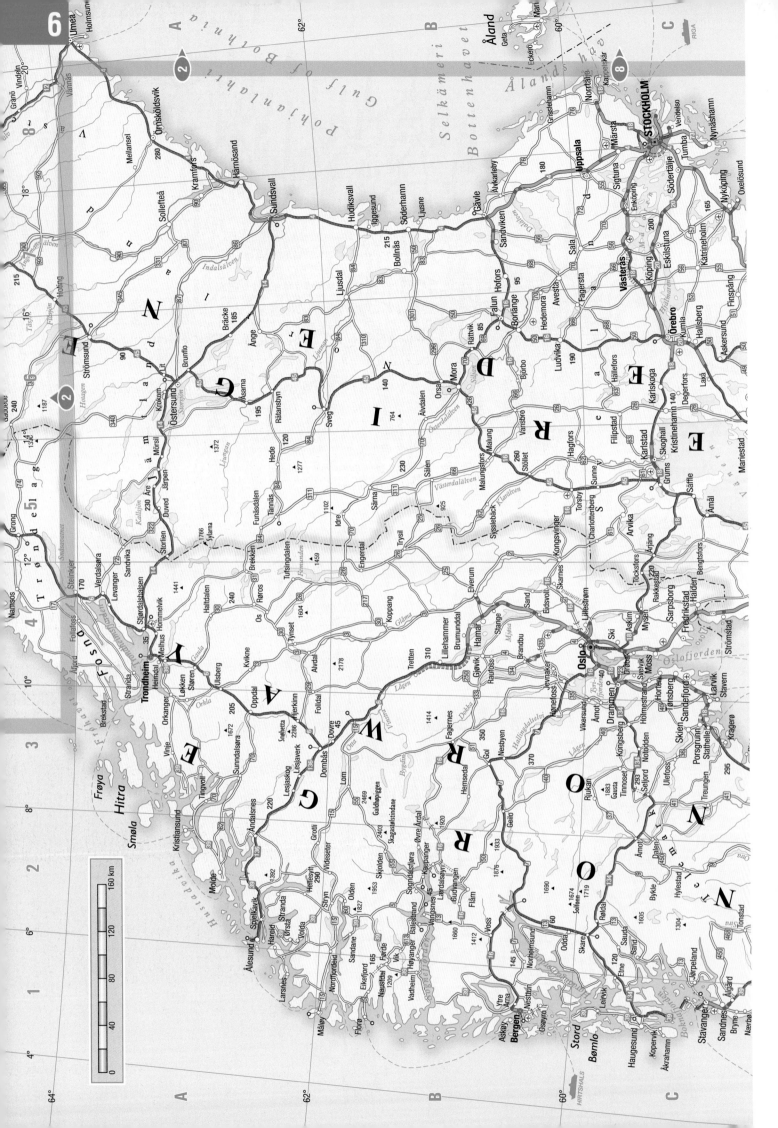

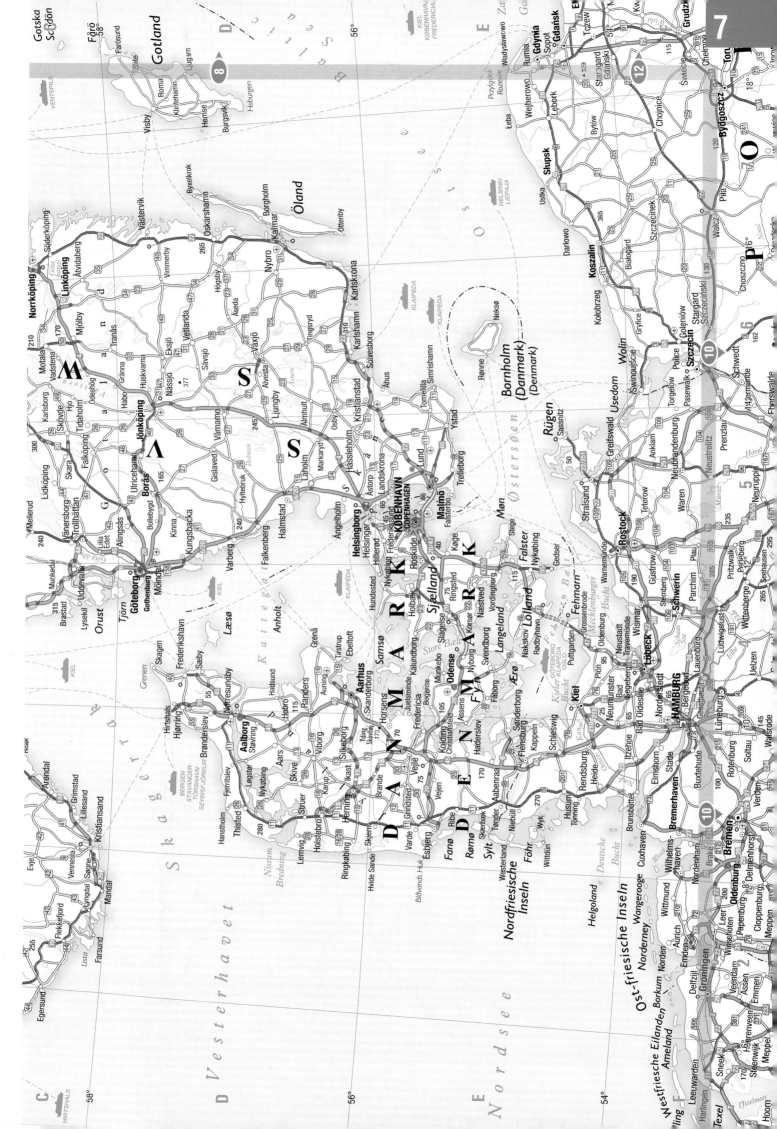

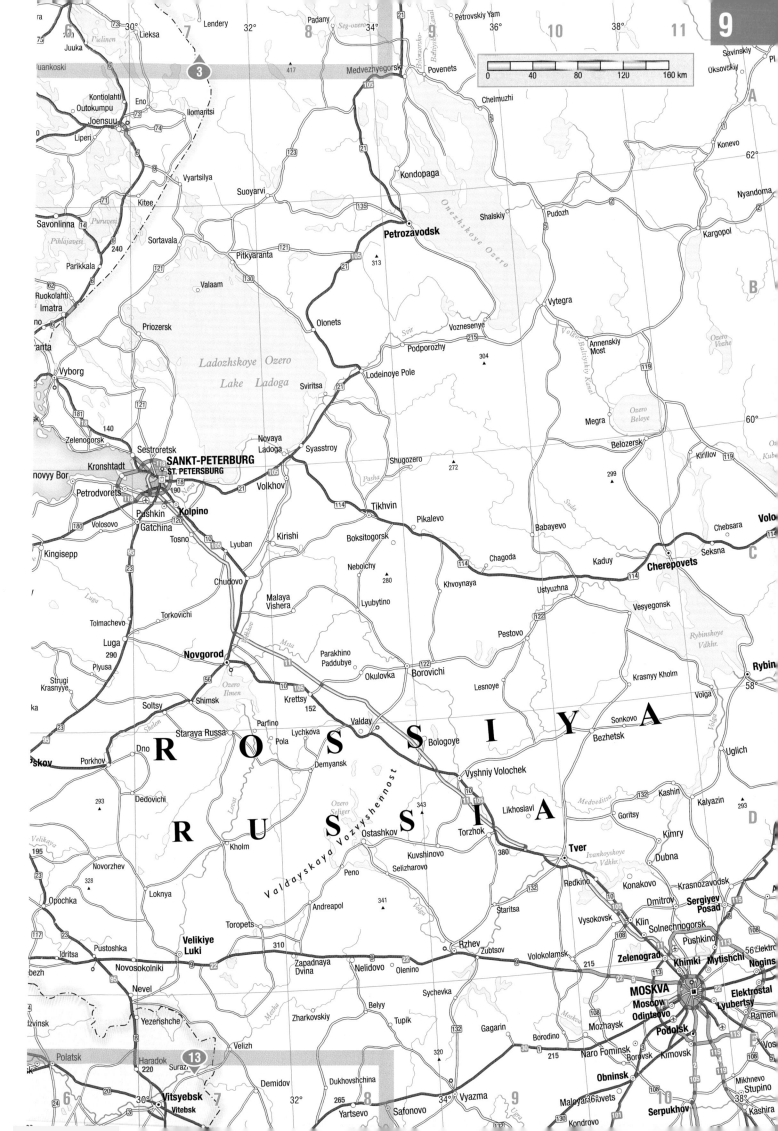

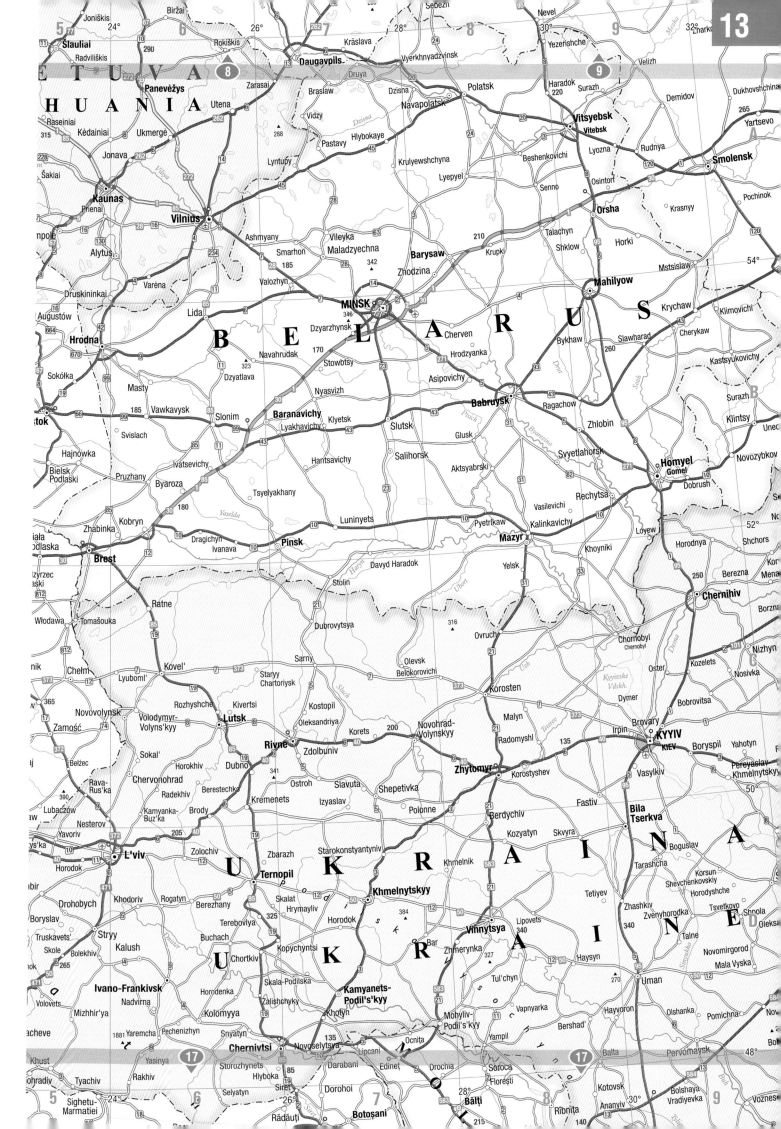

1 · 2 · 3 · 4 · 5

A B C D

50° 48° 46° 44°

ENGLISH CHANNEL

La Manche

Baie de la Seine

Bay of Biscay

Golfe de Gascogne

F R A N C E

Scale:
0 20 40 60 80 100 miles
0 40 80 120 160 km

Major places (United Kingdom):
Barnstaple, super-Mare, Mallet, Frome, Basingstoke, Woking, Dorking, Canterbury, North Foreland, Margate, Ramsgate, Minehead, Bridgwater, Glastonbury, Andover, Salisbury, Guildford, Reigate, Maidstone, Tonbridge, Dover, De Panne, Veurne, Bideford, Bude, Okehampton, Exeter, Taunton, Yeovil, Shaftesbury, Dorchester, Winchester, Southampton, Bournemouth, Gosport, Havant, Brighton, Bexhill, Hastings, Folkestone, Calais, Dunkerque, Newquay, Bodmin, Launceston, Newton Abbot, Sidmouth, Bridport, Weymouth, Poole, Newport, Portsmouth, Worthing, Eastbourne, Newhaven, Boulogne-sur-Mer, Redruth, Penzance, Truro, St. Austell, Plymouth, Torbay, Dartmouth, Exmouth, Swanage, Isle of Wight

Lands End, Lizard Pt., Start Pt., Portland Bill

France / Channel Islands:
Alderney, Guernsey, Sark, Jersey, St. Peter Port, St. Helier, Channel Is. (U.K.), Cherbourg-Octeville, Barneville-Carteret, La Haye-du-Puits, Valognes, Ste-Mère-Église, Carentan, Coutances, Granville, Avranches, Le Mont-St-Michel, Le Havre, Honfleur, Deauville, Bolbec, Yvetot, Rouen, Beauvais, Fécamp, Dieppe, Le Tréport, Abbeville, Amiens, Neufchâtel-en-Bray, Forges-les-Eaux, Gournay-en-Bray, Breteuil, Clermont, Creil, Senlis, Meaux, St-Denis, **PARIS**, Versailles, Créteil, Évry, Étampes, Melun, Fontainebleau, Nemours, Montargis

Perros-Guirec, Roscoff, Paimpol, Binic, Lannion, Guingamp, St-Brieuc, Pléneuf-Val-André, St-Malo, Dinard, Dinan, Lamballe, Brest, Le Conquet, Crozon, Morlaix, Landivisiau, Carhaix-Plouguer, Châteaulin, Douarnenez, Audierne, Quimper, Pont-l'Abbé, Concarneau, Quimperlé, Lorient, Hennebont, Auray, Vannes, Carnac, Quiberon, Belle-Île, Le Palais, Le Croisic, La Baule, St-Nazaire, Pornic, Î. de Noirmoutier, Î. d'Yeu, St-Gilles-Croix-de-Vie, Les Sables-d'Olonne, Pontivy, Loudéac, Rennes, Redon, La Roche-Bernard, Savenay, Nantes, Clisson, Cholet, Ancenis, Angers, Saumur, Chinon, Loudun, Thouars, Bressuire, Parthenay, Chantonnay, Fontenay-le-Comte, Luçon, La Roche-sur-Yon, Challans, Montaigu, Niort, Mauzé-sur-le-Mignon, La Rochelle, Î. de Ré, Rochefort, Î. d'Oléron, Royan, Saintes, Cognac, Pons, Angoulême, Barbezieux, Mirambeau, Blaye, Le Verdon-sur-Mer, C. Ferret, Arcachon, Bordeaux, Libourne, Bergerac, Périgueux, Brantôme, Thiviers, Poitiers, Chauvigny, Montmorillon, Lussac-les-Châteaux, Civray, Ruffec, Confolens, Bellac, Limoges, St-Junien, St-Léonard-de-Noblat, Guéret, Bourganeuf, Aubusson, Montluçon, Châteauroux, La Châtre, Le Blanc, Argenton-sur-Creuse, La Souterraine, Châtellerault, Tours, Amboise, Blois, Vendôme, Le Mans, Laval, Vitré, Mayenne, Alençon, Sées, Argentan, Falaise, Caen, Bayeux, St-Lô, Vire, Flers, Domfront, Mortain, Fougères, Laval, Châteaubriant, Sablé-sur-Sarthe, La Flèche, Château-du-Loir, Château-la-Vallière, Langeais, Loches, Selles-sur-Cher, Romorantin-Lanthenay, Vierzon, Bourges, Issoudun, Valençay, Orléans, Châteauneuf, Olivet, Gien, Cosne-Cours-sur-Loire, La Charité-sur-Loire, Dreux, Chartres, Nogent-le-Rotrou, Mortagne-au-Perche, Verneuil-sur-Avre, L'Aigle, Évreux, Mantes-la-Jolie, Vernon, Pontoise, Rambouillet, Pithiviers, Artenay

Terrasson-Lavilledieu, Brive-la-Gaillarde, Tulle, Argentat, Aurillac, Rocamadour, Souillac, Gourdon, Cahors, Figeac, Decazeville, Villefranche-de-Rouergue, Rodez, Lacanau, St-André-de-Cubzac, Mussidan, Langon, La Réole, Marmande, Tonneins, Aiguillon, Villeneuve-sur-Lot, Agen, Moissac, Caussade, Montauban, Gaillac, Albi, Carmaux, Castelsarrasin, Lectoure, Fleurance, Grisolles, Toulouse, Mont-de-Marsan, Tartas, St-Sever, Castets, Mimizan, Labouheyre, Bazas, Casteljaloux, Condom, Auch, L'Isle-Jourdain, Mirande, Lavaur, Graulhet, Castres, Mazamet, Bayonne, Biarritz, Donostia-San Sebastián, Irún, Hendaye, St-Jean-de-Luz, Dax, Orthez, Pau, Oloron-Ste-Marie, Tarbes, Lannemezan, Lourdes, Bagnères-de-Bigorre, St-Gaudens, St-Girons, Foix, Pamiers, Carcassonne

Spain:
Santander, Bilbao, Costa Montañesa, Llanes, San Vicente de la Barquera, Torrelavega, Reinosa, Santoña, Laredo, Castro Urdiales, Getxo, Gernika-Lumo, Durango, Amurrio, Tolosa, Beasain, Vitoria-Gasteiz, Pamplona, Picos de Europa, Potes, Oña, C. de Ajo, Costa Vasca, Costa Basque

Ferries: SANTANDER, PLYMOUTH, PORTSMOUTH, ROSSLARE, CORK

5 · 18 · 19

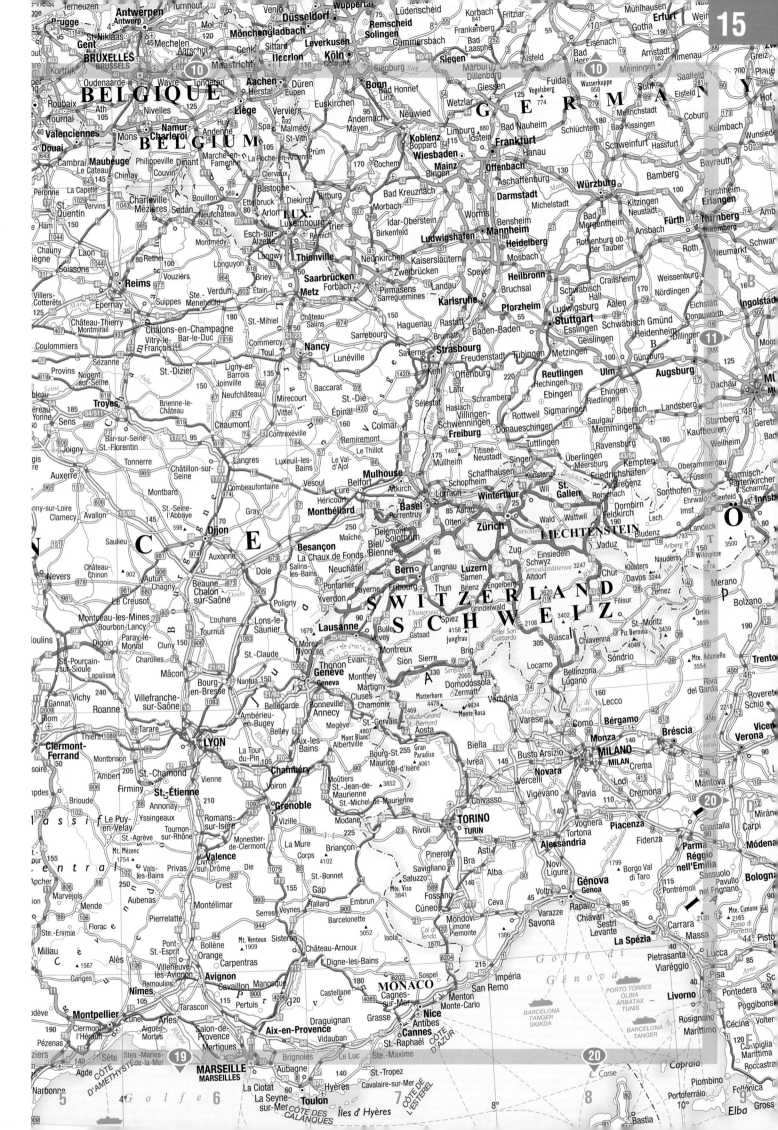

1   2   3   4

8°   6°   4°

COSTA VERDE

PORTSMOUTH

A

C. Ortegal   Ortigueira   C. de Peñas   **Gijón**   **Xixón**   Villaviciosa   **COSTA MONTAÑESA**   **Santander**   C. de Ajo

Ferrol   Ribadeo   Luarca   Avilés   Santoña   Castro Urdiales   Getxo

A Coruña   Vivero   Mondoñedo   Salas   **Oviedo**   Pola de Siero   Llanes   San Vicente de la Barquera   Laredo   **Barakaldo**   **Bilbao**

C. Touriñán   Vimianzo   Carballo   Vilalba   Tineo   Cangas de Narcea   Grado   Langreo   Mieres   Torrelavega   Reinosa   Amurrio   Orduña   Durango

Corcubión   Ordes   Baamonde   **Santiago de Compostela**   Lugo   Melide   Villablino   Pola de Lena   Picos de Europa   Potes   Oña

C. Fisterra   Noia   Lalín   Becerreá   Sarriá   Villafranca del Bierzo   La Pola de Gordón   Riaño   Briviesca

Muros   Padrón   Chantada   La Robla   Saldaña   Osorno   Miranda de

Vilagarcía de Arousa   A Estrada   Monforte de Lemos   Ponferrada   **León**   Santo Domingo de la Calzada

Marín   **Pontevedra**   O Carballiño   Astorga   Sahagún   **Burgos**   Salas de los Infantes

Redondela   Ponteareas   **Ourense**   Pobra de Trives   La Bañeza   Valencia de Don Juan   Picos de Urbión

42°   **Vigo**   Celanova   Villalón de Campos   Palencia

Baiono   Tui   Xinzo de Limia   A Gudiña   Verín   Benavente   Medina de Rioseco   Aranda de Duero   Soria

Valença   Villalpando   Burgo de Osma

Caminha   Chaves   Bragança   Alcañices   Zamora   **Valladolid**   San Esteban de Gormaz

Viana do Castelo   Vila Pouca de Aguiar   Mirandela   Miranda do Douro   Toro   Tordesillas   Cuéllar   Boceguillas

Póvoa de Varzim   **Braga**   Murça   Fermoselle   Medina del Campo   Olmedo

B   Guimarães   Vila Real   **Salamanca**   Arévalo   Segovia   Sigüenza

Vila do Conde   Amarante   Peso da Régua   Torre de Moncorvo   Ledesma   Cañizal   Peñaranda de Bracamonte   Villacastín   Medinaceli

Matosinhos   Penafiel   Lamego   Vila Nova de Foz Côa   Vitigudino   Alba de Tormes   **Ávila**   El Molar   Guadalajara   Brihuega

Porto   Vila Nova de Gaia   São João da Madeira   Pinhel   La Fuente de San Esteban   Peñaranda   El Escorial   Alcobendas

Ovar   Oliveira de Azeméis   Viseu da Beira   Celorico da Beira   Vilar Formoso   Fuentes de Oñoro   Ciudad Rodrigo   Béjar   San Martín de Valdeiglesias   **MADRID**   **Alcalá de Henares**

Abergaria-a-Velha   Águeda   Guarda   Pico Almanzor   Leganés   Arganda

Aveiro   Mangualde   Belmonte   El Barco de Ávila   Arenas de San Pedro   Navalcarnero   Getafe

Mira   Tondela   Covilhã   Plasencia   Navalmoral de la Mata   Illescas   Parla   Aranjuez   Tarancón

40°   **Coimbra**   Mealhada   Fundão   Penamacôr   Hoyos   Coria   Talavera de la Reina   Maqueda   Ocaña

Figueira da Foz   Miranda do Corvo   Castelo Branco   Alcántara   Belvís de la Jara   **Toledo**   Quintanar de la Orden

Pombal   Proença-a-Nova   Navahermosa   Orgaz   Pedro Muñoz

Leiria   Tomar   Nisa   Valencia de Alcántara   Trujillo   Guadalupe   Madridejos   Alcázar de San Juan

Caldas da Rainha   Abrantes   Gavião   Portalegre   **Cáceres**   Miajadas   Malagón   Tomelloso

Peniche   Torres Novas   Arronches   Zorita   Logrosán   Fuente el Fresno   Manzanares

C. Carvoeiro   Santarém   Almeirim   Coruche   Monforte   Campo Maior   Villanueva de la Serena   Ciudad Real   Daimiel   Valdepeñas

C   Torres Vedras   Cartaxo   Azambuja   Vila Franca de Xira   Estremoz   **Mérida**   Don Benito   Almendralejo   Castuera   Almodóvar del Campo   Almagro   Villahermosa

Mafra   Montijo   Vendas Novas   Elvas   **Badajoz**   La Albuera   Villafranca de los Barros   Hinojosa del Duque   Puertollano   Villanueva de los Infantes

Sintra   **LISBOA**   **LISBON**   Montemor-o-Novo   Olivenza   Zafra   Los Santos de Maimona   Peñarroya-Pueblonuevo   Pozoblanco   Paso Despeñaperros

C. da Roca   Estoril   Oeiras   Barreiro   Évora   Reguengos de Monsaraz   Jerez de los Caballeros   Llerena   Azuaga   Espiel   La Carolina

Almada   Setúbal   Alcácer do Sal   Viana do Alentejo   Barrancos   Fregenal de la Sierra   Fuente Obejuna   Andújar   Bailén   Linares   Villacarrillo

C. Espichel   B. de Setúbal   Grândola   Torrão   Moura   Aracena   Montoro   Úbeda

38°   Santiago do Cacém   Ferreira do Alentejo   **Beja**   Baragem de Alqueva   Cortegana   Valverde del Camino   **Córdoba**   Castro del Río   Baeza

C. de Sines   Sines   Aljustrel   Nerva   Posadas   La Carlota   Martos   **Jaén**   Huelma

Cercal   Mértola   La Palma del Condado   Palma del Río   Montilla   Baena   Cabra   Alcalá la Real   Cúllar de Baza

Odemira   Sanlúcar la Mayor   Carmona   Écija   Lucena   Estepa   Priego de Córdoba

Monchique   Portimão   Lagoa   Loulé   Vila Real de Santo António   Ayamonte   Almonte   **Sevilla**   Marchena   Osuna   Santa Fe   Guadix

D   Vila do Bispo   Albufeira   Faro   Tavira   **Huelva**   Dos Hermanas   Utrera   Morón de la Frontera   Archidona   Antequera   Vélez Málaga   **Granada**   Alhama de Granada   Orjiva   Berja   **Almería**

Sagres   Lagos   Olhão   Lebrija   Arcos de la Frontera   Campillos   Loja   Mulhacén

G. de Cádiz   **COSTA DE LA LUZ**   Sanlúcar de Barrameda   Ronda   **Málaga**   Motril

El Puerto de Santa María   **Jerez de la Frontera**   Coín   Torremolinos   Adra

LAS PALMAS DE GRAN CANARIA   **Cádiz**   San Fernando   Puerto Real   Medina Sidonia   Marbella   Fuengirola   **COSTA DEL SOL**

SANTA CRUZ DE TENERIFE   Chiclana de la Frontera   Vejer de la Frontera   Estepona   San Roque

36°   ISLAS CANARIAS   C. Trafalgar   **Algeciras**   La Línea de la Concepción   MELILLA

Str. of Gibraltar   Tarifa   Gibraltar (U.K.)   Ceuta (Esp.) (Spain)   SÈTE BARCELONA GÉNOVA   Alborán

C. Spartel   **Tanger**   Pta. de Europa   DEL SOL

Tangier   Martil

1   2   3   4

0   40   80   120   160 km

PORTUGAL   ESPAÑA   ESPAÑA   GALICIA   Castilla y León

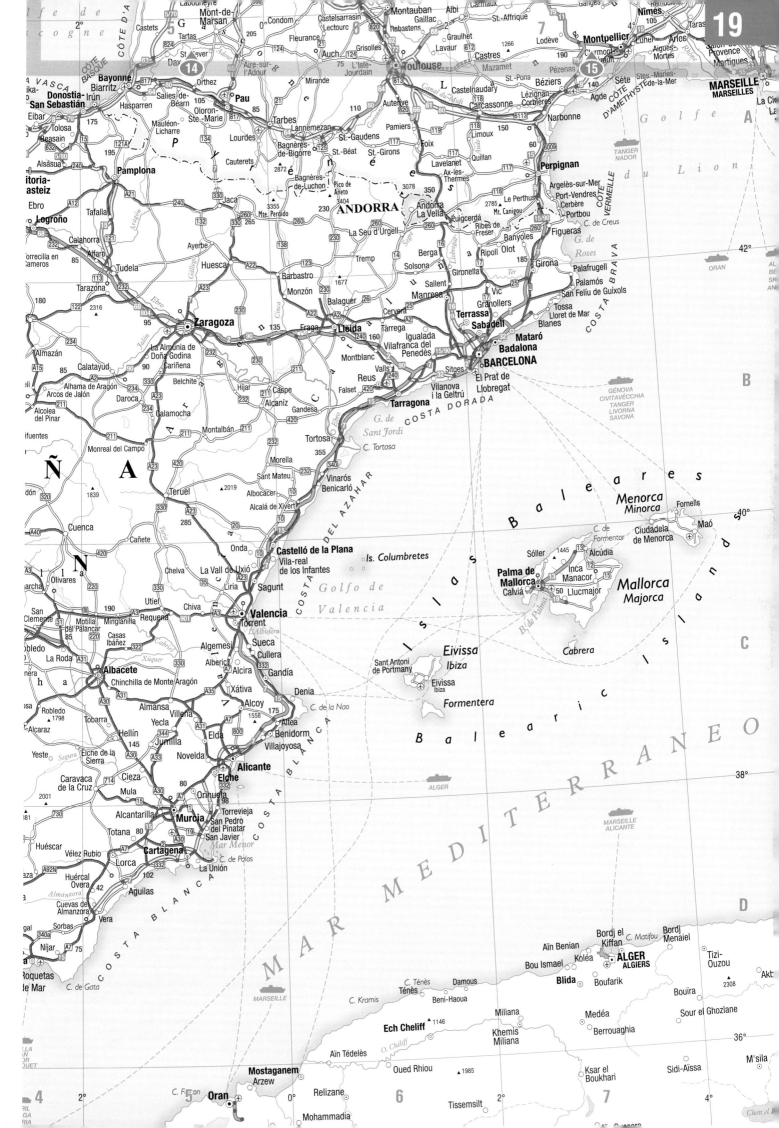

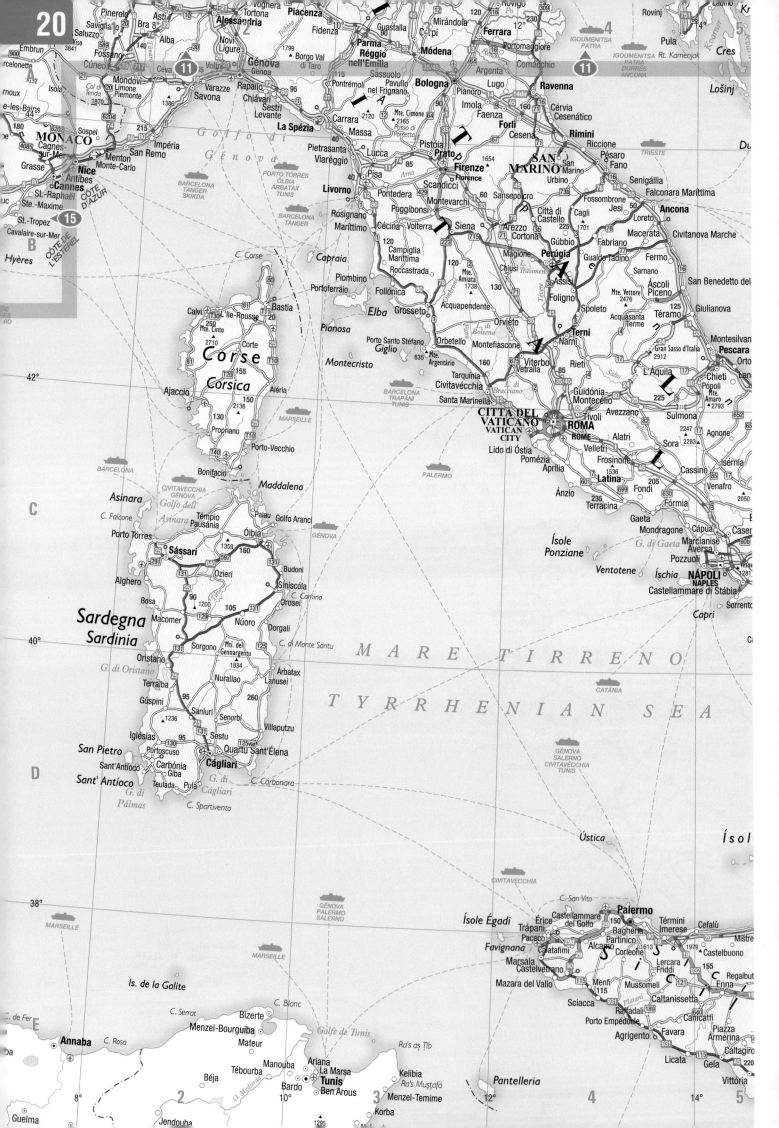

| 97 | Map pages at 1:750 000 |
| 182 | Map pages at 1:1 500 000 |

ICELAND
ÍSLAND
190 191
Reykjavik

Hammerfest
192 193
Tromsö

194
Narvik

196 197
195
FINLAND
SUOMI

Oulu

198 199 200
Umeå
Trondheim SWEDEN
SVERIGE
Vaasa

Turku
Helsinki
Saint Petersburg
Sankt Peterburg

31 32 33
Inverness Aberdeen

Gävle
46 47 48 49 50 51
Bergen Oslo Stockholm

Tallinn
ESTONIA
EESTI

RUSSIA
ROSSIYA

34 35
Glasgow Edinburgh

52 53 54 55 56 57
Stavanger Örebro
Kristiansand

Gothenburg Göteborg

Riga
LATVIA
LATVIJA

26 27 36 37
Belfast

58 60 62
Ålborg 61 63
DENMARK 59
DANMARK Copenhagen
Esbjerg København
Malmö

LITHUANIA
LIETUVA

Vilnius

IRELAND UNITED
KINGDOM
28 Dublin 38 Manchester
29 Cork 30 Liverpool 40 41
39
Cardiff Birmingham
42 43 44 45
Plymouth London
Calais

Kaliningrad RUSSIA
ROSSIYA
Gdansk
64 Kiel 65 66 67 68 69
Hamburg
Szczecin
70 71 72 73 Berlin 76 77 Warsaw
NETHERLANDS Bremen Hanover 74 75 POLAND Warszawa
NEDERLAND Hannover POLSKA Brest
Amsterdam 80 81 84 85 86 87
Rotterdam 82 83 Leipzig
Antwerp GERMANY Dresden Wroclaw Kraków
Brussels Düsseldorf DEUTSCHLAND
78 79 Cologne Frankfurt Prague
BELGIUM Köln Praha 96 97 SLOVAKIA
BELGIQUE CZECHIA Brno SLOVENSKA REP
88 89 90 91 Luxembourg Nuremberg ČESKA REPUBLIKA 98 99
Le Havre LUXEMBOURG Nürnberg 94 95
Brest 92 93 Munich Vienna Wien
Paris Strasbourg Stuttgart München AUSTRIA Bratislava Budapest
101 Salzburg ÖSTERREICH HUNGARY
Rennes 102 103 104 105 106 107 108 109 110 111 112 113 MAGYARORSZAG
100 Dijon LIECHTENSTEIN Innsbruck Graz Szeged
Nantes Basel Zürich SLOVENIA 124 125 126 ROMÂNIA
FRANCE Geneva SWITZERLAND Ljubljana SLOVENIJA Zagreb CROATIA Timişoara
114 115 116 117 Genève SCHWEIZ 120 121 122 123 HRVATSKA Belgrade Bucharest
Clermont- Lyon 118 119 Milan Venice Beograd Bucureşti
Ferrand Turin Milano Venézia BOSNIA 127
A Coruña 128 129 Torino Bologna HERZEGOVINA SERBIA BULGARIA
140 141 130 131 Genoa 134 135 BOSNA I Split SRBIJA BULGARIYA
Vigo Bordeaux Nice Génova SAN HERCEGOVINA Sofia
Porto 142 Bilbao Toulouse Marseilles 132 133 MONACO MARINO 136 137 Sarajevo 138 139 Sofiya
148 143 144 145 146 Marseille Florence ITALY MONTENEGRO KOSOVO Skopje
PORTUGAL 149 SPAIN ANDORRA 147 180 Firenze ITALIA CRNA GORA NORTH
150 151 152 153 Ajaccio Rome 168 169 170 171 MACEDONIA
154 155 ESPAÑA Zaragoza Roma Naples Bari SEVERNA
Lisbon Madrid Barcelona Nápoli 172 173 ALBANIA MAKEDONIJA
Lisboa 156 157 158 159 178 Táranto SHQIPËRIA Salonica
Valencia 174 Tirana 182 Thessaloniki 183
160 162 163 Palma 179 Tiranë GREECE
161 164 165 Alicante 166 167 Cágliari 175 ELLAS
GIBRALTAR Granada Seville Cordoba Palermo Catània Patras Athens
Málaga Sevilla 176 177 Patra Athina
MALTA 184 185

Distance table

Amsterdam

2945	**Athina**
1505 3192	**Barcelona**
1484 3742 2803	**Bergen**
650 2412 1863 1309	**Berlin**
197 2895 1308 1586 764	**Bruxelles**
2245 1219 2644 3037 1707 2181	**Bucuresti**
1420 1530 1999 2212 882 1358 852	**Budapest**
367 3100 1269 1783 956 215 2398 1573	**Calais**
533 3630 1817 270 1504 763 3021 2196 548	**Dublin**
1093 3826 1995 176 1696 941 3124 2299 726 346	**Edinburgh**
441 2499 1313 1508 550 383 1804 979 575 1123 1301	**Frankfurt**
1029 3080 2362 819 668 1145 1734 1550 1342 477 176 1067	**Göteborg**
447 2719 1780 1023 286 563 2014 1189 760 477 1486 485 582	**Hamburg**
1560 2539 2338 1063 475 1239 1834 1009 1431 1318 1236 1598 505 1113	**Helsinki**
2756 1145 2990 3653 2223 2706 690 1341 2911 3537 3657 2314 2891 2530 2350	**İstanbul**
965 2782 2090 1103 370 1081 2077 1252 1278 752 479 795 284 518 803 2593	**København**
256 2684 1376 1427 566 198 1983 1158 390 938 1116 180 986 404 1517 2499 714	**Köln**
2331 4460 1268 3723 2869 3141 3917 3222 2069 2617 2795 2400 3282 2700 3817 4342 3014 2339	**Lisboa**
480 3200 1387 458 1074 333 2591 1766 118 430 608 693 122 878 1991 3107 1188 508 2187	**London**
406 2661 1190 1613 749 209 2052 1227 424 972 1150 240 1172 590 1703 2472 900 186 2160 542	**Luxembourg**
1790 3809 617 3183 2364 1600 3262 2622 1528 1634 2254 1930 2742 2160 3276 3589 2473 1798 651 1646 1628	**Madrid**
1210 2683 509 2435 1541 1030 2154 1505 1063 1588 1789 1023 1994 1412 2525 2479 1722 1006 1777 1182 822 1126	**Marseille**
1085 2182 1038 2141 1060 890 1668 992 1072 1620 1798 683 1700 1118 1535 1993 1428 868 2315 1190 679 1655 538	**Milano**
2457 2930 3655 2223 1821 2585 1761 2099 2800 3348 3526 2312 1665 2115 1160 2605 2325 2387 4875 2918 2852 4224 3270 3027	**Moskva**
839 2106 1340 1788 594 789 1497 672 994 1524 1720 398 1347 765 1069 1907 969 580 2545 1094 555 2010 1011 473 2305	**München**
1347 3372 2680 503 960 1463 2667 1842 1660 773 729 1385 316 900 697 3089 590 1304 3604 1778 1490 3063 2312 2018 1823 1559	**Oslo**
510 2917 988 1922 1051 320 2307 1482 281 829 1007 591 1481 899 2012 2727 1209 495 1821 399 351 1280 782 857 2903 810 1799	**Paris**
950 2067 1750 1675 345 888 1362 537 1097 1635 1816 512 1013 652 770 1878 715 690 2870 1205 753 2329 1399 853 1853 388 1305 1061	**Praha**
1691 1140 1385 2706 1502 1520 1904 1263 1678 2226 2404 1289 2265 1683 1977 2237 1993 1474 2653 1796 1285 2002 876 606 3362 918 2583 1389 1309	**Roma**
2347 4223 1031 3736 2894 2150 3709 3010 2078 2626 2804 2344 3295 2713 3826 4034 3023 2318 401 2196 2178 550 1540 2078 4774 2371 3613 1830 2781 2446	**Sevilla**
2206 828 2453 3103 1673 2156 391 790 2361 2891 3087 1764 2341 1980 1800 550 2043 1949 3706 2461 1922 3037 1929 1443 2252 1367 2632 2177 1328 1687 3484	**Sofia**
1393 3418 2726 1063 1006 1509 2713 1888 1673 2254 1069 1431 505 946 167 3185 590 1350 3650 1824 1536 3109 2358 2064 1228 1600 530 1845 1351 2629 3659 2679	**Stockholm**
1256 2128 2366 1909 606 1350 1473 648 1542 2110 2268 1136 1274 886 361 1989 956 1152 3480 1680 1345 2960 2015 1469 1245 996 1506 1677 616 1853 3397 1439 1612	**Warszawa**
1168 1772 1856 1970 640 1114 1067 242 1308 1954 2034 731 1308 947 1088 1583 1010 916 3100 1524 993 2473 1353 818 2137 430 1600 1240 295 1126 2876 1033 1646 727	**Wien**
816 2426 1030 1938 863 619 1810 985 804 1352 1530 464 1497 915 2164 2323 1433 589 2296 922 410 1647 699 292 2552 303 1815 592 691 898 2061 1173 1861 1307 743	**Zürich**

548	**Dublin**	Dublin ▶ Göteborg = 477 km
726 346	**Edinburgh**	
575 1123 1301	**Frankfurt**	
1342 477 176 1067	**Göteborg**	
760 477 1486 485 582	**Hamburg**	

Distances shown in blue involve at least one ferry journey

km

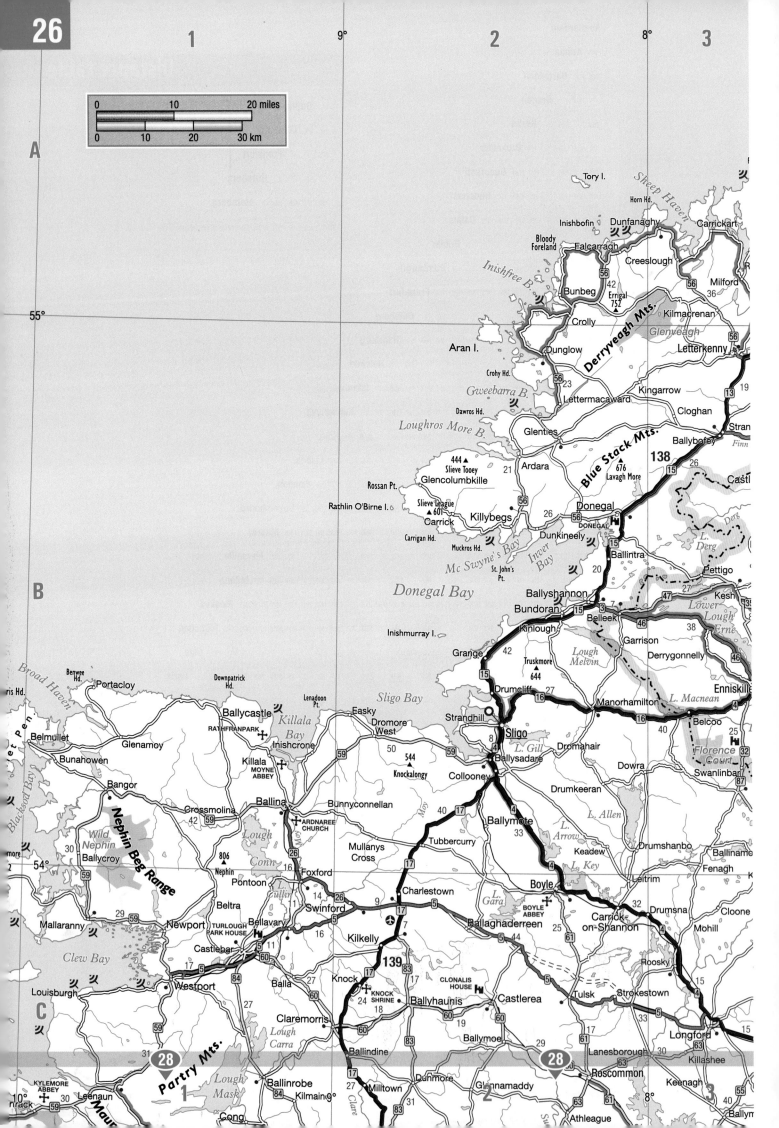

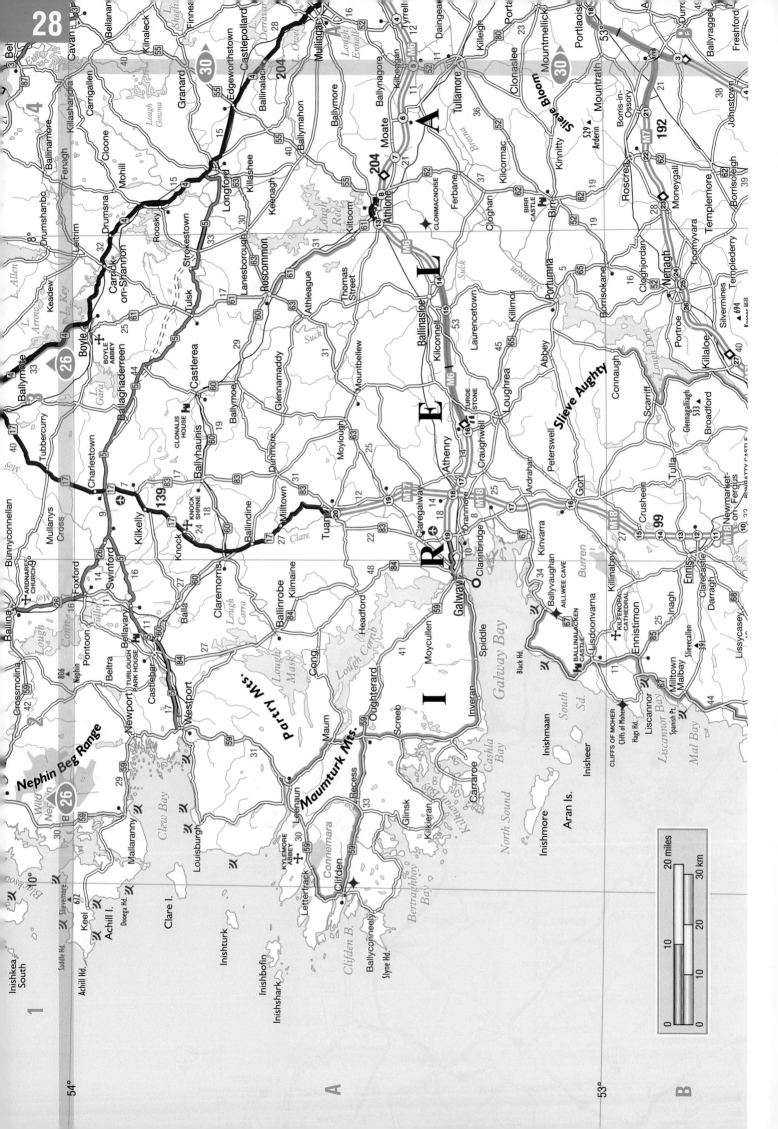

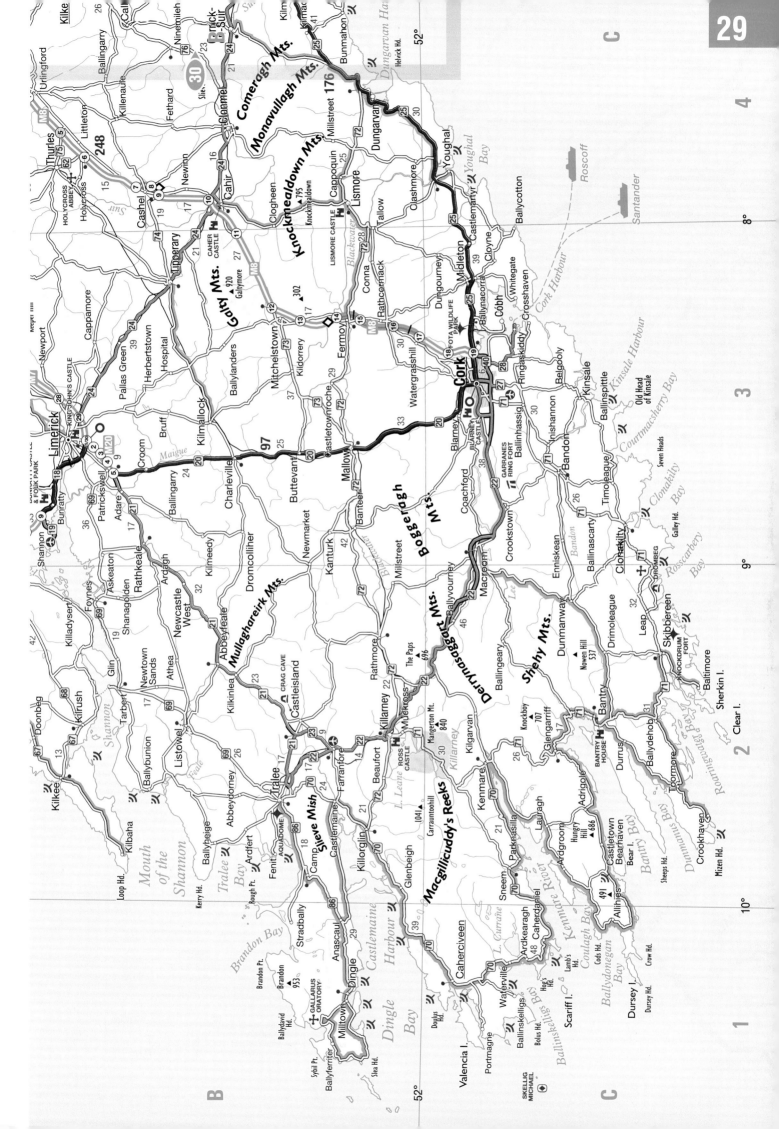

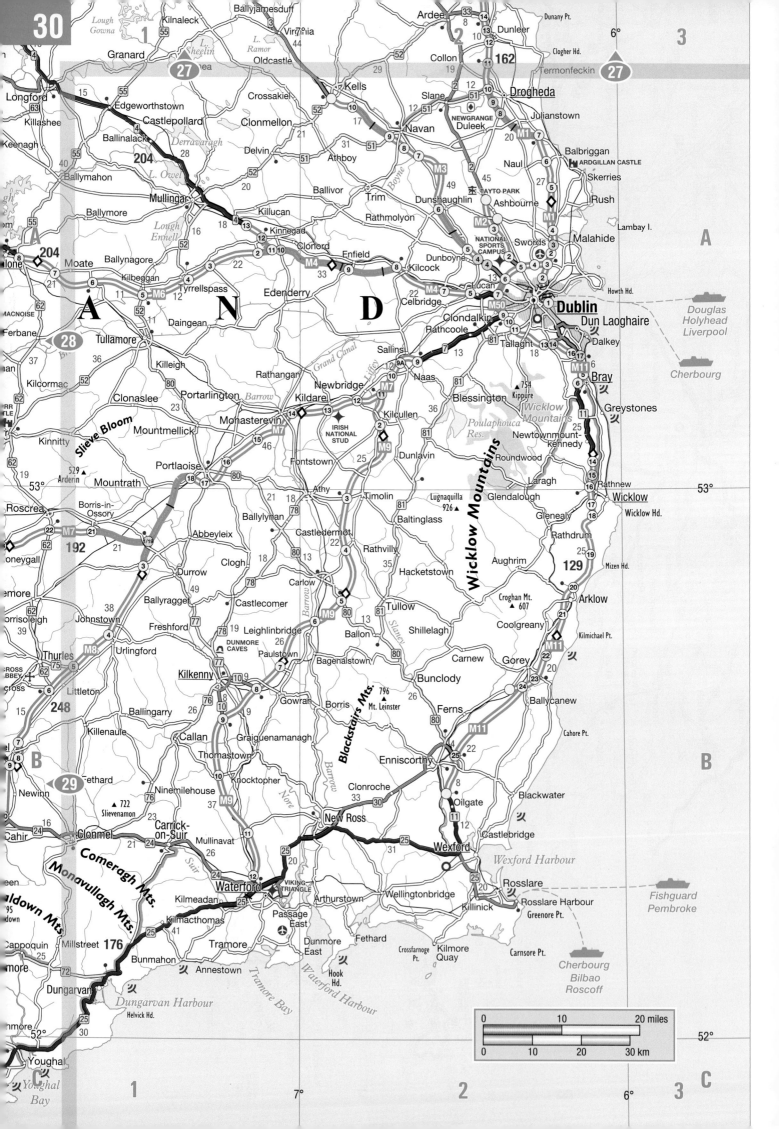

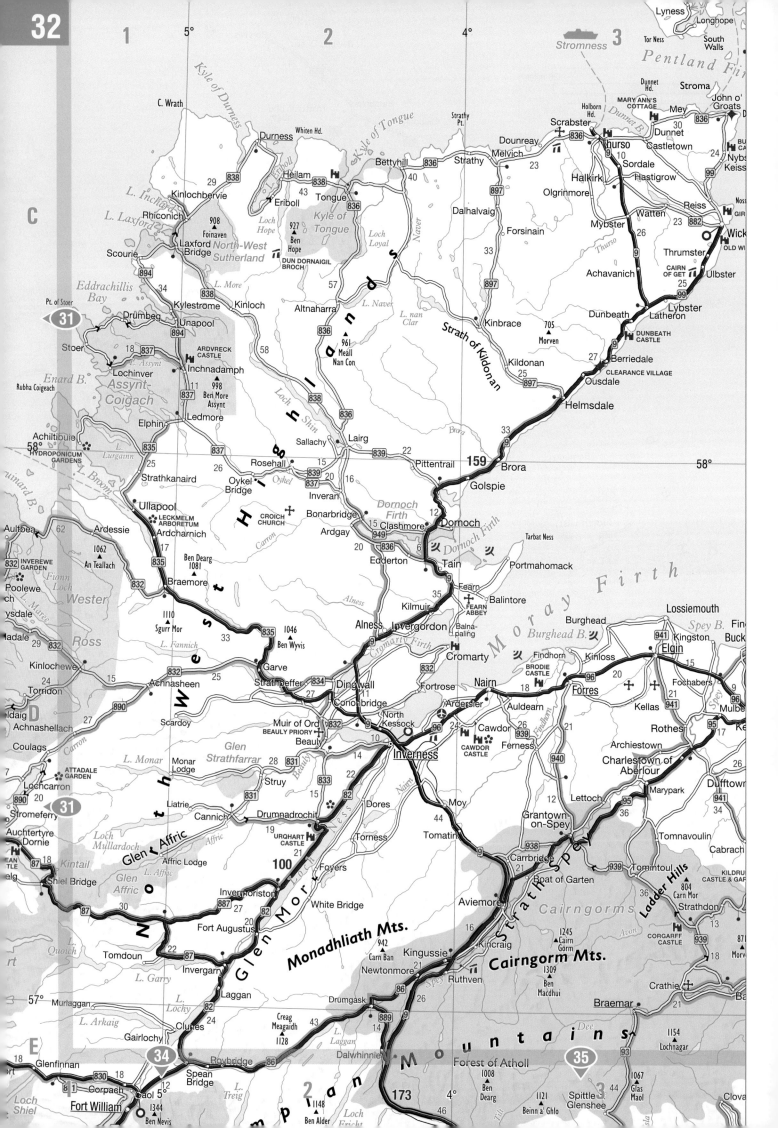

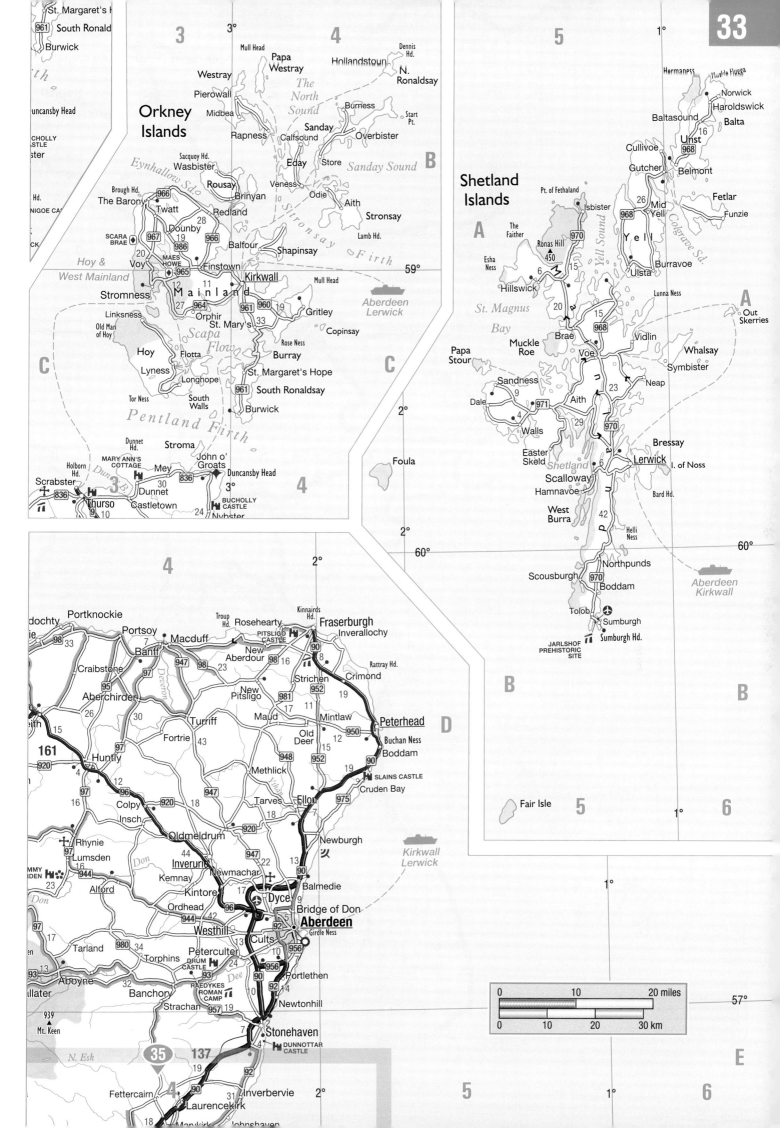

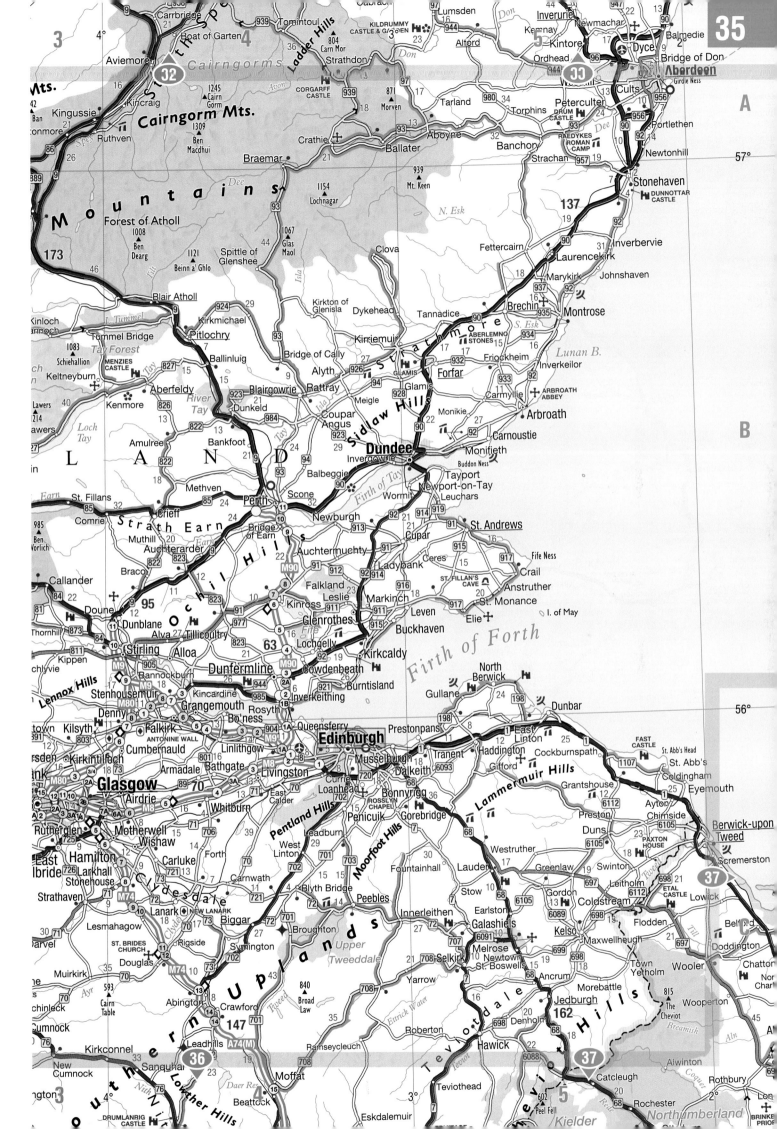

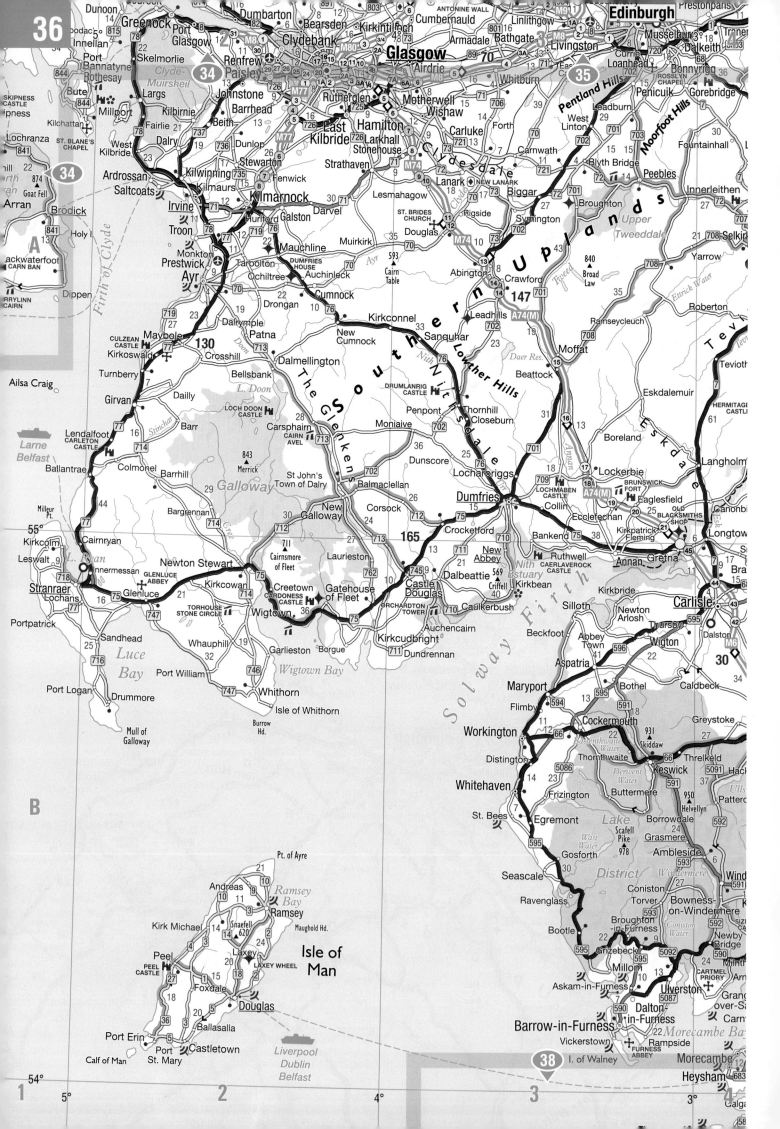

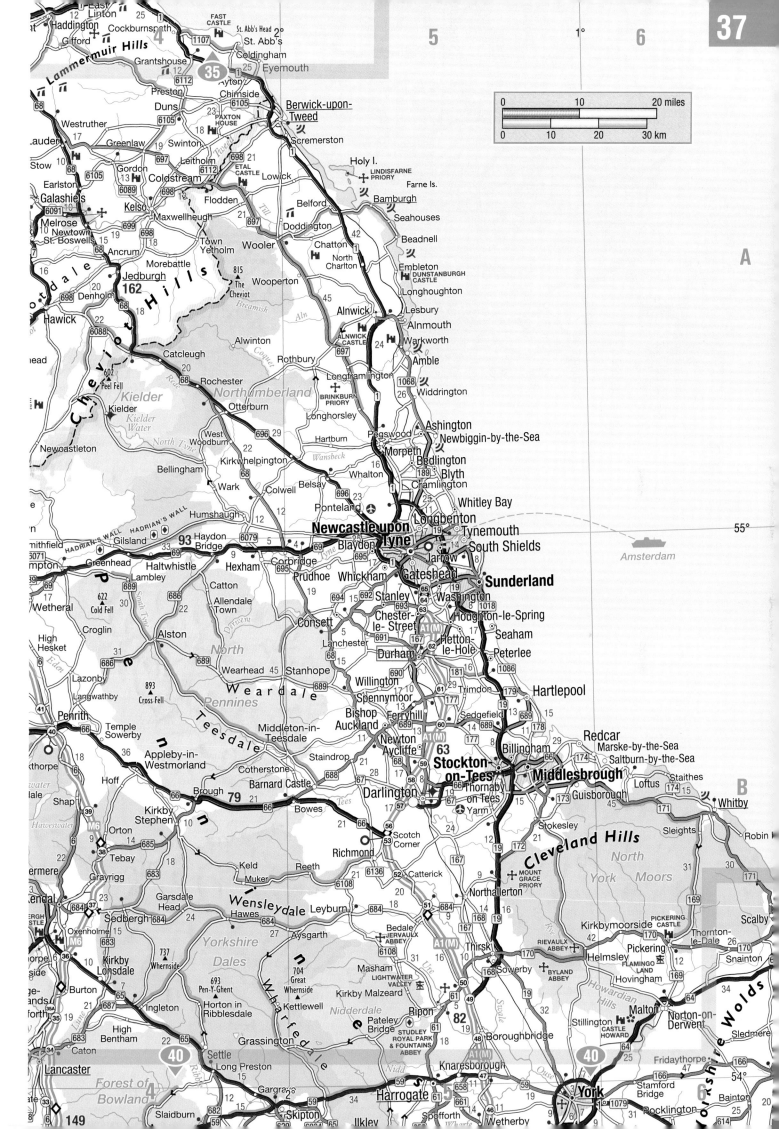

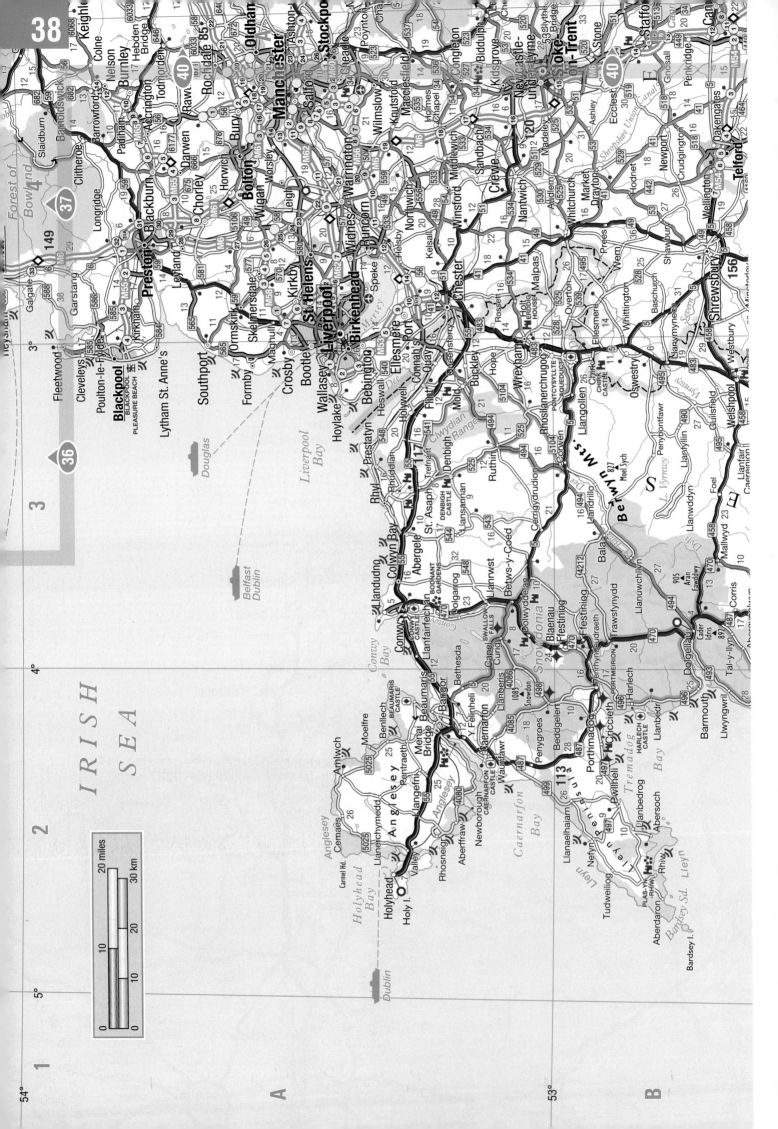

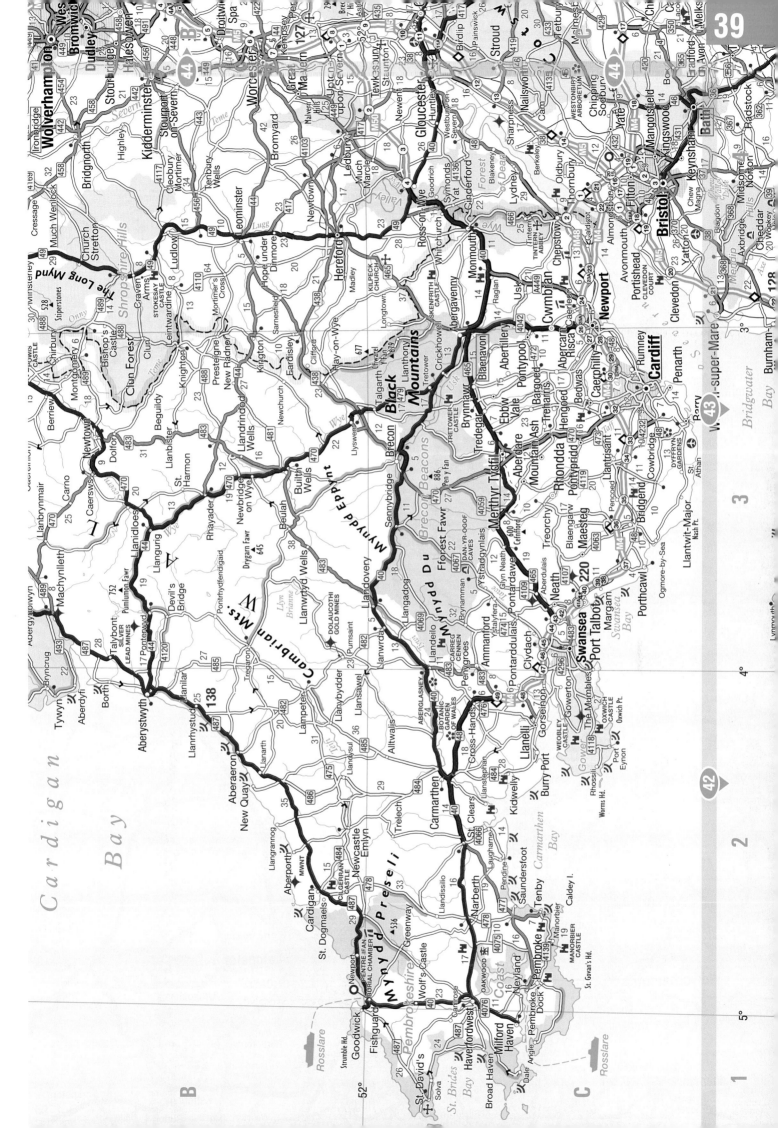

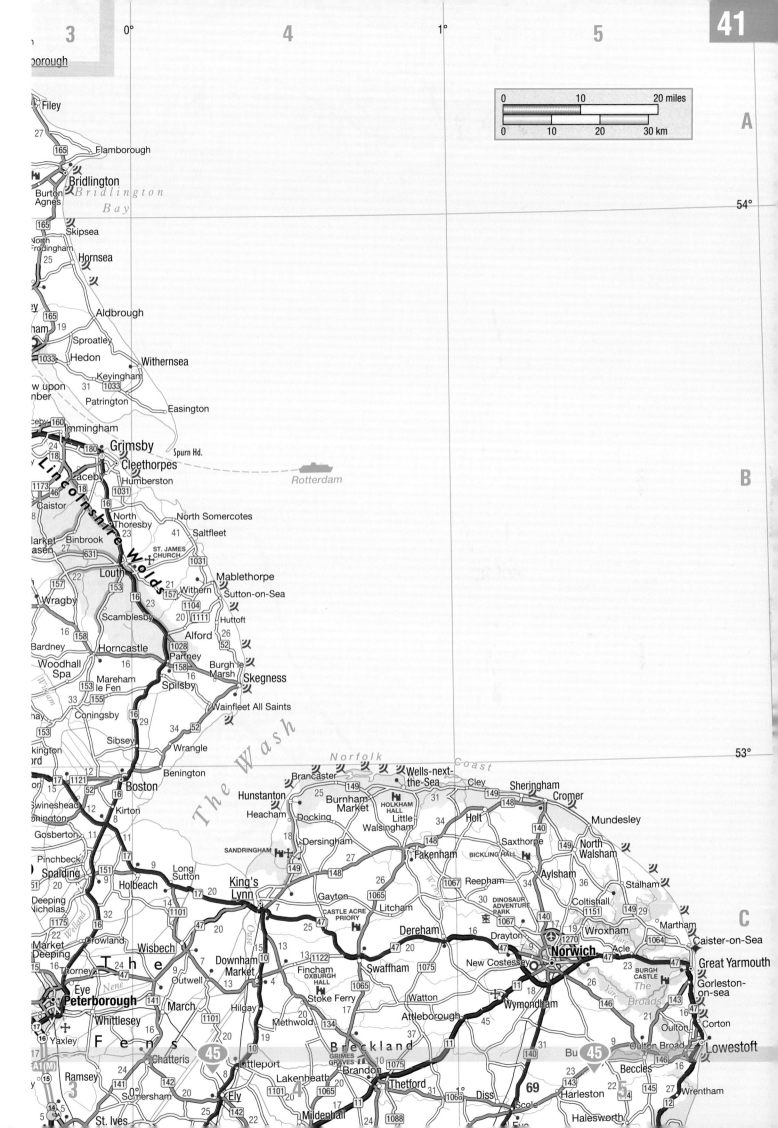

1

2

3

Pembrokeshire

St. David's Hd.
St. David's
Ramsey I.
Greenway
Wolf's Castle
Llangl
Carmarthen
Llandeilo
Mynl

St. Brides Bay
Solva
Camrose
Haverfordwest
Narberth
St. Clears
Cross-Hands
Ammanford
Ystalyfera

Skomer I.
Broad Haven
Milford Haven
Neyland
Laugharne
Llanstephan
Llanelli
Clydach
Pontarddulais

Skokholm I.
Dale
Angle
Pembroke Dock
Pembroke
Tenby
Saundersfoot
Kidwelly
Burry Port
Gorseinon

Rosslare
Manorbier
MANORBIER CASTLE
Caldey I.
Carmarthen Bay
WEOBLEY CASTLE
Gowerton
Swansea
Port Talbot
Marga

St. Govan's Hd.
Gower
Rhossili
The Mumbles
OXWICH CASTLE
Swansea Bay

Worms Hd.
Port Eynon
Oxwich Pt.
Po

A

B r i s t o l   C h a n n

Lundy
Lynmouth
Lynton
E x

Ilfracombe
Morte Pt.
Morte Bay
Woolacombe
Challac

North Devon
Croyde
Simonsb
Barnstaple

Barnstaple or Bideford Bay
Instow
Appledore

51°

Hartland Pt.
Westward Ho!
Bideford
South Molton

Clovelly
Hartland
Stibb Cross
Great Torrington
Chulml

Isles of Scilly

50°
6°
50°

Tresco
St. Martin's
Morwenstow
Venn Green
Winkleigh
North Tawton

Hugh Town
Crow Sound
St. Mary's
Bude Bay
Bude
Stratton
Hatherleigh
Coleb
South Ta

Widemouth
Holsworthy
Okehampton

6°
Poundstock
Roadford Res.

Cornwall
Boscastle
High Willhays
Chagford
Moretonhampstea

Tintagel Hd.
Tintagel
TINTAGEL CASTLE
Hallworthy
Launceston
LAUNCESTON CASTLE
Lydford
D a r t m o o r

Delabole
Port Isaac
Camelford
Marytavy
Dartmoor
Wideco
in the M

Port Isaac Bay
Pentire Pt.
St. Teath
Brown Willy
419
Bodmin Moor
Tavistock
Princetown

Padstow
176
SLATE CAVERNS
Gunnislake
Ashburto

B
Trevose Hd.
Wadebridge
Bodmin
Dobwalls
Callington
Bere Alston
BUCKFAST ABBEY
Buckfastleigh

St. Issey
Liskeard
BUCKLAND ABBEY
South Brent

Newquay
St. Columb Major
Restormel Castle
Saltash
Plymouth
Ivybridge

St. Enoder
Lostwithiel
Torpoint
Plymstock

Perranporth
EDEN PROJECT
Bodinnick
Looe
Devonport
Wembury
Newton Ferrers
Modbur

St. Agnes
St. Austell
Fowey
Polperro
Whitesand Bay
ROYAL CITADEL
Yealmpton
South

Portreath
Charlestown
Polruan
Bigbury
Bigbury Bay

HELIGAN GDNS.
Probus
Mevagissey Bay
Marlborough
Bol
Hea

Redruth
GWENNAP PIT
Truro
Mevagissey

St. Ives
Gwennap
Tregony
Gorran Haven

Carbis Bay
Hayle
Camborne
Penryn
Veryan

Pendeen
Zennor
POLDARK MINE
St. Mawes

St. Just
Marazion
Helston
Falmouth

Newlyn
Penzance
Falmouth Bay

Sennen
Mousehole
HALLIGGYE FOGOU
St. Keverne
The Manacles

Land's End
Porthleven
GOONHILLY

TREGIFFIAN BURIAL CHAMBER
Mullion
Coverack

Mount's Bay
Lizard

50°

Wolf Rock
Lizard Pt.
Roscoff Santander

1
5°
2
4°
3

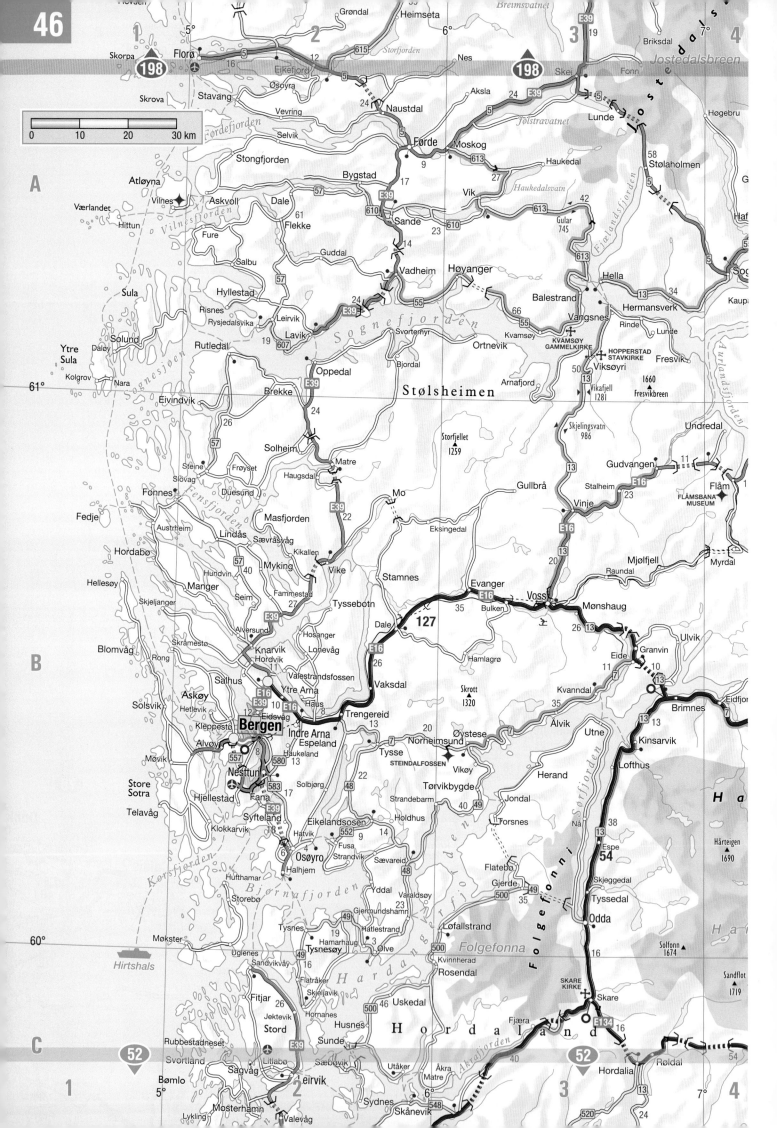

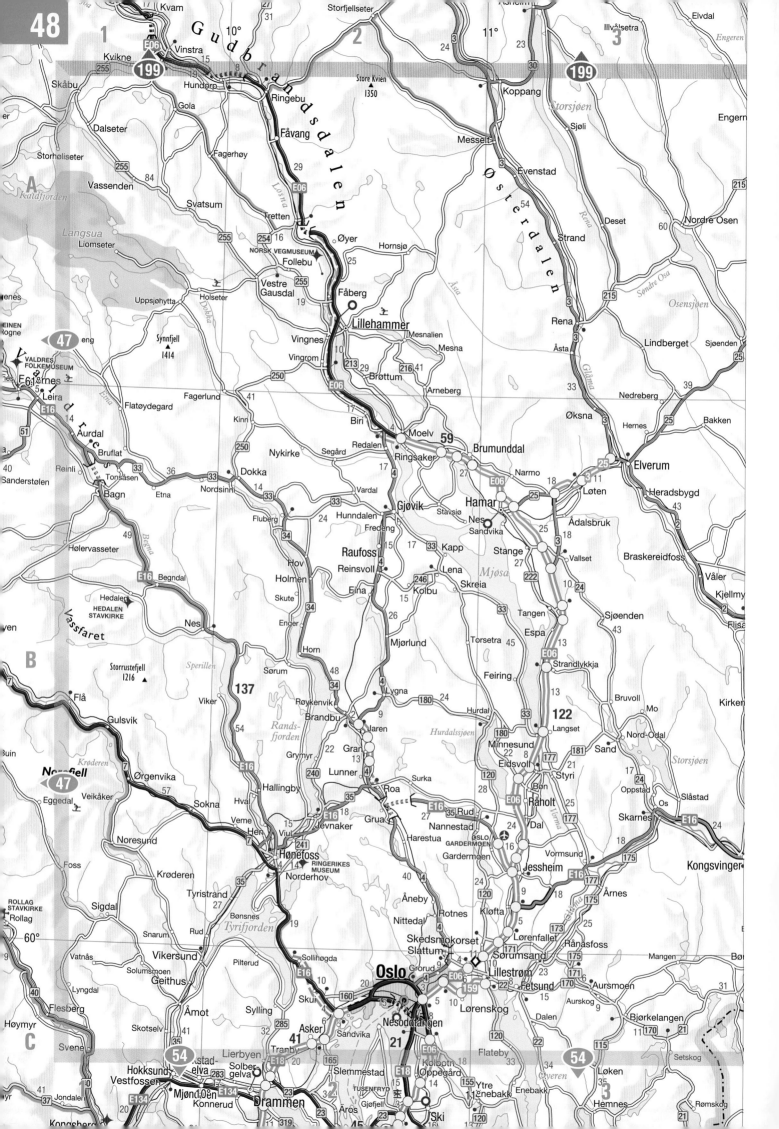

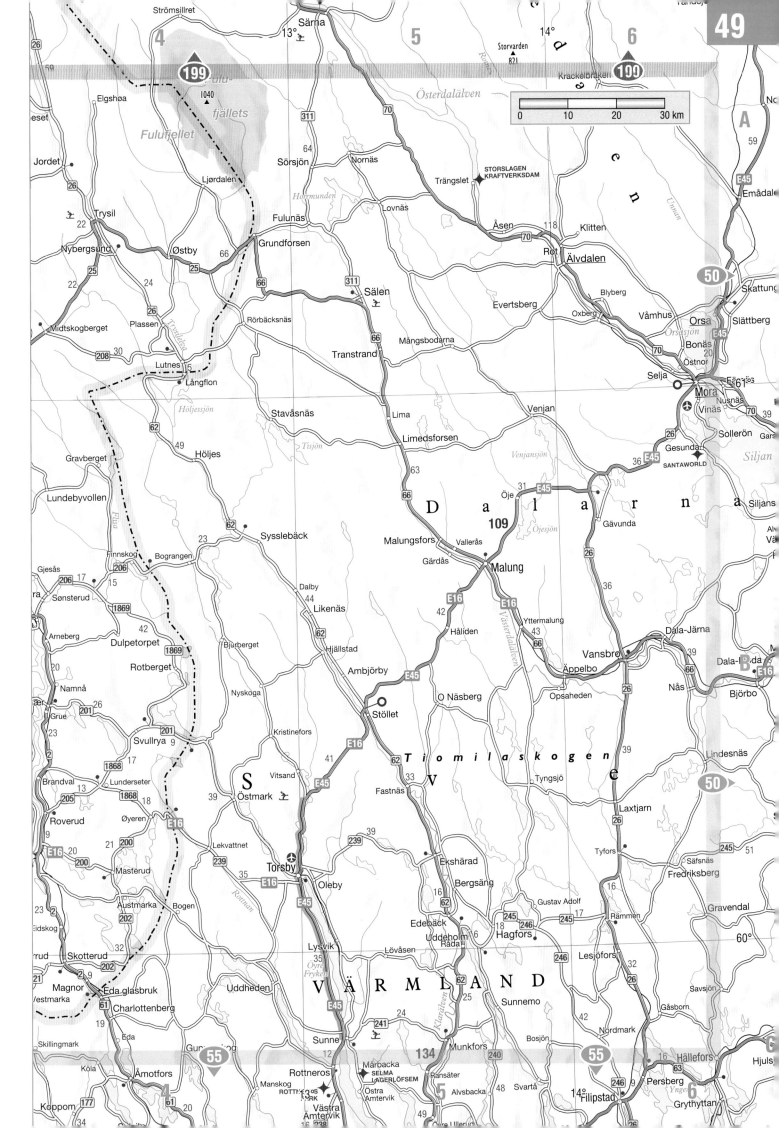

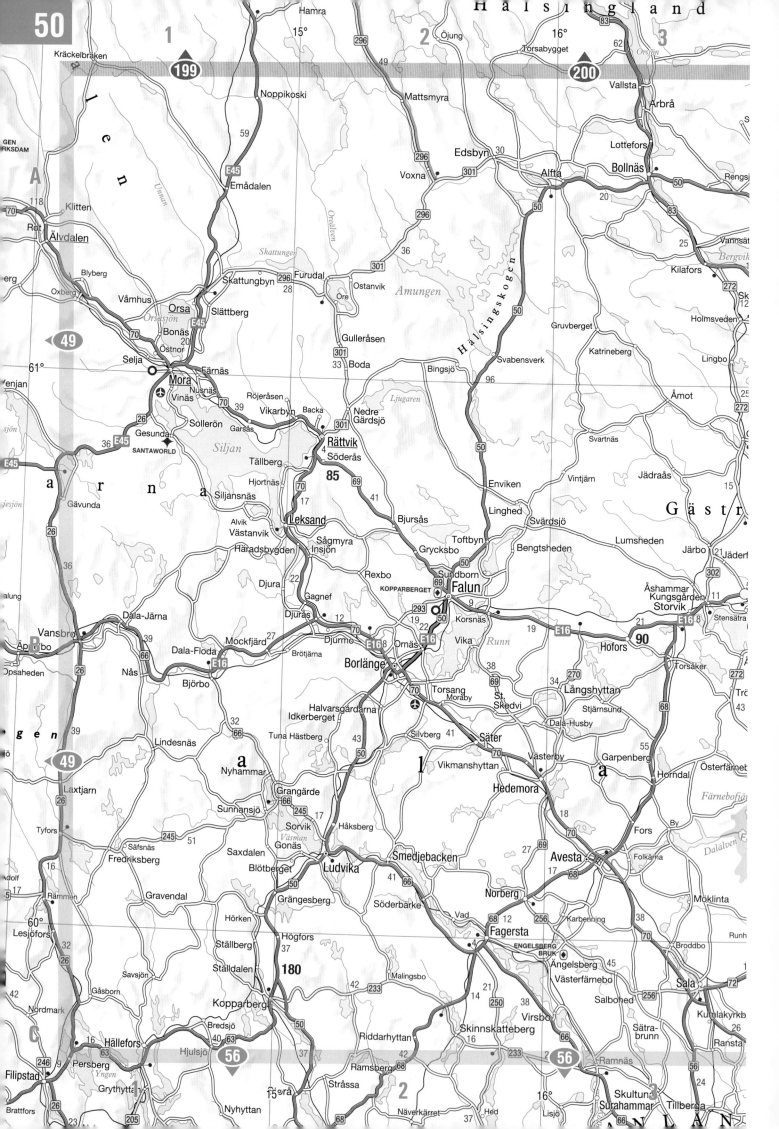

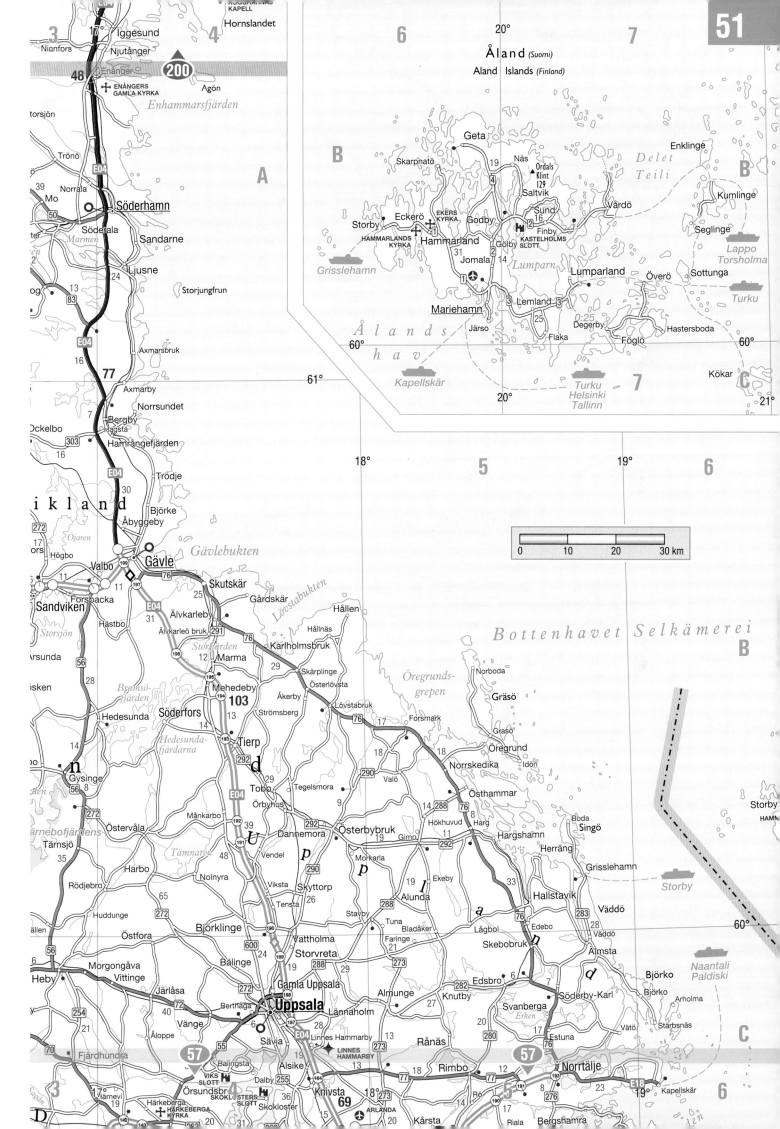

Iggesund
Njutånger
Hornslandet

ROGGKÄRRNÄS KAPELL

3 17°
Nianfors

48
ENÄNGER
ENÄNGERS GAMLA KYRKA

200

Agön

Enhammarsfjärden

4

6 20° 7

Åland (Suomi)
Aland Islands (Finland)

Enklinge

Delet
Teili

B

Kumlinge

Geta

Skarpnätö

B 19° Näs
Ordals
Klint
129
Saltvik

Sund

Vårdö

Seglinge

torsjön
Trönö

39
Mo Norrala

50
Söderala
Sandarne

Marmen

A

Söderhamn

Storby
Eckerö
EKERÖ KYRKA
HAMMARLANDS KYRKA Hammarland 1
Godby

Gölby 2 16
KASTELHOLMS SLOTT Finby

Lappo
Torsholma

2
24
Ljusne

Storjungfrun

Grisslehamn

31
Jomala 14

Lumparn

Lumparland Överö

Sottunga

Turku

og 13

83

1

Mariehamn 3 Lemland 3

25

0:25
Degerby

Hastersboda

16
E04
77

Axmarbruk

Ålands
h a v

60°

Järsö

Flaka Föglö

60°

7 Axmarby
Norrsundet

Kapellskär

20°

Turku
Helsinki
Tallinn 7

21°

Kökar
C

Bergby
Hagsta
Hamrångefjärden

303
16

Ockelbo

18° 5 19° 6

Trödje

30
E04

272
17 Ojaren
ors Högbo

i k l a n d

Björke
Åbyggeby

Gävlebukten

Scale: 0 10 20 30 km

B

Valbo 199
Gävle

11 11 197
Forsbacka
Sandviken

76

Skutskär

Gårdskär

Lövstabukten

Hållen

Hästbo
31

Älvkarleby
Älvkarleö bruk 291

76
Karlholmsbruk

Bottenhavet Selkämerei

B

Storsjön
Arsunda

56

196
12 Marma 29

Skärplinge
Österlövsta

Norboda

Gräsö

28

Bramsö-fjärden

Mehedeby
194
103

Åkerby
Strömsberg

Lövstabruk

17 Forsmark

Graso

Storfjärden

Hedesunda

Söderfors

14 13

Öregrunds-grepen

Öregrund
Idön

n
Gysinge 56
8

14

193
Tierp
292 d

Tobo

18

Valö 290

18

Norrskedika

Östhammar

272

Östervåla 192 39
Månkarbo

Örbyhus

Tegelsmora 9

14 288 76
Hökhuvud 8
Harg

Boda
Singö

Tärnsjö 191 U
Harbo 48

Vendel

290 p

Dannemora 292 Österbybruk

Morkarla

19 Gimo 292
Herräng

11
Hargshamn

Rödjebro

Nolnyra

Viksta

Skyttorp

p

19 l Ekeby

33

Grisslehamn

Storby

35

65

272
Huddunge Björklinge

26
Tensta

288
Stavby

Alunda
a

76
Edebo

Väddö
283

Storby
HAMN

56

Östfora

190
Vattholma

Tuna
Bladåker

Lågbol
Skebobruk

n

28 Väddö

60°

Heby
Morgongåva
Vittinge

600
Storvreta

24 189

288
Faringe 21

273

29

282
Edsbro 6

Almsta

d

Björkö

Naantali
Paldiski

Järlåsa

254 72

272
Gamla Uppsala
188
Berthåga
187
Uppsala

Almunge
Knutby 27

20

Söderby-Karl

Svanberga

Björkö

Arholma

70

3 17°

Fjärdhundra

57

40
Vänge
Sävja E04

Linnes Hammarby
LINNES HAMMARBY

Lännaholm 13

273

Rånäs

Erken 17 Estuna
280

Vätö Stärbsnäs

C

57
Norrtälje

E18

19 254
Härnevi

Balingsta
VIKS SLOTT

Dalby 255
SKOKLOSTERS SLOTT
Alsike

Örsundsbr
Härkeberga
HÄRKEBERGA KYRKA

4

69
Knivsta 273
18°

164

13

77 18
Rimbo 77 72
Rö
190

8 193
276
191

23 E18 19° Kapellskär

6

142 143

Skokloster

ARLANDA 20 Kårsta

Riala
Bergshamra

D

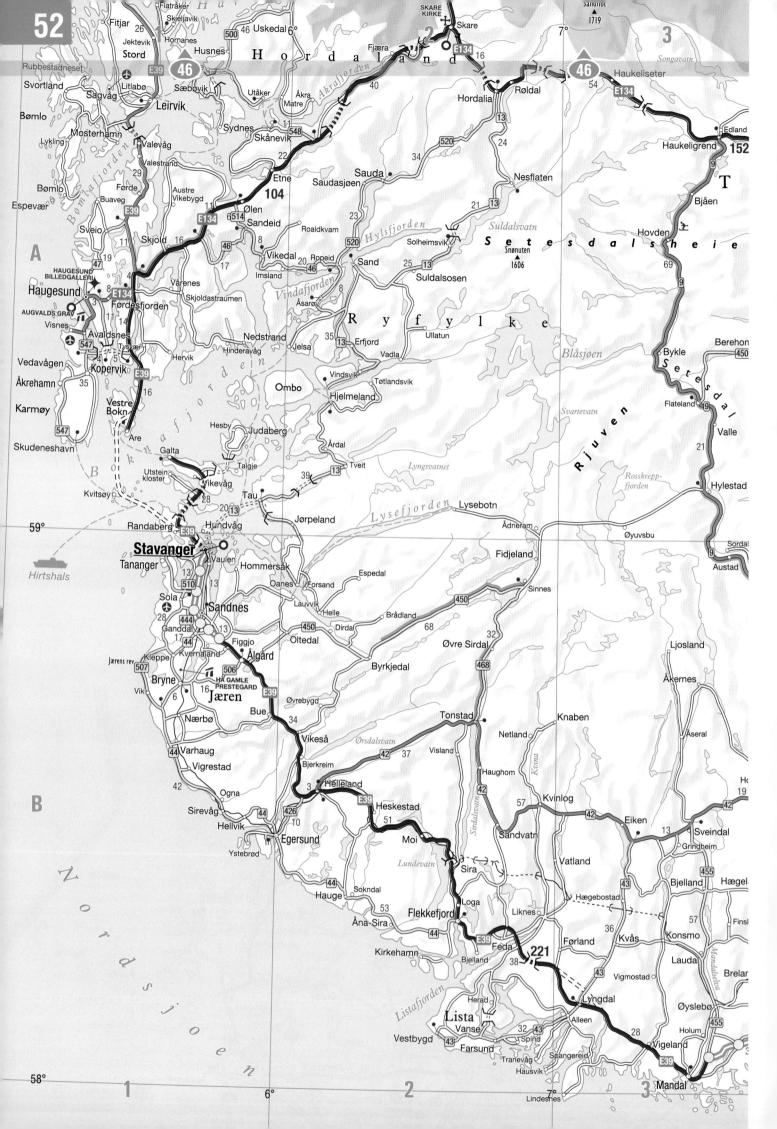

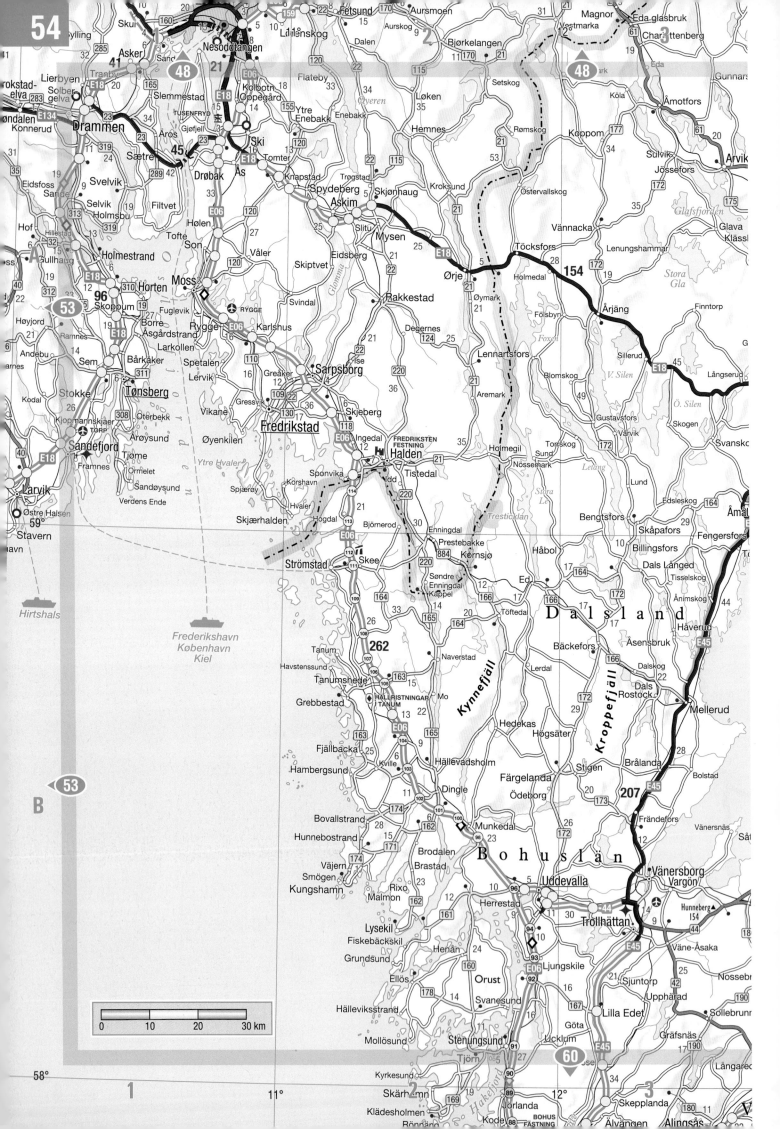

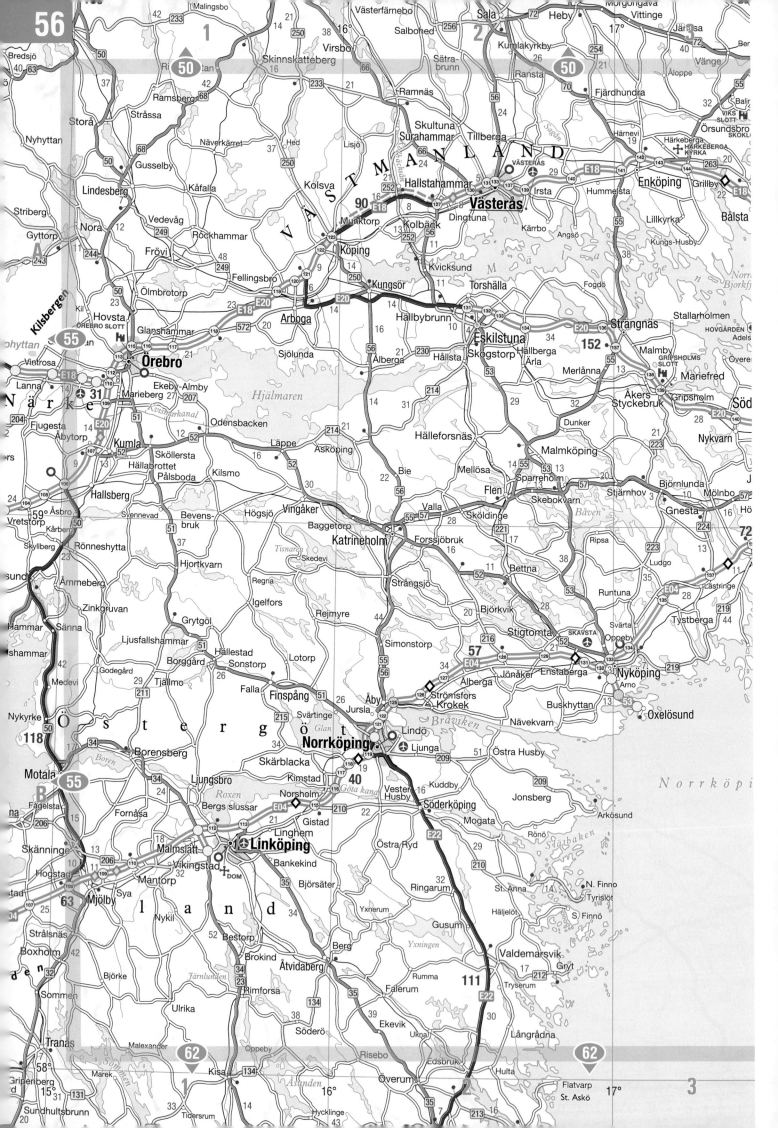

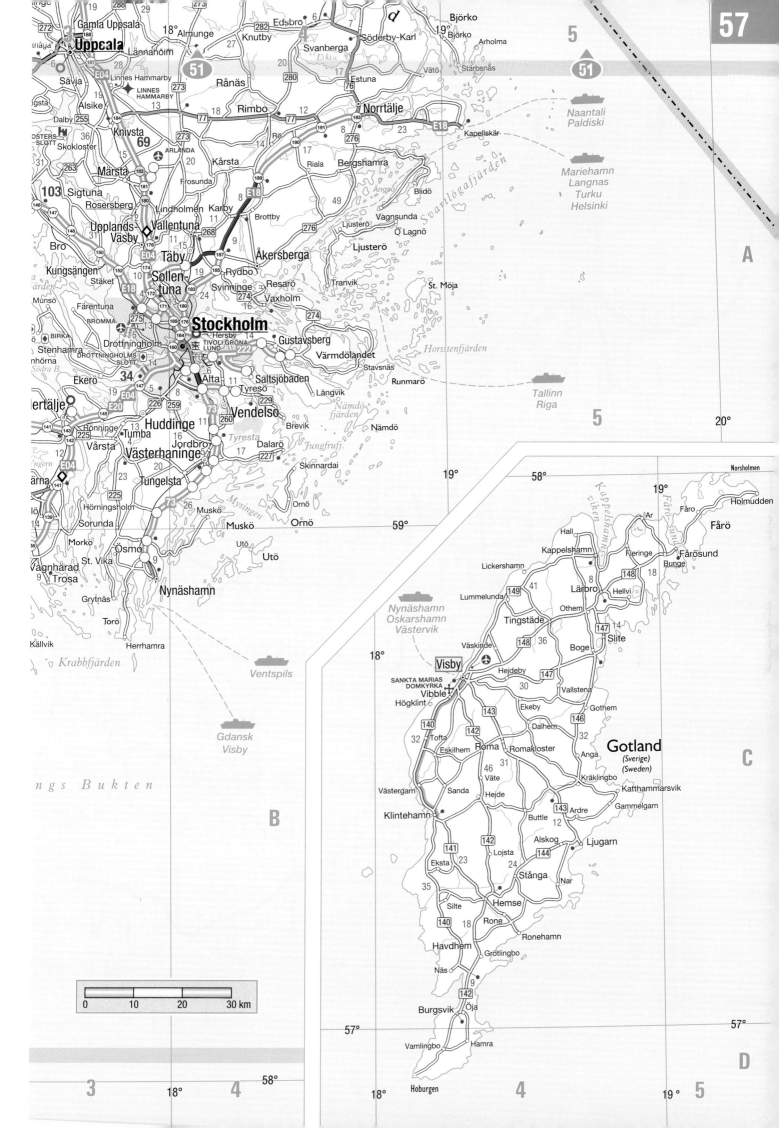

Gamla Uppsala
Uppcala
Björko
Björko
Arholma

Almunge
Edsbro
Knutby
Söderby-Karl
Svanberga
Estuna
Lännaholm
Linnes Hammarby
Rånäs
LINNES HAMMARBY
Alsike
Rimbo
Norrtälje
Kapellskär
Naantali
Paldiski
Dalby
Knivsta
Rö
Mariehamn
Langnas
Turku
Helsinki
ÖSTERS SLOTT
Skokloster
ARLANDA
Sigtuna
Rosersberg
Kårsta
Riala
Bergshamra
Märsta
Frosunda
Blidö
Upplands-Väsby
Vallentuna
Brottby
Vagnsunda
Ö Lagnö
Bro
Lindholmen
Karby
Åkersberga
Ljusterö
Ljusterö
Kungsängen
Stäket
Täby
Rydbo
Svinninge
Resarö
Tranvik
St. Möja
Sollen-tuna
Vaxholm
Färentuna
BROMMA
Stockholm
Gustavsberg
Horsstenfjärden
Stenhamra
Drottningholm
Hersby
Värmdölandet
Birka
DROTTNINGHOLMS SLOTT
Ekerö
Alta
Saltsjöbaden
Stavsnäs
Tallinn
Riga
Tyresö
Längvik
Runmarö
ertälje
Huddinge
Vendelso
Nämdö-fjärden
Nämdö
Vårsta
Tumba
Jordbro
Brevik
Tungelsta
Dalarö
Skinnardal
Ornö
Ventspils
Hörningsholm
Muskö
Musjön
Sorunda
Muskö
Ornö
Morko
St. Vika
Ösmo
Utö
Utö
Vagnhärad
Trosa
Nynäshamn
Oskarshamn
Västervik
Grytnäs
Toró
Gdansk
Visby
Källvik
Herrhamra
Krabbfjärden
ngs Bukten

Norsholmen
Hall
Kappelshamn
Ar
Fårö
Holmudden
Fårö
Lickershamn
Fleringe
Fårösund
Lummelunda
Läibro
Hellvi
Bunge
Nynäshamn
Oskarshamn
Västervik
Tingstäde
Othem
Väskinde
Slite
Visby
Boge
SANKTA MARIAS DOMKYRKA
Hejdeby
Vallstena
Vibble
Högklint
Ekeby
Gothem
Tofta
Roma
Dalhem
Gotland
(Sverige)
(Sweden)
Eskilhem
Romakloster
Anga
Kräklingbo
Väte
Katthammarsvik
Västergarn
Sanda
Hejde
Gammelgarn
Klintehamn
Ardre
Buttle
Alskog
Ljugarn
Lojsta
Eksta
Stånga
Nar
Silte
Hemse
Rone
Havdhem
Ronehamn
Näs
Grötlingbo
Burgsvik
Öja
Vamlingbo
Hamra
Hoburgen

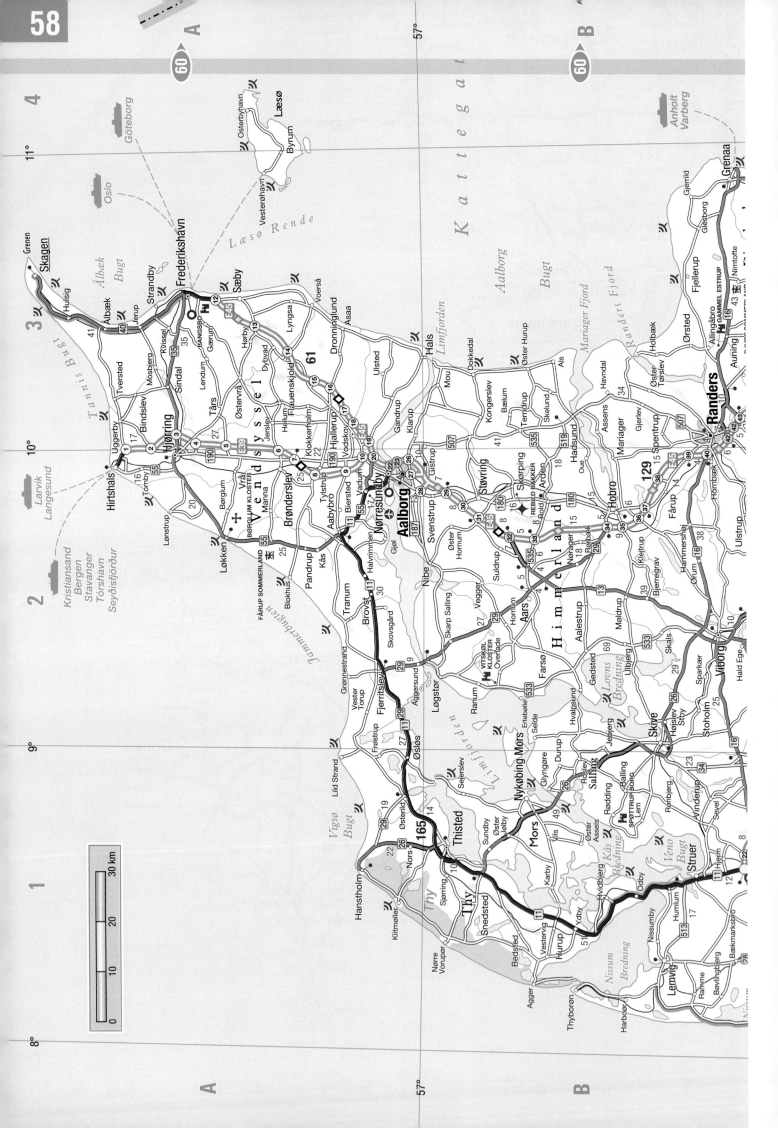

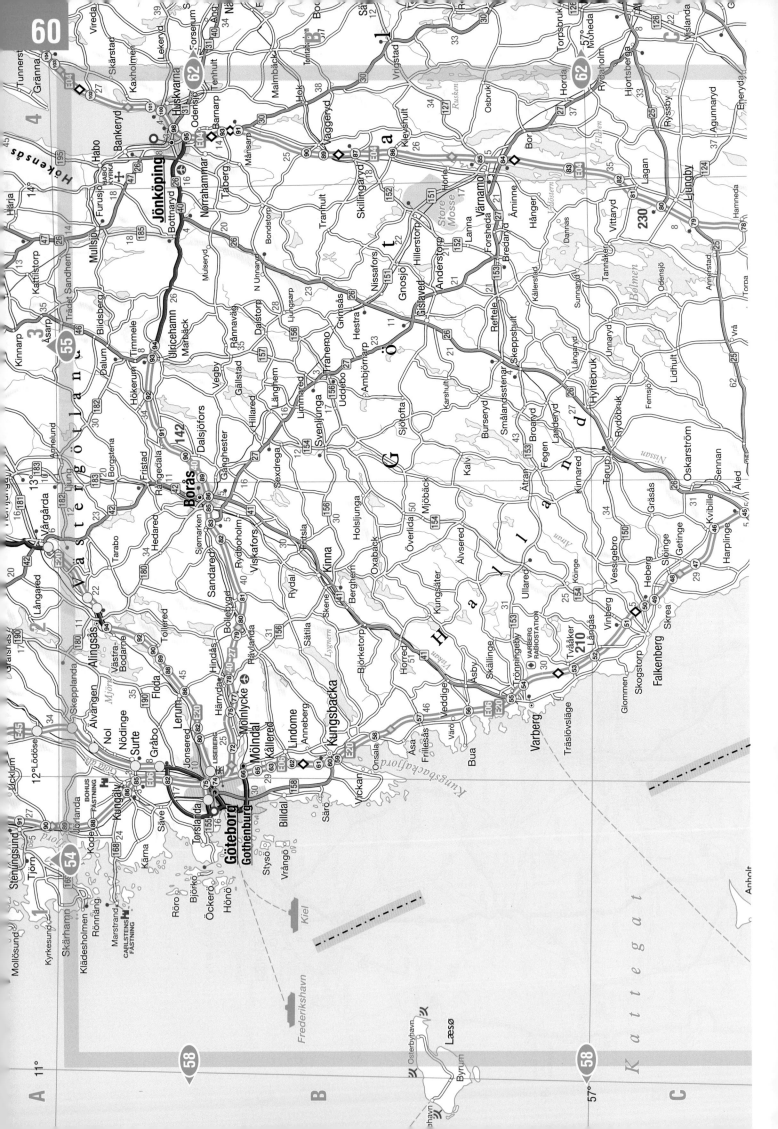

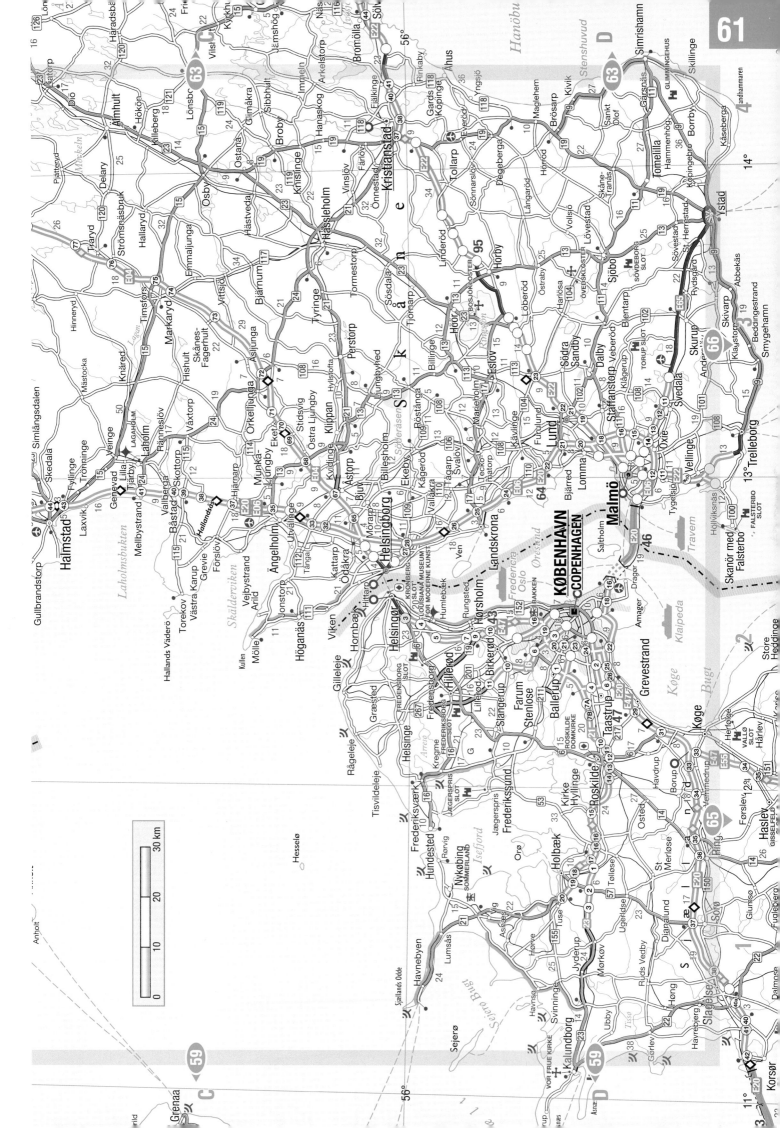

Öland
(Sverige)
(Sweden)

Gårdby
Stenåsa
Alby
Hulterstad
Seby
Eketorp
Ölands södra udde
Ottenby
Grönhögen
Degerhamn
Kastlösa
Mörbylånga
Hagby
Halltorp
Bergkvara
Torsås
Bromsebro
Fågelmara
51
136
130
48

Algutsrum
Färjestaden
Kalmar
14
Rinkabyholm
Smedby
Ljungbyholm
Vassmolösa
Trekanten
Tvärskog
Söderåkra
32
33
24

Lindsdal

E22
E22

186
Jämjö
Ramdala
Torhamn
Sturkö
Lyckeby
Aspö
Sturkö
Gdynia

Elveryd
Spjutsbygd
Holmsjö
Rödeby
Johannishus
Nättraby
Karlskrona
Hasslö

E22
28
28
44
7
5
63
61
27
23

Lyckebyån

Örsjö
Påryd
Gullabo
13
13
16

Gullabo

E

G

Eriksmåla
Skruv
Emmaboda
Johansfors
Långasjö
Vissefjärda
Eringsboda
Tving
16
16
20
120
13

N

I

K

Rävemåla
Dångebo
Konga
Hallabro
Bäckaryd
Bräkne-
Hoby
Aryd
122
120
27
30
27
41

Ronnebyån

E

Ronneby
RONNEBY
KYRKA
Kallinge
Listerby
Kuggeboda

E22

Linneryd
Tingsryd
Öljehult
Bälganet
122
120
8
31
22
24

Väckelsång
27
29

B
L
E

Mien

Urshult
Ryd
126
9
8

Åsnen

Lönashult
Häradsbäck
Fridafors
Vilshult
Kyrkhult
Olofström
Svängsta
Mörrum
Norie
Pukavik
Karlshamn
119
116
120
15
15
5
126
11
48
21
46
47

Mörrumsån

Farabol

Eneryda
Diö
Älmhult
Hökön
Killeberg
Lönsboda
Glimåkra
Sibbhult
Jämshög
Näsum
Sölvesborg
Bromölla
657
121
119
24
18
14
44
45
40
41

Ulvö

Lörby
Mjällby
Hörvik
Hanö
Hällevik
Nogersund

Pukaviks-
bukten

Hanöbukten

Klaipeda

Pjätteryd
Delary
Hallaryd
Strömsnäsbruk
Tåryd
78
77
25
26
32
120

Moskeln

maljunga

B
61
Osby

95

Hästveda
Broby
Knislinge
Hanaskog
Arkelstorp
Immeln
Fjälkinge
Kristianstad
118
118
11
19
15
23
21
32

Önnestad
Vinslöv
Färlöv
Hässleholm
119
19

Tollarp
Degeberga
Huaröd
Sönnarslöv
Everöd
Gärds
Köping
Rinkaby
Åhus
E22
40
41
38
37
9
24
19
19
19
118
118
36

Vollsjö
Löveström
Långaröd
deröd
by

Maglehem
Brösarp
Kivik
Vik
Sankt
Olof
Hammenhög
Borrby
Skillinge
Kåseberga
Sandhammaren
9
10
27
36
22
16
19
13
25

Stenshuvud

Simrishamn
Gärsnäs
Tomelilla
GLIMMINGEHUS
Köpingebro
11
11
36
9

C
61
Skåne-
Tranås

Ystad

0   10   20   30 km

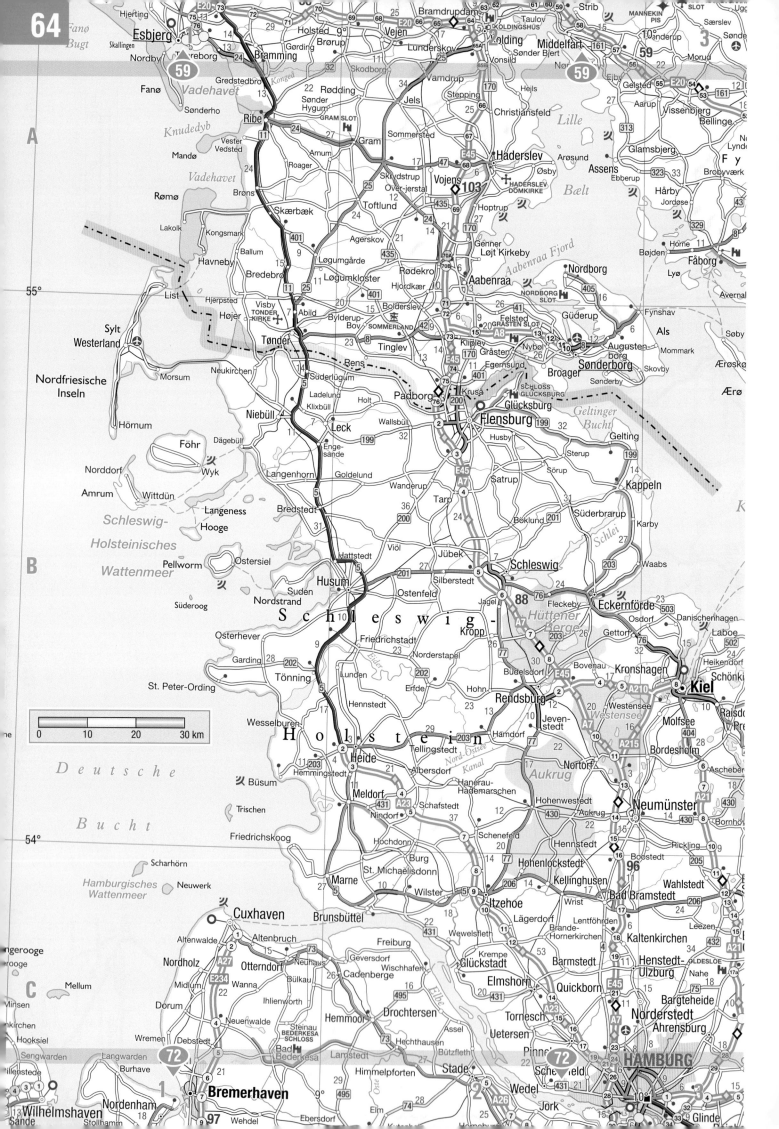

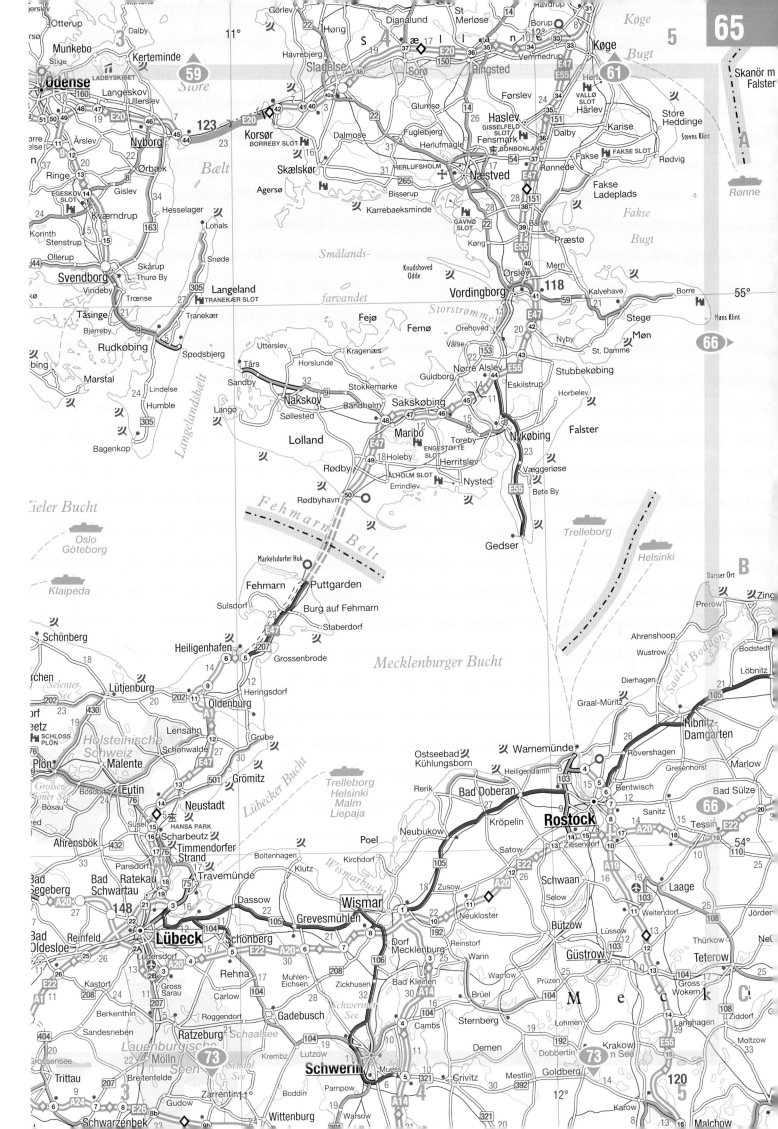

Stenshuvud

3 15° 4 16° 5

Vik

Simrishamn

MINGEHUS

Skillinge

A

0 10 20 30 km

h o l m s g a t t e t

Ertholmene

Hammeren

HAMMARSHUS

Sandvig-Allinge

Tejn

Bornholm
(Danmark)
(Denmark)

Rø

Gudhjem

Hasle

Klemensker

Nyker

Svaneke

Øster-
marie

Åkirkeby

Køge

Rønne

Nylars 38 28

Neksø

Pedersker

Snogebaek

55°

Jaroslawiec J. W

B

J. Kopań

203 64 Wieprza

Darłowo

Stary
Jaroslaw

Dąbki MUZEUM
DARŁOWO

Sławno

68

E28

Łazy J.
Bukowo 203 32 6

Ostrowiec

20

Mielno J. Jamno Jamno Lejkowo

Ustronie
Morskie Sarbinowo 11 Sianów

Ystad
Trelleborg

Kołobrzeg 11 42 Koszalin 6

Mrzezyno 5 40 6 Dobrzyca Bonin 206 35 Nacław

Niechorze Dygowo ZAMEK W.
KOSZALINIE Manowo

Rewal 102 31 102 Wrzosowo 27 163 Biesiekierz 13 15 25

Pobierowo 37 162 112 Rosnowo Mostowo

Dziwnów 103 Trzebiatów 21 6 215 Gościno 19 Karlino 166 Niedalino 37 Radew

Międzywodzie Cerkwica 18 E28 109 Białogard 167 S11 54°

Kamień
Pomorski 23 Gorawino 16 Dargiń

Wolinski 102 32 Swierzno 17 112 163 25 Bobolice

Kolczewo 12 105 Rzeszynkowo Sławoborze Tychowo 169 171

Lubin Mechowo 13 Gryfice 33 Ryman 23 Rabino 167 29 Grzmiąca

Międzyzdroje 107 Zabrowo 162 Tychówka 23 Białowąs

3 21 15 18 6 Rabino 30

Wolin 108 20 E28 Resko Rusinowo Sława 21 154 75 172 Barwice 11

E65 75 zewo 106 Płoty 35 Świdwin ZAMEK W.
POLCZYNIE Połczyn-
Zdroj

Haff Przybiernów 20 152 Starogar 4 16° 163 Ostropole 172

Zalew
Szczeciński 3 15° Żabowo 20 Brzeżno Bierzwina Szczecin

Nowe Warpno 3 Radowo
Wielkie 151 171

Nowogard Drawski

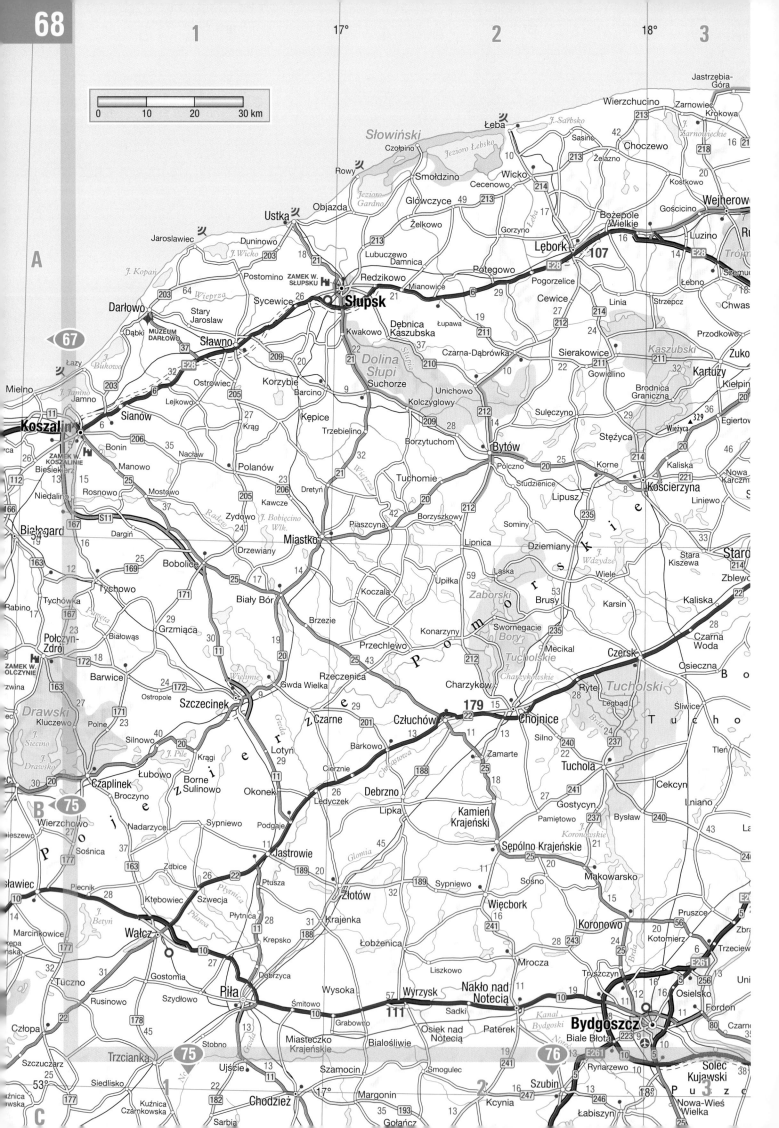

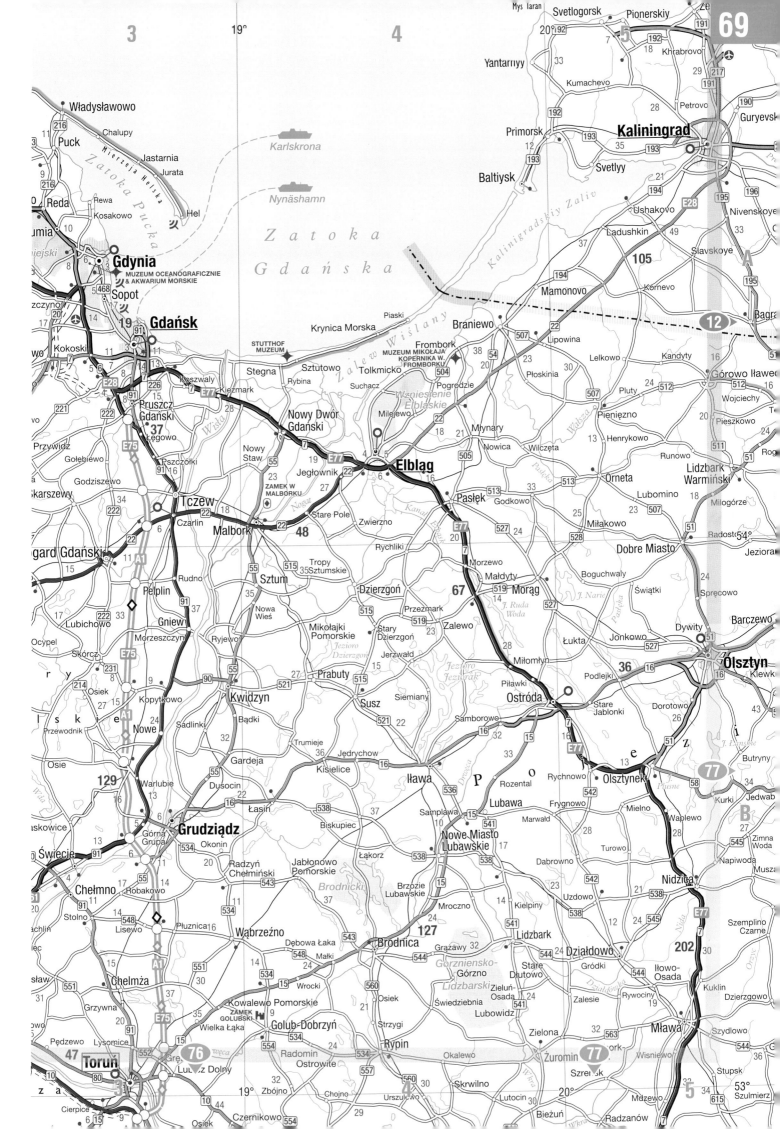

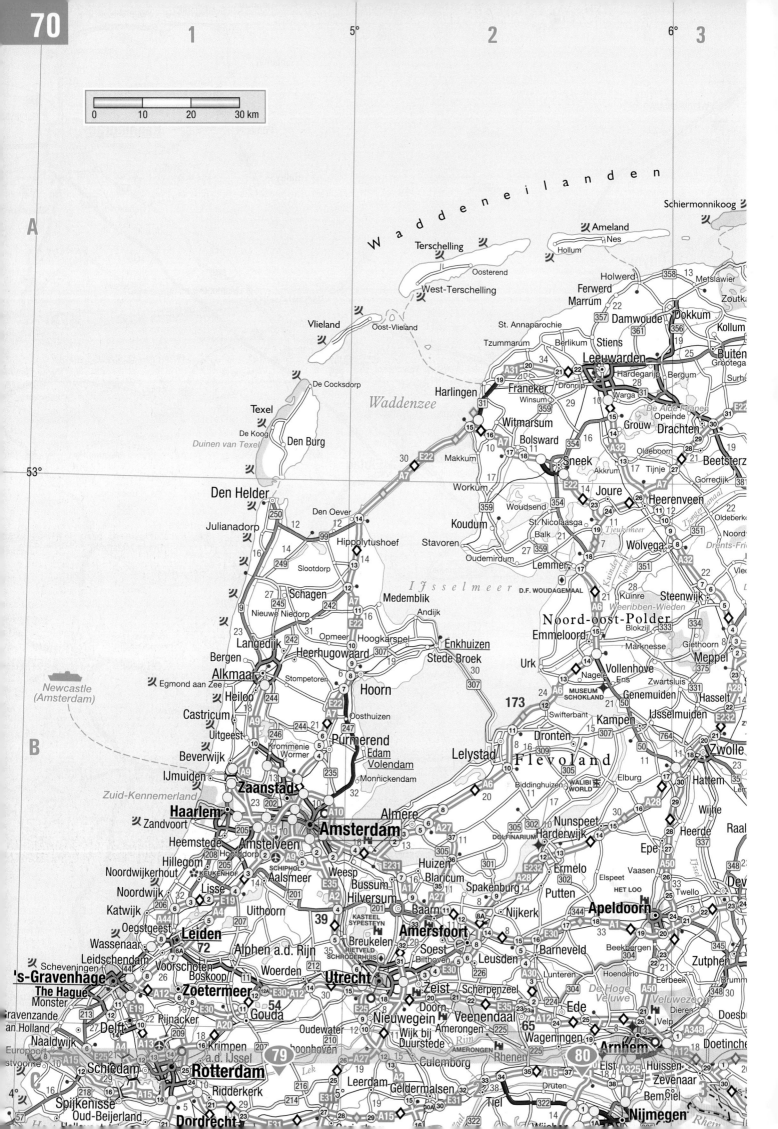

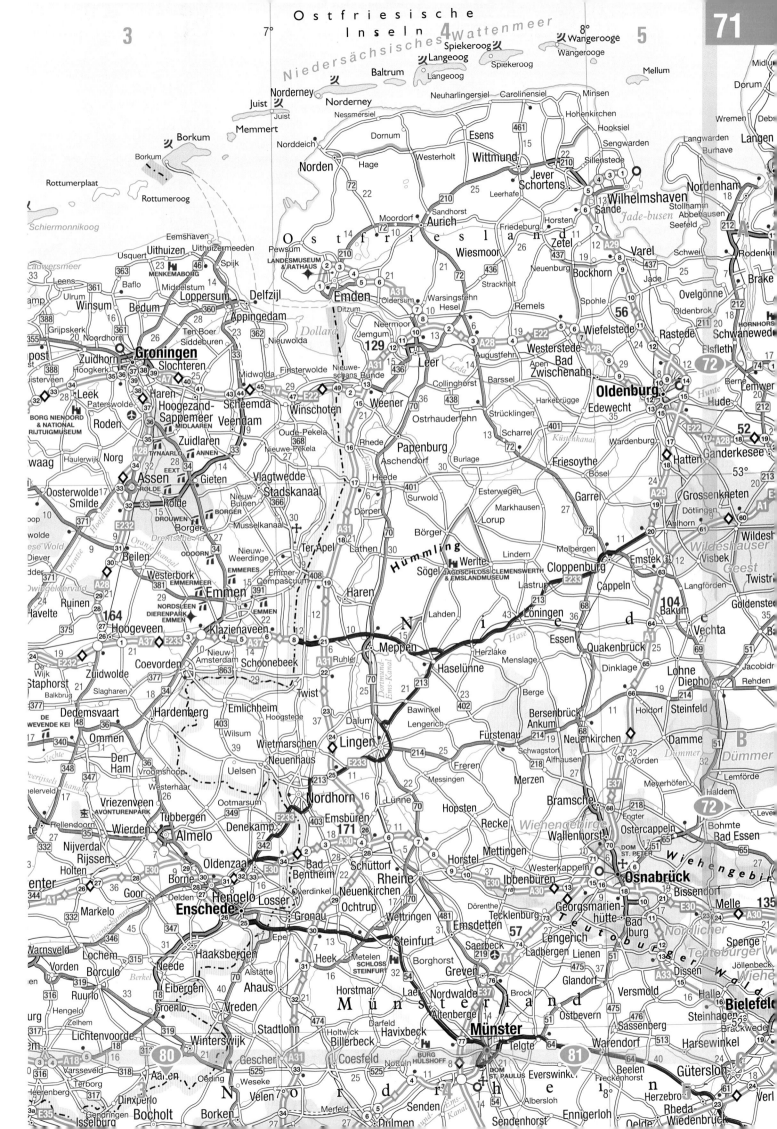

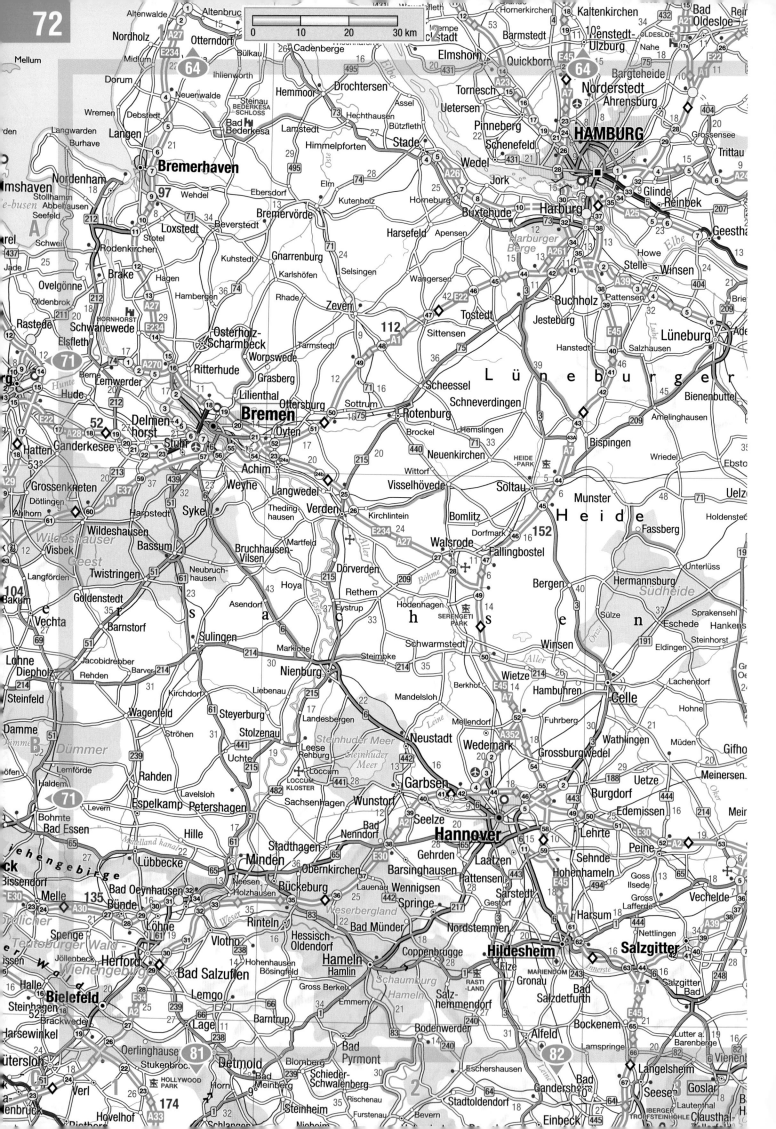

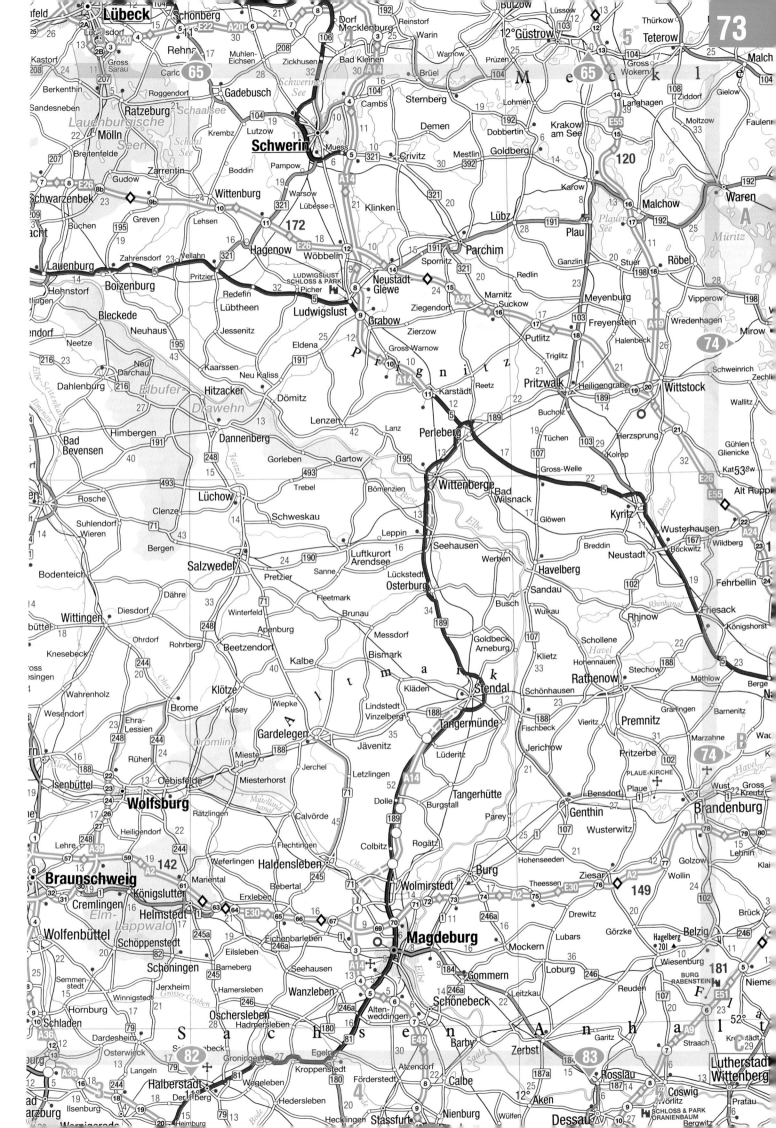

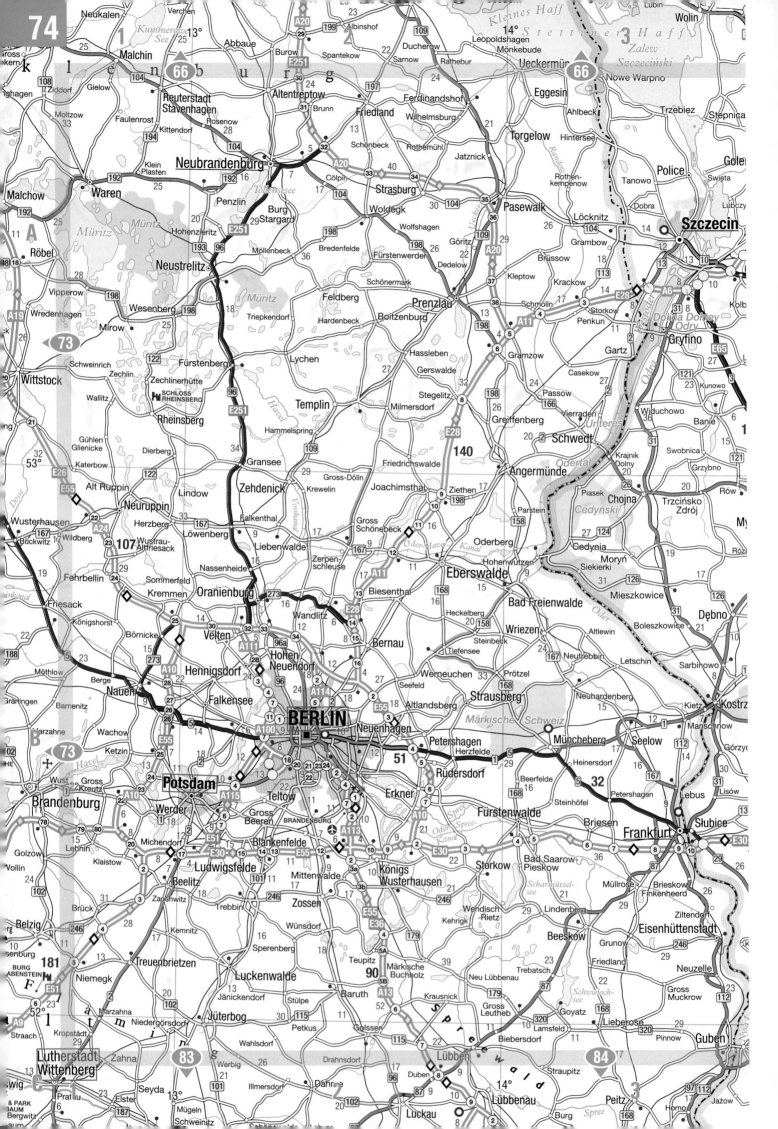

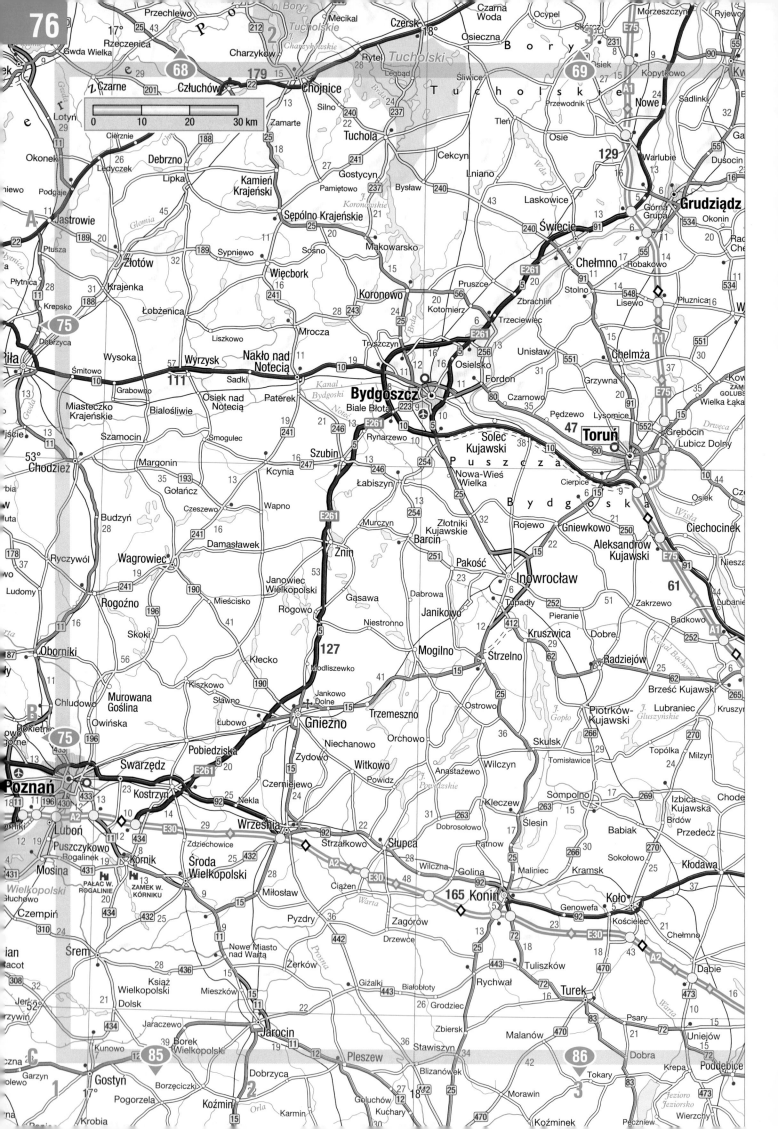

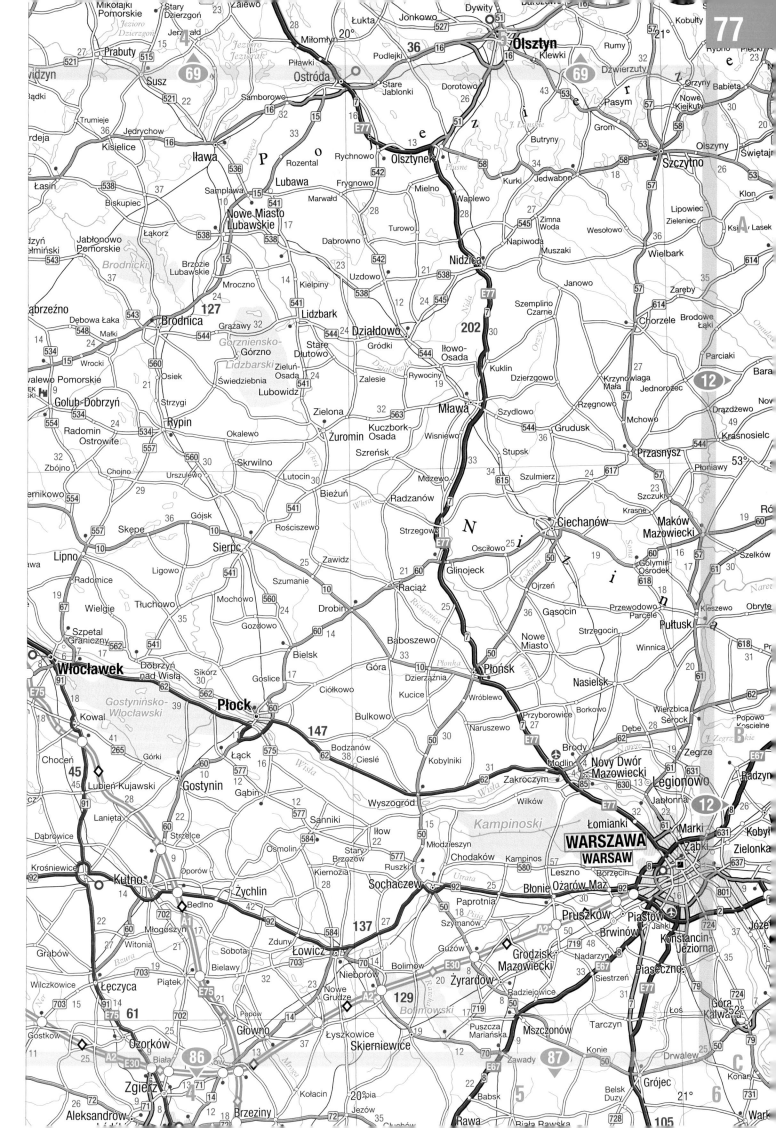

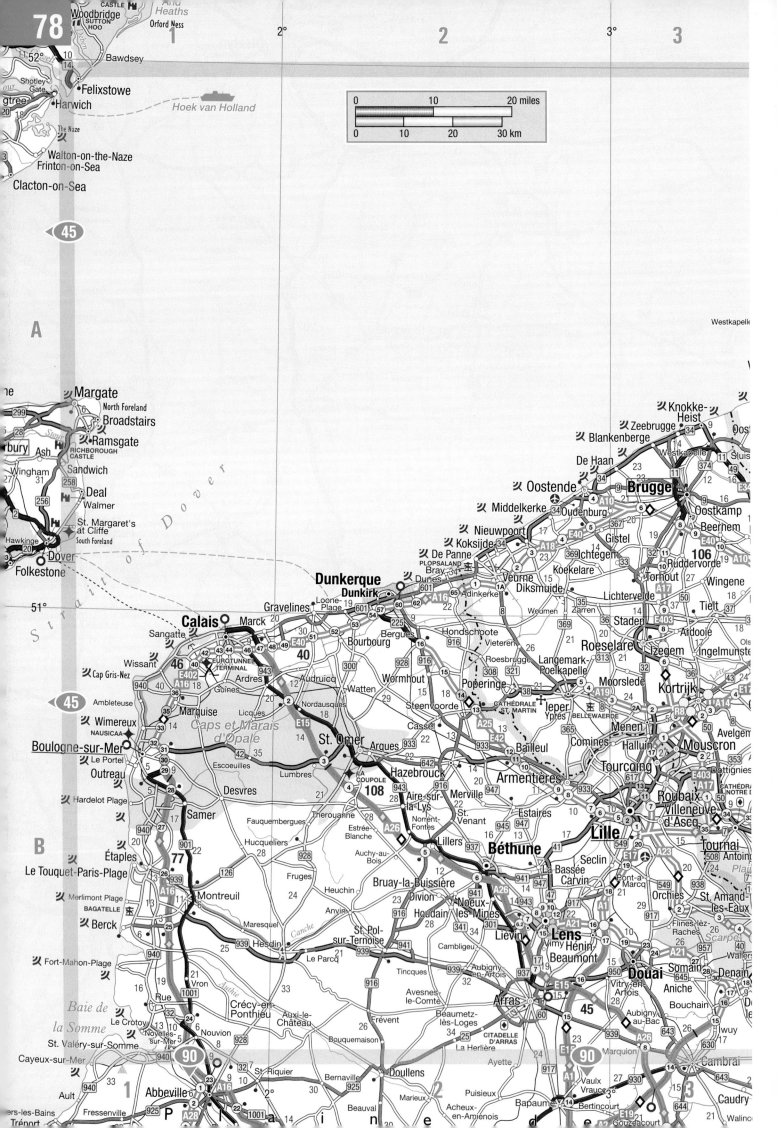

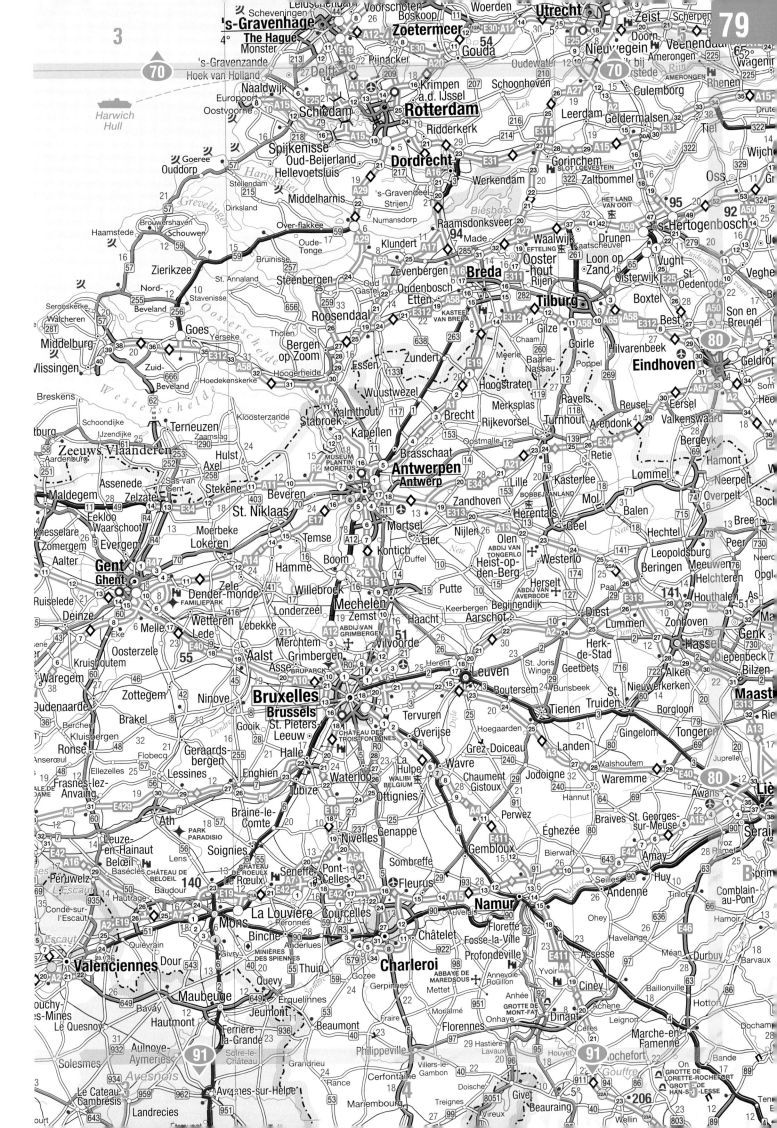

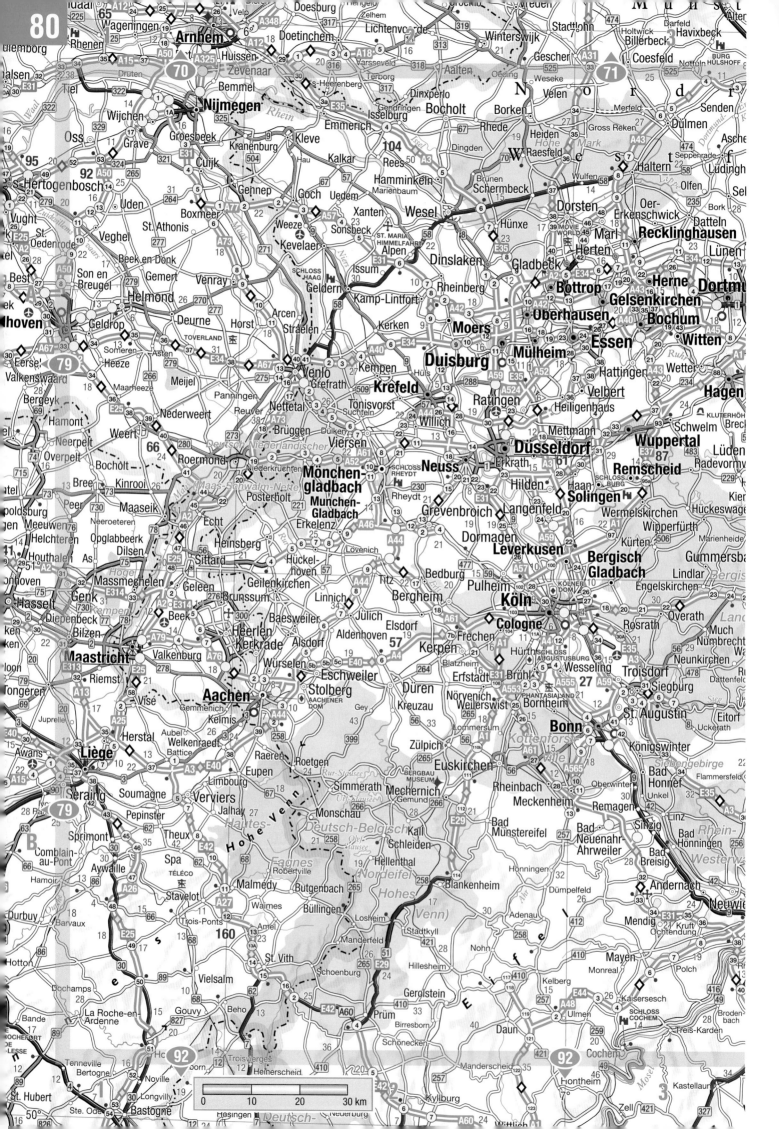

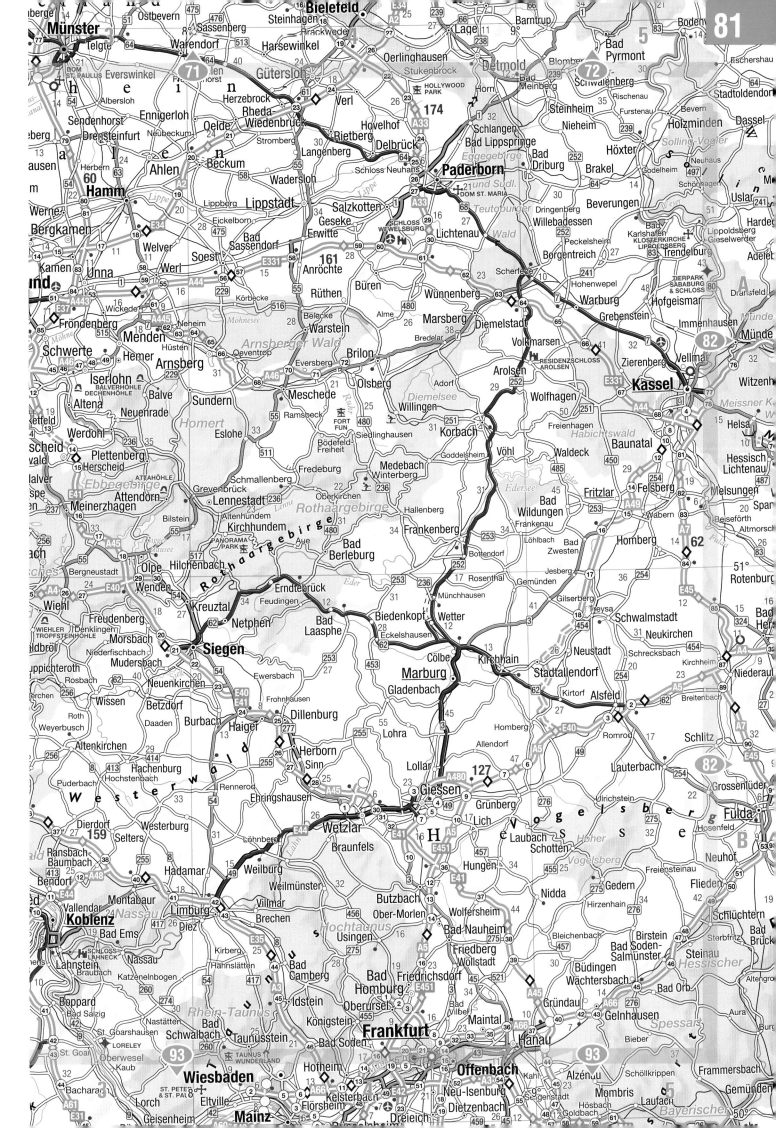

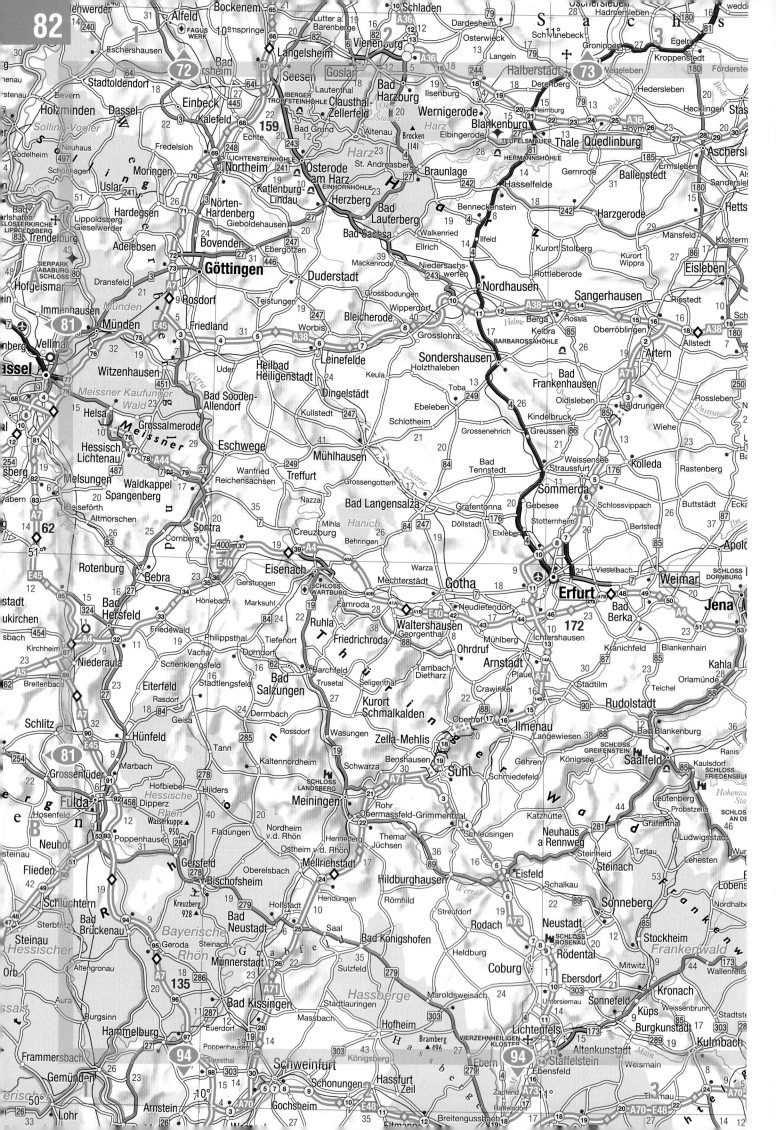

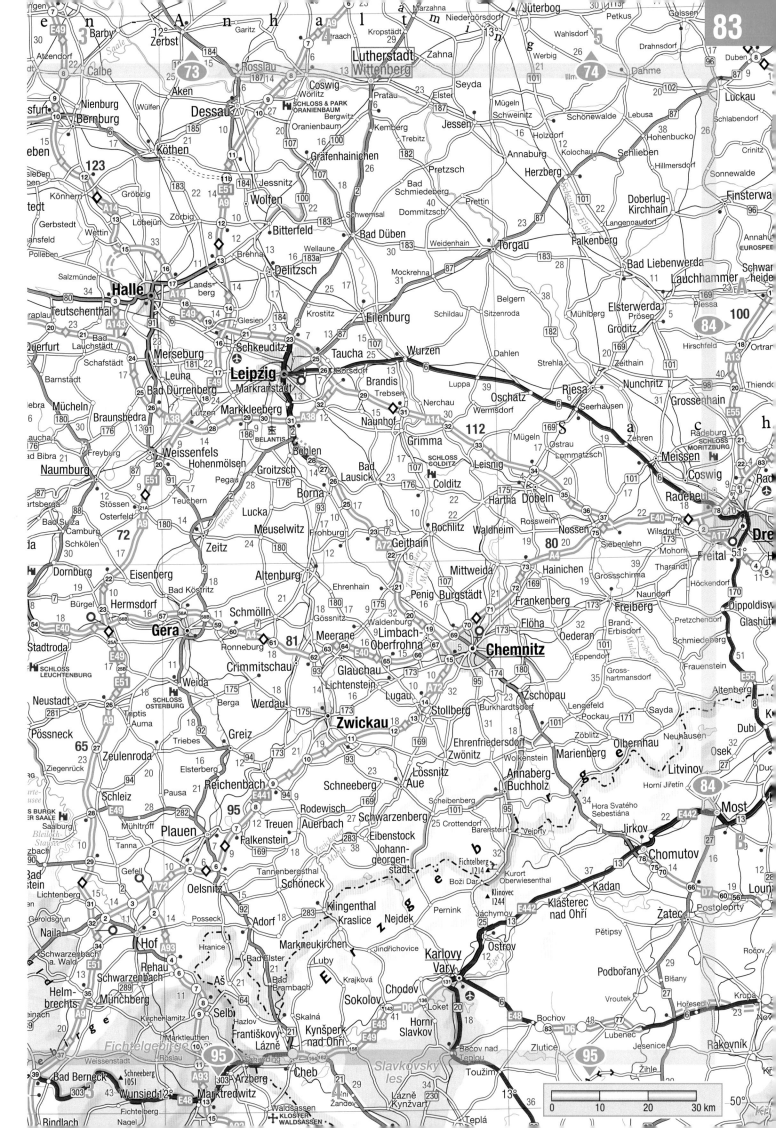

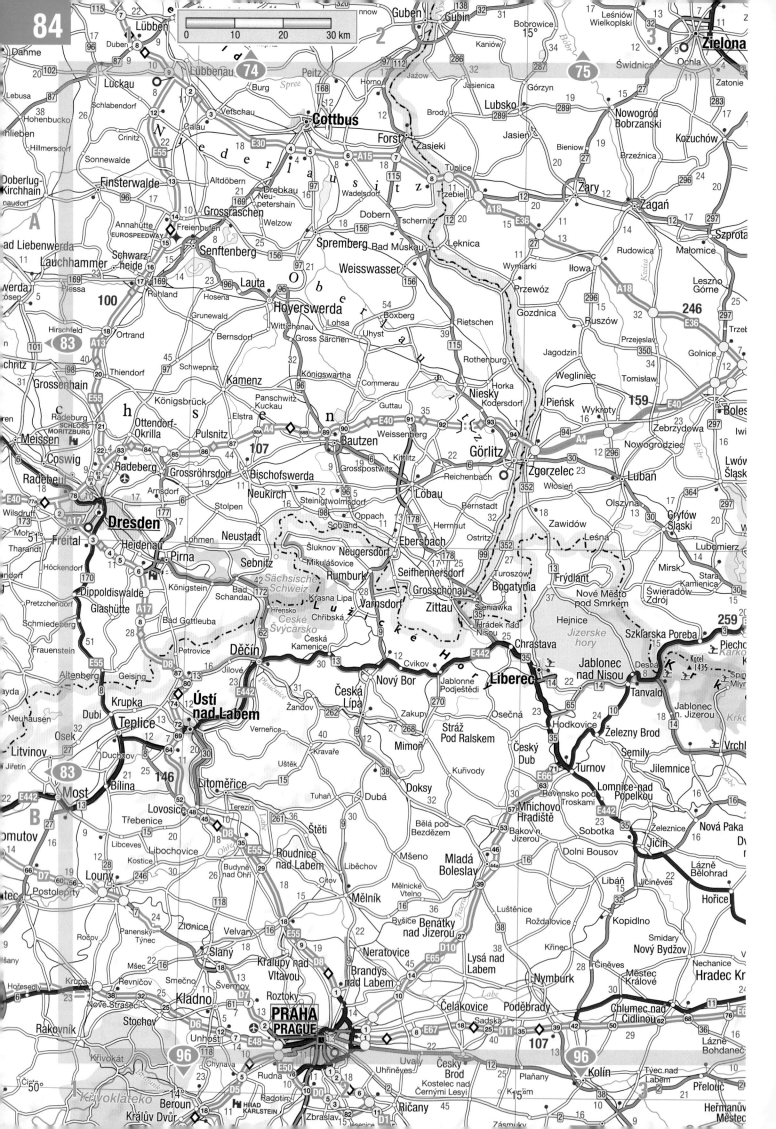

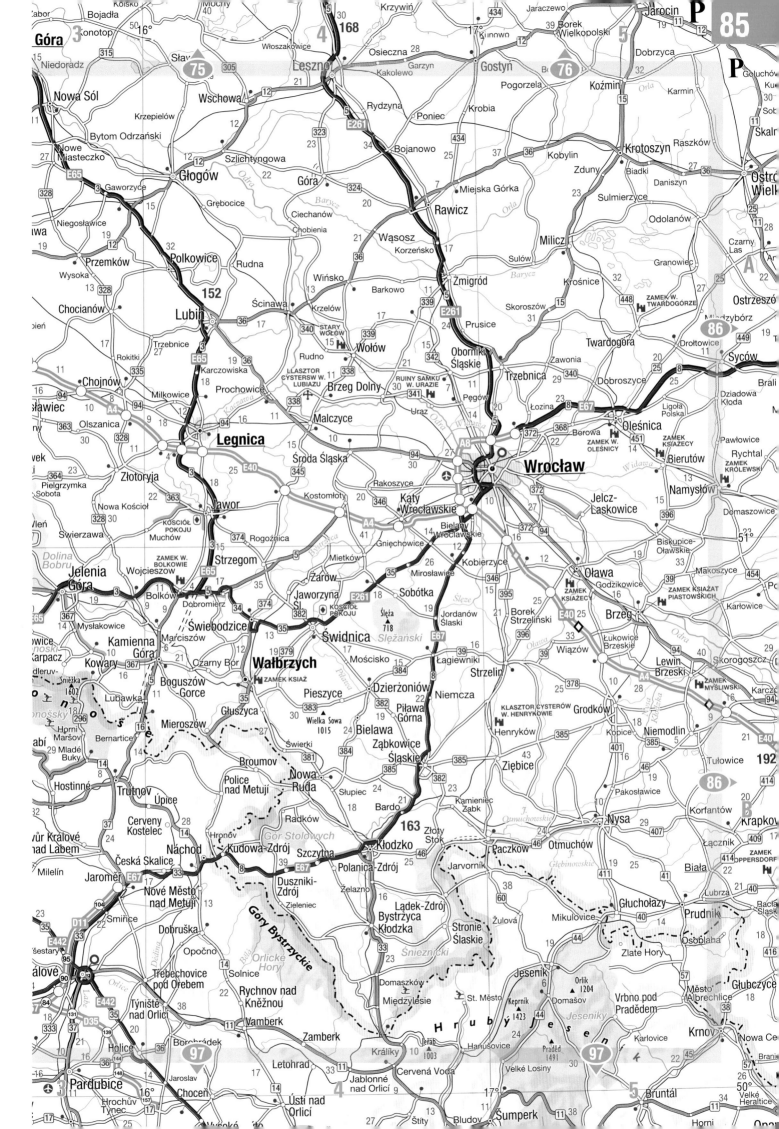

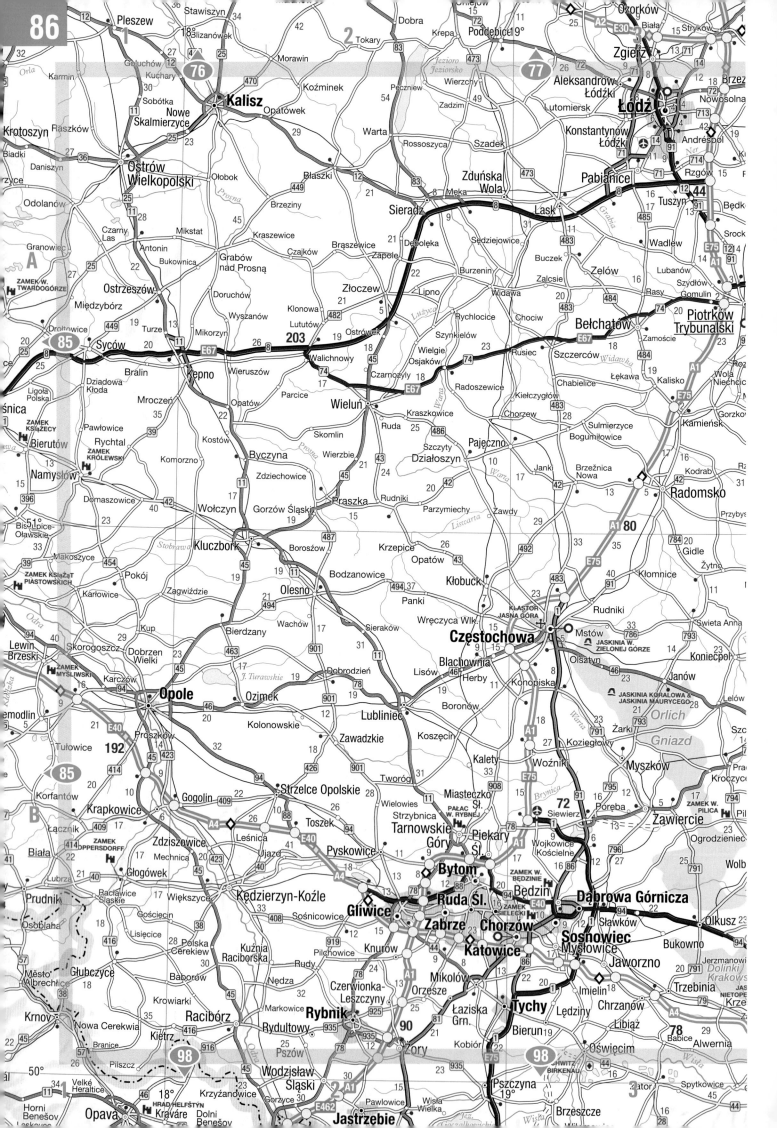

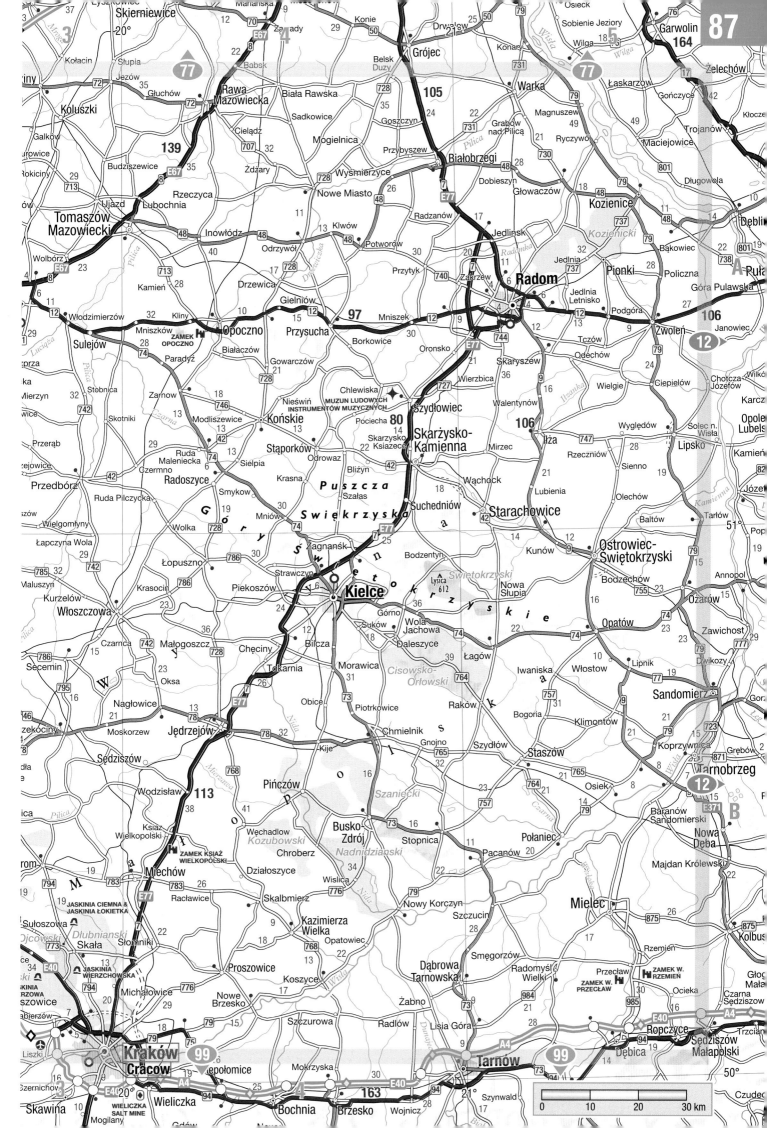

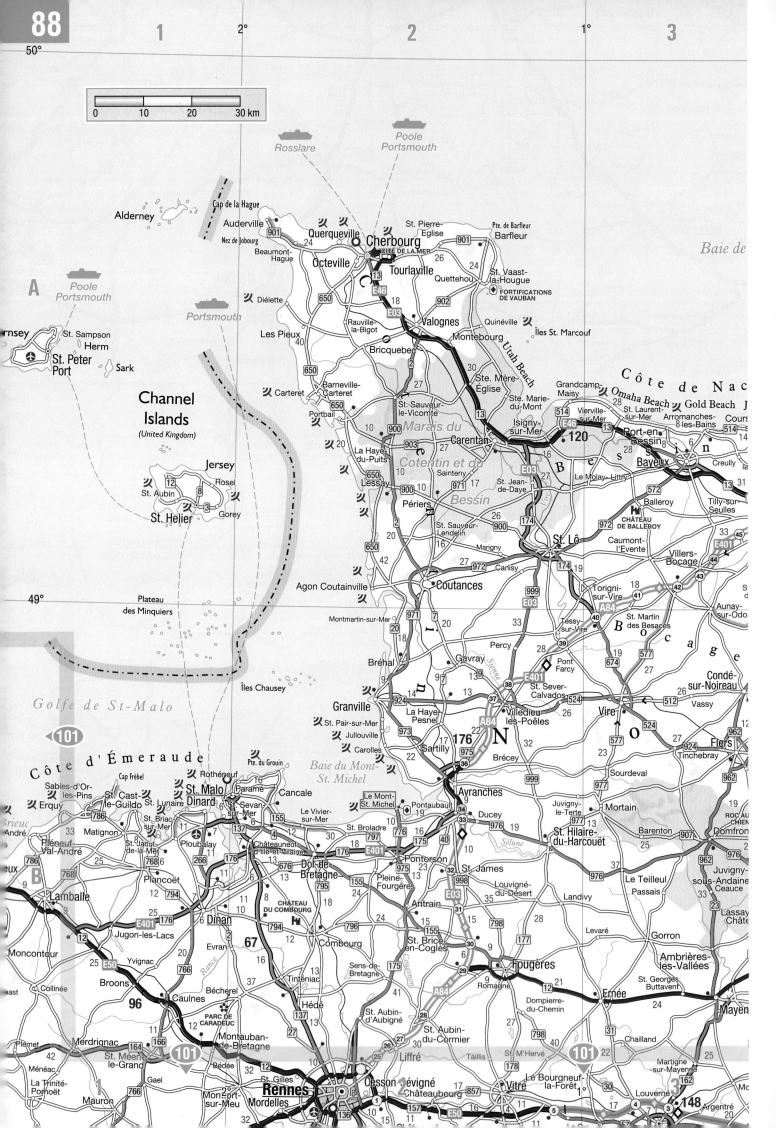

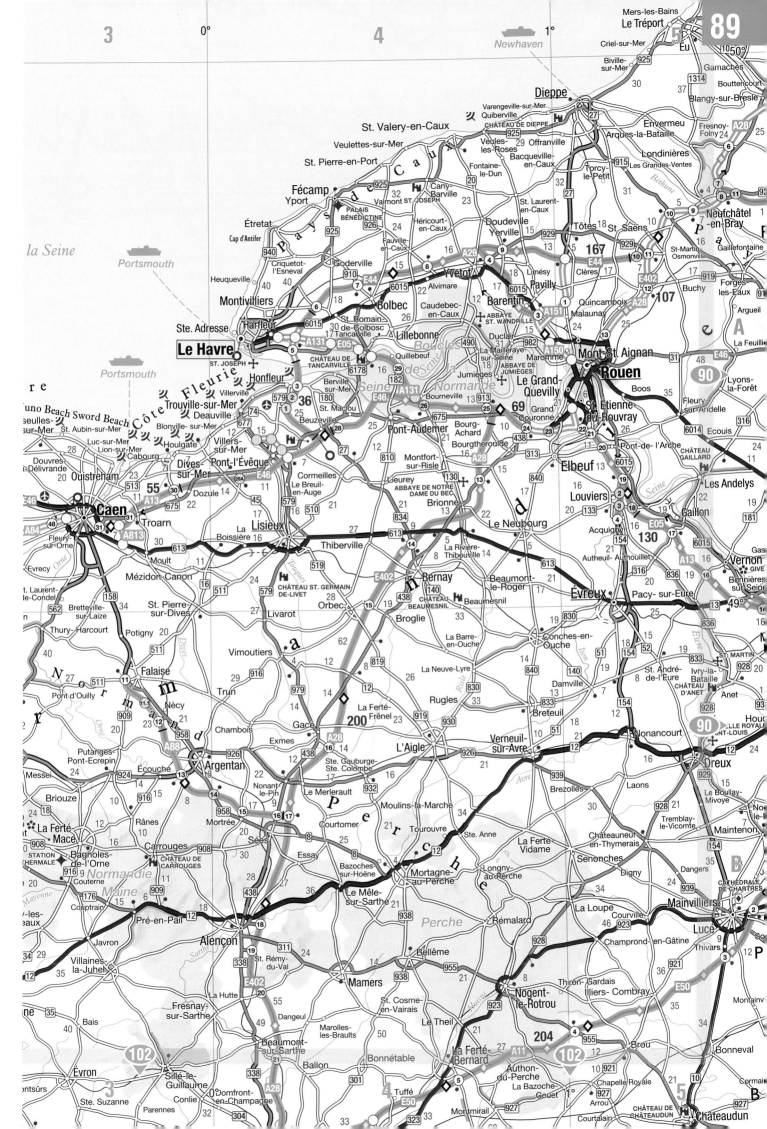

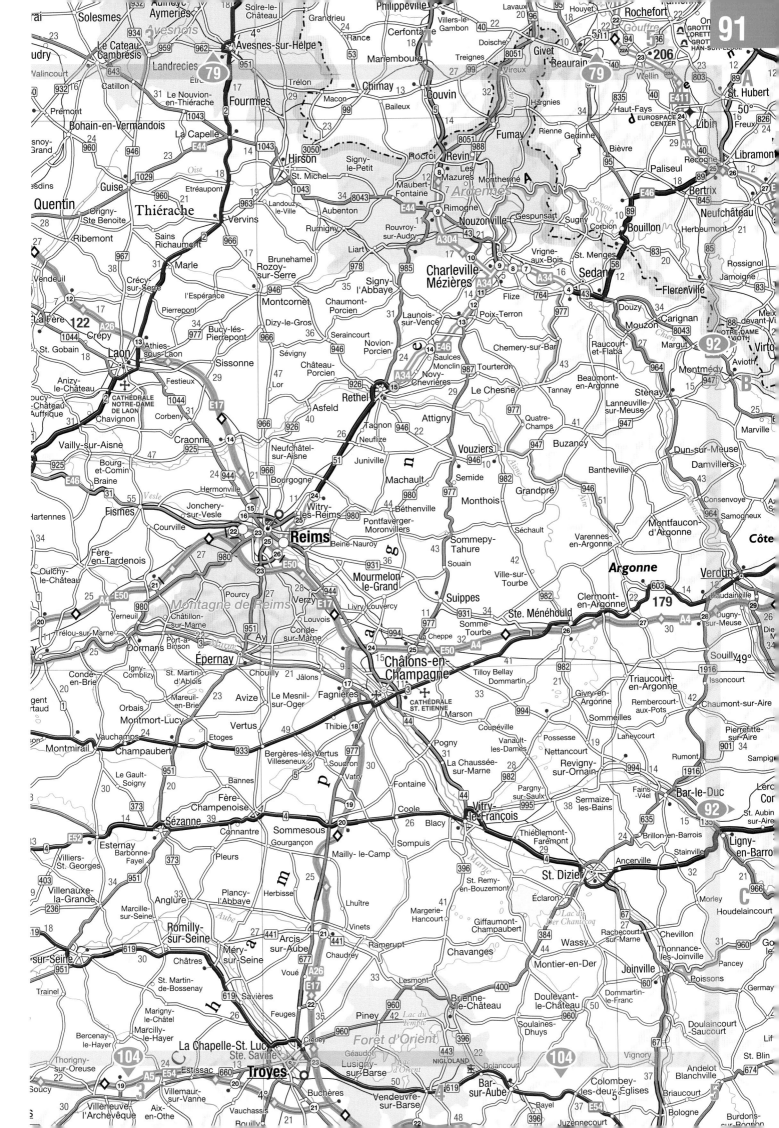

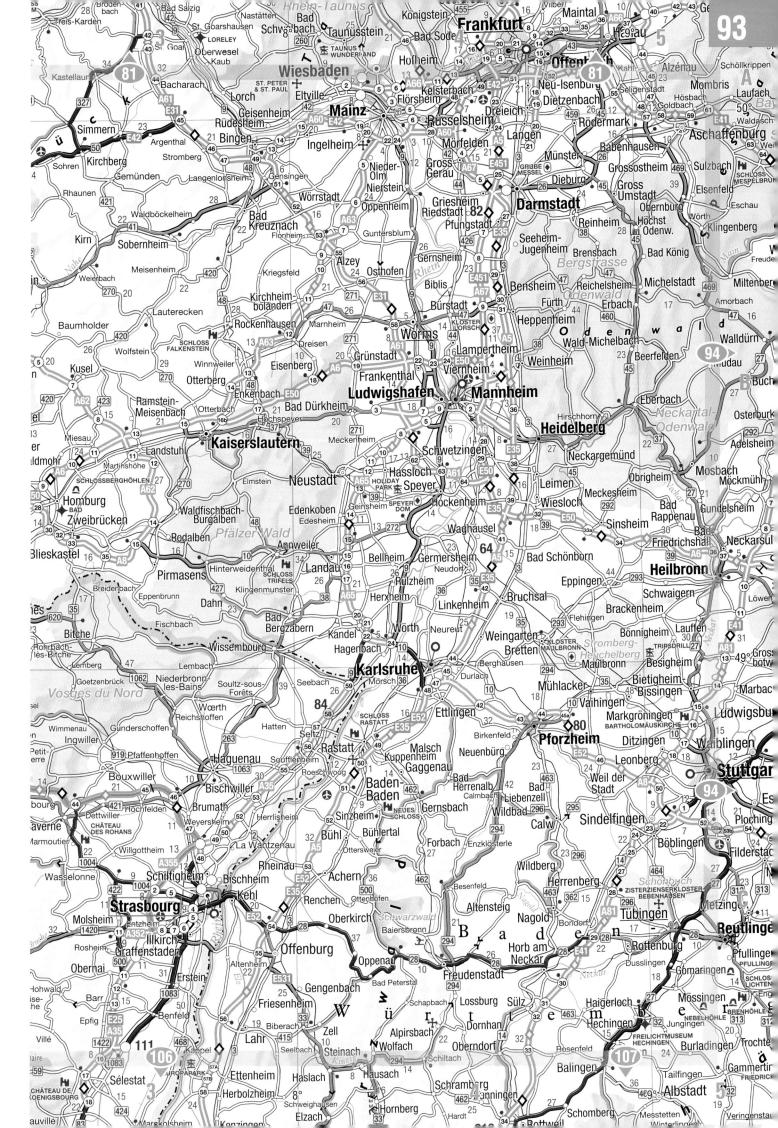

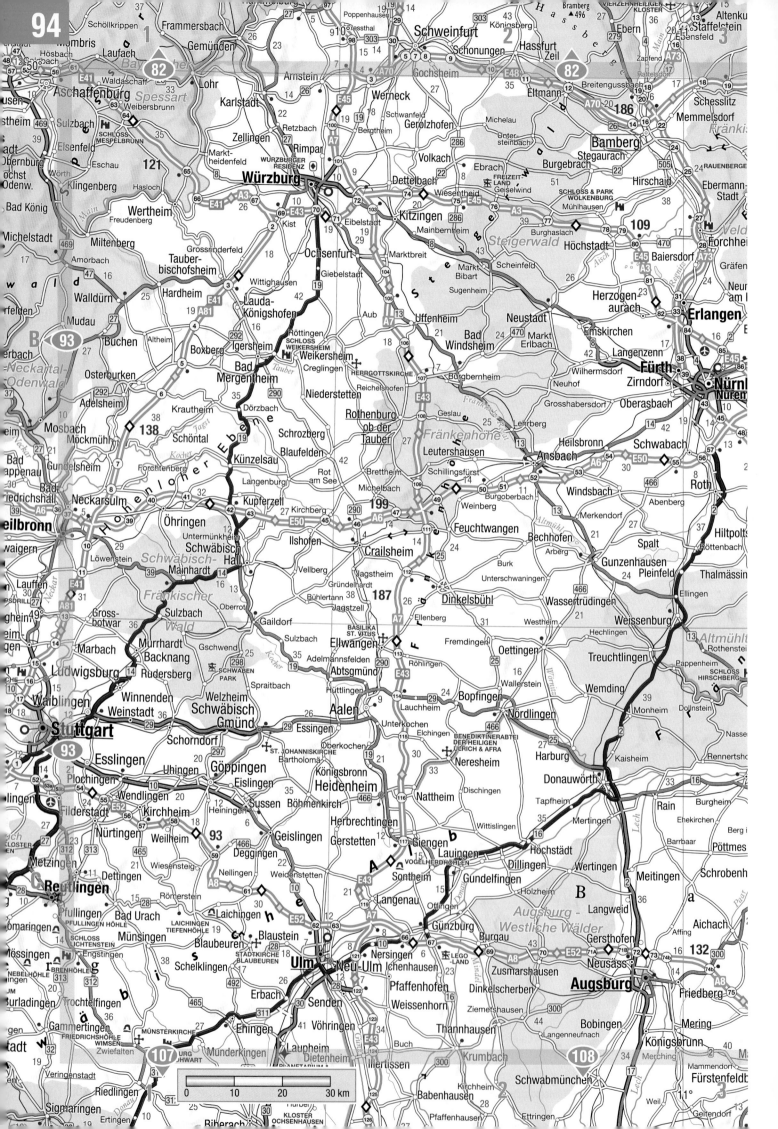

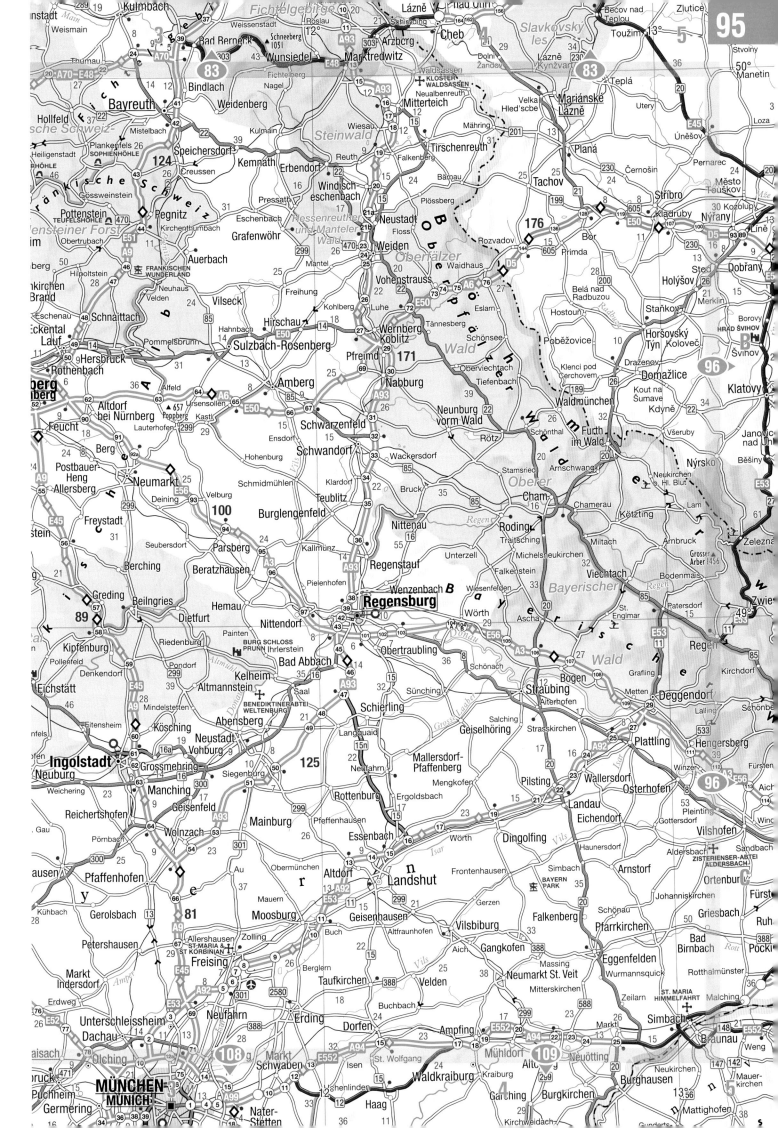

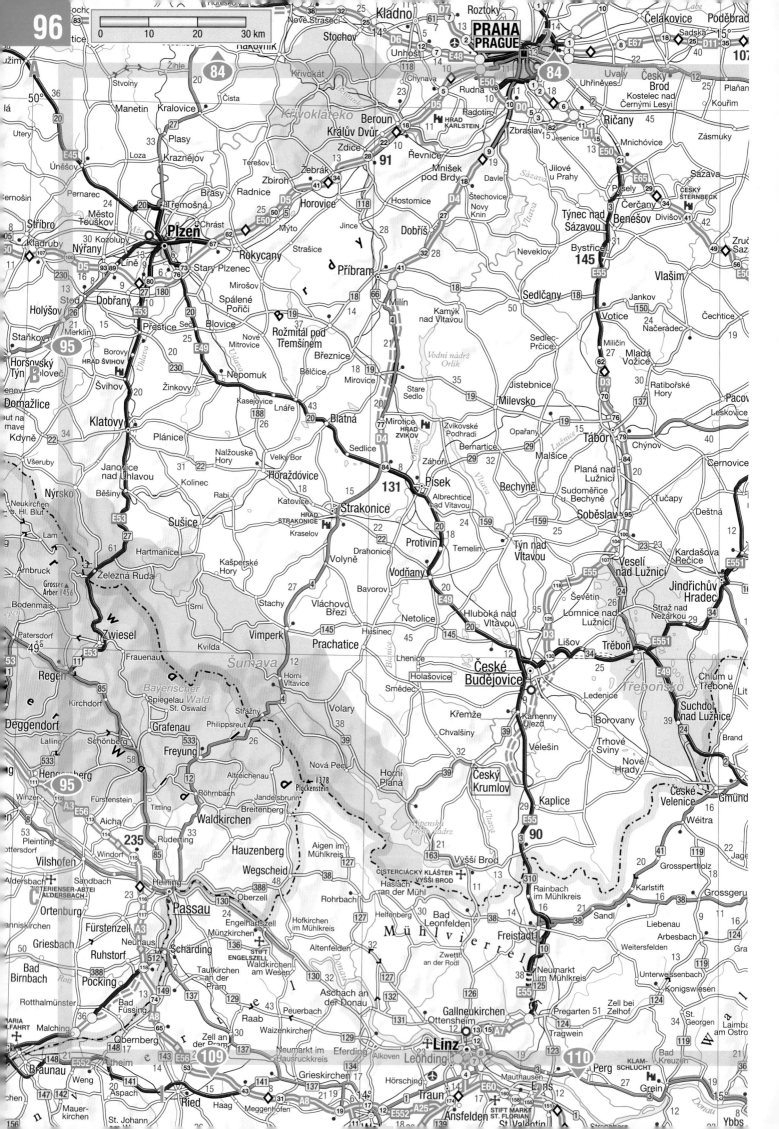

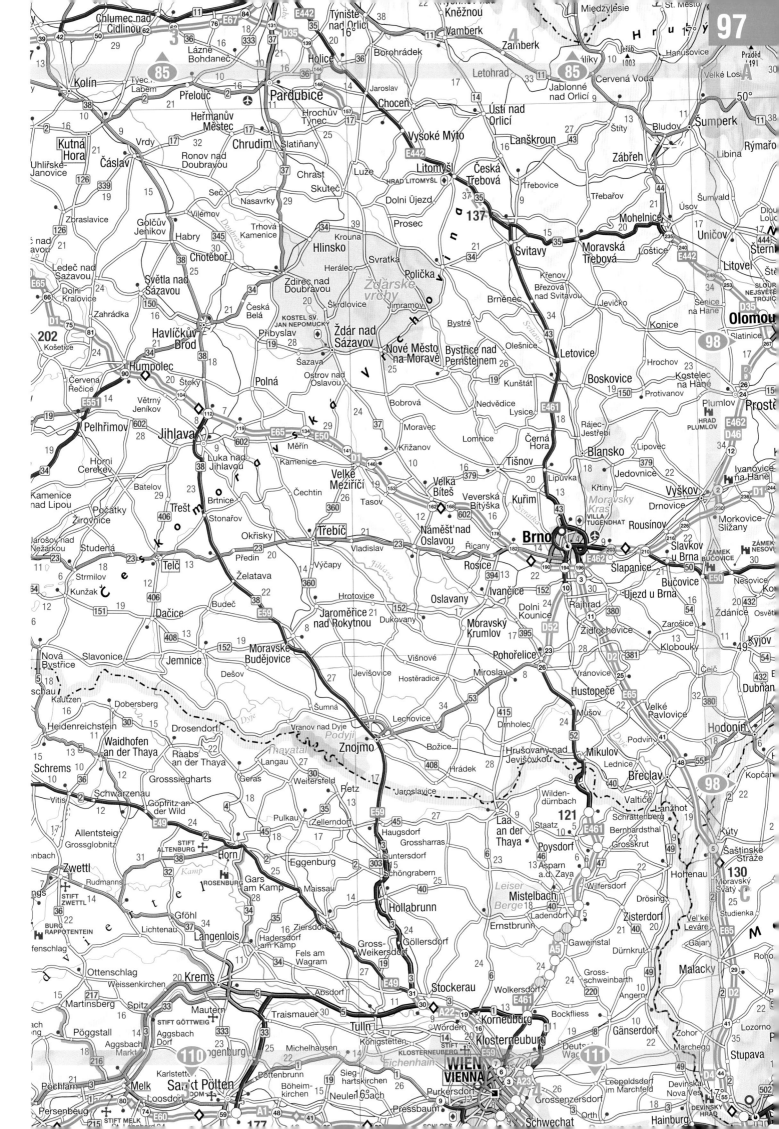

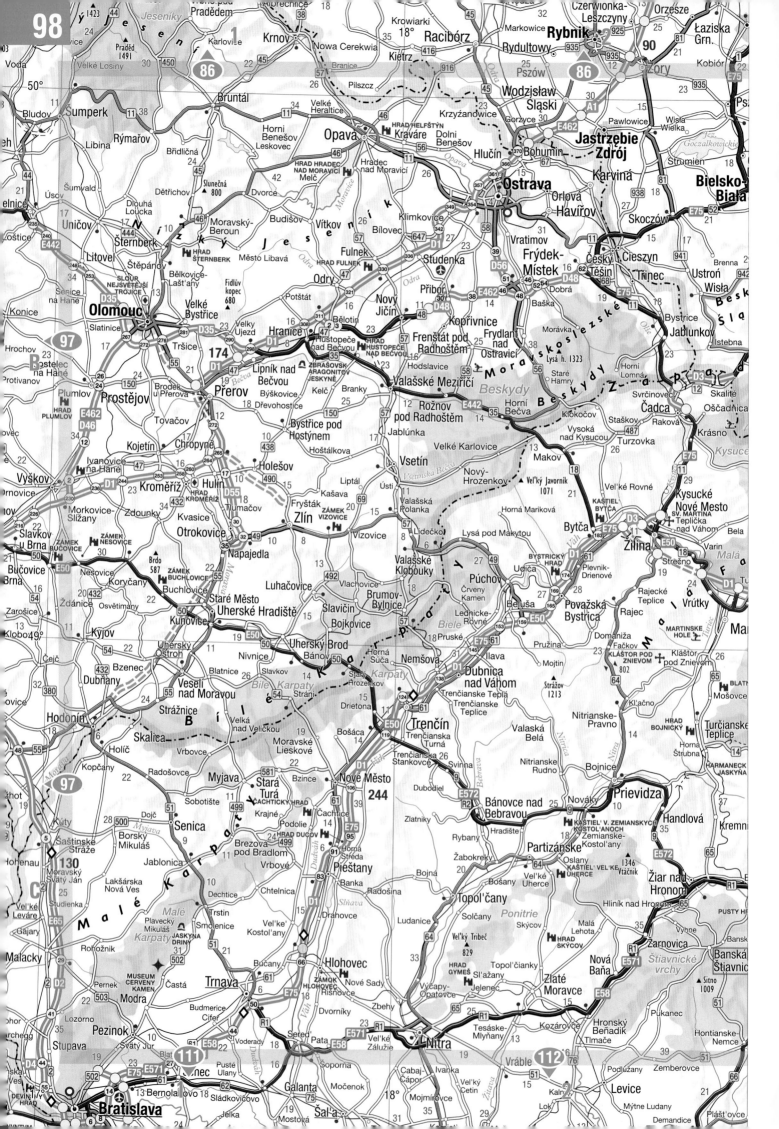

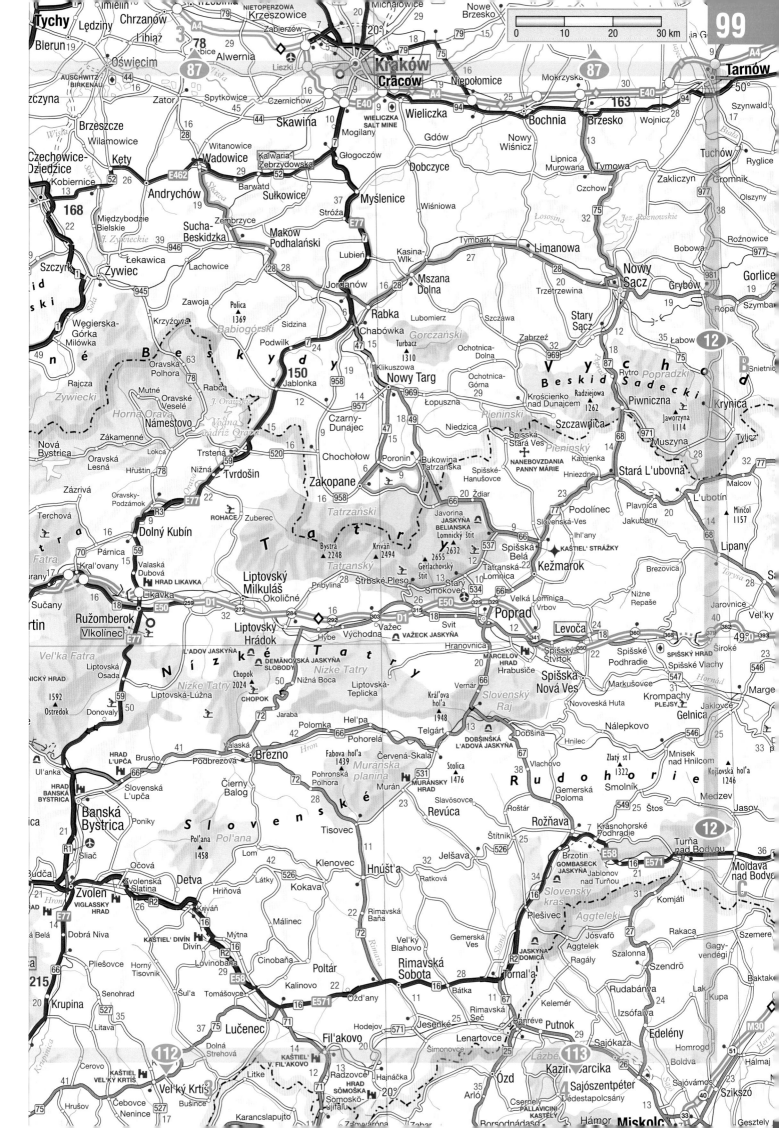

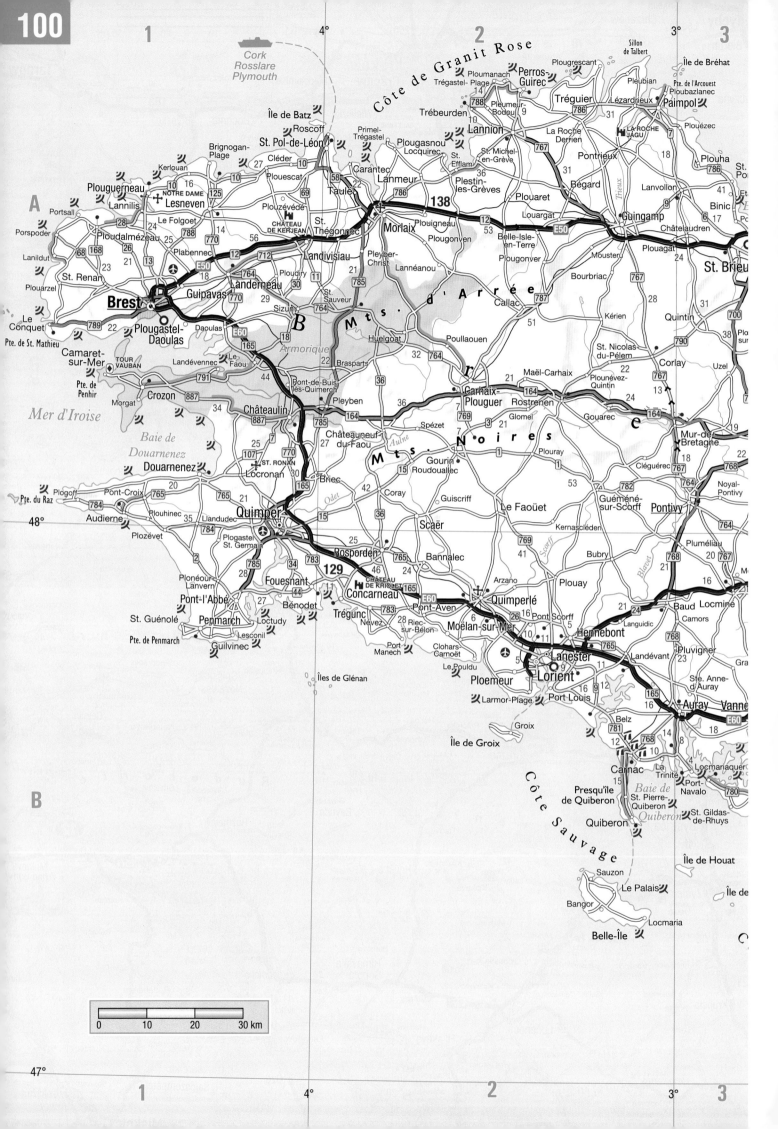

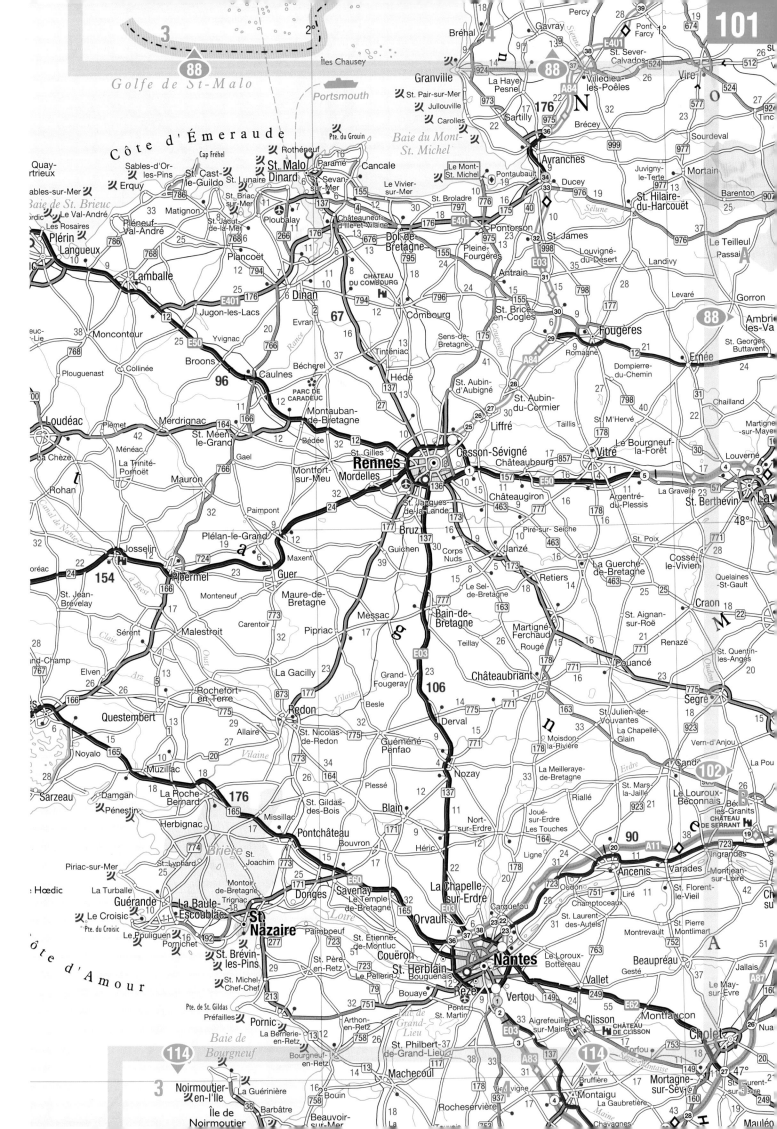

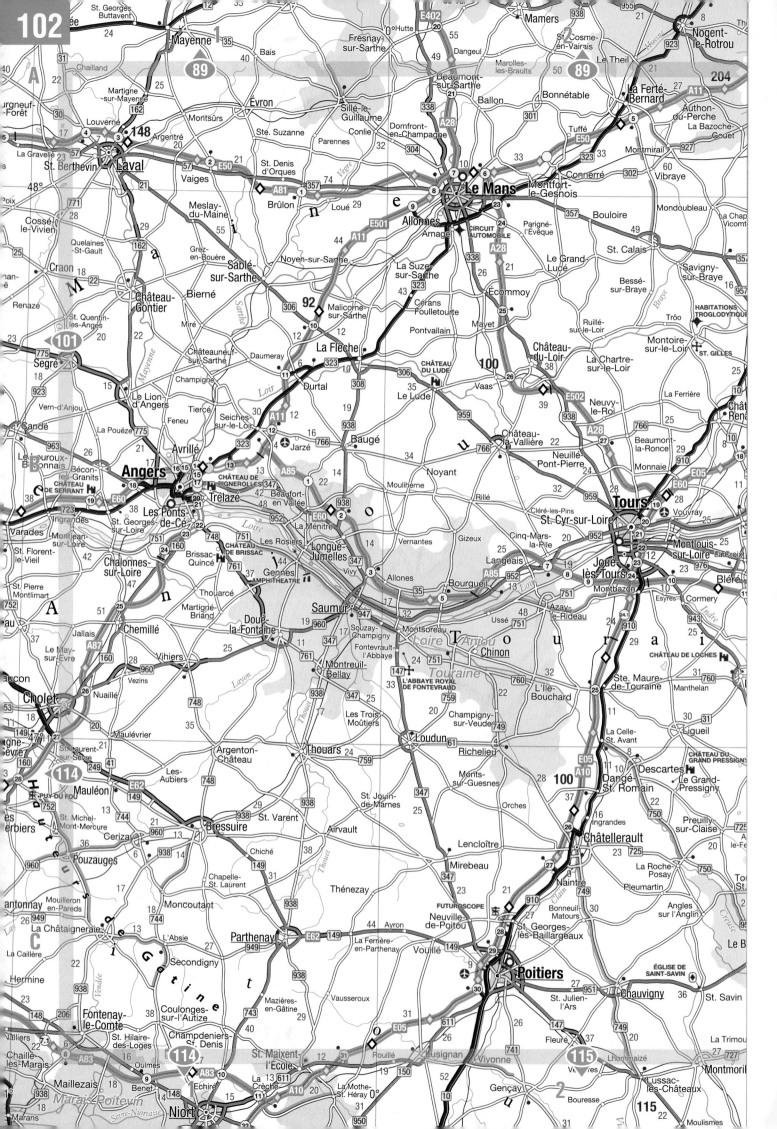

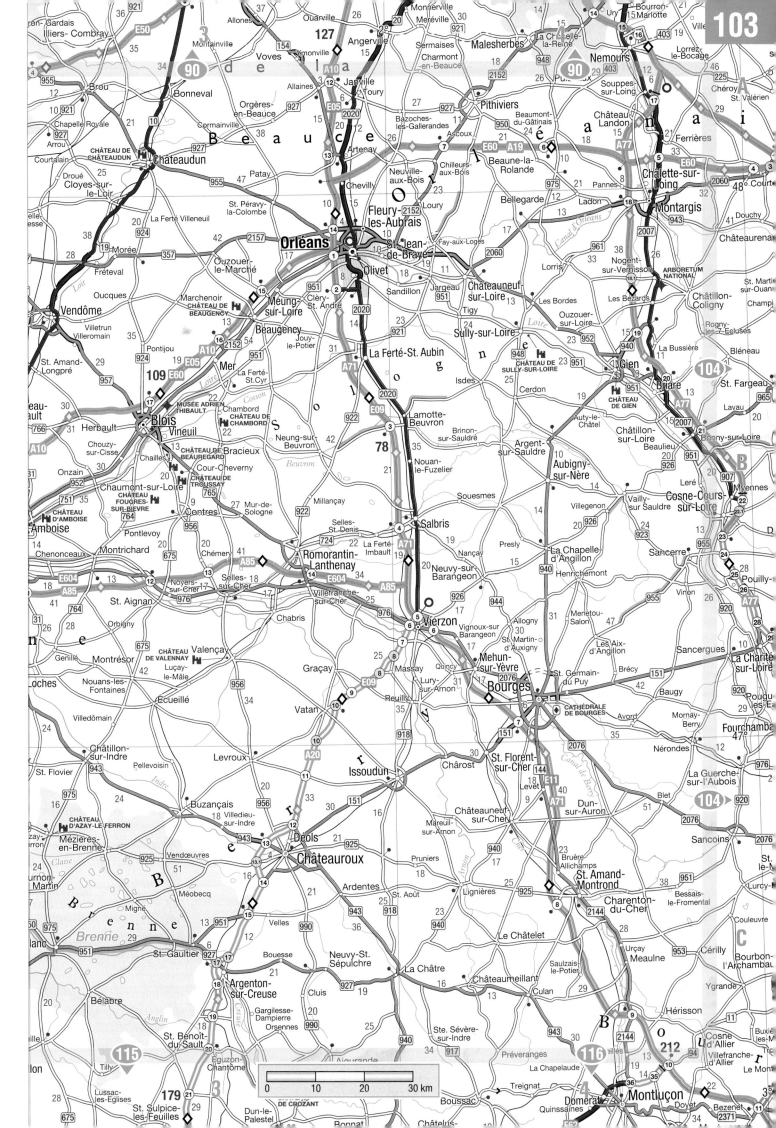

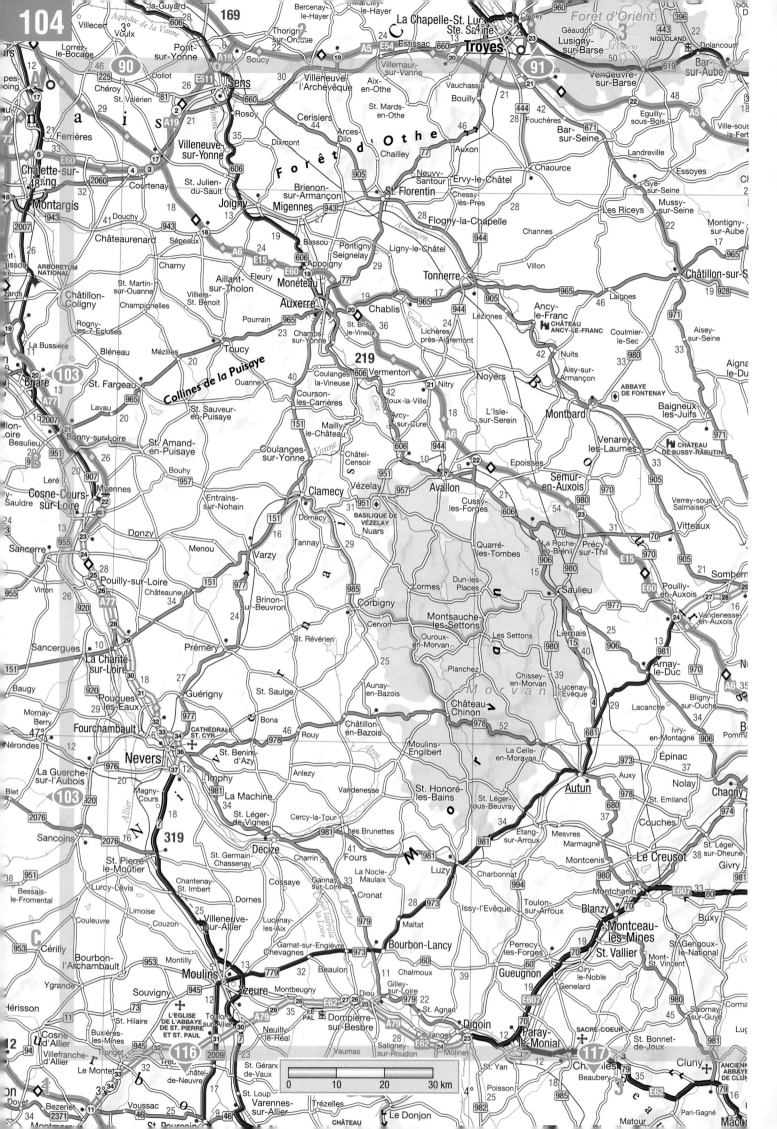

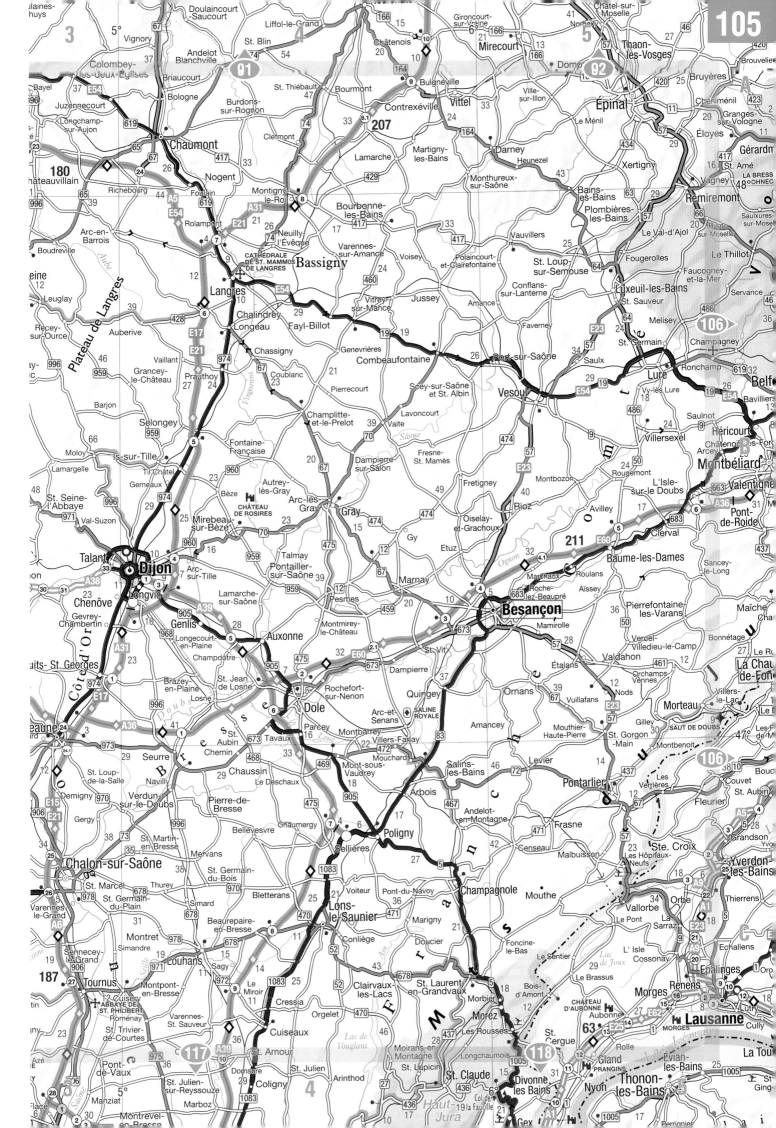

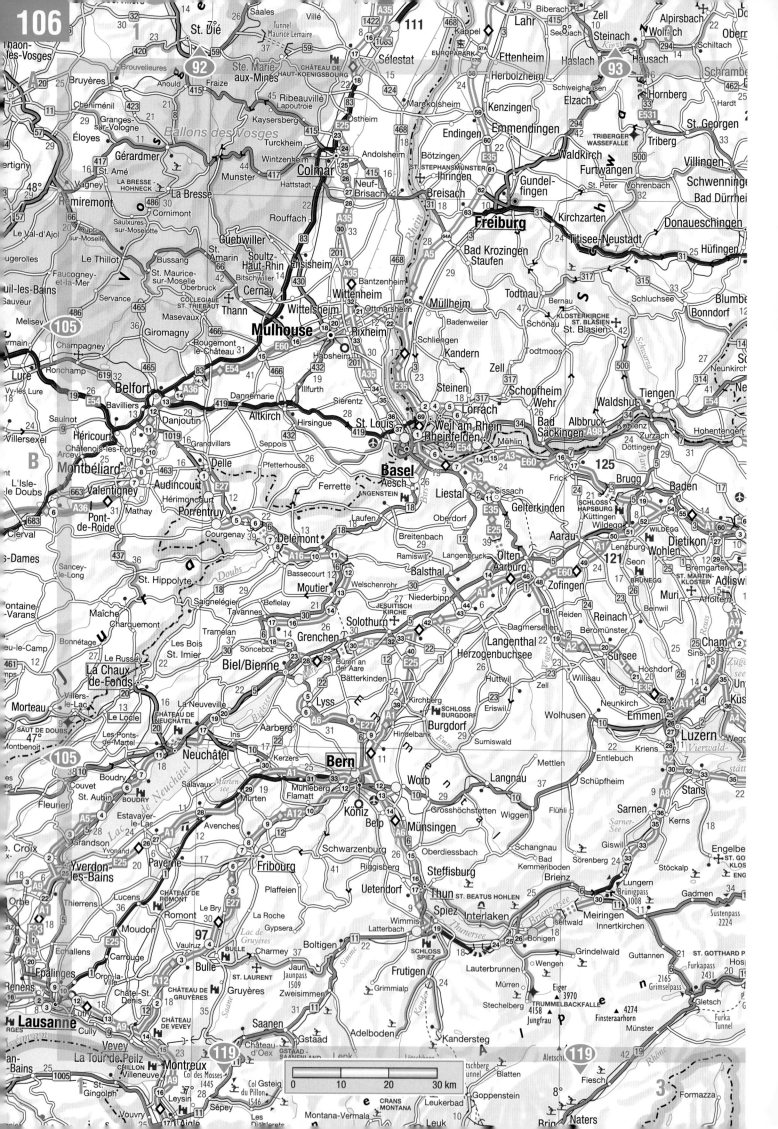

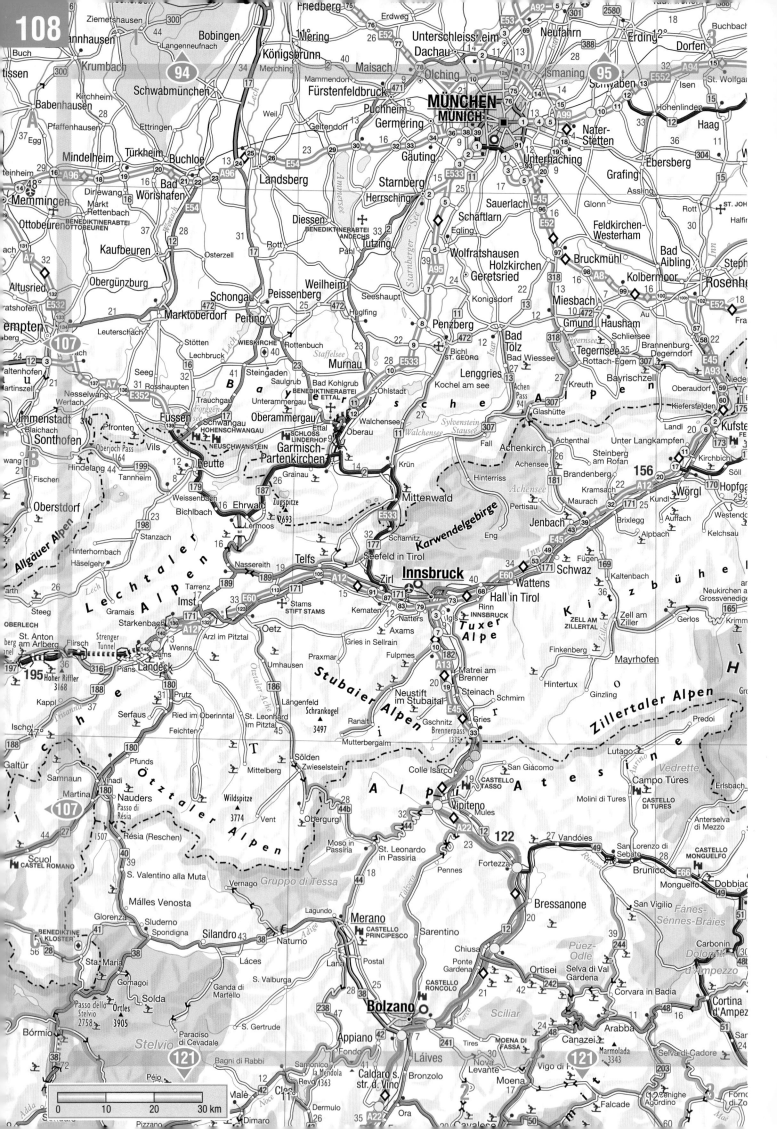

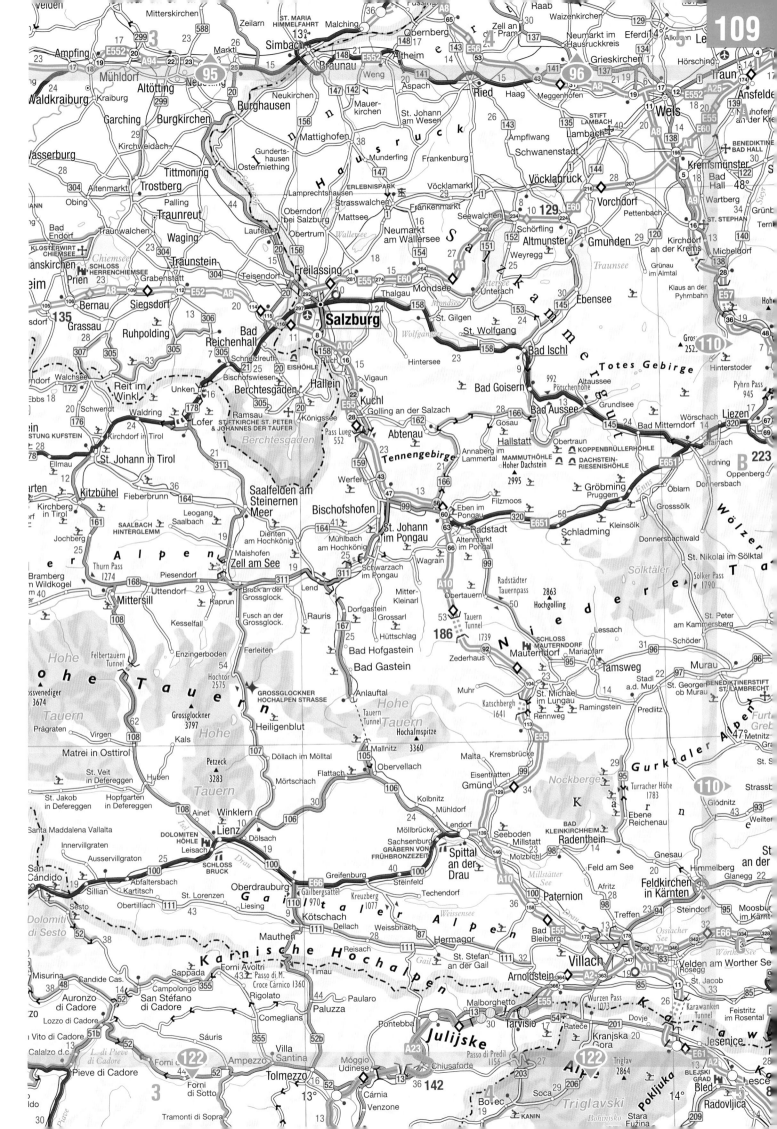

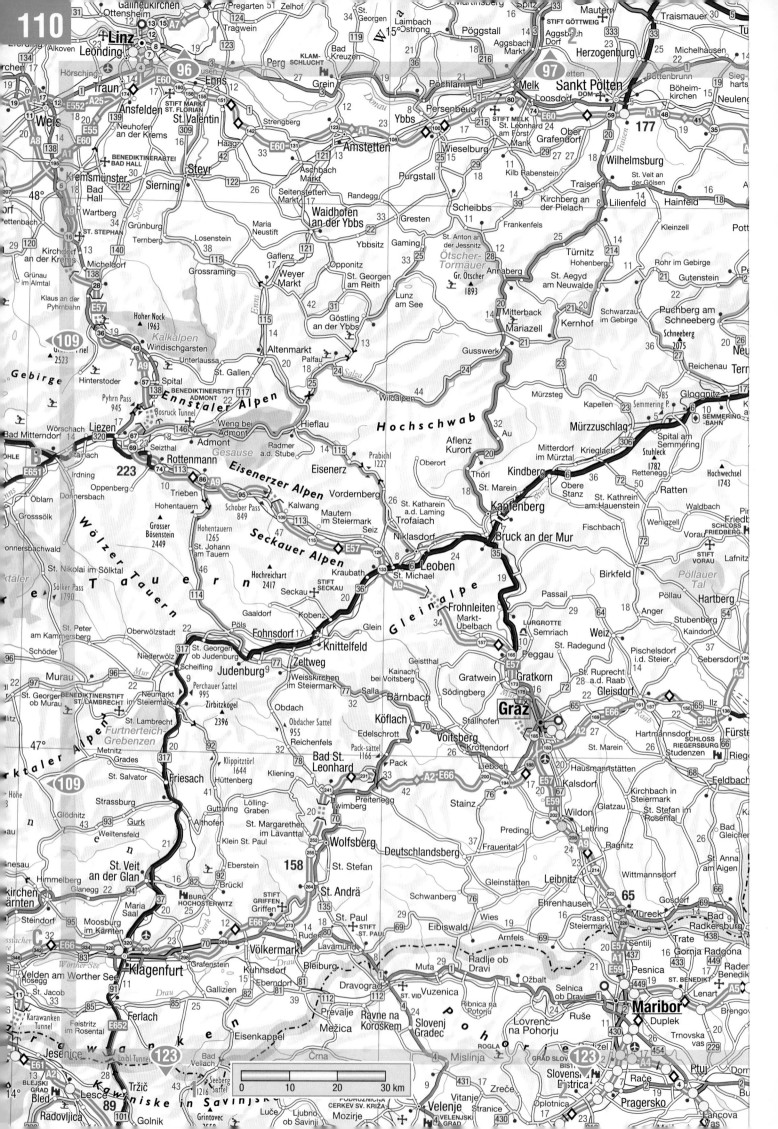

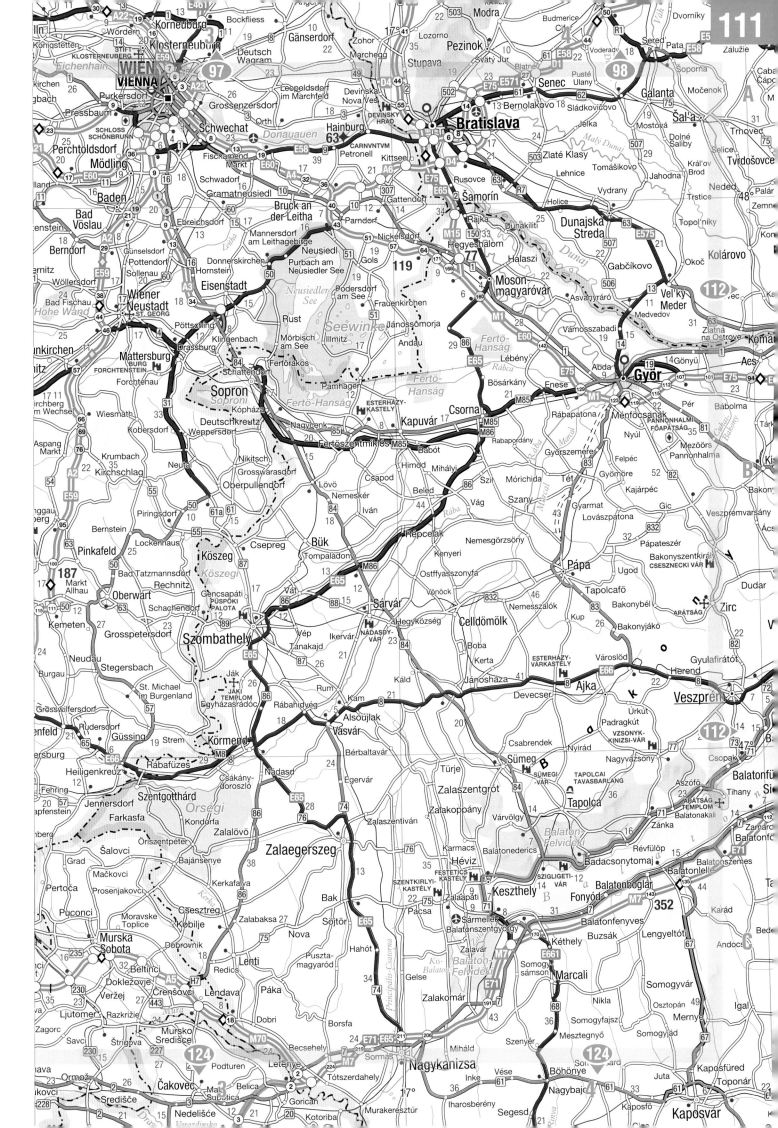

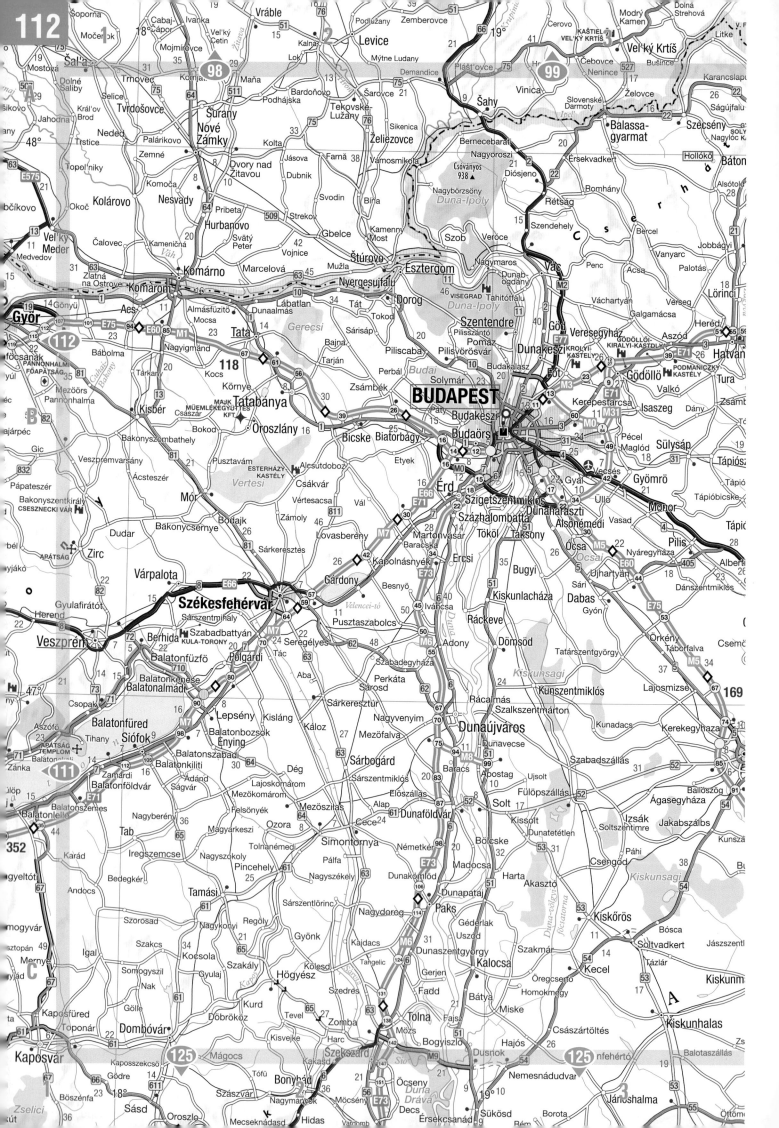

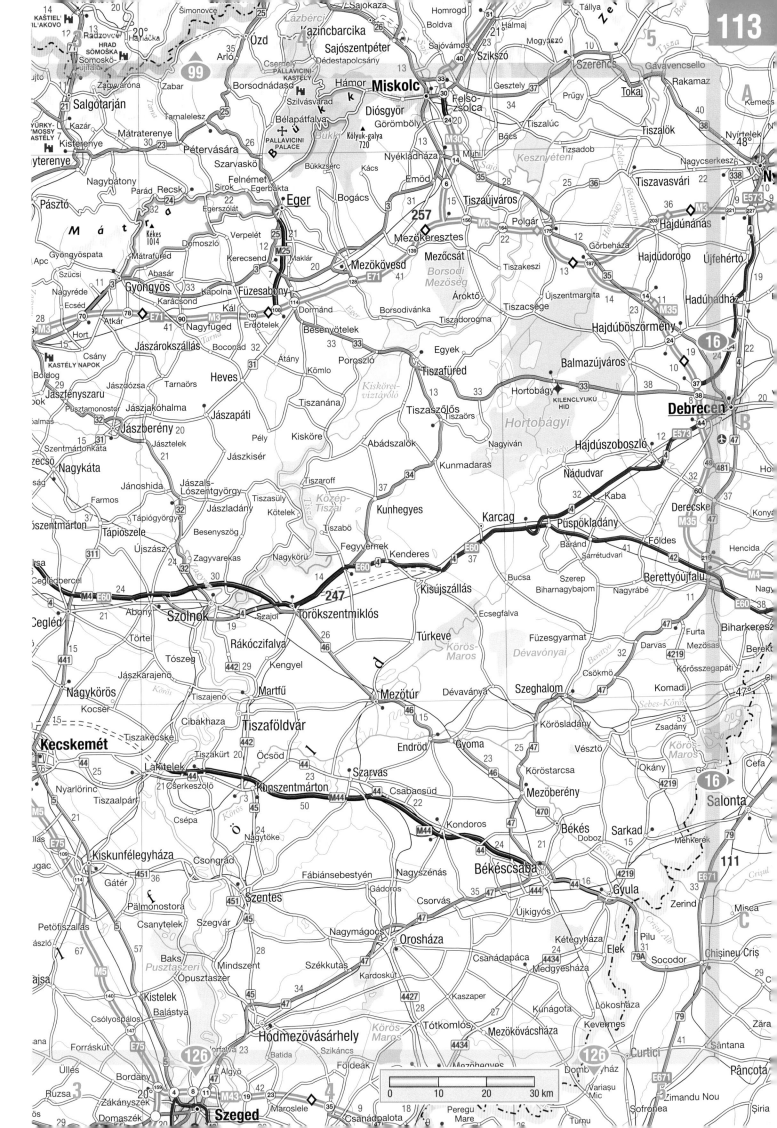

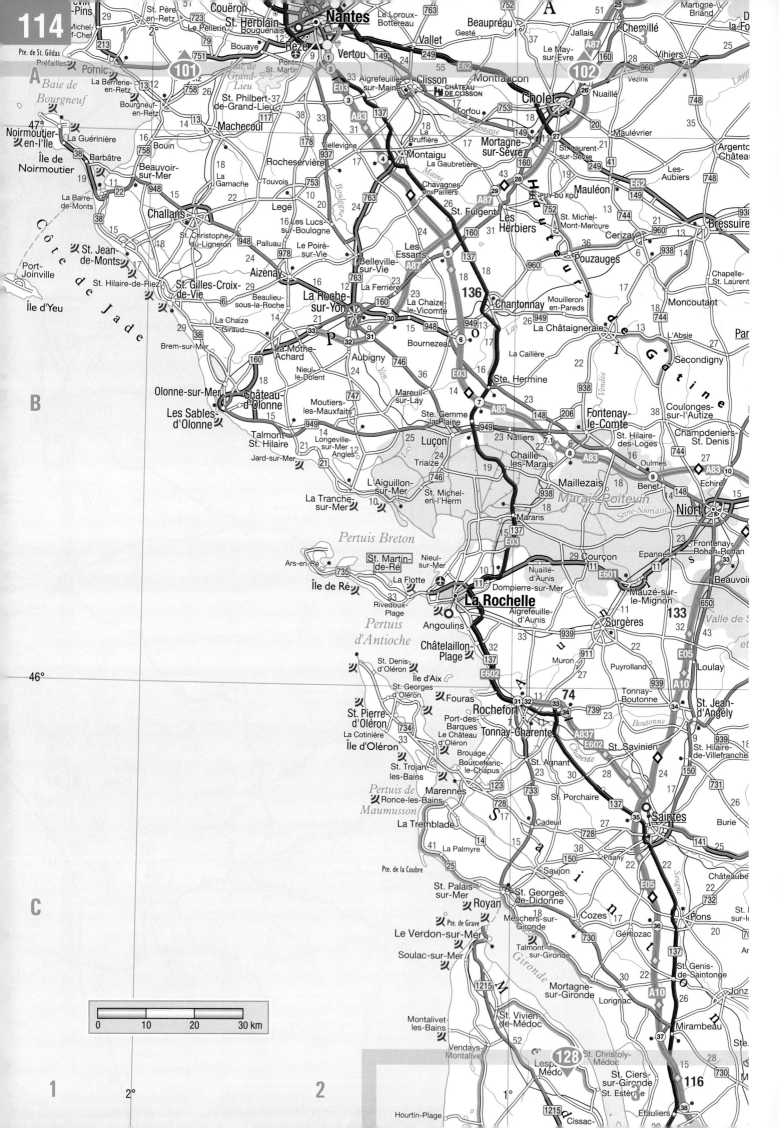

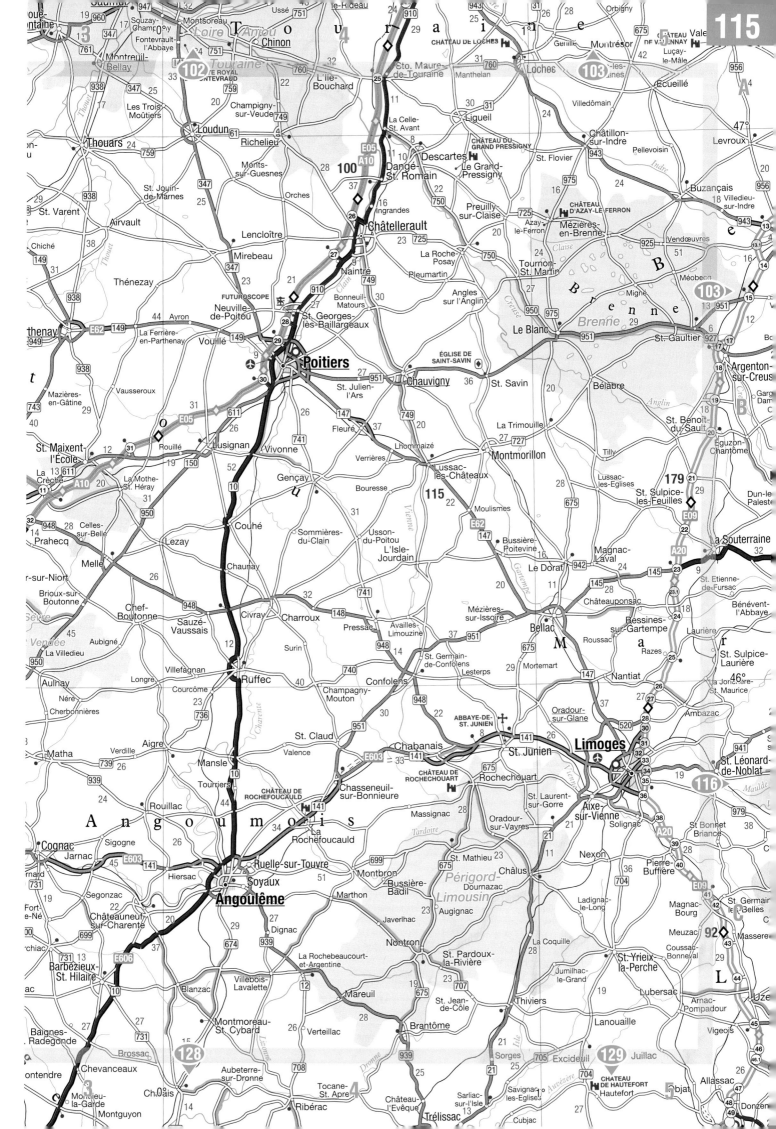

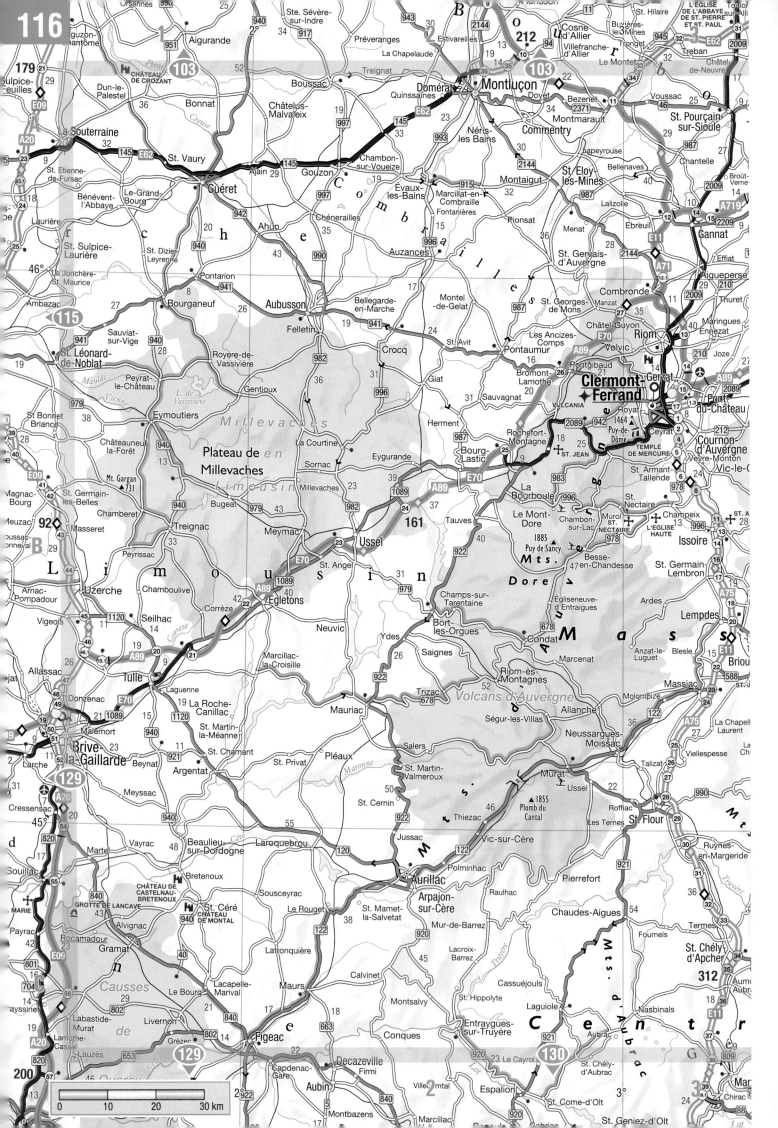

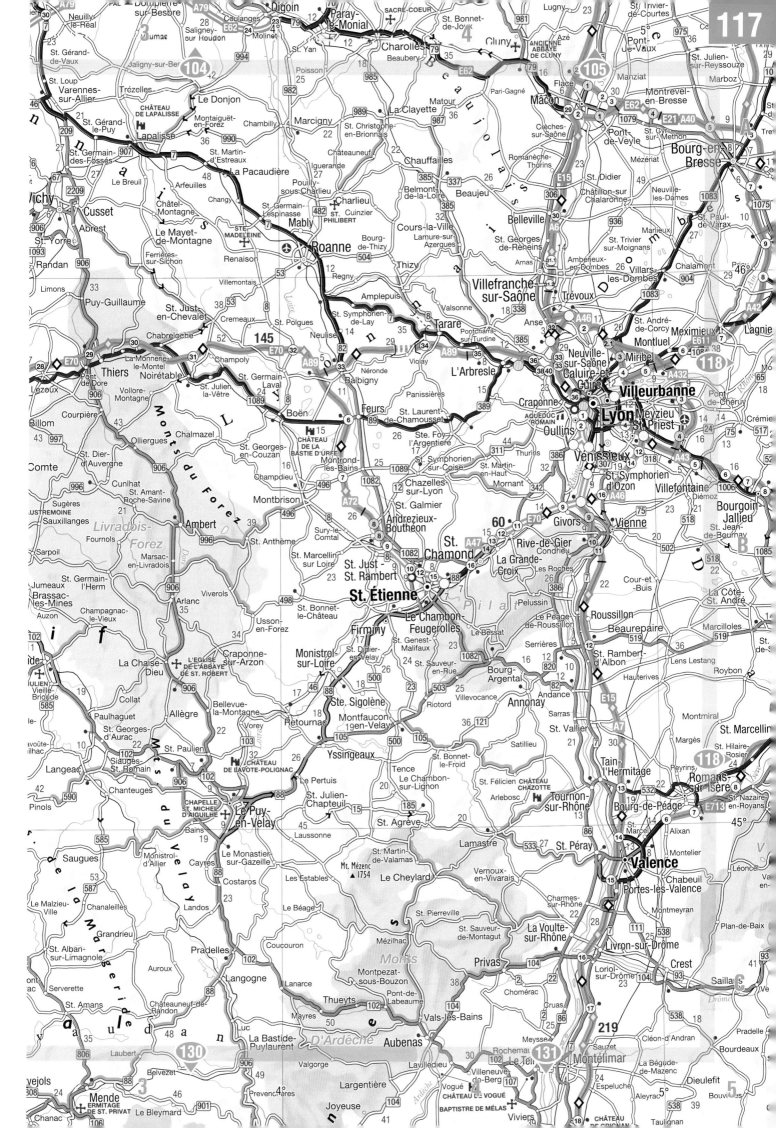

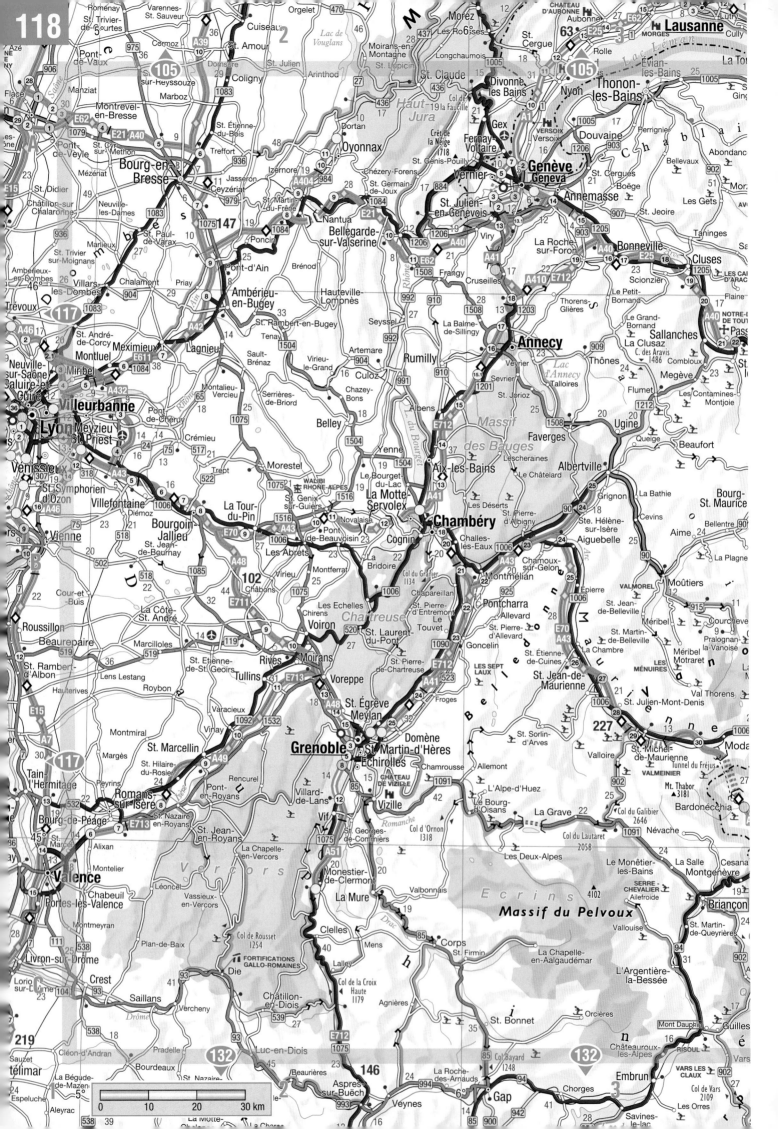

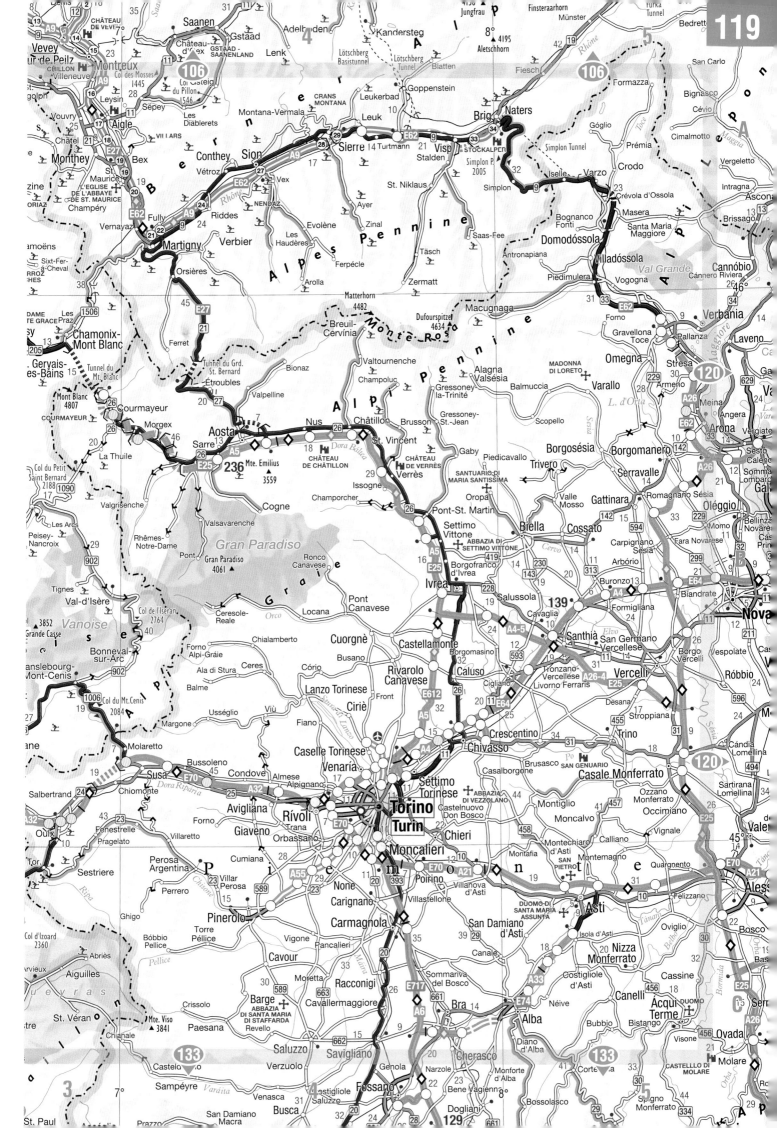

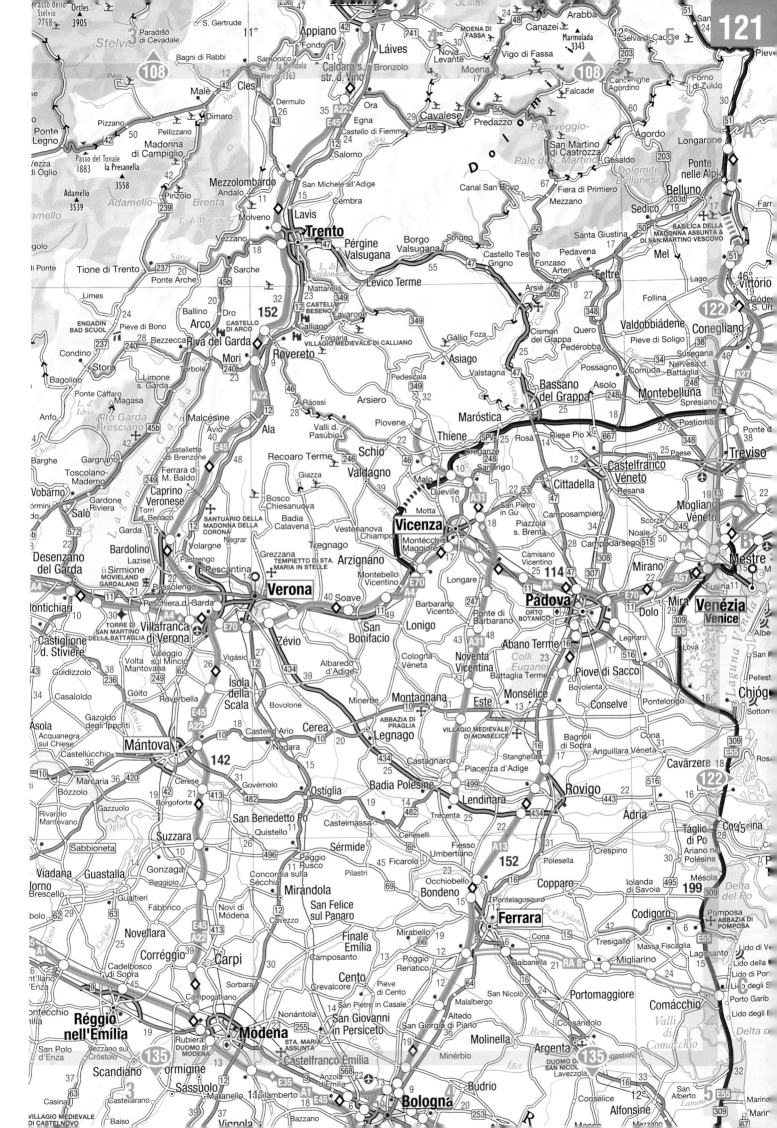

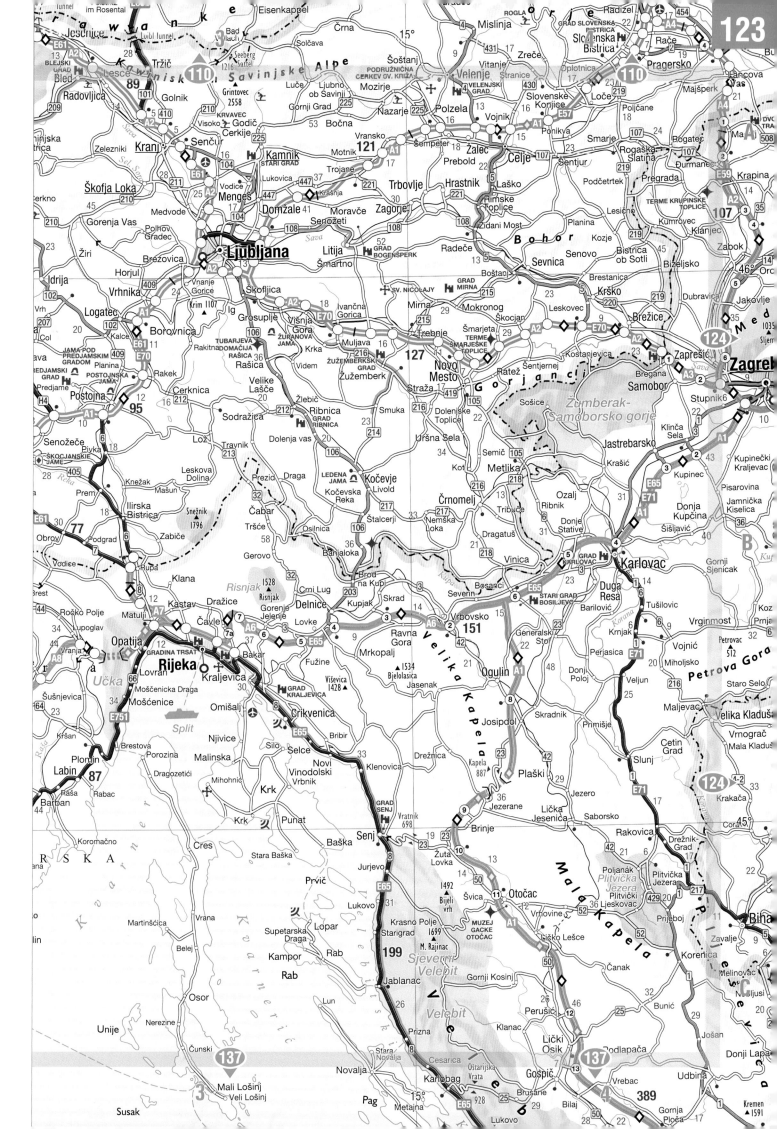

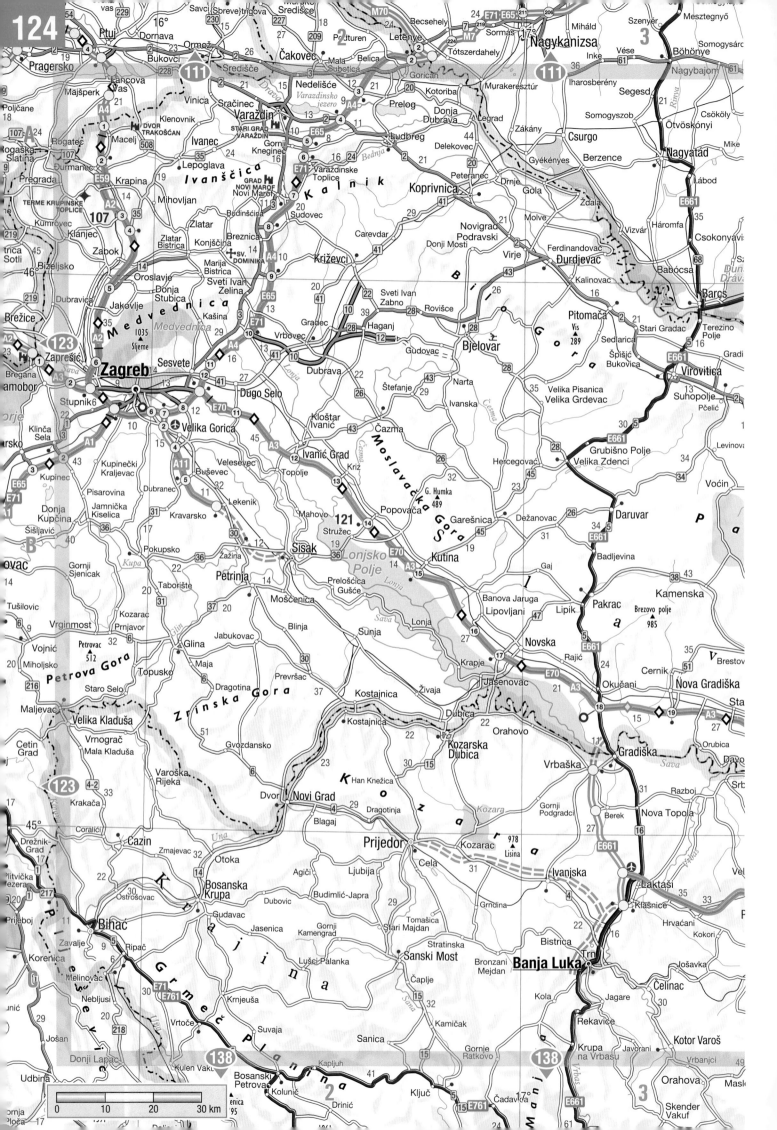

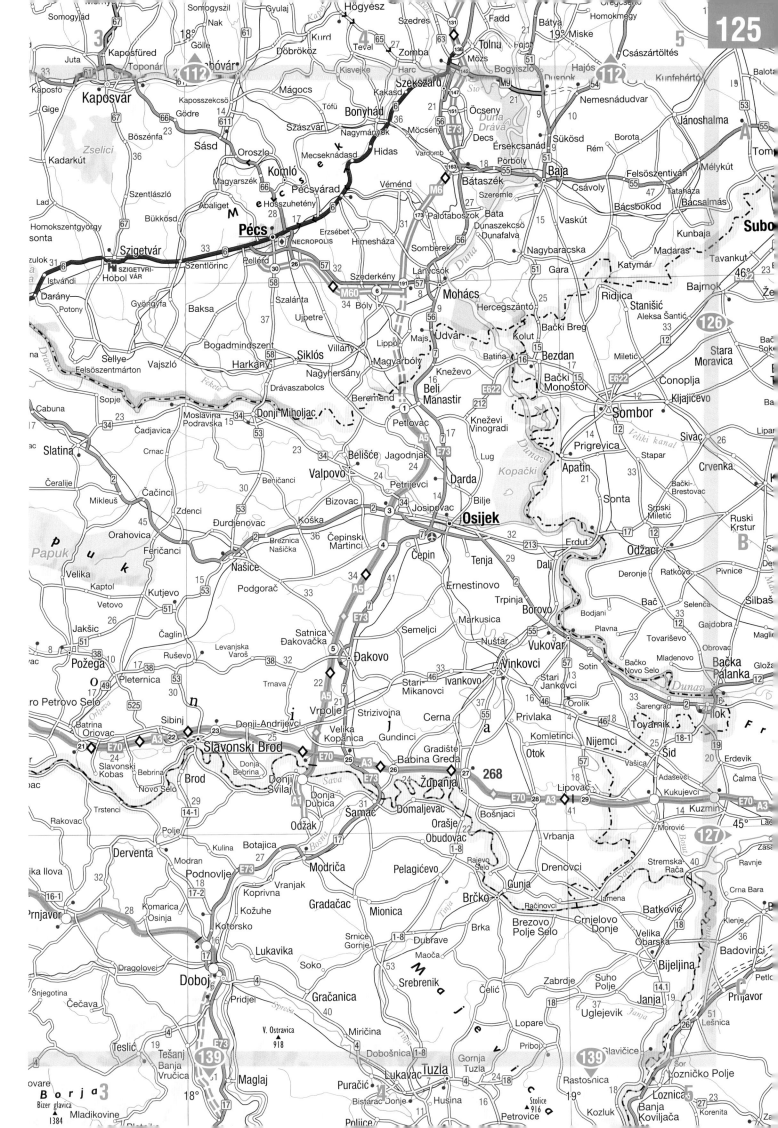

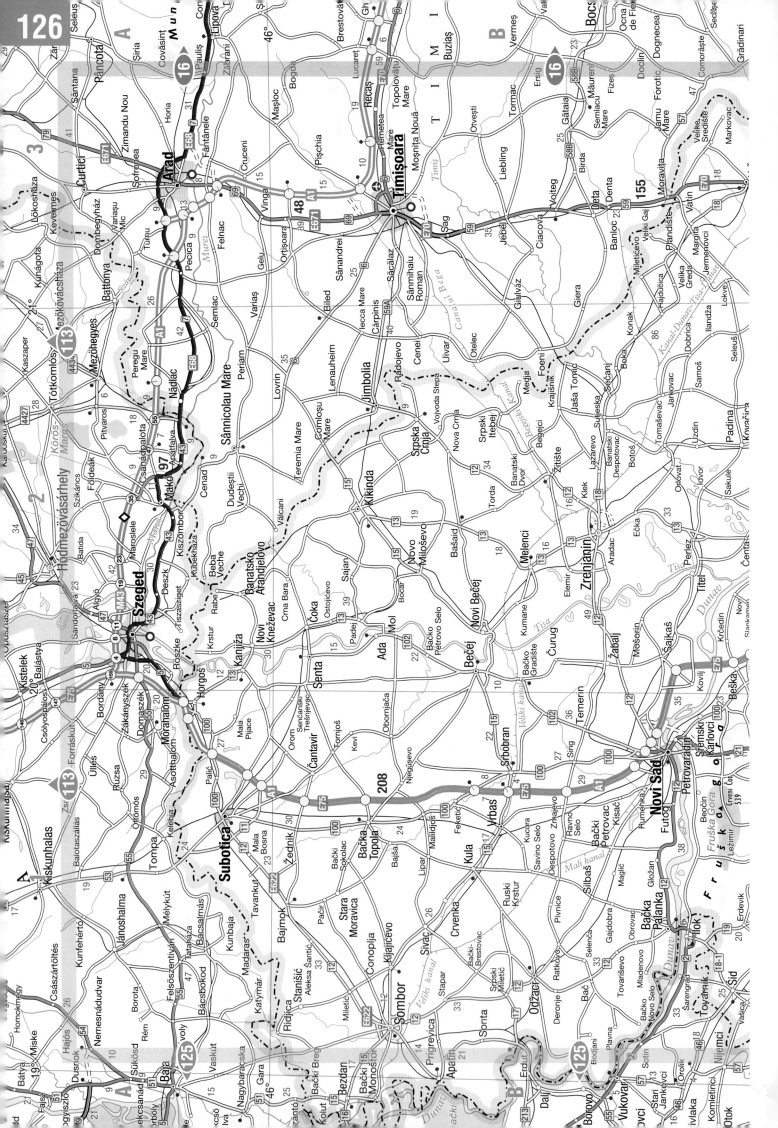

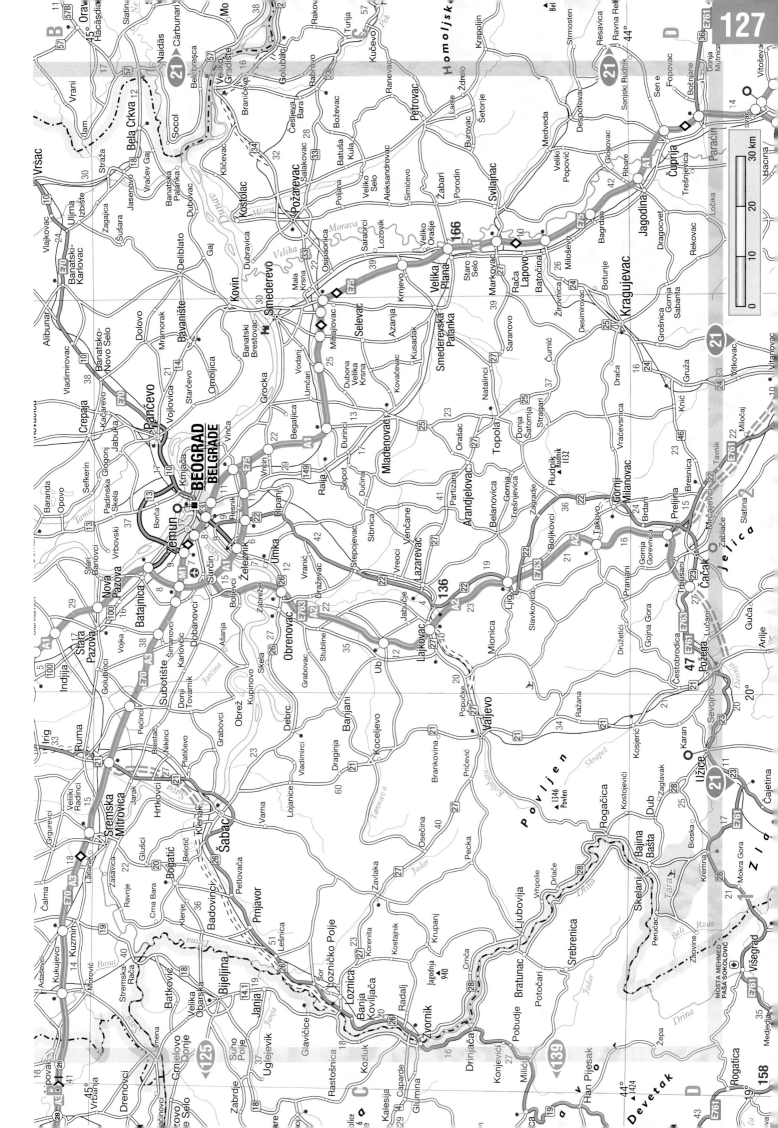

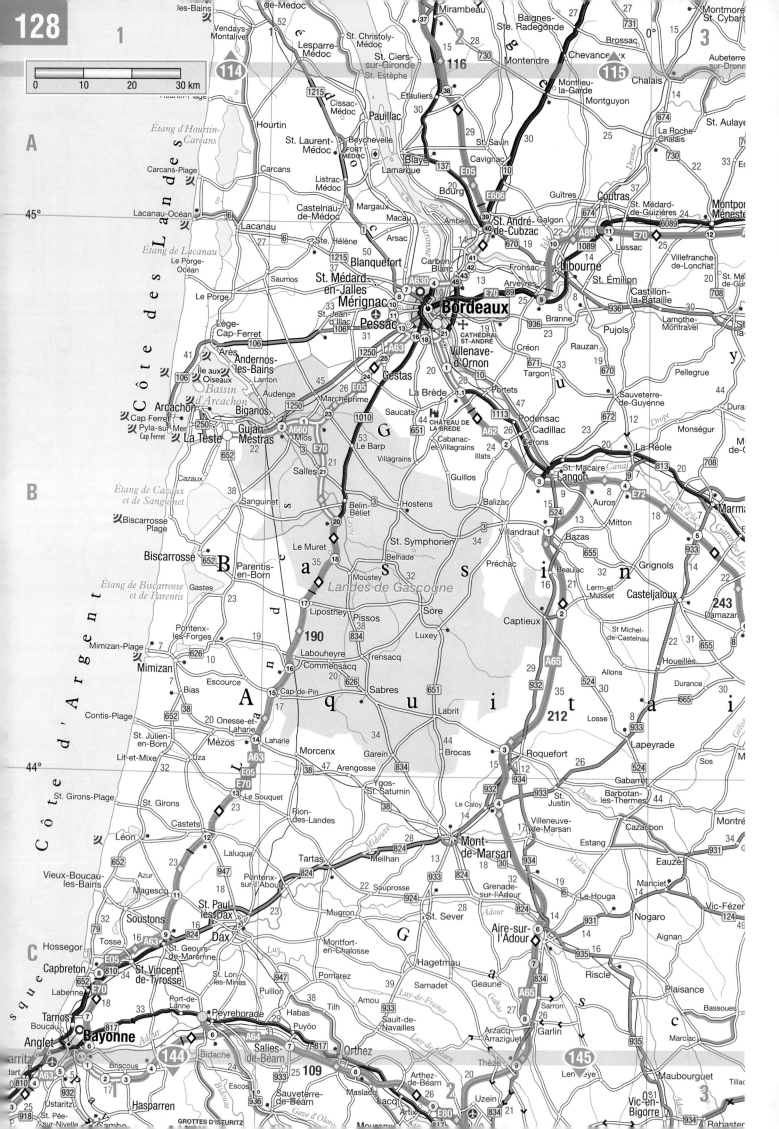

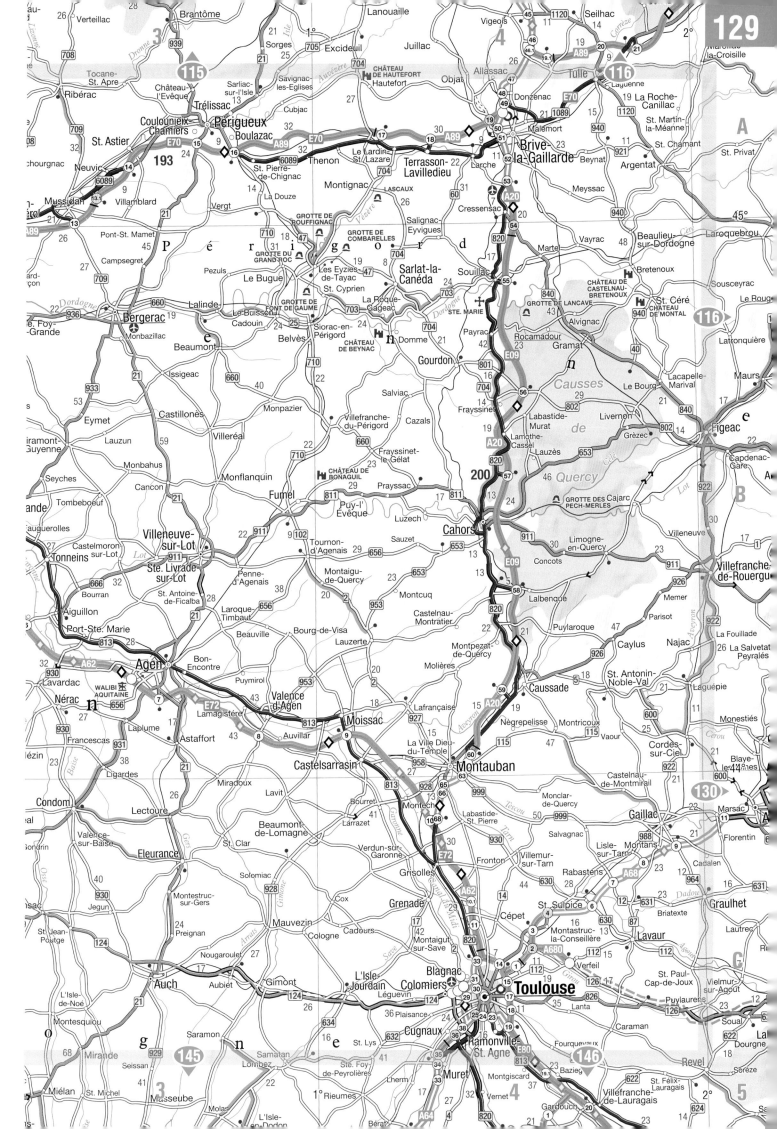

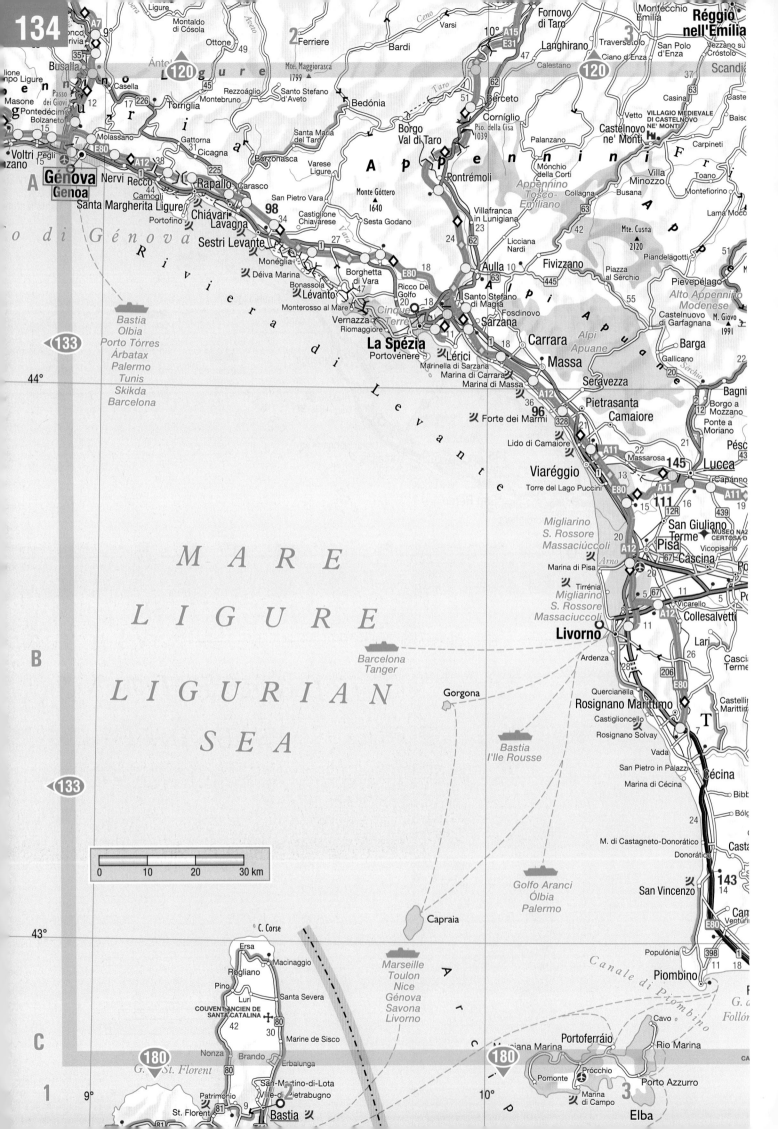

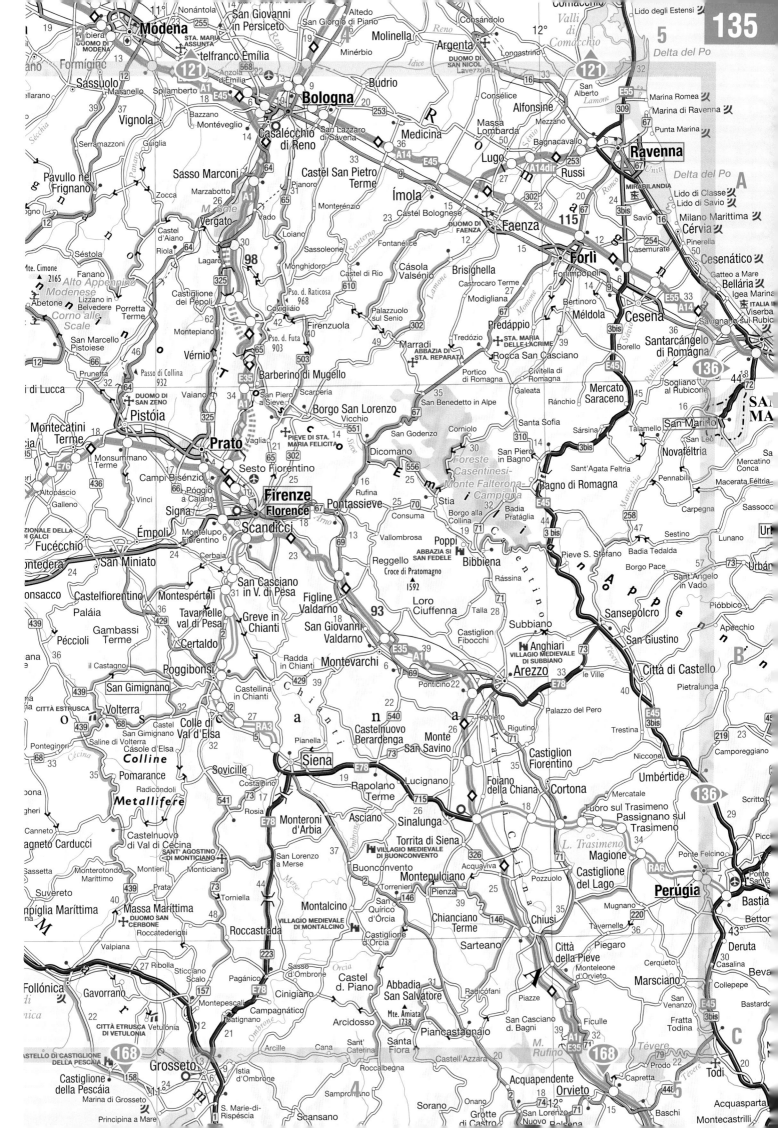

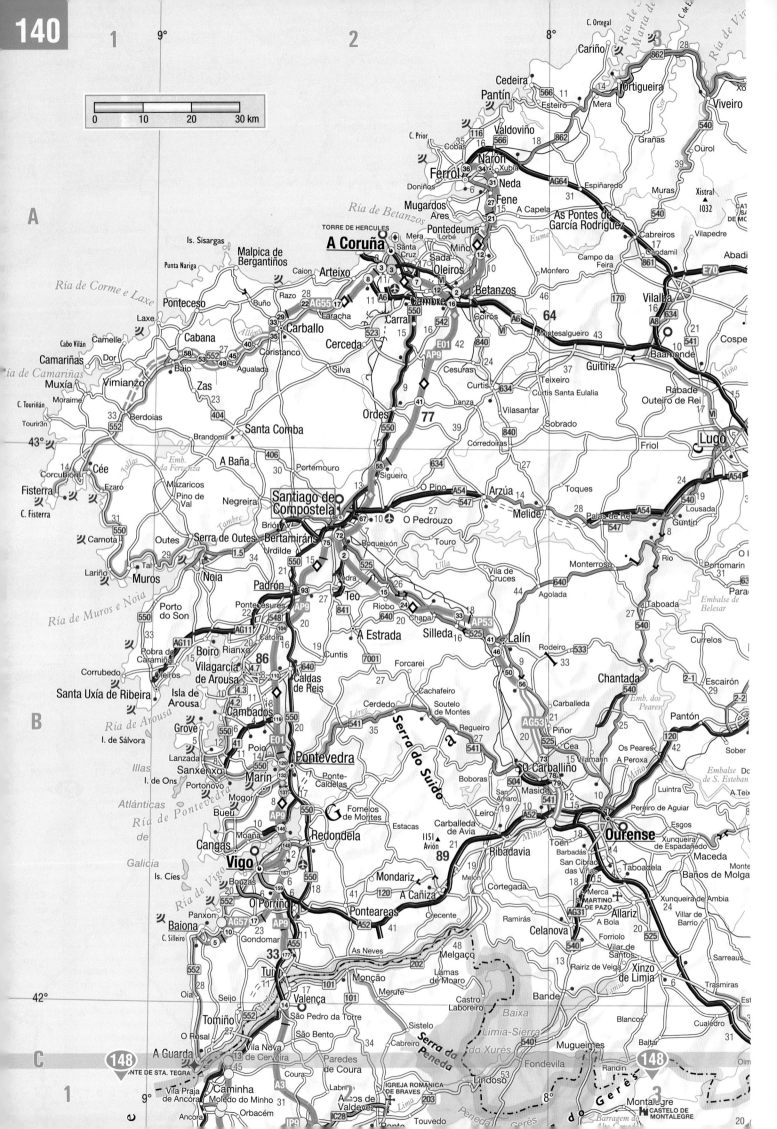

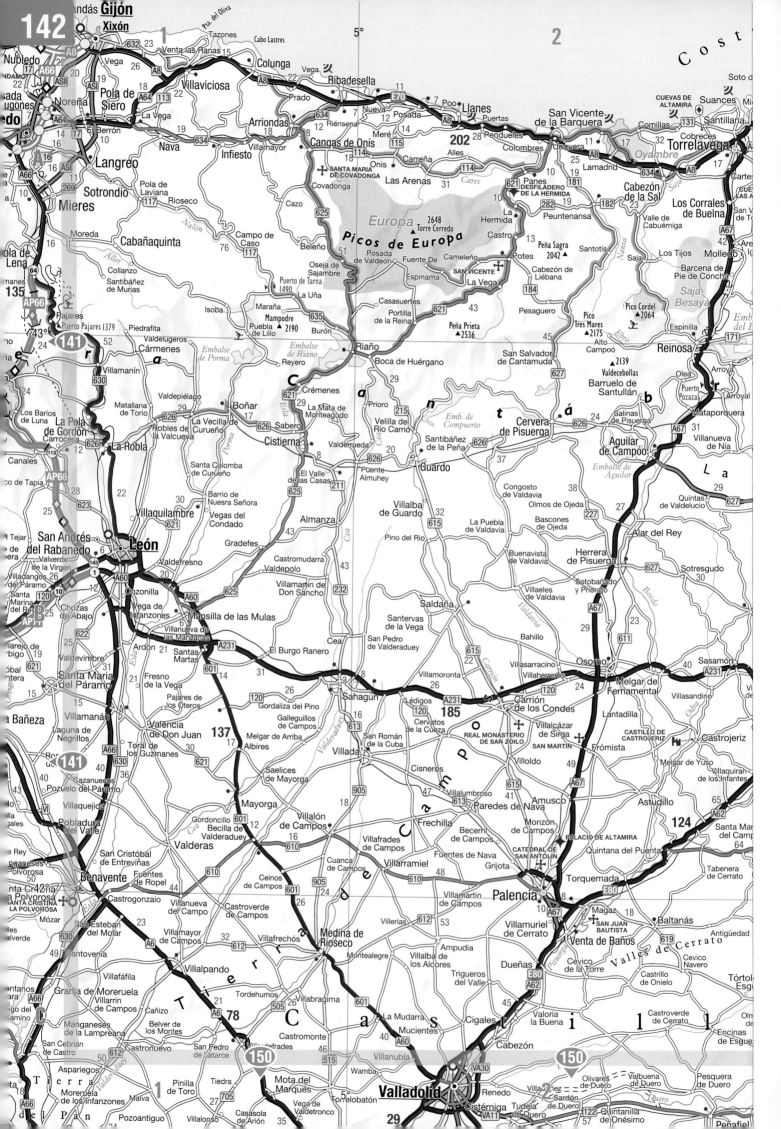

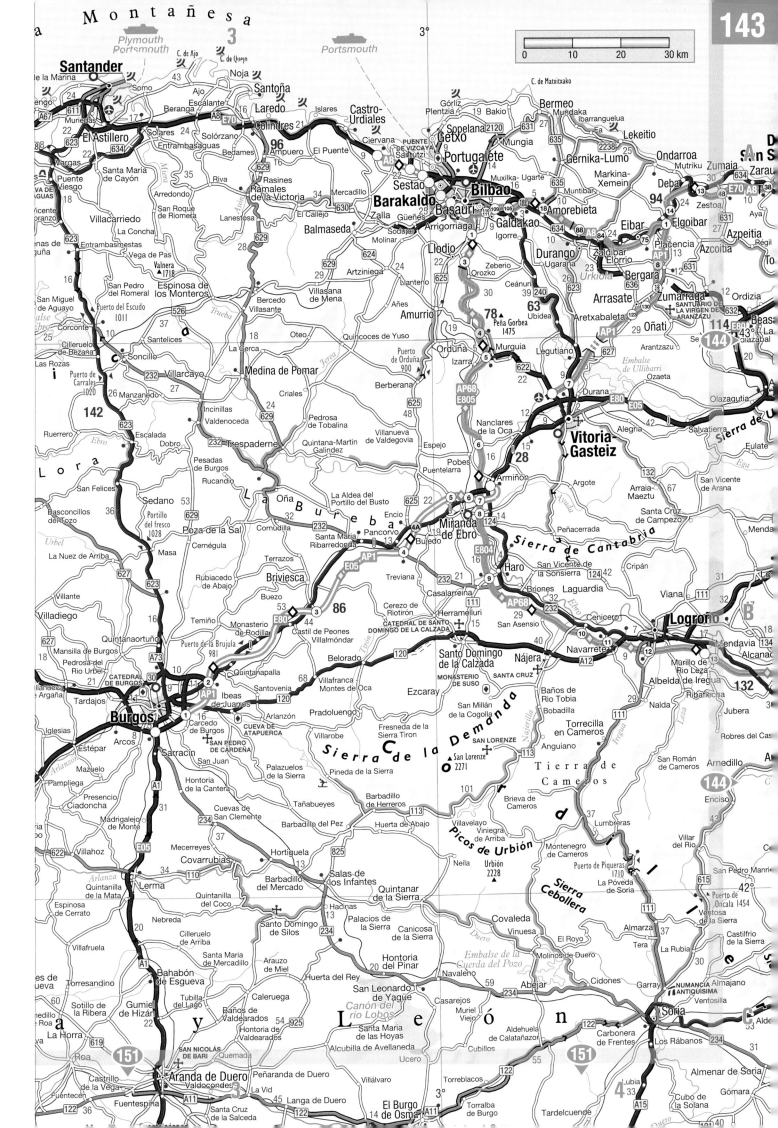

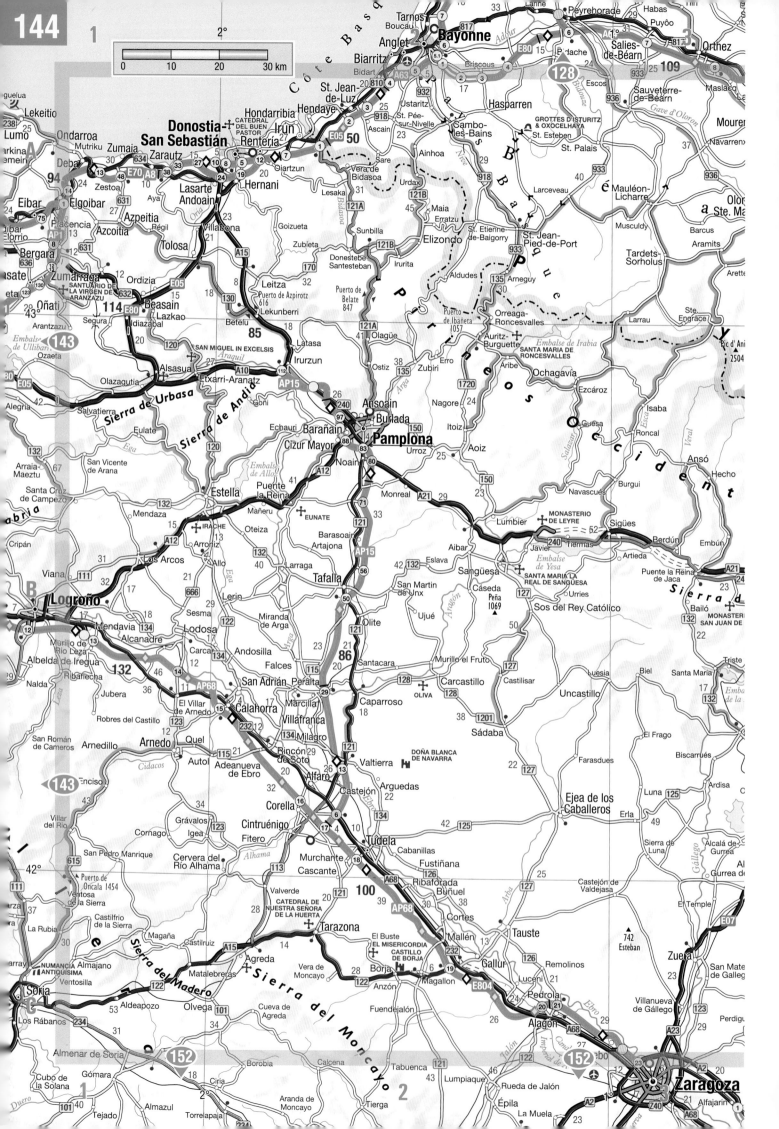

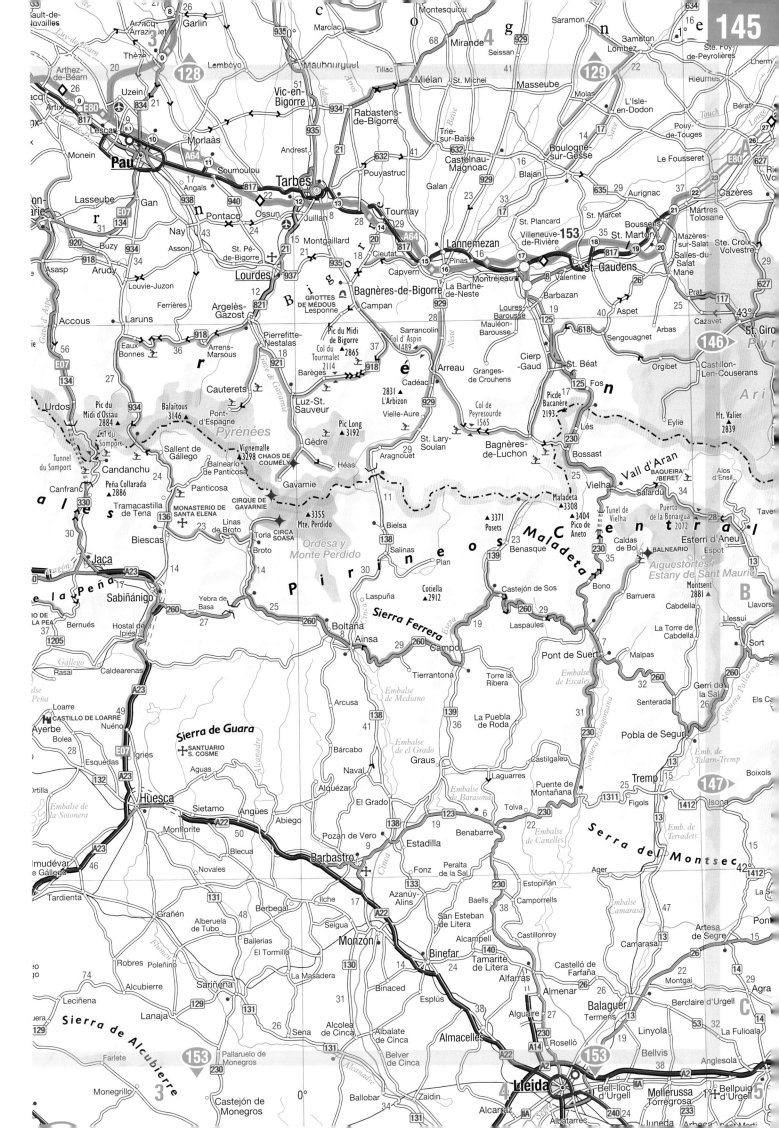

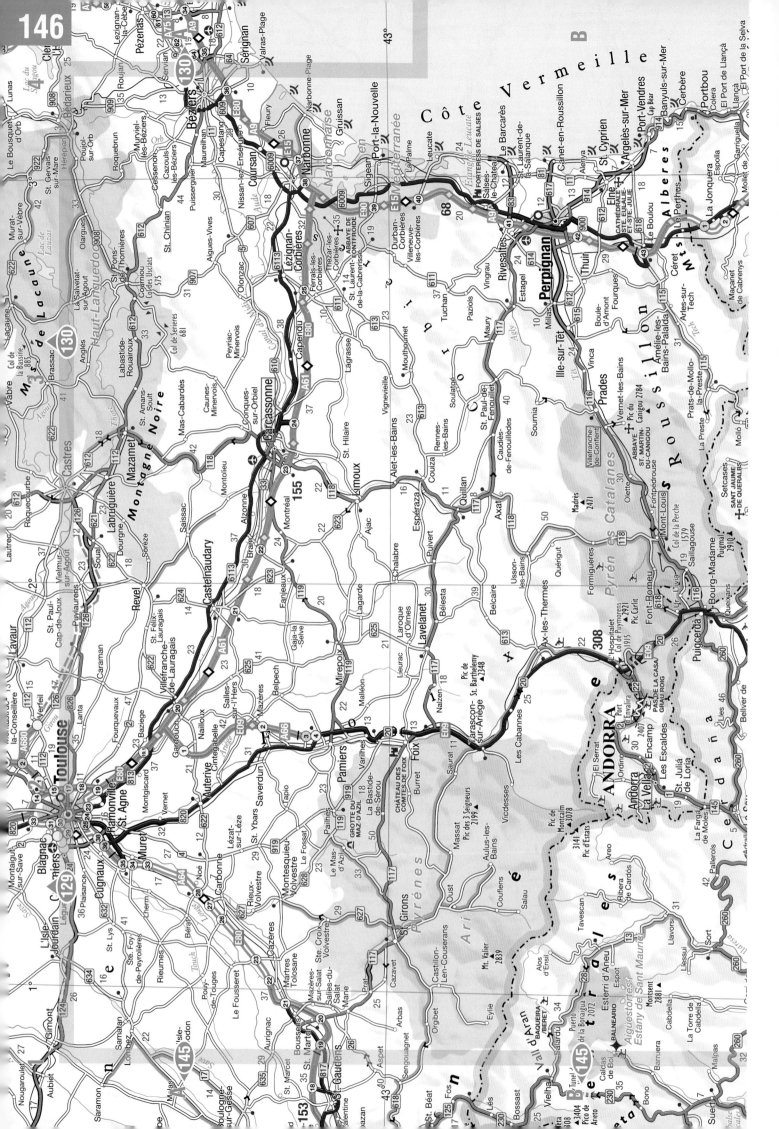

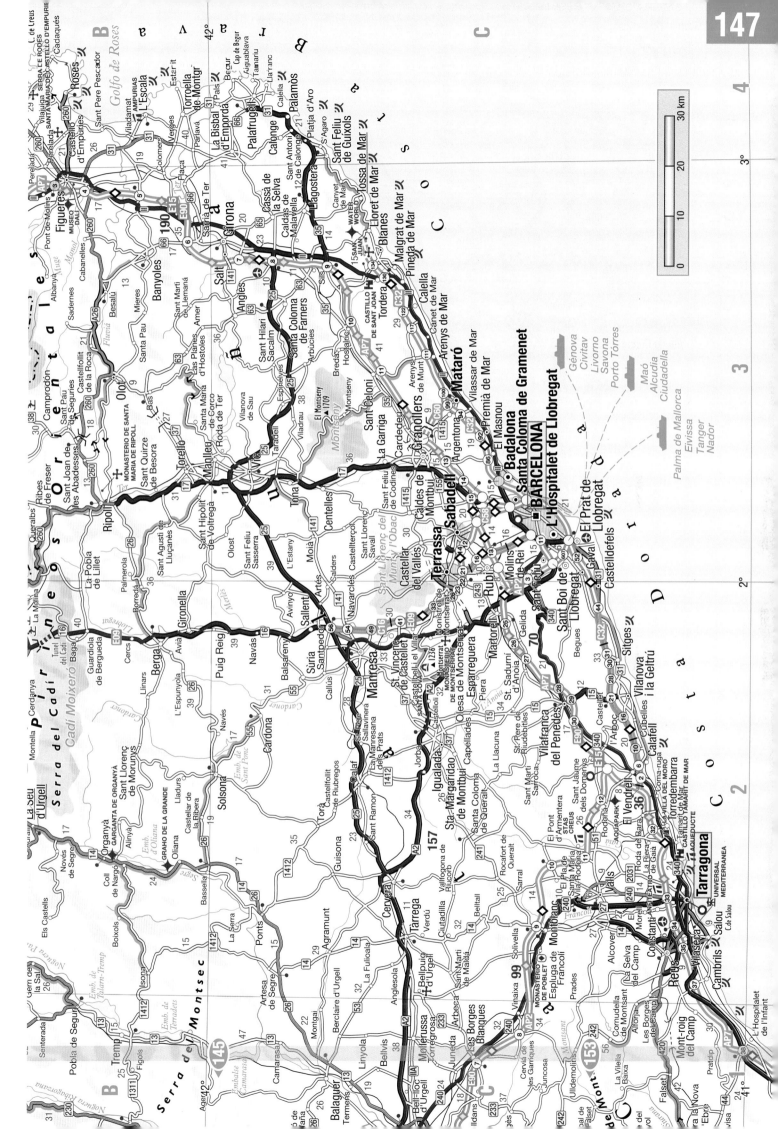

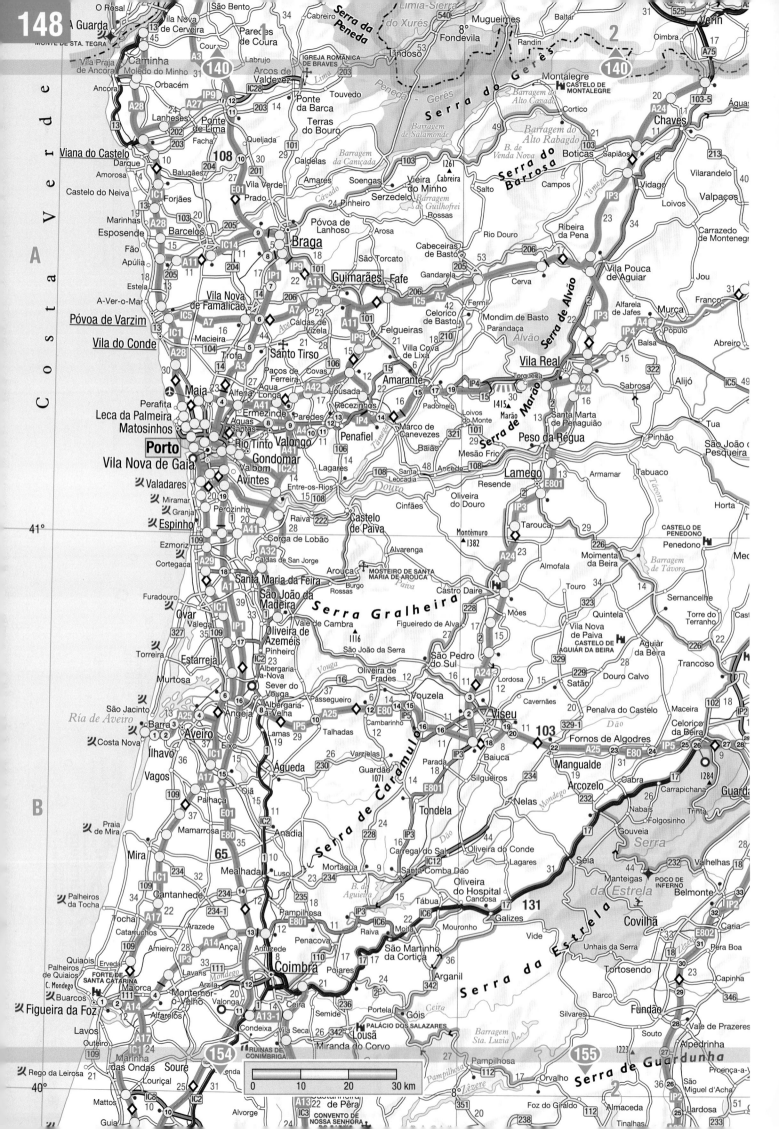

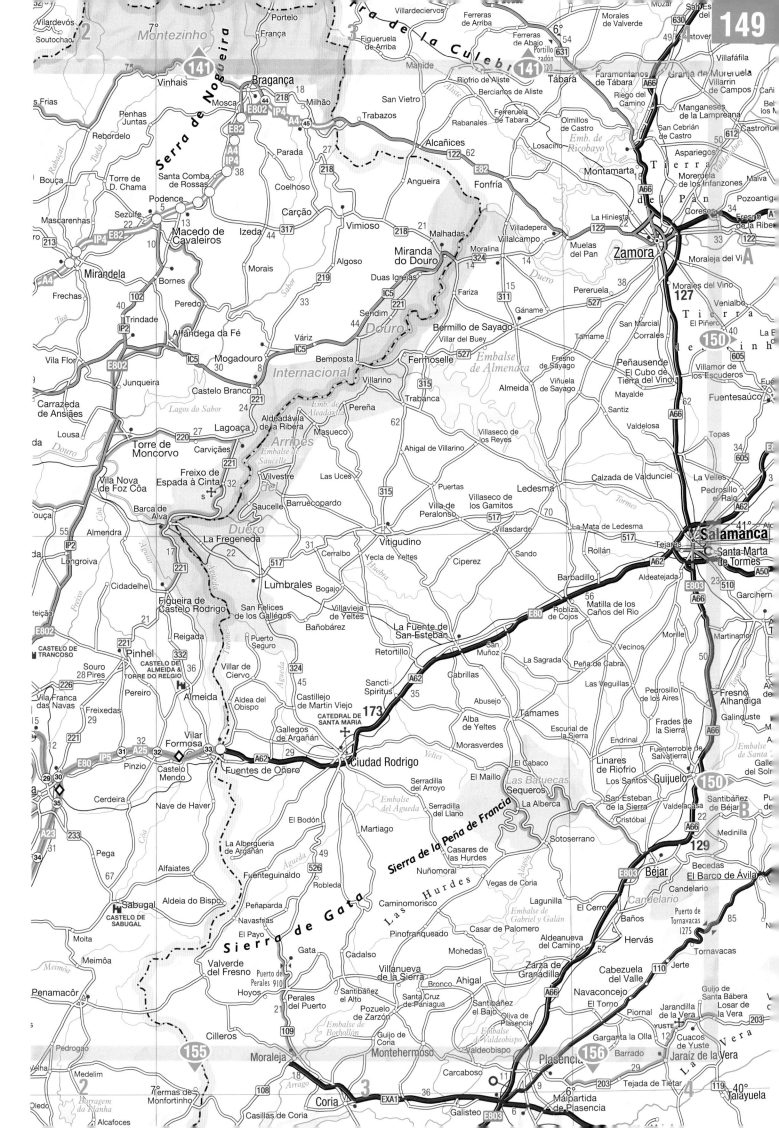

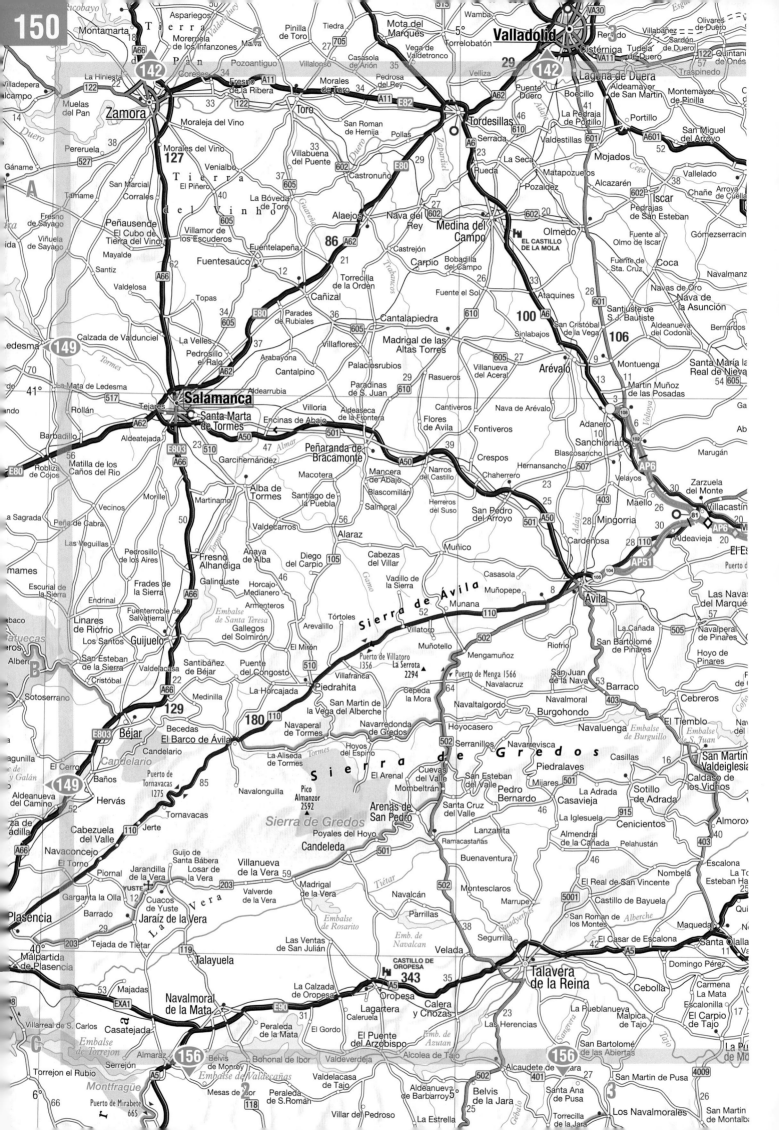

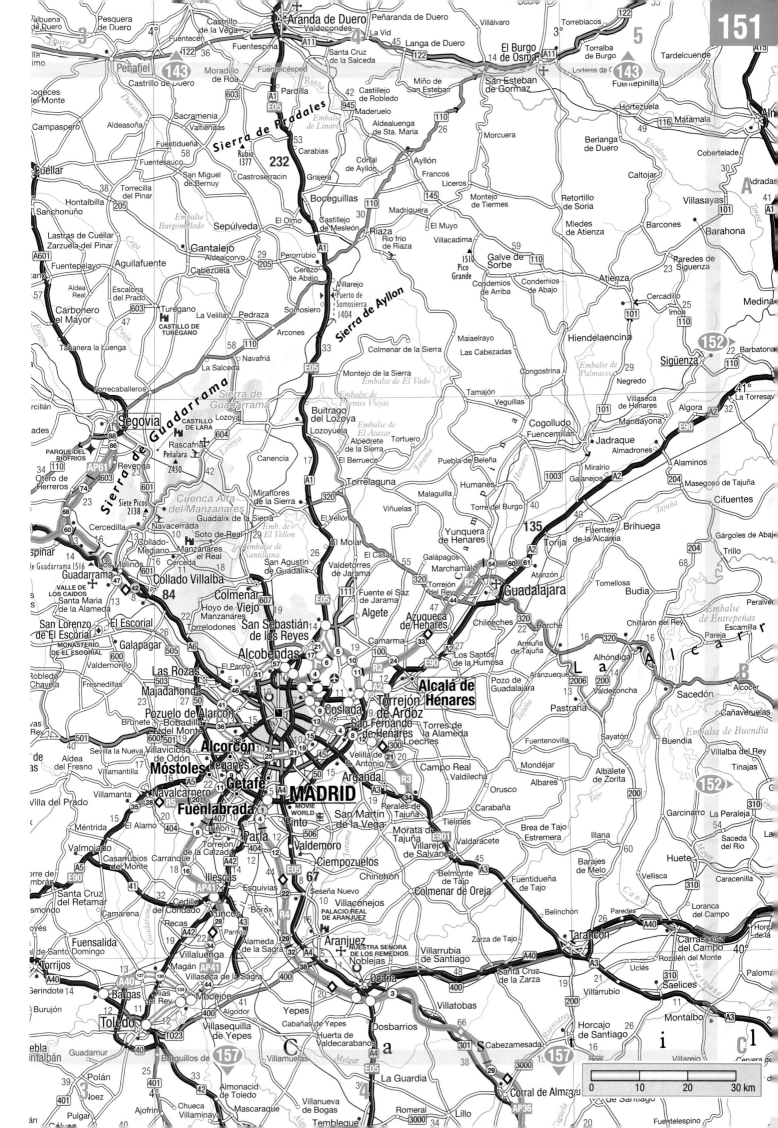

Garray · Almajano · Almajano
NUMANCIA · Mataleralas · Ágreda · Vera de Moncayo · 28 · Borja · Gallur · Remolinos
ANTIQUÍSIMA · Soria · Ventosilla · 2° · Sierra del Madero · Magallón · Luceni · 21
Carbonera de Frentes · Los Rábanos · 53 · Aldeapozo · Olvega · 101 · Cueva de Ágreda · Sierra del Moncayo · Fuendejalón · Anzón · E804 · Pedrola · 20 · 21 · 24
144 · 31 · **144** · 26 · Alagón · Utebo · 27 · 29
Lubia · 33 · Almenar de Soria · Jaray · Borobia · Calcena · Tabuenca · 43 · Lumpiaque · 122 · 46
Tardelcuende · Cubo de la Solana · Gómara · 18 · Ciria · Aranda de Moncayo · Tierga · Illueca · Rueda de Jalón · Épila · La Muela · 23
Matamala · 101 · 40 · Almazul · Torrelapaja · 234 · 20 · Villarroya de la Sierra · Cervera de la Cañada · Morata de Jalón · Ricla · Calatorao · 19 · 48 · Cadrete
A · Almazán · Escobasa de Almazán · Serón de Nájima · Deza · Villalengua · 17 · Savñán · El Frasno · La Almunia de Doña Godina · Muel
Cobertelade · Morón de Almazán · 43 · 116 · Monteagudo de las Vicarias · 47 · Calatayud · Ateca · E90 · **171** · Santa Cruz de Grío · 220 · Longares · 19 · Cariñena
Adradas · 41 · Villasayas · Barahona · Aguaviva de la Vega · 30 · Ariza · Cetina · Alhama de Aragón · Mara · 37 · Miedes de Aragón · Aguarón · Villanueva del Huerva · 44
151 · Medinaceli · Salinas de Medinaceli · Santa María de Huerta · Cabolafuente · Nuevalos · Morata de Jiloca · Fuentes de Jiloca · 1504 · Mainar · 330 · Herrera de los Navarros
Paredes de Sigüenza · 110 · 15 · Laina · Mochales · Milmarcos · PIEDRA · 202 · 58 · Villafeliche · A23 · Daroca · Badules · Villar de los Navarros
Barbatona · 110 · Alcolea del Pinar · Marachón · Labros · 210 · Campillo de Aragón · Cubel · Santa Cruz · 1423 · Santed · 211 · Báguena · Bádenas · Monforte de Moyuela
41° · La Torresaviñán · Mazarete · 60 · Anquela del Ducado · Tortuera · 213 · 53 · Laguna de Gallocanta · Gallocanta · 234 · Fonfría · Anadón
Algora · A2 · 32 · Aragoncillo · 1518 · Cillas · Odón · Bello · Calamocha · Cutanda
Caminos · Riba de Saelices · 211 · Cobeta · 10 · Rillo de Gallo · Molina de Aragón · 22 · Caminreal · Bañón · 211 · 44 · Torre los Negros
Masegoso de Tajuña · Abádanes · Sacecorbo · Huertahernando · CASTILLO DE MOLINA DE ARAGÓN · 28 · Monreal del Campo · 9 · Pancrudo
Cifuentes · Tajo · Gárgoles de Abajo · Zaorejas · El Pobo de Dueñas · 211 · Pozuel del Campo · A23 · 234 · 32 · Mezquita de Jarque · 11
Trillo · 204 · Valtablado del Rio · Villanueva de Alcorón · Terzaga · Tordesilos · Villafranco del Campo · 25 · Bueña · Visiedo · Perales de Alfambra
Peralveche · 210 · Beteta · Checa · Alustante · Ródenas · Alba · Santa Eulalia · Alfambra · 420
Embalse de Entrepeñas · Escamilla · Salmerón · Vadillos · Perelejos de las Truchas · Orea · Sierra de Albarracín · Orihuela del Tremedal · Pozondón · Bronchales · Cella · 31 · 234
Pareja · Valdeolivas · Priego · 210 · Noguera · 1856 · Sierra Alta · Gea de Albarracín · 30 · A23 · 35
B · Alcocer · Cañaveruelas · Villaconejos de Trabaque · Cañamares · Fresneda de la Sierra · San Felipe · 1835 · Villar del Cobo · Albarracín · 226
151 · 320 · 310 · 15 · Albalate de las Nogueras · Arcos de la Sierra · Guadalaviar · Frías de Albarracín · Teruel · 28
Villalba del Rey · Cañaveras · 15 · Torrecilla · Tragacete · Bezas · Villastar · 330 · 25 · Sierra de Camarena
Gascueña · Bólliga · Villar de Domingo García · Villalba de la Sierra · Huélamo · Terriente · Toril · Villel · 33 · Aldehuela · Mor
La Peraleja · 310 · La Ventosa · Losares · 1388 · CIUDAD ENCANTADA · La Toba · Javalón · 1695 · La Puebla de Valverde
Saceda del Rio · 320 · Mariana · La Toba · Laguna del Marquesado · Javalambre · 2020 · Sierra de Javalambre
Villar del Saz de Navalón · Chillarón de Cuenca · Valdecabras · Buenache de la Sierra · Valdemoro Sierra · El Hontanar · Libros · Riodeva · Cascante del Rio
Caracenilla · Naharros · A40 · 400 · Cuenca · 41 · 420 · Arcos de las Salinas
El Campo · Horcajada de la Torre · Puerto de Cabrejas · 1150 · Salvacañete · Ademuz · 23 · Santa Cruz de Moya · La Yesa
40° · Cabrejas · Júcar · Cañete · La Peraleja
A3 · 22 · Villares · 158 · 220 · Fuentes · 61 · Cañada del Hoyo · 215 · Fuentelespino de Moya · **158** · Landete · 2° · Alpuente
Palomares del Campo · Reillo · 420 · Carboneras de Guadazaón · 34 · Landete · Aras de Alpuente · 37
San Lorenzo de la Párrilla · Altarejos · Villar de Humo · Titaguas · Alpuente
1 · **2**

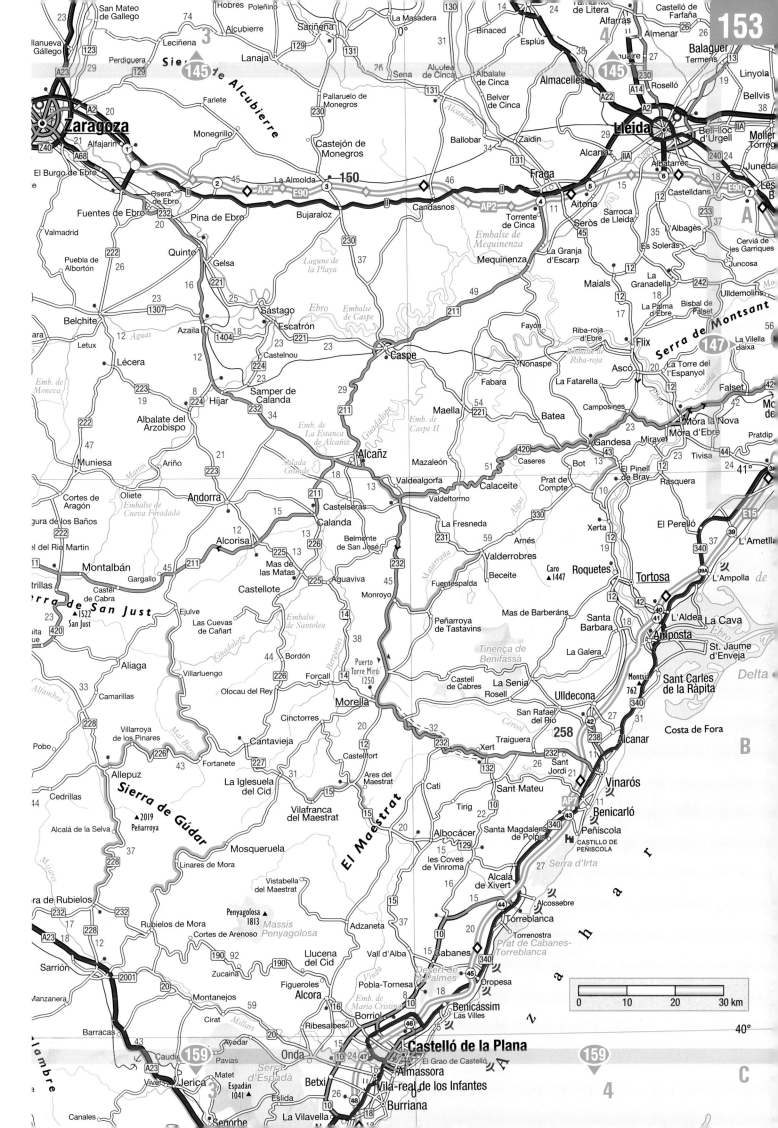

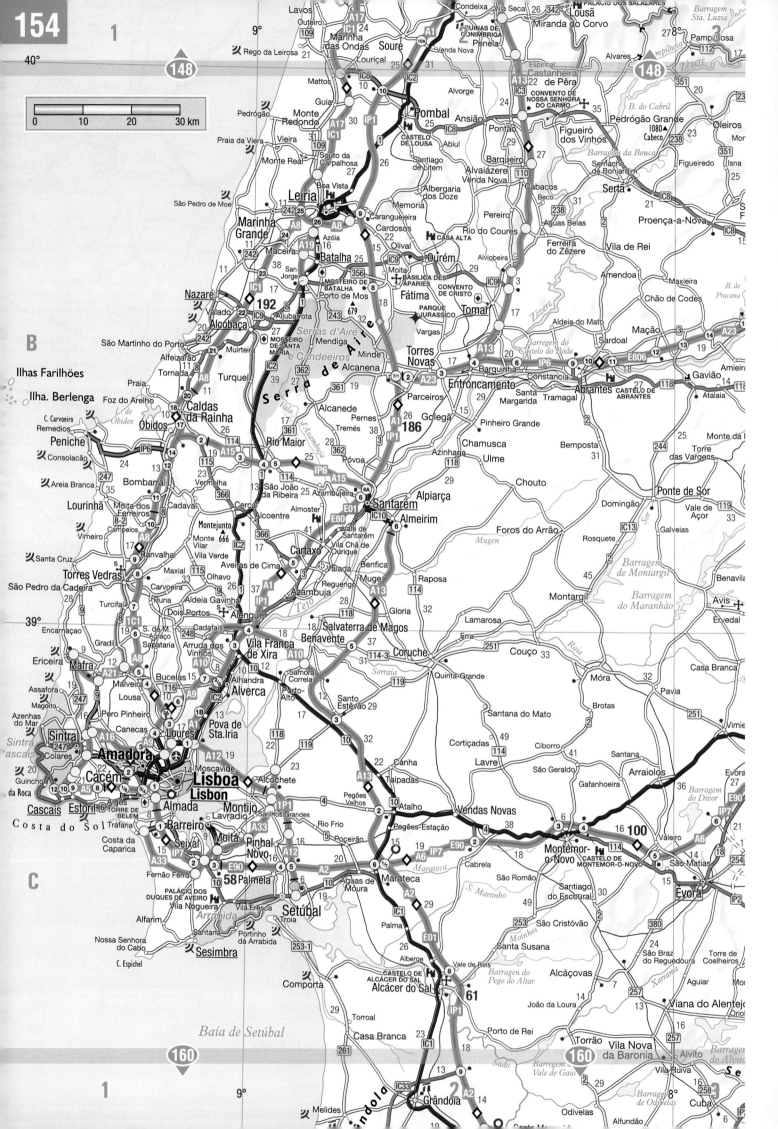

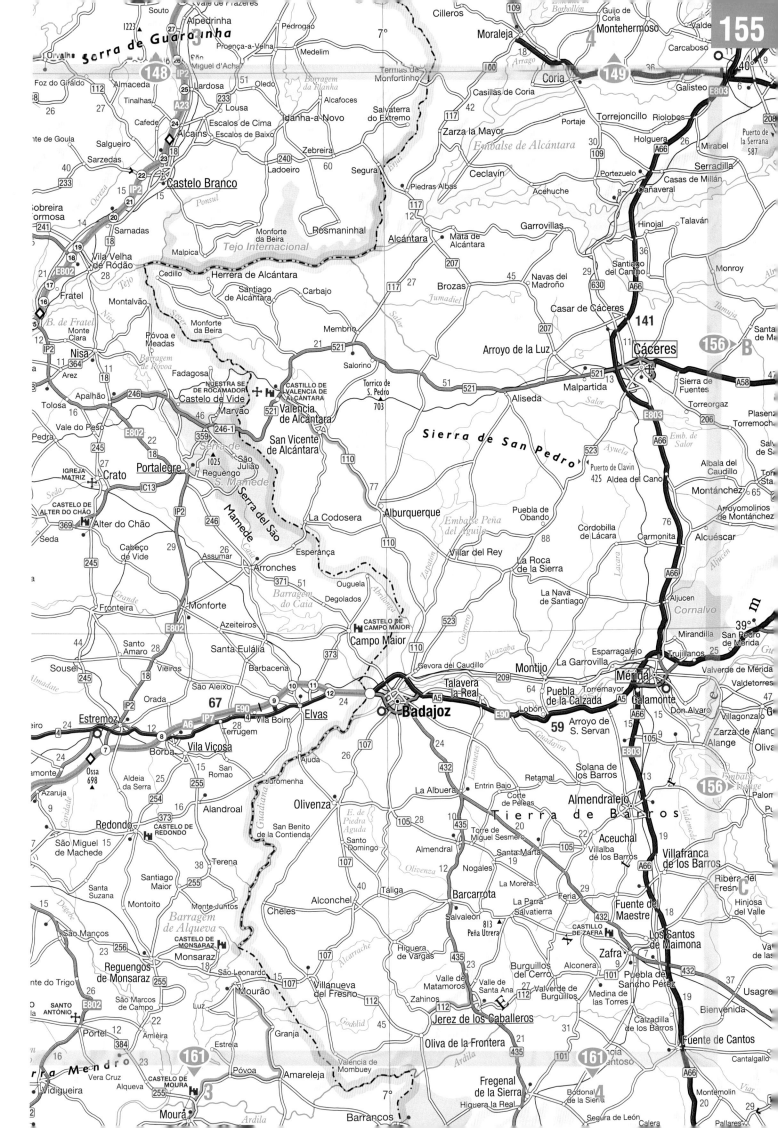

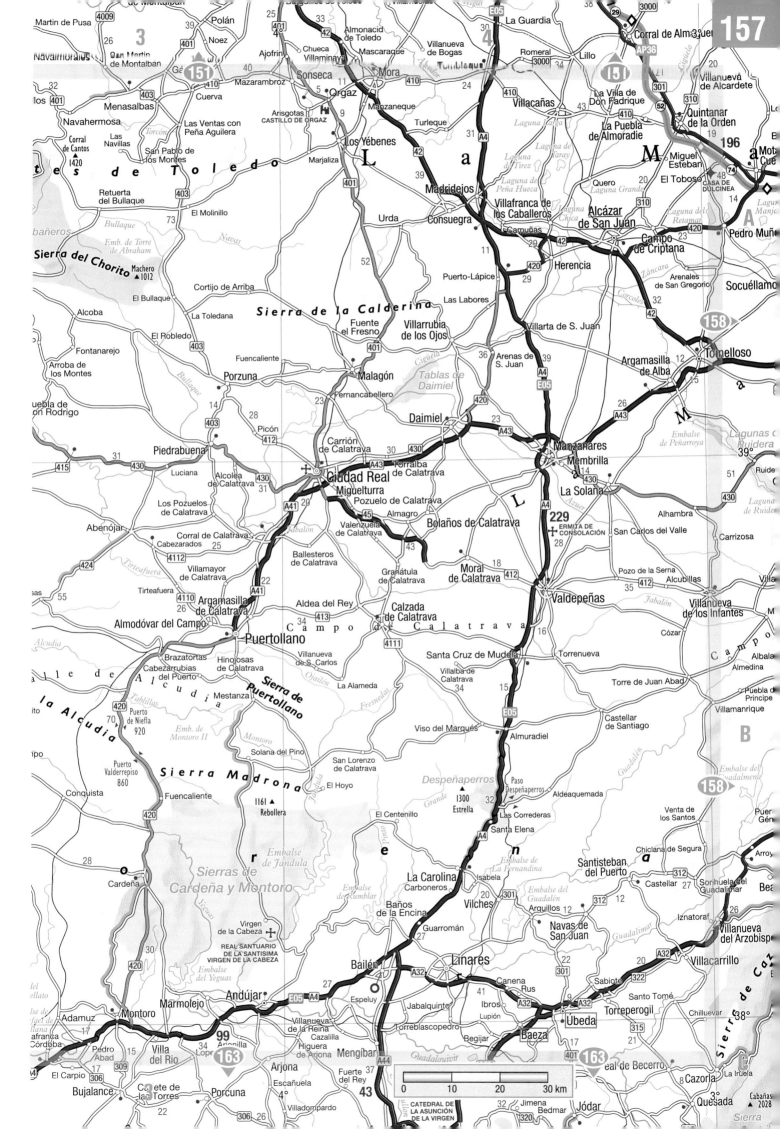

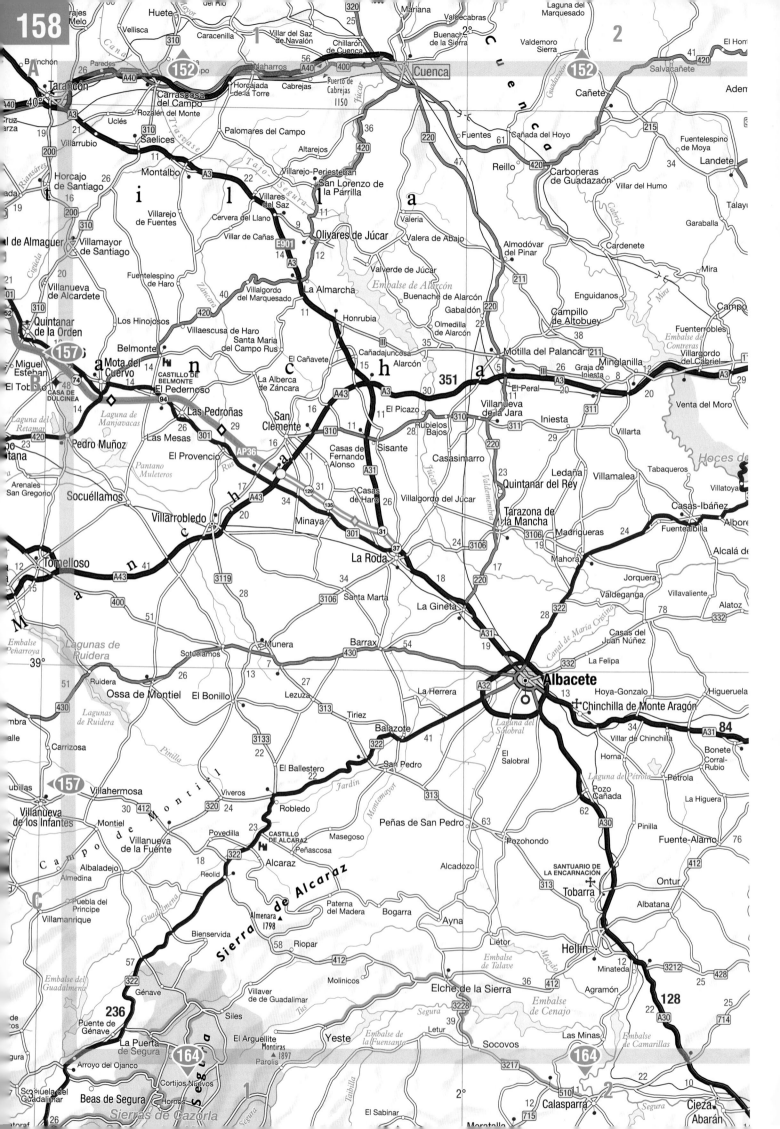

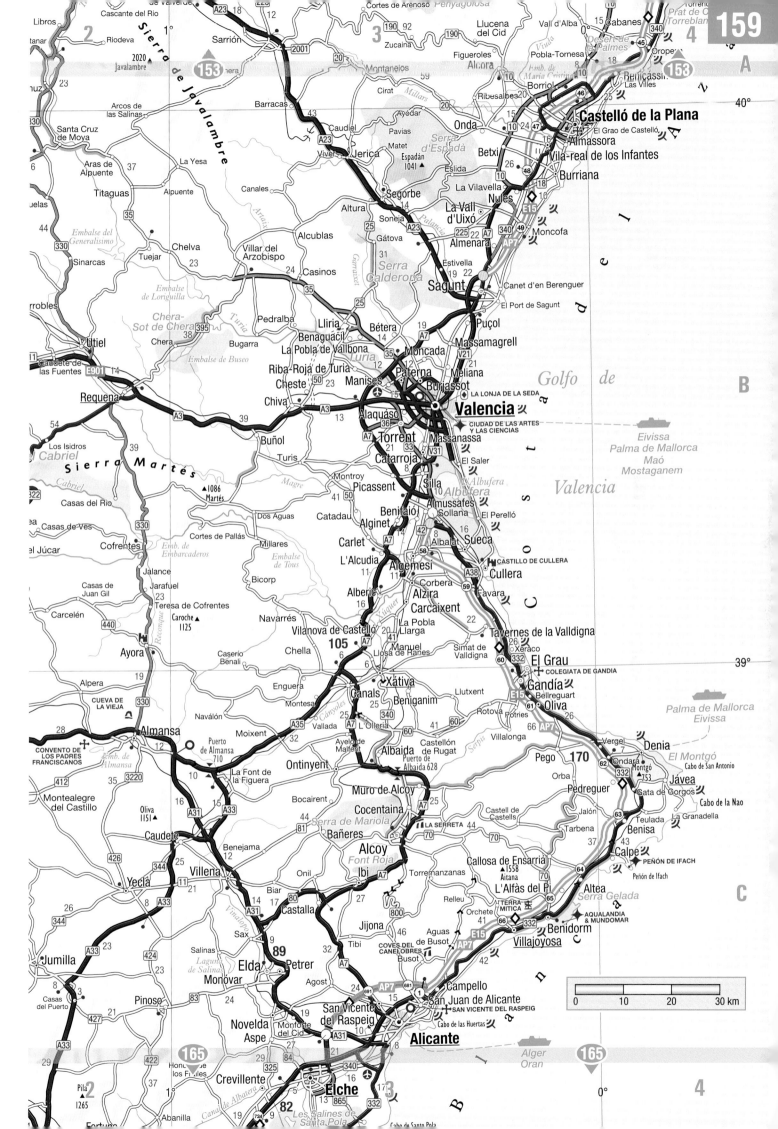

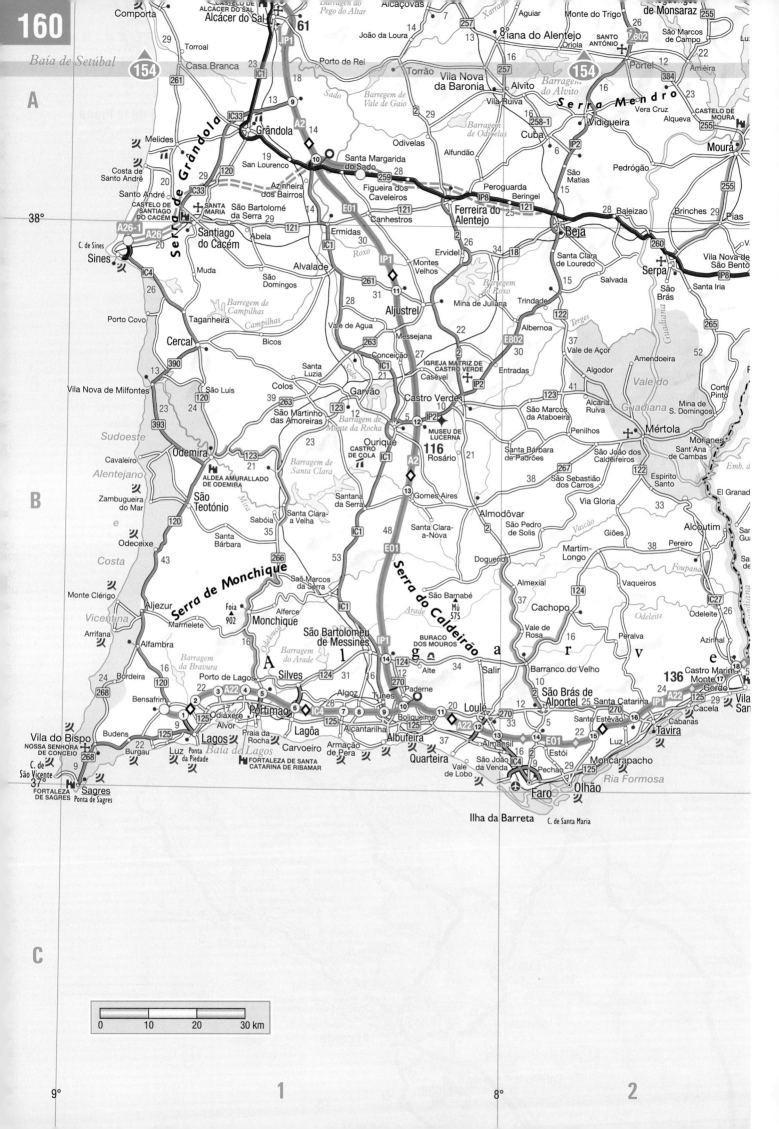

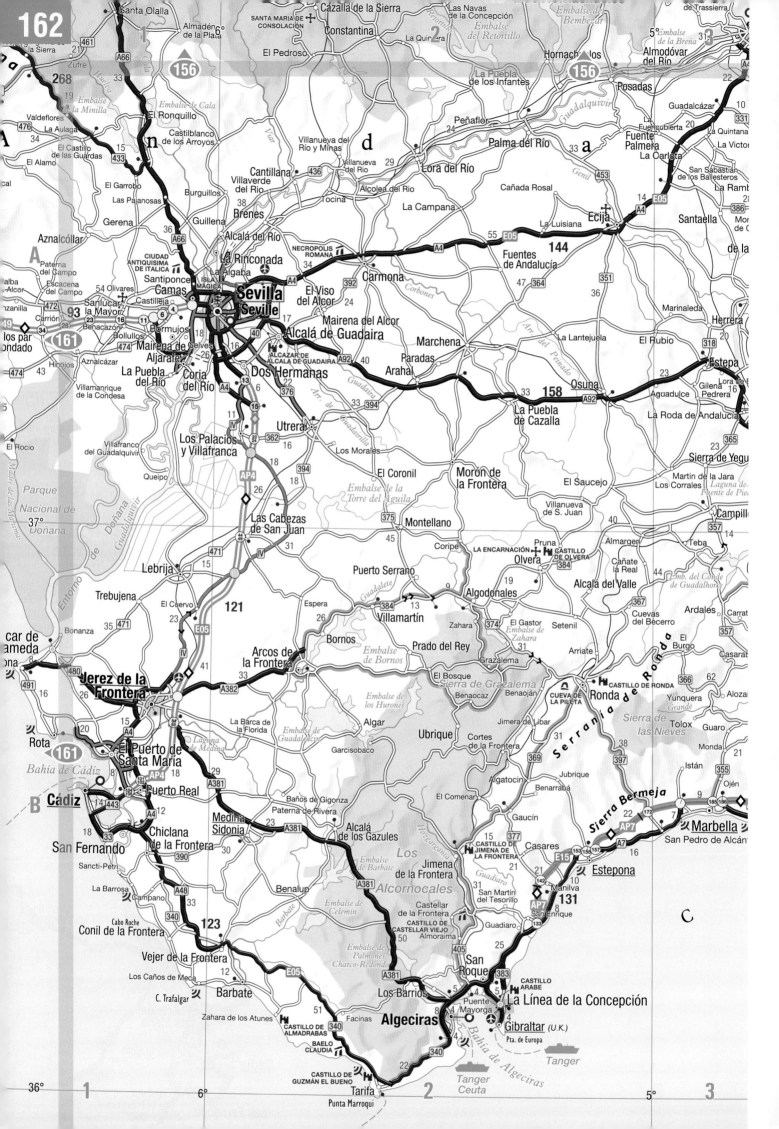

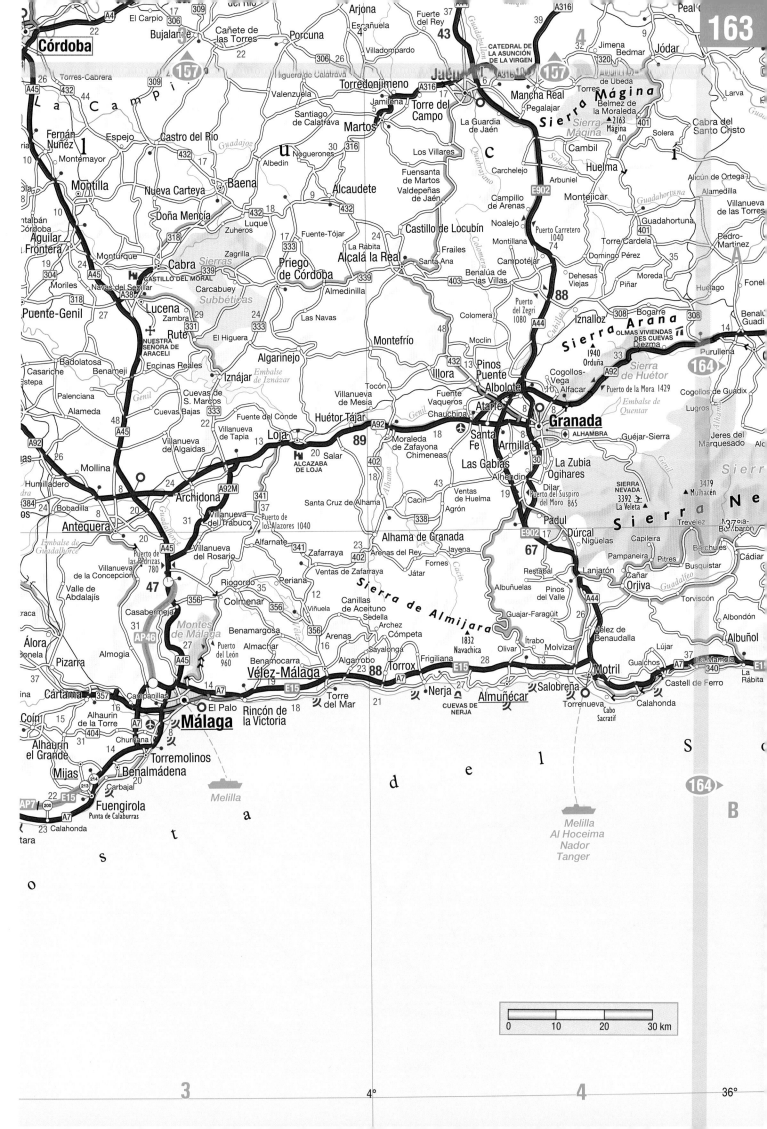

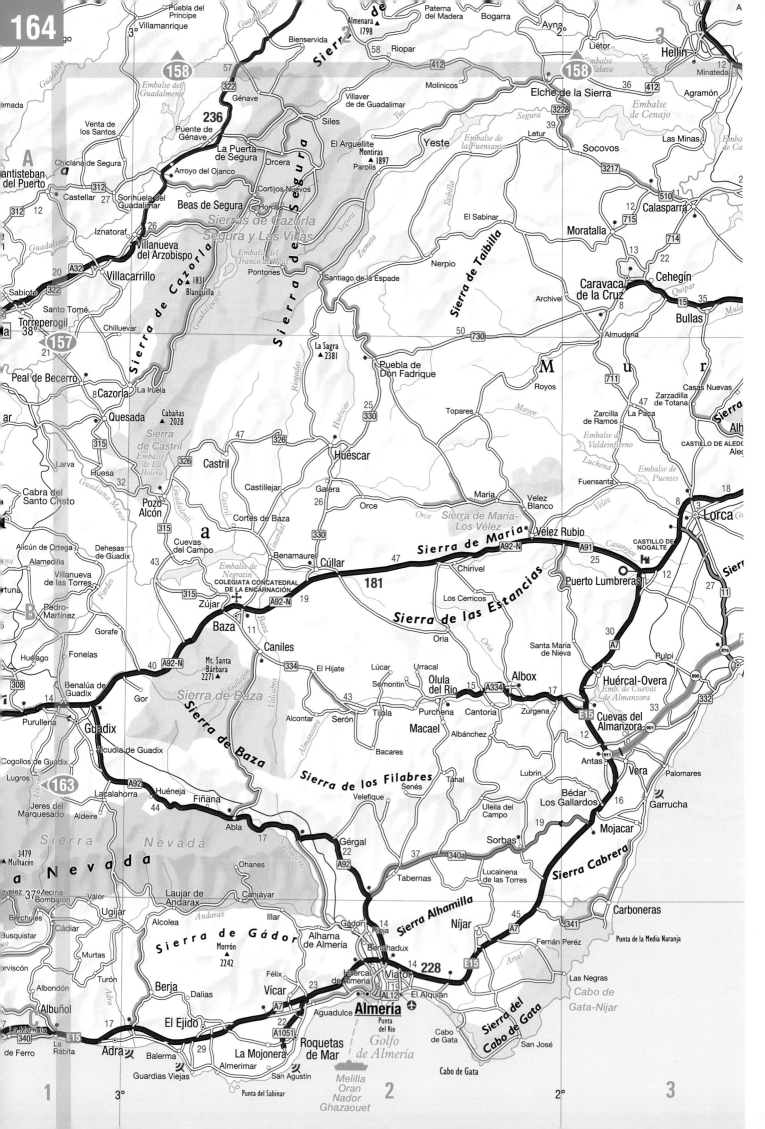

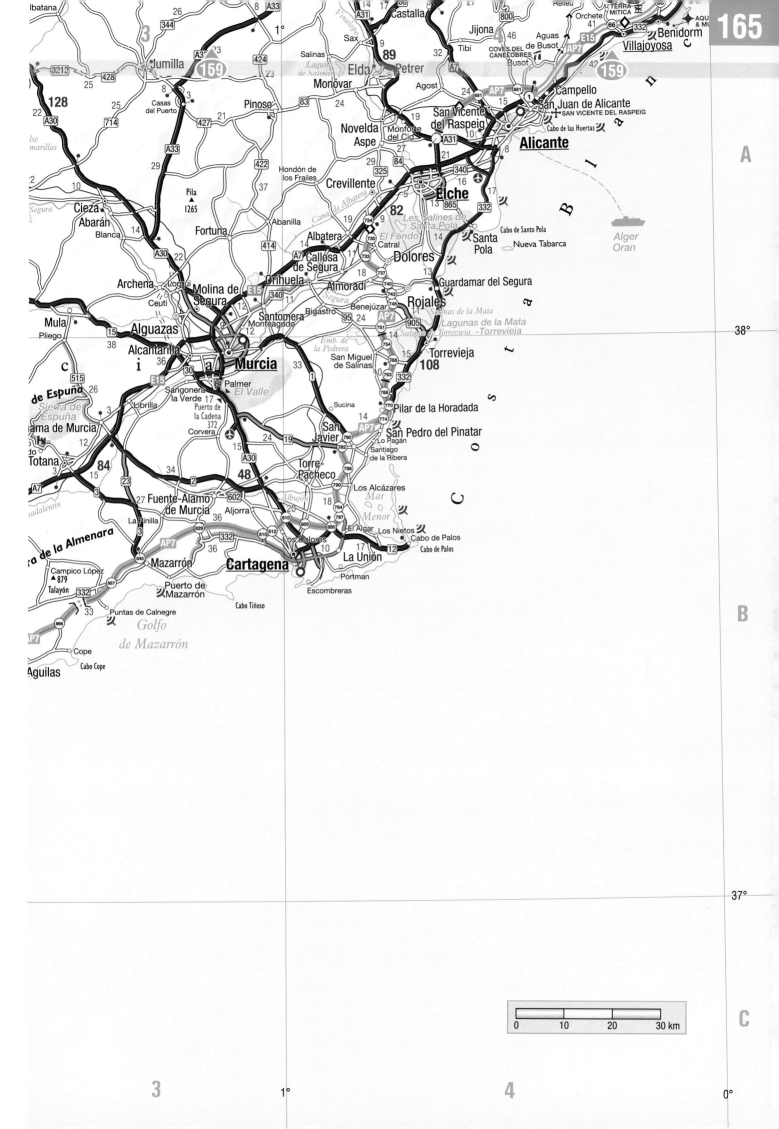

Ibatana
26
8 A33
Castalla
27
TERRA MITICA
AQU & MU

344
3
1°
A31
17
Jijona
800
Orchete
41
66
332
Benidorm

A33
23
424
23
89
Sax
9
32
Tibi
Aguas de Busot
E15
AP7
42
Villajoyosa
159

Jumilla
159
Monóvar
Elda Petrer
A7
24
691
681
15
1
Campello

3212
428
25
Casas del Puerto
8
3
83
24
Agost
15
San Juan de Alicante
SAN VICENTE DEL RASPEIG

128
A30
22
714
427
21
Pinoso
Novelda
Monforte del Cid
A31
9
10
Alicante

29
A33
422
Aspe
27
21
Cabo de las Huertas

Hondón de los Frailes
29
325
84
340
16

Pila
1265
37
Crevillente
5
Elche
865
332
Santa Pola

Cieza
Abarán
Blanca
14
Fortuna
414
Abanilla
19
724
9
82
13
Les Salines de Santa Pola
Cabo de Santo Pola
Nueva Tabarca
Alger Oran

Archena
Lorquí
Molina de Segura
E15
340
11
Albatera
14
730
733
Catral
El Fondo
Dolores
14
Guardamar del Segura

Ceutí
12
Orihuela
Almoradí
737
740
13
Rojales
905
Salinas de la Mata
Torrevieja

Mula
Pliego
15
Alguazas
9
Santomera
Monteagudo
12
Bigastro
95
24
Benejúzar
745
751
AP7
Lagunas de la Mata -Torrevieja

38°
Alcantarilla
36
30
Murcia
33
1
754
14
Salinas de Torrevieja -Torrevieja
15
Torrevieja
108

515
de Espuña
26
Sangonera la Verde
Palmer
El Valle
758
763
332

Sierra de Espuña
3
Librilla
17
Puerto de la Cadena
372
Sucina
768
770
Pilar de la Horadada

ama de Murcia
12
Corvera
15
24
19
San Javier
14
774
780
AP7
San Pedro del Pinatar

Totana
84
15
34
2
48
Torre-Pacheco
782
Lo Pagán
Santiago de la Ribera

A7
3
23
602
786
Mar Menor

Fuente-Álamo de Murcia
27
Aljorra
20
18
790
Los Alcázares

La Pinilla
3
36
810
794
797
Cabo de Palos

de la Almenara
829
332
36
815
812
805
800
El Algar
Los Nietos
Cabo de Palos

AP7
845
Mazarrón
Los Dolores
10
17
12
La Unión

Campico López
879
Talayón
857
332
Cartagena
Portman

33
Puntas de Calnegre
Puerto de Mazarrón
Escombreras
Cabo Tiñoso

866
AP7
Golfo de Mazarrón

Cope
Aguilas
Cabo Cope

A

B

37°

0   10   20   30 km

C

3
1°
4
0°

A

1

2°

2

40°

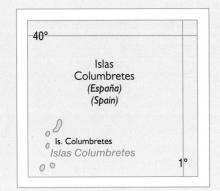

40°

Islas
Columbretes
(España)
(Spain)

Is. Columbretes
Islas Columbretes

1°

B

ISLAS BALEARES

BALEARIC ISLANDS

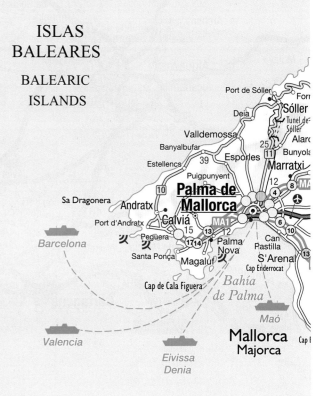

Port de Sóller
Deià   Sóller
Tunel de Sóller
Valldemossa   Alaró
Banyalbufar   25   Bunyola
Estellencs   39   Esporles   11
Puigpunyent   Marratxi
Sa Dragonera   10   12
Palma de Mallorca   4   8   MA
Andratx   Calvià   6
Port d'Andratx   15   MA1   10
13   12   Can
Barcelona   Peguera   17 14   Palma   Pastilla   13
Santa Ponça   Nova
Magaluf   S'Arenal
Cap Enderrocat
Valencia   Cap de Cala Figuera   *Bahía*
de Palma
Maó
Eivissa   **Mallorca**
Denia   Majorca   Cap

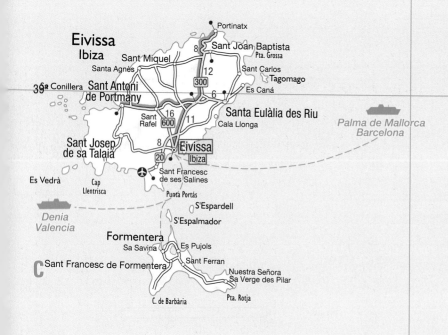

Eivissa
Ibiza

Portinatx
Sant Joan Baptista
Sant Miquel   Pta. Grossa
Santa Agnès   8   12   Sant Carlos
39° Conillera   Sant Antoni   300   Tagomago
de Portmany   6   Es Canà
16   Santa Eulàlia des Riu
Sant   600   11
Rafel   Cala Llonga   *Palma de Mallorca*
Barcelona
Sant Josep
de sa Talaia   8
20   **Eivissa**
Ibiza
Sant Francesc
de ses Salines
Es Vedrà   Cap
Llentrisca   Punta Portás
S'Espardell
Denia   S'Espalmador
Valencia
Formentera
Sa Savina   Es Pujols
Sant Ferran
C   Sant Francesc de Formentera   Nuestra Señora
Sa Verge des Pilar
C. de Barbària   Pta. Rotja

1

2°

2

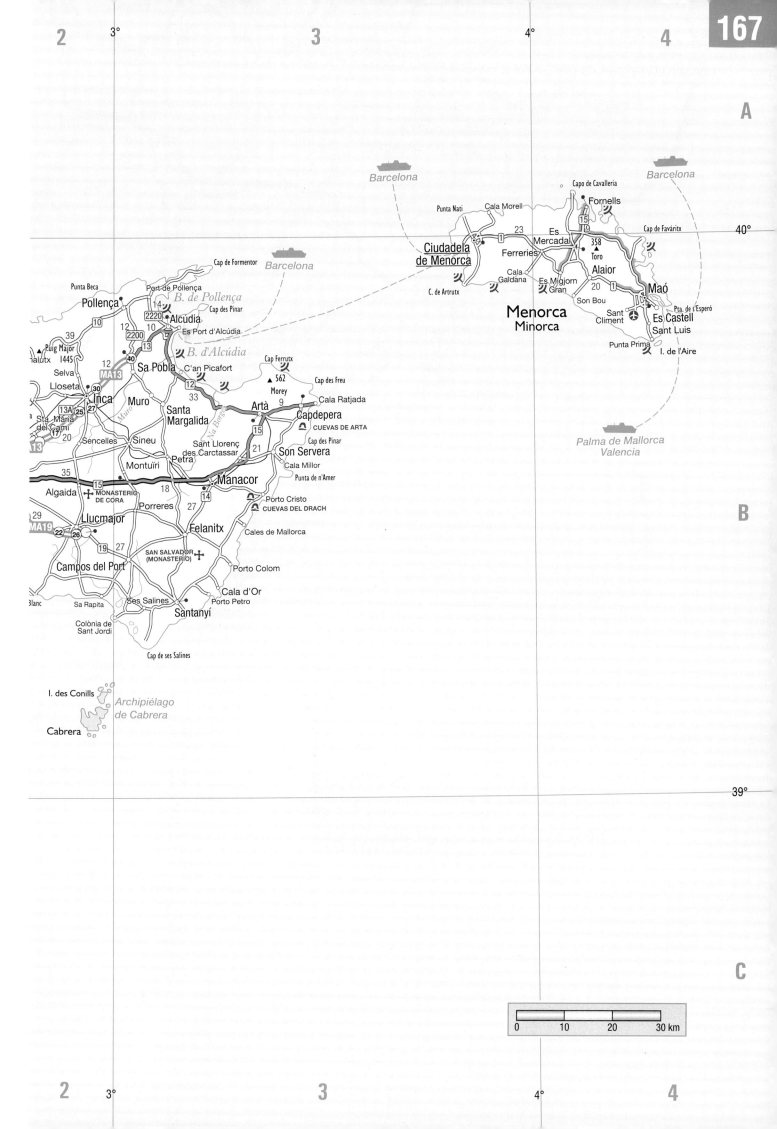

2   3°   **3**   4°   **4**

A

40°

Barcelona   *Barcelona*

Capo de Cavalleria
Fornells
Punta Nati   Cala Morell
15
Es 23
Cap de Faváritx
Ciudadela de Menorca
Mercadal
Ferreries
9
358
Toro
Barcelona
Cala Galdana
Alaior
Cap de Formentor
Es Migjorn Gran
C. de Artrutx
20
Maó
1
Son Bou
Menorca
Sant Climent
Es Castell
Minorca
Pta. de s'Esperó
Sant Luis
Punta Prima
I. de l'Aire

Punta Beca
Port de Pollença
Pollença
B. de Pollença
14
Cap des Pinar
10 2220 **Alcúdia**
12
2200 10 Es Port d'Alcúdia
13
Puig Major 1445 40 B. d'Alcúdia
nalutx 12 **Sa Pobla** C'an Picafort
Selva MA13 30 12 Cap Ferrutx
Lloseta **Inca** 33 562
13A 25 27 Muro Morey Cap des Freu
Sta. Maria 20 Santa 9 Cala Ratjada
del Camí 17 Margalida **Artà**
13 Sencelles Na Borges **Capdepera**
Sineu 15 CUEVAS DE ARTA
Petra Sant Llorenç Cap des Pinar
Montuïri des Carctassar 21 **Son Servera**
35 MONASTERIO Cala Millor
Algaida 15 DE CORA 18 Punta de n'Amer
Manacor
14
29 Porreres 27 Porto Cristo
Llucmajor CUEVAS DEL DRACH
MA19 22 26 **Felanitx** Cales de Mallorca
19 27
Campos del Port SAN SALVADOR (MONASTERIO)
Porto Colom
Blanc Ses Salines Cala d'Or
Sa Rapita Porto Petro
Santanyí
Colònia de Sant Jordi
Cap de ses Salines

B

I. des Conills
Archipiélago de Cabrera
Cabrera

39°

C

0   10   20   30 km

2   3°   **3**   4°   **4**

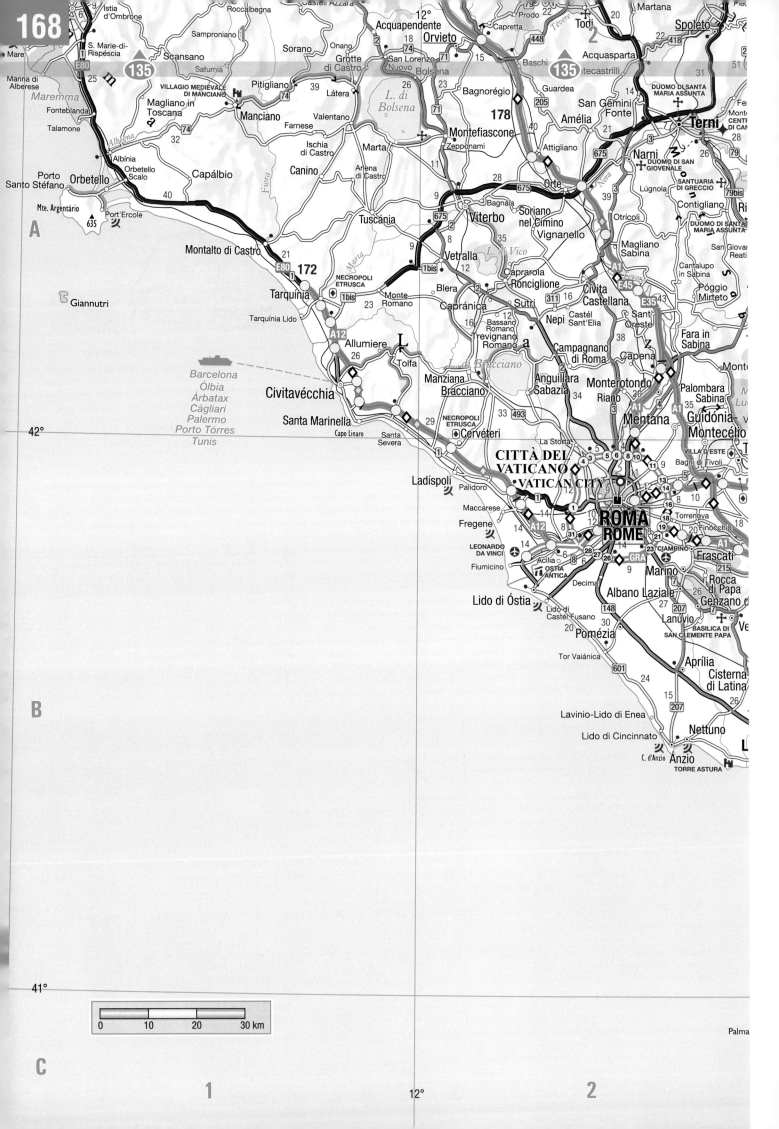

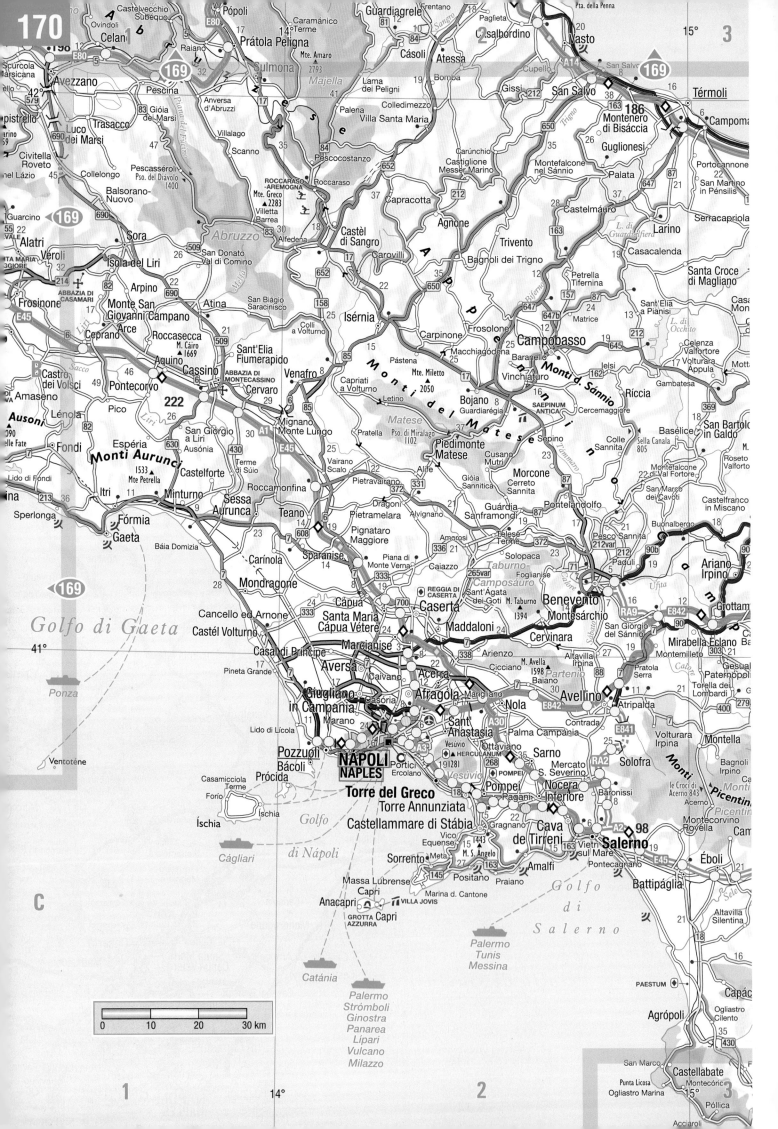

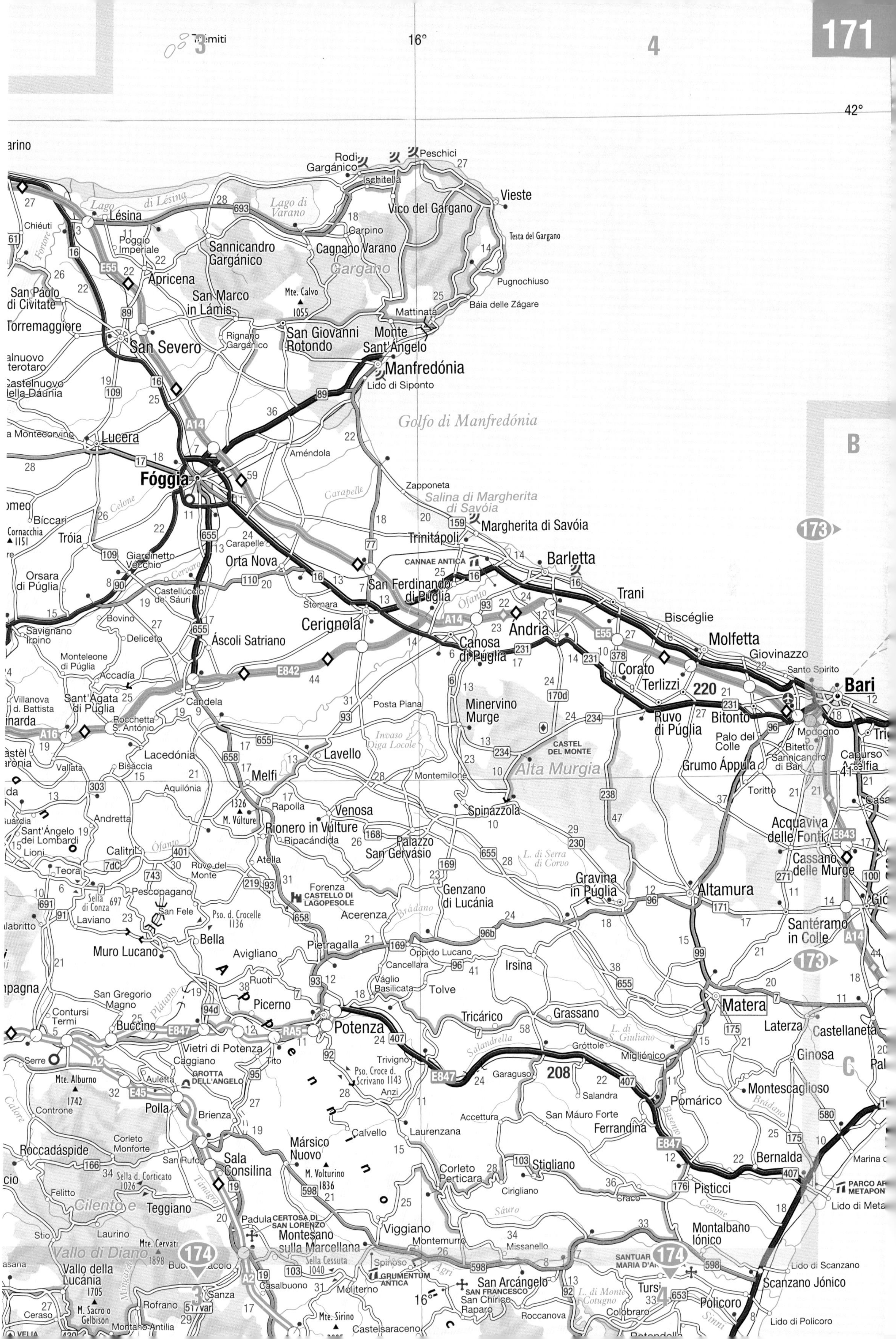

B

Témiti

Rodi Gargánico
Peschici 27
Ischitella
Vieste
Vico del Gargano
Carpino
Cagnano Varano
Testa del Gargano
Gargano
Pugnochiuso
Lésina
Lago di Varano
18
Mte. Calvo 1055
Báia delle Zágare
Poggio Imperiale
Sannicandro Gargánico
San Marco in Lámis
Mattinata 25
Apricena
Rignano Gargánico
San Giovanni Rotondo
Monte Sant'Angelo
San Páolo di Civitate
San Severo
Manfredónia
Torremaggiore
Lido di Siponto
Lucera
Améndola
Golfo di Manfredónia
Montecorvino
Fóggia
Zapponeta
Salina di Margherita di Savóia
Biccari
Tróia
Carapelle
Margherita di Savóia
Cornacchia 1151
Giardinetto Vecchio
Orta Nova
Trinitápoli
CANNAE ANTICA
Barletta
Orsara di Púglia
Castellúccio de' Sáuri
San Ferdinando di Púglia
Trani
Biscéglie
Savignano Irpino
Stornara
Cerignola
Canosa di Púglia
Andria
Molfetta
Bovino
Delicéto
Áscoli Satriano
Corato
Giovinazzo
Monteleone di Púglia
Accadía
Candela
E842
Terlizzi
220
Santo Spirito
Sant'Ágata di Púglia
Rocchetta S. António
Minervino Murge
Ruvo di Púglia
Bitonto
Bari
Villanova d. Battista
Posta Piana
CASTEL DEL MONTE
Palo del Colle
Modogno
Lacedónia
Lavello
Alta Murgia
Grumo Áppula
Bitetto
Sannicandro di Bari
Capurso
Vallata
Melfi
Montemilone
Toritto
Bisáccia
Aquilónia
Spinazzola
Acquaviva delle Fonti
Andretta
Rapolla
M. Vúlture 1326
Venosa
Cassano delle Murge
Sant'Ángelo dei Lombardi
Rionero in Vúlture
Ripacándida
Palazzo San Gervásio
Gravina in Púglia
Altamura
Calitri
Atella
Genzano di Lucánia
Santéramo in Colle
Teora
Ruvo del Monte
Forenza
Acerenza
Pescopagano
CASTELLO DI LAGOPESOLE
Sella di Conza
San Fele
Bella
Pietragalla
Oppido Lucano
Laviano
Cancellara
Irsina
Muro Lucano
Avigliano
Ruoti
Váglio Basilicata
Tolve
Matera
San Gregorio Magno
Picerno
Potenza
Tricárico
Grassano
Laterza
Contursi Termi
Buccino
Vietri di Potenza
Tito
Trivigno
Garaguso
208
Castellanéta
Serre
Caggiano
Pso. Croce d. Scrivano 1143
Anzi
Salandra
Pomárico
Ginosa
Mte. Alburno 1742
GROTTA DELL'ANGELO
Brienza
Calvello
Accettura
San Máuro Forte
Montescaglioso
Controne
Aulétta
Ferrandina
Polla
Corleto Monforte
Mársico Nuovo
M. Volturino 1836
Laurenzana
Stigliano
Bernalda
Roccadáspide
San Rufo
Sala Consilina
Cirigliano
Pisticci
PARCO METAPON
Felitto
Corleto Perticara
Craco
Lido di Meta
Teggiano
Vallo di Diano
Mte. Cervati 1898
Padula
CERTOSA DI SAN LORENZO
Montesano sulla Marcellana
Viggiano
Montemurro
Missanello
Montalbano Iónico
Vallo della Lucánia
Sella Cessuta 1040
Spinoso
GRUMENTUM ANTICA
Agri
San Arcángelo
SANTUAR MARIA D'AN
Lido di Scanzano
Stio
Laurino
Casalbuono
Moliterno
SAN FRANCESCO
San Chírico Ráparo
Tursi
Scanzano Jónico
Ceraso
M. Sacro o Gelbison
Sanza
Montano Antilia
Mte. Sirino
Castelsaraceno
Roccanova
Colábraro
Policoro
Lido di Policoro

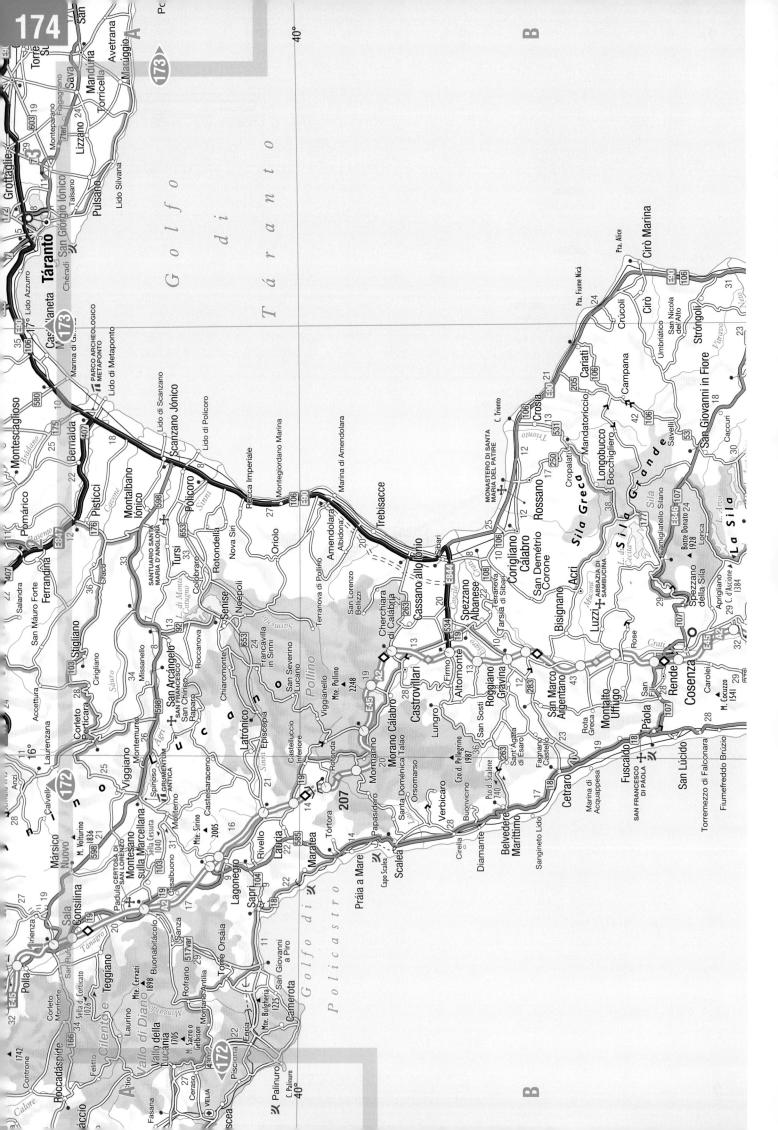

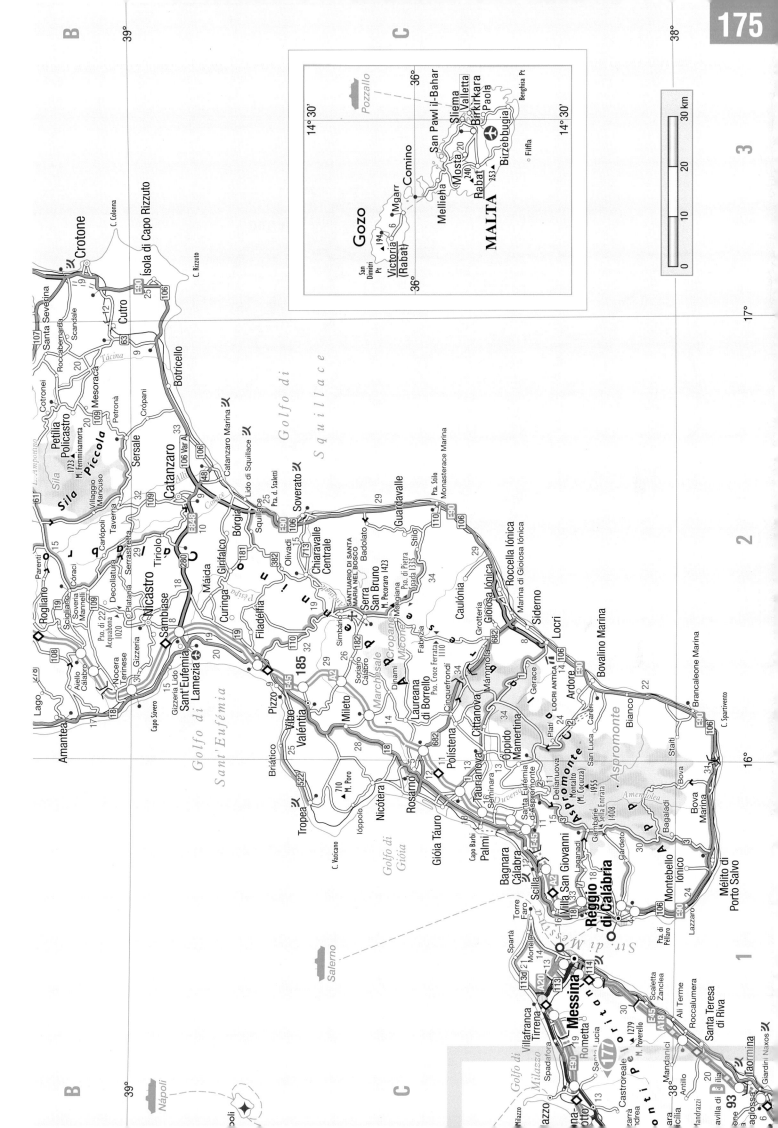

B

39°

C

38°

17°

16°

MALTA

Gozo

Pozzallo

14° 30'

36°

San Pawl il-Bahar
Sliema
Valletta
Birkirkara
Paola
Birzebbugia
Mosta 20
Rabat 253
240
Benghisa Pt
Filfla

Mellieħa

Comino

Mgarr 6

Victoria
(Rabat)

San
Dimitri
Pt
194

36°

14° 30'

17°

30 km
20
10
0

3

2

1

Crotone
C. Colonna
Isola di Capo Rizzuto
C. Rizzuto

Santa Severina
Scandale
Roccabernarda
Cotronei
Mesoraca
Petronà
Crópani
Cutro
63
9
106
E90
25

L. Ampóllino
Sila Piccola
Petilia
Policastro
M. Femminamorta 1723
Villaggio
Mancuso
Sersale
Botricello
Catanzaro
Catanzaro Marina
Lido di Squillace
Pta. d. Staletti
Squillace
Bórgia
Soverato

Golfo di
Squillace

Sila
L. Arvo
Parenti
61
15
109
33
32
109
280
48
E848
10
106
106 Var A
181
382
713
25

Rogliano
Scigliano
Soveria
Mannelli
Córaci
Decollatura
Carlópoli
Taverna
Tiriolo
Nicastro
Sambiase
Maida
Curinga
Girifalco
Filadélfia
Chiaravalle
Centrale
Olivadi
Guardavalle
Monasterace Marina
Pta. Stilo
Stilo
Badolato
Serra
San Bruno
M. Pecoraro 1423
Pso. di Pietra
Spada 1335
SANTUARIO DI SANTA
MARIA NEL BOSCO
Roccella Iónica
Marina di Gioiosa Iónica
Gioiosa Iónica
Caulónia
Siderno
Locri
LOCRI ANTICA
Bovalino Marina

Amantea
Aiello
Cálabro
Lago
Nocera
Terinese
Pso. di 22
Acquabona
Gizzeria
Gizzeria Lido
Sant'Eufemia
Lamezia
185
A2
Maida
Pizzo
Vibo
Valéntia
Briático
Tropea
C. Vaticano
Ioppolo
Nicótera
Rosarno
Gióia Táuro
Palmi
Capo Barbi
Bagnara
Cálabra
Scilla
Torre
Faro
Villa San Giovanni
Reggio
di Calábria
Pta. di Péllaro
Sparta
Mortelle

Sila
Gizzeria
Platania
Serrastretta
18
Pso. di
1020
20
E45
9
19
19
110
32
29
26
182
185
A2
29
5
34
29
682
8
106
14
E90
22
31

Golfo di
Sant'Eufémia
Golfo di
Gióia
Stretto di Messina

M. Poro 710
522
25
28
18
18
522
12
11
682
13
13
34
11
16
18
14
6
18 33
A2
16
24
2
14
24
3
30
E90
106
E90
C. Spartivento

Marchesale
Simbário
Soriano
Cálabro
Dinami
Laureana
di Borrello
Cinquefrondi
Pso. Croce Ferrata 1110
Fabrízia
Grotteria
Mámmola
Polistena
Cittanova
Taurianova
Seminara
Oppido
Mamertina
Gerace
Plati
Santa Eufémia
d'Aspromonte
Delianuova
Gambárie
Montalto
(M. Cocuzza) 1955
San Luca
Careri
Ardore
Cárdeto
Della Entrata 1408
Bianco
Staiti
Bova
Bova
Marina
Bagaladi
Montebello
Iónico
Mélito di
Porto Salvo
Lazzaro
Melograno

Aspromonte

Amendolea

Duverso

Messina
Villafranca
Tirrena
Rometta
177
E90
Romba
A20
114
113
113d
21
14
13
30
19
93

Golfo di
Milazzo
Spadafora
Villafranca Tirrena
M. Poverello 1279
Santa Lucia
Ali Terme
Roccalumera
Santa Teresa
di Riva
Giardini Naxos
Taormina
E45 A18
E90
30
20
Mandanici
Antillo
Scaletta Zanclea
Fiumara
Pe lor i tani
Monti

Napoli

Salerno

B
C

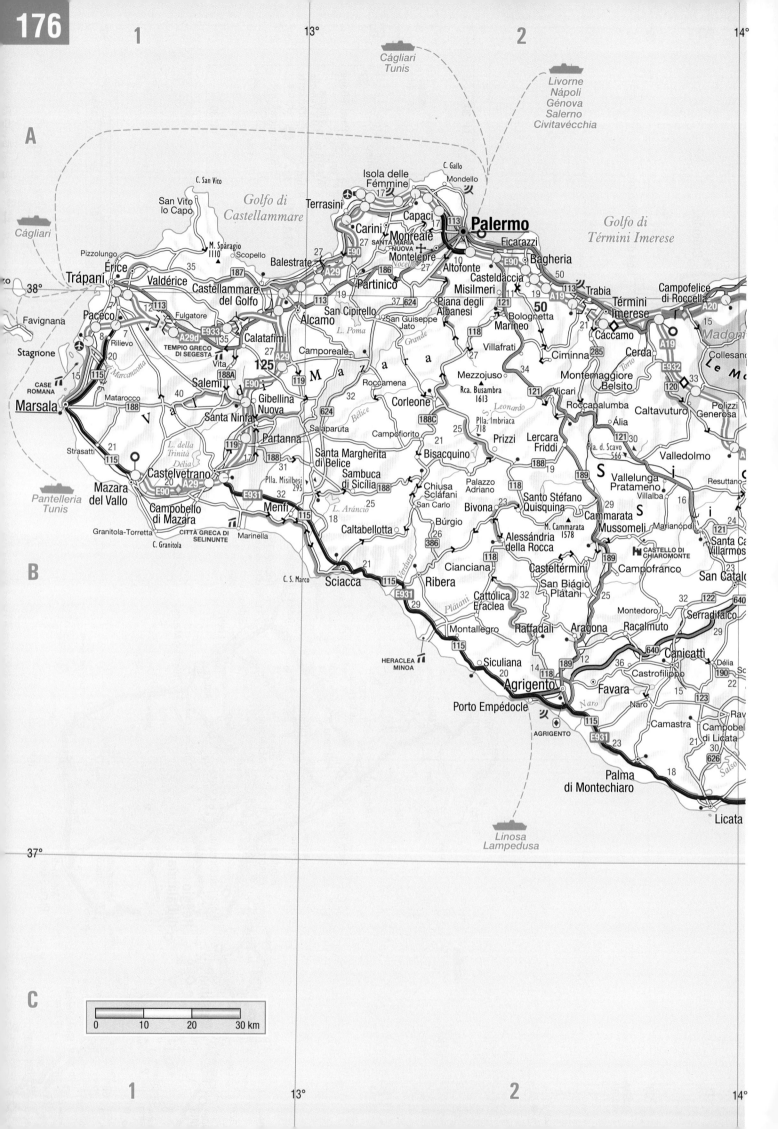

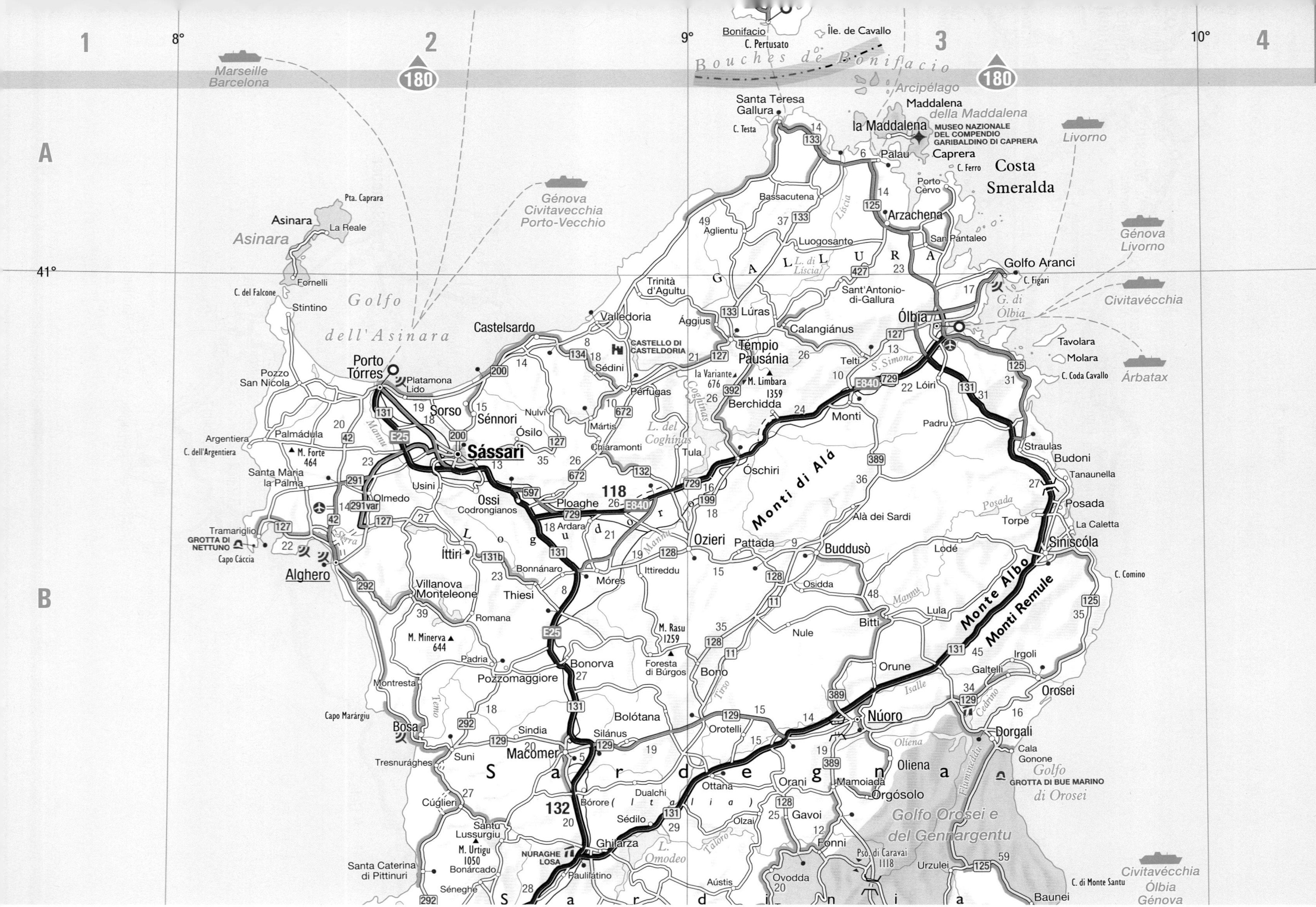

A 4 10° 3 9° 2 8° 1 41° A

B B

Bouches de Bonifacio

180

Marseille
Barcelona

Génova
Civitavecchia
Porto-Vecchio

Génova
Civitavecchia
Porto-Vecchio

île de Cavallo
Bonifacio
C. Pertusato

Arcipélago
della Maddalena

Génova
Livorno

Génova
Livorno
Civitavecchia
Árbatax

Civitavecchia
Olbia
Génova

Santa Teresa
Gallura
C. Testa

la Maddalena
MUSEO NAZIONALE
DEL COMPENDIO
GARIBALDINO DI CAPRERA
Maddalena
della Maddalena
Caprera
Costa
Smeralda

C. Ferro
Palau
Porto
Cervo
San Pantaleo
Arzachena
C. Figari
G. di
Olbia
Golfo Aranci

Pta. Caprara
La Reale
Asinara
Asinara

Stintino
Fornelli
C. del Falcone

Pozzo
San Nicola
Argentiera
C. dell'Argentiera

Palmádula
M. Forte
464
Santa Maria
la Palma

Alghero
Tramariglio
GROTTA DI
NETTUNO
Capo Cáccia

Golfo
dell'Asinara

Platamona
Lido
Porto
Tórres
Sorso
Sénnori
Sássari
Ossi
Usini
Olmedo

Castelsardo
Sedini
CASTELLO DI
CASTELDORIA
Valledoria
Trinità
d'Agultu

Aglientu
Nulvi
Ósilo
Codrongianos
Ittiri
Villanova
Monteleone

Luogosanto
Bassacútena
Ággius
Lúras
Calangiánus
Tempio
Pausánia
M. Limbara
1359
Berchidda

Sant'Antonio-
di-Gallura
Telti
S. Simone
Calangiánus
Monti
la Variante
676
Oschiri

Perfúgas
Chiaramonti
Mártis
L. del
Coghinas
Tula
Coghinas

Ploaghe
Ardara
Bonnánaro
Thiesi
Romana
Padria

Olbia

Lóiri
Padru

Straulas
Budoni
Tanaunella
Posada
La Caletta
Siniscóla
C. Comino

Monte Albo
Monti Remule
Torpè
Lodè
Lula
Irgoli
Oroséi
C. di Monte Santu
Bauneí

Posada

Galtelli
Dorgali
Cala
Gonone
GROTTA DI BUE MARINO
di Orosei
Golfo
di
Orosei

Golfo Oroséi e
del Gennargentu

Núoro
Oliena
Orgósolo
Mamoiada
Oráni
Gavoi
Fonni
Ovodda
Austis

Monti di Alà
Alà dei Sardi
Buddusò
Bitti
Osidda
Nule
Pattada
Bono
Orotelli
Ottana

M. Rasu
1259
Foresta
di Búrgos
Bolótana
Silanus
Borore
Sédilo
Ghilarza
NURAGHE
LOSA
Paulilátino

Mores
Ittireddu
Ozieri
Bonorva
Sindia
Macómer
132
131

Bonnánaro
Pozzomaggiore
Suni
Cúglieri
M. Ferru

Bosa
Tresnúraghes
Santa Caterina
di Pittínuri

M. Minerva
644
Montresta
Temo
Magomadas

M. Urtigu
1050
Sénéghe
Santu
Lussurgiu
Bonárcado

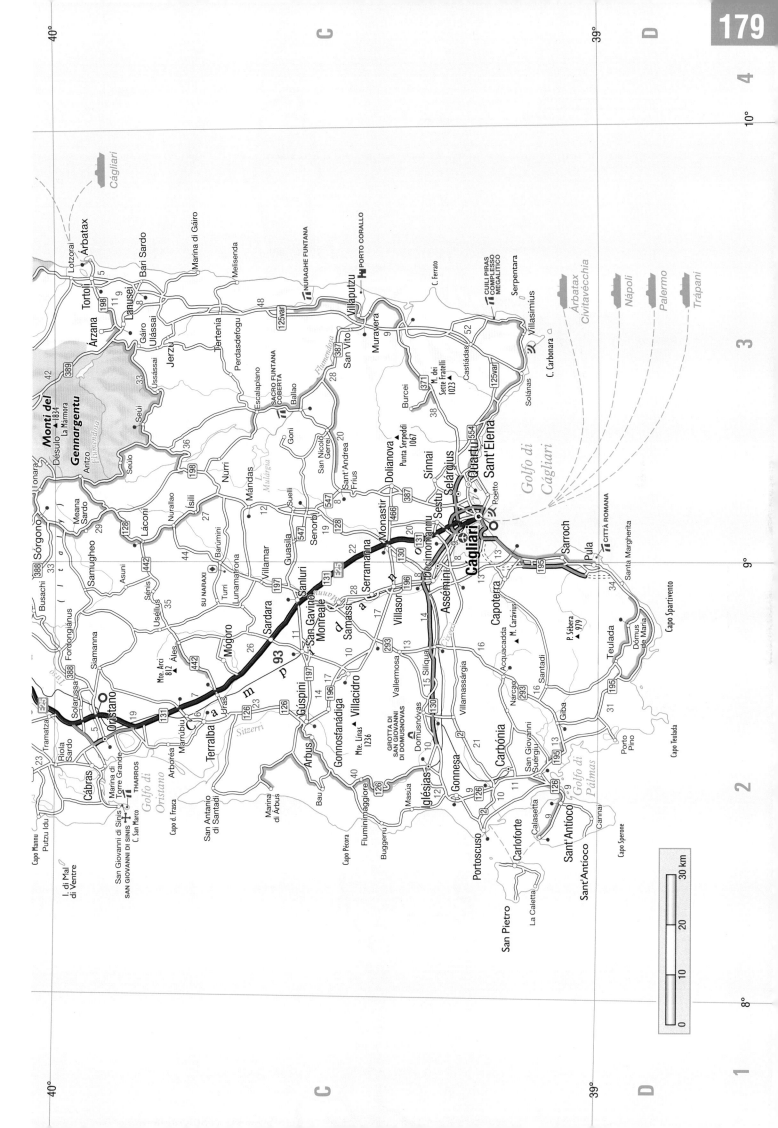

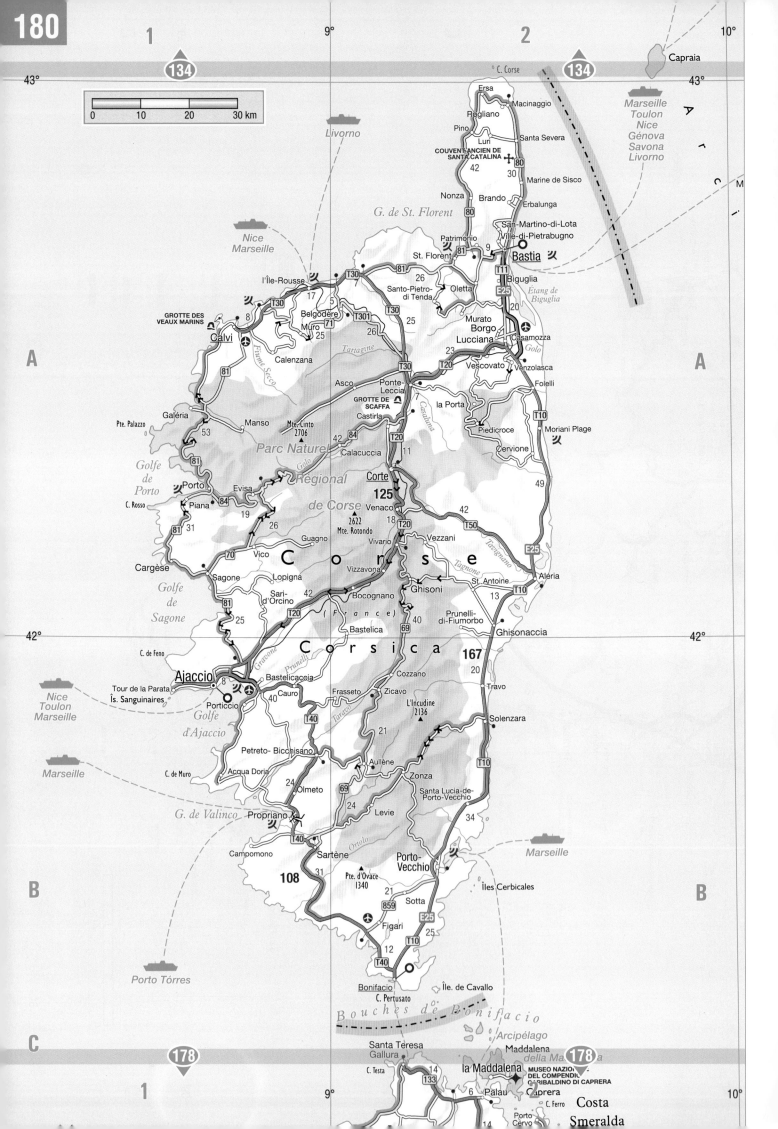

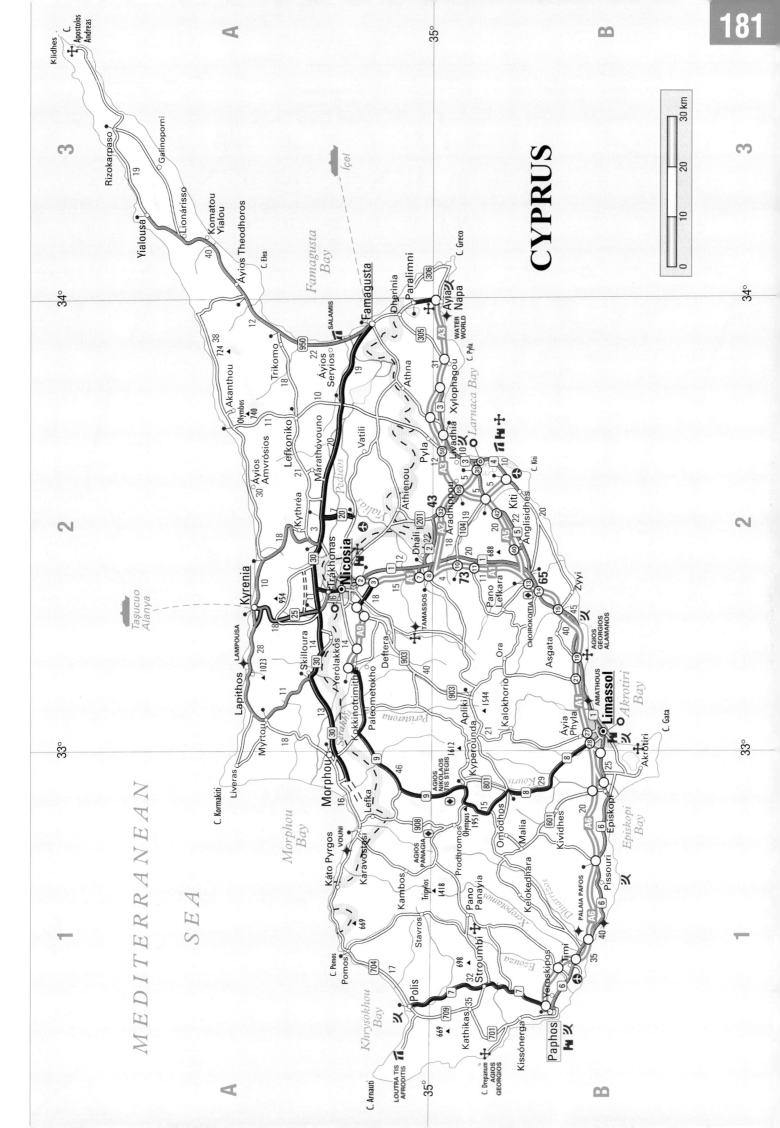

CYPRUS

MEDITERRANEAN SEA

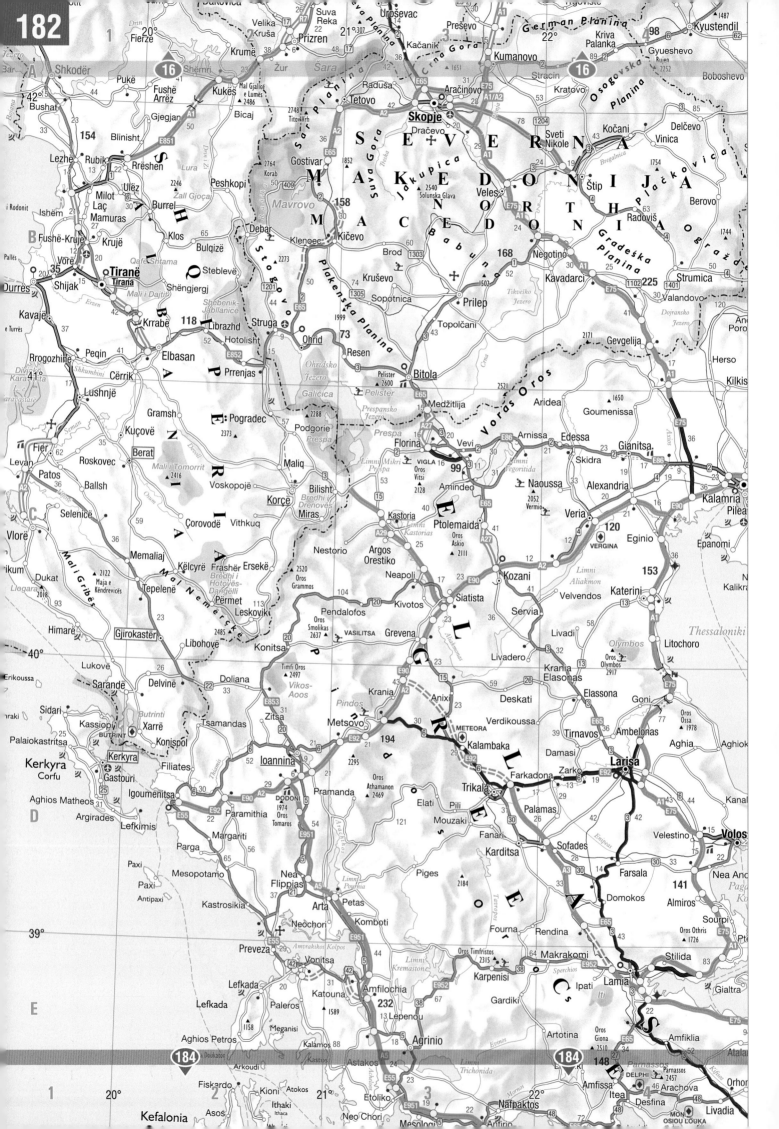

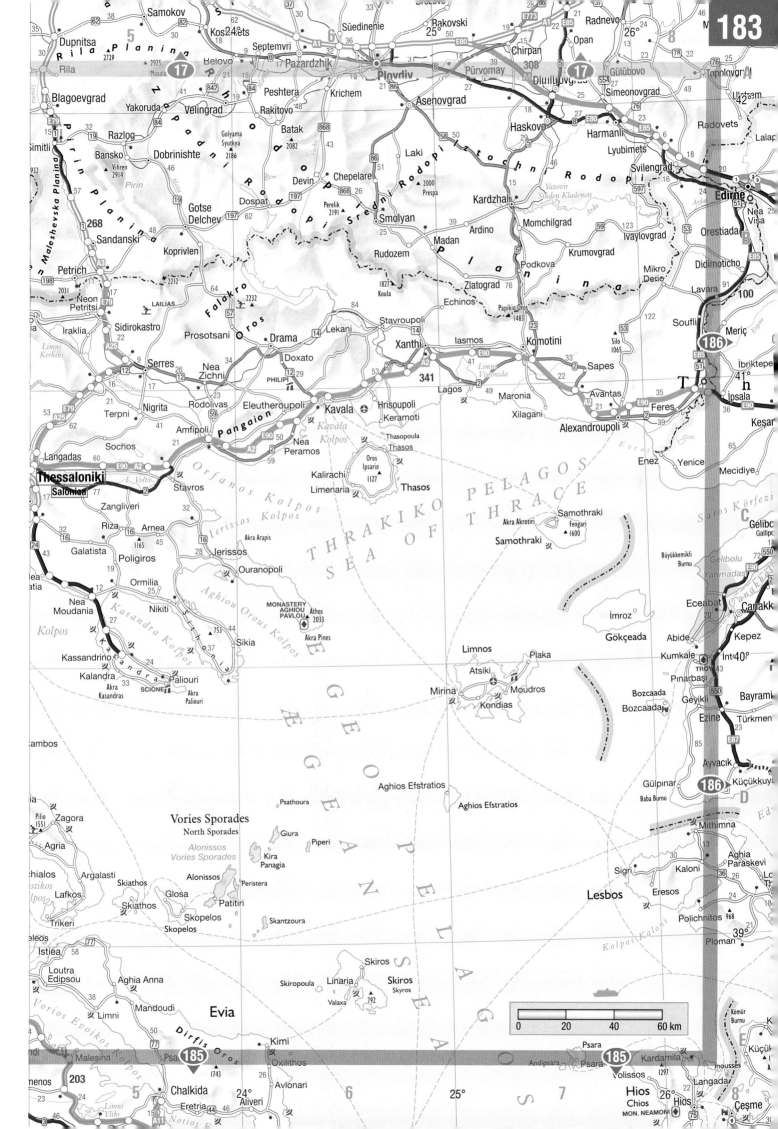

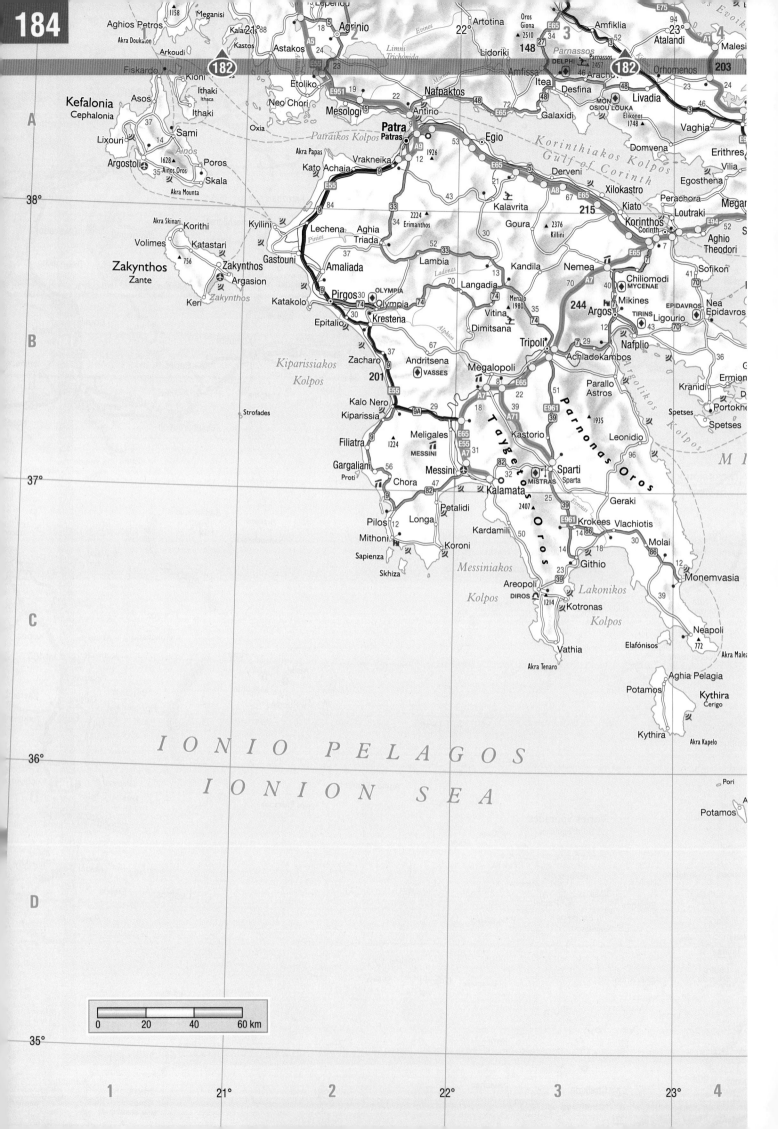

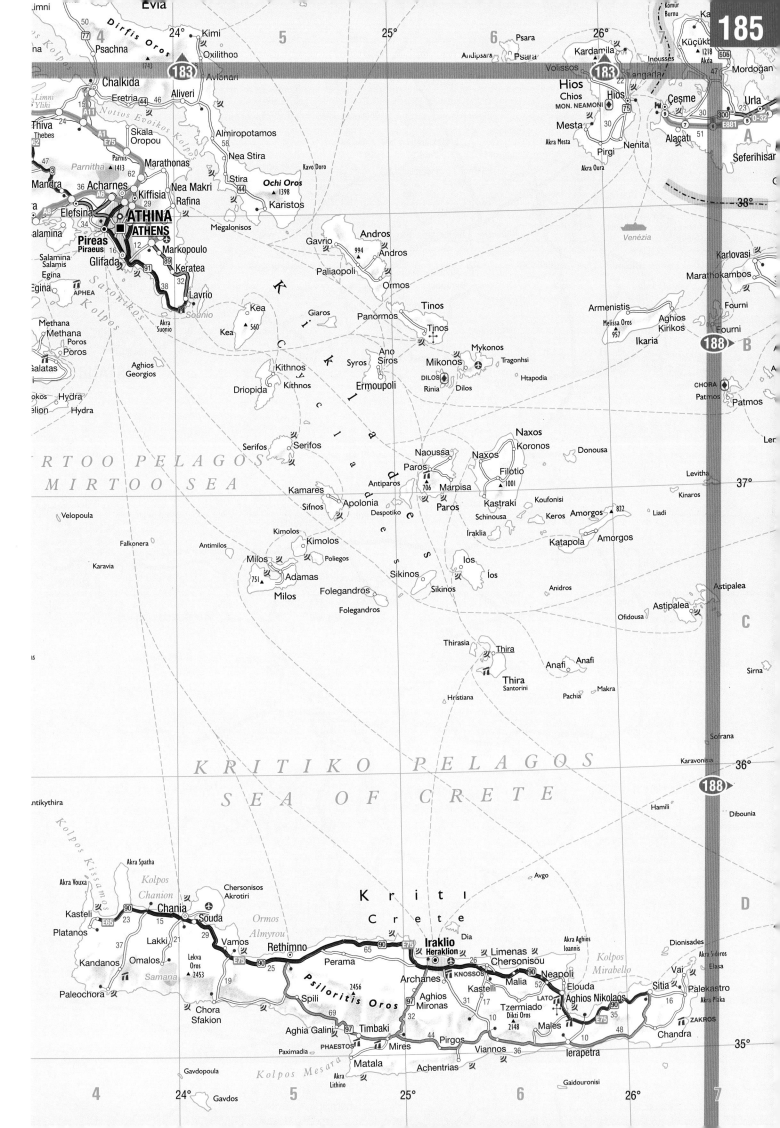

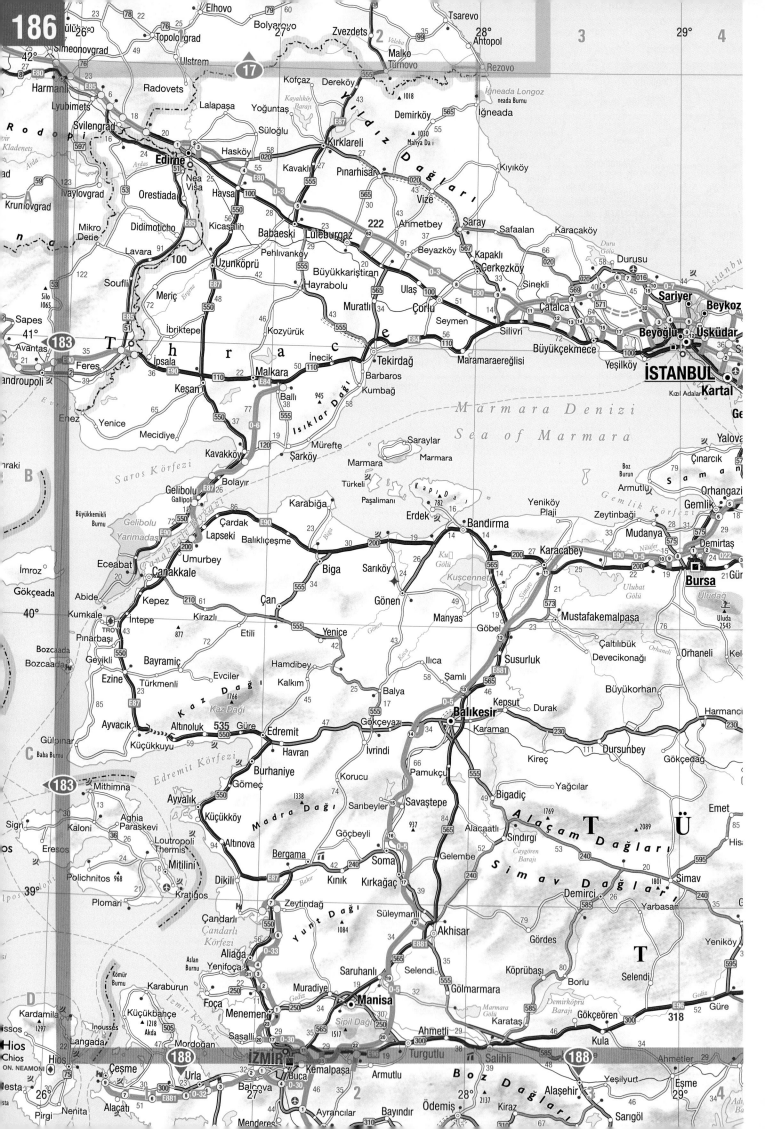

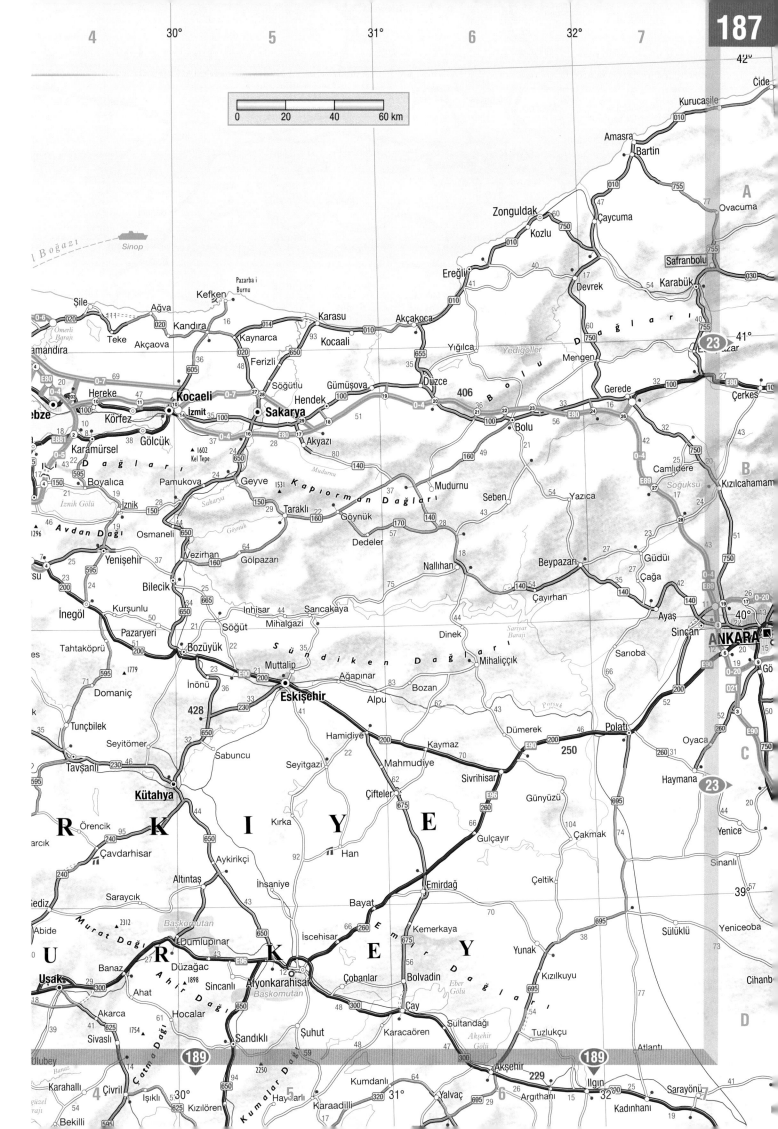

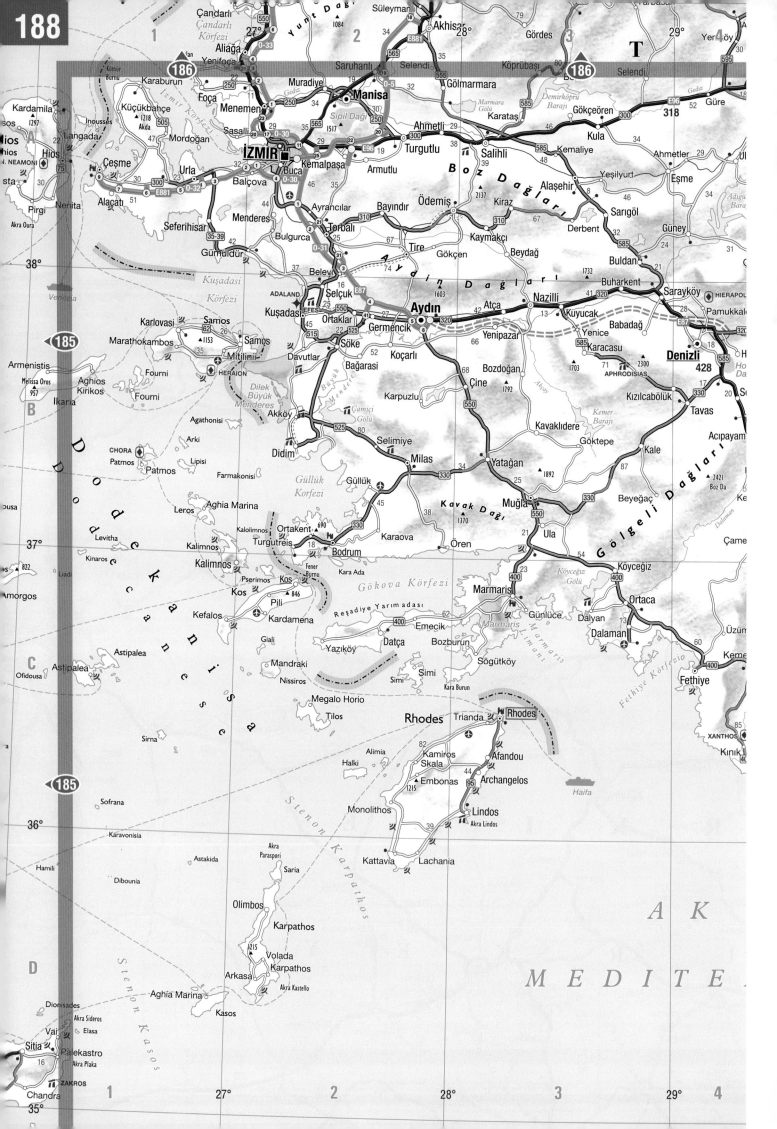

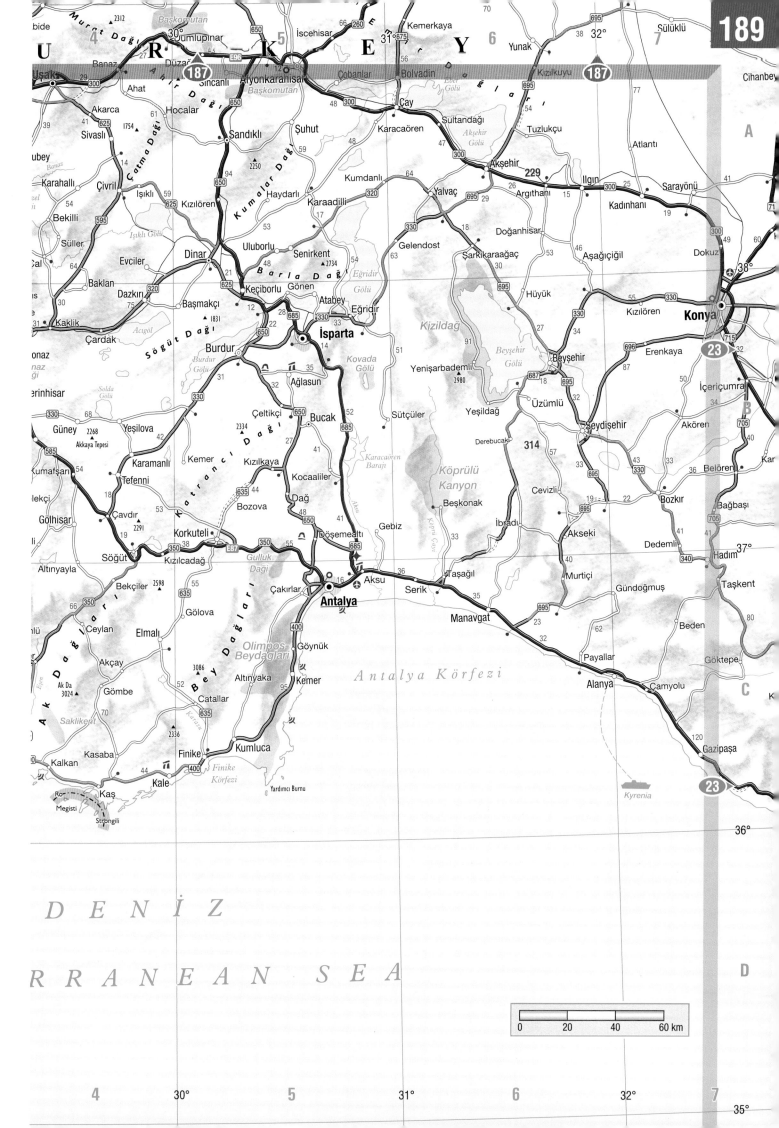

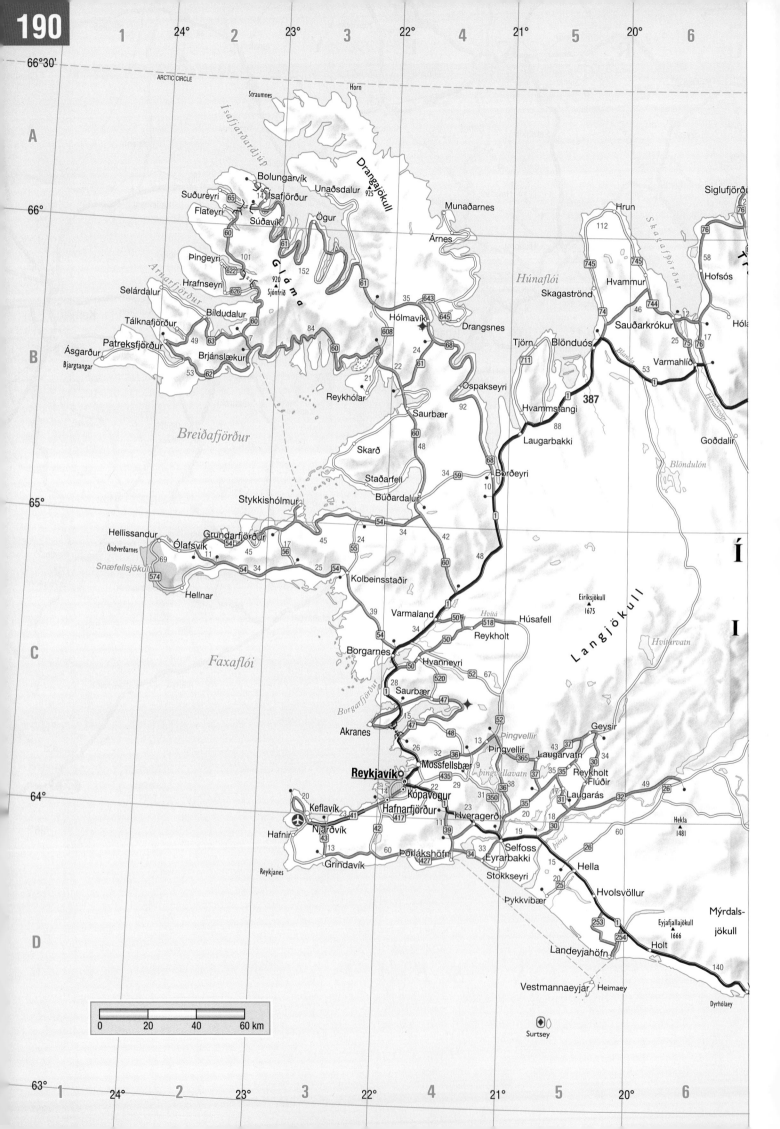

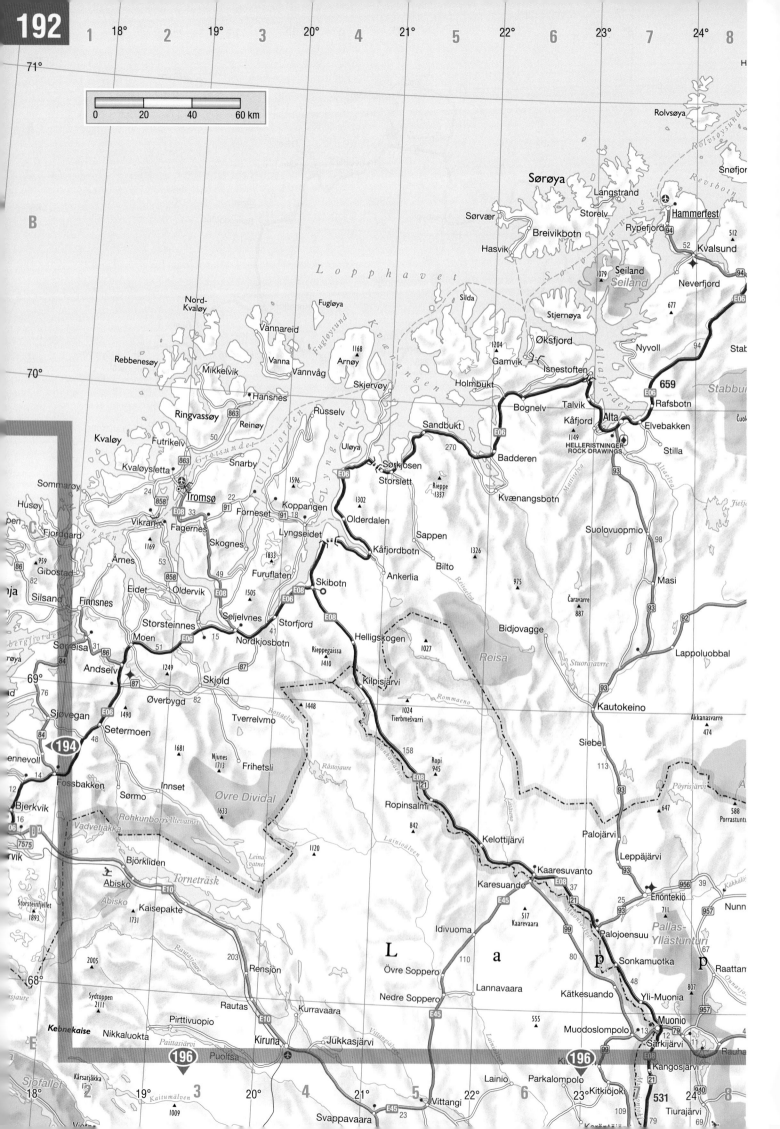

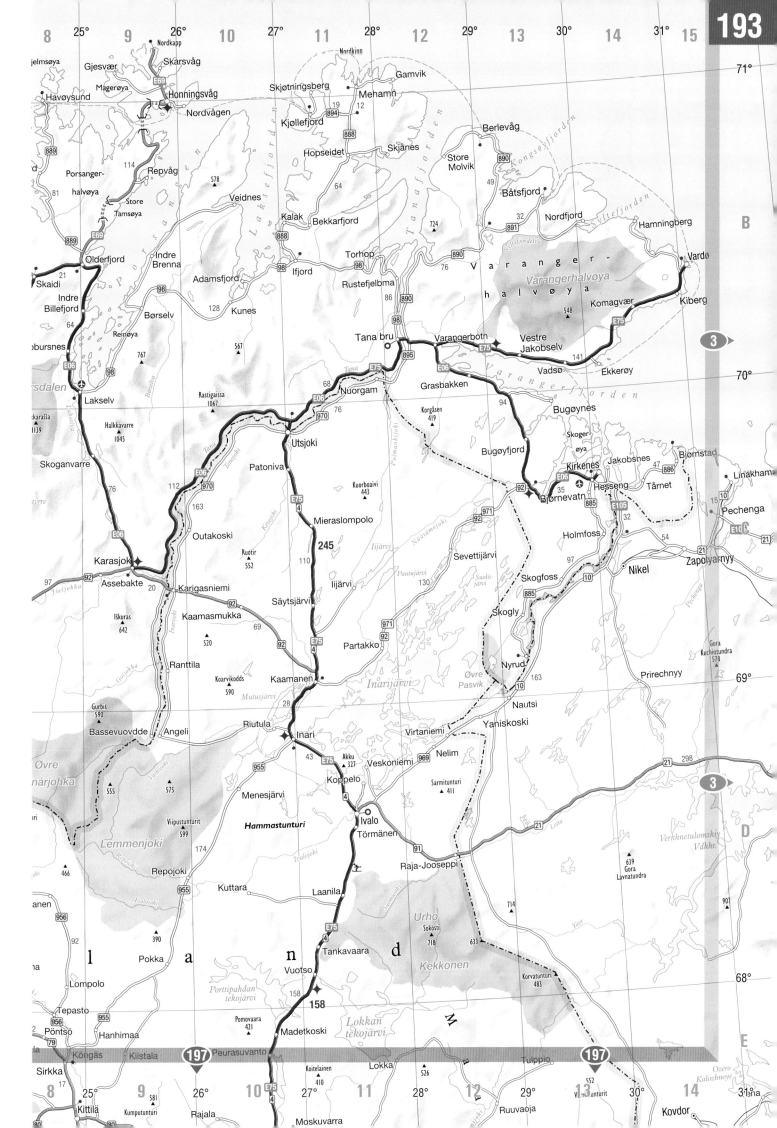

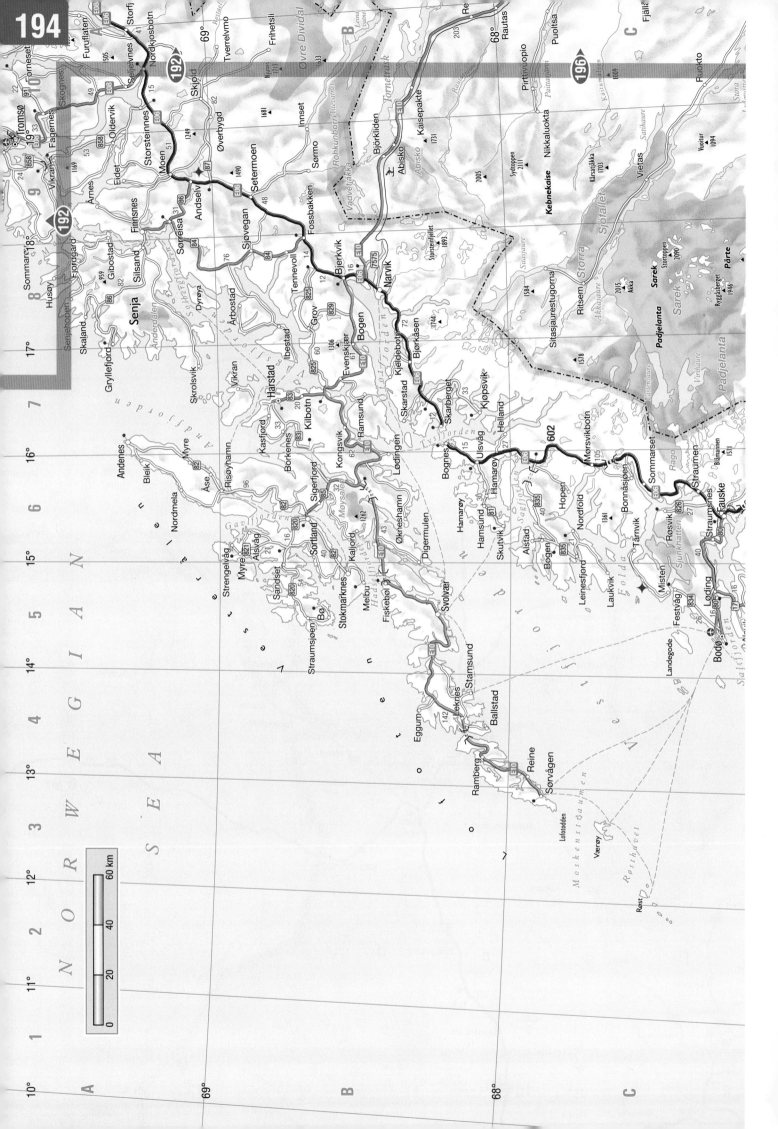

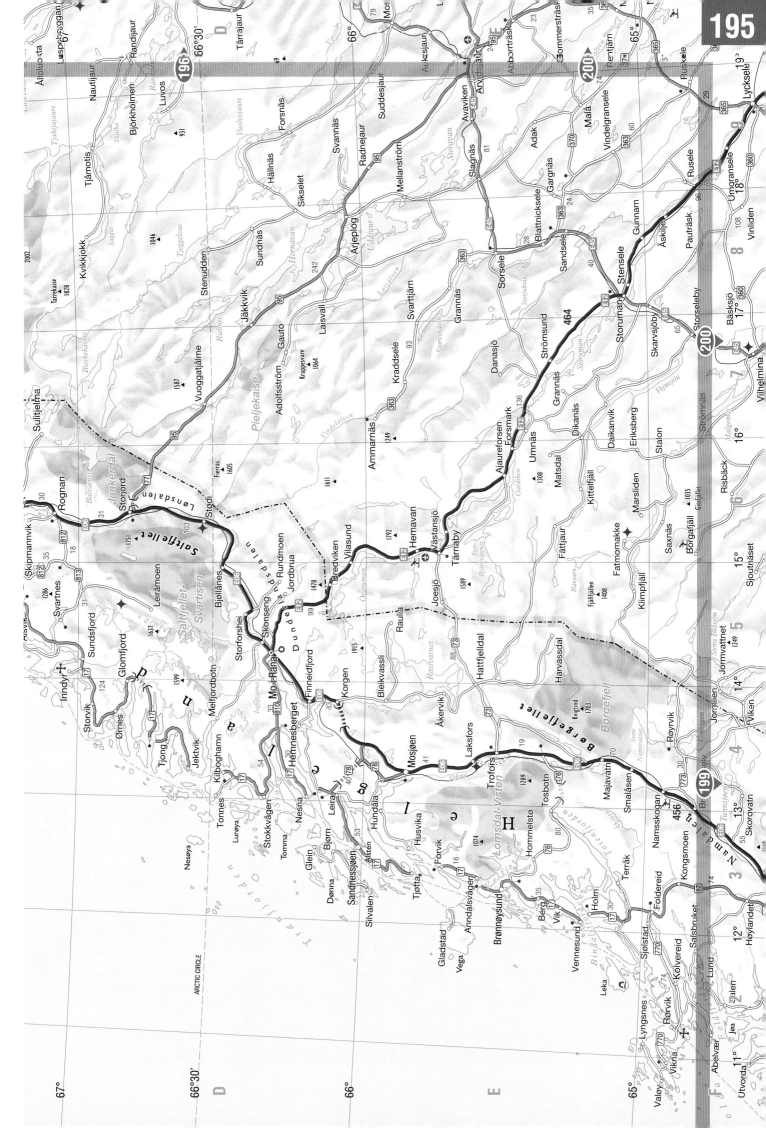

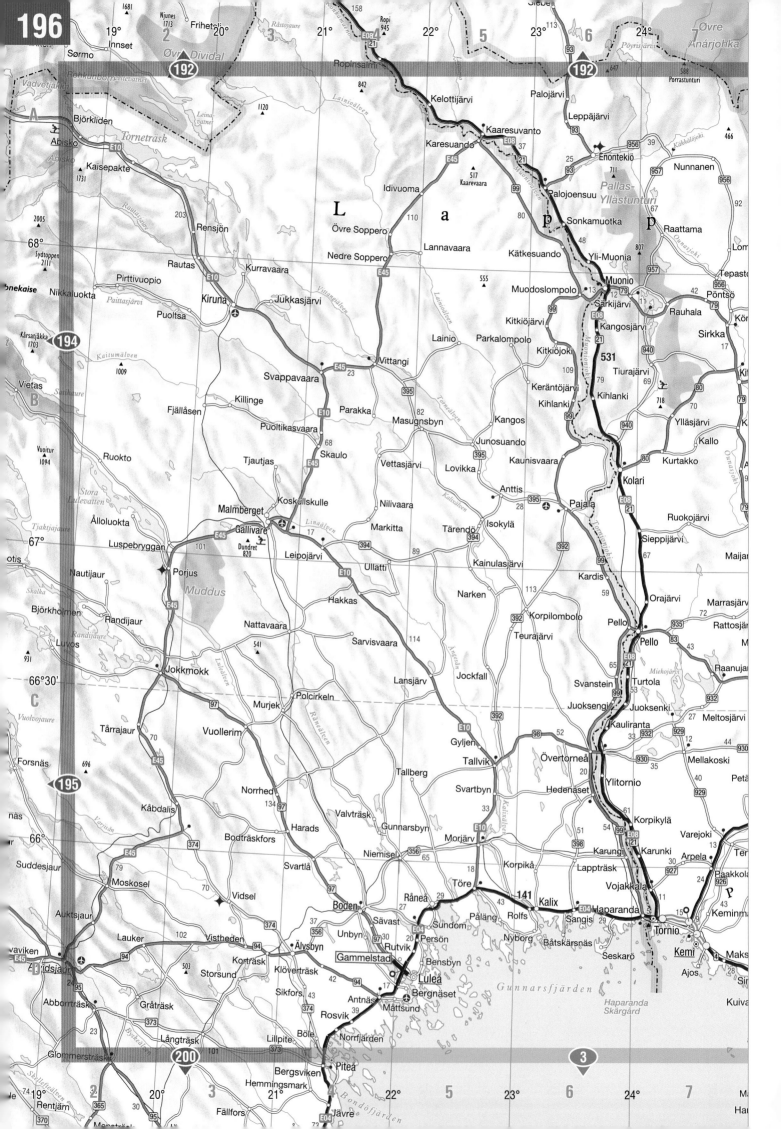

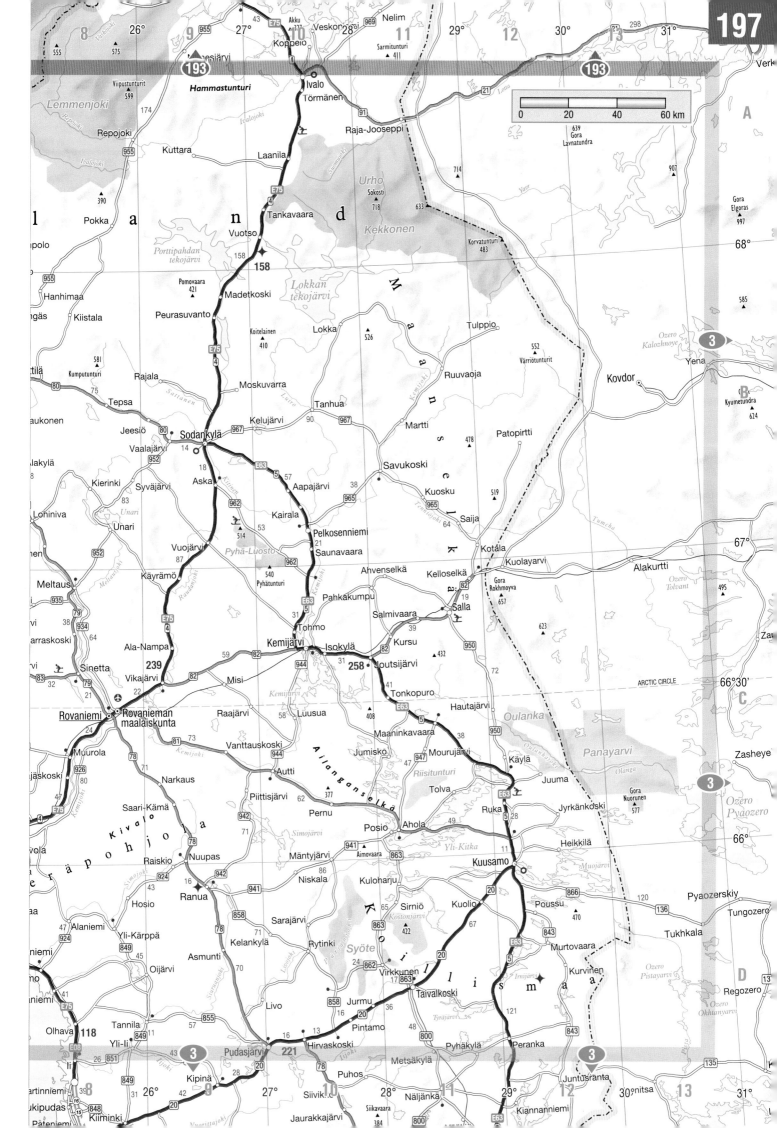

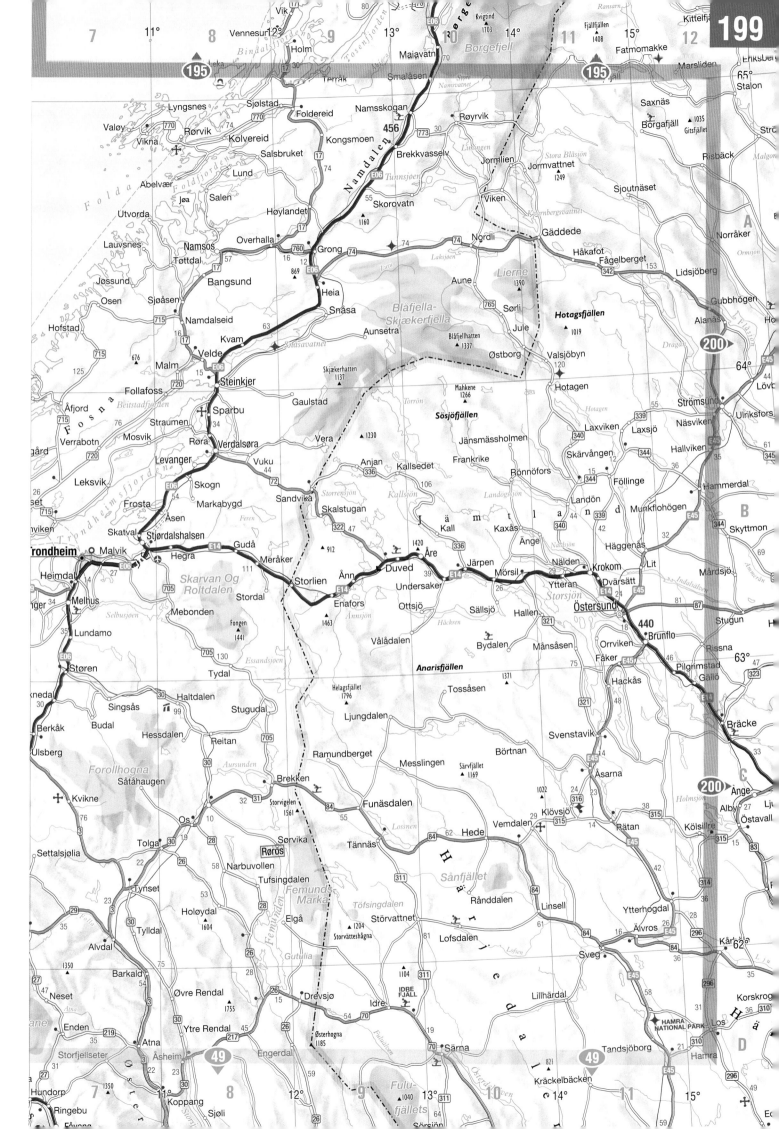

Index

(A)	Austria	Autriche	Österreich	Austria
(AL)	Albania	Albanie	Albanien	Albania
(AND)	Andorra	Andorre	Andorra	Andorra
(B)	Belgium	Belgique	Belgien	Belgio
(BG)	Bulgaria	Bulgarie	Bulgarien	Bulgaria
(BIH)	Bosnia-Herzegovin	Bosnia-Herzegovine	Bosnien-Herzegowina	Bosnia-Herzogovina
(BY)	Belarus	Belarus	Weissrussland	Bielorussia
(CH)	Switzerland	Suisse	Schweiz	Svizzera
(CY)	Cyprus	Chypre	Zypern	Cipro
(CZ)	Czechia	République Tchèque	Tschechische Republik	Repubblica Ceca
(D)	Germany	Allemagne	Deutschland	Germania
(DK)	Denmark	Danemark	Dänemark	Danimarca
(E)	Spain	Espagne	Spanien	Spagna
(EST)	Estonia	Estonie	Estland	Estonia
(F)	France	France	Frankreich	Francia
(FIN)	Finland	Finlande	Finnland	Finlandia
(FL)	Liechtenstein	Liechtenstein	Liechtenstein	Liechtenstein
(FO)	Faeroe Islands	Îles Féroé	Färoër-Inseln	Isole Faroe
(GBZ)	Gibraltar	Gibraltar	Gibraltar	Gibilterra
(GR)	Greece	Grèce	Greichenland	Grecia
(H)	Hungary	Hongrie	Ungarn	Ungheria
(HR)	Croatia	Croatie	Kroatien	Croazia
(I)	Italy	Italie	Italien	Italia
(IRL)	Ireland	Irlande	Irland	Irlanda
(IS)	Iceland	Islande	Island	Islanda
(KOS)	Kosovo	Kosovo	Kosovo	Kosovo
(L)	Luxembourg	Luxembourg	Luxemburg	Lussemburgo
(LT)	Lithuania	Lituanie	Litauen	Lituania
(LV)	Latvia	Lettonie	Lettland	Lettonia
(M)	Malta	Malte	Malta	Malta
(MC)	Monaco	Monaco	Monaco	Monaco
(MD)	Moldova	Moldavie	Moldawien	Moldavia
(MNE)	Montenegro	Monténégro	Montenegro	Montenegro
(N)	Norway	Norvège	Norwegen	Norvegia
(NL)	Netherlands	Pays-Bas	Niederlande	Paesi Bassi
(NMK)	North Macedonia	Macédoine du Nord	Nordmakedonien	Macedonia del Nord
(P)	Portugal	Portugal	Portugal	Portogallo
(PL)	Poland	Pologne	Polen	Polonia
(RO)	Romania	Roumanie	Rumanien	Romania
(RSM)	San Marino	Saint-Marin	San Marino	San Marino
(RUS)	Russia	Russie	Russland	Russia
(S)	Sweden	Suède	Schweden	Svezia
(SK)	Slovakia	République Slovaque	Slowak Republik	Repubblica Slovacca
(SLO)	Slovenia	Slovénie	Slowenien	Slovenia
(SRB)	Serbia	Serbie	Serbien	Serbia
(TR)	Turkey	Turquie	Türkei	Turchia
(UA)	Ukraine	Ukraine	Ukraine	Ucraina
(UK)	United Kingdom	Royaume Uni	Grossbritannien und Nordirland	Regno Unito

A

Aab – Aho

Aabenraa DK....64 A2
Aabybro DK.....58 A2
Aach D........107 B4
Aachen D......80 B2
Aalborg DK....58 A2
Aalen D........94 C2
Aalestrup DK ..58 B2
Aalsmeer NL...70 B1
Aalst B........79 B4
Aalten NL......71 C3
Aalter B.......79 A3
Äänekoski FIN...8 A4
Aapajärvi FIN..........197 B10
Ağapınar TR .. 187 C5
Aarau CH ... 106 B3
Aarberg CH... 106 B2
Aarburg CH... 106 B2
Aardenburg NL.79 A3
Aarhus DK.....59 B3
Aars DK........58 B2
Aarschot B.....79 B4
Aarup DK......59 C3
Aba H........112 B2
Abádanes E...152 B1
Abades E....151 B3
Abadin E......141 A3
Abádszalók H.113 B4
Abaliget H.....125 A4
Abana TR......23 A8
A Baña E......140 B2
Abanilla E....165 A3
Abano Terme I..........121 B4
Abarán E......165 A3
Abasár H......113 B4
Abbadia San Salvatore I...135 C4
Abbaue D......74 A2
Abbehausen D..72 A1
Abbekäs S....66 A2
Abbeville F.....90 A1
Abbey IRL.....28 A3
Abbeydorney IRL.............29 B2
Abbeyfeale IRL..29 B2
Abbeyleix IRL...30 B1
Abbey Town UK 36 B3
Abbiategrasso I..............120 B1

Abborrträsk S.............196 D2
Abbots Bromley UK.............40 C2
Abbotsbury UK .43 B4
Abda H........111 B4
Abejar E......143 C4
Abela P......160 B1
Abelvær N....199 A8
Abenberg D....94 B2
Abenójar E.... 157 B3
Abensberg D...95 C3
Aberaeron UK..39 C2
Abercarn UK...39 C3
Aberchirder UK 33 D4
Aberdare UK...39 C3
Aberdaron UK..38 B2
Aberdeen UK... 33 D4
Aberdulais UK ..39 C3
Aberdyfi UK....39 B2
Aberfeldy UK...35 B4
Aberffraw UK...38 A2
Aberfoyle UK ...34 B3
Abergavenny UK 39 C3
Abergele UK ...38 A3
Abergynolwyn UK.............38 B3
Aberporth UK...39 B2
Abersoch UK...38 B2
Abertillery UK ..39 C3
Abertura E.... 156 A2
Aberystwyth UK.............39 B2
Abetone I.....135 A3
Abfaltersbach A............109 C3
Abide
Çanakkale TR..........186 B1
Kütahya TR..187 D4
Abiego E......145 B3
Abild DK.......64 B1
Abingdon-on-Thames UK....44 B2
Abington UK...36 A3
Abisko S......194 B9
Abiul P........154 B2
Abla E........164 B2
Ablis F........90 C1
A Bola E.......140 B3
Abondance F..118 A3
Abony H......113 B4
Aboyne UK.....33 D4

Abrantes P....154 B2
Abreiro P.....148 A2
Abreschviller F..92 C3
Abrest F.......117 A3
Abriès F.......119 C3
Abrud RO......17 B5
Abtenau A.....109 B4
Abtsgmünd D..94 C1
Abusejo E.....149 B3
Åby
Kronoberg S ... 62 A2
Östergötland S..........56 B2
Åbyggeby S....51 B4
Åbytorp S......55 A6
A Cañiza E.....140 B2
A Capela E.....140 A2
Acate I........177 B3
Accadía I......171 B3
Accéglio I.....132 A2
Accettura I....172 B2
Acciaroli I.....170 C3
Accous F......145 A3
Accrington UK ..40 B1
Accúmoli I.....169 A3
Acedera E.....156 A2
Acehúche E...155 B4
Acered E......152 A2
Acerenza I....172 B1
Acerno I.......170 C3
Acerra I.......170 C2
Aceuchal E....155 C4
Acharacle UK ...34 B2
Acharnes GR... 185 A4
Achavanich UK..32 C3
Achene B.......79 B5
Achenkirch A.. 108 B2
Achensee A.... 108 B2
Achenthal A... 108 B2
Achentrias GR..185 E6
Acheux-en-Amienois F....90 A2
Achiltibuie UK ..32 C1
Achim D.......72 A2
Achladokambos GR.........184 B3
Achnasheen UK.............32 D1
Achnashellach UK............32 D1
Achosnich UK...34 B1
Aci Castello I... 177 B4

Aci Catena I... 177 B4
Acilia I........168 B2
Acıpayam TR.. 189 B4
Acireale I...... 177 B4
Acle UK........41 C5
A Coruña E...140 A2
Acquacadda I.. 179 C2
Acquanegra sul Chiese I......121 B3
Acquapendente I.............168 A1
Acquasanta Terme I........136 C2
Acquasparta I.168 A2
Acquaviva I...135 B4
Acquaviva delle Fonti I......171 C4
Acquaviva Picena I.............136 C2
Acquigny F....89 A5
Ácqui Terme I. 119 C5
Acri I........174 B2
Acs H.........112 B2
Acsa I.........112 B3
Ácsteszér H... 112 B1
Acy-en-Multien F............90 B2
Ada SRB...... 126 B2
Adak S.........195 E9
Ådalsbruk N...48 B3
Adamas GR... 185 C5
Adamsfjord N..........193 B10
Adamuz E.....157 B3
Adana TR......23 C8
Ádánd H......112 C2
Adanero E... 150 B3
Adare IRL......29 B3
Adaševci SRB. 125 B5
Adeanueva de Ebro E..........144 B2
Adelboden CH..........106 C2
Adelebsen D...82 A1
Adélfia I.......173 A2
Adelmannsfelden D........94 C2
Adelsheim D...94 B1
Adelsö S.......57 A3
Ademuz E.....152 B2
Adenau D......80 B2
Adendorf D....72 A3
Adinkerke B....78 A2

Adjud RO.......17 B7
Adliswil CH... 107 B3
Admont A.....110 B1
Ådneram N....52 A2
Adolfsström S.............195 D7
Adony H......112 B2
Adorf
Hessen D......81 A4
Sachsen D.....83 B4
Adra E........164 C1
Adradas E.....152 A1
Adrall E.......147 B2
Adrano I.......177 B3
Ádria I........121 B5
Adrigole IRL....29 C2
Adwick le Street UK.............40 B2
Adzaneta E ... 153 B3
Aesch CH ... 106 B2
A Estrada E... 140 B2
Afandou GR... 188 C3
Åfarnes N.....198 C4
Affing D........94 C2
Affoltern CH.. 106 B3
Affric Lodge UK............32 D1
Åfjord N......199 B7
Aflenz Kurort A............110 B2
A Fonsagrada E.............141 A3
Afritz A.......109 C4
Afyonkarahisar TR...........187 D5
Ágasegyháza H.............112 C3
Agay F........132 B2
Agazzano I....120 C2
Agde F........130 B2
Agdenes N.... 198 B6
Agen F........129 B3
Ager E........145 C4
Agerbæk DK...59 C1
Agerskov DK...64 A2
Agger DK......58 B1
Aggersund DK.58 A2
Aggius I........178 B3
Aggsbach Dorf A............97 C3
Aggsbach Markt A............97 C3
Aggtelek H.....99 C4

Aghalee UK 27 B4
Aghia GR......182 D4
Aghia Anna GR.............183 E5
Aghia Galini GR 185 D5
Aghia Marina GR............188 D1
Aghia Paraskevi GR...........186 C1
Aghia Pelagia GR...........184 C3
Aghia Triada GR............184 B2
Aghiokambos GR...........182 D4
Aghios Efstratios GR............183 D6
Aghios Kirikos GR...........185 B7
Aghios Matheos GR...........182 D1
Aghios Mironas GR...........185 D6
Aghios Nikolaos GR...........185 D6
Aghios Petros GR............182 E2
Aghio Theodori GR............184 B4
Agiči BIH...... 124 C2
Agira I........177 B3
Aglientu I......178 A3
Agnières F.....118 C2
Agno CH......120 B1
Agnone I......170 B2
Agolada E.... 140 B2
Agon Coutainville F..............88 A2
Ágordo I......121 A5
Agost E........165 A4
Agramón E....158 C2
Agramunt E...147 C2
Agreda E......144 C2
Agria GR......183 D5
Agrigento I ... 176 B2
Agrinio GR....182 E3
Agrón E........163 A4
Agrópoli I.....170 C2
Aguadulce
Almería E.....164 C2
Sevilla E......162 A3
Agualada E ... 140 A2
Agua Longa P. 148 A1

A Guarda E....140 C2
Aguarón E 152 A2
Aguas E........145 B3
Aguas Belas P. 154 B2
Aguas de Busot E............159 C3
Aguas de Moura P.............154 C2
Águas Frias P . 148 A2
Aguas Santas P.............148 A1
Aguaviva E.... 153 B3
Aguaviva de la Vega E.......152 A1
A Gudiña E.... 141 B3
Agudo E...... 156 B3
Águeda P.....148 B1
Aguessac F... 130 A2
Agugliano I... 136 B2
Aguiar P......154 C3
Aguiàr da Beira P.............148 B2
Aguilafuente E............151 A3
Aguilar de Campóo E............142 B2
Aguilar de la Frontera E ... 163 A3
Aguilas E...... 164 B3
Agunnaryd S....60 C4
Ahat TR......187 D4
Ahaus D.......71 B3
Åheim N......198 C2
Ahigal E......149 B3
Ahigal de Villarino E..........149 A3
Ahillones E... 156 B2
Ahlbeck
Mecklenburg-Vorpommern D.............66 C3
Mecklenburg-Vorpommern D.............74 A3
Ahlen D........81 A3
Ahlhorn D.....71 B5
Ahmetbey TR. 186 A2
Ahmetler TR .. 188 A4
Ahmetli TR.... 188 A2
Ahoghill UK.....27 B4
Ahola FIN 197 C11

Ahrensbök D ...65 B3
Ahrensburg D ..72 A3
Ahrenshoop D ..66 B1
Ahun F........ 116 A2
Åhus S.........63 C2
Ahvenselkä
  FIN.......... 197 C11
Aibar E....... 144 B2
Aich D 95 C4
Aicha D 96 C1
Aichach D 94 C3
Aidone I........ 177 B3
Aiello Cálabro
  I............. 175 B2
Aigen im Mühlkreis
  A............96 C1
Aigle CH 119 A3
Aignan F....... 128 C3
Aignay-le-Duc
  F............ 104 B3
Aigre F....... 115 C4
Aigrefeuille-
  d'Aunis F..... 114 B3
Aigrefeuille-sur-
  Maine F....... 101 B4
Aiguablava E . 147 C4
Aiguebelle F .. 118 B3
Aigueperse F .. 116 A3
Aigues-Mortes
  F............. 131 B3
Aigues-Vives
  F............. 130 B1
Aiguilles F 119 C3
Aiguillon F 129 B3
Aigurande F .. 103 C3
Ailefroide F... 118 C3
Aillant-sur-Tholon
  F............. 104 B2
Ailly-sur-Noye
  F............90 B2
Ailly-sur-Somme
  F............90 B2
Aimargues F .. 131 B3
Aime F........ 118 B3
Ainaži LV........8 D4
Ainet A....... 109 C3
Ainhoa F...... 144 A2
Ainsa E....... 145 B4
Airaines F......90 B1
Aird UK 34 B2
Aird Asaig
  Tairbeart UK ...31 B2
Airdrie UK..... 35 C4
Aire-sur-l'Adour
  F............. 128 C2
Aire-sur-la-Lys
  F............78 B2
Airole I....... 133 B3
Airolo CH 107 C3
Airvault F..... 102 C1
Aisey-sur-Seine
  F............. 104 B3
Aïssey F...... 105 B5
Aisy-sur-Armançon
  F............. 104 B3
Aiterhofen D....95 C4
Aith
  Orkney UK.....33 B4
  Shetland UK ... 33 A5
Aitona E...... 153 A4
Aitrach D 107 B5
Aiud RO.........17 B5
Aix-en-Othe F. 104 A2
Aix-en-Provence
  F............. 131 B4
Aixe-sur-Vienne
  F............. 115 C5
Aix-les-Bains
  F............. 118 B2
Aizenay F..... 114 B2
Aizkraukle LV....8 D4
Aizpute LV......8 D2
Ajac F........ 146 A3
Ajaccio F...... 180 B1
Ajain F....... 116 A1
Ajaureforsen
  S...........195 E6
Ajdovščina
  SLO 122 B2
Ajka H 111 B4
Ajo E......... 143 A3
Ajofrin E...... 157 A4
Ajos FIN..... 196 D7
Ajuda P...... 155 C3
Akanthou CY . 181 A2
Akarca TR ... 189 A4
Akasztó H..... 112 C3
Akçakoca TR .. 187 A6
Akçaova TR ... 187 A4
Akçay TR..... 189 C4

Aken D........83 A4
Åkerby S.....51 B4
Åkernes N 52 B3
Åkersberga S ...57 A4
Åkers styckebruk
  S............56 A3
Åkervik N....195 E4
Akhisar TR .. 186 D2
Åkirkeby DK...67 A3
Akköy TR 188 B2
Akkrum NL....70 A2
Akören TR ... 189 B7
Åkra N.........52 A2
Akranes IS ... 190 C3
Åkrehamn N...52 A1
Akrotiri CY ... 181 B1
Aksaray TR.....23 B8
Akşehir TR ... 189 A6
Akseki TR ... 189 B6
Aksu TR 189 C5
Aktsyabrski
  BY............13 B8
Akureyri IS ... 191 B7
Åkvåg N 53 B5
Akyazı TR 187 B5
ÅL N 47 B5
Ala I.......... 121 B4
Alaca TR 23 A8
Alacaatlı TR .. 186 C3
Alaçam TR 23 A8
Alaçatı TR 188 A1
Alàdei Sardi I . 178 B3
Ala di Stura I . 119 B4
Alaejos E..... 150 A2
Alagna Valsésia
  I............. 119 B4
Alagón E..... 144 C2
Alaior E...... 167 B4
Alájar E...... 161 B3
Alakurtti
  RUS....... 197 C13
Alakylä FIN .. 196 B7
Alameda E.... 163 A3
Alameda de la
  Sagra E..... 151 B4
Alamedilla E.. 163 A4
Alamillo E..... 156 B3
Alaminos E... 151 B5
Ala-Nampa
  FIN........ 197 C9
Alanäs S 199 A12
Alandroal P... 155 C3
Ålandsbro S... 200 D3
Alange E..... 156 B1
Alaniemi FIN.. 197 D8
Alanís E...... 156 B2
Alanya TR ... 189 C7
Alap H 112 C2
Alaquáso E... 159 B3
Alaraz E...... 150 B2
Alarcón E..... 158 B1
Alar del Rey E . 142 B2
Alaró E....... 167 B2
Alaşehir TR... 188 A3
Alássio I...... 133 A4
Alatoz E...... 158 B2
Alatri I....... 169 B3
Alavus FIN.....8 A3
Alba
  E........... 152 B2
  I........... 119 C5
Alba Adriática
  I............. 136 C2
Albacete E.... 158 C2
Alba de Tormes
  E........... 150 B2
Alba de Yeltes
  E........... 149 B3
Albaida E..... 159 C3
Alba-Iulia RO...17 B5
Ålbæk DK.....58 A3
Albaladejo E.. 158 C1
Albala del Caudillo
  E........... 156 A1
Albalat E..... 159 B3
Albalate de Cinca
  E........... 145 C4
Albalate del
  Arzobispo E.. 153 A3
Albalate de las
  Nogueras E .. 152 B1
Albalete de Zorita
  E........... 151 B5
Alban F....... 130 B1
Albánchez E .. 164 B2
Albánchez de
  Ubeda E..... 163 A4
Albano Laziale
  I............. 168 B2
Albanyà E..... 147 B3

Albaredo d'Adige
  I............. 121 B4
Albares E..... 151 B4
Albarracín E .. 152 B2
Albatana I.... 158 C2
Albatarrec E .. 153 A4
Albatera E.... 165 A4
Albbruck D .. 106 B3
Albedin E.... 163 A3
Albelda de Iregua
  E........... 143 B4
Albenga I..... 133 A4
Albens F..... 118 B2
Ålberga
  Södermanland
  S............ 56 A2
  Södermanland
  S............56 B2
Albergaria-a-Nova
  P........... 148 B1
Albergaria-a-Velha
  P........... 148 B1
Albergaria dos
  Doze P...... 154 B2
Alberge P..... 154 C2
Alberic E..... 159 B3
Albernoa P... 160 B2
Alberobello I.. 173 B3
Alberoni I..... 122 B1
Albersdorf D....64 B2
Albersloh D....81 A3
Albert F.......90 A2
Albertirsa H... 112 B3
Albertville F .. 118 B3
Alberuela de Tubo
  E........... 145 C3
Albi F........ 130 B1
Albidona I.... 174 B2
Albínia I...... 168 A1
Albino I....... 120 B2
Albinshof D....66 C2
Albires E..... 142 B1
Albisola Marina
  I............. 133 A4
Albocácer E .. 153 B4
Albolote E.... 163 A4
Albondón E... 164 C1
Alborea E..... 158 B2
Albox E...... 164 B2
Albrechtice nad
  Vitavou CZ....96 B2
Albstadt D.... 107 A4
Albufeira P.. 160 B1
Albuñol E..... 164 C1
Albuñuelas E.. 163 B4
Alburquerque
  E........... 155 B3
Alby
  Öland S 63 B4
  Västernorrland
  S...........200 D1
Alcácer do Sal
  P........... 154 C2
Alcáçovas P... 154 C2
Alcadozo E.... 158 C2
Alcafoces P.... 155 B3
Alcains P..... 155 B3
Alcalá de Guadaira
  E........... 162 A2
Alcalá de Gurrea
  E........... 144 B3
Alcalá de Henares
  E........... 151 B4
Alcalá la Selva
  E........... 153 B3
Alcalá del Júcar
  E........... 158 B2
Alcalá de los
  Gazules E 162 B2
Alcalá del Río
  E........... 162 A2
Alcalá del Valle
  E........... 162 B2
Alcalá de Xivert
  E........... 153 B4
Alcalá la Real
  E........... 163 A4
Álcamo I...... 176 B1
Alcampell E... 145 C4
Alcanadre E... 144 B1
Alcanar E..... 153 B4
Alcanede P.... 154 B2
Alcanena P.... 154 B2
Alcañices E.... 149 A3
Alcántara E... 155 B4
Alcantarilha P 160 B1
Alcantarilla E . 165 B3
Alcañz E..... 153 A3
Alcaracejos E . 156 B3
Alcaraz E..... 158 C1
Alcaria Ruiva
  P........... 160 B2

Alcarraz E..... 153 A4
Alcaudete E... 163 A3
Alcaudete de la
  Jara E 150 C3
Alcázar de San
  Juan E....... 157 A4
Alcazarén E... 150 A3
Alcoba E...... 157 A3
Alcobaça P... 154 B1
Alcobendas E . 151 B4
Alcocer E..... 151 B5
Alcochete P... 154 C2
Alcoentre P ... 154 B2
Alcolea
  Almería E.... 164 C2
  Córdoba E ... 156 C3
Alcolea de
  Calatrava E .. 157 B3
Alcolea de Cinca
  E........... 145 C4
Alcolea del Pinar
  E........... 152 A1
Alcolea del Rio
  E........... 162 A2
Alcolea de Tajo
  E........... 150 C2
Alcollarin E... 156 A2
Alconchel E... 155 C3
Alconera E.... 155 C4
Alcontar E.... 164 B2
Alcora E...... 153 B3
Alcorcón E.... 151 B4
Alcorisa E.... 153 B3
Alcossebre E.. 153 B4
Alcoutim P... 160 B2
Alcover E..... 147 C2
Alcoy E...... 159 C3
Alcsútdoboz
  H........... 112 B2
Alcubierre E .. 145 C3
Alcubilla de
  Avellaneda
  E........... 143 C3
Alcubilla de
  Nogales E.... 141 B5
Alcubillas E... 157 B4
Alcublas E.... 159 B3
Alcúdia E..... 167 B3
Alcúdia de Guadix
  E........... 164 B1
Alcuéscar E... 155 B4
Aldbrough UK ..41 B3
Aldea de la
  Ribera E..... 149 A3
Aldea del Cano
  E........... 155 B4
Aldea del Fresno
  E........... 151 B3
Aldea del Obispo
  E........... 149 B3
Aldea del Rey
  E........... 157 B4
Aldea de Trujillo
  E........... 156 A2
Aldealcorvo E. 151 A4
Aldealuenga de
  Santa Maria
  E........... 151 A4
Aldeamayor de San
  Martin E 150 A3
Aldeanueva de
  Barbarroya
  E........... 150 C2
Aldeanueva del
  Camino E 149 B4
Aldeanueva del
  Codonal E.... 150 A3
Aldeanueva de San
  Bartolomé E . 156 A2
Aldeapozo E.. 144 C1
Aldeaquemada
  E........... 157 B4
Aldea Real E .. 151 A3
Aldearrubia E. 150 A2
Aldeaseca de la
  Frontera E ... 150 B2
Aldeasoña E . 151 A3
Aldeatejada E. 150 B2
Aldeavieja E .. 150 B3
Aldehuela de
  Calatañazor
  E........... 143 C4
Aldeia da Serra
  P........... 155 C3
Aldeia do Bispo
  P........... 149 B3
Aldeia do Mato
  P........... 154 B2

Aldeia Gavinha
  P........... 154 B1
Aldeire E..... 164 B1
Aldenhoven D ..80 B2
Aldersbach D ..95 C5
Aldershot UK ...44 B3
Aldudes F..... 144 A2
Åled S.........60 C2
Aledo E...... 165 B3
Alegria E..... 143 B4
Aleksandrovac
  SRB.......... 127 C3
Aleksandrów
  Kujawski PL....76 B3
Aleksandrów
  Łódżki PL 86 A3
Aleksa Šantić
  SRB.......... 126 B1
Ålem S.........62 B4
Alençon F......89 B4
Alenquer P.... 154 B1
Alenya F..... 146 B3
Aléria F...... 180 A2
Alès F........ 131 A3
Åles I........ 179 C2
Alessándria I.. 120 C1
Alessándria della
  Rocca I...... 176 B2
Alessano I.... 173 C4
Ålesund N ... 198 C3
Alet-les-Bains
  F........... 146 B3
Alexandria
  GR 182 C4
  RO 17 D6
  UK 34 C3
Alexandroupoli
  GR 183 C7
Aleyrac F..... 131 A3
Alézio I....... 173 B4
Alfacar E...... 163 A4
Alfaiates P.... 149 B3
Alfajarin E.... 153 A3
Alfambra
  E........... 152 B2
  P........... 160 B1
Alfândega da Fé
  P........... 149 A3
Alfarela de Jafes
  P........... 148 A2
Alfarelos P.... 148 B1
Alfarim P..... 154 C1
Alfarnate E... 163 B3
Alfaro E...... 144 B2
Alfarrás E.... 145 C4
Alfaz del Pi E . 159 C3
Alfedena I.... 169 B4
Alfeizarão P... 154 B1
Alfeld
  Bayern D......95 B3
  Niedersachsen
  D............ 72 C2
Alfena P..... 148 A1
Alferce P..... 160 B1
Alfhausen D ...71 B4
Alfonsine I.... 135 A5
Alford
  Aberdeenshire
  UK 33 D4
  Lincolnshire
  UK 41 B4
Alforja E...... 147 C1
Alfoz E....... 141 A3
Alfreton UK....40 B2
Alfta S........50 A3
Alfundão P... 160 A1
Algaida E..... 167 B2
Algar E....... 162 B2
Älgarås S 55 B5
Ålgård N......52 B1
Algarinejo E .. 163 A3
Algarrobo E... 163 B3
Algatocin E... 162 B2
Algeciras E.... 162 B2
Algemesí E... 159 B3
Algés P...... 154 C1
Algete E...... 151 B4
Alghero I..... 178 B2
Älghult S.....62 A3
Alginet E..... 159 B3
Algodonales
  E........... 162 B2
Algodor
  E........... 151 C4
  P........... 160 B2
Algora E...... 151 B5
Algoso P..... 149 A3
Algoz P...... 160 B1
Älgsjö S..... 200 B3
Alguaire E.... 145 C4
Alguazas E.... 165 A3
Algutsrum S ...63 B4
Algyö H...... 126 A2

Alhama de Almería
  E........... 164 C2
Alhama de Aragón
  E........... 152 A2
Alhama de Granada
  E........... 163 B4
Alhama de Murcia
  E........... 165 B3
Alhambra E... 157 B4
Alhandra P.... 154 C1
Alhaurin de la Torre
  E........... 163 B3
Alhaurín el Grande
  E........... 163 B3
Alhendin E.... 163 A4
Alhóndiga E .. 151 B5
Alía E........ 156 A2
Aliaga TR 186 D1
Aliaga E...... 153 B3
Alibunar SRB.. 127 B2
Alicante E.... 165 A4
Alicún de Ortega
  E........... 164 B1
Alife I........ 170 B2
Alija del Infantado
  E........... 141 B5
Alijó P....... 148 A2
Alimena I..... 177 B3
Alingsås S.....60 B2
Alinyà E...... 147 B2
Aliseda E..... 155 B4
Aliveri GR.... 185 A5
Alixan F...... 117 C5
Aljaraque E... 161 B2
Aljezur P..... 160 B1
Aljorra E...... 165 B3
Aljubarrota P . 154 B2
Aljucen E..... 155 B4
Aljustrel P.... 160 B1
Alken B 79 B5
Alkmaar NL...70 B1
Alkoven A 96 C2
Allaines F..... 103 A3
Allaire F...... 101 B3
Allanche F.... 116 B2
Alland A 111 A3
Allariz E...... 140 B3
Allassac F.... 129 A4
Allauch F..... 131 B4
Alleen N 52 B3
Allègre F...... 117 B3
Allemont F.... 118 B3
Allendale Town
  UK 37 B4
Allendorf D....81 B4
Allentsteig A...97 C3
Allepuz E..... 153 B3
Allersberg D...95 B3
Allershausen D .95 C3
Alles E....... 142 A2
Allevard F..... 118 B3
Allgunnen S ...62 A3
Allihies IRL.....29 C1
Allingåbro DK..58 B3
Allmannsdorf
  D........... 107 B4
Allo E........ 144 B1
Alloa UK 35 B4
Allogny F..... 103 B4
Ålloluokta S .. 196 B2
Allones
  Eure et Loire
  F........... 90 C1
  Maine-et-Loire
  F........... 102 B2
Allonnes F.... 102 B2
Allons F...... 128 B2
Allos F....... 132 A2
Allstedt D.....82 A3
Alltwalis UK....39 C2
Allumiere I.... 168 A1
Almaceda P... 155 B3
Almáchar E... 163 B3
Almada P..... 154 C1
Almadén E.... 156 B3
Almadén de la Plata
  E........... 161 B3
Almadenejos
  E........... 156 B3
Almadrones E. 151 B5
Almagro E.... 157 B4
Almajano E... 144 C1
Almansa E.... 159 C2
Almansil P.... 160 B1
Almanza E.... 142 B1
Almaraz E.... 150 C2
Almargen E... 162 B2
Almarza E.... 143 C4
Almásfüzitö
  H........... 112 B2

Almassora E .. 159 B3
Almazán E.... 152 A1
Almazul E..... 152 A1
Alme D........81 A4
Almedina E... 158 C1
Almedinilla E . 163 A3
Almeida
  E........... 149 A3
  P........... 149 B3
Almeirim P.... 154 B2
Almelo NL....71 B3
Almenar E.... 145 C4
Almenara E... 159 B3
Almenar de Soria
  E........... 152 A1
Almendra P... 149 B2
Almendral E .. 155 C4
Almendral de la
  Cañada E 150 B3
Almendralejo
  E........... 155 C4
Almenno San
  Bartolomeo I. 120 B2
Almere NL....70 B2
Almería E..... 164 C2
Almerimar E .. 164 C2
Almese I...... 119 B4
Almexial P ... 160 B2
Ålmhult S.....63 B2
Almiropotamos
  GR 185 A5
Almiros GR... 182 D4
Almodôvar P.. 160 B1
Almodóvar del
  Campo E..... 157 B3
Almodóvar del
  Pinar E....... 158 B2
Almodóvar del Río
  E........... 162 A2
Almofala P.... 148 B2
Almogia E.... 163 B3
Almoharin E . 156 A1
Almonacid de la
  Sierra E...... 152 A2
Almonacid de
  Toledo E..... 157 A4
Almonaster la Real
  E........... 161 B3
Almondsbury
  UK 43 A4
Almonte E.... 161 B3
Almoradí E... 165 A4
Almoraima E . 162 B2
Almorox E.... 150 B3
Almoster P.... 154 B2
Almsele S 200 B3
Älmsta S.....51 C5
Almudena E... 164 A3
Almudévar E.. 145 B3
Almuñécar E . 163 B4
Almunge E....51 C5
Almuradiel E.. 157 B4
Almussafes E . 159 B3
Almvik S......62 A4
Alness UK 32 D2
Almunt UK....37 A5
Alnwick UK ...37 A5
Åloppe S.....51 C4
Álora E....... 163 B3
Alos d'Ensil E . 146 B2
Alosno E...... 161 B2
Alozaina E.... 162 B2
Alpbach A 108 B2
Alpedrete de la
  Sierra E...... 151 B4
Alpedrinha P.. 148 B2
Alpen D.......80 A2
Alpera E...... 159 C2
Alphen aan de Rijn
  NL............70 B1
Alpiarça P.... 154 B2
Alpignano I... 119 B4
Alpirsbach D...93 C4
Alpu TR...... 187 C5
Alpuente E.... 159 B2
Alqueva P.... 160 A2
Alquézar E.... 145 B4
Als DK.........58 B3
Alsasua E..... 144 B1
Alsdorf D......80 B2
Alsély DK.....59 C1
Alsfeld D......81 B5
Alsike S......57 A3
Alskog S......57 C4
Alsleben D.....83 A3
Alsónémedi H 112 B3
Alsótold H.... 112 B3
Alsóújlak H ... 111 B3
Alstad N..... 194 C6
Alstätte D......71 B3
Alsterbro S....62 B3
Alstermo S....62 B3
Alston UK......37 B4

Alsvåg N...... 194 B6
Alsvik N....... 194 C5
Alta N......... 192 C7
Älta S.........57 A4
Altamura I... 172 B2
Altarejos E.... 158 B1
Altaussee A... 109 B4
Altavilla Irpina
I.............. 170 B2
Altavilla Silentina
I.............. 170 C3
Altdöbern D ...84 A2
Altdorf
CH........... 107 C3
D 95 C4
Altdorf bei
Nürnberg D....95 B3
Alte P........ 160 B1
Altea E....... 159 C3
Altedo I....... 121 C4
Altena D.......81 A3
Altenau D......82 A2
Altenberg D ...84 B1
Altenberge D ...71 B4
Altenbruch D ...64 C1
Altenburg D ...83 B4
Altenfelden A...96 C1
Altengronau D..82 B1
Altenheim D ...93 C3
Altenhundem
D 81 A4
Altenkirchen
Mecklenburg-
Vorpommern
D..............66 B2
Radom P.......81 B3
Altenkunstadt
D..............82 B3
Altenmarkt
A............. 110 B1
D............. 109 A3
Altenmarkt im
Pongall A... 109 B4
Altensteig D ...93 C4
Altentreptow
D.............74 A2
Altenwalde D...64 C1
Alten-weddingen
D.............73 B4
Alter do Chão
P............. 155 B3
Altfraunhofen
D............95 C4
Altheim
A............ 109 A4
D.............94 B1
Althofen A... 110 C1
Altınoluk TR .. 186 C1
Altınova TR ... 186 C1
Altıntaş TR... 187 C5
Altınyaka TR .. 189 C5
Altınyayla TR . 189 B4
Altkirch F 106 B2
Altlandsberg D .74 B2
Altlewin D....74 B3
Altmannstein
D.............95 C3
Altmorschen D..82 A1
Altmunster A. 109 B4
Altnaharra UK ..32 C2
Alto Campoó
E............ 142 B2
Altofonte I... 176 A2
Altomonte I... 174 B2
Alton
Hampshire
UK...........44 B3
Staffordshire
UK.......... 40 C1
Altopáscio I... 135 B3
Altötting D ... 109 A3
Altreichenau D .96 C1
Alt Ruppin D ...74 B1
Altshausen D . 107 B4
Altstätten CH . 107 B4
Altura E....... 159 B3
Altusried D ... 107 B5
Alüksne LV....8 D5
Alunda S....51 B5
Alustante E... 152 B2
Alva UK.......35 B4
Alvaiázere P .. 154 B2
Alvalade P.... 160 B1
Älvängen S ...60 B2
Alvarenga P.... 148 B1
Alvares P.... 154 A2
Alvdal N ... 199 C7
Älvdalen S...49 A6
Alverca P ... 154 C1
Alversund N...46 B2
Alvesta S......62 A2
Alvignac F ... 129 B4
Alvignano I... 170 B2

Ålvik N..........46 B3
Alvik S,,,,,,,,,,50 B1
Alvimare F.....89 A4
Alviobeira P .. 154 B2
Alvito P....... 160 A2
Älvkarleby S....51 B4
Älvkarleöbruk
S............51 B4
Alvor P....... 160 B1
Alvorge P.... 154 B2
Alvøy N........46 B2
Älvros S..... 199 C11
Alvsbacka S...55 A4
Älvsbyn S... 196 D4
Älvsered S......60 B2
Alwernia PL......86 B3
Alwinton UK ...37 A4
Alyth UK 35 B4
Alytus LT......13 A6
Alzénau D 93 A5
Alzey D........93 B4
Alzira E....... 159 B3
Alzonne F.... 146 A3
Amadora P... 154 C1
Åmål S.......55 A3
Amalfi I...... 170 C2
Amaliada GR.. 184 B2
Amance F.... 105 B5
Amancey F.... 105 B5
Amándola I... 136 C2
Amantea I.... 175 B2
Amarante P... 148 A1
Amareleja P... 161 A2
Amares P.... 148 A1
Amaseno I... 169 B3
Amasra TR ... 187 A7
Amatrice I... 169 A3
Amay B.........79 B5
Ambarnyy RUS.. 3 D13
Ambazac F... 115 C5
Ambelonas
GR........... 182 D4
Amberg D......95 B3
Ambérieu-en-
Bugey F...... 118 B2
Ambérieux-en-
Dombes F... 117 A4
Ambert F..... 117 B3
Ambés F..... 128 A2
Ambjörby S.....88 B3
Ambjörnarp S..60 B3
Amble UK......37 A5
Ambleside UK..36 B4
Ambleteuse F...78 B1
Amboise F.... 102 B2
Ambrières-les-
Vallées F......88 B3
Amden CH ... 107 B4
Amel B.........80 B2
Amélia I...... 168 A2
Amélie-les-Bains-
Palalda F... 146 B3
Amelinghausen
D.............72 A3
Amendoa P ... 154 B2
Amendoeira P 160 B2
Améndola I... 171 B3
Amendolara I. 174 B2
Amer E....... 147 B3
A Merca E..... 140 B3
Amerongen NL .70 B2
Amersfoort NL..70 B2
Amersham UK ..44 B3
Amesbury UK ..44 B2
Amfiklia GR ..182 E4
Amfilochia GR .182 E3
Amfipoli GR.. 183 C5
Amfissa GR .. 184 A3
Amièira P 155 C3
Amieira P 154 B2
Amieiro P..... 148 B1
Amiens F.......90 B2
Amindeo GR .. 182 C3
Åminne S......60 B3
Åmli N.........53 B4
Amlwch UK ...38 A2
Ammanford UK.39 C3
Ammarnäs S ..195 E7
Åmmeberg S...55 B5
Amorbach D ...94 B1
Amorebieta E. 143 A4
Amorgós GR .. 185 C6
Amorosa P.... 148 A1
Amorosi I 170 B2
Åmot
Buskerud N ... 48 C1
Telemark N .. 53 A3
S............50 B3
Åmotfors S....54 A3
Åmotsdal N...53 A4
Amou F....... 128 C2
Ampezzo I.... 122 A1
Ampfing D.....95 C4

Ampflwang A. 109 A4
Amplepuis F 117 B4
Amposta E... 153 B4
Ampthill UK....44 A3
Ampudia E.... 142 C2
Ampuero E.... 143 A3
Amriswil CH .. 107 B4
Åmsele S..... 200 B5
Amstelveen NL.70 B1
Amsterdam NL..70 B1
Amstetten A.. 110 A1
Amtzell D..... 107 B4
Amulree UK...35 B4
Amurrio E.... 143 A4
Amusco E.... 142 B2
Anacapri I.... 170 C2
Anadia P...... 148 B1
Anadon E..... 152 B2
Anafi GR..... 185 C6
Anagni I...... 169 B3
Ananyiv UA....17 B8
Anascaul IRL ...29 B1
Ånäset S.......2 D7
Ana-Sira N 52 B2
Anastaźewo PL .76 B3
Anaya de Alba
E............ 150 B2
Ança P....... 148 B1
Ancaster UK....40 C3
Ancede P 148 A1
Ancenis F..... 101 B4
Ancerville F....91 C5
Anchuras E... 156 A3
Ancona I...... 136 B2
Ancora P..... 148 A1
Ancrum UK....35 C5
Ancy-le-Franc
F............ 104 B3
Andalo I...... 121 A3
Åndalsnes N .. 198 C4
Andance F.... 117 B4
Andau A...... 111 B4
Andebu N......53 A6
Andeer CH ... 107 C4
Andelfingen
CH........... 107 B3
Andelot-Blanchville
F............ 105 A4
Andelot-en-
Montagne F.. 105 C4
Andenes N... 194 A7
Andenne D.....79 B5
Anderlues B....79 B4
Andermatt
CH........... 107 C3
Andernach D...80 B3
Andernos-les-Bains
F............ 128 B1
Anderslöv S....66 A2
Anderstorp S ...60 B3
Andijk NL......70 B2
Andoain E.... 144 A1
Andocs H..... 112 C1
Andolsheim F. 106 A2
Andorra E..... 153 B3
Andorra La Vella
AND......... 146 B2
Andosilla E.... 144 B2
Andover UK....44 B2
Andratx E.... 166 B2
Andreapol RUS ..9 D8
Andreas UK....36 B2
Andréspol PL ..86 A3
Andrest F..... 145 A4
Andretta I... 172 B1
Andrezieux-
Bouthéon F .. 117 B4
Ándria I...... 171 B4
Andrijevica
MNE.........16 D3
Andritsena GR 184 B2
Andros GR... 185 B5
Andrychów PL ..99 B3
Andselv N.... 194 A9
Andújar E.... 157 B3
Anduze F..... 131 A2
Åneby N........48 B2
Aneby S........62 A2
Añes E....... 143 A3
Anet F.........90 C1
Anfo I........ 121 B3
Ang S..........62 A2
Anga S........57 C4
Angaís F..... 145 A3
Ånge S..... 199 B11
Ånge S..... 200 D1
Angeja P..... 148 B1
Angeli FIN.... 193 D9
Ängelsberg S ..50 C3
Anger A...... 110 B2
Angera I...... 120 B1

Angermünde
D............ 74 A3
Angern A 97 C4
Angers F...... 102 B1
Angerville F.....90 C2
Anghiari I.... 135 B5
Angle UK.......39 C1
Anglès E...... 147 C3
Anglés F...... 130 B1
Angles F...... 114 B2
Anglesola E... 147 C2
Angles sur l'Anglin
F............ 115 B4
Anglet F...... 128 C1
Anglisidhes
CY........... 181 B2
Anglure F......91 C3
Angoulême F . 115 C4
Angoulins F... 114 B2
Angueira P... 149 A3
Angües E..... 145 B3
Anguiano E... 143 B4
Anguillara Sabazia
I............. 168 A2
Anguillara Véneta
I............. 121 B4
Anhée B........79 B4
Anholt DK......60 C1
Aniane F...... 130 B2
Aniche F.......78 B3
Ånimskog S....54 B3
Anina RO......16 C4
Anixi GR...... 182 D3
Anizy-le-Château
F.............91 B3
Anjalankoski FIN. 8 B5
Anjan S....... 199 B9
Ankara TR.... 187 C7
Ankaran SLO.. 122 B2
Ankarsrum S...62 A4
Ankerlia N... 192 C4
Anklam D......66 C2
Ankum D......71 B4
Anlauftal A... 109 B4
Anlezy F...... 104 C2
Ånn S........ 199 B9
Annaberg A... 110 B2
Annaberg-
Buchholz D 83 B5
Annaberg im
Lammertal A. 109 B4
Annaburg D ...83 A5
Annahütte D...84 A1
Annalong UK ...27 B5
Annan UK......36 B3
Anndalsvågen
N............195 E3
Anneberg
Halland S....66 A2
Jönköping S .. 62 A2
Annecy F...... 118 B3
Annelund S.....60 B2
Annemasse F . 118 A3
Annenskiy Most
RUS...........9 B10
Annerstad S....60 C3
Annestown IRL..30 B1
Annevoie-Rouillon
B.............79 B4
Annonay F.... 117 B4
Annot F...... 132 B2
Annweiler D ...93 B3
Añora E...... 156 B3
Ano Poroia GR 183 B5
Ano Siros GR.. 185 B5
Anould F...... 106 A1
Anquela del
Ducado E ... 152 B1
Anröchte D....81 A4
Ans DK.........59 B2
Ansager DK....59 C1
Ansbach D.....94 B2
Anse F....... 117 B4
Anseroeul B....79 B3
Ansfelden A .. 110 A1
Ansião P..... 154 B2
Ansó E....... 144 B3
Ansoain E.... 144 B2
Anstruther UK ..35 B5
Antas E...... 164 B3
Antas de Alpuente
E............ 159 B2
Antegnate I... 120 B2
Antequera E.. 163 A3
Anterselva di
Mezzo I.... 108 C3
Antibes F..... 132 B3
Antigüedad E. 142 C2
Antillo I...... 177 B4
Antirio GR.... 184 A2
Antnäs S..... 196 D4
An t-Ob UK....31 B1
Antoing B......79 B3

Antonin PL.....86 A1
Antrain F......88 B2
Antrim UK.....27 B4
Antrodoco I.., 169 A3
Antronapiana
I............. 119 A5
Anttis S...... 196 B5
Antuzede P... 148 B1
Antwerp =
Antwerpen B...79 A4
Antwerpen =
Antwerp B....79 A4
Anversa d'Abruzzi
I............. 169 B3
Anvin F........78 B2
Anzat-le-Luguet
F............ 116 B3
Anzi I........ 172 B1
Ånzio I....... 168 B2
Anzola d'Emilia
I............. 135 A4
Anzón E...... 144 C2
Aoiz E....... 144 B2
Aosta I....... 119 B4
Apalhão P.... 155 B3
Apátfalva H.. 126 A2
Apatin SRB... 125 B5
Apatity RUS.....3 C13
Apc H........ 112 B3
Apécchio I... 136 B1
Apeldoorn NL...70 B2
Apen D........71 A4
Apenburg D ...73 B4
Apensen D 72 A2
A Peroxa E... 140 B3
Apiro I....... 136 B2
Apliki CY..... 181 B2
Apolda D......82 A3
Apolonia GR.. 185 C5
A Pontenova
E............ 141 A3
Apostag H.... 112 C2
Äppelbo S......49 B6
Appennino I... 136 C2
Appenzell CH . 107 B4
Appiano I..... 108 C2
Appingedam
NL............71 A3
Appleby-in-
Westmorland
UK...........37 B4
Applecross UK ..31 B3
Appledore UK...42 A2
Appoigny F... 104 B2
Apremont-la-Forêt
F.............92 C1
Aprica I...... 120 A3
Apricena I... 171 B3
Aprigliano I... 174 B2
Aprília I...... 168 B2
Apt F........ 131 B4
Apúlia P..... 148 A1
Aquiléia I.... 122 B2
Aquilónia I... 172 B1
Aquino I...... 169 B3
Ar S...........57 C4
Arabayona E.. 150 A2
Arabba I...... 108 C2
Araç TR........23 A7
Arachova GR.. 184 A3
Aračinovo
NMK........ 182 A3
Arad RO...... 126 A3
Aradac SRB... 126 B2
Aradhippou
CY........... 181 B2
Aragnouet F .. 145 B4
Aragona I.... 176 B2
Arahal E...... 162 A2
Aramits F..... 144 A3
Aramon F..... 131 B3
Aranda de Duero
E............ 143 C3
Aranda de
Moncayo E... 152 A2
Arandjelovac
SRB......... 127 C2
Aranjuez E.... 151 B4
Arantzazu E... 143 B4
Aranzueque E. 151 B4
Aras de Alpuente
E............ 159 B2
Arauzo de Miel
E............ 143 C3
Arazede P.... 148 B1
Arbas F...... 145 B4
Arbatax I..... 179 C3
Arbeca E..... 147 C1
Arberg D.......94 B2
Arbesbach A...96 C1
Arboga S......56 A1
Arbois F...... 105 C4

Arbon CH 107 B4
Arboréal I..... 170 C2
Arbostad N ... 194 B8
Arbrå S........50 A3
Arbroath UK...35 B5
Arbório I...... 119 B5
Arbúcies E.... 147 C3
Arbuniel E.... 163 A4
Arbus I...... 179 C2
Arcachon F.... 128 B1
Arce I........ 169 B3
Arcen NL......80 A2
Arc-en-Barrois
F............ 105 B3
Arces-Dilo F... 104 A2
Arc-et-Senans
F............ 105 B4
Arcévia I..... 136 B1
Arcey F...... 106 B1
Archanes GR.. 185 D6
Archangelos
GR........... 188 C3
Archena E.... 165 A3
Archez E...... 163 B4
Archiac F..... 115 C3
Archidona E... 163 A3
Archiestown
UK........... 32 D3
Archivel E.... 164 A3
Arcidosso I.... 135 C4
Arcille I...... 135 C4
Arcis-sur-Aube
F.............91 C4
Arc-lès-Gray F. 105 B4
Arco I........ 121 B3
Arcones E.... 151 A4
Arcos E...... 143 B3
Arcos de Jalón
E............ 152 A1
Arcos de la
Frontera E... 162 B2
Arcos de la Sierra
E............ 152 B1
Arcos de las Salinas
E............ 159 B2
Arcos de Valdevez
P............ 148 A1
Arcozelo P... 148 B2
Arc-sur-Tille F. 105 B4
Arcusa E..... 145 B4
Arcy-sur-Cure
F............ 104 B2
Ardagh IRL....29 B2
Ardal N........52 A2
Årdala S.......55 B4
Ardales E..... 162 B3
Ardalstangen
N............47 A4
Ardara
I........... 178 B2
IRL..........26 B2
Ardarroch UK ..31 B3
Ardbeg UK.....34 C1
Ardcharnich
UK........... 32 D1
Ardchyle UK ...34 B3
Ardee IRL......27 C4
Arden DK......58 B2
Ardentes F.... 103 C3
Ardenza I.... 134 B3
Ardersier UK .. 32 D2
Ardes F...... 116 B3
Ardessie UK.. 32 D1
Ardez CH..... 107 C5
Ardfert IRL....29 B2
Ardgay UK.... 32 D2
Ardglass UK....27 B5
Ardgroom IRL..29 C2
Ardhasig UK...31 B2
Ardino BG.... 183 B7
Ardisa E..... 144 B3
Ardkearagh
IRL..........29 C1
Ardlui UK......34 B3
Ardlussa UK...34 B2
Ardón E...... 142 B1
Ardooie B......78 B3
Ardore I...... 175 C2
Ardrahan IRL...28 A3
Ardre S........57 C4
Ardres F.......78 B1
Ardrishaig UK..34 B2
Ardrossan UK .34 C3
Åre N..........52 A1
Åre S....... 199 B10
Areia Branca
P............ 154 B1
Aremark N.....54 A2
Arenales de San
Gregorio E.. 157 A4
Arenas E..... 163 B3
Arenas de Iguña
E............ 142 A2

Arenas del Rey
E............ 163 B4
Arenas de San Juan
E............ 157 A4
Arenas de San
Pedro E.... 150 B2
Arendal N......53 B4
Arendonk B....79 A5
Arengosse F .. 128 B2
Arentorp S.....55 B3
Arenys de Mar
E............ 147 C3
Arenys de Munt
E............ 147 C3
Arenzano I.... 133 A4
Areo E....... 146 B2
Areopoli GR... 184 C3
Ares E....... 140 A2
Arès F....... 128 B1
Ares del Maestrat
E............ 153 B3
Aresvika N... 198 B5
Arette F...... 144 A3
Aretxabaleta
E............ 143 A4
Arevalillo E ... 150 B2
Arévalo E.... 150 A3
Arez P....... 155 B3
Arezzo I...... 135 B4
Arfeuilles F ... 117 A3
Argalasti GR .. 183 D5
Argallón E 156 B2
Argamasilla de
Alba E...... 157 A4
Argamasilla de
Calatrava E .. 157 B3
Arganda E.... 151 B4
Arganil P..... 148 B1
Argasion GR .. 184 B1
Argegno I.... 120 B2
Argelès-Gazost
F............ 145 A3
Argelès-
sur-Mer F .. 146 B4
Argenta I...... 121 C4
Argentan F......89 B3
Argentat F.... 116 B1
Argentera I ... 132 A2
Argenteuil F....90 C2
Argenthal D ...93 B3
Argentiera I... 178 B2
Argentona E.. 147 C3
Argenton-
Château F... 102 C1
Argenton-sur-
Creuse F.... 103 C3
Argentré F.... 102 A1
Argentré-du-
Plessis F.... 101 A4
Argent-sur-
Sauldre F... 103 B4
Argirades GR.. 182 D1
Argithani TR .. 189 A6
Argos GR..... 184 B3
Argos Orestiko
GR........... 182 C3
Argostoli GR.. 184 A1
Argote E...... 143 B4
Arguedas E... 144 B2
Argueil F.......90 B1
Arholma S....51 C6
Ariano Irpino
I............. 170 B3
Ariano nel
Polésine I.... 121 C5
Aribe E...... 144 B2
Aridea GR.... 182 C4
Arienzo I...... 170 B2
Arild S........61 C2
Arileod UK....34 B1
Arinagour
UK...........34 B1
Ariño E...... 153 A3
Arinthod F.... 118 A2
Arisaig UK.....34 B2
Arisgotas E ... 157 A4
Aritzo I...... 179 C3
Ariza E...... 152 A1
Årjäng S......54 A3
Arjeplog S... 195 D8
Arjona E..... 157 C3
Arjonilla E.... 157 C3
Arkasa GR.... 188 D2
Arkelstorp S...63 B2
Arklow IRL....30 B2
Arkösund S...56 B2
Årla S........56 A2
Arlanc F...... 117 B3
Arlanzón E... 143 B3
Arlebosc F.... 117 B4

Arlena di Castro
I..............168 A1
Arles F 131 B3
Arles-sur-Tech
F.............146 B3
Arló H.........113 A4
Arlon B.........92 B1
Armação de Pera
P............160 B1
Armadale
Highland UK....31 B3
West Lothian
UK 35 C4
Armagh UK.....27 B4
Armamar P 148 A2
Armenistis GR 185 B7
Armeno I......119 B5
Armenteros E. 150 B2
Armentières F ..78 B2
Armilla E......163 A4
Armiñón E 143 B4
Armoy UK.......27 A4
Armuña de
Tajuña E 151 B4
Armutlu
Bursa TR......186 B3
İzmir TR 188 A2
Arnac-
Pompadour F 115 C5
Arnafjord N....46 A3
Arnage F......102 B2
Arnas F 117 A4
Årnäs S 55 B4
Arnay-le-Duc
F.............104 B3
Arnborg DK....59 B2
Arnbruck D....95 B4
Arnea GR......183 C5
Arneberg
Hedmark N .. 48 A2
Hedmark N ...49 B4
Arneburg D....73 B5
Arnedillo E.... 144 B1
Arnedo E...... 144 B1
Arneguy F 144 A2
Arnés E 153 B4
Árnes IS...... 190 A4
Årnes
Akershus N 48 B3
Troms N 194 A4
Arnfels A...... 110 C2
Arnhem NL 70 C2
Arnissa GR... 182 C3
Arno S 56 B3
Arnold UK.......40 B2
Arnoldstein A. 109 C4
Arnsberg D 81 A4
Arnschwang
D 95 B4
Arnsdorf D....84 A1
Årnset N 198 B6
Arnside UK....37 B4
Arnstadt D....82 B2
Arnstein D....94 B1
Arnstorf D....95 C4
Arnum DK....59 C1
Aroche E...... 161 B3
Árokto H..... 113 B4
Arolla CH 119 A4
Arona I...... 119 B5
Äros N 54 A1
Arosa
CH 107 C4
P............148 A1
Ærøskøbing
DK............65 B3
Arøsund DK....59 C2
Arouca P......148 B1
Årøysund N....54 A1
Arpajon F 90 C2
Arpajon-sur-Cère
F............116 C2
Arpela FIN 196 C7
Arpino I...... 169 B3
Arquata del Tronto
I............136 C2
Arques F......78 B2
Arques-la-Bataille
F............89 A5
Arquillos E... 157 B4
Arraia-Maeztu
E 143 B4
Arraiolos P.... 154 C2
Arrancourt F....92 C2
Arras F......78 B2
Arrasate E.... 143 A4
Årre DK......59 C1
Arreau F 145 B4
Arredondo E.. 143 A3

Arrens-Marsous
F.............145 B3
Arriate E 162 B2
Arrifana P.... 160 B1
Arrigorriaga E 143 A4
Arriondas E... 142 A1
Arroba de los
Montes E.. 157 A3
Arrochar UK 34 B3
Arromanches-les-
Bains F........88 A3
Arronches P... 155 B3
Arroniz E.... 144 B1
Arrou F 103 A3
Arroya E 142 B2
Arroya de Cuéllar
E 150 A3
Arroyal E.... 142 B2
Arroyo de la Luz
E 155 B4
Arroyo del Ojanco
E 164 A2
Arroyo de San
Servan E... 155 C4
Arroyomolinos de
León E 141 B4
Arroyomolinos de
Montánchez
E 156 A1
Arruda dos Vinhos
P............154 C1
Arsac F...... 128 B2
Ars-en-Ré F .. 114 B2
Arsiè I...... 121 B4
Arsiero I...... 121 B4
Årslev DK......59 C3
Ársoli I...... 169 A3
Ars-sur-Moselle
F............92 B2
Årsunda S....50 B3
Artà E 167 B3
Arta GR 182 D3
Artajona E.... 144 B2
Artegna I.... 122 A2
Arteixo E.... 140 A2
Artemare F.... 118 B2
Arten I...... 121 A4
Artena I...... 169 B2
Artenay F.... 103 A3
Artern D 82 A3
Artés E...... 147 C2
Artesa de Segre
E 147 C2
Arth CH 107 B3
Arthez-de-Béarn
F............145 A3
Arthon-en-Retz
F............101 B4
Arthurstown
IRL............30 B2
Artieda E.... 144 B3
Artix F...... 145 A3
Artotina GR... 182 E4
Artsyz UA......17 B8
Artziniega E ... 143 A3
A Rúa E...... 141 B3
Arudy F...... 145 A3
Arundel UK....44 C3
Arveyres F 128 B2
Arvidsjaur S .. 196 D2
Arvieux F 118 C3
Arvika S......54 A3
Åryd
Blekinge S 63 B3
Kronoberg S 62 B2
Arzachena I... 178 A3
Arzacq-Arraziguet
F............128 C2
Árzana I...... 179 C3
Arzano F...... 100 B2
Aržano HR 138 B2
Arzberg D......95 A4
Arzignano I... 121 B4
Arzila P...... 148 B1
Arzl im Pitztal
A............108 B1
Arzúa E...... 140 B2
As B...........80 A1
Aš CZ..........83 B4
Ås N...........54 A1
Åsa S..........60 B2
Asaa DK........58 A3
Aşağiçiğil TR.. 189 A6
Ašanja SRB... 127 C2
Åsarøy N......52 A2
Åsarp S......55 B4
Asasp F...... 145 A3
Åsbro S......55 A6
Åsby S........60 B2
Asby S........62 A3
Åsbygri IS.... 191 A9
Ascain F...... 144 A2

Ascea I........172 B1
Ascha D.........95 B4
Aschach an der
Donau A 96 C2
Aschaffenburg
D 93 B5
Aschbach Markt
A............110 A1
Ascheberg
Nordrhein-
Westfalen D... 81 A3
Schleswig-Holstein
D.............65 B3
Aschendorf D...71 A4
Aschersleben
D 82 A3
Asciano I.... 135 B4
Ascó E...... 153 A4
Asco F...... 180 A2
Áscoli Piceno
I............136 C2
Áscoli Satriano
I............171 B3
Ascona CH ... 120 A1
Ascot UK......44 B3
Ascoux F.... 103 A4
Åse N...... 194 A6
Åseda S......62 A3
Åsele S........200 B3
Åsen
N............199 B8
S 49 A5
Asendorf D....72 B2
Asenovgrad
BG 183 A6
Åsensbruk S....54 B3
Åseral N......52 B3
Asfeld F........91 B4
Åsgårdstrand
N.............54 A1
Ásgarður IS .. 190 B1
Asgate CY.... 181 B2
Ash
Kent UK.......45 B5
Surrey UK....44 B3
Åshammar S....50 B3
Ashbourne
IRL 30 A2
UK............40 B2
Ashburton UK .43 B3
Ashby-de-
la-Zouch UK...40 C2
Ashchurch UK...44 B1
Åsheim N ... 199 D8
Ashford UK 45 B4
Ashington UK...37 A5
Ashley UK......38 B3
Ashmyany BY..13 A6
Ashton-under-
Lyne UK......40 B1
Ashwell UK....44 A3
Asiago I...... 121 B4
Asipovichy BY ..13 B8
Aska FIN 197 B9
Askam-in-Furness
UK............36 B3
Askeaton IRL... 29 B3
Asker N......48 C2
Askersund S 55 B5
Äskilje S 200 B3
Askim N......54 A2
Askland N......53 B4
Äsköping S 56 A2
Askvoll N 46 A2
Åsljunga S......61 C3
Asmunti FIN .. 197 D9
Asnæs DK...... 61 D1
As Neves E .. 140 B2
As Nogais E ... 141 B3
Ásola I...... 120 B3
Asolo I...... 121 B4
Asos GR...... 184 A1
Asotthalom H. 126 A1
Aspach A.... 109 A4
Aspang Markt
A............111 B3
Aspariegos E.. 149 A4
Asparn an der Zaya
A.............97 C4
Aspatria UK....36 B3
Aspberg S......55 A4
Aspe E 165 A4
Aspet F 145 A4
Äspö S.........63 B3
As Pontes de García
Rodríguez E. 140 A3
Aspres-sur-Buëch
F............132 A1
Aspsele S 200 C4
Assafora P 154 C1
Asse B..........79 B4
Assebakte N .. 193 C9
Assel D..........72 A2

Asselborn L.....92 A1
Aschà D.........95 B4
Assémini I.... 179 C2
Assen NL........71 B3
Assenede B 79 A3
Assens
Aarhus Amt.
DK............58 B3
Fyns Amt. DK .. 59 C2
Assesse B 79 B5
Assisi I 136 B1
Åsskard N.... 198 B5
Assling D 108 B3
Asso I...... 120 B2
Asson F 145 A3
Ássoro I...... 177 B3
Assumar P ... 155 B3
Åsta N........48 A3
Astaffort F... 129 B3
Astakos GR .. 184 A2
Asten NL......80 A1
Asti I...... 119 C5
Astipalea GR.. 188 C1
Astorga E.... 141 B4
Åstorp S 61 C2
Åsträsk S 200 B5
Astudillo E.... 142 B2
Asuni I...... 179 C2
Ásványráró
H............ 111 B4
Aszód H........112 B3
Aszófö H......111 C4
Atabey TR.... 189 B5
Atalaia P.... 154 B3
Atalandi GR... 182 E4
Atalho P 154 C2
Atány H...... 113 B4
Atanzón E.... 151 B4
Ataquines E.. 150 A3
Atarfe E...... 163 A4
Atça TR...... 188 B3
Ateca E...... 152 A2
A Teixeira E ... 141 B3
Atella I...... 172 B1
Atessa I...... 169 A4
Ath B..........79 B3
Athboy IRL....30 A2
Athea IRL......29 B2
Athenry IRL... 28 A3
Athens = Athina
GR 185 B4
Atherstone
UK............40 C2
Athienou CY .. 181 A2
Athies F........90 B2
Athies-sous-Laon
F.............91 B3
Athina = Athens
GR 185 B4
Athleague
IRL............28 A3
Athlone IRL... 28 A4
Athna CY...... 181 A2
Athy IRL......30 B2
Atienza E.... 151 A5
Atina I...... 169 B3
Atkár H...... 113 B3
Atlantı TR.... 189 A7
Atna N...... 199 D7
Åtorp S......55 A5
Atrå N........47 C5
Ätran S........60 B2
Atri I...... 169 A3
Atripalda I... 170 C2
Atsiki GR.... 183 D7
Attendorn D....81 A3
Attichy F........90 B3
Attigliano I... 168 A2
Attigny F........91 B4
Attleborough
UK............41 C5
Åtvidaberg S.. 56 B1
Atzendorf D...73 C4
Au
Steiermark A.. 110 B2
Vorarlberg A .. 107 B4
Bayern D 95 C3
Bayern D 108 B2
Aub D..........94 B2
Aubagne F.... 132 B1
Aubange B......92 B1
Aubel B........80 B1
Aubenas F.... 117 C4
Aubenton F....91 B4
Auberive F.... 105 B4
Aubeterre-sur-
Dronne F... 128 A3
Aubiet F...... 129 C3
Aubigné F.... 115 B3
Aubigny F.... 114 B2
Aubigny-au-Bac
F.............78 B3
Aubigny-en-Artois
F.............78 B2

Aubigny-sur-Nère
F............103 B4
Aubin F 130 A1
Aubonne CH .. 105 C5
Aubrac F 116 C2
Aubusson F... 116 B2
Auch F...... 129 C3
Auchencairn
UK............36 B3
Auchinleck UK..36 A2
Auchterarder
UK............35 B4
Auchtermuchty
UK............35 B4
Auchy-au-Bois
F.............78 B2
Audenge F.... 128 B1
Auderville F....88 A2
Audierne F.... 100 A1
Audincourt F. 106 B1
Audlem UK.....38 B4
Audruicq F......78 B2
Audun-le-Roman
F.............92 B1
Audun-le-Tiche
F.............92 B1
Aue
Nordrhein-
Westfalen D... 81 A4
Sachsen D 83 B4
Auerbach
Bayern D 95 B3
Sachsen D 83 B4
Auffach A.... 108 B3
Augher UK.....27 B3
Aughnacloy
UK............27 B4
Aughrim IRL... 30 B2
Augignac F ... 115 C4
Augsburg D... 94 C2
Augusta I 177 B4
Augusten-borg
DK............64 B2
Augustfehn D...71 A4
Augustów PL... 12 B5
Aukrug D......64 B2
Auktsjaur S ... 196 D2
Auldearn UK... 32 D3
Aulendorf D .. 107 B4
Auletta I...... 172 B1
Aulla I...... 134 A2
Aullène F 180 B2
Aulnay F 115 B3
Aulnoye-
Aymeries F....79 B3
Ault F......90 A1
Aultbea UK 31 B3
Aulum DK......59 B1
Aulus-les-Bains
F............ 146 B2
Auma D........83 B3
Aumale F......90 B1
Aumetz F......92 B1
Aumont-Aubrac
F............116 C3
Aunay-en-Bazois
F............104 B2
Aunay-sur-Odon
F.............88 A3
Aune N...... 199 A10
Auneau F......90 C1
Auneuil F......90 B1
Auning DK......58 B3
Aunsetra N... 199 A9
Aups F 132 B2
Aura D........82 B1
Auray F...... 100 B3
Aurdal N......47 B6
Aure N...... 198 B5
Aurich D......71 A4
Aurignac F.... 145 A4
Auriol F...... 132 B1
Auritz-
Burguette E.. 144 B2
Aurlandsvangen
N.............47 B4
Auronzo di Cadore
I............109 C3
Auros F...... 128 B2
Auroux F.... 117 C3
Aursmoen N ...48 C3
Ausónia I...... 169 B3
Ausservillgraton
A............109 C3
Austad N......52 B3
Austbygda N...47 B5
Auster Moland
N.............53 B4
Austre Moland

Austre Vikebygd
N............52 A1
Austrheim N 46 B1
Auterive F 146 A2
Autheuil-
Authouillet F...89 A5
Authon F...... 132 A2
Authon-du-Perche
F............102 A2
Autol E...... 144 B2
Autreville F....92 C1
Autrey-lès-Gray
F............105 B4
Autti FIN 197 C10
Autun F...... 104 C3
Auty-le-Châtel
F............103 B4
Auvelais B......79 B4
Auvillar F.... 129 B3
Auxerre F.... 104 B2
Auxi-le-Château
F.............78 B2
Auxon F...... 104 A2
Auxonne F.... 105 B4
Auxy F...... 104 C3
Auzances F... 116 A2
Auzon F...... 117 B3
Ağva TR...... 187 A4
Availles-Limouzine
F............115 B4
Avaldsnes N ...52 A1
Avallon F 104 B2
Avantas GR... 183 C7
Avaviken S.... 195 E9
Avebury UK....44 B2
A Veiga E 141 B3
Aveiras de Cima
P............154 B2
Aveiro P...... 148 B1
Avelgem B......79 B3
Avellino I 170 C2
Avenches CH.. 106 C2
A-Ver-o-Mar P 148 A1
Aversa I...... 170 C2
Avesnes-le-Comte
F.............78 B2
Avesnes-sur-Helpe
F.............91 A3
Avesta S......50 B3
Avetrana I ... 173 B3
Avezzano I... 169 A3
Avià E...... 147 B2
Aviano I...... 122 A1
Aviemore UK.. 32 D3
Avigliana I ... 119 B4
Avigliano I... 172 B1
Avignon F..... 131 B3
Ávila E...... 150 B3
Avilés E...... 141 A5
Avilley F...... 105 B5
Avintes P.... 148 A1
Avinyo E...... 147 C2
Ávio I...... 121 B3
Avioth F........92 B1
Avis P...... 154 B3
Avize F........91 C4
Avlonari GR... 185 A5
Ávola I...... 177 C4
Avon F........90 C2
Avonmouth UK .43 A4
Avord F...... 103 B4
Avranches F....88 B2
Avril F........92 B1
Avrillé F...... 102 B1
Avtovac BIH... 139 B4
Awans B........79 B5
Axams A...... 108 B2
Axat F...... 146 B3
Axbridge UK...43 A4
Axel NL......79 A3
Axmarby S......51 B4
Axmarsbruk S .51 A4
Axminster UK...43 B3
Axvall S......55 B4
Ay F........91 B4
Aya E...... 144 A1
Ayamonte E... 161 B2
Ayancık TR.... 23 A8
Ayaş TR...... 187 B7
Aydın TR.... 188 B2
Ayelo de Malferit
E............159 C3
Ayer CH...... 119 A4
Ayerbe E.... 144 B3
Ayette F........78 B2
Ayia Napa CY . 181 B2
Ayia Phyla CY. 181 B2
Áyios Amvrósios
CY 181 A2
Áyios Seryios
CY 181 A2

Áyios Theodoros
CY 181 A3
Aykirikçi TR... 187 C5
Aylesbury UK...44 B3
Ayllón E...... 151 A4
Aylsham UK....41 C5
Ayna E...... 158 C1
Ayódar E...... 159 B3
Ayora E...... 159 B2
Ayr UK........36 A2
Ayrancı TR......23 C7
Ayrancılar TR . 188 A2
Ayron F...... 115 B4
Aysgarth UK... 37 B4
Ayton UK......35 C5
Aytos BG...... 17 D7
Ayvacık TR.... 186 C1
Ayvalık TR.... 186 C1
Aywaille B......80 B1
Azaila E...... 153 A3
Azambuja P... 154 B2
Azambujeira
P............154 B2
Azanja SRB.... 127 C2
Azannes-et-
Soumazannes
F.............92 B1
Azanúy-Alins
E............145 C4
Azaruja P.... 155 C3
Azay-le-Ferron
F............115 B5
Azay-le-Rideau
F............102 B2
Azcoitia E.... 143 A4
Azé F...... 117 A4
Azeiteiros P... 155 B3
Azenhas do Mar
P............154 C1
Azinhaga P ... 154 B2
Azinhal P 160 B2
Azinheira dos
Bairros P.... 160 A1
Aznalcázar E... 161 B3
Aznalcóllar E.. 161 B3
Azóia P...... 154 B2
Azpeitia E.... 144 A1
Azuaga E...... 156 B2
Azuara E...... 153 A3
Azuqueca de
Henares E... 151 B4
Azur F...... 128 C1
Azzano Décimo
I............122 B1

B

Baad A........107 B5
Baamonde E.. 140 A3
Baar CH...... 107 B3
Bağarasi TR... 188 B2
Baarle-Nassau
B.............79 A4
Baarn NL......70 B2
Babadağ TR... 188 B3
Babadag RO....17 C8
Babaeski TR .. 186 A2
Babayevo RUS .. 9 C9
Babenhausen
Bayern D 107 A5
Hessen D 93 B4
Babiak PL......76 B3
Babice PL......87 A4
Babigoszcz PL .75 A3
Babimost PL ...75 B4
Babina Greda
HR 125 B4
Babócsa H 124 A3
Bábolma H.... 112 B3
Baborów PL ...77 B5
Baboszewo PL .77 B5
Babót H...... 111 B4
Babruysk BY ...13 B8
Babsk PL......87 A4
Bač SRB...... 125 B5
Bac UK........31 A2
Bacares E 164 B2
Bacău RO......17 B7
Baccarat F 92 C2
Bacharach D...93 A3
Backa S........50 B2
Bačka Palanka
SRB 126 B1
Backaryd S......63 B3
Bačka Topola
SRB 126 B1
Backe S...... 200 C2
Bäckebo S......62 B4
Bäckefors S....54 B3
Bäckhammar S .55 A5
Bački Breg
SRB 125 B4

Bački-Brestovac
SRB 126 B1
Bački Monoštor
SRB 125 B4
Bački Petrovac
SRB 126 B1
Bački Sokolac
SRB 126 B1
Backnang D.....94 C1
Bačko Gradište
SRB 126 B2
Bačko Novo Selo
SRB 125 B5
Bačko Petrovo Selo
SRB 126 B2
Bácoli I........ 170 C2
Bacqueville-en-
Caux F 89 A5
Bácsalmás H . . 126 A1
Bácsbokod H . 125 A5
Bad Abbach D...95 C4
Badacsonytomaj
H............ 111 C4
Bad Aibling D. 108 B3
Badajoz E 155 C4
Badalona E .. 147 C3
Badalucco I ... 133 B3
Bad Aussee A . 109 B4
Bad Bederkesa
D 72 A1
Bad Bentheim
D 71 B4
Bad Bergzabern
D 93 B3
Bad Berka D.....82 B3
Bad Berleburg
D 81 A4
Bad Berneck D ..95 A3
Bad Bevensen
D 73 A3
Bad Bibra D 82 A3
Bad Birnbach D.95 C5
Bad Blankenburg
D 82 B3
Bad Bleiberg
A........... 109 C4
Bad Brambach
D 83 B4
Bad Bramstedt
D 64 C2
Bad Breisig D ...80 B3
Bad Brückenau
D 82 B1
Bad Buchau D. 107 A4
Bad Camberg D 81 B4
Badderen N... 192 C6
Bad Doberan D .65 B4
Bad Driburg D ..81 A5
Bad Düben D...83 A4
Bad Dürkheim
D 93 B4
Bad Dürrenberg
D 83 A4
Bad Dürrheim
D 107 A3
Bad Elster D.....83 B4
Bad Ems D 81 B3
Baden
A........... 111 A3
CH 106 B3
Bádenas E 152 A2
Baden-Baden
D 93 C4
Bad Endorf D . 109 B3
Badenweiler
D 106 B2
Baderna HR... 122 B2
Bad Essen D.....71 B5
Bad Fischau A. 111 B3
Bad Frankenhausen
D 82 A3
Bad Freienwalde
D 74 B3
Bad Friedrichshall
D 93 B5
Bad Füssing D...96 C1
Bad Gandersheim
D 82 A2
Bad Gastein A. 109 B4
Bad Gleichenberg
A........... 110 C2
Bad Goisern A. 109 B4
Bad Gottleuba
D 84 B1
Bad Grund D...82 A2
Bad Hall A..... 110 A1
Bad Harzburg
D 82 A2
Bad Herrenalb
D 93 C4
Bad Hersfeld D..82 B1
Bad Hofgastein
A........... 109 B4

Bad Homburg
D 81 B4
Bad Honnef D...80 B3
Bad Hönningen
D 80 B3
Badia Calavena
I............ 121 B4
Badia Polésine
I............ 121 B4
Badia Pratáglia
I............ 135 B4
Badia Tedalda
I............ 135 B5
Bad Iburg D.....71 B5
Bad Innerlaterns
A........... 107 B4
Bad Ischl A.... 109 B4
Bad Karlshafen
D 81 A5
Bad Kemmeriboden
CH 106 C2
Bądki PL 69 B3
Bad Kissingen
D 82 B2
Bad Kleinen D...65 C4
Bad Kohlgrub
D 108 B2
Bad König D ...93 B5
Bad Königshofen
D 82 B2
Bad Köstritz D ..83 B4
Badkowo PL 76 B3
Bad Kreuzen
A........... 110 A1
Bad Kreuznach
D 93 B3
Bad Krozingen
D 106 B2
Bad Laasphe D...81 B4
Bad Langensalza
D 82 A2
Bad Lauchstädt
D 83 A3
Bad Lausick D...83 A4
Bad Lauterberg
D 82 A2
Bad Leonfelden
A...........96 C2
Bad Liebenwerda
D 83 A5
Bad Liebenzell
D 93 C4
Bad Lippspringe
D 81 A4
Badljevina HR. 124 B3
Bad Meinberg
D 81 A4
Bad Mergentheim
D 94 B1
Bad Mitterndorf
A........... 109 B4
Bad Münder D ..72 B2
Bad Münstereifel
D 80 B2
Bad Muskau D ..84 A2
Bad Nauheim D 81 B4
Bad Nenndorf
D 72 B2
Bad Neuenahr-
Ahrweiler D....80 B3
Bad Neustadt
D 82 B2
Bad Oeynhausen
D 72 B1
Badolato I 175 C2
Badolatosa E.. 163 A3
Bad Oldesloe D .65 C3
Badonviller F ...92 C2
Bad Orb D.......81 B5
Badovinci SRB 127 C1
Bad Peterstal D .93 C4
Bad Pyrmont D .72 C2
Bad Radkersburg
A........... 110 C2
Bad Ragaz CH. 107 C4
Bad Rappenau
D 93 B5
Bad Reichenhall
D 109 B3
Bad Saarow-
Pieskow D 74 B3
Bad Sachsa D...82 A2
Bad Säckingen
D 106 B2
Bad Salzdetfurth
D 72 B3
Bad Salzig D 81 B3
Bad Salzuflen
D 72 B1
Bad Salzungen
D 82 B2
Bad Sankt
Leonhard A . . 110 C1

Bad Sassendorf
D 81 A4
Bad Schandau
D 84 B2
Bad Schmiedeberg
D 83 A4
Bad Schönborn
D 93 B4
Bad Schussenried
D 107 A4
Bad Schwalbach
D 81 B4
Bad Schwartau
D 65 C3
Bad Segeberg
D 64 C3
Bad Soden D...81 B4
Bad Soden-
Salmünster D ..81 B5
Bad Sooden-
Allendorf D 82 A1
Bad Sulza D.....83 A3
Bad Sülze D.....66 B1
Bad Tatzmannsdorf
A........... 111 B3
Bad Tennstedt
D 82 A2
Bad Tölz D 108 B2
Badules E 152 A2
Bad Urach D 94 C1
Bad Vellach A . 110 C1
Bad Vilbel D.....81 B4
Bad Vöslau A. . 111 B3
Bad Waldsee
D 107 B4
Bad Wiessee
D 108 B2
Bad Wildungen
D 81 A5
Bad Wilsnack
D 73 B4
Bad Windsheim
D 94 B2
Bad Wörishofen
D 108 A1
Bad Wurzach
D 107 B4
Bad Zwesten D..81 A5
Bad Zwischenahn
D 71 A5
Baells E 145 C4
Baena E 163 A3
Baesweiler D...80 B2
Baeza E 157 C4
Baflo NL 71 A3
Baga E 147 B2
Bagaladi I 175 C1
Bagenkop DK ..65 B3
Baggetorp S 56 A2
Bagh a Chaisteil
UK 31 C1
Bagheria I.... 176 A2
Bagn N..........47 B6
Bagnacavallo
I............ 135 A4
Bagnáia I 168 A2
Bagnara Cálabra
I............ 175 C1
Bagnasco I.... 133 A4
Bagnères-de-
Bigorre F 145 A4
Bagnères-de-
Luchon F..... 145 B4
Bagni del Másino
I............ 120 A2
Bagni di Lucca
I............ 134 A3
Bagni di Rabbi
I............ 121 A3
Bagni di Tivoli
I............ 168 B2
Bagno di Romagna
I............ 135 B4
Bagnoles-de-l'Orne
F............89 B3
Bagnoli dei Trigno
I............ 170 B2
Bagnoli di Sopra
I............ 121 B4
Bagnoli Irpino
I............ 170 C3
Bagnolo Mella
I............ 120 B3
Bagnols-en-Forêt
F............ 132 B2
Bagnols-sur-Cèze
F............ 131 A3
Bagnorégio I.. 168 A2
Bagolino I.... 121 B3
Bagrationovsk
RUS 12 A4
Bagrdan SRB.. 127 C3
Báguena E 152 A2

Bahabón de
Esgueva E ... 143 C3
Bahillo E 142 B2
Báia delle Záqare
I............ 171 B4
Báia Domizia
I............ 169 B3
Baia Mare RO ...17 B5
Baiano I...... 170 C2
Baião P 148 A1
Baiersbronn D ..93 C4
Baiersdorf D ...94 B3
Baignes-Ste
Radegonde
F............ 115 C3
Baigneux-les-Juifs
F............ 104 B3
Bailén E 157 B4
Baileux B........91 A4
Bailieborough
IRL 27 C4
Bailleul F.......78 B2
Baillonville B ...79 B5
Bailó E 144 B3
Bain-de-Bretagne
F............ 101 B4
Bainton UK 40 B3
Baio E 140 A2
Baiona E 140 B2
Bais F 89 B3
Baiso I 134 A3
Baiuca P 148 B2
Baja H........ 125 A4
Bajánsenye H . 111 C3
Bajina Bašta
SRB 127 D1
Bajmok SRB... 126 B1
Bajna H 112 B2
Bajovo Polje
MNE 139 B4
Bajša SRB 126 B1
Bak H 111 C3
Bakar HR...... 123 B3
Bakewell UK 40 B2
Bakio E....... 143 A4
Bakka N........47 C6
Bakkafjörður
IS 191 A11
Bakkagerði
IS 191 B12
Bække DK......59 C2
Bakken N 48 B3
Baklan TR..... 189 B4
Bækmarksbro
DK 58 B1
Bakonybél H.. 111 B4
Bakonycsernye
H............ 112 B2
Bakonyjákó
H............ 111 B4
Bakonyszentkirály
H............ 112 B2
Bakonyszombathely
H............ 112 B1
Bakov nad Jizerou
CZ 84 B2
Bąkowiec PL ...87 A5
Baks H 113 C4
Baksa H...... 125 B4
Bakum D.......71 B5
Bâlâ TR........23 B7
Bala UK........38 B3
Balaguer E ... 145 C4
Balassagyarmat
H............ 112 A3
Balástya H ... 113 C4
Balatonakali
H............ 111 C4
Balatonalmádi
H............ 112 B2
Balatonboglár
H............ 111 C4
Balatonbozsok
H............ 112 B2
Balatonederics
H............ 111 C4
Balatonfenyves
H............ 111 C4
Balatonföldvár
H............ 112 C1
Balatonfüred
H............ 112 C1
Balatonfüzfö
H............ 112 B2
Balatonkenese
H............ 112 B2
Balatonkiliti
H............ 112 C2

Balatonlelle H 111 C4
Balatonszabadi
H............ 112 C2
Balatonszemes
H............ 111 C4
Balatonszentgyörgy
H............ 111 C4
Balazote E 158 C1
Balbeggie UK ...35 B4
Balbigny F ... 117 B4
Balboa E 141 B4
Balbriggan IRL .30 A2
Balchik BG 17 D8
Balçova TR... 188 A2
Baldock UK 44 B3
Baldone LV.....8 D4
Bale HR 122 B2
Baleira E 141 A3
Baleizao P 160 A2
Balen B 79 A5
Balerma E 164 C2
Balestrand N...46 A3
Balestrate I .. 176 A2
Balfour UK 33 B4
Bälganet S 63 B3
Balgari BG 17 D7
Balık E 144 B3
Balıkesir TR .. 186 C2
Balıklıçeşme
TR.......... 186 B2
Bälinge S 51 C4
Balingen D.... 107 A3
Balingsta S.....56 A3
Balintore UK ...32 D3
Balizac F 128 B2
Balk NL 70 B2
Balkbrug NL ...71 B3
Balla IRL 28 A2
Ballachulish UK 34 B2
Ballaghaderreen
IRL 26 C2
Ballancourt-sur-
Essonne F.....90 C2
Ballantrae UK ...36 A2
Ballao I...... 179 C3
Ballasalla UK ...36 B2
Ballater UK.... 32 D3
Ballen DK 59 C3
Ballenstedt D ...82 A3
Ballerias E ... 145 C3
Balleroy F 88 A3
Ballerup DK 61 D2
Ballesteros de
Calatrava E . 157 B4
Balli TR...... 186 B2
Ballina IRL 26 B1
Ballinalack IRL .30 A1
Ballinamore IRL 26 B3
Ballinascarty
IRL 29 C3
Ballinasloe IRL ..28 A3
Ballindine IRL ..28 A3
Balling DK 58 B1
Ballingarry
Limerick IRL...29 B3
Tipperary IRL...30 B1
Ballingeary IRL .29 C2
Ballinhassig IRL 29 C3
Ballinluig UK ...35 B4
Ballino I...... 121 B3
Ballinrobe IRL...28 A2
Ballinskelligs
IRL 29 C1
Ballinspittle IRL 29 C3
Ballintra IRL ...26 B2
Ballivor IRL 30 A2
Ballobar E 153 A4
Ballon
F............ 102 A2
IRL 30 B2
Ballószög H... 112 C3
Ballsh AL 182 C1
Ballstad N.... 194 B4
Ballum DK 64 A1
Ballybay IRL....27 B4
Ballybofey IRL .26 B3
Ballybunion IRL 29 B2
Ballycanew IRL.30 B2
Ballycarry UK ..27 B5
Ballycastle
IRL 26 B1
UK 27 A4
Ballyclare UK ...27 B5
Ballyconneely
IRL 28 A1
Ballycotton IRL..29 C3
Ballycroy IRL...29 C2
Ballydehob IRL..29 C2
Ballyferriter IRL 29 B1
Ballygawley UK 27 B3
Ballygowan UK .27 B5
Ballyhaunis IRL..28 A3
Ballyheige IRL..29 B2
Ballyjamesduff
IRL 27 C3

Ballylanders
IRL 29 B3
Ballylynan IRL...30 B1
Ballymahon
IRL 28 A4
Ballymena UK...27 B4
Ballymoe IRL...28 A3
Ballymoney UK .27 A4
Ballymore IRL ..28 A4
Ballymote IRL...26 B2
Ballynacorra
IRL 29 C3
Ballynagore
IRL 30 A1
Ballynahinch
UK 27 B5
Ballynure UK...27 B5
Ballyragget IRL .30 B1
Ballysadare IRL .26 B2
Ballyshannon
IRL 26 B2
Ballyvaughan
IRL 28 A2
Ballyvourney
IRL 29 C2
Ballywalter UK..27 B5
Balmaclellan
UK 36 A2
Balmaseda E.. 143 A3
Balmazújváros
H............ 113 B5
Balme I....... 119 B4
Balmedie UK.. 33 D4
Balmuccia I... 119 B5
Balna-paling
UK 32 D2
Balneario de
Panticosa E . 145 B3
Balotaszállás
H............ 126 A1
Balsa P....... 148 A2
Balsareny E .. 147 C2
Balsorano-Nuovo
I............ 169 B3
Bålsta S........57 A3
Balsthal CH ... 106 B2
Balta UA........17 A8
Baltanás E ... 142 C2
Baltar E 140 C3
Baltasound UK .33 A6
Bălți MD.......17 B7
Baltimore IRL ..29 C2
Baltinglass IRL .30 B2
Baltiysk RUS ...69 A4
Baltów PL......87 A5
Balugães P.... 148 A1
Bælum DK 58 B3
Balve D........81 A3
Balvi LV 8 D5
Balya TR...... 186 C2
Balzo I....... 136 C2
Bamberg D.....94 B2
Bamburgh UK...37 A5
Banatska Palanka
SRB 127 C3
Banatski Brestovac
SRB 127 C2
Banatski
Despotovac
SRB 126 B2
Banatski Dvor
SRB 126 B2
Banatski-Karlovac
SRB 127 B3
Banatsko
Arandjelovo
SRB 126 A2
Banatsko-Novo
Selo SRB 127 C2
Banaz TR..... 187 D4
Banbridge UK...27 B4
Banbury UK....44 A2
Banchory UK.. 33 D4
Bande
B.............79 B5
E............ 140 B3
Bandholm DK..65 B4
Bandırma TR.. 186 B2
Bandol F...... 132 B1
Bandon IRL 29 C3
Băneasa E 159 C3
Banff UK...... 33 D4
Bangor
F............ 100 B2
IRL 26 B1
Down UK......27 B5
Gwynedd UK... 38 A2
Bangsund N ... 199 A8
Banie PL.......74 A3
Banja Koviljača
SRB 127 C1
Banjaloka SLO 123 B3

Bač – Bar **205**

Bania Luka
BIH.......... 124 C3
Banjani SRB.. 127 C1
Banja Vručica
BIH.......... 125 C3
Banka SK.......98 C1
Bankekind S....56 B1
Bankend UK ...36 A3
Bankeryd S 62 A2
Bankfoot UK ...35 B4
Bankso BG 183 B5
Banloc RO..... 126 B3
Bannalec F.... 100 B2
Bannes F.......91 C3
Bannockburn
UK 35 B4
Bañobárez E .. 149 B3
Bañon E...... 152 B2
Banon F...... 132 A1
Baños E 149 B4
Baños de Gigonza
E............ 162 B2
Baños de la Encina
E............ 157 B4
Baños de Molgas
E............ 140 B3
Baños de Rio Tobia
E............ 143 B4
Baños de
Valdearados
E............ 143 C3
Bánov CZ 98 C1
Banova Jaruga
HR.......... 124 B2
Bánovce nad
Bebravou SK...98 C2
Banovići BIH . . 139 A4
Banovići Selo
BIH.......... 139 A4
Bánréve H 99 C4
Bansin D.......66 C3
Banská Belá
SK...........98 C2
Banská Bystrica
SK...........99 C3
Banská Štiavnica
SK...........98 C2
Bansko BG 183 B5
Banstead UK...44 B3
Banteer IRL 29 B3
Bantheville F ..91 B5
Bantry IRL......29 C2
Bantzenheim
F............ 106 B2
Banyalbufar E 166 B2
Banyoles E.... 147 B3
Banyuls-sur-Mer
F............ 146 B4
Bapaume F 90 A2
Bar
MNE 16 D3
UA 13 D7
Barabhas UK...31 A2
Barači BIH..... 138 A2
Baracs H...... 112 C2
Baracska H.... 112 B2
Barahona E ... 151 A5
Barajes de Melo
E............ 151 B5
Barakaldo E... 143 A4
Baralla E 141 B3
Barañain E.... 144 B2
Baranavichy BY 13 B7
Báránd H 113 B5
Baranda SRB.. 127 B2
Baranello I.... 170 B2
Baranów
Sandomierski
PL............87 B5
Baraqueville
F............ 130 A1
Barasoain E... 144 B2
Barbacena P .. 155 C3
Barbadás E.... 140 B3
Barbadillo E .. 149 B4
Barbadillo de
Herreros E ... 143 B3
Barbadillo del
Mercado E ... 143 B3
Barbadillo del Pez
E............ 143 B3
Barban HR.... 123 B3
Barbarano Vicento
I............ 121 B4
Barbariga HR . 122 C2
Barbaros TR... 186 B2
Barbastro E... 145 B4
Barbate E..... 162 B2
Barbatona E .. 152 A1
Barbâtre F.... 114 B1

Barbazan F . . 145 A4
Barbeitos E . . . 141 A3
Barbentane F . 131 B3
Barberino di
 Mugello I 135 A4
Barbezieux-St
 Hilaire F. 115 C3
Barbonne-Fayel
 F. 91 C3
Barbotan-les-
 Thermes F . . . 128 C2
Barby D. 73 C4
Bárcabo E 145 B4
Barca de Alva
 P. 149 A3
Barcarrota E . . . 155 C4
Barcellona-Pozzo di
 Gotto I 177 A4
Barcelona E. . . . 147 C3
Barcelonette
 F. 132 A2
Barcelos P 148 A1
Bárcena del
 Monasterio
 E. 141 A4
Barcena de Pie de
 Concha E. 142 A2
Barchfeld D. 82 B2
Barcin PL. 76 B2
Barcino PL 68 A1
Bárcis I. 122 A1
Barco P 154 B2
Barcones E. . . . 151 A5
Barcs H 124 B3
Barcus F 144 A3
Bardejov SK. . . . 12 D4
Bårdesø DK. 59 C3
Bardi I 120 C2
Bardney UK. 40 B3
Bardo PL. 85 B4
Bardolino I. . . . 121 B3
Bardonécchia
 I. 118 B3
Bardoňovo SK 112 A2
Barèges F 145 B4
Barenstein D. . . .83 B5
Barentin F. 89 A4
Barenton F. 88 B3
Barevo BIH. . . . 138 A3
Barfleur F 88 A2
Barga I. 134 A3
Bargas E 151 C3
Barge I 119 C4
Bargemon F . . 132 B2
Barghe I. 120 B3
Bargoed UK. . . .39 C3
Bargrennan UK .36 A2
Bargteheide D. .64 C3
Barham UK. 45 B5
Bari I 173 A2
Barič Draga
 HR 137 A4
Barilović HR. . . 123 B4
Bari Sardo I . . . 179 C3
Barisciano I . . . 169 A3
Barjac F. 131 A3
Barjols F 132 B1
Barjon F 105 B3
Bårkåker N. 54 A1
Barkald N 199 D7
Barkowo
 Dolnośląskie
 PL. 85 A4
 Pomorskie PL . .68 B2
Bârlad RO. 17 B7
Bar-le-Duc F . . .91 C5
Barles F 132 A2
Barletta I. 171 B4
Barlinek PL 75 B4
Barmouth UK. . .38 B2
Barmstedt D. . . .64 C2
Barnard Castle
 UK. 37 B5
Barnarp S. 62 A2
Bärnau D 95 B4
Bärnbach A . . . 110 B2
Barneberg D. . . .73 B4
Barnenitz D. 74 B1
Barnet UK. 44 B3
Barnetby le Wold
 UK. 40 B3
Barneveld NL. . .70 B2
Barneville-Carteret
 F. 88 A2
Barnoldswick
 UK. 40 B1
Barnowko PL . . .75 B3
Barnsley UK. . . .40 B2
Barnstädt D. 83 A3
Barnstaple UK . .42 A2

Barnstorf D 72 B1
Barntrup D. 72 C2
Baron F 90 B2
Baronissi I 170 C2
Barqueiro P. . . 154 B2
Barquinha P . . 154 B2
Barr
 F. 93 C3
 UK 36 A2
Barra P. 148 B1
Barracas E 159 A3
Barraco E 150 B3
Barrado E 150 B2
Barrafranca I. . . 177 B3
Barranco do Velho
 P. 160 B2
Barrancos P. . . 161 A3
Barrax E. 158 B1
Barrbaar D. 94 C2
Barre-des-
 Cevennes F . . 130 A2
Barreiro P. 154 C1
Barreiros E. . . . 141 A3
Barrême F 132 B2
Barret-le-Bas
 F. 132 A1
Barrhead UK. . . .34 C3
Barrhill UK. 36 A2
Barrio de Nuesra
 Señora E 142 B1
Barrowford UK. .40 B1
Barrow-in-Furness
 UK 36 B3
Barrow upon
 Humber UK . . .40 B3
Barruecopardo
 E. 149 A3
Barruelo de
 Santullán E . . 142 B2
Barruera E 145 B4
Barry UK 39 C3
Bårse DK. 65 A4
Barsinghausen
 D. 72 B2
Barssel D. 71 A4
Bar-sur-Aube
 F. 104 A3
Bar-sur-Seine
 F. 104 A3
Barth D. 66 B1
Bartholomä D . .94 C1
Bartin TR. 187 A7
Barton-upon-
 Humber UK . . .40 B3
Barúmini I . . . 179 C2
Baruth D. 74 B2
Barvaux B. 80 B1
Barver D. 72 B1
Barwatd PL 99 B3
Barwice PL. 68 B1
Barysaw BY 13 A8
Barzana E 141 A5
Bârzava RO 16 B4
Bárzio I 120 B2
Bas E 147 B3
Bašaid SRB . . . 126 B2
Basalúzzo I . . . 120 C1
Basarabeasca
 MD. 17 B8
Basauri E. 143 A4
Baschi I 168 A2
Baschurch UK. .38 B4
Basconcillos del
 Tozo E 143 B3
Bascones de Ojeda
 E. 142 B2
Basécles B 79 B3
Basel CH 106 B2
Baséliche I. . . . 170 B2
Basildon UK. . . .45 B4
Basingstoke UK 44 B2
Baška
 CZ. 98 B2
 HR 123 C3
Baška Voda
 HR 138 B2
Bäsksjö S 200 B3
Baslow UK. 40 B2
Başmakçı TR . . 189 B5
Basovizza I. . . . 122 B2
Bassacutena I . . 178 A3
Bassano del Grappa
 I. 121 B4
Bassano Romano
 I. 168 A2
Bassecourt CH 106 B2
Bassella E. 147 B2
Bassevuovdde
 N. 193 D9
Bassou F. 104 B2
Bassoues F. . . . 128 C3
Bassum D. 72 B1
Båstad S 61 C2

Bastardo I. 136 C1
Bastelica F 180 A2
Bastelicaccia
 F. 180 B1
Bastia
 F. 180 A2
 I. 136 B1
Bastogne B 92 A1
Baston UK. 40 C3
Bastuträsk S . . 200 B6
Bata H 125 A4
Batajnica SRB . 127 C2
Batak BG. 183 B6
Batalha P 154 B2
Bátaszék H. . . . 125 A4
Batea E 153 A4
Batelov CZ. 97 B3
Bath UK. 43 A4
Bathgate UK 35 C4
Batida H 126 A2
Batignano I . . . 135 C4
Batina HR 125 B4
Bátka SK 99 C4
Batković BIH . . 125 C5
Batley UK. 40 B2
Batnfjordsøra
 N. 198 C4
Batočina SRB. . 127 C3
Bátonyterenye
 H. 113 B3
Batrina HR 125 B3
Båtsfjord N . . . 193 B13
Båtskärsnäs
 S. 196 D6
Battaglia Terme
 I. 121 B4
Bätterkinden
 CH 106 B2
Battice B. 80 B1
Battipáglia I . . . 170 C2
Battle UK. 45 C4
Battonya H . . . 126 A3
Batuša SRB. . . . 127 C3
Bátya H 112 C2
Bau I 179 C2
Baud F. 100 B2
Baudour B 79 B3
Baugé F. 102 B1
Baugy F. 103 B4
Bauma CH 107 B3
Baume-les-Dames
 F. 105 B5
Baumholder D . .93 B3
Baunatal D. 81 A5
Baunei I. 178 B3
Bauska LV. 8 D4
Bautzen D 84 A2
Bavanište
 SRB 127 C2
Bavay F. 79 B3
Bavilliers F 106 B1
Bavorov CZ. 96 B2
Bawdsey UK. . . .45 A5
Bawinkel D. 71 B4
Bawtry UK. 40 B2
Bayat TR. 187 D5
Bayel F. 105 A3
Bayeux F. 88 A3
Bayındır TR . . . 188 A2
Bayon F. 92 C2
Bayonne F 128 C1
Bayons F. 132 A2
Bayramiç TR . . 186 C1
Bayreuth D 95 B3
Bayrischzell D . 108 B3
Baza E 164 B2
Bazas F 128 B2
Baziege F 146 A2
Bazoches-les-
 Gallerandes
 F. 103 A4
Bazoches-sur-
 Hoëne F. 89 B4
Bazzano I 135 A4
Beaconsfield
 UK. 44 B3
Beade E. 140 B2
Beadnell UK. . . .37 A5
Beaminster UK .43 B4
Bearsden UK. . . .34 C3
Beasain E 144 A1
Beas de Segura
 E. 164 A2
Beattock UK 36 A3
Beaubery F 117 A4
Beaucaire F . . . 131 B3
Beaufort
 F. 118 B3
 IRL 29 B2
Beaufort-en Vallée
 F. 102 B1
Beaugency F. . . 103 B3

Beaujeu
 Alpes-de-Haute-
 Provence F. . . 132 A2
 Rhône F. 117 A4
Beaulac F 128 B2
Beaulieu
 F. 103 B4
 UK 44 C2
Beaulieu-sous-la-
 Roche F 114 B2
Beaulieu-sur-
 Dordogne F . . 129 B4
Beaulieu-sur-Mer
 F. 133 B3
Beaulon F. 104 C2
Beauly UK. 32 D2
Beaumaris UK. . .38 A2
Beaumesnil F . . .89 A4
Beaumetz-lès-
 Loges F 78 B2
Beaumont
 B. 79 B4
 F. 129 B3
Beaumont-de-
 Lomagne F. . . 129 C3
Beaumont-du-
 Gâtinais F. . . . 103 A4
Beaumont-en-
 Argonne F. 91 B5
Beaumont-Hague
 F. 88 A2
Beaumont-
 la-Ronce F . . . 102 B2
Beaumont-
 le-Roger F 89 A4
Beaumont-
 sur-Oise F. 90 B2
Beaumont-sur-
 Sarthe F. 102 A2
Beaune F. 105 B3
Beaune-la-Rolande
 F. 103 A4
Beaupréau F . . 101 B5
Beauraing B 91 A4
Beaurepaire F. . 117 B5
Beaurepaire-en-
 Bresse F 105 C4
Beaurières F . . 132 A1
Beauvais F 90 B2
Beauval F 90 A2
Beauville F 129 B3
Beauvoir-sur-Mer
 F. 114 B1
Beauvoir-
 sur-Niort F . . . 114 B3
Beba Veche
 RO 126 A2
Bebertal D 73 B4
Bebington UK. . .38 A3
Bebra D. 82 B1
Bebrina HR. . . . 125 B3
Beccles UK 45 A5
Becedas E. 150 B2
Beceite E. 153 B4
Becerreá E. . . . 141 B3
Becerril de Campos
 E. 142 B2
Bécherel F 101 A4
Bechhofen D. . . .94 B2
Bechyně CZ. 96 B2
Becilla de
 Valderaduey
 E. 142 B1
Beckfoot UK 36 B3
Beckingham
 UK. 40 B3
Beckum D. 81 A4
Beco P 154 B2
Bécon-les-Granits
 F. 102 B1
Bečov nad Teplou
 CZ. 83 B4
Becsehely H. . . 111 C3
Bedale UK. 37 B5
Bedames E. . . . 143 A3
Bédar E 164 B3
Bédarieux F . . . 130 B2
Bédarrides F . . 131 A3
Bedburg D. 80 B2
Beddgelert UK .38 A2
Beddingestrand
 S. 66 A2
Bédée F. 101 A4
Bedegkér H. . . . 112 C2
Beden TR 189 C7
Bedford UK. 44 A3
Będków PL. 87 A3
Bedlington UK. .37 A5
Bedlno PL. 77 B4
Bedmar E 163 A4
Bédoin F 131 A4
Bedónia I 134 A2

Bedretto CH . . 107 C3
Bedsted DK 58 B1
Bedum NL 71 A3
Bedwas UK. 39 C3
Bedworth UK. . .40 C2
Będzin PL 86 B3
Beekbergen NL .70 B2
Beek en Donk
 NL 80 A1
Beelen D. 71 C5
Beelitz D. 74 B1
Beer UK. 43 B3
Beerfelde D. 74 B3
Beerfelden D . . .93 B4
Beernem B. 78 A3
Beeskow D. 74 B3
Beetsterzwaag
 NL 70 A3
Beetzendorf D. .73 B4
Beflelay CH . . . 106 B2
Begaljica SRB . 127 C2
Bégard F 100 A2
Begejci SRB . . . 126 B2
Begijar E 157 C4
Begijnendijk B. .79 A4
Begndal N 48 B1
Begues E 147 C2
Beguildy UK 39 B3
Begur E 147 C4
Beho B 80 B1
Behringen D 82 A2
Beilen NL 71 B3
Beilngries D 95 B3
Beine-Nauroy F 91 B4
Beinwil CH. . . . 106 B3
Beiseförth D 82 A1
Beith UK 34 C3
Beitostølen N . . .47 A5
Beiuş RO. 16 B5
Beja
 P. 160 A2
 E. 149 B4
Béjar E. 149 B4
Bekçiler TR. . . . 189 C4
Békés H. 113 C5
Békéscsaba H. . 113 C5
Bekilli TR. 189 A4
Bekkarfjord
 N. 193 B11
Bela SK. 98 B2
Bélábre F 115 B5
Bela Crkva
 SRB 127 C3
Belalcázar E. . . 156 B2
Belánad Radbuzou
 CZ. 95 B4
Belanovica
 SRB 127 C2
Bélapátfalva
 H. 113 A4
Bělá pod Bezdězem
 CZ. 84 B2
Belcaire F 146 B2
Bełchatów PL. . .86 A3
Belchite E. 153 A3
Beceite E. 153 B4
Bělčice CZ. 96 B1
Belcoo UK 26 B3
Bečej SRB 126 B2
Belecke D. 81 A4
Belej HR. 123 C3
Beleño E 142 A1
Bélesta F 146 B2
Belevi TR. 188 A2
Belfast UK. 27 B5
Belford UK. 37 A5
Belfort F 106 B1
Belgentier F . . 132 B1
Belgern D. 83 A5
Belgioioso I. . . . 120 B2
Belgodère F . . . 180 A2
Belgooly IRL . . .29 C3
Belgrade = Beograd
 SRB 127 C2
Belhade F 128 B2
Belica HR. 124 A2
Beli Manastir
 HR 125 B4
Belin-Béliet F . . 128 B2
Belinchón E . . . 151 B4
Beliŝće HR. 125 B4
Bělkovice-Lašťany
 CZ. 98 B1
Bella I. 172 B1
Bellac F. 115 B5
Bellágio I 120 B2
Bellananagh
 IRL. 27 C3
Bellano I 120 A2
Bellária I. 136 A1
Bellavary IRL. . . .26 C1
Belleau F. 90 B3
Belleek UK 26 B2
Bellegarde
 Gard F. 131 B3
 Loiret F 103 B4

Bellegarde-en-Diois
 F. 132 A1
Bellegarde-en-
 Marche F. 116 B2
Bellegarde-sur-
 Valserine F. . . 118 A2
Belle-Isle-
 en-Terre F. . . . 100 A2
Bellême F. 89 B4
Bellenaves F . . 116 A3
Bellentre F 118 B3
Bellevaux F . . . 118 A3
Bellevesvre F . . 105 C4
Belleville F. 117 A4
Belleville-sur-Vie
 F. 114 B2
Bellevue-la-
 Montagne F. . . 117 B3
Belley F. 118 B2
Bellheim D. 93 B4
Bellinge DK. 59 C3
Bellingham UK. .37 A4
Bellinzago
 Novarese I . . . 120 B1
Bellinzona CH. 120 A2
Bell-lloc d'Urgell
 E. 153 A4
Bello E 152 B2
Bellpuig d'Urgell
 E. 147 C2
Bellreguart E . 159 C3
Bellsbank UK . .36 A2
Belltall E 147 C2
Belluno I 121 A5
Bellver de
 Cerdanya E . . 146 B2
Bellvis E 147 C1
Bélmez E 156 B2
Belmez de la
 Moraleda E . . 163 A4
Belmont UK. . . .33 A6
Belmont-de-
 la-Loire F. 117 A4
Belmonte
 Asturias E 141 A4
 Cuenca E 158 B1
Belmonte de
 San José E. . . . 153 B3
Belmonte de
 Tajo E 151 B4
Belmont-sur-
 Rance F 130 B1
Belmullet IRL. . .26 B1
Belobreșca
 RO 127 C3
Beloeil B 79 B3
Belogradchik
 BG 16 D5
Belokorovichi
 UA 13 C8
Belorado E. . . . 143 B3
Belotič SRB. . . . 127 C1
Bělotin CZ 98 B1
Belovo BG. . . . 183 A6
Belozersk RUS . .9 C10
Belp CH 106 C2
Belpasso I. 177 B3
Belpech F. 146 A2
Belper UK. 40 B2
Belsay UK. 37 A5
Belsk Duzy PL. . .87 A4
Beluša SK 98 B2
Belvedere
 Maríttimo I. . . 174 B1
Belver de Cinca
 E. 153 A4
Belver de los
 Montes E 142 C1
Belvès F. 129 B3
Belvezet F 130 A2
Belvis de la Jara
 E. 150 C3
Belvis de Monroy
 E. 150 C2
Belyy RUS 9 E8
Belz F. 100 B2
Bełżec PL 13 C5
Belzig D. 73 B5
Bembibre E . . . 141 B4
Bembridge
 UK. 44 C2
Bemmel NL 80 A1
Bemposta
 Bragança P . . . 149 A3
 Santarém P . . . 154 B2
Benabarre E . . 145 B4
Benacazón E . . 161 B3
Benaguacil E . . 159 B3
Benahadux E . 164 C2

Benalmádena
 E. 163 B3
Benalúa de Guadix
 E. 164 B1
Benalúa de las
 Villas E. 163 A4
Benalup E. 162 B2
Benamargosa
 E. 163 B3
Benamaurel E. 164 B2
Benameji E. . . 163 A3
Benamocarra
 E. 163 B3
Benaocaz E . . . 162 B2
Benaoján E . . . 162 B2
Benarrabá E . . 162 B2
Benasque E . . . 145 B4
Benátky nad
 Jizerou CZ 84 B2
Benavente
 E. 142 B1
 P. 154 C2
Benavides de
 Órbigo E 141 B5
Benavila P 154 B3
Bendorf D 81 B3
Benedikt SLO . 110 C2
Benejama E . . . 159 C3
Benejúzar E. . . 165 A4
Benešov CZ. 96 B2
Bénestroff F . . .92 C2
Benet F 114 B3
Bene Vagienna
 I. 133 A3
Bénévent-
 l'Abbaye F . . . 116 A1
Benevento I. . . 170 B2
Benfeld F 93 C3
Benfica P. 154 B2
Bengtsfors S. . . .54 A3
Bengtsheden S .50 B2
Beničanci HR. . 125 B4
Benicarló E. . . . 153 B4
Benicàssim E. . 153 B4
Benidorm E. . . 159 C3
Benifaió E. 159 B3
Beniganim E . . 159 C3
Benington UK. . .41 B4
Benisa E. 159 C4
Benkovac HR. . 137 A4
Benllech UK. . . .38 A2
Benneckenstein
 D. 82 A2
Bénodet F 100 B1
Benquerencia de
 la Serena E . . 156 B2
Bensafrim P . . . 160 B1
Bensbyn S 196 D5
Bensdorf D 73 B5
Benshausen D . .82 B2
Bensheim D. 93 B4
Bentley UK. 44 B3
Bentwisch D . . .65 B5
Beočin SRB. . . . 126 B1
Beograd = Belgrade
 SRB 127 C2
Beragh UK 27 B3
Beranga E 143 A3
Berat AL 182 C1
Bérat F. 146 A2
Beratzhausen
 D. 95 B3
Bérbaltavár H. . 111 B3
Berbegal E 145 C3
Berbenno di
 Valtellina I . . . 120 A2
Berberana E . . 143 B3
Bercedo E 143 A3
Bercel H 112 B3
Bercenay-
 le-Hayer F 91 C3
Berceto I 134 A2
Berchem B 79 B3
Berchidda I . . . 178 B3
Berching D. 95 B3
Berchtesgaden
 D. 109 B4
Bérchules I . . . 163 B4
Bercianos de Aliste
 E. 149 A3
Berck F. 78 B1
Berclaire d'Urgell
 E. 147 C1
Berdoias E 140 A1
Berducedo E . . 141 A4
Berdún E. 144 B3
Berdychiv UA . . 13 D8
Bere Alston UK .42 B2
Bereguardo I . . 120 B2
Berehommen
 N. 53 A3
Berehove UA. . .16 A5
Berek BIH 124 B3

Beremend H . . 125 B4
Bere Regis UK . . .43 B4
Berestechko
UA 13 C6
Berettyóújfalu
H. 113 B5
Berezhany UA. . 13 D6
Berezivka UA 17 B9
Berezna UA 13 C9
Berg
D 95 B3
N. 195 E3
S. 56 B2
Berga
Sachsen-Anhalt
D. 82 A3
Thüringen D 83 B4
E. 147 B2
S. 62 A4
Bergama TR. . . 186 C2
Bérgamo I 120 B2
Bergara E 143 A4
Bergby S 51 B4
Berge
Brandenburg
D. 74 B1
Niedersachsen
D. 71 B4
Telemark N . . . 53 A4
Bergeforsen S. 200 D3
Bergen
Mecklenburg-
Vorpommern
D. 66 B2
Niedersachsen
D. 72 B2
Niedersachsen
D. 73 B3
N. 46 B2
NL 70 B1
Bergen op Zoom
NL 79 A4
Bergerac F 129 B3
Bergères-lés-Vertus
F. 91 C4
Bergeyk NL 79 A5
Berghausen D . .93 C4
Bergheim D 80 B2
Berghem S. 60 B2
Berg im Gau D . .95 C3
Bergisch Gladbach
D 80 B3
Bergkamen D . .81 A3
Bergkvara S. 63 B4
Berglern D 95 C3
Bergnäset S. . . 196 D5
Bergneustadt
D 81 A3
Bergsäng S 49 B5
Bergshamra S. . .57 A4
Bergsjö S 200 E3
Bergs slussar S. .56 B1
Bergsviken S. . 196 D4
Bergtheim D . . .94 B2
Bergues F 78 B2
Bergum NL. 70 A2
Bergün Bravuogn
CH 107 C4
Bergwitz D. 83 A4
Berhida H 112 B2
Beringel P 160 A2
Beringen B. 79 A5
Berja E 164 C2
Berkåk N 199 C7
Berkeley UK. . . .43 A4
Berkenthin D . . .65 C3
Berkhamsted
UK 44 B3
Berkheim D . . . 107 A5
Berkhof D. 72 B2
Berković BIH . . 139 B4
Berkovitsa BG. . 17 D5
Berlanga E 156 B2
Berlanga de Duero
E. 151 A5
Berlevåg N. . . . 193 B13
Berlikum NL. . . .70 A2
Berlin D. 74 B2
Berlstedt D 82 A3
Bermeo E 143 A4
Bermillo de Sayago
E. 149 A3
Bern CH. 106 C2
Bernalda I. 174 A2
Bernardos E. . . 150 A3
Bernartice
Jihočeský CZ. . . .96 B2
Vychodočeský
CZ 85 B3
Bernau
Baden-
Württemberg
D. 106 B3

Bernau continued
Bayern D 108 B3
Brandenburg
D. 74 B2
Bernaville F. 90 A2
Bernay F 89 A4
Bernburg D 83 A3
Berndorf A 111 B3
Berne D. 72 A1
Bernecebarati
H. 112 A2
Bernhardsthal
A. 97 C4
Bernkastel-Kues
D. 92 B3
Bernolakovo
SK. 111 A4
Bernsdorf D. . . .84 A2
Bernstadt D. . . .84 A2
Bernstein A . . . 111 B3
Bernués E. 145 B3
Beromünster
CH 106 B3
Beroun CZ 96 B2
Berovo NMK . . 182 B4
Berre-l'Etang
F. 131 B4
Berriedale UK. . .32 C3
Berriew UK. 39 B3
Berrocal E. 161 B3
Bersenbrück D. .71 B4
Bershad' UA . . . 13 D8
Bertamiráns E 140 B2
Berthåga S. 51 C4
Berthelming F . .92 C2
Bertincourt F . . .90 A2
Bertinoro I 135 A5
Bertogne B 92 A1
Bertrix B 91 B5
Berufjörður
IS 191 C11
Berville-sur-Mer
F. 89 A4
Berwick-upon-
Tweed UK. 37 A4
Berzasca RO 16 C4
Berzence H . . . 124 A3
Berzocana E . . 156 A2
Besalú E. 147 B3
Besançon F . . . 105 B5
Besenfeld D. . . .93 C4
Besenyötelek
H. 113 B4
Besenyszög H. 113 B4
Beshenkovichi
BY. 13 A8
Besigheim D . . .93 C5
Běšiny CZ. 96 B1
Beška SRB. . . . 126 B2
Beškonak TR . . 189 B6
Besle F 101 B4
Besnyö H 112 B2
Bessais-le-
Fromental F. . 103 C4
Bessan F 130 B2
Besse-en-
Chandesse F . 116 B2
Bessèges F . . . 131 A3
Bessé-sur-Braye
F. 102 B2
Bessines-sur-
Gartempe F. . 115 B5
Best NL 79 A5
Bestorp S 56 B1
Betanzos E. . . . 140 A2
Betelu E. 144 A2
Bétera E. 159 B3
Beteta E. 152 B1
Béthenville F . . .91 B4
Bethesda UK. . . .38 A2
Béthune F. 78 B2
Beton-Bazoches
F. 90 C3
Bettembourg L . .92 B2
Betterdorf L 92 B2
Bettna S 56 B2
Béttola I 120 C2
Bettona I. 136 B1
Bettyhill UK. . . .32 C2
Betws-y-Coed
UK 38 A3
Betxi E 159 B3
Betz F 90 B2
Betzdorf D 81 B3
Beuil F 132 A2
Beulah UK 39 B3
Beuzeville F. . . .89 A4
Bevagna I 136 C1
Bevens-bruk S . .56 A1
Beveren B. 79 A4
Beverley UK. . . .40 B3
Bevern D. 81 A5
Beverstedt D. . . .72 A1

Beverungen D . .81 A5
Beverwijk NL . . .70 B1
Bex CH. 119 A4
Boxhill UK. 45 C4
Beyazköy TR . . 186 A2
Beychevelle F. 128 A2
Beydağ TR 188 A3
Beyeğaç TR . . . 188 B3
Beykoz TR. 186 A4
Beynat F 129 A4
Beyoğlu TR 186 A4
Beypazarı TR. . 187 B6
Beyşehir TR . . . 189 B6
Bezas E 152 B2
Bezau A. 107 B4
Bezdan SRB. . . 125 B4
Bèze F 105 B4
Bezenet F 116 A2
Bezhetsk RUS . . .9 D10
Bezzecca I. . . . 121 B3
Biadki PL. 85 A5
Biała
Łódzkie PL . . . 77 C4
Opolskie PL. . . .85 B5
Białaczów PL. . .87 A4
Biała Podlaska
PL. 13 B5
Biała Rawska
PL. 87 A4
Biale Błota PL . .76 A2
Białobłoty PL. . .76 B2
Białobrzegi PL . .87 A4
Białogard PL. . . .67 C4
Białośliwie PL. . .76 A2
Białowąs PL. . . .68 B1
Biały Bór PL. . . .68 B1
Białystok PL 13 B5
Biancavilla I. . . 177 B3
Bianco I. 175 C2
Biandrate I. . . . 119 B5
Biar E 159 C3
Biarritz F. 144 A2
Bias F. 128 B1
Biasca CH 120 A1
Biatorbágy H . . 112 B2
Bibbiena I. . . . 135 B4
Bibbona I 134 B3
Biberach
Baden-
Württemberg
D. 93 C4
Baden-
Württemberg
D. 107 A4
Bibinje HR 137 A4
Bibione I. 122 B2
Biblis D 93 B4
Bibury UK. 44 B2
Bicaj AL. 182 B2
Bíccari I 171 B3
Bicester UK. . . .44 B2
Bichl D. 108 B2
Bichlbach A. . . 108 B1
Bicorp E. 159 B3
Bicos P. 160 B1
Bicske H 112 B2
Bidache F 128 C1
Bidart F 144 A2
Biddinghuizen
NL 70 B2
Biddulph UK. . . .40 B1
Bideford UK. . . .42 A2
Bidford-on-Avon
UK 44 A2
Bidjovagge N. . 192 C6
Bie S. 56 A2
Bieber D 81 B5
Biebersdorf D. .74 C2
Biedenkopf D. . .81 B4
Biel E 144 B3
Biel / Bienne
CH 106 B2
Bielany
Wroclawskie
PL. 85 A4
Bielawa PL. 85 B4
Bielawy PL. 77 B4
Biel / Bienne
CH 106 B2
Bielefeld D. 72 B1
Biella I 119 B5
Bielsa E 145 B4
Bielsk PL. 77 B4
Bielsko-Biała
PL. 99 B3
Bielsk Podlaski
PL. 13 B5
Bienenbuttel D .72 A3
Bieniow PL. 84 A3
Bienservida E. 158 C1
Bienvenida E. . 156 B1
Bierdzany PL. . .86 B2
Bierné F. 102 B1
Biersted DK. . . .58 A2

Bierun PL 86 B3
Bierwart B 79 B5
Bierzwina PL. . 75 A4
Bierzwnik PL. . .75 A4
Biescas E. 145 B3
Biesenthal D. . . .74 B2
Biesiekierz PL. . .67 B5
Bietigheim-
Bissingen D. . . .93 C5
Bièvre B. 91 B5
Biscarrués E. . . 144 B3
Bièżuń PL. 77 B4
Biga TR. 186 B2
Bigadiç TR 186 C3
Biganos F 128 B2
Bigas P. 148 B2
Bigastro E. 165 A4
Biggar UK. 36 A3
Biggin Hill UK . . .45 B4
Biggleswade
UK 44 A3
Bignasco CH . . 119 A5
Biguglia F. 180 A2
Bihać BIH 124 C1
Biharnagybajom
H. 113 B5
Bijeljani BIH. . . 139 B4
Bijeljina BIH. . . 125 C5
Bijuesca E. 152 A2
Bilaj HR 137 A4
Bila Tserkva
UA 13 D9
Bilbao E. 143 A4
Bilcza PL. 87 B4
Bíldudalur IS. . 190 B2
Bileća BIH 139 C4
Bilecik TR 187 B5
Biled RO 126 B2
Biłgoraj PL. 12 C5
Bilhorod-
Dnistrovskyy
UA 17 B9
Bílina CZ. 84 B1
Bilisht AL 182 C2
Bilje HR 125 B4
Billdal S. 60 B1
Billerbeck D. . . .71 C4
Billericay UK. . . .45 B4
Billesholm S. . . .61 C2
Billingborough
UK 40 C3
Billinge S 61 D3
Billingham UK . .37 B5
Billinghay UK. . .41 B3
Billingsfors S. . . .54 B3
Billingshurst
UK 44 B3
Billom F. 116 B3
Billsta S. 200 C4
Billund DK. 59 C2
Bílovec CZ. 98 B2
Bilstein D. 81 A4
Bilthoven NL. . . .70 B2
Bilto N 192 C5
Bilzen B. 80 B1
Biña SK. 112 B2
Binaced E. 145 C4
Binasco I. 120 B2
Binbrook UK. . . .41 B3
Binche B. 79 B4
Bindlach D. 95 B3
Bindslev DK. . . .58 A3
Binefar E. 145 C4
Bingen D. 93 B3
Bingham UK. . . .40 C3
Bingley UK. 40 B2
Bingsjö S. 50 A2
Binic F 100 A3
Binz D. 66 B2

Biržai LT. 8 D4
Birzebbuġa
M. 175 C3
Risáccia I. 172 A1
Bisacquino I . . . 176 B2
Bisbal de Falset
E. 153 A4
Biscarosse F . . . 128 B1
Biscarosse Plage
F. 128 B1
Biscarrués E. . . 144 B3
Biscéglie I. 171 B4
Bischheim F. . . .93 C3
Bischofsheim D 82 B1
Bischofshofen
A. 109 B4
Bischofswerda
D. 109 B3
Bischofszell
CH 107 B4
Bischwiller F . . .93 C3
Bisenti I. 169 A3
Bishop Auckland
UK 37 B5
Bishop's Castle
UK 39 B4
Bishops Lydeard
UK 43 A3
Bishop's Stortford
UK 45 B4
Bishop's Waltham
UK 44 C2
Bisignano I. . . . 174 B2
Bisingen D 93 C4
Biskupice-
Oławskie PL. . .85 A5
Biskupiec PL . . .69 B4
Bismark D. 73 B4
Bismo N. 198 D5
Bispgården S . 200 C2
Bispingen D . . .72 A2
Bissen L. 92 B2
Bissendorf D. . . .71 B5
Bistango I. 119 C5
Bistarac Donje
BIH. 139 A4
Bistrica ob Sotli
SLO 123 A4
Bistriţa RO 17 B6
Bitburg D 92 B2
Bitche F. 93 B3
Bitetto I. 171 B4
Bitola NMK. . . . 182 B3
Bitonto I 171 B4
Bitschwiller F . 106 B2
Bitterfeld D. . . .83 A4
Bitti I. 178 B3
Biville-sur-Mer
F. 89 A5
Bivona I. 176 B2
Biwer L. 92 B2
Bizeljsko SLO . 123 A4
Bizovac HR. . . . 125 B4
Bjåen N. 52 A3
Bjärnum S. 61 C3
Bjärred S. 61 D3
Bjästa S. 200 C4
Bjelland
Vest-Agder N. .52 B2
Vest-Agder N. .52 B3
Bjelovar HR. . . . 124 B2
Bjerkreim N. . . .52 B2
Bjerkvik N. 194 B8
Bjerreby DK. . . .65 B3
Bjerregrav DK. . .58 B2
Bjerringbro
DK 59 B2
Bjøberg N. 47 B5
Bjøllånes N . . . 195 D5
Bjørbo N. 50 B1
Bjordal N. 46 A2
Bjørg IS 191 B8
Bjørkåsen N . . 194 B7
Bjørke
Gävleborg S. . .51 B4
Østergötland S. .56 B1
Bjørkelangen
N. 48 C3
Björketorp S. . . .60 B2
Björkholmen
S. 196 C2
Bjørkliden S. . 194 B9
Björklinge S 51 B4
Björko S. 51 C6
Björkö S. 62 A2
Björköby S. 62 A2
Björkvik S. 56 B2
Bjørn N 195 D3
Björna S. 200 C4

Björneborg S . . .55 A5
Björneröd S . . . 54 A2
Björnevatn
N. 193 C13
Björnlunda S. . .56 A3
Bjørnstad N . . 193 C14
Björsäter S. 56 B2
Bjurberget S 49 B4
Bjurholm S. . . . 200 C5
Bjursås S. 50 B2
Bjurtjärn S. 55 A5
Bjuv S. 61 C2
Blachownia PL . .86 B2
Blackburn UK. . .38 A4
Blackpool UK. . .38 A3
Blackstad S. 62 A4
Blackwater IRL. .30 B2
Blackwaterfoot
UK 34 C2
Blacy F 91 C4
Bladåker S. 51 B5
Blaenau Ffestiniog
UK 38 B3
Blaenavon UK. . .39 C3
Blaengarw UK. . .39 C3
Blagaj
BIH. 124 B2
BIH. 139 B3
Blagdon UK. . . .43 A4
Blagnac F 129 C4
Blagoevgrad
BG 183 A5
Blaichach D. . . 107 B5
Blain F 101 B4
Blainville-sur-l'Eau
F. 92 C2
Blair Atholl UK. .35 B4
Blairgowrie UK. .35 B4
Blajan F 145 A4
Blakeney UK. . . .39 C4
Blakstad N. 53 B4
Blâmont F. 92 C2
Blanca E 165 A3
Blancos E 140 C3
Blandford Forum
UK 43 B4
Blanes E. 147 C3
Blangy-sur-Bresle
F. 90 B1
Blankaholm S. . .62 A4
Blankenberge
B. 78 A3
Blankenburg D .82 A2
Blankenfelde D 74 B2
Blankenhain D. .82 B3
Blankenheim D .80 B2
Blanquefort F. 128 B2
Blansko CZ. 97 B4
Blanzac F 115 C4
Blanzy F 104 C3
Blaricum NL. . . .70 B2
Blarney IRL. 29 C3
Blascomillán
E. 150 B2
Blascosancho
E. 150 B3
Błaszki PL. 86 A2
Blatná CZ. 96 B1
Blatné SK. 111 A4
Blatnica BIH . . 139 A3
Blatnika BIH . . 139 A3
Blato HR 138 C2
Blato na Cetini
HR 138 B2
Blatten CH. . . . 119 A4
Blattnicksele
S. 195 E8
Blatzheim D. . . .80 B2
Blaubeuren D. . .94 C1
Blaufelden D. . . .94 B1
Blaustein D 94 C1
Blaydon UK. 37 B5
Blaye F. 128 A2
Blaye-les-Mines
F. 130 A1
Bleckede D 73 A3
Blecua E. 145 B3
Bled SLO 123 A3
Bleialf D 80 B2
Bleibburg A. . . . 110 C1
Bleicherode D . .82 A2
Bleik N 194 A6
Bleikvassli N. . .195 E4
Bléneau F 104 B2
Blentarp S 61 D3
Blera I. 168 A2
Blérancourt F . . .90 B3
Bléré F 102 B2
Blesle F 116 B3
Blessington IRL .30 A2
Blet F 103 C4
Bletchley UK. . . .44 B3

Bletterans F. . . 105 C4
Blidö S. 57 A4
Blidsberg S. 60 B3
Blieskastel D. . . .92 B3
Bligny-sur-Ouche
F. 104 B3
Blikstorp S. 55 B5
Blinisht AL. . . . 182 B1
Blinja HR. 124 B2
Blizanówek PL. .76 C3
Bliżyn PL. 87 A4
Blois F 103 B3
Blokhus DK. 58 A2
Blokzijl NL. 70 B2
Blombacka S. . .55 A4
Blomberg D. . . .72 C2
Blomskog S. 54 A3
Blomstermåla
S. 62 B4
Blomvåg N. 46 B1
Blönduós IS . . . 190 B5
Błonie PL. 77 B5
Blonville-sur-Mer
F. 89 A4
Blötberget S . . .50 B2
Blovice CZ. 96 B1
Bloxham UK 44 A2
Blšany CZ. 83 B5
Bludenz A. 107 B4
Bludov CZ. 97 B4
Blumberg D. . . 107 B3
Blyberg S 49 A6
Blyth
Northumberland
UK 37 A5
Nottinghamshire
UK 40 B2
Blyth Bridge
UK 35 C4
Blythburgh UK. .45 A5
Blythe Bridge
UK 40 C1
Bø
Nordland N . . . 194 B5
Telemark N . . . 53 A5
Boal E. 141 A4
Boan MNE. 139 C5
Boario Terme
I. 120 B3
Boat of Garten
UK 32 D3
Boa Vista P 154 B2
Boğazkale TR . . .23 A8
Boğazlıyan TR . .23 B8
Boba H. 111 B4
Bobadilla
Logroño E . . . 143 B4
Málaga E 163 A3
Bobadilla del
Campo E 150 A2
Bobadilla del
Monte E. 151 B4
Bóbbio I 120 C2
Bóbbio Pellice
I. 119 C4
Bobigny F. 90 C2
Bobingen D. . . .94 C2
Böblingen D . . .93 C5
Bobolice PL. 68 B1
Boboras E. 140 B2
Boboshevo
BG 182 A4
Bobowa PL. 99 B4
Bobrová CZ. 97 B4
Bobrovitsa UA . .13 C9
Bobrowice PL. . .75 C4
Bobrówko PL. . .75 B4
Boca de Huérgano
E. 142 B2
Bocairent E . . . 159 C3
Bočar SRB. 126 B2
Bocchigliero I. 174 B2
Boceguillas E . 151 A4
Bochnia PL. 99 B4
Bocholt
B. 80 A1
D 80 A2
Bochov CZ. 83 B5
Bochum D. 80 A3
Bockara S. 62 A4
Bockenem D. . .72 B3
Bockfliess A. 97 C4
Bockhorn D. . . .71 A5
Bočna SLO 123 A3
Bocognano F . 180 A2
Boconád H. . . . 113 B4
Bőcs H 113 A4
Boczów PL. 75 B3
Boda S 50 A2
Böda S. 62 A5

Boda
Stockholm S 51 B5
Värmland S 55 A4
Västernorrland
S 200 D2
Bodafors S 62 A2
Boda Glasbruk
S 63 B3
Bodajk H...... 112 B2
Boddam
Aberdeenshire
UK 33 D5
Shetland UK ...33 B5
Boddin D 73 A4
Bödefeld-Freiheit
D 81 A4
Boden S....... 196 D4
Bodenmais D ...95 B5
Bodenteich D ...73 B3
Bodenwerder
D 72 C2
Bodiam UK.....45 B4
Bodinnick UK ..42 B2
Bodio CH...... 120 A1
Bodjani SRB.. 125 B5
Bodmin UK.....42 B2
Bodø N....... 194 C5
Bodonal de la
Sierra E 161 A3
Bodrum TR.... 188 B2
Bodstedt D 66 B1
Bodträskfors
S 196 C3
Bodzanów PL ...77 B5
Bodzanowice
PL.............86 B2
Bodzechów PL ..87 B5
Bodzentyn PL...87 B4
Boecillo E 150 A3
Boëge F........ 118 A3
Boën F........ 117 B3
Bogács H...... 113 B4
Bogadmindszent
H............. 125 B4
Bogajo E 149 B3
Bogarra E 158 C1
Bogarre E 163 A4
Bogatić SRB.. 127 C1
Bogatynia PL ..84 B2
Bogda RO..... 126 B3
Bogdaniec PL ..75 B4
Boge S 57 C4
Bogen
D 95 C4
Nordland N .. 194 B7
Nordland N ... 194 C6
S 49 B4
Bogense DK...59 C3
Bognanco Fonti
I............. 119 A5
Bognelv N ... 192 B6
Bognes N 194 B7
Bogno CH..... 120 A2
Bognor Regis
UK 44 C3
Bogoria PL....87 B5
Bograngen S....49 B4
Boguchwały PL .69 B5
Bogumiłowice
PL.............86 A3
Boguslav UA ... 13 D9
Boguszów-Gorce
PL.............85 B4
Bogyiszló H.. 112 C2
Bohain-en-
Vermandois F ..91 B3
Böheimkirchen
A 110 A2
Bohinjska Bistrica
SLO 122 A2
Böhlen D........83 A4
Böhmenkirch
D 94 C1
Bohmte D......71 B5
Bohonal de Ibor
E 150 C2
Böhönye H.. 124 A3
Bohumin CZ ...98 B2
Boiro E....... 140 B2
Bois-d'Amont
F............. 105 C5
Boisseron F .. 131 B3
Boitzenburg D .74 A2
Boixols E 147 B2
Boizenburg D...73 A3
Bojadła PL....75 C4
Bojano I....... 170 B2
Bojanowo PL...85 A4
Bøjden DK....64 A3
Bojkovice CZ...98 B1

Bojná SK 98 C2
Bojnice SK 98 C2
Boka SRB...... 126 B2
Böklund D 64 B2
Bokod H 112 B2
Böksholm S......62 A2
Boksitogorsk
RUS 9 C8
Bol HR 138 B2
Bolaños de
Calatrava E .. 157 B4
Bolayır TR.... 186 B1
Bolbec F 89 A4
Bölcske H..... 112 C2
Bolderslev DK...64 B2
Boldog H...... 112 B3
Boldva H...... 113 A4
Böle S....... 196 D4
Bolea E....... 145 B3
Bolekhiv UA ... 13 D5
Bolesławiec PL..84 A3
Boleszkowice
PL...........74 B3
Bolewice PL....75 B5
Bólgheri I..... 134 B3
Bolhrad UA 17 C8
Bolimów PL....77 B5
Boliden S 200 B6
Boliqueime P . 160 B1
Boljevci SRB.. 127 C2
Boljkovci SRB . 127 C2
Bolków PL 85 B4
Bollebygd S....60 B2
Bollène F...... 131 A3
Bólliga E 152 B1
Bollnäs S.....50 A3
Bollstabruk S . 200 D3
Bollullos E 161 B3
Bollullos par del
Condado E... 161 B3
Bologna I 135 A4
Bologne F..... 105 A4
Bolognetta I .. 176 B2
Bolognola I... 136 C2
Bologoye RUS...9 D9
Bolótana I..... 178 B2
Bolsena I..... 168 A1
Bolshaya
Vradiyevka
UA 17 B9
Bolsover UK...40 B2
Bolstad S 54 B3
Bolsward NL ...70 A2
Boltaña E 145 B4
Boltenhagen
D 65 C4
Boltigen CH... 106 C2
Bolton UK.....38 A4
Bolu TR 187 B6
Bolungarvík
IS 190 A2
Bolvadin TR... 187 D6
Bóly H 125 B4
Bolzaneto I ... 133 A4
Bolzano I..... 108 C2
Bomba I....... 169 A4
Bombarral P . 154 B1
Bömenzien D ...73 B4
Bomlitz D......72 B2
Bømlo N.......52 A1
Bøn N.........48 B3
Bona F....... 104 B2
Bonaduz CH... 107 C4
Bonanza E 161 C3
Boñar E 142 B1
Bonarbridge
UK 32 D2
Bonárcado I... 178 B2
Bonares E 161 B3
Bonäs S........50 A1
Bonassola I... 134 A2
Bonawe UK 34 B2
Bondal N.......53 A4
Bondeno I 121 C4
Bondorf D......93 C4
Bondstorp S ...60 B3
Bon-Encontre
F............. 129 B3
Bo'ness UK...35 B4
Bonete E..... 158 C2
Bonifacio F... 180 B2
Bonigen CH... 106 C2
Bonin PL 67 B5
Bonn D.......80 B3
Bonnånaro I .. 178 B2
Bonnåsjøen
N.......... 194 C6
Bonnat F...... 116 A1
Bonndorf D... 106 B3
Bonnétable F . 102 A2
Bonnétage F .. 106 B1
Bonneuil-
les-Eaux F......90 B2

Bonneuil-Matours
F............. 115 B4
Bonneval F.... 103 A3
Bonneval-sur-Arc
F............. 119 B4
Bonneville F . 118 A3
Bonnières-sur-
Seine F.........90 B1
Bonnieux F . 131 B4
Bönnigheim D ..93 B5
Bonnyrigg UK...35 C4
Bonny-sur-Loire
F............. 103 B4
Bono
E 145 B4
I 178 B3
Bonorva I..... 178 B2
Bønsnes N 48 B2
Bonyhád H... 125 A4
Boom B 79 A4
Boos F 89 A5
Boostedt D 64 B3
Bootle
Cumbria UK ...36 B3
Merseyside UK . 38 A3
Bopfingen D...94 C2
Boppard D......81 B3
Boqueixón E.. 140 B2
Bor
CZ 95 B4
S 62 A2
SRB 16 C5
TR........... 23 C8
Boran-sur-Oise
F..............90 B2
Borås S.......60 B2
Borba P 155 C3
Borbona I..... 169 A3
Borča SRB 127 C2
Borci BIH..... 139 B4
Borculo NL.....71 B3
Bordány H ... 126 A1
Bordeaux F ... 128 B2
Bordeira P ... 160 B1
Bordesholm D ..64 B3
Borðeyri IS..... 190 B4
Bordighera I .. 133 B3
Bording DK 59 B2
Bordón E..... 153 B3
Bore I 120 C2
Borehamwood
UK 44 B3
Borek Strzeliński
PL...........85 B5
Borek Wielkopolski
PL...........76 C2
Boreland UK ...36 A3
Borello I 135 A5
Borensberg S ..56 B1
Borgafjäll S .. 199 A12
Borgarnes IS .. 190 C4
Borgentreich
D 81 A5
Börger D......71 B4
Borger NL.....71 B3
Borggård S.....56 B1
Borghamn S ...55 B5
Borghetto di Vara
I 134 A2
Borghetto
d'Arróscia I... 133 A3
Borghetto Santo
Spirito I...... 133 A4
Borgholm S....62 B4
Borghorst D ...71 B4
Bórgia I 175 C2
Borgloon B.....79 B5
Børglum DK....58 A2
Borgo F...... 180 A2
Borgo alla Collina
I 135 B4
Borgo a Mozzano
I 134 B3
Borgoforte I .. 121 B3
Borgofranco
d'Ivrea I..... 119 B4
Borgomanero
I 119 B5
Borgomasino
I 119 B4
Borgonovo Val
Tidone I...... 120 B2
Borgo Pace I .. 135 B5
Borgorose I ... 169 A3
Borgo San
Dalmazzo I .. 133 A3
Borgo San Lorenzo
I 135 B4
Borgosésia I .. 119 B5
Borgo Val di Taro
I 134 A2
Borgo Valsugana
I 121 A4

Borgo Vercelli
I 119 B5
Borgstena S.....60 B3
Borgue UK......36 B2
Borgund N.....47 A4
Borgvik S.....55 A3
Borja E........ 144 C2
Bork D 80 A3
Borken D......80 A2
Borkenes N ... 194 B7
Borkowice PL...87 A4
Borkowo PL....77 B5
Borkum D......71 A3
Borlänge S....50 B2
Borlu TR...... 186 D3
Bormes-les-
Mimosas F ... 132 B2
Bórmio I..... 107 C5
Bormujos E ... 161 B3
Borna D........83 A4
Borne NL......71 B3
Bornes P..... 149 A2
Borne Sulinowo
PL...........68 B1
Bornheim D....80 B2
Bornhöved D ...64 B3
Börnicke D.....74 B1
Bornos E..... 162 B2
Borobia E..... 152 A2
Borodino RUS...9 E9
Borohrádek CZ ..85 B4
Boronów PL....86 B2
Bórore I 178 B2
Boroszów PL...86 B2
Borota I....... 126 A1
Boroughbridge
UK 40 A2
Borovany CZ ...96 C2
Borovichi RUS...9 C8
Borovnica
SLO 123 B3
Borovo HR ... 125 B4
Borovsk RUS... 9 E10
Borovy CZ 96 B1
Borowa PL....85 A5
Borox E 151 B4
Borrby S.......66 A3
Borre
DK 65 B5
N............. 54 A1
Borredá E..... 147 B2
Borrenes E.... 141 B4
Borriol E 159 A3
Borris
DK 59 C1
IRL 30 B2
Borris-in-Ossory
IRL 28 B4
Borrisokane IRL 28 B3
Borrisoleigh
IRL 28 B4
Borrowdale UK .36 B3
Børrud N......49 C4
Borşa RO......17 B6
Borsdorf D......83 A4
Børselv N..... 193 B9
Borsfa H 111 C3
Borský Mikuláš
SK............98 C1
Borsodivánka
H............. 113 B4
Borsodnádasd
H............. 113 A4
Börte N........53 A3
Borth UK......39 B2
Bort-les-Orgues
F............. 116 B2
Börtnan S..... 199 C10
Børtnes N.....47 B6
Borup DK 61 D1
Boryslav UA ... 13 D5
Boryspil UA 13 C9
Boryszyn PL....75 B4
Borzęciczki PL ..85 A5
Borzęcin PL....77 B5
Borzonasca I .. 134 A2
Borzyszkowy
PL...........68 A2
Borzytuchom
PL...........68 A2
Bosa I 178 B2
Bosáca SK......98 C1
Bosanci HR.... 123 B4
Bosanska Krupa
BIH........... 124 C2
Bosanski Petrovac
BIH........... 124 C2
Bosansko Grahovo
BIH........... 138 A2
Bošany SK......98 C2
Bösárkány H .. 111 B4
Bosau D........65 B3

Bósca H 112 C3
Boscastle UK...42 B2
Bosco I........ 120 C1
Bosco
Chiesanuova I 121 B4
Bösdorf D......65 B3
Bösel D 71 A4
Bosham UK....44 C3
Bösingfeld D...72 B2
Bosjön S 49 C5
Boskoop NL.....70 B1
Boskovice CZ ...97 B4
Bošnjaci HR .. 125 B4
Bošnjane SRB . 127 D3
Bossast E 145 B4
Bossolasco I .. 133 A4
Boston UK.....41 C3
Bostrak N......53 B4
Böszénfa H ... 125 A3
Bot E 153 A4
Botajica BIH... 125 C4
Bote UK........36 B3
Boticas P..... 148 A2
Botilsäter S ...55 A4
Botngård N... 198 B6
Botoš SRB.... 126 B2
Botoșani RO ... 17 B7
Botricello I ... 175 C2
Botsmark S ... 200 B6
Bottendorf D ...81 A4
Bottesford UK...40 C3
Botnaryd S.....60 B3
Bottrop D......80 A2
Botunje SRB.. 127 C3
Bötzingen D . 106 A2
Bouaye F..... 101 B4
Bouça P...... 149 A2
Boucau F..... 128 C1
Bouchain F.....78 B3
Bouchoir F.....90 B2
Boudreville F . 105 B3
Boudry CH... 106 C1
Bouesse F.... 103 C3
Bouguenais F . 101 B4
Bouhy F...... 104 B2
Bouillargues
F............. 131 B3
Bouillon B 91 B5
Bouilly F...... 104 A2
Bouin F 114 B2
Boulay-Moselle
F..............92 B2
Boulazac F.... 129 A3
Boule-d'Amont
F............. 146 B3
Bouligny F.....92 B1
Boulogne-sur-
Gesse F 145 A4
Boulogne-sur-Mer
F..............78 B1
Bouloire F.... 102 B2
Bouquemaison
F..............78 B2
Bourbon-Lancy
F............. 104 C2
Bourbon-
l'Archambault
F............. 104 C2
Bourbonne-les-
Bains F 105 B4
Bourbourg F ...78 B2
Bourbriac F... 100 A2
Bourcefranc-le-
Chapus F.... 114 C2
Bourdeaux F . 131 A4
Bouresse F.... 115 B4
Bourg F...... 128 A2
Bourg-Achard
F..............89 A4
Bourganeuf F . 116 B1
Bourg-Argental
F............. 117 B4
Bourg-de-Péage
F............. 117 B5
Bourg-de-Thizy
F............. 117 A4
Bourg-de-Visa
F............. 129 B3
Bourg-en-Bresse
F............. 118 A2
Bourg-et-Comin
F..............91 B3
Bourg-Lastic F 116 B2
Bourg-Madame
F............. 146 B2
Bourgneuf-en-Retz
F............. 114 A2
Bourgogne F...91 B4
Bourgoin-Jallieu
F............. 118 B2

Bourg-St Andéol
F............. 131 A3
Bourg-St Maurice
F............. 119 B3
Bourgtheroulde
F..............89 A4
Bourgueil F ... 102 B2
Bourmont F ... 105 A4
Bourne UK.....40 C3
Bournemouth
UK 43 B5
Bourneville F ..89 A4
Bournezeau F . 114 B2
Bourran F 129 B3
Bourret F 129 C4
Bourron-Marlotte
F..............90 C2
Bourton-on-the-
Water UK....44 B2
Boussac F..... 116 A2
Boussens F.... 145 A4
Boutersem B....79 B4
Bouttencourt F .90 B1
Bouvières F .. 131 A4
Bouvron F 101 B4
Bouxwiller F 93 C3
Bouzas E..... 140 B2
Bouzonville F ...92 B2
Boval 175 D1
Bovalino Marina
I 175 C2
Bovallstrand S ..54 B2
Bova Marina I . 175 D1
Bovec SLO 122 A2
Bóveda E..... 141 B3
Bóvegno I.... 120 B3
Bovenau D.....64 B2
Bovenden D ...82 A1
Bøverdal N... 198 D5
Boves F........90 B2
Bóves I........ 133 A3
Bovey Tracey
UK 43 B3
Bovino I...... 171 B3
Bovolenta I ... 121 B4
Bovolone I ... 121 B4
Bowes UK.....37 B5
Bowmore UK...34 C1
Bowness-on-
Windermere
UK 36 B4
Box UK.........43 A4
Boxberg
Baden-
Württemberg
D 94 B1
Sachsen D 84 A2
Boxholm S.....55 B6
Boxmeer NL....80 A1
Boxtel NL......79 A5
Boyabat TR....23 A8
Boyalıca TR . 187 B4
Boyle IRL......26 C2
Bozan TR..... 187 C6
Bozava HR 137 A3
Bozburun TR . 188 C3
Bozdoğan TR . 188 B3
Bozcaada TR . 186 C1
Bozdoğan TR . 188 B3
Bože pole Wielkie
PL...........68 A2
Boževac SRB . 127 C3
Božice CZ......97 C4
Boži Dar CZ ...83 B4
Bozkır TR..... 189 B7
Bozouls F..... 130 A1
Bozova TR ... 189 B5
Bozüyük TR... 187 C5
Bózzolo I..... 121 B3
Bra I 119 C4
Braås S........62 A3
Brabrand DK...59 B3
Bracadale UK ..31 B2
Bracciano I.... 168 A2
Bracieux F 103 B3
Bräcke S 199 C12
Brackenheim D .93 B5
Brackley UK....44 A2
Bracklin IRL....27 C4
Bracknell UK...44 B3
Braco UK......35 B4
Brad RO......16 B5
Bradford UK...40 B2
Bradford on Avon
UK 43 A4
Bradina BIH... 139 B4
Brådland N.....52 B2
Brae UK........33 A5
Braemar UK....32 D3
Braemore UK .. 32 D1

Braga P 148 A1
Bragança P ... 149 A3
Bräila RO......17 C7
Braine F........91 B3
Braine-le-Comte
B..............79 B4
Braintree UK...45 B4
Braives B......79 B5
Brake D........72 A1
Brakel
B..............79 B3
D 81 A5
Bräkne-Hoby S .63 B3
Brålanda S....54 B3
Brallo di Pregola
I 120 C2
Bram F 146 A3
Bramafan F .. 132 B2
Bramberg am
Wildkogel A . 109 B3
Bramdrupdam
DK 59 C2
Bramming DK...59 C1
Brampton UK ...37 B4
Bramsche D....71 B4
Branca I....... 136 B1
Brancaleone
Marina I..... 175 D2
Brancaster UK ..41 C4
Brand
Nieder Östereich
A 96 C3
Vorarlberg A .. 107 B4
Brandbu N.....48 B2
Brande DK....59 C2
Brande-
Hornerkirchen
D 64 C2
Brandenberg
A 108 B2
Brandenburg D 73 B5
Brand-Erbisdorf
D 83 B5
Brandis D......83 A4
Brando F..... 180 A2
Brandomil E .. 140 A2
Brandon UK...45 A4
Brandshagen D 66 B2
Brandýs nad Labem
CZ 84 B2
Braničevo
SRB 127 C3
Braniewo PL ...69 A4
Branik SLO ... 122 B2
Brankovina
SRB 127 C1
Branky CZ......98 B1
Branne F..... 128 B2
Brannenburg-
Degerndorf
D 108 B3
Brantôme F .. 115 C4
Branzi I 120 A2
Bras d'Asse F . 132 B2
Braskereidfoss
N.............48 B3
Braslaw BY.....13 A7
Braşov RO.....17 C6
Brasparts F .. 100 A2
Brassac F..... 130 B1
Brassac-les-Mines
F............. 116 B3
Brasschaat B...79 A4
Brastad S......54 B2
Břasy CZ......96 B1
Braszewice PL...86 A2
Bratislava SK.. 111 A4
Brattforsen S...55 A5
Brattvåg N... 198 C3
Bratunac BIH.. 127 C1
Braubach D....81 B3
Braunau A.....95 C5
Braunfels D....81 B4
Braunlage D ...82 A2
Braunsbedra D .83 A3
Braunschweig
D 73 B3
Bray IRL......30 A2
Bray Dunes F ..78 A2
Bray-sur-Seine
F..............90 C3
Bray-sur-Somme
F..............90 B2
Brazatortas E . 157 B3
Brazey-en-Plaine
F............. 105 B4
Brbinj HR 137 A4
Brčko BIH.... 125 C4
Brdani SRB.. 127 D2
Brdów PL......76 B3

Brea de Tajo E 151 B4
Brécev F 88 B2
Brechen D 81 B4
Brechin UK 35 B5
Brecht B 79 A4
Brecketfeld D 80 A3
Břeclav CZ 97 C4
Brecon UK 39 C3
Brécy F 103 B4
Breda
E 147 C3
NL 79 A4
Bredaryd S 60 B3
Bredbyn S 200 C4
Breddin D 73 B5
Bredebro DK 64 A1
Bredelar D 81 A4
Bredenfelde D 74 A2
Bredsjö S 50 C1
Bredstedt D 64 B1
Bredsten DK 59 C2
Bredträsk S 200 C4
Bredviken S 195 D5
Bree B 80 A1
Bregana HR 123 B4
Breganze I 121 B4
Bregenz A 107 B4
Bréhal F 88 B2
Brehna D 83 A4
Breiðdalsvík
IS 191 C11
Breidenbach F 93 B3
Breil-sur-Roya
F 133 B3
Breisach D 106 A2
Breitenbach
CH 106 B2
D 81 B5
Breitenberg D 96 C1
Breitenfelde D 73 A3
Breitengussbach
D 94 B2
Breivikbotn N 192 B6
Brejning DK 59 C2
Brekke N 46 A2
Brekken N 199 C8
Brekkestø N 53 B4
Brekkvasselv
N 199 A10
Brekstad N 198 B6
Breland N 53 B3
Bremanger N 198 D1
Bremen D 72 A1
Bremerhaven
D 72 A1
Bremervörde
D 72 A2
Bremgarten
CH 106 B3
Bremsnes N 198 B4
Brem-sur-Mer
F 114 B2
Brenderup DK 59 C2
Brenes E 162 A2
Brengova SLO 110 C2
Brenna PL 98 B2
Breno I 120 B3
Brénod F 118 A2
Brensbach D 93 B4
Brentwood UK 45 B4
Brescello I 121 C3
Bréscia I 120 B3
Breskens NL 79 A3
Bresles F 90 B2
Bresnica SRB 127 D2
Bressana I 120 B2
Bressanone I 108 C2
Bressuire F 102 C1
Brest
BY 13 B5
F 100 A1
HR 122 B2
Brestač SRB 127 C1
Brestanica
SLO 123 A4
Brestova HR 123 B3
Brestovac HR 125 B3
Bretenoux F 129 B4
Breteuil
Eure F 89 B4
Oise F 90 B2
Brétigny-
sur-Orge F 90 C2
Bretten D 93 B4
Bretteville-sur-
Laize F 89 A3
Brettheim D 94 B2
Breuil-Cervínia
I 119 B4
Breukelen NL 70 B2
Brevik
N 53 A5
Stockholm S 57 A4
Brevik *continued*
Västra Götaland
S 55 B5
Breza BIH 139 A4
Brežice SLO 123 B4
Bréziers F 132 A2
Breznica HR 124 A2
Breznica Našička
HR 125 B4
Březnice CZ 96 B1
Brezno SK 99 C3
Brezolles F 89 B5
Březová nad
Svitavou CZ 97 B4
Brezová pod
Bradlom SK 98 C1
Brezovica
SK 99 B4
SLO 123 A3
Brezovo Polje Selo
BIH 125 C4
Briançon F 118 C3
Brianconnet F 132 B2
Briare F 103 B4
Briatexte F 129 C4
Briático I 175 C2
Briaucourt F 105 A4
Bribir HR 123 B3
Bricquebec F 88 A2
Bridgend
Argyll & Bute
UK 34 C1
Bridgend UK 39 C3
Bridge of Cally
UK 35 B4
Bridge of Don
UK 33 D4
Bridge of Earn
UK 35 B4
Bridge of Orchy
UK 34 B3
Bridgnorth UK 39 B4
Bridgwater UK 43 A4
Břidličná CZ 98 B1
Bridlington UK 41 A3
Bridport UK 43 B4
Briec F 100 A1
Brie-Comte-Robert
F 90 C2
Brienne-le-Château
F 91 C4
Brienon-sur-
Armançon F 104 B2
Brienz CH 106 C3
Brienza I 172 B1
Briesen D 74 B3
Brieskow
Finkenheerd
D 74 B3
Brietlingen D 72 A3
Brieva de Cameros
E 143 B4
Briey F 92 B1
Brig CH 119 A5
Brigg UK 40 B3
Brighouse UK 40 B2
Brightlingsea
UK 45 B5
Brighton UK 44 C3
Brignogan-Plage
F 100 A1
Brignoles F 132 B2
Brigstock UK 40 C3
Brihuega E 151 B5
Brijuni HR 122 C2
Brillon-en-Barrois
F 91 C5
Brilon D 81 A4
Brimnes N 46 B3
Brinches P 160 A2
Bríndisi I 173 B3
Brinje HR 123 B4
Brinon-sur-Beuvron
F 104 B2
Brinon-sur-Sauldre
F 103 B4
Brinyan UK 33 B3
Brión E 140 B2
Briones E 143 B4
Brionne F 89 A4
Brioude F 117 B3
Brioux-sur-
Boutonne F 115 B3
Briouze F 89 B3
Briscous F 144 A2
Brisighella I 135 A4
Brissac-Quincé
F 102 B1
Brissago CH 120 A1
Bristol UK 43 A4
Brive-la-Gaillarde
F 129 A4
Briviesca E 143 B3
Brixham UK 43 B3
Brixlegg A 108 B2
Brjánslækur IS 190 B2
Brka BIH 125 C4
Brnaze HR 138 B2
Brněnec CZ 97 B4
Brno CZ 97 B4
Bro S 57 A3
Broadclyst UK 43 B3
Broadford
IRL 28 B3
UK 31 B3
Broad Haven
UK 39 C1
Broadstairs UK 45 B5
Broadstone UK 43 B4
Broadway UK 44 A2
Broager DK 64 B2
Broaryd S 60 B3
Broby S 61 C4
Brobyværk DK 59 C3
Bročanac BIH 138 B3
Brocas F 128 B2
Brock D 71 B4
Brockel D 72 A2
Brockenhurst
UK 44 C2
Broczyno PL 75 A5
Brod
BIH 125 B3
NMK 182 B3
Brodalen S 54 B2
Broddbo S 50 C3
Brodek u Přerova
CZ 98 B1
Broden-bach D 80 B3
Brodick UK 34 C2
Brod na Kupi
HR 123 B3
Brodnica PL 69 B4
Brodnica Graniczna
PL 68 A3
Brodowe Łąki
PL 77 A6
Brody
Lubuskie PL 75 B4
Lubuskie PL 84 A2
Mazowieckie
PL 77 B5
UA 13 C6
Broglie F 89 B4
Brójce PL 75 B4
Brokind S 56 B1
Brolo I 177 A3
Brome D 73 B3
Bromley UK 45 B4
Bromölla S 63 B2
Bromont-Lamothe
F 116 B2
Brömsebro S 63 B3
Bromsgrove
UK 44 A1
Bromyard UK 39 B4
Bronchales E 152 B2
Bronco E 149 B3
Brønderslev
DK 58 A2
Broni I 120 B2
Brønnøysund
N 195 E3
Brøns DK 59 C1
Bronte I 177 B3
Bronzani Mejdan
BIH 124 C2
Bronzolo I 121 A4
Broons F 101 A3
Broquies F 130 A1
Brora UK 32 C3
Brørup DK 59 C2
Brösarp S 63 C2
Brossac F 115 C3
Brostrud N 47 B5
Brotas P 154 C2
Brötjärna S 50 B2
Broto E 145 B3
Brottby S 57 A4
Brøttum N 48 A2
Brou F 103 A3
Brouage F 114 C2
Brough UK 37 B4
Broughshane
UK 27 B4
Broughton UK 35 C4
Broughton-in-
Furness UK 36 B3
Broumov CZ 85 B4
Broût-Vernet
F 116 A3
Brouvelieures
F 106 A1
Brouwershaven
NL 79 A3
Brovary UA 13 C9
Brovst DK 58 A2
Brownhills UK 40 C2
Brozas E 155 B4
Brozzo I 120 B3
Brtnice CZ 97 B3
Brtonigla HR 122 B2
Bruay-la-Buissière
F 78 B2
Bruchhausen-
Vilsen D 72 B2
Bruchsal D 93 B4
Bruck D 95 B4
Brück D 74 B1
Bruck an der
Grossglockner-
strasse A 109 B3
Bruck an der Leitha
A 111 A3
Bruck an der Mur
A 110 B2
Brückl A 110 C1
Bruckmühl D 108 B2
Brue-Auriac F 132 B1
Brüel D 65 C4
Bruen CH 107 C3
Bruère-Allichamps
F 103 C4
Bruff IRL 29 B3
Bruflat N 47 B6
Brugg CH 106 B3
Brugge B 78 A3
Brüggen D 80 A2
Brühl D 80 B2
Bruinisse NL 79 A4
Brûlon F 102 B1
Brumano I 120 B2
Brumath F 93 C3
Brummen NL 70 B3
Brumov-Bylnice
CZ 98 B2
Brumunddal N 48 B2
Brunau D 73 B4
Brunehamel F 91 B4
Brünen D 80 A2
Brunete E 151 B3
Brunflo S 199 B11
Brunico I 108 C2
Brunkeberg N 53 A4
Brunn D 74 A2
Brunnen CH 107 C3
Brunsbüttel D 64 C2
Brunssum NL 80 B1
Bruntál CZ 98 B1
Brušane HR 137 A4
Brusasco I 119 B5
Brusio CH 120 A3
Brusno SK 99 C3
Brusque F 130 B1
Brussels = Bruxelles
B 79 B4
Brusson I 119 B4
Brüssow D 74 A3
Brusy PL 68 B2
Bruton UK 43 A4
Bruvno HR 138 A1
Bruvoll N 48 B3
Bruxelles = Brussels
B 79 B4
Bruyères F 106 A1
Bruz F 101 A4
Bruzaholm S 62 A3
Brwinów PL 77 B5
Brynamman UK 39 C3
Bryncrug UK 39 B2
Bryne N 52 B1
Brynmawr UK 39 C3
Bryrup DK 59 B2
Brzeg PL 85 B5
Brzeg Dolny PL 85 A4
Brześć Kujawski
PL 76 B3
Brzesko PL 99 B4
Brzeszcze PL 99 B3
Brzezie PL 68 B1
Brzeziny
Łódzkie PL 87 A3
Wielkopolskie
PL 86 A2
Brzeźnica PL 84 A3
Brzeżnica Nowa
PL 86 A3
Brzeżno PL 75 A4
Brzotin SK 99 C4
Brzozie Lubawskie
PL 69 B4
Bua S 60 B2
Buarcos P 148 B1
Buaveg N 52 A1
Bubbio I 119 C5
Bubry F 100 B2
Buca TR 188 A2
Bucak TR 189 B5
Bučany SK 98 C1
Buccheri I 177 B3
Buccino I 172 B1
Bucelas P 154 C1
Buch
Bayern D 94 C2
Bayern D 95 C4
Buchach UA 13 D6
Bucharest =
Bucureşti RO 17 C7
Buchbach D 95 C4
Buchboden A 107 B4
Buchen D 94 B1
Büchen D 73 A3
Buchenberg
D 107 B5
Buchères F 104 A3
Buchholz D 72 A2
Buchloe D 108 A1
Buchlovice CZ 98 B1
Buchlyvie UK 34 B3
Bucholz D 73 A5
Buchs CH 107 B4
Buchy F 89 A5
Bückeburg D 72 B2
Buckfastleigh
UK 42 B3
Buckhaven UK 35 B4
Buckie UK 33 D4
Buckingham
UK 44 A3
Buckley UK 38 A3
Bückwitz D 73 B5
Bučovice CZ 97 B5
Bucsa H 113 B5
Bucureşti =
Bucharest RO 17 C7
Bucy-lés-
Pierrepont F 91 B3
Buczek PL 86 A3
Bud N 198 C3
Budakalasz H 112 B3
Budakeszi H 112 B2
Budal N 199 C7
Budaörs H 112 B2
Budapest H 112 B3
Búðardalur IS 190 B4
Budča SK 99 C3
Buddusò I 178 B3
Bude UK 42 B2
Budeč CZ 97 B3
Büdelsdorf D 64 B2
Budens P 160 B1
Budia E 151 B5
Budimlić-Japra
BIH 124 C2
Büdingen D 81 B5
Budinšćina
HR 124 A2
Budišov CZ 98 B1
Budleigh Salterton
UK 43 B3
Budmerice SK 98 C1
Budoni I 178 B3
Búdrio I 135 A4
Budva MNE 16 D3
Budyně nad Ohří
CZ 84 B2
Budziszewice
PL 87 A3
Budzyń PL 76 B1
Bue N 52 B1
Bueña E 152 B2
Buenache de
Alarcón E 158 B1
Buenache de la
Sierra E 152 B2
Buenaventura
E 150 B3
Buenavista de
Valdavia E 142 B2
Buendia E 151 B5
Bueu E 140 B2
Buezo E 143 B3
Bugac H 112 C3
Bugarra E 159 B3
Bugeat F 116 B1
Buggerru I 179 C2
Bugojno BIH 138 A3
Bugøyfjord
N 193 C13
Bugøynes N 193 C13
Bugyi H 112 B3
Buharkent TR 188 B3
Bühl
Baden-Württemberg
D 93 C4
Bayern D 107 B5
Bühlertal D 93 C4
Bühlertann D 94 B1
Buia I 122 A2
Builth Wells
UK 39 B3
Buin N 47 B6
Buis-les-Baronnies
F 131 A4
Buitenpost NL 70 A3
Buitrago del
Lozoya E 151 B4
Bujalance E 157 C3
Bujaraloz E 153 A3
Buje HR 122 B2
Bujedo E 143 B3
Bük H 111 B3
Buk PL 75 B5
Bükkösd H 125 A3
Bükkzsérc H 113 B4
Bukovci SLO 124 A1
Bukowiec PL 75 B5
Bukowina
Tatrzańska PL 99 B4
Bukownica PL 86 A2
Bukowno PL 86 B3
Bülach CH 107 B3
Búland IS 191 D7
Buldan TR 188 A3
Bulgnéville F 105 A4
Bulgurca TR 188 A2
Bülkau D 64 C1
Bulken N 46 B3
Bulkowo PL 77 B5
Bullas E 164 A3
Bulle CH 106 C2
Büllingen B 80 B2
Bullmark S 200 B6
Bulqizë AL 182 B2
Buna BIH 139 B3
Bunahowen IRL 26 B1
Bunbeg IRL 26 A2
Bunclody IRL 30 B2
Buncrana IRL 27 A3
Bunde D 71 A4
Bünde D 72 B1
Bundoran IRL 26 B2
Bunessan UK 34 B1
Bungay UK 45 A5
Bunge S 57 C5
Bunić HR 123 C4
Bunmahon IRL 30 B1
Bunnyconnellan
IRL 26 B1
Buño E 140 A2
Buñol E 159 B3
Bunratty IRL 29 B3
Bunsbeek B 79 B4
Buñuel E 144 C2
Bunyola E 166 B2
Buonabitácolo
I 172 B1
Buonalbergo I 170 B2
Buonconvento
I 135 B4
Buonvicino I 174 B1
Burano I 122 B1
Burbach D 81 B4
Burcei I 179 C3
Burdons-sur-
Rognon F 105 A4
Burdur TR 189 B5
Bureå S 2 D7
Burela E 141 A3
Büren D 81 A4
Büren an der Aare
CH 106 B2
Burford UK 44 B2
Burg
Cottbus D 84 A2
Magdeburg D 73 B4
Schleswig-Holstein
D 64 C2
Burgas BG 17 D7
Burgau
A 111 B3
D 94 C2
P 160 B1
Burg auf Fehmarn
D 65 B4
Burgbernheim
D 94 B2
Burgdorf
CH 106 B2
D 72 B3
Burgebrach D 94 B2
Bürgel D 83 B3
Burgess Hill UK 44 C3
Burghaslach D 94 B2
Burghausen
D 109 A3
Burghead UK 32 D3
Burgheim D 94 C3
Burgh le Marsh
UK 41 B4
Búrgio I 176 B2
Burgkirchen
D 109 A3
Burgkunstadt
D 82 B3
Burglengenfeld
D 95 B4
Burgo P 148 B1
Burgoberbach
D 94 B2
Burgohondo
E 150 B3
Burgos E 143 B3
Burgsinn D 82 B1
Burgstädt D 83 B4
Burgstall D 73 B4
Burg Stargard
D 74 A2
Burgsvik S 57 C4
Burgui E 144 B3
Burguillos E 162 A2
Burguillos del Cerro
E 155 C4
Burguillos de
Toledo E 151 C4
Burhaniye TR 186 C1
Burhave D 71 A5
Burie F 114 C3
Burjassot E 159 B3
Burk D 94 B2
Burkhardtsdorf
D 83 B4
Burlada E 144 B2
Burladingen
D 107 A4
Burlage D 71 A4
Burness UK 33 B4
Burnham UK 44 B3
Burnham Market
UK 41 C4
Burnham-on-
Crouch UK 45 B4
Burnham-on-Sea
UK 43 A4
Burniston UK 40 A3
Burnley UK 40 B1
Burntisland UK 35 B4
Burón E 142 A1
Buronzo I 119 B5
Burovac SRB 127 C3
Burow D 74 A2
Burravoe UK 33 A5
Burrel AL 182 B2
Burret F 146 B2
Burriana E 159 B3
Burry Port UK 39 C2
Bürs A 107 B4
Bursa TR 186 B4
Burseryd S 60 B3
Bürstadt D 93 B4
Burton UK 37 B4
Burton Agnes
UK 41 A3
Burton Bradstock
UK 43 B4
Burton Latimer
UK 44 A3
Burton upon
Stather UK 40 B3
Burton upon Trent
UK 40 C2
Burträsk S 200 B6
Burujón E 151 C3
Burwell UK 45 A4
Burwick UK 33 C4
Bury UK 40 B1
Bury St Edmunds
UK 45 A4
Burzenin PL 86 A2
Busachi I 179 B2
Busalla I 134 A1
Busana I 134 A3
Busano I 119 B4
Busca I 133 A3
Busch D 73 B4
Buševec HR 124 B2
Bushat AL 182 B1
Bushey UK 44 B3
Bushmills UK 27 A4
Bušince SK 112 A3
Buskhyttan S 56 B2
Busko-Zdrój PL 87 B4
Busot E 159 C3
Busovača BIH 139 A3
Busquistar E 163 B4
Bussang F 106 B1
Busseto I 120 C3
Bussière-Badil
F 115 C4
Bussière-Poitevine
F 115 B4
Bussolengo I 121 B3
Bussoleno I 119 B4
Bussum NL 70 B2
Busto Arsízio I 120 B1

210 Büs – Car

Büsum D 64 B1
Butera I 177 B3
Butgenbach B . . . 80 B2
Butler's Bridge
IRL 27 B3
Butryny PL 77 A5
Bütschwil CH . 107 B4
Buttermere UK . . 36 B3
Buttevant IRL . . 29 B3
Buttle S 57 C4
Buttstädt D 82 A3
Butzbach D 81 B4
Bützfleth D 72 A2
Bützow D 65 C4
Buxières-les-Mines
F 104 C1
Buxtehude D . . 72 A2
Buxton UK 40 B2
Buxy F 104 C3
Büyükçekmece
TR 186 A3
Büyükkarıştıran
TR 186 A2
Büyükorhan
TR 186 C3
Buzançais F . . . 103 C3
Buzancy F 91 B4
Buzău RO 17 C7
Buzet HR 122 B2
Buziaş RO 126 B3
Buzsák H 111 C4
Buzy F 145 A3
By S 50 B3
Byala BG 17 D6
Byaroza BY 13 B6
Byczyna PL 86 A2
Bydalen S 199 B10
Bydgoszcz PL . . 76 A3
Bygdin N 47 A5
Bygdsiljum S . . 200 B6
Bygland N 53 B3
Byglandsfjord
N 53 B3
Bygstad N 46 A2
Bykhaw BY 13 B9
Bykle N 52 A3
Bylderup-Bov
DK 64 B2
Byrkjedal N . . . 52 B2
Byrkjelo N . . . 198 D3
Byrum DK 58 A3
Byšice CZ 84 B2
Byske S 2 D7
Byškovice CZ . . 98 B1
Bysław PL 76 A2
Bystré CZ 97 B4
Bystřice CZ 96 B2
Bystrice CZ . . . 98 B2
Bystřice nad
Pernštejnem
CZ 97 B4
Bystřice pod
Hostýnem CZ . . 98 B1
Bystrzyca Kłodzka
PL 85 B4
Bytča SK 98 B2
Bytnica PL 75 B4
Bytom PL 86 B2
Bytom Odrzański
PL 85 A3
Bytów PL 68 A2
Byxelkrok S . . . 62 A5
Bzenec CZ 98 C1
Bzince SK 98 C1

C

Çağa TR 187 B7
Cabacos P 154 B2
Cabaj-Čápor
SK 98 C2
Cabana E 140 A2
Cabanac-et-
Villagrains F . 128 B2
Cabañaquinta
E 142 A1
Cabanas P . . . 160 B2
Cabañas del
Castillo E . . . 156 A2
Cabañas de Yepes
E 151 C4
Cabanelles E . . 147 B3
Cabanes E 153 B4
Cabanillas E . . . 144 B2
Čabar HR 123 B3
Cabasse F 132 B2
Cabdella E . . . 146 B2
Cabeceiras de
Basto P 148 A1

Cabeço de Vide
P 155 B3
Cabella Ligure
I 120 C2
Cabeza del Buey
E 156 B2
Cabeza la Vaca
E 161 A3
Cabezamesada
E 151 C4
Cabezarados
E 157 B3
Cabezarrubias del
Puerto E 157 B3
Cabezas del Villar
E 150 B2
Cabezas Rubias
E 161 B2
Cabezón E 142 C2
Cabezón de la Sal
E 142 A2
Cabezón de
Liébana E . . . 142 A2
Cabezuela E . . 151 A4
Cabezuela del Valle
E 149 B4
Cabo de Gata
E 164 C2
Cabo de Palos
E 165 B4
Cabolafuenta
E 152 A1
Cabourg F 89 A3
Cabra
E 163 A3
P 148 B2
Cabrach UK 32 D3
Cábras I 179 C2
Cabreiro P . . . 140 C2
Cabreiros E . . . 140 A3
Cabrejas E . . . 152 B1
Cabrela P 154 C2
Cabrillas E 149 B3
Cabuna HR . . . 125 B3
Čačak SRB 127 D2
Cáccamo I 176 B2
Caccuri I 174 B2
Cacela P 160 B2
Cacém P 154 C1
Cáceres E 155 B4
Cachafeiro E . . 140 B2
Cachopo P . . . 160 B2
Čachtice SK . . . 98 C1
Cacin E 163 A4
Cadafais P 154 C1
Cadalen F 129 C5
Cadalso E 149 B3
Cadaqués E . . . 147 B4
Cadaval P 154 B1
Cadavedo E . . . 141 A4
Čadavica BIH . . 138 A2
Čadca SK 98 B2
Cadéac F 145 B4
Cadelbosco di
Sopra I 121 C3
Cadenazzo
CH 120 A1
Cadenberge D . . 64 C2
Cadenet F 131 B4
Cadeuil F 114 C3
Cádiar E 164 C1
Cadillac F 128 B2
Cádiz E 162 B1
Čadjavica HR . . 125 B3
Cadouin F 129 B3
Cadours F 129 C4
Cadrete E 152 A3
Caen F 89 A3
Caerleon UK . . . 39 C4
Caernarfon UK . . 38 A2
Caerphilly UK . . 39 C3
Caersws UK . . . 39 B3
Cafede P 155 B3
Caggiano I 172 B1
Cagli I 136 B1
Cágliari I 179 C3
Čaglin HR 125 B3
Cagnano Varano
I 171 B3
Cagnes-sur-Mer
F 132 B3
Caher IRL 29 B4
Caherciveen
IRL 29 C1
Caherdaniel
IRL 29 C1
Cahors F 129 B4
Cahul MD 17 C8
Caiazzo I 170 B2

Caion E 140 A2
Cairndow UK . . . 34 B3
Cairnryan UK . . 36 B1
Cairo Montenotte
I 133 A4
Caister-on-Sea
UK 41 C5
Caistor UK 41 B3
Caivano I 170 C2
Cajarc F 129 B4
Čajniče BIH . . . 139 B5
Çakırlar TR . . . 189 C5
Çakmak TR 187 C6
Çal TR 189 A4
Cala E 161 B3
Calabritto I . . 172 B1
Calaceite E . . . 153 B4
Calacuccia F . . 180 A2
Cala d'Or E . . . 167 B3
Calaf E 147 C2
Calafat RO 17 C5
Calafell E 147 C2
Cala Galdana
E 167 B3
Cala Gonone I . . 178 B3
Calahonda
Granada E 163 B4
Málaga E . . . 163 B3
Calahorra E . . . 144 B2
Calais F 78 B1
Cala Llonga E . 166 C1
Calalzo di Cadore
I 109 C3
Cala Millor E . . 167 B3
Calamocha E . . . 152 B2
Calamonte E . . 155 C4
Cala Morell E . . 167 A3
Calanais UK 31 A2
Calañas E 161 B3
Calanda E 153 B3
Calangiánus I . . 178 B3
Călăraşi RO . . . 17 C7
Cala Ratjada E 167 B3
Calascibetta I . . 177 B3
Calasetta I 179 C2
Calasparra I . . 164 A3
Calatafimi I . . . 176 B1
Calatayud E . . . 152 A2
Calatorao E . . . 152 A2
Calau D 84 A1
Calbe D 73 C4
Calcena E 152 A2
Calcinelli I . . . 136 B1
Calco I 120 B2
Caldarola I . . . 136 B2
Caldaro sulla strada
del Vino I . . . 121 A4
Caldas da Rainha
P 154 B1
Caldas de Bo ì
E 145 B4
Caldas de Malavella
E 147 C3
Caldas de Reis
E 140 B2
Caldas de San Jorge
P 148 B1
Caldas de Vizela
P 148 A1
Caldaso de los
Vidrios E 150 B3
Caldbeck UK . . . 36 B3
Caldearenas E 145 B3
Caldelas P 148 A1
Calders E 147 C2
Caldes de Montbui
E 147 C3
Caldicot UK . . . 39 C4
Caldirola I 120 C2
Caledon UK 27 B4
Calella
Barcelona E . . . 147 C3
Girona E . . . 147 C4
Calenzana F . . . 180 A1
Calera de León
E 161 A3
Calera y Chozas
E 150 C3
Caleruega E . . . 143 C3
Caleruela E . . . 150 C2
Cales de Mallorca
E 167 B3
Calestano I . . . 134 A3
Calfsound UK . . 33 B4
Calimera I 173 B4
Calitri I 172 B1
Calizzano I . . . 133 A4
Callac F 100 A2
Callan IRL 30 B1
Callander UK . . . 35 B3
Callas F 132 B2

Calliano
Piemonte I 119 B5
Trentino Alto Adige
I 121 B4
Callington UK . . . 42 B2
Callosa de Ensarriá
E 159 C3
Callosa de Segura
E 165 A4
Callús E 147 C2
Čalma SRB 127 B1
Calmbach D 93 C4
Calne UK 43 A5
Calolziocorte I 120 B2
Calonge E 147 C4
Čalovec SK 112 B1
Calpe E 159 C4
Caltabellotta I 176 B2
Caltagirone I . . 177 B3
Caltanissetta I 177 B3
Caltavuturo I . . 176 B2
Çaltılıbük TR . . 186 C2
Caltojar E 151 A5
Caluire-et-Cuire
F 117 B4
Caluso I 119 B4
Calvello I 172 B1
Calvi F 180 A1
Calviá E 166 B2
Calvinet F 116 C2
Calvisson F . . . 131 B3
Calvörde D 73 B4
Calw D 93 C4
Calzada de
Calatrava E . . 157 B4
Calzada de
Valdunciel E . 150 A2
Calzadilla de los
Barros E 155 C4
Cam UK 43 A4
Camaiore I 134 B3
Camarasa E . . . 145 C4
Camarena E . . . 151 B3
Camarès F 130 B1
Camaret-sur-
Aigues F 131 A3
Camaret-sur-Mer
F 100 A1
Camarillas E . . . 153 B3
Camariñas E . . . 140 A1
Camarma E . . . 151 B4
Camarzana de Tera
E 141 B4
Camas E 162 A1
Camastra I 176 B2
Cambados E . . . 140 B2
Cambarinho P . 148 B1
Camberley UK . . 44 B3
Cambil E 163 A4
Cambligeu F . . . 78 B2
Cambo-les-Bains
F 144 A2
Camborne UK . . . 42 B1
Cambourne UK . 44 A3
Cambrai F 78 B3
Cambridge UK . 45 A4
Cambrils E 147 C2
Cambs D 65 C4
Camburg D 83 A3
Camden UK 44 B3
Cameleño E . . . 142 A2
Camelford UK . . . 42 B2
Çameli TR 189 B4
Camelle E 140 A1
Camerano I . . . 136 B2
Camerino I 136 B2
Camerota I 172 B1
Camigliatello
Silano I 174 B2
Caminha P 148 A1
Caminomorisco
E 149 B3
Caminreal E . . . 152 B2
Camisano Vicentino
I 121 B4
Camlıdere TR . . 187 B7
Cammarata I . . . 176 B2
Camogli I 134 A2
Camors F 100 B3
Camp IRL 29 B2
Campagna I . . . 172 B1
Campagnano di
Roma I 168 A2
Campagnático
I 135 C4
Campan F 145 A4
Campana I 174 B2
Campanario E . . 156 B2
Campanillas E . 163 B3
Campano E . . . 162 B1
Campaspero
E 151 A3

Campbeltown
UK 34 C2
Campello E . . . 165 A4
Campelos P . . . 154 B1
Campi Bisénzio
I 135 B4
Campico López
E 165 B3
Campíglia
Maríttima I . . . 134 B3
Campillo de
Altobuey E . . . 158 B2
Campillo de
Aragón E 152 A2
Campillo de Arenas
E 163 A4
Campillo de Llerena
E 156 B2
Campillos E . . . 162 A3
Câmpina RO 17 C6
Campi Salentina
I 173 B4
Campli I 136 C2
Campo E 145 B4
Campobasso I . 170 B2
Campobello di
Licata I 176 B2
Campobello di
Mazara I 176 B1
Campo da Feira
E 140 A3
Campodársego
I 121 B4
Campo de Bacerros
E 141 B3
Campo de Caso
E 142 A1
Campo de Criptana
E 157 A4
Campodolcino
I 120 A2
Campofelice di
Roccella I . . . 176 B2
Campofiorito
I 176 B2
Campofórmido
I 122 A2
Campofranco
I 176 B2
Campofrio E . . 161 B3
Campogalliano
I 121 C3
Campo Ligure
I 133 A4
Campolongo
I 109 C3
Campo Lugar
E 156 A2
Campo Maior
P 155 B3
Campomanes
E 141 A5
Campomarino
I 170 B3
Campo Molino
I 133 A3
Campomono
F 180 B1
Campo Real E . 151 B4
Camporeale I . 176 B2
Camporeggiano
I 136 B1
Camporrells E . 145 C4
Camporrobles
E 158 B2
Campos P 148 A2
Camposa P . . . 148 A1
Camposampiero
I 121 B4
Camposanto I . 121 C4
Campos del Port
E 167 B3
Camposines E . 153 A4
Campotéjar E . 163 A4
Campotosto I . 169 A3
Campo Túres
I 108 C2
Camprodón I . . 147 B3
Campsegret F . 129 B3
Camrose UK 39 C1
Camuñas E 157 A4
Çamyolu TR . . . 189 C7
Çan TR 186 B2
Cana I 135 C4
Cañada del Hoyo
E 158 B2
Cañadajuncosa
E 158 B1
Cañada Rosal
E 162 A2

Canales
Asturias E 141 B5
Castellón de la
Plana E 159 B3
Canals E 159 C3
Canal San Bovo
I 121 A4
Cañamares E . . . 152 B1
Cañamero E . . . 156 A2
Cañar E 163 B4
Cañete la Real
E 162 B2
Cañaveral E . . . 155 B4
Cañaveral de León
E 161 B3
Cañaveras E . . . 152 B1
Cañaveruelas
E 151 B5
Canazei I 108 C2
Cancale F 88 B2
Cancellara I . . . 172 B1
Cancello ed Arnone
I 170 B2
Cancon F 129 B3
Candamil E . . . 140 A3
Candanchu E . . . 145 B3
Candas E 141 A5
Candasnos E . . . 153 A4
Candé F 101 B4
Candela I 172 A1
Candelario E . . 150 B2
Candeleda E . . 150 B2
Cándia Lomellina
I 120 B1
Candide
Casamazzagno
I 109 C3
Candin E 141 B4
Candosa P 148 B2
Canecas P 154 C1
Canelli I 119 C5
Canena E 157 B4
Canencia E . . . 151 B4
Canero E 141 A4
Canet F 130 B2
Canet de Mar
E 147 C3
Canet d'en
Berenguer E . 159 B3
Cañete E 158 A2
Cañete de las
Torres E 163 A3
Canfranc E . . . 145 B3
Cangas
Lugo E 141 A3
Pontevedra E . 140 B2
Cangas de Narcea
E 141 A4
Cangas de Onís
E 142 A1
Canha P 154 C2
Canhestros P . . 160 A1
Canicatti I 176 B2
Canicattini Bagni
I 177 B4
Canicosa de la
Sierra E 143 C3
Caniles E 164 B2
Canillas de
Aceituno E . . . 163 B3
Canino I 168 A1
Canisy F 88 A2
Cañizal E 150 A2
Cañizo E 150 A2
Canjáyar E . . . 164 C2
Çankırı TR 23 A7
Cannai I 179 C2
Cannara I 136 B1
Cánnero Riviera
I 120 A1
Cannes F 132 B3
Canneto
Sicilia I 177 A3
Toscana I . . . 135 B3
Canneto sull'Oglio
I 120 B3
Cannich UK . . . 32 D2
Cannóbio I . . . 120 A1
Cannock UK . . . 40 C1
Canonbie UK . . . 36 A4
Canosa di Púglia
I 171 B4
Can Pastilla E . 166 B2
C'an Picafort
E 167 B3
Cantalapiedra
E 150 A2
Cantalejo E . . . 151 A4
Cantalgallo E . 161 A3

Cantalice I 169 A2
Cantalpino E . . 150 A2
Cantalupo in
Sabina I 168 A2
Cantanhede P . 148 B1
Cantavieja E . . . 153 B3
Čantavir SRB . . 126 B1
Canterbury UK . . 45 B5
Cantiano I 136 B1
Cantillana E . . . 162 A2
Cantiveros E . . . 150 B3
Cantoria E 164 B2
Cantù I 120 B2
Canvey UK 45 B4
Cany-Barville F . 89 A4
Canyet de Mar
E 147 C3
Caol UK 34 B2
Cáorle I 122 B1
Caorso I 120 B2
Capáccio I 172 B1
Capaci I 176 A2
Capálbio I 168 A1
Capánnori I . . . 134 B3
Caparde BIH . . 139 A4
Caparroso E . . . 144 B2
Capbreton F . . 128 C1
Capdenac-Gare
F 116 C2
Capdepera E . . . 167 B3
Cap-de-Pin F . . . 128 B2
Capel Curig UK . . 38 A3
Capellades E . . . 147 C2
Capena I 168 A2
Capendu F 146 A3
Capestang F . . . 130 B2
Capestrano I . . . 169 A3
Cap Ferret F . . . 128 B1
Capileira I 163 B4
Capinha P 148 B2
Ca'Pisani I 122 C1
Capistrello I . . . 169 B3
Capizzi I 177 B3
Čaplje BIH 124 C2
Čapljina BIH . . . 139 B3
Capo di Ponte
I 120 A3
Caposile I 122 B1
Capoterra I . . . 179 C2
Cappamore IRL . 29 B3
Cappeln D 71 B5
Cappoquin IRL . . 29 B4
Capracotta I . 169 B4
Capránica I . . . 168 A2
Caprarola I 168 A2
Capretta I 135 C5
Capri I 170 C2
Capriati a Volturno
I 170 B2
Caprino Veronese
I 121 B3
Captieux F 128 B2
Cápua I 170 B2
Capurso I 173 A2
Capvern F 145 A4
Carabaña E . . . 151 B4
Carabias E 151 A4
Caracal RO 17 C6
Caracenilla E . . 152 B1
Caráglio I 133 A3
Caraman F 146 A2
Caramánico Terme
I 169 A4
Caranga E 141 A4
Caranguejeira
P 154 B2
Caransebeş RO . . 16 C5
Carapelle I 171 B3
Carasco I 134 A2
Carate Brianza
I 120 B2
Caravaca de la Cruz
E 164 A3
Caravággio I . . 120 B2
Carbajal E 163 B3
Carbajo E 155 B3
Carballeda E . . 140 B3
Carballeda de Avia
E 140 B2
Carballo E 140 A2
Carbis Bay UK . . 42 B1
Carbon-Blanc
F 128 B2
Carbonera de
Frentes E 143 C4
Carboneras E . 164 C3
Carboneras de
Guadazón
E 158 B2
Carbonero el Mayor
E 151 A3
Carboneros E . 157 B4

Carbónia I 179 C2
Carbonin I 108 C3
Čarbonne F ... 146 A2
Carbost UK....31 B2
Carcaboso E .. 149 B3
Carcabuey E .. 163 A3
Carcaixent E ... 159 B3
Carcans F 128 A1
Carcans-Plage
F............. 128 A1
Carção P 149 A3
Carcar E...... 144 B2
Cárcar E..... 133 A4
Carcassonne
F............. 146 A3
Carcastillo E .. 144 B2
Carcedo de Burgos
E............. 143 B3
Carcelén E ... 159 B2
Carcès F...... 132 B2
Carchelejo E .. 163 A4
Çardak
Çanakkale
TR........... 186 B1
Denizli TR.... 189 B4
Cardedeu E ... 147 C3
Cardeña E.... 157 B3
Cardenete E... 158 B2
Cardeñosa E .. 150 B3
Cardeto I..... 175 C1
Cardiff UK....39 C3
Cardigan UK ...39 B2
Cardona E 147 C2
Cardosos P.... 154 B2
Carei RO 16 B5
Carentan F.....88 A2
Carentoir F... 101 B3
Careri I....... 175 C2
Carevdar HR .. 124 A2
Cargèse F..... 180 A1
Carhaix-Plouguer
F............. 100 A2
Caria P....... 148 B2
Cariati I...... 174 B2
Carignan F....91 B5
Carignano I... 119 C4
Cariñena E.... 152 A2
Carini I....... 176 A2
Cariño E...... 140 A3
Carínola I..... 170 B1
Carisbrooke UK 44 C2
Carlabhagh UK. .31 A2
Carlepont F..... 90 B3
Carlet E 159 B3
Carlingford IRL..27 B4
Carlisle UK....36 B4
Carloforte I ... 179 C2
Carlópoli I ... 175 B2
Carlow
D 65 C3
IRL........... 30 B2
Carlton UK....40 C2
Carluke UK....35 C4
Carmagnola I . 119 C4
Carmarthen UK .39 C2
Carmaux F.... 130 A1
Carmena E.... 150 C3
Cármenes E... 142 B1
Carmine I 133 A3
Carmona E.... 162 A2
Carmonita E .. 155 B4
Carmyllie UK...35 B5
Carnac F 100 B2
Carndonagh
IRL........... 27 A3
Carnew IRL..... 30 B2
Carnforth UK...37 B4
Cárnia I...... 122 A2
Carnlough UK...27 B5
Carno UK...... 39 B3
Carnon Plage
F............. 131 B2
Carnota E 140 B1
Carnoustie UK..35 B5
Carnwath UK...35 C4
Carolei I....... 174 B2
Carolinensiel D .71 A4
Carolles F...... 88 B2
Carona I...... 120 A2
Caronía I..... 177 A3
Carovigno I... 173 B3
Carovilli I..... 170 B2
Carpaneto
Piacentino I.. 120 C2
Carpegna I... 135 B5
Carpenédolo I 121 B3
Carpi I....... 121 C3
Carpignano Sésia
I............. 119 B5
Carpineti I 134 A3
Carpineto Romano
I............. 169 B3

Cărpinis RO ... 126 B2
Carpino I...... 171 B3
Carpinone I ... 170 B2
Carpio E...... 150 A2
Carquefou F .. 101 B4
Carqueiranne
F............. 132 B2
Carral E...... 140 A2
Carranque E .. 151 B4
Carrapichana
P............. 148 B2
Carrara I 134 A3
Carraroe IRL....28 A2
Carrascalejo
E............. 156 A2
Carrascosa del
Campo E ... 151 B5
Carratraca E .. 162 B3
Carrazeda de
Ansiães P 148 A2
Carrazedo de
Montenegro
P............. 148 A2
Carrbridge UK . 32 D3
Carregal do Sal
P............. 148 B1
Carreña E 142 A2
Carrick IRL....26 B2
Carrickart IRL..26 A3
Carrickfergus
UK........... 27 B5
Carrickmacross
IRL........... 27 C4
Carrick-on-
Shannon IRL ..26 C2
Carrick-on-Suir
IRL........... 30 B1
Carrigallen IRL ..27 C3
Carrión E..... 161 B3
Carrión de
Calatrava E .. 157 A4
Carrión de los
Condes E.... 142 B2
Carrizo de la Ribera
E............. 141 B5
Carrizosa E... 157 B5
Carro F....... 131 B4
Carrocera E .. 142 B1
Carros F...... 133 B3
Carrouge CH.. 106 C1
Carrouges F....89 B3
Carrù I 133 A3
Carryduff UK...27 B5
Carry-le-Rouet
F............. 131 B4
Carsóli I...... 169 A3
Carsphairn UK ..36 A2
Cartagena E .. 165 B4
Cártama E .. 163 B3
Cartaxo E 154 B2
Cartaya E 161 B2
Caselle Torinese
I............. 119 B4
Casella I...... 134 A2
Caselle Torinese
I............. 119 B4

Casamicciola Terme
I............. 170 C1
Casamozza F.. 180 A2
Casarabonela
E............. 162 B3
Casarano I ... 173 B4
Casar de Cáceres
E............. 155 B4
Casar de Palomero
E............. 149 B3
Casarejos E .. 143 C3
Casares E 162 B2
Casares de las
Hurdes E.... 149 B3
Casariche E .. 163 A3
Casarrubios del
Monte E..... 151 B3
Casas de Don Pedro
E............. 156 A2
Casas de Fernando
Alonso E 158 B1
Casas de Haro
E............. 158 B1
Casas de Juan Gil
E............. 159 B2
Casas del Juan
Núñez E..... 158 B2
Casas del Puerto
E............. 159 C2
Casas del Rio
E............. 159 B2
Casas de Millán
E............. 155 B4
Casas de Reina
E............. 156 B2
Casas de Ves
E............. 159 B2
Casas-Ibáñez
E............. 158 B2
Casas Nuevas
E............. 164 B3
Casasola E ... 150 B3
Casasola de Arión
E............. 150 A2
Casasuertes E. 142 A2
Casatejada E .. 150 C2
Casavieja E ... 150 B3
Casazza I..... 120 B2
Cascais P..... 154 C1
Cascante E... 144 C2
Cascante del Rio
E............. 152 B2
Cáscia I 169 A3
Casciana Terme
I............. 134 B3
Cáscina I..... 134 B3
Cáseda E..... 144 B2
Casekow D.....74 A3
Casella I...... 134 A2
Caselle Torinese
I............. 119 B4
Casemurate I . 135 A5
Casenove I.... 136 C1
Caseres E 153 A4
Caserío Benali
E............. 159 B3
Caserta I...... 170 B2
Casével P 160 B1
Cashel IRL.....29 B4
Casillas E..... 150 B3
Casillas de Coria
E............. 155 B4
Casina I...... 134 A3
Casinos E..... 159 B3
Čáslav CZ.....97 B3
Cásola Valsénio
I............. 135 A4
Cásole d'Elsa
I............. 135 B4
Cásoli I....... 169 A4
Casória I..... 170 C2
Caspe E...... 153 A3
Cassàde la Selva
E............. 147 C3
Cassagnas F . 130 A2
Cassagnes-
Bégonhès F .. 130 A1
Cassano allo Iónio
I............. 174 B2
Cassano d'Adda
I............. 120 B2
Cassano delle
Murge I...... 171 C4
Cassano Magnago
I............. 120 B1
Cassano Spinola
I............. 120 C1
Cassel F....... 78 B2
Cassíbile I..... 177 C4
Cassine I..... 119 C5
Cassino I..... 169 B3
Cassis F..... 132 B1

Cassolnovo I.. 120 B1
Cassuéjouls F . 116 C2
Castá SK 98 C1
Castagnaro I.. 121 B4
Castagneto
Carducci I.... 134 B3
Castagnola
CH........... 120 A1
Castalla E ... 159 C3
Castañar de Ibor
E............. 156 A2
Castanheira de
Pêra P....... 154 A2
Cástano Primo
I............. 120 B1
Castasegna
CH........... 120 A2
Castéggio I.... 120 B2
Casteição P ... 148 B2
Castejón E 144 B2
Castejón de
Monegros E.. 153 A3
Castejón de Sos
E............. 145 B4
Castejón de
Valdejasa E .. 144 C3
Castèl Baronia
I............. 172 A1
Castel Bolognese
I............. 135 A4
Castelbuono I. 177 B3
Casteldáccia I. 176 A2
Castel d'Aiano
I............. 135 A3
Castel d'Ario I. 121 B3
Castel de Cabra
E............. 153 B3
Casteldelfino
I............. 132 A3
Castél del Monte
I............. 169 A3
Castel del Piano
I............. 135 C4
Castel di Iúdica
I............. 177 B3
Castel di Rio I. 135 A4
Castèl di Sangro
I............. 169 B4
Castél di Tora
I............. 169 A2
Castelfidardo
I............. 136 B2
Castelfiorentino
I............. 135 B3
Castelforte I .. 169 B3
Castelfranco Emília
I............. 121 C4
Castelfranco in
Miscano I 170 B3
Castelfranco
Véneto I...... 121 B4
Castèl Frentano
I............. 169 A4
Casteljaloux F 128 B3
Castellabate I. 170 C2
Castellammare del
Golfo I....... 176 A1
Castellammare di
Stábia I 170 C2
Castellamonte
I............. 119 B4
Castellana Grotte
I............. 173 B3
Castellane F... 132 B2
Castellaneta I. 173 B2
Castellaneta
Marina I..... 173 B2
Castellar E ... 157 B4
Castellarano I. 135 A3
Castellar de la
Frontera E .. 162 B2
Castellar de la
Ribera E...... 147 C2
Castél San Pietro
Terme I...... 135 A4
Castellar del Vallés
E............. 147 C3
Castellar de
Santiago E .. 157 B4
Castell Arquato
I............. 120 C2
Castell'Azzara
I............. 135 C4
Castellbell i Villar
E............. 147 C2
Castelldans E . 153 A4
Castell de Cabres
E............. 153 B4
Castell de Castells
E............. 159 C3
Castelldefels
E............. 147 C2
Castell de Ferro
E............. 163 B4
Castelleone I.. 120 B2

Castellet E 147 C2
Castelletto di
Brenzone I... 121 B3
Castellfollit de la
Roca E 147 B3
Castellfollit de
Riubregos E.. 147 C2
Castellfort E .. 153 B3
Castellina in Chianti
I............. 135 B4
Castañar de Ibor
Castellina
Marittima I... 134 B3
Castellóde Farfaña
E............. 145 C4
Castellóde la Plana
E............. 159 B3
Castello
d'Empúries
E............. 147 B4
Castello di Fiemme
I............. 121 A4
Castelloli E... 147 C2
Castellón de Rugat
E............. 159 C3
Castellote E... 153 B3
Castello Tesino
I............. 121 A4
Castellterçol E 147 C3
Castellúcchio
I............. 121 B3
Castellúccio
de'Sáuri I.... 171 B3
Castelluccio
Inferiore I.... 174 B1
Castelmassa I. 121 B4
Castelmáuro I. 170 B2
Castelmoron-sur-
Lot F 129 B3
Castelnaudary
F............. 146 A2
Castelnau-de-
Médoc F 128 A2
Castelnau-de-
Montmirail F. 129 C4
Castelnau-Magnoac
F............. 145 A4
Castelnau-
Montratier F . 129 B4
Castelnovo E.. 153 A3
Castelnovo
ne'Monti I.... 134 A3
Castelnuovo
Berardenga I. 135 B4
Castelnuovo della
Dáunia I...... 170 B3
Castelnuovo di
Garfagnana
I............. 134 A3
Castelnuovo di Val
di Cécina I... 135 B3
Castelnuovo Don
Bosco I....... 119 B4
Castelnuovo Scrivia
I............. 120 C1
Castelo Branco
Bragança P .. 149 A3
Castelo Branco
P............. 155 B3
Castelo de Paiva
P............. 148 A1
Castelo de Vide
P............. 155 B3
Castelo do Neiva
P............. 148 A1
Castelo Mendo
P............. 149 B3
Castelraimondo
I............. 136 B2
Castel San
Gimignano I. 135 B4
Castèl San Giovanni
I............. 120 B2
Castél San Pietro
Terme I...... 135 A4
Castelsantángelo
I............. 136 C2
Castél Sant'Elia
I............. 168 A2
Castelsaraceno
I............. 174 A1
Castelsardo I.. 178 B2
Castelsarrasin
F............. 129 B4
Castelserás E.. 153 B3
Casteltérmini
I............. 176 B2
Castelvecchio
Subéquo I.... 169 A3
Castelvetrano
I............. 176 B1
Castél Volturno
I............. 170 B1
Castenédolo I. 120 B3

Castets F...... 128 C1
Castiádas I.... 179 C3
Castiglioncello
I............. 134 B3
Castiglione I.. 169 A3
Castiglione
Chiavarese I.. 134 A2
Castiglione d'Adda
I............. 120 B2
Castiglione dei
Pepoli I...... 135 A4
Castiglione del
Lago I....... 135 B5
Castiglione della
Pescáia I..... 135 C3
Castiglione delle
Stiviere I..... 121 B3
Castiglione di
Sicília I...... 177 B3
Castiglione d'Órcia
I............. 135 B4
Castiglione Messer
Marino I..... 170 B2
Castiglione Messer
Raimondo I.. 169 A3
Castiglion Fibocchi
I............. 135 B4
Castiglion
Fiorentino I.. 135 B4
Castilblanco E 156 A2
Castilblanco de los
Arroyos E.... 161 B4
Castil de Peones
E............. 143 B3
Castilfrío de la
Sierra E...... 144 C1
Castilgaleu E.. 145 B4
Castilisar E ... 144 B2
Castilleja E ... 161 B3
Castillejar E... 164 B2
Castillejo de Martin
Viejo E 149 B3
Castillejo de
Mesleón E.... 151 A4
Castillejo de
Robledo E.... 151 A4
Castillo de Bayuela
E............. 150 B3
Castillo de Locubín
E............. 163 A4
Castillonès F... 129 B3
Castillon-la-Bataille
F............. 128 B2
Castillon-Len-
Couserans F.. 146 B2
Castillonroy E. 145 C4
Castilruiz E.... 144 C1
Castione CH... 120 A2
Castions di Strada
I............. 122 B2
Castirla F...... 180 A2
Castlebar IRL...28 A2
Castlebellingham
IRL........... 27 C4
Castleblaney
IRL........... 27 B4
Castlebridge
IRL........... 30 B2
Castle Cary UK ..43 A4
Castlecomer
IRL........... 30 B1
Castlederg UK ..27 B3
Castledermot
IRL........... 30 B2
Castle Douglas
UK........... 36 B3
Castleford UK...40 B2
Castleisland IRL 29 B2
Castlemaine
IRL........... 29 B2
Castlemartyr
IRL........... 29 C3
Castlepollard
IRL........... 30 A1
Castlerea IRL...28 A3
Castleton UK...40 B3
Castletown
Highland UK.. 32 C3
Isle of Man UK .36 B2
Castletown
Bearhaven
IRL........... 29 C2
Castletownroche
IRL........... 29 B3
Castlewellan
UK........... 27 B5
Casto I 120 B3
Castrejón E ... 150 A2
Castrelo del Valle
E............. 141 B3
Castres F..... 130 B1
Castricum NL ..70 B1
Castries F 131 B2

Castrignano del
Capo I........ 173 C4
Castril E...... 164 B2
Castrillo de Duero
E............. 151 A4
Castrillo de la Vega
E............. 143 C3
Castrillo de Onielo
E............. 142 C2
Castro
E............. 142 A2
I............. 173 B4
Castrocabón
E............. 141 B5
Castro-Caldelas
E............. 141 B3
Castrocaro Terme
I............. 135 A4
Castrocontrigo
E............. 141 B4
Castro Daire P. 148 B2
Castro dei Volsci
I............. 169 B3
Castro del Río
E............. 163 A3
Castro de Rey
E............. 141 A3
Castrofilippo I 176 B2
Castrogonzaio
E............. 142 B1
Castrojeriz E .. 142 B2
Castro Laboreiro
P............. 140 B2
Castro Marim
P............. 160 B2
Castromonte
E............. 142 C1
Castromudarra
E............. 142 B1
Castronuevo
E............. 142 C1
Castronuño E . 150 A2
Castropol E ... 141 A3
Castroreale I.. 177 A4
Castroserracin
E............. 151 A4
Castro-Urdiales
E............. 143 A3
Castroverde E. 141 A3
Castro Verde
P............. 160 B1
Castroverde de
Campos E.... 142 C1
Castroverde de
Cerrato E..... 142 C2
Castrovillari I.. 174 B2
Castuera E.... 156 B2
Catadau E.... 159 B3
Cataéggio I... 120 A2
Çatalca TR.... 186 A3
Catallar TR.... 189 C5
Çatalzeytin TR .23 A8
Catánia I...... 177 B4
Catanzaro I... 175 C2
Catanzaro Marina
I............. 175 C2
Catarroja E... 159 B3
Catarruchos P. 148 B1
Catcleugh UK ...37 A4
Catenanuova
I............. 177 B3
Caterham UK ...44 B3
Cati E 153 B4
Čatići BIH 139 A4
Catignano I... 169 A3
Catillon F......91 A3
Catoira E..... 140 B2
Caton UK......37 B4
Catral E...... 165 A4
Catterick UK...37 B5
Cáttolica I.... 136 B1
Cáttolica Eraclea
I............. 176 B2
Catton UK.....37 B4
Caudebec-en-Caux
F............. 89 A4
Caudete E.... 159 C3
Caudete de las
Fuentes E.... 159 B2
Caudiel E..... 159 B3
Caudiès-de-
Fenouillèdes
F............. 146 B3
Caudry F......91 A3
Caulkerbush
UK........... 36 B3
Caulnes F..... 101 A3
Caulónia I..... 175 C2
Caumont-l'Evente
F............. 88 A3

Caunes-Minervois
F.............146 A3
Cauro F.......180 B1
Caussade F....129 B4
Causse-de-la-Selle
F.............130 B2
Cauterets F...145 B3
Cava de'Tirreni
I.............170 C2
Cavaglia I.....119 B5
Cavaillon F....131 B4
Cavalaire-sur-Mer
F.............132 B2
Cavaleiro P...160 B1
Cavalese I....121 A4
Cavallermaggiore
I.............119 C4
Cavallino I....122 B1
Cavan IRL.....27 C3
Cavárzere I...121 B5
Çavdarhisar
TR.............187 C4
Çavdır TR....189 B4
Cavernães P..148 B2
Cavezzo I....121 C4
Cavignac F....128 A2
Čavle HR....123 B3
Cavo I........134 C3
Cavour I.....119 C4
Cawdor UK...32 D3
Çay TR........187 D6
Çaycuma TR...187 A7
Cayeux-sur-Mer
F.............78 B1
Cayiralan TR...23 B8
Çayırhan TR...187 B6
Caylus F.....129 B4
Cayres F......117 C3
Cazalilla E....157 C4
Cazalla de
la Sierra E...156 C2
Cazals F.....129 B4
Cazanuecos E.142 B1
Cazaubon F...128 C2
Cazaux F.....128 B1
Cazavet F....146 A2
Cazères F....146 A2
Cazin BIH.....124 C1
Cazis CH.....107 C4
Čazma HR....124 B2
Cazo E.......142 A1
Cazorla E.....164 B2
Cazouls-lès-
Béziers F....130 B2
Cea
León E.......142 B1
Orense E.....140 B3
Ceánuri E....143 A4
Ceauce F......88 B3
Cebolla E....150 C3
Čebovce SK...112 A3
Cebreros E....150 B3
Čečava BIH...125 C3
Ceccano I.....169 B3
Cece H.......112 C2
Cecenowo PL...68 A2
Čechtice CZ....96 B3
Čechtín CZ....97 B3
Cécina I......134 B3
Ceclavín E....155 B4
Cedégolo I....120 A3
Cedeira E....140 A2
Cedillo E.....155 B3
Cedillo del
Condado E...151 B4
Cedrillas E....153 B3
Cedynia PL....74 B3
Cée E........140 B1
Cefalù I......177 A3
Céggia I......122 B1
Cegléd H.....113 B3
Ceglédbercel
H.............112 B3
Céglie
Messápica I..173 B3
Cehegín E....164 A3
Ceilhes-et-
Rocozels F...130 B2
Ceinos de Campos
E.............142 B1
Ceira P......148 B1
Čejč CZ........97 C4
Cekcyn PL....76 A3
Cela BIH......124 C2
Čelákovice
CZ.............84 B2
Celano I......169 A3
Celanova E...140 B3
Celbridge IRL...30 A2
Čelebić BIH...138 B2

Celenza
Valfortore I..170 B2
Čelić BIH......125 C4
Čelinac BIH...124 C3
Celje SLO.....123 A4
Celldömölk H..111 B4
Celle D........72 B3
Celle Ligure I..133 A4
Celles B........79 B4
Celles-sur-Belle
F.............115 B3
Cellino San Marco
I.............173 B3
Celorico da Beira
P.............148 B2
Celorico de Basto
P.............148 A1
Çeltik TR.....187 C6
Çeltikçi TR...189 B5
Cemaes UK.....38 A2
Cembra I.....121 A4
Čemerno BIH..139 B4
Cenad RO.....126 A2
Cencenighe
Agordino I...121 A4
Cenei RO.....126 B2
Ceneselli I....121 B4
Cenicero E....143 B4
Cenicientos E.150 B3
Censeau F....105 C5
Čenta SRB....126 B2
Centallo I....133 A3
Cento I.......121 C4
Centelles E....147 C3
Centúripe I...177 B3
Cepeda la Mora
E.............150 B2
Cépet F......129 C4
Čepin HR.....125 B4
Čepinski Martinci
HR.............125 B4
Cepovan SLO..122 A2
Ceprano I.....169 B3
Čeralije HR...125 B3
Cerami I......177 B3
Cerano I......120 B1
Cérans Foulletourte
F.............102 B2
Ceraso I.....172 B1
Cerbaia I.....135 B4
Cerbère F....146 B4
Cercadillo E...151 A5
Cercal
Lisboa P.....154 B1
Setúbal P....160 B1
Čerčany CZ....96 B2
Cerceda E....151 B4
Cercedilla E...151 B3
Cercemaggiore
I.............170 B2
Cercs E.......147 B2
Cercy-la-Tour
F.............104 C2
Cerda I.......176 B2
Cerdedo E....140 B2
Cerdeira P....148 B2
Cerdon F.....103 B4
Cerea I.......121 B4
Ceres
I.............119 B4
UK.............35 B5
Ceresole-Reale
I.............119 B4
Cereste F.....132 B1
Céret F......146 B3
Cerezo de Abajo
E.............151 A4
Cerezo de Riotirón
E.............143 B3
Cerfontaine B..79 B4
Cergy F........90 B2
Cerignola I...171 B3
Cérilly F.....103 C4
Cerisiers F...104 A2
Cerizay F.....114 B3
Çerkeş TR.....23 A7
Çerkezköy TR.186 A3
Cerkije SLO...123 A3
Cerknica SLO..123 B3
Cerkno SLO...122 A2
Cerkwica PL...67 B4
Cerna HR.....125 B4
Cernavodă RO..17 C8
Cernay F.....106 B2
Cerne Abbas
UK.............43 B4
Cernégula E...143 B3
Cernik HR....124 B3
Cernóbbio I...120 B2
Černošín CZ....95 B4

Cernovice CZ...96 B2
Cérons F......128 B2
Cerovlje HR...123 B3
Cerovo SK.....99 C3
Cerqueto I...135 C5
Cerralbo E....149 B3
Cerreto d'Esi I.136 B1
Cerreto Sannita
I.............170 B2
Cerrigydrudion
UK.............38 A3
Cërrik AL.....182 B1
Cerro Muriano
E.............156 B3
Certaldo I....135 B4
Certosa di Pésio
I.............133 A3
Cerva P......148 A2
Cervaro I.....169 B3
Cervatos de la
Cueza E......142 B2
Červena Řečice
CZ.............97 B3
Červená-Skala
SK.............99 C4
Cervená Voda
CZ.............97 A4
Cerveny Kostelec
CZ.............85 B4
Cervera E....147 C2
Cervera de la
Cañada E....152 A2
Cervera del Llano
E.............158 B1
Cervera del Río
Alhama E....144 B2
Cervera de
Pisuerga E...142 B2
Cervéteri I...168 B2
Cérvia I......135 A5
Cerviáde les
Garrigues E..147 C1
Cervignano del
Friuli I......122 B2
Cervinara I...170 B2
Cervione F....180 A2
Cervo E......141 A3
Cervon F.....104 B2
Cesana Torinese
I.............119 C3
Cesarica HR...137 A4
Cesarò I.....177 B3
Cesena I.....135 A5
Cesenático I..135 A5
Cēsis LV........8 D4
Česká Belá I...97 B3
Česká Kamenice
CZ.............84 B2
Česká Lípa CZ..84 B2
Česká Skalice
CZ.............85 B4
Česká Třebová
CZ.............97 B4
České Budějovice
CZ.............96 C2
České Velenice
CZ.............96 C2
Český Brod CZ..96 A2
Český Dub CZ..84 B2
Český Krumlov
CZ.............96 C2
Český Těšín CZ..98 B2
Česljeva Bara
SRB.............127 C3
Çeşme TR....188 A1
Cessenon F...130 B2
Cesson-Sévigné
F.............101 A4
Cestas F.....128 B2
Čestobrodica
SRB.............127 D2
Cesuras E....140 A2
Cetina E.....152 A2
Cetin Grad HR.123 B4
Cetinje MNE....16 D3
Cetraro I.....174 B1
Ceuti E.......165 A3
Ceva I.......133 A4
Cevico de la Torre
E.............142 C2
Cevico Navero
E.............142 C2
Cevins F.....118 B3
Cévio CH.....119 A5
Cevizli TR....189 B6
Cewice PL.....68 A2
Ceylan TR....189 C4
Ceyrat F.....116 B3
Ceyzériat F...118 A2
Chaam NL......79 A4
Chabanais F..115 C4
Chabeuil F...117 C5
Chabielice PL...86 A3

Chablis F......104 B2
Châbons F....118 B2
Chabówka PL...99 B3
Chabreloche F 117 B3
Chabris F....103 B3
Chagford UK....42 B3
Chagny F.....105 C3
Chagoda RUS....9 C9
Chaherrero E..150 B3
Chailland F.....88 B3
Chaillé-les-Marais
F.............114 B2
Chailles F....103 B3
Chailley F....104 A2
Chalabre F...146 B3
Chalais F....128 A3
Chalamont F..118 B2
Châlette-sur-Loing
F.............103 A4
Chalindrey F..105 B4
Chalkida GR..185 A4
Challacombe
UK.............42 A3
Challans F....114 B2
Challes-les-Eaux
F.............118 B2
Chalmazel F..117 B3
Chalmoux F...104 C2
Chalonnes-sur-
Loire F......102 B1
Châlons-en-
Champagne F..91 C4
Chalon-sur-Saône
F.............105 C3
Chalupy PL.....69 A3
Châlus F.....115 C4
Cham
CH.............106 B3
D.............95 B4
Chambéret F..116 B1
Chambéry F...118 B2
Chambilly F...117 A4
Chambley F....92 B1
Chambly F.....90 B2
Chambois F....89 B4
Chambon-sur-Lac
F.............116 B2
Chambon-sur-
Voueize F....116 A2
Chambord F...103 B3
Chamborigaud
F.............131 A2
Chamboulive
F.............116 B1
Chamerau D...95 B4
Chamonix-Mont
Blanc F......119 B3
Chamoux-sur-
Gelon F......118 B3
Champagnac-le-
Vieux F......117 B3
Champagney
F.............106 B1
Champagnole
F.............105 C4
Champagny-
Mouton F....115 B4
Champaubert F 91 C3
Champdeniers-St
Denis F......114 B3
Champdieu F..117 B4
Champdôtre
F.............105 B4
Champeix F...116 B3
Champéry CH. 119 A3
Champigne F..102 B1
Champignelles
F.............104 B2
Champigny-sur-
Veude F......102 B2
Champlitte-et-le-
Prelot F......105 B4
Champoluc I...119 B4
Champoly F...117 B3
Champorcher
I.............119 B4
Champrond-en-
Gâtine F......89 B5
Champs-sur-
Tarentaine F. 116 B2
Champs-sur-Yonne
F.............104 B2
Chamusca P....154 B2
Chanac F.....130 A2
Chanaleilles F. 117 C3
Chandler's Ford
UK.............44 C2
Chandra GR..185 D7
Chandrexa de
Queixa E....141 B3

Chañe E......150 A3
Changy F.....117 A3
Chania GR....185 D5
Channes F....104 B3
Chantada E...140 B3
Chantelle F...116 A3
Chantenay-
StImbert F...104 C2
Chanteuges F.117 B3
Chantilly F.....90 B2
Chantonnay
F.............114 B2
Chão de Codes
P.............154 B2
Chaource F....104 A3
Chapa E......140 B2
Chapareillan
F.............118 B2
Chapel en le Frith
UK.............40 B2
Chapelle Royale
F.............103 A3
Chapelle-St Laurent
F.............102 C1
Charbonnat F. 104 C3
Chard UK......43 B4
Charenton-du-Cher
F.............103 C4
Charlbury UK...44 B2
Charleroi B......79 B4
Charlestown
IRL.............26 C2
UK.............42 B2
Charlestown of
Aberlour UK...32 D3
Charleville IRL..29 B3
Charleville-
Mézières F....91 B4
Charlieu F....117 A4
Charlottenberg
S.............49 C4
Charlton Kings
UK.............44 B1
Charly F........90 C3
Charmes F.....92 C2
Charmes-sur-
Rhône F......117 C4
Charmey CH.. 106 C2
Charminster
UK.............43 B4
Charmont-en-
Beauce F....103 A4
Charny F.....104 B2
Charolles F...117 A4
Chârost F....103 C4
Charquemont
F.............106 B1
Charrin F.....104 C2
Charroux F...115 B4
Chartres F....90 C1
Charzykow PL..68 B2
Chasseneuil-sur-
Bonnieure F..115 C4
Chassigny F..105 B4
Château-Arnoux
F.............132 A2
Châteaubernard
F.............115 C3
Châteaubourg
F.............101 A4
Châteaubriant
F.............101 B4
Château-Chinon
F.............104 B2
Château-d'Oex
CH.............106 C2
Château-d'Olonne
F.............114 B2
Château-du-Loir
F.............102 B2
Châteaudun
F.............103 A3
Châteaugiron
F.............101 A4
Château-Gontier
F.............102 B1
Château-Landon
F.............103 A4
Château-la-Vallière
F.............102 B2
Château-l'Evêque
F.............129 A3
Châteaulin F.. 100 A1
Châteaumeillant
F.............103 C4
Châteauneuf
Nièvre F....104 B2
Saône-et-Loire
F.............117 A4
Châteauneuf-de-
Randon F....117 C3
Châteauneuf-d'Ille-
et-Vilaine F....88 B2

Châteauneuf-du-
Faou F.......100 A2
Châteauneuf-du-
Pape F.......131 A3
Châteauneuf-en-
Thymerais F....89 B5
Châteauneuf-la-
Forêt F......116 B1
Châteauneuf-le-
Rouge F......132 B1
Châteauneuf-sur-
Charente F...115 C3
Châteauneuf-sur-
Cher F.......103 C4
Châteauneuf-sur-
Loire F......103 B4
Châteauneuf-sur-
Sarthe F.....102 B1
Châteauponsac
F.............115 B5
Château-Porcien
F.............91 B4
Châteauredon
F.............132 A2
Châteaurenard
Bouches du
Rhône F....131 B3
Loiret F.....104 B1
Château-Renault
F.............102 B2
Châteauroux
F.............103 C3
Châteauroux-les-
Alpes F......118 C3
Château-Salins
F.............92 C2
Château-Thierry
F.............91 B3
Châteauvillain
F.............105 A3
Châtel F......119 A3
Châtelaillon-Plage
F.............114 B2
Châtelaudren
F.............100 A3
Châtel-Censoir
F.............104 B2
Châtel-de-Neuvre
F.............104 C2
Châtelet B......79 B4
Châtel-Guyon
F.............116 B3
Châtellerault
F.............115 B4
Châtel-Montagne
F.............117 A3
Châtel-St Denis
CH.............106 C1
Châtel-sur-Moselle
F.............92 C2
Châtelus-Malvaleix
F.............116 A2
Châtenois F...105 A4
Châtenois-les-
Forges F.....106 B1
Chatham UK....45 B4
Châtillon I....119 B4
Châtillon-Coligny
F.............103 B4
Châtillon-en-Bazois
F.............104 B2
Châtillon-en-Diois
F.............118 C2
Châtillon-sur
Chalaronne
F.............117 A4
Châtillon-sur-Indre
F.............103 C3
Châtillon-sur-Loire
F.............103 B4
Châtillon-sur-
Marne F......91 B3
Châtillon-sur-Seine
F.............104 B3
Châtres F.....91 C3
Chatteris UK...45 A4
Chatton UK....37 A5
Chauchina E...163 A4
Chaudes-Aigues
F.............116 C3
Chaudrey F...91 C4
Chauffailles F. 117 A4
Chaulnes F....90 B2
Chaument Gistoux
B.............79 B4
Chaumergy F..105 C4
Chaumont F..105 A4
Chaumont-en-
Vexin F......90 B1
Chaumont-Porcien
F.............91 B4
Chaumont-sur-Aire
F.............91 C5

Chaumont-sur-
Loire F.......103 B3
Chaunay F....115 B4
Chauny F......90 B3
Chaussin F...105 C4
Chauvigny F.. 115 B4
Chavagnes-en-
Paillers F....114 B2
Chavanges F...91 C4
Chaves P.....148 A2
Chavignon F....91 B3
Chazelles-sur-Lyon
F.............117 B4
Chazey-Bons
F.............118 B2
Cheadle
Greater
Manchester
UK.............40 B1
Staffordshire
UK.............40 C2
Cheb CZ........83 B4
Chebsara RUS...9 C11
Checa E......152 B2
Chęciny PL....87 B4
Cheddar UK...43 A4
Cheddleton UK.40 B1
Chef-Boutonne
F.............115 B3
Cheles E......155 C3
Chella E......159 B3
Chelles F......90 C2
Chełm PL......13 C5
Chełmno
Kujawsko-
Pomorskie PL. 76 A3
Wielkopolskie
PL.............76 B3
Chelmsford UK.45 B4
Chelmuzhi RUS..9 A9
Chełmża PL....76 A3
Cheltenham UK 44 B1
Chelva E......159 B2
Chémery F....103 B3
Chemery-sur-Bar
F.............91 B4
Chemillé F....102 B1
Chemin F.....105 C4
Chemnitz D....83 B4
Chénerailles F 116 A2
Cheniménil F. 105 A5
Chenonceaux
F.............103 B3
Chenôve F...105 B3
Chepelare BG. 183 B6
Chepstow UK...39 C4
Chera E......159 B3
Cherasco I....119 C4
Cherbonnières
F.............115 C3
Cherbourg F...88 A2
Cherchiara di
Calábria I...174 B2
Cherepovets
RUS.............9 C10
Chernihiv UA...13 C9
Chernivtsi UA...17 A6
Chernobyl =
Chornobyl UA.13 C9
Chernyakhovsk
RUS.............12 A4
Chéroy F.....104 A1
Cherven BY....13 B8
Chervonohrad
UA.............13 C6
Cherykaw BY...13 B9
Chesham UK....44 B3
Cheshunt UK...44 B3
Chessy-lès-Pres
F.............104 A2
Cheste E......159 B3
Chester UK....38 A4
Chesterfield UK 40 B2
Chester-le-Street
UK.............37 B5
Chevagnes F..104 C2
Chevanceaux
F.............115 C3
Chevillon F....91 C5
Chevilly F....103 A3
Chew Magna
UK.............43 A4
Chézery-Forens
F.............118 A2
Chialamberto
I.............119 B4
Chiampo I....121 B4
Chianale I....119 C4
Chianciano Terme
I.............135 B4
Chiaramonte Gulfi
I.............177 B3
Chiaramonti I..178 B2

Chiaravalle I . . 136 B2
Chiaravalle
  Centrale I 175 C2
Chiaréggio I . . 120 A2
Chiari I 120 B2
Chiaromonte
  I 174 A2
Chiasso CH 120 B2
Chiávari I 134 A2
Chiavenna I 120 A2
Chiché F 102 C1
Chichester UK . . . 44 C3
Chiclana de la
  Frontera E . . . 162 B1
Chiclana de Segura
  E 164 A1
Chiddingfold
  UK 44 B3
Chieri I 119 B4
Chiesa in
  Valmalenco
  I 120 A2
Chieti I 169 A4
Chieti Scalo I . . . 169 A4
Chiéuti I 171 B3
Chigwell UK 45 B4
Chiliomodi
  GR 184 B3
Chillarón de
  Cuenca E 152 B1
Chillarón del Rey
  E 151 B5
Chilleurs-aux-Bois
  F 103 A4
Chillón E 156 B3
Chilluevar E . . . 164 B1
Chiloeches E . . 151 B4
Chimay B 91 A4
Chimeneas E . . 163 A4
Chinchilla de Monte
  Aragón E 158 C2
Chinchón E . . . 151 B4
Chingford UK . . . 45 B4
Chinon F 102 B2
Chióggia I 122 B1
Chiomonte I . . . 119 B3
Chipiona E 161 C3
Chippenham
  UK 43 A4
Chipping Campden
  UK 44 A2
Chipping Norton
  UK 44 B2
Chipping Ongar
  UK 45 B4
Chipping Sodbury
  UK 43 A4
Chirac F 130 A2
Chirbury UK 39 B3
Chirens F 118 B2
Chirivel E 164 B2
Chirk UK 38 B3
Chirnside UK 35 C5
Chişinău =
  Khisinev MD . . . 17 B8
Chişineu Criş
  RO 113 C5
Chissey-en-
  Morvan F 104 B3
Chiusa I 108 C2
Chiusa di Pésio
  I 133 A3
Chiusaforte I . . . 122 A2
Chiusa Sclàfani
  I 176 B2
Chiusi I 135 B4
Chiva E 159 B3
Chivasso I 119 B5
Chlewiska PL . . . 87 A4
Chludowo PL . . . 75 B5
Chlumec nad
  Cidlinou CZ 84 B3
Chlum u Třeboně
  CZ 96 C2
Chmielnik PL . . . 87 B4
Chobienia PL . . 85 A4
Chobienice PL . . 75 B4
Choceň CZ 97 A4
Choceń PL 77 B4
Chochołów PL . . 99 B3
Chocianów PL . . 85 A3
Chociw PL 86 A3
Chociwel PL . . . 75 A4
Choczewo PL . . 68 A2
Chodaków PL . . 77 B5
Chodecz PL 77 B4
Chodov CZ 83 B4
Chodzież PL 75 B5
Chojna PL 74 B3
Chojnice PL 68 B2
Chojno
  Kujawsko-
  Pomorskie PL . . 77 B4

Chojno continued
  Wielkopolskie
  Pl 75 B5
Chojnów PL 85 A3
Cholet F 114 A3
Chomérac F 117 C4
Chomutov CZ . . . 83 B5
Chop UA 12 D5
Chora GR 184 B2
Chora Sfakion
  GR 185 D5
Chorges F 132 A2
Chorley UK 38 A4
Chornobyl =
  Chernobyl UA . . 13 C9
Chortkiv UA 13 D6
Chorzele PL 77 A5
Chorzew PL 86 A2
Chorzów PL 86 B2
Choszczno PL . . 75 A4
Chotěboř CZ . . . 97 B3
Chouilly F 91 B4
Chouto P 154 B2
Chouzy-sur-Cisse
  F 103 B3
Chozas de Abajo
  E 142 B1
Chrast CZ 97 B3
Chrást CZ 96 B1
Chrastava CZ . . . 84 B2
Chřibská CZ 84 B2
Christchurch
  UK 44 C2
Christiansfeld
  DK 59 C2
Chroberz PL 87 B4
Chropyně CZ . . . 98 B1
Chrudim CZ 97 B3
Chrzanów PL . . . 86 B3
Chtelnica SK . . . 98 C1
Chudovo RUS . . . 9 C7
Chueca E 157 A4
Chulmleigh UK . . 42 B3
Chur CH 107 C4
Church Stretton
  UK 39 B4
Churriana E . . . 163 B3
Churwalden
  CH 107 C4
Chvalšiny CZ . . . 96 C2
Chwaszczyno
  PL 69 A3
Chynava CZ 96 A2
Chýnov CZ 96 B2
Ciacova RO 126 B3
Ciadîr-Lunga
  MD 17 B8
Ciadoncha E . . . 143 B3
Cianciana I 176 B2
Ciano d'Enza I . . 134 A3
Ciążen PL 76 B2
Cibakháza H . . . 113 C4
Ciborro P 154 C2
Cicagna I 134 A2
Cicciano I 170 C2
Ciciliano I 169 B2
Cicognolo I 120 B3
Cidadelhe P . . . 149 B2
Cide TR 23 A7
Cidones E 143 C4
Ciechanów
  Dolnoślaskie
  PL 85 A4
  Mazowieckie
  PL 77 B5
Ciechocinek PL . 76 B3
Cielądz PL 87 A4
Ciemnik PL 75 A4
Ciempozuelos
  E 151 B4
Ciepielów PL . . . 87 A5
Čierny Balog
  SK 99 C3
Cierp-Gaud F . . 145 B4
Cierpice PL 76 B3
Ciervana E 143 A3
Cierznie PL 68 B2
Cieslé PL 77 B5
Cieszyn PL 98 B2
Cieutat F 145 A4
Cieza E 165 A3
Cifer SK 98 C1
Çifteler TR 187 C6
Cifuentes E . . . 151 B5
Cigales E 142 C2
Cigliano I 119 B5
Cihanbeyli TR . . 23 B7
Cillas E 152 B2
Cilleros E 149 B3
Cilleruelo de Arriba
  E 143 C3
Cilleruelo de
  Bezana E 143 B3

Cimalmotto
  CH 119 A5
Cìmanes del Tejar
  E 141 B5
Ciminna I 176 B2
Cimişlia MD 17 B8
Cimoláis I 122 A1
Cîmpulung RO . . 17 C6
Cinarcık TR 186 B4
Cinctorres E . . . 153 B3
Cinderford UK . . . 39 C4
Çine TR 188 B3
Čiňeves CZ 84 B3
Cinfães P 148 A1
Cingia de Botti
  I 120 B3
Cíngoli I 136 B2
Cinigiano I 135 C4
Cinobaňa SK . . . 99 C3
Cinq-Mars-la-Pile
  F 102 B2
Cinquefrondí
  I 175 C2
Cintegabelle
  F 146 A2
Cintruénigo E . . 144 B2
Ciółkowo PL 77 B4
Ciperez E 149 B3
Cirat E 153 B3
Cirella I 174 B1
Cirencester UK . . 44 B2
Cirey-sur-Vezouze
  F 92 C2
Ciria E 152 A2
Cirièl 119 B4
Cirigliano I 174 A2
Cirò I 174 B3
Cirò Marina I . . 174 B3
Ciry-le-Noble
  F 104 C3
Cisláu RO 17 C7
Cismon del Grappa
  I 121 B4
Cisneros E 142 B2
Cissac-Médoc
  F 128 A2
Čista CZ 96 A1
Cisterna di Latina
  I 169 B2
Cistérniga E . . . 150 A3
Cisternino I . . . 173 B3
Cistierna E 142 B1
Čitluk BIH 139 B3
Cítov CZ 84 B2
Cittadella I 121 B4
Cittàdella Pieve
  I 135 C5
Cittádel Vaticano =
  Vatican City
  I 168 B2
Cittàdi Castello
  I 135 B5
Cittaducale I . . . 169 A2
Cittanova I 175 C2
Città Sant'Angelo
  I 169 A4
Ciudadela de
  Menorca E . . . 167 B3
Ciudad Real E . . 157 B4
Ciudad Rodrigo
  E 149 B3
Ciutadella E . . . 147 C2
Cividale del Friuli
  I 122 A2
Cívita I 169 A3
Cívita Castellana
  I 168 A2
Civitanova Alta
  I 136 B2
Civitanova Marche
  I 136 B2
Civitavécchia
  I 168 A1
Civitella di
  Romagna I . . . 135 A4
Civitella di Tronto
  I 136 C2
Civitella Roveto
  I 169 B3
Civray F 115 B4
Çivril TR 189 A4
Cizur Mayor E . . 144 B2
Clabhach UK . . . 34 B1
Clachan UK 31 B2
Clachan na Luib
  UK 31 B1
Clacton-on-Sea
  UK 45 B5
Cladich UK 34 B2
Claggan UK 34 B2
Clairvaux-les-Lacs
  F 105 C4

Clamecy F 104 B2
Claonaig UK 34 C2
Clarecastle IRL . . 28 B3
Claregalway
  IRL 28 A3
Claremorris IRL . 28 A2
Clarinbridge
  IRL 28 A3
Clashmore
  IRL 29 B4
  UK 32 D2
Claudy UK 27 B3
Clausthal-Zellerfeld
  D 82 A2
Cláut I 122 A1
Clay Cross UK . . . 40 B2
Claye-Souilly F . . 90 C2
Cléder F 100 A1
Cleethorpes UK . 41 B3
Clefmont F 105 A4
Cléguérec F . . . 100 A2
Clelles F 118 C2
Clenze D 73 B3
Cleobury Mortimer
  UK 39 B4
Cléon-d'Andran
  F 117 C4
Cléré-les-Pins
  F 102 B2
Clères F 89 A5
Clermont F 90 B2
Clermont-en-
  Argonne F 91 B5
Clermont-Ferrand
  F 116 B3
Clermont-l'Hérault
  F 130 B2
Clerval F 105 B5
Clervaux L 92 A2
Cléry-St André
  F 103 B3
Cles I 121 A4
Clevedon UK 43 A4
Cleveleys UK . . . 38 A3
Cley UK 41 C5
Clifden IRL 28 A1
Clifford UK 39 B3
Clisson F 101 B4
Clitheroe UK . . . 40 B1
Clogh IRL 30 B1
Cloghan
  Donegal IRL . . . 26 B3
  Offaly IRL 28 A4
Clogheen IRL . . . 29 B4
Clogher UK 27 B3
Cloghjordan
  IRL 28 B3
Clohars-Carnoët
  F 100 B2
Clonakilty IRL . . 29 C3
Clonaslee IRL . . 30 A1
Clondalkin IRL . 30 A2
Clones IRL 27 B3
Clonmany IRL . . 27 A3
Clonmel IRL 29 B4
Clonmellon IRL . 30 A1
Clonord IRL 30 A1
Clonroche IRL . . 30 B2
Cloone IRL 26 C3
Cloppenburg
  D 71 B5
Closeburn UK . . . 36 A3
Clough UK 27 B5
Clova UK 35 B4
Clovelly UK 42 B2
Clowne UK 40 B2
Cloyes-sur-
  le-Loir F 103 B3
Cloyne IRL 29 C3
Cluis F 103 C3
Cluj-Napoca RO 17 B5
Clun UK 39 B3
Clunes UK 34 B3
Cluny F 117 A4
Cluses F 118 A3
Clusone I 120 B2
Clydach UK 39 C3
Clydebank UK . . 34 C3
Coachford IRL . . 29 C3
Coagh UK 27 B4
Coalisland UK . . 27 B4
Coalville UK 40 C2
Coaña E 141 A4
Cobas E 140 A2
Cobertelade E . 151 A5
Cobeta E 152 B1
Cóbh IRL 29 C3
Cobreces E 142 A2
Coburg D 82 B2
Coca E 150 A3
Cocentaina E . . 159 C3
Cochem D 80 B3

Cockburnspath
  UK 35 C5
Cockermouth
  UK 36 B3
Codigoro I 121 C3
Codognè I 120 B2
Codos E 152 A2
Codróipo I 122 B1
Codrongianos
  I 178 B2
Coelhoso P 149 A3
Coesfeld D 71 C4
Coevorden NL . . 71 B3
Cofrentes E . . . 159 B2
Cogeces del Monte
  E 150 A3
Coggeshall UK . . 45 B4
Cognac F 115 C3
Cogne I 119 B4
Cognin F 118 B2
Cogolin F 132 B2
Cogollos de Guadix
  E 164 B1
Cogollos-Vega
  E 163 A4
Cogolludo E . . . 151 B4
Coimbra P 148 B1
Coín E 163 B3
Coirós E 140 A2
Čoka SRB 126 B2
Col SLO 123 B3
Colares P 154 C1
Cölbe D 81 B4
Colbitz D 73 B4
Colchester UK . . 45 B4
Coldingham
  UK 35 C5
Colditz D 83 A4
Coldstream UK . . 35 C5
Colebrooke UK . . 43 B3
Colera E 146 B4
Coleraine UK . . . 27 A4
Colfiorito I 136 B1
Cólico I 120 A2
Coligny F 118 A2
Colindres E 143 A3
Collado-Mediano
  E 151 B3
Collado Villalba
  E 151 B4
Collagna I 134 A3
Collanzo E 142 A1
Collat F 117 B3
Coll de Nargó
  E 147 B2
Collécchio I . . . 120 C3
Colledimezzo
  I 169 B4
Colle di Val d'Elsa
  I 135 B4
Colleferro I 169 B3
Colle Isarco I . . 108 C2
Collelongo I . . . 169 B3
Collepasso I . . . 173 B4
Collepepe I . . . 136 C1
Collesalvetti I . . 134 B3
Colle Sannita I . 170 B2
Collesano I 176 B2
Colli a Volturno
  I 169 B4
Collin UK 36 A3
Collinée F 101 A3
Collingham
  Nottinghamshire
  UK 40 B2
  West Yorkshire
  UK 40 B2
Collinghorst D . . 71 A4
Collio I 120 B3
Collobrières F . 132 B2
Collon IRL 27 C4
Collooney IRL . . 26 B2
Colmar F 106 A2
Colmars F 132 A2
Colmenar E 163 B3
Colmenar de la
  Sierra E 151 A4
Colmenar de Oreja
  E 151 B4
Colmenar Viejo
  E 151 B4
Colmonel UK . . . 36 A2
Colne UK 40 B1
Colobraro I . . . 174 A2
Cologna Véneta
  I 121 B4
Cologne F 129 C3
Cologne = Köln
  D 80 B2
Cologne al Serio
  I 120 B2
Colombey-les-
  Belles F 92 C1

Colombey-les-deux-
  Églises F 105 A3
Colombres E . . . 142 A2
Colomera E 163 A4
Colomers E 147 B3
Colomiers F . . . 129 C4
Colònia de Sant
  Jordi E 167 B3
Colorno I 120 C3
Colos P 160 B1
Cölpin D 74 A2
Colpy UK 33 D4
Colsterworth
  UK 40 C3
Coltishall UK 41 C5
Colunga E 142 A1
Colwell UK 37 A4
Colwyn Bay UK . . 38 A3
Colyford UK 43 B3
Comácchio I . . . 121 C5
Coma-ruga E . . . 147 C2
Combarros E . . . 141 B4
Combeaufontaine
  F 105 B4
Comber UK 27 B5
Comblain-au-Pont
  B 80 B1
Combloux F 118 B3
Combourg F 88 B2
Combronde F . . 116 B3
Comeglians I . . 109 C3
Comillas E 142 A2
Comines F 78 B3
Cómiso I 177 C3
Comloşu Mare
  RO 126 B2
Commensacq
  F 128 B2
Commentry F . . 116 A2
Commerau D . . . 84 A2
Commercy F 92 C1
Como I 120 B2
Cómpeta E 163 B4
Compiègne F . . . 90 B2
Comporta P . . . 154 C2
Comps-sur-Artuby
  F 132 B2
Comrat MD 17 B8
Comrie UK 35 B4
Comunanza I . 136 C2
Cona
  Emilia Romagna
  I 121 C4
  Veneto I 121 B5
Concarneau F . 100 B2
Conceição P . . . 160 B1
Conches-en-Ouche
  F 89 B4
Concordia
  Sagittária I . . . 122 B1
Concordia sulla
  Sécchia I 121 C3
Concots F 129 B4
Condat F 116 B2
Condé-en-Brie
  F 91 C3
Condeixa P 148 B1
Condemios de
  Abajo E 151 A4
Condemios de
  Arriba E 151 A4
Condé-sur-l'Escaut
  F 79 B3
Conde-sur-Marne
  F 91 B4
Condé-sur-Noireau
  F 88 B3
Condino I 121 B3
Condom F 129 C3
Condove I 119 B4
Condrieu F 117 B4
Conegliano I . . 122 B1
Conflans-sur-
  Lanterne F . . . 105 B5
Confolens F . . . 115 B4
Conforto E 141 A3
Cong IRL 28 A2
Congleton UK . . 40 B1
Congosto E 141 B4
Congosto de
  Valdavia E 142 B2
Congostrina E . 151 A4
Conil de la Frontera
  E 162 B1
Coningsby UK . . 41 B3
Coniston UK 36 B3
Conlie F 102 A1
Conliège F 105 C4
Conna IRL 29 B3
Connah's Quay
  UK 38 A3
Connantre F 91 C3
Connaugh IRL . . 28 B3

Connaux F 131 A3
Connel UK 34 B2
Connerré F 102 A2
Cononbridge
  UK 32 D2
Čonoplja SRB . . 126 B1
Conques F 116 C2
Conques-
  sur-Orbiel F . . 146 A3
Conquista E . . . 157 B3
Conquista de la
  Sierra E 156 A2
Consándolo I . . 121 C4
Consélice I 135 A4
Conselve I 121 B4
Consenvoye F . . 91 B5
Consett UK 37 B5
Consolacão P . . 154 B1
Constancia P . . 154 B2
Constanța RO . . 17 C8
Constanti E . . . 147 C2
Constantina
  E 162 A2
Consuegra E . . 157 A4
Consuma I 135 B4
Contarina I 122 B1
Contay F 90 B2
Conthey CH . . . 119 A4
Contigliano I . . 168 A2
Contis-Plage
  F 128 B1
Contrada I 170 C2
Contres F 103 B3
Contrexéville
  F 105 A4
Controne I 172 B1
Contursi Termi
  I 172 B1
Conty F 90 B2
Conversano I . . 173 B3
Conwy UK 38 A3
Cookstown UK . . 27 B4
Coole F 91 C4
Coolgreany IRL . 30 B2
Cooneen UK . . . 27 B3
Cootehill IRL . . . 27 B3
Cope E 165 B3
Copenhagen =
  København
  DK 61 D2
Copertino I . . . 173 B4
Copparo I 121 C4
Coppenbrugge
  D 72 B2
Corabia RO 17 D6
Córaci I 175 B2
Coralići BIH . . . 124 C1
Corato I 171 B4
Coray F 100 A2
Corbeil-Essonnes
  F 90 C2
Corbeny F 91 B3
Corbera E 159 B3
Corbie F 90 B2
Corbigny F 104 B2
Corbion B 91 B4
Corbridge UK . . . 37 B4
Corby UK 40 C3
Corconte E 143 A3
Corcubión E . . . 140 B1
Corcumello I . . 169 A3
Cordenòns I . . . 122 B1
Cordes-sur-Ciel
  F 129 B4
Córdoba E 156 C3
Cordobilla de
  Lácara E 155 B4
Cordovado I . . . 122 B1
Corella E 144 B2
Coreses E 150 A2
Corfe Castle UK . 43 B4
Corga de Lobão
  P 148 B1
Cori I 169 B2
Coria E 155 B4
Coria del Río
  E 162 A1
Corigliano Cálabro
  I 174 B2
Corinaldo I 136 B1
Corinth = Korinthos
  GR 184 B3
Cório I 119 B4
Coripe E 162 B2
Coristanco E . . 140 A2
Cork IRL 29 C3
Corlay F 100 A2
Corleone I 176 B2
Corleto Monforte
  I 172 B1

Corleto Perticara
I.............174 A2
Çorlu TR......186 A2
Cormainville
F.............103 A3
Cormatin F....104 C3
Cormeilles F...89 A4
Cormery F....102 B2
Cormòns I.....122 B2
Cormoz F.....118 A2
Cornago E....144 B1
Cornberg D....82 A1
Cornellana E..141 A4
Corneşti MD...17 B8
Cornîglio I...134 A3
Cornimont F..106 B1
Corniolo I....135 B4
Cornuda I.....121 B5
Cornudella de
  Montsant E..147 C1
Cornudilla E..143 B3
Cornus F.....130 B2
Çorovodë AL..182 C2
Corpach UK...34 B2
Corps F.....118 C2
Corps Nuds F..101 B4
Corral de Almaguer
  E............157 A4
Corral de Ayllon
  E............151 A4
Corral de Calatrava
  E............157 B3
Corrales E....149 A4
Corral-Rubio
  E............158 C2
Corran UK.....34 B2
Corredoiras
  E............140 A2
Corréggio I...121 C3
Corrèze F.....116 B1
Corridónia I...136 B2
Corris UK.....38 B3
Corrubedo E..140 B1
Córsico I.....120 B2
Corsock UK...36 A3
Corte F.....180 A2
Corteconceptión
  E............161 B3
Corte de Peleas
  E............155 C4
Cortegaca P...148 B1
Cortegada E..140 B2
Cortegana E..161 B3
Cortemaggiore
  I............120 B2
Cortemilia I...133 A4
Corte Pinto P..160 B2
Cortes E.....144 C2
Cortes de Aragón
  E............153 B3
Cortes de Arenoso
  E............153 A3
Cortes de Baza
  E............164 B2
Cortes de la
  Frontera E..162 B2
Cortes de Pallás
  E............159 B3
Cortiçadas P..154 C2
Cortico P.....148 A2
Cortijo de Arriba
  E............157 A3
Cortijos Nuevos
  E............164 A2
Cortina d'Ampezzo
  I............108 C3
Corton UK....41 C5
Cortona I....135 B4
Coruche P....154 C2
Corullón E....141 B4
Çorum TR....23 A8
Corvara in Badia
  I............108 C2
Corvera E....165 B3
Corwen UK....38 B3
Cosenza I....174 B2
Cosham UK....44 C2
Coslada E....151 B4
Cosne-Cours-sur-
  Loire F.......104 B1
Cosne d'Allier
  F............103 C4
Cospeito E...140 A2
Cossato I.....119 B5
Cossaye F....104 C2
Cossé-le-Vivien
  F............101 B5
Cossonay CH..105 C5
Costa da Caparica
  P............154 C1

Costa de Santo
  André P......160 A1
Costalpino I...135 B4
Costa Nova P..148 B1
Costaros F....117 C3
Costeşti RO...17 C6
Costigliole d'Asti
  I............119 C5
Costigliole Saluzzo
  I............133 A3
Coswig
  Sachsen D.....83 A5
  Sachsen-Anhalt
  D.............83 A4
Cotherstone
  UK...........37 B5
Cotronei I....175 B2
Cottbus D....84 A2
Cottenham UK..45 A4
Cottingham UK.40 B3
Coublanc F...105 B4
Couches F....104 C3
Couço P.....154 C2
Coucouron F..117 C3
Coucy-le-Château-
  Auffrique F...90 B3
Couëron F....101 B4
Couflens F...146 B2
Couhé F.....115 B4
Couiza F....146 B3
Coulags UK...31 B3
Coulanges F..104 C2
Coulanges-la-
  Vineuse F....104 B2
Coulanges-sur-
  Yonne F.....104 B2
Couleuvre F..104 C1
Coulmier-le-Sec
  F............104 B3
Coulommiers F.90 C3
Coulonges-sur-
  l'Autize F....114 B3
Coulounieix-
  Chamiers F..129 A3
Coulport UK...34 B3
Coupar Angus
  UK...........35 B4
Coupéville F..91 C4
Couptrain F...89 B3
Coura P.....140 C2
Courcelles B..79 B4
Courcelles-Chaussy
  F............92 B2
Courchevel F..118 B3
Cour-Cheverny
  F............103 B3
Courcôme F...115 C4
Courçon F....114 B3
Cour-et-Buis F.117 B4
Courgenay CH.106 B2
Courmayeur I..119 B3
Courniou F....130 B1
Cournon-
  d'Auvergne
  F............116 B3
Cournonterral
  F............130 B2
Courpière F...117 B3
Coursan F....130 B2
Courseulles-sur-
  Mer F.......89 A3
Cours-la-Ville
  F............117 A4
Courson-les-
  Carrières F..104 B2
Courtalain F..103 A3
Courtenay F..104 A2
Courtomer F..89 B4
Courville
  Eure-et-Loire
  F............89 B5
  Marne F......91 B3
Coussac-Bonneval
  F............115 C5
Coutances F...88 A2
Couterne F....89 B3
Coutras F....128 A2
Couvet CH....106 C1
Couvin F.....91 A4
Couzon F....104 C2
Covadonga E..142 A1
Covaleda E...143 C4
Covarrubias E..143 B3
Covas P.....148 A1
Cove UK.....31 B3
Coventry UK..44 A2
Coverack UK..42 B1
Covigliáio I...135 A4
Covilhã P....148 B2
Cowbridge UK.39 C3
Cowdenbeath
  UK...........35 B4
Cowes UK....44 C2

Cox F.........129 C4
Cózar E.....157 B4
Cozes F......114 C3
Cozzano F....180 B2
Craco I.....174 A2
Cracow = Kraków
  PL...........99 A3
Craibstone UK..33 D4
Craighouse UK.34 C2
Craignure UK..34 B2
Crail UK......35 B5
Crailsheim D..94 B2
Craiova RO...17 C5
Cramlington
  UK...........37 A5
Cranleigh UK..44 B3
Craon F.....101 B5
Craonne F....91 B3
Craponne F...117 B4
Craponne-sur-
  Arzon F.....117 B3
Crathie UK....32 D3
Crato P.....155 B3
Craughwell IRL..28 A3
Craven Arms
  UK...........39 B4
Crawford UK..36 A3
Crawinkel D...82 B2
Crawley UK...44 B3
Creag Ghoraidh
  UK...........31 B1
Crecente I....120 B2
Crèches-sur-Saône
  F............117 A4
Crécy-en-Ponthieu
  F............78 B1
Crécy-la-Chapelle
  F............90 C2
Crécy-sur-Serre
  F............91 B3
Crediton UK...43 B3
Creeslough IRL..26 A3
Creetown UK..36 B2
Creeve UK....27 B4
Creglingen D..94 B2
Creil F......90 B2
Creissels F...130 A2
Crema I.....120 B2
Cremeaux F...117 B3
Crémenes E..142 B1
Crémieu F....118 B2
Cremlingen D...73 B3
Cremona I....120 B3
Creney F.....91 C4
Crenšovci
  SLO..........111 C3
Créon F.....128 B2
Crepaja SRB..127 B2
Crépey F.....92 C1
Crépy F......91 B3
Crépy-en-Valois
  F............90 B2
Cres HR.....123 C3
Crescentino I..119 B5
Crespino I....121 C4
Crespos E....150 B3
Cressage UK..39 B4
Cressensac F..129 A4
Cressia F....105 C4
Crest F......117 C5
Cresta CH....107 C4
Créteil F......90 C2
Creully F.....88 A3
Creussen D...95 B3
Creutzwald F..92 B2
Creuzburg D...82 A2
Crevalcore I...121 C4
Crèvecoeur-le-
  Grand F......90 B2
Crevillente E..165 A4
Crévola d'Ossola
  I............119 A5
Crewe UK....38 A4
Crewkerne UK.43 B4
Criales E.....143 B3
Crianlarich UK..34 B3
Criccieth UK...38 B2
Crickhowell UK.39 C3
Cricklade UK..44 B2
Crieff UK.....35 B4
Criel-sur-Mer F..90 A1
Crikvenica HR..123 B3
Crillon F.....90 B1
Crimmitschau
  D............83 B4
Crimond UK...33 D5
Crinitz D.....84 A1
Cripán E.....143 B4
Criquetot-l'Esneval
  F............89 A4
Crispiano I...173 B3
Crissolo I....119 C4
Cristóbal E...149 B4

Crivitz D.....73 A4
Črna SLO....110 C1
Crna Bara
  Srbija SRB....127 C1
  Vojvodina
  SRB.........126 B2
Crnac HR....125 B3
Črnča SRB....127 C1
Crni Lug
  BIH..........138 A2
  HR...........123 B3
Črni Vrh SLO..123 B3
Črnomelj SLO.123 B4
Crocketford UK.36 A3
Crocq F......116 B2
Crodo I.....119 A5
Croglin UK...37 B4
Crolly IRL....26 A2
Cromarty UK..32 D2
Cromer UK....41 C5
Cronat F....104 C2
Crookhaven
  IRL..........29 C2
Crookstown IRL.29 C3
Croom IRL....29 B3
Cropalati I...174 B2
Crópani I....175 C2
Crosbost UK...31 A2
Crosby UK....38 A3
Crosía I.....174 B3
Crossakiel IRL..27 C3
Cross-Hands
  UK...........39 C2
Crosshaven IRL.29 C3
Crosshill UK...36 A2
Crossmolina
  IRL..........26 B1
Crotone I....175 B3
Crottendorf D..83 B4
Crouy F......90 B3
Crowborough
  UK...........45 B4
Crowland UK..41 C3
Crowthorne UK.44 B3
Croyde UK....42 A2
Croydon UK...44 B3
Crozon F.....100 A1
Cruas F......117 C4
Cruceni RO...126 A3
Crúcoli I.....174 B3
Cruden Bay UK.33 D5
Crudgington
  UK...........38 B4
Cruis F......132 A1
Crumlin UK...27 B4
Cruseilles F..118 A3
Crusheen IRL..28 B3
Cruz de Incio
  E............141 B3
Crvenka SRB..126 B1
Červeny Kamen
  SK...........98 B2
Csabacsüd H..113 C4
Csabrendek
  H............111 B4
Csákánydoroszló
  H............111 C3
Csákvár H....112 B2
Csanádapáca
  H............113 C4
Csanádpalota
  H............126 A2
Csány H.....113 B3
Csanytelek H..113 C4
Csapod H....111 B3
Császár H....112 B2
Császártöltés
  H............112 C2
Csávoly H....125 A5
Csemö H....113 B3
Csengöd H...112 C3
Csépa H.....113 C4
Csepreg H...111 B3
Cserkeszölö
  H............113 C4
Csernely H...113 A4
Csesztreg H..111 C3
Csökmö H...113 B5
Csököly H...124 A3
Csokonyavisonta
  H............124 A3
Csólyospálos
  H............113 C3
Csongrád H...113 C4
Csopak H....112 C1
Csorna H....111 B4
Csorvás H...113 C4
Csurgo H....124 A3
Cuacos de Yuste
  E............150 B2
Cualedro E...140 C3

Cuanca de Campos
  E............142 B1
Cuba P......160 A2
Cubel E.....152 A2
Cubelles E...147 C2
Cubillos E...143 C4
Cubillos del Sil
  E............141 B4
Cubjac F....129 A3
Cubo de la Solana
  E............152 A1
Cuckfield UK..44 B3
Cucuron F....131 B4
Cudillero E...141 A4
Cuéllar E....151 A3
Cuenca E....152 B1
Cuers F.....132 B2
Cuerva E....157 A3
Cueva de Agreda
  E............144 C2
Cuevas Bajas
  E............163 A3
Cuevas del
  Almanzora E.164 B3
Cuevas del Becerro
  E............162 B2
Cuevas del Campo
  E............164 B2
Cuevas del Valle
  E............150 B2
Cuevas de San
  Clemente E..143 B3
Cuevas de San
  Marcos E....163 A3
Cuges-les-Pins
  F............132 B1
Cúglieri I....178 B2
Cugnaux F...129 C4
Cuijk NL.....80 A1
Cuiseaux F...105 C4
Cuisery F....105 C4
Culan F.....103 C4
Culemborg NL..79 A5
Cúllar E.....164 B2
Cullaville UK..27 B4
Cullera E....159 B3
Cullivoe UK...33 A6
Cullompton UK.43 B3
Cully CH.....106 C1
Culoz F.....118 B2
Cults UK.....33 D4
Cumbernauld
  UK...........35 C4
Cumbres de San
  Bartolomé E.161 A3
Cumbres Mayores
  E............161 A3
Cumiana I....119 C4
Cumnock UK..36 A2
Cumra TR....23 C7
Cúneo I.....133 A3
Cunlhat F....117 B3
Çunski HR....123 C3
Cuntis E.....140 B2
Cuorgnè I....119 B4
Cupar UK.....35 B4
Cupello I....170 A2
Cupra Maríttima
  I............136 B2
Cupramontana
  I............136 B2
Čuprija SRB..127 D3
Curinga I....175 C2
Currelos E...140 B3
Currie UK....35 C4
Curtea de Argeş
  RO...........17 C6
Curtici RO...126 A3
Curtis E.....140 A2
Curtis Santa Eulalia
  E............140 A2
Čurug SRB...126 B2
Cusano Mutri
  I............170 B2
Cushendall UK..27 A4
Cusset F....117 A3
Cussy-les-Forges
  F............104 B3
Custines F....92 C2
Cutanda E...152 B2
Cutro I.....175 B2
Cutrofiano I...173 B4
Cuts F......90 B3
Cuvilly F....90 B2
Cuxhaven D...64 C1
Cvikov CZ....84 B2
Cwmbran UK..39 C3
Cybinka PL...75 B3
Czacz PL.....75 B5
Czajków PL...86 A2

Czaplinek PL...75 A5
Czarlin PL....69 A3
Czarna-Dąbrówka
  PL...........68 A2
Czarna Woda
  PL...........68 B3
Czarnca PL...87 B3
Czarne PL....68 B1
Czarnków PL...75 B5
Czarnowo PL..76 A3
Czarnozyly PL..86 A2
Czarny Bór PL..85 B4
Czarny-Dunajec
  PL...........99 B3
Czarny Las PL..86 A1
Czchow PL...99 B4
Czechowice-
  Dziedzice PL..98 B2
Czempiń PL...75 B5
Czermno PL...87 A4
Czernichow PL..99 B3
Czerniejewo PL.76 B2
Czernikowo PL..76 B3
Czersk PL....68 B2
Czerwieńsk PL..75 B4
Czerwionka-
  Leszczyny PL..86 B2
Częstochowa
  PL...........86 B3
Czeszewo PL..76 B2
Człopa PL....75 A5
Człuchów PL...68 B2
Czołpino PL...68 A2

D

Dağ TR.......189 B5
Daaden D....81 B3
Dabas H.....112 B3
Dąbie PL.....76 B3
Dąbki PL.....67 B5
Dabo F......92 C3
Dabrowa PL...76 B2
Dąbrowa Górnicza
  PL...........86 B3
Dąbrowa
  Tarnowska PL..87 B4
Dąbrowice PL..77 B4
Dabrowno PL..77 A5
Dachau D....108 A2
Dačice CZ....97 B3
Daday TR....23 A7
Dagali N.....47 B5
Dägebüll D...64 B1
Dagmersellen
  CH...........106 B2
Dahlen D....83 A4
Dahlenburg D..73 A3
Dahme D....83 A5
Dahn D......93 B3
Dähre D.....73 B3
Daikanvik S...195 E7
Dail bho Dheas
  UK...........31 A2
Dailly UK....36 A2
Daimiel E....157 A4
Daingean IRL..30 A1
Đakovica KOS..16 D4
Đakovo HR...125 B4
Dal
  Akershus N...48 B3
  Telemark N..47 C5
Dalaas A.....107 B5
Dalabrog UK..31 B1
Dala-Floda S..50 B1
Dala-Husby S..50 B2
Dala-Järna S..50 B1
Dalaman TR..188 C3
Dalarö S.....57 A4
Dalbeattie UK..36 B3
Dalby
  DK...........59 C3
  Skåne S.....61 D3
  Uppsala S....57 A3
  Värmland S...49 B4
Dale
  Hordaland N..46 B2
  Sogn og Fjordane
  N.............46 A2
  Pembrokeshire
  UK...........39 C1
  Shetland UK..33 A5
Dalen
  Akershus N...48 C3
  Telemark N...53 A4
Daleszyce PL..87 B4
Dalhalvaig UK..32 C3
Dalheim L....92 B2
Dalhem S....57 C4
Dalías E.....164 C2
Dalj HR.....125 B4
Dalkeith UK...35 C4

Dalkey IRL....30 A2
Dalmally UK...34 B3
Dalmellington
  UK...........36 A2
Dalmose DK...65 A4
Daløy N......46 A1
Dalry
  Dumfries &
  Galloway UK..34 C3
  North Ayrshire
  UK...........36 A2
Dalrymple UK..36 A2
Dalseter N....47 A6
Dalsjöfors S...60 B3
Dalskog S....54 B3
Dals Långed S..54 B3
Dals Rostock S..54 B3
Dalston UK...36 B4
Dalstorp S....60 B3
Dalton-in-Furness
  UK...........36 B3
Daluis F.....132 A2
Dalum
  D............71 B4
  S............71 B4
Dalvík IS....191 B7
Dalwhinnie UK.32 E2
Dalyan TR...188 C3
Damasi GR...182 D4
Damasławek
  PL...........76 B2
Damazan F...129 B3
Damgan F....101 B3
Dammarie-les-Lys
  F............90 C2
Dammartin-en-
  Goële F......90 B2
Damme D....71 B5
Damnica PL...68 A2
Dampierre F..105 B4
Dampierre-sur-
  Salon F......105 B4
Damüls A....107 B4
Damville F....89 B5
Damvillers F..92 B1
Damwoude NL..70 A2
Danasjö S....195 E7
Danbury UK...45 B4
Dångebo S....63 B3
Dangers F....89 B5
Dangé-St Romain
  F............102 C2
Dangeul F....89 B4
Danilovgrad
  MNE.........16 D3
Danischenhagen
  D............64 B3
Daniszyn PL..85 A5
Danjoutin F...106 B1
Dannas S....60 B3
Dannemarie F.106 B2
Dannemora S..51 B4
Dannenberg D.73 A4
Dánszentmiklós
  H............112 B3
Dány H.....112 B3
Daoulas F....100 A1
Darabani RO...17 A7
Darány H....125 B3
Darda HR....125 B3
Dardesheim D..73 C3
Darfeld D....71 B4
Darfo I......120 B3
Dargin PL....68 A1
Dargun D....66 C1
Darlington UK..37 B5
Darłowo PL...68 A1
Darmstadt D...93 B4
Darney F.....105 A5
Daroca E....152 A2
Darque P....148 A1
Darragh IRL...28 B2
Dartford UK...45 B4
Dartington UK..43 B3
Dartmouth UK..43 B3
Darton UK....40 B2
Daruvar HR...124 B3
Darvas H....113 B5
Darvel UK....36 A2
Darwen UK...38 A4
Dassel D.....82 A1
Dassow D....65 C3
Datça TR....188 C2
Datteln D....80 A3
Dattenfeld D..81 B3
Daugard DK...59 C2
Daugavpils LV..8 E5
Daumeray F...102 B1
Daun D......80 B2
Daventry UK..44 A2
Davle CZ....96 B2
Davor HR....124 B3
Davos CH....107 C4

Davutlar TR . . . 188 B2
Davyd Haradok BY 13 B7
Dawlish UK 43 B3
Dax F 128 C1
Dazkırı TR 189 B4
Deal UK 45 B5
Deauville F 89 A4
Deba F 143 A4
Debar NMK . . . 182 B2
Dębe PL 77 B5
Dębica PL 87 B5
Dębnica Kaszubska PL 68 A2
Dębno PL 74 B3
Dębołęka PL 86 A2
Dębowa Łaka PL 69 B4
Debrc SRB 127 C1
Debrecen H 113 B5
Debrznica PL . . .75 B4
Debrzno PL 68 B2
Debstedt D 72 A1
Decazeville F . 130 A1
Dechtice SK 98 C1
Decima I 168 B2
Decimomannu I 179 C2
Děčín CZ 84 B2
Decize F 104 C2
De Cocksdorp NL 70 A1
Decollatura I . . 175 B2
Decs H 125 A4
Deddington UK 44 B2
Dedeler TR . . . 187 B5
Dedelow D 74 A2
Dedemli TR . . . 189 B7
Dedemsvaart NL 71 B3
Dédestapolcsány H 113 A4
Dedovichi RUS . . .9 D6
Deeping St Nicholas UK 41 C3
Deftera CY 181 A2
Dég H 112 C2
Degaña E 141 B4
Degeberga S . . . 61 D4
Degerby FIN 51 B7
Degerfors S 55 A5
Degerhamn S . . .63 B4
Degernes N 54 A2
Deggendorf D . .95 C4
Deggingen D . . .94 C1
Dego I 133 A4
Degolados P . . 155 B3
De Haan B 78 A3
Dehesas de Guadix E 164 B1
Dehesas Viejas E 163 A4
Deia E 166 B2
Deining D 95 B3
Deinze B 79 B3
Déiva Marina I 134 A2
Dej RO 17 B5
Deje S 55 A4
De Koog NL 70 A1
Delabole UK 42 B2
Delary S 61 C3
Delbrück D 81 A4
Delčevo NMK . . 182 B4
Delden NL 71 B3
Deleitosa E 156 A2
Delekovec HR . 124 A2
Delémont CH . 106 B2
Delft NL 70 B1
Delfzijl NL 71 A3
Délia I 176 B2
Delianuova I . . 175 C1
Deliblato SRB . 127 C3
Delice TR 23 B7
Deliceto I 171 B3
Delitzsch D 83 A4
Dellach A 109 C4
Delle F 106 B2
Delme F 92 C2
Delmen-horst D 72 A1
Delnice HR . . . 123 B3
Delsbo S 200 E2
Delvin IRL 30 A1
Delvinë AL 182 D2
Demandice SK 112 A2
Demen D 73 A4
Demidov RUS . . .13 A9
Demigny F 105 C3
Demirci TR 186 C3
Demirköy TR . . 186 A2
Demirtaş TR . . . 186 B4

Demmin D 66 C2
Demonte I 133 A3
Demyansk RUS . . .9 D8
Denain F 78 B3
Denbigh UK 38 A3
Den Burg NL 70 A1
Dender-monde B 79 A4
Denekamp NL . .71 B4
Den Ham NL . . .71 B3
Den Helder NL . .70 B1
Denholm UK 35 C5
Denia E 159 C4
Denizli TR 188 B4
Denkendorf D . .95 C3
Denklingen D . .81 B3
Denny UK 35 B4
Den Oever NL . . .70 B2
Denta RO 126 B3
Déols F 103 C3
De Panne B 78 A2
Derbent TR . . . 188 A3
Derby UK 40 C2
Derebucak TR 189 B6
Derecske H . . . 113 B5
Dereköy TR . . . 186 A2
Derenberg D . . .82 A2
Derinkuyu TR . .23 B8
Dermbach D . . .82 B2
Dermulo I 121 A4
Deronje SRB . . 125 B5
Derrygonnelly UK 26 B3
Derrylin UK 27 B3
Derry/Londonderry UK 27 B3
Dersingham UK 41 C4
Deruta I 136 C1
Dervaig UK 34 B1
Derval F 101 B4
Derveni GR . . . 184 A3
Derventa BIH . 125 C3
Dervock UK 27 A4
Desana I 119 B5
Descartes F . . . 102 C2
Desenzano del Garda I 121 B3
Deset N 48 A3
Deševa BIH . . . 139 B4
Desfina GR . . . 184 A3
Desimirovac SRB 127 C2
Désio I 120 B2
Deskati GR 182 D3
Deskle SLO 122 A2
Desná CZ 84 B3
Děšov CZ 97 C3
Despotovac SRB 127 C3
Despotovo SRB 126 B1
Dessau D 83 A4
Deštná CZ 96 B2
Destriana E . . . 141 B4
Désulo I 179 B3
Desvres F 78 B1
Deszk H 126 A2
Deta RO 126 B3
Detmold D 72 C1
Dětřichov CZ . . .98 B1
Dettelbach D . . .94 B2
Dettingen
Baden-Württemberg D 94 C1
Baden-Württemberg D 107 B4
Dettwiller F 93 C3
Detva SK 99 C3
Deurne NL 80 A1
Deutschkreutz A 111 B3
Deutschlandsberg A 110 C2
Deutsch Wagram A 111 A3
Deva RO 16 C5
Dévaványa H . 113 B4
Devecikonağı TR 186 C3
Devecser H . . . 111 B4
Develi TR 23 B8
Deventer NL . . .70 B3
Devil's Bridge UK 39 B3
Devin BG 183 B6
Devinska Nova Ves SK 111 A3
Devizes UK 43 A5
Devonport UK . .42 B2
Devrek TR 187 A6
Devrekâni TR . .23 A7

Đevrske HR . . . 137 B4
De Wijk NL 71 B3
Dewsbury UK . . .40 B2
Deza E 152 A1
Dežanovac HR 124 B3
Dezzo I 120 B3
Dhali CY 181 A2
Dherinia CY . . . 181 A2
Diamante I 174 B1
Dianalund DK . . 61 D1
Diano d'Alba I . 119 C5
Diano Marina I 133 B4
Dicomano I . . . 135 B4
Didcot UK 44 B2
Didim TR 188 B2
Didimoticho GR 186 A1
Die F 118 C2
Diebling F 92 B2
Dieburg D 93 B4
Diego del Carpio E 150 B2
Diekirch L 92 B2
Diélette F 88 A2
Diemelstadt D . .81 A5
Diémoz F 118 B2
Dienten am Hochkönig A 109 B3
Diepenbeck B . .79 B5
Diepholz D 71 B5
Dieppe F 89 A5
Dierberg D 74 A1
Dierdorf D 81 B3
Dieren NL 70 B3
Dierhagen D . . .66 B1
Diessen D 73 B3
Diessenhofen 108 B2
Diest B 79 B5
Dietenheim D . .94 C2
Dietfurt D 95 B3
Dietikon CH . . . 106 B3
Dietzenbach D . .93 A4
Dieue-sur-Meuse F 92 B1
Dieulefit F 131 A4
Dieulouard F . . .92 C2
Dieuze F 92 C2
Diever NL 71 B3
Diez D 81 B4
Diezma E 163 A4
Differdange L . . .92 B1
Digermulen N . 194 B6
Dignac F 115 C4
Dignano I 122 A1
Digne-les-Bains F 132 A2
Digny F 89 B5
Digoin F 104 C2
Dijon F 105 B4
Dikanäs S 195 E2
Dikili TR 186 C1
Diksmuide B . . .78 A2
Dilar E 163 A4
Dillenburg D . . .81 B4
Dillingen
Bayern D 94 C2
Saarland D 92 B2
Dilsen B 80 A1
Dimaro I 121 A3
Dimitrovgrad BG 183 A7
Dimitsana GR . 184 B3
Dinami I 175 C2
Dinan F 101 A3
Dinant B 79 B4
Dinar TR 189 A5
Dinard F 101 A3
Dinek TR 187 C6
Dingden D 80 A2
Dingelstädt D . .82 A2
Dingle
IRL 29 B1
S 54 B2
Dingolfing D . . .95 C4
Dingtuna S 56 A2
Dingwall UK . . . 32 D2
Dinkelsbühl D . .94 B2
Dinkelscherben D 94 C2
Dinklage D 71 B5
Dinslaken D 80 A2
Dinxperlo NL . . .80 A2
Diö S 63 B2
Diósgyör H . . . 113 A4
Diósjeno H 112 B3
Diou F 104 C2
Dippen UK 34 C2
Dipperz D 82 B1
Dippoldiswalde D 84 B1

Dirdal N 52 B2
Dirksland NL . . .79 A4
Dirlewang D . . . 108 B1
Dischingen D . . .94 C2
Disentis CH . . . 107 C3
Diso I 173 B4
Diss UK 45 A5
Dissen D 71 B5
Distington UK . . .36 B3
Ditzingen D 93 C5
Ditzum D 71 A4
Divača SLO 122 B2
Dives-sur-Mer F 89 A3
Divín SK 99 C3
Divion F 78 B2
Divišov CZ 96 B2
Divonne les Bains F 118 A3
Dixmont F 104 A2
Dizy-le-Gros F . .91 B4
Djúpivogur IS 191 C11
Djupvasshytta N 198 C4
Djura S 50 B1
Djuras S 50 B2
Djurmo S 50 B2
Djursdala S 62 A3
Dlouhá Loucka CZ 98 B1
Długowola PL . .87 A5
Dmitrov RUS . . .9 D10
Dno RUS 9 D6
Doade E 141 B3
Doğanhisar TR 189 A6
Dobanovci SRB 127 C2
Dobbertin D 73 A5
Dobbiaco I 108 C3
Dobczyce PL 99 B4
Dobele LV 8 D3
Doberlug-Kirchhain D 83 A5
Dobern D 84 A2
Dobersberg A . . .97 C3
Dobiegniew PL .75 B4
Dobieszyn PL . . .87 A5
Doboj BIH 125 C4
Dobošnica BIH 125 C4
Doboz H 113 C5
Dobra
Wielkopolskie PL 76 C3
Zachodnio-Pomorskie PL . 74 A3
Zachodnio-Pomorskie PL . 75 A4
Dobrá Niva SK . .99 C3
Dobřany CZ 96 B1
Dobre PL 76 B3
Dobre Miasto PL 69 B5
Dobreta-Turnu-Severin RO 16 C5
Dobri H 111 C3
Dobrica SRB . . 126 B2
Dobrich BG . . . 17 D7
Dobrinishte BG 183 B5
Dobříš CZ 96 B2
Dobro E 143 B3
Dobrodzień PL . .86 B2
Döbrököz H . . . 112 C2
Dobromierz PL . .85 B4
Dobrosołowo PL 76 B3
Dobroszyce PL . .85 A5
Dobrzany PL 75 A4
Dobrzeń Wielki PL 86 B1
Dobrzyca
Wielkopolskie PL 75 A5
Wielkopolskie PL 85 A5
Dobrzyń nad Wisłą PL 77 B4
Dobšiná SK 99 C4
Dobwalls UK 42 B2
Dochamps B 80 B1
Docking UK 41 C4
Docksta S 200 C4

Doddington UK 37 A4
Döderhult S 62 A4
Doesburg NL . . .70 B3
Doetinchem NL 71 C3
Dogliani I 133 A4
Dogueno P 160 B2
Doische B 91 A4
Dojč SK 98 C1
Dokka N 48 B2
Dokkedal DK 58 B3
Dokkum NL 70 A2
Dokležovje SLO 111 C3
Doksy CZ 84 B2
Dokuz TR 189 A7
Dolancourt F . . 104 A3
Dolceácqua I . . 133 B3
Dol-de-Bretagne F 88 B2
Dole F 105 B4
Dølemo N 53 B4
Dolenja vas SLO 123 B3
Dolenjske Toplice SLO 123 B4
Dolfor UK 39 B3
Dolgarrog UK . . .38 A3
Dolgellau UK . . .38 B3
Doliana GR 182 D2
Dolianova I . . . 179 C3
Dolice PL 75 A4
Doljani HR 138 A2
Döllach im Mölltal A 109 C3
Dolle D 73 B4
Dollnstein D 94 C3
Dollot F 104 A2
Döllstadt D 82 A2
Dolná Strehová SK 99 C3
Dolné Saliby SK 111 A4
Dolni Benešov CZ 98 B2
Dolní Bousov CZ 84 B3
Dolni Kounice CZ 97 B4
Dolni Kralovice CZ 97 B3
Dolní Újezd CZ . .97 B4
Dolní Žandov CZ 95 A4
Dolný Kubín SK .99 B3
Dolo I 121 B5
Dolores E 165 A4
Dolovo SRB . . . 127 C2
Dölsach A 109 C3
Dolsk PL 76 B2
Dolwyddelan UK 38 A3
Domaljevac BIH 125 B4
Domaniç TR . . . 187 C4
Domaniža SK . . .98 B2
Domanovići BIH 139 B3
Domašov CZ 85 B5
Domaszék H . . . 126 A1
Domaszków PL . .85 B4
Domaszowice PL 86 A1
Domat-Ems CH 107 C4
Domažlice CZ . . .95 B4
Dombås N 198 C6
Dombasle-sur-Meurthe F 92 C2
Dombegyház H 126 A3
Dombóvár H . . 112 C2
Domène F 118 B2
Domérat F 116 A2
Domfessel F 92 C3
Domfront en-Champagne F 102 A2
Domingão P . . 154 B2
Domingo Pérez
Granada E . . . 163 A4
Toledo E 150 C3
Dömitz D 73 A4
Dommartin F . . .91 C4
Dommartin-le-Franc F 91 C4
Domme F 129 B4
Dommitzsch D . .83 A4
Domodóssola I 119 A5
Dörenthe D 71 B4
Dores UK 32 D2
Domokos GR . . 182 D4

Dav – Dra 215

Dorfen D 95 C4
Dorfgastein A . 109 B4
Dorfmark D 72 B2
Dorf Mecklenburg D 65 C4
Dorgali I 178 B3
Dorking UK 44 B3
Dormagen D 80 A2
Dormánd H . . . 113 B4
Dormans F 91 B3
Dornava SLO . . 124 A1
Dornbirn A 107 B4
Dornburg D 83 A3
Dorndorf D 82 B2
Dornecy F 104 B2
Dornes F 104 C2
Dornhan D 93 C4
Dornie UK 31 B3
Dornoch UK . . . 32 D2
Dornum D 71 A4
Dorog H 112 B2
Dorohoi RO 17 B7
Dorotea S 200 B2
Dorotowo PL . . .69 B5
Dörpen D 71 B4
Dorsten D 80 A2
Dortan F 118 A2
Dortmund D 80 A3
Doruchów PL . . .86 A2
Dorum D 64 C1
Dörverden D 72 B2
Dörzbach D 94 B1
Dos Aguas E . . . 159 B3
Dosbarrios E . . 151 C4
Döşemealtı TR 189 B5
Dos Hermanas E 162 A2
Dospat BG 183 B6
Dos-Torres E . . 156 B3
Dötlingen D 72 B1
Dottignies B 78 B3
Döttingen CH . 106 B3
Douai F 78 B3
Douarnenez F . 100 A1
Douchy F 104 B2
Douchy-les-Mines F 78 B3
Doucier F 105 C4
Doudeville F 89 A4
Doué-la-Fontaine F 102 B1
Douglas
Isle of Man UK 36 B2
South Lanarkshire UK 36 A3
Doulaincourt-Saucourt F 91 C5
Doulevant-le-Château F 91 C4
Doullens F 90 A2
Dounby UK 33 B3
Doune UK 35 B3
Dounreay UK . . . 32 C3
Dour B 79 B3
Dourdan F 90 C2
Dourgne F 146 A3
Dournazac F . . . 115 C4
Douro Calvo P . 148 B2
Douvaine F 118 A3
Douvres-la-Délivrande F . . .89 A3
Douzy F 91 B5
Dover UK 45 B5
Dovje SLO 109 C4
Dovre N 198 D6
Downham Market UK 41 C4
Downhill UK 27 A4
Downpatrick UK 27 B5
Dowra IRL 26 B2
Doxato GR 183 B6
Doyet F 116 A2
Dozule F 89 A3
Drača SRB 127 C2
Dračevo
BIH 139 C4
NMK 182 B3
Drachten NL . . .70 A3
Draga S 123 C3
Drăgăşani RO . .17 C6
Dragatuš SLO . 123 B4
Dragichyn BY . .13 B6
Draginja SRB . 127 C1
Dragocvet SRB 127 D3
Dragolovci BIH 125 C3

Dragoni I...... 170 B2
Dragør DK..... 61 D2
Dragotina HR . 124 B2
Dragotinja
  BIH........ 124 B2
Dragozetići
  HR........ 123 B3
Draguignan F . 132 B2
Drahnsdorf D...74 C2
Drahonice CZ...96 B2
Drahovce SK...98 C1
Drama GR.... 183 B6
Drammen N....54 A1
Drangedal N....53 A5
Drangsnes IS.. 190 B4
Dransfeld D....82 A1
Dranske D......66 B2
Draperstown
  UK........27 B4
Drassburg A.. 111 B3
Drávaszabolcs
  H.......... 125 B4
Dravograd
  SLO......... 110 C2
Drawno PL.....75 A4
Drawsko Pomorskie
  PL........... 75 A4
Drayton UK....41 C5
Drążdżewo PL . 77 A6
Draženov CZ...95 B4
Draževac SRB . 127 C2
Dražice HR.... 123 B3
Drebkau D....84 A2
Dreieich D......93 A4
Dreisen D.....93 B4
Drenovci HR . 125 C4
Drensteinfurt
  D............81 A3
Dresden D....84 A1
Dretyń PL......68 A1
Dreux F........89 B5
Dřevohostice
  CZ..........98 B1
Drevsjø N..... 199 D9
Drewitz D......73 B5
Drezdenko PL..75 B4
Drežnica HR... 123 B4
Drežnik-Grad
  HR........ 123 C4
Drietona SK...98 C1
Driffield UK....40 A3
Drimnin UK....34 B2
Drimoleague
  IRL........29 C2
Dringenberg
  D...........81 A5
Drinić BIH.... 138 A2
Drinjača BIH.. 139 A5
Drinovci BIH... 138 B3
Driopida GR... 185 B5
Drivstua N... 198 C6
Drlače SRB.... 127 C1
Drnholec CZ...97 C4
Drniš HR.... 138 B2
Drnje HR..... 124 A2
Drnovice CZ...97 B4
Dro I....... 121 B3
Drøbak N.....54 A1
Drobin PL......77 B5
Drochia MD....17 A7
Drochtersen D. .64 C2
Drogheda IRL..30 A2
Drohobych UA. 13 D5
Droitwich Spa
  UK..........44 A1
Drołtowice PL..85 A5
Dromahair IRL. .26 B2
Dromcolliher
  IRL........29 B3
Dromore
  Down UK.....27 B5
  Tyrone UK....27 B3
Dromore West
  IRL........26 B2
Dronero I..... 133 A3
Dronfield UK...40 B2
Drongan UK...36 A2
Dronninglund
  DK..........58 A3
Dronrijp NL...70 A2
Dronten NL...70 B2
Drosendorf A...97 C3
Drösing A......97 C4
Drottningholm
  S...........57 A3
Droué F...... 103 A3
Drulingen F....92 C3
Drumbeg UK...32 C1
Drumcliff IRL...26 B2
Drumgask UK.. 32 D2

Drumkeeran
  IRL.............26 B2
Drummore UK..36 B2
Drumnadrochit
  UK............ 32 D2
Drumquin UK...27 B3
Drumshanbo
  IRL.............26 B2
Drumsna IRL....26 C2
Drunen NL.....79 A5
Druskininkai
  LT..............13 A5
Druten NL......80 A1
Druya BY........13 A7
Družetići SRB . 127 C2
Drvar BIH..... 138 A2
Drvenik HR... 138 B3
Drwalew PL....77 C6
Drymen UK....34 B3
Drynoch UK.....31 B2
Drzewce PL....76 B2
Drzewiany PL...68 B1
Drzewica PL....87 A4
Dualchi I.... 178 B2
Duas Igrejas P. 149 A3
Dub SRB...... 127 D1
Dubá CZ......84 B2
Dubăsari MD....17 B8
Duben D......74 C2
Dübendorf
  CH........ 107 B3
Dubi CZ......84 B1
Dubica HR.... 124 B2
Dublin IRL......30 A2
Dubna RUS.......9 D10
Dubňany CZ....98 C1
Dubnica nad
  Váhom SK....98 C2
Dubnik SK.... 112 B2
Dubno UA.......13 C6
Dubodiel SK ...98 C2
Dubona SRB . 127 C2
Dubovac SRB.. 127 C3
Dubranec HR.. 124 B1
Dubrava HR... 124 B2
Dubrave BIH.. 125 C4
Dubravica
  HR........ 123 B4
  SRB......... 127 C3
Dubrovnik HR. 139 C4
Dubrovytsya
  UA...........13 C7
Ducey F........88 B2
Duchcov CZ....84 B1
Ducherow D....74 A2
Dučina SRB... 127 C2
Duclair F........89 A4
Dudar H..... 112 B1
Duddington UK 40 C3
Duderstadt D...82 A2
Dudeştii Vechi
  RO........ 126 A2
Dudley UK....40 C1
Dueñas E...... 142 C2
Duesund N......46 B2
Dueville I..... 121 B4
Duffel B........79 A4
Duffield UK....40 C2
Dufftown UK... 32 D3
Duga Resa HR. 123 B4
Dugi Rat HR... 138 B2
Dugny-sur-Meuse
  F..............92 B1
Dugopolje HR. 138 B2
Dugo Selo HR. 124 B2
Duino I........ 122 B2
Dukat AL...... 182 C1
Dukovany CZ...97 B4
Duleek IRL......30 A2
Dülken D......80 A2
Dülmen D......80 A3
Dulovo BG.... 17 D7
Dulpetorpet N..49 B4
Dulverton UK...43 A3
Dumbarton UK. 34 C3
Dümerek TR.. 187 C6
Dumfries UK...36 A3
Dumlupınar
  TR........ 187 D4
Dümpelfeld D...80 B2
Dunaalmás H. 112 B2
Dunabogdány
  H.......... 112 B3
Dunafalva H.. 125 A4
Dunaföldvár
  H.......... 112 C2
Dunaharaszti
  H.......... 112 B3
Dunajská Streda
  SK........ 111 B4
Dunakeszi H.. 112 B3

Dunakiliti H... 111 B4
Dunakömlöd
  H.......... 112 C2
Dunapataj H.. 112 C2
Dunaszekcsö
  H.......... 125 A4
Dunaszentgyorgy
  H.......... 112 C2
Dunatetétlen
  H.......... 112 C3
Dunaújváros
  H.......... 112 C2
Dunavecse H.. 112 C2
Dunbar UK....35 B5
Dunbeath UK ... 32 C3
Dunblane UK ...35 B4
Dunboyne IRL. .30 A2
Dundalk IRL....27 B4
Dundee UK....35 B5
Dundrennan
  UK............36 B3
Dundrum UK...27 B5
Dunfanaghy
  IRL........26 A3
Dunfermline
  UK............35 B4
Dungannon UK .27 B4
Dungarvan IRL.. 29 B4
Dungiven UK...27 B4
Dunglow IRL....26 B2
Dungourney
  IRL........29 C3
Duninowo PL...68 A1
Dunkeld UK....35 B4
Dunker S......56 A2
Dunkerque =
  Dunkirk F.....78 A2
Dunkineely IRL .26 B2
Dunkirk =
  Dunkerque F...78 A2
Dun Laoghaire
  IRL........30 A2
Dunlavin IRL....30 A2
Dunleer IRL....27 C4
Dun-le-Palestel
  F.......... 116 A1
Dun-les-Places
  F.......... 104 B3
Dunlop UK.....36 A2
Dunloy UK.....27 A4
Dunmanway
  IRL........29 C2
Dunmore IRL....28 A3
Dunmore East
  IRL........30 B2
Dunmurry UK...27 B4
Dunnet UK.... 32 C3
Dunningen D . 107 A3
Dunoon UK....34 C3
Duns UK......35 C5
Dunscore UK...36 A3
Dunsford UK....43 B3
Dunshaughlin
  IRL........30 A2
Dunstable UK...44 B3
Dunster UK....43 A3
Dun-sur-Auron
  F.......... 103 C4
Dun-sur-Meuse
  F............91 B5
Dunvegan UK...31 B2
Duplek SLO... 110 C2
Dupnitsa BG.. 17 D5
Durağan TR...23 A8
Durach D.... 107 B5
Durak TR..... 186 C3
Durana E..... 143 B4
Durance F.... 128 B3
Durango E.... 143 A4
Durankulak BG 17 D8
Duras F...... 128 B3
Durban-Corbières
  F.......... 146 B3
Dürbheim D... 107 A3
Durbuy B......79 B5
Dúrcal E..... 163 B4
Đurdjenovac
  HR........ 125 B4
Đurdjevac HR. 124 A3
Đurdjevik BIH. 139 A4
Düren D......80 B2
Durham UK....37 B5
Đurinci SRB... 127 C2
Durlach D......93 C4
Đurmanec HR. 124 A1
Durness UK... 32 C2
Dürnkrut A....97 C4
Dürrboden
  CH........ 107 C4
Dürrenboden
  CH........ 107 C3
Dürrës AL.... 182 B1
Durrow IRL....30 B1

Durrus IRL.......29 C2
Dursunbey TR. 186 C3
Durtal F....... 102 B1
Durup DK......58 B1
Durusu TR.... 186 A3
Dusina BIH... 139 B3
Dusnok H..... 112 C2
Dusocin PL.....69 B3
Düsseldorf D...80 A2
Dusslingen D..93 C5
Duszniki PL....75 B5
Duszniki-Zdrój
  PL........... 85 B4
Dutovlje SLO.. 122 B2
Duvebo S.....55 B5
Duved S...... 199 B9
Düzağaç TR... 187 D5
Düzce TR.... 187 B6
Dvärsätt S... 199 B11
Dvor HR...... 124 B2
Dvorce CZ......98 B1
Dvorníky SK...98 C1
Dvory nad Žitavou
  SK........ 112 B2
Dvůr Královénad
  Labem CZ....85 B3
Dybvad DK.....58 A3
Dyce UK..... 33 D4
Dygowo PL....67 B4
Dykehead UK...35 B4
Dymchurch UK. .45 B5
Dymer UA......13 C9
Dyrnes N.... 198 B4
Dywity PL......69 B5
Dzierząźnia PL. 77 B5
Dzierzgoń PL...69 B4
Dzierzgowo PL. .77 A5
Dzierżoniów
  PL........... 85 B4
Dzisna BY.......13 A8
Dziwnów PL....67 B3
Dźwierzuty PL. .77 A5
Dzyarzhynsk
  BY.............13 B7
Dzyatlava BY....13 B6

E

Ea E......... 143 A4
Eaglesfield UK . .36 A3
Ealing UK.....44 B3
Eardisley UK....39 B3
Earls Barton UK .44 A3
Earl Shilton UK. 40 C2
Earlston UK....35 C5
Easington UK...41 B4
Easky IRL......26 B2
Eastbourne UK. .45 C4
East Calder UK . .35 C4
East Dereham
  UK............41 C4
Easter Skeld
  UK............ 33 A5
East Grinstead
  UK............45 B4
East Ilsley UK...44 B2
East Kilbride
  UK............36 A2
Eastleigh UK....44 C2
East Linton UK . 35 C5
East Markham
  UK............40 B3
Easton UK.....43 B4
East Wittering
  UK............44 C3
Eaton Socon
  UK............44 A3
Eaux-Bonnes
  F.......... 145 B3
Eauze F...... 128 C3
Ebberup DK....59 C2
Ebbs A....... 108 B3
Ebbw Vale UK ...39 C3
Ebeleben D....82 A2
Ebene Reichenau
  A......... 109 C4
Eben im Pongau
  A......... 109 B4
Ebensee A.... 109 B4
Ebensfeld D....94 A2
Eberbach D....93 B4
Ebergötzen D...82 A2
Ebermann-Stadt
  D............94 B3

Ebern D........82 B2
Eberndorf A .. 110 C1
Ebersbach D...84 A2
Ebersberg D .. 108 A2
Ebersdorf
  Bayern D....82 B3
  Niedersachsen
  D............ 72 A2
Eberstein A ... 110 C1
Eberswalde D...74 B2
Ebnat-Kappel
  CH........ 107 B4
Éboli I......... 170 C3
Ebrach D......94 B2
Ebreichsdorf
  A........... 111 B3
Ebreuil F...... 116 A3
Ebstorf D......72 A3
Eccleshall UK...40 C1
Eceabat TR... 186 B1
Echallens CH .. 106 C1
Echauri E..... 144 B2
Echinos GR... 183 B7
Echiré F....... 114 B3
Echirolles F ... 118 B2
Echourgnac F . 128 A3
Echt NL........80 A1
Echte D........82 A2
Echternach L...92 B2
Ecija E....... 162 A2
Ečka SRB.... 126 B2
Eckartsberga D. 82 A3
Eckelshausen D 81 B4
Eckental D.....94 B3
Eckernförde D..64 B2
Eckerö FIN..... 51 B6
Eckington UK...40 B2
Éclaron F......91 C4
Écommoy F... 102 B2
Écouché F......89 B3
Écouis F.......90 B1
Ecséd H...... 113 B3
Ecsegfalva H.. 113 B4
Écueillé F..... 103 B3
Ed S..........54 B2
Eda S..........49 C4
Eda glasbruk S. .49 C4
Edam NL......70 B2
Edane S.......55 A3
Edderton UK... 32 D2
Ede NL........70 B2
Edebäck S.....49 B5
Edebo S.......51 B5
Edelény H......99 C4
Edelschrott A . 110 B2
Edemissen D...72 B3
Edenbridge UK .45 B4
Edenderry IRL...30 A1
Edenkoben D...93 B4
Edesheim D....93 B4
Edessa GR.... 182 C4
Edewecht D....71 A4
Edgeworthstown
  IRL........30 A1
Edinburgh UK...35 C4
Edineţ MD.....17 A7
Edirne TR.... 186 A1
Edland N......52 A3
Edolo I...... 120 A3
Edøy N...... 198 B5
Edremit TR... 186 C2
Edsbro S......51 C5
Edsbruk S.....56 B2
Edsbyn S......50 A2
Edsele S..... 200 C2
Edsleskog S....54 A3
Edsvalla S.....55 A4
Eekloo B.......79 A3
Eemshaven NL. .71 A3
Eerbeek NL....70 B3
Eersel NL......79 A5
Eferding A.....96 C2
Effiat F....... 116 A3
Efteløt N......53 A5
Egeln D.......73 C4
Eger H....... 113 B4
Egerbakta H . 113 B4
Egernsund DK. .64 B2
Egersund N....52 B2
Egerszólát H. . 113 B4
Egervár H.... 111 C3
Egg
  A......... 107 B4
  D......... 107 A5
Eggby S.......55 B4
Eggedal N......47 B6
Eggenburg A...97 C3
Eggenfelden D. .95 C4
Eggesin D......74 A3
Eggum N..... 194 B4
Egham UK.....44 B3
Éghezée B......79 B4

Egiertowo PL ...68 A3
Egilsstaðir IS . 191 B11
Egina GR..... 185 B4
Eginio GR.... 182 C4
Egio GR...... 184 A3
Égletons F ... 116 B2
Egling D..... 108 B2
Eglinton UK....27 A3
Eglisau CH... 107 B3
Église-neuve-
  d'Entraigues
  F.......... 116 B2
Eglofs D..... 107 B4
Egmond aan Zee
  NL...........70 B1
Egna I....... 121 A4
Egosthena GR. 184 A4
Egremont
  UK............36 B3
Egtved DK.....59 C2
Eguilles F.... 131 B4
Eguilly-sous-Bois
  F.......... 104 A3
Éguzon-Chantôme
  F.......... 103 C3
Egyek H..... 113 B4
Egyházasrádóc
  H.......... 111 B3
Ehekirchen D ...94 C3
Ehingen D.....94 C1
Ehra-Lessien D. .73 B3
Ehrang D......92 B2
Ehrenfriedersdorf
  D............83 B4
Ehrenhain D ...83 B4
Ehrenhausen
  A........... 110 C2
Ehringshausen
  D............81 B4
Ehrwald A.... 108 B1
Eibar E....... 143 A4
Eibelstadt D ...94 B2
Eibenstock D ...83 B4
Eibergen NL....71 B3
Eibiswald A ... 110 C2
Eichenbarleben
  D............73 B4
Eichendorf D ...95 C4
Eichstätt D......95 C3
Eickelborn D...81 A4
Eide
  Hordaland N....46 B3
  Møre og Romsdal
  N......... 198 C4
Eidet N....... 194 A9
Eidfjord N......46 B4
Eidsberg N.....54 A2
Eidsbugarden
  N...........47 A5
Eidsdal N.... 198 C4
Eidsfoss N.....53 A6
Eidskog N.....49 B4
Eidsvåg
  Hordaland N....46 B2
  Møre og Romsdal
  N......... 198 C5
Eidsvoll N.....48 B3
Eikefjord N.....46 A2
Eikelandsosen
  N...........46 B2
Eiken N.......52 B3
Eikesdal N.... 198 C5
Eikstrand N....53 A5
Eilenburg D....83 A4
Eilsleben D.....73 B4
Eina N........48 B2
Einbeck D......82 A1
Eindhoven NL. .79 A5
Einsiedeln CH. 107 B3
Einville-au-Jard
  F............92 C2
Eisenach D.....82 B2
Eisenberg
  Rheinland-Pfalz
  D............93 B4
  Thüringen D. .83 B3
Eisenerz A.... 110 B1
Eisenhüttenstadt
  D............74 B3
Eisenkappel A 110 C1
Eisenstadt A . 111 B3
Eisentratten
  A......... 109 C4
Eisfeld D......82 B2
Eisleben D......82 A3
Eislingen D....94 C1
Eitensheim D...95 C3
Eiterfeld D.....82 B1
Eitorf D........80 B3
Eivindvik N....46 A2
Eivissa = Ibiza
  E.......... 166 C1
Eixo P....... 148 B1
Ejby DK.......59 C2

Ejea de los
  Caballeros E . 144 B2
Ejstrupholm
  DK..........59 C2
Ejulve E...... 153 B3
Eke B.........79 B3
Ekeby
  Gotland S..... 57 C4
  Skåne S....... 61 D2
  Uppsala S... 51 B5
Ekeby-Almby S .56 A1
Ekenäs S.....55 B4
Ekenässjön S...62 A3
Ekerö S.......57 A3
Eket S........61 C3
Eketorp S......63 B4
Ekevik S......56 B2
Ekkerøy N.... 193 B14
Eknäs S.......55 B4
Ekshärad S....49 B5
Eksingedal N...46 B2
Eksjö S........62 A2
Eksta S........57 C4
Ekträsk S.... 200 B5
El Alamo
  Madrid E..... 151 B4
  Sevilla E..... 161 B3
El Algar E..... 165 B4
El Almendro E. 161 B2
El Alquián E .. 164 C2
Élancourt F....90 C1
El Arenal E.... 150 B2
El Arguellite E. 164 A2
El Astillero E .. 143 A3
Elati GR...... 182 D3
El Ballestero E. .158 C1
El Barco de Ávila
  E.......... 150 B2
Elbasan AL.... 182 B2
El Berrón E.... 142 A1
El Berrueco E.. 151 B4
Elbeuf F.......89 A4
Elbingerode D. .82 A2
Elbląg PL......69 A4
El Bodón E... 149 B3
El Bonillo E.... 158 C1
El Bosque E... 162 B2
El Bullaque E.. 157 A3
Elburg NL.....70 B2
El Burgo E.... 162 B3
El Burgo de Ebro
  E.......... 153 A3
El Burgo de Osma
  E.......... 151 A4
El Burgo Ranero
  E.......... 142 B1
El Buste E.... 144 C2
El Cabaco E ... 149 B3
El Callejo E ... 143 A3
El Campillo E.. 161 B3
El Campillo de la
  Jara E...... 156 A2
El Cañavete E . 158 B1
El Carpio E.... 157 C3
El Carpio de Tajo
  E.......... 150 C3
El Casar E ... 151 B4
El Casar de
  Escalona E... 150 B3
El Castillo de las
  Guardas E... 161 B3
El Centenillo E 157 B4
El Cerro E ... 149 B4
El Cerro de
  Andévalo E .. 161 B3
Elche de la Sierra
  E.......... 158 C1
Elchingen D....94 C2
El Comenar E . 162 B2
El Coronil E.... 162 A2
El Crucero E... 141 A4
El Cubo de Tierra
  del Vino E... 149 A4
El Cuervo E... 162 B1
Elda E....... 159 C3
Eldena D......73 A4
Eldingen D....72 B3
Elefsina GR... 185 A4
El Ejido E.... 164 C2
Elek H....... 113 C5
Elemir SRB.... 126 B2
El Escorial E .. 151 B3
El Espinar E .. 151 B3
Eleutheroupoli
  GR........ 183 C6
El Frago E.... 144 B3
El Franco E.... 141 A4
El Frasno E.... 152 A2
Elgå N....... 199 C8
El Garrobo E.. 161 B3
El Gastor E... 162 B2

Elgin UK. 32 D3
Elgoibar E. 143 A4
Elgol UK. 31 B2
El Gordo F. 150 C2
El Grado E. 145 B4
El Granado E. . . 161 B2
El Grao de Castelló
　E. 159 B4
El Grau E 159 C3
Elgshøa N. 49 A4
El Higuera E. . . 163 A3
El Hijate E. 164 B2
El Hontanar E. . 152 B2
Elhovo BG. 17 D7
El Hoyo E. 157 B4
Elie UK 35 B5
Elizondo E 144 A2
Ełk PL 12 B5
Ellenberg D 94 B2
Ellesmere UK. . .38 B4
Ellesmere Port
　UK 38 A4
Ellezelles B. 79 B3
Ellingen D 94 B2
Ellmau A 109 B3
Ellon UK. 33 D4
Ellös S. 54 B2
Ellrich D. 82 A2
Ellwangen D . . .94 C2
Elm
　CH 107 C4
　D 72 A2
Elmadağ TR 23 B7
El Madroño E. . 161 B3
El Maillo E. . . . 149 B3
Elmalı TR. 189 C4
El Masnou E. . . 147 C3
El Mirón E. 150 B2
El Molar E. 151 B4
El Molinillo E. . 157 A3
El Morell E 147 C2
Elmshorn D. . . .64 C2
Elmstein D. 93 B3
El Muyo E 151 A4
Elne F 146 B3
Elnesvågen N. 198 C4
El Olmo E 151 A4
Elorrio E 143 A4
Elöszállás H . . . 112 C2
Elouda GR. . . . 185 D6
Éloyes F. 105 A5
El Palo E. 163 B3
El Pardo E. . . . 151 B4
El Payo E 149 B3
El Pedernoso
　E. 158 B1
El Pedroso E. . . 162 A2
El Peral E. 158 B2
El Perelló
　Tarragona E . . 153 B4
　Valencia E . . . 159 B3
Elphin UK 32 C1
El Picazo E 158 B1
El Pinell de Bray
　E. 153 A4
El Piñero E 150 A2
El Pla de Santa
　Maria E 147 C2
El Pobo E. 153 B3
El Pobo de Dueñas
　E. 152 B2
El Pont
　d'Armentera
　E. 147 C2
El Port de la Selva
　E. 147 B4
El Port de Llançà
　E. 146 B4
El Port de Sagunt
　E. 159 B3
El Prat de Llobregat
　E. 147 C3
El Provencio E. 158 B1
El Puente E. . . . 143 A3
El Puente del
　Arzobispo E. . 150 C2
El Puerto E 141 A4
El Puerto de Santa
　María E 162 B1
El Real de la Jara
　E. 161 B3
El Real de San
　Vincente E . . . 150 B3
El Robledo E . . 157 A3
El Rocio E 161 B3
El Rompido E. . 161 B2
El Ronquillo E. 161 B3
El Royo E. 143 C4
El Rubio E. 162 A3
El Sabinar E . . . 164 A2
El Saler E. 159 B3
El Salobral E. . 158 C2
El Saucejo E. . . 162 A2

Els Castells E . . 147 B2
Elsdorf D. 80 B2
Elsenfeld D 93 B5
El Serrat AND . 146 B2
Elsfleth D 72 A1
Elspeet NL 70 B2
Elst NL 70 C2
Elstead UK 44 B3
Elster D 83 A4
Elsterberg D . . .83 B4
Elsterwerda D . .83 A5
Elstra D 84 A2
El Temple E . . . 144 C3
El Tiemblo E. . . 150 B3
Eltmann D 94 B2
El Toboso E . . . 157 A5
El Tormillo E . . 145 C3
El Torno E 149 B4
Eltville D. 93 A4
El Valle de las Casas
　E. 142 B1
Elvas P. 155 C3
Elvebakken N. 192 C7
El Vellón E. . . . 151 B4
Elven F. 101 B3
El Vendrell E . . 147 C2
Elverum N 48 B3
El Villar de Arnedo
　E. 144 B1
Elvington UK. . .40 B3
El Viso del Alcor
　E. 162 A2
Elxleben D 82 A2
Ely UK. 45 A4
Elzach D 106 A3
Elze D. 72 B2
Emådalen S. . . .50 A1
Embleton UK. . .37 A5
Embonas GR . . 188 C2
Embrun F. 132 A2
Embún E 144 B3
Emden D. 71 A4
Emecik TR. . . . 188 C2
Emet TR. 186 C4
Emirdağ TR . . . 187 C6
Emlichheim D. . .71 B3
Emmaboda S . . .63 B3
Emmaljunga S . .61 C3
Emmeloord NL. .70 B2
Emmen
　CH 106 B3
　NL 71 B3
Emmendingen
　D 106 A2
Emmer-
　Compascuum
　NL 71 B4
Emmerich D . . .80 A2
Emmern D. 72 B2
Emöd H 113 B4
Émpoli I. 135 B3
Emsbüren D 71 B4
Emsdetten D. . . .71 B4
Emsfors S 62 A4
Emskirchen D. . .94 B2
Emstek D 71 B5
Emsworth UK . .44 C3
Emyvale IRL. . . .27 B4
Enafors S 199 B9
Enånger S. 51 A4
Encamp AND. . 146 B2
Encarnação P. . 154 C1
Encinas de Abajo
　E. 150 B2
Encinas de Esgueva
　E. 142 C2
Encinasola E . . 161 A3
Encinas Reales
　E. 163 A3
Encio E. 143 B3
Enciso E. 144 B1
Enden N 199 D7
Endingen D . . . 106 A2
Endrinal E. 149 B4
Endröd H 113 C4
Enebakk N 54 A2
Eneryda S. 63 B2
Enese H. 111 B4
Enez TR 183 C8
Enfield IRL. 30 A2
Eng A 108 B2
Engelberg CH. 106 C3
Engelhartszell
　A. 96 C1
Engelskirchen
　D 80 B3
Engen D 107 B3
Enger N. 48 B2
Engerdal N. . . . 199 D8
Engerneset N . .49 A4
Enge-sande D. . .64 B1
Engesvang DK . .59 B2

Enghien B. 79 B4
Engstingen D . .94 C1
Engter D 71 B5
Enguera E. 159 C3
Enguidanos E. 158 B2
Enkenbach D . . .93 B3
Enkhuizen NL. . .70 B2
Enklinge FIN. . . .51 B7
Enköping S 56 A3
Enna I. 177 B3
Ennezat F. 116 B3
Ennigerloh D . . .81 A4
Enningdal N 54 B2
Ennis IRL. 28 B3
Enniscorthy IRL.30 B2
Enniskean IRL...29 C3
Enniskillen UK . .27 B3
Ennistimon IRL..28 B2
Enns A 110 A1
Eno FIN 9 A7
Enontekiö
　FIN. 196 A6
Ens NL 70 B2
Enschede NL. . . .71 B3
Ensdorf D. 95 B3
Ensisheim F. . . 106 B2
Enstaberga S . . .56 B2
Enstone UK 44 B2
Entlebuch CH . 106 B3
Entrácque I . . . 133 A3
Entradas P. . . . 160 B1
Entrains-sur-
　Nohain F. . . . 104 B2
Entrambasaguas
　E. 143 A3
Entrambasmestas
　E. 143 A3
Entraygues-sur-
　Truyère F. . . . 116 C2
Entre-os-Rios
　P. 148 A1
Entrevaux F. . . 132 B2
Entrin Bajo E. . 155 C4
Entroncamento
　P. 154 B2
Entzheim F. 93 C3
Envermeu F. . . .89 A5
Enviken S. 50 B2
Enying H. 112 C2
Enzingerboden
　A. 109 B3
Enzklösterle D . .93 C4
Épagny F. 90 B3
Epalinges CH . 106 C1
Epannes F. 114 B3
Épanomi GR . . 182 C4
Epe
　D 71 B4
　NL 70 B2
Épernay F. 91 B3
Épernon F. 90 C1
Epfig F 93 C3
Épierre F 118 B3
Épila E 152 A2
Épinac F 104 C3
Épinal F 105 A5
Episcopia I 174 A2
Episkopi CY . . . 181 B1
Epitalio GR. . . . 184 B2
Epoisses F 104 B3
Eppenbrunn D. .93 B3
Eppendorf D. . . .83 B5
Epping UK 45 B4
Eppingen D 93 B4
Epsom UK. 44 B3
Epworth UK. . . .40 B3
Eraclea I 122 B1
Eraclea Mare I. . 122 B1
Erba I 120 B2
Erbach
　Baden-
　Württemberg
　D. 94 C1
　Hessen D 93 B4
Erbalunga F. . . 180 A2
Erbendorf D 95 B4
Érchie I. 173 B3
Ercolano I 170 C2
Ercsi H 112 B2
Érd H. 112 B2
Erdek TR 186 B2
Erdemli TR 23 C8
Erdevik SRB. . . 126 B1
Erding D. 95 C3
Erdötelek H. . . . 113 B4
Erdut HR. 125 B5
Erdweg D 95 C3
Ereğli
　Konya TR 23 C8
　Zonguldak
　TR. 187 A6
Erenkaya TR . . 189 B7
Eresfjord N . . . 198 C5

Eresos GR 183 D7
Eretria GR. 185 A4
Erfde D 64 B2
Ercoz F. 111 A2
Erfjord N. 52 A2
Erfstadt D. 80 B2
Erfurt D. 82 B3
Ergli LV. 8 D4
Ergoldsbach D. .95 C4
Eriboll UK. 32 C2
Érice I. 176 A1
Ericeira P. 154 C1
Eğridir TR. 189 B5
Eriksberg S . . . 195 E6
Eriksmåla S 62 B3
Eringsboda S . . .63 B3
Erithres GR. . . . 185 A4
Erkelenz D 80 A2
Erkner D 74 B2
Erkrath D 80 A2
Erla E 144 B3
Erlangen D. 94 B3
Erli I. 133 A4
Erlsbach A 109 C3
Ermelo NL. 70 B2
Ermenak TR. 23 C7
Ermenonville
　F. 90 B2
Ermezinde P. . . 148 A1
Ermidas P. 160 A1
Ermioni GR. . . . 184 B4
Ermoupoli GR. 185 B5
Ermsleben D. . . .82 A3
Erndtebrück D. .81 B4
Ernée F 88 B3
Ernestinovo
　HR. 125 B4
Ernstbrunn A . . .97 C4
Erolzheim D . . . 107 A5
Erquelinnes B...79 B4
Erquy F. 101 A3
Erra P 154 C2
Erratzu E. 144 A2
Errindlev DK . . .65 B4
Erro E 144 B2
Ersa F 180 A2
Érsekcsanád
　H. 125 A4
Ersekë AL. 182 C2
Érsekvadkert
　H. 112 B3
Ersmark S. 200 C6
Erstein F 93 C3
Erstfeld CH. . . . 107 C3
Ertebølle DK . . .58 B2
Ertingen D. . . . 107 A4
Ervedal
　Coimbra P . . . 148 B1
　Portalegre P . 154 B3
Ervenik HR. . . . 138 A1
Ervidel P. 160 B1
Ervy-le-Châtel
　F. 104 A2
Erwitte D. 81 A4
Erxleben D. 73 B4
Erzsébet H 125 A4
Esbjerg DK. 59 C1
Esbly F. 90 C2
Escacena del
　Campo E. . . . 161 B3
Escairón E. . . . 140 B3
Escalada E 143 B3
Escalante E . . . 143 A3
Escalaplano I . 179 C3
Escalona E . . . 150 B3
Escalona del Prado
　E. 151 A3
Escalonilla E . . 150 C3
Escalos de Baixo
　P. 155 B3
Escalos de Cima
　P. 155 B3
Escamilla E. . . . 152 B1
Es Caná E. 166 B1
Escañuela E . . . 157 C3
Escatrón E 153 A3
Eschach D. 107 B4
Eschau D. 94 B1
Eschede D. 72 B3
Eschenau D. 95 B3
Eschenbach D...95 B3
Eschenz CH. . . . 107 B3
Eschershausen
　D 72 C2
Esch-sur-Alzette
　L. 92 B1
Esch-sur-Sûre L .92 B1
Eschwege D. . . .82 A2
Eschweiler D. . . .80 B2
Escobasa de
　Almazán E . . . 152 A1
Escoeuilles F. . . .78 B1

Escombreras
　E. 165 B4
Escource F 128 B1
Escragnolles F . 132 B2
Escrick UK. 40 B2
Escurial E. 156 A2
Escurial de la Sierra
　E. 149 B4
Esens D 71 A4
Esgos E. 140 B3
Esher UK 44 B3
Eskdalemuir
　UK. 36 A3
Eskifjörður
　IS 191 B12
Eskilhem S. 57 C4
Eskilsäter S. . . .55 B4
Eskilstrup DK . . .65 B4
Eskilstuna S. . . .56 A2
Eskipazar TR. . . 187 B7
Eskişehir TR. . . 187 C5
Eslarn D. 95 B4
Eslava E. 144 B2
Eslida E. 159 B3
Eslohe D 81 A4
Eslöv S 61 D3
Esme TR. 188 A3
Es Mercadal E. 167 B4
Es Migjorn Gran
　E. 167 B4
Espa N 48 B3
Espalion F 130 A1
Esparragalejo
　E. 155 C4
Esparragosa del
　Caudillo E. . . 156 B2
Esparragossa de la
　Serena E 156 B2
Esparreguera
　E. 147 C2
Esparron F. . . . 132 B1
Espe N. 46 B3
Espedal N. 52 B2
Espejo
　Alava E 143 B3
　Córdoba E . . . 163 A3
Espeland N. 46 B2
Espelkamp D . . .72 B1
Espeluche F. . . 131 A3
Espeluy E 157 B4
Espera E. 162 B2
Esperança P. . . 155 B3
Espéraza F. . . . 146 B3
Espéria I. 169 B3
Espevær N 52 A1
Espiel E. 156 B2
Espinama E. . . . 142 A2
Espiñaredo E. . 140 A3
Espinasses F . . 132 A2
Espinelves E . . 147 C3
Espinhal P 154 A2
Espinho P. 148 A1
Espinilla E. 142 A2
Espinosa de Cerrato
　E. 143 C3
Espinosa de los
　Monteros E . . 143 A3
Espinoso del Rey
　E. 156 A3
Espirito Santo
　P. 160 B2
Espluga de Francolí
　E. 147 C2
Esplús E. 145 C4
Espolla E. 146 B3
Espoo FIN. 8 B4
Esporles E. 166 B2
Es Port d'Alcúdia
　E. 167 B3
Esposende P. . . 148 A1
Espot E. 146 B2
Es Pujols E 166 C1
Esquedas E. . . . 145 B3
Esquivias E. . . . 151 B4
Essay F. 89 B4
Essen
　D 79 A4
　Niedersachsen
　D. 71 B4
　Nordrhein-
　Westfalen D. . . 80 A3
Essenbach D. . . .95 C4
Essertaux F 90 B2
Essingen D. 94 C2
Esslingen D. 94 C1
Es Soleràs E . . . 153 A4
Essoyes F 104 A3
Estacas E. 140 B2
Estadilla E. 145 B4
Estaires F. 78 B2
Estang F 128 C2

Estarreja P 148 B1
Estartit E. 147 B4
Estavayer-le-Lac
　CH 106 C1
Este I 121 B4
Esteiro E 140 A2
Estela P. 148 A1
Estella E. 144 B1
Estellencs E . . . 166 B2
Estepa E 162 A3
Estépar E. 143 B3
Estepona E. . . . 162 B2
Esternay F 91 C3
Esterri d'Aneu
　E. 146 B2
Esterwegen D. . .71 B4
Estissac F 104 A2
Estivadas E . . . 140 B3
Estivareilles F. 116 A2
Estivella E. 159 B3
Estói P 160 B2
Estopiñán E. . . 145 C4
Estoril P. 154 C1
Estoublon F. . . 132 B2
Estrée-Blanche
　F. 78 B2
Estrées-St Denis
　F. 90 B2
Estrela P 155 C3
Estremera E. . . 151 B4
Estremoz P. . . . 155 C3
Estuna S. 51 C5
Esyres F. 102 B2
Esztergom H. . 112 B2
Étables-sur-Mer
　F. 100 A3
Étain F 92 B1
Étalans F 105 B5
Étalle B 92 B1
Étampes F 90 C2
Etang-sur-Arroux
　F. 104 C3
Étaples F. 78 B1
Etauliers F 128 A2
Etili TR 186 C1
Etna N. 48 B1
Etne N 52 A1
Etoges F 91 C3
Etoliko GR 184 A2
Eton UK 44 B3
Étréaupont F. . .91 B3
Étrechy F. 90 C2
Étrépagny F. . . .90 B1
Étretat F 89 A4
Étroeungt F. 91 A3
Étroubles I 119 B3
Ettal D 108 B2
Ettelbruck L. . . .92 B2
Etten NL 79 A4
Ettenheim D . . 106 A2
Ettington UK. . .44 A2
Ettlingen D 93 C4
Ettringen D . . . 108 A1
Etuz F 105 B4
Etxarri-Aranatz
　E. 144 B1
Etyek H 112 B2
Eu F 90 A1
Euerdorf D. 82 B2
Eulate E. 144 B1
Eupen B. 80 B2
Europoort NL. . .79 A4
Euskirchen D . . .80 B2
Eutin D 65 B3
Evanger N 46 B3
Évaux-les-Bains
　F. 116 A2
Evciler
　Afyon TR. 189 A4
　Çanakkale TR . 186 C1
Evenskjær N . . 194 B7
Evenstad N. 48 A3
Evercreech UK . .43 A4
Evergem B 79 A3
Everöd S 61 D4
Eversberg D 81 A4
Everswinkel D . .71 C4
Evertsberg S. . . .49 A5
Evesham UK. . . .44 A2
Évian-les-Bains
　F. 118 A3
Evisa F 180 A1
Evje N. 53 B3
Evolène CH . . . 119 A4
Évora P 154 C2
Evoramonte P. 155 C3
Evran F. 101 A4
Evrecy F. 89 A3
Évreux F. 89 A4
Évron F. 102 A1
Évry F. 90 C2
Ewell UK 44 B3
Ewersbach D. . . .81 B4

Excideuil F 115 C5
Exeter UK 43 D3
Exmes F. 89 B4
Exminster UK . . .43 B3
Exmouth UK 43 B3
Eydehamn N 53 B4
Eye
　Peterborough
　　UK 41 C3
　Suffolk UK . . . 45 A5
Eyemouth UK . . .35 C5
Eyguians F 132 A1
Eyguières F . . . 131 B3
Eygurande F . . . 116 B2
Eylie F 145 B4
Eymet F. 129 B3
Eymoutiers F . . 116 B1
Eynsham UK 44 B2
Eyrarbakki IS . . 190 D4
Eystrup D. 72 B2
Ezaro E. 140 B1
Ezcaray E 143 B4
Ezcároz E 144 B2
Ezine TR. 186 C1
Ezmoriz P 148 B1

F

Fabara E 153 A4
Fábbrico I. 121 C3
Fåberg N. 48 A2
Fabero E 141 B4
Fábiánsebestyén
　H. 113 C4
Fåborg DK 64 A3
Fabrègues F . . . 130 B2
Fabriano I 136 B1
Fabrizia I. 175 C2
Facha P 148 A1
Facinas E. 162 B2
Fačkov SK. 98 B2
Fadagosa P . . . 155 B3
Fadd H 112 C2
Faédis I 122 A2
Faenza I. 135 A4
Fafe P 148 A1
Fagagna I 122 A2
Fågelberget
　S. 199 A11
Fågelfors S. 62 A3
Fågelmara S 63 B3
Fågelsta S. 55 B6
Fagerås S 55 A4
Fagerheim N . . .47 B4
Fagerhøy N 48 A1
Fagerhult S 62 A3
Fagerlund N 48 B2
Fagernes
　Oppland N. 47 B6
　Troms N 192 C3
Fagersanna S . . .55 B5
Fagersta S 50 B2
Fåglavik S. 55 B4
Fagnano Castello
　I. 174 B2
Fagnières F 91 C4
Faido CH 107 C3
Fains-Véel F. . . .91 C5
Fairford UK 44 B2
Fairlie UK 34 C3
Fajsz H 112 C2
Fakenham UK. . .41 C4
Fåker S. 199 B11
Fakse DK. 65 A5
Fakse Ladeplads
　DK. 65 A5
Falaise F 89 B3
Falcade I. 121 A4
Falcarragh IRL . .26 A2
Falces E 144 B2
Falconara
　Maríttima I. . . 136 B2
Falcone I. 177 A4
Faldingworth
　UK. 40 B3
Falerum S. 56 B2
Fălești RO. 17 B7
Falkenberg
　Bayern D 95 B4
　Bayern D 95 C4
　Brandenburg
　　D. 83 A5
　S. 60 C2
Falkensee D. 74 B2
Falkenstein
　Bayern D 95 B4

Falkenstein
continued
Sachsen D 83 B4
Falkenthal D...74 B2
Falkirk UK......35 B4
Falkland UK....35 B4
Falköping S.....55 B4
Fall D 108 B2
Falla S...........56 B1
Fallingbostel D .72 B2
Falmouth UK....42 B1
Falset E 147 C1
Fălticeni RO....17 B7
Falun S.........50 B2
Famagusta CY 181 A2
Fammestad N...46 B2
Fana N.........46 B2
Fanano I 135 A3
Fanari GR 182 D3
Fanjeaux F.....146 A3
Fano I.........136 B2
Fântânele RO .126 A3
Fão P..........148 A1
Fara in Sabina
  I.............168 A2
Faramontanos de
  Tábara E 149 A4
Fara Novarese
  I.............119 B5
Farasdues E...144 B2
Fårbo S........62 A4
Fareham UK....44 C2
Färentuna S....57 A3
Färgelanda S ..54 B2
Färila S........61 C4
Faringdon UK..44 B2
Faringe S.......51 C5
Farini I.......120 C2
Fariza E 149 A3
Färjestaden S...63 B4
Farkadona GR .182 D4
Farkasfa H 111 C3
Farlete E 153 A3
Färlöv S........61 C4
Farmos H 113 B3
Farnă SK 112 B2
Färnäs S 50 B1
Farnborough
  UK............44 B3
Farnese I......168 A1
Farnham UK ...44 B3
Farnroda D 82 B2
Faro P.........160 B2
Fåro S..........57 C5
Fårösund S.....57 C5
Farra d'Alpago
  I.............122 A1
Farranfore IRL..29 B2
Farre DK.......59 B2
Farsala GR 182 D4
Farsø DK.......58 B2
Farsund N......52 B2
Farum DK......61 D2
Fårup DK.......58 B2
Fasana I......172 B1
Fasano I......173 B3
Fáskrúðsfjörður
  IS 191 C11
Fassberg D.....72 B3
Fastiv UA......13 C8
Fastnäs S......49 B5
Fátima P 154 B2
Fatmomakke
  S............195 E6
Fättjaur S.....195 E6
Faucogney-et-la-
  Mer F 105 B5
Fauguerolles
  F............128 B3
Faulenrost D...74 A1
Faulquemont F .92 B2
Fauquembergues
  F.............78 B2
Fauske N......194 C6
Fauville-en-Caux
  F.............89 A4
Fauvillers B 92 B1
Fåvang N.......48 A2
Favara
  E 159 B3
  I............176 B2
Faverges F....118 B3
Faverney F....105 B5
Faversham UK .45 B4
Favignana I ...176 B1
Fawley UK 44 C2
Fay-aux-Loges
  F 103 B4
Fayence F.....132 B2
Fayet F........130 B1

Fayl-Billot F...105 B4
Fayón E 153 A4
Fearn UK.......32 D3
Fécamp F......89 A4
Feda N.........52 B2
Fedje N........46 B1
Feeny UK......27 B3
Fegen S........60 B3
Fegyvernek H. 113 B4
Fehrbellin D ...74 B1
Fehring A 111 C3
Feichten A 108 B1
Feiring N.......48 B3
Feistritz im
  Rosental A ...110 C1
Feketić SRB ...126 B1
Felanitx E 167 B3
Feld am See A .109 C4
Feldbach A....110 C2
Feldberg D.....74 A2
Feldkirch A ...107 B4
Feldkirchen in
  Kärnten A....109 C5
Feldkirchen-
  Westerham
  D 108 B2
Felgueiras P ..148 A1
Felitto I 172 B1
Félix E 164 C2
Felixstowe UK .45 B5
Felizzano I ...119 C5
Felletin F......116 B2
Fellingsbro S...56 A1
Felnac S......126 A3
Felnémet H ...113 B4
Felpéc H 111 B4
Fels am Wagram
  A............97 C3
Felsberg D.....81 A5
Felsőnyék H ..112 C2
Felsőszentiván
  H...........126 A1
Felsőszentmárton
  H...........125 B3
Felsőzsolca H. 113 A4
Felsted DK.....64 B2
Feltre I 121 A4
Femsjö S.......60 C3
Fenagh IRL....26 B3
Fene E 140 A2
Fenestrelle I ..119 B4
Fénétrange F ..92 C3
Feneu F.......102 B1
Fengersfors S...54 B3
Fenit IRL......29 B2
Fensmark DK ..65 A4
Fenwick UK ...36 A2
Feolin Ferry
  UK...........34 C1
Ferbane IRL....28 A4
Ferdinandovac
  HR 124 A3
Ferdinandshof
  D 74 A2
Fère-Champenoise
  F............91 C3
Fère-en-Tardenois
  F............91 B3
Ferentillo I ...168 A2
Ferentino I ...169 B3
Feres GR 183 C8
Feria E 154 C4
Feričanci HR .125 B3
Ferizli TR......187 B5
Ferla I........177 B3
Ferlach A 110 C1
Ferleiten A ...109 B3
Fermil P......148 A2
Fermo I 136 B2
Fermoselle E..149 A3
Fermoy IRL....29 B3
Fernancabellero
  E 157 A4
Fernán Nuñéz
  E 163 A3
Fernán Peréz
  E 164 C2
Fernão Ferro
  P...........154 C1
Fernay-Voltaire
  F...........118 A3
Ferndown UK ..43 B5
Ferness UK.....32 D3
Fernhurst UK ..44 B3
Ferns IRL......30 B2
Ferpécle CH...119 A4
Ferrals-les-
  Corbières F ..146 A3
Ferrandina I ..172 B2
Ferrara I 121 C4
Ferrara di Monte
  Baldo I......121 B3
Ferreira E 141 A3

Ferreira do
  Alentejo P ...160 A1
Ferreira do Zêzere
  P............154 B2
Ferreras de Abajo
  E 141 C4
Ferreras de Arriba
  E 141 C4
Ferreries E ...167 B4
Ferreruela E ..152 A2
Ferreruela de
  Tabara E 149 A3
Ferret CH 119 B4
Ferrette F 106 B2
Ferriere I 120 C2
Ferrière-la-Grande
  F............79 B3
Ferrières
  Hautes-Pyrénées
  F...........145 A3
  Loiret F 103 A4
  Oise F 90 B2
Ferrières-sur-
  Sichon F 117 A3
Ferrol E 140 A2
Ferryhill UK....37 B5
Fertörakos H..111 B3
Fertöszentmiklós
  H...........111 B3
Ferwerd NL....70 A2
Festieux F......91 B3
Festøy N......198 C3
Festvåg N.....194 C5
Feteşti RO......17 C7
Fethard
  Tipperary IRL...29 B4
  Wexford IRL...30 B2
Fethiye TR 188 C4
Fetsund N......48 C3
Fettercairn UK .35 B5
Feucht D.......95 B3
Feuchtwangen
  D............94 B2
Feudingen D...81 B4
Feuges F.......91 C4
Feuquières F...90 B1
Feurs F.......117 B4
Fevik N........46 C2
Ffestiniog UK ..38 B3
Fiamignano I. 169 A3
Fiano I 119 B4
Ficarazzi I 176 A2
Ficarolo I.....121 C4
Fichtelberg D ..95 A3
Ficulle I 135 C5
Fidenza I 120 C3
Fidjeland N ...52 B2
Fieberbrunn
  A............109 B3
Fier AL 182 C1
Fiera di Primiero
  I............121 A4
Fiesch CH 119 A5
Fiesso Umbertiano
  I............121 C4
Figari F 180 B2
Figeac F.......116 C2
Figeholm S.....62 A4
Figgjo N........52 B1
Figline Valdarno
  I............135 B4
Figols S 145 B4
Figueira da Foz
  P............148 B1
Figueira de Castelo
  Rodrigo P ...149 B3
Figueira dos
  Caveleiros P .160 A1
Figueiredo P...154 B3
Figueiredo de Alva
  P...........148 B2
Figueiródos Vinhos
  P............154 B2
Figueres E ...147 B3
Figueroles E ..153 B3
Figuerela de
  Arriba E.....141 C4
Filadélfia I ...175 C2
Fil'akovo SK...99 C3
Fildertstadt D...94 C1
Filey UK.......41 A3
Filiaşi RO......17 C5
Filiates GR ...182 D2
Filiatra GR ...184 B2
Filipstad S.....55 A5
Filisur CH 107 C4
Fillan N......198 B5
Filotio GR 185 B6
Filottrano I ..136 B2
Filskov DK 59 C2
Filton UK......43 A4
Filtvet N.......54 A1
Filzmoos A....109 B4

Finale Emília I. 121 C4
Finale Lígure I. 133 A4
Fiñana E 164 B2
Finby FIN.......51 B7
Fincham UK....41 C4
Finchingfield
  UK............45 B4
Findhorn UK ...32 D3
Findochty UK ..33 D4
Finike TR......189 C5
Finkenberg A. 108 B2
Finnea IRL......27 C3
Finneidfjord
  N............195 D4
Finnerödja S...55 B5
Finnskog N 49 B4
Finnsnes N....194 A9
Finntorp S.....54 A3
Finocchio I ...168 B2
Finsjö S........62 A4
Finsland N.....52 B3
Finspång S.....56 B1
Finsterwalde D .84 A1
Finsterwolde
  NL............71 A4
Finstown UK ...33 B3
Fintona UK.....27 B3
Fionnphort UK .34 B1
Fiorenzuola d'Arda
  I............120 C2
Firenze = Florence
  I............135 B4
Firenzuola I...135 A4
Firmi F.......130 A1
Firminy F......117 B4
Firmo I........174 B2
Fischamend Markt
  A............111 A3
Fischbach
  A............110 B2
  D............93 B3
Fischbeck D....73 B5
Fischen D.....107 B5
Fishbourne UK .44 C2
Fishguard UK ..39 C2
Fiskardo GR ...184 A1
Fiskebäckskil
  S............54 B2
Fiskebøl N 194 B5
Fismes F 91 B3
Fisterra E 140 B1
Fitero E 144 B2
Fitjar N........46 C2
Fiuggi I 169 B3
Fiumata I 169 A3
Fiumefreddo
  Brúzio I 174 B2
Fiumefreddo di
  Sicília I......177 B4
Fiumicino I....168 B2
Fivemiletown
  UK............27 B3
Fivizzano I ...134 A3
Fjälkinge S.....63 B2
Fjällåsen S....196 B3
Fjällbacka S...54 B2
Fjæra N.......46 C3
Fjärdhundra S .56 A2
Fjellerup DK....58 B3
Fjerritslev DK..58 A2
Fjordgard N...194 A8
Fjugesta S.....55 A5
Flå N..........47 B6
Flåbygd N.....53 A4
Flaça E 147 B3
Flace F........117 A4
Fladungen D...82 B2
Flaine F.......118 A3
Flaka FIN......51 B7
Flåm N........46 B4
Flamatt CH....106 C2
Flamborough
  UK............41 A3
Flammersfeld
  D............81 B3
Flassans-sur-Issole
  F 132 B2
Flatdal N......53 A4
Flatebø N......46 B3
Flateby N......48 C3
Flateland N....52 A3
Flateyri IS.....190 A2
Flatøydegard
  N............47 B6
Flatråker N....46 C2
Flattach A.....109 C4
Flatvarp S.....62 A4
Flauenskjold
  DK............58 A3
Flavigny-sur-
  Moselle F....92 C2
Flavy-le-Martel
  F............90 B3

Flawil CH 107 B4
Flayosc F......132 B2
Flechtingen D...73 B4
Fleckeby D......64 B2
Fleetmark D ...73 B4
Fleetwood UK..38 A3
Flehingen D....93 B4
Flekke N.......46 A2
Flekkefjord N...52 B2
Flen S..........56 A2
Flensburg D ...64 B2
Fleringe S......57 C4
Flerohopp S ...62 B3
Flers F.........88 B3
Flesberg N.....47 C6
Fleurance F ...129 C3
Fleuré F 115 B4
Fleurier CH....105 C5
Fleurus B......79 B4
Fleury
  Hérault F 130 B2
  Yonne F 104 B2
Fleury-les-Aubrais
  F 103 B3
Fleury-sur-Andelle
  F............89 A5
Fleury-sur-Orne
  F............89 A3
Flieden D......81 B5
Flimby UK......36 B3
Flims CH 107 C4
Flines-lèz-Raches
  F............78 B3
Flint UK.......38 A3
Flirey F........92 C1
Flirsch A 108 B1
Flisa N.........49 B4
Flisby S........62 A2
Fliseryd S......62 A4
Flix E 153 A4
Flixecourt F....90 A2
Flize F.........91 B4
Flobecq B......79 B3
Floby S........55 B4
Floda S........60 B2
Flodden UK 37 A4
Flogny-la-Chapelle
  F............104 B2
Flöha D 83 B5
Flonheim D....93 B4
Florac F 130 A2
Floreffe B......79 B4
Florence = Firenze
  I............135 B4
Florennes B....79 B4
Florensac F ...130 B2
Florentin F....129 C5
Florenville B...91 B5
Flores de Avila
  E 150 B2
Floresta I 177 B3
Floreşti MD....17 B8
Florída I 177 B4
Florina GR 182 C3
Florø N........46 A2
Flörsheim D....93 A4
Floss D........95 B4
Fluberg N......48 B2
Flúðir IS.......190 C5
Flühli CH......106 C3
Flumet F......118 B3
Fluminimaggiore
  I............179 C2
Flums CH 107 B4
Flyeryd S......63 B3
Flygsfors S.....62 B3
Flöglö FIN......51 B7
Foča BIH......139 B4
Foça TR.......186 D1
Fochabers UK..32 D3
Focşani RO.....17 C7
Foel UK........38 B3
Foeni RO......126 B2
Fogdö S........56 A2
Föggia I.......171 B3
Foglianise I...170 B2
Föglö FIN......51 B7
Fohnsdorf A ..110 B1
Foiano della
  Chiana I......135 B4
Foix F.........146 B2
Fojnica
  BIH..........139 B3
  BIH..........139 B4
Fokstua N.....198 C6
Földeák H.....126 A2
Foldereid N...199 A9
Földes H 113 B5
Folegandros
  GR 185 C5
Folelli F 180 A2
Folgaria I 121 B4
Folgosinho P. 148 B2

Folgoso de la
  Ribera E......141 B4
Folgoso do Courel
  E 141 B3
Foligno I 136 C1
Folkärna S.....50 B3
Folkestad N...198 C3
Folkestone UK .45 B5
Follafoss N....199 B8
Folldal N......198 C6
Follebu N......48 A2
Follina I.......121 B5
Follónica I 135 C3
Fölsbyn S......54 A3
Foncebadón
  E 141 B4
Foncine-le-Bas
  F............105 C5
Fondevila E...140 C2
Fondi I........169 B3
Fondo I 121 A4
Fonelas E 164 B1
Fonfría
  Teruel E......152 B2
  Zamora E....149 A3
Fonn N........46 A3
Fonnes N......46 B1
Fonni I........178 B3
Fontaine F 91 C4
Fontainebleau
  F............90 C2
Fontaine de
  Vaucluse F ...131 B4
Fontaine-Française
  F............105 B4
Fontaine-le-Dun
  F............89 A4
Fontan F 133 A3
Fontanarejo E 157 A3
Fontane I 133 A3
Fontanélice I .135 A4
Fontanières F. 116 A2
Fontanosas E . 157 B3
Fonteblanda I. 168 A1
Fontenay-le-Comte
  F............114 B3
Fontenay-Trésigny
  F............90 C2
Fontevrault-
  l'Abbaye F...102 B2
Fontiveros E...150 B3
Fontoy F.......92 B1
Fontpédrouse
  F............146 B3
Font-Romeu F 146 B3
Fontstown IRL .30 A2
Fonyód H 111 C4
Fonz E 145 B4
Fonzaso I 121 A4
Fóppolo I......120 A2
Föra S.........62 A4
Forbach
  D 93 C4
  F.............92 B2
Forcall E 153 B3
Forcalquier F .132 B1
Forcarei E 140 B2
Forchheim D...94 B3
Forchtenau A .111 B3
Forchtenberg
  D............94 B1
Ford UK.......34 B2
Førde
  Hordaland N... 52 A1
  Sogn og Fjordane
  N. 46 A2
Förderstedt D..83 A3
Førdesfjorden
  N............52 A1
Fordham UK ...45 A4
Fordingbridge
  UK............44 C2
Fordon PL......76 B3
Fordongiánus
  I............179 C2
Forenza I......172 B1
Foresta di Búrgos
  I............178 B2
Forfar UK......35 B5
Forges-les-Eaux
  F............90 B1
Foría I 172 B1
Forío I 170 C1
Forjães P......148 A1
Førland N.....52 B3
Forl I.........135 A5
Forlimpopoli I 135 A5
Formazza I....119 A5
Formby UK.....38 A3
Formerie F 90 B1
Fórmia I.......169 B3
Formígine I ...135 A3

Formigliana I . 119 B5
Formiguères
  F 146 B3
Fornalutx E ...166 B2
Fornåsa S......56 B1
Fornelli I......178 B2
Fornells E 167 A4
Fornelos de Montes
  E 140 B2
Forneset N....192 C3
Forni Avoltri I. 109 C3
Forni di Sopra
  I............122 A1
Forni di Sotto
  I............122 A1
Forno
  Piemonte I...119 B4
  Piemonte I...119 B5
Forno Alpi-Gráie
  I............119 B4
Forno di Zoldo
  I............121 A5
Fornos de Algodres
  P............148 B2
Fornovo di Taro
  I............120 C3
Foros do Arrão
  P............154 B2
Forráskút H...126 A1
Forres UK 32 D3
Forriolo E 140 B3
Fors S.........50 B3
Forsand N.....52 B2
Forsbacka S...51 B3
Forserum S....62 A2
Forshaga S....55 A4
Forsheda S.....60 B3
Forsinain UK...32 C3
Førslev DK.....65 A4
Förslöv S......61 C2
Forsmark
  Uppsala S......51 B5
  Västerbotten
  S............195 E6
Forsmo S......200 C3
Forsnäs S 195 D9
Forsnes N.....198 B5
Forssa FIN......8 B3
Forssjöbruk S..56 B2
Forst D.........84 A2
Forsvik S......55 B5
Fortanete E ...153 B3
Fort Augustus
  UK............32 D2
Forte dei Marmi
  I............134 B3
Fortezza I.....108 C2
Forth UK......35 C4
Fort-Mahon-Plage
  F............78 B1
Fortrie UK.....33 D4
Fortrose UK....32 D2
Fortun N.......47 A4
Fortuna E 165 A3
Fortuneswell
  UK............43 B4
Fort William UK 34 B2
Forvik N......195 E3
Fos F 145 B4
Fosdinovo I ...134 A3
Foss N........47 B6
Fossacésia I...169 A4
Fossano I 133 A3
Fossato di Vico
  I............136 B1
Fossbakken N. 194 B8
Fosse-la-Ville B .79 B4
Fossombrone
  I............136 B1
Fos-sur-Mer F. 131 B3
Fot H.........112 B3
Fouchères F....104 A3
Fouesnant F ...100 B1
Foug F.........92 C1
Fougères F.....88 B2
Fougerolles F. 105 B5
Foulain F......105 A4
Fountainhall
  UK............35 C5
Fouras F 114 C2
Fourchambault
  F............104 B2
Fourfourás GR .91 A4
Fourna GR 182 D3
Fournels F 116 C2
Fourni GR.....188 B1
Fournols F 117 B3
Fourques F....146 B3
Fourquevaux
  F 146 A2
Fours F........104 C2
Fowey UK......42 B2

Foxdale UK 36 B2
Foxford IRL 26 C1
Foyers UK 32 D2
Foynes IRL 29 B2
Foz E 141 A3
Foza I 121 B4
Foz do Arelho P 154 B1
Foz do Giraldo P 155 B3
Frabosa Soprana I 133 A3
Frades de la Sierra E 149 B4
Fraga E 153 A4
Fragagnano I 173 B3
Frailes E 163 A4
Fraire B 79 B4
Fraize F 106 A1
Framlingham UK 45 A5
Frammersbach D 94 A1
Framnes N 54 A1
França P 141 C4
Francaltroff F 92 C2
Francavilla al Mare I 169 A4
Francavilla di Sicília I 177 B4
Francavilla Fontana I 173 B3
Francavilla in Sinni I 174 A2
Francescas F 129 B3
Franco P 148 A2
Francofonte I 177 B3
Francos E 151 A4
Frändefors S 54 B3
Franeker NL 70 A2
Frangy F 118 A2
Frankenau D 81 A4
Frankenberg
Hessen D 81 A4
Sachsen D 83 B5
Frankenburg A 109 A4
Frankenfels A 110 B2
Frankenmarkt A 109 B4
Frankenthal D 93 B4
Frankfurt
Brandenburg D 74 B3
Hessen D 81 B4
Frankrike S 199 B10
Fränsta S 200 D2
Františkovy Lázně CZ 83 B4
Franzburg D 66 B1
Frascati I 168 B2
Frasdorf D 109 B3
Fraserburgh UK 33 D4
Frashër AL 182 C2
Frasne F 105 C5
Frasnes-lez-Anvaing B 79 B3
Frasseto F 180 B2
Frastanz A 107 B4
Fratel P 155 B3
Fratta Todina I 135 C5
Frauenau D 96 C1
Frauenfeld CH 107 B3
Frauenkirchen A 111 B3
Frauenstein D 83 B5
Frauental A 110 C2
Frayssinet F 129 B4
Frayssinet-le-Gélat F 129 B4
Frechas P 149 A2
Frechen D 80 B2
Frechilla E 142 B2
Freckenhorst D 71 C4
Fredeburg D 81 A4
Fredelsloh D 82 A1
Fredeng N 48 B2
Fredensborg DK 61 D2
Fredericia DK 59 C2
Frederiks DK 59 B2
Frederikshavn DK 58 A3
Frederikssund DK 61 D2
Frederiksværk DK 61 D2
Fredrika S 200 B4
Fredriksberg S 50 B1
Fredriksdal S 62 A2
Fredrikstad N 54 A1
Fregenal de la Sierra E 161 A3
Fregene I 168 B2
Freiberg D 83 B5
Freiburg
Baden-Württemberg D 106 B2
Niedersachsen D 64 C2
Freienhagen D 81 A5
Freienhufen D 84 A1
Freiensteinau D 81 B5
Freihung D 95 B3
Freilassing D 109 B3
Freisen D 92 B3
Freising D 95 C3
Freistadt A 96 C2
Freital D 84 A1
Freixedas P 149 B2
Freixo de Espada à Cinta P 149 A3
Fréjus F 132 B2
Fremdingen D 94 C2
Frenštát pod Radhoštěm CZ 98 B2
Freren D 71 B4
Freshford IRL 30 B1
Freshwater UK 44 C2
Fresnay-sur-Sarthe F 89 B4
Fresneda de la Sierra E 152 B1
Fresneda de la Sierra Tiron E 143 B3
Fresnedillas E 151 B3
Fresnes-en-Woevre F 92 B1
Fresne-St Mamès F 105 B4
Fresno Alhandiga E 150 B2
Fresno de la Ribera E 150 A2
Fresno de la Vega E 142 B1
Fresno de Sayago E 149 A4
Fresnoy-Folny F 90 B1
Fresnoy-le-Grand F 91 B3
Fressenville F 90 A1
Fresvik N 46 A3
Fréteval F 103 B3
Fretigney F 105 B4
Freudenberg
Baden-Württemberg D 94 B1
Nordrhein-Westfalen D 81 B3
Freudenstadt D 93 C4
Freux B 92 B1
Frévent F 78 B2
Freyburg D 83 A3
Freyenstein D 73 A5
Freyming-Merlebach F 92 B2
Freystadt D 95 B3
Freyung D 96 C1
Frias de Albarracin E 152 B2
Fribourg CH 106 C2
Frick CH 106 B3
Fridafors S 63 B2
Fridaythorpe UK 40 A3
Friedberg
A 111 B3
Bayern D 94 C2
Hessen D 81 B4
Friedeburg D 71 A4
Friedewald D 82 B1
Friedland
Brandenburg D 74 B3
Mecklenburg-Vorpommern D 74 A2
Niedersachsen D 82 A1
Friedrichroda D 82 B2
Friedrichsdorf D 81 B4
Friedrichshafen D 107 B4
Friedrichskoog D 64 B1
Friedrichstadt D 64 B2
Friedrichswalde D 74 A2
Friesach A 110 C1
Friesack D 73 B5
Friesenheim D 93 C3
Friesoythe D 71 A4
Friggesund S 200 E2
Frigiliana E 163 B4
Frihetsli N 192 D3
Frillesås S 60 B2
Frinnaryd S 62 A2
Frinton-on-Sea UK 45 B5
Friockheim UK 35 B5
Friol E 140 A3
Fristad S 60 B2
Fritsla S 60 B2
Fritzlar D 81 A5
Frizington UK 36 B3
Frödinge S 62 A4
Froges F 118 B2
Frohburg D 83 A4
Frohnhausen D 81 B4
Frohnleiten A 110 B2
Froissy F 90 B2
Frombork PL 69 A4
Frome UK 43 A4
Frómista E 142 B2
Fröndenberg D 81 A3
Fronsac F 128 B2
Front I 119 B4
Fronteira P 155 B3
Frontenay-Rohan-Rohan F 114 B3
Frontenhausen D 95 C4
Frontignan F 130 B2
Fronton F 129 C4
Fröseke S 62 B3
Frosinone I 169 B3
Frosolone I 170 B2
Frosta N 199 B7
Frøstrup DK 58 A1
Frosunda S 57 A4
Frouard F 92 C2
Frövi S 56 A1
Frøyset N 46 B2
Fruges F 78 B2
Frutigen CH 106 C2
Frýdek-Místek CZ 98 B2
Frýdlant CZ 84 B3
Frydlant nad Ostravicí CZ 98 B2
Frygnowo PL 77 A5
Fryšták CZ 98 B1
Fucécchio I 135 B3
Fuencaliente
Ciudad Real E 157 A4
Ciudad Real E 157 B3
Fuencemillán E 151 B4
Fuendejalón E 144 C2
Fuengirola E 163 B3
Fuenlabrada E 151 B4
Fuenlabrada de los Montes E 156 A3
Fuensalida E 151 B3
Fuensanta E 164 B3
Fuensanta de Martos E 163 A4
Fuente-Alamo E 158 C2
Fuente-Álamo de Murcia E 165 B3
Fuentealbilla E 158 B2
Fuente al Olmo de Iscar E 150 A3
Fuentecén E 151 A4
Fuente Dé E 142 A2
Fuente de Cantos E 155 C4
Fuente del Arco E 156 B2
Fuente del Conde E 163 A3
Fuente del Maestre E 155 C4
Fuente de Santa Cruz E 150 A3
Fuente el Fresno E 157 A4
Fuente el Saz de Jarama E 151 B4
Fuente el Sol E 150 A3
Fuenteguinaldo E 149 B3
Fuentelapeña E 150 A2
Fuentelcésped E 151 A4
Fuentelespino de Haro E 158 B1
Fuentelespino de Moya E 158 B2
Fuentenovilla E 151 B4
Fuente Obejuna E 156 B2
Fuente Palmera E 162 A2
Fuentepelayo E 151 A3
Fuentepinilla E 151 A5
Fuenterroble de Salvatierra E 150 B2
Fuenterrobles E 158 B2
Fuentes E 158 B1
Fuentesauco E 151 A3
Fuentesaúco E 150 A2
Fuentes de Andalucía E 162 A2
Fuentes de Ebro E 153 A3
Fuentes de Jiloca E 152 A2
Fuentes de la Alcarria E 151 B5
Fuentes de León E 161 A3
Fuentes de Nava E 142 B2
Fuentes de Oñoro E 149 B3
Fuentes de Ropel E 142 B1
Fuentespalda E 153 B4
Fuentespina E 151 A4
Fuente-Tójar E 163 A3
Fuente Vaqueros E 163 A4
Fuentidueña E 151 A4
Fuentidueña de Tajo E 151 B4
Fuerte del Rey E 157 C4
Fügen A 108 B2
Fuglebjerg DK 65 A4
Fuglevik N 54 A1
Fuhrberg D 72 B2
Fulda D 82 B1
Fulgatore I 176 B1
Fully CH 119 A4
Fulnek CZ 98 B1
Fülöpszállás H 112 C3
Fulpmes A 108 B2
Fulunäs S 49 A5
Fumay F 91 B4
Fumel F 129 B3
Funäsdalen S 199 C9
Fundão P 148 B2
Funzie UK 33 A6
Furadouro P 148 B1
Fure N 46 A2
Fürstenau D 71 B4
Furstenau D 81 A5
Fürstenberg D 74 A2
Fürstenfeld A 111 B3
Fürstenfeldbruck D 108 A2
Fürstenstein D 96 C1
Fürstenwalde D 74 B3
Fürstenwerder D 74 A2
Fürstenzell D 96 C1
Furta H 113 B5
Fürth
Bayern D 94 B2
Hessen D 93 B4
Furth im Wald D 95 B4
Furtwangen D 106 A3
Furuby S 62 B3
Furudal S 50 A2
Furuflaten N 192 C4
Furulund S 61 D3
Furusjö S 60 B3
Fusa N 46 B2
Fuscaldo I 174 B2
Fusch an der Grossglockner-strasse A 109 B3
Fushë Arrëz AL 182 A2
Fushë-Krujë AL 182 B1
Fusina I 122 B1
Fusio CH 107 C3
Füssen D 108 B1
Fustiñana E 144 B2
Futog SRB 126 B1
Futrikelv N 192 C3
Füzesabony H 113 B4
Füzesgyarmat H 113 B5
Fužine HR 123 B3
Fyllinge S 61 C2
Fynshav DK 64 B2
Fyresdal N 53 A4

G

Gaaldorf A 110 B1
Gabaldón E 158 B2
Gabarret F 128 C2
Gabčíkovo SK 111 B4
Gąbin PL 77 B4
Gabriac F 130 A1
Gabrovo BG 17 D6
Gaby I 119 B4
Gacé F 89 B4
Gacko BIH 139 B4
Gäddede S 199 A11
Gadebusch D 65 C4
Gadmen CH 106 C3
Gádor E 164 C2
Gádoros H 113 C4
Gael F 101 A3
Găeşti RO 17 C6
Gaeta I 169 B3
Gafanhoeira P 154 C2
Gaflenz A 110 B1
Gagarin RUS 9 E9
Gaggenau D 93 C4
Gagliano Castelferrato I 177 B3
Gagliano del Capo I 173 C4
Gagnet S 50 B2
Gaibanella I 121 C4
Gaildorf D 94 B1
Gaillac F 129 C4
Gaillefontaine F 90 B1
Gaillon F 89 A5
Gainsborough UK 40 B3
Gairloch UK 31 B3
Gairlochy UK 34 B3
Gáiro I 179 C3
Gaj
HR 124 B3
SRB 127 C3
Gaja-la-Selve F 146 A2
Gajanejos E 151 B5
Gajary SK 97 C4
Gajdobra SRB 126 B1
Galan F 145 A4
Galanta SK 111 A4
Galapagar E 151 B3
Galápagos E 151 B4
Galaroza E 161 B3
Galashiels UK 35 C5
Galatas GR 185 B4
Galaţi RO 17 C8
Galatina I 173 B4
Galatista GR 183 C5
Galátone I 173 B4
Galaxidi GR 184 A3
Galdakao E 143 A4
Galeata I 135 B4
Galende E 141 B4
Galera E 164 B2
Galéria F 180 A1
Galgamácsa H 112 B3
Galgate UK 38 A4
Galgon F 128 B2
Galinduste E 150 B2
Galinoporni CY 181 A3
Galisteo E 155 B4
Galizes P 148 B2
Galków PL 87 A3
Gallarate I 120 B1
Gallardon F 90 C1
Gallegos de Argañán E 149 B3
Gallegos del Solmirón E 150 B2
Galleguillos de Campos E 142 B1
Galleno I 135 B3
Galliate I 120 B1
Gallicano I 134 A3
Gállio I 121 B4
Gallípoli I 173 B3
Gallipoli = Gelibolu TR 186 B1
Gällivare S 196 B3
Gallizien A 110 C1
Gallneukirchen A 96 C2
Gällö S 199 C12
Gallocanta E 152 B2
Gällstad S 60 B3
Gallur E 144 C2
Galmisdale UK 31 C2
Galmpton UK 43 B3
Galston UK 36 A2
Galta N 52 A1
Galtelli I 178 B3
Galten DK 59 B2
Galtür A 107 C5
Galve de Sorbe E 151 A4
Galveias P 154 B2
Gálvez E 157 A3
Galway IRL 28 A2
Gamaches F 90 B1
Gámbara I 120 B3
Gambárie I 175 C1
Gambassi Terme I 135 B3
Gambatesa I 170 B2
Gambolò I 120 B1
Gaming A 110 B2
Gamla Uppsala S 51 C4
Gamleby S 62 A4
Gamlingay UK 44 A3
Gammelgarn S 57 C4
Gammelstad S 196 D5
Gammertingen D 107 A4
Gams CH 107 B4
Gamvik
Finnmark N 192 B6
Finnmark N 193 A12
Gan F 145 A3
Gáname E 149 A3
Ganda di Martello I 108 C1
Gandarela P 148 A1
Ganddal N 52 B1
Ganderkesee D 72 A1
Gandesa E 153 A4
Gandía E 159 C3
Gandino I 120 B2
Gandrup DK 58 A3
Ganges F 130 B2
Gånghester S 60 B3
Gangi I 177 B3
Gangkofen D 95 C4
Gannat F 116 A3
Gannay-sur-Loire F 104 C2
Gänserdorf A 97 C4
Ganzlin D 73 A5
Gap F 132 A2
Gara H 125 A5
Garaballa E 158 B2
Garaguso I 172 B2
Garbayuela E 156 A2
Garbhallt UK 34 B2
Garbsen D 72 B2
Garching D 109 A3
Garciaz E 156 A2
Garcihernández E 150 B2
Garcillán E 151 B3
Garcinarro E 151 B5
Garcisobaco E 162 B2
Garda I 121 B3
Gardanne F 131 B4
Gärdås S 49 B5
Gårdby S 63 B4
Gardeja PL 69 B3
Gardelegen D 73 B4
Gardermoen N 48 B3
Gardiki GR 182 E3
Garding D 64 B1
Gardone Riviera I 121 B3
Gardone Val Trómpia I 120 B3
Gárdony H 112 B2
Gardouch F 146 A2
Gårdsjö S 55 B5
Gårdskär S 51 B4
Gards Köpinge S 63 C2
Garein F 128 B2
Garelochhead UK 34 B3
Garéoult F 132 B2
Garešnica HR 124 B2
Garéssio I 133 A4
Garforth UK 40 B2
Gargaliani GR 184 B2
Gargaligas E 156 A2
Gargallo E 153 B3
Garganta la Olla E 150 B2
Gargantiel E 156 B3
Gargellen A 107 C4
Gargilesse-Dampierre F 103 C3
Gargnano I 121 B3
Gargnäs S 195 E8
Gárgoles de Abajo E 152 B1
Gargrave UK 40 B1
Garitz D 73 C5
Garlasco I 120 B1
Garlieston UK 36 B2
Garlin F 128 C2
Garlitos E 156 B2
Garmisch-Partenkirchen D 108 B2
Garnat-sur-Engièvre F 104 C2
Garpenberg S 50 B3
Garphyttan S 55 A5
Garray E 143 C4
Garrel D 71 B5
Garriguella E 146 B4
Garrison UK 26 B2
Garrovillas E 155 B4
Garrucha E 164 B3
Gars-am-Kamp A 97 C3
Garsås S 50 B1
Garsdale Head UK 37 B4
Gärsnäs S 63 C2
Garstang UK 38 A4
Gartow D 73 A4
Gartz D 74 A3
Gærum DK 58 A3
Garvagh UK 27 B4
Garvão P 160 B1
Garve UK 32 D2
Garwolin PL 12 C4
Garz D 66 B2
Garzyn PL 85 A4
Gąsawa PL 76 B2
Gåsborn S 49 C6
Gaschurn A 107 C5
Gascueña E 152 B1
Gasny F 90 B1
Gąsocin PL 77 B5
Gastes F 128 B1
Gastouni GR 184 B2
Gastouri GR 182 D1
Gata
E 149 B3
HR 138 B2
Gata de Gorgos E 159 C4
Gătaia RO 126 B3
Gatchina RUS 9 C7
Gatehouse of Fleet UK 36 B2
Gátér H 113 C3
Gateshead UK 37 B5
Gátova E 159 B3
Gattendorf A 111 A3
Gatteo a Mare I 136 A1
Gattinara I 119 B5
Gattorna I 134 A2
Gaucín E 162 B2
Gaulstad N 199 B9
Gaupne N 47 A4
Gautefall N 53 A4
Gauting D 108 A2
Gauto S 195 D7
Gava E 147 C3
Gavardo I 121 B3
Gavarnie F 145 B3
Gåvavencsello H 113 A5
Gavi I 120 C1
Gavião P 154 B3
Gavirate I 120 B1
Gävle S 51 B4

Gavoi I 178 B3
Gavorrano I . . . 135 C3
Gavray F 88 B2
Gavrio GR 185 B5
Gävunda S 49 B6
Gaweinstal A . . .97 C4
Gaworzyce PL . .85 A3
Gawroniec PL . .75 A5
Gaydon UK 44 A2
Gayton UK 41 C4
Gazipaşa TR . . . 189 C7
Gazoldo degli
 Ippoliti I 121 B3
Gazzuolo I 121 B3
Gbelce SK 112 B2
Gdańsk PL 69 A3
Gdinj HR 138 B2
Gdov RUS 8 C5
Gdów PL 99 B4
Gdynia PL 69 A3
Gea de Albarracin
 E 152 B2
Geary UK 31 B2
Géaudot F 91 C4
Geaune F 128 C2
Gebesee D 82 A2
Gebiz TR 189 B5
Gebze TR 187 B4
Géderlak H 112 C2
Gedern D 81 B5
Gedinne B 91 B4
Gediz TR 187 D4
Gèdre F 145 B4
Gedser DK 65 B4
Gedsted DK 58 B2
Geel B 79 A4
Geesthacht D . . .72 A3
Geetbets B 79 B5
Gefell D 83 B3
Gehrden D 72 B2
Gehren D 82 B3
Geilenkirchen
 D 80 B2
Geilo N 47 B5
Geinsheim D 93 B4
Geisa D 82 B1
Geiselhöring
 D 95 C4
Geiselwind D . . .94 B2
Geisenfeld D 95 C3
Geisenhausen
 D 95 C4
Geisenheim D . . .93 B4
Geising D 84 B1
Geisingen D . . . 107 B3
Geislingen D 94 C1
Geistthal A 110 B2
Geiterygghytta
 N 47 B4
Geithain D 83 A4
Geithus N 48 C1
Gela I 177 B3
Geldermalsen
 NL 79 A5
Geldern D 80 A2
Geldrop NL 80 A1
Geleen NL 80 B1
Gelembe TR . . . 186 C2
Gelendost TR . 189 A6
Gelibolu = Gallipoli
 TR 186 B1
Gelida E 147 C2
Gelnhausen D . .81 B5
Gelnica SK 99 C4
Gelsa E 153 A3
Gelse H 111 C3
Gelsenkirchen
 D 80 A3
Gelsted DK 59 C2
Geltendorf D . 108 A2
Gelterkinden
 CH 106 B2
Gelting D 64 B2
Gelu RO 126 A3
Gelves E 162 A1
Gembloux B 79 B4
Gemeaux F . . . 105 B4
Gémenos F 132 B1
Gemerská Poloma
 SK 99 C4
Gemerská Ves
 SK 99 C4
Gemert NL 80 A1
Gemla S 62 B2
Gemlik TR 186 B4
Gemmenich B . .80 B1
Gemona del Friuli
 I 122 A2
Gémozac F 114 C3
Gemund D 80 B2

Gemünden
 Bayern D 94 A1
 Hessen D 81 B4
 Rheinland-Pfalz
 D 93 B3
Genappe B 79 B4
Génave E 164 A2
Genazzano I . . . 169 B2
Gençay F 115 B4
Gencsapáti H . . 111 B3
Gendringen NL .80 A2
Genelard F 104 C3
Genemuiden
 NL 70 B3
Generalski Stol
 HR 123 B4
Geneva = Genève
 CH 118 A3
Genevad S 61 C3
Genève = Geneva
 CH 118 A3
Genevriéres F . 105 B4
Gengenbach D . .93 C4
Genillé F 103 B3
Genk B 80 B1
Genlis F 105 B4
Gennep NL 80 A1
Genner DK 64 A2
Gennes F 102 B1
Genoa = Génova
 I 134 A1
Genola I 133 A3
Génova = Genoa
 I 134 A1
Genowefa PL . . .76 B3
Gensingen D 93 B3
Gent = Ghent B. .79 A3
Genthin D 73 B5
Gentioux F 116 B1
Genzano di Lucánia
 I 172 B2
Genzano di Roma
 I 168 B2
Georgenthal D . .82 B2
Georgsmarienhütte
 D 71 B5
Gera D 83 B4
Geraards-bergen
 B 79 B3
Gerace I 175 C2
Geraci Sículo I . 177 B3
Geraki GR 184 C3
Gérardmer F . . 106 A1
Geras A 97 C3
Gerbéviller F . . .92 C2
Gerbini I 177 B3
Gerbstedt D 83 A3
Gerði IS 191 C9
Gerede TR 187 B7
Gerena E 161 B3
Geretsried D . . 108 B2
Gérgal E 164 B2
Gergy F 105 C3
Gerindote E . . . 150 C3
Gerjen H 112 C2
Gerlos A 108 B3
Germay F 92 C1
Germencik TR . 188 B2
Germering D . . 108 A2
Germersheim
 D 93 B4
Gernika-Lumo
 E 143 A4
Gernrode D 82 A3
Gernsbach D 93 C4
Gernsheim D 93 B4
Geroda D 82 B1
Gerola Alta I . . 120 A2
Geroldsgrun D . .83 B3
Gerolsbach D . . .95 C3
Gerolstein D 80 B2
Gerolzhofen D . .94 B2
Gerovo HR 123 B3
Gerpinnes B 79 B4
Gerrards Cross
 UK 44 B3
Gerri de la Sal
 E 147 B2
Gersfeld D 82 B1
Gerstetten D 94 C2
Gersthofen D . . .94 C2
Gerstungen D . . .82 B2
Gerswalde D 74 A2
Gerzat F 116 B3
Gerze TR 23 A8
Gerzen D 95 C4
Gescher D 71 C4
Geseke D 81 A4
Geslau D 94 B2
Gespunsart F . . .91 B4
Gesté F 101 B4
Gestorf D 72 B2
Gesualda I 170 C3

Gesunda S 50 B1
Gesztely H 113 A4
Geta FIN 51 B6
Getafe E 151 B4
Getinge S 60 C2
Getxo E 143 A4
Geversdorf D . . .64 C2
Gevgelija
 NMK 182 B4
Gevora del Caudillo
 E 155 C4
Gevrey-Chambertin
 F 105 B3
Gex F 118 A3
Gey D 80 B2
Geyikli TR 186 C1
Geysir IS 190 C5
Geyve TR 187 B5
Gföhl A 97 C3
Ghedi I 120 B3
Ghent = Gent B. .79 A3
Gheorgheni
 RO 17 B6
Ghigo I 119 C4
Ghilarza I 178 B2
Ghisonaccia F. 180 A2
Ghisoni F 180 A2
Gialtra GR 182 E4
Gianitsa GR . . . 182 C4
Giardinetto Vécchio
 I 171 B3
Giardini Naxos
 I 177 B4
Giarratana I . . . 177 B3
Giarre I 177 B4
Giat F 116 B2
Giaveno I 119 B4
Giazza I 121 B4
Gíycko PL 179 C2
Giba I 179 C2
Gibellina Nuova
 I 176 B1
Gibostad N . . . 194 A9
Gibraleón E . . . 161 B3
Gibraltar GBZ . 162 B2
Gic H 111 B4
Gideå S 200 C5
Gideåkroken
 S 200 B3
Gidle PL 86 B3
Giebelstadt D . . .94 B1
Gieboldehausen
 D 82 A2
Gielniów PL 87 A4
Gielow D 74 A1
Gien F 103 B4
Giengen D 94 C2
Giens F 132 B2
Giera RO 126 B2
Gieselwerder D .81 A5
Giessen D 81 B4
Gieten NL 71 A3
Giethoorn NL . .70 B3
Giffaumont-
 Champaubert
 F 91 C4
Gifford UK 35 C5
Gifhorn D 73 B3
Gige H 125 A3
Gignac F 130 B2
Gijón = Xixón
 E 142 A1
Gilena E 162 A3
Gilford UK 27 B4
Gillberga S 55 A3
Gilleleje DK 61 C2
Gilley F 105 B5
Gilley-sur-Loire
 F 104 C2
Gillingham
 Dorset UK 43 A4
 Medway UK 45 B4
Gilocourt F 90 B2
Gilserberg D 81 B5
Gilsland UK 37 B4
Gilze NL 79 A4
Gimåt S 200 C4
Gimo S 51 B5
Gimont F 129 C3
Ginasservis F . 132 B1
Gingelom B 79 B5
Gingst D 66 B2
Ginosa I 171 C4
Ginzling A 108 B2
Giões P 160 B2
Gióia dei Marsi
 I 169 B3
Gióia del Colle
 I 173 B2
Gióia Sannítica
 I 170 B2
Gióia Táuro I . 175 C1
Gioiosa Iónica
 I 175 C2

Gioiosa Marea
 I 177 A3
Giosla UK 31 A2
Giovinazzo I . . 171 B4
Girifalco I 175 C2
Giromagny F . . 106 B1
Girona E 147 C3
Gironcourt-sur-
 Vraine F 92 C1
Gironella E 147 B2
Gironville-sous-les-
 Côtes F 92 C1
Girvan UK 36 A2
Gislaved S 60 B3
Gislev DK 59 C3
Gisors F 90 B1
Gissi I 170 A2
Gistad S 56 B1
Gistel B 78 A2
Gistrup DK 58 B3
Githio GR 184 C3
Giugliano in
 Campania I . . 170 C2
Giulianova I . . . 136 C2
Giulväz RO 126 B2
Giurgiu RO 17 D6
Give DK 59 C2
Givet F 91 A4
Givors F 117 B4
Givry
 B 79 B4
 F 104 C3
Givry-en-Argonne
 F 91 C4
Givskud DK 59 C2
Giżalki PL 76 B2
Gizeux F 102 B2
Gizycko PL 12 A4
Gizzeria I 175 C2
Gizzeria Lido I . 175 C2
Gjedved DK 59 C2
Gjegjan AL 182 B2
Gjendesheim N .47 A5
Gjerde N 46 B3
Gjerlev DK 58 B3
Gjermundshamn
 N 46 B2
Gjerrild DK 58 B3
Gjerstad N 53 B5
Gjesås N 49 B4
Gjesvær N . . . 193 A9
Gjirokastër AL 182 C2
Gjøfjell N 54 A1
Gjøl DK 58 A2
Gjøra N 198 C6
Gjøvik N 48 B2
Gladbeck D 80 A2
Gladenbach D . . .81 B4
Gladstad N . . . 195 E2
Glamis UK 35 B4
Glamoč BIH . . . 138 A2
Glamsbjerg DK. .59 C3
Gland CH 105 C5
Glandorf D 71 B4
Glanegg A 110 C1
Glanshammar
 S 56 A1
Glarus CH 107 B4
Glasgow UK 35 C3
Glashütte
 Bayern D 108 B2
 Sachsen D 84 B1
Glastonbury
 UK 43 A4
Glatzau A 110 C2
Glauchau D 83 B4
Glava S 54 A3
Glavatičevo
 BIH 139 B4
Glavičice BIH . . 127 C1
Gŭlŭbovo BG . 183 A7
Glein
 A 110 B1
 N 195 D3
Gleinstätten
 A 110 C2
Gleisdorf A . . . 110 B2
Glenamoy IRL . .26 B1
Glenarm UK 27 B5
Glenavy UK 27 B4
Glenbarr UK 34 C2
Glenbeigh IRL . .29 B2
Glenbrittle UK . .31 B2
Glencoe UK 34 B2
Glencolumbkille
 IRL 26 B2
Glendalough
 IRL 30 A2
Glenealy IRL . . .30 B2
Glenelg UK 31 B3
Glenfinnan UK . .34 B2
Glengarriff IRL . .29 C2

Glenluce UK 36 B2
Glennamaddy
 IRL 28 A3
Glenrothes UK . .35 B4
Glenties IRL 26 B2
Glesborg DK 58 B3
Glesien D 83 A4
Gletsch CH 106 C3
Glewitz D 66 B1
Glifada GR 185 B4
Glimåkra S 63 B2
Glin IRL 29 B2
Glina HR 124 B2
Glinde D 72 A3
Glinojeck PL 77 B5
Glinsk IRL 28 A2
Glissjöberg S . . .50 A1
Gliwice PL 86 B2
Glödnitz A 109 C5
Gloggnitz A . . . 110 B2
Głogoczów PL . .99 B3
Glogonj SRB . . 127 C2
Glogovac SRB . 127 C3
Głogów PL 85 A4
Głogówek PL . . .86 B1
Glomel F 100 A2
Glomfjord N . . 195 D4
Glommen S 60 C2
Glommersträsk
 S 196 D2
Glonn D 108 B2
Glorenza I 108 C1
Gloria P 154 B2
Glosa GR 183 D5
Glossop UK 40 B2
Głowaczów PL . .87 A5
Główczyce PL . . .68 A2
Glöwen D 73 B5
Głowno PL 77 C4
Gložan SRB . . . 126 B1
Głubczyce PL . . .86 B1
Głuchołazy PL . .85 B5
Głuchów PL 87 A4
Głuchowo PL . . .75 B5
Glücksburg D . . .64 B2
Glückstadt D 64 C2
Glumina BIH . . 139 A5
Glumsø DK 65 A4
Glušci SRB 127 C1
Glusk BY 13 B8
Głuszyca PL 85 B4
Glyngøre DK 58 B1
Glyn Neath UK . .39 C3
Gmünd
 Karnten A 109 C4
 Nieder Östereich
 A 96 C2
Gmund D 108 B2
Gmunden A . . . 109 B4
Gnarp S 200 D3
Gnarrenburg D .72 A2
Gnesau A 109 C4
Gnesta S 56 A3
Gniechowice
 PL 85 A4
Gniew PL 69 B3
Gniewkowo PL . .76 B3
Gniezno PL 76 B2
Gnoien D 66 C1
Gnojnice BIH . . 139 B3
Gnojno PL 87 B4
Gnosall UK 40 C1
Gnosjö S 60 B3
Göbel TR 186 B3
Göçbeyli TR . . . 186 C2
Goch D 80 A2
Gochsheim D . . .94 A2
Göd H 112 B3
Godalming UK . .44 B3
Godby FIN 51 B6
Goðdalir IS 190 B6
Goddelsheim D .81 A4
Gódega di
 Sant'Urbano
 I 122 B1
Godegård S 56 B1
Godelheim D 81 A5
Goderville F 89 A4
Godiasco I 120 C2
Godič SLO 123 A3
Godkowo PL 69 A4
Godmanchester
 UK 44 A3
Gödöllő H 112 B3
Gödre H 125 A3
Godshill UK 44 C2
Godzikowice
 PL 85 B5
Godziszewo PL .69 A3
Goes NL 79 A3
Goetzenbrück
 F 93 C3
Goppenstein
 CH 119 A4

Gogolin PL 86 B2
Göhren D 66 B2
Goirle NL 79 A5
Góis P 148 B1
Góito I 121 B3
Goizueta E 144 A2
Gojna Gora
 SRB 127 D2
Gójsk PL 77 B4
Gökçedağ TR . . 186 C3
Gökçen TR 188 A2
Gökçeören
 TR 188 A3
Gökçeyazı TR . 186 C2
Göktepe TR . . . 188 B3
Gol N 47 B5
Gola
 HR 124 A3
 N 48 A1
Gołańcz PL 76 B2
Gölbaşı TR 23 B7
Gölby FIN 51 B6
Gölcük
 Kocaeli TR 187 B4
 Niğde TR 23 B8
Golčův Jeníkov
 CZ 97 B3
Gołczewo PL . . .67 C3
Goldach CH . . . 107 B4
Goldbach D 93 A5
Goldbeck D 73 B4
Goldberg D 73 A5
Goldelund D 64 B2
Goldenstedt D . .72 B1
Gołębiewo PL . . .69 A3
Golegã P 154 B2
Goleniów PL 75 A3
Golfo Aranci I . 178 B3
Gölhisar TR . . . 189 B4
Golina PL 76 B3
Gölle H 112 C2
Göllersdorf A . . .97 C4
Golling an der
 Salzach A 109 B4
Gölmarmara
 TR 186 D2
Golnice PL 84 A3
Golnik SLO 123 A3
Gölova TR 189 C5
Gölpazarı TR . . 187 B5
Gols A 111 B3
Golspie UK 32 D3
Golssen D 74 C2
Golub-Dobrzyń
 PL 77 A4
Golubinci SRB. 127 C2
Goluchów PL . . .86 A1
Golymin-Ośrodek
 PL 77 B5
Golzow D 73 B5
Gomagoi I 108 C1
Gómara E 152 A1
Gomaringen D . .93 C5
Gömbe TR 189 C4
Gömeç TR 186 C1
Gomel = Homyel
 BY 13 B9
Gomes Aires P 160 B1
Gómezserracin
 E 150 A3
Gommern D 73 B4
Gomulin PL 86 A3
Gonäs S 50 B2
Goncelin F 118 B3
Gończyce PL 87 A5
Gondomar
 E 140 B2
 P 148 A1
Gondrecourt-le-
 Château F 92 C1
Gondrin F 128 C3
Gönen
 Balıkesir TR . . . 186 B2
 Isparta TR 189 B5
Gonfaron F . . . 132 B2
Goñi E 144 B2
Goni
 GR 182 D4
 I 179 C3
Gonnesa I 179 C2
Gonnosfanádiga
 I 179 C2
Gönyü H 111 B4
Gonzaga I 121 C3
Goodwick UK . . .39 B1
Goodwood UK . .44 C3
Gooik B 79 B4
Goole UK 40 B3
Goor NL 71 B3
Göpfritz an der
 Wild A 97 C3

Göppingen D . . .94 C1
Gor E 164 B2
Góra
 Dolnośląskie
 PL 85 A4
 Mazowieckie
 PL 77 B5
Gorafe E 164 B1
Gorawino PL . . .67 C4
Goražde BIH . . 139 B4
Görbeháza H. . 113 B5
Gordaliza del Pino
 E 142 B1
Gördes TR 186 D3
Gørding DK 59 C1
Górdola CH . . . 120 A1
Gordon UK 35 C5
Gordoncillo E . 142 B1
Gorebridge UK . .35 C4
Gorenja Vas
 SLO 123 A3
Gorenje Jelenje
 HR 123 B3
Gorey
 IRL 30 B2
 UK 88 A1
Gorgonzola I . . 120 B2
Gorica HR 137 A4
Gorican HR. . . . 124 A2
Gorinchem NL . .79 A4
Goring UK 44 B2
Goritsy RUS 9 D10
Göritz D 74 A2
Gorízia I 122 B2
Górki PL 77 B4
Gorleben D 73 B4
Gorleston-on-sea
 UK 41 C5
Gørlev DK 61 D1
Görlitz D 84 A2
Górliz E 143 A4
Görmin D 66 C2
Górna Grupa
 PL 69 B3
Gorna Oryahovitsa
 BG 17 D6
Gornja Gorevnica
 SRB 127 D2
Gornja Ploča
 HR 137 A4
Gornja Radgona
 SLO 110 C2
Gornja Sabanta
 SRB 127 D3
Gornja Trešnjevica
 SRB 127 C2
Gornja Tuzla
 BIH 125 C4
Gornje Polje
 MNE 139 C4
Gornje Ratkovo
 BIH 124 C2
Gornji Grad
 SLO 123 A3
Gornji Humac
 HR 138 B2
Gornji Jasenjani
 BIH 139 B3
Gornji Kamengrad
 BIH 124 C2
Gornji Kneginec
 HR 124 A2
Gornji Kosinj
 HR 123 C4
Gornji Milanovac
 SRB 127 C2
Gornji Podgradci
 BIH 124 B2
Gornji Ravno
 BIH 138 B3
Gornji Sjenicak
 HR 124 B1
Gornji Vakuf
 BIH 138 B3
Górno D 87 B4
Görömböly
 H 113 A4
Górowo Iławeckie
 PL 69 A5
Gorran Haven
 UK 42 B2
Gorredijk NL . . .70 A3
Gorron F 88 B3
Gorseinon UK . .39 C2
Gort IRL 28 A3
Gortin UK 27 B3
Görzke D 73 B5
Gorzkowice PL. .86 A3
Gorzów
 Kujawsko-
 Pomorskie PL . 77 A4
 Zachodnio-
 Pomorskie PL . 75 A4

Gorzów Śląski PL 86 A2
Gorzów Wielkopolski PL 75 B4
Górzyca PL 74 B3
Gorzyce PL 98 B2
Górzyn PL 84 A2
Gorzyń PL 75 B4
Gorzyno PL 68 A2
Gosaldo I 121 A4
Gosau A 109 B4
Gosberton UK 41 C3
Gościcino PL 68 A3
Gościęcin PL 86 B2
Gościm PL 75 B4
Gościno PL 67 B4
Gosdorf A 110 C2
Gosforth UK 36 B3
Goslar D 82 A2
Goslice PL 77 B4
Gospič HR 137 A4
Gosport UK 44 C2
Gössäter S 55 B4
Gossau CH 107 B4
Goss Ilsede D 72 B3
Gössnitz D 83 B4
Gössweinstein D 95 B3
Gostivar NMK 182 B2
Gostkow PL 77 C4
Göstling an der Ybbs A 110 B1
Gostomia PL 75 A5
Gostycyn PL 76 A2
Gostyń PL 85 A5
Gostynin PL 77 B4
Goszczyn PL 87 A4
Göta S 54 B3
Göteborg = Gothenburg S 60 B1
Götene S 55 B4
Gotha D 82 B2
Gothem S 57 C4
Gothenburg = Göteborg S 60 B1
Gotse Delchev BG 183 B5
Gottersdorf D 95 C4
Göttingen D 82 A1
Gottne S 200 C4
Götzis A 107 B4
Gouarec F 100 A2
Gouda NL 70 B1
Goudhurst UK 45 B4
Goumenissa GR 182 C4
Goura GR 184 B3
Gourdon F 129 B4
Gourgançon F 91 C4
Gourin F 100 A2
Gournay-en-Bray F 90 B1
Gourock UK 34 C3
Gouveia P 148 B2
Gouvy B 80 B1
Gouzeacourt F 90 A3
Gouzon F 116 A2
Govedari HR 138 C3
Govérnolo I 121 B3
Gowarczów PL 87 A4
Gowerton UK 39 C2
Gowidlino PL 68 A2
Gowran IRL 30 B1
Goyatz D 74 B3
Göynük
TR 187 B5
Antalya TR 189 C5
Gozdnica PL 84 A3
Gozdowo PL 77 B4
Gozee B 79 B4
Graal-Müritz D 65 B5
Grabenstätt D 109 B3
Grabhair UK 31 A2
Gråbo S 60 B2
Grabovac
HR 138 B2
SRB 127 C2
Grabovci SRB 127 C1
Grabow D 73 A4
Grabów PL 77 B4
Grabow nad Pilicą PL 87 A5
Grabów nad Prosną PL 86 A2
Grabowno PL 76 A2
Grabs CH 107 B4
Gračac HR 138 A1
Gračanica BIH 125 C4
Graçay F 103 B3
Grad SLO 111 C3
Gradac
BIH 139 C4
HR 138 B3
MNE 139 B5
Gradačac BIH 125 C4
Gradec HR 124 B2
Gradefes E 142 B1
Grades A 110 C1
Gradil P 154 C1
Gradina
HR 124 B3
MNE 139 B5
Gradisca d'Isonzo I 122 B2
Gradiška BIH 124 B3
Gradište HR 125 B4
Grado
E 141 A4
I 122 B2
Grafenau D 96 C1
Gräfenberg D 95 B3
Gräfenhainichen D 83 A4
Grafenschlag A 97 C3
Grafenstein A 110 C1
Gräfenthal D 82 B3
Grafentonna D 82 A2
Grafenwöhr D 95 B3
Grafing D 108 A2
Grafling D 95 C4
Gräfsnäs S 54 B3
Gragnano I 170 C2
Grahovo SLO 122 A2
Graiguenamanagh IRL 30 B2
Grain UK 45 B4
Grainau D 108 B2
Graja de Iniesta E 158 B2
Grajera E 151 A4
Gram DK 59 C2
Gramais A 108 B1
Gramat F 129 B4
Gramatneusiedl A 111 A3
Grambow D 74 A3
Grammichele I 177 B3
Gramsh AL 182 C2
Gramzow D 74 A3
Gran N 48 B2
Granada E 163 A4
Granard IRL 27 C3
Grañas E 140 A3
Granátula de Calatrava E 157 B4
Grancey-le-Château F 105 B4
Grandas de Salime E 141 A4
Grandcamp-Maisy F 88 A2
Grand-Champ F 100 B3
Grand Couronne F 89 A5
Grand-Fougeray F 101 B4
Grândola P 160 A1
Grandpré F 91 B4
Grandrieu
B 79 B4
F 117 C3
Grandson CH 106 C1
Grandvillars F 106 B1
Grandvilliers F 90 B1
Grañén E 145 C3
Grangärde S 50 B1
Grange IRL 26 B2
Grangemouth UK 35 B4
Grange-over-Sands UK 36 B4
Grängesberg S 50 B1
Granges-de Crouhens F 145 B4
Granges-sur-Vologne F 106 A1
Gräningen D 73 B5
Granitola-Torretta I 176 B1
Granja
Évora P 155 C3
Porto P 148 A1
Granja de Moreruela E 142 C1
Granja de Torrehermosa E 156 B2
Gränna S 55 B5
Grannäs
Västerbotten S 195 E7
Grannäs *continued*
Västerbotten S 195 E8
Granö S 200 B5
Granollers E 147 C3
Granowiec PL 85 A5
Granowo PL 75 B5
Gransee D 74 A2
Gransherad N 53 A5
Grantham UK 40 C3
Grantown-on-Spey UK 32 D3
Grantshouse UK 35 C5
Granville F 88 B2
Granvin N 46 B3
Grærup Strand DK 59 C1
Gräsås S 60 C2
Grasbakken N 193 B12
Grasberg D 72 A2
Grasmere UK 36 B3
Gräsmyr S 200 C5
Grasö S 51 B5
Grassano I 172 B2
Grassau D 109 B3
Grasse F 132 B2
Grassington UK 40 A2
Græsted DK 61 C2
Gråsten DK 64 B2
Grästorp S 54 B3
Gratkorn A 110 B2
Gråträsk S 196 D2
Gratwein A 110 B2
Graulhet F 129 C4
Graus E 145 B4
Grávalos E 144 B2
Gravberget N 49 B4
Grave NL 80 A1
Gravedona I 120 A2
Gravelines F 78 A2
Gravellona Toce I 119 B5
Gravendal S 50 B1
Gravens DK 59 C2
Gravesend UK 45 B4
Graveson F 131 B3
Gravina in Púglia I 172 B2
Gray F 105 B4
Grayrigg UK 37 B4
Grays UK 45 B4
Grayshott UK 44 B3
Graz A 110 B2
Grazalema E 162 B2
Grążawy PL 69 B4
Grazzano Visconti I 120 C2
Greåker N 54 A2
Great Dunmow UK 45 B4
Great Malvern UK 39 B4
Great Torrington UK 42 B2
Great Waltham UK 45 B4
Great Yarmouth UK 41 C5
Grebbestad S 54 B2
Grebenstein D 81 A5
Grębocice PL 85 A4
Grębocin PL 76 A3
Greding D 95 B3
Gredstedbro DK 59 C1
Greencastle IRL 27 A3
Greenhead UK 37 B4
Greenisland UK 27 B5
Greenlaw UK 35 C5
Greenock UK 34 C3
Greenway UK 39 C2
Greenwich UK 45 B4
Grefrath D 80 A2
Greifenburg A 109 C4
Greiffenberg D 74 A2
Greifswald D 66 B2
Grein A 110 A1
Greipstad N 53 B3
Greiz D 83 B4
Grenaa DK 58 B3
Grenade F 129 C4
Grenade-sur-l'Adour F 128 C2
Grenchen CH 106 B2
Grendi N 53 B3
Grenivík IS 191 B7
Grenoble F 118 B2
Gréoux-les-Bains F 132 B1
Gresenhorst D 66 B1
Gressoney-la-Trinité I 119 B4
Gressoney-St-Jean I 119 B4
Gressthal D 82 B2
Gressvik N 54 A1
Gresten A 110 B2
Gretna UK 36 B3
Greussen D 82 A2
Greve in Chianti I 135 B4
Greven
Mecklenburg-Vorpommern D 73 A3
Nordrhein-Westfalen D 71 B4
Grevena GR 182 C3
Grevenbroich D 80 A2
Grevenbrück D 81 A4
Grevenmacher L 92 B2
Grevesmühlen D 65 C4
Grevestrand DK 61 D2
Grevie S 61 C2
Greystoke UK 36 B4
Greystones IRL 30 A2
Grez-Doiceau B 79 B4
Grèzec F 129 B4
Grez-en-Bouère F 102 B1
Grezzana I 121 B4
Grgar SLO 122 A2
Grgurevci SRB 127 B1
Gries A 108 B2
Griesbach D 96 C1
Griesheim D 93 B4
Gries in Sellrain A 108 B2
Grieskirchen A 109 A4
Griffen A 110 C1
Grignan F 131 A3
Grignano I 122 B2
Grigno I 121 A4
Grignols F 128 B2
Grignon F 118 B3
Grijota E 142 B2
Grijpskerk NL 71 A3
Grillby S 56 A3
Grimaud F 132 B2
Grimbergen B 79 B4
Grimma D 83 A4
Grimmen D 66 B2
Grimmialp CH 106 C2
Grimsås S 60 B3
Grimsby UK 41 B3
Grimslöv S 62 B2
Grímsstaðir IS 191 B9
Grimstad N 53 B4
Grimstorp S 62 A2
Grindavík IS 190 D3
Grindelwald CH 106 C3
Grindheim N 52 B3
Grindsted DK 59 C1
Griñón E 151 B4
Gripenberg S 62 A2
Gripsholm S 56 A3
Grisolles F 129 C4
Grisslehamn S 51 B5
Gritley UK 33 C4
Grizebeck UK 36 B3
Grndina BIH 124 C2
Gröbming A 109 B4
Gröbzig D 83 A3
Grocka SRB 127 C2
Gröditz D 83 A5
Gródki PL 77 A5
Grodków PL 85 B5
Grodziec PL 76 B3
Grodzisk Mazowiecki PL 77 B5
Grodzisk Wielkopolski PL 75 B5
Groenlo NL 71 B3
Groesbeek NL 80 A1
Grohote HR 138 B2
Groitzsch D 83 A4
Groix F 100 B2
Grójec PL 77 C5
Grom PL 77 A5
Gromiljca BIH 139 B4
Grömitz D 65 B3
Gromnik PL 99 B4
Gromo I 120 B2
Gronau
Niedersachsen D 72 B2
Nordrhein-Westfalen D 71 B4
Grønbjerg DK 59 B1
Grönenbach D 107 B5
Grong N 199 A9
Grönhögen S 63 B4
Groningen
D 73 C4
NL 71 A3
Grønnestrand DK 58 A2
Grono CH 120 A2
Grönskåra S 62 A3
Grootegast NL 71 A3
Gropello Cairoli I 120 B1
Grorud N 48 C2
Grósio I 120 A3
Grošnica SRB 127 D2
Grossalmerode D 82 A1
Grossarl A 109 B4
Gross Beeren D 74 B2
Gross Berkel D 72 B2
Grossbodungen D 82 A2
Gross-botwar D 94 C1
Grossburgwedel D 72 B2
Grosschönau D 84 B2
Gross-Dölln D 74 A2
Grossenbrode D 65 B4
Grossenehrich D 82 A2
Grossengottern D 82 A2
Grossenhain D 83 A5
Grossenkneten D 71 B5
Grossenlüder D 81 B5
Grossensee D 72 A3
Grossenzersdorf A 111 A3
Grosseto I 135 C4
Gross-Gerau D 93 B4
Grossgerungs A 96 C2
Grossglobnitz A 97 C3
Grosshabersdorf D 94 B2
Grossharras A 97 C4
Grosshartmansdorf D 83 B5
Grosshöchstetten CH 106 C2
Gross Kreutz D 74 B1
Grosskrut A 97 C4
Gross Lafferde D 72 B3
Gross Leutheb D 74 B3
Grosslohra D 82 A2
Grossmehring D 95 C3
Gross Muckrow D 74 B3
Gross Oesingen D 72 B3
Grossostheim D 93 B5
Grosspertholz A 96 C2
Grosspetersdorf A 111 B3
Grosspostwitz D 84 A2
Grossraming A 110 B1
Grossräschen D 84 A2
Gross Reken D 80 A3
Grossrinderfeld D 94 B1
Grossröhrsdorf D 84 A2
Gross Sarau D 65 C3
Gross Särchen D 84 A2
Grossschirma D 83 B5
Gross Schönebeck D 74 B2
Grossschweinbarth A 97 C4
Grosssiegharts A 97 C3
Grosssölk A 109 B4
Gross Umstadt D 93 B4
Grosswarasdorf A 111 B3
Gross Warnow D 73 A4
Gross-Weikersdorf A 97 C3
Gross-Welle D 73 A5
Grosswilfersdorf A 110 B2
Gross Wokern D 65 C5
Grostenquin F 92 C2
Grosuplje SLO 123 B3
Grotli N 198 C4
Grötlingbo S 57 C4
Grottáglie I 173 B3
Grottaminarda I 170 B3
Grottammare I 136 C2
Grotte di Castro I 168 A1
Grotteria I 175 C2
Gróttole I 172 B2
Grouw NL 70 A2
Grov N 194 B8
Grova N 53 A4
Grove E 140 B2
Grua N 48 B2
Grube D 65 B4
Grubišno Polje HR 124 B3
Grude BIH 138 B3
Grudusk PL 77 A5
Grudziądz PL 69 B3
Grue N 49 B4
Gruissan F 130 B2
Grullos E 141 A4
Grumo Áppula I 171 B4
Grums S 55 A4
Grünau im Almtal A 109 B4
Grünberg D 81 B4
Grünburg A 110 B1
Grundarfjörður IS 190 C2
Gründau D 81 B5
Gründelhardt D 94 B1
Grundforsen S 49 A4
Grundlsee A 109 B4
Grundsund S 54 B2
Grunewald D 84 A1
Grungedal N 53 A3
Grunow D 74 B3
Grünstadt D 93 B4
Gruvberget S 50 A3
Gruyères CH 106 C2
Gruža SRB 127 D2
Grybów PL 99 B4
Grycksbo S 50 B2
Gryfice PL 67 C4
Gryfino PL 74 A3
Gryfów Śląski PL 84 A3
Gryllefjord N 194 A8
Grymyr N 48 B2
Gryt S 56 B2
Grytgöl S 56 B1
Grythyttan S 55 A5
Grytnäs S 57 B3
Grzmiąca PL 68 B1
Grzybno PL 74 A3
Grzywna PL 76 A3
Gschnitz A 108 B2
Gschwend D 94 C1
Gstaad CH 106 C2
Gsteig CH 119 A4
Guadahortuna E 163 A4
Guadalajara E 151 B4
Guadalaviar E 152 B2
Guadalcanal E 156 B2
Guadalcázar E 162 A3
Guadalix de la Sierra E 151 B4
Guadálmez E 156 B3
Guadalupe E 156 A2
Guadamur E 151 C3
Guadarrama E 151 B3
Guadiaro E 162 B2
Guadix E 164 B1
Guagnano I 173 B3
Guagno F 180 A1
Guajar-Faragüit E 163 B4
Gualchos E 163 B4
Gualdo Tadino I 136 B1
Gualtieri I 121 C3
Guarcino I 169 B3
Guarda P 149 B2
Guardamar del Segura E 165 A4
Guardão P 148 B1
Guardavalle I 175 C2
Guardea I 168 A2
Guárdia I 172 B1
Guardiagrele I 169 A4
Guardiarégia I 170 B2
Guárdia Sanframondi I 170 B2
Guardias Viejas E 164 C2
Guardiola de Bergueda E 147 B2
Guardo E 142 B2
Guareña E 156 B1
Guaro E 162 B3
Guarromán E 157 B4
Guasila I 179 C3
Guastalla I 121 C3
Gubbhögen S 199 A12
Gúbbio I 136 B1
Guben D 74 C3
Gubin PL 74 C3
Gudå N 199 B8
Gudavac BIH 124 C2
Guddal N 46 A2
Güderup DK 64 B2
Gudhem S 55 B4
Gudhjem DK 67 A3
Gudovac HR 124 B2
Gudow D 73 A3
Güdül TR 187 B7
Gudvangen N 46 B3
Guebwiller F 106 B2
Guéjar-Sierra E 163 A4
Guéméné-Penfao F 101 B4
Guéméné-sur-Scorff F 100 A2
Güeñes E 143 A3
Guer F 101 B3
Guérande F 101 B3
Guéret F 116 A1
Guérigny F 104 B2
Guesa E 144 B2
Gueugnon F 104 C3
Guglionesi I 170 B2
Gühlen Glienicke D 74 A1
Guia P 154 B2
Guichen F 101 B4
Guidizzolo I 121 B3
Guidónia-Montecélio I 168 B2
Guiglia I 135 A3
Guignes F 90 C2
Guijo E 156 B3
Guijo de Coria E 149 B3
Guijo de Santa Bábera E 150 B2
Guijuelo E 150 B2
Guildford UK 44 B3
Guillaumes F 132 A2
Guillena E 162 A1
Guillestre F 118 C3
Guillos F 128 B2
Guilsfield UK 38 B3
Guilvinec F 100 B1
Guimarães P 148 A1
Guincho P 154 C1
Guînes F 78 B1
Guingamp F 100 A2
Guipavas F 100 A1
Guisborough UK 37 B5
Guiscard F 90 B3
Guiscriff F 100 A2
Guise F 91 B3
Guisona E 147 C2
Guitiriz E 140 A3
Guîtres F 128 A2
Gujan-Mestras F 128 B1
Gulbene LV 8 D5
Gulçayır TR 187 C6
Guldborg DK 65 B4
Gullabo S 63 B3
Gullane UK 35 B5

Gullbrå N 46 B3
Gullbrandstorp
  S. 61 C2
Gulleråsen S 50 A2
Gullhaug N 53 A6
Gullringen S 62 A3
Gullspång S 55 B5
Gullstein N. . . . 198 B5
Güllük TR 188 B2
Gülnar TR 23 C7
Gülpınar TR . . . 186 C1
Gülşehir TR 23 B8
Gulsvik N 48 B1
Gumiel de Hizán
  E. 143 C3
Gummersbach
  D 81 A3
Gümüldür TR . . 188 A2
Gümüşhacıköy
  TR. 23 A8
Gümüşova
  TR. 187 B5
Gundelfingen
  D 94 C2
Gundel-fingen
  D 106 A2
Gundelsheim D 93 B5
Gunderschoffen
  F. 93 C3
Gundertshausen
  A. 109 A3
Gundinci HR . . 125 B4
Gündoğmuş
  TR. 189 C7
Güney
  Burdur TR. 189 B4
  Denizli TR. 188 A4
Gunja HR. 125 C4
Günlüce TR 23 C8
Gunnarn S 195 E8
Gunnarsbyn S 196 C4
Gunnarskog S . .49 C4
Gunnebo S. 62 A4
Gunnislake UK . .42 B2
Günselsdorf A 111 B3
Guntersblum D .93 B4
Guntersdorf A . .97 C4
Guntin E 140 B3
Günyüzü TR . . . 187 C6
Günzburg D. 94 C2
Gunzenhausen
  D 94 B2
Güre
  Balıkesir TR . . 186 C1
  Uşak TR 186 D4
Gurk A 110 C1
Gurrea de Gállego
  E. 144 B3
Gürsu TR. 186 B4
Gušče HR 124 B2
Gusev RUS 12 A5
Gúspini I 179 C2
Gusselby S. 56 A1
Güssing A. 111 B3
Gusswerk A. . . . 110 B2
Gustav Adolf S. .49 B5
Gustavsberg S . .57 A4
Gustavsfors S . .54 A3
Güstrow D 65 C5
Gusum S 56 B2
Gutcher UK 33 A5
Gutenstein A . . 110 B2
Gütersloh D. 81 A4
Guttannen CH 106 C3
Guttaring A 110 C1
Guttau D. 84 A2
Güttingen CH. 107 B4
Gützkow D. 66 C2
Guzów PL 77 B5
Gvardeysk RUS .12 A4
Gvarv N. 53 A5
Gvozd MNE . . . 139 C5
Gvozdansko
  HR 124 B2
Gwda Wielka
  PL. 68 B1
Gwennap UK . . .42 B1
Gy F. 105 B4
Gyál H 112 B3
Gyarmat H 111 B4
Gyékényes H. . 124 A3
Gyé-sur-Seine
  F. 104 A3
Gyljen S. 196 C5
Gylling DK 59 C3
Gyoma H. 113 C4
Gyömöre H 111 B4
Gyömrö H. 112 B3
Gyón H. 112 B3
Gyöngyfa H. . . . 125 B3

Gyöngyös H . . 113 B3
Gyöngyöspata
  H. 113 B3
Gyönk H 112 C2
Györ H 111 B4
Györszemere
  H. 111 B4
Gypsera CH . . 106 C2
Gysinge S. 51 B3
Gyttorp S. 55 A5
Gyula H 113 C5
Gyulafirátót
  H. 112 B1
Gyulaj H 112 C2

H

Haacht B 79 B4
Haag
  Nieder Östereich
    A. 110 A1
  Ober Östereich
    A. 109 A4
  D 108 A3
Haaksbergen
  NL 71 B3
Haamstede NL . .79 A3
Haan D. 80 A3
Haapajärvi FIN. . 3 E9
Haapsalu EST . . . 8 C3
Haarlem NL 70 B1
Habas F 128 C2
Habay B. 92 B1
Habo S 62 A2
Håbol S 54 B3
Habry CZ. 97 B3
Habsheim F. . . 106 B2
Hachenburg D . .81 B3
Hacıbektaş TR . .23 B8
Hacılar TR. 23 B8
Hacinas E 143 C3
Hackås S 199 C11
Hacketstown
  IRL 30 B2
Hackthorpe UK .37 B4
Hadamar D 81 B4
Hädanberg S. . 200 C4
Haddington UK .35 C5
Hadersdorf am
  Kamp A 97 C3
Haderslev DK . . .59 C2
Haderup DK. 59 B1
Hadım TR 23 C7
Hadleigh
  Essex UK. 45 B4
  Suffolk UK 45 A4
Hadlow UK. 45 B4
Hadmersleben
  D 73 B4
Hadsten DK. 59 B3
Hadsund DK. 58 B3
Hadžići BIH . . . 139 B4
Hafnarfjörður
  IS 190 C4
Hafnir IS 190 D3
Hafslo N 47 A4
Haganj HR 124 B2
Hagby S. 63 B4
Hage D. 71 A4
Hægebostad N. .52 B3
Hægeland N 53 B3
Hagen
  Niedersachsen
    D. 72 A1
  Nordrhein-
    Westfalen D. . . 80 A3
Hagenbach D . .93 B4
Hagenow D 73 A4
Hagetmau F . . 128 C2
Hagfors S 49 B5
Häggenås S . . 199 B11
Hagondange F. .92 B2
Hagsta S. 51 B4
Haguenau F. 93 C3
Hahnbach D 95 B3
Hahnstätten D . .81 B4
Hahót H. 111 C3
Haiger D 81 B4
Haigerloch D. . . .93 C4
Hailsham UK 45 C4
Hainburg A 111 A3
Hainfeld A . . . 110 A2
Hainichen D. . . .83 B5
Hajdúböszörmény
  H. 113 B5
Hajdučica SRB 126 B2
Hajdúdorog
  H. 113 B5
Hajdúnánás
  H. 113 B5
Hajdúszoboszló
  H. 113 B5

Hajnáčka SK . . 113 A3
Hajnówka PL. . . .13 B5
Hajós H 112 C3
Håkafot S . . . 199 A11
Hakkas S 196 C4
Håksberg S. 50 B2
Halaszi H. 111 B4
Halberstadt D. . .82 A3
Halberton UK. . . .43 B3
Hald Ege DK. . . .58 B2
Haldem D. 71 B5
Halden N. 54 A2
Haldensleben
  D 73 B4
Halenbeck D. . . .73 A5
Halesowen UK . .40 C1
Halesworth UK. .45 A5
Halfing D. 109 B3
Halhjem N 46 B2
Håliden S 49 B5
Halifax UK 40 B2
Häljelöt S. 56 B2
Halkirk UK 32 C3
Hall S 57 C4
Hälla S 200 C3
Hallabro S 63 B3
Hällabrottet S . .56 A1
Halland UK. 45 C4
Hälläryd S. 63 B2
Hallaryd S. 61 C3
Hällberga S 56 A2
Hällbybrunn S . .56 A2
Halle
  B. 79 B4
  Nordrhein-
    Westfalen D. . .72 B1
  Sachsen-Anhalt
    D. 83 A3
Hålleberga S. . . .62 B3
Hällefors S 55 A5
Hälleforsnäs S . .56 A2
Hallein A. 109 B4
Hällekis S. 55 B4
Hallen S. 199 B11
Hällen S. 51 B4
Hallenberg D . . .81 A4
Hällestad S 56 B1
Hällevadsholm
  S 54 B2
Hällevik S. 63 B2
Hälleviksstrand
  S 54 B2
Hallingby N 48 B2
Hallingeberg S. .62 A4
Hallingen N. 47 B6
Hall in Tirol A. . . 108 B2
Hällnäs S 195 D9
Hällnäs S. 51 B4
Hällnäs S. 200 B5
Hallormsstaður
  IS 191 B11
Hallsberg S 56 A1
Hallsta S 56 A2
Hallstahammar
  S 56 A2
Hallstatt A 109 B4
Hallstavik S 51 B5
Halltorp S. 63 B4
Halluin F. 78 B3
Hallviken S . . . 199 B12
Hallworthy UK . .42 B2
Halmstad S 61 C2
Hals DK 58 A3
Halsa N 198 B5
Halstead UK. 45 B4
Haltdalen N. . . . 199 C8
Haltern D 80 A3
Haltwhistle UK . .37 B4
Halvarsgårdarna
  S 50 B2
Halver D 80 A3
Halvrimmen
  DK 58 A2
Ham F. 90 B3
Hamar N 48 B3
Hamarhaug N. . .46 B2
Hamarøy N 194 B6
Hambach F 92 B3
Hambergen D. . .72 A1
Hambergsund
  S 54 B2
Hambledon UK .44 C2
Hambuhren D . .72 B2
Hamburg D. 72 A2
Hamdibey TR . 186 C2
Hamdorf D. 64 B2
Hämeenlinna
  FIN. 8 B4
Hameln = Hamlin
  D. 72 B2
Hamersleben D 73 B4
Hamidiye TR . . 187 C5
Hamilton UK 36 A2

Hamina FIN 8 B5
Hamlagrø N. 46 B3
Hamlin = Hameln
  D. 72 B2
Hamm D 81 A3
Hammar S 55 B5
Hammarland
  FIN. 51 B6
Hammarö S. 55 A4
Hammarstrand
  S. 200 C2
Hamme B. 79 A4
Hammel DK. 59 B2
Hammelburg D .82 B1
Hammelspring
  D 74 A2
Hammenhög S. .66 A3
Hammerdal
  S. 199 B12
Hammerfest
  N. 192 B7
Hammershøj
  DK. 58 B2
Hammerum DK .58 B2
Hamminkeln D .80 A2
Hamnavoe UK . .33 A5
Hamneda S 60 C3
Hamningberg
  N. 193 B14
Hamoir B. 80 B1
Hamont B. 80 A1
Hámor H 113 A4
Hamra
  Gävleborg
    S. 199 D12
  Gotland S. 57 D4
Hamrångefjärden
  S. 51 B4
Hamstreet UK. . .45 B4
Hamsund N 194 B6
Han TR 187 C5
Hanaskog S. 61 C4
Hanau D 81 B4
Händelöp S 62 A4
Handlová SK. . . .98 C2
Hanerau-
  Hademarschen
    D 64 B2
Hånger S. 60 B3
Hanhimaa FIN. 197 B8
Hanken S 55 B5
Hankensbüttel
  D 73 B3
Han Knežica
  BIH. 124 B2
Hanko FIN 8 C3
Hannover D. 72 B2
Hannut B. 79 B5
Han Pijesak
  BIH. 139 A4
Hansnes N 192 C3
Hanstedt D 72 A3
Hanstholm DK . .58 A1
Hantsavichy BY .13 B7
Hanušovice CZ. .85 B4
Haparanda S. . 196 D7
Haradok BY. 13 A8
Harads S 196 C4
Häradsbäck S . .63 B2
Häradsbygden
  S. 50 B2
Harbo S. 51 B4
Harboør DK. 58 B1
Harburg
  Bayern D 94 C2
  Hamburg D. . . . 72 A2
Hårby DK. 59 C3
Harc H 112 C2
Hardegarijp NL .70 A2
Hardegsen D. . . .82 A1
Hardelot Plage
  F. 78 B1
Hardenbeck D . .74 A2
Hardenberg NL .71 B3
Harderwijk NL . .70 B2
Hardheim D. 94 B1
Haren
  D 71 B4
  NL 71 A3
Harestua N. 48 B2
Harfleur F. 89 A4
Harg S 51 B5
Hargicourt F. 90 B3
Hargnies F. 91 A4
Hargshamn S. . . .51 B5
Härja S. 55 B4
Harkány H 125 B4
Harkebrügge
  D 71 A4
Harlech UK. 38 B2

Harleston UK . . .45 A5
Hårlev DK. 65 A5
Harlingen NL . . .70 A2
Harlösa S 61 D3
Harlow UK 45 B4
Harmancık
  TR. 186 C4
Harmånger S . .200 E3
Harmanli BG. . 183 B7
Härnevi S 56 A3
Härnösand S . . 200 D3
Haro E 143 B4
Haroldswick
  UK 33 A6
Háromfa H 124 A3
Haroué F. 92 C2
Harpenden UK . .44 B3
Harplinge S. 60 C2
Harpstedt D 72 B1
Harrogate UK. . .40 A2
Harrow UK. 44 B3
Härryda S. 60 B2
Harsefeld D. 72 A2
Harsewinkel D . .71 C5
Hârşova. 17 C7
Harstad N. 194 B7
Harsum D. 72 B2
Harsvik N 199 A7
Harta H 112 C3
Hartberg A. . . . 110 B2
Hartburn UK 37 A5
Hartennes F 90 B3
Hartest UK 45 A4
Hartha D. 83 A4
Hartland UK 42 B2
Hartlepool UK . .37 B5
Hartmanice CZ. .96 B1
Hartmannsdorf
  A. 110 B2
Harvassdal N . .195 E5
Harwell UK. 44 B2
Harwich UK 45 B5
Harzgerode D. . .82 A3
Häselgehr A . . . 108 B1
Haselünne D 71 B4
Haskovo BG. . . 183 B7
Hasköy TR 186 A1
Haslach D. 106 A3
Haslach an der
  Mühl A. 96 C2
Hasle DK. 67 A3
Haslemere UK . .44 B3
Haslev DK. 65 A4
Hasloch D. 94 B1
Hasparren F . . 144 A2
Hassela S 200 D2
Hasselfelde D. . .82 A2
Hasselfors S. . . .55 A5
Hasselt
  B. 79 B5
  NL 70 B3
Hassfurt D. 94 A2
Hassleben D 74 B2
Hässleholm S . .61 C3
Hasslö S 63 B3
Hassloch D. 93 B4
Hästbo S. 51 B4
Hastière-Lavaux
  B. 79 B4
Hastigrow UK . . .32 C3
Hastings UK. 45 C4
Hästveda S. 61 C3
Hasvik N 192 B6
Hatfield
  Hertfordshire
    UK 44 B3
  South Yorkshire
    UK 40 B3
Hatherleigh UK .42 B2
Hathersage UK. .40 B2
Hatlestrand N. . .46 B2
Hattem NL 70 B3
Hatten
  D 71 A5
  F. 93 C3
Hattfjelldal N .195 E4
Hatting DK. 59 C2
Hattingen D 80 A3
Hattstadt D. 64 B3
Hatvan H 112 B3
Hatvik N 46 B2
Hau D. 80 A2
Haudainville F. .92 B1
Hauganes IS . . 190 B7
Haugastøl N. . . .47 B4
Hauge N 52 B2
Haugesund N. . .52 A1
Haughom N. 52 B2
Haugsdal N 46 B2

Haugsdorf A . . .97 C4
Haukedal N 46 A3
Haukeland N. . . .46 B2
Haukeligrend
  N. 52 A3
Haukeliseter N. .52 A3
Haukipudas FIN. .3 D9
Haulerwijk NL . .71 A3
Haunersdorf D. .95 C4
Haus N 46 B2
Hausach D. . . . 106 A3
Hausham D . . . 108 B2
Hausmannstätten
  A. 110 C2
Hausvik N. 52 B2
Hautajärvi
  FIN. 197 C12
Hauterives F. . 117 B5
Hauteville-
  Lompnès F. . . . 118 B2
Hautmont F. 79 B3
Hautrage B 79 B3
Hauzenberg D . .96 C1
Havant UK 44 C3
Havdhem S 57 C4
Havdrup DK. . . . 61 D2
Havelange B. . . .79 B5
Havelberg D 73 B5
Havelte NL 70 B3
Haverfordwest
  UK 39 C2
Haverhill UK 45 A4
Havering UK 45 B4
Håverud S. 54 B3
Havířov CZ. 98 B2
Havixbeck D 71 C4
Havndal DK. 58 B3
Havneby DK 64 A1
Havnebyen DK. 61 D1
Havnsø DK. 61 D1
Havøysund N . 193 A8
Havran TR. 186 C2
Havrebjerg DK. 61 D1
Havsa TR. 186 A1
Havstenssund
  S. 54 B2
Havza TR. 23 A8
Hawes UK 37 B4
Hawick UK 35 C5
Hawkhurst UK . .45 B4
Hawkinge UK . . .45 B5
Haxey UK 40 B3
Hayange F 92 B2
Haydarlı TR . . . 189 A5
Haydon Bridge
  UK 37 B4
Hayle UK. 42 B1
Haymana TR . . 187 C7
Hay-on-Wye UK 39 B3
Hayrabolu TR . 186 A2
Haysyn UA 13 D8
Hayvoron UA . . 13 D8
Haywards Heath
  UK 44 C3
Hazebrouck F. .78 B2
Hazlov CZ. 83 B4
Heacham UK . . .41 C4
Headcorn UK. . . .45 B4
Headford IRL. . . .28 A2
Heanor UK 40 B2
Héas F 145 B4
Heathfield UK. . .45 C4
Hebden Bridge
  UK 40 B1
Heberg S. 60 C2
Heby S 51 C3
Hechingen D. . . .93 C4
Hechlingen D. . . .94 C2
Hecho E. 144 B3
Hechtel B 79 A5
Hechthausen D .72 A2
Heckelberg D . . .74 B2
Heckington UK . .41 C3
Hecklingen D . . .82 A3
Hed S 56 A1
Hedalen N 48 B2
Hedared S 60 B2
Heddal N 53 A5
Hédé F. 101 A4
Hede S 199 C10
Hedekas S. 54 B2
Hedemora S 50 B2
Hedenäset S . . 196 C6
Hedensted DK . .59 C2
Hedersleben D. .82 A3
Hedesunda S . . .51 B4
Hedge End UK . .44 C2
Hedon UK 41 B3

Heek D. 71 B4
Heemstede NL . .70 B1
Heerde NL 70 B3
Heerenveen NL .70 B2
Heerhugowaard
  NL 70 B1
Heerlen NL. 80 B1
Heeze NL 80 A1
Heggenes N. 47 A6
Hegra N. 199 B8
Hegyeshalom
  H. 111 B4
Hegyközség
  H. 111 B3
Heia N 199 A9
Heide D. 64 B2
Heidelberg D . . .93 B4
Heiden D. 80 A2
Heidenau D. 84 B1
Heidenheim D . .94 C2
Heidenreichstein
  A. 97 C3
Heikendorf D . . .64 B3
Heikkilä FIN. . 197 C12
Heilam UK 32 C2
Heiland N. 53 B4
Heilbad
  Heiligenstadt
    D. 82 A2
Heilbronn D 93 B5
Heiligenblut
  A. 109 B3
Heiligendamn
  D 65 B4
Heiligendorf D. .73 B3
Heiligengrabe
  D 73 A5
Heiligenhafen
  D 65 B3
Heiligenhaus D .80 A2
Heiligenkreuz
  A. 111 C3
Heiligenstadt
  D 94 B3
Heiloo NL 70 B1
Heilsbronn D . . .94 B2
Heim N. 198 B6
Heimburg D 82 A2
Heimdal N. 199 B7
Heinerscheid L. .92 A2
Heinersdorf D . .74 B3
Heining D. 96 C1
Heiningen D. 94 C1
Heinola FIN 8 B5
Heinsberg D 80 A2
Heist-op-den-Berg
  B. 79 A4
Hejde S 57 C4
Hejdeby S. 57 C4
Hejls DK. 59 C2
Hejnice CZ. 84 B3
Hel PL. 69 A3
Helchteren B. . . .79 A5
Heldburg D 82 B2
Heldrungen D . .82 A3
Helechosa E. . . 156 A3
Helensburgh
  UK 34 B3
Helfenberg A . . .96 C2
Helgen N 53 A5
Helgeroa N 53 B5
Hella
  IS 190 D5
  N. 46 A3
Helland N 194 B7
Hellas S 55 B3
Helle N. 52 B2
Helleland N. 52 B2
Hellendoorn
  NL 71 B3
Hellenthal D 80 B2
Hellesøy N 46 B1
Hellesylt N. . . . 198 C3
Hellevoetsluis
  NL 79 A4
Helligskogen
  N. 192 C4
Hellín E 158 C2
Hellissandur
  IS 190 C2
Hellnar IS 190 C2
Hellum D 58 A3
Hellvi S 57 C4
Hellvik N. 52 B1
Helm-brechts D 83 B3
Helmond NL 80 A1
Helmsdale UK. . .32 C3
Helmsley UK 37 B5
Helmstedt D 73 B3
Hel'pa SK 99 C3
Helsa D. 82 A1
Helsby UK. 38 A4
Helsingborg S . .61 C2

Hel – Hor 223

Helsinge DK 61 C2
Helsingør DK 61 C2
Helsinki FIN 8 B4
Helston UK 42 B1
Hemau D 95 B3
Hemavan S 195 E6
Hemel Hempstead UK 44 B3
Hemer D 81 A3
Héming F 92 C2
Hemmet DK 59 C1
Hemmingstedt D 64 B2
Hemmoor D 64 C2
Hemnes N 54 A2
Hemnesberget N 195 D4
Hemse S 57 C4
Hemsedal N 47 B5
Hemslingen D 72 A2
Hemsworth UK 40 B2
Hen N 48 B2
Henån S 54 B2
Hendaye F 144 A2
Hendek TR 187 B5
Hendungen D 82 B2
Henfield UK 44 C3
Hengelo
Gelderland NL 71 B3
Overijssel NL 71 B3
Hengersberg D 95 C5
Hengoed UK 39 C3
Hénin-Beaumont F 78 B2
Henley-on-Thames UK 44 B3
Hennan S 200 D1
Henneberg D 82 B2
Hennebont F 100 B2
Henne Strand DK 59 C1
Hennigsdorf D 74 B2
Hennset N 198 B5
Hennstedt D 64 B2
Henrichemont F 103 B4
Henryków PL 85 B5
Henrykowo PL 69 A5
Hensås N 47 A5
Henstedt-Ulzburg D 64 C2
Heppenheim D 93 B4
Herad
Buskerud N 47 B6
Vest-Agder N 52 B2
Heradsbygd N 48 B3
Heraklion = Iraklio GR 185 D6
Herálec CZ 97 B4
Herand N 46 B3
Herbault F 103 B3
Herbern D 81 A3
Herbertstown IRL 29 B3
Herbeumont B 91 B5
Herbignac F 101 B3
Herbisse F 91 C4
Herbitzheim F 92 B3
Herbolzheim D 106 A2
Herborn D 81 B4
Herbrechtingen D 94 C2
Herby PL 86 B2
Herceg-Novi MNE 16 D3
Hercegovać HR 124 B3
Hercegszántó H 125 B4
Herchen D 80 B3
Heréd H 112 B3
Hereford UK 39 B4
Herefoss N 53 B4
Hereke TR 187 B4
Herencia E 157 A4
Herend H 111 B4
Herent B 79 B4
Herentals B 79 A4
Hérépian F 130 B2
Herfølge DK 61 D2
Herford D 72 B1
Herguijuela E 156 A2
Héric F 101 B4
Héricourt F 106 B1
Héricourt-en-Caux F 89 A4
Hérimoncourt F 106 B1
Heringsdorf D 65 B4
Herisau CH 107 B4
Hérisson F 103 C4
Herk-de-Stad B 79 B5
Herlufmagle DK 65 A4
Hermagor A 109 C4
Hermannsburg D 72 B3
Hermansverk N 46 A3
Heřmanův Městec CZ 97 B3
Herment F 116 B2
Hermeskeil D 92 B2
Hermisende E 141 C4
Hermonville F 91 B3
Hermsdorf D 83 B3
Hernani E 144 A2
Hernansancho E 150 B3
Herne D 80 A3
Herne Bay UK 45 B5
Hernes N 48 B3
Herning DK 59 B1
Herøya N 53 A5
Herramelluri E 143 B3
Herräng S 51 B5
Herre N 53 A5
Herrenberg D 93 C4
Herrera E 162 A3
Herrera de Alcántara E 155 B3
Herrera del Duque E 156 A2
Herrera de los Navarros E 152 A2
Herrera de Pisuerga E 142 B2
Herreros del Suso E 150 B2
Herrestad S 54 B2
Herrhamra S 57 B3
Herritslev DK 65 B4
Herrlisheim F 93 C3
Herrljunga S 55 B4
Herrnhut D 84 A2
Herrsching D 108 A2
Hersbruck D 95 B3
Hersby S 57 A4
Herscheid D 81 A3
Herselt B 79 A4
Herso GR 182 B4
Herstal B 80 B1
Herstmonceux UK 45 C4
Herten D 80 A3
Hertford UK 44 B3
Hervás E 149 B4
Hervik N 52 A1
Herxheim D 93 B4
Herzberg
Brandenburg D 74 B1
Brandenburg D 83 A5
Niedersachsen D 82 A2
Herzebrock D 81 A4
Herzfelde D 74 B2
Herzlake D 71 B4
Herzogenaurach D 94 B2
Herzogenbuchsee CH 106 B2
Herzogenburg A 110 A2
Herzsprung D 73 A5
Hesby N 52 A1
Hesdin F 78 B2
Hesel D 71 A4
Heskestad N 52 B2
Hessdalen N 199 C8
Hesselager DK 65 A3
Hesseng N 193 C13
Hessisch Lichtenau D 82 A1
Hessisch-Oldendorf D 72 B2
Hestra S 60 B3
Heswall UK 38 A3
Hetlevik N 46 B2
Hettange-Grande F 92 B2
Hetton-le-Hole UK 37 B5
Hettstedt D 82 A3
Heuchin F 78 B2
Heudicourt-sous-les-Côtes F 92 C1
Heunezel F 105 A5
Heuqueville F 89 A4
Heves H 113 B4
Héviz H 111 C4
Hexham UK 37 B4
Heysham UK 36 B4
Heytesbury UK 43 A4
Hidas H 125 A4
Hieflau A 110 B1
Hiendelaencina E 151 A5
Hiersac F 115 C4
High Bentham UK 37 B4
Highclere UK 44 B2
High Hesket UK 37 B4
Highley UK 39 B4
High Wycombe UK 44 B3
Higuera de Arjona E 157 C4
Higuera de Calatrava E 163 A3
Higuera de la Serena E 156 B2
Higuera de la Sierra E 161 B3
Higuera de Vargas E 155 C4
Higuera la Real E 161 A3
Higuers de Llerena E 156 B1
Higueruela E 158 C2
Híjar E 153 A3
Hilchenbach D 81 A4
Hildburghausen D 82 B2
Hilden D 80 A2
Hilders D 82 B1
Hildesheim D 72 B2
Hilgay UK 41 C4
Hillared S 60 B3
Hille D 72 B1
Hillegom NL 70 B1
Hillerød DK 61 D2
Hillerstorp S 60 B3
Hillesheim D 80 B2
Hillestad N 53 A6
Hillmersdorf D 83 A5
Hillsborough UK 27 B4
Hillswick UK 33 A5
Hilpoltstein D 95 B3
Hiltpoltstein D 94 B3
Hilvarenbeek NL 79 A5
Hilversum NL 70 B2
Himarë AL 182 C1
Himbergen D 73 A3
Himesháza H 125 A4
Himmelberg A 109 C5
Himmelpforten D 72 A2
Himód H 111 B4
Hinckley UK 40 C2
Hindås S 60 B2
Hindelang D 108 B1
Hindelbank CH 106 B2
Hinderavåg N 52 A1
Hindhead UK 44 B3
Hinjosa del Valle E 156 B1
Hinnerup DK 59 B3
Hinneryd S 61 C3
Hinojal E 155 B4
Hinojales E 161 B3
Hinojos E 161 B3
Hinojosa del Duque E 156 B2
Hinojosas de Calatrava E 157 B3
Hinterhornbach A 108 B1
Hinterriss A 108 B2
Hintersee
A 109 B4
D 74 A3
Hinterstoder A 110 B1
Hintertux A 108 B2
Hinterweidenthal D 93 B3
Hinwil CH 107 B3
Hios GR 185 A7
Hippolytushoef NL 70 B1
Hirschaid D 94 B2
Hirschau D 95 B3
Hirschfeld D 83 A5
Hirschhorn D 93 B4
Hirsingue F 106 B2
Hirson F 91 B4
Hirtshals DK 58 A2
Hirvaskoski FIN 197 D10
Hirzenhain D 81 B5
Hisarcık TR 186 C4
Hishult S 61 C3
Hissjön S 200 C6
Hitchin UK 44 B3
Hitra N 198 B5
Hittarp S 61 C2
Hittisau A 107 B4
Hittun N 46 A1
Hitzacker D 73 A4
Hjallerup DK 58 A3
Hjällstad S 49 B5
Hjältevad S 62 A3
Hjärnarp S 61 C2
Hjartdal N 53 A4
Hjellestad N 46 B2
Hjelmeland N 52 A2
Hjelset N 198 C4
Hjerkinn N 198 C6
Hjerm DK 58 B1
Hjerpsted DK 64 A1
Hjerting DK 59 C1
Hjo S 55 B5
Hjordkær DK 64 A2
Hjørring DK 58 A2
Hjorted S 62 A4
Hjortkvarn S 56 B1
Hjortnäs S 50 B1
Hjortsberga S 62 B2
Hjukse N 53 A5
Hjuksebø N 53 A5
Hjulsjö S 55 A5
Hliník nad Hronom SK 98 C2
Hlinsko CZ 97 B3
Hlío IS 191 A10
Hlohovec SK 98 C1
Hlubokánad Vltavou CZ 96 B2
Hlučín CZ 98 B2
Hlyboka UA 17 A6
Hlybokaye BY 13 A7
Hniezdne SK 99 B4
Hnilec SK 99 C4
Hnúšťa SK 99 C3
Hobol H 125 A3
Hobro DK 58 B2
Hobscheid L 92 B1
Hocalar TR 189 A4
Hochdonn D 64 B2
Hochdorf CH 106 B3
Hochfelden F 93 C3
Hochspeyer D 93 B3
Höchstadt D 94 B2
Höchstädt D 94 C2
Hochstenbach D 81 B3
Höchst im Odenwald D 93 B5
Höckendorf D 83 B5
Hockenheim D 93 B4
Hoddesdon UK 44 B3
Hodejov SK 99 C3
Hodenhagen D 72 B2
Hodkovice CZ 84 B3
Hódmezövásárhely H 113 C4
Hodnet UK 38 B4
Hodonín CZ 98 C1
Hodslavice CZ 98 B2
Hoedekenskerke NL 79 A3
Hoegaarden B 79 B4
Hoek van Holland NL 79 A4
Hoenderlo NL 70 B2
Hof
D 83 B3
N 53 A6
Hofbieber D 82 B1
Hoff UK 37 B4
Hofgeismar D 81 A5
Hofheim
Bayern D 82 B2
Hessen D 93 A4
Hofkirchen im Mühlkreis A 96 C1
Höfn IS 191 C10
Hofors S 50 B3
Hofsós IS 190 B6
Hofstad N 199 A7
Höganäs S 61 C2
Högbo S 51 B3
Hogdal S 54 A2
Høgebru N 46 A4
Högfors S 50 C2
Högklint S 57 C4
Högsäter S 54 B3
Högsby S 62 A4
Högsjö S 56 A1
Hogstad S 55 B6
Högyész H 112 C2
Hohenau A 97 C4
Hohenberg A 110 B2
Hohenbucko D 83 A5
Hohenburg D 95 B3
Hohendorf D 66 B1
Hohenems A 107 B4
Hohenhameln D 72 B3
Hohenhausen D 72 B1
Hohenkirchen D 71 A4
Hohenlinden D 108 A2
Hohenlockstedt D 64 C2
Hohenmölsen D 83 A4
Hohennauen D 73 B5
Hohen Neuendorf D 74 B2
Hohenseeden D 73 B5
Hohentauern A 110 B1
Hohentengen D 106 B3
Hohenwepel D 81 A5
Hohenwestedt D 64 B2
Hohenwutzen D 74 B3
Hohenzieritz D 74 A2
Hohn D 64 B2
Hohne D 72 B3
Hohnstorf D 73 A3
Højer DK 64 B1
Højslev Stby DK 58 B2
Hok S 62 A2
Hökerum S 60 B3
Hökhuvud S 51 B5
Hokksund N 53 A5
Hökön S 63 B2
Hol N 47 B5
Hólar IS 190 B6
Holašovice CZ 96 C2
Holbæk
Aarhus Amt. DK 58 B3
Vestsjællands Amt. DK 61 D1
Holbeach UK 41 C4
Holdenstedt D 73 B3
Holdhus N 46 B2
Holdorf D 71 B5
Holeby DK 65 B4
Hølen N 54 A1
Hølervasseter N 47 B6
Holešov CZ 98 B1
Holguera E 155 B4
Holíč SK 98 C1
Holice
CZ 97 A3
SK 111 B4
Höljes S 49 B4
Hollabrunn A 97 C4
Hollandstoun UK 33 B4
Høllen N 53 B3
Hollfeld D 95 B3
Hollókő H 112 B3
Hollstadt D 82 B2
Hollum NL 70 A2
Höllviksnäs S 66 A1
Holm N 195 E3
Hólmavík IS 190 B4
Holmbukt N 192 B5
Holmedal S 54 A2
Holmegil N 54 A2
Holmen N 48 B2
Holme-on-Spalding-Moor UK 40 B3
Holmes Chapel UK 38 A4
Holmestrand N 54 A1
Holmfirth UK 40 B2
Holmfoss N 193 C14
Holmsbu N 54 A1
Holmsjö S 63 B3
Holmsund S 200 C6
Holmsveden S 50 A3
Holmudden S 57 C5
Hölö S 57 A3
Holøydal N 199 C8
Holsbybrunn S 62 A3
Holseter N 48 A1
Holsljunga S 60 B2
Holstebro DK 59 B1
Holsted DK 59 C1
Holsworthy UK 42 B2
Holt
D 64 B2
Holt *continued*
IS 190 D6
N 53 B4
Norfolk UK 41 C5
Wrexham UK 38 A4
Holten NL 71 B3
Holtwick D 71 B4
Holum N 52 B3
Holwerd NL 70 A2
Holycross IRL 29 B4
Holyhead UK 38 A2
Holýšov CZ 95 B5
Holywell UK 38 A3
Holywood UK 27 B5
Holzdorf D 83 A5
Holzhausen D 72 B1
Holzheim D 94 C2
Holzkirchen D 108 B2
Holzminden D 81 A5
Holzthaleben D 82 A2
Homberg
Hessen D 81 A5
Hessen D 81 B5
Homburg D 93 B3
Hommelstø N 195 E3
Hommersåk N 52 B1
Homokmegy H 112 C3
Homokszentgyörgy H 124 A3
Homyel = Gomel BY 13 B9
Honaz TR 188 B4
Hondarribia E 144 A2
Hondón de los Frailes E 165 A4
Hondschoote F 78 B2
Hönebach D 82 B1
Hønefoss N 48 B2
Honfleur F 89 A4
Høng DK 61 D1
Honiton UK 43 B3
Hönningen D 80 B2
Honningsvåg N 193 B9
Hönö S 60 B1
Honrubia E 158 B1
Hontalbilla E 151 A3
Hontheim D 92 A2
Hontianske-Nemce SK 98 C2
Hontoria de la Cantera E 143 B3
Hontoria del Pinar E 143 C3
Hontoria de Valdearados E 143 C3
Hoofddorp NL 70 B1
Hoogerheide NL 79 A4
Hoogeveen NL 71 B3
Hoogezand-Sappemeer NL 71 A3
Hoogkarspel NL 70 B2
Hoogkerk NL 71 A3
Hoogstede D 71 B3
Hoogstraten B 79 A4
Hook UK 44 B3
Hooksiel D 71 A5
Höör S 61 D3
Hoorn NL 70 B2
Hope UK 38 A3
Hopen N 194 C6
Hope under Dinmore UK 39 B4
Hopfgarten A 108 B3
Hopfgarten in Defereggen A 109 C3
Hopseidet N 193 B11
Hopsten D 71 B4
Hoptrup DK 59 C2
Hora Svatého Sebestiána CZ 83 B5
Horaždovice CZ 96 B1
Horb am Neckar D 93 C4
Horbelev DK 65 B5
Hørby DK 58 A3
Hörby S 61 D3
Horcajada de la Torre E 158 A1
Horcajo de los Montes E 156 A3
Horcajo de Santiago E 151 C4
Horcajo-Medianero E 150 B2
Horche E 151 B4
Horda S 62 A2
Hordabø N 46 B1
Hordalia N 52 A2
Hordvik N 46 B2
Hořesedly CZ 83 B5
Horezu RO 17 C6
Horgen CH 107 B3
Horgoš SRB 126 A1
Horia RO 126 A3
Hořice CZ 84 B3
Horjul SLO 123 A3
Horka D 84 A2
Hörken S 50 B1
Horki BY 13 A9
Hörle S 60 B4
Horn
A 97 C3
D 81 A4
N 48 B2
S 62 A3
Horna E 158 C2
Hornachos E 156 B1
Hornachuelos E 162 A2
Horná Mariková SK 98 B2
Hornanes N 46 C2
Horná Streda SK 98 C1
Horná Štrubna SK 98 C2
Horná Súča SK 98 C1
Hornbæk
Aarhus Amt. DK 58 B2
Frederiksværk DK 61 C2
Hornberg D 106 A3
Hornburg D 73 B3
Horncastle UK 41 B3
Horndal S 50 B3
Horndean UK 44 C2
Horne
Fyns Amt. DK 64 A3
Ribe Amt. DK 59 C1
Hörnebo S 55 B5
Horneburg D 72 A2
Hörnefors S 200 C5
Horní Bečva CZ 98 B2
Horni Benešov CZ 98 B1
Horni Cerekev CZ 97 B3
Horní Jiřetín CZ 83 B5
Horní Lomná CZ 98 B2
Horni Maršov CZ 85 B3
Hornindal N 198 D3
Hørning DK 59 B3
Hörningsholm S 57 A3
Horní Planá CZ 96 C2
Horni Slavkov CZ 83 B4
Horni Vltavice CZ 96 C1
Hornnes N 53 B3
Horno D 84 A2
Hornos E 164 A2
Hornoy-le-Bourg F 90 B1
Hornsea UK 41 B3
Hornsjø N 48 A2
Hornslet DK 59 B3
Hornstein A 111 B3
Hörnum D 64 B1
Hornum DK 58 B2
Horný Tisovnik SK 99 C3
Horodenka UA 13 D6
Horodnya UA 13 C9
Horodok
Khmelnytskyy UA 13 D7
Lviv UA 13 D5
Horokhiv UA 13 C6
Horovice CZ 96 B1
Horred S 60 B2
Hörröd S 61 D4
Hörsching A 110 A1
Horsens DK 59 C2
Horsham UK 44 B3
Hørsholm DK 61 D2
Horslunde DK 65 B4

Horšovský Týn
CZ 95 B4
Horst NL 80 A2
Horstel D 71 B4
Horsten D 71 A4
Horstmar D 71 B4
Hort H 113 B3
Horta P 148 A2
Horten N. 54 A1
Hortezuela E. . 151 A5
Hortiguela E . . 143 B3
Hortobágy H. . . 113 B5
Horton in
 Ribblesdale
 UK. 37 B4
Hørve DK 61 D1
Hörvik S 63 B2
Horwich UK 38 A4
Hosanger N. 46 B2
Hösbach D 93 A5
Hosena D 84 A2
Hosenfeld D 81 B5
Hosingen L 92 A2
Hosio FIN 197 D8
Hospental CH. 107 C3
Hospital IRL. 29 B3
Hossegor F. . . . 128 C1
Hosszúhetény
 H. 125 A4
Hostal de Ipiés
 E. 145 B3
Hoštálkova CZ . .98 B1
Hostalric E 147 C3
Hostens F 128 B2
Hostěradice CZ .97 C4
Hostinné CZ 85 B3
Hostomice CZ. . .96 B2
Hostouň CZ 95 B4
Hotagen S 199 B11
Hoting S 200 B2
Hotolisht AL . . 182 B2
Hotton B 79 B5
Houdain F 78 B2
Houdan F 90 C1
Houdelaincourt
 F. 92 C1
Houeillès F. . . . 128 B3
Houffalize B 92 A1
Houghton-le-
 Spring UK. 37 B5
Houlberg DK. . .59 B2
Houlgate F. 89 A3
Hounslow UK . . .44 B3
Hourtin F 128 A1
Hourtin-Plage
 F. 128 A1
Houthalen B 79 A5
Houyet B. 79 B4
Hov
 DK. 59 C3
 N. 48 B2
Hova S 55 B5
Høvåg N 53 B4
Hovborg DK 59 C1
Hovda N 47 B6
Hovden N. 52 A3
Hove UK 44 C3
Hovedgård DK. .59 C2
Hovelhof D 81 A4
Hoven DK. 59 C1
Hovet N. 47 B5
Hovingham UK .40 A3
Hovmantorp S . .62 B3
Hovsta S 56 A1
Howden UK 40 B3
Howe D 72 A3
Höxter D 81 A5
Hoya D. 72 B2
Hoya de Santa
 Maria E 161 B3
Hoya-Gonzalo
 E. 158 C2
Høyanger N. 46 A3
Hoyerswerda
 D 84 A2
Høyjord N 53 A6
Hoylake UK 38 A3
Høylandet N . . 199 A9
Hoym D. 82 A2
Høymyr N. 47 C6
Hoyocasero E. 150 B3
Hoyo de
 Manzanares
 E. 151 B4
Hoyo de Pinares
 E. 150 B3
Hoyos E 149 B3
Hoyos del Espino
 E. 150 B2
Hrabušice SK. . . .99 C4

Hradec Králové
 CZ 85 B3
Hradec nad
 Moravicí CZ 98 B1
Hrádek CZ 97 C4
Hrádek nad Nisou
 CZ 84 B2
Hradiště SK 98 C2
Hrafnagil IS . . 191 B7
Hrafnseyri IS . . 190 B2
Hranice
 Severomoravsky
 CZ 98 B1
 Západočeský
 CZ 83 B4
Hranovnica SK . .99 C4
Hrasnica BIH . . 139 B4
Hrastnik SLO . . 123 A4
Hřensko CZ 84 B2
Hriňová SK. 99 C3
Hrisoupoli GR. 183 C6
Hrochov CZ. . . .97 B4
Hrochův Tynec
 CZ 97 B3
Hrodna BY 13 B5
Hrodzyanka BY .13 B8
Hronov CZ. 85 B4
Hronský Beňadik
 SK. 98 C2
Hrotovice CZ. . .97 B4
Hrtkovci SRB. . 127 C1
Hrun IS 190 A5
Hrušov SK. 112 A3
Hrušovany nad
 Jevišovkou
 CZ 97 C4
Hřuštín SK 99 B3
Hrvačani BIH. . 124 C3
Hrvace HR 138 B2
Hrymayliv UA. . .13 D7
Huben A 109 C3
Hückel-hoven
 D 80 A2
Hückeswagen
 D 80 A3
Hucknall UK. . . .40 B2
Hucqueliers F. .78 B1
Huddersfield
 UK 40 B2
Huddinge S 57 A3
Huddunge S 51 B3
Hude D 72 A1
Hudiksvall S . . 200 E3
Huélago E. 163 A4
Huélamo E. . . . 152 B2
Huelgoat F. . . . 100 A2
Huelma E 163 A4
Huelva E 161 B3
Huéneja E. 164 B2
Huércal de Almeria
 E. 164 C2
Huércal-Overa
 E. 164 B3
Huerta de Abajo
 E. 143 B3
Huerta del Rey
 E. 143 C3
Huerta de
 Valdecarabanos
 E. 151 C4
Huertahernando
 E. 152 B1
Huesa E 164 B1
Huesca E 145 B3
Huéscar E. 164 B2
Huete E 151 B5
Huétor Tájar
 E. 163 A3
Hüfingen D . . . 106 B3
Hufthamar N. . .46 B2
Hugh Town UK . .42 B1
Huglfing D. . . . 108 B2
Huissen NL. 70 C2
Huittinen FIN 8 B3
Huizen NL. 70 B2
Hulín CZ 98 B1
Hüls D. 80 A2
Hulsig DK 58 A3
Hulst NL 79 A4
Hult S 62 A3
Hulta S. 56 B2
Hulteby S. 55 A5
Hulterstad S 63 B4
Hultsfred S. 62 A3
Humanes E. . . . 151 B4
Humberston
 UK 41 B3
Humble DK 65 B3
Humilladero E 163 A3
Humlebæk DK . 61 D2
Humlum DK. . . .58 B1
Hummelsta S . . .56 A2

Humpolec CZ . . .97 B3
Humshaugh
 UK 37 A4
Hundåla N . . . 195 E3
Hundested DK . 61 D1
Hundorp N. 48 A1
Hundvåg N 52 A1
Hundvin N. 46 B2
Hunedoara RO. .17 C5
Hünfeld D. 82 B1
Hungen D. 81 B4
Hungerford UK .44 B2
Hunndalen N . . .48 B2
Hunnebostrand
 S. 54 B2
Hunstanton
 UK 41 C4
Huntingdon
 UK 44 A3
Huntley UK 39 C4
Huntly UK 33 D4
Hünxe D 80 A2
Hurbanovo SK 112 B2
Hürbel D 107 A4
Hurdal N. 48 B3
Hurezani RO . . .17 C5
Hurlford UK. . . .36 A2
Hurstbourne
 Tarrant UK 44 B2
Hurstpierpoint
 UK 44 C3
Hürth D. 80 B2
Hurum N. 47 A5
Hurup DK 58 B1
Húsafell IS . . . 190 C5
Húsavík IS . . . 191 A8
Husbands
 Bosworth UK. .44 A2
Husby
 D 64 B2
 DK 59 B1
Husey IS 191 B11
Huşi RO 17 B8
Husina BIH . . . 139 A4
Husínec CZ. 96 B1
Husinish UK. . . .31 B1
Huskvarna S 62 A2
Husnes N. 46 C2
Husøy N 194 A8
Hustad N. 198 C4
Hüsten D. 81 A3
Hustopeče CZ. . .97 C4
Hustopeče nad
 Bečvou CZ 98 B1
Husum
 D 64 B2
 S. 200 C5
Husvika N. 195 E3
Huta PL. 75 B5
Hutovo BIH . . . 139 C3
Hüttenberg A. 110 C1
Hüttlingen D. . .94 C2
Huttoft UK. 41 B4
Hutton Cranswick
 UK 40 B3
Hüttschlag A. . 109 B4
Huttwil CH. . . . 106 B2
Hüyük TR. 189 B6
Hval N. 48 B2
Hvåle N 47 B6
Hvaler N 54 A2
Hvalpsund DK . .58 B2
Hvammstangi
 IS 190 B5
Hvammur IS . . 190 B6
Hvanneyri IS . . 190 C4
Hvar HR. 138 B2
Hvarnes N 53 A5
Hveragerði IS . 190 D4
Hvidbjerg DK . .58 B1
Hvide Sande
 DK 59 C1
Hvittingfoss N . .53 A6
Hvolsvöllur IS. 190 D5
Hybe SK. 99 B3
Hycklinge S. 62 A3
Hydra GR 185 B4
Hyen N. 198 D2
Hyères F 132 B2
Hyéres Plage
 F. 132 B2
Hylestad N. 52 A3
Hylke DK. 59 C2
Hyllestad N. . . .46 A2
Hyllstofta S 61 C3
Hyltebruk S. . . .60 B3
Hynnekleiv N. . .53 B4
Hythe
 Hampshire
 UK 44 C2
 Kent UK 45 B5
Hyvinkää FIN 8 B3

I

Iam RO 127 B3
Iaşi RO 17 B7
Iasmos GR . . . 183 B7
Ibahernando
 E. 156 A2
Ibarranguelua
 E. 143 A4
Ibbenbüren D. . .71 B4
Ibeas de Juarros
 E. 143 B3
Ibestad N 194 B8
Ibi E 159 C3
Ibiza = Eivissa
 E. 166 C1
İbradı TR 189 B6
Ibros E 157 B4
Ibstock UK 40 C2
İçel TR. 23 C8
Ichenhausen D. .94 C2
Ichtegem B 78 A3
Ichtershausen
 D 82 B2
Idanha-a-Novo
 P. 155 B3
Idar-Oberstein
 D 93 B3
Idd N. 54 A2
Idiazábal E. . . . 144 B1
Idivuoma S . . . 196 A4
Idön S. 51 B5
Idre S 199 D9
Idrija SLO 123 A3
Idritsa RUS. 9 D6
Idstein D. 81 B4
Idvor SRB. 126 B2
Iecca Mare RO. 126 B2
Ielsi I. 170 B2
Ieper = Ypres B. .78 B2
Ierapetra GR . 185 D6
Ierissos GR . . . 183 C5
Ifjord N 193 B11
Ig SLO 123 B3
Igal H 112 C1
Igea E 143 A4
Igea Marina I. . 136 A1
Igelfors S 56 B1
Igersheim D. . . .94 B1
Iggesund S. . . . 200 E3
Iglesias E. 143 B3
Iglésias I 179 C2
Igls A. 108 B2
Igny-Comblizy
 F. 91 B3
Igorre E 143 A4
Igoumenitsa
 GR 182 D2
Igries E. 145 B3
Igualada E 147 C2
Igüeña E 141 B4
Iguerande F. . . 117 A4
Iharosberény
 H. 124 A3
Ihl'any SK. 99 B4
Ihlienworth D. . .64 C1
Ihringen D. . . . 106 A2
Ihrlerstein D . . .95 C3
İhsaniye TR . . . 187 C5
Ii FIN 197 D8
Iijärvi FIN . . . 193 C11
Iisalmi FIN 3 E10
IJmuiden NL . . .70 B1
IJsselmuiden
 NL. 70 B2
IJzendijke NL. . .79 A3
Ikast DK. 59 B2
Ikervár H. 111 B3
Ilandža SRB . . 126 B2
Ilanz CH. 107 C4
Ilava SK. 98 C2
Iława PL. 69 B4
il Castagno I. . . 135 B3
Ilche E 145 C4
Ilchester UK. . . .43 B4
Ilfeld D. 82 A2
Ilfracombe UK . .42 A2
Ilgaz TR 23 A7
Ilğın TR 189 A6
Ílhavo P. 148 B1
Ilıca TR. 186 C2
Ilidža BIH. 139 B4
Ilijaš BIH 139 B4
Ilirska Bistrica
 SLO 123 B3
Ilkeston UK 40 C2
Ilkley UK. 40 B2
Illana E. 151 B5
Illano E. 141 A4
Illar E 164 C2

Illas E 141 A5
Illats F 128 B2
Illertissen D. . . .94 C2
Illescas E. 151 B4
Ille-sur-Têt F . . 146 B3
Illfurth F 106 B2
Illichivsk UA . . .17 B9
Illiers-Combray
 F. 89 B5
Illkirch-
 Graffenstaden
 F. 93 C3
Illmersdorf D. .74 C2
Illmitz A. 111 B3
Íllora E. 163 A4
Illueca E. 152 A2
Ilmajoki FIN. 8 A3
Ilmenau D. 82 B2
Ilminster UK . . .43 B4
Ilok HR. 126 B1
Ilomantsi FIN . . .9 A7
Iłów PL. 77 B5
Iłowa PL. 84 A3
Iłowo-Osada
 PL. 77 A5
Ilsenburg D 82 A2
Ilshofen D. 94 B1
Ilz A. 110 B2
Iłża PL. 87 A5
Imatra FIN 9 B6
Imielin PL. 86 B3
Imingen N 47 B5
Immeln S 63 B2
Immenhausen
 D 81 A5
Immenstadt D 107 B5
Immingham UK 41 B3
Ímola I. 135 A4
Imon E. 151 A5
Imotski HR. . . . 138 B3
Impéria I 133 B4
Imphy F 104 C2
İmroz TR 183 C7
Imsland N. 52 A1
Imst A. 108 B1
Inagh IRL. 28 B2
Inari FIN. 193 D10
Inca E 167 B2
Inchnadamph
 UK 32 C2
Incinillas E 143 B3
Indal S 200 D3
Indjija SRB . . . 127 B2
Indre Arna N. . .46 B2
Indre Billefjord
 N. 193 B9
Indre Brenna
 N. 193 B9
İğneada TR. . . 186 A2
İnebolu TR 23 A7
İnecik TR 186 B2
İnegöl TR 187 B4
Inerthal CH . . . 107 B3
Infiesto E 142 A1
Ingatorp S 62 A3
Ingedal N 54 A2
Ingelheim D . . .93 B4
Ingelmunster B .78 B2
Ingelstad S. 62 B2
Ingleton UK. . . .37 B4
Ingolfsland N . .47 C5
Ingolstadt D . . .95 C3
Ingrandes
 Maine-et-Loire
 F. 101 B5
 Vienne F 102 C2
Ingwiller F. 93 C3
Inhisar TR. 187 B5
Iniesta E 158 B2
Inishannon IRL. .29 C3
Inishcrone IRL. .26 B1
Inke H. 124 A3
Inndyr N 195 C5
Innellan UK 34 C3
Innerleithen
 UK 35 C4
Innermessan
 UK 36 B2
Innertkirchen
 CH 106 C3
Innervillgraten
 A. 109 C3
Innset N. 194 B9
Innvik N 198 D3
İnönü TR. 187 C5
Inowłódz PL . . .87 A4
Inowrocław PL. .76 B3
Ins CH. 106 B2
Insch UK 33 D4
Insjön S. 50 B2
Ińsko PL. 75 A4
Instow UK. 42 A2

İntepe TR 186 B1
Interlaken CH. 106 C2
Intragna CH. . . 120 A1
Introbio I. 120 B2
Inverallochy
 UK 33 D5
Inveran
 IRL 28 A2
 UK 32 D2
Inveraray UK . . .34 B2
Inverbervie UK. .35 B5
Invergarry UK. . 32 D2
Invergordon
 UK 32 D2
Invergowrie UK 35 B4
Inverkeilor UK . .35 B5
Inverkeithing
 UK 35 B4
Invermoriston
 UK 32 D2
Inverness UK. . 32 D2
Inveruno I 120 B1
Inverurie UK . . 33 D4
Ioannina GR . . 182 D2
Iolanda di Savoia
 I. 121 C4
Ion Corvin RO. .17 C7
Ióppolo I. 175 C1
Ios GR 185 C6
Ipati GR. 182 E4
İpsala TR 186 B1
Ipswich UK. 45 A5
Iraklia GR 183 B5
Iraklio = Heraklion
 GR 185 D6
Irdning A 110 B1
Irgoli I. 178 B3
Irig SRB 127 B1
Ironbridge UK . .39 B4
Irpin UA 13 C9
Irrel D. 92 B2
Irsina I 172 B2
Irsta S 56 A2
Irthlingborough
 UK 44 A3
Iruela E 141 B4
Irún E 144 A2
Irurita E 144 A2
Irurzun E 144 B2
Irvine UK. 36 A2
Irvinestown
 UK 27 B3
Isaba E. 144 B3
Isabela E. 157 B4
İsane N. 198 D2
Isaszeg H 112 B3
Isbister UK 33 A5
Íscar E. 150 A3
İscehisar TR . . . 187 D5
Ischgl A 107 B5
Ischia I 170 C1
Ischia di Castro
 I. 168 A1
Ischitella I. . . . 171 B3
Isdes F 103 B4
Ise N 54 A2
Iselle I 119 A5
Iseltwald CH . . 106 C2
Isen D. 108 A3
Isenbüttel D . . .73 B3
Iseo I. 120 B3
Iserlohn D 81 A3
Isérnia I 170 B2
Isfjorden N. . . 198 C4
Ishëm AL. 182 B1
Isigny-sur-Mer
 F. 88 A2
Işıklı TR 189 A4
Ísili I 179 C3
İskilip TR 23 A8
Isla Canela E . . 161 B2
Isla Cristina E . 161 B2
Islares E. 143 A3
Isleham UK. 45 A4
Isle of Whithorn
 UK 36 B2
Ismaning D . . . 108 A2
Isna P. 154 B3
Isnestoften N . 192 B6
Isny D. 107 B5
Isoba E. 142 A1
Isokylä
 FIN 197 C10
 S. 196 B5
Isola F 132 A3
Isola d'Asti I . . 119 C5
Isola del Gran Sasso
 d'Itália I. 169 A3
Ísola della Scala
 I. 121 B4

Isola delle
 Fémmine I . . 176 A2
Ísola del Liri I. . 169 B3
Ísola di Capo
 Rizzuto I 175 C3
Isona E. 147 B2
Ispagnac F . . . 130 A2
Isparta TR. 189 B5
Isperih BG. 17 D7
Íspica I 177 C3
Isselburg D 80 A2
Issigeac F 129 B3
Issogne I. 119 B4
Issoire F 116 B3
Issoncourt F. . . .91 C5
Issoudun F. . . . 103 C4
Issum D 80 A2
Is-sur-Tille F. . . 105 B4
Issy-l'Evêque
 F. 104 C2
Istán E 162 B3
İstanbul TR. . . . 186 A3
Istebna PL 98 B2
Ístia d'Ombrone
 I. 135 C4
Istiea GR 183 E5
Istres F. 131 B3
Istvándi H. 125 A3
Itea GR 184 A3
Ithaki GR. 184 A1
Itoiz E. 144 B2
Itrabo E 163 B4
Itri I 169 B3
Ittireddu I. 178 B2
Íttiri I 178 B2
Itzehoe D 64 C2
Ivalo FIN . . . 193 D11
Iván H. 111 B3
Ivanava BY 13 B6
Ivančice CZ 97 B4
Ivančna Gorica
 SLO 123 B3
Iváncsa H 112 B2
Ivanec HR 124 A2
Ivanić Grad
 HR 124 B2
Ivanjska BIH . . 124 C3
Ivanka SK 98 C2
Ivankovo HR. . 125 B4
Ivano-Frankivsk
 UA 13 D6
Ivanovice na Hané
 CZ 98 B1
Ivanska HR. . . . 124 B2
Ivatsevichy BY . .13 B6
Ivaylovgrad
 BG 183 B8
Iveland N 53 B3
Ivoz Ramet B. . .79 B5
Ivrea I 119 B4
İvrindi TR 186 C2
Ivry-en-Montagne
 F. 104 C3
Ivry-la-Bataille
 F. 90 C1
Ivybridge UK. . . .42 B3
Iwaniska PL. 87 B5
Iwiny PL. 85 A3
Iwuy F 78 B3
Ixworth UK. 45 A4
Izarra E 143 B4
Izbica Kujawska
 PL. 76 B3
Izbište SRB . . . 127 B3
Izeda P. 149 A3
Izegem B. 78 B3
Izernore F. 118 A2
Izmayil UA. 17 C8
İzmir TR. 188 A2
İzmit = Kocaeli
 TR. 187 B4
Iznájar E 163 A3
Iznalloz E 163 A4
Iznatoraf E. . . . 164 A1
İznik TR 187 B4
Izola SLO. 122 B2
Izsák H. 112 C3
Izsófalva H. 99 C4
Izyaslav UA 13 C7

J

Jabalquinto E. 157 B4
Jablanac HR. . . 123 C3
Jablanica BIH . 139 B3
Jablonec nad
 Jizerou CZ 84 B3
Jablonec nad Nisou
 CZ 84 B3
Jablonica SK . . .98 C1
Jabłonka PL. . . .99 B3
Jabłonna PL. . . .77 B5

Jab – Kar 225

Jablonné nad Orlicí CZ 97 A4
Jablonné Podještědí CZ 84 B2
Jablonov nad Turňou SK 99 C4
Jabłonowo Pomorskie PL 69 B4
Jablúnka CZ 98 B1
Jablunkov CZ 98 B2
Jabučje SRB 127 C2
Jabugo E 161 B3
Jabuka SRB 127 C2
Jabukovac HR 124 B2
Jaca E 145 B3
Jáchymov CZ 83 B4
Jacobidrebber D 72 B1
Jade D 71 A5
Jäderfors S 50 B3
Jädraås S 50 B3
Jadraque E 151 B5
Jaén E 163 A4
Jagare BIH 124 C3
Jagel D 64 B2
Jagenbach A 96 C3
Jægerspris DK 61 D1
Jagodina SRB 127 D3
Jagodnjak HR 125 B4
Jagodzin PL 84 A3
Jagstheim D 94 B2
Jagstzell D 94 B2
Jahodna SK 111 A4
Jajce BIH 138 A3
Ják H 111 B3
Jakabszálbs H 112 C3
Jäkkvik S 195 D8
Jakobsnes N 193 C14
Jakovlje HR 124 B1
Jakšic HR 125 B3
Jakubany SK 99 B4
Jalance E 159 B2
Jalasjärvi FIN 8 A3
Jalhay B 80 B1
Jaligny-sur-Besbre F 117 A3
Jallais F 102 B1
Jalón E 159 C3
Jâlons F 91 C4
Jamena SRB 125 C5
Jamilena E 163 A4
Jämjö S 63 B3
Jamnička Kiselica HR 124 B1
Jamno PL 67 B5
Jamoigne B 92 B1
Jämsä FIN 8 B4
Jämshög S 63 B2
Jamu Mare RO 126 B3
Janakkala FIN 8 B4
Jandelsbrunn D 96 C1
Jänickendorf D 74 B2
Janikowo PL 76 B3
Janja BIH 125 C5
Janjina HR 138 C3
Janki
  Łódzkie PL 86 A3
  Mazowieckie PL 77 B5
Jankov CZ 96 B2
Jankowo Dolne PL 76 B2
Jánoshalma H 126 A1
Jánosháza H 111 B4
Jánoshida H 113 B4
Jánossomorja H 111 B4
Janovice nad Uhlavou CZ 96 B1
Janów PL 86 B3
Janowiec Wielkopolski PL 76 B2
Janowo PL 77 A5
Jänsmässholmen S 199 B10
Janville F 103 A3
Janzé F 101 B4
Jarabá SK 99 C3
Jaraczewo PL 76 C2
Jarafuel E 159 B2
Jaraicejo E 156 A2
Jaraíz de la Vera E 150 B2
Jarak SRB 127 C1
Jarandilla de la Vera E 150 B2
Jaray E 152 A1
Järbo S 50 B3
Jard-sur-Mer F 114 B2
Jaren N 48 B2
Jargeau F 103 B4
Jarkovac SRB 126 B2
Järlåsa S 51 C4
Jarmen D 66 C2
Järna S 57 A3
Jarnac F 115 C3
Järnäs S 200 C5
Järnforsen S 62 A3
Jarny F 92 B1
Jarocin PL 76 C2
Jaroměř CZ 85 B3
Jaroměřice nad Rokytnou CZ 97 B3
Jaroslav CZ 97 A4
Jaroslavice CZ 97 C4
Jarosław PL 12 C5
Jaroslawiec PL 68 A1
Jarošov nad Nežarkou CZ 96 B3
Järpås S 55 B3
Järpen S 199 B10
Jarrow UK 37 B5
Järso FIN 51 B6
Järvenpää FIN 8 B4
Jarvorník CZ 85 B4
Järvsö S 200 E2
Jarzé F 102 B1
Jaša Tomic SRB 126 B2
Jasenak HR 123 B4
Jasenica BIH 124 C2
Jasenice HR 137 A4
Jasenovac HR 124 B2
Jasenovo SRB 127 C3
Jasień PL 84 A3
Jasienica PL 84 A2
Jasło PL 12 D4
Jásova SK 112 B2
Jasseron F 118 A2
Jastarnia PL 69 A3
Jastrebarsko HR 123 B4
Jastrowie PL 68 B1
Jastrzębia-Góra PL 68 A3
Jastrzębie Zdrój PL 98 B2
Jászals-Lószentgyörgy H 113 B4
Jászapáti H 113 B4
Jászárokszállás H 113 B3
Jászberény H 113 B3
Jászdózsa H 113 B4
Jászfényszaru H 113 B3
Jászjakóhalma H 113 B4
Jászkarajenö H 113 B4
Jászkisér H 113 B4
Jászladány H 113 B4
Jászszentlászló H 113 C3
Jásztelek H 113 B4
Játar E 163 B4
Jättendal S 200 E3
Jatznick D 74 A2
Jaun CH 106 C2
Jausiers F 132 A2
Jávea E 159 C4
Jävenitz D 73 B4
Javerlhac F 115 C4
Javier E 144 B2
Javorani BIH 124 C3
Javorina SK 99 B4
Javron F 89 B3
Jawor PL 85 A4
Jaworzno PL 86 B3
Jaworzyna Śl. PL 85 B4
Jayena E 163 B4
Jażow PL 84 A2
Jebel RO 126 B3
Jebjerg DK 58 B2
Jedburgh UK 35 C5
Jedlinsk PL 87 A5
Jedlnia PL 87 A5
Jedlnia Letnisko PL 87 A5
Jednorożec PL 77 A6
Jedovnice CZ 97 B4
Jędrychow PL 69 B4
Jędrzejów PL 87 B4
Jedwabno PL 77 A5
Jeesiö FIN 197 B9
Jegłownik PL 69 A4
Jegun F 129 C3
Jēkabpils LV 8 D4
Jektevik N 46 C2
Jektvik N 195 D4
Jelcz-Laskowice PL 85 A5
Jelenec SK 98 C2
Jelenia Góra PL 85 B3
Jelgava LV 8 D3
Jelka SK 111 A4
Jelling DK 59 C2
Jels DK 59 C2
Jelsa
  HR 138 B2
  N 52 A2
Jelšava SK 99 C4
Jemgum D 71 A4
Jemnice CZ 97 B3
Jena D 82 B3
Jenaz CH 107 C4
Jenbach A 108 B2
Jenikow PL 75 A4
Jennersdorf A 111 C3
Jenny S 62 A4
Jerchel D 73 B4
Jeres del Marquesado E 164 B1
Jerez de la Frontera E 162 B1
Jerez de los Caballeros E 155 C4
Jerica E 159 B3
Jerichow D 73 B5
Jerka PL 75 B5
Jermenovci SRB 126 B3
Jerslev DK 58 A3
Jerte E 150 B2
Jerup DK 58 A3
Jerxheim D 73 B3
Jerzmanowice PL 87 B3
Jerzu I 179 C3
Jerzwałd PL 69 B4
Jesberg D 81 B5
Jesenice
  Středočeský CZ 83 B5
  Středočeský CZ 96 B2
  SLO 109 C5
Jeseník CZ 85 B5
Jesenké SK 99 C4
Jesi I 136 B2
Jésolo I 122 B1
Jessen D 83 A4
Jessenitz D 73 A4
Jessheim N 48 B3
Jessnitz D 83 A4
Jesteburg D 72 A2
Jeumont F 79 B4
Jeven-stedt D 64 B2
Jever D 71 A4
Jevičko CZ 97 B4
Jevišovice CZ 97 C3
Jevnaker N 48 B2
Jezerane HR 123 B4
Jezero
  BIH 138 A3
  HR 123 B4
Jezów PL 87 A3
Jičín CZ 84 B3
Jičiněves CZ 84 B3
Jihlava CZ 97 B3
Jijona E 159 C3
Jilemnice CZ 84 B3
Jilové CZ 84 B2
Jilovéu Prahy CZ 96 B2
Jimbolia RO 126 B2
Jimena E 163 A4
Jimena de la Frontera E 162 B2
Jimera de Libar E 162 B2
Jimramov CZ 97 B4
Jince CZ 96 B1
Jindřichovice CZ 83 B4
Jindřichův Hradec CZ 96 B3
Jirkov CZ 83 B5
Jistebnice CZ 96 B2
Joachimsthal D 74 B2
João da Loura P 154 C2
Jobbágyi H 112 B3
Jochberg A 109 B3
Jockfall S 196 C5
Jódar E 163 A4
Jodoigne B 79 B4
Joensuu FIN 9 A6
Joesjö S 195 E5
Joeuf F 92 B1
Jõgeva EST 8 C5
Johanngeorgenstadt D 83 B4
Johannishus S 63 B3
Johanniskirchen D 95 C4
Johansfors S 63 B3
John o'Groats UK 32 C3
Johnshaven UK 35 B5
Johnstone UK 34 C3
Johnstown IRL 30 B1
Jõhvi EST 8 C5
Joigny F 104 B2
Joinville F 91 C5
Jokkmokk S 196 C2
Jöllenbeck D 72 B1
Jomala FIN 51 B6
Jönåker S 56 B2
Jonava LT 13 A6
Jonchery-sur-Vesle F 91 B3
Jondal N 46 B3
Jondalen N 53 A5
Joniškis LT 8 D3
Jönköping S 62 A2
Jonkowo PL 69 B5
Jønnbu N 53 A5
Jonsberg S 56 B2
Jonsered S 60 B2
Jonstorp S 61 C2
Jonzac F 114 C3
Jorba E 147 C2
Jordanów PL 99 B3
Jordanowo PL 75 B4
Jordanów Ślaski PL 85 B4
Jordbro S 57 A4
Jordbrua N 195 D5
Jördenstorf D 66 C1
Jordet N 49 A4
Jordøse DK 59 C3
Jork D 72 A2
Jörlanda S 60 B1
Jormlien S 199 A10
Jormvattnet S 199 A11
Jörn S 200 A6
Jørpeland N 52 A2
Jorquera E 158 B2
Jošan HR 123 C4
Jošavka BIH 124 C3
Josipdol HR 123 B4
Josipovac HR 125 B4
Jössefors S 54 A3
Josselin F 101 B3
Jøssund N 199 A7
Jostedal N 47 A4
Jósvafö H 99 C4
Jou P 148 A2
Jouarre F 90 C3
Joué-lès-Tours F 102 B2
Joué-sur-Erdre F 101 B4
Joure NL 70 B2
Joutseno FIN 9 B6
Joutsijärvi FIN 197 C10
Joux-la-Ville F 104 B2
Jouy F 90 C1
Jouy-le-Châtel F 90 C3
Jouy-le-Potier F 103 B3
Joyeuse F 131 A3
Joze F 116 B3
Juankoski FIN 8 A6
Juan-les-Pins F 132 B3
Jübek D 64 B2
Jubera E 144 B1
Jubrique E 162 B2
Jüchsen D 82 B2
Judaberg N 52 A1
Judenburg A 110 B1
Juelsminde DK 59 C3
Jugon-les-Lacs F 101 A3
Juillac F 129 A4
Juillan F 145 A4
Juist D 71 A4
Jukkasjärvi S 196 B3
Jule N 199 A10
Julianadorp NL 70 B1
Julianstown IRL 30 A2
Jülich D 80 B2
Jullouville F 88 B2
Jumeaux F 117 B3
Jumièges F 89 A4
Jumilhac-le-Grand F 115 C5
Jumilla E 159 C2
Jumisko FIN 197 C11
Juncosa E 153 A4
Juneda E 147 C1
Jung S 55 B4
Jungingen D 93 C5
Junglingster L 92 B2
Juniville F 91 B4
Junosuando S 196 B5
Junqueira P 149 A2
Junsele S 200 C2
Juoksengi S 196 C6
Juoksenki FIN 196 C6
Juprelle B 80 B1
Jurata PL 69 A3
Jurbarkas LT 12 A5
Jurjevo HR 123 C3
Jūrmala LV 8 D3
Jurmu FIN 197 D10
Juromenha P 155 C3
Jursla S 56 B2
Jussac F 116 C2
Jussey F 105 B4
Jussy F 90 B3
Juta H 125 A3
Jüterbog D 74 C2
Juuka FIN 3 E11
Juuma FIN 197 C12
Juvigny-le-Terte F 88 B2
Juvigny-sous-Andaine F 89 B3
Juzennecourt F 105 A3
Jyderup DK 61 D1
Jyrkänkoski FIN 197 C12
Jyväskylä FIN 8 A4

K

Kaamanen FIN 193 C11
Kaamasmukka FIN 193 C10
Kaaresuvanto FIN 192 D6
Kaarssen D 73 A4
Kaatscheuvel NL 79 A5
Kaba H 113 B5
Kåbdalis S 196 C3
Kačarevo SRB 127 C2
Kács H 113 B4
Kadan CZ 83 B5
Kadarkút H 125 A3
Kadınhanı TR 189 A7
Kaduy RUS 9 C10
Kåfalla S 56 A1
Kåfjord N 192 C7
Kåfjordbotn N 192 C4
Kågeröd S 61 D3
Kahl D 93 A5
Kahla D 82 B3
Kainach bei Voitsberg A 110 B2
Kaindorf A 110 B2
Kainulasjärvi S 196 C5
Kairala FIN 197 B10
Kaisepakte S 192 D3
Kaisersesch D 80 B3
Kaiserslautern D 93 B3
Kaisheim D 94 C2
Kajaani FIN 3 D10
Kajárpéc H 111 B4
Kajdacs H 112 C2
Kakanj BIH 139 A4
Kakasd H 125 A4
Kaklik TR 189 B4
Kakolewo PL 85 A4
Kál H 113 B4
Kalajoki FIN 3 D8
Kalak N 193 B11
Kalamata GR 184 B3
Kalambaka GR 182 D3
Kalamria GR 182 C4
Kalandra GR 183 D5
Kälarne S 200 D2
Kalavrita GR 184 A3
Kalbe D 73 B4
Kalce SLO 123 B3
Káld H 111 B4
Kale
  Antalya TR 189 C4
  Denizli TR 188 B3
Kalecik TR 23 A7
Kalefeld D 82 A2
Kalesija BIH 139 A4
Kalety PL 86 B2
Kalevala RUS 3 D12
Kalhovd N 47 B5
Kalí HR 137 A4
Kalimnos GR 188 C2
Kaliningrad RUS 69 A5
Kalinkavichy BY 13 B8
Kalinovac HR 124 A3
Kalinovik BIH 139 B4
Kalinovo SK 99 C3
Kalirachi GR 183 C6
Kaliska
  Pomorskie PL 68 A3
  Pomorskie PL 68 B3
Kalisko PL 86 A3
Kalisz PL 86 A2
Kalisz Pomorski PL 75 A4
Kaljord N 194 B6
Kalkan TR 189 C4
Kalkar D 80 A2
Kalkım TR 186 C2
Kall
  D 80 B2
  S 199 B10
Källby S 55 B4
Kållered S 60 B2
Kållerstad S 60 B3
Kallinge S 63 B3
Kallmünz D 95 B3
Kallo FIN 196 B7
Kallsedet S 199 B9
Källvik S 56 B3
Kalmar S 63 B4
Kalmthout B 79 A4
Kalná SK 112 A2
Kalocsa H 112 C2
Kalokhorio CY 181 B2
Kalo Nero GR 184 B2
Kaloni GR 186 C1
Káloz H 112 C2
Kals A 109 B3
Kalsdorf A 110 C2
Kaltbrunn CH 107 B4
Kaltenbach A 108 B2
Kaltenkirchen D 64 C2
Kaltennordheim D 82 B2
Kalundborg DK 61 D1
Kalush UA 13 D6
Kalv S 60 B3
Kalvåg N 198 D1
Kalvehave DK 65 A5
Kalwang A 110 B1
Kalwaria-Zebrzydowska PL 99 B3
Kalyazin RUS 9 D10
Kam H 111 B3
Kaman TR 23 B7
Kamares GR 185 C5
Kambos CY 181 A1
Kamen D 81 A3
Kamenice CZ 97 B3
Kamenice nad Lipou CZ 96 B3
Kamenicná SK 112 B2
Kamenný Most SK 112 B2
Kamenny Ujezd CZ 96 C2
Kamenska HR 124 B3
Kamensko HR 138 B2
Kamenz D 84 A2
Kamičak BIH 124 C2
Kamień PL 87 A4
Kamieniec Zabk PL 85 B4
Kamienka SK 99 B4
Kamień Krajeński PL 76 A2
Kamienna Góra PL 85 B4
Kamień Pomorski PL 67 C3
Kamieńsk PL 86 A3
Kamiros Skala GR 188 C2
Kamnik SLO 123 A3
Kampen NL 70 B2
Kampinos PL 77 B5
Kamp-Lintfort D 80 A2
Kampor HR 123 C3
Kamyanets-Podil's'kyy UA 13 D7
Kamyanka-Buz'ka UA 13 C6
Kamýk nad Vltavou CZ 96 B2
Kanal SLO 122 A2
Kanalia GR 182 D4
Kandalaksha RUS 3 C13
Kandanos GR 185 D4
Kandel D 93 B4
Kandern D 106 B2
Kandersteg CH 106 C2
Kandila GR 184 B3
Kandıra TR 187 A5
Kandyty PL 69 A5
Kanfanar HR 122 B2
Kangasala FIN 8 B4
Kangos S 196 B5
Kangosjärvi FIN 196 B6
Kaniów PL 75 C3
Kanjiža SRB 126 A2
Kankaanpää FIN 8 B3
Kannus FIN 3 E8
Kanturk IRL 29 B3
Kapaklı TR 186 A2
Kapellen
  A 110 B2
  B 79 A4
Kapellskär S 57 A5
Kapfenberg A 110 B2
Kapfenstein A 110 C2
Kaplice CZ 96 C2
Kapljuh BIH 124 C2
Kápolna H 113 B4
Kápolnásnyék H 112 B2
Kaposfö H 125 A3
Kaposfüred H 125 A3
Kaposszekcsö H 125 A4
Kaposvár H 125 A3
Kapp N 48 B2
Kappel D 93 C3
Kappeln D 64 B2
Kappelshamn S 57 C4
Kappl A 107 B5
Kappstad S 55 A4
Kaprun A 109 B3
Kaptol HR 125 B3
Kapuvár H 111 B4
Karaadilli TR 189 A5
Karabiğa TR 186 B2
Karabük TR 187 A7
Karaburun TR 186 D1
Karacabey TR 186 B3
Karacaköy TR 186 A3
Karacaören TR 189 A5
Karacasu TR 188 B3
Karácsond H 113 B4
Karád H 112 C1
Karahallı TR 189 A4
Karaisali TR 23 C8
Karaman
  Balıkesir TR 186 C3
  Karaman TR 23 C7
Karamanlı TR 189 B4
Karamürsel TR 187 B4
Karan SRB 127 D1
Karancslapujto H 113 A3
Karaova TR 188 B2
Karapınar TR 23 C7
Karasjok N 193 C9
Karasu TR 187 A5
Karataş
  Adana TR 23 C8
  Manisa TR 188 A3
Karatoprak TR 188 B2
Karavostasi CY 181 A1
Karbenning S 50 B3
Kårberg S 55 B5
Kårböle S 199 D12
Karby
  D 64 B2
  DK 58 B1
Kårby S 62 A4
Karby S 57 A4
Karcag H 113 B4
Karczów PL 86 B1
Karczowiska PL 85 A4
Kardamena GR 188 C2
Kardamila GR 185 A7
Kardamili GR 184 C3

Kardašova Řečice
CZ 96 B2
Kardis S 196 C6
Karditsa GR . . . 182 D3
Kärdla EST 8 C3
Kardoskút H . . 113 C4
Kardzhali BG. . 183 B7
Karesuando
S 192 D6
Kargı TR. 23 A8
Kargopol RUS . . .9 B11
Kargowa PL 75 B4
Karigasniemi
FIN. 193 C9
Karise DK 65 A5
Karistos GR . . . 185 A5
Karkkila FIN. 8 B4
Karlholmsbruk
S 51 B4
Karlino PL. 67 B4
Karlobag HR . . 137 A4
Karlovac HR. . . 123 B4
Karlovasi GR . . 188 B1
Karlovčic SRB . 127 C2
Karlovice CZ 85 B5
Karlovo BG. 17 D6
Karlovy Vary
CZ 83 B4
Karłowice PL. . . .86 B1
Karlsborg S 55 B5
Karlshamn S 63 B2
Karlshöfen D. . . .72 A2
Karlshus N 54 A1
Karlskoga S 55 A5
Karlskrona S 63 B3
Karlsrud N 47 B5
Karlsruhe D 93 B4
Karlstad S 55 A4
Karlstadt D 94 B1
Karlstetten A . . 110 A2
Karlstift A. 96 C2
Karlstorp S 62 A3
Karmacs H 111 C4
Karmin PL. 85 A5
Kärna S 60 B1
Karnobat BG . . . 17 D7
Karojba HR. . . . 122 B2
Karow D 73 A5
Karpacz PL. 85 B3
Karpathos GR . 188 D2
Karpenisi GR. . .182 E3
Karpuzlu TR. . . 188 B2
Kärrbo S 56 A2
Karrebaeksminde
DK 65 A4
Karshult S. 60 B3
Karsin PL. 68 B2
Kårsta S. 57 A4
Karstädt D 73 A4
Kartal TR. 186 B4
Kartitsch A. . . . 109 C3
Kartuzy PL. 68 A3
Karungi S 196 C6
Karunki FIN. . . 196 C7
Karup DK 59 B2
Karviná CZ. 98 B2
Kås DK 58 A2
Kaş TR. 189 C4
Kasaba TR. 189 C4
Kašava CZ. 98 B1
Kåseberga S 66 A3
Kasejovice CZ. . .96 B1
Kasfjord N 194 B7
Kashin RUS. 9 D10
Kašina HR. 124 B2
Kasina-Wielka
PL. 99 B4
Kaskinen FIN. . . .8 A2
Kašperské Hory
CZ 96 B1
Kassandrino
GR 183 C5
Kassel D 81 A5
Kassiopi GR . . . 182 D1
Kastamonu TR . .23 A7
Kastav HR. 123 B3
Kasteli GR. 185 D4
Kastellaun D. . . .93 A3
Kastelli GR. . . . 185 D6
Kaštel-Stari
HR 138 B2
Kaštel Zegarski
HR 138 A1
Kasterlee B 79 A4
Kastl D 95 B3
Kastlösa S. 63 B4
Kastorf D 65 C3
Kastoria GR . . . 182 C3
Kastorio GR. . . 184 B3
Kastraki GR . . . 185 C6

Kastrosikia
GR 182 D2
Kastsyukovichy
BY. 13 B10
Kaszaper H . . . 113 C4
Katakolo GR . . . 184 B2
Katapola GR . . . 188 B4
Katastari GR . . 184 B1
Katerbow D. . . .74 B1
Katerini GR . . . 182 C4
Kathikas CY . . . 181 B1
Kätkesuando
S. 196 A6
Katlenburg-Lindau
D. 82 A2
Kato Achaia
GR 184 A2
Káto Pyrgos
CY 181 A1
Katouna GR. . . .182 E3
Katovice CZ. 96 B1
Katowice PL. . . .86 B3
Katrineberg S. . .50 A3
Katrineholm S . .56 B2
Kattarp S 61 C2
Kattavia GR . . . 188 D2
Katthammarsvik
S. 57 C4
Kattilstorp S . . .55 B4
Katwijk NL 70 B1
Katymár H 125 A5
Kąty Wrocławskie
PL. 85 A4
Katzenelnbogen
D. 81 B3
Katzhütte D. 82 B3
Kaub D. 93 A3
Kaufbeuren D. . 108 B1
Kauhajoki FIN. . . .8 A3
Kauhava FIN 8 A3
Kaukonen FIN. . 196 B7
Kauliranta FIN . 196 C7
Kaulsdorf D. 82 B3
Kaunas LT. 13 A5
Kaunisvaara S 196 B6
Kaupanger N . . .47 A4
Kautokeino N . 192 C7
Kautzen A. 97 C3
Kavadarci
NMK 182 B4
Kavajë AL 182 B1
Kavakköy TR. . . 186 B1
Kavaklı TR 186 A2
Kavaklıdere
TR. 188 B3
Kavala GR. 183 C6
Kavarna BG 17 D8
Kävlinge S 61 D3
Kawcze PL 68 A1
Kaxås S 199 B10
Kaxholmen S . . .62 A2
Käylä FIN. . . . 197 C12
Kaymakçı TR. . 188 A3
Kaymaz TR. . . . 187 C6
Kaynarca TR . . 187 A5
Käyrämö FIN. . 197 C9
Kayseri TR 23 B8
Kaysersberg F 106 A2
Kazanlak BG . . . 17 D6
Kazár H 113 A3
Kazimierza Wielka
PL. 87 B4
Kazincbarcika
H. 113 A4
Kaźmierz PL 75 B5
Kcynia PL 76 A2
Kdyně CZ 95 B5
Kea GR 185 B5
Keadew IRL 26 B2
Keady UK 27 B4
Kecel H 112 C3
Keçiborlu TR . . 189 B5
Kecskemét H. . . 113 C3
Kėdainiai LT. 13 A5
Kędzierzyn-Koźle
PL. 86 B2
Keel IRL 28 A1
Keenagh IRL 28 A4
Keerbergen B . . .79 A4
Kefalos GR 188 C1
Kefken TR. 187 A5
Keflavík IS 190 C3
Kegworth UK. . .40 C2
Kehl D 93 C3
Kehrigk D. 74 B2
Keighley UK. 40 B2
Keila EST 8 C4
Keillmore UK. . . .34 C2
Keiss UK 32 C3
Keith UK 33 D4
Kelankylä
FIN. 197 D10
Kelberg D. 80 B2

Kelbra D 82 A3
Kelč CZ. 98 B1
Kelchsau A. . . . 108 B3
Këlcyrë AL 182 C2
Keld UK 37 B4
Kelebia H 126 A1
Kelekçi TR. 188 B4
Kelemér H 99 C4
Keles TR. 186 C4
Kelheim D 95 C3
Kell D 92 B2
Kellas UK. 32 D3
Kellinghusen D .64 C2
Kelloselkä
FIN. 197 C11
Kells
IRL 27 C4
UK 27 B4
Kelmis B 80 B2
Kelokedhara
CY 181 B1
Kelottijärvi
FIN. 192 D6
Kelsall UK. 38 A4
Kelso UK 35 C5
Kelsterbach D. . .93 A4
Keltneyburn
UK 35 B3
Kelujärvi FIN. 197 B10
Kemaliye TR . . 188 A3
Kemalpaşa
TR. 188 A2
Kematen A. 108 B2
Kemberg D 83 A4
Kemer
Antalya TR. . . 189 C5
Burdur TR. . . . 189 B5
Muğla TR 189 C4
Kemerkaya
TR. 187 D6
Kemeten A. 111 B3
Kemi FIN 196 D7
Kemijärvi
FIN. 197 C10
Keminmaa
FIN. 196 D7
Kemnath D 95 B3
Kemnay UK . . . 33 D4
Kemnitz
Brandenburg
D. 74 B1
Mecklenburg-
Vorpommern
D. 66 B2
Kempen D 80 A2
Kempsey UK 39 B4
Kempten D 107 B5
Kemptthal CH. . 107 B3
Kendal UK 37 B4
Kenderes H . . . 113 B4
Kengyel H 113 B4
Kenilworth UK . .44 A2
Kenmare IRL 29 C2
Kenmore UK 35 B4
Kennacraig UK. .34 C2
Kenyeri H 111 B4
Kenzingen D. . . 106 A2
Kepez TR. 186 B1
Kępice PL 68 A1
Kępno PL. 86 A2
Kepsut TR. 186 C3
Keramoti GR . . 183 C6
Keräntöjärvi
S. 196 B6
Keratea GR. . . . 185 B4
Kerava FIN 8 B4
Kerecsend H . . 113 B4
Kerekegyhaza
H. 112 C3
Kerepestarcsa
H. 112 B3
Keri GR. 184 B1
Kérien F. 100 A2
Kerkafalva H . . 111 C3
Kerken D. 80 A2
Kerkrade NL 80 B2
Kerkyra GR. . . . 182 D1
Kernascléden
F. 100 A2
Kernhof A. 110 B2
Kerns CH. 106 C3
Kerpen D 80 B2
Kerrysdale UK . .31 B3
Kerta H 111 B4
Kerteminde DK .59 C3
Kerzers CH. . . . 106 C2
Keşan TR. 186 B1
Kesgrave UK 45 A5
Kesh UK 26 B3
Keskin TR. 23 B7
Kesselfall A . . . 109 B3
Kestenga RUS. . .3 D12

Keswick UK 36 B3
Keszthely H. . . 111 C4
Kétegyháza H. 113 C5
Kéthely H 111 C4
Kętrzyn PL 12 A4
Kettering UK. . . .44 A3
Kettlewell UK . . .40 A1
Kęty PL 99 B3
Ketzin D. 74 B1
Keula D 82 A2
Keuruu FIN. 8 A4
Kevelaer D. 80 A2
Kevermes H. . . . 113 C5
Kevi SRB 126 B1
Keyingham UK. .41 B3
Keynsham UK. . .43 A4
Kežmarok SK. . . .99 B4
Khimki RUS 9 E10
Khisinev =
Chişinău MD . . .17 B8
Khmelnik UA. . . 13 D7
Khmelnytskyy
UA 13 D7
Khodoriv UA . . . 13 D6
Kholm RUS. 9 D7
Khotyn UA. 13 D7
Khoyniki BY. 13 C8
Khust UA. 17 A5
Khvalynsk RUS. .9 C9
Kiato GR 184 A3
Kibæk DK 59 B1
Kiberg N 193 B14
Kicasalih TR. . . 186 A1
Kičevo NMK. . . 182 B2
Kidderminster
UK 39 B4
Kidlington UK. .44 B2
Kidsgrove UK . . .40 B1
Kidwelly UK. 39 C2
Kiefersfelden
D 108 B3
Kiel D 64 B3
Kielce PL. 87 B4
Kiełczygłów
PL. 86 A3
Kielder UK 37 A4
Kiełpino PL. 68 A3
Kielpiny PL. 77 A4
Kierinki FIN . . . 197 B8
Kiernozia PL 77 B4
Kierspe D 81 A3
Kietrz PL. 86 B2
Kietz D. 74 B3
Kiev = Kyiv
UA 13 C9
Kiezmark PL 69 A3
Kiffisia GR. 185 A4
Kifino Selo
BIH. 139 B4
Kihlanki
FIN. 196 B6
S 196 B6
Kiistala FIN. . . . 197 B8
Kije PL 87 B4
Kijevo HR 138 B2
Kikallen N. 46 B2
Kikinda SRB. . . 126 B2
Kil
N. 53 B5
Örebro S. 55 A6
Värmland S . . . 55 A4
Kila S. 55 A3
Kilafors S. 50 A3
Kilbaha IRL. 28 B2
Kilbeggan IRL. . .30 A1
Kilberry UK 34 C2
Kilbirnie UK. 34 C3
Kilboghamn
N. 195 D4
Kilbotn N 194 B7
Kilb Rabenstein
A. 110 A2
Kilchattan UK. . .34 C2
Kilchoan UK. 34 B1
Kilcock IRL 30 A2
Kilconnell IRL . . .28 A3
Kilcormac IRL . . .28 A4
Kilcreggan UK . .34 C3
Kilcullen IRL. . . .30 A2
Kilcurry IRL 27 B4
Kildare IRL 30 A2
Kildinstroy RUS . 3 B13
Kildonan UK 32 C3
Kildorrery IRL . . .29 B3
Kilegrend N. 53 A4
Kilen N. 53 A4
Kilgarvan IRL . . .29 C2
Kiliya UA 17 C8
Kilkee IRL 28 B2
Kilkeel UK. 27 B4
Kilkelly IRL. 26 C2
Kilkenny IRL 30 B1
Kilkieran IRL. . . .28 A2

Kilkinlea IRL 29 B2
Kilkis GR 182 B4
Killadysert IRL . .29 B2
Killala IRL 26 B1
Killaloe IRL 28 B3
Killarney IRL 29 B2
Killashandra
IRL. 27 B3
Killashee IRL 28 A4
Killearn UK. 34 B3
Killeberg S. 61 C4
Killeigh IRL. 30 A1
Killenaule IRL . . .29 B4
Killimor IRL 28 A3
Killin UK 34 B3
Killinaboy IRL. . .28 B2
Killinge S 196 B3
Killinick IRL 30 B2
Killorglin IRL. . . .29 B2
Killucan IRL 30 A1
Killybegs IRL 26 B2
Killyleagh UK . . .27 B5
Kilmacrenan
IRL 26 A3
Kilmacthomas
IRL 30 B1
Kilmaine IRL . . .28 A2
Kilmallock IRL. . .29 B3
Kilmarnock UK. .36 A2
Kilmartin UK. . . .34 B2
Kilmaurs UK 36 A2
Kilmeadan IRL . .30 B1
Kilmeedy IRL. . . .29 B3
Kilmelford UK. . .34 B2
Kilmore Quay
IRL 30 B2
Kilmuir UK 32 D2
Kilnaleck IRL 27 C3
Kilninver UK. . . .34 B2
Kilpisjärvi FIN. 192 C4
Kilrea UK. 27 B4
Kilrush IRL 29 B2
Kilsmo S. 56 A1
Kilsyth UK. 35 C3
Kiltoom IRL 28 A3
Kilwinning UK . .36 A2
Kimasozero
RUS 3 D12
Kimi GR 185 A5
Kimolos GR . . . 185 C5
Kimovsk RUS. . .9 E10
Kimratshofen
D 107 B5
Kimry RUS 9 D10
Kimstad S. 56 B1
Kinbrace UK 32 C3
Kincardine UK . .35 B4
Kincraig UK . . . 32 D3
Kindberg A . . . 110 B2
Kindelbrück D. .82 A3
Kingarrow IRL. . .26 B2
Kingisepp RUS. . .9 C6
Kingsbridge UK 43 B3
Kingsclere UK. . .44 B2
Kingscourt IRL. .27 C4
King's Lynn UK. .41 C4
Kingsteignton
UK 43 B3
Kingston
Greater London
UK 44 B3
Moray UK. 32 D3
Kingston Bagpuize
UK 44 B2
Kingston upon Hull
UK 40 B3
Kingswear UK. . .43 B3
Kingswood UK . .43 A4
Kington UK 39 B3
Kingussie UK. . . 32 D2
Kınık
Antalya TR. . . 188 C4
İzmir TR 186 C2
Kinloch
Highland UK. . .31 B2
Highland UK . . 32 C2
Kinlochbervie
UK 32 C1
Kinlochewe UK. 32 D1
Kinlochleven
UK 34 B3
Kinlochmoidart
UK 34 B2
Kinloch Rannoch
UK 35 B3
Kinloss UK 32 D3
Kinlough IRL 26 B2
Kinn N 48 B2
Kinna S 60 B2
Kinnared S. 60 B3
Kinnarp S. 55 B4
Kinnegad IRL . . .30 A1
Kinne-Kleva S. . .55 B4

Kinnitty IRL 28 A4
Kinrooi B. 80 A1
Kinross UK 35 B4
Kinsale IRL 29 C3
Kinsarvik N 46 B3
Kintarvie UK 31 A2
Kintore UK 33 D4
Kinvarra IRL. 28 A3
Kioni GR 184 A1
Kiparissia GR. . 184 B2
Kipfenburg D . . .95 C3
Kippen UK 35 B3
Kiraz TR 188 A3
Kirazlı TR. 186 B1
Kirberg D 81 B4
Kirchbach in
Steiermark
A. 110 C2
Kirchberg
CH. 106 B2
Baden-
Württemberg
D. 94 B1
Rheinland-Pfalz
D. 93 B3
Kirchberg am
Wechsel A. . . . 110 B2
Kirchberg an der
Pielach A. 110 A2
Kirchberg in Tirol
A. 109 B3
Kirchbichl A. . . . 108 B3
Kirchdorf
Bayern D 96 C1
Mecklenburg-
Vorpommern
D. 65 C4
Niedersachsen
D. 72 B1
Kirchdorf an der
Krems A. 109 B5
Kirchdorf in Tirol
A. 109 B3
Kirchenlamitz
D 83 B3
Kirchenthumbach
D 95 B3
Kirchhain D. 81 B4
Kirchheim
Baden-
Württemberg
D. 94 C1
Bayern D 108 A1
Hessen D. 81 B5
Kirchheimbolanden
D 93 B4
Kirchhundem
D 81 A4
Kirchlintein D. . .72 B2
Kirchschlag A. . 111 B3
Kirchweidach
D 109 A3
Kirchzarten D. 106 B2
Kircubbin UK. . . .27 B5
Kireç TR. 186 C3
Kırıkkale TR. 23 B7
Kirillov RUS 9 C11
Kirishi RUS 9 C8
Kırka TR. 187 C5
Kırkağaç TR . . . 186 C2
Kirkbean UK 36 B3
Kirkbride UK 36 B3
Kirkby UK. 38 A4
Kirkby Lonsdale
UK 37 B4
Kirkby Malzeard
UK 40 A2
Kirkbymoorside
UK 37 B6
Kirkby Stephen
UK 37 B4
Kirkcaldy UK. . . .35 B4
Kirkcolm UK 36 B1
Kirkconnel UK . .36 A2
Kirkcowan UK. . .36 B2
Kirkcudbright
UK 36 B2
Kirkehamn N . . .52 B2
Kirke Hyllinge
DK 61 D1
Kirkenær N 49 B4
Kirkenes N . . . 193 C14
Kirkham UK 38 A4
Kirkintilloch
UK 35 C3
Kirkjubæjarklaustur
IS 191 D7
Kirkkonummi
FIN. 8 B4
Kırklareli TR. . . 186 A2
Kirkmichael UK .35 B4
Kirk Michael
UK 36 B2

Kirkoswald UK . .36 A2
Kirkpatrick Fleming
UK 36 A3
Kirkton of Glenisla
UK 35 B4
Kirkwall UK 33 C4
Kirkwhelpington
UK 37 A5
Kirn D. 93 B3
Kirovsk RUS. 3 C13
Kirriemuir UK . . .35 B5
Kırşehir TR 23 B8
Kirton UK 41 C3
Kirton in Lindsey
UK 40 B3
Kirtorf D 81 B5
Kiruna S 196 B3
Kisa S 62 A3
Kisač SRB 126 B1
Kisbér H 112 B2
Kiseljak BIH . . . 139 B4
Kisielice PL. 69 B4
Kiskőre H 113 B4
Kiskőrös H 112 C3
Kiskunfélegyháza
H. 113 C3
Kiskunhalas H 112 C3
Kiskunlacháza
H. 112 B2
Kiskunmajsa
H. 113 C3
Kisláng H 112 C2
Kisslegg D 107 B4
Kissolt H 112 C3
Kissónerga
CY 181 B1
Kist D. 94 B1
Kistanje HR . . . 138 B1
Kistelek H. 113 C3
Kisterenye H. . . 113 A3
Kisújszállás
H. 113 B4
Kisvárda H 16 A5
Kisvejke H 112 C2
Kiszkowo PL 76 B2
Kiszombor H. . . 126 A2
Kitee FIN. 9 A7
Kithnos GR 185 B5
Kiti CY 181 B2
Kitkiöjärvi S . . . 196 B6
Kitkiöjoki S 196 B6
Kittelfjäll S. 195 E6
Kittendorf D. . . .74 A1
Kittilä FIN. 196 B7
Kittlitz D. 84 A2
Kittsee A. 111 A4
Kitzbühel A 109 B3
Kitzingen D. 94 B2
Kiuruvesi FIN . . .3 E10
Kivertsi UA. 13 C6
Kividhes CY . . . 181 B1
Kivik S. 63 C2
Kivotos GR. . . . 182 C3
Kıyıköy TR 186 A3
Kızılcabölük
TR. 188 B4
Kızılcadağ
TR. 189 B4
Kızılcahamam
TR. 23 A7
Kızılırmak TR. . . .23 A7
Kızılkaya TR . . . 189 B5
Kızılkuyu TR . . 187 D6
Kızılören
Afyon TR 189 A5
Konya TR 189 B7
Kjeldebotn N . . 194 B7
Kjellerup DK 59 B2
Kjellmyra N 49 B4
Kjøllefjord N . . 193 B11
Kjopmannskjaer
N. 54 A1
Kjøpsvik N 194 B7
Kl'ačno SK 98 C2
Kladanj BIH . . . 139 A4
Kläden D. 73 B4
Klädesholmen
S. 60 B1
Kladnice HR. . . . 138 B2
Kladno CZ 84 B2
Kladruby CZ 95 B4
Klagenfurt A . . . 110 C1
Klågerup S 61 D3
Klagstorp S 66 A2
Klaipėda LT 8 E2
Klaistow D. 74 B1
Klaksvík FO. 4 A3
Klana HR. 123 B3
Klanac HR. 123 C4
Klanjec HR 123 A4
Klardorf D. 95 B4
Klarup DK. 58 A3
Klašnice BIH. . . 124 C3

Klässbol S 55 A3
Klášterec nad Ohří
CZ 83 B5
Kláštor pod
Znievom SK 98 C2
Klatovy CZ 96 D1
Klaus an der
Pyhrnbahn
A. 110 B1
Klazienaveen
NL 71 B3
Kłecko PL 76 B2
Kleczew PL. 76 B3
Klein Plasten D. .74 A1
Klein Sankt Paul
A. 110 C1
Kleinsölk A . . . 109 B4
Kleinzell A 110 B2
Klejtrup DK 58 B2
Klek SRB 126 B2
Klemensker DK .67 A3
Klenak SRB. . . 127 C1
Klenci pod
Cerchovem CZ 95 B4
Klenica PL. 75 C4
Klenje SRB 127 C1
Klenoec NMK . .182 B2
Klenovec SK. . . .99 C3
Klenovica HR . . 123 B3
Klenovnik HR . . 124 A2
Kleppe N. 52 B1
Kleppestø N . . .46 B2
Kleptow D 74 A2
Kleszewo PL 77 B6
Kleve D 80 A2
Klevshult S 60 B4
Klewki PL 77 A5
Kličevac SRB . . 127 C3
Kliening A 110 C1
Klietz D 73 B5
Klikuszowa PL . .99 B3
Klimkovice CZ . .98 B2
Klimontów PL. . .87 B5
Klimovichi BY . . .13 B9
Klimpfjäll S 195 E5
Klin RUS. 9 D10
Klinča Sela
HR 123 B4
Klingenbach
A. 111 B3
Klingenberg D . .93 B5
Klingenmunster
D 93 B4
Klingenthal D. . .83 B4
Klinken D 73 A4
Klintehamn S . . .57 C4
Kliny PL 87 A4
Kliplev DK 64 B2
Klippan S 61 C3
Klis HR 138 B2
Klitmøller DK . . .58 A1
Klitten S 49 A6
Klixbüll D 64 B1
Kljajićevo
SRB 126 B1
Ključ BIH 138 A2
Klobouky CZ . . .97 C4
Kłobuck PL. 86 B2
Klockestrand
S 200 D3
Kłodawa
Lubuskie PL. . . .75 B4
Wielkopolskie
PL. 76 B3
Kłodzko PL 85 B4
Kløfta N. 48 B3
Klokkarvik N. . . .46 B2
Klokkerholm
DK 58 A3
Klokočov SK. . . .98 B2
Kłomnice PL 86 B3
Klonowa PL. 86 A2
Kloosterzande
NL 79 A4
Kłopot PL 74 B3
Klos AL. 182 B2
Kloštar Ivanić
HR 124 B2
Kloster
D 66 B2
DK 59 B1
Klösterle A. 107 B5
Klostermansfeld
D 82 A3
Klosterneuburg
A. 97 C4
Klosters CH 107 C4
Kloten CH. 107 B3
Klötze D 73 B4
Klöverträsk S . 196 D4
Klövsjö S. 199 C11
Kluczbork PL. . . .86 B2
Kluczewo PL. . . .75 A5

Kluisbergen B. . .79 B3
Klundert NL. 79 A4
Klutz D. 65 C4
Kłiwów PL 87 A4
Klyetsk BY 13 B7
Knaben N 52 B2
Knaften S 200 B4
Knapstad N. 54 A2
Knäred S. 61 C3
Knaresborough
UK 40 A2
Knarvik N. 46 B2
Knebel DK 59 B3
Knebworth UK . .44 B3
Knesebeck D. . . .73 B3
Knesselare B . . .78 A3
Kneža SLO 123 B3
Kneževi Vinogradi
HR 125 B4
Kneževo HR. . . . 125 B4
Knić SRB 127 D2
Knighton UK 39 B3
Knin HR 138 A2
Knislinge S. 61 C4
Knittelfeld A. . . 110 B1
Knivsta S. 57 A3
Knock IRL 28 A3
Knocktopher
IRL 30 B1
Knokke-Heist B .78 A3
Knowle UK 44 A2
Knurów PL 86 B2
Knutby S. 51 C5
Knutsford UK . . .38 A4
Kobarid SLO . . 122 A2
København =
Copenhagen
DK 61 D2
Kobenz A 110 B1
Kobersdorf A . . 111 B3
Kobiernice PL. . .99 B3
Kobierzyce PL. .85 B4
Kobilje SLO . . . 111 C3
Kobiór PL 86 B2
Koblenz
CH 106 B3
D 81 B3
Kobryn BY 13 B6
Kobylanka PL. . .75 A3
Kobylin PL 85 A5
Kobylniki PL. . . .77 B5
Kocaali TR. 187 A5
Kocaaliler TR. . 189 B5
Kocaeli = İzmit
TR. 187 B4
Kočani NMK. . . .182 B4
Koçarlı TR. 188 B2
Koceljevo SRB. 127 C1
Kočerin BIH . . . 138 B3
Kočevje SLO . . 123 B3
Kočevska Reka
SLO 123 B3
Kochel am see
D 108 B2
Kocs H 112 B2
Kocsér H 113 B3
Kocsola H. 112 C2
Kodal N 53 A6
Kode S 60 B1
Kodersdorf D . . .84 A2
Kodrab PL. 86 A3
Koekelare B. 78 A2
Kofçaz TR. 186 A2
Köflach A 110 B2
Køge DK 61 D2
Kohlberg D 95 B4
Kohtla-Järve
EST. 8 C5
Köinge S 60 B2
Kojetín CZ 98 B1
Kökar FIN 51 C7
Kokava SK 99 C3
Kokkinotrimithia
. . . . 181 A2
Kokkola FIN. 3 E8
Kokori BIH 124 C3
Kokoski PL. 69 A3
Koksijde B 78 A2
Kola
BIH. 124 C3
RUS 3 B13
Köla S. 54 A3
Kołacin PL 87 A3
Kolari FIN 196 B6
Kolárovo SK. . . . 112 B1
Kolašin MNE . . .16 D3
Kolbäck S 56 A2
Kolbacz PL. 75 A3
Kolbeinsstaðir
IS 190 C2
Kolbermoor D . .108 B3
Kolbnitz A 109 C4

Kolbotn N. 54 A1
Kolbu N. 48 B2
Kolby Kås DK, , , .59 C3
Kolczewo PL. . . .67 C3
Kolczyglowy
PL. 68 A2
Kolding DK 59 C2
Kölesd H. 112 C2
Kolgrov N 46 A1
Kolín CZ 97 A3
Kolind DK. 59 B3
Kolinec CZ 96 B1
Koljane HR. 138 B2
Kølkær DK 59 B2
Kölleda D 82 A3
Kollum NL 70 A3
Köln = Cologne
D 80 B2
Koło PL 76 B3
Kołobrzeg PL . . .67 B4
Kolochau D 83 A5
Kolomyya UA . . .13 D6
Kolonowskie
PL. 86 B2
Koloveč CZ. 95 B5
Kolpino RUS 9 C7
Kolrep D 73 A5
Kölsillre S. 199 C12
Kolsko PL 75 C4
Kolsva S. 56 A1
Kolta SK 112 A2
Kolunič BIH . . . 138 A2
Koluszki PL 87 A3
Kolut SRB 125 B4
Kolvereid N. . . . 199 A8
Kølvrå DK. 59 B2
Komadi H 113 B5
Komagvær N. 193 B14
Komarica BIH . 125 C3
Komárno SK . . . 112 B2
Komárom H. . . . 112 B2
Komatou Yialou
CY 181 A3
Komboti GR. . . .182 D3
Komen SLO . . . 122 B2
Komin HR. 138 B3
Komiža HR 138 B2
Komjáti H 99 C4
Komjatice SK. . 112 A2
Komletinci HR 125 B4
Komló H 125 A4
Komoča SK. . . . 112 B2
Komorniki PL . . .75 B5
Komorzno PL. . . .86 A2
Komotini GR . . .183 B7
Konak SRB 126 B2
Konakovo RUS . .9 D10
Konarzyny PL. . .68 B2
Kondias GR 183 D7
Kondopaga RUS .9 A9
Kondorfa H 111 C3
Kondoros H. . . . 113 C4
Konevo RUS. 9 A11
Køng DK 65 A4
Konga S. 63 B3
Köngäs FIN 196 B7
Kongerslev DK. .58 B3
Kongsberg N. . . .53 A5
Kongshamn N .53 B4
Kongsmark DK. .64 A1
Kongsmoen N 199 A9
Kongsvik N 194 B7
Kongsvinger N. .48 B3
Konice CZ. 97 B4
Koniecpol PL. . . .86 B3
Königsberg D. . .82 B2
Königsbronn D .94 C2
Königsbrück D . .84 A1
Königsbrunn D .94 C2
Königsdorf D . . 108 B2
Königsee D 82 B3
Königshorst D . .74 B1
Königslutter D. .73 B3
Königssee D . . . 109 B3
Königstein
Hessen D 81 B4
Sachsen D 84 B2
Königstetten A .97 C4
Königswartha
D 84 A2
Konigswiesen
A. 96 C2
Königswinter
D 80 B3
Königs
Wusterhausen
D. 74 B2
Konin PL. 76 B3
Konispol AL. . . .182 D2
Konitsa GR. 182 C2
Köniz CH. 106 C2

Konjevići BIH . 139 A5
Konjevrate HR 138 B2
Konjic BIH 139 B3
Konjšćina HR. . 124 A2
Könnern D. 83 A3
Konnerud N. 53 A6
Konopiska PL. . .86 B2
Konotop PL 75 C4
Końskie PL. 87 A4
Konsmo N 52 B3
Konstancin-
Jeziorna PL 77 B6
Konstantynów
Łódźki PL 86 A3
Konstanz D 107 B4
Kontich B 79 A4
Kontiolahti FIN . .9 A6
Konya TR. 189 B7
Konz D. 92 B2
Kópasker IS . . . 191 A9
Kopavogur IS . 190 C4
Kopčany SK. 98 C1
Koper SLO 122 B2
Kopervik N. 52 A1
Kópháza H 111 B3
Kopice PL. 85 B5
Kopidlno CZ. . . .84 B3
Köping S. 56 A1
Köpingebro S . . .66 A2
Köpingsvik S. . . .62 B4
Köpmanholmen
S 200 C4
Koppang N. 48 A3
Koppangen N. 192 C4
Kopparberg S. . .50 C1
Kopparberg S . 193 D11
Koppl A 109 B4
Koprivlen BG . . 183 B5
Koprivna BIH. . 125 C4
Koprivnica HR 124 A1
Koprivnice CZ. .98 B2
Köprübaşı
TR. 186 D3
Koprzywnica
PL. 87 B5
Kopstal L. 92 B2
Kopychyntsi
UA 13 D6
Kopytkowo PL. .69 B3
Korbach D 81 A4
Körbecke D. 81 A4
Korçë AL. 182 C2
Korczyców PL. . .75 B3
Korenica HR . . 123 C4
Korenita SRB . 127 C1
Korets UA 13 C7
Korfantów PL. . .85 B5
Korfez TR 187 B4
Korgen N 195 D4
Korinth DK 64 A3
Korinthos = Corinth
GR 184 B3
Korita
BIH. 138 A2
HR 139 C3
Korithi GR. 184 B1
Korkuteli TR. . . 189 B5
Körmend H 111 B3
Korne PL. 68 A2
Korneuburg A . .97 C4
Kornevo RUS. . . .69 A5
Kórnik PL. 76 B2
Kornsjø N. 54 B2
Kornwestheim
D 94 C1
Környe H. 112 B2
Koromačno
HR 123 C3
Koroni GR. 184 C2
Koronos GR. . . .185 B6
Koronowo PL. . .76 A2
Körösladány
H. 113 C5
Köröstarcsa
H. 113 C5
Korosten UA . . .13 C8
Korostyshev
UA 13 C8
Korpikå S 196 D6
Korpikylä FIN . 196 C6
Korpilombolo
S 196 C6
Korsberga
Jönköping S . . .62 A3
Skaraborg S. . . .55 B5
Korshavn N 54 A1
Korskrogen S . .200 E1
Korsnäs S 50 B2
Korsør DK. 65 A4
Korsun
Shevchenkovskiy
UA 13 D9
Korträsk S 196 D3
Kortrijk B 78 B3

Korucu TR. 186 C2
Koryčany CZ . . .98 B1
Korzeńsko PL . .85 A4
Korzybie PL. 68 A1
Kos GR 188 C2
Kosakowo PL. . .69 A3
Kosanica MNE. 139 B5
Kösching D 95 C3
Kościan PL. 75 B5
Kościelec PL. . . .76 B3
Kościerzyna PL.68 A2
Košetice CZ 97 B3
Kosjerić SRB. . 127 D1
Košice SK 12 D4
Koška HR 125 B4
Koskullskulle
S 196 B3
Kosovska Mitrovica
KOS 16 D4
Kosta S. 62 B3
Kostajnica
BIH. 124 B2
HR 124 B2
Kostajnik SRB. 127 C1
Kostanjevica
SLO 123 B4
Kostelec nad
Černými Lesy
CZ 96 B2
Kostelec na Hané
CZ 97 B5
Kostice CZ 84 B1
Kostkowo PL. . . .68 A3
Kostojevići
SRB 127 C1
Kostolac SRB. . 127 C3
Kostomłoty PL. .85 A4
Kostopil UA 13 C7
Kostów PL 86 A2
Kostrzyn
Lubuskie PL. . . .74 B3
Wielkopolskie
PL. 76 B2
Koszalin PL 67 B5
Koszęcin PL. . . .86 B2
Köszeg H. 111 B3
Koszwaly PL. . . .69 A3
Koszyce PL. 87 B4
Kot SLO 123 B4
Kotala FIN. 197 B11
Kötelek H 113 B4
Köthen D 83 A3
Kotka FIN 8 B5
Kotomierz PL. . .76 A3
Kotor MNE 16 D3
Kotoriba HR. . . 124 A2
Kotorsko BIH. . 125 C4
Kotor Varoš
BIH. 124 C3
Kotovsk UA 17 B8
Kótronas GR . . 184 C3
Kötschach A . . 109 C3
Kötzting D 95 B4
Koudum NL 70 B2
Kourim CZ. 96 A2
Kout na Šumave
CZ 95 B5
Kouvola FIN. 8 B5
Kovačevac
SRB 127 C2
Kovačica SRB. . 126 B2
Kovdor RUS . . . 197 B13
Kovel' UA 13 C6
Kovilj SRB 126 B2
Kovin SRB. 127 C2
Kowal PL. 77 B4
Kowalewo
Pomorskie PL. .69 B3
Kowalów PL. . . .75 B3
Kowary PL. 85 B3
Köyceğiz TR. . . 188 C3
Kozani GR. 182 C3
Kozarac
BIH. 124 C2
HR 124 B1
Kozárovce SK . . .98 C2
Kozarska Dubica
BIH. 124 B2
Kozelets UA. . . .13 C9
Kozica HR. 138 B3
Koziegłowy PL. .86 B3
Kozienice PL. . . .87 A5
Kozina SLO. 122 B2
Kozje SLO 123 A4
Kozlu TR 187 A6
Kozluk BIH 139 A5
Koźmin PL. 85 A5
Koźminek PL. . . .86 A2
Kozolupy CZ 96 B1
Kožuchov PL. . . .85 A3
Kožuhe BIH . . . 125 C4
Kozyatyn UA. . . .13 D8

Kozyürük TR . . 186 A1
Kräckelbräken
S. 49 A6
Krackow D 74 A3
Kraddsele S . . .195 E7
Krąg PL 68 A1
Kragenæs DK . .65 B4
Kragerø N. 53 B5
Krągi PL. 68 B1
Kragujevac
SRB 127 C2
Kraiburg D. . . . 109 A3
Krajenka PL. 68 B1
Krajišnik SRB. . 126 B2
Krajková CZ. . . .83 B4
Krajné SK 98 C1
Krajnik Dolny
PL. 74 A3
Krakača BIH . . . 124 B1
Kräklingbo S. . . .57 C4
Kraków = Cracow
PL. 99 A3
Krakow am See
D 73 A5
Králíky CZ. 85 B4
Kraljevica HR . 123 B3
Kraljevo SRB . . 16 D4
Kral'ovany SK. . .99 B3
Kral'ov Brod
SK. 111 A4
Kralovice CZ . . .96 B1
Kralupy nad
Vltavou CZ. . . .84 B2
Králův Dvůr CZ. .96 B2
Kramfors S. . . . 200 D3
Kramsach A . . . 108 B2
Kramsk PL 76 B3
Kranenburg D . .80 A2
Krania GR. 182 D3
Krania Elasonas
GR 182 D4
Kranichfeld D. . .82 B3
Kranidi GR 184 B4
Kranj SLO 123 A3
Kranjska Gora
SLO 109 C4
Krapanj HR. . . . 138 B1
Krapina HR. . . . 124 A1
Krapje HR. 124 B2
Krapkowice PL. .86 B1
Kraselov CZ. 96 B1
Krašić HR. 123 B4
Kraslava LV 8 E5
Kraslice CZ. 83 B4
Krasna PL. 87 A4
Krasna Lipa CZ. .84 B2
Krasne PL 77 B5
Kraśnik PL. 12 C5
Krašnja SLO. . . 123 A3
Krásno SK. 98 B2
Krásnohorské
Podhradie SK . .99 C4
Krasno Polje
HR 123 C4
Krasnozavodsk
RUS 9 D11
Krasnystaw PL. .13 C5
Krasnyy RUS . . .13 A9
Krasnyy Kholm
RUS 9 C10
Krasocin PL 87 B4
Kraszewice PL. .86 A2
Kraszkowice PL .86 A2
Kratigos GR . . . 186 C1
Kratovo NMK. . 182 A4
Kraubath A . . . 110 B1
Krausnick D 74 B2
Krautheim D . . .94 B1
Kravaře CZ. 84 A2
Kraváre CZ. 98 B2
Kravarsko HR . 124 B2
Kraznějov CZ . . .96 B1
Krčedin SRB. . . 126 B2
Kŭrdzhali BG. . .183 B7
Krefeld D 80 A2
Kregme DK. 61 D2
Krembz D 73 A4
Kremenets UA . .13 C6
Kremmen D. 74 B2
Kremna SRB. . . 127 D1
Kremnica SK . . .98 C2
Krempe D 64 C2
Krems A 97 C3
Kremsbrücke
A. 109 C4
Kremsmünster
A. 110 A1
Křemže CZ. 96 C2
Křenov CZ. 97 B4
Krepa PL. 76 C3
Krępa Krajeńska
PL. 75 A5

Krepsko PL. 68 B1
Krešovo BIH. . . 139 B4
Kressbronn D. . 107 B4
Krestena GR . . 184 B2
Kretinga LT 8 E2
Krettsy RUS 9 C8
Kreuth D. 108 B2
Kreuzau D 80 B2
Kreuzlingen
CH 107 B4
Kreuztal D 81 B3
Krewelin D. 74 B2
Krezluk BIH . . . 138 A3
Krichem BG. . . .183 A6
Krieglach A. . . . 110 B2
Kriegsfeld D 93 B3
Kriens CH 106 B3
Krimml A 108 B3
Krimpen aan de
IJssel NL 79 A4
Křinec CZ. 84 B3
Kristdala S 62 A4
Kristiansand N. .53 B4
Kristianstad S. . .61 C4
Kristiansund
N. 198 B4
Kristiinankaupunki
FIN 8 A2
Kristinefors S . . .49 B4
Kristinehamn S .55 A5
Kriváň SK 99 C3
Kriva Palanka
NMK. 182 A4
Křivoklát CZ. . . .96 A1
Kríž HR. 124 B2
Křižanov CZ. . . .97 B4
Križevci HR. . . . 124 A2
Krk HR 123 B3
Krka SLO. 123 B3
Krnjača SRB. . . 127 C2
Krnjak HR. 123 B4
Krnjeuša BIH . . 124 C2
Krnjevo SRB. . . 127 C3
Krnov CZ. 98 A1
Krobia PL. 85 A4
Kroczyce PL. 86 B3
Krøderen N 48 B1
Krokees GR . . . 184 C3
Krokek S 56 B2
Krokom S 199 B11
Krokowa PL. 68 A3
Krokstad-elva
N. 53 A5
Kroksund N 54 A2
Kroměříž CZ 98 B1
Krommenie NL. .70 B1
Krompachy SK . .99 C4
Kronach D 82 B3
Kronshagen D . .64 B3
Kronshtadt RUS. .9 C6
Kröpelin D 65 B4
Kropp D. 64 B2
Kroppenstedt
D 73 C4
Kropstädt D 74 C1
Krościenko nad
Dunajcem PL. . .99 B4
Kröslin D. 66 B2
Krośnice PL. 85 A5
Krośniewice PL .77 B4
Krosno PL 12 D4
Krosno Odrzańskie
PL. 75 B4
Krostitz D 83 A4
Krotoszyn PL. . . .85 A5
Krottendorf A. 110 B2
Krouna CZ 97 B4
Krowiarki PL. . . .86 B2
Krrabë AL. 182 B1
Kršan HR. 123 B3
Krško SLO. 123 B4
Krstac MNE . . . 139 B4
Křtiny CZ 97 B4
Kruft D. 80 B3
Kruishoutem B. .79 B3
Krujë AL 182 B1
Krulyewshchyna
BY. 13 A7
Krumbach
A. 111 B3
D 94 C2
Krumovgrad
BG 183 B7
Krün D. 108 B2
Krupá CZ. 84 B1
Krupa na Vrbasu
BIH. 124 C3
Krupanj SRB . . 127 C1
Krupina SK. 99 C3

Krupka CZ.....84 B1
Krupki BY......13 A8
Kruså DK.......64 B2
Krušćica BIH .. 139 A3
Kruševac SRB . 16 D4
Kruševo NMK . 182 B3
Kruszwica PL...76 B3
Kruszyn PL......77 B4
Krychaw BY...13 B9
Krynica PL.....99 B4
Krynica Morska PL............69 A4
Krzęcin PL 75 A4
Krzelów PL......85 A4
Krzepice PL....86 B2
Krzepielów PL..85 A4
Krzeszowice PL.86 B3
Krzeszyce PL....75 B4
Krzynowlaga Mała PL............77 A5
Krzywiń PL.....75 C5
Krzyżanowice PL............98 B2
Krzyżowa PL....99 B3
Krzyż Wielkopolski PL............75 B5
Ksiaz Wielkopolski PL............87 B4
Książ Wielkopolski PL............76 B2
Ktębowiec PL...75 A5
Kübekháza H . 126 A2
Küblis CH 107 C4
Kuchary PL.....86 A1
Kuchl A 109 B4
Kucice PL......77 B5
Kuciste HR 138 C3
Kuçovë AL 182 C1
Küçükbahçe TR............ 188 A1
Küçükköy TR.. 186 C1
Küçükkuyu TR............ 186 C1
Kucura SRB.... 126 B1
Kuczbork-Osada PL............77 A5
Kuddby S 56 B2
Kudowa-Zdrój PL............85 B4
Kufstein A 108 B3
Kuggeboda S ...63 B3
Kuggörana S...200 E3
Kühbach D 95 C3
Kuhmo FIN.....3 D11
Kuhmoinen FIN .. 8 B4
Kuhnsdorf A .. 110 C1
Kuhstedt D 72 A1
Kuinre NL.......70 B2
Kuivaniemi FIN...........197 D8
Kuivastu EST.....8 C3
Kukës AL...... 182 A2
Kuklin PL.......77 A5
Kukljica HR ... 137 B4
Kukujevci SRB. 127 B1
Kula
Srbija SRB 127 C3
Vojvodina SRB 126 B1
TR.......... 188 A3
Kuldīga LV.....8 D2
Kulen Vakuf BIH........... 124 C2
Kulina BIH.... 125 C4
Kullstedt D....82 A2
Kulmain D 95 B3
Kulmbach D 82 B3
Kuloharju FIN...........197 D11
Kulu TR 23 B7
Kumachevo RUS..........69 A5
Kumafşarı TR . 189 B4
Kumane SRB .. 126 B2
Kumanovo NMK 182 A3
Kumbağ TR .. 186 B2
Kumdanlı TR . 189 A5
Kumkale TR... 186 C1
Kumla S........56 A1
Kumlakyrkby S .50 C3
Kumlinge FIN ..51 B7
Kumluca TR.. 189 C5
Kumrovec HR . 123 A4
Kunadacs H... 112 C1
Kunágota H.. 113 C4
Kunbaja H ... 126 A1
Kunda EST 8 C5
Kundl A....... 108 B2
Kunes N...... 193 B10

Kunfehértó H . 126 A1
Kungälv S......60 B1
Kungsängen S ..57 A3
Kungsäter S.....60 B2
Kungsbacka S...60 B2
Kungsgården S .50 B3
Kungshamn S...54 B2
Kungs-Husby S .56 A3
Kungsör S.......56 A2
Kunhegyes H . 113 B4
Kunmadaras H............. 113 B4
Kunovice CZ ...98 B1
Kunów PL.......87 B5
Kunowo
Wielkopolskie PL........... 76 C2
Zachodnio-Pomorskie PL . 74 A3
Kunštát CZ.....97 B4
Kunszállás H... 113 C3
Kunszentmárton H............. 113 C4
Kunszentmiklós H............. 112 B3
Kunžak CZ.....97 B3
Künzelsau D....94 B1
Kuolajarvi RUS......... 197 C12
Kuolio FIN....197 D11
Kuopio FIN......8 A5
Kuosku FIN... 197 B11
Kup
H............. 111 B4
PL............86 B1
Kupferzell D ...94 B1
Kupinec HR ... 123 B4
Kupinečki Kraljevac HR . 124 B1
Kupinovo SRB. 127 C2
Kupirovo HR .. 138 A2
Kupjak HR 123 B3
Kuppenheim D .93 C4
Kupres BIH.... 138 B3
Küps D.........82 B3
Kurd H........ 112 C2
Küre TR 23 A7
Kuressaare EST ..8 C3
Kurikka FIN.....8 A3
Kuřim CZ.......97 B4
Kuřivody CZ....84 B2
Kurki PL........77 A5
Kurort Oberwiesenthal D 83 B4
Kurort Schmalkalden D 82 B2
Kurort Stolberg D 82 A2
Kurort Wippra D 82 A3
Kurów PL......12 C5
Kurowice PL....86 A3
Kurravaara S... 196 B3
Kursu FIN 197 C11
Kurşunlu
Bursa TR...... 187 B4
Çankırı TR 23 A7
Kurtakko FIN.. 196 B7
Kürten D........80 A3
Kurucaşile TR . 187 A7
Kurvinen FIN 197 D12
Kurzelów PL....87 B3
Kusadak SRB.. 127 C2
Kuşadası TR... 188 B2
Kusel D.........93 B3
Kusey D........73 B4
Küsnacht CH .. 106 B3
Kütahya TR ... 187 C4
Kutenholz D ...72 A2
Kutina HR 124 B2
Kutjevo HR.... 125 B3
Kutná Hora CZ ..97 B3
Kutno PL.......77 B4
Kuttara FIN .. 193 D10
Küttingen CH . 106 B3
Kúty SK 98 C1
Kuusamo FIN...........197 D12
Kuusankoski FIN............8 B5
Kuvshinovo RUS .9 D9
Kuyucak TR ... 188 B3
Kuzmin SRB... 127 B1
Kuźnia Raciborska PL............86 B2
Kuźnica Czarnkowska PL............75 B5
Kuźnica Żelichowska PL............75 B5

Kvaløysletta N............. 192 C2
Kvalsund N ... 192 B7
Kvam
Nord-Trøndelag N............. 199 A8
Oppland N.... 198 D6
Kvamsøy N......46 A3
Kvanndal N.....46 B3
Kvänum S......55 B4
Kværndrup DK..59 C3
Kvås N 52 B3
Kvasice CZ......98 B1
Kvelde N........53 A5
Kvenna N..... 198 C5
Kvernaland N...52 B1
Kvibille S........60 C2
Kvicksund S....56 A2
Kvidinge S......61 C3
Kvikkjokk S ... 195 D8
Kvikne
Hedmark N ... 199 C7
Oppland N.... 47 A6
Kvilda CZ.......96 B1
Kville S.........54 B2
Kvillsfors S.....62 A3
Kvinlog N.......52 B2
Kvinnherad N...46 C3
Kvissel DK......58 A3
Kvissleby S.... 200 D3
Kviteseid N 53 A4
Kvitsøy N.......52 A1
Kwakowo PL....68 A2
Kwidzyn PL.....69 B3
Kwilcz PL.......75 B5
Kyjov CZ........98 C1
Kyleakin UK....31 B3
Kyle of Lochalsh UK............31 B3
Kylerhea UK ...31 B3
Kylestrome UK..32 C1
Kyllburg D......92 A2
Kyllini GR......184 B2
Kynšperk nad Ohří CZ............83 B4
Kyperounda CY........... 181 B1
Kyrenia CY... 181 A2
Kyritz D.........73 B5
Kyrkesund S...60 A1
Kyrkhult S......63 B2
Kyrksæterøra N............. 198 B6
Kysucké Nové Mesto SK......98 B2
Kythira GR.... 184 C3
Kythréa CY.... 181 A2
Kyustendil BG . 16 D5
Kyyiv = Kiev UA............13 C9
Kyyjärvi FIN......8 A4

L

Laa an der Thaya A.............97 C4
La Adrada E... 150 B3
Laage D.........65 C5
La Alameda E . 157 B4
La Alberca E... 149 B3
La Alberca de Záncara E 158 B1
La Albergueria de Argañán E ... 149 B3
La Albuera E .. 155 C4
La Aldea del Portillo del Busto E............. 143 B3
La Algaba E... 162 A1
La Aliseda de Tormes E..... 150 B2
La Almarcha E. 158 B1
La Almolda E.. 153 A3
La Almunia de Doña Godina E............. 152 A2
Laanila FIN... 193 D11
Laarne B.......79 A4
La Antilla E... 161 B2
La Arena E.... 141 A4
Laatzen D.......72 B2
La Aulaga E .. 161 B3
La Balme-de-Sillingy F..... 118 B3
La Bañeza E... 141 B5
La Barca de la Florida E..... 162 B2
La Barre-de-Monts F............. 114 B1
La Barre-en-Ouche F............89 B4

La Barrosa E... 162 B1
La Barthe-de-Neste F ... 145 A4
La Bassée F 78 B2
La Bastide-de-Sèrou F 146 A2
La Bastide-des-Jourdans F... 132 B1
Labastide-Murat F............. 129 B4
La Bastide-Puylaurent F. 117 C3
Labastide-Rouairoux F.. 130 B1
Labastide-St Pierre F............. 129 C4
La Bathie F ... 118 B3
La Bazoche-Gouet F............. 102 A2
La Bégude-de-Mazenc F.... 131 A3
Labenne F.... 128 C1
La Bernerie-en-Retz F............. 114 A1
La Bisbal d'Empordà E............. 147 C4
Lablachère F. 131 A3
Lábod H...... 124 A3
Laboe D........64 B3
La Boissière F ..89 A4
Labouheyre F. 128 B2
La Bourboule F............. 116 B2
La Bóveda de Toro E............. 150 A2
Łabowa PL.....99 B4
La Brède F.... 128 B2
La Bresse F... 106 A1
La Bridoire F.. 118 B2
La Brillanne F. 132 B1
Labrit F....... 128 B2
Labros E...... 152 A2
La Bruffière F. 114 A2
Labruguière F............. 130 B1
Labrujo P..... 148 B1
L'Absie F..... 114 B3
La Bussière F.. 103 B4
Laç AL........ 182 B1
Lacalahorra E. 164 B1
La Caletta
Cágliari I...... 179 C2
Núoro I...... 178 B3
La Calmette F. 131 B3
La Calzada de Oropesa E... 150 C2
La Campana E. 162 A2
La Cañada E... 150 B3
Lacanau F.... 128 B1
Lacanau-Océan F............. 128 A1
Lacanche F... 104 B3
La Canourgue F............. 130 A2
La Capelle F....91 B3
Lacapelle-Marival F............. 129 B4
La Cardanchosa E............. 156 B2
La Caridad E.. 141 A4
La Carlota E... 162 A3
La Carolina E.. 157 B4
Lacaune F.... 130 B1
La Cava E..... 153 B4
La Cavalerie F. 130 A2
Laceby UK......41 B3
Lacedónia I... 172 A1
La Celle-en-Moravan F.... 104 B3
La Celle-St Avant F............. 102 B2
La Cerca E.... 143 B3
Láces I....... 108 C1
La Chaise-Dieu F............. 117 B3
La Chaize-Giraud F............. 114 B2
La Chaize-le-Vicomte F.... 114 B2
La Chambre F. 118 B3
Lachania GR . 188 D2
La Chapelaude F............. 116 A2
La Chapelle-d'Angillon F.. 103 B4

La Chapelle-en-Aalgaudémar F............. 118 C3
La Chapelle-en-Vercors F..... 118 C2
La Chapelle-Glain F............. 101 B4
La Chapelle-la-Reine F........90 C2
La Chapelle-Laurent F.... 116 B3
La Chapelle-St Luc F......91 C4
La Chapelle-sur-Erdre F....... 101 B4
La Chapelle-Vicomtesse F............. 103 B3
La Charce F ... 132 A1
La Charité-sur-Loire F............. 104 B2
La Chartre-sur-le-Loir F.. 102 B2
La Châtaigneraie F............. 114 B3
La Châtre F.... 103 C3
La Chaussée-sur-Marne F.......91 C4
La Chaux-de-Fonds CH........... 106 B1
Lachen CH.... 107 B3
Lachendorf D..72 B3
La Cheppe F....91 B4
La Chèze F.... 101 A3
Lachowice PL ..99 B3
La Ciotat F.... 132 B1
La Clayette F.. 117 A4
La Clusaz F... 118 B3
La Codosera E. 155 B3
La Concha E... 143 A3
La Condamine-Châtelard F.. 132 A2
La Contienda E............. 161 A3
La Coquille F.. 115 C4
La Coronada E 156 B2
La Côte-St André F... 118 B2
La Cotinière F. 114 C2
La Courtine F. 116 B2
Lacq F........ 145 A3
La Crau F..... 132 B2
La Crèche F ... 115 B3
La Croix F.... 102 B2
La Croix-Barrez F............. 116 C2
Lacroix-St Ouen F.............90 B2
Lacroix-sur-Meuse F.............92 C1
La Croix-Valmer F............. 132 B2
La Cumbre E . 156 A2
Łącznik PL......86 B1
Lad H......... 125 A3
Ladbergen D...71 B4
Lądek-Zdrój PL............85 B4
Ladelund D....64 B2
Ladendorf A....97 C4
Ladignac-le-Long F............. 115 C5
Ladíspoli I.... 168 B2
Ladoeiro P.... 155 B3
Ladon F....... 103 B4
La Douze F.... 129 A3
Ladushkin RUS..69 A5
Ladybank UK...35 B4
Laer D.........71 B4
La Espina E... 141 A4
La Estrella E... 156 A2
La Farga de Moles E............. 146 B2
La Fatarella E . 153 A4
La Felipa E.... 158 B2
La Fère F.......90 B3
La Ferrière
Indre-et-Loire F............. 117 B3
Vendée F 114 B2
La Ferrière-en-Parthenay F. 115 B3
La-Ferté-Alais F.............90 C2
La Ferté-Bernard F............. 102 B2
La Ferté-Frênel F............89 B4

La Ferté-Gaucher F.............90 C3
La Ferté-Imbault F............. 103 B3
La Ferté-Macé F.............89 B3
La Ferté-Milon F.............90 B3
La Ferté-sous-Jouarre F......90 C3
La Ferté-St-Aubin F............. 103 B3
La Ferté-St-Cyr F............. 103 B3
La Ferté-Vidame F.............89 B4
La Ferté Villeneuil F............. 103 B3
La Feuillie F.....90 B1
La Flèche F.... 102 B1
La Flotte F.... 114 B2
Lafnitz A...... 111 B3
Lafkos GR.... 183 D5
Lafrançaise F . 129 B4
La Fregeneda E............. 149 B3
La Fresneda E. 153 B4
La Fuencubierta E............. 162 A3
La Fuente de San Esteban E ... 149 B3
La Fulioala E .. 147 C2
La Gacilly F.... 101 B3
La Galera E... 153 B4
Lagan S........60 C3
Laganadi I.... 175 C1
Lagarde F..... 146 A2
La Garde-Freinet F............. 132 B2
Lagares
Coimbra P 148 B2
Porto P...... 148 A1
La Garnache F. 114 B2
Lagaro I...... 135 A4
La Garriga E... 147 C3
La Garrovilla E............. 155 C4
Lagartera E... 150 C2
La Gaubretière F............. 114 B2
Lågbol S........51 B5
Lage D.........72 C1
Lägerdorf D....64 C2
Lagg UK........34 C2
Laggan UK.... 32 D2
Laggartorp S ...55 A5
La Gineta E... 158 B1
Láglio I....... 120 B2
Lagnieu F..... 118 B2
Lagny-sur-Marne F.............90 C2
Lago
Calabria I..... 175 B2
Veneto I..... 121 B5
Lagôa P...... 160 B1
Lagoaça P.... 149 A3
Lagonegro I... 174 A1
Lagosanto I... 121 C5
Lagos
GR........... 183 B7
P............ 160 B1
Łagów
Lubuskie PL.... 75 B4
Świętokrzyskie PL............87 B5
La Granadella
Alicante E.... 159 C4
Lleida E...... 153 A4
La Grand-Combe F............. 131 A3
La Grande-Croix F............. 117 B4
La Grande-Motte F............. 131 B3
La Granja d'Escarp E............. 153 A4
La Granjuela E 156 B2
Lagrasse F.... 146 A3
La Grave F.... 118 B3
La Gravelle F.. 101 A4
Laguardia E... 143 B4
La Guardia E.. 151 C4
La Guardia de Jaén E............. 163 A4
Laguarres E... 145 B4
Laguenne F... 116 B1
Laguépie F.... 129 B4
La Guerche-de-Bretagne F... 101 B4

La Guerche-sur-l'Aubois F 104 C1
La Guérinière F............. 114 B1
Laguiole F 116 C2
Laguna de Duera E............. 150 A3
Laguna del Marquesado E............. 152 B2
Laguna de Negrillos E............. 142 B1
Lagundo I..... 108 C2
Lagunilla E.... 149 B3
La Haba E..... 156 B2
Laharie F..... 128 B1
La Haye-du-Puits F............88 A2
La Haye-Pesnel F............88 B2
Lahden D......71 B4
La Herlière F ...78 B2
La Hermida E.. 142 A2
La Herrera E... 158 C1
Laheycourt F ...91 C5
La Higuera E .. 158 C2
La Hiniesta E.. 149 A4
Lahnstein D....81 B3
Laholm S......61 C3
La Horcajada E............. 150 B2
La Horra E.... 143 C3
Lahr D.........93 C3
Lahti FIN........8 B4
La Hulpe B 79 B4
La Hutte F......89 B4
Laichingen D ...94 C1
L'Aigle F.......89 B4
La Iglesuela E . 150 B3
La Iglesuela del Cid E............. 153 B3
Laignes F..... 104 B3
Laiguéglia I... 133 B4
L'Aiguillon-sur-Mer F............. 114 B2
Laimbach am Ostrong A.....97 C3
Laina E....... 152 A1
Lainio S...... 196 B5
Lairg UK.......32 C2
La Iruela E.... 164 B2
Laissac F..... 130 A1
Laisvall S..... 195 D8
Láives I....... 121 A4
La Javie F..... 132 A2
Lajkovac SRB. 127 C2
La Jonchère-St Maurice F.... 116 A1
La Jonquera E. 146 B3
Łagiewniki PL...85 B4
Lajoskomárom H............. 112 C2
Lajosmizse H . 112 B3
Lak H...........99 C4
Lakenheath UK .45 A4
Laki BG...... 183 B6
Lakitelek H... 113 C4
Lakki GR..... 185 D4
Lakolk DK......64 A1
Łąkorz PL......69 B4
Lakšárska Nová Ves SK........98 C1
Lakselv N.... 193 B8
Laksfors N... 195 E4
Laktaši BIH... 124 C3
La Lantejuela E............. 162 A2
Lalapaşa TR .. 186 A1
L'Albagès E... 153 A4
Lalbenque F .. 129 B4
L'Alcúdia E... 159 B3
L'Aldea E..... 153 B4
Lalín E....... 140 B2
Lalinde F..... 129 B3
La Línea de la Concepción E............. 162 B2
Lalizolle F.... 116 A3
La Llacuna E .. 147 C2
Lalley F....... 118 C2
Lalling D.......95 C5
Lalm N....... 198 D6
La Londe-les-Maures F.... 132 B2
La Loupe F.....89 B4
La Louvière B ..79 B4
L'Alpe-d'Huez F............. 118 B3
La Luisiana E . 162 A2
Laluque F..... 128 C1
Lam D..........95 B5
La Machine F.. 104 C2
la Maddalena I............. 178 A3

Lama dei Peligni
  I 169 A4
Lamadrid E . . . 142 A2
Lamagistère F 129 B3
La Mailleraye-sur-
  Seine F 89 A4
La Malène F . . . 130 A2
Lama Mocogno
  I 135 A3
La Mamola E . . 163 B4
La Manresana dels
  Prats E 147 C2
Lamarche F . . . 105 A4
Lamarche-sur-
  Saône F 105 B4
Lamargelle F . . 105 B3
Lamarosa P 154 B2
Lamarque F . . 128 A2
Lamas P 148 B1
La Masadera
  E 145 C3
Lamas de Moaro
  P 140 B2
Lamastre F 117 C4
La Mata E 150 C3
La Mata de
  Ledesma E . . 149 A4
La Mata de
  Monteagudo
  E 142 B1
Lambach A 109 A4
Lamballe F 101 A3
Lamberhurst
  UK 45 B4
Lambesc F 131 B4
Lambia GR 184 B2
Lambley UK 37 B4
Lambourn UK . . . 44 B2
Lamego P 148 A2
La Meilleraye-de-
  Bretagne F . . . 101 B4
La Ménitré F . . 102 B1
L'Ametlla de Mar
  E 153 B4
Lamia GR 182 E4
Lammhult S . . . 62 A2
La Mojonera E 164 C2
La Mole F 132 B2
La Molina E . . . 147 B2
La Monnerie-le-
  Montel F 117 B3
La Morera E . . . 155 C4
La Mothe-Achard
  F 114 B2
Lamothe-Cassel
  F 129 B4
Lamothe-
  Montravel F . . 128 B3
La Mothe-St Héray
  F 115 B3
Lamotte-Beuvron
  F 103 B4
La Motte-
  Chalançon F . 131 A4
La Motte-du-Caire
  F 132 A2
La Motte-Servolex
  F 118 B2
Lampertheim D 93 B4
Lampeter UK . . . 39 B2
L'Ampolla de Mar E 153 B4
Lamprechtshausen
  A 109 B3
Lamsfeld D . . . 74 C3
Lamspringe D . . 72 C3
Lamstedt D . . . 72 A2
La Mudarra E . . 142 C2
La Muela E . . . 152 A2
La Mure F 118 C2
Lamure-sur-
  Azergues F . . . 117 A4
Lana I 108 C2
Lanaja E 145 C3
Lanarce F 117 C3
Lanark UK 36 A3
La Nava E 161 B3
La Nava de
  Ricomalillo E. 156 A3
La Nava de
  Santiago E . . . 155 B4
Lancaster UK . . 37 B4
Lanchester UK . 37 B5
Lanciano I 169 A4
Lancing UK 44 C3
Lançon-Provence
  F 131 B4
Lancova Vas
  SLO 124 A1
Landau
  Bayern D 95 C4
  Rheinland-Pfalz
  D 93 B4
Landeck A 108 B1

Landen B 79 B5
Landerneau F . . 100 A1
Landervd S . . . 60 D3
Landesbergen
  D 72 B2
Landete E 158 B2
Landévant F . . 100 B2
Landévennec
  F 100 A1
Landeyjahöfn
  . . . . 190 D5
Landivisiau F . 100 A1
Landivy F 88 B2
Landl A 108 B3
Landön S . . . 199 B11
Landos F 117 C3
Landouzy-le-Ville
  F 91 B4
Landquart CH. 107 C4
Landrecies F . . . 91 A3
Landreville F . . 104 A3
Landriano I . . . 120 B2
Landsberg D . . 108 A1
Lands-berg D . . 83 A4
Landsbro S . . . 62 A2
Landscheid D . . 92 B2
Landshut D . . . 95 C4
Landskrona S . . 61 D2
Landstuhl D . . . 93 B3
Lanesborough
  IRL 28 A4
Lanester F 100 B2
Lanestosa E . . . 143 A3
La Neuve-Lyre
  F 89 B4
La Neuveville
  CH 106 B2
Langå DK 59 B2
Langada GR . . 185 A7
Langadas GR . . 183 C5
Langa de Duero
  E 151 A4
Langadia GR . . 184 B3
Langangen N . . 53 A5
Långared S . . . 60 A2
Långaröd S . . . 61 D3
Långaryd S . . . 60 B3
Långås S 60 C2
Långasjö S 63 B3
Langau A 97 C3
Langeac F 117 B3
Langeais F 102 B2
Langedijk NL . . 70 B1
Langeln D 73 C3
Langelsheim D . 72 C3
Langemark-
  Poelkapelle B . 78 B2
Langen
  Hessen D 93 B4
  Niedersachsen
  D 72 A1
Langenau D . . . 94 C2
Langenberg D . 81 A4
Langenbruck
  CH 106 B2
Langenburg D . 94 B1
Längenfeld A . 108 B1
Langenfeld D . . 80 A2
Langenhorn D . 64 B1
Langenlois A . . 97 C3
Langenlonsheim
  D 93 B3
Langennaudorf
  D 83 A5
Langenneufnach
  D 94 C2
Langenthal
  CH 106 B2
Langenzenn D . 94 B2
Langeoog D . . . 71 A4
Langeskov DK . 59 C3
Langesund N . . 53 A5
Langewiesen D . 82 B2
Långflon S . . . 49 A4
Långförden D . . 71 B5
Langhagen D . . 73 A5
Länghem S . . . 60 B3
Langhirano I . . 120 C3
Langholm UK . . 36 A4
Langholt IS . . 191 D7
Langnau CH . . 106 C2
Langø DK 65 B4
Langogne F . . . 117 C3
Langon F 128 B2
Langquaid D . . 95 C4
Långrådna S . . 56 B2
Langreo E 142 A1
Langres F 105 B4
Långsele S . . . 200 C3
Långserud S . . 54 A3
Langset N 48 B3
Långshyttan S . 50 B3

Langstrand N . 192 B7
Långträsk S . . 196 D3
Langueux F . . . 101 A3
Languidic F . . . 100 B2
Längvik S 57 A4
Langwarden D . 71 A5
Langwathby
  UK 37 B5
Langwedel D . . 72 B2
Langweid D . . . 94 C2
Langwies CH . . 107 C4
Lanheses P . . . 148 A1
Lanięta PL 77 B4
Lanildut F . . . 100 A1
Lanjarón E . . . 163 B4
Lanmeur F . . . 100 A2
Lanna
  Jönköping S . . 60 B3
  Örebro S 55 A5
Lännaholm S . . 51 C4
Lannavaara S . 196 A4
Lannéanou F . 100 A2
Lannemezan
  F 145 A4
Lanneuville-sur-
  Meuse F 91 B5
Lannilis F 100 A1
Lannion F 100 A2
La Nocle-Maulaix
  F 104 C2
Lanouaille F . . 115 C5
Lansjärv S . . . 196 C5
Lanškroun CZ . 97 B4
Lanslebourg-Mont-
  Cenis F 119 B3
Lanta F 129 C4
Lantadilla E . . 142 B2
Lanton F 128 B1
Lantosque F . . 133 B3
La Nuez de Arriba
  E 143 B3
Lanusei I 179 C3
Lanúvio I 168 B2
Lanvollon F . . . 100 A3
Lánycsók H . . . 125 A4
Lanz D 73 A4
Lanza E 140 A2
Lanzada E 140 B2
Lanzahíta E . . 150 B3
Lanžhot CZ . . . 97 C4
Lanzo Torinese
  I 119 B4
Laole SRB 127 C3
Laon F 91 B3
Laons F 89 B5
La Paca E 164 B3
La Pacaudière
  F 117 A3
Lapalisse F . . . 117 A3
La Palma d'Ebre
  E 153 A4
La Palma del
  Condado E . . . 161 B3
La Palme F . . . 146 B4
La Palmyre F . . 114 C2
La Parra E 155 C4
Łapczyna Wola
  PL 87 B3
La Pedraja de
  Portillo E . . . 150 A3
La Peraleja E . . 152 B1
La Petit-Pierre
  F 93 C3
Lapeyrade F . . 128 B2
Lapeyrouse F . 116 A2
Lapford UK . . . 42 B3
La Pinilla E . . . 165 B3
Lapithos CY . . 181 A2
La Plagne F . . . 118 B3
La Plaza E 141 A4
Laplume F . . . 129 B3
La Pobla de Lillet
  E 147 B2
La Pobla de
  Vallbona E . . . 159 B3
La Pobla Llarga
  E 159 B3
La Pola de Gordón
  E 142 B1
la Porta F 180 A2
La Pouëze F . . 102 B1
La Póveda de Soria
  E 143 B4
Lapovo SRB . . 127 C3
Läppe S 56 A1
Lappeenranta
  FIN 8 B6
Lappoluobbal
  N 192 C7
Lappträsk S . . 196 C6
La Preste F . . . 146 B3
La Primaube F 130 A1

Lapseki TR 186 B1
Lapua FIN 8 A3
La Puebla de
  Almoradie E . 157 A4
La Puebla de
  Cazalla E 162 A2
La Puebla de los
  Infantes E . . . 162 A2
La Puebla del Río
  E 162 A1
La Puebla de
  Montalbán
  E 150 C3
La Puebla de Roda
  E 145 B4
La Puebla de
  Valdavia E . . . 142 B2
La Puebla de
  Valverde E . . . 152 B3
La Pueblanueva
  E 150 C3
La Puerta de
  Segura E 164 A2
La Punt CH . . . 107 C4
L'Áquila I 169 A3
La Quintana
  E 162 A3
La Quintera E . 162 A2
La Rábita
  Granada E . . . 164 C1
  Jaén E 163 A3
Laracha E 140 A2
Laragh IRL . . . 30 A2
Laragne-Montéglin
  F 132 A1
La Rambla E . . 163 A3
l'Arboç E 147 C2
L'Arbresle F . . 117 B4
Lärbro S 57 C4
Larceveau F . . 144 A2
Larche
  Alpes-de-Haute-
  Provence F . . 132 A2
  Corrèze F 129 A4
Lårdal N 53 A4
Lærdalsøyri N . 47 A4
Lardosa P 155 B3
La Reale I 178 A2
Laredo E 143 A3
La Redondela
  E 161 B2
La Réole F 128 B2
Largentière F . 131 A3
L'Argentière-la-
  Bessée F 118 C3
La Seca E 150 A3
La Selva del Camp
  E 147 C2
La Senia E 153 B4
La Serra E 147 C2
La Seu d'Urgell
  E 146 B2
La Seyne-sur-Mer
  F 132 B1
Lariño E 140 B1
Larino I 170 B2
Larisa GR 182 D4
La Rivière-
  Thibouville F . 89 A4
Larkhall UK . . . 36 A3
Larkollen N . . . 54 A1
Larmor-Plage
  F 100 B2
Larnaca CY . . . 181 B2
Larne UK 27 B5
La Robla E 142 B1
La Roca de la Sierra
  E 155 B4
La Roche CH . . 106 C2
La
  Rochebeaucourt-
  Argentine F . . 115 C4
La Roche-Bernard
  F 101 B3
La Roche-Canillac
  F 116 B1
La Roche-Chalais
  F 128 A3
La Roche Derrien
  F 100 A2
La Roche-des-
  Arnauds F . . . 132 A1
La Roche-en-
  Ardenne B 80 B1
La Roche-en-Brénil
  F 104 B3
La Rochefoucauld
  F 115 C4
La Roche-Guyon
  F 90 B1
La Rochelle F . . 114 B2
La Roche-Posay
  F 115 B4
La Roche-sur-Foron
  F 118 A3

La Roche-sur-Yon
  F 114 B2
Larochette L . . . 92 B2
La Rochette F . 131 A4
La Roda
  Albacete E . . . 158 B1
  Oviedo E 141 A4
La Roda de
  Andalucía E . . 162 A3
Laroquebrou
  F 116 C2
La Roquebrussanne
  F 132 B1
Laroque d'Olmes
  F 146 B2
La Roque-Gageac
  F 129 B4
La Roque-Ste
  Marguerite
  F 130 A2
Laroque-Timbaut
  F 129 B3
Larouco E 141 B3
Larraga E 144 B2
Larrau F 144 A3
Larrazet F 129 C4
Larsnes N 198 C2
La Rubia E 143 C4
Laruns F 145 A3
Larva E 164 B1
Larvik N 53 A6
La Sagrada E . . 149 B3
La Salceda E . . 151 A4
Lasalle F 131 A2
La Salle F 118 C3
la Salute di Livenza
  I 122 B1
La Salvetat-
  Peyralés F . . . 130 A1
La Salvetat-sur-
  Agout F 130 B1
Las Arenas E . . 142 A2
La Sarraz CH . . 105 C5
Lasarte E 144 A1
Låsby DK 59 B2
Las Cabezadas
  E 151 A4
Las Cabezas de San
  Juan E 162 B2
Las Correderas
  E 157 B4
Las Cuevas de
  Cañart E 153 B3
La Seca E 150 A3
La Selva del Camp
  E 147 C2
La Senia E 153 B4
La Serra E 147 C2
La Seu d'Urgell
  E 146 B2
La Seyne-sur-Mer
  F 132 B1
Las Gabias E . . 163 A4
Las Herencias
  E 150 C3
Las Herrerias
  E 161 B2
Łasin PL 69 B4
Lask PL 86 A3
Laska PL 68 B2
Łaskarzow PL . 87 A5
Łasko SLO . . . 123 A4
Laskowice PL . 76 A3
Las Labores E . 157 A4
Las Mesas E . . 158 B1
Las Minas E . . 164 A3
Las Navas E . . 163 A3
Las Navas de la
  Concepción
  E 156 C2
Las Navas del
  Marqués E . . . 150 B3
Las Navillas E . 157 A3
Las Negras E . 164 C3
La Solana E . . . 157 B4
La Souterraine
  F 116 A1
Las Pajanosas
  E 161 B3
Laspaules E . . 145 B4
Las Pedroñas
  E 158 B1
La Spézia I . . . 134 A2
Las Planes
  d'Hostoles E . 147 B3
Laspuña E . . . 145 B4
Las Rozas
  Cantabria E . 142 B2
  Madrid E 151 B4
Lassan D 66 C2
Lassay-les-
  Châteaux F . . 89 B3
Lasseube F . . . 145 A3

Lassigny F 90 B2
La Storta I 168 B2
Lastovo HR . . 138 C2
Lastras de Cuéllar
  E 151 A3
Lästringe S . . . 56 B3
Lastrup D 71 B4
Las Uces E . . . 149 A3
La Suze-sur-Sarthe
  F 102 B2
Las Veguillas
  E 149 B4
Las Ventas con
  Peña Aguilera
  E 157 A3
Las Ventas de San
  Julián E 150 B2
Las Villes E . . . 153 B4
Latasa E 144 B2
Látera I 168 A1
Laterza I 171 C4
La Teste F 128 B1
Lathen D 71 B4
Latheron UK . . 32 C3
La Thuile I 119 B3
Latiano I 173 B3
Latina I 169 B2
Latisana I 122 B2
Látky SK 99 C3
La Toba E 152 B2
La Toledana E . 157 A3
La Torre de
  Cabdella E . . 146 B1
La Torre de Esteban
  Hambrán E . . 151 B3
La Torre del
  l'Espanyol E . 153 A4
La Torresaviñán
  E 152 B1
La Tour d'Aigues
  F 132 B1
La Tour de Peilz
  CH 106 C1
La Tour-du-Pin
  F 118 B2
La Tranche-sur-Mer
  F 114 B2
La Tremblade
  F 114 C2
La Trimouille
  F 115 B5
La Trinité F . . . 101 B3
La Trinité-Porhoët
  F 101 A3
Latrónico I . . . 174 A2
Latronquière
  F 116 C2
Latterbach CH 106 C2
La Turballe F . . 101 B3
Laubach D 81 B4
Laubert F 117 C3
Laucha D 83 A3
Lauchhammer
  D 84 A1
Lauchheim D . 94 C2
Lauda-
  Königshofen
  D 94 B1
Laudal N 52 B3
Lauder UK 35 C5
Lauenau D . . . 72 B2
Lauenburg D . . 73 A3
Lauf D 95 B3
Laufach D 94 A1
Laufen
  CH 106 B2
  D 109 B3
Lauffen D 93 B5
Laugar IS 191 B8
Laugarás IS . . 190 C5
Laugarbakki
  IS 190 B5
Laugarvatn IS. 190 C5
Laugharne UK . 39 C2
Lauingen D . . . 94 C2
Laujar de Andarax
  E 164 C2
Laukaa FIN 8 A4
Lauker S 196 D2
Laukvik N 194 C5
La Uña E 142 A1
Launceston UK. 42 B2
La Unión E . . . 165 B4
Launois-sur-Vence
  F 91 B4
Laupheim D . . 94 C1
Lauragh IRL . . 29 C2
Laureana di
  Borrello I . . . 175 C2
Laurencekirk
  UK 35 B5
Laurencetown
  IRL 28 A3

Laurenzana I . . 172 B1
Lauria I 174 A1
Laurière F 116 A1
Laurieston UK . . 36 B2
Laurino I 172 B1
Lausanne CH . . 106 C1
Laussonne F . . 117 C4
Lauta D 84 A2
Lautenthal D . . 82 A2
Lauterach A . . 107 B4
Lauterbach D . . 81 B5
Lauterbrunnen
  CH 106 C2
Lauterecken D . 93 B3
Lauterhofen D . 95 B3
Lautrec F 130 B1
Lauvsnes N . . . 199 A7
Lauvvlk N 52 B2
Lauzerte F . . . 129 B4
Lauzès F 129 B4
Lauzun F 129 B3
Lavagna I 134 A2
Laval F 102 A1
La Vall d'Uixó
  E 159 B3
Lavamünd A . . 110 C1
Lavara GR 186 A1
Lavardac F . . . 129 B3
Lavaris P 148 B1
Lavarone I 121 B4
Lavau F 104 B1
Lavaur F 129 C4
La Vecilla de
  Curueño E . . . 142 B1
La Vega
  Asturias E . . . 141 A5
  Asturias E . . . 142 A1
  Cantabria E . . 142 A2
Lavelanet F . . . 146 B2
La Velilla E . . . 151 A4
La Velles E . . . 150 A2
Lavello I 172 A1
Lavelsloh D . . . 72 B1
Lavenham UK . . 45 A4
Laveno I 120 B1
La Ventosa E . . 152 B1
Lavezzola I . . . 135 A4
Laviano I 172 B1
La Victoria E . . 162 A3
La Vid E 151 A4
Lavik N 46 A2
La Vilavella E . 159 B3
La Vilella Baixa
  E 147 C1
La Villa de Don
  Fadrique E . . 157 A4
Lavilledieu F . . 131 A3
La Villedieu F . 115 B3
La Ville Dieu-du-
  Temple F 129 B4
Lavinio-Lido di
  Enea I 168 B2
Lavis I 121 A4
Lavit F 129 C3
Lavoncourt F . . 105 B4
Lavos P 148 B1
La Voulte-sur-
  Rhône F 117 C4
Lavoûte-Chilhac
  F 117 B3
Lavradio P . . . 154 C1
Lavre P 154 C2
Lavrio GR 185 B5
La Wantzenau
  F 93 C3
Lawers UK 35 B3
Ławy PL 75 B3
Laxå S 55 B5
Laxamýri IS . . 191 B8
Laxe E 140 A2
Laxey UK 36 B2
Laxford Bridge
  UK 32 C1
Laxhall S 55 B4
Laxsjö S 199 B11
Laxtjarn S 49 B6
Laxvik S 61 C2
Laxviken S . . 199 B11
La Yesa E 159 B3
Laza E 141 B3
Lazarevac
  SRB 127 C2
Lazarevo SRB . 126 B2
Lazise I 121 B3
Łaziska Grn. PL. 86 B2
Lazkao E 144 A1
Lázně Bělohrad
  CZ 84 B3
Lázně Bohdaneč
  CZ 97 A3

Lázně Kynžvart
CZ 95 A4
Lazonby UK 37 B4
La Zubia E 163 A4
Łazy PL 67 B5
Lazzaro I 175 D1
Lea UK 40 B3
Leadburn UK 35 C4
Leadhills UK 36 A3
Leap IRL 29 C2
Leatherhead
UK 44 B3
Łeba PL 68 A2
Lebach D 92 B2
Le Barcarès F . . 146 B4
Le Barp F 128 B2
Le Bar-sur-Loup
F 132 B2
Le Béage F . . . 117 C4
Le Beausset F . 132 B1
Lebekke B 79 A4
Lébény H 111 B4
Le Bessat F 117 B4
Le Blanc F 115 B5
Le Bleymard F . 130 A2
Łebno PL 68 A3
Leboreiro E . . . 140 B3
Lębork PL 68 A2
Le Boullay-Mivoye
F 89 B5
Le Boulou F . . . 146 B3
Le Bourg F 129 B4
Le Bourg-d'Oisans
F 118 B3
Le Bourget-du-Lac
F 118 B2
Le Bourgneuf-la-
Forêt F 101 A5
Le Bousquet d'Orb
F 130 B2
Le Brassus CH . 105 C5
Le Breuil F 117 A3
Le Breuil-en-Auge
F 89 A4
Lebrija E 162 B1
Lebring A 110 C2
Le Brusquet F . 132 A2
Le Bry CH 106 C2
Le Bugue F 129 B3
Le Buisson F . . . 129 B3
Lebus D 74 B3
Lebusa D 83 A5
Leca da Palmeira
P 148 A1
Le Caloy F 128 C2
Le Cap d'Agde
F 130 B2
Le Cateau
Cambrésis F . . .91 A3
Le Caylar F 130 B2
Le Cayrol F 116 C2
Lecce I 173 B4
Lecco I 120 B2
Lécera E 153 A3
Lećevica HR . . . 138 B2
Lech A 107 B5
Le Chambon-
Feugerolles
F 117 B4
Le Chambon-sur-
Lignon F . . . 117 B4
Le Château
d'Oléron F . . . 114 C2
Le Châtelard
F 118 B3
Le Châtelet F . . 103 C4
Le Chatelet-en-Brie
F 90 C2
Lechbruck D . . . 108 B1
Lechena GR . . . 184 B2
Le Chesne F 91 B4
Le Cheylard F . . 117 C4
Lechlade UK 44 B2
Lechovice CZ . . .97 C4
Leciñena E 145 C3
Leck D 64 B1
Le Collet-de-Deze
F 131 A2
Le Conquet F . . 100 A1
Le Creusot F . . . 104 C3
Le Croisic F 101 B3
Le Crotoy F 78 B1
Lectoure F 129 C3
Łęczyca
Łódzkie PL 77 B4
Zachodnio-
Pomorskie PL . 75 A4
Ledaña E 158 B2
Ledbury UK 39 B4
Lede B 79 B3

Ledečnad Sazavou
CZ 97 B3
Ledenice CZ 96 C2
Le Deschaux F 105 C4
Ledesma E . . . 149 A3
Lédignan F . . . 131 B3
Lédigos E 142 B2
Ledmore UK 32 C2
Lednice CZ 97 C4
Lednicke-Rovné
SK 98 B2
Le Donjon F . . . 117 A3
Le Dorat F 115 B5
Lędyczek PL 68 B1
Lędziny PL 86 B3
Leeds UK 40 B2
Leek
NL 71 A3
UK 40 B1
Leenaun IRL 28 A2
Leens NL 71 A3
Leer D 71 A4
Leerdam NL 79 A5
Leerhafe D 71 A4
Leese D 72 B2
Leeuwarden
NL 70 A2
Leezen D 64 C3
Le Faou F 100 A1
Le Faoüet F . . . 100 A2
Lefka CY 181 A1
Lefkada GR . . . 182 E2
Lefkimis GR . . . 182 D2
Lefkoniko CY . 181 A2
Le Folgoet F . . . 100 A1
Le Fossat F 146 A2
Le Fousseret
F 146 A2
Le Fugeret F . . 132 A2
Leganés E 151 B4
Legau D 107 B5
Le Gault-Soigny
F 91 C3
Legbąd PL 68 B2
Legé F 114 B2
Lège-Cap-Ferret
F 128 B1
Legionowo PL . .77 B5
Léglise B 92 B1
Legnago I 121 B4
Legnano I 120 B1
Legnaro I 121 B4
Legnica PL 85 A4
Łęgowo PL 69 A3
Legrad HR 124 A2
Le Grand-Bornand
F 118 B3
Le-Grand-Bourg
F 116 A1
Le Grand-Lucé
F 102 B2
Le Grand-Pressigny
F 102 C2
Le Grand-Quevilly
F 89 A5
Le Grau-du-Roi
F 131 B3
Léguevin F 129 C4
Legutiano E . . . 143 B4
Le Havre F 89 A4
Lehesten D 82 B3
Lehnice SK 111 A4
Lehnin D 74 B1
Le Hohwald F . .93 C3
Le Houga F . . . 128 C2
Lehrberg D 94 B2
Lehre D 73 B3
Lehrte D 72 B2
Lehsen D 73 A4
Leibnitz A 110 C2
Leicester UK 40 C2
Leiden NL 70 B1
Leidschendam
NL 70 B1
Leigh UK 38 A4
Leighlinbridge
IRL 30 B2
Leighton Buzzard
UK 44 B3
Leignon B 79 B5
Leikanger N . . . 198 C2
Leimen D 93 B4
Leinefelde D 82 A2
Leines fjord N . 194 C6
Leintwardine
UK 39 B4
Leipojärvi S . . . 196 B4
Leipzig D 83 A4
Leira
Nordland N . . 195 D4
Oppland N 47 B6
Leirâmoen N . . 195 D5
Leiria P 154 B2

Leirvassbu N 47 A5
Leirvik
Hordaland N . . 52 A1
Sogn og Fjordane
N 46 A2
Leisach A 109 C3
Leisnig D 83 A4
Leiston UK 45 A5
Leitholm UK 35 C5
Leitrim IRL 26 C2
Leitza E 144 A2
Leitzkau D 73 B4
Lejkowo PL 68 A1
Lekani GR 183 B6
Łękawa PL 86 A3
Lekeitio E 143 A4
Lekenik HR . . . 124 B2
Lekeryd S 62 A2
Leknes N 194 B4
Łęknica PL 84 A2
Leksand S 50 B1
Leksvik N 199 B7
Lekunberri E . . 144 A2
Lekvattnet S 49 B4
Le Lardin-St Lazare
F 129 A4
Le Lauzet-Ubaye
F 132 A2
Le Lavandou
F 132 B2
Le Lion-d'Angers
F 102 B1
Lelkowo PL 69 A5
Le Locle CH . . . 106 B1
Le Loroux-
Bottereau F . . 101 B4
Le Louroux-
Béconnais F . . 101 B5
Lelów PL 86 B3
Le Luc F 132 B2
Le Lude F 102 B2
Lelystad NL 70 B2
Lem
Ringkøbing
DK 59 B1
Viborg Amt.
DK 58 B1
Le Malzieu-Ville
F 116 C3
Le Mans F 102 A2
Le Mas-d'Azil
F 146 A2
Le Massegros
F 130 A2
Le Mayet-de-
Montagne F . . 117 A3
Le May-sur-Evre
F 101 B5
Lembach F 93 B3
Lemberg F 93 B3
Lembèye F 145 A3
Lemelerveld NL 71 B3
Le Mêle-sur-Sarthe
F 89 B4
Le Ménil F 105 A5
Le Merlerault F . .89 B4
Le Mesnil-sur-Oger
F 91 C4
Lemförde D 71 B5
Lemgo D 72 B1
Le Miroir F 105 C4
Lemland FIN 51 B7
Lemmer NL 70 B2
Le Molay-Littry
F 88 A3
Le Monastier-sur-
Gazeille F . . . 117 C3
Le Monêtier-les-
Bains F 118 C3
Le Mont-Dore
F 116 B2
Le Montet F . . . 116 A3
Le Mont-St Michel
F 88 B2
Lempdes F 116 B3
Le Muret F 128 B2
Le Muy F 132 B2
Lemvig DK 58 B1
Lemwerder D . . .72 A1
Lena E 48 B2
Lenart SLO . . . 110 C2
Lenauheim
RO 126 B2
Lencloître F . . . 102 C2
Lend A 109 B4
Lendalfoot UK . .36 A2
Lendava SLO . . 111 C3
Lendery RUS 3 E12
Lendinara I . . . 121 B4
Lendorf A 109 C4
Lendum DK 58 A3

Le Neubourg F . .89 A4
Lengefeld D 83 B5
Lengerich
Niedersachsen
D 71 B4
Nordrhein-
Westfalen D . . .71 B4
Lenggries D . . . 108 B2
Lengyeltóti H . 111 C4
Lenhovda S 62 B3
Lenk CH 106 C2
Lennartsfors S . .54 A2
Lennestadt D . . .81 A4
Lennoxtown
UK 35 C3
Leno I 120 B3
Lénola I 169 B3
Le Nouvion-en-
Thiérache F . . .91 A3
Lens
B 79 B3
F 78 B2
Lensahn D 65 B3
Lens Lestang
F 117 B5
Lensvik N 198 B6
Lentellais E . . . 141 B3
Lentföhrden D . .64 C2
Lenti I 111 C3
Lentini I 177 B3
Lenungshammar
S 54 A3
Lenzburg CH . . 106 B3
Lenzen D 73 A4
Lenzerheide
CH 107 C4
Leoben A 110 B2
Leogang A 109 B3
Leominster UK . .39 B4
León E 142 B1
Léon F 128 C1
Leonberg D 93 C5
Léoncel F 118 C2
Leonding A 96 C2
Leonessa I 169 A2
Leonforte I 177 B3
Leonidio GR . . . 184 B3
Leopoldsburg
B 79 A5
Leopoldsdorf im
Marchfeld A . . 111 A3
Leopoldshagen
D 74 A2
Leova MD 17 B8
Le Palais F 100 B2
Le Parcq F 78 B2
Lepe E 161 B2
Le Péage-de-
Roussillon F . . 117 B4
Le Pellerin F . . . 101 B4
Lepenou GR . . .182 E3
Le Perthus F . . 146 B3
Le Pertuis F . . . 117 B4
Le Petit-Bornand
F 118 B3
Lephin UK 31 B2
L'Épine F 132 A1
Le Poët F 132 A1
Lepoglava HR . 124 B2
Le Poirè-sur-Vie
F 114 B2
Le Pont CH 105 C5
Le Pont-de-
Montvert F . . 130 A2
Le Porge F 128 B1
Le Porge-Océan
F 128 B1
Le Portel F 78 B1
Le Pouldu F . . . 100 B2
Le Pouliguen
F 101 B3
Leppäjärvi
FIN 192 D7
Leppävirta FIN . . .8 A5
Leppin D 73 B4
le Prese I 120 A3
Lepsény H 112 C2
Le Puy-en-Velay
F 117 B3
Le Puy-Ste
Réparade F . . 131 B4
Le Quesnoy F . . .79 B3
Léquile I 173 B4
Le Rayol F 132 B2
Lercara Friddi
I 176 B2
Lerdal S 54 B2
Leré F 103 B4
Léric I 134 A2
Lerin E 144 B2
Lerma E 143 B3
Lerm-et-Musset
F 128 B2

Lermoos A 108 B1
Le Roeulx B 79 B4
Le Rouget F . . . 116 C2
Lérouville F 92 C1
Le Rozier F 130 A2
Le Russey F . . . 106 B1
Lervik N 54 A1
Lerwick UK 33 A5
Lés E 145 B4
Les Abrets F . . . 118 B2
Les Aix-d'Angillon
F 103 B4
Les Ancizes-Comps
F 116 B2
Les Andelys F . . .90 B1
Les Arcs
Savoie F 119 B3
Var F 132 B2
Les-Aubiers F . . 102 C1
Les Baux-de-
Provence F . . . 131 B3
Les Bézards F . . 103 B4
Les Bois CH . . . 106 B1
Les Bordes F . . 103 B4
Les Borges
Blanques E . . . 147 C1
Les Borges del
Camp E 147 C2
Les Brunettes
F 104 C2
Les Cabannes
CH 107 C4
**Les Contamines-
Montjoie** F . . . 118 B3
les Coves de
Vinroma E . . . 153 B4
Les Déserts F . . 118 B2
Les Deux-Alpes
F 118 C3
Les Diablerets
CH 119 A4
Lesdins F 90 B3
Les Echelles F . . 118 B2
Le Sel-de-Bretagne
F 101 B4
Les Escaldes
AND 146 B2
Les Essarts F . . 114 B2
Les Estables
F 117 C4
Les Eyzies-
de-Tayac F . . . 129 B4
Les Gets F 118 A3
Les Grandes-Ventes
F 89 A5
Les Haudères
CH 119 A4
Les Herbiers F . 114 B2
Les Hôpitaux-Neufs
F 105 C5
Lesično SLO . . . 123 A4
Lésina I 171 B3
Lesjaskog N . . . 198 C5
Lesjöfors S 49 C6
Leskovac SRB . . 16 D4
Leskova Dolina
SLO 123 B3
Leskovec
CZ 98 B1
SLO 123 B4
Leskovice CZ . . .97 B3
Leskovik AL . . . 182 C2
Leslie UK 35 B4
Les Lucs-sur-
Boulogne F . . 114 B2
Les Mages F . . . 131 A3
Lesmahagow
UK 36 A3
Les Mazures F . .91 B4
Les Mées F 132 A1
Lesmont F 91 C4
Les Mureaux F . .90 C1
Lesna PL 84 A3
Lesneven F 100 A1
Lešnica PL 86 B2
Lešnica SRB . . . 127 C1
Lesný
Wielkopolski
PL 75 C4
Lesnoye RUS 9 C9
Lesogo I 132 A1
Les Omergues
F 132 A1

Les Ormes-sur-
Voulzie F 90 C3
Les Orres F 132 A2
Le Souquet F . . 128 C1
Lesparre-Médoc
F 128 A2
l'Espérance F . . .91 B3
l'Esperou F 130 A2
Les Pieux F 88 A2
Lesponne F . . . 145 A4
Les Ponts-de-Cé
F 102 B2
Les Ponts-de-
Martel CH . . . 106 C1
Les Praz F 119 B3
L'Espunyola E . 147 B2
Les Riceys F . . . 104 B3
Les Roches F . . 117 B4
Les Rosaires F . 101 A3
Les Rosiers F . . 102 B1
Les Rousses F . 105 C5
Les Sables-
d'Olonne F . . 114 B2
Lessach A 109 B4
Lessay F 88 A2
Lessebo S 62 B3
Les Settons F . . 104 B3
Lessines B 79 B3
L'Estany E 147 C3
Les Ternes F . . . 116 B2
Lesterps F 115 B4
Les Thilliers en-
Vexin F 90 B1
Les Touches F . 101 B4
Les Trois Moûtiers
F 102 B2
L'Escala E 147 B4
Lescar F 145 A3
L'Escarène F . . 133 B3
Lesce SLO 123 A3
Lescheraines
F 118 B3
Leswalt UK 36 B1
Les Vans F 131 A3
Les Verrières
CH 105 C5
Les Vignes F . . 130 A2
Leszno
Mazowieckie
PL 77 B5
Wielkopolskie
PL 85 A4
Leszno Górne
PL 84 A3
Letchworth UK . .44 B3
Le Teil F 131 A3
Le Teilleul F 88 B3
Le Temple-de-
Bretagne F . . 101 B4
Letenye H 111 C3
Le Theil F 89 B4
Le Thillot F 106 B1
Letino I 170 B2
Letohrad CZ . . .97 A4
Le Touquet-Paris-
Plage F 78 B1
Le Touvet F . . . 118 B2
Letovice CZ 97 B4
Le Translay F 90 B1
Le Tréport F 90 A1
Letschin D 74 B3
Letterfrack IRL . .28 A2
Letterkenny
IRL 26 B3
Lettermacaward
IRL 26 B2
Lettoch UK 32 D3
Letur E 164 A2
Letux E 153 A3
Letzlingen D 73 B4
Leucate F 146 B4
Leuchars UK 35 B5
Leuglay F 105 B3
Leuk CH 119 A4
Leukerbad CH 119 A4
Leumrabhagh
UK 31 A2
Leuna D 83 A4
Leusden NL 70 B2
Leutenberg D . . .82 B3
Leuterschach
D 108 B1
Leutershausen
D 94 B2
Leutkirch D . . . 107 B5
Leuven B 79 B4
Leuze-en-Hainaut
B 79 B3
Le Val F 132 B2
Le Val-André
F 101 A3
Le Val-d'Ajol
F 105 B5
Levan AL 182 C1
Levanger N . . . 199 B8
Levanjska Varoš
HR 125 B4
Lévanto I 134 A2
Levaré F 88 B2

Levata I 120 B3
Leveld N 47 B5
Leven
East Yorkshire
UK 41 B3
Fife UK 35 B5
Leverano I 173 B3
Le Verdon-sur-Mer
F 114 C2
Leverkusen D . . .80 A2
Levern D 72 B1
Le Vernet F 132 A2
Levet F 103 C4
Levice SK 112 A2
Lévico Terme
I 121 A4
Levie F 180 B2
Levier F 105 C5
Le Vigan F 130 B2
Lévignen F 90 B2
le Ville I 135 B5
Levinovac HR . 124 B3
Le Vivier-
sur-Mer F 88 B2
Levoča SK 99 B4
Levroux F 103 C3
Lewes UK 45 C4
Lewin Brzeski
PL 85 B5
Lewisham UK . . .44 B3
Leyburn UK 37 B5
Leyland UK 38 A4
Leysdown-
on-Sea UK 45 B4
Leysin CH 119 A4
Lezajsk PL 12 C5
Lézardrieux F . . 100 A2
Lézat-sur-Léze
F 146 A2
Lezay F 115 B3
Lezhë AL 182 B1
Lézignan-
Corbières F . . 130 B1
Lezignan-la-Cèbe
F 130 B2
Ležimir SRB . . . 126 B1
Lézinnes F 104 B3
Lezoux F 117 B3
Lezuza E 158 C1
Lhenice CZ 96 C2
Lherm F 146 A2
Lhommaizé F . . 115 B4
L'Hospitalet F . 146 B2
L'Hospitalet de
l'Infant E 147 D1
L'Hospitalet de
Llobregat E . . 147 C3
L'Hospitalet-du-
Larzac F 130 B2
Lhuître F 91 C4
Liancourt F 90 B2
Liart F 91 B4
Liatorp S 63 B2
Liatrie UK 32 D2
Libáň CZ 84 B3
Libceves CZ 84 B1
Libčhov CZ 84 B2
Liber E 141 B3
Liberec CZ 84 B3
Libiąż PL 86 B3
Libina CZ 98 B1
Libochovice
CZ 84 B2
Libohovë AL . . 182 C2
Libourne F 128 B2
Libramont B 92 B1
Librazhd AL . . . 182 B2
Librilla E 165 B3
Libros E 152 B2
Licata I 176 B2
Licciana Nardi
I 134 A3
Licenza I 169 A2
Liceros E 151 A4
Lich D 81 B4
Lichères-près-
Aigremont F . 104 B2
Lichfield UK 40 C2
Lichtenau
A 97 C3
D 81 A4
Lichtenberg D . .83 B3
Lichtenfels D . . .82 B3
Lichtensteig
CH 107 B4
Lichtenstein D . .83 B4
Lichtenvoorde
NL 71 C3
Lichtervelde B . .78 A3
Lička Jesenica
HR 123 B4
Lickershamn S . .57 C4
Lički Osik HR . . 123 C4

Ličko Lešce
HR 123 C4
Licodía Eubéa
I. 177 B3
Licques F. 78 B1
Lida BY. 13 B6
Lidar N. 47 A6
Lidečko CZ. 98 B2
Liden S. 200 D2
Lidhult S 60 C3
Lidköping S. 55 B4
Lido I 122 B1
Lido Azzurro I. . . 173 B3
Lido degli Estensi
I. 122 C1
Lido degli Scacchi
I. 122 C1
Lido della Nazioni
I. 122 C1
Lido di Camaiore
I. 134 B3
**Lido di
Casalbordino**
I. 169 A4
**Lido di Castél
Fusano** I. 168 B2
Lido di Cincinnato
I. 168 B2
Lido di Classe
I. 135 A5
Lido di Fermo
I. 136 B2
Lido di Fondi I. 169 B3
Lido di Jésolo
I. 122 B1
Lido di Lícola
I. 170 C2
Lido di Metaponto
I. 174 A2
Lido di Óstia I. 168 B2
Lido di Policoro
I. 174 A2
Lido di Pomposa
I. 122 C1
Lido di Savio I. 135 A5
Lido di Scanzano
I. 174 A2
Lido di Siponto
I. 171 B3
Lido di Squillace
I. 175 C2
Lido di Volano
I. 122 C1
Lido Riccio I. . . 169 A4
Lidoriki GR. . . 184 A3
Lido Silvana I . 173 B3
Lidsjöberg S . 199 A12
Lidzbark PL 77 A4
**Lidzbark
Warmiński** PL . .69 A5
Liebenau
A. 96 C2
D. 72 B2
Liebenwalde D. .74 B2
Lieberose D. 74 C3
Liebling RO. . . 126 B3
Lieboch A. 110 C2
Liège B. 80 B1
Lieksa FIN. 3 E12
Lienen D 71 B4
Lienz A. 109 C3
Liepāja LV. 8 D2
Lier B 79 A4
Lierbyen N. 54 A1
Liernais F. 104 B3
Liesing A. 109 C3
Liestal CH. . . . 106 B2
Liétor E 158 C2
Lieurac F. 146 B2
Lieurey F. 89 A4
Liévin F 78 B2
Liezen A 110 B1
Liffol-le-Grand
F. 92 C1
Lifford IRL. 27 B3
Liffré F. 101 A4
Ligardes F . . . 129 B3
**Lignano
Sabbiadoro** I. 122 B2
Ligne F. 101 B4
Lignières F . . . 103 C4
Ligny-en-Barrois
F. 92 C1
Ligny-le-Châtel
F. 104 B2
Ligoła Polska
PL. 85 A5
Ligourio GR . . 184 B4
Ligowo PL. 77 B4
Ligueil F 102 B2
Likenäs S. 49 B5
Likhoslavl RUS . .9 D9

Liknes N 52 B2
Lild Strand DK . .58 A1
L'Île Bouchard
F 102 B2
l'Île-Rousse F . 180 A1
Linsell S 199 C10
Lilienfeld A . . . 110 A2
Lilienthal D 72 A1
Lilla Edet S 54 B3
Lilla Tjärby S 61 C3
Lille
B. 79 A4
F. 78 B3
Lillebonne F . . .89 A4
Lillehammer N. .48 A2
Lillerød DK. . . . 61 D2
Lillers F 78 B2
Lillesand N. 53 B4
Lillestrøm N . . .48 C3
Lillhärdal S . . 199 D11
Lillkyrka S 56 A3
Lillo E 157 A4
Lillögda S 200 B3
Lillpite S 196 D4
Lima S 49 B5
Limanowa PL . . .99 B4
Limassol CY. . . 181 B2
Limavady UK. . .27 A4
**Limbach-
Oberfrohna** D. .83 B4
Limbaži LV. 8 D4
Limbourg B 80 B1
Limburg D 81 B4
Lime DK. 58 B3
Limedsforsen S .49 B5
Limenaria GR . 183 C6
**Limenas
Chersonisou**
GR 185 D6
Limerick IRL. . . .29 B3
Limes I 121 B3
Limésy F 89 A4
Limmared S. 60 B3
Limni GR. 183 E5
Limoges F. . . . 115 C5
Limogne-en-Quercy
F. 129 B4
Limoise F 104 C2
Limone Piemonte
I. 133 A3
Limone sul Garda
I. 121 B3
Limons F. 117 B3
Limours F. 90 C2
Limoux F. 146 A3
Linares E. 157 B4
Linares de Mora
E. 153 B3
Linares de Riofrio
E. 149 B4
Linaria GR. . . . 183 E6
Linas de Broto
E. 145 B3
Lincoln UK 40 B3
Lind DK 59 B1
Lindås N 46 B2
Lindau D 107 B4
Lindberget N . . .48 A3
Lindelse DK. 65 B3
Lindenberg D . . .74 B3
**Lindenberg im
Allgäu** D 107 B4
Lindern D 71 B4
Linderöd S. 61 D3
Lindesberg S. . . .56 A1
Lindesnäs S. 50 B1
Lindholmen S. . . .57 A4
Lindknud DK. . . .59 C2
Lindlar D. 80 A3
Lindö S 56 B2
Lindome S 60 B2
Lindos GR. . . . 188 C3
Lindoso P 148 A1
Lindow D 74 B1
Lindsdal S 62 B4
Lindshammar
S. 62 A3
Lindstedt D 73 B4
Lindved DK. 59 C2
Líně CZ. 96 B1
Lingbo S 50 A3
Lingen D 71 B4
Linghed S 50 B2
Linghem S 56 B1
Linguaglossa
I. 177 B4
Linia PL 68 A2
Linie PL 74 A3
Liniewo PL. 68 A3
Linkenheim D. . .93 B4
Linköping S. 56 B1
Linksness UK. . .33 C3
Linlithgow UK . .35 C4

Linneryd S 63 B3
Linnes Hammarby
S. 51 C4
Linnich D 80 B2
Linsell S 199 C10
Linslade UK. 44 B3
Linthal CH . . . 107 C4
Linyola E. 147 C1
Linz
A. 96 C2
D. 80 B3
Liomseter N. 47 A6
Lionárisso CY . 181 A3
Lioni I. 172 B1
Lion-sur-Mer F . .89 A3
Lipany SK. 99 B4
Lipar SRB. 126 B1
Lipari I 177 A3
Lipcani MD. 17 A7
Liperi FIN 9 A6
Liphook UK. 44 B3
Lipiany PL 75 A3
Lipik HR. 124 B3
Lipka PL 68 B2
Lipki Wielkie
PL. 75 B4
Lipnica PL. 68 B2
Lipnica Murowana
PL. 99 B4
Lipnik PL. 87 B5
Lipník nad Bečvou
CZ 98 B1
Lipno
*Kujawsko-
Pomorskie* PL . .77 B4
Łódzkie PL 86 A2
Liposthey F . . . 128 B2
Lipovac HR. . . . 125 B5
Lipovec CZ. 97 B4
Lipovets UA. . . . 13 D8
Lipovljani HR . 124 B2
Lipowiec PL. 77 A6
Lipowina PL. 69 A4
Lippborg D 81 A4
Lippó H 125 B4
Lippoldsberg
D 81 A5
Lippstadt D 81 A4
Lipsko PL 87 A5
Liptál CZ. 98 B1
Liptovská-Lúžna
SK. 99 C3
Liptovská Osada
SK. 99 C3
Liptovská-Teplička
SK. 99 C4
Liptovský Hrádok
SK. 99 B3
Liptovský Milkuláš
SK. 99 B3
Lipusz PL 68 A2
Lipůvka CZ. 97 B4
Liré F. 101 B4
Lisac BIH 139 A3
Lisbellaw UK. . . .27 B3
Lisboa = Lisbon
P. 154 C1
Lisbon = Lisboa
P. 154 C1
Lisburn UK. 27 B4
Liscannor IRL. . . .28 B2
Lisdoonvarna
IRL. 28 A2
Lisewo PL. 69 B3
Lisia Góra PL. . . .87 B5
Lisięcice PL. 86 B1
Lisieux F 89 A4
Lisjö S 56 A2
Liskeard UK. 42 B2
L'Isle CH. 105 C5
L'Isle-Adam F . .90 B2
L'Isle-de-Noé
F. 129 C3
L'Isle-en-Dodon
F 145 A4
L'Isle-Jourdain
Gers F 129 C4
Vienne F 115 B4
L'Isle-sur-la-Sorgue
F. 131 B3
L'Isle-sur-le-Doubs
F 105 B5
L'Isle-sur-Serein
F 104 B3
Lisle-sur-Tarn
F 129 C4
Lismore IRL. . . .29 B4
Lisnaskea UK . . .27 B3
Lišov CZ. 96 B2
Lisów
Lubuskie PL. . . .74 B3
Śląskie PL. 86 B2
Lisse NL 70 B1

Lissycasey IRL. . .28 B2
List D 64 A1
Listerby S 63 B3
Listowel IRL. 29 B2
Liszki PL. 99 A3
Liszkowo PL. 76 A2
Lit S. 199 B11
Litava SK. 99 C3
Litcham UK. 41 C4
Lit-et-Mixe F . . 128 B1
Litija SLO. 123 A3
Litke H 112 A3
Litlabø N. 52 A1
Litochoro GR. . 182 C4
Litoměřice CZ. . .84 B2
Litomyšl CZ. 97 B4
Litovel CZ. 98 B1
Litschau A. 96 C3
Littlehampton
UK. 44 C3
Littleport UK. . .45 A4
Littleton IRL. 29 B4
Little Walsingham
UK. 41 C4
Litvinov CZ 83 B5
Livadero GR. . . 182 C3
Livadhia CY. . . 181 B2
Livadi GR 182 C4
Livadia GR 184 A3
Livarot F 89 A4
Liveras CY 181 A1
Livernon F 129 B4
Liverovici
MNE 139 C5
Liverpool UK. . .38 A4
Livigno I 107 C5
Livingston UK. . .35 C4
Livno BIH 138 B2
Livo FIN 197 D9
Livold SLO 123 B3
Livorno I 134 B3
Livorno Ferraris
I. 119 B5
Livron-sur-Drôme
F. 117 C4
Livry-Louvercy
F. 91 B4
Lixheim F 92 C3
Lixouri GR 184 A1
Lizard UK 42 C1
Lizy-sur-Ourcq
F. 90 B3
Lizzano I 173 B3
**Lizzano in
Belvedere** I . . 135 A3
Ljig SRB 127 C2
Ljørdalen N. . . .49 A4
Ljosland N. 52 B3
Ljubija BIH 124 C2
Ljubinje BIH. . . 139 C4
Ljubljana SLO. . 123 A3
Ljubno ob Savinji
SLO 123 A3
Ljubovija SRB. . 127 C1
Ljubuški BIH . . . 138 B3
Ljugarn S 57 C4
Ljung S 60 B3
Ljunga S 56 B2
Ljungaverk S . 200 D2
Ljungby S 60 C3
Ljungbyhed S. . . .61 C3
Ljungbyholm
S. 63 B4
Ljungdalen S . 199 C9
Ljungsarp S. 60 B3
Ljungsbro S. 56 B1
Ljungskile S 54 B2
Ljusdal S. 200 E2
Ljusfallshammar
S. 56 B1
Ljusne S 51 A4
Ljusterö S 57 A4
Ljutomer SLO. . 111 C3
Lüki BG 183 B6
Lladurs E 147 B2
Llafranc I 147 C4
Llagostera E . . . 147 C3
Llanaelhaiarn
UK. 38 B2
Llanarth UK . . .39 B2
Llanbedr UK . . .38 B2
Llanbedrog UK. .38 B2
Llanberis UK . . .38 A2
Llanbister UK . . .39 B3
Llanbrynmair
UK. 38 B2
Llançà E 146 B4
Llandeilo UK . . .39 C3
Llandissilio UK. .39 C2
Llandovery UK. .39 C3
Llandrillo UK . . .38 B3

Llandrindod Wells
UK. 39 B3
Llandudno UK. . .38 A3
Llandysul UK. . . .39 D2
Llanelli UK 39 C2
Llanerchymedd
UK. 38 A2
Llanes E. 142 A2
Llanfair Caereinion
UK. 38 B3
Llanfairfechan
UK. 38 A3
Llanfyllin UK. . . .38 B3
Llangadog UK. . .39 C3
Llangefni UK. . . .38 A2
Llangollen UK. . .38 B3
Llangrannog
UK. 39 B2
Llangurig UK. . . .39 B3
Llanidloes UK. . .39 B3
Llanilar UK. 39 B2
Llanrhystud UK.39 B2
Llanrwst UK. . . .38 A3
Llansannan UK. .38 A3
Llansawel UK. . .39 B2
Llanstephan
UK. 39 C2
Llanteno E. . . . 143 A3
Llanthony UK. . .39 C3
Llantrisant UK. .39 C3
Llantwit-Major
UK. 39 C3
Llanuwchllyn
UK. 38 B3
Llanwddyn UK. .38 B3
Llanwrda UK. . . .39 C3
Llanwrtyd Wells
UK. 39 B3
Llanybydder
UK. 39 B2
Llanymynech
UK. 38 B3
Llavorsi E. 146 B2
Lleida E. 153 A4
Llera E 156 B1
Llerena E. 156 B1
Lles E 146 B2
Llessui E 146 B2
Llinars E 147 B2
Lliria E 159 B3
Llivia E 146 B2
Llodio E. 143 A4
Lloret de Mar
E. 147 C3
Llosa de Ranes
E. 159 B3
Llucena del Cid
E. 153 B3
Llucmajor E. . . 167 B2
Llutxent E. . . . 159 C3
Llwyngwril UK. .38 B2
Llyswen UK. . . .39 B3
Lnáře CZ 96 B1
Lniano PL. 76 A3
Loanhead UK. . .35 C4
Loano I. 133 A4
Loarre E. 145 B3
Löbau D. 84 A2
Löbejün D. 83 A3
Löberöd S. 61 D3
Łobez PL. 75 A4
Löbnitz D. 66 B1
Lobón E. 155 C4
Loburg D 73 B5
Łobżenica PL. . .76 A2
Locana I. 119 B4
Locarno CH. . . 120 A1
Loccum D. 72 B2
Loče SLO. 123 A4
Lochailort UK. . .34 B2
Lochaline UK. . .34 B2
Lochans UK. . . .36 B1
Locharbriggs
UK. 36 A3
Lochau A. 107 B4
Loch Baghasdail
UK. 31 B1
Lochcarron UK. .31 B3
Lochearnhead
UK. 34 B3
Lochem NL. 71 B3
Loches F. 102 B2
Lochgelly UK. . .35 B4
Lochgilphead
UK. 34 B2
Lochgoilhead
UK. 34 B3
Lochinver UK. . .32 C1
Loch nam Madadh
UK. 31 B1
Lochranza UK. . .34 C2

Ločika SRB 127 D3
Lockenhaus A. 111 B3
Lockerbie UK . . .36 A3
Löcknitz D 74 A3
Locmaria F . . . 100 B2
Locmariaquer
F. 100 B3
Locminé F. . . . 100 B3
Locorotondo I 173 B3
Locquirec F . . . 100 A2
Locri I 175 C2
Locronan F. . . . 100 A1
Loctudy F 100 B1
Lodares de Osma
E. 151 A5
Lodé I 178 B3
Lodeinoye Pole
RUS 9 B8
Lodève F. 130 B2
Lodi I 120 B2
Lödöse S 54 B3
Łódź PL. 86 A3
Loeches E 151 B4
Løfallstrand N . .46 B3
Lofer A. 109 B3
Lofsdalen S . . 199 C10
Loftahammar S .62 A4
Lofthus N 46 B3
Loftus UK 37 B6
Loga N 52 B2
Logatec SLO . . . 123 B3
Lögdeå S 200 C5
Lograto I 120 B3
Logroño E. 143 B4
Logrosán E. . . . 156 A2
Løgstør DK. 58 B2
Løgumgårde
DK. 64 A1
Løgumkloster
DK. 64 A1
Lohals DK. 65 A3
Lohiniva FIN. . . 197 B8
Lohja FIN 8 B4
Löhlbach D 81 A4
Lohmen
*Mecklenburg-
Vorpommern*
D 65 C5
Sachsen D 84 B2
Löhnberg D 81 B4
Lohne D 71 B5
Löhne D 72 B1
Lohr D 94 B1
Lohra D 81 B4
Lohsa D 84 A2
Loiano I. 135 A4
Loimaa FIN. 8 B3
Lóiri I 178 B3
Loitz D 66 C2
Loivos E 148 A2
Loivos do Monte
P. 148 A2
Loja E 163 A3
Lojanice SRB . . 127 C1
Lojsta S 57 C4
Lokca SK. 99 B3
Lokeren B. 79 A3
Loket CZ. 83 B4
Lokka FIN 197 B10
Løkken
DK. 58 A2
N. 198 B6
Loknya RUS 9 D7
Lökosháza H. . 113 C5
Lokve SRB. . . . 126 B3
Lollar D 81 B4
L'Olleria E. . . . 159 C3
Lölling-Graben
A. 110 C1
Lom
BG. 17 D5
N. 198 D5
SK. 99 C3
Lombez F 146 A1
Lomello I. 120 B1
Łomianki PL . . .77 B5
Lomma S 61 D3
Lommaryd S. . . .62 A2
Lommatzsch D. .83 A5
Lommel B 79 A5
Lommersum D. .80 B2
**Lomnice nad
Lužnici** CZ. 96 B2
**Lomnice-nad-
Popelkou** CZ. . .84 B3

Lompolo FIN . . 196 A7
Łomża PL 12 B5
Lönashult S. 63 B2
Lønborg DK. 59 C1
Londerzeel B. . .79 A4
Londinières F . . .89 A5
London UK. 44 B3
Lonevåg N. 46 B2
Longa GR 184 C2
Longare I 121 B4
Longares E. . . . 152 A2
Longarone I . . . 121 A5
Longastrino I . 135 A5
Long Bennington
UK. 40 C3
Longbenton
UK. 37 A5
**Longchamp-sur-
Aujon** F 105 A3
Longchaumois
F. 118 A2
Long Eaton UK. .40 C2
Longeau F. . . . 105 B4
**Longecourt-en-
Plaine** F. 105 B4
**Longeville-les-St
Avold** F 92 B2
Longeville-sur-Mer
F. 114 B2
Longford IRL. . . .28 A4
Longframlington
UK. 37 A5
Longhope UK. . .33 C3
Longhorsley
UK. 37 A5
Longhoughton
UK. 37 A5
Longi I. 177 A3
Long Melford
UK. 45 A4
Longny-au-Perche
F. 89 B4
Longobucco I. 174 B2
Long Preston
UK. 40 A1
Longré F 115 B3
Longridge UK. . .38 A4
Longroiva P. . . 149 B2
Long Sutton
UK. 41 C4
Longtown
Cumbria UK . . . 36 A4
Herefordshire
UK. 39 C4
Longueau F. . . .90 B2
Longué-Jumelles
F. 102 B1
Longuyon F. . . .92 B1
Longvic F. 105 B4
Longvilly B. 92 A1
Longwy F. 92 B1
Lonigo I 121 B4
Löningen D 71 B4
Lonja HR 124 B2
Lönneberga S. .62 A3
Lönsboda S. 63 B2
Lønset N 198 C6
Lons-le-Saunier
F. 105 C4
Lønstrup DK . . .58 A2
Looe UK. 42 B2
Loone-Plage F .78 A2
Loon op Zand
NL. 79 A5
Loosdorf A. . . . 110 A2
Lo Pagán E. . . . 165 B4
Lopar HR. 123 C3
Lopare BIH. . . . 125 C4
Lopera E 157 C3
Lopigna F 180 A1
Loppersum NL. .71 A3
Łopuszna PL. . . .99 B4
Łopuszno PL. . . .87 B4
Lor F. 91 B4
Lora N. 198 C5
Lora de Estepa
E. 162 A3
Lora del Río E . 162 A2
Loranca del Campo
E. 151 B5
Lorbé E. 140 A2
Lörby S 63 B2
Lorca E. 164 B3
Lorch D 93 A3
Lørenfallet N . . .48 B3
Lørenskog N. . . .48 C2
Loreo I 122 B1
Loreto I 136 B2
Lorgues F. 132 B2
Lorica I 174 B2

Lorient F......100 B2
Lorignac F....114 C3
Lörinci H......112 B3
Loriol-sur-Drôme
F......117 C4
Lormes F......104 B2
Loro Ciuffenna
I.........135 B4
Lorqui E.......165 A3
Lörrach D.....106 B2
Lorrez-le-Bocage
F.........103 A4
Lorris F....103 B4
Lorup D......71 B4
Łoś PL......77 C5
Los S.........199 D12
Losacino E....149 A3
Los Alcázares
E.........165 B4
Los Arcos E....144 B1
Losar de la Vera
E.........150 B2
Los Barios de Luna
E.........141 B5
Los Barrios E.. 162 B2
Los Caños de Meca
E.........162 B1
Los Cerricos E. 164 B2
Los Corrales E. 162 A3
Los Corrales de
Buelna E.....142 A2
Los Dolores E.. 165 B3
Losenstein A.. 110 B1
Los Gallardos
E.........164 B3
Losheim
Nordrhein-
Westfalen D....80 B2
Saarland D....92 B2
Los Hinojosos
E.........158 B1
Los Isidros E... 159 B2
Los Molinos E. 151 B3
Los Morales E.. 162 A2
Los Navalmorales
E.........156 A3
Los Navalucillos
E.........156 A3
Losne F.....105 B4
Los Nietos E... 165 B4
Løsning DK....59 C2
Los Palacios y
Villafranca E. 162 A2
Los Pozuelos de
Calatrava E.. 157 B3
Los Rábanos
E.........143 C4
Los Santos E... 149 B4
Los Santos de la
Humosa E.. 151 B4
Los Santos de
Maimona E... 155 C4
Lossburg D....93 C4
Losse F.......128 B2
Losser NL......71 B4
Lossiemouth
UK......32 D3
Lössnitz D....83 B4
Loštice CZ......97 B4
Los Tijos E..... 142 A2
Lostwithiel UK. 42 B2
Los Villares E.. 163 A4
Los Yébenes E. 157 A4
Løten N......48 B3
Lotorp S......56 B1
Lottefors S....50 A3
Löttorp S......62 A5
Lotyń PL......68 B1
Lotzorai I...... 179 C3
Louargat F.... 100 A2
Loudéac F..... 101 A3
Loudun F......102 B2
Loué F.......102 B1
Loughborough
UK.........40 C2
Loughbrickland
UK.........27 B4
Loughrea IRL... 28 A3
Louhans F.....105 C4
Louisburgh IRL. 28 A2
Loukhi RUS....3 C13
Loulay F.....114 B3
Loulé P.......160 B1
Louny CZ......84 B1
Lourdes F.....145 A3
Lourenzá E....141 A3
Loures P.....154 C1
Loures-Barousse
F.........145 A4
Louriçal P.....154 A2

Lourinhã P....154 B1
Lourmarin F... 131 B4
Loury F......103 B4
Lousa
Bragança P... 149 A2
Castelo Branco
P.........155 B3
Lousã P.....148 B1
Lousa P.....154 C1
Lousada
P.........148 A1
Louth UK........41 B3
Loutra Edipsou
GR.........183 E5
Loutraki GR... 184 B3
Loutropoli Thermis
GR.........186 C1
Louverné F....102 A1
Louvie-Juzon
F.........145 A3
Louviers F......89 A5
Louvigné-du-
Désert F.......88 B2
Louvois F.......91 B4
Loval I........121 B5
Lovasberény
H.........112 B2
Lövåsen S......49 C5
Lovászpatona
H.........111 B4
Lövberga S....200 C1
Lövenich D....80 A2
Lovere I.......120 B3
Lövestad S....61 D3
Loviisa FIN......8 B5
Lovikka S....196 B5
Lovinobaña
SK.........99 C3
Loviste HR....138 B3
Lovke HR.....123 B3
Lovnäs S......49 A5
Lövö H.......111 B3
Lovosice CZ....84 B2
Lovozero RUS..3 C14
Lovran HR....123 B3
Lovreć HR.....138 B2
Lovrenc na Pohorju
SLO.........110 C2
Lovrin RO....126 B2
Lövstabruk S.. 51 B4
Löwenberg D.. 74 B2
Lowestoft UK.. 41 C5
Lowick UK.......37 A5
Łowicz PL......77 B4
Loxstedt D.....72 A1
Loyew BY....13 C9
Lož SLO......123 B3
Loza CZ......96 B1
Łozina PL......85 A5
Loznica SRB... 127 C1
Lozničko Polje
SRB.........127 C1
Lozorno SK.... 111 A4
Lozovik SRB... 127 C3
Lozoya E.....151 B4
Lozoyuela E... 151 B4
Lozzo di Cadore
I.........109 C3
Luanco E.....141 A5
Luarca E.....141 A4
Lubaczów PL.. 13 C5
Lubań PL......84 A3
Lubanie PL......76 B3
Lubanów PL....86 A3
Lubars D......73 B5
Lubasz PL.....75 B5
Lubawa PL.....69 B4
Lubawka PL.... 85 B4
Lübbecke D....72 B1
Lübben D......74 C2
Lübbenau D....84 A1
Lubczyna PL.. 74 A3
Lübeck D......65 C3
Lubenec CZ....83 B5
Lubersac F.... 115 C5
Lübesse D.....73 A4
Lubia E.......152 A1
Lubian E.......141 B4
Lubiatowo PL.. 75 A4
Lubichowo PL. 69 B3
Lubicz Dolny
PL.........76 A3
Lubień PL......99 B3
Lubienia PL....87 A5
Lubień Kujawski
PL.........77 B4
Lubieszewo PL. 75 A4
Lubin
Dolnośląskie
PL.........85 A4

Lubin continued
Zachodnio-
Pomorskie PL. 67 C3
Lublin.........12 C5
Lubliniec PL.....86 B2
Lubmin D......66 B2
Lubniewice PL . 75 B4
Lubochnia PL. 87 A4
Lubomierz
Dolnośląskie
PL.........84 A3
Małopolskie
PL.........99 B4
Lubomino PL.. 69 A5
Luboń PL......76 B1
Lubowidz PL.. 77 A4
Łubowo
Wielkopolskie
PL.........76 B2
Zachodnio-
Pomorskie PL.. 68 B1
Lubraniec PL.. 76 B3
Lubrin E......164 B2
Lubrza PL......85 B5
Lubsko PL......84 A2
Lübtheen D....73 A4
Lubuczewo PL. 68 A2
Luby CZ......83 B4
Lübz D.......73 A5
Luc F.........117 C3
Lucainena de las
Torres E.....164 B2
Lucan IRL......30 A2
Lučani SRB... 127 D2
Lúcar E......164 B2
Luçay-le-Mâle
F.........103 B3
Lucca I.......134 B3
Lucciana F... 180 A2
Lucé F.........90 C1
Luče SLO.....123 A3
Lucena
Córdoba E.... 163 A3
Huelva E... 161 B3
Lucenay-les-Aix
F.........104 C2
Lucenay-l'Evêque
F.........104 B3
Luc-en-Diois F 118 C2
Lučenec SK.....99 C3
Luceni E......144 C2
Lucens CH....106 C1
Lucera I......171 B3
Luceram F....133 B3
Luciana E.....157 B3
Lucignano I... 135 B4
Lucija SLO.... 122 B2
Lucka D.......83 A4
Luckau D......84 A1
Luckenwalde D. 74 B2
Lückstedt D....73 B4
Luco dei Marsi
I.........169 B3
Luçon F......114 B2
Luc-sur-Mer F.. 89 A3
Ludanice SK....98 C2
Ludbreg HR... 124 A2
Lüdenscheid D.. 81 A3
Lüderitz D.....73 B4
Lüdersdorf D.. 65 C3
Ludgershall UK. 44 B2
Ludgo S......56 B3
Lüdinghausen
D.........80 A3
Ludlow UK.....39 B4
Ludomy PL.....75 B5
Ludvika S......50 B2
Ludweiler Warndt
D.........92 B2
Ludwigsburg D. 94 C1
Ludwigsfelde D 74 B2
Ludwigshafen
D.........93 B4
Ludwigslust D .73 A4
Ludwigsstadt
D.........82 B3
Ludza LV......8 D5
Luesia E......144 B2
Luftkurort
Arendsee D 73 B4
Lug
BIH.........139 C4
HR.........125 B4
Luga RUS......9 C6
Lugagnano Val
d'Arda I......120 C2
Lugano CH.... 120 A1
Lugau D.......83 B4
Lugnas S......55 B4
Lúgnola I..... 168 A2
Lugny F......105 C3

Lugo
E.........140 A3
I.........135 A4
Lugoj RO......16 C4
Lugones E.....141 A5
Lugros E......163 A4
Luhačovice CZ. .98 B1
Luhe D........95 B4
Luino I.......120 B1
Luintra E.....140 B3
Lújar E......163 B4
Luka nad Jihlavou
CZ.........97 B3
Lukavac BIH... 125 C4
Lukavika BIH.. 125 C4
Lukovë AL.... 182 D1
Lukovica SLO . 123 A3
Lukovit BG......17 D6
Lukovo HR.... 123 C3
Lukovo Šugorje
HR.........137 A4
Łuków PL......12 C5
Łukowice Brzeskie
PL.........85 B5
Luksefjell N....53 A5
Łukta PL......69 B5
Lula I........178 B3
Luleå S......196 D5
Lüleburgaz
TR.........186 A2
Lumbarda HR. 138 C3
Lumbier E.....144 B2
Lumbrales E.. 149 B3
Lumbreras E.. 143 B4
Lumbres F.....78 B2
Lummelunda S .57 C4
Lummen B......79 B5
Lumparland
FIN.........51 B7
Lumpiaque E.. 152 A2
Lumsås DK......61 D1
Lumsden UK... 33 D4
Lumsheden S... 50 B3
Lun HR.......123 C3
Luna E.......144 B3
Lunamatrona
I.........179 C2
Lunano I......136 B1
Lunas F......130 B2
Lund
N.........199 A8
Skåne S......61 D3
Västra Götaland
S.........54 A3
Lundamo N... 199 B7
Lunde
DK.........59 C1
Sogn og Fjordane
N.........46 A3
Telemark N.. 53 A5
S.........200 D3
Lundebyvollen
N.........49 B4
Lunden D......64 B2
Lunderseter N .. 49 B4
Lunderskov DK. 59 C2
Lundsberg S... 55 A5
Lüneburg D....72 A3
Lunel F......131 B3
Lünen D......81 A3
Lunéville F.....92 C2
Lungern CH.. 106 C3
Lungro I......174 B2
Luninets BY....13 B7
Lünne D......71 B4
Lunner N......48 B2
Lunteren NL... 70 B2
Lunz am See
A.........110 B2
Luogosanto I. 178 A3
Łupawa PL.....68 A2
Lupión E......157 B4
Lupoglav HR.. 123 B3
Luppa D.......83 A4
Luque E......163 A3
Lurago d'Erba
I.........120 B2
Lúras I......178 B3
Lurcy-Lévis F.. 104 C1
Lure F......105 B5
Lurgan UK......27 B4
Luri F........180 A2
Lury-sur-Arnon
F.........103 B4
Lušci Palanka
BIH.........124 C2
Lüsevera I.... 122 A2
Lushnjë AL.... 182 C1
Lusignan F.... 115 B4
Lusigny-sur-Barse
F.........104 A3
Lusnić BIH.... 138 B2
Luso P......148 B1

Lusówko PL.....75 B5
Luspebryggan
S.........196 B2
Luss UK.......34 B3
Lussac F......128 B2
Lussac-les-
Châteaux F... 115 B4
Lussac-les-Eglises
F.........115 B5
Lussan F......131 A3
Lüssow D......65 C5
Lustenau A... 107 B4
Luštěnice CZ...84 B2
Luster N......47 A4
Lutago I......108 C2
Lutherstadt
Wittenberg D .83 A4
Lütjenburg D ...65 B3
Lutnes N......49 A4
Lutocin PL......77 B4
Lutomiersk PL. 86 A3
Luton UK......44 B3
Lutry CH.....106 C1
Lutter am
Barenberge D. .72 C3
Lutterworth UK 40 C2
Lututów PL......86 A2
Lützen D......83 A4
Lutzow D......73 A4
Luusua FIN... 197 C10
Luvos S......196 C1
Luxembourg L ..92 B2
Luxeuil-les-Bains
F.........105 B5
Luxey F......128 B2
Luz
Évora P......155 C3
Faro P......160 B1
Faro P........160 B2
Luzarches F.....90 B2
Luže CZ.......97 B4
Luzech F......129 B4
Luzino PL......68 A3
Luz-St Sauveur
F.........145 B3
Luzy F......104 C2
Lužy F.......174 B2
L'viv UA......13 D6
Lwówek PL.....75 B5
Lwówek Śląski
PL.........84 A3
Lyakhavichy BY 13 B7
Lybster UK......32 C3
Lychen D......74 A2
Lyckeby S.....63 B3
Lycksele S....200 B4
Lydd UK.......45 C4
Lydford UK.....42 B2
Lydney UK.....39 C4
Lyepyel BY....13 A8
Lygna S......48 B2
Lykkja N......47 B5
Lykling N......52 A1
Lyme Regis UK. 43 B4
Lymington UK. .44 C2
Lympne UK.....45 B5
Lyndhurst UK.. 44 C2
Lyneham UK... 43 A5
Lyness UK......33 C3
Lyngdal
Buskerud N .. 47 C6
Vest-Agder N.. 52 B3
Lyngør N......53 B5
Lyngsa DK.....58 A3
Lyngseidet N . 192 C4
Lyngsnes N... 199 A8
Lynmouth UK.. 42 A3
Lynton UK......42 A3
Lyntupy BY....13 A7
Lyon F......117 B4
Lyons-la-Forêt
F.........90 B1
Lyozna BY......13 A9
Lyrestad S.....55 B5
Lysánad Labem
CZ.........84 B2
Lysápod Makytou
SK.........98 B2
Lysebotn N....52 A2
Lysekil S......54 B2
Lysice CZ......97 B4
Lysomice PL.. 76 A3
Lysøysund N.. 198 B6
Lyss CH.....106 B2
Lystrup DK.....59 B3
Lysvik S......49 B5
Łyszkowice PL. .77 C4
Lytham St Anne's
UK.........38 A3

Lyubertsy RUS . . 9 E10
Lyubimets BG. 183 B8
Lyuboml' UA...13 C6
Lyubytino RUS... 9 C8

M

Maaninkavaara
FIN.........197 C11
Maarheeze NL..80 A1
Maaseik B......80 A1
Maastricht NL... 80 B1
Mablethorpe
UK.........41 B4
Mably F......117 A4
Macael E......164 B2
Maçanet de
Cabrenys E... 146 B3
Mação P......154 B2
Macau F......128 A2
Maccagno-Agra
I.........120 A1
Maccarese I... 168 B2
Macchiagódena
I.........170 B2
Macclesfield
UK.........40 B1
Macduff UK.... 33 D4
Maceda E......140 B3
Macedo de
Cavaleiros P . 149 A3
Maceira
Guarda P.... 148 B2
Leiria P......154 B2
Macelj HR.... 124 A1
Macerata I... 136 B2
Macerata Féltria
I.........136 B1
Machault F.....91 B4
Machecoul F.. 114 B2
Machrihanish
UK.........34 C2
Machynlleth
UK.........39 B3
Macieira P.... 148 A1
Maciejowice PL. 87 A5
Macinaggio F. 180 A2
Mackenrode D. 82 A2
Mačkovci SLO. 111 C3
Macomer I.... 178 B2
Macon B......91 A4
Mâcon F......117 A4
Macotera E.... 150 B2
Macroom IRL... 29 C3
Macugnaga I.. 119 B4
Madan BG... 183 B6
Madängsholm
S.........55 B4
Madaras H.... 126 A1
Maddaloni I... 170 B2
Made NL......79 A4
Madeley UK.... 38 B4
Maderuelo E.. 151 A4
Madetkoski
FIN.........197 B9
Madley UK.....39 B4
Madocsa H.... 112 C2
Madona LV......8 D5
Madonna di
Campiglio I. 121 A3
Madrid E......151 B4
Madridejos E.. 157 A4
Madrigal de las
Altas Torres
E.........150 A2
Madrigal de la Vera
E.........150 B2
Madrigalejo E. 156 A2
Madrigalejo de
Monte E...... 143 B3
Madriguera E. 151 A4
Madrigueras
E.........158 B2
Madroñera E.. 156 A2
Maël-Carhaix
F.........100 A2
Maella E......153 A4
Maello E......150 B3
Maesteg UK.... 39 C3
Mafra P......154 C1
Magacela E... 156 B2
Magallon E... 144 C2
Magaluf E.... 166 B2
Magán E......151 C4
Magaña E.... 144 C1
Magasa I......121 B3
Magaz E......142 C2
Magdeburg D... 73 B4
Magenta I.... 120 B1
Magescq F.... 128 C1
Maghera UK.... 27 B4
Magherafelt UK 27 B4

Maghull UK.....38 A4
Magilligan UK...27 A4
Magione I..... 135 B5
Magioto P.... 154 C1
Maglaj BIH.... 125 C4
Maglehem S ...63 C2
Magliano de'Marsi
I.........169 A3
Magliano in
Toscana I... 168 A1
Magliano Sabina
I.........168 A2
Maglić SRB... 126 B1
Máglie I......173 B4
Maglód H.... 112 B3
Magnac-Bourg
F.........115 C5
Magnac-Laval
F.........115 B5
Magnieres F ... 92 C2
Magnor N......49 C4
Magnuszew PL. .87 A5
Magny-Cours
F.........104 C2
Magny-en-Vexin
F.........90 B1
Mágocs H.... 125 A4
Maguilla E.... 156 B2
Maguiresbridge
UK.........27 B3
Magyarbóly
H.........125 B4
Magyarkeszi
H.........112 C2
Magyarszék
H.........125 A4
Mahide E.... 141 C4
Mahilyow BY....13 B9
Mahmudiye
TR.........187 C5
Mahora E..... 158 B2
Mahovo HR... 124 B2
Mähring D......95 B4
Maia
E.........144 A2
P.........148 A1
Maiaelrayo E.. 151 A4
Maials E...... 153 A4
Maîche F......106 B1
Máida I......175 C2
Maiden Bradley
UK.........43 A4
Maidenhead
UK.........44 B3
Maiden Newton
UK.........43 B4
Maidstone UK...45 B4
Maienfeld CH. 107 B4
Maignelay
Montigny F... 90 B2
Maijanen FIN . 197 B8
Maillezais F... 114 B3
Mailly-le-Camp
F.........91 C4
Mailly-le-Château
F.........104 B2
Mainar E..... 152 A2
Mainbernheim
D.........94 B2
Mainburg D....95 C3
Mainhardt D....94 B1
Maintal D......81 B4
Maintenon F....90 C1
Mainvilliers F ...90 C1
Mainz D......93 A4
Maiorca P.... 148 B1
Mairena de Aljarafe
E.........162 A1
Mairena del Alcor
E.........162 A2
Maisach D.... 108 A2
Maishofen A.. 109 B3
Maison-Rouge
F.........90 C3
Maissau A......97 C3
Maisse F......90 C2
Maizières-lès-Vic
F.........92 C2
Maja HR..... 124 B2
Majadahonda
E.........151 B4
Majadas E.... 150 C2
Majavatn N 195 E4
Majs H.......125 B4
Majšperk SLO. 123 A4
Makarska HR.. 138 B3
Makkum NL... 70 A2
Maklár H...... 113 B4
Makó H...... 126 A2
Makoszyce PL.. 85 B5
Makov SK......98 B2
Mąkowarsko
PL.........76 A2

Maków Mazowiecki PL.............77 B6
Maków Podhalański PL.............99 B3
Makrakomi GR.........182 E4
Maksniemi FIN..........196 D7
Malá S.........195 E9
Mala Bosna SRB.........126 A1
Malacky SK.....97 C5
Maladzyechna BY.............13 A7
Málaga E......163 B3
Malagón E....157 A4
Malaguilla E..151 B4
Malahide IRL....30 A2
Mala Kladuša BIH.........124 B1
Mala Krsna SRB.........127 C3
Malalbergo I..121 C4
Malá Lehota SK..98 C2
Malanów PL...76 C3
Mala Pijace SRB.........126 A1
Mala Subotica HR.........124 A2
Malaucène F..131 A4
Malaunay F.....89 A5
Malaya Vishera RUS.............9 C8
Malborghetto I.............109 C4
Malbork PL.....69 A4
Malborn D.....92 B2
Malbuisson F..105 C5
Malcésine I....121 B3
Malchin D......74 A1
Malching D.....96 C1
Malchow D.....73 A5
Malcocinado E.............156 B2
Malczyce PL....85 A4
Maldegem B....79 A3
Maldon UK.....45 B4
Małdyty PL.....69 B4
Malè I.........121 B3
Malemort F...129 A4
Malente D......65 B3
Målerås S......62 B3
Males GR......185 D6
Malesherbes F..90 C2
Malesina GR...183 E5
Malestroit F...101 B3
Maletto I......177 B3
Malexander S...56 B1
Malgrat de Mar E.............147 C3
Malhadas P...149 A3
Malia CY.........181 B1
GR.........185 D6
Malicorne-sur-Sarthe F......102 B1
Malijai F......132 A2
Malildjoš SRB.126 B1
Målilla S......62 A3
Mali Lošinj HR.........137 A3
Malin IRL......27 A3
Málinec SK.....99 C5
Malingsbo S...50 C2
Maliniec PL.....76 B3
Malinska HR...123 B3
Maliq AL.....182 C2
Maljevac HR..123 B4
Malkara TR...186 B1
Małki PL.......69 B4
Malko Tarnovo BG............17 D7
Mallaig UK......34 A2
Mallaranny IRL..28 A2
Mallemort F..131 B4
Mallén E......144 C2
Malléon F....146 A2
Mallersdorf-Pfaffenberg D..95 C4
Málles Venosta I.............108 C1
Malling DK......59 B3
Mallnitz A.....109 C4
Mallow IRL......29 B3
Mallwyd UK.....38 B3
Malm N........199 A8
Malmbäck S.....62 A2
Malmberget S.196 B3
Malmby S......56 A3
Malmédy B......80 B2
Malmesbury UK.....43 A4

Malmköping S..56 A2
Malmö S.......61 D3
Malmon S......54 B2
Malmslätt S.....56 B1
Malnate I......120 B1
Malo I.........121 B4
Małogoszcz PL..87 B4
Maloja CH......120 A2
Małomice PL...84 A3
Måløy N.......198 D2
Malpartida E...155 B4
Malpartida de la Serena E.....156 B2
Malpartida de Plasencia E...150 C1
Malpas E.............145 B4
UK..........38 A4
Malpica P......155 B3
Malpica de Bergantiños E.............140 A2
Malpica de Tajo E.............150 C3
Malsch D.......93 C4
Malšice CZ......96 B2
Malta A.......109 C4
Maltat F.......104 C2
Maltby UK......40 B2
Malung S......49 B5
Malungsfors S..49 B5
Maluszów PL...75 B4
Maluszyn PL....87 B3
Malva E.......142 C1
Malvaglia CH..120 A1
Malveira P....154 C1
Malvik N......199 B7
Malyn UA......13 C8
Mamarrosa P..148 B1
Mamer L......92 B2
Mamers F......89 B4
Mamirolle F...105 B5
Mammendorf D.............108 A2
Mámmola I...175 C2
Mamoiada I...178 B3
Mamonovo RUS............69 A4
Mamuras AL...182 B1
Maňa SK......112 A2
Manacor E....167 B3
Manavgat TR..189 C6
Mancera de Abajo E.............150 B2
Mancha Real E.............163 A4
Manchester UK............40 B1
Manching D.....95 C3
Manchita E....156 B1
Manciano I....168 A1
Manciet F.....128 C3
Mandal N......52 B3
Mandanici I...177 A4
Mándas I......179 C3
Mandatoríccio I.............174 B2
Mandayona E..151 B5
Mandelieu-la-Napoule F....132 B2
Mandello del Lário I.............120 B2
Mandelsloh D...72 B2
Manderfeld B...80 B2
Manderscheid D.............80 B2
Mandino Selo BIH............138 B3
Mandoudi GR..183 E5
Mandra GR....185 A4
Mandraki GR..188 C2
Mandúria I....173 B3
Mane
Alpes-de-Haute-Provence F...132 B1
Haute-Garonne F.............145 A4
Manérbio I....120 B3
Mañeru E....144 B2
Manetin CZ.....96 B1
Manfredónia I.............171 B3
Mangalia RO...17 D8
Manganeses de la Lampreana E.............149 A4
Manganeses de la Polvorosa E..141 B5
Mangen N.....48 C3
Manger N......46 B2
Mangiennes F..92 B1
Mangotsfield UK............43 A4

Mångsbodarna S.............49 A5
Mangualde P..148 D2
Maniago I.....122 A1
Manilva E.....162 B2
Manisa TR.....186 D2
Manises E......159 B3
Mank A.......110 A2
Månkarbo S....51 B4
Manlleu E.....147 C3
Manna DK......58 A2
Männedorf CH.............107 B3
Mannersdorf am Leithagebirge A.............111 B3
Mannheim D....93 B4
Manningtree UK............45 B5
Manoppello I..169 A4
Manorbier UK..39 C2
Manorhamilton IRL............26 B2
Manosque F...132 B1
Manowo PL.....67 B5
Manresa E....147 C2
Månsarp S.....62 A2
Månsåsen S..199 B11
Manschnow D..74 B3
Mansfeld D....82 A3
Mansfield UK...40 B2
Mansilla de Burgos E.............143 B3
Mansilla de las Mulas E......142 B1
Manskog S.....55 A3
Mansle F......115 C4
Manso F......180 A1
Manteigas P...148 B2
Mantel D.......95 B4
Mantes-la-Jolie F.............90 C1
Mantes-la-Ville F.............90 C1
Manthelan F...102 B2
Mantorp S......56 B1
Mántova I.....121 B3
Mänttä FIN......8 A4
Mäntyjärvi FIN......197 C10
Manuel E......159 B3
Manyas TR....186 B2
Manzanal de Arriba E.............141 B4
Manzanares E..157 A4
Manzanares el Real E.............151 B4
Manzaneda
León E......141 B4
Orense E....141 B3
Manzanedo E..143 B3
Manzaneque E.............157 A4
Manzanera E..153 B3
Manzanilla E..161 B3
Manzat F......116 B2
Manziana I....168 A2
Manziat F......117 A4
Maó E........167 B4
Maoča BIH....125 C4
Maqueda E....150 B3
Mara E........152 A2
Maramaereğlisi TR.............186 B2
Maraña E.....142 A1
Maranchón E..152 A1
Maranello I...135 A3
Marano I......170 C2
Marano Lagunare I.............122 B2
Marans F.....114 B2
Marateca P...154 C2
Marathokambos GR.............188 B1
Marathonas GR.............185 A4
Marathóvouno CY............181 A2
Marazion UK....42 B1
Marbach
Baden-Württemberg D.............94 C1
Hessen D......82 B1
F..........92 C2
Marbäck S.....60 B3
Mårbacka S....55 A4
Marbella E....162 B3
Marboz F.....118 A2
Marburg D......81 B4
Marcali H.....111 C4
Marčana HR...122 C2

Marcaria I.....121 B3
Marcelová SK..112 B2
Marcenat F...116 B2
March UK......41 C4
Marchamalo E.151 B4
Marchaux F...105 B5
Marche-en-Famenne B.....79 B5
Marchegg A....111 A3
Marchena E...162 A2
Marchenoir F..103 B3
Marcheprime F.............128 B2
Marciac F.....128 C3
Marciana Marina I.............134 C3
Marcianise I...170 B2
Marcigny F....117 A4
Marcilla E.....144 B2
Marcillac-la-Croisille F.....116 B2
Marcillac-Vallon F.............130 A1
Marcillat-en-Combraille F.116 A2
Marcille-sur-Seine F...........91 C3
Marcilloles F...118 B2
Marcilly-le-Hayer F...........91 C3
Marcinkowice PL.............75 A5
Marciszów PL...85 B4
Marck F.........78 B1
Marckolsheim F.............106 A2
Marco de Canevezes P.148 A1
Mårdsele S....200 B5
Mårdsjö S....200 C1
Mareham le Fen UK............41 B3
Marek S.......62 A3
Marennes F...114 C2
Maresquel F...78 B1
Mareuil F....115 C4
Mareuil-en-Brie F...........91 C3
Mareuil-sur-Arnon F...........103 C4
Mareuil-sur-Lay F.............114 B2
Mareuil-sur-Ourcq F...........90 B3
Margam UK....39 C3
Margariti GR..182 D2
Margate UK....45 B5
Margaux F....128 A2
Margerie-Hancourt F...........91 C4
Margès F......117 B5
Margherita di Savóia I......171 B4
Margita SRB...126 B3
Margone I.....119 B4
Margonin PL...76 B2
Marguerittes F.............131 B3
Margut F.......91 B5
Maria E.......164 B2
Mariager DK...58 B2
Mariana E.....152 B1
Maria Neustift A.............110 B1
Mariannelund S.............62 A3
Marianópoli I..176 B2
Mariánské Lázně CZ............95 B4
Mariapfarr A...109 B4
Maria Saal A..110 C1
Mariazell A...110 B2
Maribo DK.....65 B4
Maribor SLO...110 C2
Marieberg S...56 A1
Mariefred S...56 A3
Mariehamn FIN.51 B6
Marieholm S...61 D3
Mariembourg B.............91 A4
Marienbaum D..80 A2
Marienberg D...83 B5
Marienheide D..81 A3
Mariental D....73 B3
Mariestad S...55 B4
Marieux F.....90 A2
Marigliano I...170 C2
Marignane F..131 B4
Marigny
Jura F........105 C4
Manche F......88 A2
Marigny-le-Châtel F...........91 C3

Marija Bistrica HR...........124 A2
Marijampolė LT............13 A5
Marín E......140 B2
Marina HR....138 B2
Marina del Cantone I.............170 C2
Marina di Acquappesa I.............174 B1
Marina di Alberese I.............168 A1
Marina di Amendolara I.............174 B2
Marina di Árbus I.............179 C2
Marina di Campo I.............134 C3
Marina di Carrara I.............134 A3
Marina di Castagneto-Donorático I.134 B3
Marina di Cécina I.............134 B3
Marina di Gáiro I.............179 C3
Marina di Ginosa I.............173 B2
Marina di Gioiosa Iónica I.....175 C2
Marina di Grosseto I.............135 C3
Marina di Léuca I.............173 C4
Marina di Massa I.............134 A3
Marina di Nováglie I.............173 C4
Marina di Pisa I.............134 B3
Marina di Ragusa I.............177 C3
Marina di Ravenna I.............135 A5
Marina di Torre Grande I.....179 C2
Marinaleda E.162 A3
Marina Romea I.............135 A5
Marine de Sisco F.............180 A2
Marinella I....176 B1
Marinella di Sarzana I.....134 A3
Marineo I.....176 B2
Marines F......90 B1
Maringues F...116 B3
Marinha das Ondas P.............154 A2
Marinha Grande P.............154 B2
Marinhas P...148 A1
Marino I......168 B2
Marjaliza E...157 A4
Markabygd N..199 B8
Markaryd S....61 C3
Markdorf D....107 B4
Markelo NL....71 B3
Market Deeping UK............40 C3
Market Drayton UK............38 B4
Market Harborough UK............40 C3
Markethill UK...27 B4
Market Rasen UK............40 B3
Market Warsop UK............40 B2
Market Weighton UK............40 B3
Markgröningen D.............93 C5
Markhausen D..71 B4
Marki PL......77 B6
Markina-Xemein E.............143 A4
Markinch UK...35 B4
Märkische Buchholz D...74 B2
Markitta S.....196 B4
Markkleeberg D.............83 A4
Marklohe D....72 B2
Marknesse NL..70 B2
Markneukirchen D.............83 B4
Markopoulo GR............185 B4

Markovac
Srbija SRB....127 C3
Vojvodina SRB.........126 B3
Markowice PL...86 B2
Markranstädt D.............83 A4
Marksuhl D.....82 B2
Markt Allhau A.............111 B3
Markt Bibart D..94 B2
Marktbreit D....94 B2
Markt Erlbach D.............94 B2
Markt-heidenfeld D.............94 B1
Markt Indersdorf D.............95 C3
Marktl D.......95 C4
Marktleuthen D.............83 B3
Marktoberdorf D.............108 B1
Marktredwitz D.............95 A4
Markt Rettenbach D.............108 B1
Markt Schwaben D.............108 A2
Markt-Übelbach A.............110 B2
Markusica HR..125 B4
Markušovce SK..99 C4
Marl D..........80 A3
Marlborough
Devon UK.......42 B3
Wiltshire UK....44 B2
Marle F.........91 B3
Marlieux F....117 A5
Marlow
D..........66 B1
UK............44 B3
Marma S......51 B4
Marmagne F..104 C3
Marmande F..128 B3
Marmara TR...186 B2
Marmaris TR..188 C3
Marmelete P..160 B1
Marmolejo E...157 B3
Marmoutier F..93 C3
Marnay F.....105 B4
Marne D.......64 C2
Marnheim D...93 B4
Marnitz D......73 A4
Maroldsweisach D.............82 B2
Marolles-les-Braults F.......89 B4
Maromme F.....89 A5
Marone I......120 B3
Maronia GR...183 C7
Maroslele H...126 A2
Maróstica I...121 B4
Marotta I......136 B2
Marpisa GR...185 B6
Marquion F....78 B3
Marquise F....78 B1
Marradi I......135 A4
Marrasjärvi FIN.............197 C8
Marraskoski FIN.............197 C8
Marratxi E....166 B2
Marrúbiu I....179 C2
Marrum NL....70 A2
Marrupe E....150 B3
Marsac F.....129 C5
Marsac-en-Livradois F...117 B3
Marságlia I...120 C2
Marsala I......176 B1
Marsberg D....81 A4
Marsciano I...135 C5
Marseillan F...130 B2
Marseille = Marseilles F...131 B4
Marseille en Beauvaisis F...90 B1
Marseilles = Marseille F...131 B4
Mársico Nuovo I.............172 B1
Marske-by-the-Sea UK............37 B5
Mars-la-Tours F.92 B1
Marslet DK....58 B3
Marsliden S..195 E6
Marson F......91 C4
Märsta S......57 A3
Marstal DK....65 B3
Marstrand S...60 B1
Marta I......168 A1
Martano I....173 B4
Martel F.....129 B4

Martelange B...92 B1
Martfeld D......72 B2
Martfű H......113 B4
Martham UK...41 C5
Marthon F....115 C4
Martiago E...149 B3
Martigné-Briand F.............102 B1
Martigné-Ferchaud F.............101 B4
Martigne-sur-Mayenne F...102 A1
Martigny CH...119 A4
Martigny-les-Bains F.............105 A4
Martigues F...131 B4
Martim-Longo P.............160 B2
Martin SK.......98 B2
Martina CH...108 C1
Martina Franca I.............173 B3
Martinamor E.150 B2
Martin de la Jara E.............162 A3
Martinengo I..120 B2
Martin Muñoz de las Posadas E.............150 A3
Martinsberg A..97 C3
Martinšćica HR.............123 C3
Martinshöhe D..93 B3
Martinsicuro I.136 C2
Martinszell D..107 B5
Mártis I.......178 B2
Martofte DK....59 C3
Martonvásár H.............112 B2
Martorell E...147 C2
Martos E......163 A4
Martres Tolosane F.............146 A1
Martti FIN....197 B11
Marugán E....150 B3
Marúggio I...173 B3
Marvão P.....155 B3
Marvejols F...130 A2
Marville F......92 B1
Marwałd PL....77 B4
Marykirk UK...35 B5
Marypark UK...32 D3
Maryport UK...36 B3
Marytavy UK....42 B2
Marzabotto I..135 A4
Marzahna D....74 C1
Marzahne D....73 B5
Marzamemi I...177 C4
Marzocca I....136 B2
Masa E.......143 B3
Mas-Cabardès F.............146 A3
Máscali I......177 B4
Mascaraque E.157 A4
Mascarenhas P.............149 A2
Mascioni I....169 A3
Mas de Barberáns E.............153 B4
Mas de las Matas E.............153 B3
Masegoso E...158 C1
Masegoso de Tajuña E......151 B5
Masera I......119 A5
Masevaux F...106 B1
Masfjorden N...46 B2
Masham UK....37 B5
Masi N.......192 C7
Maside E.....140 B2
Maslacq F....144 A3
Maslinica HR..138 B2
Maşloc RO....126 B3
Maslovare BIH.138 A3
Masone I......133 A4
Massa I......134 A3
Massa Fiscáglia I.............121 C5
Massafra I....173 B3
Massa Lombarda I.............135 A4
Massa Lubrense I.............170 C2
Massamagrell E.............159 B3
Massa Maríttima I.............135 B3
Massa Martana I.............136 C1
Massanassa E.159 B3

Massarosa I... 134 B3
Massat F...... 146 B2
Massay F...... 103 B3
Massbach D....82 B2
Masseret F... 116 B1
Masseube F... 145 A4
Massiac F...... 116 B3
Massignac F... 115 C4
Massing D...... 95 C4
Massmechelen
  B............80 B1
Masterud N.....49 B4
Mästocka S.....61 C3
Masty BY.......13 B6
Masúa I....... 179 C2
Masueco E.... 149 A3
Masugnsbyn
  S........ 196 B5
Mašun SLO.... 123 B3
Maszewo
  Lubuskie PL.....75 B3
  Zachodnio-
  Pomorskie PL. 75 A4
Mata de Alcántara
  E......... 155 B4
Matala GR.....185 E5
Matalascañas
  E......... 161 B3
Matalebreras
  E......... 144 C1
Matallana de Torio
  E......... 142 B1
Matamala E... 151 A5
Mataporquera
  E......... 142 B2
Matapozuelos
  E......... 150 A3
Mataró E...... 147 C3
Matarocco I... 176 B1
Matélica I.... 136 B2
Matera I....... 172 B2
Mátészalka H...16 B5
Matet E....... 159 B3
Matfors S..... 200 D3
Matha F....... 115 C3
Mathay F...... 106 B1
Matignon F... 101 A3
Matilla de los
  Caños del Rio
  E......... 149 B4
Matlock UK.....40 B2
Matosinhos P. 148 A1
Matour F...... 117 A4
Mátrafüred H. 113 B3
Mátraterenye
  H........ 113 A3
Matre
  Hordaland N...46 B2
  Hordaland N... 52 A1
Matrei am Brenner
  A........... 108 B2
Matrei in Osttirol
  A........... 109 B3
Matrice I..... 170 B2
Matsdal S.....195 E6
Mattarello I... 121 A4
Mattersburg
  A........... 111 B3
Mattighofen
  A........... 109 A4
Mattinata I... 171 B4
Mattos P...... 154 B2
Mattsee A.... 109 B4
Mattsmyra S...50 A2
Måttsund S... 196 D5
Matulji HR.... 123 B3
Maubert-Fontaine
  F........... 91 B4
Maubeuge F...79 B3
Maubourguet
  F.......... 145 A4
Mauchline UK...36 A2
Maud UK....... 33 D4
Mauer-kirchen
  A........... 109 A4
Mauern D......95 C3
Mauguio F... 131 B3
Maulbronn D...93 C4
Maule F.......90 C1
Mauléon F.... 114 B3
Mauléon-Barousse
  F.......... 145 A4
Mauléon-Licharre
  F.......... 144 A3
Maulévrier F. 114 A3
Maum IRL.....28 A2
Maurach A.... 108 B2
Maure-de-Bretagne
  F........... 101 B4
Maureilhan F. 130 B2

Mǎureni RO... 126 B3
Mauriac F..... 116 B2
Mauron F..... 101 A3
Maurs F...... 116 C2
Maury F...... 146 B3
Maussane-les-
  Alpilles F... 131 B3
Mautern A......97 C3
Mauterndorf
  A........... 109 B4
Mautern im
  Steiermark
  A........... 110 B1
Mauthausen
  A........... 110 A1
Mauthen A.... 109 C3
Mauvezin F... 129 C3
Mauzé-sur-le-
  Mignon F... 114 B3
Maxent F..... 101 B3
Maxey-sur-Vaise
  F...........92 C1
Maxial P..... 154 B1
Maxieira P... 154 B2
Maxwellheugh
  UK...........35 C5
Mayalde E.... 149 A4
Maybole UK....36 A2
Mayen D.......80 B3
Mayenne F.....88 B3
Mayet F...... 102 B2
Mayorga E.... 142 B1
Mayres F..... 117 C4
Mayrhofen A.. 108 B2
Mazagón E.... 161 B3
Mazaleón E... 153 A4
Mazamet F.... 130 B1
Mazan F...... 131 A4
Mazara del Vallo
  I........... 176 B1
Mazarambroz
  E.......... 157 A3
Mazarete E... 152 B1
Mazaricos E... 140 B2
Mazarrón E... 165 B3
Mažeikiai LT....8 D3
Mazères F.... 146 A2
Mazères-sur-Salat
  F.......... 145 A4
Mazières-en-Gâtine
  F.......... 115 B3
Mazin HR..... 138 A1
Mazuelo E.... 143 B3
Mazyr BY.......13 B8
Mazzarino I... 177 B3
Mazzarrà
  Sant'Andrea
  I........... 177 A4
Mazzo di Valtellina
  I........... 120 A3
Mchowo PL.....77 A5
Mdzewo PL.....77 B5
Mealabost UK...31 A2
Mealhada P... 148 B1
Méan B........79 B5
Meana Sardo I 179 C3
Meaulne F.... 103 C4
Meaux F.......90 C2
Mebonden N. 199 B8
Mecerreyes E . 143 B3
Mechelen B.....79 A4
Mechernich D...80 B2
Mechnica PL....86 B2
Mechowo PL....67 C4
Mechterstädt
  D...........82 B2
Mecidiye TR... 186 B1
Mecikal PL.....68 B2
Mecina-Bombarón
  E.......... 164 C1
Mecitözü TR...23 A8
Meckenbeuren
  D.......... 107 B4
Meckenheim
  Rheinland-Pfalz
  D............80 B3
Meckesheim D..93 B4
Mecseknádasd
  H.......... 125 A4
Meda
  I........... 120 B2
  P........... 149 B2
Medak HR..... 137 A4
Medel I...... 120 B1
Medebach D....81 A4
Medelim P.... 155 A3
Medemblik NL..70 B2
Medena Selista
  BIH........ 138 A2
Medesano I... 120 C3
Medevi S.......55 B5

Medgidia RO....17 C8
Medgyesháza
  H........... 113 C5
Medhamn S.....55 A4
Mediaş RO......17 B6
Medicina I.... 135 A4
Medinaceli E.. 152 A1
Medina de las
  Torres E..... 155 C4
Medina del Campo
  E.......... 150 A3
Medina de Pomar
  E.......... 143 B3
Medina de Ríoseco
  E.......... 142 C1
Medina Sidonia
  E.......... 162 B2
Medinilla E... 150 B2
Medja SRB.... 126 B2
Medjedja BIH. 139 B5
Medulin HR... 122 C2
Meduno I..... 122 A1
Medveda SRB. 127 C3
Medvedov SK. 111 B4
Medvezhyegorsk
  RUS..........9 A9
Medvide HR... 137 A4
Medvode SLO.. 123 A3
Medzev SK......99 C4
Medžitlija
  NMK........ 182 C3
Meerane D......83 B4
Meerle B......79 A4
Meersburg D.. 107 B4
Meeuwen B.....79 A5
Megalo Horio
  GR.......... 188 C2
Megalopoli
  GR.......... 184 B3
Megara GR.... 185 A4
Megève F..... 118 B3
Meggenhofen
  A........... 109 A4
Megra RUS......9 B10
Megyaszó H... 113 A5
Mehamn N.... 193 A11
Mehedeby S...51 B4
Méhkerék H... 113 C5
Mehun-sur-Yèvre
  F.......... 103 B4
Meigle UK......35 B4
Meijel NL......80 A1
Meilen CH.... 107 B3
Meilhan F.... 128 C2
Meimôa P..... 149 B2
Meina I...... 119 B5
Meine D.......73 B3
Meinersen D....72 B3
Meinerzhagen
  D............81 A3
Meiningen D....82 B2
Meira E...... 141 A3
Meiringen CH. 106 C3
Meisenheim D..93 B3
Meissen D......83 A5
Meitingen D....94 C2
Meix-devant-
  Virton B......92 B1
Męka PL.......86 A2
Meka Gruda
  BIH........ 139 B4
Mel I....... 121 A5
Melbu N...... 194 B5
Melč CZ........98 B1
Meldal N..... 198 B6
Méldola I.... 135 A5
Meldorf D......64 B2
Melegnano I... 120 B2
Melenci SRB... 126 B2
Melendugno
  I........... 173 B4
Melfi I....... 172 B1
Melfjordbotn
  N.......... 195 D4
Melgaço P.... 140 B2
Melgar de Arriba
  E.......... 142 B1
Melgar de
  Fernamental
  E.......... 142 B2
Melgar de Yuso
  E.......... 142 B2

Mélito di Porto
  Salvo I...... 175 D1
Melk A....... 110 A2
Melksham UK...43 A4
Mellakoski
  FIN......... 196 C7
Mellanström
  S...........195 E9
Mellbystrand S .61 C2
Melle
  B............79 A3
  D.............71 B5
  F............ 115 B3
Mellendorf D...72 B2
Mellerud S.....54 B3
Mellieha M.... 175 C3
Mellösa S......56 A2
Mellrichstadt
  D............82 B2
Mělnické Vtelno
  CZ...........84 B2
Mělník CZ......84 B2
Melón E....... 140 B2
Melrose UK.....35 C5
Mels CH...... 107 B4
Melsungen D...82 A1
Meltaus FIN... 197 C8
Meltham UK....40 B2
Melton Mowbray
  UK...........40 C3
Meltosjärvi
  FIN......... 196 C7
Melun F.......90 C2
Melvaig UK.....31 B3
Melvich UK.....32 C3
Mélykút H.... 126 A1
Melzo I...... 120 B2
Memaliaj AL.. 182 C1
Membrilla E.. 157 B4
Membrio E.... 155 B3
Memer F..... 129 B4
Memmelsdorf
  D............94 B2
Memmingen
  D.......... 107 B5
Memoria P.... 154 B2
Menággio I... 120 A2
Menai Bridge
  UK...........38 A2
Menasalbas E. 157 A3
Menat F...... 116 A2
Mendavia E... 144 B1
Mendaza E.... 144 B1
Mende F...... 130 A2
Menden D......81 A3
Menderes TR.. 188 A2
Mendig D......80 B3
Mendiga P... 154 B2
Mendrisio CH. 120 B1
Ménéac F.... 101 A3
Menemen TR.. 188 A2
Menen B.......78 B3
Menesjärvi
  FIN.........193 D10
Menetou-Salon
  F.......... 103 B4
Menfi I...... 176 B1
Ménföcsanak
  H.......... 111 B4
Mengamuñoz
  E.......... 150 B3
Mengen
  D........... 107 A4
  TR.......... 187 B7
Mengeš SLO... 123 A3
Mengíbar E... 157 C4
Mengkofen D...95 C4
Menou F...... 104 B2
Mens F....... 118 C2
Menslage D....71 B4
Mensträsk S.. 200 A5
Mentana I... 168 A2
Menton F..... 133 B3
Méntrida E... 151 B3
Méobecq F... 115 B5
Méounes-les-
  Montrieux F. 132 B1
Meppel NL.....70 B3
Meppen D......71 B4
Mequinenza E 153 A4
Mer F........ 103 B3
Mera
  Coruña E.... 140 A2
  Coruña E.... 140 A3
Meråker N.... 199 B8
Merano I..... 108 C2
Merate I...... 120 B2
Mercadillo E . 143 A3
Mercatale E... 135 B5
Mercatino Conca
  I........... 136 B1
Mercato San
  Severino I... 170 C2

Mercato Saraceno
  I........... 135 B5
Merching D... 108 A1
Merchtem B....79 B4
Merdrignac F. 101 A3
Merdžanići
  BIH........ 139 B3
Meré E....... 142 A2
Mere UK.......43 A4
Meréville F....90 C2
Merfeld D......80 A3
Méribel F.... 118 B3
Méribel Motraret
  F.......... 118 B3
Meriç TR..... 186 A1
Mérida E..... 155 C4
Mérignac F... 128 B2
Mérignat F... 118 A2
Měřín CZ........97 B3
Mering D......94 C2
Merkendorf D..94 B2
Merklín CZ.....96 B1
Merksplas B....79 A4
Merlånna S 56 A2
Merlimont Plage
  F............78 B1
Mern DK.......65 A5
Mernye H..... 111 C4
Mersch L......92 B2
Merseburg D...83 A3
Mers-les-Bains
  F............90 A1
Merthyr Tydfil
  UK...........39 C3
Mertingen D...94 C2
Mértola P.... 160 B2
Méru F........90 B2
Merufe P..... 140 B2
Mervans F.... 105 C4
Merville F.....78 B2
Méry-sur-Seine
  F............91 C3
Merzen D......71 B4
Merzifon TR...23 A8
Merzig D......92 B2
Mesagne I.... 173 B3
Mesão Frio P. 148 A2
Mesas de Ibor
  E.......... 156 A2
Meschede D....81 A4
Meschers-sur-
  Gironde F.... 114 C3
Meslay-du-Maine
  F.......... 102 B1
Mesna N.......48 A2
Mesnalien N....48 A2
Mesocco CH... 120 A2
Mésola I..... 122 C1
Mesologi GR . 184 A2
Mesopotamo
  GR.......... 182 D2
Mesoraca I... 175 B2
Messac F..... 101 B4
Messancy B....92 B1
Messdorf D....73 B4
Messei F......88 B3
Messejana P . 160 B1
Messelt N......48 A3
Messina I..... 177 A4
Messingen D...71 B4
Messini GR... 184 B3
Messkirch D.. 107 B4
Messlingen S . 199 C9
Messstetten D . 107 A3
Mesta GR..... 185 A6
Mestanza E... 157 B3
Město Albrechtice
  CZ...........85 B5
Město Libavá
  CZ...........98 B1
Město Touškov
  CZ...........96 B1
Mestre I...... 122 B1
Mesvres F.... 104 C3
Mesztegnyő
  H.......... 111 C4
Meta I....... 170 C2
Metajna HR... 137 A4
Metelen D......71 B4
Methana GR . 185 B4
Methlick UK... 33 D4
Methven UK....35 B4
Methwold UK..41 C4
Metković HR.. 139 B3
Metlika SLO.. 123 B4
Metnitz A.... 110 C1
Metsäkylä
  FIN......... 197 D11
Metslawier NL..70 A3
Metsovo GR.. 182 D3
Metten D......95 C4

Mettendorf D...92 B2
Mettet B.......79 B4
Mettingen D...71 B4
Mettlach D.....92 B2
Mettlen CH... 106 C2
Mettmann D...80 A2
Metz F........92 B2
Metzervisse F..92 B2
Metzingen D...94 C1
Meulan F......90 B1
Meung-sur-Loire
  F.......... 103 B3
Meuselwitz D...83 A4
Meuzac F..... 115 C5
Mevagissey
  UK...........42 B2
Mexborough
  UK...........40 B2
Meximieux F.. 118 B2
Mey UK........32 C3
Meyenburg D...73 A5
Meyerhöfen D..71 B5
Meylan F..... 118 B2
Meymac F..... 116 B2
Meyrargues F. 132 B1
Meyrueis F... 130 A2
Meyssac F.... 129 A4
Meysse F..... 117 C4
Meyzieu F.... 117 B4
Mèze F....... 130 B2
Mézériat F... 117 A5
Mézidon-Canon
  F............89 A3
Mézières-en-
  Brenne F.... 115 B5
Mézières-sur-
  Issoire F.... 115 B4
Mézilhac F... 117 C4
Mézilles F.... 104 B2
Mézin F...... 128 B3
Mezőberény
  H.......... 113 C5
Mezőcsát H... 113 B4
Mezőfalva H.. 112 C2
Mezőhegyes
  H.......... 126 A2
Mezőkeresztes
  H.......... 113 B4
Mezőkomárom
  H.......... 112 C2
Mezőkövácsháza
  H.......... 113 C4
Mezőkövesd
  H.......... 113 B4
Mezőörs H.... 111 B4
Mézos F...... 128 B1
Mezőszilas H.. 112 C2
Mezőtúr H.... 113 B4
Mezquita de Jarque
  E.......... 153 B3
Mezzano
  Emilia Romagna
  I........... 135 A5
  Trentino Alto Adige
  I........... 121 A4
Mezzojuso I... 176 B2
Mezzoldo I.... 120 A2
Mezzolombardo
  I........... 121 A4
Mgarr M..... 175 C3
Miajadas E.... 156 A2
Miały PL.......75 B5
Mianowice PL..68 A2
Miasteczko
  Krajeńskie PL..76 A2
Miasteczko Śl.
  PL...........86 B2
Miastko PL......68 A1
Michalovce SK. 12 D4
Michałowice
  PL...........87 B3
Michelau D....94 B2
Michelbach D . 94 B1
Michelhausen
  A........... 110 A2
Michelsneukirchen
  D............95 B4
Michelstadt D..93 B5
Michendorf D..74 B2
Mickleover UK..40 C2
Midbea UK.....33 B4
Middelburg NL .79 A3
Middelfart DK..59 C2
Middelharnis
  NL...........79 A4
Middelkerke B..78 A2
Middelstum NL.71 A3
Middlesbrough
  UK...........37 B5
Middleton Cheney
  UK...........44 A2

Middleton-in-
  Teesdale UK...37 B4
Middletown UK 27 B4
Middlewich UK..38 A4
Middlezoy UK..43 A4
Midhurst UK...44 C3
Midleton IRL...29 C3
Midlum D......64 C1
Midsomer Norton
  UK...........43 A4
Midtgulen N . 198 D2
Midtskogberget
  N............49 A4
Midwolda NL...71 A4
Mid Yell UK....33 A5
Miechów PL....87 B4
Miedes de Aragón
  E.......... 152 A2
Miedes de Atienza
  E.......... 151 A4
Międzybodzie
  Bielskie PL...99 B3
Międzybórz PL..85 A5
Międzychód PL .75 B4
Międzylesie PL..85 B4
Międzyrzec
  Podlaski PL...12 C5
Międzyrzecz PL .75 B4
Międzywodzie
  PL...........67 B3
Międzyzdroje
  PL...........67 C3
Miejska Górka
  PL...........85 A4
Miélan F..... 145 A4
Mielec PL......87 B5
Mielęcin PL.....75 A3
Mielno
  Warmińsko-
  Mazurskie PL . 77 A5
  Zachodnio-
  Pomorskie PL ..67 B5
Miengo E..... 143 A3
Mieraslompolo
  FIN.........193 C11
Miercurea Ciuc
  RO...........17 B6
Mieres
  Asturias E.... 141 A5
  Girona E..... 147 B3
Mieroszów PL..85 B4
Mierzyn PL.....86 A3
Miesau D.......93 B3
Miesbach D... 108 B2
Mieścisko PL...76 B2
Mieste D.......73 B4
Miesterhorst D.73 B4
Mieszków PL...76 B2
Mieszkowice
  PL...........74 B3
Mietków PL....85 B4
Migennes F... 104 B2
Miggiano I... 173 C4
Migliánico I... 169 A4
Migliarino I... 121 C4
Miglionico I... 172 B2
Mignano Monte
  Lungo I..... 169 B3
Migné F...... 115 B5
Miguel Esteban
  E.......... 157 A4
Miguelturra E. 157 B4
Mihajlovac
  SRB........ 127 C2
Miháld H..... 111 C4
Mihalgazi TR.. 187 B5
Mihaliççık TR. 187 C6
Mihályi H.... 111 B4
Mihla D.......82 A2
Mihohnić HR . 123 B3
Miholjsko HR . 123 B4
Mihovljan HR . 124 A1
Mijares E..... 150 B3
Mijas E....... 163 B3
Mike H....... 124 A3
Mikines GR... 184 B3
Mikkeli FIN.....8 B5
Mikkelvik N... 192 B3
Mikleuš HR... 125 B3
Mikołajki
  Pomorskie PL..69 B4
Mikołów PL....86 B2
Mikorzyn PL...86 A2
Mikro Derio
  GR.......... 183 B8
Mikstat PL.....86 A1
Mikulášovice
  CZ...........84 B2
Mikulov CZ.....97 C4
Mikulovice CZ..85 B5
Milagro E.... 144 B2
Miłakowo PL...69 A5

Milan = Milano I 120 B2
Miland N 47 C5
Milano = Milan I 120 B2
Milano Marittima I 135 A5
Milas TR 188 B2
Milazzo I 177 A4
Mildenhall UK 45 A4
Milejewo PL 69 A4
Milelín CZ 85 B3
Miletić SRB 125 B5
Miletićevo SRB 126 B3
Mileto I 175 C2
Milevsko CZ 96 B2
Milford IRL 26 A3
Milford Haven UK 39 C1
Milford on Sea UK 44 C2
Milhão P 149 A3
Milići BIH 139 A5
Miličin CZ 96 B2
Milicz PL 85 A5
Milín CZ 96 B2
Militello in Val di Catánia I 177 B3
Miljevina BIH 139 B4
Milkowice PL 85 A4
Millançay F 103 B3
Millares E 159 B3
Millas F 146 B3
Millau F 130 A2
Millesimo I 133 A4
Millevaches F 116 B2
Millom UK 36 B3
Millport UK 34 C3
Millstatt A 109 C4
Millstreet
Cork IRL 29 B2
Waterford IRL 29 B4
Milltown
Galway IRL 28 A3
Kerry IRL 29 B1
Milltown Malbay IRL 28 B2
Milly-la-Forêt F 90 C2
Milmarcos E 152 A2
Milmersdorf D 74 A2
Milna HR 138 B2
Milnthorpe UK 37 B4
Milogórze PL 69 A5
Miłomłyn PL 69 B4
Milos GR 185 C5
Miloševo SRB 127 C3
Miłosław PL 76 B2
Milot AL 182 B1
Milówka PL 99 B3
Miltach D 95 B4
Miltenberg D 94 B1
Milton Keynes UK 44 A3
Miltzow D 66 B2
Milverton UK 43 A3
Milzyn PL 76 B3
Mimice HR 138 B2
Mimizan F 128 B1
Mimizan-Plage F 128 B1
Mimoň CZ 84 B2
Mina de Juliana P 160 B1
Mina de São Domingos P 160 B2
Minas de Riotinto E 161 B3
Minateda E 158 C2
Minaya E 158 B1
Minde P 154 B2
Mindelheim D 108 A1
Mindelstetten D 95 C3
Minden D 72 B1
Mindszent H 113 C4
Minehead UK 43 A3
Mineo I 177 B3
Minerbe I 121 B4
Minérbio I 121 C4
Minervino Murge I 171 B4
Minglanilla E 158 B2
Mingorria E 150 B3
Minnesund N 48 B3
Miño E 140 A2
Miño de San Esteban E 151 A4
Minsen D 71 A4
Minsk BY 13 B7
Mińsk Mazowiecki PL 12 B4
Minsterley UK 39 B4
Mintlaw UK 33 D4
Minturno I 169 B3
Mionica
BIH 126 C1
SRB 127 C2
Mios F 128 B2
Mira
E 158 B2
I 121 B5
P 148 B1
Mirabel E 155 B4
Mirabel-aux-Baronnies F 131 A4
Mirabella Eclano I 170 B3
Mirabella Imbáccari I 177 B3
Mirabello I 121 C4
Miradoux F 129 B3
Miraflores de la Sierra E 151 B4
Miralrio E 151 B5
Miramar P 148 A1
Miramare I 136 A1
Miramas F 131 B3
Mirambeau F 114 C3
Miramont-de-Guyenne F 129 B3
Miranda de Arga E 144 B2
Miranda de Ebro E 143 B4
Miranda do Corvo P 148 B1
Miranda do Douro P 149 A3
Mirande F 129 C3
Mirandela P 149 A2
Mirandilla E 155 C4
Mirándola I 121 C4
Miranje HR 137 A4
Mirano I 121 B5
Miras AL 182 C2
Miravet E 153 A4
Miré F 102 B1
Mirebeau F 102 C2
Mirebeau-sur-Bèze F 105 B4
Mirecourt F 105 A5
Mirepoix F 146 A2
Mires GR 185 D5
Miribel F 117 B4
Miričina BIH 125 C4
Mirina GR 183 D7
Mirna SLO 123 B4
Miroslav CZ 97 C4
Mirosławice PL 85 B4
Mirosławiec PL 75 A5
Mirošov CZ 96 B1
Mirotice CZ 96 B2
Mirovice CZ 96 B2
Mirow D 74 A1
Mirsk PL 84 B3
Mirzec PL 87 A5
Misi FIN 197 C9
Misilmeri I 176 A2
Miske H 112 C3
Miskolc H 113 A4
Mislinja SLO 110 C2
Missanello I 174 A2
Missillac F 101 B3
Mistelbach
A 97 C4
D 95 B3
Misten N 194 C5
Misterbianco I 177 B4
Misterhult S 62 A4
Mistretta I 177 B3
Misurina I 109 C3
Mitchelstown IRL 29 B3
Mithimna GR 186 C1
Mithoni GR 184 C2
Mitilini GR 186 C1
Mitilinii GR 188 B1
Mittelberg
Tirol A 108 C1
Vorarlberg A 107 B5
Mittenwald D 108 B2
Mittenwalde D 74 B2
Mitterback A 110 B2
Mitterdorf im Mürztal A 110 B2
Mitter-Kleinarl A 109 B4
Mittersheim F 92 C2
Mittersill A 109 B3
Mitterskirchen D 95 C4
Mitterteich D 95 B4
Mitton F 128 B2
Mittweida D 83 B4
Mitwitz D 82 B3
Mizhhir'ya UA 13 D5
Mjällby S 63 B2
Mjåvatn N 53 B4
Mjöbäck S 60 B2
Mjölby S 56 B1
Mjølfjell N 46 B3
Mjøndalen N 53 A6
Mjørlund N 48 B2
Mladá Boleslav CZ 84 B2
Mladá Vožice CZ 96 B2
Mladé Buky CZ 85 B3
Mladenovac SRB 127 C2
Mladenovo SRB 126 B1
Mladikovine BIH 139 A3
Mława PL 77 A5
Mlinište BIH 138 A2
Młodzieszyn PL 77 B5
Młogoszyn PL 77 B4
Młynary PL 69 A4
Mnichóvice CZ 96 B2
Mnichovo Hradiště CZ 84 B2
Mniów PL 87 A4
Mnisek nad Hnilcom SK 99 C4
Mníšek pod Brdy CZ 96 B2
Mniszek PL 87 A4
Mniszków PL 87 A4
Mo
Hedmark N 48 B3
Hordaland N 46 B2
Møre og Romsdal N 198 C5
Telemark N 53 A3
Gävleborg S 51 A3
Västra Götaland S 54 B2
Moaña E 140 B2
Moate IRL 28 A4
Mocejón E 151 C4
Močenok SK 111 A4
Mochales E 152 A1
Mochowo PL 77 B4
Mochy PL 75 B5
Mockern D 73 B4
Mockfjärd S 50 B1
Möckmühl D 94 B1
Mockrehna D 83 A4
Moclin E 163 A4
Mocsa H 112 B2
Möcsény H 125 A4
Modane F 118 B3
Modbury UK 42 B3
Módena I 121 C3
Módica I 177 C3
Modigliana I 135 A4
Modlin PL 77 B5
Mödling A 111 A3
Modliszewice PL 87 A4
Modliszewko PL 76 B2
Modogno I 171 B4
Modra SK 98 C1
Modran BIH 125 C3
Modriča BIH 125 C4
Möðrudalur IS 191 B10
Modrý Kamen SK 99 C3
Moëlan-sur-Mer F 100 B2
Moelfre UK 38 A2
Moelv N 48 B2
Moen N 194 A9
Moena I 121 A4
Moerbeke B 79 A3
Moers D 80 A2
Móes P 148 B2
Moffat UK 36 A3
Mogadouro P 149 A3
Mogata S 56 B2
Móggio Udinese I 122 A2
Mogielnica PL 87 A4
Mogilany PL 99 B3
Mogilno PL 76 B2
Mogliano I 136 B2
Mogliano Véneto I 122 B1
Mogor E 140 B2
Mógoro I 179 C2
Moguer E 161 B3
Mohács H 125 B4
Moheda S 62 A2
Mohedas E 149 B3
Mohedas de la Jara E 156 A2
Mohelnice CZ 97 B4
Mohill IRL 26 C3
Möhlin CH 106 B2
Moholm S 55 B5
Mohorn D 83 A5
Mohyliv-Podil's'kyy UA 13 D7
Moi N 52 B2
Moià E 147 C3
Móie I 136 B2
Moimenta da Beira P 148 B2
Mo i Rana N 195 D5
Moirans F 118 B2
Moirans-en-Montagne F 118 A2
Moisaküla EST 8 C4
Moisdon-la-Rivière F 101 B4
Moissac F 129 B4
Moita
Coimbra P 148 B1
Guarda P 149 B2
Santarém P 154 B2
Setúbal P 154 C1
Moita dos Ferreiros P 154 B1
Moixent E 159 C3
Mojacar E 164 B3
Mojados E 150 A3
Mojmírovce SK 112 A2
Mojtin SK 98 C2
Möklinta S 50 B3
Mokošica HR 139 C4
Mokronog SLO 123 B4
Mokro Polje HR 138 A2
Mokrzyska PL 99 A4
Møkster N 46 B2
Mol
B 79 A5
SRB 126 B2
Mola di Bari I 173 A3
Molai GR 184 C3
Molare I 133 A4
Molaretto I 119 B4
Molas F 145 A4
Molassano I 134 A1
Molbergen D 71 B4
Mold UK 38 A3
Molde N 198 C4
Møldrup DK 58 B2
Moledo do Minho P 148 A1
Molfetta I 171 B4
Molfsee D 64 B3
Moliden S 200 C4
Molières F 129 B4
Molina de Aragón E 152 B2
Molina de Segura E 165 A3
Molinar E 143 A3
Molinaseca E 141 B4
Molinella I 121 C4
Molinet F 104 C2
Molinicos E 158 C1
Molini di Tures I 108 C2
Molinos de Duero E 143 C4
Molins de Rei E 147 C3
Moliterno I 174 A1
Molkom S 55 A4
Möllbrücke A 109 C4
Mölle S 61 C2
Molledo E 142 A2
Möllenbeck D 74 A2
Mollerussa E 147 C1
Mollet de Perelada E 146 B3
Mollina E 163 A3
Mölln D 73 A3
Molló E 146 B3
Mollösund S 54 B2
Mölltorp S 55 B5
Mölnbo S 56 A3
Mölndal S 60 B2
Mölnlycke S 60 B2
Molompize F 116 B3
Moloy F 105 B3
Molsheim F 93 C3
Moltzow D 73 A5
Molve HR 124 A3
Molveno I 121 A3
Molvizar E 163 B4
Molzbichl A 109 C4
Mombaróccio I 136 B1
Mombeltrán E 150 B2
Mombris D 93 A5
Mombuey E 141 B4
Momchilgrad BG 183 B7
Mommark DK 64 B3
Momo I 119 B5
Monaghan IRL 27 B4
Monar Lodge UK 32 D2
Monasterace Marina I 175 C2
Monasterevin IRL 30 A1
Monasterio de Rodilla E 143 B3
Monastir I 179 C3
Monbahus F 129 B3
Monbazillac F 129 B3
Moncada E 159 B3
Moncalieri I 119 B4
Moncalvo I 119 B5
Monção P 140 B2
Moncarapacho P 160 B2
Moncel-sur-Seille F 92 C2
Monchegorsk RUS 3 C13
Mönchengladbach = Munchen-Gladbach D 80 A2
Mónchio della Corti I 134 A3
Monchique P 160 B1
Monclar-de-Quercy F 129 C4
Moncofa E 159 B3
Moncontour F 101 A3
Moncoutant F 114 B3
Monda E 162 B3
Mondariz E 140 B2
Mondavio I 136 B1
Mondéjar E 151 B4
Mondello I 176 A2
Mondim de Basto P 148 A2
Mondolfo I 136 B2
Mondoñedo E 141 A3
Mondorf-les-Bains L 92 B2
Mondoubleau F 102 B2
Mondovì I 133 A3
Mondragon F 131 A3
Mondragone I 170 B1
Mondsee A 109 B4
Monéglia I 134 A2
Monegrillo E 153 A3
Monein F 145 A3
Monemvasia GR 184 C4
Mónesi I 133 A3
Monesiglio I 133 A4
Monesterio E 161 A3
Monestier-de-Clermont F 118 C2
Monestiés F 130 A1
Monéteau F 104 B2
Moneygall IRL 28 B4
Moneymore UK 27 B4
Monfalcone I 122 B2
Monfero E 140 A2
Monflanquin F 129 B3
Monflorite E 145 B3
Monforte P 155 B3
Monforte da Beira
E 155 B3
P 155 B3
Monforte d'Alba I 133 A3
Monforte del Cid E 165 A4
Monforte de Lemos E 140 B3
Monforte de Moyuela E 152 A2
Monghidoro I 135 A4
Mongiana I 175 C2
Monguelfo I 108 C3
Monheim D 94 C2
Moniaive UK 36 A3
Monifieth UK 35 B5
Monikie UK 35 B5
Monistrol-d'Allier F 117 C3
Monistrol de Montserrat E 147 C2
Monistrol-sur-Loire F 117 B4
Mönkebude D 74 A2
Monkton UK 36 A2
Monmouth UK 39 C4
Monnaie F 102 B2
Monnerville F 90 C2
Monnickendam NL 70 B2
Monolithos GR 188 C2
Monópoli I 173 B3
Monor H 112 B3
Monóvar E 159 C3
Monpazier F 129 B3
Monreal
D 80 B3
E 144 B2
Monreal del Campo E 152 B2
Monreale I 176 A2
Monroy E 155 B4
Monroyo E 153 B3
Mons B 79 B3
Monsaraz P 155 C3
Monschau D 80 B2
Monségur F 128 B3
Monsélice I 121 B4
Mønshaug N 46 B3
Monster NL 70 B1
Mönsterås S 62 A4
Monsummano Terme I 135 B3
Montabaur D 81 B3
Montafia I 119 C5
Montagnac F 130 B2
Montagnana I 121 B4
Montaigu F 114 B2
Montaigu-de-Quercy F 129 B4
Montaiguët-en-Forez F 117 A3
Montaigut F 116 A2
Montaigut-sur-Save F 129 C4
Montainville F 90 C1
Montalbán E 153 B3
Montalbán de Córdoba E 163 A3
Montalbano Elicona I 177 A4
Montalbano Iónico I 174 A2
Montalbo E 158 B1
Montalcino I 135 B4
Montaldo di Cósola I 120 C2
Montalegre P 148 A2
Montalieu-Vercieu F 118 B2
Montalivet-les-Bains F 114 C2
Montallegro I 176 B2
Montalto delle Marche I 136 C2
Montalto di Castro I 168 A1
Montalto Pavese I 120 C2
Montalto Uffugo I 174 B2
Montalvão P 155 B3
Montamarta E 149 A4
Montana BG 17 D5
Montana-Vermala CH 119 A4
Montánchez E 156 A1
Montanejos E 153 B3
Montano Antilia I 172 B1
Montans F 129 C4
Montargil P 154 B2
Montargis F 103 B4
Montastruc-la-Conseillère F 129 C4
Montauban F 129 B4
Montauban-de-Bretagne F 101 A3
Montbard F 104 B3
Montbarrey F 105 B4
Montbazens F 130 A1
Montbazon F 102 B2
Montbéliard F 106 B1
Montbenoit F 105 C5
Montbeugny F 104 C2
Montblanc E 147 C2
Montbozon F 105 B5
Montbrison F 117 B4
Montbron F 115 C4
Montbrun-les-Bains F 131 A4
Montceau-les-Mines F 104 C3
Montcenis F 104 C3
Montchanin F 104 C3
Montcornet F 91 B4
Montcuq F 129 B4
Montdardier F 130 B2
Mont-de-Marsan F 128 C2
Montdidier F 90 B2
Monteagudo E 165 A3
Monteagudo de las Vicarias E 152 A1
Montealegre E 142 C2
Montealegre del Castillo E 159 C2
Montebello Iónico I 175 D1
Montebello Vicentino I 121 B4
Montebelluna I 121 B5
Montebourg F 88 A2
Montebruno I 134 A2
Monte-Carlo MC 133 B3
Montecarotto I 136 B2
Montecassiano I 136 B2
Montecastrilli I 168 A2
Montecatini Terme I 135 B3
Montécchio I 136 B1
Montécchio Emilia I 121 C3
Montécchio Maggiore I 121 B4
Montech F 129 C4
Montechiaro d'Asti I 119 B5
Monte Clara P 155 B3
Monte Clérigo P 160 B1
Montecórice I 170 C2
Montecorvino Rovella I 170 C2
Monte da Pedra P 155 B3
Monte de Goula P 155 B3
Montederramo E 141 B3
Montedoro I 176 B2
Monte do Trigo P 155 C3
Montefalco I 136 C1
Montefalcone di Val Fortore I 170 B3
Montefalcone nel Sánnio I 170 B2
Montefano I 136 B2
Montefiascone I 168 A2
Montefiorino I 134 A3
Montefortino I 136 C2
Montefranco I 168 A2
Montefrío E 163 A4
Montegiordano Marina I 174 A2
Montegiórgio I 136 B2
Monte Gordo P 160 B2
Montegranaro I 136 B2
Montehermoso E 149 B3
Montejicar E 163 A4
Montejo de la Sierra E 151 A4
Montejo de Tiermes E 151 A4
Monte Juntos P 155 C3
Montel-de-Gelat F 116 B2
Monteleone di Púglia I 171 B3
Monteleone di Spoleto I 169 A2
Monteleone d'Orvieto I 135 C5
Montelepre I 176 A2

Montelibretti I 168 A2
Montelier F 117 C5
Montélimar F 131 A3
Montella
E 146 B2
I 170 C3
Montellano E 162 A2
Montelupo Fiorentino I 135 B4
Montemaggiore Belsito I 176 B2
Montemagno I 119 C5
Montemayor E 163 A3
Montemayor de Pinilla E 150 A3
Montemésola I 173 B3
Montemilleto I 170 B2
Montemilone I 172 A1
Montemolín E 161 A3
Montemónaco I 136 C2
Montemor-o-Novo P 154 C2
Montemor-o-Velho P 148 B1
Montemurro I 174 A1
Montendre F 128 A2
Montenegro de Cameros E 143 B4
Montenero di Bisáccia I 170 B2
Monteneuf F 101 B3
Monteparano I 173 B3
Montepescali I 135 C4
Montepiano I 135 A4
Monte Porzio I 136 B2
Montepulciano I 135 B4
Monte Real P 154 B2
Montereale I 169 A3
Montereale Valcellina I 122 A1
Montereau-Faut-Yonne F 90 C2
Monte Redondo P 154 B2
Monterénzio I 135 A4
Monte Romano I 168 A1
Monteroni d'Arbia I 135 B4
Monteroni di Lecce I 173 B4
Monterosso al Mare I 134 A2
Monterosso Almo I 177 B3
Monterosso Grana I 133 A3
Monterotondo I 168 A2
Monterotondo Maríttimo I 135 B3
Monterrey E 141 C3
Monterroso E 140 B3
Monterrubio de la Serena E 156 B2
Monterubbiano I 136 B2
Montesa E 159 C3
Montesalgueiro E 140 A2
Monte San Giovanni Campano I 169 B3
Montesano sulla Marcellana I 174 A1
Monte San Savino I 135 B4
Monte Sant'Ángelo I 171 B3
Montesárchio I 170 B2
Montescaglioso I 171 C4
Montesclaros E 150 B3
Montesilvano I 169 A4
Montespértoli I 135 B4
Montesquieu-Volvestre F 146 A2
Montesquiou F 129 C3
Montestruc-sur-Gers F 129 C3
Montes Velhos P 160 B1
Montevarchi I 135 B4
Montevéglio I 135 A4
Monte Vilar P 154 B1
Montfaucon F 101 B4
Montfaucon-d'Argonne F 91 B5
Montfaucon-en-Velay F 117 B4
Montferrat
Isère F 118 B2
Var F 132 B2
Montfort-en-Chalosse F 128 C2
Montfort-l'Amaury F 90 C1
Montfort-le-Gesnois F 102 A2
Montfort-sur-Meu F 101 A4
Montfort-sur-Risle F 89 A4
Montgai E 147 C1
Montgaillard F 145 A4
Montgenèvre F 118 C3
Montgiscard F 146 A2
Montgomery UK 39 B3
Montguyon F 128 A2
Monthermé F 91 B4
Monthey CH 119 A3
Monthois F 91 B4
Monthureux-sur-Saône F 105 A4
Monti I 178 B3
Monticelli d'Ongina I 120 B2
Montichiari I 120 B3
Monticiano I 135 B4
Montiel E 158 C1
Montier-en-Der F 91 C4
Montieri I 135 B4
Montiglio I 119 B5
Montignac F 129 A4
Montigny-le-Roi F 105 B4
Montigny-lès-Metz F 92 B2
Montigny-sur-Aube F 105 B3
Montijo
E 155 C4
P 154 C2
Montilla E 163 A3
Montillana E 163 A4
Montilly F 104 C2
Montivilliers F 89 A4
Montjaux F 130 A1
Montjean-sur-Loire F 102 B1
Montlhéry F 90 C2
Montlieu-la-Garde F 128 A2
Mont-Louis F 146 B3
Montlouis-sur-Loire F 102 B2
Montluçon F 116 A2
Montluel F 117 B5
Montmarault F 116 A2
Montmartin-sur-Mer F 88 B2
Montmédy F 92 B1
Montmélian F 118 B3
Montmeyan F 132 B2
Montmeyran F 117 C4
Montmirail
Marne F 91 C3
Sarthe F 102 A2
Montmiral F 118 B2
Montmirat F 131 B3
Montmirey-le-Château F 105 B4
Montmoreau-St Cybard F 115 C4
Montmorency F 90 C2
Montmorillon F 115 B4
Montmort-Lucy F 91 C3
Montoir-de-Bretagne F 101 B3
Montoire-sur-le-Loir F 102 B2
Montoito P 155 C3
Montolieu F 146 A3
Montório al Vomano I 169 A3
Montoro E 157 B3
Montpellier F 131 B2
Montpezat-de-Quercy F 129 B4
Montpezat-sous-Bouzon F 117 C4
Montpon-Ménestérol F 128 A3
Montpont-en-Bresse F 105 C4
Montréal
Aude F 146 A3
Gers F 128 C3
Montredon-Labessonnié F 130 B1
Montréjeau F 145 A4
Montrésor F 103 B3
Montresta I 178 B2
Montret F 105 C4
Montreuil
Pas de Calais F 78 B1
Seine St Denis F 90 C2
Montreuil-aux-Lions F 90 B3
Montreuil-Bellay F 102 B1
Montreux CH 106 C1
Montrevault F 101 B4
Montrevel-en-Bresse F 118 A2
Montrichard F 103 B3
Montricoux F 129 B4
Mont-roig del Camp E 147 C1
Montrond-les-Bains F 117 B4
Montrose UK 35 B5
Montroy E 159 B3
Montsalvy F 116 C2
Montsauche-les-Settons F 104 B3
Montseny E 147 C3
Montsoreau F 102 B2
Mont-sous-Vaudrey F 105 C4
Monts-sur-Guesnes F 102 C2
Mont-St Aignan F 89 A5
Mont-St Vincent F 104 C3
Montsûrs F 102 A1
Montuenga E 150 A3
Montuïri E 167 B3
Monturque E 163 A3
Monza I 120 B2
Monzón E 145 C4
Monzón de Campos E 142 B2
Moorbad Lobenstein D 83 B3
Moordorf D 71 A4
Moorslede B 78 B3
Moos D 107 B3
Moosburg D 95 C3
Moosburg im Kärnten A 110 C1
Mór H 112 B2
Mora E 157 A4
Móra P 154 C2
Mora S 50 A1
Moraby S 50 B2
Mòra d'Ebre E 153 A4
Mora de Rubielos E 153 B3
Moradillo de Roa E 151 A4
Morąg PL 69 B4
Mórahalom H 126 A1
Moraime E 140 A1
Morais P 149 A3
Mòra la Nova E 153 A4
Moral de Calatrava E 157 B4
Moraleda de Zafayona E 163 A4
Moraleja E 149 B3
Moraleja del Vino E 150 A2
Morales del Vino E 150 A2
Morales de Toro E 150 A2
Morales de Valverde E 141 C5
Moralina E 149 A3
Morano Cálabro I 174 B2
Mörarp S 61 C2
Morasverdes E 149 B3
Morata de Jalón E 152 A2
Morata de Jiloca E 152 A2
Morata de Tajuña E 151 B4
Moratalla E 164 A3
Moravče SLO 123 A3
Moravec CZ 97 B4
Moraviţa RO 126 B3
Morávka CZ 98 B2
Moravská Třebová CZ 97 B4
Moravské Budějovice CZ 97 B3
Moravské Lieskové SK 98 C1
Moravske Toplice SLO 111 C3
Moravský-Beroun CZ 98 B1
Moravský Krumlov CZ 97 B4
Moravský Svätý Ján SK 98 C1
Morawica PL 87 B4
Morawin PL 86 A2
Morbach D 92 B3
Morbegno I 120 A2
Morbier F 105 C5
Mörbisch am See A 111 B3
Mörbylånga S 63 B4
Morcenx F 128 B2
Morciano di Romagna I 136 B1
Morcone I 170 B2
Morcuera E 151 A4
Mordelles F 101 A4
Mordoğan TR 188 A1
Moréac F 100 B3
Morebattle UK 35 C5
Morecambe UK 36 B4
Moreda
Granada E 163 A4
Oviedo E 142 A1
Morée F 103 B3
Moreles de Rey E 141 B5
Morella E 153 B3
Moreruela de los Infanzones E 149 A4
Morés E 152 A2
Móres I 178 B2
Morestel F 118 B2
Moretonhampstead UK 43 B3
Moreton-in-Marsh UK 44 B2
Moret-sur-Loing F 90 C2
Moretta I 119 C4
Moreuil F 90 B2
Morez F 105 C5
Mörfelden D 93 B4
Morgat F 100 A1
Morges CH 105 C5
Morgex I 119 B4
Morgongåva S 51 C3
Morhange F 92 C2
Morhet B 92 B1
Mori I 121 B3
Morialmé B 79 B4
Morianes P 160 B2
Moriani Plage F 180 A2
Mórichida H 111 B4
Moriles E 163 A3
Morille E 150 B2
Moringen D 82 A1
Morjärv S 196 C5
Morkarla S 51 B4
Mørke DK 59 B3
Mørkøv DK 61 D1
Morkovice-Slížany CZ 98 B1
Morlaàs F 145 A3
Morlaix F 100 A2
Morley F 91 C5
Mörlunda S 62 A3
Mormanno I 174 B1
Mormant F 90 C2
Mornant F 117 B4
Mornay-Berry F 103 B4
Morón de Almazán E 152 A1
Morón de la Frontera E 162 A2
Morović SRB 125 B5
Morozzo I 133 A3
Morpeth UK 37 A5
Morphou CY 181 A1
Mörrum S 63 B2
Morsbach D 81 B3
Mörsch D 93 C4
Mörsil S 199 B10
Morsum D 64 B1
Mørsvikbotn N 194 C6
Mortagne-au-Perche F 89 B4
Mortagne-sur-Gironde F 114 C3
Mortagne-sur-Sèvre F 114 B3
Mortágua P 148 B1
Mortain F 88 B3
Mortara I 120 B1
Morteau F 105 B5
Mortegliano I 122 B2
Mortelle I 177 A4
Mortemart F 115 B4
Mortimer's Cross UK 39 B4
Mortrée F 89 B4
Mörtschach A 109 C3
Mortsel B 79 A4
Morud DK 59 C3
Morwenstow UK 42 B2
Moryń PL 74 B3
Morzeszczyn PL 69 B3
Morzewo PL 69 B4
Morzine F 118 A3
Mosbach D 93 B5
Mosbjerg DK 58 A3
Mosby N 53 B3
Mosca P 149 A3
Moscavide P 154 C1
Moščenica HR 124 B2
Mošćenice HR 123 B3
Moščenicka Draga HR 123 B3
Mosciano Sant'Ángelo I 136 C2
Mościsko PL 85 B4
Moscow = Moskva RUS 9 E10
Mosina PL 75 B5
Mosjøen N 195 E4
Moskog N 46 A3
Moskorzew PL 87 B3
Moskosel S 196 D2
Moskuvarra FIN 197 B9
Moskva = Moscow RUS 9 E10
Moslavina Podravska HR 125 B3
Moşniţa Nouă RO 126 B3
Moso in Passíria I 108 C2
Mosonmagyaróvár H 111 B4
Mošorin SRB 126 B2
Mošovce SK 98 C2
Mosqueruela E 153 B3
Moss N 54 A1
Mossfellsbær IS 190 C4
Mössingen D 93 C5
Møsstrand N 47 C5
Most CZ 83 B5
Mosta M 175 C3
Mostar BIH 139 B3
Mosterhamn N 52 A1
Mostki PL 75 B4
Most na Soči SLO 122 A2
Móstoles E 151 B4
Mostová SK 111 A4
Mostowo PL 68 A1
Mostuéjouls F 130 A2
Mosty PL 75 A3
Mostys'ka UA 13 D5
Mosvik N 199 B7
Mota del Cuervo E 158 B1
Mota del Marqués E 150 A2
Motala S 55 B6
Motherwell UK 35 C4
Möthlow D 74 B1
Motilla del Palancar E 158 B2
Motnik SLO 123 A3
Motovun HR 122 B2
Motril E 163 B4
Motta I 121 B4
Motta di Livenza I 122 B1
Motta Montecorvino I 170 B3
Motta Visconti I 120 B1
Mottisfont UK 44 B2
Móttola I 173 B3
Mou DK 58 B3
Mouchard F 105 C4
Moudon CH 106 C1
Moudros GR 183 D7
Mougins F 132 B2
Mouilleron-en-Pareds F 114 B3
Mouliherne F 102 B2
Moulinet F 133 B3
Moulins F 104 C2
Moulins-Engilbert F 104 C2
Moulins-la-Marche F 89 B4
Moulismes F 115 B4
Moult F 89 A3
Mountain Ash UK 39 C3
Mountbellew IRL 28 A3
Mountfield UK 27 B3
Mountmellick IRL 30 A1
Mountrath IRL 30 A1
Mountsorrel UK 40 C2
Moura P 160 A2
Mourão P 155 C3
Mourenx F 145 A3
Mouriés F 131 B3
Mourmelon-le-Grand F 91 B4
Mouronho P 148 B1
Mourujärvi FIN 197 C11
Mouscron B 78 B3
Mousehole UK 42 B1
Moussac F 131 B3
Moussey F 92 C2
Mousteru F 100 A2
Moustey F 128 B2
Moustiers-Ste Marie F 132 B2
Mouthe F 105 C5
Mouthier-Haute-Pierre F 105 B5
Mouthoumet F 146 B3
Moutier CH 106 B2
Moûtiers F 118 B3
Moutiers-les-Mauxfaits F 114 B2
Mouy F 90 B2
Mouzaki GR 182 D3
Mouzon F 91 B5
Møvik N 46 B2
Moville IRL 27 A3
Moy
Highland UK 32 D2
Tyrone UK 27 B4
Moycullen IRL 28 A2
Moyenmoutier F 92 C2
Moyenvic F 92 C2
Moylough IRL 28 A3
Mózar E 141 C5
Mozhaysk RUS 9 E10
Mozirje SLO 123 A3
Mözs H 112 C2
Mozzanica I 120 B2
Mramorak SRB 127 C2
Mrčajevci SRB 127 D2
Mrkonjić Grad BIH 138 A3
Mrkopalj HR 123 B3
Mrocza PL 76 A2
Mroczeń PL 86 A1
Mroczno PL 69 B4
Mrzezyno PL 67 B4
Mšec CZ 84 B1
Mšeno CZ 84 B2
Mstów PL 86 B3
Mstsislaw BY 13 A9
Mszana Dolna PL 99 B4
Mszczonów PL 77 C5
Muć HR 138 B2
Múccia I 136 B2
Much D 80 B3
Mücheln D 83 A3
Much Marcle UK 39 C4
Muchów PL 85 A4
Much Wenlock UK 39 B4
Mucientes E 142 C2
Muckross IRL 29 B2
Mucur TR 23 B8
Muda P 160 B1
Mudanya TR 186 B3
Mudau D 93 B5
Müden D 72 B3
Mudersbach D 81 B3
Mudurnu TR 187 B6
Muel E 152 A2
Muelas del Pan E 149 A4
Muess D 73 A4
Muff IRL 27 A3
Mugardos E 140 A2
Muge P 154 B2
Mügeln
Sachsen D 83 A5
Sachsen-Anhalt D 83 A5
Múggia I 122 B2
Mugnano I 135 B5
Mugron F 128 C2
Mugueimes E 140 C3
Muhi H 113 B4
Mühlacker D 93 C4
Mühlbach am Hochkönig A 109 B4
Mühlberg
Brandenburg D 83 A5
Thüringen D 82 B2
Mühldorf
A 109 C4
D 95 C4
Muhleberg CH 106 C2
Mühleim D 107 A3
Muhlen-Eichsen D 65 C4
Mühlhausen
Bayern D 94 B2
Thüringen D 82 A2
Mühltroff D 83 B3
Muhos FIN 3 D10
Muhr A 109 B4
Muine Bheag IRL 30 B2
Muirkirk UK 36 A2
Muir of Ord UK 32 D2
Muirteira P 154 B1
Mukacheve UA 12 D5
Muker UK 37 B4
Mula E 165 A3
Muğla TR 188 B3
Mulben UK 32 D3
Mulegns CH 107 C4
Mules I 108 C2
Mülheim D 80 A2
Mulhouse F 106 B2
Muljava SLO 123 B3
Mullanys Cross IRL 26 B2
Müllheim D 106 B2
Mullhyttan S 55 A5
Mullinavat IRL 30 B1
Mullingar IRL 30 A1
Mullion UK 42 B1
Müllrose D 74 B3
Mullsjö S 60 B3
Mulseryd S 60 B3
Munaðarnes IS 190 A4
Munana E 150 B2
Muñás E 141 A4
Münchberg D 83 B3
Müncheberg D 74 B3
München = Munich D 108 A2
Munchen-Gladbach = Mönchengladbach D 80 A2
Münchhausen D 81 B4
Mundaka E 143 A4

Münden D 82 A1
Munderfing A. 109 A4
Munderkingen
D 107 A4
Mundesley UK ...41 C5
Munera E 158 B1
Mungia E 143 A4
Munich = München
D 108 A2
Muñico E..... 150 B2
Muniesa E..... 153 A3
Munka-Ljungby
S............61 C2
Munkebo DK....59 C3
Munkedal S....54 B2
Munkflohögen
S............ 199 B11
Munkfors S 49 C5
Munktorp S....56 A2
Münnerstadt D .82 B2
Muñopepe E.. 150 B3
Muñotello E... 150 B2
Münsingen
CH 106 C2
D 94 C1
Munsö S 57 A3
Münster
CH 106 C3
Hessen D 93 B4
Munster D 72 B3
Münster D 71 C4
Munster F... 106 A2
Muntibar E... 143 A4
Münzkirchen A .96 C1
Muodoslompolo
S........... 196 B6
Muonio FIN ... 196 B6
Muotathal CH. 107 C3
Muradiye TR . 186 D2
Murakeresztúr
H............ 124 A2
Murán SK 99 C4
Murano I...... 122 B1
Muras E...... 140 A3
Murat F...... 116 B2
Muratlı TR.... 186 A2
Murato F...... 180 A2
Murat-sur-Vèbre
F............ 130 B1
Murau A 109 B5
Muravera I.... 179 C3
Murazzano I.. 133 A4
Murça P....... 148 B2
Murchante E.. 144 B2
Murchin D 66 C2
Murcia E.... 165 B3
Murczyn PL ...76 B2
Mur-de-Barrez
F............ 116 C2
Mur-de-Bretagne
F............ 100 A2
Mur-de-Sologne
F............ 103 B3
Mureck A 110 C2
Mürefte TR... 186 B2
Muret F...... 146 A2
Murg CH...... 107 B4
Murguia E... 143 B4
Muri CH...... 106 B3
Murias de Paredes
E............ 141 B4
Muriedas E.... 143 A3
Muriel Viejo E. 143 C4
Murillo de Rio Leza
E............ 143 B4
Murillo el Fruto
E............ 144 B2
Murjek S..... 196 C3
Murlaggan UK ..34 B2
Murmansk RUS .3 B13
Murmashi RUS . 3 B13
Murnau D..... 108 B2
Muro
E........... 167 B3
F........... 180 A1
Muro de Alcoy
E........... 159 C3
Murol F...... 116 B2
Muro Lucano I 172 B1
Muron F...... 114 B3
Muros E...... 140 B1
Muros de Nalón
E............ 141 A4
Murowana Goślina
PL............76 B2
Mürren CH.... 106 C2
Murrhardt D ...94 C1
Murska Sobota
SLO 111 C3
Mursko Središce
HR 111 C3
Murtas E..... 164 C1
Murten CH.... 106 C2

Murter HR 137 B4
Murtiçi TR..... 189 C6
Murtosa P..... 148 B1
Murtovaara
FIN....... 197 D12
Murvica HR ... 137 A4
Murviel-lès-Béziers
F............. 130 B2
Mürzsteg A .. 110 B2
Murzynowo PL...75 B4
Mürzzuschlag
A........... 110 B2
Musculdy F ... 144 A3
Muskö S 57 A4
Mušov CZ.......97 C4
Musselburgh
UK 35 C4
Musselkanaal
NL 71 B4
Mussidan F ... 129 A3
Mussomeli I... 176 B2
Musson B 92 B1
Mussy-sur-Seine
F............. 104 B3
Mustafakemalpaşa
TR.......... 186 B3
Muszaki PL.....77 A5
Muszyna PL.....99 B4
Mut TR 23 C7
Muta SLO 110 C2
Muthill UK 35 B4
Mutné SK 99 B3
Mutriku E 143 A4
Muttalip TR ... 187 C5
Mutterbergalm
A........... 108 B2
Muurola FIN .. 197 C8
Muxía E...... 140 A1
Muxilka-Ugarte
E............ 143 A4
Muzillac F..... 101 B3
Mužla SK..... 112 B2
Muzzano del
Turgnano I... 122 B2
Mybster UK 32 C3
Myckelgensjö
S........... 200 C3
Myennes F.... 104 B1
Myjava SK.....98 C1
Myking N 46 B2
Mykland N.....53 B4
Myra N........53 B5
Myrdal N......46 B4
Myre
Nordland N ... 194 A6
Nordland N ... 194 B6
Myresjö S 62 A2
Mýri IS 191 B8
Myrtou CY ... 181 A2
Mysen N 54 A2
Mysłakowice
PL............85 B3
Myślenice PL....99 B3
Myślibórz PL...75 B3
Mysłowice PL...86 B3
Myszków PL ...86 B3
Mytishchi RUS . 9 E10
Mýtna SK 99 C3
Mýtne Ludany
SK........... 112 A2
Mýto CZ........96 B1

N

Nå N 46 B3
Naaldwijk NL ...79 A4
Naantali FIN 8 B2
Naas IRL......30 A2
Nabais P 148 B2
Nabbelund S....62 A5
Nabburg D..... 95 B4
Načeradec CZ...96 B2
Náchod CZ.....85 B4
Nacław PL......68 A1
Nadarzyce PL...75 A5
Nadarzyn PL....77 B5
Nádasd H..... 111 C3
Nădlac RO.... 126 A2
Nádudvar H... 113 B5
Næfels CH 107 B4
Nafpaktos
GR....... 184 A2
Nafplio GR.... 184 B3
Nagel D....... 95 B3
Nagele NL......70 B2
Naggen S 200 D2
Nagłowice PL..87 B4
Nagold D 93 C4
Nagore E...... 144 B2
Nagyatád H... 124 A3
Nagybajom H. 124 A3

Nagybaracska
H............ 125 A4
Nagybátony
H............ 113 B3
Nagyberény
H............ 112 C2
Nagybörzsöny
H............ 112 B2
Nagycenk H... 111 B3
Nagycserkesz
H............ 113 B5
Nagydorog H . 112 C2
Nagyfüged H . 113 B4
Nagyhersány
H............ 125 B4
Nagyigmánd
H............ 112 B2
Nagyiván H... 113 B4
Nagykanizsa
H............ 111 C3
Nagykáta H... 113 B3
Nagykonyi H.. 112 C2
Nagykörös H.. 113 B3
Nagykörü H... 113 B4
Nagylóc H.... 112 A3
Nagymágocs
H............ 113 C4
Nagymányok
H............ 125 A4
Nagymaros H. 112 B2
Nagyoroszi H . 112 A3
Nagyrábé H... 113 B5
Nagyréde H... 113 B3
Nagyszékely
H............ 112 C2
Nagyszénás H. 113 C4
Nagyszokoly
H............ 112 C2
Nagytőke H... 113 C4
Nagyvázsony
H............ 111 C4
Nagyvenyim
H............ 112 C2
Naharros E.... 152 B1
Nahe D.........64 C3
Naila D........83 B3
Nailloux F..... 146 A2
Nailsworth UK .43 A4
Naintré F...... 115 B4
Nairn UK 32 D3
Najac F....... 129 B4
Nájera E...... 143 B4
Nak H........ 112 C2
Nakksjø N......53 A5
Nakło nad Notecią
PL............76 A2
Nakskov DK....65 B4
Nalda E 143 B4
Nälden S 199 B11
Nálepkovo SK. .99 C4
Nalliers F..... 114 B2
Nallıhan TR ... 187 B6
Nalzen F...... 146 B2
Nalžouské Hory
CZ...........96 B1
Namdalseid N 199 A8
Náměšt'nad
Oslavou CZ ...97 B4
Námestovo SK..99 B3
Namná S.......49 B4
Namsos N..... 199 A8
Namsskogan
N........... 199 A10
Namur B..... 79 B4
Namysłów PL...86 A1
Nançay F..... 103 B4
Nanclares de la Oca
E............ 143 B4
Nancy F.......92 C2
Nangis F.......90 C3
Nannestad N....48 B3
Nant F....... 130 A2
Nanterre F.....90 C2
Nantes F..... 101 B4
Nanteuil-le-
Haudouin F ...90 B2
Nantiat F..... 115 B5
Nantua F..... 118 A2
Nantwich UK...38 A4
Naoussa
Cyclades GR . 185 B6
Imathia GR ... 182 C4
Napajedla CZ...98 B1
Napiwoda PL ...77 A5
Naples = Nápoli
I............ 170 C2
Nápoli = Naples
I............ 170 C2
Nar S..........57 C4
Nara N.........46 A1
Naraval E..... 141 A4
Narberth UK ...39 C2
Nærbø N.......52 B1

Narbonne F... 130 B1
Narbonne-Plage
F............. 130 B2
Narbuvollen
N............ 199 C8
Narcao I....... 179 C2
Nardò I....... 173 B4
Narkaus FIN... 197 C9
Narken S..... 196 C5
Narmo N.......48 B3
Narni I....... 168 A2
Naro I....... 176 B2
Naro Fominsk
RUS........... 9 E10
Narón E...... 140 A2
Narros del Castillo
E............ 150 B2
Narta HR..... 124 B2
Naruszewo PL...77 B5
Narva EST....... 8 C6
Narvik N 194 B8
Narzole I..... 133 A3
Näs FIN 51 B7
Nås S..........50 B1
Näs S..........57 C4
Näsåker S.... 200 C2
Năsăud RO......17 B6
Nasavrky CZ ...97 B3
Nasbinals F ... 116 C3
Næsbjerg DK....59 C1
Näshull S.......62 A3
Našice HR 125 B4
Nasielsk PL 77 B5
Naso I....... 177 A3
Nassau D......81 B3
Nassenfels D...95 C3
Nassenheide D. .74 B2
Nassereith A.. 108 B1
Nässjö S.......62 A2
Nastätten D....81 B3
Næstved DK ...65 A4
Näsum S.......63 B2
Näsviken S... 199 B12
Natalinci SRB . 127 C2
Naters CH.... 119 A5
Nater-Stetten
D 108 A2
Nattavaara S.. 196 C3
Natters A..... 108 B2
Nattheim D....94 C2
Nättraby S.....63 B3
Naturno I..... 108 C1
Naucelle F.... 130 A1
Nauders A.... 108 C1
Nauen D.......74 B1
Naul IRL.......30 A2
Naumburg D...83 A3
Naundorf D....83 B5
Naunhof D.....83 A4
Naustdal N.....46 A2
Nautijaur S ... 196 C2
Nautsi RUS . 193 D13
Nava E 142 A1
Navacerrada
E............ 151 B3
Navaconcejo
E............ 149 B4
Nava de Arévalo
E............ 150 B3
Nava de la
Asunción E... 150 A3
Nava del Rey
E............ 150 A2
Navafría E.... 151 A4
Navahermosa
E............ 157 A3
Navahrudak BY .13 B6
Naval E 145 B4
Navalacruz E.. 150 B3
Navalcán E.... 150 B2
Navalcarnero
E............ 151 B3
Navaleno E ... 143 C3
Navalmanzano
E............ 151 A3
Navalmoral E . 150 B3
Navalmoral de la
Mata E...... 150 C2
Navalón E.... 159 C3
Navalonguilla
E............ 150 B2
Navalperal de
Pinares E..... 150 B3
Navalpino E... 157 A3
Navaltalgordo
E............ 150 B3
Navaltoril E... 156 A3
Navaluenga E. 150 B3
Navalvillar de Pela
E............ 156 A2
Navan IRL.....30 A2
Navaperal de
Tormes E..... 150 B2

Navapolatsk
BY............13 A8
Navarclés E ... 147 C2
Navarredonda de
Gredos E.... 150 B2
Navarrenx F .. 144 A3
Navarrés E.... 159 B3
Navarrete E... 143 B4
Navarrevisca
E............ 150 B3
Navás E...... 147 C2
Navascués E .. 144 B2
Navas del Madroño
E............ 155 B4
Navas del Rey
E............ 151 B3
Navas del Sepillar
E............ 163 A3
Navas de Oro
E............ 150 A3
Navas de San Juan
E............ 157 B4
Navasfrias E .. 149 B3
Nave I....... 120 B3
Nave de Haver
P............ 149 B3
Navekvarn S...56 B2
Navelli I...... 169 A3
Navenby UK ...40 B3
Näverkärret S...56 A1
Naverstad S....54 B2
Navés E...... 147 C2
Navezuelas E . 156 A2
Navia E 141 A4
Navia de Suarna
E............ 141 B4
Navilly F..... 105 C4
Năvodari RO ...17 C8
Naxos GR 185 B6
Nay F 145 A3
Nazaré P..... 154 B1
Nazarje SLO... 123 A3
Nazilli TR..... 188 B3
Nazza D........82 A2
Nea Anchialos
GR.......... 182 D4
Nea Epidavros
GR.......... 184 B4
Nea Flippias
GR.......... 182 D2
Nea Kalikratia
GR.......... 183 C5
Nea Makri GR . 185 A4
Nea Moudania
GR.......... 183 C5
Neap UK 33 A5
Nea Peramos
GR.......... 183 C6
Neapoli
Kozani GR ... 182 C3
Kriti GR......185 D6
Lakonia GR .. 184 C4
Nea Stira GR . 185 A5
Neath UK 39 C3
Nea Visa GR ... 186 A1
Nea Zichni GR. 183 B5
Nebljusi HR... 124 C1
Neblo SLO.... 122 A2
Nebolchy RUS....9 C8
Nebra D........82 A3
Nebreda E.... 143 C3
Nechanice CZ...84 B3
Neckargemünd
D 93 B4
Neckarsulm D..94 B1
Neda E....... 140 A2
Neded SK..... 112 A1
Nedelišce HR. 124 A2
Nederweert NL .80 A1
Nedreberg N....48 B3
Nedre Gärdsjö
S............50 B2
Nedre Soppero
S........... 196 A4
Nedstrand N...52 A1
Nedvědice CZ...97 B4
Nędza PL......86 B2
Neede NL......71 B3
Needham Market
UK 45 A5
Needingworth
UK 44 A3
Neermoor D ...71 A4
Neeroeteren B. .80 A1
Neerpelt B.....79 A5
Neesen D......72 B1
Neetze D.......73 A3
Nefyn UK......38 B2
Negotin SRB ...16 C5
Negotino
NMK........ 182 B4
Negrar I...... 121 B3
Negredo E.... 151 A5

Negreira E 140 B2
Nègrepelisse
F............ 129 B4
Nègru Vodă
RO........... 17 D8
Negueira de Muñiz
E............ 141 A4
Neheim D......81 A3
Neila E....... 143 B4
Néive I....... 119 C5
Nejdek CZ......83 B4
Nekla PL.......76 B2
Neksø DK......67 A4
Nelas P...... 148 B2
Nelaug N......53 B4
Nelidovo RUS ...9 D8
Nelim FIN 193 D12
Nellingen D....94 C1
Nelson UK......40 B1
Neman RUS....12 A5
Nemea GR 184 B3
Nemesgörzsöny
H............ 111 B4
Nemeskér H.. 111 B3
Nemesnádudvar
H............ 125 A5
Nemesszalók
H............ 111 B4
Nemšová SK ...98 C2
Nenagh IRL 28 B3
Nenince SK.... 112 A3
Nenita GR..... 185 A7
Nenzing A 107 B4
Neochori GR .. 182 D3
Neo Chori GR. 184 A2
Neon Petritsi
GR.......... 183 B5
Nepi I....... 168 A2
Nepomuk CZ...96 B1
Nérac F 129 B3
Neratovice CZ ..84 B2
Nerchau D 83 A4
Néré F 115 C3
Neresheim D...94 C2
Nereto I...... 136 C2
Nerezine HR .. 123 C3
Nerežišća HR . 138 B2
Neringa LT 12 A4
Néris-les Bains
F............ 116 A2
Nerito I....... 169 A3
Nerja E....... 163 B4
Néronde F.... 117 B4
Nérondes F ... 103 C4
Nerpio E...... 164 A2
Nersingen D ...94 C2
Nerva E...... 161 B3
Nervesa della
Battáglia I.... 121 B5
Nervi I....... 134 A2
Nes
Buskerud N....48 B1
Hedmark N....48 B2
Sogn og Fjordane
N........... 46 A3
Sør-Trøndelag
N........... 198 B6
NL 70 A2
Nesbyen N......47 B6
Neset N...... 199 D7
Nesflaten N....52 A2
Nesjahverfi
IS.......... 191 C10
Neskaupstaður
IS.......... 191 B12
Nesland N 53 A3
Neslandsvatn
N............53 B5
Nesle F........90 B2
Nesna N..... 195 D4
Nesoddtangen
N............48 C2
Nesovice CZ...98 B1
Nesselwang D 108 B1
Nesslau CH.... 107 B4
Nessmersiel D .71 A4
Nesso I....... 120 B2
Nesterov UA ...13 C5
Nestorio GR... 182 C3
Nesttun N......46 B2
Nesvady SK... 112 B2
Nesvatnstemmen
N............53 B4
Nether Stowey
UK 43 A3
Netland N......52 B2
Netolice CZ.....96 B2
Netphen D.....81 B4
Netstal CH.... 107 B4

Nettancourt F...91 C4
Nettetal D.....80 A2
Nettlingen D...72 B3
Nettuno I..... 168 B2
Neualbenreuth
D 95 B4
Neubeckum D .81 A4
Neubrandenburg
D 74 A2
Neubruchhausen
D 72 B1
Neubukow D....65 B4
Neuburg D..... 94 C3
Neuchâtel CH. 106 C1
Neu Darchau
D 73 A3
Neudau A..... 111 B3
Neudietendorf
D 82 B2
Neudorf D..... 93 B4
Neuenbürg D .. 93 C4
Neuenburg D ..71 A4
Neuendorf D....66 B2
Neuenhagen D .74 B2
Neuenhaus D...71 B3
Neuenkirchen
Niedersachsen
D..............71 B5
Niedersachsen
D............ 72 A2
Nordrhein-
Westfalen D....71 B4
Nordrhein-
Westfalen D....81 B3
Neuenrade D ..81 A3
Neuenwalde D..64 C1
Neuerburg D...92 A2
Neufahrn
Bayern D 95 C3
Bayern D 95 C4
Neuf-Brisach
F............ 106 A2
Neufchâteau
B............ 92 B1
F............ 92 C1
Neufchâtel-
en-Bray F 90 B1
Neufchâtel-sur-
Aisne F.......91 B4
Neuflize F......91 B4
Neugersdorf
D 84 B2
Neuhardenberg
D 74 B3
Neuharlingersiel
D 71 A4
Neuhaus
Bayern D 95 B3
Bayern D 96 C1
Niedersachsen
D............ 64 C2
Niedersachsen
D............ 73 A3
Niedersachsen
D............ 81 A5
Neuhaus a
Rennweg D ...82 B2
Neuhausen
CH 107 B3
D 83 B5
Neuhausen ob Eck
D 107 B3
Neuhof
Bayern D 94 B2
Hessen D 82 B1
Neuhofen an der
Krems A..... 110 A1
Neuillé-Pont-Pierre
F............ 102 B2
Neuilly-en-Thelle
F.............90 B2
Neuilly-le-Réal
F............ 104 C2
Neuilly-l'Évêque
F............ 105 B4
Neuilly-St Front
F.............90 B3
Neu-Isenburg
D 93 A4
Neukalen D....66 C1
Neu Kaliss D ...73 A4
Neukirch D....84 A2
Neukirchen
A............ 109 A4
Hessen D 81 B5
Schleswig-Holstein
D............ 64 B1
Neukirchen am
Grossvenediger
A............ 109 B3

Neukirchen bei
Heiligen Blut
D 95 B4
Neukloster D . . . 65 C4
Neulengbach
A 110 A2
Neulise F 117 B4
Neu Lübbenau
D 74 B2
Neum BIH 139 C3
Neumagen D 92 B2
Neumarkt D 95 B3
Neumarkt am
Wallersee A . . 109 B4
Neumarkt im
Hausruckkreis
A 109 A4
Neumarkt im
Mühlkreis A . . . 96 C2
Neumarkt im
Steiermark
A 110 B1
Neumarkt Sankt
Veit D 95 C4
Neumünster D . . 64 B2
Neunburg vorm
Wald D 95 B4
Neung-sur-Beuvron
F 103 B3
Neunkirch
Luzern CH . . . 106 B3
Schaffhausen
CH 107 B3
Neunkirchen
A 111 B3
Nordrhein-
Westfalen D 80 B3
Saarland D 92 B3
Neunkirchen am
Brand D 94 B3
Neuötting D 95 C4
Neupetershain
D 84 A2
Neuravensburg
D 107 B4
Neureut D 93 B4
Neuruppin D 74 B1
Neusäss D 94 C2
Neusiedl A 111 B3
Neuss D 80 A2
Neussargues-
Moissac F 116 B2
Neustadt
Bayern D 94 B2
Bayern D 95 B4
Bayern D 95 C3
Brandenburg
D 73 B5
Hessen D 81 B5
Niedersachsen
D 72 B2
Rheinland-Pfalz
D 93 B4
Sachsen D 84 A2
Schleswig-Holstein
D 65 B3
Thüringen D 82 B3
Thüringen D 83 B3
Neustadt-Glewe
D 73 A4
Neustift im
Stubaital A . . . 108 B2
Neustrelitz D . . . 74 A2
Neutal A 111 B3
Neutrebbin D . . . 74 B3
Neu-Ulm D 94 C2
Neuves-Maisons
F 92 C2
Neuvic
Corrèze F . . . 116 B2
Dordogne F . . 129 A3
Neuville-aux-Bois
F 103 A4
Neuville-de-Poitou
F 115 B4
Neuville-les-Dames
F 117 A5
Neuville-sur-Saône
F 117 B4
Neuvy-le-Roi
F 102 B2
Neuvy-Santour
F 104 A2
Neuvy-St Sépulcre
F 103 C3
Neuvy-sur-
Barangeon F . 103 B4
Neuwied D 80 B3
Neuzelle D 74 B3
Névache F 118 B3

Neveklov CZ 96 B2
Nevel RUS 9 D6
Neverfjord N . . 192 B7
Nevers F 104 C2
Nevesinje BIH . 139 B4
Névez F 100 B2
Nevlunghavn
N 53 B5
Nevşehir TR 23 B8
New Abbey UK . . 36 B3
New Aberdour
UK 33 D4
New Alresford
UK 44 B2
Newark-on-Trent
UK 40 B3
Newbiggin-by-the-
Sea UK 37 A5
Newbliss IRL . . . 27 B3
Newborough
UK 38 A2
Newbridge IRL . . 30 A2
Newbridge on Wye
UK 39 B3
Newburgh
Aberdeenshire
UK 33 D4
Fife UK 35 B4
Newbury UK 44 B2
Newby Bridge
UK 36 B4
Newcastle UK . . 27 B5
Newcastle Emlyn
UK 39 B2
Newcastleton
UK 37 A4
Newcastle-under-
Lyme UK 40 B1
Newcastle upon
Tyne UK 37 B5
Newcastle West
IRL 29 B2
Newchurch UK . . 39 B3
New Costessey
UK 41 C5
New Cumnock
UK 36 A2
Newent UK 39 C4
New Galloway
UK 36 A2
Newham UK 45 B4
Newhaven UK . . 45 C4
Newington UK . . 45 B5
Newinn IRL 29 B4
Newlyn UK 42 B1
Newmachar UK . 33 D4
Newmarket
IRL 29 B2
Suffolk UK . . . 45 A4
Western Isles
UK 31 A2
Newmarket-on-
Fergus IRL . . . 28 B3
New Mills UK . . . 40 B2
New Milton UK . . 44 C2
New Pitsligo
UK 33 D4
Newport
Mayo IRL 28 A2
Tipperary IRL . . 29 B3
Isle of Wight
UK 44 C2
Newport UK . . . 39 C4
Pembrokeshire
UK 39 B2
Telford & Wrekin
UK 38 B4
Newport-on-Tay
UK 35 B5
Newport Pagnell
UK 44 A3
Newquay UK . . . 42 B1
New Quay UK . . 39 B2
New Radnor
UK 39 B3
New Romney
UK 45 C4
New Ross IRL . . 30 B2
Newry UK 27 B4
New Scone UK . . 35 B4
Newton Abbot
UK 43 B3
Newton Arlosh
UK 36 B3
Newton Aycliffe
UK 37 B5
Newton Ferrers
UK 42 B2
Newtonhill UK . 33 D4
Newtonmore
UK 32 D2
Newton Stewart
UK 36 B2

Newtown
Herefordshire
UK 39 B4
Powys UK 39 B3
Newtownabbey
UK 27 B5
Newtownards
UK 27 B5
Newtownbutler
UK 27 B3
Newtown
Cunningham
IRL 27 B3
Newtownhamilton
UK 27 B4
Newtownmount-
kennedy IRL . . . 30 A2
Newtown St
Boswells UK . . . 35 C5
Newtown Sands
IRL 29 B2
Newtownstewart
UK 27 B3
Nexon F 115 C5
Neyland UK 39 C2
Nibbiano I 120 C2
Nibe DK 58 B2
Nicastro I 175 C2
Niccone I 135 B5
Nice F 133 B3
Nickelsdorf A . 111 B4
Nicolosi I 177 B4
Nicosia
CY 181 A2
I 177 B3
Nicótera I 175 C1
Nidda D 81 B5
Niğde TR 23 C8
Nidzica PL 77 A5
Niebla E 161 B3
Nieborów PL . . . 77 B5
Niebüll D 64 B1
Niechanowo PL . 76 B2
Niechorze PL . . . 67 B4
Niedalino PL . . . 67 B5
Niederaula D . . . 82 B1
Niederbipp
CH 106 B2
Niederbronn-les-
Bains F 93 C3
Niederfischbach
D 81 B3
Niedergörsdorf
D 74 C1
Niederkrüchten
D 80 A2
Niederndorf A 108 B3
Nieder-Olm D . . 93 B4
Niedersachswerfen
D 82 A2
Niederstetten
D 94 B1
Niederurnen
CH 107 B4
Niederwölz A . 110 B1
Niedoradz PL . . . 85 A3
Niedzica PL 99 B4
Niegosławice
PL 85 A3
Nieheim D 81 A5
Niemcza PL 85 B4
Niemegk D 74 B1
Niemisel S 196 C5
Niemodlin D . . . 85 B5
Nienburg
Niedersachsen
D 72 B2
Sachsen-Anhalt
D 83 A3
Niepołomice
PL 99 A4
Nierstein D 93 B4
Niesky D 84 A2
Niestronno PL . . 76 B2
Nieświń PL 87 A4
Nieszawa PL . . . 76 B3
Nieul-le-Dolent
F 114 B2
Nieul-sur-Mer
F 114 B2
Nieuw-Amsterdam
NL 71 B3
Nieuw-Buinen
NL 71 B3
Nieuwegein NL . 70 B2
Nieuwe Niedorp
NL 70 B1
Nieuwe-Pekela
NL 71 A3
Nieuwerkerken
B 79 B5
Nieuwe-schans
NL 71 A4

Nieuwolda NL . . 71 A3
Nieuwpoort B . . 78 A2
Nieuw-Weerdinge
NL 71 B3
Nigrita GR 183 C5
Nigüelas E 163 B4
Níjar E 164 C2
Nijemci HR 125 B5
Nijkerk NL 70 B2
Nijlen B 79 A4
Nijmegen NL . . . 80 A1
Nijverdal NL 71 B3
Nikel RUS 193 C14
Nikinci SRB . . . 127 C1
Nikiti GR 183 C5
Nikitsch A 111 B3
Nikkaluokta
S 196 B2
Nikla H 111 C4
Niklasdorf A . . 110 B2
Nikšić MNE . . . 139 C4
Nilivaara S 196 B4
Nîmes F 131 B3
Nimis I 122 A2
Nimtofte DK . . . 58 B3
Nin HR 137 A4
Nindorf D 64 B2
Ninemilehouse
IRL 30 B1
Ninove B 79 B4
Niort F 114 B3
Niš SRB 16 D4
Nisa P 155 B3
Niscemi I 177 B3
Niskala FIN . . 197 D10
Nissafors S 60 B3
Nissan-lez-
Ensérune F . . 130 B2
Nissedal N 53 A4
Nissumby DK . . 58 B1
Nisterud N 53 A5
Niton UK 44 C2
Nitra SK 98 C2
Nitrianske-
Pravno SK 98 C2
Nitrianske
Rudno SK 98 C2
Nitry F 104 B2
Nittedal N 48 B2
Nittenau D 95 B4
Nittendorf D . . . 95 B3
Nivala FIN 3 E9
Nivelles B 79 B4
Nivnice CZ 98 C1
Nižná SK 99 B3
Nižná Boca SK . . 99 C3
Nižne Repaše
SK 99 B4
Nizza Monferrato
I 119 C5
Njarðvík IS . . . 190 D3
Njeguševo
SRB 126 B1
Njivice HR 123 B3
Njurundabommen
S 200 D3
Njutånger S . . . 200 E3
Noailles F 90 B2
Noain E 144 B2
Noale I 121 B5
Noalejo E 163 A4
Noblejas E 151 C4
Noceda E 141 B4
Nocera Inferiore
I 170 C2
Nocera Terinese
I 175 B2
Nocera Umbra
I 136 B1
Noci I 173 B3
Nociglia I 173 B4
Nodeland N 53 B3
Nödinge S 60 B2
Nods F 105 B5
Noé F 146 A2
Noépoli I 174 A2
Noeux-les-Mines
F 78 B2
Noez E 157 A3
Nogales E 155 C4
Nogara I 121 B4
Nogarejas E . . . 141 B4
Nogaro F 128 C2
Nogent F 105 A4
Nogent l'Artaud
F 90 C3
Nogent-le-Roi
F 90 C1
Nogent-le-Rotrou
F 89 B4
Nogent-sur-Seine
F 91 C3

Nogent-sur-
Vernisson F . . 103 B4
Nogersund S 63 B2
Noguera E 152 B2
Noguerones E . 163 A3
Nohfelden D . . . 92 B3
Nohn D 80 B2
Noia E 140 B2
Noicáttaro I . . . 173 A2
Noirétable F . . 117 B3
Noirmoutier-en-
l'Île F 114 A1
Noja E 143 A3
Nojewo PL 75 B5
Nokia FIN 8 B3
Nol S 60 B2
Nola I 170 C2
Nolay F 104 C3
Noli I 133 A4
Nolnyra S 51 B4
Nombela E 150 B3
Nomeny F 92 C2
Nomexy F 92 C2
Nonancourt F . . 89 B5
Nonant-le-Pin
F 89 B4
Nonántola I . . . 121 C4
Nonaspe E 153 A4
None I 119 C4
Nontron F 115 C4
Nonza F 180 A2
Noordhorn NL . . 71 A3
Noordwijk NL . . 70 B1
Noordwijkerhout
NL 70 B1
Noordwolde NL 70 B3
Noppikoski S . . . 50 A1
Nora S 55 A6
Nørager DK 58 B2
Norberg S 50 B2
Norboda S 51 B5
Nórcia I 136 C2
Nordagutu N . . . 53 A5
Nordanås S . . . 200 B4
Nordausques F . 78 B2
Nordborg DK . . . 64 A2
Nordby
Aarhus Amt.
DK 59 C3
Ribe Amt. DK . . 59 C1
Norddeich D . . . 71 A4
Norddorf D 64 B1
Norden D 71 A4
Nordenham D . . 72 A1
Norderhov N . . . 48 B2
Norderney D . . . 71 A4
Norderstapel
D 64 B2
Norderstedt D . 64 C3
Nordfjord N . . 193 B14
Nordfjordeid
N 198 D3
Nordfold N . . . 194 C6
Nordhalben D . . 82 B3
Nordhausen D . 82 A2
Nordheim vor der
Rhön D 82 B2
Nordholz D 64 C1
Nordhorn D 71 B4
Nordkjosbotn
N 192 C3
Nordli N 199 A10
Nördlingen D . . 94 C2
Nordmaling S . 200 C5
Nordmark S 49 C6
Nordmela N . . . 194 A6
Nord-Odal N . . . 48 B3
Nordre Osen N . 48 A3
Nordsinni N 48 B1
Nørdstedalsseter
N 198 D4
Nordstemmen
D 72 B2
Nordvågen
N 193 B10
Nordwalde D . . . 71 B4
Noreña E 142 A1
Noresund N 48 B1
Norg NL 71 A3
Norheimsund
N 46 B3
Norie S 63 B2
Norma I 169 B2
Nornäs S 49 A5
Norra S 62 A2
Norråker S 200 B1
Norrala S 51 A3
Norra Vi S 62 A3
Nørre Aaby DK . 59 C2
Nørre Alslev
DK 65 B4

Nørre Lyndelse
DK 59 C3
Nørre Nebel
DK 59 C1
Nørre Snede
DK 59 C2
Nørresundby
DK 58 A2
Nørre Vorupør
DK 58 B1
Norrfjärden S . 196 D4
Norrhed S 196 C3
Norrhult
Klavreström
S 62 A3
Norrköping S . . 56 B2
Norrskedika S . . 51 B5
Norrsundet S . . 51 B4
Norrtälje S 57 A4
Nors DK 58 A1
Norsbron S 55 A4
Norsholm S 56 B1
Norsjö S 200 B5
Nörten-
Hardenberg
D 82 A1
Northallerton
UK 37 B5
Northampton
UK 44 A3
North Berwick
UK 35 B5
North Charlton
UK 37 A5
North Frodingham
UK 40 B3
North Kessock
UK 32 D2
Northleach UK . 44 B2
North Molton
UK 42 A3
North Petherton
UK 43 A3
Northpunds UK 33 B5
North Somercotes
UK 41 B4
Northstowe UK . 45 A4
North Tawton
UK 42 B3
North Thoresby
UK 41 B3
North Walsham
UK 41 C5
Northwich UK . . 38 A4
Norton UK 40 A3
Nortorf D 64 B2
Nort-sur-Erdre
F 101 B4
Nörvenich D . . . 80 B2
Norwich UK 41 C5
Norwick UK 33 A6
Nøsen N 47 B5
Nossa Senhora do
Cabo P 154 C1
Nossebro S 55 B3
Nössemark S . . . 54 A2
Nossen D 83 B5
Notaresco I . . . 169 A3
Noto I 177 C4
Notodden N . . . 53 A5
Nottingham UK 40 C2
Nottuln D 71 C4
Nouan-le-Fuzelier
F 103 B4
Nouans-les-
Fontaines F . . 103 B3
Nougaroulet
F 129 C3
Nouvion F 78 B1
Nouzonville F . . 91 B4
Nova H 111 C3
Nová Baňa SK . . 98 C2
Nová Bystrica
SK 99 B3
Nová Bystřice
CZ 97 B3
Nova Crnja
SRB 126 B2
Novaféltria I . . 135 B5
Nova Gorica
SLO 122 B2
Nova Gradiška
HR 124 B3
Nováky SK 98 C2
Novalaise F . . . 118 B2
Novales E 145 B3
Nova Levante
I 108 C2
Novalja HR . . . 137 A3

Nová Paka CZ . . 84 B3
Nova Pazova
SRB 127 C2
Nová Pec CZ . . . 96 C1
Novara I 120 B1
Novara di Sicília
I 177 A4
Nova Siri I 174 A2
Novate Mezzola
I 120 A2
Nova Topola
BIH 124 B3
Novaya Ladoga
RUS 9 B8
Nova Zagora
BG 17 D6
Nové Hrady CZ . 96 C2
Novelda E 165 A4
Novellara I 121 C3
Nové Město SK . 98 C1
Nové Město nad
Metují CZ 85 B4
Nové Město na
Moravě CZ . . . 97 B4
Nové Město pod
Smrkem CZ . . . 84 B3
Nové Mitrovice
CZ 96 B1
Noventa di Piave
I 122 B1
Noventa Vicentina
I 121 B4
Novés E 151 B3
Noves F 131 B3
Nové Sady SK . . 98 C1
Noves de Segre
E 147 B2
Nové Strašeci
CZ 84 B1
Nové Zámky
SK 112 B2
Novgorod RUS . . 9 C7
Novi Bečej
SRB 126 B2
Novi di Módena
I 121 C3
Novigrad
Istarska HR . . 122 B2
Zadarsko-Kninska
HR 137 A4
Novi Grad BIH . 124 B2
Novigrad Podravski
HR 124 A2
Novi Kneževac
SRB 126 A2
Novi Lígure I . . 120 C1
Noville B 92 A1
Novi Marof
HR 124 A2
Novion-Porcien
F 91 B4
Novi Pazar
BG 17 D7
SRB 16 D4
Novi Sad SRB . . 126 B1
Novi Slankamen
SRB 126 B2
Novi Travnik
BIH 139 A3
Novi Vinodolski
HR 123 B3
Novohrad-
Volynskyy UA . . 13 C7
Novo Mesto
SLO 123 B4
Novo Miloševo
SRB 126 B2
Novorzhev RUS . 9 D6
Novo Selo BIH . 125 B3
Novoselytsya
UA 17 A7
Novosokolniki
RUS 9 D6
Novoveská Huta
SK 99 C4
Novovolynsk
UA 13 C6
Novska HR 124 B2
Nový Bor CZ . . . 84 B2
Nový Bydžov
CZ 84 B3
Novy-Chevrières
F 91 B4
Nový Dwór
Mazowiecki
PL 77 B5
Nový-Hrozenkov
CZ 98 B2
Nový Jičín CZ . . 98 B2
Nový Knin CZ . . 96 B2
Nowa Cerekwia
PL 86 B1
Nowa Dęba PL . 87 B5

Nowa Karczma
PL............68 A3
Nowa Kościoł
PL............85 A3
Nowa Ruda PL ..85 B4
Nowa Słupia
PL............87 B5
Nowa Sól PL....85 A3
Nowa Wieś PL...69 B4
Nowa-Wieś Wielka
PL............76 B3
Nowe PL 69 B3
Nowe Brzesko
PL............87 B4
Nowe Grudze
PL............77 B4
Nowe Kiejkuty
PL............77 A6
Nowe Miasteczko
PL............85 A3
Nowe Miasto
Mazowieckie
PL............77 B5
Mazowieckie
PL............ 87 A4
Nowe Miasto
Lubawskie PL ..69 B4
Nowe Miasto nad
Wartą PL....76 B2
Nowe Skalmierzyce
PL............86 A2
Nowe Warpno
PL............74 A3
Nowica PL......69 A4
Nowogard PL ...75 A4
Nowogród
Bobrzanski PL .84 A3
Nowogrodziec
PL............84 A3
Nowosolna PL ..86 A3
Nowy Dwór
Gdański PL.....69 A4
Nowy Korczyn
PL............87 B4
Nowy Sącz PL ...99 B4
Nowy Staw PL...69 A4
Nowy Targ PL ...99 B4
Nowy Tomyśl
PL............75 B5
Nowy Wiśnicz
PL............99 B4
Noyalo F 101 B3
Noyal-Pontivy
F............ 100 A3
Noyant F...... 102 B2
Noyelles-sur-Mer
F............78 B1
Noyen-sur-Sarthe
F............ 102 B1
Noyers F...... 104 B2
Noyers-sur-Cher
F............ 103 B3
Noyers-sur-Jabron
F............ 132 A1
Noyon F........90 B2
Nozay F...... 101 B4
Nuaillé F 102 B1
Nuaillé-d'Aunis
F............ 114 B3
Nuars F...... 104 B2
Nubledo E ... 141 A5
Nuéno E 145 B3
Nuestra Señora Sa
Verge des Pilar
E............ 166 C1
Nueva E...... 142 A2
Nueva Carteya
E............ 163 A3
Nuevalos E... 152 A2
Nuits F 104 B3
Nuits-St Georges
F............ 105 B3
Nule I 178 B3
Nules E 159 B3
Nulvi I....... 178 B2
Numana I 136 B2
Numansdorp
NL...........79 A4
Nümbrecht D ...81 B3
Nunchritz D....83 A5
Nuneaton UK ...40 C2
Nunnanen FIN 196 A7
N Unnaryd S ...60 B3
Nuñomoral E.. 149 B3
Nunspeet NL...70 B2
Nuorgam FIN 193 B11
Núoro I 178 B3
Nurallao I 179 C3
Nuremberg =
Nürnberg D....94 B3
Nurmes FIN ...3 E11
Nürnberg =
Nuremberg D..94 B3

Nurri I........ 179 C3
Nürtingen D ...94 C1
Nus I......... 119 D1
Nusnäs S.......50 B1
Nusplingen D. 107 A3
Nuštar HR.... 125 B4
Nuupas FIN ... 197 C9
Nyåker S 200 C5
Nyáregyháza
H........... 112 B3
Nyarlörinc H .. 113 C3
Nyasvizh BY.....13 B7
Nybble S.......55 A5
Nybergsund N ..49 A4
Nybøl DK 64 B2
Nyborg
DK 59 C3
S............ 196 D6
Nybro S........62 B3
Nybster UK 32 C3
Nyby DK 65 B5
Nye S 62 A3
Nyékládháza
H........... 113 B4
Nyergesujfalu
H........... 112 B2
Nyhammar S...50 B1
Nyhyttan S.....55 A5
Nyirád H 111 B4
Nyírbátor H....16 B5
Nyíregyháza H..16 B4
Nyker DK 67 A3
Nykil S 56 B1
Nykirke N......48 B2
Nykøbing
Falster DK 65 B4
Vestsjællands Amt.
DK 61 D1
Nykøbing Mors
DK 58 B1
Nyköping S 56 B3
Nykroppa S....55 A5
Nykvarn S.....56 A3
Nykyrke S.....55 B5
Nyland S 200 C3
Nylars DK......67 A3
Nymburk CZ ...84 B3
Nynäshamn S...57 B3
Nyon CH 118 A3
Nyons F 131 A4
Nýřany CZ 96 B1
Nýrsko CZ......95 B5
Nyrud N...... 193 C13
Nysa PL........85 B5
Nysäter S 55 A3
Nyseter N 198 C5
Nyskoga S.....49 B4
Nysted DK 65 B4
Nystrand N 53 A5
Nyúl H 111 B4
Nyvoll N 192 B7

O

Oadby UK 40 C2
Oakengates UK .38 B4
Oakham UK 40 C3
Oanes N 52 B2
Obalj BIH..... 139 B4
O Barco E 141 B4
Obbola S 200 C6
Obdach A 110 B1
Obejo E 156 B3
Oberammergau
D........... 108 B2
Oberasbach D ..94 B2
Oberau D 108 B2
Oberaudorf D. 108 B3
Oberbruck F .. 106 B1
Oberdiessbach
CH 106 C2
Oberdorf CH.. 106 B2
Oberdrauburg
A........... 109 C3
Oberelsbach
D............82 B2
Obere Stanz A 110 B2
Ober Grafendorf
A........... 110 A2
Obergünzburg
D........... 108 B1
Obergurgl A .. 108 C2
Oberhausen D ..80 A2
Oberhof D 82 B2
Oberkirch D....93 C4
Oberkirchen D..81 A4
Oberkochen D..94 C2
Obermassfeld-
Grimmenthal
D............82 B2
Ober-Morlen D .81 B4

Obermünchen
D.............95 C3
Obernai F......93 C3
Obernberg A....96 C1
Obernburg D ...93 B5
Oberndorf D...93 C4
Oberndorf bei
Salzburg A.. 109 B3
Obernkirchen
D.............72 B2
Oberort A..... 110 B2
Oberpullendorf
A........... 111 B3
Oberriet CH... 107 B4
Oberröblingen
D.............82 A3
Oberrot D......94 B1
Oberstaufen
D........... 107 B5
Oberstdorf D. 107 B5
Obertauern A. 109 B4
Obertilliach A. 109 C3
Obertraubling
D.............95 C4
Obertraun A.. 109 B4
Obertrubach D .95 B3
Obertrum A... 109 B4
Oberursel D....81 B4
Obervellach A 109 C4
Oberviechtach
D.............95 B4
Oberwart A... 111 B3
Oberwesel D...93 A3
Oberwinter D...80 B3
Oberwölzstadt
A........... 110 B1
Oberzell D.....96 C1
Obice PL.......87 B4
Óbidos P...... 154 B1
Obing D....... 109 B3
Objat F....... 129 A4
Objazda PL 68 A2
Öblarn A..... 109 B5
Obninsk RUS... 9 E10
O Bolo E...... 141 B3
Oborniki PL....75 B5
Oborniki Śląskie
PL............85 A4
Obornjača
SRB 126 B1
Obrenovac
SRB 127 C2
Obrež SRB.... 127 C1
Obrigheim D...93 B5
Obrov SLO.... 123 B3
Obrovac
HR 137 A4
SRB 126 B1
Obrovac Sinjski
HR 138 B2
Obruk TR......23 B7
Obrzycko PL ...75 B5
Obudovac BIH 125 C4
Ocaña E...... 151 C4
O Carballiño
E............ 140 B2
Occhiobello I.. 121 C4
Occimiano I... 119 B5
Očevlja BIH ... 139 A4
Ochagavía E .. 144 B2
Ochiltree UK...36 A2
Ochla PL.......84 A3
Ochotnica-Dolna
PL............99 B4
Ochotnica-Górna
PL............99 B4
Ochsenfurt D ..94 B2
Ochsenhausen
D........... 107 A4
Ochtendung D..80 B3
Ochtrup D 71 B4
Ocieka PL......87 B5
Ockelbo S.....50 B3
Ockerö S.......60 B1
Ocniţa MD.....17 A7
O Corgo E 141 B3
Očová SK......99 C3
Ócsa H 112 B3
Ócseny H 125 A4
Ócsöd H....... 113 C4
Octeville F.....88 A2
Ocypel PL......69 B3
Ödåkra S.......61 C2
Odby DK 58 B1
Odda N........46 B2
Odder DK 59 C3
Ödeborg S.....54 B2
Odeceixe P.... 160 B1
Odechów PL...87 A5
Odeleite P.... 160 B2
Odemira P.... 160 B1
Ödemiş TR.... 188 A2
Odensbacken S 56 A1

Odense DK.....59 C3
Odensjö
Jönköping S .. 62 A2
Kronoberg S ... 60 C3
Oderberg D....74 B3
Oderzo I 122 B1
Odesa = Odessa
UA...........17 B9
Ödeshög S 55 B5
Odessa = Odesa
UA...........17 B9
Odiáxere P.... 160 B1
Odie UK........33 B4
Odiham UK 44 B3
Odintsovo RUS..9 E10
Odivelas P.... 160 A1
Odolanów PL ..85 A5
Odón E....... 152 B2
Odorheiu Secuiesc
RO 17 B6
Odrowaz PL....87 A4
Odry CZ........98 B1
Odrzywół PL...87 A4
Ødsted DK 59 C2
Odžaci SRB... 126 B1
Odžak BIH.... 125 B4
Oebisfelde D...73 B3
Oederan D.....83 B5
Oeding D......71 C3
Oegstgeest NL..70 B1
Oelde D........81 A4
Oelsnitz D.....83 B4
Oer-Erkenschwick
D.............80 A3
Oerlinghausen
D.............72 C1
Oettingen D ...94 C2
Oetz A....... 108 B1
Oeventrop D...81 A4
Offanengo I... 120 B2
Offenbach D...81 B4
Offenburg D ...93 C3
Offida I 136 C2
Offingen D.....94 C2
Offranville F ...89 A5
Ofte N 53 A4
Ofterschwang
D........... 107 B5
Oggiono I..... 120 B2
Ogihares E... 163 A4
Ogliastro Cilento
I............ 170 C3
Ogliastro Marina
I............ 170 C2
Ogmore-by-Sea
UK 39 C3
Ogna N........52 B1
Ogre LV 8 D4
Ogrodzieniec
PL............86 B3
Ogulin HR.... 123 B4
Ögur IS....... 190 A3
Ohanes E 164 B2
Ohey B........79 B5
Ohlstadt D... 108 B2
Ohrdorf D.....73 B3
Ohrdruf D.....82 B2
Ohrid NMK... 182 B2
Öhringen D....94 B1
Ohlava FIN... 197 D8
Ohavo P...... 154 B1
Oiana E...... 147 B3
Oia E........ 151 C4
Oiã P........ 148 B1
Oiartzun E ... 144 A2
Oijärvi FIN ... 197 D8
Oilgate IRL....30 B2
Oimbra E..... 148 A2
Oiselay-et-
Grachoux F .. 105 B4
Oisemont F ...90 B1
Oisterwijk NL ..79 A5
Öja S..........57 C4
Öje S 49 B5
Ojén E 162 B3
Ojrzeń PL......77 B5
Ojuelos Altos
E............ 156 B2
Okalewo PL....77 A4
Okány H 113 C5
Okehampton
UK 42 B2
Oklaj HR 138 B2
Økneshamn N 194 B6
Okoč SK...... 111 B4
Okolićne SK....99 B3
Okonek PL.....68 B1
Okonin PL......69 B3
Okřisky CZ 97 B3
Oksa PL........87 B4
Oksbøl DK 59 C1
Oksby DK 59 C1
Øksfjord N ... 192 B6
Øksna N 48 B3
Okučani HR... 124 B3
Okulovka RUS ...9 C8

Ólafsfjörður
IS........... 191 A7
Ólafsvík IS ... 190 C2
Üllerup DK.....65 A3
ÖLagnö S 57 A4
Olagüe E..... 144 B2
Oland N........53 B4
Olargues F.... 130 B1
Oława PL.......85 B5
Olazagutia E.. 144 B1
Olbernhau D...83 B5
Ólbia I....... 178 B3
Olching D.... 108 A2
Oldbury UK ...43 A4
Oldcastle IRL...27 C3
Old Deer UK... 33 D4
Oldeberkoop
NL...........70 B3
Oldeboorn NL..70 A2
Olden N...... 198 D3
Oldenbrok D...71 A5
Oldenburg
Niedersachsen
D........... 71 A5
Schleswig-Holstein
D............65 B3
Oldenzaal NL ..71 B3
Olderdalen N . 192 C4
Olderfjord N.. 193 B9
Oldersum D...71 A4
Oldervik N.... 192 C2
Oldham UK....40 B1
Oldisleben D...82 A3
Oldmeldrum
UK 33 D4
Olea E....... 142 B2
Oleby S........49 B5
Olsberg D......81 A4
Olsene B.......79 B3
Olserud S......55 A4
Olshammar S...55 B5
Olshanka UA... 13 D9
Olszanica PL...85 A3
Olsztyn
Śląskie PL.....86 B3
Warmińsko-
Mazurskie PL ..69 B5
Olsztynek PL...77 A5
Olszyna PL.....84 A3
Olszyny PL.....77 A6
Oltedal N......52 B2
Olten CH..... 106 B2
Olteniţa RO....17 C7
Olula del Rio E 164 B2
Ølve N 46 B2
Olvega E..... 144 C2
Olvera E...... 162 B2
Olympia GR... 184 B2
Olzai I....... 178 B3
Omagh UK.....27 B3
Omalos GR.... 185 D4
Omegna I..... 119 B5
Omiš HR...... 138 B2
Omišalj HR... 123 B3
Ommen NL.....71 B3
Omodhos CY.. 181 B1
Omoljica SRB . 127 C2
On B 79 B5
Oña E........ 143 B3
Onano I...... 168 A1
O Näsberg S....49 B5
Oñati E....... 143 A4
Onda E....... 159 B3
Ondara E..... 159 C4
Ondarroa E ... 143 A4
Onesse-et-Laharie
F............ 128 B1
Oneşti RO.....17 B7
Onhaye B 79 B4
Onich UK......34 B2
Onil E........ 159 C3
Onis E....... 142 A2
Önnestad S 61 C4
Onsala S.......60 B2
Ontinyent E... 159 C3
Ontur E...... 158 C2
Onzain F...... 103 B3
Onzonilla E ... 142 B1
Oostburg NL...79 A3
Oostende B....78 A2
Oosterend NL...70 A2
Oosterhout NL..79 A4
Oosterwolde
NL...........71 B3
Oosterzele B....79 B3
Oosthuizen NL..70 B2
Oostkamp B....78 A3
Oostmalle B....79 A4
Oost-Vlieland
NL...........70 A2
Oostvoorne NL .79 A4
Ootmarsum NL .71 B3
Opalenica PL...75 B5
O Páramo E....140 B3
Opařany CZ....96 B2
Opatija HR ... 123 B3

Opatów
Śląskie PL......86 B2
Świętokrzyskie
PL............87 B5
Wielkopolskie
PL............ 86 A2
Opatówek PL ..86 A2
Opatowiec PL..87 B4
Opava CZ......98 B1
O Pedrouzo E . 140 B2
Opeinde NL....70 A3
Oper Thalkirchdorf
D........... 107 B5
Opglabbeerk B .80 A1
Opicina I...... 122 B2
O Pino E...... 140 B2
Oplotnica SLO 123 A4
Opmeer NL....70 B1
Opochka RUS ...9 D6
Opočno CZ.....85 B4
Opoczno PL....87 A4
Opole PL.......86 B1
Oporów PL.....77 B4
O Porriño E.... 140 B2
Opovo SRB... 127 B2
Oppach D......84 A2
Oppdal N 198 C6
Oppeby
Östergötland
S.............56 B1
Södermanland
S.............56 B2
Oppedal N 46 A2
Oppegård N ...54 A1
Oppenau D....93 C4
Oppenberg A . 110 B1
Oppenheim D...93 B4
Óppido Lucano
I............ 172 B1
Óppido Mamertina
I............ 175 C1
Opponitz A ... 110 B1
Oppstad N.....48 B3
Oprtalj HR ... 122 B2
Opsaheden S ..49 B5
Ópusztaszer
H........... 113 C4
Opuzen HR.... 138 B3
Ora
CY 181 B2
I............ 121 A4
Orada P...... 155 C3
Oradea RO.... 16 B4
Oradour-sur-Glane
F............ 115 C5
Oradour-sur-Vayres
F............ 115 C4
Oragonja SLO. 122 B2
Orah BIH..... 139 C4
Orahova BIH.. 138 A3
Orahovica HR. 125 B3
Orahovo BIH.. 124 B3
Oraison F..... 132 B1
Orajärvi FIN .. 196 C7
Orange F...... 131 A3
Orani I....... 178 B3
Oranienbaum
D............83 A4
Oranienburg D .74 B2
Oranmore IRL...28 A3
Orašac SRB... 127 C2
Orašje BIH ... 125 B4
Oravská Lesná
SK............99 B3
Oravská Polhora
SK............99 B3
Oravské Veselé
SK............99 B3
Oravsky-Podzámok
SK............99 B3
Orba E....... 159 C3
Orbacém P.... 148 A1
Orbais F.......91 C3
Ørbæk DK......59 C3
Orbassano I... 119 B4
Orbe CH..... 105 C5
Orbec F........89 A4
Orbetello I.... 168 A1
Orbetello Scalo
I............ 168 A1
Orbigny F.... 103 B3
Ørby DK........59 B3
Örbyhus S 51 B4
Orce E....... 164 B2
Orcera E..... 164 A2
Orchamps-Vennes
F............ 105 B5
Orches F...... 102 B2
Orchete E..... 159 C3
Orchies F......78 B3

Orchowo PL....76 B3
Orcières F.....118 C3
Ordes E.......140 A2
Ordhead UK... 33 D4
Ordino AND... 146 B2
Ordizia E......144 A1
Orduña E 143 B4
Ore S..........50 A2
Orea E 152 B2
Orebić HR.... 138 C3
Örebro S........56 A1
Öregcsertő H . 112 C3
Öregrund S 51 B5
Orehoved DK...65 B4
Orellana E ... 156 A2
Orellana de la
  Sierra E 156 A2
Ören TR 188 B2
Örencik TR.... 187 C4
Orestiada GR.. 186 A1
Organyà E 147 B2
Orgaz E 157 A4
Orgelet F..... 105 C4
Ørgenvika N....48 B1
Orgères-en-Beauce
  F............ 103 A3
Orgibet F 145 B4
Orgnac-l'Aven
  F............ 131 A3
Orgon F....... 131 B3
Orgósolo I 178 B3
Orhaneli TR... 186 C3
Orhangazi TR . 187 B4
Orhei MD 17 B8
Orhomenos
  GR 184 A3
Oria E 164 B2
Ória I......... 173 B3
Origny-Ste Benoite
  F............. 91 B3
Orihuela E 165 A4
Orihuela del
  Tremedal E .. 152 B2
Orikum AL.... 182 C1
Oriola P....... 154 C3
Oriolo I 174 A2
Oriovac HR.... 125 B3
Orissaare EST 8 C3
Oristano I 179 C2
Öriszentpéter
  H............ 111 C3
Ørje N..........54 A2
Orjiva E 163 B4
Orkanger N ... 198 B6
Örkelljunga S...61 C3
Örkény H 112 B3
Orlamünde D...82 B3
Orléans F 103 B3
Orlová CZ......98 B2
Orlovat SRB... 126 B2
Ormea I....... 133 A3
Ormelet N 54 A1
Oremeyr N 53 A5
Ormília GR.... 183 C5
Ormos GR.... 185 B5
Ormož SLO... 124 A2
Ormskirk UK...38 A4
Ornans F 105 B5
Ornäs S 50 B2
Ørnes N...... 195 D4
Orneta PL......69 A5
Ørnhoj DK.....59 B1
Ornö S.........57 A4
Örnsköldsvik
  S........... 200 C4
Orolik HR 125 B4
Orom SRB.... 126 B1
Oron-la-Ville
  CH 106 C1
Oronsko PL 87 A4
Oropa I....... 119 B4
Oropesa
  Castellón de la
  Plana E 153 B4
  Toledo E..... 150 C2
O Rosal E..... 140 C2
Orosei I 178 B3
Orosháza H ... 113 C4
Oroslavje HR.. 124 B1
Oroszlány H ... 112 B2
Oroszlo H..... 125 A4
Orotelli I 178 B3
Orozko E...... 143 A4
Orphir UK......33 C3
Orpington UK...45 B4
Orreaga-
  Roncesvalles
  E........... 144 A2
Orrefors S......62 B4
Orrviken S ... 199 B11

Orsa S..........50 A1
Orsara di Púglia
  I............ 171 B3
Orsay F 90 C2
Orscholz D 92 B2
Orsennes F.... 103 C3
Orserum S 55 B5
Orsha BY.......13 A9
Orsières CH ... 119 A4
Örsjö S.........63 B3
Ørslev DK......65 A4
Örslösa S......55 B3
Orsogna I 169 A4
Orsomarso I... 174 B1
Orşova RO 16 C5
Ørsta N 198 C3
Ørsted DK......58 B3
Örsundsbro S...56 A3
Ortaca TR 188 C3
Ortakent TR.. 188 B2
Ortaklar TR ... 188 B2
Ortaköy TR.....23 B8
Orta Nova I ... 171 B3
Orte I 168 A2
Ortenburg D ...96 C1
Orth A 111 A3
Orthez F 128 C2
Ortigueira E... 140 A3
Ortilla E 145 B3
Ortisei I 108 C2
Orţişoara RO... 126 B3
Ortnevik N.....46 A3
Orton UK.......37 B4
Ortona I...... 169 A4
Ortrand D......84 A1
Orubica HR ... 124 B3
Ørum DK.......58 B2
Orune I....... 178 B3
Orusco E 151 B4
Orvalho P..... 155 A3
Orvault F 101 B4
Ørvella N 53 A5
Orvieto I 168 A2
Orvínio I 169 A2
Oryahovo BG .. 17 D5
Orzesze PL......86 B2
Orzinuovi I ... 120 B2
Orzivécchi I ... 120 B2
Orzyny PL......77 A6
Os
  Hedmark N 48 B3
  Hedmark N .. 199 C8
Osann-Monzel
  D............92 B2
Osbruk S......62 A2
Øsby DK 59 C2
Osby S 61 C3
Oščadnica SK ...98 B2
Oschatz D......83 A5
Oschersleben
  D............73 B4
Óschiri I 178 B3
Oscilowo PL....77 B5
Osdorf D......64 B3
Osečina SRB... 127 C1
Osečná CZ......84 B2
Oseja de Sajambre
  E........... 142 A1
Osek CZ......84 B1
Osen N 199 A7
Osera de Ebro
  E........... 153 A3
Osidda I...... 178 B3
Osie PL........69 B3
Osieczna
  Pomorskie PL ..68 B3
  Wielkopolskie
  PL 75 C5
Osieczno PL....75 A4
Osiek
  Kujawsko-
  Pomorskie PL ..76 B3
  Kujawsko-
  Pomorskie PL . 77 A4
  Pomorskie PL ..69 B3
  Świętokrzyskie
  PL 87 B5
Osiek nad Notecią
  PL............76 A2
Osielsko PL....76 A3
Osijek HR 125 B4
Osilnica SLO .. 123 B3
Ósilo I......... 178 B2
Ósimo I...... 136 B2
Osinja BIH 125 C3
Osintorf BY ...13 A9
Osipaonica
  SRB 127 C3
Osjaków PL....86 A2
Oskamull UK...34 B1
Oskarshamn S...62 A4
Oskarström S...60 C2
Oslany SK......98 C2

Oslavany CZ....97 B4
Ošlje HR....... 139 C3
Oslo N 48 C2
Osløs DK.......58 A1
Osmancık TR....23 A8
Osmaneli TR .. 187 B4
Ösmo S........57 B3
Osmolin PL....77 B4
Osnabrück D...71 B5
Ośno Lubuskie
  PL............75 B3
Osoblaha CZ....85 B5
Osor HR...... 123 C3
Osorno E...... 142 B2
Øsoyra N.......46 A2
Osøyro N.......46 B2
Óspakseyri IS . 190 B4
Os Peares E ... 140 B3
Ospedaletti I .. 133 B3
Ospitaletto I .. 120 B3
Oss NL.........80 A1
Ossa de Montiel
  E........... 158 C1
Ossi I......... 178 B2
Ossjøen N......47 B5
Ossun F....... 145 A3
Ostanå S......61 C4
Ostanvik S.....50 A2
Ostashkov RUS ..9 D8
Östavall S..... 200 D1
Ostbevern D ...71 B4
Østborg N .. 199 A10
Østby N 49 A4
Osted DK...... 61 D1
Ostenfeld D......64 B2
Oster UA.......13 C9
Øster Assels DK.58 B1
Osterburg D ...73 B4
Osterburken D..94 B1
Österbybruk S ..51 B4
Österbyhavn
  DK 58 A4
Österbymo S...62 A3
Ostercappeln D 71 B5
Österfärnebo S ..51 B3
Osterfeld D.....83 A3
Österforse S .. 200 C3
Osterhever D...64 B1
Osterhofen D...95 C5
Osterholz-
  Scharmbeck
  D............72 A1
Øster Hornum
  DK 58 B2
Øster Hurup DK 58 B3
Østerild DK....58 A1
Øster Jølby DK..58 B1
Österlövsta S ..51 B4
Øster-marie DK .67 A4
Ostermiething
  A........... 109 A3
Osterode am Harz
  D............82 A2
Ostersiel D......64 B1
Östersund S.. 199 B11
Øster Tørslev
  DK 58 B3
Östervåla S 51 B4
Östervallskog
  S............54 A2
Ostervrå DK....58 A3
Osterwieck D...73 C3
Osterzell D..... 108 B1
Ostffyasszonyfa
  H........... 111 B4
Östfora S......51 C4
Östhammar S...51 B5
Ostheim F..... 106 A2
Ostheim vor der
  Rhön D........82 B2
Osthofen D.....93 B4
Ostiano I..... 120 B3
Ostíglia I..... 121 B4
Ostiz E 144 B2
Östmark S......49 B4
Östnor S........50 A1
Ostojićevo
  SRB 126 B2
Ostra I....... 136 B2
Östra Amtervik
  S............55 A4
Östraby S...... 61 D3
Ostrach D..... 107 B4
Östra Husby S...56 B2
Östra Ljungby
  S............61 C3
Östra Ryd S....56 B2
Ostrau D......83 A5
Ostrava CZ......98 B2
Ostritz D......84 A2

Ostróda PL......69 B4
Ostroh UA.......13 C7
Ostrołęka PL....12 B4
Ostropole PL....68 B1
Ostroróg PL....75 B5
Ostrošovac
  BIH.......... 124 C1
Ostrov
  CZ............83 B4
  RUS 8 D6
Ostrov nad Oslavou
  CZ............97 B3
Ostrówek PL....86 A2
Ostrowiec PL....68 A1
Ostrowiec-
  Świętokrzyski
  PL............87 B5
Ostrowite PL....77 A4
Ostrów
  Mazowiecka
  PL............12 B4
Ostrowo PL 76 B3
Ostrów
  Wielkopolski
  PL............86 A1
Ostrožac BIH .. 139 B3
Ostrzeszów PL ..86 A1
Ostseebad
  Kühlungsborn
  D............65 B4
Ostuni I...... 173 B3
Osuna E 162 A2
Osvětimany CZ .98 B1
Oswestry UK....38 B3
Oświęcim PL....86 B3
Osztopán H ... 111 C4
Oteiza E 144 B2
Otelec RO..... 126 B2
Oteo E 143 A3
Oterbekk N 54 A1
Otero de Herreros
  E........... 151 B3
Otero de O Bodas
  E........... 141 C4
Othem S.......57 C4
Otley UK.......40 B2
Otmuchów PL...85 B5
Otočac HR..... 123 C4
Otok
  Splitsko-
  Dalmatinska
  HR 138 B2
  Vukovarsko-
  Srijemska
  HR 125 B4
Otoka BIH..... 124 C2
Otranto I..... 173 B4
Otrić HR...... 138 A2
Otrícoli I 168 A2
Otrokovice CZ ..98 B1
Otta N 198 D6
Ottana I...... 178 B3
Ottaviano I ... 170 C2
Ottenby S......63 B4
Ottendorf-Okrilla
  D............84 A1
Ottenhöfen D...93 C4
Ottenschlag A ..97 C3
Ottensheim A...96 C2
Otterbach D....93 B3
Otterbäcken S ..55 B5
Otterberg D....93 B3
Otterburn UK ..37 A4
Otter Ferry UK .34 B2
Otterndorf D...64 C1
Ottersburg D ..72 A2
Ottersweier D...93 C4
Otterup DK....59 C3
Ottery St Mary
  UK 43 B3
Ottignies B.....79 B4
Ottmarsheim
  F............ 106 B2
Ottobeuren D. 107 B5
Ottone I...... 120 C2
Ottsjö S..... 199 B10
Ottweiler D.....92 B3
Otvešti RO.... 126 B3
Ötvöskónyi H. 124 A3
Otwock PL......12 B4
Ouanne F..... 104 B2
Ouarville F......90 C1
Oucques F 103 B3
Oud-Beijerland
  NL............79 A4
Ouddorp NL....79 A3
Oudemirdum
  NL............70 B2
Oudenaarde B ..79 B3
Oudenbosch
  NL............79 A4
Oudenburg B ..78 A3

Oude-Pekela
  NL............71 A4
Oude-Tonge
  NL............79 A4
Oudewater NL ..70 B1
Oud Gastel NL ..79 A4
Oudon F...... 101 B4
Oue DK.........58 B2
Oughterard IRL .28 A2
Ouguela P 155 B3
Ouistreham F...89 A3
Oulainen FIN.....3 D9
Oulchy-le-Château
  F............. 91 B3
Oullins F 117 B4
Oulmes F 114 B3
Oulton UK 41 C5
Oulton Broad
  UK 41 C5
Oulu FIN 3 D9
Oulx I........ 119 B3
Oundle UK 40 C3
Ouranopoli
  GR 183 C6
Ourém P 154 B2
Ourense E..... 140 B3
Ourique P..... 160 B1
Ourol E....... 140 A3
Ouroux-en-Morvan
  F............ 104 B2
Ousdale UK 32 C3
Oust F 146 B2
Outakoski
  FIN......... 193 C10
Outeiro P 148 A1
Outeiro de Rei
  E........... 140 A3
Outes E 140 B2
Outokumpu FIN. .9 A6
Outreau F......78 B1
Outwell UK.....41 C4
Ouzouer-le-Marché
  F............ 103 B3
Ouzouer-sur-Loire
  F............ 103 B4
Ovada I...... 133 A4
Ovar P 148 B1
Ovelgönne D ...72 A1
Overath D......80 B3
Overbister UK...33 B4
Overdinkel NL ..71 B4
Överenhörna S .56 A3
Overhalla N... 199 A8
Overijse B......79 B4
Over-jerstal DK .59 C2
Overlade DK....58 B2
Överlida S 60 B2
Överö FIN......51 B7
Overpelt B......79 A5
Overton UK.....38 B4
Övertorneå S. 196 C6
Överum S......62 A4
Ovidiopol UA...17 B9
Oviedo E...... 141 A5
Oviglio I 119 C5
Ovíndoli I 169 A3
Ovodda I..... 178 B3
Øvre Årdal N...47 A4
Øvrebygd N....52 B2
Øvre Rendal
  N........... 199 D8
Øvre Sirdal N ...52 B2
Övre Soppero
  S........... 196 A4
Øvre Ullerud S .55 A4
Övruch UA......13 C8
Ovtrup DK......59 C1
Owińska PL 76 B1
Oxaback S......60 B2
Oxberg S.......49 A6
Oxelösund S...56 B3
Oxenholme UK. .37 B4
Oxford UK 44 B2
Oxie S........ 61 D3
Oxilithos GR .. 185 A5
Oxted UK.......45 B4
Oyaca TR..... 187 C7
Øye N 47 A5
Øyenkilen N ...54 A1
Øyeren N 48 A2
Øyfjell N.......53 A4
Øygärdslia N...53 B4
Oykel Bridge
  UK 32 D2
Øymark N......54 A2
Oyonnax F 118 A2
Øyslebø N 52 B3
Øystese N......46 B3
Oyten D........72 A2
Øyuvsbu N.....52 A3
Ozaeta E 143 B4

Ozalj HR 123 B4
Ożarów PL......87 B5
Ożarów Maz
  PL............77 B5
Ožbalt SLO.... 110 C2
Ózd H......... 113 A4
Ożd'any SK.....99 C3
Ozieri I....... 178 B3
Ozimek PL......86 B2
Ozimica BIH... 139 A4
Ozora H....... 112 C2
Ozorków PL....77 C4
Ozzano Monferrato
  I............ 119 B5

P

Paakkola FIN.. 196 D7
Paal B..........79 A5
Pabianice PL....86 A3
Pacanów PL....87 B5
Paceco I...... 176 B1
Pachino I..... 177 C4
Pačir SRB..... 126 B1
Pack A 110 B2
Paços de Ferreira
  P............ 148 A1
Pacov CZ......96 B3
Pacsa H 111 C4
Pacy-sur-Eure
  F............. 89 A5
Paczków PL....85 B5
Padany RUS.... 3 E13
Padborg DK....64 B2
Padej SRB.... 126 B2
Padene HR 138 A2
Paderborn D...81 A4
Paderne P.... 160 B1
Padiham UK....40 B1
Padina SRB.... 126 B2
Padinska Skela
  SRB 127 C2
Padornelo P .. 148 A1
Padova I...... 121 B4
Padragkút H .. 111 B4
Padria I....... 178 B2
Padrón E...... 140 B2
Padru I....... 178 B3
Padstow UK....42 B2
Padul E 163 A4
Padula I...... 172 B1
Paduli I...... 170 B2
Paesana I 119 C4
Paese I....... 121 B5
Pag HR 137 A4
Pagani I...... 170 C2
Pagánica I.... 169 A3
Pagánico I ... 135 C4
Pagl'ieta I ... 169 A4
Pagny-sur-Moselle
  F............. 92 C2
Páhi H 112 C3
Pahkakumpu
  FIN......... 197 C11
Pahl D....... 108 B2
Paide EST 8 C4
Paignton UK ...43 B3
Pailhès F 146 A2
Paimboeuf F .. 101 B3
Paimio FIN 8 B3
Paimpol F..... 100 A2
Paimpont F ... 101 A3
Painswick UK ..43 A4
Painten D......95 C3
Paisley UK.....34 C3
Pajala S 196 B6
Pajares de los
  Oteros E 142 B1
Pajęczno PL....86 A2
Páka H 111 C3
Pakość PL......76 B3
Pakosławice
  PL............85 B5
Pakoštane HR. 137 B4
Pakrac HR.... 124 B3
Paks H 112 C2
Palacios de la Sierra
  E........... 143 C3
Palaciòs de la
  Valduerna E.. 141 B5
Palacios del Sil
  E........... 141 B4
Palacios de
  Sanabria E .. 141 B4
Palaciosrubios
  E........... 150 A2
Palafrugell E .. 147 C4
Palagiano I ... 173 B3
Palagonía I ... 177 B3
Paláia I....... 135 B3
Palaiokastritsa
  GR 182 D1

Palaiseau F 90 C2
Palamas GR ... 182 D4
Palamòs E..... 147 C4
Påläng S 196 D5
Palanga LT 8 E2
Palanzano I ... 134 A3
Palárikovo SK. 112 A2
Palas de Rei E . 140 B3
Palata I....... 170 B2
Palau I....... 178 A3
Palavas-les-Flots
  F............ 131 B2
Palazuelos de la
  Sierra E 143 B3
Palazzo Adriano
  I............ 176 B2
Palazzo del Pero
  I............ 135 B4
Palazzolo Acréide
  I............ 177 B3
Palazzolo sull Oglio
  I............ 120 B2
Palazzo San
  Gervásio I.... 172 B1
Palazzuolo sul
  Senio I...... 135 A4
Paldiski EST......8 C4
Pale BIH...... 139 B4
Palekastro GR. 185 D7
Palena I...... 169 B4
Palencia E..... 142 B2
Palenciana E .. 163 A3
Paleochora
  GR 185 D4
Paleometokho
  CY 181 A2
Palermo I..... 176 A2
Paleros GR....182 E2
Palestrina I.... 169 B2
Pálfa H 112 C2
Palfau A....... 110 B1
Palhaça P 148 B1
Palheiros da Tocha
  P............ 148 B1
Palheiros de
  Quiaios P.... 148 B1
Paliaopoli GR . 185 B5
Palić SRB..... 126 A1
Palidoro I 168 B2
Palinuro I 172 B1
Paliouri GR.... 183 D5
Paliseul B......91 B5
Pallanza I.... 119 B5
Pallares E 161 A3
Pallaruelo de
  Monegros E .. 153 A3
Pallas Green
  IRL 29 B3
Pallerols E 146 B2
Palling D...... 109 A3
Palluau F 114 B2
Palma P....... 154 C2
Palma Campánia
  I............ 170 C2
Palma del Río
  E........... 162 A2
Palma de Mallorca
  E........... 166 B2
Palma di
  Montechiaro
  I............ 176 B2
Palmádula I... 178 B2
Palmanova I .. 122 B2
Palma Nova E . 166 B2
Palmela P 154 C2
Palmerola E... 147 B3
Palmi I....... 175 C1
Pälmonostora
  H........... 113 C3
Palo del Colle
  I............ 171 B4
Palojärvi FIN . 192 D7
Palojoensuu
  FIN......... 196 A6
Palomares E .. 164 B3
Palomares del
  Campo E 158 B1
Palombara Sabina
  I............ 168 A2
Palos de la Frontera
  E........... 161 B3
Palotaboszok
  H........... 125 A4
Palotás H 112 B3
Pals E 147 C4
Pålsboda S.....56 A1
Paluzza I 109 C4
Pamhagen A... 111 B3
Pamiers F..... 146 A2
Pamiętowo PL ..76 A2
Pampaneira I. 163 B4
Pamparato I .. 133 A3

Pampilhosa
Aveiro P **148** B1
Coimbra P . . . **148** B2
Pampliega E . . **143** B3
Pamplona E . . **144** B2
Pampow D **73** A4
Pamukçu TR . . **186** C2
Pamukkale TR **188** B4
Pamukova TR . **187** B5
Panagyurishte
BG **17** D6
Pancalieri I . . . **119** C4
Pančevo SRB . . **127** C2
Pancey F **91** C5
Pancorvo E . . . **143** B3
Pancrudo E . . . **152** B2
Pandino I **120** B2
Pandrup DK **58** A2
Panenský-Týnec
CZ **84** B1
Panes E **142** A2
Panevėžys LT **8** E4
Pangbourne
UK **44** B2
Panissières F . . **117** B4
Panki PL **86** B2
Pannes F **103** A4
Panningen NL . . **80** A1
Pannonhalma
H **111** B4
Pano Lefkara
CY **181** B2
Pano Panayia
CY **181** B1
Panormos GR . **185** B6
Panschwitz-Kuckau
D **84** A2
Pansdorf D **65** C3
Pantano de Cíjara
E **156** A3
Pantín E **140** A2
Pantoja E **151** B4
Pantón E **140** B3
Panxon E **140** B2
Páola I **174** B2
Paola M **175** C3
Pápa H **111** B4
Papasídero I . . **174** B1
Pápateszér H . **111** B4
Papenburg D . . **71** A4
Paphos CY **181** B1
Pappenheim D . . **94** C2
Paprotnia PL . . . **77** B5
Parábita I **173** B4
Paraćin SRB . . **127** D3
Parád H **113** B4
Parada
Bragança P . . **149** A3
Viseu P **148** B1
Paradas E **162** A2
Paradela E **140** B3
Parades de
Rubiales E . . . **150** A2
Paradinas de San
Juan E **150** B2
Paradiso di
Cevadale . . . **108** C1
Paradyż PL **87** A4
Parainen FIN **8** B3
Parakhino
Paddubye RUS . . **9** C8
Parakka S **196** B4
Paralimni CY . . **181** A2
Parallo Astros
GR **184** B3
Paramé F **88** B2
Paramithia
GR **182** D2
Páramo E **141** A4
Páramo del Sil
E **141** B4
Parandaça P . . **148** A2
Paravadella E . **141** A3
Paray-le-Monial
F **104** C3
Parceiros P . . . **154** B2
Parcey F **105** B4
Parchim D **73** A4
Parciaki PL **77** A6
Parcice PL **86** A2
Pardilla E **151** A4
Pardubice CZ . . **97** A3
Paredes
E **151** B5
P **148** A1
Paredes de Coura
P **140** C2
Paredes de Nava
E **142** B2
Paredes de
Siguenza E . . **151** A5
Pareja E **151** B4

Parennes F **102** A1
Parenti I **175** B2
Parentis-en-Born
F **128** B1
Parey D **73** B4
Parfino RUS **9** D7
Parga GR **182** D2
Pargny-sur-Saulx
F **91** C4
Pari-Gagné F . . **117** A4
Parigné-l'Évêque
F **102** B2
Parikkala FIN **9** B6
Paris F **90** C2
Parisot F **129** B4
Parkalompolo
S **196** B5
Parkano FIN **8** A3
Parknasilla IRL . . **29** C2
Parla E **151** B4
Parlavá E **147** B4
Parma I **120** C3
Parndorf A **111** B3
Párnica SK **99** B3
Parnu EST **8** C4
Parolis E **164** A2
Paros GR **185** B6
Parrillas E **150** B2
Parsberg D **95** B3
Parstein D **74** B3
Partakko FIN. **193** C11
Partanna I **176** B1
Parthenay F . . . **102** C1
Partinico I **176** A2
Partizani SRB . **127** C2
Partizánske SK . **98** C2
Partney UK **41** B4
Påryd S **63** B3
Parzymiechy
PL **86** A2
Paşcani RO **17** B7
Pasewalk D **74** A2
Pašina Voda
MNE **139** B5
Påskallavik S . . . **62** A4
Pasłęk PL **69** A4
Pašman HR **137** B4
Passage East
IRL **30** B2
Passail A **110** B2
Passais F **88** B3
Passau D **96** C1
Passegueiro P. **148** B1
Passignano sul
Trasimeno I . . **135** B5
Passo di Tréia
I **136** B2
Passopisciaro
I **177** B4
Passow D **74** A3
Passy F **118** B3
Pastavy BY **13** A7
Pástena I **170** B2
Pastrana E **151** B5
Pastrengo I . . . **121** B3
Pasym PL **77** A5
Pásztó H **113** B3
Pata SK **98** C1
Patay F **103** A3
Pateley Bridge
UK **40** A2
Paterek PL **76** A2
Paterna E **159** B3
Paterna del Campo
E **161** B3
Paterna del Madera
E **158** C1
Paterna de Rivera
E **162** B2
Paternion A . . . **109** C4
Paternò I **177** B3
Paternópoli I . . **170** C3
Patersdorf D **95** B4
Paterswolde
NL **71** A3
Patitiri GR **183** D5
Patmos GR **188** B1
Patna UK **36** A2
Patoniva FIN . **193** C11
Patopirtti
FIN **197** B12
Patos AL **182** C1
Patra = Patras
GR **184** A2
Patras = Patra
GR **184** A2
Patreksfjörður
IS **190** B2
Patrickswell IRL **29** B3
Patrimonio F . . **180** A2
Patrington UK . . **41** B3
Pattada I **178** B3

Pattensen
Niedersachsen
D **72** A3
Niedersachsen
D **72** B2
Patterdale UK . . **36** B4
Patti I **177** A3
Páty H **112** B2
Pau F **145** A3
Pauillac F **128** A2
Paularo I **109** C4
Paulhaguet F . **117** B3
Paulhan F **130** B2
Paulilátino I . . **178** B2
Pauliström S . . . **62** A3
Paullo I **120** B2
Paulstown IRL . . **30** B1
Pausa D **83** B3
Pauträsk S **200** B3
Pavia
I **120** B2
P **154** C2
Pavias E **159** B3
Pavilly F **89** A4
Pāvilosta LV **8** D2
Pavullo nel
Frignano I . . . **135** A3
Pawłowice PL . . **86** A1
Pawlowice PL . . **98** B2
Paxi GR **182** D2
Payallar TR . . . **189** C6
Payerne CH . . . **106** C1
Paymogo E **161** B2
Payrac F **129** B4
Pazardzhik
BG **183** A6
Pazaryeri TR . . **187** B4
Pazin HR **122** B2
Paziols F **146** B3
Pčelić HR **124** B3
Peal de Becerro
E **164** B1
Peasmarsh UK . . **45** C4
Peć KOS **16** D4
Péccioli I **135** B3
Pécel H **112** B3
Pechao P **160** B2
Pechenga RUS . . **3** B12
Pechenizhyn
UA **13** D6
Pecica RO **126** A3
Pećinci SRB . . . **127** C1
Pecka SRB **127** C1
Peckelsheim D . **81** A5
Peczniew PL . . . **86** A2
Pedaso I **136** B2
Pedavena I . . . **121** A4
Pedérobba I . . **121** B4
Pedersker DK . . **67** A3
Pedescala I . . . **121** B4
Pedrafita E . . . **141** B3
Pedrajas de San
Esteban E . . . **150** A3
Pedralba E **159** B3
Pedralba de la
Praderia E . . . **141** B4
Pedraza E **151** A4
Pedreguer E . . **159** C4
Pedrera E **162** A3
Pedro Abad E . **157** C3
Pedro Bernardo
E **150** B3
Pedrógão P . . . **160** A2
Pedrogao P . . . **149** B2
Pedrógão P . . . **154** B2
Pedrógão Grande
P **154** B2
Pedrola E **144** C2
Pedro-Martinez
E **164** B1
Pedro Muñoz
E **158** B1
Pedrosa del Rey
E **150** A2
Pedrosa del Rio
Urbel E **143** B3
Pedrosa de
Tobalina E . . . **143** B3
Pedrosillo de los
Aires E **150** B2
Pedrosillo el Ralo
E **150** A2
Pędzewo PL . . . **76** A3
Peebles UK **35** C4
Peel UK **36** B2
Peenemünde D . **66** B2
Peer B **79** A5
Pega P **149** B2
Pegalajar E . . . **163** A4

Pegau D **83** A4
Peggau A **110** B2
Pegli I **133** A4
Pegnitz D **95** B3
Pego E **159** C3
Pegões-Estação
P **154** C2
Pegões Velhos
P **154** C2
Pegswood UK . . **37** A5
Peguera E **166** B2
Pehlivanköy
TR **186** A1
Peine D **72** B3
Peisey-Nancroix
F **118** B3
Peissenberg D **108** B2
Peiting D **108** B1
Peitz D **84** A2
Péjo I **121** A3
Pelagićevo
BIH **125** C4
Pelahustán E . . **150** B3
Pełczyce PL **75** A4
Pelhřimov CZ . . **97** B3
Pélissanne F . . **131** B4
Pelkosenniemi
FIN **197** B10
Pellegrino
Parmense I . . **120** C2
Pellegrue F . . . **128** B3
Pellérd H **125** A4
Pellestrina I . . **122** B1
Pellevoisin F . . **103** C3
Pellizzano I . . . **121** A3
Pello
FIN **196** C7
S **196** C6
Peloche E **156** A2
Pelplin PL **69** B3
Pelussin F **117** B4
Pély H **113** B4
Pembroke UK . . **39** C2
Pembroke Dock
UK **39** C2
Peñacerrada
E **143** B4
Penacova P . . . **148** B1
Peña de Cabra
E **149** B4
Peñafiel E **151** A3
Penafiel P **148** A1
Peñaflor E **162** A2
Peñalba de
Santiago E . . . **141** B4
Peñalsordo E . . **156** B2
Penalva do Castelo
P **148** B2
Penamacôr P . **149** B2
Peñaparda E . . **149** B3
Peñaranda de
Bracamonte
E **150** B2
Peñaranda de
Duero E **143** C3
Peñarroya de
Tastavins E . . **153** B4
Peñarroya-
Pueblonuevo
E **156** B2
Penarth UK **39** C3
Peñascosa E . . **158** C1
Peñas de San Pedro
E **158** C2
Peñausende
E **149** A4
Penc H **112** B3
Pencoed UK . . . **39** C3
Pendalofos
GR **182** C3
Pendeen UK . . . **42** B1
Pendine UK . . . **39** C2
Pendueles E . . **142** A2
Penedono P . . . **148** B2
Penela P **154** A2
Pénestin F **101** B3
Penhas Juntas
P **149** A2
Peniche P **154** B1
Penicuik UK . . . **35** C4
Penig D **83** B4
Penilhos P **160** B2
Peñíscola E . . . **153** B4
Penistone UK . . **40** B2
Penkridge UK . . **40** C1
Penkun D **74** A3
Penmarch F . . . **100** B1
Pennabilli I . . . **135** B5
Penne I **169** A3
Penne-d'Agenais
F **129** B3

Pennes I **108** C2
Pennyghael UK . **34** B1
Peno RUS **9** D8
Penpont UK **36** A3
Penrhyndeudraeth
UK **38** B2
Penrith UK **37** B4
Penryn UK **42** B1
Pentraeth UK . . **38** A2
Penybontfawr
UK **38** B3
Penygroes
Carmarthenshire
UK **39** C2
Gwynedd UK . . **38** A2
Penzance UK . . . **42** B1
Penzberg D . . . **108** B2
Penzlin D **74** A2
Pepinster B **80** B1
Peqin AL **182** B1
Pér H **111** B4
Pera Boa P **148** B2
Perachora GR . **184** A3
Perafita P **148** A1
Peraleda de la Mata
E **150** C2
Peraleda del
Zaucejo E . . . **156** B2
Peraleda de San
Román E **156** A2
Perales de
Alfambra E . . **152** B2
Perales del Puerto
E **149** B3
Perales de Tajuña
E **151** B4
Peralta E **144** B2
Peralta de la Sal
E **145** C4
Peralva P **160** B2
Peralveche E . . **152** B1
Perama GR . . . **185** D5
Peranka FIN . **197** D12
Perbál H **112** B2
Perchtoldsdorf
A **111** A3
Percy F **88** B2
Perdasdefogu
I **179** C3
Perdiguera E . . **145** C3
Peredo P **149** A3
Peregu Mare
RO **126** A2
Pereiro
Faro P **160** B2
Guarda P . . . **149** B2
Santarém P . . **154** B2
Pereiro de Aguiar
E **140** B3
Perelada E **147** B4
Perelejos de las
Truchas E . . . **152** B2
Pereña E **149** A3
Pereruela E . . . **149** A4
Pérfugas I **178** B2
Perg A **110** A1
Pérgine Valsugana
I **121** A4
Pérgola I **136** B1
Pergusa I **177** B3
Periam RO **126** A2
Periana E **163** B3
Périers F **88** A2
Périgueux F . . . **129** A3
Perino I **120** C2
Perjasica HR . . **123** B4
Perkáta H **112** B2
Perković HR . . . **138** B2
Perleberg D **73** A4
Perlez SRB **126** B2
Përmet AL **182** C2
Pernarec CZ . . . **95** B5
Pernek SK **98** C1
Pernes P **154** B2
Pernes-les-
Fontaines F . . **131** A4
Pernik BG **17** D5
Pernink CZ **83** B4
Pernitz A **110** B2
Pernu FIN . . . **197** C10
Peroguarda P . **160** A1
Pérols F **131** B2
Péronne F **90** B2
Péronnes B **79** B4
Pero Pinheiro
P **154** C1
Perorrubio E . . **151** A4
Perosa Argentina
I **119** C4
Perozinho P . . . **148** A1
Perpignan F . . . **146** B3
Perranporth
UK **42** B1

Perranzabuloe
UK **42** B1
Perrecy-les-Forges
F **104** C3
Perrero I **119** C4
Perrignier F . . . **118** A3
Perros-Guirec
F **100** A2
Persan F **90** B2
Persberg S **55** A5
Persenbeug A. **110** A2
Pershore UK . . . **44** A1
Persön S **196** D5
Perstorp S **61** C3
Perth UK **35** B4
Pertisau A **108** B2
Pertoča SLO . . . **111** C3
Pertuis F **131** B4
Perućac SRB . . **127** D1
Perúgia I **136** B1
Perušić HR **123** C4
Péruwelz B **79** B3
Pervomaysk
UA **13** D9
Perwez B **79** B4
Pesadas de Burgos
E **143** B3
Pesaguero E . . **142** A2
Pésaro I **136** B1
Pescantina I . . **121** B3
Pescara I **169** A4
Pescasséroli I . **169** B3
Peschici I **171** B4
Peschiera del Garda
I **121** B3
Péscia I **135** B3
Pescina I **169** A3
Pescocostanzo
I **169** B4
Pescopagano
I **172** B1
Pesco Sannita
I **170** B2
Peshkopi AL . . **182** B2
Peshtera BG . . **183** A6
Pesmes F **105** B4
Pesnica SLO . . . **110** C2
Peso da Régua
P **148** A2
Pesquera de Duero
E **142** C2
Pessac F **128** B2
Pestovo RUS **9** C9
Petäjäskoski
FIN **197** C8
Petalidi GR . . . **184** C2
Pétange L **92** B1
Petas GR **182** D3
Peteranec HR . **124** A2
Peterborough
UK **41** C3
Peterculter UK . **33** D4
Peterhead UK . . **33** D5
Peterlee UK **37** B5
Petersfield UK . . **44** B3
Petershagen
Brandenburg
D **74** B2
Brandenburg
D **74** B3
Nordrhein-
Westfalen D . . . **72** B1
Petershausen
D **95** C3
Peterswell IRL . . **28** A3
Pétervására
H **113** A4
Petília Policastro
I **175** B2
Petín E **141** B3
Petkus D **74** C2
Petlovac HR . . . **125** B4
Petlovača SRB . **127** C1
Petöfiszallás
H **113** C3
Petra E **167** B3
Petralia Sottana
I **177** B3
Petrčane HR . . . **137** A4
Petrella Tifernina
I **170** B2
Petreto-Bicchisano
F **180** B1
Petrich BG **183** B5
Petrijevci HR . . **125** B4
Petrinja HR . . . **124** B2
Petrodvorets
RUS **9** C6
Pétrola E **158** C2
Petronà I **175** B2
Petronell A . . . **111** A3

Petroşani RO . . . **17** C5
Petrovac SRB . . **127** C3
Petrovaradin
SRB **126** B1
Petrovice
BIH **139** A4
CZ **84** B1
Petrovo RUS **69** A5
Petrozavodsk
RUS **9** B9
Pettenbach A . . **109** B5
Pettigo IRL **26** B3
Petworth UK . . . **44** C3
Peuerbach A . . . **96** C1
Peuntenansa
E **142** A2
Peurasuvanto
FIN **197** B9
Pevensey Bay
UK **45** C4
Peveragno I . . . **133** A3
Pewsey UK **44** B2
Pewsum D **71** A4
Peyrat-le-Château
F **116** B1
Peyrehorade
F **128** C1
Peyriac-Minervois
F **146** A3
Peyrins F **117** B5
Peyrissac F . . . **116** B1
Peyrolles-en-
Provence F . . **132** B1
Peyruis F **132** A1
Pézarches F **90** C2
Pézenas F **130** B2
Pezinok SK . . . **111** A4
Pezuls F **129** B3
Pfaffenhausen
D **108** A1
Pfaffenhofen
Bayern D **94** C2
Bayern D **95** C3
Pfaffenhoffen
F **93** C3
Pfäffikon CH . . **107** B3
Pfarrkirchen D . . **95** C4
Pfeffenhausen
D **95** C3
Pfetterhouse
F **106** B2
Pforzheim D . . . **93** C4
Pfreimd D **95** B4
Pfronten D **108** B1
Pfullendorf D . . **107** B4
Pfullingen D . . . **94** C1
Pfunds A **108** C1
Pfungstadt D . . . **93** B4
Pfyn CH **107** B3
Phalsbourg F . . . **92** C3
Philippeville B . . **79** B4
Philippsreut D . . **96** C1
Philippsthal D . . **82** B1
Piacenza I **120** B2
Piacenza d'Adige
I **121** B4
Piádena I **120** B3
Piana F **180** A1
Piana Crixia I . . **133** A4
Piana degli
Albanesi I . . . **176** B2
Piana di Monte
Verna I **170** B2
Piancastagnáio
I **135** C4
Piandelagotti
I **134** A3
Pianella
Abruzzi I **169** A4
Toscana I **135** B4
Pianello Val Tidone
I **120** C2
Pianoro I **135** A4
Pians A **108** B1
Pías E **141** B4
Pias P **160** A2
Piaseczno PL . . . **77** B6
Piasek PL **74** B3
Piaski PL **69** A4
Piastów PL **77** B5
Piaszczyna PL . . **68** A2
Piątek PL **77** B4
Piatra Neamț
RO **17** B7
Piazza al Sérchio
I **134** A3
Piazza Armerina
I **177** B3
Piazza Brembana
I **120** B2

Piazze I 135 C4
Piazzola sul Brenta
  I. 121 B4
Picassent E. . . . 159 B3
Piccione I 136 B1
Picerno I 172 B1
Picher D 73 A4
Pickering UK. . . .40 A3
Pico I. 169 B3
Picón E. 157 A3
Picquigny F 90 B2
Piechowice PL . .84 B3
Piecnik PL. 75 A5
Piedicavallo I . 119 B4
Piedicroce F. . . 180 A2
Piedimonte Etneo
  I. 177 B4
Piedimonte Matese
  I. 170 B2
Piedimulera I . 119 A5
Piedipaterno I 136 C1
Piedrabuena
  E. 157 A3
Piedraescrita
  E. 156 A3
Piedrafita E . . . 142 A1
Piedrahita E. . . 150 B2
Piedralaves E . 150 B3
Piedras Albas
  E. 155 B4
Piedras Blancas
  E. 141 A5
Piegaro I 135 C5
Piekary Śl. PL . . .86 B2
Piekoszów PL . . .87 B4
Pieksämäki FIN . .8 A5
Pielenhofen D . .95 B3
Pielgrzymka PL .85 A3
Pieniężno PL. . . .69 A5
Pieńsk PL 84 A3
Pienza I 135 B4
Piera E 147 C2
Pieranie PL. 76 B3
Pierowall UK. . . .33 B4
Pierre-Buffière
  F 115 C5
Pierrecourt F. . 105 B4
Pierre-de-Bresse
  F 105 C4
Pierrefeu-du-Var
  F 132 B2
Pierrefitte-Nestalas
  F 145 B3
Pierrefitte-sur-Aire
  F 92 C1
Pierrefonds F . . .90 B2
Pierrefontaine-les-
  Varans F 105 B5
Pierrefort F . . . 116 C2
Pierrelatte F . . . 131 A3
Pierrepont
  Aisne F 91 B3
  Meurthe-et-Moselle
  F 92 B1
Piesendorf A. . . 109 B3
Pieštany SK 98 C1
Pieszkowo PL. . .69 A5
Pieszyce PL 85 B4
Pietarsaari FIN . . 3 E8
Pietragalla I. . . 172 B1
Pietra Ligure I . 133 A4
Pietralunga I. . . 136 B1
Pietramelara I 170 B2
Pietraperzía I . . 177 B3
Pietrasanta I . . 134 B3
Pietravairano
  I. 170 B2
Pieve del Cáiro
  I. 120 B1
Pieve di Bono
  I. 121 B3
Pieve di Cadore
  I. 122 A1
Pieve di Cento
  I. 121 C4
Pieve di Soligo
  I. 121 B5
Pieve di Teco
  I. 133 A3
Pievepélago I . 134 A3
Pieve Santo
  Stefano I 135 B5
Pieve Torina I . 136 B2
Piges GR 182 D3
Píglio I. 169 B3
Pigna I 133 B3
Pignan F 130 B2
Pignataro
  Maggiore I. . . 170 B2
Piittisjärvi FIN 197 C9

Pijnacker NL 70 B1
Pikalevo RUS. 9 C9
Piła PL 75 A5
Pilar de la
  Horadada E . . 165 B4
Pilas E. 161 B3
Pilastri I. 121 C4
Piława Górna
  PL. 85 B4
Piławki PL. 69 B4
Pilchowice PL . . .86 B2
Pilea GR. 183 C5
Pilgrimstad
  S. 199 C12
Pili
  Dodekanisa
  GR 188 C2
  Trikala GR . . . 182 D3
Pilica PL. 86 B3
Pilis H. 112 B3
Piliscaba H. . . . 112 B2
Pilisszántó H. . 112 B2
Pilisvörösvár
  H. 112 B2
Pilos GR. 184 C2
Pilsting D 95 C4
Pilszcz PL 98 A1
Pilterud N. 48 C2
Pilu RO. 113 C5
Pina de Ebro
  E. 153 A3
Piñar E. 163 A4
Pınarbaşı TR . . 186 C1
Pınarhisar TR . 186 A2
Pinas F 145 A4
Pincehely H. . . 112 C2
Pinchbeck UK. . .41 C3
Pińczów PL. 87 B4
Pineda de la Sierra
  E. 143 B3
Pineda de Mar
  E. 147 C3
Pinerella I 135 A5
Pinerolo I 119 C4
Pineta Grande
  I. 170 C1
Pineto I 169 A4
Piney F. 91 C4
Pinggau A 111 B3
Pinhal Novo P. 154 C2
Pinhão P 148 A2
Pinheiro
  Aveiro P 148 A1
  Aveiro P 148 B1
Pinheiro Grande
  P. 154 B2
Pinhel P. 149 B2
Pinhoe UK 43 B3
Pinilla E 158 C2
Pinilla de Toro
  E. 150 A2
Pinkafeld A . . . 111 B3
Pinneberg D 72 A2
Pinnow D 74 C3
Pino F. 180 A2
Pino del Rio E . 142 B2
Pino de Val E . . 140 B2
Pinofranqueado
  E. 149 B3
Pinols F 117 B3
Piñor E. 140 B2
Pinos del Valle
  E. 163 B4
Pinoso E 159 C2
Pinos Puente
  E. 163 A4
Pinsk BY 13 B7
Pintamo FIN . 197 D10
Pinto E. 151 B4
Pinzano al
  Tagliamento
  I. 122 A1
Pinzio P 149 B2
Pinzolo I 121 A3
Pióbbico I. 136 B1
Piombino I. . . . 134 C3
Pionki PL. 87 A5
Pionsat F 116 A2
Pióraco I 136 B1
Piornal E. 150 B2
Piotrkowice
  PL. 87 B4
Piotrków-Kujawski
  PL. 76 B3
Piotrków
  Trybunalski
  PL. 86 A3
Piotrowo PL. . . .75 B5
Piove di Sacco
  I. 121 B5
Piovene I 121 B4
Piperskärr S. . . .62 A4
Pipriac F 101 B4

Piraeus = Pireas
  GR 185 B4
Piran SLO 122 B2
Pireas = Piraeus
  GR 185 B4
Piré-sur-Seiche
  F 101 A4
Pirgi GR 185 A6
Pirgos
  Ilia GR. 184 B2
  Kriti GR 185 D6
Piriac-sur-Mer
  F 101 B3
Piringsdorf A . . 111 B3
Pirmasens D 93 B3
Pirna D. 84 B1
Pirnmill UK. 34 C2
Pirot SRB. 16 D5
Pirovac HR. . . . 137 B4
Pirttivuopio S. 196 B2
Pisa I. 134 B3
Pisany F. 114 C3
Pisarovina HR. 124 B1
Pischelsdorf in der
  Steiermark
  A. 110 B2
Pişchia RO . . . 126 B3
Pisciotta I. 172 B1
Písek CZ. 96 B2
Pisogne I. 120 B3
Pissos F 128 B2
Pissouri CY. . . . 181 B1
Pisticci I. 174 A2
Pistóia I 135 B3
Piteå S 196 D4
Piteşti RO 17 C6
Pithiviers F. . . . 103 A4
Pitigliano I 168 A1
Pitkyaranta RUS . 9 B7
Pitlochry UK 35 B4
Pitomača HR . . 124 B3
Pitres F 163 B4
Pittentrail UK . . 32 D2
Pitvaros H 126 A2
Pivka SLO 123 B3
Pivnice SRB . . . 126 B1
Piwniczna PL. . .99 B4
Pizarra E 163 B3
Pizzano I 121 A3
Pizzighettone
  I. 120 B2
Pizzo I. 175 C2
Pízzoli I 169 A3
Pizzolungo I . . 176 A1
Pjätteryd S. 61 C4
Plabennec F . . . 100 A1
Placencia E. . . . 143 A4
Plaffeien CH . . 106 C2
Plaisance
  Gers F 128 C3
  Haute-Garonne
  F 129 C4
  Tarn F 130 B1
Plaka GR 183 D7
Plan E 145 B4
Planá CZ. 95 B4
Planánad Lužnici
  CZ. 96 B2
Plaňany CZ 96 A3
Planchez F 104 B3
Plancoët F 101 A3
Plancy-l'Abbaye
  F 91 C3
Plan-de-Baix
  F 118 C2
Plan-d'Orgon
  F 131 B3
Plánice CZ 96 B1
Planina
  SLO 123 A4
  SLO 123 B3
Plankenfels D. . .95 B3
Plasencia E. . . . 143 B3
Plasenzuela E. . 156 A1
Plaški HR. 123 B4
Plassen
  Buskerud N 47 B4
  Hedmark N . . . 49 A4
Plášt'ovce SK . . 112 A3
Platamona Lido
  I. 178 B2
Platania I 175 B2
Platanos GR. . . 185 D4
Platí I 175 C2
Platičevo SRB . 127 C1
Platja d'Aro E . . 147 C4
Plattling D. 95 C4
Plau D. 73 A5
Plaue
  Brandenburg
  D. 73 B5

Plaue *continued*
  Thüringen D . . .82 B2
Plauen D. 83 B4
Plavecký Mikuláš
  SK. 98 C1
Plavinas LV. 8 D4
Plavna SRB. . . . 125 B5
Plavnica SK 99 B4
Plavno HR. 138 A2
Pléaux F 116 B2
Pleine-Fougères
  F 88 B2
Pleinfeld D. 94 B2
Pleinting D 95 C5
Plélan-le-Grand
  F 101 B3
Plémet F 101 A3
Pléneuf-Val-André
  F 101 A3
Plentzia E. 143 A4
Plérin F 101 A3
Plešivec SK. 99 C4
Plessa D. 83 A5
Plessé F 101 B4
Plestin-les-Grèves
  F 100 A2
Pleszew PL. 76 C2
Pleternica HR . 125 B3
Plettenberg D . .81 A3
Pleubian F 100 A2
Pleumartin F. . 115 B4
Pleumeur-Bodou
  F 100 A2
Pleurs F. 91 C3
Pleven BG. 17 D6
Plevnik-Drienové
  SK. 98 B2
Pleyben F 100 A2
Pleyber-Christ
  F 100 A2
Pliego E. 165 B3
Pliešovce SK . . .99 C3
Plitvička Jezera
  HR 123 C4
Plitvički Ljeskovac
  HR 123 C4
Ploaghe I 178 B2
Ploče HR 138 B3
Plochingen D . . .94 C1
Płock PL. 77 B4
Ploemeur F . . . 100 B2
Ploërmel F 101 B3
Ploeuc-sur-Lie
  F 101 A3
Plogastel St
  Germain F . . . 100 B1
Plogoff F 100 A1
Ploieşti RO 17 C7
Plomari GR. . . . 186 D1
Plombières-les-
  Bains F 105 B5
Plomin HR 123 B3
Plön D 65 B3
Plonéour-Lanvern
  F 100 B1
Płonia PL. 74 A3
Płoniawy PL. . . .77 B6
Płońsk PL. 77 B5
Płoskinia PL. . . .69 A4
Plössberg D. 95 B4
Płoty PL. 67 C4
Plouagat F 100 A2
Plouaret F 100 A2
Plouarzel F. . . . 100 A1
Plouay F 100 B2
Ploubalay F . . . 101 A3
Ploubazlanec
  F 100 A2
Ploudalmézeau
  F 100 A1
Ploudiry F. 100 A1
Plouescat F . . . 100 A1
Plouézec F 100 A2
Plougasnou F . 100 A2
Plougastel-Daoulas
  F 100 A1
Plougonven F . 100 A2
Plougonver F . 100 A2
Plougrescant
  F 100 A2
Plouguenast
  F 101 A3
Plouguerneau
  F 100 A1
Plouha F 100 A2
Plouhinec F . . . 100 A1
Plouigneau F . . 100 A2
Ploumanac'h F 100 A2
Plounévez-Quintin
  F 100 A2
Plouray F. 100 A2
Plouzévédé F . 100 A1
Plovdiv BG. . . . 183 A6

Plozévet F 100 B1
Plumbridge UK .27 B3
Pluméliau F. . . 100 B3
Plumlov CZ 97 B5
Plungė LT 8 E2
Pluty PL. 69 A5
Pluvigner F . . . 100 B3
Plužine
  BIH. 139 B4
  MNE 139 B4
Płuznica PL 69 B3
Plymouth UK. . .42 B2
Plymstock UK. . .42 B2
Plytnica PL. 68 B1
Plyusa RUS. 9 C6
Plzeň CZ 96 B1
Pniewy PL. 75 B5
Pobes E 143 B4
Poběžovice CZ. .95 B4
Pobiedziska PL .76 B2
Pobierowo PL. . .67 B3
Pobla de Segur
  E. 145 B4
Pobladura del Valle
  E. 142 B1
Pobla-Tornesa
  E. 153 B4
Pobra de Trives
  E. 141 B3
Pobra do Brollón
  E. 141 B3
Pobra do
  Caramiñal E. . 140 B2
Pobudje BIH . . 139 A5
Počátky CZ. 97 B3
Poceirão P 154 C2
Pöchlarn A 110 A2
Pociecha PL. . . .87 A4
Pockau D 83 B5
Pocking D. 96 C1
Pocklington UK 40 B3
Podbořany CZ . .83 B5
Podbrdo SLO. . 122 A2
Podbrezová SK .99 C3
Podčetrtek
  SLO 123 A4
Poddębice PL. . .76 C3
Poděbrady CZ . .84 B3
Podence F 149 A3
Podensac F . . . 128 B2
Podenzano I . . 120 C2
Podersdorf am See
  A. 111 B3
Podgaje PL. 68 B1
Podgora HR. . . 138 B3
Podgóra PL. 87 A5
Podgorač HR. . 125 B4
Podgorica MNE 16 D3
Podgorie AL . . 182 C2
Podgrad SLO. . 123 B3
Podhájska SK . . 112 A2
Podkova BG. . . 183 B7
Podlapača HR. . 123 C4
Podlejki PL. 69 B5
Podlužany SK. . .98 C2
Podnovlje BIH 125 C4
Podolie SK 98 C1
Podolínec SK. . .99 B4
Podolsk RUS . . .9 E10
Podporozhy RUS. 9 B9
Podromanija
  BIH. 139 B4
Podturen HR. . 111 C3
Podvin F. 97 C4
Podwilk PL. 99 B3
Poetto I 179 C3
Poggardo I 173 B4
Poggibonsi I. . . 135 B4
Póggio a Caiano
  I. 135 B4
Poggio Imperiale
  I. 171 B3
Póggio Mirteto
  I. 168 A2
Póggio Moiano
  I. 169 A2
Póggio Renatico
  I. 121 C4
Póggio Rusco
  I. 121 C4
Pogny F 91 C4
Pogorzela PL. . . .85 A5
Pogorzelice PL. .68 A2
Pogradec AL . . 182 C2
Pogrodzie PL. . .69 A4
Pohorelá SK. . . .99 C4
Pohořelice CZ. . .97 C4
Pohronská Polhora
  SK. 99 C3
Poiares P. 148 B1
Poio E 140 B2

Poirino I 119 C4
Poisson F 117 A4
Poissons F 91 C5
Poissy F. 90 C2
Poitiers F 115 B4
Poix-de-Picardie
  F 90 B1
Poix-Terron F . . .91 B4
Pokka FIN 197 A8
Pokój PL 86 B1
Pokupsko HR . 124 B1
Pol E 141 A3
Pola RUS 9 D7
Pol a Charra UK .31 B1
Pola de Allande
  E. 141 A4
Pola de Laviana
  E. 142 A1
Pola de Lena
  E. 141 A5
Pola de Siero
  E. 142 A1
Pola de Somiedo
  E. 141 A4
Polaincourt-et-
  Clairefontaine
  F 105 B5
Połajewo PL 75 B5
Polán E 151 C3
Polanica-Zdrój
  PL. 85 B4
Połaniec PL 87 B5
Polanów PL 68 A1
Polatı TR 187 C7
Polatsk BY 13 A8
Polch D 80 B3
Polcirkeln S . . . 196 C4
Pólczno PL. 68 A2
Połczyn-Zdrój
  PL. 67 C5
Polegate UK 45 C4
Poleñino E. . . . 145 C3
Polesella I 121 C4
Polessk RUS. . . .12 A4
Polgár H 113 B5
Polgárdi H 112 B2
Polhov Gradec
  SLO 123 A3
Police PL. 74 A3
Police nad Metují
  CZ. 85 B4
Polichnitos
  GR 186 C1
Polička CZ 97 B4
Poličnik HR . . . 137 A4
Policoro I 174 A2
Policzna PL 87 A5
Poligiros GR . . 183 C5
Polignano a Mare
  I. 173 B3
Poligny F 105 C4
Polis CY 181 A1
Polístena I 175 C2
Polizzi Generosa
  I. 176 B3
Poljana SRB . . . 127 C3
Poljanak HR. . . 123 C4
Poljčane SLO. . 123 A4
Polje BIH 125 C3
Poljice
  BIH. 138 A2
  BIH. 139 B4
Polkowice PL . . .85 A4
Polla I 172 B1
Pollas E 150 A2
Pöllau A. 110 B2
Polleben D. 82 A3
Pollença E 167 B3
Pollenfeld D 95 C3
Pollfoss N 198 D4
Póllica I 170 C3
Polminhac F . . 116 C2
Polná CZ. 97 B3
Polna RUS. 9 C6
Polne PL. 75 A5
Polomka SK 99 C3
Polonne UA 13 C7
Polperro UK 42 B2
Polruan UK. 42 B2
Pöls A 110 B1
Polska Cerekiew
  PL. 86 B2
Poltár SK 99 C3
Põltsamaa EST . .8 C4
Polyarny RUS . . 3 B13
Polyarnyye Zori
  RUS 3 C13
Polzela SLO . . . 123 A4
Pomarance I . . 135 B3
Pomarez F 128 C2
Pomárico I 172 B2
Pomáz H 112 B3
Pombal P 154 B2

Pomeroy UK 27 B4
Pomézia I 168 B2
Pommard F . . . 105 B3
Pommelsbrunn
  D. 95 B3
Pomonte I 134 C3
Pomorie BG. . . . 17 D7
Pomos CY 181 A1
Pompei I 170 C2
Pompey F. 92 C2
Pomposa I 122 C1
Poncin F 118 A2
Pondorf D 95 C3
Ponferrada E. . 141 B4
Poniec PL 85 A4
Ponikva SLO . . 123 A4
Poniky SK 99 C3
Pons F 114 C3
Ponsacco I 134 B3
Pont I 119 B4
Pont-a-Celles B .79 B4
Pontacq F 145 A3
Pontailler-sur-
  Saône F 105 B4
Pont-a-Marcq F .78 B3
Pont-à-Mousson
  F 92 C2
Pontão F. 154 B2
Pontardawe UK 39 C3
Pontarddulais
  UK 39 C2
Pontarion F . . . 116 B1
Pontarlier F. . . 105 C5
Pontassieve I . 135 B4
Pontaubault F . .88 B2
Pont-Audemer
  F 89 A4
Pontaumur F. . 116 B2
Pont-Aven F . . 100 B2
Pont Canavese
  I. 119 B4
Pontcharra F . . 118 B3
Pontcharra-sur-
  Turdine F 117 B4
Pontchâteau
  F 101 B3
Pont-Croix F . . 100 A1
Pont-d'Ain F . . 118 A2
Pont-de-Beauvoisin
  F 118 B2
Pont-de-Buis-lès-
  Quimerch F . . 100 A1
Pont-de-Chéruy
  F 118 B2
Pont de Dore
  F 117 B3
Pont-de-Labeaume
  F 117 C4
Pont-de-l'Arche
  F 89 A5
Pont de Molins
  E. 147 B3
Ponte-de-Roide
  F 106 B1
Pont-de-Salars
  F 130 A1
Pont-d'Espagne
  F 145 B3
Pont de Suert
  E. 145 B4
Pont-de-Vaux
  F 117 A4
Pont-de-Veyle
  F 117 A4
Pont d'Ouilly F . .89 B3
Pont-du-Château
  F 116 B3
Pont-du-Navoy
  F 105 C4
Ponte a Moriano
  I. 134 B3
Ponte Arche I . 121 A3
Ponteareas E. . 140 B2
Pontebba I . . . 109 C4
Ponte Cáffaro
  I. 121 B3
Pontecagnano
  I. 170 C2
Ponte-Caldelas
  E. 140 B2
Ponteceso E. . . 140 A2
Pontecorvo I . . 169 B3
Ponte da Barca
  P. 148 A1
Pontedássio I . 133 B4
Pontedécimo
  I. 133 A4
Ponte de Lima
  P. 148 A1
Ponte dell'Ólio
  I. 120 C2

Pontedera I . . . 134 B3
Ponte de Sor
  P. 154 B2
Pontedeume
  E. 140 A2
Ponte di Barbarano
  I. 121 B4
Ponte di Legno
  I. 121 A3
Ponte di Nava
  I. 133 A3
Ponte di Piave
  I. 122 B1
Ponte Felcino
  I. 136 B1
Pontefract UK . . .40 B2
Ponte Gardena
  I. 108 C2
Ponteginori I . 135 B3
Pontelagoscuro
  I. 121 C4
Ponteland UK . . .37 A5
Pontelandolfo
  I. 170 B2
Ponte-Leccia
  F. 180 A2
Pontelongo I . . 121 B5
Ponte nelle Alpi
  I. 122 A1
Pont-en-Royans
  F. 118 B2
Pontenure I . . . 120 C2
Pontenx-les-Forges
  F. 128 B1
Ponterwyd UK . .39 B3
Ponte San Giovanni
  I. 136 B1
Ponte San Pietro
  I. 120 B2
Pontevedra E . . 140 B2
Pontevico I. . . . 120 B3
Pont Farcy F. . . .88 B2
Pontfaverger-
  Moronvillers
  F. 91 B4
Pontgibaud F . 116 B2
Ponticino I 135 B4
Pontigny F 104 B2
Pontijou F 103 B3
Pontínia I 169 B3
Pontinvrea I . . 133 A4
Pontivy F 100 A3
Pont-l'Abbé F . 100 B1
Pont-l'Évêque
  F. 89 A4
Pontlevoy F. . . . 103 B3
Pontoise F. 90 B2
Pontones E . . . 164 A2
Pontonx-sur-
  l'Abour F 128 C2
Pontoon IRL. . . .26 C1
Pontorson F 88 B2
Pontrémoli I . . 134 A2
Pont-Remy F . . .90 A1
Pontresina CH 107 C4
Pontrhydfendigaid
  UK 39 B3
Pontrieux F . . . 100 A2
Ponts E 147 C2
Ponts-aux-Dames
  F. 90 C2
Pont Scorff F . . 100 B2
Pöntsö FIN . . . 196 B7
Pont-Ste Maxence
  F. 90 B2
Pont-St Esprit
  F. 131 A3
Pont-St Mamet
  F. 129 B3
Pont-St Martin
  F. 101 B4
  I. 119 B4
Pont-St Vincent
  F. 92 C2
Pont-sur-Yonne
  F. 104 A2
Pontvallain F . 102 B2
Pontypool UK . .39 C3
Pontypridd UK . .39 C3
Ponza I. 169 C2
Poo E 142 A2
Poole UK. 43 B5
Poolewe UK. 31 B3
Poperinge B 78 B2
Pópoli I 169 A3
Popovac SRB . . 127 D3
Popovača HR . . 124 B2
Popow PL. 77 B4
Poppel B 79 A5
Poppenhausen
  Bayern D 82 B2
  Hessen D 82 B1
Poppi I. 135 B4

Poprad SK. 99 B4
Popučke SRB . . 127 C1
Pópulo P. 148 A2
Populónia I . . . 134 C3
Pörböly H. 125 A4
Porcuna E. 163 A3
Pordenone I . . . 122 B1
Pordic F. 100 A3
Poręba PL. 86 B3
Poreč HR 122 B2
Pori FIN 8 B2
Porjus S. 196 C2
Porkhov RUS. 9 D6
Porlezza I. 120 A2
Porlock UK. 43 A3
Pörnbach D 95 C3
Pornic F. 101 B3
Pornichet F . . . 101 B3
Porodin SRB . . 127 C3
Poronin PL. 99 B3
Poros
  Attiki GR. 185 B4
  Kefalonia GR . 184 A1
Poroszló H. . . . 113 B4
Porozina HR . . 123 B3
Porquerolles
  F. 132 C2
Porrentruy CH 106 B2
Porreres E. 167 B3
Porretta Terme
  I. 135 A3
Porsgrunn N . . .53 A5
Porspoder F . . 100 A1
Port-a-Binson
  F. 91 B3
Portacloy IRL. . .26 B1
Portadown UK . .27 B4
Portaferry UK . .27 B5
Portaje E 155 B4
Portalegre P . . 155 B3
Portarlington
  IRL. 30 A1
Port Askaig UK .34 C1
Portavadie UK . .34 C2
Portavogie UK . .27 B5
Portbail F 88 A2
Port Bannatyne
  UK 34 C2
Portbou E 146 B4
Port-Camargue
  F. 131 B3
Port Charlotte
  UK 34 C1
Port d'Andratx
  E. 166 B2
Port-de-Bouc
  F. 131 B3
Port-de-Lanne
  F. 128 C1
Port de Pollença
  E. 167 B3
Port-des-Barques
  F. 114 C2
Port de Sóller
  E. 166 B2
Portegrandi I . . 122 B1
Portel P. 155 C3
Portela P. 148 B1
Port Ellen UK. . .34 C1
Portelo P. 141 C4
Portemouro E. 140 B2
Port-en-Bessin
  F. 88 A3
Port'Ercole I . . 168 A1
Port Erin UK. . . .36 B2
Portes-lès-Valence
  F. 117 C4
Portets F. 128 B2
Port Eynon UK . .39 C2
Portezuelo E . . 155 B4
Port Glasgow
  UK 34 C3
Portglenone
  UK 27 B4
Porthcawl UK . .39 C3
Port Henderson
  UK 31 B3
Porthleven UK . .42 B1
Porthmadog
  UK 38 B2
Porticcio F 180 B1
Portici I 170 C2
Portico di Romagna
  I. 135 A4
Portilla de la Reina
  E. 142 A2
Portillo E. 150 A3
Portimão P. . . . 160 B1
Portinatx E. . . . 166 B1
Portinho da
  Arrabida P . . 154 C1
Port Isaac UK . .42 B2
Portishead UK . .43 A4

Port-Joinville
  F. 114 B1
Portknockie
  UK 33 D4
Port-la-Nouvelle
  F. 130 B2
Portlaoise IRL. . .30 A1
Portlethen UK . .33 D4
Port Logan UK . .36 B2
Port Louis F. . . 100 B2
Portmagne IRL. .29 C1
Portmahomack
  UK 32 D3
Portman E 165 B4
Port Manech F 100 B2
Portnacroish
  UK 34 B2
Portnahaven
  UK 34 C1
Port Nan Giuran
  UK 31 A2
Port-Navalo F. 100 B3
Port Nis UK. 31 A2
Porto
  F. 180 A1
  P. 148 A1
Porto-Alto P . . 154 C2
Porto Azzurro
  I. 134 C3
Portocannone
  I. 170 B3
Porto Cerésio
  I. 120 B1
Porto Cervo I. . 178 A3
Porto Cesáreo
  I. 173 B3
Porto Colom E 167 B3
Porto Covo P. . 160 B1
Porto Cristo E 167 B3
Porto d'Áscoli
  I. 136 C2
Porto de Lagos
  P. 160 B1
Porto de Mos
  P. 154 B2
Porto de Rei P. 154 C2
Porto do Son
  E. 140 B2
Porto Empédocle
  I. 176 B2
Portoferráio I. . 134 C3
Portofino I. . . . 134 A2
Porto Garibaldi
  I. 122 C1
Portogruaro I. 122 B1
Portokhelion
  GR 184 B4
Portomaggiore
  I. 121 C4
Portomarin E . 140 B3
Porton UK. 44 B2
Portonovo E . . 140 B2
Portopalo di Capo
  Passero I 177 C4
Porto Petro E . 167 B3
Porto Pino I. . . 179 D2
Porto Potenza
  Picena I 136 B2
Portør N. 53 B5
Porto Recanati
  I. 136 B2
Porto San Giórgio
  I. 136 B2
Porto Sant'Elpídio
  I. 136 B2
Porto Santo
  Stéfano I 168 A1
Portoscuso I . . 179 C2
Porto Tolle I. . . 122 C1
Porto Tórres I . 178 B2
Porto-Vecchio
  F. 180 B2
Portovénere I. 134 A2
Portpatrick UK .36 B1
Portreath UK. . .42 B1
Portree UK. 31 B2
Portroe IRL. 28 B3
Portrush UK. . . .27 A4
Port St Mary UK 36 B2
Portsall F 100 A1
Portsmouth UK .44 C2
Portsoy UK 33 D4
Port-Ste Marie
  F. 129 B3
Portstewart
  UK 27 A4
Port-St-Louis-du-
  Rhône F. 131 B3
Port-sur-Saône
  F. 105 B5
Port Talbot UK . .39 C3
Portugalete E . 143 A4
Portumna IRL. . .28 A3

Port-Vendres
  F. 146 B4
Port William UK .36 B2
Porvoo FIN. 8 B4
Porzuna E. 157 A3
Posada
  Oviedo E. 141 A5
  Oviedo E. 142 A2
  I. 178 B3
Posada de Valdeón
  E. 142 A2
Posadas E 162 A2
Poschiavo CH . 120 A3
Posedarje HR . 137 A4
Posio FIN. 197 C11
Positano I. 170 C2
Possagno I. . . . 121 B4
Posseck D. 83 B4
Possesse F. 91 C4
Pössneck D 83 B3
Posta I. 169 A3
Postal I. 108 C2
Posta Piana I . . 172 A1
Postbauer-Heng
  D. 95 B3
Posterholt NL. . .80 A2
Postioma I 121 B5
Postira HR 138 B2
Postojna SLO . . 123 B3
Postoloprty CZ .84 B1
Postomino PL. . .68 A1
Posušje BIH . . . 138 B3
Potamos
  Attiki GR. 184 C3
  Attiki GR. 184 D4
Potegowo PL . . .68 A2
Potenza I 172 B1
Potenza Picena
  I. 136 B2
Potes E. 142 A2
Potigny F 89 B3
Potočari BIH . . 127 C1
Potoci
  BIH. 138 A2
  BIH. 139 B3
Potony H. 125 B3
Potries E 159 C3
Potsdam D. 74 B2
Pottenbrunn
  A. 110 A2
Pottendorf A. . 111 B3
Pottenstein
  A. 111 B3
  D. 95 B3
Potters Bar UK . .44 B3
Pöttmes D 94 C3
Pöttsching A. . 111 B3
Potworów PL . . .87 A4
Pouancé F 101 B4
Pougues-les-Eaux
  F. 104 B2
Pouilly-en-Auxois
  F. 104 B3
Pouilly-sous
  Charlieu F. . . . 117 A4
Pouilly-sur-Loire
  F. 104 B1
Poujol-sur-Orb
  F. 130 B2
Poullaouen F . 100 A2
Poulton-le-Fylde
  UK 38 A4
Poundstock UK .42 B2
Pourcy F 91 B3
Pourrain F 104 B2
Poussu FIN. . . 197 D12
Pouyastruc F. . 145 A4
Pouy-de-Touges
  F. 146 A2
Pouzauges F . . 114 B3
Pova de Santa Iria
  P. 154 C1
Považská Bystrica
  SK. 98 B2
Povedilla E. . . . 158 C1
Povenets RUS. . . . 9 A9
Povlja HR 138 B2
Povljana HR. . . 137 A4
Póvoa
  Beja P 161 A2
  Santarém P . . 154 B2
Póvoa de Lanhoso
  P. 148 A1
Póvoa de Varzim
  P. 148 A1
Póvoa e Meadas
  P. 155 B3
Powidz PL. 76 B2
Poyales del Hoyo
  E. 150 B2
Poynton UK. 40 B1
Poyntz Pass UK .27 B4

Poysdorf A. 97 C4
Poza de la Sal
  E. 143 B3
Pozaldez E 150 A3
Pozán de Vero
  E. 145 B4
Pozanti TR 23 C8
Požarevac
  SRB 127 C3
Požega
  HR 125 B3
  SRB 127 D2
Pozo Alcón E . . 164 B2
Pozoantiguo
  E. 150 A2
Pozoblanco E. 156 B3
Pozo Cañada
  E. 158 C2
Pozo de
  Guadalajara
  E. 151 B4
Pozo de la Serna
  E. 157 B4
Pozohondo E . . 158 C2
Pozondón E. . . 152 B2
Pozuel del Campo
  E. 152 B2
Pozuelo de Alarcón
  E. 151 B4
Pozuelo de
  Calatrava E . . 157 B4
Pozuelo del
  Páramo E. . . . 142 B1
Pozuelo de Zarzón
  E. 149 B3
Pozzallo I 177 C3
Pozzomaggiore
  I. 178 B2
Pozzo San Nicola
  I. 178 B2
Pozzuoli I. 170 C2
Pozzuolo I. 135 B4
Prabuty PL. 69 B4
Prača BIH 139 B4
Prachatice CZ . .96 B1
Prada E. 141 B3
Pradelle F 118 C2
Pradelles F. . . . 117 C2
Prades
  E. 147 C1
  F. 146 B3
Pradła PL 86 B3
Prado
  E. 142 A1
  P. 148 A1
Prado del Rey
  E. 162 B2
Pradoluengo
  E. 143 B3
Pragelato I. . . . 119 B3
Pragersko
  SLO 123 A4
Prägraten A. . . 109 B3
Prague = Praha
  CZ 84 B2
Praha = Prague
  CZ 84 B2
Prahecq F. 115 B3
Praia P 154 B1
Práia a Mare I . 174 B1
Praia da Rocha
  P. 160 B1
Praia da Viera
  P. 154 B2
Praia de Mira
  P. 148 B1
Praiano I. 170 C2
Pralboino I. . . . 120 B3
Pralognan-la-
  Vanoise F . . . 118 B3
Pramanda GR. 182 D3
Pranjani SRB . . 127 C2
Prapatnica HR 138 B2
Præstø DK. 65 A5
Praszka PL. 86 A2
Prat F 146 A1
Prata I. 135 B3
Prata di Pordenone
  I. 122 B1
Pratau D 83 A4
Prat de Compte
  E. 153 B4
Pratdip E. 147 C1
Pratella I. 170 B2
Prato I. 135 B4
Prátola Peligna
  I. 169 A3
Prátola Serra I. 170 C2
Pratovecchio I. 135 B4
Prats-de-Mollo-la-
  Preste F 146 B3

Prauthoy F. . . . 105 B4
Pravia E. 141 A4
Praxmar A . . . 108 B2
Prayssac F 129 B4
Prazzo I 132 A2
Prebold SLO . . 123 A4
Préchac F 128 B2
Précy-sur-Thil
  F. 104 B3
Predáppio I . . . 135 A4
Predazzo I 121 A4
Predding A. . . . 110 C2
Predjame SLO. 123 B3
Predlitz A 109 B4
Predoi I 108 B3
Pré-en-Pail F . . .89 B3
Prees UK 38 B4
Preetz D 64 B3
Préfailles F. . . . 101 B3
Pregarten A. . . .96 C2
Pregrada HR . . 123 A4
Preignan F. . . . 129 C3
Preili LV. 8 D5
Preitenegg A . 110 C1
Prekaja BIH . . . 138 A2
Preko HR 137 A4
Preljina SRB . . 127 D2
Prelog HR 124 A2
Prelošćica HR . 124 B2
Přelouč CZ. 97 A3
Prem SLO 123 B3
Premantura
  HR 122 C2
Prémery F 104 B2
Prémia I. 119 A5
Premià de Mar
  E. 147 C3
Premnitz D 73 B5
Prémont F 91 A3
Prenzlau D. 74 A2
Preodac BIH. . . 138 A2
Přerov CZ. 98 B1
Prerow D 66 B1
Presencio E . . . 143 B3
Presicce I. 173 C4
Presly F 103 B4
Prešov SK. 12 D4
Pressac F 115 B4
Pressath D 95 B3
Pressbaum A. . 111 A3
Prestatyn UK. . .38 A3
Prestebakke N . .54 B2
Presteigne UK . .39 B3
Přeštice CZ. 96 B1
Prevalje SLO. . . 110 C1
Prevenchères
  F. 131 A2
Préveranges
  F. 116 A2
Preveza GR. . . 182 E2
Prevršac HR. . . 124 B2
Prezid HR 123 B3
Priaranza del
  Bierzo E 141 B4
Priay F 118 A2
Pribeta SK 112 B2
Priboj
  BIH. 125 C4
  SRB 16 D3
Přibor CZ 98 B2
Příbram CZ 96 B2
Pribylina SK. . . .99 B3
Pričević SRB . . 127 C1
Preston
  Lancashire
  UK 38 A4
  Scottish Borders
  UK 35 C5
Prestonpans
  UK 35 C5
Prestwick UK. . .36 A2
Prettin D. 83 A4
Preturo I 169 A3
Pretzchendorf
  D. 83 B5
Pretzier D. 73 B4
Pretzsch D. 83 A4
Preuilly-sur-Claise
  F. 115 B4
Pridjel BIH . . . 125 C4
Priego E. 152 B1
Priego de Córdoba
  E. 163 A3
Priekule LV. 8 D2
Prien D. 109 B3
Prienai LT. 13 A5
Prievidza SK . . .98 C2
Prigradica HR. 138 C2
Prigrevica SRB 125 B5
Prijeboj HR . . . 123 C4

Prijedor BIH. . . 124 C2
Prijepolje SRB . 16 D3
Prilep NMK. . . 182 B3
Priluka BIH. . . . 138 B2
Primda CZ 95 B4
Primel-Trégastel
  F. 100 A2
Primišje HR . . . 123 B4
Primorsk
  Kaliningrad
  RUS 69 A5
  Severo-Zapadnyy
  RUS 9 B6
Primošten HR. 138 B1
Primstal D 92 B2
Princes Risborough
  UK 44 B3
Princetown UK. .42 B2
Principina a Mare
  I. 135 C4
Priolo Gargallo
  I. 177 B4
Prioro E. 142 B2
Priozersk RUS. . . 9 B7
Prirechnyy
  RUS 193 C14
Prisoje BIH . . . 138 B3
Priština KOS . . 16 D4
Pritzerbe D. 73 B5
Pritzier D 73 A4
Pritzwalk D 73 A5
Privas F 117 C4
Priverno I 169 B3
Privlaka
  Vukovarsko-
  Srijemska
  HR 125 B4
  Zadarska HR . 137 A4
Prizna HR 123 C3
Prizren KOS . . . 16 D4
Prizzi I 176 B2
Prnjavor
  BIH. 125 C3
  HR 124 B1
  SRB 127 C1
Proaza E 141 A4
Probstzella D . .82 B3
Probus UK 42 B2
Prócchio I. 134 C3
Prochowice PL. .85 A4
Prócida I 170 C2
Prodhromos
  CY 181 B1
Prodo I. 135 C5
Proença-a-Nova
  P. 154 B3
Proença-a-Velha
  P. 155 A3
Profondeville B 79 B4
Prokuplje SRB. 16 D4
Propriano F . . . 180 B1
Prosec CZ 97 B4
Prösen D. 83 A5
Prosenjakovci
  SLO 111 C3
Prosotsani GR. 183 B5
Prostějov CZ. . .98 B1
Prószków PL . . .86 B1
Proszowice PL . .87 B4
Protić BIH 138 A2
Protivanov CZ .97 B4
Protivín CZ. 96 B2
Prötzel D. 74 B2
Provins F. 90 C3
Prozor BIH . . . 139 B3
Prrenjas AL . . . 182 B2
Prudhoe UK. . . .37 B5
Prudnik PL. 85 B5
Pruggern A . . . 109 B4
Průgy H. 113 A5
Prüm D 80 B2
Pruna E 162 B2
Prunelli-di-
  Fiumorbo F . . 180 A2
Prunetta I. 135 A3
Pruniers F. 103 C4
Prusice PL. 85 A4
Pruské SK. 98 B2
Pruszcz PL 76 A3
Pruszcz Gdański
  PL. 69 A3
Pruszków PL. . . .77 B5
Prutz A. 108 B1
Prüzen D. 65 C5
Pruzhany BY . . . 13 B6
Pružina SK. 98 B2
Půrvomay BG. 183 A7
Pryzłęg PL. 75 B4
Przasnysz PL. . . .77 A5
Przechlewo PL. .68 B2

Przecław PL....87 B5
Przedbórz PL ...87 A3
Przedecz PL...76 B3
Przejęslav PL ...84 A3
Przemków PL ..85 A3
Przemocze PL...75 A3
Przemyśl PL.... 12 D5
Przerąb PL 87 A3
Przewodnik PL..69 B3
Przewodowo
  Parcele PL.....77 B5
Przewóz PL.....84 A2
Przezmark PL...69 B4
Przodkowo PL ..68 A3
Przybiernów
  PL..........75 A3
Przyborowice
  PL..........77 B5
Przybyszew PL..87 A4
Przybyszów PL..86 A3
Przyłęg PL 75 B4
Przysucha PL ...87 A4
Przytóczna PL...75 B4
Przytyk PL 87 A4
Przywidz PL....68 A3
Psachna GR .. 185 A4
Psara GR 185 A6
Psary PL.......76 C3
Pskov RUS 8 C3
Pszczew PL....75 B4
Pszczółki PL....69 A3
Pszczyna PL....98 B2
Pszów PL.......86 B2
Pteleos GR 182 D4
Ptolemaida
  GR 182 C3
Ptuj SLO...... 124 A1
Ptusza PL 68 B1
Puch A 109 B4
Puchberg am
  Schneeberg
  A 110 B2
Puchevillers F...90 A2
Puchheim D... 108 A2
Púchov SK 98 B2
Pučišća HR 138 B2
Puck PL 69 A3
Puçol E........ 159 B3
Puconci SLO... 111 C3
Pudasjärvi
  FIN......197 D10
Puderbach D...81 B3
Pudozh RUS....9 B10
Puebla de Albortón
  E 153 A3
Puebla de Alcocer
  E 156 B2
Puebla de Beleña
  E 151 B4
Puebla de Don
  Fadrique E .. 164 B2
Puebla de Don
  Rodrigo E ... 156 A3
Puebla de Guzmán
  E 161 B2
Puebla de la
  Calzada E ... 155 C4
Puebla de la Reina
  E 156 B1
Puebla de Lillo
  E 142 A1
Puebla del Maestre
  E 161 A3
Puebla del Principe
  E 158 C1
Puebla de Obando
  E 155 B4
Puebla de Sanabria
  E 141 B4
Puebla de Sancho
  Pérez E 155 C4
Puente Almuhey
  E 142 B2
Puente de Domingo
  Flórez E ... 141 B4
Puente de Génave
  E 164 A2
Puente del
  Congosto E .. 150 B2
Puente de
  Montañana
  E 145 B4
Puente Duero
  E 150 A3
Puente-Genil
  E 162 A3
Puente la Reina
  E 144 B2
Puente la Reina de
  Jaca E........ 144 B3

Puentelarra E . 143 B3
Puente Mayorga
  E............. 162 B2
Puente Viesgo
  E............. 143 A3
Puertas
  Asturias E .. 142 A2
  Salamanca E.. 149 A3
Puerto de
  Mazarrón E .. 165 B3
Puerto de Santa
  Cruz E........ 156 A2
Puerto de San
  Vicente E 156 A2
Puerto-Lápice
  E............. 157 A4
Puertollano E . 157 B3
Puerto Lumbreras
  E............. 164 B3
Puerto Moral
  E............. 161 B3
Puerto Real E . 162 B1
Puerto Rey E .. 156 A2
Puerto Seguro
  E............. 149 B3
Puerto Serrano
  E............. 162 B2
Puget-Sur-Argens
  F............. 132 B2
Puget-Théniers
  F............. 132 B2
Puget-ville F .. 132 B2
Pugnochiuso I 171 B4
Puigcerdà E... 146 B2
Puigpunyent
  E............. 166 B2
Puig Reig E.... 147 C2
Puillon F...... 128 C2
Puimichel F... 132 B2
Puimoisson F . 132 B2
Puiseaux F 103 A4
Puisieux F......90 A2
Puisserguier F 130 B2
Puivert F...... 146 B3
Pujols F....... 128 B2
Pukanec SK 98 C2
Pukavik S......63 B2
Pukë AL....... 182 A1
Pula
  HR 122 C2
  I 179 C2
Puławy PL......12 C4
Pulborough UK .44 C3
Pulfero I 122 A2
Pulgar E....... 157 A3
Pulheim D 80 A2
Pulkau A.......97 C3
Pulpí E 164 B3
Pulsano I 173 B3
Pulsnitz D......84 A2
Pułtusk PL 77 B6
Pumpsaint UK .39 B3
Punat HR...... 123 B3
Punta Marina
  I 135 A5
Punta Prima E. 167 B4
Punta Sabbioni
  I 122 B1
Puntas de Calnegre
  E............. 165 B3
Punta Umbria
  E............. 161 B3
Puolanka FIN ..3 D10
Puoltikasvaara
  S 196 B4
Puoltsa S..... 196 B2
Puračić BIH... 125 C4
Purbach am
  Neusiedler See
  A 111 B3
Purchena E.... 164 B2
Purfleet UK 45 B4
Purgstall A.... 110 A2
Purkersdorf A. 111 A3
Purmerend NL ..70 B1
Purullena E ... 164 B1
Pushkin RUS 9 C7
Pushkino RUS..9 D10
Püspökladány
  H.......... 113 B5
Pusté Ulany
  SK.......... 111 A4
Pustoshka RUS...9 D6
Puszcza Mariańska
  PL............77 C5
Puszczykowo
  PL............76 B1
Pusztamagyaród
  H.......... 111 C3
Pusztamonostor
  H.......... 113 B3
Pusztaszabolcs
  H.......... 112 B2

Pusztavám H.. 112 B2
Putanges-Pont-
  Ecrepin F......89 B3
Putbus D.......66 B2
Putignano I ... 173 B3
Putlitz D 73 A5
Putnok H 99 C4
Putte B.........79 A4
Puttelange-aux-
  Lacs F 92 B2
Putten NL......70 B2
Puttgarden D...65 B4
Püttlingen D....92 B2
Putzu Idu I 179 B2
Puy-Guillaume
  F............. 117 B3
Puylaroque F . 129 B4
Puylaurens F.. 146 A3
Puy-l'Évêque
  F............. 129 B4
Puymirol F..... 129 B3
Puyôo F....... 128 C2
Puyrolland F.. 114 B3
Pwllheli UK 38 B2
Pyetrikaw BY .. 13 B8
Pyhäjärvi FIN ... 3 E9
Pyhäkylä
  FIN..........197 D11
Pyla CY....... 181 A2
Pyla-sur-Mer
  F............. 128 B1
Pyrzyce PL......75 A3
Pysely CZ......96 B2
Pyskowice PL...86 B2
Pytalovo RUS ...8 D5
Pyzdry PL.......76 B2

Q

Quakenbrück
  D 71 B4
Quargnento I . 119 C5
Quarré-les-Tombes
  F............. 104 B2
Quarteira P ... 160 B1
Quartu Sant'Élena
  I 179 C3
Quatre-Champs
  F.............91 B4
Quedlinburg D..82 A3
Queensferry
  Edinburgh
  UK 35 C4
  Flintshire UK ... 38 A3
Queige F...... 118 B3
Queipo E...... 161 B3
Queixans E.... 146 B2
Quel E........ 144 B1
Quelaines-St-Gault
  F............. 102 B1
Queljada P.... 148 A1
Quemada E ... 143 C3
Queralbs E.... 147 B3
Quercianella I. 134 B3
Querfurt D......82 A3
Quérigut F.... 146 B3
Quero
  E............. 157 A4
  I 121 B4
Querqueville F..88 A2
Quesada E 164 B1
Questembert
  F............. 101 B3
Quettehou F ...88 A2
Quevauvillers F 90 B2
Quevy B........79 B4
Quiaios P..... 148 B1
Quiberon F ... 100 B2
Quiberville F ..89 A4
Quickborn D....64 C2
Quiévrain B....79 B3
Quillan F...... 146 B3
Quillebeuf F ...89 A4
Quimper F 100 A1
Quimperlé F .. 100 B2
Quincampoix
  F.............89 A5
Quincoces de Yuso
  E............. 143 B3
Quincy F...... 103 B4
Quinéville F....88 A2
Quingey F.... 105 B4
Quinson F..... 132 B2
Quinssaines F . 116 A2
Quinta-Grande
  P 154 C2
Quinta de la
  Serena E 156 B2
Quintana del
  Castillo E.... 141 B4
Quintana del Marco
  E............. 141 B5

Quintana del
  Puenta E 142 B2
Quintana-Martin
  Galindez E .. 143 B3
Quintanaortuño
  E............. 143 B3
Quintanapalla
  E............. 143 B3
Quintanar de la
  Orden E 157 A4
Quintanar de la
  Sierra E 143 C3
Quintanar del Rey
  E............. 158 B2
Quintanilla de la
  Mata E 143 C3
Quintanilla del
  Coco E 143 C3
Quintanilla de
  Onésimo E ... 150 A3
Quintanilla de
  Somoza E 141 B4
Quintas de
  Valdelucio E . 142 B2
Quintela P 148 B2
Quintin F 100 A3
Quinto E 153 A3
Quinzano d'Oglio
  I 120 B3
Quiroga E..... 141 B3
Quismondo E . 150 B3
Quissac F 131 B2
Quistello I..... 121 B3

R

Raab A.........96 C1
Raabs an der Thaya
  A.............97 C3
Raahe FIN........3 D9
Raajärvi FIN... 197 C9
Raalte NL......71 B3
Raamsdonksveer
  NL 79 A4
Raanujarvi
  FIN......... 196 C7
Raattama FIN . 196 A7
Rab HR....... 123 C3
Rabac HR..... 123 B3
Rábade E..... 140 A3
Rábafüzes H .. 111 C3
Rábahidvég H 111 B3
Rabanales E... 149 A3
Rábapatona
  H.......... 111 B4
Rabapordány
  H.......... 111 B4
Rabastens F... 129 C4
Rabastens-de-
  Bigorre F.... 145 A4
Rabat M...... 175 C3
Rabat = Victoria
  M 175 C3
Rabča SK......99 B3
Rabe SRB..... 126 A2
Rabi CZ........96 B1
Rabino PL......67 C4
Rabka PL......99 B3
Rabrovo SRB . 127 C3
Rača SRB..... 127 C3
Rácale I 173 C4
Rácalmás H ... 112 B2
Racalmuto I .. 176 B2
Racconigi I ... 119 C4
Rače SLO..... 123 A4
Rachecourt-sur-
  Marne F.......91 C5
Raciąż PL......77 B5
Raciborz PL.....86 B2
Račinovci HR.. 125 C4
Ráckeve H 112 B2
Racławice PL...87 B4
Racławice Śląskie
  PL............86 B1
Racot PL.......75 B5
Råda
  Skaraborg S...55 B4
  Värmland S....49 B5
Radalj SRB.... 127 C1
Rădăuți RO....17 B6
Radda in Chianti
  I 135 B4
Raddusa I 177 B3
Radeberg D....84 A1
Radebeul D....84 A1
Radeburg D....84 A1
Radeče SLO... 123 A4
Radekhiv UA... 13 C6
Radenci SLO.. 111 C3
Radenthein A. 109 C4
Radevormwald
  D 80 A3

Radicófani I... 135 C4
Radicóndoli I . 135 B4
Radišići BIH.... 138 B3
Radizel SLO... 110 C2
Radków PL.....85 B4
Radlje ob Dravi
  SLO 110 C2
Radlów PL.....87 B4
Radmer an der
  Stube A 110 B1
Radnejaur S... 195 E9
Radnice CZ.....96 B1
Radohova BIH. 138 A3
Radojevo SRB . 126 B2
Radolfzell D .. 107 B3
Radom PL......87 A5
Radomice PL...77 B4
Radomin PL....77 A4
Radomsko PL..86 A3
Radomyshl UA.13 C8
Radomyśl Wielki
  PL............87 B5
Radošina SK ...98 C1
Radošovce SK..98 C1
Radoszewice
  PL............86 A2
Radoszyce PL ..87 A4
Radotin CZ.....96 B2
Radovets BG.. 186 A1
Radoviš NMK.. 182 B4
Radovljica
  SLO 123 A3
Radowo Wielkie
  PL............75 A4
Radstadt A.... 109 B4
Radstock UK ...43 A4
Raduc HR..... 137 A4
Raduša NMK.. 182 A3
Radviliškis LT ... 8 E3
Radzanów
  Mazowieckie
  PL............77 B5
  Mazowieckie
  PL............ 87 A4
Radziejów PL..76 B3
Radziejowice
  PL............77 B5
Radzovce SK .. 113 A3
Radzyń Chełmiński
  PL............69 B3
Raeren B.......80 B2
Raesfeld D.....80 A2
Raffadali I..... 176 B2
Rafina GR..... 185 A4
Rafsbotn N.... 192 B7
Ragachow BY .. 13 B9
Ragály H.......99 C4
Rageleje DK....61 C2
Raglan UK 39 C4
Ragnitz A..... 110 C2
Ragusa I 177 C3
Rahden D......72 B1
Råholt N.......48 B3
Raiano I...... 169 A3
Raigada E..... 141 B3
Rain D.........94 C2
Rainbach im
  Mühlkreis A...96 C2
Rainham UK ...45 B4
Rairiz de Veiga
  E............. 140 B3
Raisdorf D.....64 B3
Raisio FIN......8 B3
Raiskio FIN... 197 D9
Raiva
  Aveiro P 148 A1
  Coimbra P .. 148 B1
Raja-Joosseppi
  FIN......... 193 D12
Rajala FIN.... 197 B9
Rajcza PL......99 B3
Rajec SK.......98 B2
Rájec-Jestřebi
  CZ 97 B4
Rajecké Teplice
  SK............98 B2
Rajevo Selo
  HR 125 C4
Rajhrad CZ.....97 B4
Rajić HR...... 124 B3
Rajka H....... 111 B4
Rakaca H.......99 C4
Rakamaz H ... 113 A5
Rakek SLO... 123 B3
Rakhiv UA......17 A6
Rakitna SLO... 123 B3
Rakitovo BG .. 183 B6
Rakkestad N...54 A2
Rákóczifalva
  H.......... 113 B4
Rakoniewice PL 75 B5
Rakoszyce PL...85 A4
Raková SK.....98 B2

Rakovac BIH .. 125 B3
Rakovica HR .. 123 C4
Rakovník CZ ...96 A1
Rakow D.......66 B2
Raków PL......87 B5
Rakvere EST......8 C5
Ralja SRB..... 127 C2
Ramacastañas
  E............. 150 B2
Ramacca I 177 B3
Ramales de la
  Victoria E 143 A3
Ramberg N ... 194 B4
Rambervillers
  F.............92 C2
Rambouillet F...90 C1
Rambucourt F ..92 C1
Ramdala S......63 B3
Ramerupt F....91 C4
Ramingstein
  A 109 B4
Ramirás E..... 140 B2
Ramiswil CH .. 106 B2
Ramkvilla S.....62 A2
Ramme DK.....58 B1
Rämmen S.....49 B6
Ramnäs S......56 A2
Ramnes N......54 A1
Râmnicu Vâlcea
  RO 17 C6
Ramonville-St Agne
  F............. 129 C4
Rampside UK ...36 B3
Ramsau D..... 109 B3
Ramsbeck D...81 A4
Ramsberg S....56 A1
Ramsele S..... 200 C2
Ramsey
  Cambridgeshire
  UK 44 A3
  Isle of Man UK .36 B2
Ramsgate UK ...45 B5
Ramsjö S..... 200 D1
Ramstein-
  Meisenbach D .93 B3
Ramsund N ... 194 B7
Ramundberget
  S 199 C9
Ramvik S..... 200 D3
Ranalt A 108 B2
Rånäs S.......51 C5
Rånåsfoss N...48 B3
Rance B........91 A4
Ránchio I..... 135 B5
Randaberg N ..52 A1
Randalstown
  UK 27 B4
Randan F...... 117 A3
Randazzo I.... 177 B3
Randders DK...58 B3
Randijaur S... 196 C2
Randin E...... 140 C3
Randsverk N.. 198 D6
Råneå S...... 196 D5
Rânes F........89 B3
Rångedala S...60 B3
Ranis D........82 B3
Rankweil A.... 107 B4
Rånnaväg S....60 B3
Ränneslöv S....61 C3
Rannoch Station
  UK 34 B3
Ranovac SRB . 127 C3
Ransäter S.....55 A4
Ransbach-
  Baumbach D..81 B3
Ransta S......56 A2
Ranttila FIN... 193 C9
Ranua FIN.... 197 D9
Ranum DK.....58 B2
Ranvalhal P... 154 B1
Raon-l'Étape F .92 C2
Ráossi I 121 B4
Rapallo I 134 A2
Rapla EST......8 C4
Rapness UK 33 B4
Rapolano Terme
  I 135 B4
Rapolla I 172 B1
Raposa P..... 154 B2
Rapperswil
  CH 107 B3
Raša HR...... 123 B3
Rascafria E ... 151 B4
Rasdorf D......82 B1
Raseiniai LT 8 A5
Rašica SLO... 123 B3

Rasines E 143 A3
Rasquera E.... 153 A4
Rássina I 135 B4
Rastatt D......93 C4
Rastede D......71 A5
Rastenberg D..82 A3
Rastošnica
  BIH......... 125 C4
Rastovac MNE. 139 C4
Rasueros E.... 150 A2
Rasy PL.......86 A3
Raszków PL....86 A1
Rätan S...... 199 C11
Rateče SLO... 109 C4
Ratekau D......65 C3
Ratež SLO.... 123 B4
Rathangan IRL..30 A2
Rathcoole IRL...30 A2
Rathcormack
  IRL 29 B3
Rathdrum IRL..30 B2
Rathebur D....74 A2
Rathenow D ...73 B5
Rathfriland UK..27 B4
Rathkeale IRL..29 B3
Rathmelton IRL.27 A3
Rathmolyon
  IRL 30 A2
Rathmore IRL..29 B2
Rathmullan IRL.27 A3
Rathnew IRL...30 B2
Rathvilly IRL ...30 B2
Ratibořské Hory
  CZ 96 B2
Ratingen D.....80 A2
Ratková SK....99 C4
Ratkovo SRB . 126 B1
Ratne UA...... 13 C6
Rattelsdorf D ..94 A2
Ratten A 110 B2
Rattosjärvi
  FIN......... 196 C7
Rattray UK 35 B4
Rättvik S.......50 B2
Ratvika N..... 199 B7
Ratzeburg D ...65 C3
Rätzlingen D....73 B4
Raucourt-et-Flaba
  F.............91 B4
Raudeberg N . 198 D2
Raufarhöfn
  IS 191 A10
Raufoss N......48 B2
Rauhala FIN... 196 B7
Rauland N 53 A4
Raulhac F 116 C2
Raulia N......195 E5
Rauma FIN......8 B2
Raundal N......46 B3
Raunds UK 44 A3
Rauris A...... 109 B4
Rautas S...... 196 B2
Rautavaara FIN .3 E11
Rauville-la-Bigot
  F.............88 A2
Rauzan F...... 128 B2
Ravanusa I ... 176 B2
Rava-Rus'ka
  UA 13 C5
Ravča HR..... 138 B3
Ravels B.......79 A4
Rävemåla S....63 B3
Ravenglass UK .36 B3
Ravenna I 135 A5
Ravensburg D 107 B4
Rävlanda S....60 B2
Ravna Gora
  HR 123 B3
Ravne na
  Koroškem
  SLO 110 C1
Ravnje SRB.... 127 C1
Ravno BIH.... 139 C3
Ravno Selo
  SRB 126 B1
Rawa Mazowiecka
  PL............87 A4
Rawicz PL......85 A4
Rawtenstall UK .40 B1
Rayleigh UK....45 B4
Ražana SRB... 127 C1
Ražanac HR... 137 A4
Razbojna BIH.. 124 B3
Razes F....... 115 B5
Razgrad BG.... 17 D7
Razkrižje SLO. 111 C3
Razlog BG.... 183 B5
Razo E....... 140 A2
Reading UK....44 B3
Réalmont F ... 130 B1
Rebais F.......90 C3
Reboly RUS 3 E12
Rebordelo P .. 149 A2

Recanati I..... 136 B2
Recas E....... 151 B4
Recco I....... 134 A2
Recess IRL.....28 A2
Recey-sur-Ource
F............. 105 B3
Recezinhos P . 148 A1
Rechnitz A 111 B3
Rechytsa BY.....13 B9
Recke D.......71 B4
Recklinghausen
D 80 A3
Recoaro Terme
I............. 121 B4
Recogne B ...92 B1
Recoules-
Prévinquières
F............. 130 A1
Recsk H....... 113 B4
Recz PL 75 A4
Reda PL 69 A3
Redalen N 48 B2
Redange L 92 B1
Redcar UK.......37 B5
Redditch UK ...44 A2
Redefin D.......73 A4
Redhill UK 44 B3
Redics H 111 C3
Redkino RUS ...9 D10
Redland UK 33 B3
Redlin D 73 A5
Redon F....... 101 B3
Redondela E .. 140 B2
Redondo P.... 155 C3
Red Point UK...31 B3
Redruth UK 42 B1
Redzikowo PL..68 A2
Reepham UK....41 C5
Rees D 80 A2
Reeth UK........37 B5
Reetz D 73 A4
Reftele S.......60 B3
Regalbuto I 177 B3
Regen D 95 C5
Regensburg D ..95 B4
Regenstauf D ...95 B4
Reggello I..... 135 B4
Réggio di Calábria
I............. 175 C1
Reggiolo I..... 121 C3
Réggio nell'Emília
I............. 121 C3
Reghin RO 17 B6
Régil E 144 A1
Regna S........56 B1
Regniéville F....92 C1
Regny F....... 117 B4
Rego da Leirosa
P............. 154 A2
Regöly H...... 112 C2
Regueiro E..... 140 B2
Reguengo
Portalegre P .. 155 B3
Santarém P ... 154 B2
Reguengos de
Monsaraz P .. 155 C3
Rehau D 83 B4
Rehburg D.....72 B2
Rehden D.......72 B1
Rehna D 65 C4
Reichelsheim D 93 B4
Reichelshofen
D 94 B2
Reichenau A .. 110 B2
Reichenbach
Sachsen D 83 B4
Sachsen D 84 A2
Reichenfels A . 110 B1
Reichensachsen
D 82 A2
Reichertshofen
D 95 C3
Reichshoffen F..93 C3
Reiden CH 106 B2
Reigada
E............. 141 A4
P............. 149 B3
Reigate UK.....44 B3
Reillanne F.... 132 B1
Reillo E....... 158 B2
Reims F.......91 B4
Reinach CH ... 106 B3
Reinbek D 72 A3
Reinberg D.....66 B2
Reine N 194 C4
Reinfeld D.....65 C3
Reinheim D 93 B4
Reinli N 47 B6
Reinosa E 142 A2
Reinstorf D 65 C4
Reinsvoll N 48 B2
Reisach A 109 C4
Reiss UK.......32 C3

Reitan N 199 C8
Reit im Winkl
D 109 B3
Rejmyre S......56 B1
Rekavice BIH .. 124 C3
Rekovac SRB . 127 D3
Relleu E....... 159 C3
Rém H 125 A5
Remagen D 80 B3
Rémalard F 89 B4
Rembercourt-aux-
Pots F.......91 C5
Remedios P ... 154 B1
Remels D 71 A4
Remetea Mare
RO 126 B3
Remich L........92 B2
Rémilly F........92 B2
Remiremont
F............. 105 A5
Remolinos E .. 144 C2
Remoulins F .. 131 B3
Remscheid D...80 A3
Rena N........48 A3
Renaison F.... 117 A3
Renazé F..... 101 B4
Renchen D 93 C4
Rencurel F 118 B2
Rende I 174 B2
Rendina GR .. 182 D3
Rendsburg D...64 B2
Renedo E 150 A3
Renens CH ... 105 C5
Renfrew UK 34 C3
Rengsjö S......50 A3
Reni UA 17 C8
Rennebu N ... 198 C6
Rennerod D....81 B4
Rennertshofen
D 94 C3
Rennes F...... 101 A4
Rennes-les-Bains
F............. 146 B3
Rennweg A ... 109 B4
Rens DK........64 B2
Rensjön S 196 A2
Rentería E.... 144 A2
Rentjärn S 200 A4
Répcelak H.... 111 B4
Repojoki FIN . 193 D9
Repvåg N 193 B9
Requena E 159 B2
Réquista F 130 A1
Rerik D........65 B4
Resana I...... 121 B4
Resarö S 57 A4
Reschen = Résia
I............. 108 C1
Resen NMK.... 182 B3
Resende P 148 A2
Résia = Reschen
I............. 108 C1
Reşiţa
RO 16 C4
RO 126 B3
Resko PL.......67 C4
Resnik SRB.... 127 C2
Ressons-sur-Matz
F............. 90 B2
Restábal E 163 B4
Resuttano I ... 177 B3
Retamal E.... 155 C4
Retford UK.....40 B3
Rethel F........91 B4
Rethem D.......72 B2
Rethimno GR . 185 D5
Retie B 79 A5
Retiers F...... 101 B4
Retortillo E 149 B3
Retortillo de Soria
E............. 151 A4
Retuerta del
Bullaque E ... 157 A3
Retz A.........97 C3
Retzbach D 94 B1
Reuden D 73 B5
Reuilly F 103 B4
Reus E 147 C2
Reusel NL......79 A5
Reuterstadt
Stavenhagen
D 74 A1
Reuth D........95 B4
Reutlingen D .. 94 C1
Reutte A 108 B1
Reuver NL......80 A2
Revel F....... 146 A2
Revello I 119 C4
Revenga E 151 B3

Revest-du-Bion
F............. 132 A1
Révfülöp H,,,, 111 C4
Revigny-sur-Ornain
F............. 91 C4
Revin F........91 B4
Řevnice CZ.....96 B2
Řevničov CZ ...84 B1
Revo I........ 121 A4
Revsnes N......47 A4
Revúca SK......99 C4
Rewa PL.......69 A3
Rewal PL.......67 B4
Rexbo S........50 B2
Reyðarfjörður
IS 191 B11
Reyero E 142 B1
Reykhólar IS .. 190 B3
Reykholt
Árnessýsla
IS 190 C5
Borgarfjarðarsýsla
IS 190 C4
Reykjahlið IS.. 191 B9
Reykjavík IS... 190 C4
Rezé F........ 101 B4
Rēzekne LV 8 D5
Rezovo BG 17 E8
Rezzato I..... 120 B3
Rezzoáglio I... 134 A2
Rhade D 72 A2
Rhaunen D 93 B3
Rhayader UK...39 B3
Rheda-
Wiedenbrück
D 81 A4
Rhede
Niedersachsen
D........... 71 A4
Nordrhein-
Westfalen D... 80 A2
Rheinau D 93 C3
Rheinbach D...80 B2
Rheinberg D...80 A2
Rheine D.......71 B4
Rheinfelden D 106 B2
Rheinsberg D...74 A1
Rhêmes-Notre-
Dame I...... 119 B4
Rhenen NL.....70 C2
Rhens D........81 B3
Rheydt D.......80 A2
Rhiconich UK ..32 C2
Rhinow D 73 B5
Rhiw UK........38 B2
Rho I......... 120 B2
Rhodes GR.... 188 C3
Rhondda UK ...39 C3
Rhosllanerchrugog
UK 38 A3
Rhosneigr UK ..38 A2
Rhossili UK......39 C2
Rhubodach UK..34 C2
Rhuddlan UK...38 A3
Rhyl UK 38 A3
Rhynie UK......33 D4
Riala S 57 A4
Riallé F....... 101 B4
Riaño E 142 B1
Riano I....... 168 A2
Rians F....... 132 B1
Rianxo E 140 B2
Riaza E....... 151 A4
Ribadavia E... 140 B2
Ribadeo E..... 141 A3
Riba de Saelices
E............. 152 B1
Ribadesella E . 142 A1
Ribaflecha E .. 143 B4
Ribaforada E.. 144 C2
Ribare SRB.... 127 C3
Riba-roja d'Ebre
E............. 153 A4
Riba-Roja de Turia
E............. 159 B3
Ribe DK........59 C1
Ribeauvillé F... 106 A2
Ribécourt-
Dreslincourt F .90 B2
Ribeira da Pena
P............. 148 A2
Ribeira de Piquín
E............. 141 A3
Ribemont F 91 B3
Ribera I....... 176 B2
Ribérac F..... 129 A3
Ribera de Cardós
E............. 146 B2
Ribera del Fresno
E............. 156 B1
Ribesalbes E .. 159 A3
Ribes de Freser
E............. 147 B3

Ribiers F 132 A1
Ribnica
BIH 139 A4
SLO 123 B3
Ribnica na Potorju
SLO 110 C2
Ribnik BIH 123 B4
Ribnița MD.....17 B8
Ribnitz-Damgarten
D 66 B1
Ribolla I...... 135 C4
Říčany CZ......97 B4
Ričany CZ......96 B2
Ríccia I....... 170 B2
Riccione I 136 A1
Ricco Del Golfo
I............. 134 A2
Richebourg F . 105 A4
Richelieu F.... 102 B2
Richisau CH... 107 B3
Richmond
Greater London
UK 44 B3
North Yorkshire
UK 37 B5
Richtenberg D ..66 B1
Richterswil
CH 107 B3
Rickling D.......64 B3
Rickmansworth
UK 44 B3
Ricla E....... 152 A2
Riddarhyttan S .50 C2
Ridderkerk NL ..79 A4
Riddes CH..... 119 A4
Ridjica SRB... 125 B5
Riec-sur-Bélon
F............. 100 B2
Ried A 109 A4
Riedenburg D...95 C3
Ried im Oberinntal
A............. 108 B1
Riedlingen D.. 107 A4
Riedstadt D.....93 B4
Riegersburg A 110 C2
Riego de la Vega
E............. 141 B5
Riego del Camino
E............. 149 A4
Riello E....... 141 B5
Riemst B 80 B1
Rienne B........91 B4
Riénsena E.... 142 A2
Riesa D........83 A5
Riese Pio X I .. 121 B4
Riesi I........ 177 B3
Riestedt D......82 A3
Rietberg D.....81 A4
Rieti I........ 169 A2
Rietschen D.....84 A2
Rieumes F 146 A2
Rieupeyroux
F............. 130 A1
Rieux-Volvestre
F............. 146 A2
Riez F........ 132 B2
Rignac F...... 130 A1
Rignano Gargánico
I............. 171 B3
Rigolato I..... 109 C3
Rigside UK......36 A3
Rigutino I..... 135 B4
Riihimäki FIN ...8 B4
Rijeka HR 123 B3
Rijen NL........79 A4
Rijkevorsel B....79 A4
Rijssen NL......71 B3
Rila BG....... 183 A5
Rilić BIH...... 138 B3
Rilievo I...... 176 B1
Rillé F........ 102 B2
Rillo de Gallo
E............. 152 B2
Rimavská Baňa
SK............99 C3
Rimavská Seč
SK............99 C4
Rimavská Sobota
SK............99 C4
Rimbo S........57 A4
Rimforsa S.....56 B1
Rímini I...... 136 A1
Rîmnicu Sărat
RO 17 C7
Rimogne F......91 B4
Rimpar D.......94 B1
Rimske Toplice
SLO 123 A4
Rincón de la
Victoria E 163 B3

Rincón de Soto
E............. 144 B2
Rindal N 190 D6
Rinde N........46 A3
Ringarum S....56 B2
Ringaskiddy
IRL 29 C3
Ringe DK.......59 C3
Ringebu N 48 A2
Ringkøbing DK .59 B1
Ringsaker N....48 B2
Ringsted DK .. 61 D1
Ringwood UK...44 C2
Rinkaby S......63 C2
Rinkabyholm S .63 B4
Rinlo E....... 141 A3
Rinn A 108 B2
Rinteln D 72 B2
Rio E......... 140 B3
Riobo E....... 140 B2
Riodeva E..... 152 B2
Rio do Coures
P............. 154 B2
Rio Douro P... 148 A2
Riofrio E...... 150 B3
Rio Frio P 154 C2
Riofrio de Aliste
E............. 149 A3
Rio frio de Riaza
E............. 151 A4
Riogordo E.... 163 B3
Rioja E....... 164 C2
Riola I....... 135 A4
Riola Sardo I .. 179 C2
Riolobos E 155 B4
Riom F....... 116 B3
Riomaggiore I 134 A2
Rio Maior P ... 154 B2
Rio Marina I... 134 C3
Riom-ès-
Montagnes F. 116 B2
Rion-des-Landes
F............. 128 C2
Rionegro del
Puente E 141 B4
Rionero in Vúlture
I............. 172 B1
Riopar E 158 C1
Riós E 141 C3
Rioseco E 142 A1
Rioseco de Tapia
E............. 141 B5
Rio Tinto E.... 148 A1
Riotord F...... 117 B4
Riotorto E..... 141 A3
Rioz F........ 105 B5
Ripač BIH..... 124 C1
Ripacándida I. 172 B1
Ripanj SRB.... 127 C2
Ripatransone
I............. 136 C2
Ripley UK......40 B2
Ripoll E 147 B3
Ripon UK.......40 A2
Riposto I...... 177 B4
Ripsa S........56 B2
Risan MNE 16 D3
Risbäck S 200 B1
Risca UK........39 C3
Rischenau D ...81 A5
Riscle F....... 128 C2
Risebo S 56 B2
Risnes N 46 A2
Rišňovce SK....98 C1
Risør N........53 B5
Risøyhamn N . 194 B6
Rissna S...... 199 B12
Ritsem S...... 194 C8
Ritterhude D...72 A1
Riutula FIN .. 193 D10
Riva E....... 143 A3
Riva del Garda
I............. 121 B3
Riva Lígure I .. 133 B3
Rivanazzano I. 120 C2
Rivarolo Canavese
I............. 119 B4
Rivarolo
Mantovano I. 121 B3
Rive-de-Gier F 117 B4
Rivedoux-Plage
F............. 114 B2
Rivello I...... 174 A1
Rivergaro I.... 120 C2
Rives F....... 118 B2
Rivesaltes F... 146 B3
Rivignano I ... 122 B2
Rivne UA......13 C7
Rívoli I....... 119 B4
Rivolta d'Adda
I............. 120 B2
Rixheim F..... 106 B2
Rixo S.........54 B2

Riza GR 183 C5
Rizokarpaso
CY 181 A3
Rjukan N.......47 C5
Rø DK.........67 A3
Rö S...........57 A4
Roa
E............. 143 C3
N.............48 B2
Roade UK......44 A3
Roager DK 59 C1
Roaldkvam N ..52 A2
Roanne F 117 A4
Röbäck S...... 200 C6
Robakowo PL...69 B3
Róbbio I 120 B1
Röbel D........73 A5
Roberton UK....35 C5
Robertsfors S . 200 B6
Robertville B....80 B2
Robin Hood's Bay
UK 37 B6
Robleda E..... 149 B3
Robledillo de
Trujillo E 156 A2
Robledo
Albacete E 158 C1
Orense E...... 141 B4
Robledo de Chavela
E............. 151 B3
Robledo del Buey
E............. 156 A3
Robledo del Mazo
E............. 156 A3
Robledollano
E............. 156 A2
Robles de la
Valcueva E ... 142 B1
Robliza de Cojos
E............. 149 B4
Robres E 145 C3
Robres del Castillo
E............. 144 B1
Rocafort de Queralt
E............. 147 C2
Rocamadour
F............. 129 B4
Roccabernarda
I............. 175 B2
Roccabianca
I............. 120 B3
Roccadáspide
I............. 172 B1
Rocca di Mezzo
I............. 169 A3
Rocca di Papa
I............. 168 B2
Roccagorga I.. 169 B3
Rocca Imperiale
I............. 174 A2
Roccalbegna I. 135 C4
Roccalumera I 177 B4
Roccamena I.. 176 B2
Roccamonfina
I............. 170 B1
Roccanova I... 174 A2
Roccapalumba
I............. 176 B2
Roccapassa I.. 169 A3
Rocca Priora I . 136 B2
Roccaraso I... 169 B4
Rocca San Casciano
I............. 135 A4
Roccasecca I.. 169 B3
Rocca Sinibalda
I............. 169 A2
Roccastrada I . 135 B4
Roccatederighi
I............. 135 B4
Roccella Iónica
I............. 175 C2
Rocchetta
Sant'António
I............. 172 A1
Rocester UK....40 C2
Rochdale UK....40 B1
Rochechouart
F............. 115 C4
Rochefort
B.............79 B5
Rochefort-en-Terre
F............. 101 B3
Rochefort-
Montagne F.. 116 B2
Rochefort-sur-
Nenon F..... 105 B4
Roche-lez-Beaupré
F............. 105 B5
Rochemaure
F............. 131 A3
Rocheservière
F............. 114 B2

Rochester
Medway UK.....45 B4
Northumberland
UK 37 A4
Rochlitz D.......83 A4
Rociana del
Condado F ... 161 B3
Rockenhausen
D 93 B3
Rockhammar S .56 A1
Rockneby S.....62 B4
Ročko Polje
HR 123 B3
Ročov CZ.......84 B1
Rocroi F........91 B4
Rodach D.......82 B2
Roda de Bara
E............. 147 C2
Roda de Ter E . 147 C3
Rodalben D 93 B3
Rødberg N.....47 B5
Rødby DK......65 B4
Rødbyhavn DK..65 B4
Rødding
Sonderjyllands
Amt. DK 59 C2
Viborg Amt.
DK............58 B1
Rödeby S.......63 B3
Rodeiro E 140 B3
Rødekro DK....64 A2
Roden NL......71 A3
Ródenas E 152 B2
Rodenkirchen
D 72 A1
Rödental D 82 B3
Rödermark D ...93 B4
Rodewisch D...83 B4
Rodez F....... 130 A1
Rodi Gargánico
I............. 171 B3
Roding D 95 B4
Rödjebro S......51 B4
Rødkærsbro DK 59 B2
Rodolivas GR . 183 C5
Rodoña E 147 C2
Rødvig DK......65 A5
Roermond NL...80 A1
Roesbrugge B...78 B2
Roeschwoog F .93 C4
Roeselare B.....78 B3
Roetgen D 80 B2
Roffiac F...... 116 B3
Röfors S.......55 B5
Rofrano I...... 172 B1
Rogač HR...... 138 B2
Rogačica SRB . 127 C1
Rogalinek PL....76 B1
Rogaška Slatina
SLO 123 A4
Rogatec SLO .. 123 A4
Rogatica BIH .. 139 B5
Rogatyn UA.... 13 D6
Rogätz D........73 B4
Roggendorf D ..65 C4
Roggiano Gravina
I............. 174 B2
Roghadal UK...31 B2
Rogliano
F............. 180 A2
I............. 175 B2
Rognan N 195 C6
Rogne N 47 A6
Rognes F...... 131 B4
Rogny-les-7-Ecluses
F............. 103 B4
Rogowo PL.....76 B2
Rogoznica HR. 138 B1
Rogóznica PL...85 A4
Rogoźno PL....76 B1
Rohan F....... 101 A3
Röhlingen D ...94 C2
Rohožnik SK ...98 C1
Rohr D.........82 B2
Rohrbach A 96 C1
Rohrbach-lès-
Bitche F.......92 B3
Rohrberg D.....73 B4
Rohr im Gebirge
A............. 110 B2
Röhrnbach D ..96 C1
Roisel F........90 B3
Roja LV.........8 D3
Rojales E 165 A4
Röjeråsen S.....50 B1
Rojewo PL......76 B3
Rokiciny PL....87 A3
Rokietnica PL...75 B5
Rokiškis LT......8 E4
Rokitki PL......85 A3

Rokycany CZ....96 B1
Rolampont F.. 105 B4
Rold DK........58 B2
Røldal N 52 A2
Rolde NL.......71 B3
Rolfs S ... 196 D6
Rollag N 47 B6
Rollán E...... 149 B4
Rolle CH ... 105 C5
Roma S 57 C4
Roma = Rome
I............. 168 B2
Romagnano Sésia
I............. 119 B5
Romagné F....88 B2
Romakloster S ..57 C4
Roman RO 17 B7
Romana I 178 B2
Romanèche-
Thorins F..... 117 A4
Romano di
Lombardia I.. 120 B2
Romanshorn
CH 107 B4
Romans-sur-Isère
F............. 118 B2
Rombas F.......92 B2
Rome = Roma
I............. 168 B2
Romeán E..... 141 B3
Romenay F.... 105 C4
Romeral E..... 157 A4
Römerstein D...94 C1
Rometta I..... 177 A4
Romford UK....45 B4
Romhány H ... 112 B3
Römhild D 82 B2
Romilly-sur-Seine
F.............91 C3
Romont CH ... 106 C1
Romorantin-
Lanthenay F.. 103 B3
Romrod D......81 B5
Romsey UK....44 C2
Rømskog N 54 A2
Rønbjerg DK...58 B1
Roncal E 144 B3
Ronce-les-Bains
F............. 114 C2
Ronchamp F .. 106 B1
Ronchi dei
Legionari I... 122 B2
Ronciglione I.. 168 A2
Ronco Canavese
I............. 119 B4
Ronco Scrivia
I............. 120 C1
Ronda E...... 162 B2
Rønde DK......59 B3
Rone S.........57 C4
Ronehamn S...57 C4
Rong N........46 B1
Rönnäng S.....60 B1
Rønne DK......67 A3
Ronneburg D...83 B4
Ronneby S.....63 B3
Rönneshytta S ..55 B6
Rönninge S.....57 C4
Rönnöfors S . 199 B10
Rönö S........56 B2
Ronov nad
Doubravou
CZ...........97 B3
Ronse B........79 B3
Roosendaal NL..79 A4
Roosky IRL......26 C3
Ropczyce PL...87 B5
Ropeid N......52 A2
Ropinsalmi
FIN........... 192 D5
Ropuerelos del
Páramo E.. 141 B5
Roquebilière
F............. 133 A3
Roquebrun F.. 130 B2
Roquecourbe
F............. 130 B1
Roquefort F... 128 B2
Roquemaure
F............. 131 A3
Roquesteron
F............. 132 B2
Roquetas de Mar
E............. 164 C2
Roquetes E... 153 B4
Roquevaire F.. 132 B1
Røra N....... 199 B8
Rörbäcksnäs S..49 A4
Rørbæk DK....58 B2
Rore BIH 138 A2

Röro S 60 B1
Røros N 199 C8
Rorschach CH. 107 B4
Rørvig DK...... 61 D1
Rørvik N 199 A8
Rörvik S........62 A2
Rosà I........ 121 B4
Rosal de la Frontera
E............. 161 B2
Rosalina Mare
I............. 122 B1
Rosa Marina I . 173 B3
Rosans F...... 132 A1
Rosário P 160 B1
Rosarno I.... 175 C1
Rosbach D 81 B3
Rosche D.......73 B3
Rościszewo PL ..77 B4
Roscoff F..... 100 A2
Roscommon
IRL...........28 A3
Roscrea IRL ...28 B4
Rosdorf D.......82 A1
Rose I........ 174 B2
Rosegg A 109 C5
Rosehall UK... 32 D2
Rosehearty UK. 33 D4
Rosel UK......88 A1
Rosell E 153 B4
Roselló E 153 A4
Rosendal N 46 C3
Rosenfeld D....93 C4
Rosenfors S 62 A3
Rosenheim D . 108 B3
Rosenow D.....74 A2
Rosenthal D ...81 A4
Rosersberg S...57 A3
Roses E 147 B4
Roseto degli
Abruzzi I..... 169 A4
Roseto Valfortore
I............. 170 B3
Rosheim F 93 C3
Rosia I........ 135 B4
Rosice CZ......97 B4
Rosières-en-
Santerre F 90 B2
Rosignano
Maríttimo I... 134 B3
Rosignano Solvay
I............. 134 B3
Roşiori-de-Vede
RO...........17 C6
Roskhill UK ...31 B2
Roskilde DK... 61 D2
Roskovec AL.. 182 C1
Röslau D 83 B3
Roslev DK......58 B1
Rosmaninhal
P............ 155 B3
Rosnowo PL...67 B5
Rosolini I..... 177 C3
Rosova MNE .. 139 B5
Rosoy F...... 104 A2
Rosporden F.. 100 B2
Rosquete P ... 154 B2
Rosrath D......80 B3
Rossa CH 120 A2
Rossano I.... 174 B2
Rossas
Aveiro P 148 B1
Braga P....... 148 A1
Rossdorf D.....82 B2
Rossett UK.....38 A4
Rosshaupten
D............ 108 B1
Rossignol B....92 B1
Rossla D 82 A3
Rosslare IRL ...30 B2
Rosslare Harbour
IRL...........30 B2
Rosslau D......83 A4
Rosslea UK.....27 B3
Rossleben D ...82 A3
Rossön S...... 200 C2
Ross-on-Wye
UK...........39 C4
Rossoszyca PL .86 A2
Rosswein D 83 A5
Röstånga S..... 61 C3
Roštár SK......99 C4
Rostock D......65 B5
Rostrenen F... 100 A2
Røsvik N 194 C6
Rosvik S...... 196 D4
Rosyth UK..... 35 B4
Röszke H..... 126 A2
Rot S..........49 A6
Rota E....... 161 C3
Rota Greca I.. 174 B2
Rot am See D...94 B2
Rotberget N ...49 B4

Rotella I....... 136 C2
Rotenburg
Hessen D 82 B1
Niedersachsen
D 72 A2
Roth
Bayern D 94 B3
Rheinland-Pfalz
D............81 B3
Rothbury UK...37 A5
Rothemühl D ..74 A2
Röthenbach D ..95 B3
Rothenburg D..84 A2
Rothenburg ob der
Tauber D......94 B2
Rothéneuf F ...88 B2
Rothenklempenow
D 74 A3
Rothenstein D ..94 C3
Rotherham UK..40 B2
Rothes UK.....32 D3
Rothesay UK...34 C2
Rothwell UK....44 A3
Rotnes N......48 B2
Rotonda I.... 174 B2
Rotondella I.. 174 A2
Rotova E..... 159 C3
Rott
Bayern D 108 B1
Bayern D 108 B3
Rottach-Egern
D 108 B2
Röttenbach D...94 B3
Rottenbuch D. 108 B1
Rottenburg
Baden-
Württemberg
D............ 93 C4
Bayern D 95 C4
Rottenmann
A............. 110 B1
Rotterdam NL..79 A4
Rotthalmünster
D............96 C1
Rottingdean
UK...........44 C3
Röttingen D ...94 B1
Rottleberode D 82 A2
Rottne S......62 A2
Rottneros S....55 A4
Rottofreno I.. 120 B2
Rottweil D.... 107 A3
Rötz D........95 B4
Roubaix F.....78 B3
Roudnice nad
Labem CZ....84 B2
Roudouallec F 100 A2
Rouen F.......89 A5
Rouffach F.... 106 B2
Rougé F...... 101 B4
Rougemont F. 105 B5
Rougemont-le-
Château F... 106 B1
Rouillac F.... 115 C3
Rouillé F..... 115 B4
Roujan F..... 130 B2
Roulans F.... 105 B5
Roundwood
IRL...........30 A2
Rousínov CZ....97 B4
Roussac F.... 115 B5
Roussennac F. 130 A1
Rousses F..... 130 B2
Roussillon F... 117 B4
Rouvroy-sur-Audry
F............91 B4
Rouy F...... 104 B2
Rovanieman
maalaiskunta
FIN........... 197 C8
Rovaniemi
FIN........... 197 C8
Rovato I..... 120 B2
Rovensko pod
Troskami CZ...84 B3
Roverbella I... 121 B3
Rovereto I.... 121 B4
Rövershagen D .65 B5
Roverud N.....49 B4
Rovigo I..... 121 B4
Rovinj HR..... 122 B2
Rovišce HR... 124 B2
Rów PL.......74 B3
Rowy PL......68 A2
Royal Leamington
Spa UK.......44 A2
Royal Tunbridge
Wells UK.....45 B4
Royan F..... 114 C2
Royat F...... 116 B3
Roybon F..... 118 B2
Roybridge UK..34 B3
Roye F........90 B2

Royère-de-
Vassivière F.. 116 B1
Røykenvik N...48 B2
Royos E...... 164 B2
Røyrvik N 199 A10
Royston UK 44 A3
Rozadas E.....11 A4
Rozalén del Monte
E............. 151 C5
Rózańsko PL ...75 B3
Rozay-en-Brie
F............90 C2
Roždalovice CZ.84 B3
Rozdilna UA.....17 B9
Rozental PL....69 B4
Rozhyshche UA .13 C6
Rožmitál pod
Třemšínem
CZ...........96 B1
Rožňava SK.....99 C4
Rožnov pod
Radhoštěm
CZ...........98 B2
Rozoy-sur-Serre
F............91 B4
Rozprza PL....86 A3
Roztoky CZ....84 B2
Rozvadov CZ...95 B4
Rozzano I.... 120 B2
Rrëshen AL ... 182 B1
Rrogozhine
AL 182 B1
Ruanes E...... 156 A2
Rubbestaddneset
N.............46 C2
Rubi E....... 147 C3
Rubiá E...... 141 B4
Rubiacedo de
Abajo E 143 B3
Rubielos Bajos
E............. 158 B1
Rubielos de Mora
E............. 153 B3
Rubiera I..... 121 C3
Rubik AL..... 182 B1
Rucandio E... 143 B3
Rud
Akershus N 48 B3
Buskerud N ...48 B2
Ruda
PL........... 86 A2
S 62 A4
Ruda Maleniecka
PL...........87 A4
Ruda Pilczycka
PL...........87 A4
Ruda Śl. PL...86 B2
Ruddervorde B .78 A3
Ruden A 110 C1
Rudersberg D...94 C1
Rudersdorf A . 111 B3
Rüdersdorf D ...74 B2
Ruderting D....96 C1
Rüdesheim D ..93 B3
Rudkøbing DK ..65 B3
Rudmanns A ...97 C3
Rudna
CZ 96 A2
PL........... 85 A4
Rudnik SRB... 127 C2
Rudniki
Opolskie PL ... 86 A2
Śląskie PL......86 B3
Rudno
Dolnośląskie
PL........... 85 A4
Pomorskie PL ..69 B3
Rudnya RUS.....13 A9
Rudolstadt D ...82 B3
Rudowica PL...84 A3
Rudozem BG .. 183 B6
Rudskoga S....55 A5
Rudston UK....40 A3
Ruds Vedby DK 61 D1
Rudy PL.......86 B2
Rue F.........78 B1
Rueda E...... 150 A3
Rueda de Jalón
E............. 152 A2
Ruelle-sur-Touvre
F............. 115 C4
Ruerrero E.... 143 B3
Ruffano I..... 173 C4
Ruffec F...... 115 B4
Rufina I...... 135 B4
Rugby UK......44 A2
Rugeley UK....40 C2
Ruggstrop S....62 B4
Rugles F......89 B4
Rugozero RUS .3 D13
Rühen D.......73 B3
Ruhla D........82 B2

Ruhland D 84 A1
Ruhle D.......71 B4
Ruhpolding D. 109 B3
Ruhstorf D.....96 C1
Ruidera E..... 158 C1
Ruillé-sur-le-Loir
F............. 102 B2
Ruinen NL......71 B3
Ruiselede B 78 A3
Ruka FIN..... 197 C12
Rulles B........92 B1
Rülzheim D 93 B4
Rum H 111 B3
Ruma SRB.... 127 B1
Rumboci BIH.. 138 B3
Rumburk CZ....84 B2
Rumenka SRB. 126 B1
Rumia PL......69 A3
Rumigny F.....91 B4
Rumilly F 118 B2
Rumma S......56 B2
Rumney UK....39 C3
Rumont F......91 C5
Runa P....... 154 B1
Runcorn UK....38 A4
Rundmoen N . 195 D5
Rungsted DK... 61 D2
Runhällen S...51 B3
Runowo PL....69 A5
Runtuna S 56 B3
Ruokojärvi
FIN........... 196 B7
Ruokolahti FIN...9 B6
Ruokto S..... 196 B2
Ruoms F..... 131 A3
Ruoti I....... 172 B1
Rupa HR 123 B3
Ruppichteroth
D............80 B3
Rupt-sur-Moselle
F............. 106 B1
Rus E........ 157 B4
Ruse BG...... 17 D7
Ruše SLO..... 110 C2
Rusele S..... 200 B4
Rusevo HR.... 125 B4
Rush IRL.......30 A2
Rushden UK....44 A3
Rusiec PL......86 A2
Rusinowo
Zachodnio-
Pomorskie PL . 67 C4
Zachodnio-
Pomorskie PL . 75 A5
Ruskele S..... 200 B4
Ruski Krstur
SRB......... 126 B1
Ruskington UK..40 B3
Rusovce SK ... 111 A4
Rüsselsheim D .93 B4
Russelv N 192 C4
Russi I....... 135 A5
Rust A 111 B3
Rustefjelbma
N........... 193 B12
Rustrel F..... 131 B4
Ruszki PL......77 B5
Ruszów PL.....84 A3
Rute E....... 163 A3
Rüthen D......81 A4
Rutherglen UK.35 C3
Ruthin UK.....38 A3
Ruthven UK... 32 D2
Ruthwell UK...36 B3
Rüti CH 107 B3
Rutigliano I... 173 A3
Rutledal N 46 A2
Rutvik S...... 196 D5
Ruurlo NL......71 B3
Ruuvaoja FIN 197 B11
Ruvo del Monte
I............. 172 B1
Ruvo di Púglia
I............. 171 B4
Ruynes-en-
Margeride F.. 116 C3
Ružic HR..... 138 B2
Ružomberok
SK............99 B3
Ružsa H...... 126 A1
Ry DK.........59 B2
Rybany SK.....98 C2
Rybina PL......69 A4
Rybnik PL......86 B2
Rychliki PL.....69 B4
Rychlocice PL ..86 A2
Rychnov nad
Kněžnou CZ...85 B4
Rychnowo PL ..77 A5
Rychtal PL......86 A1
Rychwał PL....76 B3
Ryczywół PL....87 A5
Ryczywół PL ...75 B5

Ryd S 63 B2
Rydaholm S....62 B2
Rydal S.........60 B2
Rydbo S........57 A4
Rydboholm S...60 B2
Ryde UK........44 C2
Rydöbruk S.....60 C3
Rydsgård S.....66 A2
Rydsnäs S......62 A3
Rydultowy PL...86 B2
Rydzyna PL.....85 A4
Rye UK.........45 C4
Rygge N........54 A1
Ryjewo PL......69 B3
Rykene N.......53 B4
Rymań PL......67 C4
Rýmařov CZ....98 B1
Rynarzewo PL..76 A2
Ryomgård DK...59 B3
Rypefjord N... 192 B7
Rypin PL.......77 A4
Rysjedalsvika
N.............46 A2
Ryssby S.......60 C4
Rytel PL........68 B2
Rytro PL........99 B4
Rywociny PL....77 A5
Rzeczenica PL..68 B2
Rzeczniów PL...87 A5
Rzeczyca PL....87 A4
Rzegnowo PL...77 A5
Rzejowice PL...87 A3
Rzemień PL....87 B5
Rzepin PL......75 B3
Rzesznikowo
PL............67 C4
Rzeszów PL....12 C4
Rzgów PL......86 A3
Rzhev RUS.......9 D9

S

Saal
Bayern D 82 B2
Bayern D 95 C3
Saalbach A.... 109 B3
Saalburg D.....83 B3
Saales F........92 C3
Saalfeld D......82 B3
Saalfelden am
Steinernen Meer
A............. 109 B3
Saanen CH.... 106 C2
Saarbrücken D. 92 B2
Saarburg D.....92 B2
Saarijärvi FIN....8 A4
Saari-Kämä
FIN........... 197 C9
Saarlouis D.....92 B2
Saas-Fee CH .. 119 A4
Šabac SRB.... 127 C1
Sabadell E.... 147 C3
Sabáudia I.... 169 B3
Sabbioneta I.. 121 C3
Sabero E..... 142 B1
Sabiñánigo E . 145 B3
Sabiote E..... 157 B4
Sablé-sur-Sarthe
F............. 102 B1
Saboia P..... 160 B1
Sabóia P..... 148 B2
Sabrosa P.... 148 A2
Sabugal P.... 149 B2
Sabuncu TR .. 187 C5
Sæby DK......58 A3
Săcălaz RO... 126 B3
Sacecorbo E .. 152 B1
Saceda del Rio
E............. 151 B5
Sacedón E 151 B5
Săcele RO......17 C6
Saceruela E... 156 B3
Sachsenburg
A............. 109 C4
Sachsenhagen
D............72 B2
Sacile I....... 122 B1
Sacramenia E. 151 A4
Sada E....... 140 A2
Sádaba E..... 144 B2
Sadernes E... 147 B3
Sadki PL.......76 A2
Sadkowice PL..87 A4
Sadlinki PL.....69 B3
Sadów PL......75 B3
Sadská CZ.....84 B2

Saelices E..... 151 C5
Saelices de
Mayorga E ... 142 B1
Saerbeck D 71 B4
Saeul L........92 B1
Safaalan TR ... 186 A3
Safara P...... 161 A2
Säffle S........55 A3
Saffron Walden
UK...........45 A4
Safranbolu TR 187 A7
Säfsnäs S......50 B1
Şag RO....... 126 B3
Sagard D......66 B2
S'Agaró E 147 C4
Sågmyra S.....50 B2
Sagone F..... 180 A1
Sagres E..... 160 C1
Sagunt E..... 159 B3
Sagvåg N......52 A1
Ságvár H..... 112 C2
Sagy F....... 105 C4
Sahagún E ... 142 B1
Šahy SK...... 112 A2
Saignelégier
CH........... 106 B1
Saignes F..... 116 B2
Saija FIN..... 197 B11
Saillagouse F. 146 B3
Saillans F.... 118 C2
Sains Richaumont
F............91 B3
St Abb's UK.....35 C5
St Affrique F .. 130 B1
St Agnan F.... 104 C2
St Agnant F... 114 C3
St Agnes UK....42 B1
St Agrève F... 117 B4
St Aignan F... 103 B3
St Aignan-sur-Roë
F............. 101 B4
St Albans UK...44 B3
St Alban-sur-
Limagnole F . 117 C3
St Amand-en-
Puisaye F 104 B2
St Amand-les-Eaux
F............79 B3
St Amand-Longpré
F............. 103 B3
St Amand-
Montrond F.. 103 C4
St Amans F... 117 C3
St Amans-Soult
F............. 130 B1
St Amant-Roche-
Savine F 117 B3
St Amarin F... 106 B1
St Ambroix F. 131 A3
St Amé F..... 106 A1
St Amour F... 118 A2
St André-de-Corcy
F............. 117 B4
St André-de-Cubzac
F............. 128 B2
St André-de-l'Eure
F............89 B5
St André-de-
Roquepertuis
F............. 131 A3
St André-de-
Sangonis F.. 130 B2
St Andre-de-
Valborgne F.. 130 A2
St André-les-Alpes
F............. 132 B2
St Andrews UK . 35 B5
St Angel F.... 116 B2
St Anthème F . 117 B3
St Antoine F.. 180 A2
St Antoine-de-
Ficalba F..... 129 B3
St Antönien
CH........... 107 C4
St Antonin-Noble-
Val F........ 129 B4
St Armant-Tallende
F............. 116 B3
St Arnoult F....90 C1
St Asaph UK...38 A3
St Astier F.... 129 A3
St Athan UK....39 C3
St Auban F... 132 B2
St Aubin
CH........... 106 C1
F............. 105 B4
UK........... 88 A1
St Aubin-d'Aubigne
F............. 101 A4
St Aubin-du-
Cormier F.... 101 A4

St Aubin-sur-Aire
F..............92 C1
St Aubin-sur-Mer
F..............89 A3
St Aulaye F... 128 A3
St Austell UK....42 B2
St Avit F........ 116 B2
St Avold F........92 B2
St Aygulf F..... 132 B2
St Bauzille-de-
Putois F..... 130 B2
St Béat F...... 145 B4
St Beauzély F. 130 A1
St Bees UK.......36 B3
St Benim-d'Azy
F.............104 C2
St Benoît-du-Sault
F.............115 B5
St Benoit-en-
Woëvre F......92 C1
St Berthevin F. 102 A1
St Blaise-la-Roche
F..............92 C3
St Blazey UK....42 B2
St Blin F....... 105 A4
St Bonnet F.... 118 C3
St Bonnet Briance
F............. 115 C5
St Bonnet-de-Joux
F.............104 C3
St Bonnet-le-
Château F.... 117 B4
St Bonnet-le-Froid
F.............117 B4
St Brévin-les-Pins
F............. 101 B3
St Briac-sur-Mer
F............. 101 A3
St Brice-en-Coglès
F..............88 B2
St Brieuc F.... 101 A3
St Bris-le-Vineux
F.............104 B2
St Broladre F...88 B2
St Calais F..... 102 B2
St Cannat F... 131 B4
St Cast-le-Guildo
F............. 101 A3
St Céré F...... 129 B4
St Cergue CH.. 118 A3
St Cergues F .. 118 A3
St Cernin F.... 116 B2
St Chamant F. 116 B1
St Chamas F... 131 B4
St Chamond F. 117 B4
St Chély-d'Apcher
F............. 116 A2
St Chély-d'Aubrac
F............. 116 C2
St Chinian F... 130 B1
St Christol F... 131 A4
St Christol-lès-Alès
F............. 131 B3
St Christoly-Médoc
F............. 114 C3
St Christophe-du-
Ligneron F.. 114 B2
St Christophe-en-
Brionnais F. 117 A4
St Ciers-sur-
Gironde F... 128 A2
St Clair-sur-Epte
F..............90 B1
St Clar F...... 129 C3
St Claud F..... 115 C4
St Claude F.... 118 A2
St Clears UK.....39 C2
St Columb Major
UK..............42 B2
St Come-d'Olt
F............. 130 A1
St Cosme-en-
Vairais F......89 B4
St Cyprien
Dordogne F... 129 B4
Pyrénées-
Orientales F.. 146 B4
St Cyr-sur-Loire
F............. 102 B2
St Cyr-sur-Mer
F............. 132 B1
St Cyr-sur-Methon
F............. 117 A4
St David's UK...39 C1
St Denis F.......90 C2
St Denis-d'Oléron
F............. 114 B2
St Denis d'Orques
F............. 102 A1
St Didier F..... 117 A4
St Didier-en-Velay
F............. 117 B4
St Dié F........92 C2

St Dier-d'Auvergne
F............. 117 B3
St Dizier F.......91 C4
St Dizier-Leyrenne
F............. 116 A1
St Dogmaels
UK..............39 B2
Ste Adresse F ..89 A4
Ste Anne F......89 B4
Ste Anne-d'Auray
F............. 100 B3
Ste Croix CH .. 105 C5
Ste Croix-Volvestre
F............. 146 A2
Ste Engrâce F .. 144 A3
Ste Enimie F... 130 A2
Ste Efflam F 100 A2
Ste Foy-de-
Peyrolières
F............. 146 A2
Ste Foy-la-Grande
F............. 128 B3
Ste Foy l'Argentiere
F............. 117 B4
Ste Gauburge-Ste
Colombe F 89 B4
Ste Gemme la
Plaine F..... 114 B2
Ste Geneviève
F..............90 B2
St Égrève F.... 118 B2
Ste Hélène F .. 128 B2
Ste Hélène-sur-
Isère F....... 118 B3
Ste Hermine F. 114 B2
Ste Jalle F..... 131 A4
Ste Livrade-sur-Lot
F............. 129 B3
St Eloy-les-Mines
F............. 116 A2
Ste Marie-aux-
Mines F...... 106 A2
Ste Marie-du-Mont
F..............88 A2
Ste Maure-de-
Touraine F... 102 B2
Ste Maxime F . 132 B2
Ste Ménéhould
F..............91 B4
Ste Mère-Église
F..............88 A2
St Emiland F .. 104 C3
St Émilion F... 128 B2
St Enoder UK....42 B2
Sainteny F.....88 A2
Ste Ode B......92 A1
Saintes F..... 114 C3
Ste Savine F....91 C4
Ste Sévère-sur-
Indre F...... 103 C4
Ste Sigolène F. 117 B4
St Esteben F... 144 A2
St Estèphe F... 128 A2
Ste Suzanne F. 102 A1
St Étienne F... 117 B4
St Etienne-de-
Baigorry F... 144 A2
St Étienne-de-
Cuines F..... 118 B3
St Étienne-de-
Fursac F..... 116 A1
St Etienne-de-
Montluc F.... 101 B4
St Etienne-de-St
Geoirs F..... 118 B2
St Étienne-de-Tinée
F............. 132 A1
St Étienne-du-Bois
F............. 118 A2
St Étienne-du-
Rouvray F....89 A5
St Etienne-les-
Orgues F..... 132 A1
Ste Tulle F..... 132 B1
St Fargeau F... 104 B2
St Félicien F... 117 B4
St Felix-de-Sorgues
F............. 130 B1
St Félix-Lauragais
F............. 146 A2
Saintfield UK....27 B5
St Fillans UK....35 B3
St Firmin F.... 118 C3
St Florent F.... 180 A2
St Florentin F . 104 B2
St Florent-le-Vieil
F............. 101 B4
St Florent-sur-Cher
F............. 103 C4
St Flour F 116 B3
St Flovier F.... 103 C3
St Fort-sur-le-Né
F............. 115 C3

St Fulgent F... 114 B2
St Galmier F... 117 B4
St Gaudens F.. 145 A4
St Gaultier F... 115 B5
St Gély-du-Fesc
F............. 130 B2
St Genest-Malifaux
F............. 117 B4
St Gengoux-le-
National F ... 104 C3
St Geniez F.... 132 A2
St Geniez-d'Olt
F............. 130 A1
St Genis-de-
Saintonge F.. 114 C3
St Genis-Pouilly
F............. 118 A3
St Genix-sur-Guiers
F............. 118 B2
St Georges
Buttavent F 88 B3
St Georges-d'Aurac
F............. 117 B3
St Georges-de-
Commiers F.. 118 B2
St Georges-de-
Didonne F ... 114 C3
St Georges-de-
Luzençon F . 130 A1
St Georges-de
Mons F....... 116 B2
St Georges-de-
Reneins F ... 117 A4
St Georges
d'Oléron F ... 114 C2
St Georges-en-
Couzan F.... 117 B3
St Georges-lès-
Baillargeaux
F............. 115 B4
St Georges-sur-
Loire F....... 102 B1
St Georges-sur-
Meuse B........79 B5
St Geours-de-
Maremne F .. 128 C1
St Gérand-de-Vaux
F............. 117 A3
St Gérand-le-Puy
F............. 117 A3
St Germain F... 105 B5
St Germain-
Chassenay F . 104 C2
St Germain-de-
Calberte F.... 130 A2
St Germain-de-
Confolens F.. 115 B4
St Germain-de-Joux
F............. 118 A2
St Germain-des-
Fossés F..... 117 A3
St Germain-du-Bois
F............. 105 C4
St Germain-du-
Plain F...... 105 C3
St Germain-du-Puy
F............. 103 B4
St Germain-en-Laye
F..............90 C2
St Germain-Laval
F............. 117 B4
St Germain-
Lembron F... 116 B3
St Germain-les-
Belles F..... 116 B1
St Germain-
Lespinasse F . 117 A3
St Germain-l'Herm
F............. 117 B3
St Gervais-
d'Auvergne
F............. 116 A2
St Gervais-les-Bains
F............. 118 B3
St Gervais-sur-Mare
F............. 130 B2
St Gildas-de-Rhuys
F............. 100 B3
St Gildas-des-Bois
F............. 101 B3
St Gilles
Gard F....... 131 B3
Ille-et-Vilaine
F............. 101 A4
St Gilles-Croix-de-
Vie F........ 114 B2
St Gingolph F . 119 A3
St Girons
Ariège F...... 146 B2
Landes F..... 128 C1
St Girons-Plage
F............. 128 C1
St Gobain F 91 B3

St Gorgon-Main
F............. 105 B5
St Guénolé F ... 100 B1
St Harmon
UK..............39 B3
St Helens UK ...38 A4
St Helier UK.....88 A1
St Herblain F . 101 B4
St Hilaire
Allier F....... 104 C2
Aude F....... 146 A3
St Hilaire-de-Riez
F............. 114 B2
St Hilaire-des-
Loges F..... 114 B3
St Hilaire-de-
Villefranche
F............. 114 C3
St Hilaire-du-
Harcouët F....88 B2
St Hilaire-du-Rosier
F............. 118 B2
St Hippolyte
Aveyron F..... 116 C2
Doubs F...... 106 B1
St Hippolyte-du-
Fort F....... 130 B2
St Honoré-les-Bains
F............. 104 C2
St Hubert B....92 A1
St Imier CH.... 106 B2
St Issey UK......42 B2
St Ives
Cambridgeshire
UK....... 44 A3
Cornwall UK ...42 B1
St Izaire F..... 130 B1
St Jacques-de-
la-Lande F... 101 A4
St Jacut-de-la-Mer
F............. 101 A3
St James F.......88 B2
St Jaume d'Enveja
E............. 153 B4
St Jean-Brévelay
F............. 101 B3
St Jean-d'Angély
F............. 114 C3
St Jean-de-
Belleville F... 118 B3
St Jean-de-Bournay
F............. 118 B2
St Jean-de-Braye
F............. 103 B3
St Jean-de-Côle
F............. 115 C4
St Jean-de-Daye
F..............88 A2
St Jean de Losne
F............. 105 B4
St Jean-de-Luz
F............. 144 A2
St Jean-de-
Maurienne F. 118 B3
St Jean-de-Monts
F............. 114 B1
St Jean-d'Illac
F............. 128 B2
St Jean-du-Bruel
F............. 130 A2
St Jean-du-Gard
F............. 131 A2
St Jean-en-Royans
F............. 118 B2
St Jean-la-Riviere
F............. 133 B3
St Jean-Pied-de-
Port F....... 144 A2
St Jean-Poutge
F............. 129 C3
St Jeoire F..... 118 A3
St Joachim F .. 101 B3
St Johnstown
IRL............27 B3
St Jorioz F..... 118 B3
St Joris Winge
B.............79 B4
St Jouin-de-Marnes
F............. 102 C1
St Juéry F..... 130 B1
St Julien F..... 118 A2
St Julien-Chapteuil
F............. 117 B4
St Julien-de-
Vouvantes F . 101 B4
St Julien-du-Sault
F............. 104 A2
St Julien-du-
Verdon F..... 132 B2
St Julien-en-Born
F............. 128 B1
St Julien-en-
Genevois F... 118 A3

St Julien-l'Ars
F............. 115 B4
St Julien la-Vêtre
F............. 117 B3
St Julien-Mont-
Denis F....... 118 B3
St Julien-sur-
Reyssouze F . 118 A2
St Junien F..... 115 C4
St Just
F............. 131 A3
UK..............42 B1
St Just-en-
Chaussée F.....90 B2
St Just-en-Chevalet
F............. 117 B3
St Justin F..... 128 C2
St Just-St Rambert
F............. 117 B4
St Keverne UK...42 B1
St Lary-Soulan
F............. 145 B4
St Laurent-
d'Aigouze F . 131 B3
St Laurent-de-
Chamousset
F............. 117 B4
St Laurent-de-
Condel F......89 A3
St Laurent-de-la-
Cabrerisse F . 146 A3
St Laurent-de-la-
Salanque F... 146 B3
St Laurent-des-
Autels F..... 101 B4
St Laurent-du-Pont
F............. 118 B2
St Laurent-en-Caux
F..............89 A4
St Laurent-en-
Grandvaux F . 105 C4
St Laurent-Médoc
F............. 128 A2
St Laurent-sur-
Gorre F....... 115 C4
St Laurent-sur-Mer
F............. 101 B3
St Laurent-sur-
Sèvre F....... 114 B3
St Leger B.......92 B1
St Léger-de-Vignes
F............. 104 C2
St Léger-sous-
Beuvray F.... 104 C3
St Léger-sur-
Dheune F.... 104 C3
St Léonard-de-
Noblat F..... 116 B1
St Leonards UK..45 C4
St Lô F.........88 A2
St Lon-les-Mines
F............. 128 C1
St Louis F..... 106 B2
St Loup F..... 117 A3
St Loup-de-la-Salle
F............. 105 C3
St Loup-sur-
Semouse F... 105 B5
St Lunaire F ... 101 A3
St Lupicin F... 118 A2
St Lyphard F . 101 B3
St Lys F....... 146 A2
St Macaire F... 128 B2
St Maclou F.....89 A4
St Maixent-l'École
F............. 115 B3
St Malo F........88 B1
St Mamet-la-
Salvetat F.... 116 C2
St Mandrier-sur-
Mer F....... 132 B1
St Marcel
Drôme F...... 117 C4
Saône-et-Loire
F............. 105 C3
St Marcellin F . 118 B2
St Marcellin sur
Loire F....... 117 B4
St Marcet F.... 145 A4
St Mards-en-Othe
F............. 104 A2
St Margaret's-at-
Cliffe UK.......45 B5
St Margaret's Hope
UK..............33 C4
St Mars-la-Jaille
F............. 101 B4
St Martin-d'Ablois
F..............91 C3
St Martin-
d'Auxigny F . 103 B4
St Martin-de-
Belleville F... 118 B3

St Julien-l'Ars
F............. 115 B4
St Martin-de-
Bossenay F...91 C3
St Martin-de-Crau
F............. 131 B3
St Martin-de-
Londres F 130 B2
St Martin-
d'Entraunes
F............. 132 A2
St Martin-de-
Queyrières F . 118 C3
St Martin-de-Ré
F............. 114 B2
St Martin des
Besaces F......88 A3
St Martin-
d'Estreaux F . 117 A3
St Martin-de-
Valamas F.... 117 C4
St Martin-d'Hères
F............. 118 B2
St Martin-du-Frêne
F............. 118 A2
St Martin-en-Bresse
F............. 105 C4
St Martin-en-Haut
F............. 117 B4
St Martin-la-
Méanne F 116 B1
St Martin-
Osmonville F...90 B1
St Martin-sur-
Ouanne F.... 104 B2
St Martin-
Valmeroux F . 116 B2
St Martin-Vésubie
F............. 133 A3
St Martory F .. 145 A4
St Mary's UK....33 C4
St Mathieu F . 115 C4
St Mathieu-de-
Tréviers F.... 131 B2
St Maurice CH. 119 A3
St Maurice-
Navacelles F . 130 B2
St Maurice-sur-
Moselle F 106 B1
St Mawes UK....42 B1
St Maximin-la-Ste
Baume F..... 132 B1
St Méard-de-
Gurçon F..... 128 B3
St Médard-de-
Guizières F... 128 A2
St Médard-en-Jalles
F............. 128 B2
St Méen-le-Grand
F............. 101 A3
St Menges F.....91 B4
St Merløse DK.. 61 D1
St Mesto CZ....85 B4
St M'Hervé F . 101 A4
St Michel
Aisne F.......91 B4
Gers F........ 145 A4
St Michel-Chef-Chef
F............. 101 B3
St Michel-de-
Castelnau F .. 128 B2
St Michel-de-
Maurienne F . 118 B3
St Michel-en-Grève
F............. 100 A2
St Michel-en-l'Herm
F............. 114 B2
St Michel-Mont-
Mercure F.... 114 B3
St Mihiel F......92 C1
St Monance UK..35 B5
St Montant F.. 131 A3
St Moritz CH .. 107 C4
St Nazaire F... 101 B3
St Nazaire-en-
Royans F..... 118 B2
St Nazaire-le-
Désert F...... 131 A4
St Nectaire F .. 116 B2
St Neots UK 44 A3
St Nicolas-de-Port
F..............92 C2
St Nicolas-de-
Redon F..... 101 B3
St Nicolas-du-
Pélem F..... 100 A2
St Niklaas B 79 A4
St Omer F......78 B2
St Pair-sur-Mer
F..............88 B2
St Palais F..... 144 A2
St Palais-sur-Mer
F............. 114 C2
St Pardoux-la-
Rivière F..... 115 C4

St A – St R 247

St Paul-Cap-de-
Joux F....... 129 C4
St Paul-de-
Fenouillet F.. 146 B3
St Paul-de-Varax
F............. 118 A2
St Paulien F ... 117 B3
St Paul-le-Jeune
F............. 131 A3
St Paul-lès-Dax
F............. 128 C1
St Paul-Trois-
Châteaux F... 131 B3
St Pé-de-Bigorre
F............. 145 A3
St Pée-sur-Nivelle
F............. 144 A2
St Péravy-la-
Colombe F ... 103 B3
St Péray F..... 117 C4
St Père-en-Retz
F............. 101 B3
St Peter Port
UK..............88 A1
St Petersburg =
Sankt-Peterburg
RUS...........9 C7
St Philbert-de-
Grand-Lieu
F............. 114 A2
St Pierre F..... 130 B1
St Pierre-d'Albigny
F............. 118 B3
St Pierre-d'Allevard
F............. 118 B3
St Pierre-de-
Chartreuse F. 118 B2
St Pierre-de-
Chignac F.... 129 A3
St Pierre-de-la-Fage
F............. 130 B2
St Pierre-
d'Entremont
F............. 118 B2
St Pierre-d'Oléron
F............. 114 C2
St Pierre-Eglise
F..............88 A2
St Pierre-en-Port
F..............89 A4
St Pierre-le-
Moûtier F.... 104 C2
St Pierre
Montlimart
F............. 101 B4
St Pierre-Quiberon
F............. 100 B2
St Pierre-sur-Dives
F..............89 A3
St Pierreville
F............. 117 C4
St Pieters-Leeuw
B.............79 B4
St Plancard F.. 145 A4
St Poix F...... 101 B4
St Pol-de-Léon
F............. 100 A2
St Polgues F... 117 B3
St Pol-sur-Ternoise
F..............78 B2
St Pons-de-
Thomières F . 130 B1
St Porchaire F. 114 C3
St Pourçain-sur-
Sioule F..... 116 A3
St Priest F..... 117 B4
St Privat F..... 116 B2
St Quay-Portrieux
F............. 100 A3
St Quentin F 90 B3
St Quentin-la-
Poterie F..... 131 A3
St Quentin-les-
Anges F...... 102 B1
St Rambert-d'Albon
F............. 117 B4
St Rambert-en-
Bugey F..... 118 B2
St Raphaël F . 132 B2
St Rémy-de-
Provence F... 131 B3
St Rémy-du-Val
F..............89 B4
St Remy-en-
Bouzemont F ..91 C4
St Renan F..... 100 A1
St Révérien F... 104 B2
St Riquier F....90 A1
St Romain-de-
Colbosc F.....89 A4

St Rome-de-Cernon
F............130 A1
St Rome-de-Tarn
F............130 A1
St Sadurní-d'Anoia
E............147 C2
St Saëns F......89 A5
St Sampson UK..88 A1
St Samson-la-
Poterie F......90 B1
St Saturnin-de-
Lenne F....130 A2
St Saturnin-lès-Apt
F............131 B4
St Sauflieu F ..90 B2
St Saulge F....104 B2
St Sauveur
Finistère F 100 A2
Haute-Saône
F............105 B5
St Sauveur-de-
Montagut F..117 C4
St Sauveur-en-
Puisaye F 104 B2
St Sauveur-en-Rue
F............117 B4
St Sauveur-
Lendelin F....88 A2
St Sauveur-le-
Vicomte F.....88 A2
St Sauveur-sur-
Tinée F.......132 A3
St Savin
Gironde F.....128 A2
Vienne F......115 B4
St Savinien F..114 C3
St Savournin
F............131 B4
St Seine-l'Abbaye
F............105 B3
St Sernin-sur-Rance
F............130 B1
St Sevan-sur-Mer
F............88 B1
St Sever F.....128 C2
St Sever-Calvados
F............88 B2
St Sorlin-d'Arves
F............118 B3
St Soupplets F..90 B2
St Sulpice F...129 C4
St Sulpice-Laurière
F............116 A1
St Sulpice-les-
Feuilles F....115 B5
St Symphorien
F............128 B2
St Symphoriende-
Lay F.........117 B4
St Symphorien
d'Ozon F.....117 B4
St Symphoriensur-
Coise F.......117 B4
St Teath UK...42 B2
St Thégonnec
F............100 A2
St Thiébault F. 105 A4
St Trivier-de-
Courtes F....118 A2
St Trivier-sur-
Moignans F..117 A4
St Trojan-les-Bains
F............114 C2
St Tropez F....132 B2
St Truiden B....79 B5
St Vaast-la-Hougue
F............88 A2
St Valérien F..104 A2
St Valery-en-Caux
F............89 A4
St Valéry-sur-
Somme F.....78 B1
St Vallier
Drôme F......117 B4
Saône-et-Loire
F............104 C3
St Vallier-de-Thiey
F............132 B2
St Varent F....102 C1
St Vaury F....116 A1
St Venant F....78 B2
St Véran F.....119 C3
St Vincent I....119 B4
St Vincent-de-
Tyrosse F....128 C1
St Vit F.......105 B4
St Vith B........80 B2
St Vivien-de-Médoc
F............114 C2
St Yan F.......117 A4

St Ybars F.....146 A2
St Yorre F.....117 A3
St Yrieix-la-Perche
F............115 C5
Saissac F......146 A3
Saja E.........142 A2
Sajan SRB.....126 B2
Šajkaš SRB....126 B2
Sajókaza H.....99 C4
Sajószentpéter
H............113 A4
Sajóvámos H.. 113 A4
Sakarya TR....187 B5
Šakiai LT......13 A5
Sakskøbing DK.65 B4
Sakule SRB....126 B2
Sala S.........50 C3
Šal'a SK.......111 A4
Sala Baganza
I............120 C3
Sala Consilina
I............172 B1
Salakovac SRB 127 C3
Salamanca E...150 B2
Salamina GR...185 B4
Salandra I.....172 B2
Salaparuta I...176 B1
Salar E........163 A3
Salardú E.....145 B4
Salas E........141 A4
Salas de los
Infantes E.... 143 B3
Salau F........146 B2
Salavaux CH...106 C2
Salbertrand I..119 B3
Salbohed S....50 C3
Salbris F......103 B4
Salbu N........46 A2
Salce E........141 B4
Salching D.....95 C4
Salcombe UK...43 B3
Saldaña E.....142 B2
Saldus LV......8 D3
Sale I.........120 C1
Saleby S.......55 B4
Salem D.......107 B4
Salemi I.......176 B1
Salen N.......199 A8
Sälen S........49 A5
Salen
Argyll & Bute
UK...........34 B2
Highland UK...34 A1
Salernes F....132 B2
Salerno I......170 C2
Salers F.......116 B2
Salford UK.....40 B1
Salgótarján
H............113 A3
Salgueiro P...155 B3
Salhus N.......46 B2
Sali HR........137 B4
Sálice Salentino
I............173 B3
Salientes E....141 B4
Salies-de-Béarn
F............144 A3
Salies-du-Salat
F............145 A4
Salignac-Eyvigues
F............129 B4
Saligney-sur-
Roudon F....104 C2
Salihli TR.....188 A3
Salihorsk BY ...13 B7
Salinas
Alicante E....159 C3
Huesca E.....145 B4
Salinas de
Medinaceli E. 152 A1
Salinas de Pisuerga
E............142 B2
Salindres F....131 A3
Saline di Volterra
I............135 B3
Salins-les-Bains
F............105 C4
Salir P........160 B1
Salisbury UK...44 B2
Salla
A............110 B1
FIN..........197 C11
Sallachy UK...32 C2
Sallanches F...118 B3
Sallent E......147 C2
Sallent de Gállego
E............145 B3
Salles F.......128 B2
Salles-Curan
F............130 A1
Salles-sur-l'Hers
F............146 A2
Sallins IRL.....30 A2

Sällsjö S......199 B10
Salmerón E ...152 B1
Salmiech F....130 A1
Salmivaara
FIN..........197 C11
Salmoral E....150 B2
Salo FIN.......8 B3
Salò I.........121 B3
Salobreña E...163 B4
Salon-de-Provence
F............131 B4
Salonica =
Thessaloniki
GR...........182 C4
Salonta RO.....16 B4
Salorino E.....155 B3
Salornay-sur-Guye
F............104 C3
Salorno I......121 A4
Salou E........147 C2
Šalovci SLO....111 C3
Salsbruket N...199 A8
Salses-le-Chateau
F............146 B3
Salsomaggiore
Terme I......120 C2
Salt E.........147 C3
Saltaire UK....40 B2
Saltara I......136 B1
Saltash UK.....42 B2
Saltburn-by-the-
Sea UK........37 B6
Saltcoats UK...34 C3
Saltfleet UK...41 B4
Salto P........148 A2
Saltrød N......53 B4
Saltsjöbaden S..57 A4
Saltvik
FIN...........51 B7
S.............62 A4
Saludécio I....136 B1
Salussola I....119 B5
Saluzzo I......119 C4
Salvacañete E. 152 B2
Salvada P......160 B2
Salvagnac F...129 C4
Salvaleon E...155 C4
Salvaterra de
Magos P......154 B2
Salvaterra do
Extremo P ...155 B4
Salvatierra
Avila E........143 B4
Badajoz E.....155 C4
Salvatierra de
Santiago E....156 A1
Salviac F......129 B4
Salzburg A....109 B4
Salzgitter D....72 B3
Salzgitter Bad
D............72 B3
Salzhausen D..72 A3
Salzhemmendorf
D............72 B2
Salzkotten D...81 A4
Salzmünde D...83 A3
Salzwedel D....73 B4
Šamac BIH.....125 B4
Samadet F....128 C2
Samandıra
TR...........186 B4
Samassi I......179 C2
Samatan F....146 A1
Sambiase I....175 C2
Sambir UA.....13 D5
Samborowo PL .69 B4
Sambuca di Sicília
I............176 B2
Samedan CH...107 C4
Samer F........78 B1
Sami GR.......184 A1
Šamlı TR......186 C2
Sammichele di Bari
I............173 B2
Samnaun CH...107 C5
Samobor HR...123 B4
Samoëns F....118 A3
Samogneux F...92 B1
Samokov BG....17 D5
Samora Correia
P............154 C2
Šamorín SK....111 A4
Samos
E............141 B3
GR...........188 B1
Samoš SRB....126 B2
Samothraki
GR...........183 C7
Samper de Calanda
E............153 A3
Sampéyre I....133 A3
Sampieri I.....177 C3
Sampigny F....92 C1

Samplawa PL...69 B4
Samproniano
I............168 A1
Samtens D......66 B2
Samugheo I...179 C2
San Adrián E..144 B2
San Agustín E. 164 C2
San Agustin de
Guadalix E...151 B4
Sanaigmore UK 34 C1
San Alberto I..135 A5
San Amaro E..140 B2
Sânandrei RO. 126 B3
San Andrês del
Rabanedo E.. 142 B1
San Antanio di
Santadi I.....179 C2
San Antolín de Ibias
E............141 A4
San Arcángelo
I............174 A2
San Asensio E. 143 B4
San Bartolomé de
las Abiertas
E............150 C3
San Bartolomé de la
Torre E.......161 B2
San Bartolomé
Pinares E.....150 B3
San Bartolomeo in
Galdo I.......170 B3
San Benedetto del
Tronto I......136 C2
San Benedetto in
Alpe I........135 B4
San Benedetto Po
I............121 B3
San Benito E.. 156 B3
San Benito de la
Contienda E.. 155 C3
San Biágio Plátani
I............176 B2
San Biágio
Saracinisco I. 169 B3
San Bonifacio
I............121 B4
San Calixto E.. 156 C2
San Cándido I. 109 C3
San Carlo
CH...........119 A5
I............176 B2
San Carlos del Valle
E............157 B4
San Casciano dei
Bagni I.......135 C4
San Casciano in Val
di Pesa I.....135 B4
San Cataldo
Puglia I......173 B4
Sicília I......176 B2
San Cebrián de
Castro E......149 A4
Sancergues F ..104 B1
Sancerre F.....103 B4
San Cesário di
Lecce I.......173 B4
Sancey-le-Long
F............105 B5
Sanchiorian E. 150 B3
San Chírico Raparo
I............174 A2
Sanchonuño
E............151 A3
San Cibrao das
Viñas E.......140 B3
San Cipirello I. 176 B2
San Ciprián E.. 141 A3
San Clemente
E............158 B1
San Clodio E.. 141 B3
Sancoins F....104 C1
San Colombano al
Lambro I.....120 B2
San Costanzo
I............136 B2
San Crisóbal de
Entreviñas E. 142 B1
San Cristóbal de la
Polantera E.. 141 B5
San Cristóbal de la
Vega E.......150 A3
San Cristovo E 141 C3
Sancti-Petri E. 162 B1
Sancti-Spiritus
E............149 B3
Sand
Hedmark N ...48 B3
Rogaland N....52 A2
Sanda S........57 C4
San Damiano d'Asti
I............119 C5

San Damiano Macra
I............133 A3
Sandane N....198 D3
San Daniele del
Friuli I.......122 A2
Sandanski BG. 183 B5
Sandared S....60 B2
Sandarne S....51 A4
Sandau D......73 B5
Sandbach
D............96 C1
UK...........38 A4
Sandbank UK..34 C3
Sandbanks UK .43 B5
Sandbukt N...192 C5
Sandby DK.....65 B4
Sande
D............71 A5
Sogn og Fjordane
N............46 A2
Vestfold N....54 A1
Sandefjord N..54 A1
Sandeid N.....52 A1
San Demétrio
Corone I.....174 B2
San Demétrio né
Vestini I......169 A3
Sandersleben
D............82 A3
Sanderstølen
N............47 B6
Sandes N......53 B3
Sandesneben
D............65 C3
Sandhead UK..36 B2
Sandhem S....60 B3
Sandhorst D...71 A4
Sandhurst UK..44 B3
Sandıklı TR....189 A5
Sandillon F...103 B4
Sandl A.......96 C2
Sandnes N.....51 B3
Sandness UK...33 A5
Sandnessjøen
N............195 D3
Sando E.......149 B3
Sandomierz PL..87 B5
San Dónaci I .. 173 B3
San Donàdi Piave
I............122 B1
San Donato Val di
Comino I.....169 B3
Sándorfalva
H............126 A2
Sandown UK....44 C2
Sandøysund N..54 A1
Sandrigo I.....121 B4
Sandsele S....195 E8
Sandset N.....194 B5
Sandsjöfors S..62 A2
Sandstad N...198 B6
Sandvatn N....52 B2
Sandvig-Allinge
DK...........67 A3
Sandvika
Akershus N....48 C2
Hedmark N....48 B3
Nord-Trøndelag
N............199 B9
Sandviken S...51 B3
Sandvikvåg N..46 C2
Sandwich UK...45 B5
Sandy UK......44 A3
San Emiliano
E............141 B5
San Enrique E. 162 B2
San Esteban E. 141 A4
San Esteban de
Gormaz E....151 A4
San Esteban de la
Sierra E......149 B4
San Esteban de
Litera E.......145 C4
San Esteban del
Molar E.......142 C1
San Esteban del
Valle E........150 B3
San Esteban de
Valdueza E...141 B4
San Fele I......172 B1
San Felice Circeo
I............169 B3
San Felices E.. 143 B3
San Felices de los
Gallégos E....149 B3
San Felice sul
Panaro I......121 C4
San Ferdinando di
Púglia I......171 B4
San Fernando
E............162 B1
San Fernando de
Henares E... 151 B4

San Fili I.......174 B2
San Foca I.....173 B4
San Fratello I..177 B3
Sangatte F.....78 B1
San Gavino
Monreale I...179 C2
San Gémini Fonte
I............168 A2
Sangerhausen
D............82 A3
San Germano
Vercellese I .. 119 B5
San Giácomo
Trentino Alto
Adige I.......108 C2
Umbria I......136 C1
San Gimignano
I............135 B4
San Ginésio I.. 136 B2
Sangineto Lido
I............174 B1
San Giórgio a Liri
I............169 B3
San Giorgio della
Richinvelda
I............122 A1
San Giórgio del
Sánnio I......170 B2
San Giórgio di
Lomellina I...120 B1
San Giorgio di
Nogaro I......122 B2
San Giorgio di
Piano I.......121 C4
San Giórgio Iónico
I............173 B3
San Giovanni a Piro
I............172 B1
San Giovanni
Bianco I......120 B2
San Giovanni di
Sinis I........179 C2
San Giovanni in
Croce I.......120 B3
San Giovanni in
Fiore I........174 B2
San Giovanni in
Persiceto I ...121 C4
San Giovanni
Reatino I.....169 A2
San Giovanni
Rotondo I....171 B3
San Giovanni
Suérgiu I.....179 C2
San Giovanni
Valdarno I...135 B4
Sangis S.......196 D6
San Giuliano Terme
I............134 B3
San Giustino I.135 B5
San Godenzo I 135 B4
Sangonera la Verde
E............165 B3
San Gregorio
Magno I......172 B1
Sangüesa E...144 B2
Sanguinet F...128 B1
San Guiseppe Jato
I............176 B2
Sanica BIH.....124 C2
Sanitz D.......65 B5
San Javier E...165 B4
San Jorge P ...154 B2
San José E.....164 C2
San Juan E....143 B3
San Juan de
Alicante E....165 A4
San Juan de la Nava
E............150 B3
San Justo de la
Vega E........141 B4
Sankt Aegyd am
Neuwalde A.. 110 B2
Sankt Andrä
A............110 C1
Sankt Andreasberg
D............82 A2
Sankt Anna S...56 B2
Sankt Anna am
Aigen A......110 C2
Sankt Anton am
Arlberg A....107 B5
Sankt Anton an der
Jessnitz A....110 B2
Sankt Augustin
D............80 B3
Sankt Blasien
D............106 B3
Sankt Englmar
D............95 B4
Sankt Gallen
A............110 B1
CH...........107 B4

Sankt Gallenkirch
A............107 B4
Sankt Georgen
A............96 C2
D............106 A3
Sankt Georgen am
Reith A.......110 B1
Sankt Georgen ob
Judenburg A. 110 B1
Sankt Georgen ob
Murau A.....109 B5
Sankt Gilgen
A............109 B4
Sankt Goar D....81 B3
Sankt Goarshausen
D............81 B3
Sankt Ingbert
D............92 B3
Sankt Jacob A. 109 C5
Sankt Jakob in
Defereggen
A............109 C3
Sankt Johann am
Tauern A.....110 B1
Sankt Johann im
Wesen A.....109 A4
Sankt Johann im
Pongau A....109 B4
Sankt Johann in
Tirol A........109 B3
Sankt Katharein an
der Laming
A............110 B2
Sankt Kathrein am
Hauenstein
A............110 B2
Sankt Lambrecht
A............110 B1
Sankt Leonhard am
Forst A.......110 A2
Sankt Leonhard im
Pitztal A......108 B1
Sankt Lorenzen
A............109 C3
Sankt Marein
A............110 B2
Sankt Margarethen
im Lavanttal
A............110 C1
Sankt Margrethen
CH...........107 B4
Sankt Michael
A............110 B2
Sankt Michael im
Burgenland
A............111 B3
Sankt Michael im
Lungau A....109 B4
Sankt
Michaelisdonn
D............64 C2
Sankt Niklaus
CH...........119 A4
Sankt Nikolai im
Sölktal A.....109 B5
Sankt Olof S....63 C2
Sankt Oswald
D............96 C1
Sankt Paul
A............110 C1
F............132 A2
Sankt Peter D. 106 A3
Sankt Peter am
Kammersberg
A............110 B1
Sankt-Peterburg =
St Petersburg
RUS...........9 C7
Sankt Peter-Ording
D............64 B1
Sankt Pölten
A............110 A2
Sankt Radegund
A............110 B2
Sankt Ruprecht an
der Raab A... 110 B2
Sankt Salvator
A............110 C1
Sankt Stefan
A............110 C1
Sankt Stefan an der
Gail A........109 C4
Sankt Stefan im
Rosental A.... 110 C2
Sankt Valentin
A............110 A1
Sankt Veit an der
Glan A.......110 C1
Sankt Veit an der
Gölsen A..... 110 A2
Sankt Veit in
Defereggen
A............109 C3

Sankt Wendel D 92 B3
Sankt Wolfgang A 109 D4
D 108 A3
San Lazzaro di Sávena I 135 A4
San Leo I 135 B5
San Leonardo de Yagüe E 143 C3
San Leonardo in Passiria I 108 C2
San Lorenzo al Mare I 133 B3
San Lorenzo a Merse I 135 B4
San Lorenzo Bellizzi I 174 B2
San Lorenzo de Calatrava E .. 157 B4
San Lorenzo de El Escorial E .. 151 B3
San Lorenzo de la Parrilla E .. 158 B1
San Lorenzo di Sebato I 108 C2
San Lorenzo in Campo I 136 B1
San Lorenzo Nuovo I .. 168 A1
San Lourenco P 160 A1
San Luca I 175 C2
Sanlúcar de Barrameda E. 161 C3
Sanlúcar de Guadiana E .. 160 B2
Sanlúcar la Mayor E 161 B3
San Lúcido I... 174 B2
Sanluri I.......179 C2
San Marcello I. 136 B2
San Marcello Pistoiese I.... 135 A3
San Marcial E. 149 A4
San Marco I ... 170 C2
San Marco Argentano I.. 174 B2
San Marco dei Cavoti I 170 B2
San Marco in Lámis I 171 B3
San Marino RSM. 136 B1
San Martin de Castañeda E. 141 B4
San Martín de la Vega E 151 B4
San Martin de la Vega del Alberche E 150 B2
San Martín del Tesorillo E ... 162 B2
San Martin de Luiña E.......141 A4
San Martin de Montalbán E 157 A3
San Martin de Oscos E 141 A4
San Martin de Pusa E 150 C3
San Martin de Unx E 144 B2
San Martín de Valdeiglesias E 150 B3
San Martino di Campagna I.. 122 A1
San Martino di Castrozza I... 121 A4
San-Martino-di-Lota F.......180 A2
San Martino in Pénsilis I 170 B3
San Mateo de Gallego E .. 144 C3
San Máuro Forte I.............172 B2
San Michele all'Adige I... 121 A4
San Michele di Ganzaria I.... 177 B3
San Michele Mondovi I ... 133 A3
San Miguel de Aguayo E .. 142 A2
San Miguel de Bernuy E .. 151 A4
San Miguel del Arroyo E .. 150 A3
San Miguel de Salinas E 165 B4

Sânmihaiu Roman RO 126 B3
San Millán de la Cogulla E 143 B4
San Miniato I.............135 B3
San Muñoz E.. 149 B3
Sänna S.......55 B5
Sannazzaro de'Burgondi I.............120 B1
Sanne D........73 B4
Sannicandro di Bari I..... 171 B4
Sannicandro Gargánico I.. 171 B3
San Nicola del'Alto I.............174 B2
San Nicolás del Puerto E ... 156 C2
Sânnicolau Mare RO 126 A2
San Nicolò I ... 121 C4
San Nicolò Gerrei I.............179 C3
Sannidal N.....53 B5
Sanniki PL 77 B4
Sanok PL...... 12 D5
San Pablo de los Montes E... 157 A3
San Pancrázio Salentino I... 173 B3
San Pantaleo I.............178 A3
San Páolo di Civitate I..... 171 B4
San Pawl il-Bahar M 175 C3
San Pedro Albacete E 158 C1
Oviedo E.....141 A4
San Pedro de Alcántara E .. 162 B3
San Pedro de Ceque E 141 B4
San Pedro del Arroyo E 150 B2
San Pedro de Latarce E..... 142 C1
San Pedro del Pinatar E.... 165 B4
San Pedro del Romeral E... 143 A3
San Pedro de Merida E 156 B1
San Pedro de Valderaduey E 142 B2
San Pedro Manrique E .. 144 B1
San Pellegrino Terme I 120 B2
San Piero a Sieve I.............135 B4
San Piero in Bagno I.............135 B4
San Piero Patti I.............177 A3
San Pietro I ... 177 B3
San Pietro in Casale I.............121 C4
San Pietro in Gu I.............121 B4
San Pietro in Palazzi I...... 134 B3
San Pietro in Volta I.............122 B1
San Pietro Vara I.............134 A2
San Pietro Vernótico I... 173 B3
San Polo d'Enza I.............121 C3
Sanquhar UK 36 B3
San Quírico d'Órcia I............. 135 B4
San Rafael del Rio E 153 B4
San Remo I.... 133 B3
San Román de Cameros E ... 143 B4
Sân Roman de Hernija E.... 150 A2
San Román de la Cuba E 142 B2
San Roman de los Montes E.... 150 B3
San Romao P.... 155 C3
San Roque E .. 162 B2
San Roque de Riomera E... 143 A3
San Rufo I..... 172 B1

San Sabastián de los Ballesteros E 162 A3
San Salvador de Cantamuda E 142 B2
San Salvo I.... 170 A2
San Salvo Marina I.............170 A2
San Sebastián de los Reyes E .. 151 B4
San Sebastiano Curone I 120 C2
San Secondo Parmense I... 120 C3
Sansepolcro I . 135 B5
San Serverino Marche I.... 136 B2
San Severino Lucano I 174 A2
San Severo I... 171 B3
San Silvestre de Guzmán E.... 161 B2
Sanski Most BIH.............124 C2
San Sosti I..... 174 B2
San Stéfano di Cadore I.....109 C3
San Stino di Livenza I.....122 B1
Santa Agnès E.............166 B1
Santa Amalia E.............156 A1
Santa Ana Cáceres E ... 156 A2
Jaén E........163 A4
Santa Ana de Pusa E 150 C3
Santa Barbara E 153 B4
Santa Bárbara P 160 B1
Santa Barbara de Casa E 161 B2
Santa Bárbara de Padrões P.... 160 B2
Santacara E... 144 B2
Santa Catarina P.............160 B2
Santa Caterina di Pittinuri I... 178 B2
Santa Caterina Villarmosa I.. 177 B3
Santa Cesárea Terme I 173 B4
Santa Clara-a-Nova P.............160 B1
Santa Clara-a-Velha P.............160 B1
Santa Clara de Louredo P.... 160 B2
Santa Coloma de Farners E .. 147 C3
Santa Coloma de Gramenet E.. 147 C3
Santa Coloma de Queralt E..... 147 C2
Santa Colomba de Curueño E... 142 B1
Santa Colomba de Somoza E ... 141 B4
Santa Comba E 140 A2
Santa Comba Dáo P.............148 B1
Santa Comba de Rossas P 149 A3
Santa Cristina I 120 B2
Santa Cristina de la Polvorosa E.. 141 B5
Santa Croce Camerini... 177 C3
Santa Croce di Magliano I... 170 B2
Santa Cruz E.............140 A2
E.............154 B1
Santa Cruz de Alhama E.... 163 A4
Santa Cruz de Campezo E... 143 B4
Santa Cruz de Grio E 152 A2
Santa Cruz de la Salceda E... 151 A4
Santa Cruz de la Sierra E 156 A2
Santa Cruz de la Zarza E 151 C4
Santa Cruz del Retamar E... 151 B3

Santa Cruz del Valle E 150 B2
Santa Cruz de Moya E.............159 B2
Santa Cruz de Mudela E... 157 B4
Santa Cruz de Paniagua E... 149 B3
Santadi I...... 179 C2
Santa Doménica Talao I..... 174 B1
Santa Doménica Vittória I..... 177 B3
Santa Elena E . 157 B4
Santa Elena de Jamuz E..... 141 B5
Santaella E.... 162 A3
Santa Eufemia E 156 B3
Santa Eufémia d'Aspromonte I.............175 C1
Santa Eulalia E.............152 B2
Santa Eulália P 155 C3
Santa Eulalia de Oscos E 141 A3
Santa Eulàlia des Riu E 166 C1
Santa Fe E....... 163 A4
Santa Fiora I .. 135 C4
Sant'Ágata dei Goti I.............170 B2
Sant'Ágata di Ésaro I.............174 B1
Sant'Ágata di Puglia I 171 B3
Sant'Agata Feltria I.............135 B5
Sant'Ágata Militello I.............177 A3
Santa Gertrude I.............108 C1
Santa Giustina I.............121 A5
Sant Agusti de Lluçanès E ... 147 B3
Santa Iria P.... 160 B2
Santa Leocadia P.............148 A1
Santa Lucia del Mela I....... 177 A4
Santa Lucia-de-Porto-Vecchio F.............180 B2
Santa Luzia P . 160 B1
Santa Maddalena Vallalta I.... 108 C3
Santa Magdalena de Polpis E ... 153 B4
Santa Margalida E.............167 B3
Santa Margarida P.............154 B2
Santa Margarida do Sado P 160 A1
Santa Margaridao de Montbui E.............147 C2
Santa Margherita I.............179 D2
Santa Margherita di Belice I....... 176 B2
Santa Margherita Ligure I 134 A2
Santa Maria CH.............108 C1
E.............144 B3
Santa Maria al Bagno I..... 173 B3
Santa Maria Cápua Vétere I 170 B2
Santa Maria da Feira P..... 148 B1
Santa Maria de Cayón E..... 143 A3
Santa Maria de Corco E 147 B3
Santa Maria de Huerta E .. 152 A1
Santa Maria de la Alameda E ... 151 B3
Santa Maria de las Hoyas E 143 C3
Santa Maria del Camí E 167 B2
Santa Maria del Campo E 143 B3
Santa Maria del Campo Rus E. 158 B1
Santa Maria della Versa I 120 C2

Santa Maria del Páramo E 142 B1
Santa Maria del Taro I..... 134 A2
Santa Maria de Mercadillo E . 143 C3
Santa Maria de Nieva E..... 164 B3
Santa Maria de Trassierra E .. 156 C3
Santa Maria di Licodia I..... 177 B3
Santa Maria-di-Rispéscia I ... 168 A1
Santa Maria la Palma I....... 178 B2
Santa María la Real de Nieva E.... 150 A3
Santa Maria Maggiore I... 119 A5
Santa Maria Ribarredonda E 143 B3
Santa Marina del Rey E....... 141 B5
Santa Marinella I.............168 A1
Santa Marta Albacete E 158 B1
Badajoz E..... 155 C4
Santa Marta de Magasca E ... 156 A1
Santa Marta de Penaguião P . 148 A2
Santa Marta de Tormes E.... 150 B2
Santana Évora P....... 154 C2
Setúbal P 154 C1
Sântana RO ... 126 A3
Santana da Serra P............. 160 B1
Sant'Ana de Cambas P 160 B2
Santana do Mato P............. 154 C2
Sant'Anastasia I.............170 C2
Santander E.... 143 A3
Sant'Andrea Fríus I.............179 C3
Sant'Ángelo dei Lombardi I... 172 B1
Sant'Angelo in Vado I........ 136 B1
Sant'Angelo Lodigiano I... 120 B2
Santa Ninfa I... 176 B1
Sant'Antíoco I. 179 C2
Sant Antoni de Calonge E.... 147 C4
Sant Antoni de Portmany E.. 166 C1
Sant'Antonio-di-Gallura I 178 B3
Santanyí E.... 167 B3
Santa Olalla Huelva E.... 161 B3
Toledo E...... 150 B3
Santa Pau E.... 147 B3
Santa Pola E ... 165 A4
Santa Ponça E. 166 B2
Santarcángelo di Romagna I. 136 A1
Santarém P ... 154 B2
Santa Severa F............. 180 A2
I............. 168 A1
Santa Severina I............. 175 B2
Santas Martas E............. 142 B1
Santa Sofia I ... 135 B4
Santa Susana P............. 154 C2
Santa Suzana P............. 155 C3
Santa Teresa di Riva I....... 177 B4
Santa Teresa Gallura I..... 178 A3
Santa Uxía E ... 140 B2
Santa Valburga I............. 108 C1
Santa Vittória in Matenano I .. 136 B2
Sant Boi de Llobregat E.. 147 C3
Sant Carles de la Ràpita E...... 153 B4
Sant Carlos E.. 166 B1
Sant'Caterina I............. 135 C4

Sant Celoni E... 147 C3
Sant Climent E............. 167 B4
Santed E....... 152 A2
Sant'Egídio alla Vibrata I 136 C2
Sant'Elia a Pianisi I............. 170 B2
Sant'Elia Fiumerapido I............. 169 B3
Santelices E.... 143 A3
San Telmo E.... 161 B3
Sant'Elpídio a Mare I............. 136 B2
Santervas de la Vega E 142 B2
Sant'Eufemia Lamezia I...... 175 C2
Sant Feliú E ... 147 C3
Sant Feliu de Codines E.... 147 C3
Sant Feliu de Guíxols E.... 147 C4
Sant Feliu Sasserra E............. 147 C3
Sant Ferran E . 166 C1
Sant Francesc de Formentera I............. 166 C1
Sant Francesc de ses Salines E . 166 C1
Santhià I....... 119 B5
Sant Hilari Sacalm E............. 147 C3
Sant Hipòlit de Voltregà E ... 147 B3
Santiago de Alcántara E .. 155 B3
Santiago de Calatrava E .. 163 A3
Santiago de Compostela E............. 140 B2
Santiago de la Espade E..... 164 A2
Santiago de la Puebla E..... 150 B2
Santiago de la Ribera E...... 165 B4
Santiago del Campo E 155 B4
Santiago de Litem P............. 154 B2
Santiago do Cacém P............. 160 B1
Santiago do Escoural P.... 154 C2
Santiago Maior P............. 155 C3
Santibáñez de Béjar E...... 150 B2
Santibáñez de la Peña E 142 B2
Santibáñez de Murias E...... 142 A1
Santibáñez de Vidriales E... 141 B4
Santibáñez el Alto E............. 149 B3
Santibáñez el Bajo E............. 149 B3
Santillana E.... 142 A2
Santiponce E.. 162 A1
San Tirso de Abres E........ 141 A3
Santisteban del Puerto E.... 157 B4
Santiuste de San Juan Bautiste E............. 150 A3
Santiz E....... 149 A4
Sant Jaume dels Domenys E.. 147 C2
Sant Joan Baptista E............. 166 B1
Sant Joan de les Abadesses E . 147 B3
Sant Jordi E.... 153 B4
Sant Josep de sa Talaia E 166 C1
Sant Juliáde Loria AND 146 B2
Sant'Ilario d'Enza I............. 121 C3
Sant Llorençde Morunys E.... 147 B2
Sant Llorençdes Carctassar E... 167 B3
Sant Llorenç Savall E............. 147 C3

Sant Luis E 167 B4
Sant Mart ide Llemaná E 147 B3
Sant Marti de Maldá E....... 147 C2
Sant Marti Sarroca E............. 147 C2
Sant Mateu E.. 153 B4
Sant Miquel E. 166 B1
Santo Aleixo P............. 161 A2
Santo Amado P............. 161 A2
Santo Amaro P............. 155 C3
Santo André P............. 160 A1
Santo Domingo E............. 155 C3
Santo Domingo de la Calzada E.. 143 B4
Santo Domingo de Silos E............. 143 C3
Santo Estêvão Faro E 160 B2
Santarém P ... 154 C2
Santok PL.......75 B4
Santomera E... 165 A3
Santoña E...... 143 A3
Santo-Pietro-di-Tenda F...... 180 A2
Sant'Oreste I.. 168 A2
Santo Spirito I 171 B4
Santo Stefano d'Aveto I..... 134 A2
Santo Stéfano di Camastra I ... 177 A3
Santo Stefano di Magra I...... 134 A2
Santo Stéfano Quisquina I .. 176 B2
Santo Tirso P.. 148 A1
Santotis E..... 142 A2
Santo Tomé E . 164 A1
Santovenia Burgos E...... 143 B3
Zamora E..... 142 C1
Sant Pau de Seguries E ... 147 B3
Santpedor E .. 147 C2
Sant Pere de Riudebitles E............. 147 C2
Sant Pere Pescador E............. 147 B4
Sant Pere Sallavinera E. 147 C2
Sant Quirze de Besora E 147 B3
Sant Rafel E.. 166 C1
Sant Ramon E. 147 C2
Santu Lussurgiu I............. 178 B2
Santutzi E..... 143 A3
Sant Vincençde Castellet E .. 147 C2
San Valentino alla Muta I....... 108 C1
San Venanzo I. 135 C5
San Vicente de Alcántara E .. 155 B3
San Vicente de Arana E 144 B1
San Vicente de la Barquera E.. 142 A2
San Vicente de la Sonsierra E... 143 B4
San Vicente de Toranzo E.... 143 A3
San Vietro E... 149 A3
San Vigílio I... 108 C2
San Vincente del Raspeig E.... 165 A4
San Vincenzo I............. 134 B3
San Vito I...... 179 C3
San Vito al Tagliamento I............. 122 B1
San Vito Chietino I............. 169 A4
San Vito dei Normanni I... 173 B3
San Vito di Cadore I............. 108 C3
San Vito lo Capo I............. 176 A1
San Vito Romano I............. 169 B2
Sanxenxo E ... 140 B2

Sanza I........ 172 B1
São Aleixo P . 155 C3
São Barnabé
P............. 160 B1
São Bartoloméda
Serra P....... 160 A1
São Bartolomeu de
Messines P... 160 B1
São Bento P... 140 C2
São Brás P..... 160 B2
São Brás de
Alportel P.... 160 B2
São Braz do
Reguedoura
P............. 154 C2
São Cristóvão
P............. 154 C2
São Domingos
P............. 160 B1
São Geraldo P. 154 C2
São Jacinto P.. 148 B1
São João da
Madeira P.... 148 B1
São João da
Pesqueira P.. 148 A2
São João da
Ribeira P..... 154 B2
São João da Serra
P............. 148 B1
São João da Venda
P............. 160 B2
São João dos
Caldeireiros
P............. 160 B2
São Julião P... 155 B3
São Leonardo
P............. 155 C3
São Luis P..... 160 B1
São Manços P. 155 C3
São Marcos da
Ataboeira P.. 160 B2
Saõ Marcos da
Serra P....... 160 B1
São Marcos de
Campo P..... 155 C3
São Martinho da
Cortiça P..... 148 B1
São Martinho das
Amoreiras P.. 160 B1
São Martinho do
Porto P....... 154 B1
São Matias
Beja P 160 A2
Évora P....... 154 C2
São Miguel d'Acha
P............. 155 A3
São Miguel de
Machede P... 155 C3
São Pedro da Torre
P............. 140 C2
São Pedro de
Cadeira P 154 B1
São Pedro de Moel
P............. 154 B1
São Pedro de Solis
P............. 160 B2
São Pedro do Sul
P............. 148 B1
Saorge F 133 B3
São Romão P.. 154 C2
São Sebastião dos
Carros P...... 160 B2
São Teotónio
P............. 160 B1
São Torcato P . 148 A1
Sapataria P ... 154 C1
Sapes GR..... 183 B7
Sapiãos P..... 148 A2
Sa Pobla E..... 167 B3
Sappada I..... 109 C3
Sappen N 192 C5
Sapri I........ 174 A1
Sarajärvi FIN 197 D10
Sarajevo BIH ... 139 B4
Saramon F.... 129 C3
Sarandë AL ... 182 D2
Saranovo SRB . 127 C2
Saraorci SRB . 127 C3
Sa Rapita E.... 167 B3
Saray TR 186 A2
Saraycık TR ... 187 C4
Sarayköy TR ... 188 B3
Saraylar TR ... 186 B2
Sarayönü TR .. 189 A7
Sarbia PL.....75 B5
Sarbinowo
Zachodnio-
Pomorskie PL ..67 B4
Zachodnio-
Pomorskie PL ..74 B3

Sárbogárd H .. 112 C2
Sarcelles F 90 B2
Sarche I....... 121 A3
Sardara I...... 179 C2
Sardoal P 154 B2
Sardón de Duero
E............. 150 A3
Sare F........ 144 A2
S'Arenal E..... 166 B2
Šarengrad HR.. 125 B5
Sarentino I.... 108 C2
Sarezzo I...... 120 B3
Sargans CH... 107 B4
Sárī H........ 112 B3
Sarıbeyler TR . 186 C2
Sarıcakaya
TR........... 187 B5
Sari-d'Orcino
F............. 180 A1
Sarıgöl TR..... 188 A3
Sarıkaya TR ...23 B8
Sarıköy TR 186 B2
Sarilhos Grandes
P............. 154 C2
Sariñena E 145 C3
Sarıoba TR 187 C7
Sárisáp H 112 B2
Sariyer TR..... 186 A4
Sarkad H...... 113 C5
Sárkeresztes
H............. 112 B2
Sárkeresztúr
H............. 112 B2
Särkijärvi FIN . 196 B6
Şarkikaraağaç
TR........... 189 A6
Şarköy TR..... 186 B2
Sarlat-la-Canéda
F............. 129 B4
Sarliac-sur-l'Isle
F............. 129 A3
Sármellék H... 111 C4
Särna S 199 D10
Sarnadas P.... 155 B3
Sarnano I..... 136 B2
Sarnen CH ... 106 C3
Sarnesfield UK . .39 B4
Sárnico I...... 120 B2
Sarno I....... 170 C2
Sarnonico I ... 121 A4
Sarnow D......74 A2
Sarny UA......13 C7
Särö S.........60 B1
Saronno I..... 120 B2
Sárosd H...... 112 B2
Šarovce SK.... 112 A2
Sarpoil F...... 117 B3
Sarpsborg N ...54 A2
Sarracín E..... 143 B3
Sarral E....... 147 C2
Sarralbe F......92 B3
Sarrancolin F . 145 B4
Sarras F....... 117 B4
Sarre I........ 119 B4
Sarreaus E 140 B3
Sarrebourg F ..92 C3
Sarreguemines
F............. .92 B3
Sárrétudvari
H............. 113 B5
Sarre-Union F. .92 C3
Sarria E 141 B3
Sarriable Ter E. 147 B3
Sarrión E..... 153 B3
Sarroca de Lleida
E............. 153 A4
Sarroch I...... 179 C3
Sarron F...... 128 C2
Sársina I...... 135 B5
Særslev DK.....59 C3
Sarstedt D......72 B2
Sárszentlörinc
H............. 112 C2
Sárszentmihaly
H............. 112 B2
Sárszentmiklós
H............. 112 C2
Sarteano I..... 135 C4
Sartène F 180 B1
Sartilly F.......88 B2
Sartirana Lomellina
I............. 120 B1
Saruhanlı TR .. 186 D2
Sárvár H 111 B3
Sarvisvaara S . 196 C4
Sarzana I...... 134 A2
Sarzeau F..... 101 B3
Sarzedas P.... 155 B3
Sasalli TR..... 188 A1
Sasamón E.... 142 B2
Sa Savina E... 166 C1
Sásd H....... 125 A4
Sasino PL......68 A2

Sássari I....... 178 B2
Sassello I..... 133 A4
Sassenberg D. .71 C5
Sassetta I..... 134 B3
Sassnitz D 66 B2
Sassocorvaro
I............. 136 B1
Sasso d'Ombrone
I............. 135 C4
Sassoferrato I. 136 B1
Sassoleone I.. 135 A4
Sasso Marconi
I............. 135 A4
Sassuolo I..... 135 A3
Sástago E 153 A3
Šaštinske Stráže
SK........... .98 C1
Sas van Gent
NL........... .79 A3
Såtåhaugen
N........... 199 C7
Satão P 148 B2
Såtenäs S......55 B3
Säter S........50 B2
Sätila S........60 B2
Satillieu F..... 117 B4
Satnica Đakovačka
HR.......... 125 B4
Sátoraljaújhely
H............. .16 A4
Satow D......65 C4
Sätra-brunn S. . .50 C3
Sætre N........54 A1
Satrup D......64 B2
Satteins A..... 107 B4
Satu Mare RO ...17 B5
Saturnia I..... 168 A1
Saucats F 128 B2
Saucelle E..... 149 A3
Sauda N........52 A2
Sauðárkrókur
IS........... 190 B6
Saudasjøen N. . .52 A2
Sauerlach D... 108 B2
Saugues F..... 117 C3
Sauherad N....53 A5
Saujon F...... 114 C3
Sauland N.....53 A4
Saulces Monclin
F............. .91 B4
Saulgau D ... 107 A4
Saulgrub D ... 108 B2
Saulieu F...... 104 B3
Saulnot F 106 B1
Sault F....... 131 A4
Sault-Brénaz
F............. 118 B2
Sault-de-Navailles
F............. 128 C2
Saulx F....... 105 B5
Saulxures-sur-
Moselotte F. . 106 B1
Saulzais-le-Potier
F............. 103 C4
Saumos F..... 128 B1
Saumur F..... 102 B1
Saunavaara
FIN.......... 197 B10
Saundersfoot
UK........... .39 C2
Saurat F...... 146 B2
Saurbær
Borgarfjarðarsýsla
IS........... 190 C4
Dalasýsla IS... 190 B4
Eyjafjarðarsýsla
IS........... 191 B7
Sáuris I....... 109 C3
Sausset-les-Pins
F............. 131 B4
Sauteyrargues
F............. 131 B2
Sauvagnat F . . 116 B2
Sauve F 131 B2
Sauveterre-de-
Béarn F 144 A3
Sauveterre-de-
Guyenne F... 128 B2
Sauviat-sur-Vige
F............. 116 B1
Sauxillanges
F............. 117 B3
Sauzet
Drôme F 117 C4
Lot F 129 B4
Sauzé-Vaussais
F............. 115 B4
Sauzon F..... 100 B2
Sava I........ 173 B3
Savaari I...... 173 B3
Savalou F....... 131 B4
Sauxillanges

Savaştepe TR . 186 C2
Savci SLO 111 C3
Säve S........60 B1
Savelletri I.... 173 B3
Savelli I....... 174 B2
Savenay F.... 101 B4
Saverdun F ... 146 A2
Saverne F......93 C3
Savières F......91 C3
Savigliano I... 119 C4
Savignac-les-
Eglises F 129 A3
Savignano Irpino
I............. 171 B3
Savignano sul
Rubicone I ... 136 A1
Savigny-sur-Braye
F............. 102 B2
Saviñán E 152 A2
Savines-le-lac
F............. 132 A2
Savino Selo
SRB 126 B1
Savio I....... 135 A5
Sävja S........51 C4
Savognin CH.. 107 C4
Savona I...... 133 A4
Savonlinna FIN . . 9 B6
Savournon F.. 132 A1
Sævråsvåg N. . .46 B2
Savsjö S.......62 A2
Savsjön S......50 C1
Sävsjöström S. . 62 A3
Savudrija HR. . 122 B2
Savukoski
FIN.......... 197 B11
Sawbridgeworth
UK........... .45 B4
Sawtry UK 44 A3
Sax E........ 159 C3
Saxdalen S..... 50 B1
Saxilby UK.....40 B3
Saxmundham
UK........... .45 A5
Saxnäs S..... 195 F6
Saxthorpe UK. .41 C5
Sayalonga E . . 163 B3
Sayatón E..... 151 B5
Sayda D.......83 B5
Säytsjärvi
FIN.......... 193 C11
Sázava CZ......97 B3
Sázava CZ......96 B2
Scaër F....... 100 A2
Scafa I....... 169 A4
Scalasaig UK...34 B1
Scalby UK......40 A3
Scalea I....... 174 B1
Scaletta Zanclea
I............. 177 A4
Scalloway UK . . 33 A5
Scamblesby
UK........... .41 B3
Scandale I..... 175 B2
Scandiano I... 121 C3
Scandicci I.... 135 B4
Scandolara Ravara
I............. 120 B3
Scanno I...... 169 B3
Scansano I.... 168 A1
Scanzano Jónico
I............. 174 A2
Scarborough
UK........... .40 A3
Scardovari I... 122 C1
Scardoy UK ...32 D2
Scarperia I.... 135 B4
Scarriff IRL......28 B3
Scey-sur-Saône-et-
St Albin F ... 105 B4
Schachendorf
A........... 111 B3
Schaffhausen
CH........... 107 B3
Schafstädt D....83 A3
Schafstedt D....64 B2
Schäftlarn D.. 108 B2
Schagen NL....70 B1
Schalkau D....82 B3
Schangnau
CH........... 106 C2
Schapbach D. ..93 C4
Scharbeutz D. . .65 B3
Schärding A....96 C1
Scharnitz A ... 108 B2
Scharrel D......71 A4
Schattendorf
A........... 111 B3
Scheemda NL. .71 A3
Scheessel D.....72 A2
Schéggia I.... 136 B1
Scheibbs A.... 110 B2

Scheibenberg
D............. .83 B4
Scheidegg D.. 107 B4
Scheifling A... 110 B1
Scheinfeld D....94 B2
Schelklingen D .94 C1
Schenefeld
Schleswig-
Holstein D 64 B2
Schleswig-Holstein
D........... .72 A2
Schenklengsfeld
D............. .82 B1
Scherfede D....81 A5
Schermbeck D. .80 A2
Scherpenzeel
NL........... .70 B2
Schesslitz D.....94 B3
Scheveningen
NL........... .70 B1
Schiedam NL...79 A4
Schieder-
Schwalenberg
D............. .72 C2
Schierling D....95 C4
Schiers CH.... 107 C4
Schildau D.....83 A4
Schillingen D..92 B2
Schillingsfürst
D............. .94 B2
Schilpário I... 120 A3
Schiltach D....93 C4
Schiltigheim F .93 C3
Schio I....... 121 B4
Schirmeck F. ...92 C3
Schirnding D. ..83 B4
Schkeuditz D. .83 A4
Schkölen D....83 A3
Schlabendorf
D............. .84 A1
Schladen D....73 B3
Schladming A. 109 B4
Schlangen D....81 A4
Schleiden D.....80 B2
Schleiz D......83 B3
Schleswig D....64 B2
Schleusingen D 82 B2
Schlieben D....83 A5
Schliengen D . 106 B2
Schliersee D.. 108 B2
Schlitz D 81 B5
Schloss Neuhans
D............. .81 A4
Schlossvippach
D............. .82 A3
Schlotheim D. ..82 A2
Schluchsee D . 106 B3
Schlüchtern D ..81 B5
Schmallenberg
D............. .81 A4
Schmelz D......92 B2
Schmidmühlen
D............. .95 B3
Schmiedeberg
D............. .84 B1
Schmiedefeld
D............. .82 B2
Schmirn A ... 108 B2
Schmölln
Brandenburg
D........... 74 A3
Sachsen D.....83 B4
Schnaittach D. .95 B3
Schneeberg D .83 B4
Schneizlreuth
D............. 109 B3
Schneverdingen
D............. .72 A2
Schöder A.... 109 B5
Schoenberg B.. .80 B2
Schollene D....73 B5
Schöllkrippen
A........... 111 B3
Schomberg D. 107 A3
Schönach D....95 C4
Schönau
Baden-
Württemberg
D........... 106 B2
Bayern D 95 C4
Schönbeck D....74 A2
Schönberg
Bayern D 96 C1
Mecklenburg-
Vorpommern
D........... 65 C3
Schleswig-Holstein
D........... .65 B3
Schönebeck D .73 B4
Schöneck D....83 B4
Schönecken- D..80 B2
Schönermark
D............. .74 A2

Schönewalde
D............. .83 A5
Schongau D... 108 B1
Schöngrabern
A............. .97 C4
Schönhagen D. .81 A5
Schönhausen
D............. .73 B5
Schöningen D . .73 B3
Schönkirchen
D............. .64 B3
Schönsee D.....95 B4
Schöntal D.....94 B1
Schönthal D....95 B4
Schonungen D.94 A2
Schönwalde D. .65 B3
Schoondijke
NL........... .79 A3
Schoonebeek
NL........... .71 B3
Schoonhoven
NL........... .79 A4
Schopfheim D 106 B2
Schöppenstedt
D............. .73 B3
Schörfling A . . 109 B4
Schorndorf D ...94 C1
Schortens D....71 A4
Schotten D......81 B5
Schramberg
D............. .93 C4
Schraplau D....83 A3
Schrattenberg
A............. .97 C4
Schrecksbach
D............. .81 B5
Schrems A 96 C3
Schrobenhausen
D............. .95 C3
Schröcken A . . 107 B5
Schrozberg D. . .94 B1
Schruns A..... 107 B4
Schüpfheim
CH........... 106 C3
Schüttorf D.....71 B4
Schwaan D....65 C5
Schwabach D ...94 B3
Schwäbisch
Gmünd D....94 C1
Schwäbisch Hall
D............. .94 B1
Schwabmünchen
D........... 108 A1
Schwadorf A.. 111 A3
Schwagstorf D. .71 B4
Schwaigern D. .93 B5
Schwalmstadt
D............. .81 B5
Schwanberg
A........... 110 C2
Schwanden
CH........... 107 C4
Schwandorf D. .95 B4
Schwanebeck
D............. .73 C4
Schwanenstadt
A........... 109 A4
Schwanewede
D............. .72 A1
Schwanfeld D...94 B2
Schwangau D. 108 B1
Schwarmstedt
D............. .72 B2
Schwarza D....82 B2
Schwarzach im
Pongau D 109 B4
Schwarzau im
Gebirge A.... 110 B2
Schwarzenau A .97 C3
Schwarzenbach
D............. .83 B3
Schwarzenbach am
Wald D......83 B3
Schwarzenbek
D............. .72 A3
Schwarzenberg
D............. .83 B4
Schwarzenburg
CH........... 106 C2
Schwarzenfeld
D............. .95 B4
Schwarz-heide
D............. .84 A1
Schwaz A 108 B2
Schwechat A. . 111 A3
Schwedt D....74 A3
Schwei D......71 A5
Schweich D....92 B2
Schweighausen
D............. 106 A3
Schweinfurt D . .94 A2
Schweinitz D. ..83 A5
Schweinrich D. .74 A1

Schwelm D.....80 A3
Schwemsal D. . .83 A4
Schwendt A... 109 B3
Schwenningen
D............. 107 A3
Schwepnitz D. . .84 A1
Schwerin D 73 A4
Schwerte D.....81 A3
Schweskau D . ..73 B4
Schwetzingen
D............. .93 B4
Schwyz CH.... 107 C3
Sciacca I...... 176 B2
Sciara I....... 176 B2
Scicli I....... 177 C3
Sciechów PL ...75 B3
Scigliano I.... 175 B2
Ścinawa PL.....85 A4
Scionzier F.... 118 A3
Scoglitti I..... 177 C3
Scole UK 45 A5
Sconser UK.....31 B2
Scopello
Piemonte I ... 119 B5
Sicilia I...... 176 A1
Scordia I...... 177 B3
Scorzè I....... 121 B5
Scotch Corner
UK........... .37 B5
Scotter UK.....40 B3
Scourie UK.....32 C1
Scousburgh UK .33 B5
Scrabster UK. . .32 C3
Screeb IRL......28 A2
Scremerston
UK........... .37 A5
Scritto I....... 136 B1
Scunthorpe UK .40 B3
Scuol CH..... 107 C5
Scúrcola Marsicana
I............. 169 A3
Seaford UK.....45 C4
Seaham UK.....37 B5
Seahouses UK. .37 A5
Seascale UK....36 B3
Seaton UK 43 B3
Sebazac-Concourès
F............. 130 A1
Seben TR..... 187 B6
Sebersdorf A.. 110 B2
Sebezh RUS.....8 D6
Sebnitz D......84 B2
Seborga I..... 133 B3
Seby S........63 B4
Seč
Vychodočeský
CZ........... .97 B3
Západočeský
CZ........... .96 B1
Sečanj SRB.... 126 B2
Secemin PL.....87 B3
Séchault F......91 B4
Seckau A..... 110 B1
Seclin F....... .78 B3
Secondigny F . 114 B3
Seda P....... 155 B3
Sedan F.......91 B4
Sedano E...... 143 B3
Sedbergh UK. . .37 B4
Sedella I...... 163 B3
Séderon F..... 131 A4
Sedgefield UK ..37 B5
Sedico I...... 121 A5
Sédilo I...... 178 B2
Sédini I...... 178 B2
Sedlarica HR.. 124 B3
Sedlčany CZ....96 B2
Sedlec-Prčice
CZ........... .96 B2
Sędziejowice
PL........... .86 A3
Sędziszów PL ...87 B3
Sędziszów
Małopolski
PL........... .87 B5
Seebach F......93 C3
Seeboden A... 109 C4
Seefeld
Brandenburg
D........... .74 B2
Niedersachsen
D........... 71 A5
Seefeld in Tirol
A........... 108 B2
Seeg D....... 108 B2
Seehausen D. . .73 B4
Seeheim-
Jugenheim D ..93 B4
Seelbach D.....93 C3
Seelow D......74 B3
Seelze D.......72 B2
Seerhausen D. .83 A5

Sóos F 09 D4
Seesen D 82 A2
Seeshaupt D 108 B2
Seewalchen A 109 B4
Seferihisar TR 188 A1
Sefkerin SRB 127 B2
Segård N 48 B2
Segerstad S 55 A4
Segesd H 124 A3
Seglinge FIN 51 B7
Segmon S 55 A4
Segonzac F 115 C3
Segorbe E 159 B3
Segovia E 151 B3
Segré F 101 B5
Segura
 E 144 B1
 P 155 B3
Segura de León
 E 161 A3
Segura de los
 Baños E 152 B3
Ségur-les-Villas
 F 116 B2
Segurrilla E 150 B3
Sehnde D 72 B2
Seia P 148 B2
Seiches-sur-le-Loir
 F 102 B1
Seifhennersdorf
 D 84 B2
Seignelay F 104 B2
Seijo E 140 C2
Seilhac F 116 B1
Seilles B 79 B5
Seim N 46 B2
Seinäjoki FIN 8 A3
Seissan F 145 A4
Seitenstetten Markt
 A 110 A1
Seixal P 154 C1
Seiz A 110 B1
Seizthal A 110 B1
Sejerslev DK 58 B1
Seksna RUS 9 C11
Selárdalur IS 190 B1
Selárgius I 179 C3
Selb D 83 B4
Selby UK 40 B2
Selca HR 138 B2
Selce HR 123 B3
Selçuk TR 188 B2
Selde DK 58 B2
Selenča SRB 126 B1
Selendi
 Manisa TR 186 D2
 Manisa TR 186 D3
Selenicë AL 182 C1
Sélestat F 106 A2
Seleuš SRB 126 B2
Selevac SRB 127 C2
Selfoss IS 190 D5
Selgua E 145 C4
Selice SK 112 A1
Seligenstadt D 93 A4
Seligenthal D 82 B2
Selimiye TR 188 B2
Selizharovo RUS 9 D8
Selja S 50 A1
Selje N 198 C2
Seljelvnes N 192 C3
Seljord N 53 A4
Selkirk UK 35 C5
Sellano I 136 C1
Selles-St Denis
 F 103 B3
Selles-sur-Cher
 F 103 B3
Sellières F 105 C4
Sellin D 66 B2
Sellye H 125 B3
Selm D 80 A3
Selnica ob Dravi
 SLO 110 C2
Selongey F 105 B4
Selonnet F 132 A2
Selow D 65 C4
Selsey UK 44 C3
Selsingen D 72 A2
Selters D 81 B3
Seltz F 93 C4
Selva I 167 B2
Selva di Cadore
 I 108 C3
Selva di Val
 Gardena I 108 C2
Selvik
 Sogn og Fjordane
 N 46 A2
 Vestfold N 54 A1
Selvino I 120 B2
Selyatyn UA 17 B6
Sem N 54 A1

Semeljci HR 125 B4
Semič SLO 123 B4
Semide
 F 91 D4
 P 148 B1
Semily CZ 84 B3
Seminara I 175 C1
Semlac RO 126 A2
Semlacu Mare
 RO 126 B3
Semmen-stedt
 D 73 B3
Šempeter SLO 123 A4
Semriach A 110 B2
Semur-en-Auxois
 F 104 B3
Sena E 145 C3
Sena de Luna
 E 141 B5
Senarpont F 90 B1
Sénas F 131 B4
Senćanski
 Trešnjevac
 SRB 126 B1
Sencelles E 167 B2
Senčur SLO 123 A3
Senden
 Bayern D 94 C2
 Nordrhein-
 Westfalen D 80 A3
Sendenhorst D 81 A3
Sendim P 149 A3
Senec SK 111 A4
Seneffe B 79 B4
Séneghe I 178 B2
Senés E 164 B2
Senez F 132 B2
Senftenberg D 84 A1
Sengouagnet
 F 145 B4
Sengwarden D 71 A5
Senica SK 98 C1
Senice na Hané
 CZ 98 B1
Senigállia I 136 B2
Senirkent TR 189 A5
Sénis I 179 C2
Senise I 174 A2
Senj HR 123 C3
Senje SRB 127 D3
Senjehopen N 194 A8
Senjski Rudnik
 SRB 127 D3
Senlis F 90 B2
Sennan S 60 C2
Sennecey-le-Grand
 F 105 C3
Sennen UK 42 B1
Senno BY 13 A8
Sénnori I 178 B2
Sennwald CH 107 B4
Sennybridge
 UK 39 C3
Senohrad SK 99 C3
Senonches F 89 B5
Senones F 92 C2
Senorbì I 179 C3
Senovo SLO 123 A4
Senožeče
 SLO 123 B3
Senožeti SLO 123 A3
Sens F 104 A2
Sens-de-Bretagne
 F 101 A4
Senta SRB 126 B2
Senterada E 145 B4
Sentilj SLO 110 C2
Šentjernej
 SLO 123 B4
Šentjur SLO 123 A4
Senumstad N 53 B4
Seoane E 141 B3
Seon CH 106 B3
Sépeaux F 104 B2
Sépey CH 119 A4
Sepino I 170 B2
Sępólno Krajeńskie
 PL 76 A2
Seppenrade D 80 A3
Seppois F 106 B2
Septemvri BG 183 A6
Sepúlveda E 151 A4
Sequals I 122 A1
Sequeros E 149 B3
Seraincourt F 91 B4
Seraing B 80 B1
Seravezza I 134 B3
Sered' SK 98 C1
Seredka RUS 8 C6
Seregélyes H 112 B2

Seregno I 120 B2
Sérent F 101 B3
Serfaus A 108 B1
Sergiyev Posad
 RUS 9 D11
Seriate I 120 B2
Sérifontaine F 90 B1
Serifos GR 185 B5
Sérignan F 130 B2
Serik TR 189 C6
Serina I 120 B2
Serinhisar TR 188 B4
Sermaises F 90 C2
Sérmide I 121 C4
Sermoneta I 169 B2
Sernache de
 Bonjardim P 154 B2
Sernancelhe P 148 B2
Serock PL 77 B6
Serón E 164 B2
Serón de Najima
 E 152 A1
Serooskerke
 NL 79 A3
Seròs E 153 A4
Serpa P 160 B2
Serracapriola
 I 171 B3
Serrada E 150 A3
Serra de Outes
 E 140 B2
Serradifalco I 176 B2
Serradilla E 155 B4
Serradilla del
 Arroyo E 149 B3
Serradilla del Llano
 E 149 B3
Serramanna I 179 C2
Serramazzoni
 I 135 A3
Serranillos E 150 B3
Serrapetrona
 I 136 B2
Serra San Bruno
 I 175 C2
Serra San Quírico
 I 136 B2
Serrastretta I 175 B2
Serravalle
 Piemonte I 119 B5
 Umbria I 136 C2
Serravalle di
 Chienti I 136 B1
Serravalle Scrívia
 I 120 C1
Serre I 172 B1
Serrejón E 150 C2
Serres
 F 132 A1
 GR 183 B5
Serrières F 117 B4
Serrières-de-Briord
 F 118 B2
Sersale I 175 B2
Sertã P 154 B2
Sertig Dörfli
 CH 107 C4
Servance F 106 B1
Serverette F 117 C3
Servia GR 182 C4
Servian F 130 B2
Serviers F 131 A3
Servigliano I 136 B2
Serzedelo P 148 A1
Seseña Nuevo
 E 151 B4
Sesimbra P 154 C1
Seskarö S 196 D6
Seskinore UK 27 B3
Sesma E 144 B1
Sessa Aurunca
 I 170 B1
Ses Salines E 167 B3
Sesta Godano
 I 134 A2
Šestanovac
 HR 138 B2
Sestao E 143 A4
Sestino I 135 B5
Sesto I 109 C3
Sesto Calende
 I 120 B1
Sesto Fiorentino
 I 135 B4
Séstola I 135 A3
Sesto San Giovanni
 I 120 B2
Sestriere I 119 C3
Sestri Levante
 I 134 A2
Sestroretsk RUS 9 B7

Sestu I 179 C3
Sesvete HR 124 B2
Séte F 130 B2
Setcases E 146 B3
Sètenil E 162 B2
Setermoen N 194 B9
Setonje SRB 127 C3
Setskog N 54 A2
Settalsjølia N 199 C7
Séttimo Torinese
 I 119 B4
Settimo Vittone
 I 119 B4
Settle UK 40 A1
Setúbal P 154 C2
Seubersdort D 95 B3
Seúl I 179 C3
Seúlo I 179 C3
Seurre F 105 C4
Sevel DK 58 B1
Sevenoaks UK 45 B4
Sévérac-le-Château
 F 130 A2
Sever do Vouga
 P 148 B1
Severin HR 123 B4
Severomorsk
 RUS 3 B13
Séveso I 120 B2
Ševětin CZ 96 B2
Sevettijärvi
 FIN 193 C12
Sévigny F 91 B4
Sevilla = Seville
 E 162 A2
Sevilla la Nueva
 E 151 B3
Seville = Sevilla
 E 162 A2
Sevilleja de la Jara
 E 156 A3
Sevlievo BG 17 D6
Sevnica SLO 123 A4
Sevojno SRB 127 D1
Sevrier F 118 B3
Sexdrega S 60 B3
Seyches F 129 B3
Seyda D 83 A4
Seydişehir TR 189 B6
Seyðisfjörður
 IS 191 B12
Seyitgazi TR 187 C5
Seyitömer TR 187 C4
Seymen TR 186 A2
Seyne F 132 A2
Seynes F 131 A3
Seyssel F 118 B2
Sežana SLO 122 B2
Sézanne F 91 C3
Sezulfe P 149 A2
Sezze I 169 B3
Sfântu Gheorghe
 RO 17 C6
Sforzacosta I 136 B2
Sgarasta Mhor
 UK 31 B1
's-Gravendeel
 NL 79 A4
's-Gravenhage =
 The Hague NL 70 B1
's-Gravenzande
 NL 79 A4
Shaftesbury UK 43 A4
Shaldon UK 43 B3
Shalskiy RUS 9 B9
Shanagolden
 IRL 29 B2
Shanklin UK 44 C2
Shap UK 37 B4
Sharpness UK 43 A4
Shawbury UK 38 B4
's-Heerenberg
 NL 80 A2
Sheerness UK 45 B4
Sheffield UK 40 B2
Shefford UK 44 A3
Shëmri AL 182 A2
Shenfield UK 45 B4
Shëngjergj AL 182 B2
Shepetivka UA 13 C7
Shepshed UK 40 C2
Shepton Mallet
 UK 43 A4
Sherborne UK 43 B4
Shercock IRL 27 C4
Sheringham UK 41 C5
's-Hertogenbosch
 NL 79 A5
Shiel Bridge
 UK 32 D1
Shieldaig UK 31 B3
Shijak AL 182 B1
Shillelagh IRL 30 B1

Shimsk RUS 9 C7
Shipston-on-Stour
 UK 44 A2
Shklow BY 13 A9
Shkodër AL 182 A1
Shoeburyness
 UK 45 B4
Shoreham-by-Sea
 UK 44 C3
Shotley Gate
 UK 45 B5
Shrewsbury UK 38 B4
Shugozero RUS 9 C9
Shumen BG 17 D7
Siabost UK 31 A2
Siamanna I 179 C2
Sianów PL 67 B5
Siatista GR 182 C3
Siauges-St Romain
 F 117 B3
Šiauliai LT 8 E3
Sibari I 174 B2
Sibbhult S 63 B2
Šibenik HR 138 B1
Siberstedt D 64 B2
Sibinj HR 125 B3
Sibiu RO 17 C6
Sibnica SRB 127 C2
Sibsey UK 41 B4
Siculiana I 176 B2
Šid SRB 125 B5
Sidari GR 182 D1
Siddeburen NL 71 A3
Sidensjö S 200 C4
Siderno I 175 C2
Sidirokastro
 GR 183 B5
Sidmouth UK 43 B3
Sidzina PL 99 B3
Siebe N 192 D7
Siebenlehn D 83 A5
Siedlce PL 12 B5
Siedlice PL 75 A4
Siedlinghausen
 D 81 A4
Siedlisko PL 75 B5
Siegburg D 80 B3
Siegen D 81 B4
Siegenburg D 95 C3
Sieghartskirchen
 A 111 A3
Siegsdorf D 109 B3
Siekierki PL 74 B3
Sielpia PL 87 A4
Siemiany PL 69 B4
Siena I 135 B4
Sieniawka PL 84 B2
Sienno PL 87 A5
Sieppijärvi
 FIN 196 B7
Sieradz PL 86 A2
Sieraków
 Śląskie PL 86 B2
 Wielkopolskie
 PL 75 B5
Sierakowice PL 68 A2
Sierck-les-Bains
 F 92 B2
Sierentz F 106 B2
Sierning A 110 A1
Sierpc PL 77 B4
Sierra de Fuentes
 E 155 B4
Sierra de Luna
 E 144 B3
Sierra de Yeguas
 E 162 A3
Sierre CH 119 A4
Siestrzeń PL 77 B5
Sietamo E 145 B3
Siewierz PL 86 B3
Sigdal N 48 B1
Sigean F 130 B1
Sigerfjord N 194 B6
Sighetu-Marmatiei
 RO 17 B5
Sighişoara RO 17 B6
Sigillo I 136 B1
Siglufjörður
 IS 191 A7
Sigmaringen
 D 107 A4
Signa I 135 B4
Signes F 132 B1
Signy-l'Abbaye
 F 91 B4
Signy-le-Petit F 91 B4
Sigogne F 115 C3
Sigri GR 183 D7
Sigtuna S 57 A3
Sigueiro E 140 B2
Sigüenza E 151 A5
Sigües E 144 B2

Sigulda LV 8 D4
Siilinjärvi FIN 8 A5
Sikenica SK 112 A2
Sikfors S 196 D4
Sikia GR 183 C5
Sikinos GR 185 C6
Sikkilsdalseter
 N 47 A6
Siklós H 125 B4
Sikórz PL 77 B4
Sikselet S 195 D8
Silandro I 108 C1
Silánus I 178 B2
Silbaš SRB 126 B1
Šile TR 187 A4
Siles E 164 A2
Silgueiros P 148 B2
Silifke TR 23 C7
Síliqua I 179 C2
Silistra BG 17 C7
Siljan N 53 A5
Siljansnäs S 50 B1
Silkeborg DK 59 B2
Silla E 159 B3
Sillamäe EST 8 C5
Silleda E 140 B2
Sillé-le-Guillaume
 F 102 A1
Sillenstede D 71 A4
Sillerud S 54 A3
Sillian A 109 C3
Silloth UK 36 B3
Silno PL 68 B2
Silnowo PL 68 B1
Silo HR 123 B3
Sils E 147 C3
Silsand N 194 A8
Silte S 57 C4
Šilute LT 12 A4
Silvalen N 195 E3
Silvaplana CH 107 C4
Silvares P 148 B2
Silvberg S 50 B2
Silverdalen S 62 A3
Silvermines IRL 28 B3
Silverstone UK 44 A2
Silverton UK 43 B3
Silves P 160 B1
Silvi Marina I 169 A4
Simandre F 105 C3
Šimanovci SRB 127 C2
Simard F 105 C4
Simat de Valldigna
 E 159 B3
Simav TR 186 C3
Simbach
 Bayern D 95 C4
 Bayern D 95 C5
Simbário I 175 C2
Simeonovgrad
 BG 183 A7
Simeria RO 17 C5
Simi GR 188 C2
Simićevo SRB 127 C3
Simitli BG 183 B5
Simlångsdalen
 S 60 C3
Simmerath D 80 B2
Simmerberg
 D 107 B4
Simmern D 93 B3
Simo FIN 197 D8
Šimonovce SK 99 C4
Simonsbath UK 43 A3
Simonstorp S 56 B2
Simontornya
 H 112 C2
Simplon CH 119 A5
Simrishamn S 63 C2
Sinaia RO 17 C6
Sinalunga I 135 B4
Sinarcas E 159 B2
Sincan TR 187 C7
Sincanlı TR 187 D5
Sindal DK 58 A3
Sindelfingen D 93 C4
Sindia I 178 B2
Sındırgı TR 186 C3
Sinekli TR 186 A3
Sines P 160 B1
Sinetta FIN 197 C8
Sineu E 167 B3
Singen D 107 B3
Singleton UK 44 C3
Singsås N 199 C7
Siniscóla I 178 B2
Sinj HR 138 B2
Sinlabajos E 150 A3
Sinn D 81 B4
Sínnai I 179 C3
Sinnes N 52 B2

Sinop TR 23 A8
Sins CH 106 B3
Sinsheim D 93 B4
Sint Annaland
 NL 79 A4
Sint Annaparochie
 NL 70 A2
Sint Athonis NL 80 A1
Sint Nicolaasga
 NL 70 B2
Sint Oedenrode
 NL 79 A5
Sintra P 154 C1
Sinzheim D 93 C4
Sinzig D 80 B3
Siófok H 112 C2
Sion CH 119 A4
Sion Mills UK 27 B3
Siorac-en-Périgord
 F 129 B3
Šipanska Luka
 HR 139 C3
Šipovo BIH 138 A3
Sira N 52 B2
Siracusa I 177 B4
Siret RO 17 B7
Sirevåg N 52 B1
Sirig SRB 126 B1
Sirkka FIN 196 B7
Sirmione I 121 B3
Sirniö FIN 197 D11
Sirok H 113 B4
Široké SK 99 C4
Široki Brijeg
 BIH 139 B3
Sirolo I 136 B2
Sirvena E 156 B2
Sisak HR 124 B2
Sisante E 158 B1
Šišljavić HR 123 B4
Sissach CH 106 B2
Sissonne F 91 B3
Sistelo P 140 C2
Sisteron F 132 A1
Sistiana I 122 B2
Sistranda N 198 B5
Sitasjaurestugorna
 S 194 C8
Sitges E 147 C2
Sitia GR 185 D7
Sittard NL 80 A1
Sittensen D 72 A2
Sittingbourne
 UK 45 B4
Sitzenroda D 83 A4
Sivac SRB 126 B1
Sivaslı TR 189 A4
Siverić HR 138 B2
Sivrihisar TR 187 C6
Sixt-Fer-á-Cheval
 F 119 A3
Siziano I 120 B2
Sizun F 100 A1
Sjenica SRB 16 D3
Sjoa N 198 D6
Sjøåsen N 199 A8
Sjöbo S 61 D3
Sjøenden
 Hedmark N 48 A3
 Hedmark N 48 B3
Sjøholt N 198 C3
Sjøli N 48 A3
Sjølstad N 199 A9
Sjölunda S 56 A1
Sjømarken S 60 B2
Sjørring DK 58 B1
Sjötofta S 60 B3
Sjötorp S 55 B4
Sjoutnäset S 199 A11
Sjøvegan N 194 B8
Sjuntorp S 54 B3
Skåbu N 47 A6
Skafså N 53 A4
Skaftafell IS 191 D9
Skagaströnd
 IS 190 B5
Skagen DK 58 A3
Skagersvik S 55 B5
Skaidi N 193 B8
Skala GR 184 A1
Skała PL 87 B3
Skaland N 194 A8
Skala Oropou
 GR 185 A4
Skala-Podilska
 UA 13 D7
Skalat UA 13 D6
Skalbmierz PL 87 B4
Skålevik N 53 B4

Skalica SK......98 C1
Skalité SK......98 B2
Skällinge S.....60 B2
Skalná CZ......83 B4
Skals DK......58 B2
Skælskør DK...65 A4
Skalstugan S.. 199 B9
Skanderborg
DK..............59 B2
Skånes-Fagerhult
S...............61 C3
Skåne-Tranås
S........ 61 D3
Skånevik N 52 A1
Skänninge S 55 B6
Skanör med
Falsterbo S.....66 A1
Skåpafors S....54 A3
Skæpe PL......75 B4
Skara S........55 B4
Skærbæk DK....64 A1
Skarberget N . 194 B7
Skärblacka S...56 B1
Skarð IS...... 190 B3
Skarda S..... 200 B4
Skare N........46 C3
Skåre S........55 A4
Skärhamn S.....60 B1
Skarnes N......48 B3
Skärplinge S...51 B4
Skarpnatö FIN ..51 B6
Skarp Salling
DK............58 B2
Skarrild DK 59 C1
Skarstad N.... 194 B7
Skärstad S.....62 A2
Skarsvåg N ... 193 A9
Skarszewy PL ..69 A3
Skårup DK.....65 A3
Skärvången
S........... 199 B11
Skarvsjöby S..195 F8
Skaryszew PL ..87 A5
Skarżysko-
Kamienna PL...87 A4
Skarzysko Ksiazece
PL............87 A4
Skatøy N........53 B5
Skattkärr S.....55 A4
Skattungbyn S..50 A1
Skatval N 199 B7
Skaulo S 196 B4
Skave DK.......59 B1
Skawina PL 99 B3
Skebobruk S...51 C5
Skebokvarn S...56 A2
Skedala S.....61 C2
Skedevi S......56 B1
Skedsmokorset
N............48 B3
Skee S........54 B2
Skegness UK ...41 B4
Skei N..........46 A3
Skela SRB 127 C2
Skelani BIH....127 D1
Skellefteå S....2 D7
Skelleftehamn S.2 D7
Skelmersdale
UK...........38 A4
Skelmorlie UK ..34 C3
Skelund DK....58 B3
Skender Vakuf
BIH.......... 138 A3
Skene S.......60 B2
Skæpe PL......77 B4
Skepplanda S...60 B2
Skeppshult S...60 B3
Skerries IRL 30 A2
Ski N..........54 A1
Skiathos GR... 183 D5
Skibbereen IRL..29 C2
Skibotn N 192 C4
Skidra GR 182 C4
Skien N 53 A5
Skierniewice
PL............77 C5
Skillingaryd S...60 B4
Skillinge S.....63 C2
Skillingmark S..49 C4
Skilloura CY... 181 A2
Skinnardai S...57 A4
Skinnskatteberg
S............50 C2
Skipmannvik
N............ 195 C6
Skipness UK ...34 C2
Skipsea UK.....41 B3
Skipton UK.....40 B1
Skiptvet N 54 A2
Skiros GR 183 E6

Skivarp S 66 A2
Skive DK........58 B2
Skjånes N 193 B12
Skjærhalden N ..54 A2
Skjeberg N.....54 A2
Skjeggedal N ..46 B3
Skjeljanger N ..46 B1
Skjeljavik N....46 C2
Skjern DK......59 C1
Skjervøy N.... 192 B4
Skjold
Rogaland N.... 52 A1
Troms N 192 C3
Skjoldastraumen
N.............52 A1
Skjolden N......47 A4
Skjønhaug N...54 A2
Skjøtningsberg
N............ 193 A11
Škocjan SLO .. 123 B4
Skoczów PL....98 B2
Skodborg DK ...59 C2
Škofja Loka
SLO 123 A3
Škofljica SLO.. 123 B3
Skog S........51 A3
Skoganvarre
N............ 193 C9
Skogen S......54 A3
Skogfoss N... 193 C13
Skoghall S 55 A4
Skogly N..... 193 C13
Skogn N 199 B8
Skognes N 192 C3
Skogstorp
Halland S...... 60 C2
Södermanland
S.............. 56 A2
Skoki PL 76 B2
Skokloster S ...57 A3
Sköldinge S....56 A2
Skole UA 13 D5
Skollenborg N ..53 A5
Sköllersta S....56 A1
Skomlin PL.....86 A2
Skonseng N... 195 D5
Skopelos GR . 183 D5
Skopje NMK... 182 A3
Skoppum N....54 A1
Skórcz PL 69 B3
Skorogoszcz PL 86 B1
Skoroszów PL...85 A5
Skorovatn N . 199 A10
Skorped S.... 200 C3
Skørping DK...58 B2
Skotfoss N 53 A5
Skotniki PL 87 A3
Skotselv N.....48 C1
Skotterud N ...49 C4
Skottorp S 61 C2
Skovby DK.....64 B2
Skövde S......55 B4
Skovsgård DK..58 A2
Skrad HR..... 123 B3
Skradin HR... 138 B1
Skradnik HR .. 123 B4
Skråmestø N ...46 B1
Škrdlovice CZ...97 B3
Skrea S........60 C2
Skreia N.......48 B2
Skrolsvik N ... 194 A7
Skruv S........63 B3
Skrwilno PL....77 A4
Skrydstrup DK ..59 C2
Skucani BIH ... 138 B2
Skudeneshavn
N.............52 A1
Skui N........48 C2
Skulsk PL 76 B3
Skultorp S 55 B4
Skultuna S.....56 A2
Skuodas LT.....8 D2
Skute N........48 B2
Skuteč CZ......97 B3
Skutskär S.....51 B4
Skutvik N 194 B6
Skvyra UA 13 D8
Skwierzyna PL ..75 B4
Skýcov SK......98 C2
Skyllberg S.....55 B5
Skyttmon S... 200 C1
Skyttorp S 51 B4
Sládkovičovo
SK.......... 111 A4
Slagelse DK ...61 D1
Slagharen NL ..71 B3
Slagnäs S....195 E9
Slaidburn UK ..40 B1
Slane IRL 30 A2
Slano HR..... 139 C3
Slantsy RUS......8 C6

Slaný CZ......84 B2
Slap SLO 122 A2
Šlapanice CZ...97 B4
Slåstad N 48 B3
Slatina
BIH.......... 139 B3
HR 125 B3
RO 17 C6
Slatiňany CZ...97 B3
Slatinice CZ.....98 B1
Slättberg S.....50 A1
Slattum N......48 C2
Slavičín CZ.....98 B1
Slavkov CZ.....98 C1
Slavkovica
SRB 127 C2
Slavkov u Brna
CZ...........97 B4
Slavonice CZ...97 C3
Slavonski Brod
HR 125 B4
Slavonski Kobas
HR 125 B3
Slavõsovce SK ..99 C4
Slavskoye RUS ..69 A5
Slavuta UA......13 C7
Sława
Lubuskie PL.... 85 A4
Zachodnio-
Pomorskie PL . 67 C4
Slawharad BY ...13 B9
Sławków PL.....86 B3
Sławno
Wielkopolskie
PL.............76 B2
Zachodnio-
Pomorskie PL . 68 A1
Sławoborze PL..67 C4
Sl'ažany SK 98 C2
Sleaford UK....40 C3
Sleðbrjótur
IS 191 B11
Sledmere UK...40 A3
Sleights UK 37 B6
Slemmestad N ..54 A1
Ślesin PL.......76 B3
Sliač SK 99 C3
Sliema M..... 175 C3
Sligo IRL 26 B2
Slite S.........57 C4
Slitu N 54 A2
Sliven BG 17 D7
Śliwice PL......68 B3
Slobozia RO....17 C7
Slochteren NL..71 A3
Slöinge S......60 C2
Słomniki PL.....87 B4
Slonim BY......13 B6
Słońsk PL 75 B3
Slootdorp NL ...70 B1
Slottsbron S ...55 A4
Slough UK 44 B3
Slövag N.......46 B2
Slovenj Gradec
SLO 110 C2
Slovenska Bistrica
SLO 123 A4
Slovenská L'upča
SK...........99 C3
Slovenská-Ves
SK...........99 B4
Slovenské Darmoty
SK.......... 112 A3
Slovenske Konjice
SLO 123 A4
Słubice PL......74 B3
Sluderno I 108 C1
Sluis NL 78 A3
Šluknov CZ.....84 A2
Slunj HR 123 B4
Słupca PL......76 B2
Słupia PL......87 A3
Słupiec PL.....85 B4
Słupsk PL......68 A2
Slutsk BY......13 B7
Smålandsstenar
S............60 B3
Smalåsen N...195 E4
Smardzewo PL..75 B4
Smarhon BY.....13 A7
Šmarje SLO ... 123 B4
Šmarješka Toplice ... 123 B4
Šmartno SLO.. 123 A3
Smečno CZ.....84 B2
Smedby S......63 B4
Smědec CZ.....96 C2
Smederevo
SRB 127 C2
Smederevska
Palanka SRB.. 127 C2
Smedjebacken
S.............50 B2
Smęgorzów PL..87 B5

Smeland N.....53 B4
Smidary CZ....84 B3
Śmigiel PL.....75 B5
Smilde NL.....71 B3
Smiřice CZ.....85 B3
Smithfield UK ..36 B4
Śmitowo PL....75 A5
Smøgen S......54 B2
Smogulec PL...76 A2
Smołdzino PL...68 A2
Smolenice SK ..98 C1
Smolensk RUS 13 A10
Smolník SK.....99 C4
Smolyan BG... 183 B6
Smuka SLO... 123 B3
Smygehamn S ..66 A2
Smykow PL.....87 A4
Snainton UK ...40 A3
Snaith UK......40 B2
Snaptun DK....59 C3
Snarby N...... 192 C3
Snarum N......48 B1
Snåsa N 199 A9
Snedsted DK...58 B1
Sneek NL......70 A2
Sneem IRL 29 C2
Snejbjerg DK...59 B1
Snillfjord N .. 198 B6
Šnjegotina
BIH.......... 125 C3
Snøde DK......65 A3
Snøfjord N....193 B8
Snogebaek DK..67 A4
Snyatyn UA ... 13 D6
Soave I........ 121 B4
Sober E 140 B3
Sobernheim D .93 B3
Soběslav CZ ...96 B2
Sobota
Dolnośląskie
PL............ 85 A3
Łódzkie PL.....77 B4
Sobotište SK ...98 C1
Sobotka CZ.....84 B3
Sobótka
Dolnośląskie
PL............85 B4
Wielkopolskie
PL............ 86 A1
Sobra HR..... 139 C3
Sobrado
Coruña E 140 A2
Lugo E....... 141 B3
Sobral da Adica
P............ 161 A2
Sobral de Monte
Agraço P.... 154 C1
Sobreira Formosa
P............ 154 B3
Søby DK.......64 B3
Soca SLO..... 122 A2
Sochaczew PL..77 B5
Sochos GR ... 183 C5
Socodor RO... 113 C5
Socol RO..... 127 C3
Socovos E.... 164 A3
Socuéllamos E 158 B1
Sodankylä
FIN.......... 197 B9
Söderåkra S....63 B4
Söderala S.....51 A3
Söderås S......50 B2
Söderbärke S..50 B2
Söderby-Karl S..51 C5
Söderfors S....51 B4
Söderhamn S ..51 A4
Söderköping S..56 B2
Söderö S......56 B1
Södertälje S....57 A3
Södra Finnö S ..56 B2
Södra Ny S.....55 A4
Södra Sandby
S............ 61 D3
Södra Vi S......62 A3
Sodražica SLO. 123 B3
Sodupe E 143 A3
Soengas P 148 A1
Soest
D............ 81 A4
NL...........70 B2
Sofades GR .. 182 D4
Sofia BG...... 17 D5
Sofikon GR.... 184 B4
Şofronea RO .. 126 A3
Sögel D........71 B4
Sogliano al
Rubicone I .. 135 A5
Sogndalsfjøra
N.............46 A4
Søgne N........53 B3
Sögütköy TR . 188 C3

Soham UK......45 A4
Sohland D......84 A2
Sohren D.......93 B3
Soignies B 79 B4
Soissons F 90 B3
Söjtör H...... 111 C3
Sokal' UA 13 C6
Söke TR 188 B2
Sokna N........48 B1
Sokndal N 52 B2
Soknedal N ... 199 C7
Soko BIH..... 125 C4
Sokolac BIH ... 139 B4
Sokółka PL.....13 B5
Sokolov CZ.....83 B4
Sokołowo PL...76 B3
Sokołów Podlaski
PL............12 B5
Sola N.........52 B1
Solana de los
Barros E..... 155 C4
Solana del Pino
E............ 157 B3
Solánas I..... 179 C3
Solares E..... 143 A3
Solarino I 177 B4
Solarussa I ... 179 C2
Solas UK.......31 B1
Solberg S 200 C3
Solberga S.....62 A2
Solber-gelva N..53 A6
Solbjørg N.....46 B2
Solčany SK.....98 C2
Solčava SLO... 123 A3
Solda I........ 108 C1
Sölden A...... 108 C2
Solec Kujawski
PL............76 A3
Soleils F...... 132 B2
Solenzara F... 180 B2
Solera E 163 A4
Solesmes F....79 B3
Soleto I....... 173 B4
Solgne F.......92 C2
Solheim N 46 B2
Solheimsvik N .52 A2
Solignac F 115 C5
Solihull UK.....44 A2
Solin HR...... 138 B2
Solingen D......80 A3
Solivella E 147 C2
Solkan SLO... 122 B2
Söll A 108 B3
Sollana E..... 159 B3
Sollebrunn S...54 B3
Sollefteå S ... 200 C3
Sollenau A 111 B3
Sollen-tuna S ..57 A3
Sóller E 166 B2
Sollerön S.....50 B1
Søllested DK...65 B4
Solliès-Pont F. 132 B2
Sollihøgda N...48 C2
Solnechnogorsk
RUS.........9 D10
Solnice CZ.....85 B4
Solofra I...... 170 C2
Solomiac F.... 129 C3
Solopaca I ... 170 B2
Solórzano E... 143 A3
Solothurn CH ..106 B2
Solre-le-Château
F............79 B4
Solsona E 147 C2
Solsvik N......46 B1
Solt H 112 C3
Soltau D........72 B2
Soltsy RUS......9 C7
Soltszentimre
H........... 112 C3
Soltvadkert H. 112 C3
Solumsmoen N .48 C1
Solund N......46 A1
Solva UK 39 C1
Sölvesborg S...63 B2
Solymár H.... 112 B2
Soma TR 186 C2
Somain F........78 B3
Somberek H . 125 A4
Sombernon F . 104 B3
Sombor SRB.. 125 B5
Sombreffe B ...79 B4
Someren NL....80 A1
Somero FIN......8 B3
Somersham UK .44 A3
Somerton UK ..43 A4
Sömmerda D...82 A3
Sommersted
DK............59 C2
Sommesous F...91 C4
Somme-Tourbe
F.............91 B4
Sommières F.. 131 B3
Sommières-du-
Clain F 115 B4
Somo E 143 A3
Somogyfajsz
H........... 111 C4
Somogyjád H . 111 C4
Somogysámson
H........... 111 C4
Somogysárd
H........... 125 A3
Somogyszil H . 112 C2
Somogyszob
H........... 124 A3
Somogyvár H . 111 C4
Somontin E ... 164 B2
Somosierra E . 151 A4
Somoskőújifalu
H........... 113 A3
Sompolno PL ...76 B3
Sompuis F 91 C4
Son N 54 A1
Son Bou E ... 167 B4
Soncillo E 143 B3
Soncino I..... 120 B2
Sóndalo I..... 120 A3
Søndeled N 53 B5
Sønder Bjert
DK............59 C2
Sønderborg
DK............64 B2
Sønderby DK...64 B2
Sønder Felding
DK............59 C1
Sønderho DK ..59 C1
Sønder Hygum
DK............59 C1
Sønder Omme
DK............59 C1
Søndersø DK....59 C3
Søndervig DK...59 B1
Søndre Enningdal
Kappel N.....54 B2
Sóndrio I..... 120 A2
Soneja E 159 B3
Son en Breugel
NL...........80 A1
Songe N........53 B5
Songeons F....90 B1
Sonkamuotka
FIN.......... 196 A6
Sonkovo RUS ..9 D10
Sönnarslöv S...61 D4
Sonneberg D ..82 B3
Sonnefeld D ..82 B3
Sonnewalde D..84 A1
Sonnino I 169 B3
Sonogno CH .. 120 A1
Sonsbeck D....80 A2
Sonseca E 157 A4
Son Servera E. 167 B3
Sonstorp S.....56 B1
Sonta SRB.... 125 B5
Sontheim D....94 C2
Sonthofen D .. 107 B5
Sontra D.......82 A1
Sopelana E ... 143 A4
Sopje HR..... 125 B3
Sopoćani SK .. 111 A4
Sopot
PL.......... 69 A3
SRB 127 C2
Sopotnica
NMK........ 182 B3
Sopron H..... 111 B3
Šoporňa SK ... 111 A4
Sopuerta E ... 143 A3
Sora I........ 169 B3
Soragna I..... 120 C3
Söråker S..... 200 D3
Sorano I...... 168 A1
Sorbara I..... 121 C4
Sörbo S...... 200 D2
Sorbas E 164 B2
Sórbolo I..... 121 C3
Sörbygden S.. 200 D2
Sordal N.......52 B3
Sordale UK 32 C3
Sore F........ 128 B2

Sommatino I.. 176 B2
Sommeilles F ..91 C4
Sommen S 55 B5
Sommepy-Tahure
F.............91 B4
Sömmerda D...82 A3
Sommerfeld D ..74 B2
Sommersted
DK............59 C2
Sommesous F...91 C4
Somme-Tourbe
F.............91 B4
Sommières F.. 131 B3
Sommières-du-
Clain F 115 B4
Somo E 143 A3
Somogyfajsz
H........... 111 C4
Somogyjád H . 111 C4
Somogysámson
H........... 111 C4
Somogysárd
H........... 125 A3
Somogyszil H . 112 C2
Somogyszob
H........... 124 A3
Somogyvár H . 111 C4
Somontin E ... 164 B2
Somosierra E . 151 A4
Somoskőújifalu
H........... 113 A3
Sompolno PL ...76 B3
Sompuis F 91 C4
Son N 54 A1
Son Bou E ... 167 B4
Soncillo E 143 B3
Soncino I..... 120 B2
Sóndalo I..... 120 A3
Søndeled N 53 B5
Sønder Bjert
DK............59 C2
Sønderborg
DK............64 B2
Sønderby DK...64 B2
Sønder Felding
DK............59 C1
Sønderho DK ..59 C1
Sønder Hygum
DK............59 C1
Sønder Omme
DK............59 C1
Søndersø DK....59 C3
Søndervig DK...59 B1
Søndre Enningdal
Kappel N.....54 B2
Sóndrio I..... 120 A2
Soneja E 159 B3
Son en Breugel
NL...........80 A1
Songe N........53 B5
Songeons F....90 B1
Sonkamuotka
FIN.......... 196 A6
Sonkovo RUS ..9 D10
Sönnarslöv S...61 D4
Sonneberg D ..82 B3
Sonnefeld D ..82 B3
Sonnewalde D..84 A1
Sonnino I 169 B3
Sonogno CH .. 120 A1
Sonsbeck D....80 A2
Sonseca E 157 A4
Son Servera E. 167 B3
Sonstorp S.....56 B1
Sonta SRB.... 125 B5
Sontheim D....94 C2
Sonthofen D .. 107 B5
Sontra D.......82 A1
Sopelana E ... 143 A4
Sopje HR..... 125 B3
Sopoćani SK .. 111 A4
Sopot
PL.......... 69 A3
SRB 127 C2
Sopotnica
NMK........ 182 B3
Sopron H..... 111 B3
Šoporňa SK ... 111 A4
Sopuerta E ... 143 A3
Sora I........ 169 B3
Soragna I..... 120 C3
Söråker S..... 200 D3
Sorano I...... 168 A1
Sorbara I..... 121 C4
Sörbo S...... 200 D2
Sorbas E 164 B2
Sórbolo I..... 121 C3
Sörbygden S.. 200 D2
Sordal N.......52 B3
Sordale UK 32 C3
Sore F........ 128 B2

Sörenberg CH. 106 C3
Soresina I.... 120 B2
Sorèze F 146 A3
Sörforsa S.... 200 E3
Sorges F 115 C4
Sórgono I 179 B3
Sorgues F 131 A3
Sorgun TR.... 23 B8
Soria E 143 C4
Soriano Cálabro
I............ 175 C2
Soriano nel Cimino
I............ 168 A2
Sorihuela del
Guadalimar
E............ 164 A1
Sorisdale UK ...34 B1
Sørkjosen N... 192 C4
Sørli N....... 199 A10
Sormás H 111 C3
Sörmjöle S ... 200 C6
Sornac F 116 B2
Sorø DK....... 61 D1
Soroca MD....17 A8
Sørreisa N ... 194 A9
Sorrento I 170 C2
Sorsele S.....195 E8
Sörsjön S 49 A5
Sorso I....... 178 B2
Sort E 146 B2
Sortavala RUS... 9 B7
Sortino I 177 B4
Sortland N ... 194 B6
Sørum N 48 B3
Sørumsand N...48 C3
Sorunda S......57 A3
Sörup D........64 B2
Sørvågen N ... 194 C3
Sørvær N ... 192 B6
Sorvik S.......50 B2
Sørvika N 199 C8
Sos F........ 128 B3
Sösdala S 61 C3
Sos del Rey
Católico E ... 144 B2
Sošice HR ... 123 B4
Sośnica PL 75 A5
Sośnicowice PL .86 B2
Sośno PL.......76 A2
Sosnovyy Bor
RUS...........9 C6
Sosnowiec PL ..86 B3
Sospel F 133 B3
Šoštanj SLO ... 123 A4
Sotaseter N ... 198 D4
Sotillo de Adrada
E............ 150 B3
Sotillo de la Ribera
E............ 143 C3
Sotin HR 125 B5
Sotkamo FIN...3 D11
Soto de la Marina
E............ 143 A3
Soto del Barco
E............ 141 A4
Soto de los Infantes
E............ 141 A4
Soto de Real E. 151 B4
Soto de Ribera
E............ 141 A5
Sotoserrano E. 149 B3
Soto y Amío E . 141 B5
Sotresgudo E . 142 B2
Sotrondio E .. 142 A1
Sotta F....... 180 B2
Sottomarina I. 122 B1
Sottrum D 72 A2
Sottunga FIN...51 B7
Sotuelamos E. 158 B1
Souain F 91 B4
Soual F....... 146 A3
Soucy F...... 104 A2
Souda GR 185 D5
Soudron F 91 C4
Souesmes F... 103 B4
Souffelweyersheim F .93 C3
Soufli GR..... 186 A1
Souillac F 129 B4
Souilly F.......91 B5
Soulac-sur-Mer
F............ 114 C2
Soulaines-Dhuys
F.............91 C4
Soulatgé F ... 146 B3
Soultz-Haut-Rhin
F............ 106 B2
Soultz-sous-Forêts
F.............93 C3
Soumagne B ...80 B1
Soumoulou F . 145 A3

Sou – Str 253

Souppes-sur-Loing F 103 A4
Souprosse F 128 C2
Sourdeval F 88 B3
Soure P 154 A2
Sournia F 146 B3
Souro Pires P 149 B2
Sourpi GR 182 D4
Sours F 90 C1
Sousceyrac F 116 C2
Sousel P 155 C3
Soustons F 128 C1
Söğüt
Bilecik TR 187 B5
Burdur TR 189 B4
Soutelo de Montes E 140 B2
Southam UK 44 A2
Southampton UK 44 C2
Southborough UK 45 B4
South Brent UK 42 B3
South Cave UK 40 B3
Southend UK 34 C2
Southend-on-Sea UK 45 B4
South Hayling UK 44 C3
South Molton UK 42 A3
South Ockendon UK 45 B4
South Petherton UK 43 B4
Southport UK 38 A3
South Shields UK 37 B5
South Tawton UK 42 B3
Southwell UK 40 B3
Southwold UK 45 A5
South Woodham Ferrers UK 45 B4
Söğütlu TR 187 B5
Souto P 148 B2
Soutochao E 141 C3
Souto da Carpalhosa P 154 B2
Souvigny F 104 C2
Souzay-Champigny F 102 B1
Soverato I 175 C2
Soveria Mannelli I 175 B2
Sövestad S 66 A2
Sovetsk RUS 12 A4
Sovići BIH 138 B3
Sovicille I 135 B4
Søvik N 198 C3
Sowerby UK 37 B5
Soyaux F 115 C4
Sozopol BG 17 D7
Spa B 80 B1
Spadafora I 177 A4
Spaichingen D 107 A3
Spakenburg NL 70 B2
Spalding UK 41 C3
Spálené Poříčí CZ 96 B1
Spalt D 94 B2
Spangenberg D 82 A1
Spangereid N 52 B3
Spantekow D 74 A2
Sparanise I 170 B2
Sparbu N 199 B8
Sparkær DK 58 B2
Sparkford UK 43 A4
Sparreholm S 56 A2
Spartà I 177 A4
Sparta = Sparti GR 184 B3
Sparti = Sparta GR 184 B3
Spean Bridge UK 34 B3
Speicher D 92 B2
Speichersdorf D 95 B3
Speke UK 38 A4
Spello I 136 C1
Spenge D 72 B1
Spennymoor UK 37 B5
Spentrup DK 58 B3
Sperenberg D 74 B2
Sperlinga I 177 B3
Sperlonga I 169 B3
Spetalen N 54 A1
Spetses GR 184 B4
Speyer D 93 B1
Spézet F 100 A2
Spezzano Albanese I 174 B2
Spezzano della Sila I 174 B2
Spiddle IRL 28 A2
Spiegelau D 96 C1
Spiekeroog D 71 A4
Spiez CH 106 C2
Spigno Monferrato I 133 A4
Spijk NL 71 A3
Spijkenisse NL 79 A4
Spilamberto I 135 A4
Spili GR 185 D5
Spilimbergo I 122 A1
Spilsby UK 41 B4
Spinazzola I 172 B2
Spincourt F 92 B1
Spind N 52 B2
Spindleruv-Mlyn CZ 84 B3
Spinoso I 174 A1
Špišjć Bukovica HR 124 B3
Spišská Belá SK 99 B4
Spišská Nová Ves SK 99 C4
Spisská Stará Ves SK 99 B4
Spišské-Hanušovce SK 99 B4
Spišské Podhradie SK 99 C4
Spišské Vlachy SK 99 C4
Spišský-Štvrtok SK 99 C4
Spital A 110 B1
Spital am Semmering A 110 B2
Spittal an der Drau A 109 C4
Spittle of Glenshee UK 35 B4
Spitz A 97 C3
Spjald DK 59 B1
Spjærøy N 54 A1
Spjelkavik N 198 C3
Spjutsbygd S 63 B3
Split HR 138 B2
Splügen CH 107 C4
Spodsbjerg DK 65 B3
Spofforth UK 40 B2
Spohle D 71 A5
Spoleto I 136 C1
Spoltore I 169 A4
Spondigna I 108 C1
Sponvika N 54 A2
Spornitz D 73 A4
Spotorno I 133 A4
Spraitbach D 94 C1
Sprakensehl D 72 B3
Spręcowo PL 69 B5
Spremberg D 84 A2
Spresiano I 122 B1
Sprimont B 80 B1
Springe D 72 B2
Sproatley UK 41 B3
Spydeberg N 54 A2
Spytkowice PL 99 B3
Squillace I 175 C2
Squinzano I 173 B4
Sračinec HR 124 A2
Srbac BIH 124 B3
Srbobran SRB 126 B1
Srebrenica BIH 127 C1
Srebrenik BIH 125 C4
Sredets BG 17 D7
Središče SLO 124 A2
Śrem PL 76 B2
Sremska Mitrovica SRB 127 C1
Sremski Karlovci SRB 126 B1
Srní CZ 96 B1
Srnice Gornje BIH 125 C4
Srock PL 86 A3
Środa Śląska PL 85 A4
Środa Wielkopolski PL 76 B2
Srpska Crnja SRB 126 B2
Srpski Itebej SRB 126 B2
Srpski Miletić SRB 125 B5
Staatz A 97 C4
Stabbursnes N 193 B8
Staberdorf D 65 B4
Stabroek B 79 A4
Stachy CZ 96 B1
Staðarfell IS 190 B3
Stade D 72 A2
Staden B 78 B3
Stadl an der Mur A 109 B4
Stadskanaal NL 71 B3
Stadtallendorf D 81 B5
Stadthagen D 72 B2
Stadtilm D 82 B3
Stadtkyll D 80 B2
Stadtlauringen D 82 B2
Stadtlengsfeld D 82 B2
Stadtlohn D 71 C3
Stadtoldendorf D 82 A1
Stadtroda D 83 B3
Stadtsteinach D 82 B3
Stäfa CH 107 B3
Staffanstorp S 61 D3
Staffelstein D 82 B2
Staffin UK 31 B2
Stafford UK 40 C1
Stainach A 110 B1
Staindrop UK 37 B5
Staines-upon-Thames UK 44 B3
Stainville F 91 C5
Stainz A 110 C2
Staithes UK 37 B6
Staíti I 175 D2
Stäket S 57 A3
Stakroge DK 59 C1
Štalcerji SLO 123 B3
Stalden CH 119 A4
Stalham UK 41 C5
Stalheim N 46 B3
Stallarholmen S 56 A3
Ställberg S 50 C1
Ställdalen S 50 C1
Stallhofen A 110 B2
Stalon S 195 F6
Stalowa Wola PL 12 C5
Stamford UK 40 C3
Stamford Bridge UK 40 B3
Stamnes N 46 B2
Stams A 108 B1
Stamsried D 95 B4
Stamsund N 194 B4
Stanford le Hope UK 45 B4
Stånga S 57 C4
Stange N 48 B3
Stanghella I 121 B4
Stanhope UK 37 B4
Stanišić SRB 125 B5
Staňkov CZ 95 B5
Stankovci HR 137 B4
Stanley UK 37 B5
Stans CH 106 C3
Stansted Mountfitchet UK 45 B4
Stanzach A 108 B1
Stapar SRB 125 B5
Staphorst NL 70 B3
Staplehurst UK 45 B4
Stąporków PL 87 A4
Stara Baška HR 123 C3
Starachowice PL 87 A5
Stara Fužina SLO 122 A2
Stara Kamienica PL 84 B3
Stara Kiszewa PL 68 B3
Stará L'ubovnă SK 99 B4
Stara Moravica SRB 126 B1
Stara Novalja HR 137 A3
Stara Pazova SRB 127 C2
Stará Turá SK 98 C1
Staraya Russa RUS 9 D7
Stara Zagora BG 17 D6
Stärbsnäs S 51 C6
Starčevo SRB 127 C2
Stare Dłutowo PL 77 A4
Staré Hamry CZ 98 B2
Stare Jablonki PL 69 B5
Staré Město CZ 98 B1
Stare Pole PL 69 A4
Stare Sedlo CZ 96 B2
Stare Strącze PL 85 A4
Stargard Szczeciński PL 75 A4
Stårheim N 198 D2
Stari Banovci SRB 127 C2
Starigrad
Ličko-Senjska HR 123 C3
Splitsko-Dalmatinska HR 138 B2
Stari Gradac HR 124 B3
Starigrad-Paklenica HR 137 A4
Stari Jankovci HR 125 B4
Stari Majdan BIH 124 C2
Stari-Mikanovci HR 125 B4
Staritsa RUS 9 D9
Starkenbach A 108 B1
Starnberg D 108 B2
Starogard PL 75 A4
Starogard Gdański PL 69 B3
Starokonstyantyniv UA 13 D7
Staro Petrovo Selo HR 124 B3
Staro Selo
HR 124 B1
SRB 127 C3
Stary Brzozów PL 77 B5
Stary Dzierzgoń PL 69 B4
Starý Hrozenkov CZ 98 C1
Stary Jaroslaw PL 68 A1
Stary Plzenec CZ 96 B1
Stary Sącz PL 99 B4
Starý Smokovec SK 99 B4
Staryy Chartoriysk UA 13 C6
Staškov SK 98 B2
Stassfurt D 82 A3
Staszów PL 87 B5
Stathelle N 53 A5
Staufen D 106 B2
Staunton UK 39 C4
Stavang N 46 A2
Stavanger N 52 B1
Stavåsnäs S 49 B4
Stavby S 51 B5
Staveley UK 40 B2
Stavelot B 80 B1
Stavenisse NL 79 A4
Stavern N 53 B6
Stavnäs S 55 A3
Stavoren NL 70 B2
Stavros
CY 181 A1
GR 183 C5
Stavroupoli GR 183 B6
Stavseng N 47 A6
Stavsiø N 48 B2
Stavsnäs S 57 A4
Stawiszyn PL 76 C3
Steane N 53 A4
Steblevë AL 182 B2
Stechelberg CH 106 C2
Štěchovice CZ 96 B2
Stechow D 73 B5
Steckborn CH 107 B3
Stede Broek NL 70 B2
Steeg A 107 B5
Steenbergen NL 79 A4
Steenvoorde F 78 B2
Steenwijk NL 70 B3
Štefanje HR 124 B2
Steffisburg CH 106 C2
Stegaurach D 94 B2
Stege DK 65 B5
Stegelitz D 74 A2
Stegersbach A 111 B3
Stegna PL 69 A4
Steimbke D 72 B2
Stein UK 31 B2
Steinach
Baden-Württemberg D 106 A3
Bayern D 82 B2
Thüringen D 82 B3
Stein an Rhein CH 107 B3
Steinau
Bayern D 81 B5
Niedersachsen D 64 C1
Steinbeck D 74 B2
Steinberg am Rofan A 108 B2
Steindorf A 109 C5
Steine N 46 B2
Steinen D 106 B2
Steinfeld
A 109 C4
D 71 B5
Steinfurt D 71 B4
Steingaden D 108 B1
Steinhagen D 72 B1
Steinheid D 82 B3
Steinheim
Bayern D 107 A5
Nordrhein-Westfalen D 81 A5
Steinhöfel D 74 B3
Steinhorst D 72 B3
Steinigtwolmsdorf D 84 A2
Steinkjer N 199 A8
Steinsholt N 53 A5
Stekene B 79 A4
Stelle D 72 A3
Stellendam NL 79 A4
Stenåsa S 63 B4
Stenay F 91 B5
Stenberga S 62 A3
Stendal D 73 B4
Stenhammar S 55 B4
Stenhamra S 57 A3
Stenhousemuir UK 35 B4
Stenlose DK 61 D2
Stensätra S 50 B3
Stensele S 195 E8
Stenstorp S 55 B4
Stenstrup DK 65 A3
Stenudden S 195 D8
Stenungsund S 54 B2
Štěpánov CZ 98 B1
Stephanskirchen D 108 B3
Stepnica PL 74 A3
Stepojevac SRB 127 C2
Stepping DK 59 C2
Sterbfritz D 82 B1
Sternberg D 65 C4
Šternberk CZ 98 B1
Sterup D 64 B2
Stes Maries-de-la-Mer F 131 B3
Stęszew PL 75 B5
Štěti CZ 84 B2
Stevenage UK 44 B3
Stewarton UK 36 A2
Steyerburg D 72 B2
Steyning UK 44 C3
Steyr A 110 A1
Stężyca PL 68 A2
Stezzano I 120 B2
Stia I 135 B4
Stibb Cross UK 42 B2
Sticciano Scalo I 135 C4
Stidsvig S 61 C3
Stiens NL 70 A2
Stige DK 59 C3
Stigen S 54 B3
Stigliano I 174 A2
Stigtomta S 56 B2
Stilida GR 182 E4
Stilla N 192 C7
Stillington UK 40 A2
Stilo I 175 C2
Stintino I 178 B2
Stio I 172 B1
Štip NMK 182 B4
Stira GR 185 A5
Stirling UK 35 B4
Štítnik SK 99 C1
Štíty CZ 97 B4
Stjärnhov S 56 A3
Stjärnsund S 50 B3
Stjørdalshalsen N 199 B7
Stobnica PL 87 A3
Stobno PL 75 A5
Stobreč HR 138 B2
Stochov CZ 84 B1
Stockach D 107 B4
Stöckalp CH 106 C3
Stockaryd S 62 A2
Stockbridge UK 44 B2
Stockerau A 97 C4
Stockheim D 82 B3
Stockholm S 57 A4
Stockport UK 40 B1
Stocksbridge UK 40 B2
Stockton-on-Tees UK 37 B5
Stod CZ 96 B1
Stöde S 200 D2
Stødi N 195 D6
Stöðvarfjörður IS 191 C12
Stoer UK 32 C1
Stoholm DK 58 B2
Stoke Ferry UK 41 C4
Stoke Fleming UK 43 B3
Stoke Mandeville UK 44 B3
Stoke-on-Trent UK 40 B1
Stokesley UK 37 B5
Stokke N 54 A1
Stokkemarke DK 65 B4
Stokken N 53 B4
Stokkseyri IS 190 D4
Stokkvågen N 195 D4
Stokmarknes N 194 B5
Štoky CZ 97 B3
Stolac BIH 139 B3
Stølaholmen N 46 A3
Stolberg D 80 B2
Stolin BY 13 C7
Stollberg D 83 B4
Stöllet S 49 B5
Stollhamm D 71 A5
Stolno PL 76 A3
Stolpen D 84 A2
Stolzenau D 72 B2
Stompetoren NL 70 B1
Ston HR 139 C3
Stonařov CZ 97 B3
Stone UK 40 C1
Stonehaven UK 33 E4
Stonehouse UK 36 A3
Stongfjorden N 46 A2
Stonndalen N 47 B4
Stony Stratford UK 44 A3
Stopnica PL 87 B4
Storå S 56 A1
Storås N 198 B6
Storby FIN 51 B6
Stordal
Møre og Romsdal N 198 C4
Nord-Trøndelag N 199 B8
Store UK 33 B4
Storebø N 46 B2
Storebro S 62 A3
Store Damme DK 65 B5
Store Heddinge DK 65 A5
Store Herrestad S 66 A2
Store Levene S 55 B3
Storelv N 192 B6
Store Molvik N 193 B12
Støren N 199 B7
Store Skedvi S 50 B2
Store Vika S 57 B3
Storfjellseter N 199 D7
Storfjord N 192 C3
Storfjorden N 198 C3
Storfors S 55 A5
Storforshei N 195 D5
Storhøliseter N 47 A6
Storjord N 193 D6
Storkow
Brandenburg D 74 B2
Mecklenburg-Vorpommern D 74 A3
Storli N 198 C6
Storlien S 199 B9
Stornara I 171 B3
Stornoway UK 31 A2
Storo I 121 B3
Storozhynets UA 17 A6
Storrington UK 44 C3
Storseleby S 200 B2
Storsjön S 50 A3
Storslett N 192 C5
Storsteinnes N 192 C3
Storsund S 196 D3
Storuman S 195 E8
Störvattnet S 199 C9
Storvik
N 195 D4
S 50 B3
Storvreta S 51 C4
Štos SK 99 C4
Stössen D 83 A3
Stotel D 72 A1
Stötten D 108 B1
Stotternheim D 82 A3
Stouby DK 59 C2
Stourbridge UK 40 C1
Stourport-on-Severn UK 39 B4
Støvring DK 58 B2
Stow UK 35 C5
Stowbtsy BY 13 B7
Stowmarket UK 45 A5
Stow-on-the-Wold UK 44 B2
Straach D 73 C5
Strabane UK 27 B3
Strachan UK 33 D4
Strachur UK 34 B2
Stracin NMK 182 A4
Strackholt D 71 A4
Stradbally IRL 29 B1
Stradella I 120 B2
Straelen D 80 A2
Stragari SRB 127 C2
Strakonice CZ 96 B1
Strålsnäs S 55 B6
Stralsund D 66 B2
Strand N 48 A3
Stranda N 198 C3
Strandby DK 58 A3
Strandebarm N 46 B3
Strandhill IRL 26 B2
Strandlykkja N 48 B3
Strandvik N 46 B2
Strangford UK 27 B5
Strängnäs S 56 A3
Strångsjö S 56 B2
Stráni CZ 98 C1
Stranice SLO 123 A4
Stranorlar IRL 26 B3
Stranraer UK 36 B1
Strasatti I 176 B1
Strasbourg F 93 C3
Strasburg D 74 A2
Strašice CZ 96 B1
Stråssa S 56 A1
Strassburg A 110 C1
Strass im Steiermark A 110 C2
Strasskirchen D 95 C4
Strasswalchen A 109 B4
Stratford-upon-Avon UK 44 A2
Strathaven UK 36 A2
Strathdon UK 32 D3
Strathkanaird UK 32 D1
Strathpeffer UK 32 D2
Strathy UK 32 C3
Strathyre UK 34 B3
Stratinska BIH 124 C2
Stratton UK 42 B2
Straubing D 95 C4
Straulas I 178 B3
Straume N 53 A5

Straumen
Nordland N . . . 194 C6
Nord-Trøndelag
N. 199 B8
Straumsjøen
N. 194 B5
Straumsnes N. 194 C6
Straupitz D 74 C3
Strausberg D . . 74 B2
Straussfurt D . . 82 A3
Strawczyn PL . . 87 B4
Straža
SLO 123 B4
SRB 127 C3
Stražnad Nezárkou
CZ 96 B2
Strážnice CZ . . 98 C1
Strážný CZ 96 C1
Stráž Pod Ralskem
CZ 84 B2
Štrbské Pleso
SK. 99 B4
Strečno SK 98 B2
Street UK 43 A4
Strehla D 83 A5
Strekov SK . . . 112 B2
Strem A 111 B3
Stremska-Rača
SRB 127 C1
Strengberg A . 110 A1
Strengelvåg
N. 194 B6
Stresa I 119 B5
Streufdorf D . . . 82 B2
Strib DK. 59 C2
Striberg S 55 A5
Stříbro CZ. 95 B4
Strichen UK . . . 33 D4
Strigno I 121 A4
Štrigova HR . . . 111 C3
Strijen NL 79 A4
Strizivojna HR 125 B4
Strmica HR . . . 138 A2
Strmilov CZ . . . 97 B3
Ströhen D. 72 B1
Strokestown
IRL 28 A3
Stromberg
Nordrhein-
Westfalen D. . . 81 A4
Rheinland-Pfalz
D. 93 B3
Stromeferry UK 31 B3
Strömnäs S . . . 200 B2
Stromness UK. . 33 C3
Strömsberg S . . 51 B4
Strömsbruk S . 200 E3
Strömsfors S . . 56 B2
Strömsnäsbruk
S. 61 C3
Strömstad S . . . 54 B2
Strömsund
Jämtland
S. 199 B12
Västerbotten
S. 195 E7
Stronachlachar
UK 34 B3
Stróngoli I 174 B3
Stronie Ślaskie
PL. 85 B4
Strontian UK. . . 34 B2
Stroppiana I . . 119 B5
Stroud UK 43 A4
Stroumbi CY . . 181 B1
Stróża PL. 99 B3
Strücklingen D. 71 A4
Struer DK. 58 B1
Struga NMK. . . 182 B2
Strugi Krasnyye
RUS 9 C6
Strumica NMK 182 B4
Strumien PL. . . . 98 B2
Struy UK 32 D2
Stružec HR . . . 124 B2
Stryków PL. . . . 77 C4
Stryn N 198 D3
Stryy UA 13 D5
Strzałkowo PL . 76 B2
Strzegocin PL . . 77 B5
Strzegom PL. . . 85 B4
Strzegowo PL. . 77 B5
Strzelce PL. . . . 77 B4
Strzelce Krajeńskie
PL. 75 B4
Strzelce Kurowo
PL. 75 B4
Strzelce Opolskie
PL. 86 B2
Strzelin PL 85 B5

Strzelno PL 76 B3
Strzepcz PL 68 A3
Strzybnica PL . . 86 B2
Strzygi PL. 77 A4
Stubbekøbing
DK. 65 B5
Stuben A. 107 B5
Stubenberg A. 110 B2
Stubline SRB . . 127 C2
Studená CZ 97 B3
Studenci HR. . . 138 B3
Studenka CZ. . . 98 B2
Studenzen A . . 110 B2
Studienka SK . . 98 C1
Studland UK . . . 43 B5
Studley UK. . . . 44 A2
Studzienice PL. . 68 A2
Stuer D 73 A5
Stugudal N . . . 199 C8
Stugun S 200 C1
Stuhr D 72 A1
Stukenbrock
D 81 A4
Stülpe D 74 B2
Stupava SK . . . 111 A4
Stupnik HR . . . 124 B1
Stupsk PL 77 A5
Sturkö S 63 B3
Sturminster
Newton UK. . . 43 B4
Štúrovo SK. . . . 112 B2
Sturton UK. . . . 40 B3
Stuttgart D 94 C1
Stvolny CZ. 96 A1
Stykkishólmur
IS 190 B3
Styri N 48 B3
Stysö S. 60 B1
Suances E. 142 A2
Subbiano I 135 B4
Subiaco I. 169 B3
Subotica SRB. . 126 A1
Subotište SRB. 127 C1
Sučany SK. 98 B2
Suceava RO. . . . 17 B7
Sucha-Beskidzka
PL. 99 B3
Suchacz PL. . . . 69 A4
Suchań PL. 75 A4
Suchdol nad
Lužnice CZ. . . 96 C2
Suchedniów
PL. 87 A4
Suchorze PL. . . 68 A2
Suchteln D 80 A2
Sucina E 165 B4
Suckow D 73 A4
Sućuraj HR . . . 138 B3
Súðavík IS 190 A3
Sudbury UK . . . 45 A4
Suddesjaur S 195 E10
Suden D 64 B1
Süderbrarup D. 64 B2
Süderlügum D. . 64 B1
Sudoměřice u
Bechyně CZ. . 96 B2
Sudovec HR . . . 124 A2
Sueca E 159 B3
Suelli I 179 C3
Sugenheim D . . 94 B2
Sugères F 117 B3
Sugny B. 91 B4
Suhl D 82 B2
Suhlendorf D . . 73 B3
Suho Polje
BIH. 125 C5
Şuhut TR. 189 A5
Šuica BIH. 138 B3
Suippes F 91 B4
Sukošan HR . . . 137 A4
Sükösd H 125 A4
Suków PL. 87 B4
Šul'a SK 99 C3
Suldalsosen N . 52 A2
Suldrup DK. . . . 58 B2
Sulechów PL. . . 75 B4
Sulęcin PL. 75 B4
Sulęczyno PL. . . 68 A2
Sulejów PL. 87 A3
Süleymanlı
TR. 186 D2
Sulgen CH 107 B4
Sulibórz PL. . . . 75 A4
Sulina RO 17 C8
Sulingen D. 72 B1
Suliszewo PL. . . 75 A4
Sulitjelma N . . 195 C7
Sułkowice PL. . . 99 B3
Süller TR. 189 A4
Sully-sur-Loire
F. 103 B4

Sulmierzyce
Łódzkie PL. . . . 86 A3
Wielkopolskie
PL. 85 A5
Sulmona I. 169 A3
Süloğlu TR 186 A1
Sułoszowa PL. . . 87 B3
Sulów PL. 85 A5
Sulsdorf D 65 B4
Sultandağı
TR. 189 A6
Sülüklü TR 187 D7
Suluova TR. 23 A8
Sulvik S 54 A3
Sülysáp H 112 B3
Sülz D. 93 C4
Sulzbach
Baden-
Württemberg
D. 94 B1
Baden-
Württemberg
D. 94 C1
Bayern D 93 B5
Saarland D . . . 92 B3
Sulzbach-
Rosenberg D. . 95 B3
Sülze D. 72 B3
Sulzfeld D. 82 B2
Sumartin HR . . 138 B2
Sumburgh UK. . . 33 B5
Sümeg H. 111 C4
Sumiswald CH 106 B2
Šumná CZ. 97 C3
Šumperk CZ . . . 97 B1
Šumvald CZ 98 B1
Sunbilla E 144 A2
Sünching D 95 C4
Sund
FIN. 51 B7
S. 54 A2
Sundborn S 50 B2
Sundby DK. 58 B1
Sunde N. 46 C2
Sunde bru N . . . 53 B5
Sunderland UK . 37 B5
Sundern D 81 A4
Sundhultsbrunn
S. 62 A2
Sundnäs S 195 D8
Sundom S. 196 D5
Sunds DK. 59 B2
Sundsfjord N . 195 D5
Sundsvall S . . . 200 D3
Sungurlu TR. . . . 23 A8
Suni I. 178 B2
Sunja HR. 124 B2
Sunnansjö S . . . 50 B1
Sunnaryd S 60 B3
Sunndalsøra
N. 198 C5
Sunne S. 49 C5
Sunnemo S 49 C5
Sunnersberg S . 55 B4
Suolovuopmio
N. 192 C7
Suomussalmi
FIN. 3 D11
Suoyarvi RUS . . 9 A8
Super Sauze F. 132 A2
Supetar HR . . . 138 B2
Supetarska Draga
HR 123 C3
Supino I. 169 B3
Šuplja Stijena
MNE 139 B5
Surahammar S . 56 A2
Šurany SK. 112 A2
Surazh BY. 13 A9
Surbo I. 173 B4
Surčin SRB . . . 127 C2
Surgères F 114 B3
Surhuisterveen
NL. 70 A3
Súria E. 147 C2
Surin F 115 B4
Surka N 48 B2
Surnadalsøra
N. 198 C5
Sursee CH. 106 B3
Surte S. 60 B2
Surwold D 71 B4
Sury-le-Comtal
F. 117 B4
Susa I 119 B4
Šušara SRB . . . 127 C3
Susch CH. 107 C5
Susegana I. . . . 122 B1
Süsel D. 65 B3
Sušice CZ 96 B1
Šušnjevica
HR 123 B3
Sussen D. 94 C1

Susurluk TR . . . 186 C3
Susz PL. 69 B4
Sütçüler TR . . . 189 B5
Sutivan HR. . . . 138 B2
Sutjeska SRB . . 126 B2
Sutri I 168 A2
Sutton UK. 44 B3
Sutton Coldfield
UK 40 C2
Sutton-in-Ashfield
UK 40 B2
Sutton-on-Sea
UK 41 B4
Sutton-on-Trent
UK 40 B3
Sutton Scotney
UK 44 B2
Sutton Valence
UK 45 B4
Suvaja BIH 124 C2
Suvereto I. 135 B3
Suwałki PL. 12 A5
Suze-la-Rousse
F. 131 A3
Suzzara I 121 C3
Svabensverk S. . 50 A2
Svalbarð IS. . . 191 A10
Sülze D 72 B3
Svalöv S 61 D3
Svanabyn S . . . 200 B2
Svanberga S . . . 51 C5
Svaneke DK. . . . 67 A4
Svanesund S . . . 54 B2
Svängsta S 63 B2
Svannäs S 195 D9
Svanskog S 54 A3
Svanstein S . . . 196 C6
Svappavaara
S. 196 B4
Svärdsjö S 50 B2
Svarstad N 53 A5
Svärta S 56 B3
Svartå S 55 A4
Svartbyn S 196 C5
Svärtinge S 56 B2
Svartlå S 196 D4
Svartnäs S 50 B3
Svartnes N 195 C5
Svarttjärn S . . . 195 E7
Svatsum N. 48 A1
Svätý Jur SK. . . 111 A4
Svätý Peter
SK. 112 B2
Svedala S 61 D3
Sveg S 199 C11
Sveindal N 52 B3
Sveio N 52 A1
Svejbæk DK. . . . 59 B2
Svelgen N. 198 D2
Svelvik N. 54 A1
Svendborg DK . . 65 A3
Svene N. 53 A5
Svenljunga S . . . 60 B3
Svennevad S . . . 56 A1
Svenstavik S . 199 C11
Svenstrup DK. . . 58 B2
Švermov CZ. . . . 84 B2
Sveti Ivan Zabno
HR 124 B2
Sveti Ivan Zelina
HR 124 B2
Sveti Nikole
NMK 182 B3
Sveti Rok HR . . 137 A4
Světla nad Sázavou
CZ 97 B3
Svetlyy RUS 69 A5
Svetvinčenat
HR 122 B2
Švica HR 123 C4
Svidník SK 12 D4
Švihov CZ. 96 B1
Svilajnac SRB . 127 C3
Svilengrad
BG 183 B8
Svindal N. 54 A2
Svinhult S. 62 A3
Svinna SK. 98 C2
Svinninge
DK 61 D1
S. 57 A4
Sviritsa RUS. . . . 9 B8
Svishtov BG. . . . 17 D6
Svislach BY. 13 B6
Svit SK 99 B4
Svitavy CZ 97 B4
Svodin SK 112 B2
Svolvær N 194 B5
Svortemyr N . . . 46 A2
Svortland N 52 A1
Svratka CZ. 97 B4
Svrčinovec SK. . 98 B2
Svullrya N. 49 B4

Svyetlahorsk
BY. 13 B8
Swadlincote
UK 40 C2
Swaffham UK . . 41 C4
Swanage UK . . . 43 B5
Swanley UK. . . . 45 B4
Swanlinbar IRL. 26 B3
Swansea UK. . . . 39 C3
Swarzędz PL . . . 76 B2
Swatragh UK. . . 27 B4
Świątki PL. 69 B5
Świdnica
Dolnośląskie
PL. 85 B4
Lubuskie PL. . . 84 A3
Świdnik PL. 12 C5
Świdwin PL. . . . 75 A4
Świebodzice PL 85 B4
Świebodzin PL. . 75 B4
Świecie PL. 76 A3
Świedziebnia
PL. 77 A4
Świeradów Zdrój
PL. 84 B3
Świerki PL 85 B4
Świerzawa PL. . . 85 A3
Świerzno PL. . . . 67 C3
Święta PL 74 A3
Święta Anna PL . 86 B3
Świętno PL. 75 B5
Swifterbant NL . 70 B2
Swindon UK. . . . 44 B2
Swineshead UK . 41 C3
Swinford IRL . . . 26 C2
Świnoujście PL. . 66 C3
Swinton UK 35 C5
Swobnica PL . . . 74 A3
Swords IRL 30 A2
Swornegacie
PL. 68 B2
Sya S 56 B1
Sycewice PL. . . . 68 A1
Sychevka RUS. . . 9 E9
Syców PL. 86 A1
Sycowice PL. . . . 75 B4
Sydnes N. 52 A1
Syfteland N 46 B2
Syke D 72 B1
Sykkylven N . . . 198 C3
Sylling N 48 C2
Sylte N. 198 C4
Symbister UK . . 33 A5
Symington UK . . 36 A3
Symonds Yat
UK 39 C4
Sypniewo
Kujawsko-
Pomorskie PL . 76 A2
Wielkopolskie
PL. 68 B1
Syserum S 62 A4
Sysslebäck S . . . 49 B4
Syväjärvi FIN. . 197 B8
Szabadbattyán
H. 112 B2
Szabadegyháza
H. 112 B2
Szabadszállás
H. 112 C3
Szadek PL. 86 A2
Szajol H 113 B4
Szakály H 112 C2
Szakcs H 112 C2
Szakmár H 112 C3
Szalánta H 125 B4
Szałas PL. 87 A4
Szalkszentmárton
H. 112 C3
Szalonna H 99 C4
Szamocin PL . . . 76 A2
Szamotuły PL. . . 75 B5
Szany H 111 B4
Szarvas H 113 C4
Szarvaskö H . . . 113 B4
Szászvár H 125 A4
Százhalombatta
H. 112 B2
Szczawa PL 99 B4
Szczawnica PL . . 99 B4
Szczecin PL. 74 A3
Szczecinek PL. . . 68 B1
Szczekociny PL . 87 B3
Szczerców PL. . . 86 A3
Szczucin PL. . . . 87 B5
Szczuczarz PL . . 75 A5
Szczuki PL. 77 B5
Szczurowa PL. . . 87 B4
Szczyrk PL. 99 B3
Szczytna PL. . . . 85 B4
Szczytno PL. . . . 77 A5
Szczyty PL. 86 A2

Szécsény H . . . 112 A3
Szederkény H. 125 B4
Szedres H. 112 C2
Szeged H 126 A2
Szeghalom H . 113 B5
Szegvár H. 113 C4
Székesfehérvár
H. 112 B2
Székkutas H . . 113 C4
Szekszárd H . . 125 A4
Szemplino Czarne
PL. 77 A5
Szemud PL. 68 A3
Szendehely H. 112 B3
Szendrö H 99 C4
Szentendre H. 112 B3
Szentes H 113 C4
Szentgotthárd
H. 111 C3
Szentlászló H . 125 A3
Szentlörinc H . 125 A3
Szentmártonkáta
H. 113 B3
Szenyér H. 111 C4
Szeremle H 125 A4
Szerencs H 113 A5
Szerep H 113 B5
Szigetszentmiklós
H. 112 B3
Szigetvár H . . . 125 A3
Szikáncs H 126 A2
Szikszó H 113 A4
Szil H 111 B4
Szilvásvárad
H. 113 A4
Szklarska Poreba
PL. 84 B3
Szlichtyngowa
PL. 85 A4
Szob H 112 B2
Szolnok H. 113 B4
Szombathely
H. 111 B3
Szorosad H . . . 112 C2
Szpetal Graniczny
PL. 77 B4
Szprotawa PL. . . 84 A3
Szreńsk PL. 77 A5
Sztum PL. 69 B4
Sztutowo PL . . . 69 A4
Szubin PL 76 A2
Szücsi H. 113 B3
Szulmierz PL. . . 77 B5
Szulok H 124 A3
Szumanie PL. . . 77 B4
Szwecja PL 75 A5
Szydłów
Łódzkie PL. . . . 86 A3
Świętokrzyskie
PL. 87 B5
Szydłowiec PL. . 87 A4
Szydlowo PL. . . 77 A5
Szydlowo PL. . . 77 A5
Szymanów PL. . 77 B5
Szynkielów PL . . 86 A2

T

Taastrup DK. . . . 61 D2
Tab H 112 C2
Tabanera la Luenga
E. 151 A3
Tabaqueros E . 158 B2
Tábara E 149 A4
Tabenera de
Cerrato E . . . 142 B2
Taberg S 62 A2
Tabernas E 164 B2
Tabiano Bagni
I. 120 C3
Taboada E 140 B3
Taboadela E . . . 140 B3
Tábor CZ. 96 B2
Táborfalva H . . 112 B3
Taborište HR . . 124 B2
Tábua P. 148 B1
Tabuaco P. 148 A2
Tabuenca E 152 A2
Tabuyo del Monte
E. 141 B4
Täby S 57 A4
Tác H 112 B2
Tachov CZ. 95 B4
Tadcaster UK. . . 40 B2
Tadley UK. 44 B2
Tafalla E 144 B2
Tafjord N. 198 C4
Taganheira P . . 160 B1
Tågarp S 61 D2
Tággia I. 133 B3
Tagliacozzo I . . 169 A3
Táglio di Po I . . 121 B5

Tagnon F. 91 B4
Tahal E. 164 B2
Tahitótfalu H . 112 B3
Tahtaköprü
TR. 187 C4
Tailfingen D. . . 107 A4
Taillis F. 101 A4
Tain UK 32 D2
Tain-l'Hermitage
F. 117 B4
Taipadas P 154 C2
Taivalkoski
FIN. 197 D11
Takene S. 55 A4
Takovo SRB . . . 127 C2
Taksony H 112 B3
Tal E 140 B2
Talachyn BY. . . . 13 A8
Talamello I. . . . 135 B5
Talamone I. . . . 168 A1
Talant F 105 B3
Talarrubias E. . 156 A2
Talaván E 155 B4
Talavera de la
Reina E. 150 C3
Talavera la Real
E. 155 C4
Talayuela E . . . 150 C2
Talayuelas E . . 159 B2
Talgarth UK 39 C3
Talgje N. 52 A1
Talhadas P 148 B1
Táliga E 155 C3
Talizat F. 116 B3
Tálknafjörður
IS 190 B2
Talla I 135 B4
Talladale UK . . . 31 B3
Tallaght IRL . . . 30 A2
Tallard F 132 A2
Tällberg S. 50 B1
Tallberg S. 196 C5
Tallinn EST 8 C4
Talloires F. 118 B3
Tallow IRL. 29 B3
Tallsjö S 200 B4
Tallvik S 196 C5
Talmay F 105 B4
Talmont-St Hilaire
F. 114 B2
Talmont-sur-
Gironde F . . . 114 C3
Talne UA 13 D9
Talsano I 173 B3
Talsi LV. 8 D3
Talvik N 192 B6
Talybont UK. . . . 39 B3
Tal-Y-Llyn UK. . . 38 B3
Tamajón E 151 B4
Tamame E 149 A4
Tamames E 149 B3
Tamarit de Mar
E. 147 C2
Tamarite de Litera
E. 145 C4
Tamariu E. 147 C4
Tamási H. 112 C2
Tambach-Dietharz
D. 82 B2
Tameza E 141 A4
Tammisaari FIN . 8 B3
Tampere FIN 8 B3
Tamsweg A . . . 109 B4
Tamurejo E . . . 156 B3
Tamworth UK . . 40 C2
Tana bru N . . . 193 B12
Tañabueyes E . 143 B3
Tanakajd H 111 B3
Tananger N 52 B1
Tananulla I. . . . 178 B3
Tancarville F. . . . 89 A4
Tandsjöborg
S. 199 D11
Tånga S. 61 C2
Tangelic H 112 C2
Tangen N 48 B3
Tangerhütte D. . 73 B4
Tangermünde
D. 73 B4
Tanhua FIN. . . 197 B10
Taninges F 118 A3
Tankavaara
FIN. 197 A10
Tann D. 82 B2
Tanna D. 83 B3
Tannadice UK . . 35 B5
Tännåker S 60 C3
Tännäs S 199 C9
Tannay
Ardennes F . . . 91 B4
Nièvre F 104 B2
Tannenbergsthal
D. 83 B4

Tännesberg D...95 B4
Tannheim A.... 108 B1
Tannila FIN.... 197 D0
Tanowo PL 74 A3
Tanum S 54 B2
Tanumshede
  S..............54 B2
Tanus F 130 A1
Tanvald CZ.....84 B3
Taormina I 177 B4
Tapa EST 8 C5
Tapfheim D 94 C2
Tapia de Casariego
  E.............. 141 A4
Tapio F 146 A2
Tápióbicske
  H............. 112 B3
Tápiógyörgye
  H............. 113 B3
Tápióság H ... 112 B3
Tápiószecsö
  H............. 112 B3
Tápiószele H... 113 B3
Tápiószentmárton
  H............. 112 B3
Tapolca H 111 C4
Tapolcafö H.... 111 B4
Tar HR....... 122 B2
Tarabo S 60 B2
Taradell E 147 C3
Taraklı TR 187 B5
Taramundi E... 141 A3
Tarancón E... 151 B4
Táranto I...... 173 B3
Tarare F...... 117 B4
Tarascon F 131 B3
Tarascon-sur-
  Ariège F...... 146 B2
Tarashcha UA .. 13 D9
Tarazona E..... 144 C2
Tarazona de la
  Mancha E 158 B2
Tarbena E..... 159 C3
Tarbert
  IRL 29 B2
  UK 34 C2
Tarbes F....... 145 A4
Tarbet UK......34 B3
Tarbolton UK ...36 A2
Tarcento I..... 122 A2
Tarčin BIH..... 139 B4
Tarczyn PL 77 C5
Tardajos E 143 B3
Tardelcuende
  E............. 151 A5
Tardets-Sorholus
  F............. 144 A3
Tardienta E ... 145 C3
Tärendö S.... 196 B5
Targon F 128 B2
Targovishte
  BG 17 D7
Târgoviște RO ..17 C6
Târgu-Jiu RO...17 C5
Târgu Mureş
  RO 17 B6
Târgu Ocna RO..17 B7
Târgu Secuiesc
  RO 17 C7
Tarifa E...... 162 B2
Tariquejas E... 161 B2
Tarján H...... 112 B2
Tárkany H 112 B2
Tarland UK.... 33 D4
Tarłów PL......87 A5
Tarm DK 59 C1
Tarmstedt D ...72 A2
Tärnaby S....195 E6
Tarnalelesz H . 113 A4
Tarnaörs H..... 113 B4
Târnăveni RO ...17 B6
Tårnet N 193 C14
Tarnobrzeg PL ..87 B5
Tarnos F 128 C1
Tarnów
  Lubuskie PL...75 B3
  Małopolskie
  PL............87 B4
Tarnowo Podgórne
  PL............75 B5
Tarnowskie Góry
  PL............86 B2
Tärnsjö S.......51 B3
Tårnvik N ... 194 C6
Tarouca P 148 A2
Tarp D 64 B2
Tarquínia I 168 A1
Tarquínia Lido
  I............. 168 A1
Tarragona E... 147 C2
Târrajaur S... 196 C2
Tàrrega E 147 C2
Tarrenz A 108 B1

Tårs
  Nordjyllands
  DK 58 A3
  Storstrøms DK ..65 B4
Tarsia I 174 B2
Tarsus TR 23 C8
Tartas F 128 C2
Tartu EST........ 8 C5
Tarves UK 33 D4
Tarvísio I..... 109 C4
Taşağıl TR..... 189 C6
Täsch CH..... 119 A4
Tasov CZ......97 B4
Tasovčići BIH.. 139 B3
Tașucuo TR.....23 C7
Tát H......... 112 B2
Tata H........ 112 B2
Tatabánya H .. 112 B2
Tataháza H.... 126 A1
Tatarbunary
  UA 17 C8
Tatárszentgyörgy
  H............. 112 B3
Tatranská-Lomnica
  SK............99 B4
Tau N 52 A1
Tauberbischofsheim
  D 94 B1
Taucha D........83 A4
Taufkirchen D...95 C4
Taufkirchen an der
  Pram A........96 C1
Taulé F........ 100 A2
Taulignan F ... 131 A3
Taulov DK......59 C2
Taunton UK 43 A3
Taunusstein D ..81 B4
Tauragė LT 12 A5
Taurianova I .. 175 C2
Taurisano I.... 173 C4
Tauste E....... 144 C2
Tauves F 116 B2
Tavankut SRB . 126 A1
Tavannes CH.. 106 B2
Tavarnelle val di
  Pesa I 135 B4
Tavas TR 188 B4
Tavaux F 105 B4
Tävelsås S 62 B2
Taverna I..... 175 B2
Taverne CH... 120 A1
Tavernelle I... 135 B5
Tavernes de la
  Valldigna E .. 159 B3
Tavérnola
  Bergamasca
  I............. 120 B3
Taverny F 90 B2
Tavescan E.... 146 B2
Taviano I..... 173 C4
Tavira P...... 160 B2
Tavistock UK....42 B2
Tavşanlı TR.... 187 C4
Tayinloan UK ...34 C2
Taynuilt UK 34 B2
Tayport UK..... 35 B5
Tázlár H....... 112 C3
Tazones E..... 142 A1
Tczew PL......69 A3
Tczów PL......87 A5
Teangue UK....31 B3
Teano I....... 170 B2
Teba E 162 B3
Tebay UK 37 B4
Techendorf A. 109 C4
Tecklenburg D ..71 B4
Tecko-matorp
  S 61 D3
Tecuci RO......17 C7
Tefenni TR ... 189 B4
Tegelsmora S ...51 B4
Tegernsee D .. 108 B2
Teggiano I.... 172 B1
Tegoleto I..... 135 B4
Teichel D........82 B3
Teignmouth UK 43 B3
Teillay F....... 101 B4
Teillet F....... 130 B1
Teisendorf D.. 109 B3
Teistungen D ...82 A2
Teixeiro E.... 140 A2
Tejada de Tiétar
  E............. 150 B2
Tejado E 152 A1
Tejares E...... 150 B2
Tejn DK........67 A3
Teke TR 187 A4
Tekirdağ TR... 186 B2
Tekovské-Lužany
  SK........... 112 A2
Telavåg N.......46 B1
Telč CZ........97 B3

Telese Terme I 170 B2
Telford UK 38 B4
Telfs A 108 B2
Telgárt SK,.....99 C4
Telgte D 71 C4
Tellingstedt D ..64 B2
Telšiai LT........ 8 E3
Telti I 178 B3
Teltow D........74 B2
Tembleque E.. 157 A4
Temelín CZ.....96 B2
Temerin SRB .. 126 B1
Temiño E..... 143 B3
Témpio Pausánia
  I............. 178 B2
Templederry
  IRL 28 B3
Templemore
  IRL 28 B4
Temple Sowerby
  UK 37 B4
Templin D 74 A2
Temse B........79 A4
Tenay F 118 B2
Ten Boer NL....71 A3
Tenbury Wells
  UK 39 B4
Tenby UK 39 C2
Tence F 117 B4
Tende F 133 A3
Tenhult S 62 A2
Tenja H....... 125 B4
Tenneville B ...92 A1
Tennevoll N... 194 B8
Tensta S........51 B4
Tenterden UK...45 B4
Teo E......... 140 B2
Teora I........ 172 B1
Tepasto FIN... 196 B7
Tepelenë AL .. 182 C2
Teplá CZ........95 B4
Teplice CZ......84 B1
Teplička nad
  Váhom SK......98 B2
Tepsa FIN ... 197 B8
Tera E........ 143 C4
Téramo I 169 A3
Ter Apel NL 71 B4
Terborg NL 71 C3
Terchová SK ...99 B3
Terebovlya UA. 13 D6
Teremia Mare
  RO 126 B2
Terena P 155 C3
Teresa de Cofrentes
  E............. 159 B2
Terešov CZ.....96 B1
Terezín CZ 84 B2
Terezino Polje
  HR 124 B3
Tergnier F......90 B3
Teriberka RUS ..3 B14
Terlizzi I 171 B4
Termas de
  Monfortinho
  P............. 155 A4
Terme di Súio
  I............. 169 B3
Terme di Valdieri
  I............. 133 A3
Termens E ... 145 C4
Termes F...... 116 C3
Términi Imerese
  I............. 176 B2
Terminillo I ... 169 A2
Térmoli I...... 170 B3
Termonfeckin
  IRL 27 C4
Ternberg A ... 110 B1
Terndrup DK....58 B3
Terneuzen NL...79 A3
Terni I........ 168 A2
Ternitz A...... 111 B3
Ternopil UA... 13 D6
Terpni GR.... 183 C5
Terracina I.... 169 B3
Terråk N 195 E3
Terralba I..... 179 C2
Terranova di
  Pollino I...... 174 B2
Terranova di Sibari
  I............. 174 B2
Terras do Bouro
  P............. 148 A1
Terrasini I.... 176 A2
Terrassa E..... 147 C3
Terrasson-
  Lavilledieu F. 129 A4
Terrazos E 143 B3
Terriente E... 152 B2
Terrugem P ... 155 C3
Tertenía I 179 C3
Teruel E...... 152 B2

Tervola FIN ... 196 C7
Tervuren B......79 B4
Terzaga E 152 B2
Tešani BIH ,,,, 125 C3
Tesáske-Mlyňany
  SK............98 C2
Teslić BIH 125 C3
Tessin D 66 B1
Tessy-sur-Vire
  F.............88 B2
Tét H......... 111 B4
Tetbury UK 43 A4
Teterchen F.....92 B2
Teterow D 65 C5
Teteven BG ... 17 D6
Tetiyev UA 13 D8
Tetovo NMK .. 182 A2
Tettau D........82 B3
Tettnang D ... 107 B4
Teublitz D 95 B4
Teuchern D 83 A4
Teulada
  E............. 159 C4
  I............. 179 D2
Teupitz D 74 B2
Teurajärvi S... 196 C5
Teutschenthal
  D 83 A3
Tevel H 112 C2
Teviothead UK..36 A4
Tewkesbury UK 39 C4
Thale D 82 A3
Thalfang D......92 B2
Thalgau A..... 109 B4
Thalkirch CH ...107 C4
Thalmässing D..95 B3
Thalwil CH ... 107 B3
Thame UK......44 B3
Thann F...... 106 B2
Thannhausen
  D 94 C2
Thaon-les-Vosges
  F............. 105 A5
Tharandt D 83 B5
Tharsis E 161 B2
Thasos GR ... 183 C6
Thatcham UK ..44 B2
Thaxted UK 45 B4
Thayngen CH . 107 B3
Theale UK......44 B2
The Barony UK ..33 B3
Thebes = Thiva
  GR 185 A4
Theding-hausen
  D 72 B2
Theessen D 73 B5
The Hague = 's-
  Gravenhage
  NL 70 B1
Themar D........82 B2
The Mumbles
  UK 39 C3
Thénezay F ... 102 C1
Thenon F 129 A4
Therouanne F...78 B2
Thessaloniki =
  Salonica GR .. 182 C4
Thetford UK....45 A4
Theux B........80 B1
Thézar-les-
  Corbières F .. 146 A3
Thèze F 145 A3
Thiberville F ...89 A4
Thibie F........91 C4
Thiéblemont-
  Farémont F ...91 C4
Thiendorf D....84 A1
Thiene I...... 121 B4
Thierrens CH.. 106 C1
Thiers F...... 117 B3
Thiesi I....... 178 B2
Thiessow D 66 B2
Thiezac F 116 B2
Thionville F....92 B2
Thira GR 185 C6
Thiron-Gardais
  F.............89 B4
Thirsk UK......37 B5
Thisted DK.....58 B1
Thiva = Thebes
  GR 185 A4
Thivars F......90 C1
Thiviers F ... 115 C4
Thizy F....... 117 A4
Tholen NL......79 A4
Tholey D........92 B3
Thomas Street
  IRL 28 A3
Thomastown
  IRL 30 B1
Thônes F..... 118 B3

Thonnance-les-
  Joinville F......91 C5
Thonon les Bains
  F............. 118 A3
Thorame-Basse
  F............. 132 A2
Thorame-Haute
  F............. 132 A2
Thorens-Glières
  F............. 118 A3
Thorigny-sur-
  Oreuse F......91 C3
Thörl A........ 110 B2
Þorlákshöfn
  IS 190 D4
Thornaby on Tees
  UK 37 B5
Thornbury UK...43 A4
Thorne UK 40 B3
Thorney UK.....41 C3
Thornhill
  Dumfries &
  Galloway UK.. 36 A3
  Stirling UK......35 B3
Thorning DK....59 B2
Thornthwaite
  UK 36 B3
Thornton-le-Dale
  UK 40 A3
Þórshöfn IS .. 191 A10
Thouarcé F.... 102 B1
Thouars F..... 102 C1
Thrapston UK...44 A3
Threlkeld UK...36 B3
Thrumster UK...32 C3
Thueyts F 117 C4
Thuin B 79 B4
Thumau D 95 A3
Thun CH 106 C2
Thuret F 116 B3
Thurey F...... 105 C4
Thüringen A .. 107 B4
Thurins F 117 B4
Thürkow D......65 C5
Thurles IRL.....29 B4
Thurmaston UK 40 C2
Thurø By DK ...65 A3
Thursby UK....36 B3
Thurso UK 32 C3
Thury-Harcourt
  F.............89 B3
Thusis CH..... 107 C4
Thyborøn DK...58 B1
Þykkvibær IS.. 190 D5
Thyregod DK... 59 C2
Tibi E 159 C3
Tibro S........55 B5
Tidaholm S.....55 B4
Tidan S........55 B5
Tidersrum S.....62 A3
Tiedra E 150 A2
Tiefenbach D ...95 B4
Tiefencastel
  CH 107 C4
Tiefenort D 82 B2
Tiefensee D 74 B2
Tiel NL 79 A5
Tielmes E 151 B4
Tielt B 78 A3
Tienen B 79 B4
Tiengen D 106 B3
Tiercé F...... 102 B1
Tierga E 152 A2
Tiermas E 144 B2
Tierp S........51 B4
Tierrantona E . 145 B4
Tighina MD....17 B8
Tighnabruaich
  UK 34 C2
Tignes F...... 119 B3
Tigy F 103 B4
Tihany H..... 112 C1
Tijnje NL.......70 A2
Tijola E 164 B2
Tikhvin RUS 9 C8
Tilburg NL......79 A5
Til Châtel F ... 105 B4
Tilh F 128 C2
Tillberga S 56 A2
Tille F 90 B2
Tillicoultry UK...35 B4
Tilloy Bellay F ...91 B4
Tilly F....... 115 B5
Tilly-sur-Seulles
  F.............88 A3
Tim DK 59 B1
Timau I....... 109 C4
Timbaki GR .. 185 D5
Timi CY...... 181 B1
Timişoara RO ...16 C4
Timmele S 60 B3

Timmendorfer
  Strand D 65 C3
Timmernabben
  S.............62 B4
Timmersdala S ..55 B4
Timoleague IRL .29 C3
Timolin IRL.....30 B2
Timrå S...... 200 D3
Timsfors S......61 C3
Timsgearraidh
  UK 31 A1
Tinajas E 152 B1
Tinalhas P.... 155 B3
Tinchebray F...88 B3
Tincques F......78 B2
Tineo E 141 A4
Tinglev DK.....64 B2
Tingsryd S 63 B2
Tingstäde S 57 C4
Tinlot B 79 B5
Tinnoset N 53 A5
Tinos GR 185 B6
Tintagel UK 42 B2
Tinténiac F ... 101 A4
Tintern UK 39 C4
Tintigny B.......92 B1
Tione di Trento
  I............. 121 A3
Tipperary IRL...29 B3
Tiptree UK 45 B4
Tirana = Tiranë
  AL 182 B1
Tiranë = Tirana
  AL 182 B1
Tirano I 120 A3
Tiraspol MD....17 B8
Tire TR 188 A2
Tires I........ 108 C2
Tiriez E....... 158 C1
Tirig E....... 153 B4
Tiriolo I 175 C2
Tirnavos GR... 182 D4
Tirrénia I..... 134 B3
Tirschenreuth
  D 95 B4
Tirstrup DK.....59 B3
Tirteafuera E.. 157 B3
Tisno HR 137 B4
Tišnov CZ......97 B4
Tisovec SK......99 C3
Tisselskog S....54 B3
Tistedal N......54 A2
Tistrup DK......59 C1
Tisvildeleje DK..61 C2
Tiszaalpár H .. 113 C3
Tiszabö H 113 B4
Tiszacsége H .. 113 B5
Tiszadorogma
  H............. 113 B4
Tiszaföldvár
  H............. 113 C4
Tiszafüred H .. 113 B4
Tiszajenö H ... 113 B4
Tiszakécske H. 113 C4
Tiszakeszi H... 113 B4
Tiszakürt H ... 113 C4
Tiszalök H 113 A5
Tiszalúc H 113 A5
Tiszanána H... 113 B4
Tiszaörs H 113 B4
Tiszaroff H 113 B4
Tiszasüly H.... 113 B4
Tiszasziget H.. 126 A2
Tiszaszőlős H . 113 B4
Tiszaújváros
  H............. 113 B5
Tiszavasvári
  H............. 113 B5
Titaguas E.... 159 B2
Titel SRB..... 126 B2
Titisee-Neustadt
  D 106 B3
Tito I........ 172 B1
Titran N 198 B5
Tittling D 96 C1
Tittmoning D . 109 A3
Titz D.........80 A2
Tiurajärvi FIN. 196 B7
Tived S........55 B5
Tiverton UK....43 B3
Tivisa E 153 A4
Tívoli I........ 168 B2
Tizsadob H.... 113 A5
Tjällmo S......56 B1
Tjåmotis S ... 195 D9
Tjæreborg DK...59 C1
Tjautjas S ... 196 B3
Tjøme N........54 A1
Tjong N....... 195 D4
Tjonnefoss N ...53 B4
Tjörn IS 190 B5
Tjörnarp S 61 D3

Tiøtta N,,,,,,,,195 E3
Tkon HR..... 137 B4
Tleń PL.........68 B3
Tlmače SK......98 C2
Tłuchowo PL....77 B4
Tlumačov CZ...98 B1
Tóalmas H 112 B3
Toano I....... 134 A3
Toba D.........82 A2
Tobarra E 158 C2
Tobermore UK. .27 B4
Tobermory UK ..34 B1
Toberonochy
  UK 34 B2
Tobha Mor UK .31 B1
Tobo S........51 B4
Tocane-St Apre
  F............. 129 A3
Tocha P 148 B1
Tocina E 162 A2
Töcksfors S 54 A2
Tocón E 163 A4
Todal N 198 C5
Todi I 136 C1
Todmorden UK .40 B1
Todorici BIH... 138 A3
Todtmoos D .. 106 B3
Todtnau D ... 106 B3
Toén E 140 B3
Tofta
  Gotland S..... 57 C4
  Skaraborg S...55 B4
Toftbyn S......50 B2
Tofte N 54 A1
Töftedal S......54 B2
Tofterup DK....59 C1
Toftlund DK....59 C2
Tófü H 125 A4
Tohmo FIN... 197 C10
Tokaj H....... 113 A5
Tokarnia PL....87 B4
Tokary PL......76 C3
Tokod H 112 B2
Tököl H 112 B2
Tolastadh bho
  Thuath UK ...31 A2
Toledo E 151 C3
Tolentino I.... 136 B2
Tolfa I........ 168 A1
Tolg S.........62 A2
Tolga N....... 199 C8
Tolkmicko PL ...69 A4
Tollarp S 61 D3
Tollered S......60 B2
Tølløse DK.... 61 D1
Tolmachevo
  RUS 9 C6
Tolmezzo I.... 122 A2
Tolmin SLO ... 122 A2
Tolna H...... 112 C2
Tolnanémedi
  H............. 112 C2
Tolob UK.......33 B5
Tolosa
  E............. 144 A1
  P............. 155 B3
Tolox E 162 B3
Tolpuddle UK...43 B4
Tolva
  E............. 145 B4
  FIN......... 197 C11
Tolve I....... 172 B2
Tomar P....... 154 B2
Tomaševac
  SRB 126 B2
Tomašica BIH . 124 C2
Tomášikovo
  SK........... 111 A4
Tomašouka BY..13 C5
Tomášovce SK ..99 C3
Tomaszów
  Mazowiecki
  PL............87 A4
Tomatin UK.... 32 D3
Tombeboeuf
  F............. 129 B3
Tomdoun UK... 32 D1
Tomelilla S......66 A2
Tomellosa E... 151 B5
Tomelloso E .. 157 A4
Tomiño E 140 C2
Tomintoul UK.. 32 D3
Tomislavgrad
  BIH 138 B3
Tomisław PL....84 A3
Tomisławice
  PL............76 B3
Tomnavoulin
  UK 32 D3
Tompa H...... 126 A1

Tompaládony
  H............111 B3
Tomra N 198 C3
Tomter N 54 A1
Tona E 147 C3
Tonara I......179 B3
Tonbridge UK...45 B4
Tondela P......148 B1
Tønder DK.....64 B1
Tongeren B.....79 B5
Tongue UK......32 C2
Tönisvorst D....80 A2
Tønjum N......47 A4
Tonkopuro
  FIN..........197 C11
Tonnay-Boutonne
  F.............114 C3
Tonnay-Charente
  F.............114 C3
Tonneins F....129 B3
Tonnerre F....104 B2
Tonnes N 195 D4
Tönning D 64 B1
Tonsåsen N 47 B6
Tønsberg N 54 A1
Tonstad N 52 B2
Toomyvara IRL..28 B3
Toormore IRL...29 C2
Topares E 164 B2
Topas E 150 A2
Toplița RO 17 B6
Topola SRB....127 C2
Topolčani
  NMK.........182 B3
Topol'čany SK...98 C2
Topol'čianky
  SK...........98 C2
Topolje HR....124 B2
Topólka PL....76 B3
Topol'niky SK.111 B4
Topolováțu Mare
  RO 126 B3
Toponár H....125 A3
Toporów PL...75 B4
Topsham UK....43 B3
Topusko HR...124 B1
Toques E......140 B3
Torà E.........147 C2
Toral de los
  Guzmanes E .142 B1
Toral de los Vados
  E.............141 B4
Torbalı TR.....188 A2
Torbjörntorp S..55 B4
Torbole I.....121 B3
Torchiarolo I..173 B4
Torcross UK....43 B3
Torcy-le-Petit
  F.............89 A5
Torda SRB.....126 B2
Tørdal N 53 A4
Tordehumos
  E............142 C1
Tordera E......147 C3
Tordesillas E...150 A2
Tordesilos E...152 B2
Töre S.......196 D5
Töreboda S....55 B5
Toreby DK......65 B4
Torekov S.....61 C2
Torella dei
  Lombardi I...170 C3
Torellò E.....147 B3
Toreno E......141 B4
Torfou F......114 A2
Torgau D.......83 A5
Torgelow D....74 A3
Torgueda P...148 A2
Torhamn S.....63 B3
Torhop N 193 B11
Torhout B......78 A3
Torigni-sur-Vire
  F............88 A3
Torija E 151 B4
Toril E.......152 B2
Torino = Turin
  I............119 B4
Toritto I......171 C4
Torkovichi RUS..9 C7
Torla E 145 B3
Tormac RO....126 B3
Törmänen
  FIN..........193 D11
Tormestorp S...61 C3
Tórmini I.....121 B3
Tornada P.....154 B1
Tornal'a SK.....99 C4
Tornavacas E .150 B2
Tornby DK.....58 A2
Tornesch D 72 A2

Torness UK.....32 D2
Torniella I.....135 B4
Tornimparte I.169 A3
Tornio FIN 196 D7
Tornjoš SRB...126 B1
Tornos E......152 B2
Toro E........150 A2
Törökszentmiklós
  H.............113 B4
Toropets RUS....9 D7
Torpa S.......61 C3
Torpè I.......178 B3
Torphins UK...33 D4
Torpo N.......47 B5
Torpoint UK....42 B2
Torpsbruk S...62 A2
Torquay UK.....43 B3
Torquemada
  E............142 B2
Torralba de Burgo
  E............151 A5
Torralba de
  Calatrava E .157 A4
Torrão P.....154 C2
Torre Annunziata
  I............170 C2
Torreblacos E.143 C4
Torreblanca E.153 B4
Torreblascopedro
  E............157 B4
Torrecaballeros
  E............151 A3
Torrecampo E.156 B3
Torre Canne I .173 B3
Torre Cardela
  E............163 A4
Torrecilla E ...152 B1
Torrecilla de la Jara
  E............156 A3
Torrecilla de la
  Orden E......150 A2
Torrecilla del Pinar
  E............151 A3
Torrecilla en
  Cameros E ...143 B4
Torrecillas de la
  Tiesa E 156 A2
Torre das Vargens
  P............154 B3
Torre de Coelheiros
  P............154 C3
Torre de Dom
  Chama P 149 A2
Torre de Juan Abad
  E............157 B4
Torre del Bierzo
  E............141 B4
Torre del Burgo
  E............151 B4
Torre del Campo
  E............163 A4
Torre del Greco
  I............170 C2
Torre del Lago
  Puccini I......134 B3
Torre dell'Orso
  I............173 B4
Torre del Mar
  E............163 B3
Torredembarra
  E............147 C2
Torre de Miguel
  Sesmero E ...155 C4
Torre de Moncorvo
  P............149 A2
Torre de Santa
  Maria E 156 A1
Torredonjimeno
  E............163 A4
Torre do Terranho
  P............148 B2
Torre Faro I ...177 A4
Torregrosa E..147 C1
Torreira P....148 B1
Torrejoncillo
  E............155 B4
Torrejón de Ardoz
  E............151 B4
Torrejón de la
  Calzada E 151 B4
Torrejón del Rey
  E............151 B4
Torrejon el Rubio
  E............156 A1
Torrelaguna E.151 B4
Torrelapaja E.152 A2
Torre la Ribera
  E............145 B4
Torrelavega E.142 A2
Torrelobatón
  E............150 A2
Torrelodones
  E............151 B4

Torre los Negros
  E............152 B2
Torremaggiore
  I............171 B3
Torremanzanas
  E............159 C3
Torremayor E.155 C4
Torremezzo di
  Falconara I...174 B2
Torremocha E.156 A1
Torremolinos
  E............163 B3
Torrenieri I....135 B4
Torrenostra E.153 B4
Torrenova I...168 B2
Torrent E......159 B3
Torrente de Cinca
  E............153 A4
Torrenueva
  Ciudad Real
  E............157 B4
  Granada E....163 B4
Torreorgaz E.155 B4
Torre Orsáia I.172 B1
Torre-Pacheco
  E............165 B4
Torre Péllice I.119 C4
Torreperogil E 157 B4
Torres E......163 A4
Torresandino
  E............143 C3
Torre Santa
  Susanna I....173 B3
Torres-Cabrera
  E............163 A3
Torres de la
  Alameda E ...151 B4
Torres Novas
  P............154 B2
Torres Vedras
  P............154 B1
Torrevieja E...165 B4
Torricella I....173 B3
Torri del Benaco
  I............121 B3
Torridon UK....31 B3
Torriglia I....134 A2
Torrijos E.....151 C3
Tørring DK.....59 C2
Torrita di Siena
  I............135 B4
Torroal P......154 C2
Torroella de
  Montgrì E....147 B4
Torrox E......163 B4
Torrskog S....54 A3
Torsåker S....50 B3
Torsang S....50 B2
Torsås S......63 B4
Torsby S......49 B4
Torsetra N....48 B2
Torshälla S....56 A2
Tórshavn FO....4 A3
Torslanda S....60 B1
Torsminde DK.59 B1
Torsnes N.....46 B3
Törtel H......113 B3
Tórtoles E....150 B2
Tórtoles de
  Esgueva E...142 C2
Tortol i I.....179 C3
Tortona I.....120 C1
Tórtora I.....174 B1
Tortoreto Lido
  I............136 C2
Tortorici I....177 A3
Tortosa E.....153 B4
Tortosendo P.148 B2
Tortuera E....152 B2
Tortuero E....151 B4
Toruń PL......76 A3
Torup S......60 C3
Tor Vaiánica I.168 B2
Torver UK.....36 B3
Tørvikbygde N..46 B3
Torviscón E...163 B4
Torzhok RUS....9 D9
Torzym PL.....75 B4
Tosbotn N....195 E3
Toscolano-
  Maderno I...121 B3
Tosno RUS.....9 C7
Tossa de Mar
  E............147 C3
Tossåsen S...199 C10
Tosse F......128 C1
Tössë S.......54 B3
Tossicia I.....169 A3
Tostedt D.....72 A2
Tószeg H......113 B4
Toszek PL......86 B2
Totana E......165 B3

Totebo S.......62 A4
Tôtes F........89 A5
Tótkomlós H..113 C4
Totland N....198 D2
Tøtlandsvik N...52 A2
Totnes UK......43 B3
Tótszerdahely
  H.............124 A2
Tøttdal N 199 A8
Totton UK......44 C2
Touça P......149 A2
Toucy F......104 B2
Toul F........92 C1
Toulon F......132 B1
Toulon-sur-Allier
  F............104 C2
Toulon-sur-Arroux
  F............104 C2
Toulouse F...129 C4
Tourcoing F....78 B3
Tour de la Parata
  F............180 B1
Tourlaville F...88 A2
Tournai B......78 B3
Tournan-en-Brie
  F............90 C2
Tournay F....145 A4
Tournon-d'Agenais
  F............129 B3
Tournon-St Martin
  F............115 B4
Tournon-sur-
  Rhône F......117 B4
Tournus F....105 C3
Touro
  E............140 B2
  P............148 B2
Tourouvre F...89 B4
Tourriers F...115 C4
Tours F......102 B2
Tourteron F...91 B4
Tourves F....132 B1
Toury F......103 A3
Touvedo P....148 A1
Touvois F....114 B2
Toužim CZ.....83 B4
Tovačov CZ....98 B1
Tovariševo
  SRB.........126 B1
Tovarnik HR..125 B5
Tovdal N......53 B4
Towcester UK...44 A3
Town Yetholm
  UK...........35 C5
Tråastølen N....47 B4
Trabada E....141 A3
Trabadelo E..141 B4
Trabanca E...149 A3
Trabazos E...149 A3
Traben-Trarbach
  D............92 B3
Trabia I......176 B2
Tradate I.....120 B1
Trafaria P....154 C1
Tragacete E...152 B2
Tragwein A....96 C2
Traiguera E...153 B4
Trainel F......91 C3
Traisen A.....110 A2
Traismauer A..97 C3
Traitsching D...95 B4
Trákhonas CY.181 A2
Tralee IRL......29 B2
Tramacastilla de
  Tena E 145 B3
Tramagal P...154 B2
Tramariglio I..178 B2
Tramatza I...179 B2
Tramelan CH..106 B2
Tramonti di Sopra
  I............122 A1
Tramore IRL....30 B1
Trampot F.....92 C1
Trana I......119 B4
Tranås S......55 B5
Trancoso P...148 B2
Tranebjerg DK.59 C3
Traneby N.....54 A1
Tranemo S....60 B3
Tranent UK.....35 C5
Tranevåg N....52 B2
Trängslet S....49 A5
Tranhult S....60 B3
Trani I.......171 B4
Trans-en-Provence
  F............132 B2
Tranum DK....58 A2
Tranvik S......57 A4
Trápani I......176 A1

Trappes F......90 C2
Traryd S......61 C3
Trasacco I....169 B3
Trasierra E....156 B1
Träslövsläge S..60 B2
Trasmiras E...140 B3
Traspinedo E.150 A3
Trate SLO....110 C2
Trauchgau D..108 B1
Traun A......110 A1
Traunreut D...109 B3
Traunstein D..109 B3
Traunwalchen
  D............109 B3
Travemünde D.65 C3
Traversétolo I.120 C3
Travnik
  BIH.........139 A3
  SLO.........123 B3
Travo
  I............180 B2
  I............120 C2
Trawsfynydd
  UK...........38 B3
Trbovlje SLO..123 A4
Trbušani SRB..127 D2
Treban F......116 A3
Trebatsch D....74 B3
Trebbin D.....74 B2
Trebechovice pod
  Orebem CZ...85 B3
Trebel D......73 B4
Třebenice CZ...84 B1
Trébeurden F.100 A2
Třebíč CZ......97 B3
Trebisacce I...174 B2
Trebitz D......83 A4
Trebnje SLO...123 B4
Třeboň CZ.....96 B2
Trebovice CZ...97 B4
Trebsen D.....83 A4
Trebujena E...161 C3
Trecastagni I..177 B4
Trecate I.....120 B1
Trecenta I....121 B4
Tredegar UK....39 C3
Tredózio I....135 A4
Treffen A.....109 C4
Treffort F.....118 A2
Treffurt D......82 A2
Trefnant UK....38 A3
Tregaron UK...39 B3
Trégastel-Plage
  F............100 A2
Tregnago I....121 B4
Tregony UK....42 B2
Tréguier F....100 A2
Trégunc F....100 B2
Treharris UK...39 C3
Trehörningsjö
  S............200 C4
Tréia I.......136 B2
Treignac F....116 B1
Treignat F....116 A2
Treignes B.....91 A4
Treis-Karden D.80 B3
Trekanten S....63 B4
Trélazé F.....102 B1
Trelleborg S....66 A2
Trélon F......91 A4
Trélou-sur-Marne
  F............91 B3
Tremblay-le-
  Vicomte F.....89 B5
Tremés P....154 B2
Tremezzo I...120 B2
Tremp E......145 B4
Třemošná CZ...96 B1
Tremp E......145 B4
Trenčianska
  Stankovce SK..98 C1
Trenčianska Turná
  SK...........98 C2
Trenčianske Teplá
  SK...........98 C2
Trenčianske
  Teplice SK....98 C2
Trenčín SK.....98 C2
Trendelburg D..81 A5
Trengereid N...46 B2
Trensacq F....128 B2
Trent D.......66 B2
Trento I......121 A4
Treorchy UK...39 C3
Trept F......118 B2
Trepuzzi I....173 B3
Trescore Balneário
  I............120 B2
Tresenda I....120 A3

Tresfjord N ...198 C4
Tresigallo I....121 C4
Tresnjevica
  SRB.........127 D3
Tresnuràghes
  I............178 B2
Trespaderne E 143 B3
Třešt CZ......97 B3
Trestina I.....135 B5
Tretower UK...39 C3
Trets F.......132 B1
Tretten N......48 A2
Treuchtlingen
  D............94 C2
Treuen D......83 B4
Treuenbrietzen
  D............74 B1
Treungen N....53 A4
Trevelez E....163 B4
Trevi I.......136 C1
Treviana E....143 B3
Treviglio I....120 B2
Trevignano
  Romano I....168 A2
Trevi nel Lázio
  I............169 B3
Treviso I......122 B1
Trévoux F....117 B4
Treysa D......81 B5
Trézelles F....117 A3
Trezzo sull'Adda
  I............120 B2
Trhová Kamenice
  CZ...........97 B3
Trhové Sviny
  CZ...........96 C2
Triacastela E..141 B3
Triaize F......114 B2
Trianda GR...188 C3
Triaucourt-en-
  Argonne F 91 C5
Tribanj Krušćica
  HR..........137 A4
Triberg D.....106 A3
Tribsees D......66 B1
Tribuče SLO...123 B4
Tricárico I....172 B2
Tricase I......173 C4
Tricésimo I....122 A2
Trieben A.....110 B1
Triebes D......83 B4
Triepkendorf D.74 A2
Trier D........92 B2
Trieste I......122 B2
Trie-sur-Baïse
  F............145 A4
Triggiano I....173 A2
Triglitz D......73 A5
Trignac F....101 B3
Trigueros E...161 B3
Trigueros del Valle
  E............142 C2
Trikala
  GR..........182 B3
Trikeri GR....183 D5
Trikomo CY...181 A2
Trilj HR......138 B2
Trillo E.......152 B1
Trilport F......90 C2
Trim IRL......30 A2
Trimdon UK...37 B5
Trindade
  Beja P 160 B2
  Bragança P ..149 A2
Trinec CZ......98 B2
Tring UK......44 B3
Trinità d'Agultu
  I............178 B2
Trinitápoli I...171 B4
Trino I.......119 B5
Trinta P......148 B2
Tripoli GR....184 B3
Triponzo I....136 C1
Triptis D......83 B3
Triste E......144 B3
Trittau D......72 A3
Trivento I....170 B2
Trivero I......119 B5
Trivigno I....172 B1
Trn BIH.......124 B2
Trnava
  HR..........125 B4
  SK...........98 C1
Trnovec SK...112 A1
Trnovo BIH...139 B4
Trnovska vas
  SLO.........110 C2
Troarn F......89 A3
Trochtelfingen
  D............94 C1
Trödje S......51 B4
Troense DK....65 A3
Trofa P......148 A1

Trofaiach A ...110 B2
Trofors N 195 E4
Trogir HR.....138 B2
Trøgstad N.....54 A2
Tróia I.......171 B3
Troia P.......154 C2
Troina I......177 B3
Troisdorf D....80 B3
Trois-Ponts B..80 B1
Troisvierges L..92 A2
Trojane SLO...123 A3
Troldhede DK...59 C1
Trollhättan S...54 B3
Trolog BIH...138 B2
Tromello I....120 B1
Tromøy N.....53 B4
Tromsø N 192 C3
Trondheim N .199 B7
Tronget F......116 A3
Trönninge S...61 C2
Trönningeby S..60 B2
Trönö S.......51 A3
Tronzano-
  Vercellese I ..119 B5
Trôo F.......102 B2
Troon UK......36 A2
Tropea I......175 C1
Tropy Sztumskie
  PL............69 B4
Trosa S.......57 B3
Trösken S.....50 B3
Trosly-Breuil F..90 B3
Trossingen D .107 A3
Trostberg D...109 A3
Trouville-sur-Mer
  F............89 A4
Trowbridge UK.43 A4
Troyes F.....104 A3
Trpanj HR....138 B3
Trpinja HR...125 B4
Tršće HR......123 B3
Tršice CZ......98 B1
Trstená SK.....99 B3
Trstenci BIH...125 B3
Trsteno HR...139 C3
Trstice SK....111 A4
Trstin SK......98 C1
Trubia E.......141 A5
Trubjela MNE .139 C4
Truchas E....141 B4
Trujillanos E ..155 C4
Trujillo E.....156 A2
Trumieje PL....69 B4
Trun
  CH...........107 C3
  F............89 A4
Truro UK......42 B1
Trusetal D......82 B2
Truskavets' UA.13 D5
Trustrup DK....59 B3
Trutnov CZ.....85 B3
Tryserum S....56 B2
Trysil N.......49 A4
Tryszczyn PL...76 A2
Trzcianka PL...75 A5
Trzciel PL.....75 B4
Trzcińsko Zdrój
  PL............74 B3
Trzebiatów PL..67 B4
Trzebiel PL....84 A2
Trzebielino PL .68 A2
Trzebień PL....84 A3
Trzebiez PL....74 A3
Trzebinia PL...86 B3
Trzebnica PL...85 A5
Trzebnice PL...85 A4
Trzeciewiec PL.76 B2
Trzemeszno PL .76 B2
Trzemeszno-
  Lubuskie PL....75 B4
Trzetrzewina
  PL............99 B4
Tržič SLO......123 A3
Tsamandas
  GR..........182 D2
Tschagguns A.107 B4
Tschernitz D...84 A2
Tsebrykove UA..17 B9
Tsyelyakhany
  BY............13 B6
Tua P.......148 A2
Tuam IRL......28 A3
Tubbercurry
  IRL...........26 B2
Tubbergen NL .71 B3
Tubilla del Lago
  E............143 C3
Tübingen D....93 C5
Tubize B......79 B4
Tučapy CZ.....96 B2
Tučepi HR....138 B2
Tuchan F.....146 B3
Tüchen D......73 A5

Tuchola PL 76 A2
Tuchomie PL 68 A2
Tuchów PL 99 B5
Tuczno PL 75 A5
Tuddal N 53 A4
Tudela E 144 B2
Tudela de Duero E 150 A3
Tudweiliog UK 38 B2
Tuejar E 159 B2
Tuffé F 102 A2
Tufsingdalen N 199 C8
Tuhaň CZ 84 B2
Tui E 140 B2
Tukhkala RUS 197 D13
Tukums LV 8 D3
Tula I 178 B2
Tulcea RO 17 C8
Tul'chyn UA 13 D8
Tulette F 131 A3
Tuliszków PL 76 B3
Tulla IRL 28 B3
Tullamore IRL 30 A1
Tulle F 116 B1
Tullins F 118 B2
Tulln A 97 C4
Tullow IRL 30 B2
Tułowice PL 85 B5
Tulppio FIN 197 B12
Tulsk IRL 28 A3
Tumba S 57 A3
Tummel Bridge UK 35 B3
Tun S 55 B3
Tuna
Kalmar S 62 A4
Uppsala S 51 B5
Tuna Hästberg S 50 B2
Tunçbilek TR 187 C4
Tunes P 160 B1
Tungelsta S 57 A4
Tunnerstad S 55 B5
Tunnhovd N 47 B5
Tunstall UK 45 A5
Tuohikotti FIN 8 B5
Tuoro sul Trasimeno I 135 B5
Tupadły PL 76 B3
Tupanari BIH 139 A4
Tupik RUS 9 E8
Tuplice PL 84 A2
Tura H 112 B3
Turanj HR 137 B4
Turany SK 99 B3
Turbe BIH 139 A3
Turbenthal CH 107 B3
Turcia E 141 B5
Turčianske Teplice SK 98 C2
Turcifal P 154 B1
Turckheim F 106 A2
Turda RO 17 B5
Turégano E 151 A4
Turek PL 76 B3
Turgutlu TR 188 A2
Turgutreis TR 188 B2
Turi I 173 B3
Turin = Torino I 119 B4
Turis E 159 B3
Türje H 111 C4
Turka UA 12 D5
Túrkeve H 113 B4
Türkheim D 108 A1
Türkmenli TR 186 C1
Turku FIN 8 B3
Turleque E 157 A4
Turňa nad Bodvou SK 99 C4
Turnberry UK 36 A2
Turnhout B 79 A4
Türnitz A 110 B2
Turnov CZ 84 B3
Turnu RO 126 A3
Turnu Măgurele RO 17 D6
Turón E 164 C1
Turoszów PL 84 B2
Turowo PL 77 A5
Turquel P 154 B1
Turri I 179 C2
Turries F 132 A2
Turriff UK 33 D4
Tursi I 174 A2
Turtmann CH 119 A4
Turtola FIN 196 C6
Turze PL 86 A1
Turzovka SK 98 B2
Tusa I 177 B3
Tuscània I 168 A1
Tuse DK 61 D1
Tušilovic HR 123 B4
Tuszyn PL 86 A3
Tutow D 66 C2
Tutrakan BG 17 C7
Tuttlingen D 107 B3
Tutzing D 108 B2
Tuzla
BIH 125 C4
TR 23 C8
Tuzlukçu TR 189 A6
Tvååker S 60 B2
Tvärålund S 200 B5
Tvärskog S 63 B4
Tvedestrand N 53 B4
Tveit
Hordaland N 47 B4
Rogaland N 52 A2
Tver RUS 9 D9
Tverrelvmo N 192 D3
Tversted DK 58 A3
Tving S 63 B3
Tvrdošin SK 99 B3
Tvrdošovce SK 112 A2
Twardogóra PL 85 A5
Twatt UK 33 B3
Twello NL 70 B3
Twimberg A 110 C1
Twist D 71 B4
Twistringen D 72 B1
Tworóg PL 86 B2
Twyford
Hampshire UK 44 B2
Wokingham UK 44 B3
Tyachiv UA 17 A5
Tychówka PL 67 C5
Tychowo PL 67 C5
Tychy PL 86 B2
Tydal N 199 B8
Týec nad Labem CZ 97 A3
Tyfors S 49 B6
Tygelsjö S 61 D2
Tylldal N 199 C7
Tylstrup DK 58 A2
Tymbark PL 99 B4
Tymowa PL 99 B4
Tyndrum UK 34 B3
Týnec nad Sázavou CZ 96 B2
Tynemouth UK 37 A5
Tyngsjö S 49 B5
Týništěnad Orlicí CZ 85 B4
Týn nad Vltavou CZ 96 B2
Tynset N 199 C7
Tyresö S 57 A4
Tyringe S 61 C3
Tyrislöt S 56 B2
Tyristrand N 48 B2
Tyrrellspass IRL 30 A1
Tysnes N 46 B2
Tysse N 46 B2
Tyssebotn N 46 B2
Tyssedal N 46 B3
Tystberga S 56 B3
Tysvær N 52 A1
Tywyn UK 39 B2
Tzermiado GR 185 D6
Tzummarum NL 70 A2

U

Ub SRB 127 C2
Ubby DK 61 D1
Úbeda E 157 B4
Überlingen D 107 B4
Ubidea E 143 A4
Ubli HR 138 C2
Ubrique E 162 B2
Ucero E 143 C3
Uchaud F 131 B3
Uchte D 72 B1
Uckerath D 80 B3
Uckfield UK 45 C4
Ucklum S 54 B2
Uclés E 151 C5
Ucria I 177 A3
Udbina HR 137 A4
Uddebo S 60 B3
Uddeholm S 49 B5
Uddevalla S 54 B2
Uddheden S 49 C4
Uden NL 80 A1
Uder D 82 A2
Udiča SK 98 B2
Údine I 122 A2
Udvar H 125 B4
Ueckermünde D 74 A3
Uedem D 80 A2
Uelsen D 71 B3
Uelzen D 73 B3
Uetendorf CH 106 C2
Uetersen D 72 A2
Uetze D 72 B3
Uffculme UK 43 B3
Uffenheim D 94 B2
Ugarana E 143 A4
Ugento I 173 C4
Ugerldse DK 61 D1
Uggerby DK 58 A3
Uggerslev DK 59 C3
Uggiano la Chiesa I 173 B4
Ugíjar E 164 C1
Ugine F 118 B3
Uglejevik BIH 125 C5
Uglenes N 46 B2
Uglich RUS 9 D11
Ugljane HR 138 B2
Ugod H 111 B4
Uherské Hradiště CZ 98 B1
Uherský Brod CZ 98 B1
Uherský Ostroh CZ 98 C1
Uhingen D 94 C1
Uhlířské-Janovice CZ 96 B3
Uhřiněves CZ 96 A2
Uhyst D 84 A2
Uig UK 31 B2
Uitgeest NL 70 B1
Uithoorn NL 70 B1
Uithuizen NL 71 A3
Uithuizermeeden NL 71 A3
Uivar RO 126 B2
Ujazd
Łódzkie PL 87 A3
Opolskie PL 86 B2
Ujezd u Brna CZ 97 B4
Ujhartyán H 112 B3
Újkigyós H 113 C5
Ujpetre H 125 B4
Ujście PL 75 A5
Ujsolt H 112 C3
Újszász H 113 B4
Újszentmargita H 113 B5
Ujué E 144 B2
Ukanc SLO 122 A2
Ukmergė LT 13 A6
Ukna S 56 B2
Ula TR 188 B3
Ul'anka SK 99 C3
Ulaş TR 186 A2
Ulássai I 179 C3
Ulbjerg DK 58 B2
Ulbster UK 32 C3
Ulceby UK 40 B3
Ulcinj MNE 16 E3
Uldum DK 59 C2
Ulefoss N 53 A5
Uleila del Campo E 164 B2
Ulëz AL 182 B1
Ulfborg DK 59 B1
Uljma SRB 127 B3
Ullånger S 200 C4
Ullapool UK 32 D1
Ullared S 60 B2
Ullatti S 196 B4
Ullatun N 52 A2
Ulldecona E 153 B4
Ulldemolins E 147 C1
Ullerslev DK 59 C3
Ullervad S 55 B4
Üllés H 126 A1
Üllö H 112 B3
Ulm D 94 C1
Ulme P 154 B2
Ulmen D 80 B2
Ulnes N 47 B6
Ulog BIH 139 B4
Ulricehamn S 60 B3
Ulrichstein D 81 B5
Ulrika S 56 B1
Ulriksfors S 200 C1
Ulrum NL 71 A3
Ulsberg N 198 C6
Ulsta UK 33 A5
Ulsted DK 58 A3
Ulsteinvik N 198 C2
Ulstrup
Vestsjællands Amt. DK 59 C3
Viborg Amt. DK 59 B2
Ulsvåg N 194 B6
Ulubey TR 188 A4
Uluborlu TR 189 A5
Ulukışla TR 23 C8
Ulverston UK 36 B3
Ulvik N 46 B3
Umag HR 122 B2
Uman UA 13 D9
Umba RUS 3 C14
Umbértide I 135 B5
Umbriático I 174 B2
Umčari SRB 127 C2
Umeå S 200 C6
Umgransele S 200 B4
Umhausen A 108 B1
Umka SRB 127 C2
Umljanovic HR 138 B2
Umnäs S 195 E7
Umurbey TR 186 B1
Unaðsdalur IS 190 A3
Unapool UK 32 C1
Unari FIN 197 B8
Unbyn S 196 D4
Uncastillo E 144 B2
Undenäs S 55 B5
Undersaker S 199 B10
Undredal N 46 B4
Unešić HR 138 B2
Úněšov CZ 96 B1
Ungheni MD 17 B7
Unhais da Serra P 148 B2
Unhošt CZ 84 B2
Unichowo PL 68 A2
Uničov CZ 98 B1
Uniejów PL 76 C3
Unisław PL 76 A3
Unkel D 80 B3
Unken A 109 B3
Unna D 81 A3
Unnaryd S 60 C3
Unquera E 142 A2
Unterach A 109 B4
Unterägeri CH 107 B3
Unterammergau D 108 B2
Unterhaching D 108 A2
Unteriberg CH 107 B3
Unterkochen D 94 C2
Unter Langkampfen A 108 B3
Unterlaussa A 110 B1
Unterlüss D 72 B3
Untermünkheim D 94 B1
Unterschächen CH 107 C3
Unterschleissheim D 95 C3
Unterschwaningen D 94 B2
Untersiemau D 82 B2
Unter-steinbach D 94 B2
Unterweissenbach A 96 C2
Unterzell D 95 B4
Upavon UK 44 B2
Úpice CZ 85 B4
Upiłka PL 68 B2
Upphärad S 54 B3
Uppingham UK 40 C3
Upplands-Väsby S 57 A3
Uppsala S 51 C4
Uppsjøhytta N 48 A1
Upton-upon-Severn UK 39 B4
Ur F 146 B2
Uras I 179 C2
Uraz PL 85 A4
Urbánia I 136 B1
Urbino I 136 B1
Urçay F 103 C4
Urda E 157 A4
Urdax E 144 A2
Urdilde E 140 B2
Urdos F 145 B3
Urk NL 70 B2
Úrkút H 111 B4
Urla TR 188 A1
Urlingford IRL 30 B1
Urnäsch CH 107 B4
Urnes N 47 A4
Uroševac KOS 16 D4
Urracal E 164 B2
Urries E 144 B2
Urroz E 144 B2
Ursensollen D 95 B3
Urshult S 63 B2
Uršna Sela SLO 123 B4
Urszulewo PL 77 B4
Ury F 90 C2
Urziceni RO 17 C7
Urzulei I 178 B3
Usagre E 156 B1
Uşak TR 187 D4
Usedom D 66 C2
Useldange L 92 B1
Uséllus I 179 C2
Ushakovo RUS 69 A5
Usingen D 81 B4
Usini I 178 B2
Usk UK 39 C4
Uskedal N 46 C2
Üsküdar TR 186 A4
Uslar D 82 A1
Úsov CZ 97 B5
Usquert NL 71 A3
Ussássai I 179 C3
Ussé F 102 B2
Usséglio I 119 B4
Ussel
Cantal F 116 B2
Corrèze F 116 B2
Usson-du-Poitou F 115 B4
Usson-en-Forez F 117 B3
Usson-les-Bains F 146 B3
Ustaoset N 47 B5
Ustaritz F 144 A2
Uštěk CZ 84 B2
Uster CH 107 B3
Ústi CZ 98 B1
Ustikolina BIH 139 B4
Ústínad Labem CZ 84 B2
Ústínad Orlicí CZ 97 B4
Ustipračà BIH 139 B5
Ustka PL 68 A1
Ust Luga RUS 8 C6
Ustroń PL 98 B2
Ustronie Morskie PL 67 B4
Ustyuzhna RUS 9 C10
Uszód H 112 C2
Utåker N 52 A1
Utansjö S 200 D3
Utebo E 152 A3
Utena LT 13 A6
Utery CZ 95 B4
Uthaug N 198 B6
Utiel E 159 B2
Utne N 46 B3
Utö S 57 B4
Utrecht NL 70 B2
Utrera E 162 A2
Utrillas E 153 B3
Utsjoki FIN 193 C11
Utstein kloster N 52 A1
Uttendorf A 109 B3
Uttenweiler D 107 A4
Utterslev DK 65 B4
Uttoxeter UK 40 C2
Utvälinge S 61 C2
Utvorda N 199 A7
Uusikaarlepyy FIN 3 E8
Uusikaupunki FIN 8 B2
Uvaly CZ 96 A2
Uvdal N 47 B5
Uza F 128 B1
Uzdin SRB 126 B2
Uzdowo PL 77 A5
Uzein F 145 A3
Uzel F 100 A3
Uzerche F 116 B1
Uzès F 131 A3
Uzhhorod UA 12 D5
Uzhok UA 12 D5
Užice SRB 127 D1
Uznach CH 107 B3
Üzümlü
Konya TR 189 B6
Muğla TR 188 C4
Uzunköprü TR 186 A1

V

Vaalajärvi FIN 197 B9
Vaas F 102 B2
Vaasa FIN 8 A2
Vaasen NL 70 B2
Vabre F 130 B1
Vác H 112 B3
Vacha D 82 B2
Váchartyán H 112 B3
Väckelsång S 63 B2
Vacqueyras F 131 A3
Vad S 50 B2
Vada I 134 B3
Väddö S 51 C5
Väderstad S 55 B5
Vadheim N 46 A2
Vadillo de la Sierra E 150 B2
Vadillos E 152 B1
Vadla N 52 A2
Vado I 135 A4
Vado Lígure I 133 A4
Vadsø N 193 B13
Vadstena S 55 B5
Vadum DK 58 A2
Vaduz FL 107 B4
Vafos N 53 B5
Vág H 111 B4
Vågåmo N 198 D6
Væggerløse DK 65 B4
Vaggeryd S 62 A2
Vaghia GR 184 A4
Vaglia I 135 B4
Váglio Basilicata I 172 B1
Vagney F 106 A1
Vagnhärad S 57 B3
Vagnsunda S 57 A4
Vagos P 148 B1
Vai GR 185 D7
Vaiano I 135 B4
Vaiges F 102 A1
Vaihingen D 93 C4
Vaillant F 105 B4
Vailly-sur-Aisne F 91 B3
Vailly-sur Sauldre F 103 B4
Vairano Scalo I 170 B2
Vaison-la-Romaine F 131 A4
Vaite F 105 B4
Väjern S 54 B2
Vajszló H 125 B3
Vaksdal N 46 B2
Vál H 112 B2
Valaam RUS 9 B7
Valada P 154 B2
Vålådalen S 199 B10
Valadares P 148 A1
Valado P 154 B1
Valandovo NMK 182 B4
Valaská SK 99 C3
Valaská Belá SK 98 C2
Valaská Dubová SK 99 B3
Valašská Polanka CZ 98 B1
Valašské Klobouky CZ 98 B2
Valašské Meziříčí CZ 98 B1
Valberg F 132 A2
Vålberg S 55 A4
Valbo S 51 B4
Valbom P 148 A1
Valbondione I 120 A3
Valbonnais F 118 C2
Valbuena de Duero E 142 C2
Vălcani RO 126 B2
Valdagno I 121 B4
Valdahon F 105 B5
Valdaracete E 151 B4
Valday RUS 9 D8
Valdealgorfa E 153 B3
Valdecaballeros E 156 A2
Valdecabras E 152 B1
Valdecarros E 150 B2
Valdeconcha E 151 B5
Valdeflores E 161 B3
Valdefresno E 142 B1
Valdeganga E 158 B2
Valdelacasa E 150 B2
Valdelacasa de Tajo E 156 A2
Valdelarco E 161 B3
Valdelosa E 149 A4
Valdeltormo E 153 B4
Valdelugeros E 142 B1
Valdemanco de Esteras E 156 B3
Valdemarsvik S 56 B2
Valdemorillo E 151 B3
Valdemoro E 151 B4
Valdemoro Sierra E 152 B2
Valdenoceda E 143 B3
Valdeobispo E 149 B3
Valdeolivas E 152 B1
Valdepeñas E 157 B4
Valdepeñas de Jaén E 163 A4
Valdepiélago E 142 B1
Valdepolo E 142 B1
Valderas E 142 B1
Valdérice I 176 A1
Valderrobres E 153 B4
Valderrueda E 142 B2
Val de San Lorenzo E 141 B4
Val de Santo Domingo E 150 B3
Val d'Esquières F 132 B2
Valdestillas E 150 A3
Valdetorres E 156 B1
Valdetorres de Jarama E 151 B4
Valdeverdeja E 150 C2
Valdevimbre E 142 B1
Valdieri I 133 A3
Valdilecha E 151 B4
Val-d'Isère F 119 B3
Valdobbiádene I 121 B4
Valdocondes E 143 C3
Valdoviño E 140 A2
Valea lui Mihai RO 16 B5
Vale de Açor
Beja P 160 B2
Portalegre P 154 B3
Vale de Agua P 160 B1
Vale de Cambra P 148 B1
Vale de Lobo P 160 B1
Vale de Prazeres P 148 B2
Vale de Reis P 154 C2
Vale de Rosa P 160 B2
Vale de Santarém P 154 B2
Vale de Vargo P 160 B2
Vale do Peso P 155 B3
Valega P 148 B1
Valéggio sul Mincio I 121 B3
Valeiro P 154 C2
Valença P 140 B2
Valençay F 103 B3
Valence
Charente F 115 C4
Drôme F 117 C4
Valence d'Agen F 129 B3
Valence d'Albigeois F 130 A1
Valence-sur-Baise F 129 C3
Valencia E 159 B3
Valencia de Alcántara E 155 B3
Valencia de Don Juan E 142 B1
Valencia de las Torres E 156 B1
Valencia del Ventoso E 161 A3
Valencia de Mombuey E 161 A2

Valenciennes F .79 B3
Valensole F ... 132 B1
Valentano I ... 168 A1
Valentigney F. 106 B1
Valentine F ... 145 A4
Valenza I 120 B1
Valenzuela E .. 163 A3
Valenzuela de
  Calatrava E .. 157 B4
Våler
  Hedmark N 48 B3
  Østfold N 54 A1
Valera de Abajo
  E............ 158 B1
Valeria E 158 B1
Valestrand N....52 A1
Valestrandsfossen
  N.............46 B2
Valevåg N........52 A1
Valfabbrica I .. 136 B1
Valflaunes F .. 131 B2
Valga EST 8 D5
Valgorge F ... 131 A3
Valgrisenche I 119 B4
Valguarnera
  Caropepe I ... 177 B3
Valhelhas P ... 148 B2
Valjevo SRB ... 127 C1
Valka LV........8 D4
Valkeakoski FIN.. 8 B4
Valkenburg NL..80 B1
Valkenswaard
  NL...........79 A5
Valkó H 112 B3
Valla S 56 A2
Vallada E 159 C3
Vallado E...... 141 A4
Valladolid E... 150 A3
Vallåkra S......61 D2
Vallata I....... 172 A1
Vallberga S....61 C3
Vall d'Alba E .. 153 B3
Valldemossa
  E............ 166 B2
Valle N.........52 A3
Valle Castellana
  I............ 136 C2
Valle de Abdalajís
  E............ 163 B3
Valle de
  Cabuérniga
  E............ 142 A2
Valle de la Serena
  E............ 156 B2
Valle de Matamoros
  E............ 155 C4
Valle de Santa Ana
  E............ 155 C4
Valledolmo I... 176 B2
Valledoria I ... 178 B2
Vallelado E.... 150 A3
Vallelunga
  Pratameno I . 176 B2
Valle Mosso I.. 119 B5
Vallendar D.....81 B3
Vallentuna S....57 A4
Valleräs S 49 B5
Valleraugue F. 130 B2
Vallermosa I... 179 C2
Vallet F 101 B4
Valletta M..... 175 C3
Valley UK 38 C1
Vallfogona de
  Riucorb I 147 C2
Valli del Pasúbio
  I............ 121 B4
Vallo della Lucánia
  I............ 172 B1
Valloire F 118 B3
Vallombrosa I. 135 B4
Vallon-Pont-d'Arc
  F............ 131 A3
Vallorbe CH... 105 C5
Vallouise F 118 C3
Valls E 147 C2
Vallset N........48 B3
Vallsta S........50 A3
Vallstena S......57 C4
Valmadrid E... 153 A3
Valmiera LV......8 D4
Valmojado E.. 151 B3
Valmont F......89 A4
Valmontone I. 169 B2
Valö S..........51 B5
Valognes F.....88 A2
Valonga P..... 148 B1
Valongo P..... 148 A1
Válor E........ 164 C1
Valoria la Buena
  E............ 142 C2

Valøy N 199 A7
Valozhyn BY ...13 A7
Valpaços P.... 148 A2
Valpelline I.... 119 B4
Valpiana I..... 135 B3
Valpovo HR ... 125 B4
Valras-Plage F 130 B2
Valréas F 131 A3
Vals CH 107 C4
Valsavarenche
  I............ 119 B4
Vålse DK........65 B4
Valsequillo E.. 156 B2
Valsjöbyn S .. 199 A11
Vals-les-Bains
  F............ 117 C4
Valsonne F.... 117 B4
Valstagna I.... 121 B4
Val-Suzon F... 105 B3
Valtablado del Rio
  E............ 152 B1
Valþjofsstaður
  IS 191 B11
Val Thorens F . 118 B3
Valtice CZ......97 C4
Valtiendas E .. 151 A4
Valtierra E ... 144 B2
Valtopina I.... 136 B1
Valtorta I..... 120 B2
Valtournenche
  I............ 119 B4
Valverde E 144 C2
Valverde de
  Burguillos E.. 155 C4
Valverde de Júcar
  E............ 158 B1
Valverde de la Vera
  E............ 150 B2
Valverde de la
  Virgen E..... 142 B1
Valverde del
  Camino E 161 B3
Valverde del Fresno
  E............ 149 B3
Valverde de Llerena
  E............ 156 B2
Valverde de Mérida
  E............ 156 B1
Valvträsk S 196 C4
Vamberk CZ....85 B4
Vamdrup DK...59 C2
Våmhus S......50 A1
Vamlingbo S... 57 D4
Vammala FIN 8 B3
Vamos GR..... 185 D5
Vámosmikola
  H........... 112 B2
Vámosszabadi
  H........... 111 B4
Vanault-les-Dames
  F............91 C4
Vandel DK 59 C2
Vandenesse F. 104 C2
Vandenesse-en-
  Auxois F 104 B3
Vandóies I 108 C2
Vâne-Åsaka S...54 B3
Vänersborg S...54 B3
Vänersnäs S ...54 B3
Vang N.........47 A5
Vänge S........51 C4
Vangsnes N 46 A3
Vänjaurbäck
  S 200 B4
Vännacka S 54 A3
Vannareid N .. 192 B3
Vännäs S 200 C5
Vannes F 101 B3
Vannsätter S...51 A3
Vannvåg N.... 192 B3
Vansbro S......49 B6
Vanse N........52 B2
Vantaa FIN...... 8 B4
Vanttauskoski
  FIN.......... 197 C9
Vanviken N ... 199 B7
Vanyarc H..... 112 B3
Vaour F....... 129 B4
Vapnyarka UA . 13 D8
Vaprio d'Adda
  I............ 120 B2
Vaqueiros P... 160 B2
Vara S..........55 B3
Varacieux F... 118 B2
Varades F..... 101 B4
Varages F..... 132 B1
Varaldsøy N....46 B2
Varallo I...... 119 B5
Varangerbotn
  N........... 193 B12
Varano de'Melegari
  I............ 120 C3
Varaždin HR .. 124 A2

Varaždinske
  Toplice HR .. 124 A2
Varazze I...... 133 A4
Varberg S......60 B2
Vardal N........48 B2
Varde DK.......59 C1
Vårdö FIN......51 B7
Vardø N...... 193 B15
Vardomb H ... 125 A4
Varejoki FIN... 196 C7
Varel D........71 A5
Varèna LT.......13 A6
Vårenes N......52 A1
Varengeville-sur-
  Mer F 89 A4
Varenna I 120 A2
Varennes-en-
  Argonne F 91 B5
Varennes-le-Grand
  F............ 105 C3
Varennes-St
  Sauveur F .. 105 C4
Varennes-sur-Allier
  F............ 117 A3
Varennes-sur-
  Amance F ... 105 B4
Vareš BIH 139 A4
Varese I....... 120 B1
Varese Ligure
  I............ 134 A2
Vårfurile RO ...16 B5
Vårgårda S......60 A2
Vargas
  E............ 143 A3
  P............ 154 B2
Vargön S........54 B3
Varhaug N......52 B1
Variaş RO 126 A2
Variaşu Mic
  RO 126 A3
Varilhes F 146 A2
Varin SK........98 B2
Väring S........55 B4
Váriz P........ 149 A3
Varkaus FIN...... 8 A5
Varmahlíð IS . 190 B6
Varmaland IS . 190 C4
Värmlands Bro
  S 55 A4
Värmskog S....55 A3
Varna
  BG 17 D7
  SRB 127 C1
Värnamo S......60 B4
Varnhem S......55 B4
Varnsdorf CZ ..84 B2
Varö S..........60 B2
Varoška Rijeka
  BIH.......... 124 B2
Városlöd H.... 111 B4
Várpalota H... 112 B2
Varreddes F....90 C2
Vars F......... 118 C3
Varsi I........ 120 C2
Varsseveld NL..71 C3
Vårsta S........57 A3
Vartdal N 198 C3
Vartofta S......55 B4
Varvarin SRB.. 127 C3
Varzi I........ 120 C2
Varzjelas P.... 148 B1
Varzo I....... 119 A5
Varzy F....... 104 B2
Vasad H....... 112 B3
Väse S..........55 A4
Vašica SRB 125 B5
Vasilevichi BY...13 B8
Vasiliki GR......57 C4
Vaskút H...... 125 A4
Vaslui RO 17 B7
Vassbotn N 53 B4
Vassenden N...47 A6
Vassieux-en-
  Vercors F 118 C2
Vassmolösa S...63 B4
Vassy F.........88 B3
Västansjö S .. 195 E6
Västanvik S....50 B1
Västerås S 56 A2
Västerby S......50 B2
Västerfärnebo
  S 50 C3
Västergarn S...57 C4
Västerhaninge
  S 57 A4
Västervik S.....62 A4
Vasto I....... 170 A2
Västra Ämtervik
  S 55 A4
Västra-Bodarne
  S 60 B2
Västra Karup S ..61 C2

Vasvár H...... 111 B3
Vasylkiv UA....13 C9
Vát H......... 111 B3
Vatan F....... 103 B3
Väte S.........57 C4
Vathia GR 184 C3
Vatican City =
  Cittádel Vaticano
  I............ 168 B2
Vatili CY...... 181 A2
Vatin SRB 126 B3
Vatland N......52 B3
Vatnar N.......53 A5
Vatnås N.......48 C1
Vatne N........53 B3
Vatnestrøm N...53 B4
Vätö S..........51 C5
Vatra-Dornei
  RO...........17 B6
Vatry F.........91 C4
Vattholma S ...51 B4
Vättis CH...... 107 C4
Vauchamps F...91 C3
Vauchassis F .. 104 A2
Vaucouleurs F .92 C1
Vaudoy-en-Brie
  F............90 C3
Vaulen S........52 B1
Vaulruz CH.... 106 C1
Vaulx Vraucourt
  F............90 A2
Vaumas F 104 C2
Vausseroux F . 115 B3
Vauvenargues
  F............ 132 B1
Vauvert F 131 B3
Vauvillers F ... 105 B5
Vaux-sur-Sure
  B............92 B1
Vawkavysk BY .13 B6
Vaxholm S 57 A4
Växjö S 62 B2
Våxtorp S......61 C3
Vayrac F 129 B4
Važec SK 99 B3
Veberöd S......61 D3
Vechelde D 72 B3
Vechta D.......71 B5
Vecinos E 149 B4
Vecsés H 112 B3
Vedavågen N ...52 A1
Veddige S......60 B2
Vedersø DK....59 B1
Vedeseta I.... 120 B2
Vedevåg S 56 A1
Vedra E 140 B2
Vedum S 55 B3
Veendam NL...71 A3
Veenendaal NL.70 B2
Vega E........ 142 A1
Vega de Espinareda
  E............ 141 B4
Vega de Infanzones
  E............ 142 B1
Vegadeo E 141 A3
Vega de Pas E . 143 A3
Vega de Valcarce
  E............ 141 B4
Vega de
  Valdetronco
  E............ 150 A2
Vegårshei N ...53 B4
Vegas de Coria
  E............ 149 B3
Vegas del Condado
  E............ 142 B1
Vegby S........60 B3
Vegger DK 58 B2
Veggli N 47 B6
Veghel NL......80 A1
Veglast D......66 B1
Véglie I....... 173 B3
Veguillas E.... 151 B4
Vegusdal N 53 B4
Veidholmen N 198 B4
Veidnes N.... 193 B10
Veikåker N......48 B1
Veinge S.......61 C3
Vejbystrand S..61 C2
Vejen DK.......59 C2
Vejer de la Frontera
  E............ 162 B2
Vejle DK 59 C2
Vejprty CZ 83 B5
Velada E 150 B3
Vela Luka HR.. 138 C2
Velayos E 150 B3
Velbert D......80 A3
Velburg D......95 B3
Velde N 199 A8
Velden
  Bayern D 95 B3
  Bayern D ... 95 C4

Velden am Worther
  See A 109 C5
Velefique E ... 164 B2
Velen D........80 A2
Velenje SLO... 123 A4
Veles NMK 182 B3
Velesevec HR . 124 B2
Velešin CZ 96 C2
Velestino GR.. 182 D4
Velez Blanco
  E............ 164 B2
Vélez de
  Benaudalla E. 163 B4
Vélez-Málaga
  E............ 163 B3
Vélez Rubio E . 164 B2
Veliiki Radinci
  SRB 127 B1
Velika HR 125 B3
Velika Gorica
  HR 124 B2
Velika Grdevac
  HR 124 B3
Velika Greda
  SRB 126 B3
Velika Ilova
  BIH.......... 125 C3
Velika Kladuša
  BIH.......... 124 B1
Velika Kopanica
  HR 125 B4
Velika Krsna
  SRB 127 C2
Velika Obarska
  BIH.......... 125 C5
Velika Pisanica
  HR 124 B3
Velika Plana
  SRB 127 C3
Velika Zdenci
  HR 124 B3
Velike Lašče
  SLO 123 B3
Velike Središte
  SRB 126 B3
Veliki Gaj SRB. 126 B3
Veliki Popović
  SRB 127 C3
Velikiye Luki
  RUS 9 D7
Veliko Gradište
  SRB 127 C3
Veliko Orašje
  SRB 127 C3
Veliko Selo
  SRB 127 C3
Veliko Tarnovo
  BG 17 D6
Velilla del Río
  Carrió E 142 B2
Velilla de San
  Antonio E.... 151 B4
Veli Lošinj
  HR 137 A3
Velingrad BG . 183 A5
Velizh RUS 9 E7
Veljun HR 123 B4
Velká Bíteš CZ ..97 B4
Velka Hled'scbe
  CZ 95 B4
Velká Lomnica
  SK............99 B4
Velkánad Veličkou
  CZ 98 C1
Velké Bystřice
  CZ 98 B1
Velké Heraltice
  CZ 98 B1
Velké Karlovice
  CZ 98 B2
Vel'ke'Kostol'any
  SK............98 C1
Vel'ké Leváre
  SK............97 C5
Velké Losiny
  CZ 98 A1
Velké Meziříčí
  CZ 97 B4
Velké Pavlovice
  CZ 97 C4
Vel'ké Rovné
  SK............98 B2
Vel'ké Uherce
  SK............98 C2
Vel'ké Zálužie
  SK............98 C1
Velayos→
Velké Karlovice
  CZ 98 B2
Velburg→
Velky Bor CZ ...96 B1
Vel'ký Cetin
  SK............112 A2
Vel'ký Krtíš
  SK............112 A3

Vel'ký Meder
  SK........... 111 B4
Velky Ujezd CZ..98 B1
Vellahn D......73 A3
Vellberg D......94 B1
Velles F 103 C3
Velletri I 168 B2
Vellinge S......66 A2
Vellisca E 151 B5
Velliza E 150 A3
Vellmar D......81 A5
Velp NL........70 B2
Velten D 74 B2
Velvary CZ......84 B2
Velvendos GR. 182 C4
Vemb DK.......59 B1
Vemdalen S.. 199 C10
Veme N........48 B2
Véménd H ... 125 A4
Vemmedrup
  DK........... 61 D2
Vena S.........62 A3
Venaco F...... 180 A2
Venafro I...... 169 B4
Venarey-les-
  Laumes F ... 104 B3
Venaría I 119 B4
Venasca I..... 133 A3
Venčane SRB.. 127 C2
Vence F....... 132 B3
Venda Nova
  Coimbra P... 154 A2
  Leiria P ... 154 B2
Vendas Novas
  P............ 154 C2
Vendays-
  Montalivet F. 114 C2
Vendel S.......51 B4
Vendelso S.....57 A4
Vendeuil F 91 B3
Vendeuvre-sur-
  Barse F....... 104 A3
Vendoeuvres
  F............ 115 B5
Vendôme F ... 103 B3
Venelles F..... 131 B4
Veness UK......33 B4
Venézia = Venice
  I............ 122 B1
Venialbo E 150 A2
Venice = Venézia
  I............ 122 B1
Vénissieux F .. 117 B4
Venjan S.......49 B5
Venlo NL.......80 A2
Vennesla N 53 B3
Vennesund N ..195 E3
Vennezey F.....92 C2
Venn Green UK..42 B2
Venosa I...... 172 B1
Venray NL......80 A1
Vent A........ 108 C1
Venta de Baños
  E............ 142 C2
Venta del Moro
  E............ 158 B2
Venta de los Santos
  E............ 157 B4
Venta las Ranas
  E............ 142 A1
Ventanueva E. 141 A4
Ventas de Huelma
  E............ 163 A4
Ventas de
  Zafarraya E .. 163 B3
Ventavon F ... 132 A1
Ventimíglia I. 133 B3
Ventnor UK....44 C2
Ventosa de la Sierra
  E............ 143 C4
Ventosilla E... 143 C4
Ventspils LV......8 D2
Venturina I.... 134 B3
Venzolasca F.. 180 A2
Venzone I..... 122 A2
Vép H 111 B3
Vera
  E............ 164 B3
  N........... 199 B9
Vera Cruz P ... 160 A2
Vera de Bidasoa
  E............ 144 A2
Vera de Moncayo
  E............ 144 C2
Verbánia I 119 B5
Verberie F......90 B2
Verbicaro I.... 174 B1
Verbier CH.... 119 A4
Vercelli I...... 119 B5
Vercel-Villedieu-le-
  Camp F 105 B5
Verchen D......66 C1
Vercheny F.... 118 C2

Verclause F ... 131 A4
Verdalsøra N.. 199 B8
Verden D 72 B2
Verdens Ende
  N.............54 A1
Verdikoussa
  GR 182 D3
Verdille F 115 C3
Verdú E....... 147 C2
Verdun F.......92 B1
Verdun-sur-
  Garonne F ... 129 C4
Verdun-sur-le-
  Doubs F...... 105 C4
Veresegyház
  H........... 112 B3
Verfeil F 129 C4
Vergato I...... 135 A4
Vergel E 159 C4
Vergeletto
  CH 120 A1
Verges E 147 B4
Vergiate I..... 120 B1
Vergt F........ 129 A3
Veria GR 182 C4
Verín E....... 141 C3
Veringenstadt
  D............ 107 A4
Verl D..........81 A4
Verma N 198 C5
Vermand F......90 B3
Vermelha P .. 154 B1
Vermenton F.. 104 B2
Vernago I..... 108 C1
Vernante I 133 A3
Vernantes F... 102 B2
Vernár SK......99 C4
Vernasca I 120 C2
Vernayaz CH.. 119 A4
Vernazza I 134 A2
Vern-d'Anjou
  F............ 102 B1
Verneřice CZ...84 B2
Vernet F 146 A2
Vernet-les-
  Bains F....... 146 B3
Verneuil F......91 B3
Verneuil-sur-Avre
  F.............89 B4
Vernier CH.... 118 A3
Vérnio I...... 135 A4
Vérnole I...... 173 B4
Vernon F.......90 B1
Vernoux-en-
  Vivarais F 117 C4
Veróce H...... 112 B3
Verolanuova I. 120 B3
Véroli I....... 169 B3
Verona I 121 B4
Verpelèt H.... 113 B4
Verrabotn N .. 199 B7
Verrès I....... 119 B4
Verrey-sous-
  Salmaise F ... 104 B3
Verrières F.... 115 B4
Versailles F 90 C2
Versam CH.... 107 C4
Verseg H...... 112 B3
Versmold D....71 B5
Versoix CH.... 118 A3
Verteillac F ... 115 C3
Vértesacsa H.. 112 B2
Vertou F 101 B4
Vertus F.......91 C3
Verviers B......80 B1
Vervins F......91 B3
Verwood UK ...43 B5
Veryan UK 42 B2
Veržej SLO ... 111 C3
Verzuolo I..... 133 A3
Verzy F........91 B4
Vescovato F... 180 A2
Vése H 124 A3
Veselie BG 17 D7
Veselínad Lužnicí
  CZ 96 B2
Veselínad Moravou
  CZ 98 C1
Vésime I...... 119 C5
Veskoniemi
  FIN......... 193 D11
Vesoul F 105 B5
Vespolate I ... 120 B1
Vessigebro S...60 C2
Vestbygd N ...52 B2
Vestenanova I 121 B4
Vester Husby S..56 B2
Vester Nebel
  DK...........59 C2
Vesterøhavn
  DK...........58 A3
Vester Torup
  DK...........58 A2

Vester Vedsted
DK 59 C1
Vestervig DK....58 B1
Vestfossen N....53 A5
Vestmannaeyjar
IS 190 D5
Vestmarka N....48 C3
Vestnes N.....198 C4
Vestone I 120 B3
Vestre Gausdal
N............48 A2
Vestre Jakobselv
N...........193 B13
Vestre Slidre N..47 A5
Vesyegonsk
RUS............9 C10
Veszprém H....112 B1
Veszprémvarsány
H............112 B1
Vésztö H......113 C5
Vetlanda S.....62 A3
Vetovo HR....125 B3
Vetralla I......168 A2
Větrný Jeníkov
CZ..........97 B3
Vétroz CH.....119 A4
Vetschau D....84 A2
Vettasjärvi S..196 B4
Vetto I.......134 A3
Vetulónia I....135 C3
Veules-les-Roses
F...........89 A4
Veulettes-sur-Mer
F...........89 A4
Veum N.......53 A4
Veurne B......78 A2
Veverská Bítýška
CZ..........97 B4
Vevey CH.....106 C1
Vevi GR.......182 C3
Vevring N......46 A2
Vex CH......119 A4
Veynes F......132 A1
Veyre-Monton
F...........116 B3
Veyrier F......118 B3
Vézelay F.....104 B2
Vézelise F......92 C2
Vézenobres F.131 A3
Vezins F......102 B1
Vézins-de-Lévézou
F...........130 A1
Vezirhan TR...187 B5
Vezirköprü
TR............23 A8
Vezza di Óglio
I............120 A3
Vezzani F.....180 A2
Vezzano I....121 A4
Vezzano sul
Cróstolo I....121 C3
Vi S.........200 D3
Viadana I....121 C3
Via Gloria P..160 B2
Viana E.......143 B4
Viana do Alentejo
P...........154 C2
Viana do Bolo
E...........141 B3
Viana do Castelo
P...........148 A1
Vianden L......92 B2
Viannos GR...185 D6
Viaréggio I...134 B3
Viator E......164 C2
Vibble S.......57 C4
Viborg DK.....58 B2
Vibo Valéntia
I............175 C2
Vibraye F.....102 A2
Vic E.......147 C3
Vícar E......164 C2
Vicari I......134 B3
Vicari I......176 B2
Vicchio I......135 B4
Vicdesses F..146 B2
Vic-en-Bigorre
F...........145 A4
Vicenza I.....121 B4
Vic-Fézensac
F...........129 C3
Vichy F.......117 A3
Vickan S 60 B2
Vickerstown
UK...........36 B3
Vic-le-Comte
F...........116 B3
Vico F.......180 A1
Vico del Gargano
I............171 B3
Vico Equense
I............170 C2
Vicopisano I..134 B3

Vicosoprano
CH..........120 A2
Vicovaro I....169 A2
Vic-sur-Aisne F..90 B3
Vic-sur-Cère F.116 C2
Victoria = Rabat
M..........175 C3
Vidago P.....148 A2
Vidauban F...132 B2
Vide P.......148 B2
Videbæk DK...59 B1
Videm SLO...123 B3
Videseter N...198 D4
Vidigueira P...160 A2
Vidin BG......16 D5
Vidsel S......196 D3
Vidzy BY......13 A7
Viechtach D....95 B4
Vieille-Brioude
F...........117 B3
Vieira P......154 B2
Vieira do Minho
P...........148 A1
Vieiros P.....155 C3
Vielha E......145 B4
Vielle-Aure F..145 B4
Viellespesse F.116 B3
Viellevigne F..114 B2
Vielmur-sur-Agout
F...........130 B1
Vielsalm B....80 B1
Viels Maison F..91 C3
Vienenburg D..73 C3
Vienna = Wien
A..........111 A3
Vienne F.....117 B4
Vieritz D......73 B5
Viernheim D...93 B4
Vierraden D...74 A3
Viersen D.....80 A2
Vierville-sur-Mer
F...........88 A3
Vierzon F.....103 B4
Vieselbach D...82 B3
Vieste I......171 B4
Vietas S......194 C9
Vieteren B 78 B2
Vietri di Potenza
I............172 B1
Vietri sul Mare
I............170 C2
Vieux-Boucau-les-
Bains F.......128 C1
Vif F.........118 B2
Vig DK........61 D1
Vigásio I.....121 B3
Vigaun A......109 B4
Vigeland N.....52 B3
Vigeois F......116 B1
Vigévano I....120 B1
Viggianello I..174 B2
Viggiano I....174 A1
Vigliano I.....169 A3
Vigmostad N...52 B3
Vignale I.....119 B5
Vignanello I...168 A2
Vigneulles-lès-
Hattonchâtel
F...........92 C1
Vignevieille F.146 B3
Vignola I.....135 A4
Vignory F.....105 A4
Vignoux-sur-
Barangeon F.103 B4
Vigo E........140 B2
Vigo di Fassa I.121 A4
Vigone I......119 C4
Vigrestad N....52 B1
Vihiers F......102 B1
Viitasaari FIN...8 A4
Vík IS........190 D6
Vik
Nordland N ..195 E3
Rogaland N....52 B1
Sogn og Fjordane
N............46 A3
Vika S........50 B2
Vikajärvi FIN..197 C9
Vikane N......54 A1
Vikarbyn S....50 B2
Vike N........46 B2
Vikedal N.....52 A1
Vikeland N....53 B3
Viken
Jämtland
S...........199 A10
Skåne S.......61 C2
Viker N......48 B2
Vikersund N ...48 C1
Vikeså N......52 B2
Vikevåg N.....52 A1

Vikingstad S ...56 B1
Vikmanshyttan
S............50 B2
Vikna N......199 A7
Vikøy N.......46 B3
Vikran
Troms N 192 C2
Troms N 194 B7
Viksjö S......200 D3
Viksøyri N.....46 A3
Viksta S.......51 B4
Vila Boim P...155 C3
Vila Châde Ourique
P...........154 B2
Viladamat E...147 B4
Vila de Cruces
E...........140 B2
Vila de Rei P..154 B2
Vila do Bispo
P...........160 B1
Vila do Conde
P...........148 A1
Viladrau E.....147 C3
Vila Flor P....149 A2
Vila Franca das
Navas P.....149 B2
Vilafranca del
Maestrat E...153 B3
Vilafranca del
Penedès E...147 C2
Vila Franca de Xira
P...........154 C1
Vila Fresca P..154 C1
Vilagarcía de
Arousa E.....140 B2
Vilajuiga E...147 B4
Vilalba E......140 A3
Vilamarin E...140 B3
Vilamartín de
Valdeorras E.141 B3
Vila Nogueira
P...........154 C1
Vila Nova da
Baronia P....154 C2
Vilanova de
Castelló E....159 B3
Vila Nova de
Cerveira P....140 C2
Vila Nova de
Famalicão P..148 A1
Vila Nova de Foz
Côa P........149 A2
Vila Nova de Gaia
P...........148 A1
Vila Nova de
Milfontes P ..160 B1
Vila Nova de Paiva
P...........148 B2
Vila Nova de São
Bento P......161 B2
Vilanova de Sau
E...........147 C3
Vilanova i la Geltrú
E...........147 C2
Vilapedre E...140 A3
Vila Pouca de
Aguiar P.....148 A2
Vila Praja de
Ancora P.....148 A1
Vilarandelo P.148 A2
Vilar de Santos
E...........140 B3
Vilardevós E..141 C3
Vila Real P....148 A2
Vila-real de los
Infantes E....159 B3
Vila Real de Santo
António P....160 B2
Vilar Formosa
P...........149 B3
Vila-Rodona E.147 C2
Vila Ruiva P...160 A2
Vilasantar E...140 A2
Vilaseca E....147 C2
Vila Seca P...148 B1
Vilassar de Mar
E...........147 C3
Vilasund S...195 D5
Vila Velha de
Ródão P......155 B3
Vila Verde
Braga P.....148 A1
Lisboa P......154 B1
Vila Verde de
Filcalho P....161 B2
Vila Viçosa P..155 C3
Vilches E.....157 B4
Vildbjerg DK...59 B1
Vilémov CZ....97 B3
Vileyka BY.....13 A7
Vilhelmina S ..200 B2
Vilia GR......184 A4
Viljandi EST....8 C4

Villabáñez E...150 A3
Villablanca E..161 B2
Villablino E...141 B4
Villabona E...144 A1
Villabragima
E...........142 C1
Villabuena del
Puente E.....150 A2
Villacadima E..151 A4
Villacañas E...157 A4
Villacarriedo
E...........143 A3
Villacarrillo E.164 A1
Villa Castelli I.173 B3
Villacastín E...150 B3
Villach A......109 C4
Villacidro I....179 C2
Villaconejos E.151 B4
Villaconejos de
Trabaque E...152 B1
Villa Cova de Lixa
P...........148 A1
Villada E......142 B2
Villadangos del
Páramo E....141 B5
Villadecanes
E...........141 B4
Villa del Prado
E...........150 B3
Villa del Rio E.157 C3
Villadepera E.149 A3
Villa de Peralonso
E...........149 A3
Villa di Chiavenna
I............120 A2
Villadiego E...142 B2
Villadompardo
E...........163 A3
Villadóssola I.119 A5
Villaeles de
Valdavia E ...142 B2
Villaescusa de Haro
E...........158 B1
Villafáfila E...142 C1
Villafeliche E..152 A2
Villaflores E...150 A2
Villafrades de
Campos E....142 B2
Villafranca
Avila E.......150 B2
Navarra E.....144 B2
Villafranca de
Córdoba E...157 C3
Villafranca del
Bierzo E......141 B4
Villafranca de los
Barros E......155 C4
Villafranca de los
Caballeros E.157 A4
Villafranca di
Verona I.....121 B3
Villafranca in
Lunigiana I...134 A2
Villafranca-Montes
de Oca E.....143 B3
Villafranca Tirrena
I............177 A4
Villafranco del
Campo E.....152 B2
Villafranco del
Guadalquivir
E...........161 B3
Villafrati I....176 B2
Villafrechós E.142 C1
Villafruela E...143 C3
Villagarcia de las
Torres E......156 B1
Villaggio Mancuso
I............175 B2
Villagonzalo E.150 B2
Villagotón E..141 B4
Villagrains F ..128 B2
Villaharta E...156 B3
Villahermosa
E...........158 C1
Villaherreros
E...........142 B2
Villahoz E....143 B3
Villaines-la-Juhel
F...........89 B3
Villajoyosa E..159 C3
Villalago I....169 B3
Villalba I......176 B2
Villalba de
Calatrava E ..157 B4
Villalba de Guardo
E...........142 B2
Villalba del Alcor
E...........161 B3
Villalba de la Sierra
E...........152 B1
Villalba de los
Alcores E.....142 C2

Villalba de los
Barros E......155 C4
Villalba del Rey
E...........151 B5
Villalcampo E.149 A3
Villalcázar de Sirga
E...........142 B2
Villalengua E..152 A2
Villalgordo del
Júcar E......158 B1
Villalgordo del
Marquesado
E...........158 B1
Villalmóndar
E...........143 B3
Villalón de Campos
E...........142 B1
Villalonga E..159 C3
Villalonso E...150 A2
Villalpando E.142 C1
Villaluenga E..151 B4
Villalumbroso
E...........142 B2
Villálvaro E...143 C3
Villamalea E..158 B2
Villamanán E..142 B1
Villamanín E..142 B1
Villamanrique
E...........157 B5
Villamanrique de la
Condesa E...161 B3
Villamanta E..151 B3
Villamantilla
E...........151 B3
Villamar I....179 C2
Villamartín E.162 B2
Villamartin de
Campos E....142 B2
Villamartin de Don
Sancho E.....142 B1
Villamassárgia
I............179 C2
Villamayor E..142 A1
Villamayor de
Calatrava E ..157 B3
Villamayor de
Campos E....142 C1
Villamayor de
Santiago E...157 A5
Villamblard F.129 A3
Villamejil E...141 B4
Villamesias E..156 A2
Villaminaya E.157 A4
Villa Minozzo
I............134 A3
Villamor de los
Escuderos E..150 A2
Villamoronta
E...........142 B2
Villamuelas E.151 C4
Villamuriel de
Cerrato E.....142 C2
Villandraut F..128 B2
Villanova I....173 B3
Villanova d'Asti
I............119 C4
Villanova del
Battista I.....171 B3
Villanova Mondovì
I............133 A3
Villanova
Monteleone
I............178 B2
Villante E.....143 B3
Villántério I...120 B2
Villanubla E..142 C2
Villanueva de
Alcardete E..157 A4
Villanueva de
Alcorón E....152 B1
Villanueva de
Algaidas E...163 A3
Villanueva de
Argaña E.....143 B3
Villanueva de
Bogas E......157 A4
Villanueva de
Córdoba E...156 B3
Villanueva de
Gállego E....144 C3
Villanueva del
Aceral E......150 A3
Villanueva de la
Concepcion
E...........163 B3
Villanueva de la
Fuente E.....158 C1
Villanueva de la
Jara E.......158 B2
Villanueva de la
Reina E......157 B4
Villanueva del
Arzobispo E..164 A2

Villanueva de la
Serena E 156 B2
Villanueva de la
Sierra F 149 B3
Villanueva de las
Manzanas E..142 B1
Villanueva de las
Peras E......141 C5
Villanueva de las
Torres E......164 B1
Villanueva de la
Vera E........150 B2
Villanueva del
Campo E.....142 C1
Villanueva del
Duque E 156 B3
Villanueva del
Fresno E.....155 C3
Villanueva del
Huerva E.....152 A2
Villanueva de los
Castillejos E..161 B2
Villanueva de los
Infantes E....157 B5
Villanueva del Rey
E...........156 B2
Villanueva del Rio
E...........162 A2
Villanueva del Río y
Minas E......162 A2
Villanueva del
Rosario E.....163 B3
Villanueva del
Trabuco E....163 A3
Villanueva de
Mesia E......163 A4
Villanueva de Nía
E...........142 B2
Villanueva de
Oscos E......141 A4
Villanueva de San
Carlos E......157 B4
Villanueva de San
Juan E.......162 A2
Villanueva de Tapia
E...........163 A3
Villanueva de
Valdegovia
E...........143 B3
Villány H.....125 B4
Villaputzu I...179 C3
Villaquejida E.142 B1
Villaquilambre
E...........142 B1
Villaquiran de los
Infantes E....142 B2
Villaralto E...156 B3
Villarcayo E...143 B3
Villard-de-Lans
F...........118 B2
Villar de Barrio
E...........140 B3
Villar de Cañas
E...........158 B1
Villar de Chinchilla
E...........158 C2
Villar de Ciervo
E...........149 B3
Villardeciervos
E...........141 C4
Villar de Domingo
Garcia E.....152 B1
Villardefrades
E...........142 C1
Villar del Arzobispo
E...........159 B3
Villar del Buey
E...........149 A3
Villar del Cobo
E...........152 B2
Villar del Humo
E...........158 B2
Villar de los
Navarros E...152 A2
Villar del Pedroso
E...........156 A2
Villar del Rey
E...........155 B4
Villar del Rio E.143 B4
Villar del Saz de
Navalón E...152 B1
Villar de Rena
E...........156 A2
Villarejo E....151 A4
Villarejo de Fuentes
E...........158 B1
Villarejo de Orbigo
E...........141 B5
Villarejo de
Salvanes E ..151 B4
Villarejo-
Periesteban
E...........158 B1

Villares del Saz
E...........158 B1
Villaretto I ...119 B4
Villargordo del
Cabriel E.....158 B2
Villarino E....149 A3
Villarino de Conso
E...........141 B3
Villarluengo E 153 B3
Villarobe E....143 B3
Villarosa I....177 B3
Villar Perosa I.119 C4
Villarramiel E.142 B2
Villarrasa E....161 B3
Villarreal de San
Carlos E......150 C1
Villarrin de Campos
E...........142 C1
Villarrobledo
E...........158 B1
Villarroya de la
Sierra E......152 A2
Villarroya de los
Pinares E.....153 B3
Villarrubia de los
Ojos E.......157 A4
Villarrubia de
Santiago E...151 C4
Villarrubio E..151 C5
Villars-les-Dombes
F...........117 A5
Villarta E.....158 B2
Villarta de los
Montes E.....156 A3
Villarta de San Juan
E...........157 A4
Villasana de Mena
E...........143 A3
Villasandino E 142 B2
Villa San Giovanni
I............175 C1
Villa Santa Maria
I............169 B4
Villasante E...143 A3
Villa Santina I.122 A1
Villasarracino
E...........142 B2
Villasayas E...151 A5
Villasdardo E.149 A3
Villaseca de
Henares E....151 B5
Villaseca de Laciana
E...........141 B4
Villaseca de la
Sagra E......151 C4
Villaseco de los
Gamitos E...149 A3
Villaseco de los
Reyes E......149 A3
Villasequilla de
Yepes E......151 C4
Villasimíus I...179 C3
Villasmundo I.177 B4
Villasor I.....179 C2
Villastar E....152 B2
Villastellone I.119 C4
Villatobas E...151 C4
Villatorp E....150 B2
Villatoya E....158 B2
Villavaliente
E...........158 B2
Villavelayo E..143 B4
Villavella E....141 B3
Villaver de de
Guadalimar
E...........158 C1
Villaverde del Rio
E...........162 A2
Villaviciosa E.142 A1
Villaviciosa de
Córdoba E...156 B3
Villaviciosa de
Odón E.......151 B4
Villavieja de Yeltes
E...........149 B3
Villayón E....141 A4
Villé F........93 C3
Villebois-Lavalette
F...........115 C4
Villecerf F.....90 C2
Villecomtal F.130 A1
Villedieu-les-Poêles
F...........88 B2
Villedieu-sur-Indre
F...........103 C3
Ville-di-
Pietrabugno
F...........180 A2
Villedômain F.103 B3
Villefagnan F.115 B4

Villefontaine
F.............. 118 B2
Villefort F..... 131 A2
Villefranche-
d'Albigeois
F.............. 130 B1
Villefranche-
d'Allier F 116 A2
Villefranche-de-
Lauragais F .. 146 A2
Villefranche-de-
Lonchat F 128 B3
Villefranche-de-
Panat F 130 A1
Villefranche-de-
Rouergue F .. 130 A1
Villefranche-du-
Périgord F ... 129 B4
Villefranche-sur-
Cher F........ 103 B3
Villefranche-sur-
Mer F 133 B3
Villefranche-sur-
Saône F 117 A4
Villegenon F .. 103 B4
Villel E 152 B2
Villemaur-sur-
Vanne F...... 104 A2
Villemontais
F.............. 117 B3
Villemur-sur-Tarn
F............. 129 C4
Villena E 159 C3
Villenauxe-la-
Grande F......91 C3
Villenave-d'Ornon
F............. 128 B2
Villeneuve
CH 119 A3
F............. 129 B5
Villeneuve-d'Ascq
F.............78 B3
Villeneuve-de-Berg
F............. 131 A3
Villeneuve-de-
Marsan F...... 128 C2
Villeneuve-de-
Rivière F 145 A4
Villeneuve-la-
Guyard F......90 C3
Villeneuve-
l'Archevêque
F............. 104 A2
Villeneuve-le-
Comte F.......90 C2
Villeneuve-lès-
Avignon F.... 131 B3
Villeneuve-les-
Corbières F .. 146 B3
Villeneuve-
St Georges F ...90 C2
Villeneuve-sur-
Allier F 104 C2
Villeneuve-sur-Lot
F............. 129 B3
Villeneuve-sur-
Yonne F 104 A2
Villeréal F..... 129 B3
Villerias E 142 C2
Villeromain F . 103 B3
Villers-Bocage
Calvados F.. 88 A3
Somme F 90 B2
Villers-Bretonneux
F.............90 B2
Villers-Carbonnel
F.............90 B2
Villers-Cotterêts
F.............90 B3
Villersexel F... 105 B5
Villers-Farlay
F............. 105 C4
Villers-le-Gambon
B.............79 B4
Villers-le-Lac
F............. 106 B1
Villers-sur-Mer
F.............89 A3
Villerupt F 92 B1
Villerville F ...89 A4
Villesenneux F ...91 C4
Ville-sous-la-Ferté
F............. 105 A3
Ville-sur-Illon
F............. 105 A5
Ville-sur-Tourbe
F.............91 B4
Villetrun F ... 103 B3
Villetta Barrea
I............. 169 B3

Villeurbanne
F............. 117 B4
Villeveyrac F .. 130 B2
Villevocance
F............. 117 B4
Villiers-St-Benoit
F............. 104 B2
Villiers-St-Georges
F..............91 C3
Villingen D.... 106 A3
Villmar D.......81 B4
Villoldo E 142 B2
Villon F 104 B3
Villoria E 150 B2
Vilnes N.......46 A1
Vilnius LT 13 A6
Vils
A........... 108 B1
DK.............58 B1
Vilsbiburg D ...95 C4
Vilseck D.......95 B3
Vilshofen D.....96 C1
Vilshult S 63 B2
Vilusi MNE 139 C4
Vilvestre E 149 A3
Vilvoorde B 79 B4
Vimeiro P 154 B1
Vimercate I ... 120 B2
Vimianzo E.... 140 A1
Vimieiro P 154 C3
Vimioso P..... 149 A3
Vimmerby S.....62 A3
Vimoutiers F....89 B4
Vimperk CZ.....96 B1
Vimy F.........78 B2
Vinadi CH 108 C1
Vinadio I 133 A3
Vinaixa E..... 147 C1
Vinarós E 153 B4
Vinäs S.........50 B1
Vinay F........ 118 B2
Vinberg S.......60 C2
Vinča SRB 127 C2
Vinchiaturo I... 170 B2
Vinci I........ 135 B3
Vindeby DK.....65 A3
Vindelgransele
S............195 E9
Vindeln S 200 B5
Vinderup DK....58 B1
Vindsvik N......52 A2
Vinets F........91 C4
Vineuil F 103 B3
Vinga RO..... 126 A3
Vingåker S.....56 A1
Vingnes N......48 A2
Vingrom N......48 A2
Vinhais P..... 149 A3
Vinica
HR 124 A2
NMK 182 B4
SK............ 112 A3
SLO 123 B4
Viniegra de Arriba
E............. 143 B4
Vinje
Hordaland N....46 B3
Sør-Trøndelag
N............. 198 B6
Telemark N .. 53 A3
Vinkovci HR... 125 B4
Vinliden S..... 200 B3
Vinninga S.....55 B4
Vinnytsya UA .. 13 D8
Vinon F 103 B4
Vinon-sur-Verdon
F............. 132 B1
Vinslöv S.......61 C3
Vinstra N.......48 A1
Vintjärn S.......50 B3
Vintrosa S......55 A5
Viñuela E ... 163 B3
Viñuela de Sayago
E............. 149 A4
Viñuelas E ... 151 B4
Vinuesa E ... 143 C4
Vinzelberg D....73 B4
Viöl D..........64 B2
Viola I........ 133 A3
Violay F 117 B4
Vipava SLO.... 122 B2
Vipiteno I..... 108 C2
Vipperow D.....74 A1
Vir
BIH.......... 138 B3
HR 137 A4
Vira CH....... 120 A1
Vire F..........88 B3
Vireda S........62 A2
Vireux F.......91 A4
Virgen A...... 109 B3

Virgen de la Cabeza
E............. 157 B3
Virginia IRL 27 C3
Virieu F....... 118 B2
Virieu-le-Grand
F............. 118 B2
Virje HR........ 124 A2
Virkkunen
FIN..........197 D10
Virklund DK.....59 B2
Virovitica HR... 124 B3
Virsbo S.......50 C3
Virserum S......62 A3
Virtaniemi
FIN..........193 D12
Virton B.........92 B1
Virtsu EST.......8 C3
Vis HR........ 138 B2
Visbek D........71 B5
Visby
DK............ 64 A1
S............. 57 C4
Visé B...........80 B1
Višegrad BIH.. 139 B5
Viserba I 136 A1
Viseu P....... 148 B2
Visiedo E..... 152 B2
Viskafors S......60 B2
Visland N 52 B2
Vislanda S......62 B2
Visnes N 52 A1
Višnja Gora
SLO 123 B3
Višnjan HR.... 122 B2
Višnové CZ......97 C4
Visnums-Kil S...55 A5
Viso del Marqués
E............. 157 B4
Visoko
BIH.......... 139 B4
SLO 123 A3
Visone I 119 C5
Visp CH 119 A4
Vissefjärda S....63 B3
Visselhövede
D...............72 B2
Vissenbjerg DK .59 C3
Visso I........ 136 C2
Vistabella del
Maestrat E ... 153 B3
Vistheden S... 196 D3
Vita I......... 176 B1
Vitanje SLO ... 123 A4
Vitebsk = Vitsyebsk
BY............13 A9
Viterbo I 168 A2
Vitez BIH...... 139 A3
Vithkuq AL.... 182 C2
Vitigudino E .. 149 A3
Vitina
BIH.......... 138 B3
GR 184 B3
Vitis A..........97 C3
Vitkov CZ.......98 B1
Vitoria-Gasteiz
E............. 143 B4
Vitré F 101 A4
Vitrey-sur-Mance
F............. 105 B4
Vitry-en-Artois
F.............78 B2
Vitry-le-François
F..............91 C4
Vitry-sur-Seine
F.............90 C2
Vitsand S.......49 B4
Vitsyebsk = Vitebsk
BY............13 A9
Vittangi S 196 B4
Vittaryd S.......60 C3
Vitteaux F..... 104 B3
Vittel F 105 A4
Vittinge S.......51 C4
Vittória I 177 C3
Vittório Véneto
I............. 122 B1
Vittsjö S........61 C3
Viù I.......... 119 B4
Viul N..........48 B2
Vivario F 180 A2
Viveiro E 140 A3
Vivel del Rio Martin
E............. 152 B3
Viver E....... 159 B3
Viverols F..... 117 B3
Viveros E..... 158 C1
Viviers F...... 131 A3
Vivonne F..... 115 B4
Vivy F........ 102 B1
Vize TR........ 186 A2
Vizille F 118 B2
Viziñada HR... 122 B2

Viziru RO........17 C7
Vizovice CZ 98 B1
Vizvár H 124 A3
Vizzavona F... 180 A2
Vizzini I 177 B3
Vlachiotis GR .. 184 C3
Vlachovice CZ ..98 B1
Vlachovo SK....99 C4
Vláchovo Březí
CZ...........96 B1
Vladimirci
SRB 127 C1
Vladimirovac
SRB 127 B2
Vladislav CZ....97 B3
Vlagtwedde NL .71 A4
Vlajkovac SRB. 127 B3
Vlasenica BIH .. 139 A4
Vlašim CZ.......96 B2
Vledder NL......70 B3
Vlieland NL.....70 A1
Vlissingen NL...79 A3
Vlkolínec SK....99 B3
Vlorë AL...... 182 C1
Vlotho D........72 B1
Vnanje Gorice
SLO 123 B3
Vobarno I..... 121 B3
Voćin HR..... 124 B3
Vöcklabruck
A........... 109 A4
Vöcklamarkt
A........... 109 B4
Vodanj SRB ... 127 C2
Voderady SK....98 C1
Vodice
Istarska HR ... 123 B3
Šibenska HR .. 137 B4
SLO 123 A3
Vodňany CZ 96 B2
Vodnjan HR... 122 C2
Vodskov DK.....58 A3
Voe UK.........33 A5
Voerså DK.......58 A3
Voghera I 120 C2
Vogogna I 119 A5
Vogošća BIH .. 139 B4
Vogué F....... 131 A3
Vohburg D......95 C3
Vohenstrauss
D.............95 B4
Vöhl D..........81 A4
Vöhrenbach
D........... 106 A3
Vöhringen D....94 C2
Void-Vacon F ...92 C1
Voiron F...... 118 B2
Voise F.........90 C1
Voisey F...... 105 B4
Voiteg RO..... 126 B3
Voiteur F..... 105 C4
Voitsberg A... 110 B2
Vojakkala FIN. 196 D7
Vojens DK.......59 C2
Vojka SRB..... 127 C2
Vojlovica SRB . 127 C2
Vojnić HR..... 123 B4
Vojnice SK..... 112 B2
Vojnik SLO.... 123 A4
Vojvoda Stepa
SRB 126 B2
Volada GR 188 D2
Volargne I..... 121 B3
Volary CZ......96 C1
Volče SLO..... 122 A2
Volda N....... 198 C3
Volendam NL...70 B2
Volga RUS......9 C11
Volimes GR ... 184 B1
Volissos GR ... 185 A6
Volkach D.......94 B2
Völkermarkt
A........... 110 C1
Volkhov RUS....9 C8
Völklingen D.....92 B2
Volkmarsen D ..81 A5
Voll N........ 198 C4
Vollenhove NL...70 B2
Vollore-Montagne
F............. 117 B3
Vollsjö S 61 D3
Volodymyr-
Volyns'kyy
UA............13 C6
Volokolamsk
RUS...........9 D9
Volos GR...... 182 D4
Volosovo RUS...9 C6
Volovets UA ... 13 D5
Voltággio I.... 120 C1
Volta Mantovana
I............. 121 B3
Volterra I 135 B3

Voltri I 133 A4
Volturara Áppula
I............. 170 B3
Volturara Irpina
I............. 170 C2
Volvic F....... 116 B3
Volx F........ 132 B1
Volyně CZ......96 B1
Vonitsa GR....182 E2
Vönöck H 111 B4
Vonsild DK.....59 C2
Voorschoten
NL............70 B1
Vopnafjörður
IS 191 B11
Vorau A 110 B2
Vorbasse DK....59 C2
Vorchdorf A ... 109 B4
Vorden
D..............71 B5
NL............71 B3
Vordernberg
A........... 110 B1
Vordingborg
DK............65 A4
Vorë AL...... 182 B1
Voreppe F 118 B2
Vorey F....... 117 B3
Vorgod DK......59 B1
Vormsund N....48 B3
Võru EST........8 D5
Voskopojë AL. 182 C2
Voss N..........46 B3
Votice CZ.......96 B2
Voué F..........91 C4
Vouillé F 115 B4
Voulx F.........90 C2
Voussac F..... 116 A3
Vouvray F..... 102 B2
Vouvry CH 119 A3
Vouzela P..... 148 B1
Vouziers F......91 B4
Voves F....... 103 A3
Voxna S.........50 A2
Voy UK.........33 B3
Voynitsa RUS ...3 D12
Voznesenye RUS. 9 B9
Vrå
DK............ 58 A2
S............. 60 C3
Vráble SK.......98 C2
Vračenovići
MNE 139 C4
Vračev Gaj
SRB 127 C3
Vračevsnica
SRB 127 C2
Vrådal N........53 A4
Vrakneika GR . 184 A2
Vrana HR...... 123 C3
Vranduk BIH .. 139 A3
Vrångö S.......60 B1
Vrani RO...... 127 B3
Vranić SRB ... 127 C2
Vraniči BIH ... 139 B4
Vranja HR.... 123 B3
Vranjak BIH ... 125 C4
Vranje SRB... 16 D4
Vranovice CZ ...97 C4
Vranov nad Dyje
CZ............97 C3
Vransko SLO ... 123 A3
Vrapčići BIH... 139 B3
Vratimov CZ....98 B2
Vratsa BG.... 17 D5
Vrbanja HR... 125 C4
Vrbanjci BIH ... 124 C2
Vrbas SRB.... 126 B1
Vrbaška BIH... 124 B3
Vrbnik
Primorsko-
Goranska
HR 123 B3
Zadarsko-Kninska
HR 138 A2
Vrbno pod
Pradědem CZ ..85 B5
Vrboska HR... 138 B2
Vrbov SK......99 B4
Vrbovce SK.....98 C1
Vrbovec HR... 124 B2
Vrbovski SRB.. 127 C2
Vrbovsko HR.. 123 B4
Vrchlabí CZ.....84 B3
Vrčin SRB.... 127 C2
Vrdy CZ........97 B3
Vrebac HR......137 A4
Vreden D........71 B3
Vreoci SRB... 127 C2
Vretstorp S.....55 A5
Vrginmost HR. 124 B1
Vrgorac HR... 138 B3

Vrhnika SLO .. 123 B3
Vrhovine HR ... 123 C4
Vrhpolje SRB.. 127 C1
Vriezenveen
NL............71 B3
Vrigne-aux-Bois
F..............91 B4
Vrigstad S......62 A2
Vrlika HR...... 138 B2
Vrnograč BIH.. 124 B1
Vron F.........78 B1
Vroomshoop
NL............71 B3
Vroutek CZ 83 B5
Vrpolje HR.... 125 B4
Vršac SRB 126 B3
Vrsar HR...... 122 B2
Vrsi HR....... 137 A4
Vrtoče BIH ... 124 C2
Vrútky SK......98 B2
Všeruby CZ....95 B4
Všestary CZ.....85 B3
Vsetín CZ......98 B1
Vučkovica
SRB 127 D2
Vught NL.......79 A5
Vuillafans F ... 105 B5
Vukovar HR ... 125 B5
Vuku N....... 199 B8
Vulcan RO......17 C5
Vulcăneşti MD ..17 C8
Vuoggatjålme
S............195 D7
Vuojärvi FIN . 197 B9
Vuolijoki FIN ...3 D10
Vuollerim S ... 196 C3
Vuotso FIN ... 197 A10
Vuzenica SLO . 110 C2
Vyartsilya RUS ...9 A7
Vyborg RUS......9 B6
Výčapy CZ......97 B3
Výčapy-Opatovce
SK............98 C2
Východna SK...99 B3
Vydrany SK ... 111 A4
Vyerkhnyadzvinsk
BY............13 A7
Vyhne SK 98 C2
Vy-lès Lure F .. 105 B5
Vylkove UA.....17 C8
Vynohradiv UA .17 A5
Vyshniy Volochek
RUS...........9 D9
Vyškov CZ......97 B5
Vysokánad
Kysucou SK....98 B2
Vysoké Mýto
CZ............97 B4
Vysokovsk RUS .9 D10
Vyšší Brod CZ...96 C2
Vytegra RUS 9 B10

W

Waabs D........64 B2
Waalwijk NL....79 A5
Waarschoot B...79 A3
Wabern D.......81 A5
Wąbrzeźno PL .. 69 B3
Wąchock PL.....87 A5
Wachow D......74 B1
Wachów PL.....86 B2
Wächtersbach
D.............81 B5
Wackersdorf D. .95 B4
Waddington
UK............40 B3
Wadebridge
UK............42 B2
Wadelsdorf D...84 A2
Wädenswil
CH 107 B3
Wadern D.......92 B2
Wadersloh D....81 A4
Wadlew PL......86 A3
Wadowice PL....99 B3
Wagenfeld D....72 B1
Wageningen
NL............70 C2
Waghäusel D ...93 B4
Waging A..... 109 B3
Wagrain A ... 109 B4
Wagrowiec PL ..76 B2
Wahlsdorf D....74 C2
Wahlstedt D....64 C3
Wahrenholz D .. 73 B3
Waiblingen D....94 C1
Waidhaus D.....95 B4
Waidhofen an der
Thaya A.......97 C3
Waidhofen an der
Ybbs A 110 B1

Waimes B.......80 B2
Wainfleet All Saints
UK............41 B4
Waizenkirchen
A.............96 C1
Wakefield UK...40 B2
Wałbrzych PL...85 B4
Walchensee D 108 B2
Walchsee A ... 109 B3
Waldaschaff D ..94 B1
Waldbach A... 110 B2
Waldböckelheim
D.............93 B3
Waldbröl D.....81 B3
Waldeck D......81 A5
Waldenburg D .83 B4
Waldfischbach-
Burgalben D ..93 B3
Waldheim D....83 A5
Waldkappel D ..82 A1
Waldkirch D .. 106 A2
Waldkirchen D. .96 C1
Waldkirchen am
Wesen A......96 C1
Waldkraiburg
D........... 109 A3
Wald-Michelbach
D.............93 B4
Waldmohr D....93 B3
Waldmünchen
D.............95 B4
Waldring A ... 109 B3
Waldsassen D...95 A4
Waldshut D... 106 B3
Waldstatt CH . 107 B4
Waldwisse F....92 B2
Walenstadt
CH 107 B4
Walentynów
PL............87 A5
Walichnowy PL .86 A2
Walincourt F....90 A3
Walkenried D...82 A2
Walkeringham
UK............40 B3
Wallasey UK ...38 A3
Walldürn D.....94 B1
Wallenfells D...82 B3
Wallers F.......78 B3
Wallersdorf D...95 C4
Wallerstein D...94 C2
Wallingford UK .44 B2
Wallitz D.......74 A1
Walls UK.......33 A5
Wallsbüll D.....64 B2
Walmer UK.....45 B5
Walsall UK.....40 C2
Walshoutem B...79 B5
Walsrode D.....72 B2
Waltenhofen
D........... 107 B5
Waltershausen
D...........82 B2
Waltham Abbey
UK............45 B4
Waltham on the
Wolds UK.....40 C3
Walton-on-Thames
UK............44 B3
Walton-on-the-
Naze UK.......45 B5
Wamba E 142 C2
Wanderup D....64 B2
Wandlitz D......74 B2
Wanfried D.....82 A2
Wangen im Allgäu
D........... 107 B4
Wangerooge D .71 A4
Wangersen D...72 A2
Wängi CH..... 107 B3
Wanna D.......64 C1
Wansford UK...40 C3
Wantage UK ...44 B2
Wanzleben D ...73 B4
Waplewo PL.....77 A5
Wapnica PL.....75 A4
Wapno PL......76 B2
Warburg D......81 A5
Wardenburg D .71 A5
Ware UK.......44 B3
Waregem B.....79 B3
Wareham UK...43 B4
Waremme B.....79 B5
Waren D........74 A1
Warendorf D....71 C4
Warga NL.......70 A2
Warin D........65 C4
Wark UK.......37 A4
Warka PL......87 A5
Warkworth UK .37 A5

Warlubie PL.....69 B3
Warminster UK .43 A4
Warnemünde
D 65 B5
Warnow D 65 C4
Warnsveld NL...70 B3
Warrenpoint
UK 27 B4
Warrington UK..38 A4
Warsaw =
Warszawa PL...77 B6
Warsingsfehn
D 71 A4
Warsow D.......73 A4
Warstein D......81 A4
Warszawa =
Warsaw PL.....77 B6
Warta PL........86 A2
Wartberg A ...110 B1
Warth A......107 B5
Warwick UK.....44 A2
Warza D 82 B2
Wasbister UK ..33 B3
Washington UK 37 B5
Wąsosz PL......85 A4
Wasselonne F...93 C3
Wassen CH....107 C3
Wassenaar NL...70 B1
Wasserauen
CH 107 B4
Wasserburg D 108 A3
Wassertrüdingen
D 94 B2
Wassy F........91 C4
Wasungen D.....82 B2
Watchet UK.....43 A3
Waterford IRL...30 B1
Watergrasshill
IRL 29 B3
Waterloo B......79 B4
Waterville IRL...29 C1
Watford UK.....44 A3
Wathlingen D...72 B3
Watten
F..............78 B2
UK 32 C3
Wattens A 108 B2
Watton UK......41 C4
Wattwil CH....107 B4
Waunfawr UK...38 A2
Wavignies F.....90 B2
Wavre B........79 B4
Wearhead UK...37 B4
Węchadlow PL..87 B4
Wedel D 72 A2
Wedemark D...72 B2
Weedon Bec
UK 44 A2
Weener D......71 A4
Weert NL.......80 A1
Weesp NL.......70 B2
Weeze D........80 A2
Weferlingen D..73 B4
Wegeleben D...82 A3
Weggis CH....106 B3
Węgierska-Górka
PL............99 B3
Węgliniec PL...84 A3
Węgorzyno PL..75 A4
Węgrzynice PL..75 B4
Wegscheid D...96 C1
Wehdel D......72 A1
Wehr D 106 B2
Weibersbrunn
D 94 B1
Weichering D...95 C3
Weida D........83 B4
Weiden D.......95 B4
Weidenberg D..95 B3
Weidenhain D..83 A4
Weidenstetten
D 94 C1
Weierbach D...93 B3
Weikersheim D.94 B1
Weil D 108 A1
Weil am Rhein
D 106 B2
Weilburg D....81 B4
Weil der Stadt
D 93 C4
Weilerswist D..80 B2
Weilheim
Baden-
Württemberg
D........... 94 C1
Bayern D ...108 B2
Weilmünster D.81 B4
Weiltensfeld
A...........110 C1
Weimar D......82 B3
Weinberg D.....94 B2
Weinfelden
CH 107 B4

Weingarten
Baden-Württemberg
D.............93 B4
Baden-Württemberg
D............107 B4
Weinheim D ...93 B4
Weinstadt D ...94 C1
Welsmaln D.....82 B3
Weissbriach A 109 C4
Weissenbach
A............108 B1
Weissenberg
D 84 A2
Weissenbrunn
D 82 B3
Weissenburg D .94 B2
Weissenfels D...83 A3
Weissenhorn D .94 C2
Weissenkirchen
A..............97 C3
Weissensee D...82 A3
Weissenstadt
D 83 B3
Weisskirchen im
Steiermark
A............110 B1
Weisstannen
CH 107 C4
Weisswasser D..84 A2
Weitendorf D...65 C5
Weitersfeld A ..97 C3
Weitersfelden
A..............96 C2
Weitnau D 107 B5
Wéitra A 96 C2
Weiz A 110 B2
Wejherowo PL ..68 A3
Welkenraedt B..80 B1
Wellaune D.....83 A4
Wellin B........91 A5
Wellingborough
UK 44 A3
Wellington
Somerset UK....43 B3
Telford & Wrekin
UK 38 B4
Wellingtonbridge
IRL 30 B2
Wells UK 43 A4
Wells-next-the-Sea
UK 41 C4
Wels A 109 A5
Welschenrohr
CH 106 B2
Welshpool UK..38 B3
Welver D.......81 A3
Welwyn Garden
City UK........44 B3
Welzheim D....94 C1
Welzow D......84 A2
Wem UK 38 B4
Wembury UK ..42 B2
Wemding D....94 C2
Wenden D.....81 B3
Wendisch Rietz
D 74 B3
Wendlingen D ..94 C1
Weng A 109 A4
Weng bei Admont
A............110 B1
Wengen CH ...106 C2
Wenigzell A...110 B2
Wennigsen D ...72 B2
Wenns A 108 B1
Wenzenbach D .95 B4
Weppersdorf
A............111 B3
Werben D......73 B4
Werbig D......74 C2
Werdau D......83 B4
Werder D......74 B1
Werdohl D.....81 A3
Werfen A 109 B4
Werkendam NL .79 A4
Werl D........81 A3
Werlte D 71 B4
Wermelskirchen
D 80 A3
Wermsdorf D ..83 A4
Wernberg Köblitz
D 95 B4
Werne D 81 A3
Werneck D.....94 B2
Werneuchen D .74 B2
Wernigerode D .82 A2
Wertach D 108 B1
Wertheim D....94 B1
Wertingen D...94 C2
Weseke D......80 A2
Wesel D........80 A2
Wesenberg D...74 A1
Wesendorf D ...73 B3
Wesołowo PL...77 A5

Wesselburen D .64 B1
Wesseling D 80 B2
West Bridgford
UK 40 C2
West Bromwich
UK 40 C2
Westbury
Shropshire
UK 38 B4
Wiltshire UK ...43 A4
Westbury-on-
Severn UK.....39 C4
Westendorf A. 108 B3
Westensee D....64 B2
Westerbork NL..71 B3
Westerburg D...81 B3
Westerhaar NL..71 B3
Westerholt D ...71 A4
Westerkappeln
D 71 B4
Westerland D...64 B1
Westerlo B......79 A4
Westerstede D..71 A4
West Haddon
UK 44 A2
Westheim D 94 B2
Westhill UK 33 D4
Westkapelle
B............. 78 A3
NL 79 A3
West Kilbride
UK 34 C3
West Linton UK .35 C4
West Lulworth
UK 43 B4
West Mersea
UK 45 B4
Westminster
UK 44 B3
Weston UK......40 C1
Weston-super-Mare
UK 43 A4
Westport IRL....28 A2
Westruther UK..35 C5
West-Terschelling
NL 70 A2
Westward Ho!
UK 42 A2
West Woodburn
UK 37 A4
Wetheral UK ...37 B4
Wetherby UK ...40 B2
Wetter
Hessen D 81 B4
Nordrhein-
Westfalen D... 80 A3
Wetteren B 79 A3
Wettin D........83 A3
Wettringen D...71 B4
Wetzikon CH.. 107 B3
Wetzlar D......81 B4
Wewelsfleth D..64 C2
Wexford IRL.....30 B2
Weybridge UK ..44 B3
Weyerbusch D..81 B3
Weyer Markt
A............110 B1
Weyersheim F ..93 C3
Weyhe D.......72 B1
Weyhill UK.....44 B2
Weymouth UK ..43 B4
Weyregg A.....109 B4
Wężyska PL.....75 B3
Whalton UK....37 A5
Whauphill UK..36 B2
Wheatley UK...44 B2
Whickham UK..37 B5
Whipsnade UK..44 B3
Whitburn UK...35 C4
Whitby UK 37 B6
Whitchurch
Hampshire
UK 44 B2
Herefordshire
UK 39 C4
Shropshire UK..38 B4
White Bridge
UK 32 D2
Whitegate IRL..29 C3
Whitehaven UK 36 B3
Whitehead UK..27 B5
Whithorn UK...36 B2
Whitley Bay UK .37 A5
Whitstable UK ..45 B5
Whittington UK 38 B4
Whittlesey UK..41 C3
Wiązów PL......85 B5
Wick UK........32 C3
Wickede D......81 A3
Wickford UK ...45 B4
Wickham UK....44 C2
Wickham Market
UK 45 A5

Wicklow IRL.....30 B2
Wicko PL........68 A2
Widawa PL......86 A2
Widdrington
UK 37 A5
Widecombe in the
Moor UK.......42 B3
Widemouth
UK 42 B2
Widnes UK......38 A4
Widuchowo PL..74 A3
Więcbork PL ...76 A2
Wiefelstede D...71 A5
Wiehe D........82 A3
Wiehl D........81 B3
Wiek D.........66 B2
Większyce PL...86 B1
Wielbark PL....77 A5
Wiele PL 68 B2
Wieleń PL 75 B5
Wielgie
Kujawsko-
Pomorskie PL ..77 B4
Łódzkie PL..... 86 A2
Mazowieckie
PL........... 87 A5
Wielgomłyny
PL............87 A3
Wielichowo PL..75 B5
Wieliczka PL ...99 B4
Wielka Łąka PL..76 A3
Wielowies PL...86 B2
Wieluń PL......86 A2
Wien = Vienna
A............ 111 A3
Wiener Neustadt
A............ 111 B3
Wiepke D 73 B4
Wierden NL.....71 B3
Wieren D.......73 B3
Wieruszów PL...86 A2
Wierzbica
Mazowieckie
PL............77 B6
Mazowieckie
PL........... 87 A5
Wierzbie PL.....86 A2
Wierzbięcin PL..75 A4
Wierzchowo PL .75 A5
Wierzchucino
PL............68 A3
Wierzchy PL....86 A2
Wies A 110 C2
Wiesau D.......95 B4
Wiesbaden D ...93 A4
Wieselburg A ..110 A2
Wiesen CH 107 C4
Wiesenburg D ..73 B5
Wiesenfelden
D 95 B4
Wiesensteig D ..94 C1
Wiesentheid D..94 B2
Wiesloch D......93 B4
Wiesmath A.. 111 B3
Wiesmoor D ...71 A4
Wietmarschen
D 71 B4
Wietze D.......72 B2
Wigan UK 38 A4
Wiggen CH.... 106 C2
Wigston UK....40 C2
Wigton UK.....36 B3
Wigtown UK....36 B2
Wijchen NL.....80 A1
Wijhe NL.......70 B3
Wijk bij Duurstede
NL 70 C2
Wil CH 107 B4
Wilamowice PL .99 B3
Wilczęta PL 69 A4
Wilczkowice PL .77 B4
Wilczna PL......76 B3
Wilczyn PL......76 B3
Wildalpen A .. 110 B1
Wildbad D 93 C4
Wildberg
Baden-
Württemberg
D 93 C4
Brandenburg
D 74 B1
Wildendürnbach
A..............97 C4
Wildeshausen
D 72 B1
Wildon A...... 110 C2
Wilfersdorf A ..97 C4
Wilhelmsburg
A............ 110 A2
D 74 A2
Wilhelmsdorf
D 107 B4

Wilhelmshaven
D 71 A5
Wilków PL 77 B5
Willebadessen
D 81 A5
Willebroek B....79 A4
Willgottheim F..93 C3
Willhermsdorf
D 94 B2
Willich D........80 A2
Willingen D.....81 A4
Willington UK...37 B5
Willisau CH ...106 B3
Wilmslow UK...40 B1
Wilsdruff D.....83 A5
Wilster D.......64 C2
Wilsum D 71 B3
Wilton UK......44 B2
Wiltz L 92 B1
Wimborne Minster
UK 43 B5
Wimereux F 78 B1
Wimmenau F ...93 C3
Wimmis CH ...106 C2
Wincanton UK ..43 A4
Winchcombe
UK 44 B2
Winchelsea UK..45 C4
Winchester UK..44 B2
Windermere
UK 36 B4
Windischeschenbach
D 95 B4
Windischgarsten
A............ 110 B1
Windorf D......96 C1
Windsbach D ...94 B2
Windsor UK.....44 B3
Wingene B......78 A3
Wingham UK...45 B5
Winkleigh UK ..42 B3
Winklern A..... 109 C3
Winnenden D ..94 C1
Winnica PL.....77 B5
Winnigstedt D .73 B3
Winnweiler D...93 B3
Winschoten NL .71 A4
Winsen
Niedersachsen
D........... 72 A3
Niedersachsen
D........... 72 B2
Winsford UK ...38 A4
Wińsko PL......85 A4
Winslow UK.....44 B3
Winsum
Friesland NL ... 70 A2
Groningen NL.. 71 A3
Winterberg D...81 A4
Winterfeld D....73 B4
Winterswijk NL .71 C3
Winterthur
CH 107 B3
Wintzenheim
F............ 106 A2
Winzer D.......95 C5
Wipperdorf D..82 A2
Wipperfürth D..80 A3
Wirksworth UK .40 B2
Wisbech UK....41 C4
Wischhafen D..64 C2
Wishaw UK.....35 C4
Wisła PL.......98 B2
Wisła Wielka
PL............98 B2
Wislica PL......87 B4
Wismar D......65 C4
Wisniewo PL...77 A5
Wiśniowa PL...99 B4
Wissant F.......78 B1
Wissembourg F 93 B3
Wissen D.......81 B3
Witanowice PL..99 B3
Witham UK.....45 B4
Withern UK 41 B4
Withernsea UK .41 B4
Witkowo PL....76 B2
Witmarsum NL..70 A2
Witney UK......44 B2
Witnica PL......75 B3
Witnica PL......77 B4
Witry-les-Reims
F.............91 B4
Wittdün D......64 B1
Wittelsheim F. 106 B2
Witten D........80 A3
Wittenberge D..73 A4
Wittenburg D..73 A4
Wittenheim F. 106 B2
Wittichenau D..84 A2
Wittighausen D 94 B1
Wittingen D....73 B3
Wittislingen D ..94 C2

Wittlich D.......92 B2
Wittmannsdorf
A............. 110 C2
Wittmund D ...71 A4
Wittorf D 72 A2
Wittstock D....73 A5
Witzenhausen
D 82 A1
Wivenscombe
UK 43 A3
Wivenhoe UK ..45 B4
Władysławowo
PL............69 A3
Wleń PL........84 A3
Włocławek PL..77 B4
Włodawa PL ...13 C5
Włodzimierzów
PL............87 A3
Włosień PL.....84 A3
Włostow PL.....87 B5
Włoszakowice
PL............75 C5
Włoszczowa
PL............87 B3
Wöbbelin D....73 A4
Woburn UK 44 B3
Wodzisław PL...87 B4
Wodzisław Śląski
PL............98 B2
Woerden NL ...70 B1
Woerth F........93 C3
Wohlen CH.... 106 B3
Woippy F 92 B2
Wojcieszow PL..85 B3
Wojkowice
Kościelne PL...86 B3
Wojnicz PL......99 B4
Woking UK......44 B3
Wokingham UK 44 B3
Wola Jachowa
PL............87 B4
Wola Niechcicka
PL............86 A3
Wolbórz PL 87 A3
Wolbrom PL....87 B3
Wołczyn PL 86 A2
Woldegk D......74 A2
Wolfach D 93 C4
Wolfegg D 107 B4
Wolfen D.......83 A4
Wolfenbüttel D 73 B3
Wolfersheim D..81 B4
Wolfhagen D...81 A5
Wolfratshausen
D 108 B2
Wolfsberg A .. 110 C1
Wolfsburg D ...73 B3
Wolf's Castle
UK 39 C2
Wolfshagen D..74 A2
Wolfstein D....93 B3
Wolfurt A 107 B4
Wolgast D......66 B2
Wolhusen CH . 106 B3
Wolin PL 67 C3
Wolka PL.......87 A4
Wolkenstein D..83 B5
Wolkersdorf A ..97 C4
Wöllersdorf A. 111 B3
Wollin D 73 B5
Wöllstadt D....81 B4
Wolmirstedt D..73 B4
Wolnzach D....95 C3
Wołów PL......85 A4
Wolsztyn PL....75 B5
Wolvega NL....70 B2
Wolverhampton
UK 40 C1
Wolverton UK..44 A3
Wombwell UK..40 B2
Woodbridge
UK 45 A5
Woodhall Spa
UK 41 B3
Woodstock UK..44 B2
Wookey Hole
UK 43 A4
Wool UK 43 B4
Woolacombe
UK 42 A2
Wooler UK 37 A4
Woolwich UK ..45 B4
Wooperton UK .37 A5
Worb CH 106 C2
Worbis D.......82 A2
Worcester UK ..39 B4
Wördern A.....97 C4
Wörgl A 108 B3
Workington UK .36 B3
Worksop UK....40 B2
Workum NL....70 B2
Wörlitz D.......83 A4
Wormer NL.....70 B1

Wormhout F 78 B2
Wormit UK.....35 B5
Worms D........93 B4
Worpswede D...72 A1
Wörrstadt D ...93 B4
Wörschach A... 110 B1
Worsley UK.....38 A4
Wörth
Bayern D 93 B5
Bayern D 95 B4
Bayern D 95 C4
Rheinland-Pfalz
D............93 B4
Worthing UK...44 C3
Woudsend NL...70 B2
Woumen B......78 A2
Woźniki PL......86 B3
Wragby UK.....41 B3
Wrangle UK.....41 B4
Wręczyca Wlk.
PL............86 B2
Wredenhagen
D 73 A5
Wremen D 72 A1
Wrentham UK..45 A5
Wrexham UK...38 A3
Wriedel D......72 A3
Wriezen D......74 B3
Wrist D.........64 C2
Wróblewo
Mazowieckie
PL............77 B5
Wielkopolskie
PL............75 B5
Wrocki PL......69 B4
Wrocław PL....85 A5
Wronki PL......75 B5
Wroxham UK...41 C5
Września PL....76 B2
Wrzosowo PL...67 B4
Wschowa PL ...85 A4
Wulfen D.......80 A3
Wülfen D.......83 A3
Wulkau D......73 B5
Wünnenberg D .81 A4
Wünsdorf D....74 B2
Wunsiedel D...95 A4
Wunstorf D.....72 B2
Wuppertal D...80 A3
Wurmannsquick
D 95 C4
Würselen D....80 B2
Wurzbach D ...82 B3
Würzburg D....94 B1
Wurzen D......83 A4
Wust D.........74 B1
Wusterhausen
D 73 B5
Wusterwitz D...73 B5
Wustrau-Altfriesack
D 74 B1
Wustrow D.....66 B1
Wuustwezel B..79 A4
Wye UK........45 B4
Wyględów PL...87 A5
Wyk D.........64 B1
Wykroty PL.....84 A3
Wylye UK......43 A5
Wymiarki PL...84 A3
Wymondham
UK 41 C5
Wyrzysk PL.....76 A2
Wyśmierzyce
PL............87 A4
Wysoka
Dolnośląskie
PL........... 85 A3
Wielkopolskie
PL.......... 76 A2
Wyszanów PL..86 A3
Wyszogród PL ..77 B5

X

Xanten D........80 A2
Xanthi GR..... 183 B6
Xarrë AL 182 D2
Xátiva E 159 C3
Xeraco E 159 B3
Xert E 153 B4
Xerta E 153 B4
Xertigny F 105 A5
Xilagani GR ... 183 C7
Xilokastro GR .184 A3
Xinzo de Limia
E 140 B3
Xixón = Gijón
E 142 A1
Xove E 140 A3

Xubia E 140 A2
Xunqueira de
 Ambia E 140 B3
Xunqueira de
 Espadañedo
 E 140 B3
Xylophagou
 CY 181 B2

Y

Yablanitsa BG . . 17 D6
Yağcılar TR 186 C3
Yahyalı TR 23 B8
Yakoruda BG . . 183 A5
Yalova TR 187 B4
Yalvaç TR 189 A6
Yambol BG 17 D7
Yampil UA 13 D8
Yaniskoski
 RUS 193 D12
Yantarnyy RUS . 69 A4
Yarbasan TR . . . 186 D3
Yarcombe UK . . . 43 B3
Yaremcha UA . . 13 D6
Yarm UK 37 B5
Yarmouth UK . . . 44 C2
Yarrow UK 35 C4
Yasinya UA 17 A6
Yatağan TR 188 B3
Yate UK 43 A4
Yatton UK 43 A4
Yavoriv UA 13 D5
Yaxley UK 41 C3
Yazıca TR 187 B6
Yazıköy TR 188 C2
Ybbs A 110 A2
Ybbsitz A 110 B1
Ydby DK 58 B1
Yddal N 46 B2
Ydes F 116 B2
Yealmpton UK . . 42 B3
Yebra de Basa
 E 145 B3
Yecla E 159 C2
Yecla de Yeltes
 E 149 B3
Yelsk BY 13 C8
Yelverton UK . . . 42 B2
Yena RUS 197 B14
Yenice
 Ankara TR 23 B7
 Aydın TR 188 B3
 Çanakkale TR . 186 C2
 Edirne TR 183 C8
Yenifoça TR . . . 186 D1
Yeniköy TR 186 D4
Yeniköy Plaji
 TR 186 B3
Yenipazar TR . . 188 B3
Yenişarbademli
 TR 189 B6
Yenişehir TR . . 187 B4
Yenne F 118 B2
Yeovil UK 43 B4
Yepes E 151 C4
Yerköy TR 23 B8
Yerólakkos
 CY 181 A2
Yeroskipos CY 181 B1
Yerseke NL 79 A4
Yerville F 89 A4
Yeşildağ TR . . . 189 B6
Yeşilhisar TR . . . 23 B8
Yeşilköy TR . . . 186 B3
Yeşilova TR . . . 189 B4
Yeşilyurt TR . . . 188 A3
Yeste E 164 A2
Yezerishche BY . . 9 E6
Y Felinheli UK . . 38 A2
Ygos-St-Saturnin
 F 128 C2
Ygrande F 104 C1
Yialousa CY . . . 181 A3
Yığılca TR 187 B6
Yli-Ii FIN 197 D8
Yli-Kärppä
 FIN 197 D8
Yli-Muonia
 FIN 196 A6

Ylitornio FIN . . 196 C6
Ylivieska FIN 3 D9
Ylläsjärvi FIN . . 196 B7
Ymonville F . . . 103 A3
Yngsjö S 63 C2
York UK 40 B2
Youghal IRL 29 C4
Yoğuntaş TR . . 186 A2
Yozgat TR 23 B8
Yport F 89 A4
Ypres = Ieper B . . 78 B2
Yssingeaux F . . 117 B4
Ystad S 66 A2
Ystalyfera UK . . 39 C3
Ystebrød N 52 B1
Ystradgynlais
 UK 39 C3
Ytre Arna N 46 B2
Ytre Enebakk N .54 A2
Ytre Rendal N . 199 D8
Ytteran S 199 B11
Ytterhogdal
 S 199 C11
Yttermalung S . . 49 B5
Yunak TR 187 D6
Yuncos E 151 B4
Yunquera E . . . 162 B3
Yunquera de
 Henares E . . . 151 B4
Yushkozero
 RUS 3 D13
Yverdon-les-Bains
 CH 106 C1
Yvetot F 89 A4
Yvignac F 101 A3
Yvoir B 79 B4
Yvonand CH . . 106 C1
Yxnerum S 56 B2
Yzeure F 104 C2

Z

Zaamslag NL . . . 79 A3
Zaanstad NL . . . 70 B1
Žabalj SRB . . . 126 B2
Zabar H 113 A4
Žabari SRB . . . 127 C3
Zabiče SLO . . . 123 B3
Zabierzów PL . . 87 B3
Ząbki PL 77 B6
Ząbkowice Śląskie
 PL 85 B4
Zablaće HR . . . 138 B1
Žabljak MNE . . 139 B5
Żabno PL 87 B4
Zabok HR 124 A1
Žabokreky SK . . 98 C2
Zabor PL 75 C4
Żabowo PL 75 A4
Zabrdje BIH . . . 125 C4
Zábřeh CZ 97 B4
Zabreže SRB . . 127 C2
Ząbrowo PL 67 C4
Zabrze PL 86 B2
Zabrzeź PL 99 B4
Zachara GR . . . 184 B2
Zadar HR 137 A4
Zadzim PL 86 A2
Zafarraya E . . . 163 B3
Zafferana Etnea
 I 177 B4
Zafra E 155 C4
Žaga SLO 122 A2
Żagań PL 84 A3
Zaglav HR 137 B4
Zaglavak SRB . 127 D1
Zagnańsk PL . . . 87 B4
Zagora GR 183 D5
Zagorc SLO . . . 110 C2
Zagoričani
 BIH 138 B3
Zagorje SLO . . . 123 A4
Zagórów PL 76 B2
Zagradje SRB . 127 C2
Zagreb HR 124 B1
Zagrilla E 163 A3
Zagvozd HR . . . 138 B3
Zagwiżdże PL . . 86 B1
Zagyvarékas
 H 113 B4
Zagyvaróna
 H 113 A3

Zahara E 162 B2
Zahara de los
 Atunes E 162 B2
Zahinos E 155 C4
Zahna D 83 A4
Záhoří CZ 96 B2
Zahrádka CZ . . . 97 B3
Zahrensdorf D . .73 A3
Zaidin E 153 A4
Zaječar SRB . . . 16 D5
Zákamenné SK . .99 B3
Zákány H 124 A2
Zákányszék
 H 126 A1
Zakliczyn PL . . . 99 B4
Zakopane PL . . . 99 B3
Zakroczym PL . . 77 B5
Zakrzew PL 87 A5
Zakrzewo PL . . . 76 B3
Zakupy CZ 84 B2
Zakynthos GR . 184 B1
Zalaapáti H . . . 111 C4
Zalabaksa H . . 111 C3
Zalaegerszeg
 H 111 C3
Zalakomár H . . 111 C4
Zalakoppány
 H 111 C4
Zalalövö H 111 C3
Zalamea de la
 Serena E 156 B2
Zalamea la Real
 E 161 B3
Zalaszentgrót
 H 111 C4
Zalaszentiván
 H 111 C3
Zalău RO 17 B5
Zalavár H 111 C4
Zalcsie PL 86 A3
Žalec SLO 123 A4
Zalesie PL 77 A5
Zalewo PL 69 B4
Zalishchyky UA 13 D6
Zalla E 143 A3
Zaltbommel
 NL 79 A5
Zamárdi H 112 C1
Zamarte PL 68 B2
Zamberk CZ . . . 85 B4
Zambra E 163 A3
Zambugueira do
 Mar P 160 B1
Zámoly H 112 B2
Zamora E 149 A4
Zamość PL 13 C5
Zamoście PL . . . 86 A3
Zams A 108 B1
Zandhoven B . . . 79 A4
Žandov CZ 84 B2
Zandvoort NL . . 70 B1
Zangliveri GR . 183 C5
Zánka H 111 C4
Zaorejas E 152 B1
Zaovine SRB . . 127 D1
Zapadnaya Dvina
 RUS 9 D8
Zapfend D 94 A2
Zapole PL 86 A2
Zapolyarnyy
 RUS 193 C14
Zapponeta I . . . 171 B3
Zaprešić HR . . . 124 B1
Zaragoza E 153 A3
Zarasai LT 13 A7
Zarautz E 144 A1
Zarcilla de Ramos
 E 164 B3
Zaręby PL 77 A6
Żarki PL 86 B3
Zarko GR 182 D4
Zarnowiec PL . . 68 A3
Žarnovica SK . . 98 C2
Zarnow PL 87 A4
Zarnowiec PL . . 68 A3
Zarošice CZ 97 B4
Zarren B 78 A2
Zarrentin D 73 A3
Żary PL 84 A3
Zarza Capilla
 E 156 B2
Zarza de Alange
 E 156 B1

Zarza de Granadilla
 E 149 B3
Zarza de Tajo
 E 151 B4
Zarzadilla de
 Totana E 164 B3
Zarza la Mayor
 E 155 B4
Zarzuela del Monte
 E 150 B3
Zarzuela del Pinar
 E 151 A3
Zas E 140 A2
Zasavica SRB . 127 C1
Zasieki PL 84 A2
Zásmuky CZ . . . 96 B3
Žatec CZ 83 B5
Zaton HR 139 C4
Zatonie PL 84 A3
Zator PL 99 A3
Zauchwitz D . . . 74 B2
Zavala BIH 139 C3
Zavalje BIH . . . 124 C1
Zavattarello I . . 120 C2
Zavidovići
 BIH 139 A4
Zavlaka SRB . . 127 C1
Zawady PL 77 C5
Zawadzkie PL . . 86 B2
Zawdy PL 86 A2
Zawidów PL 84 A3
Zawidz PL 77 B4
Zawiercie PL . . . 86 B3
Zawoja PL 99 B3
Zawonia PL 85 A5
Zázrivá SK 99 B3
Zbarazh UA . . . 13 D6
Zbąszyń PL 94 B1
Zbąszynek PL . . 75 B4
Zbehy SK 98 C2
Zbiersk PL 76 C3
Zbiroh CZ 96 B1
Zblewo PL 69 B3
Zbójno PL 77 A4
Zbrachlin PL . . . 76 A3
Zbraslav CZ 96 B2
Zbraslavice CZ . 97 B3
Ždala HR 124 A3
Ždánice CZ 98 B1
Žďár nad Sázavou
 CZ 97 B3
Zdbice PL 75 A5
Zdenci HR 125 B3
Ždiar SK 99 B4
Zdice CZ 96 B1
Zdirec nad
 Doubravou
 CZ 97 B3
Zdolbuniv UA . . 13 C7
Zdounky CZ 98 B1
Ždrelo SRB . . . 127 C3
Zduńska Wola
 PL 86 A2
Zduny PL 86 A2
Zdziechowice
 Opolskie PL . . . 86 A2
Zdziszowice PL . 86 B2
Zeberio E 143 A4
Žebrák CZ 96 B1
Zebreira P 155 B3
Zebrzydowa PL .84 A3
Zechlin D 74 A1
Zechlinerhütte
 D 74 A1
Zederhaus A . . 109 B4
Žednik SRB . . . 126 B1
Zeebrugge B . . . 78 A3
Zegrze PL 77 B6
Zehdenick D . . . 74 B2
Zehren D 83 A5
Zeil D 94 A2
Zeilarn D 95 C4
Zeist NL 70 B2
Zeithain D 83 A5
Zeitz D 83 A4
Želatava CZ 97 B3
Żelazno PL 68 A2

Zele B 79 A4
Zelenoborskiy
 RUS 3 C13
Zelenogorsk
 RUS 9 B6
Zelenograd
 RUS 9 D10
Zelenogradsk
 RUS 12 A4
Železná Ruda
 CZ 96 B1
Železnice CZ . . . 84 B3
Železnik SRB . . 127 C2
Zelezniki SLO . 123 A3
Železny Brod
 CZ 84 B3
Zelhem NL 71 B3
Želiezovce SK . 112 A2
Żelkowo PL 68 A2
Zell
 CH 106 B2
 Baden-
 Württemberg
 D 93 C4
 Baden-
 Württemberg
 D 106 B2
 Rheinland-Pfalz
 D 92 A3
Zella-Mehlis D . 82 B2
Zell am See A . . 109 B3
Zell am Ziller
 A 108 B2
Zell an der Pram
 A 96 C1
Zell bei Zellhof
 A 96 C2
Zellerndorf A . . 97 C3
Zellingen D 94 B1
Želovce SK . . . 112 A3
Zelów PL 86 A3
Zeltweg A 110 B1
Zelzate B 79 A3
Zemberovce SK 98 C2
Zembrzyce PL . . 99 B3
Zemianske-
 Kostol'any SK . 98 C2
Zemitz D 66 C2
Zemné SK 112 B1
Zemst B 79 B4
Zemun SRB . . . 127 C2
Zemunik Donji
 HR 137 A4
Zenica BIH . . . 139 A3
Zennor UK 42 B1
Žepa BIH 139 B5
Žepče BIH 139 A4
Zepponami I . . 168 A2
Zerbst D 73 C5
Zerf D 92 B2
Zerind RO 113 C5
Żerków PL 76 B2
Zermatt CH . . . 119 A4
Zernez CH 107 C5
Zerpen-schleuse
 D 74 B2
Zestoa E 144 A1
Zetel D 71 A4
Zeulenroda D . . 83 B3
Zeven D 72 A2
Zevenaar NL . . . 70 C3
Zevenbergen
 NL 79 A4
Zévio I 121 B4
Zeytinbağı TR . 186 B3
Zeytindağ TR . 186 D2
Zgierz PL 86 A3
Zgorzelec PL . . . 84 A3
Zgošća BIH . . . 139 A4
Zhabinka BY . . . 13 B6
Zharkovskiy
 RUS 9 E8
Zhashkiv UA . . 13 D9
Zhlobin BY 13 B9
Zhmerynka UA . 13 D8
Zhodzina BY . . 13 A8
Zhytomyr UA . . 13 C8
Žiar nad Hronom
 SK 98 C2
Zicavo F 180 B2
Zickhusen D . . . 65 C4
Zidani Most
 SLO 123 A4
Ziddorf D 73 A5

Židlochovice
 CZ 97 B4
Ziębice PL 85 B5
Ziegendorf D . . 73 A4
Ziegenrück D . . 83 B3
Zieleniec
 Dolnośląskie
 PL 85 B4
 Warmińsko-
 Mazurskie PL . 77 A6
Zachodnio-
 Pomorskie PL . 75 A4
Zielona PL 77 A4
Zielona Góra
 PL 75 C4
Zieluń-Osada
 PL 77 A4
Ziemetshausen
 D 94 C2
Zierenberg D . . 81 A5
Zierikzee NL . . . 79 A3
Ziersdorf A 97 C3
Zierzow D 73 A4
Ziesar D 73 B5
Ziesendorf D . . . 65 C5
Ziethen D 74 B2
Žihle CZ 96 A1
Žilina SK 98 B2
Ziltendorf D . . . 74 B3
Zimandu Nou
 RO 126 A3
Zimna Woda
 PL 77 A5
Zimnicea RO . . . 17 D6
Zinal CH 119 A4
Zinasco I 120 B2
Zingst D 66 B1
Zinkgruvan S . . 55 B6
Žinkovy CZ 96 B1
Zinnowitz D . . . 66 B2
Zirc H 112 B1
Zirchow D 66 B2
Žiri SLO 123 A3
Zirl A 108 B2
Zirndorf D 94 B2
Žirovnica SRB . 127 C3
Žirovnice CZ . . . 97 B3
Zisterdorf A 97 C4
Žitište SRB . . . 126 B2
Zitsa GR 182 D2
Zittau D 84 B2
Živaja HR 124 B2
Živinice BIH . . . 139 A4
Zlatar HR 124 A2
Zlatar Bistrica
 HR 124 A2
Zlate Hory CZ . . 85 B5
Zlaté Klasy SK . 111 A4
Zlaté Moravce
 SK 98 C2
Zlatna Ostrove
 SK 112 B1
Zlatograd BG . 183 B7
Žlebič SLO . . . 123 B3
Zlín CZ 98 B1
Złocieniec PL . . 75 A5
Złoczew PL 86 A2
Zlonice CZ 84 B2
Złotniki Kujawskie
 PL 76 B3
Złotoryja PL . . . 85 A3
Złotów PL 68 B2
Złoty Stok PL . . 85 B4
Zlutice CZ 83 B5
Zmajevac BIH . 124 C2
Zmajevo SRB . 126 B1
Żmigród PL 85 A4
Zmijavci HR . . . 138 B3
Žminj HR 122 B2
Žnin PL 76 B2
Znojmo CZ 97 C4
Zöblitz D 83 B5
Zocca I 135 A3
Zoetermeer NL . 70 B1
Zofingen CH . . 106 B2
Zognol 120 B2
Zohor SK 111 A3
Zolling D 95 C3
Zolochiv UA . . . 13 D6
Zomba H 112 C2
Zomergem B . . . 79 A3
Zoñán E 141 A3
Zonguldak TR . 187 A6
Zonhoven B . . . 79 B5

Zonza F 180 B2
Zörbig D 83 A4
Zorita E 156 A2
Żory PL 98 A2
Zossen D 74 B2
Zottegem B 79 B3
Zoutkamp NL . . 71 A3
Zovi Do BIH . . . 139 B4
Zreče SLO 123 A4
Zrenjanin SRB . 126 B2
Žrnovica HR . . 138 B2
Zručnad Sazavou
 CZ 97 B3
Zsadány H . . . 113 C5
Zsámbék H . . . 112 B2
Zsámbok H . . . 112 B3
Zsana H 126 A1
Zschopau D . . . 83 B5
Zuberec SK 99 B3
Zubieta E 144 A2
Zubiri E 144 B2
Zubtsov RUS . . . 9 D9
Zucaina E 153 B3
Zudar D 66 B2
Zuera E 144 C3
Zufre E 161 B3
Zug CH 107 B3
Zuheros E 163 A3
Zuidhorn NL . . . 71 A3
Zuidlaren NL . . 71 A3
Zuidwolde NL . 71 B3
Zújar E 164 B2
Žukowo PL 69 A3
Žuljana HR . . . 138 C3
Žulová CZ 85 B5
Zülpich D 80 B2
Zumaia E 144 A1
Zumárraga E . . 143 A4
Zundert NL 79 A4
Županja HR . . . 125 B4
Zurgena E 164 B2
Zürich CH 107 B3
Žuromin PL 77 A4
Zurzach CH . . . 106 B3
Zusmarshausen
 D 94 C2
Zusow D 65 C4
Züssow D 66 C2
Žuta Lovka
 HR 123 C4
Zutphen NL 70 B3
Žužemberk
 SLO 123 B3
Zvenyhorodka
 UA 13 D9
Zvíkovské Podhradí
 CZ 96 B2
Zvolen SK 99 C3
Zvolenská Slatina
 SK 99 C3
Zvornik BIH . . . 139 A5
Zwartsluis NL . . 70 B3
Zweibrücken D .93 B3
Zweisimmen
 CH 106 C2
Zwettl A 97 C3
Zwettl an der Rodl
 A 96 C2
Zwickau D 83 B4
Zwiefalten D . . 107 A4
Zwieryn PL 75 B4
Zwierzno PL . . . 69 A4
Zwiesel D 96 B1
Zwieselstein
 A 108 C2
Zwoleń PL 87 A5
Zwolle NL 70 B3
Zwönitz D 83 B4
Żychlin PL 77 B4
Zydowo
 Wielkopolskie
 PL 76 B2
Zachodnio-
 Pomorskie PL . 68 A1
Żyrardów PL . . . 77 B5
Żytno PL 86 B3
Żywiec PL 99 B3
Zyyi CY 181 B2